The 400th:
From Slavery to Hip Hop

JOHN BURL SMITH

RiverHouse Publishing, LLC

The 400th: From Slavery to Hip Hop

Copyright © 2021 by John Burl Smith

All rights reserved. No part of this book may be reproduced or transmitted in any form or by any means without written permission of the author.

The opinions expressed in this published work are those of the author and do not reflect the opinions of RiverHouse Publishing, LLC or its Editors. Information contained in our published works have been obtained by RiverHouse Publishing, LLC from sources believed to be reliable.

ISBN 978-1-7335622-5-6

www.riverhousepublishingllc.com

I dedicate *"The 400th"* to life and love for and with my wife Dot and the wonderful life we had together. She reflected both qualities for me before and now, even though she passed in 2013. She gave me both her love and her life while inspiring me to be and do far more than I ever imagined or dreamed possible. Without her love, tutelage, and encouragement, *"The 400th"* would not ever have become an idea. *"The 400th"* represents the culmination and reflects the 42 years of life working and loving together. It is my truest conviction God gave me one of his angels to teach me how to submit to His Will!!

Acknowledgments

There are so many people, who played truly important roles in the process of bringing ***"The 400th"*** to life that I cannot possibly name and thank all of them here. However, some made such incredibly important contributions, as well as sacrifices, which made the project a success, who I must mention, knowing I will overlook some, so I beg their indulgence in advance. In terms of support, family comes first. My loving family daughter Laquitta, grandchildren—Tristyn, Tahlia, Toi, Tyrus and Trevius, Mudear, Mrs. Willie May Gray, my cheer leading brothers and sisters, Tommy Cal, Willie May, Bernice and William Brandon, Molly and Harvey Al-Ghani, Rev. Kilen and Cassandra Gray, Kim and Bridgitte Gray, niece and nephews Roslyn Jackson, Darryl, Gerald, and Terry Buford always played important roles anytime I asked.

Then when I reached out to the larger world, some friends and supporters were there at the very beginning pushing me and helping out. Nevertheless, some of these supporters, like Wylene Carol, who was so instrumental and without her insight and inspiration, early on, when ***"The 400th"*** was just an idea without real direction, helped make it the narrative you are about to read. Then there is Arish A. Khan, my road buddy "King" Khan. Arish and his family Lil, Saba Lou, and Bella, were there at the beginning and supported me throughout. They became a second family.

The following friends and supporters were more than cheerleaders, some helped bring ***"The 400th"*** into focus as I developed the idea completely. My deepest gratitude begins with Daisy McGowan, Floyd D. Tunson, Rainbow Robert, Maria Owczarz, Michael Fritz, Bob van Huer, Dawn Hailburton-Rudy, *Black Lips*, Maichael Eaton, Dr. Reginal Moss and wife Barbara, all played key roles at key points along the way to make ***"The 400th"*** a reality.

I will end on my man Vincent Taylor; he has had my back through good and very bad times. He picked up the slack for me since 1974. I have leaned on many truly wonderful friends and others getting ***"The 400th"*** to the public and it pains me not to name them individually. But, I will end on all those who know they were in my corner from day one, giving me their ears and time, listening to me, as I struggled to develop the idea of ***"The 400th"***. They offered their hearts and minds, so I give them my most heartfelt appreciation, while saying thanks and God bless!!!!!!!!!!

How We Got to The 400th

A slave's life amounted to a desperate voyage in treacherous tempest-tossed waters, chained and locked in the hole of a leaky ship. With water pouring in on them, slaves drowned, even though the ship didn't sink. Surviving their ordeal, crossing the *"Middle Passage,"* most enslaved Africans ended up someplace in the Western Hemisphere. A slave's reward for enduring those perils was a life of perpetual bondage and servitude. Would it have been better to drown?

Shanghaied Africans that ended up in North America began the journey descendants of American slavery made to ***"The 400th"***. First and foremost, ***"The 400th"*** is a love story. Yet, it is a saga filled with tragedy, horror, mayhem, treachery, and war. The love for self and family drives the action and storyline of ***"The 400th"***. It is the adventure of a people who fell in love with being themselves and were willing to brave the most incredible odds, holding on to the idea of who they are.

Their story takes place on a world stage. Mighty armies and powerful kings, emperors, and nations battled on four continents (Europe, Africa, North, and South America) to gain the wealth their services produced. Tyrants rose and fell, striving to control the wealth enslaved African's produced, while their fate hung in the balance, teetering on the brink of disaster for over 400 years (sic 1452-1865). The most powerful and economically dominant empires and nations grew rich, garnering even more power, as slavery became the dominant socio-economic and political system of that world. Kidnapped, shackled, and driven to produce wealth for the world, enslaved Africans were free enterprise—***Black Gold***—for Europeans.

Enslaved Africans' epic journey into bondage became known as the ***Trans-Atlantic Slave Trade.*** Once trapped in this horrific system of domination and subjugation, enslaved Africans endured to survive by placing their hopes in the next generation. Surviving the horrors of slavery, kidnapped Africans' propelled their progeny toward ***"The 400th"***, which is the terminal end of the longest-running instance of genocide in the history of humankind. Yes, we made it; 2019 marked the 400th year, some historians have designated as the year enslaved Africans first stepped foot on North American terra firma.

When speaking of ***"The 400th"***, one is not talking about the full breadth and life of slavery. That gruesome and torturous voyage across the Atlantic Ocean to the Western Hemisphere did not begin the horrors of slavery. For that story, one must look back another 247 years.

"The 400th" looks back at American slavery, which establishes that every descendant of American slavery alive today is a survivor of the most treacherous, brutal, deadly, and gruesome existence of any human beings that still exist today—those survivors are the last vestiges of the **Trans-Atlantic slave Trade's** dirty business. *"The 400th"* is a look back over those dark years, and it details a horrid existence without mercy, while their survival teetered on the brink of disaster. Somehow enslaved Africans found the will to hold on to who they were.

Telling their story, I pay homage to the heroic struggle of millions, who did not survive that *"desperate voyage in treacherous tempest-tossed waters, chained and locked in the holds of leaky ships."* Once ashore in North America, enslaved Africans began the time we will commemorate to honor the lives of all those who did not survive the horrors reaching North America, as part of *"The 400th"*. Celebrating the struggles of those who made it, we honor all enslaved Africans who were kidnapped and dragged aboard slave ships that ended up any place outside of Africa. Those of us, who reverence *"The 400th"*, as the greatest survival act of any people, which needed all the magic and togetherness that could be conjured to deliver their progeny to where they now offer *"The 400th"*, as a fitting eulogy, which they never received.

Peering into that dark past, I see faint images of my great-great-great-grandparents, like flickering specters barely perceptible, and without names. The first name my family found among the millions of kidnapped enslaved Africans that arrived in the Western Hemisphere is Burl Lee. Burl was my great-great-grandfather; he was the last Lee born in slavery. His son, Burl Lee, Jr., was the first Lee born after the bondage of slavery ended. They are the points of light that illuminate my family's connection to the voyage from **"The Door of No Return," Goreé Island, Dakar, Senegal**. These faint flickers were emitted by the first survivors of that mournful voyage, across the *"Middle Passage"* that made it to North America, sometime in our far distant past but are unknown.

My name is John Burl Smith. My middle name, Burl, is for the two patriarchs I've just introduced. John Smith, my father's great-grandfather, was a white riverboat captain. I did not know John, but I knew Burl Lee, Jr., my mother's grandfather. Rev. Lee rode a circuit out of Jackson, Mississippi, preaching and ministering to members of what was called then the *"Colored Methodist Episcopal Church (CME)."* He also ministered to any needy souls wherever he found them.

During my childhood, I listened to Rev. Lee preparing and practicing his sermons on Saturday evenings. His favorite sermon was, *"Can these dry bones live again?"* Ezekiel (37:1-14). *(Ezekiel was a great prophet among the Children of Israel. He ranks alongside Isaiah and Jeremiah. He was educated and trained to be a priest in the kingdom of Judah. But, as a young man, he was a captive of King Nebuchadnezzar in Babylon. Separated from the temple in Jerusalem, Ezekiel questioned if his education and training would ever be of real value? But through a vision, God showed Ezekiel a valley filled with dry bones and asked, "Can these dry bones live?"* Ezekiel's vision or metaphor was God's way of revealing his ability to work His Will, and change the circumstances of life, no matter how hopeless and bleak the situation may appear.)

The 400th: From Slavery to Hip Hop

Beginning this discussion of *"The 400th"*, I am reminded of how Rev. Lee spoke of former slaves after emancipation (1863), as though they were in the grave. He told me of listening to his father, the first Burl, and older men around campfires, talking of their times as slaves. These stories were about emancipation, life during Civil War, and their contraband period as they dreamed of freedom, which never came. He said, *"Tears would fill my father's eyes when he talked of the loss promises of freedom and how so many were worked to death as slaves, even though they were supposed to be free."* Rev. Lee would ask rhetorically, *"Can these dry bones live again?"*

Until age eleven, I had the great fortune of hearing Rev. Lee preach and tell stories about his and his father's life. Growing up, most of these stories became shadowy memories that slipped into the deep recesses of my mind, but back then, I had questions about, *"How did that happen and why?"* I know now slavery happened, and for one to fully understand the world slavery created, one must understand the world it replaced!

Telling the story of something unknown but knowable as slavery, one must begin at the very edge of what is known. The problem is; if one stretches the known beyond where it supports the weight that uncertain speculation places on it, one can slips into the void of their imaginings, trying to explain the unknown. The solution for me, regarding the unknowns of slavery, was to take the one indisputable fact of my existence and look back at the origin of how it began, who was involved, why were they involved and what was gained from their involvement to provide a solution. Answering these questions led to the first facts of my family's legacy, which began in slavery. There is a caveat to the mountain of interrogatives I had to ascend addressing these questions and assembling the information that came at a courtesy of the culprits, who, in most cases, perpetrated the dirty deed. Consequently, my case is only as reliable and factual as that evidence permits. So, I begin.

The Catholic Church and the Slave Trade

Comprehending the economic impact of slavery and clarifying the major culprits involved requires readers to visualize Europe at the beginning of the 5th century. The historical record indicates the people of Europe were dirt poor, ignorant, and brutish. Europe was ruled by warring factions lead by feudal lords. World history, as taught in American history books, is viewed through the eyes of Europeans. They thought the Earth was flat, and in their cosmology, the ocean flowed over the edge of the earth and off into an abyss. This benighted time is designated as the *"Middle or Dark Age."*

Some historians point to Italian scholar Petrarch (1304 -1374), who referred to the Latin *saeculum obscurum*, in identifying this time. Caesar Baronius (1538-1607), an Italian cardinal and ecclesiastical historian of the Roman Catholic Church, applied this designation to the tumultuous period of the 10th and 11th centuries, but Baronius' designation came to include periods before the 10th Century. Characterizing this period, he was referring to the demographic, cultural, and economic deterioration that occurred in Western Europe, following the withdrawal and decline of the Roman Empire, as *"a dark period,"* hence its designation **"Dark Age."** The Greco-Roman society that flourished in the Mediterranean, during these times, wielded great power, and influence throughout Europe, North Africa, and Western Asia, because of the Roman Empire, which became the Roman Catholic Church. This time is considered the Classical Age or Classical Antiquity.

As a result of the First Crusade (1095–1099), which occurred during this time, Europeans began venturing beyond the borders of their closed "flat world." Emerging from their flat earth **"Dark Age"** view of their existence, Europeans realized there was a larger and different world beyond their limited horizon. Europeans first adventurous peek outside their closed world was precipitated by Pope Urban II, during the Council of Clermont in 1095.

Pope Urban demanded Christians recapture the *Holy Land*. Christendom had lost the *Holy Land* to Islamic expansion by the Seljuq Turks back in the 7th century. Needing to get to the *Near East* to fight the Crusade, Europeans did not sail into the Mediterranean aboard ships, they walked. Believers in "flat earth" cosmology, Europeans feared the ocean's unknowns—sailing off the edge of the earth was their greatest fear. They were not seafarers.

Nevertheless, the results of that military expedition, known as *the Princes' Crusade*, allowed Christendom to not only re-captured the Holy Land—the Levant—they also liberated Anatolia, a Byzantine Christians stronghold. *(The Byzantine Empire or Eastern Roman Empire was the name given the eastern remnant of the*

Roman Empire, which survived until the Middle Age. Its capital was Constantinople, which today is Istanbul in Turkey. Unlike the Western Roman Empire, the most important language was Greek, not Latin, and Greek culture and identity dominated, until its fall to the Seljuq Turks).

Historians say the *First Crusade* was a result of a combination of factors happening both in Europe and the *Near East*. However, for my purposes, the most pertinent facts are the military and religious confrontations of Christianity and Islam in the Mediterranean. These confrontations laid the foundation for the next 500 years. As such, going back to the 7th to 8th centuries Christianity was adopted throughout the Roman Empire, but the Umayyad Caliphate *(The Umayyad Caliphate, was the second of four major caliphates established after Muhammad's death. The Umayyad caliphate ruled from Mecca)* rose up and conquered Syria, Egypt, and North Africa from the predominantly Byzantine Greek Christian Empire, and Hispania from the Visigothic Kingdom *(The Visigothic Kingdom occupied what is now southwestern France and the Iberian Peninsula from the 5th to the 8th centuries).* The Umayyads continued the Muslim conquests, incorporating Transoxiana, Sindh, the Maghreb and the Iberian Peninsula *(Al-Andalus), (bringing them into the Muslim sphere. At its greatest extent, the Umayyad Caliphate covered 11,100,000 km (4,300,000 sq mi) and 62 million people {29% of the world's population}*, making it one of the largest empires in history in both area and world proportion (<u>*The End of the Jihad State, the Reign of Hisham Ibn 'Abd-al Malik and the collapse of the Umayyads*</u>, Khalid Yahya Blankinship, 1994, State University of New York Press).

The idea here is to clarify the power blocks that produced the geopolitical changes that created the political map, which made slavery possible. During this period, Popes utilized knights to defend and protect Christendom, not only from political enemies of the Papacy but also against Al-Andalus or theoretically against the *Seljuq dynasty* in the east. The *Seljuqs* established both the *Seljuk Empire and the Sultanate of Rum*, which at their heights stretched from Anatolia through Iran. This area was the target of the First Crusade (<u>*The Atlas of the Crusades*</u>, Jonathan Riley-Smith; Import, 1991).

Beyond gaining more land and people, *the Crusades* brought Europeans out of the *"Dark Age"* and in contact with many new commodities and ideas that were limited or nonexistent in Europe—silver, gold, oils, fragrances, spices, salt, silk and new ideas to name a few. A spherical world was the major "new" idea that effectively brought Europe out of the *"Dark Age."* The Christian Byzantine Greek Empire had supplied these commodities to Europe, but the Ottoman Empire took control of Constantinople in 1453.

They blocked Europe's access to trade routes, stopping the flow of goods from the Far East to Europe. Also, it blocked access to North Africa and the Red Sea, two very important trade routes to the Far East for Europeans. The need to reach the Far East brought the new idea of a spherical world into prominence with Europeans, because of the blockade. Navigation—the ability to sail beyond the sight of land—became the technology and key to prosperity for Europeans.

Looking back to the beginning of these changes, the battle for the Iberian Peninsula began with Hannibal Barca. A Carthaginian, Hannibal is known for marching an army, which included war elephants, from Iberia over the Pyrenees and the Alps mountains into Italy. The Carthaginians lost the Iberian Peninsula to Rome when Hannibal was recalled from Italy by the war party in Carthage in 202 BC. The Iberian Peninsula remained in the hands of Portugal and Spain (*the Visigothic Kingdom*) until, Moorish (Muslim) Arab and Moors of Berber descent sailed across the Strait of Gibraltar and landed an invasion force on the Iberian Peninsula, renewing the battle for control of it in 700 AD.

Following a series of battles, the Moors conquered *Visigothic Christian Hispania* in 711 AD. Moors were seafaring people; they taught Portuguese and Spanish mariners modern navigation technology, based on a spherical world. Europeans were ignorant of modern navigation techniques; they believed in a flat earth. Even Vikings navigated by staying in sight of land. Moorish knowledge allowed Portuguese mariners to take the lead among Europeans, exploring for new routes to the Far East, which began what Europeans historians called *"The Age of Discovery."*

The need to find new routes to the Far East forced Europeans, basically Portugal and then Spain, to begin build ships and developing navies as leaders in Europe. *The Age of Discovery* is a term loosely applied to the period of European expansion by water, which brings this narrative to the early 1400s. At this point, it is very important to remember that at the dawning of the 1400s, Europe was among the wretchedly poor regions of the world, compared to the Mediterranean, India, or the Far East. Slavery and the revenues it generated, turned Europe, a continent of serfs ruled by autocratic backward feudalistic warlords, into the political, economic, and cultural standard of the world. Without the preceding discussion, before talking about the wealth and opulence Europeans came to lavish upon themselves, readers, like Europeans, would be without the ability to imagine the tremendous changes slavery brought their world.

Slavery brings this narrative back to the point of my childhood questions, *"How did slavery happen and why?"* Slavery did not pop up out of nowhere, and certainly powerless renegades, plotting in some obscure tavern, could not have masterminded such a world-changing enterprise. The real question is, *"How and why did the advent of African enslavement develop into the world's economic system?"*

For that answer, this narrative must return to Europe's emergence from the *"Dark Age"* (5th to 10th centuries), during those caliginous times, European Kings had been fighting over land and people since before the arrival of the Roman Empire. Conquering people and land was the bases of wealth across Europe and most of the known world. Amidst feuding monarchs, the Catholic Church was a countervailing force between warring powers. Once Portuguese explorers learned the earth was not *"flat,"* as Europeans believed, and after gaining knowledge of navigation from Moors, they began exploring the African coast (13 to early 1400s centuries), followed later by Spain.

According to many writers, slavery across the Sahara had been ongoing for centuries. It had commenced between African rulers, who supplied labor (slaves) to Arabs from the Mediterranean. The human trade was very small compared to what would develop, beginning with Portuguese and Spanish exploration. Tradition says African Rulers saw this trade as a way of dealing with defeated enemies or a way of controlling the power base of rivals. This process grew into a lucrative but small slave trade across the Sahara.

These writers believed African chiefs saw no difference in trading people to the Portuguese than to Arabs. Portugal's slave trade in African is believed began in the mid-1300s. During this time, the Portuguese began shipping slaves from West Africa to Europe and the Azores. It also shipped slaves into the Indian Ocean—Spicy Islands, as they established colonies. *(The Spice Islands—Indonesia—were known for the nutmeg, mace, and cloves that were originally and exclusively found there. These spices were Portugal's road to riches in Europe).* Discovering such commodities created the need for lots of labor. Slavery grew in Europe and the Atlantic islands (Azores), which were owned by Portugal and its main markets for slaves. Once Spain and Portugal "discovered" what they named the Americas and Islands in the Caribbean, slavery expanded to the Western Hemisphere.

I reiterate, understanding the enormous changes slavery brought to the world, especially Europe, one needs to comprehend fully the kind of world it replaced. The Catholic Church had accumulated great wealth over this period brokering peace among Christian Monarchs and giving church sanction for "exclusive" rights to pillage and plunder infidels (non-Christians). Popes Nicholas V issued a *Papal Bull* (an edit), the *Dum Diversas* on June 18, 1452, to aid Christians on the Iberian Peninsula (Portugal and Spain), which was under control of Moors (Arabs). Pope Nicholas V's *Dum Diversas* started it all by authorizing Alfonso V of Portugal to enslave captured Saracens and pagans, as *"perpetual slaves."*

Although the world's enslavement of Africans was not the intent, Europeans expanded Pope Nicholas V's authorization to include Africans; they were considered pagans. The Catholic Church sanctioning slavery made black skin *"free enterprise!"* for those with white skin. The Pope's words made people along the West Coast of Africa tantamount to Wildebeests (Gnus), free for the taking by any white man who desired. The Pope's words eventually gave birth to the **Trans-Atlanta Slave Trade,** which began its ascent sometime around 1452s.

The Trans-Atlanta Slave Trade made slavery more than just a way of dealing with defeated enemies and rivals. But, at this point, slavery was a practice, not the industry it became. Eventually, slavery became an open grave for millions, including the first of my family. The opening to **The Door of No Return, Goreé Island, Dakar, Senegal,** became an orifice that shallowed enslaved

Africans, as they disappeared into dark holes of ships. The Catholic Church is responsible for creating the open grave of slavery; a hold never to be filled, always hungry for more bodies. Its insatiable appetite consumed millions of Africans, as the **Trans-Atlantic Slave Trade** ran non-stop for approximately over 400 years, transporting enslaved Africans, *"black gold,"* across the *"Middle Passage"* and around the horn of African. The **Trans-Atlantic Slave Trade** began the commoditization of African human beings: a process that turned human being into black gold, oil to grease the wheels of the world's economy.

This epic saga for millions of families— ***"The 400th"*** –is a scenario that describes the survival struggle of countless human seeds planted in the grave of slavery at **The Door of No Return, Goreé Island, Dakar, Senegal.** These seeds were transported across the *"Middle Passage"* to the Western Hemisphere. As I said in my opening statement, *"A slave's life amounted to a desperate voyage in treacherous tempest-tossed waters, chained and locked in the hole of a leaky ship."* Many slave seeds did not survive the harrowing journey across the *"Middle Passage."* My family's seed did, which began its survival struggle getting to me.

Lost among millions of other slaves at this point, my family has no idea when the first slave carrying the Lee seed touched terra firma in North America. Burl, my great-great-grandfather, is the first name we know. Whether that seed was among the first slaves that arrived over 600 years ago or was among the last to arrive in early 1807, Burl is the first name we know that carried the Lee seed. The flickering specters before him left no clues, which is why he became the beacon that lit and guided my family's path on the way to ***"The 400th".*** The line from him, to me and beyond, is the point of this narrative. Slave families, like individuals, faced different circumstances, trials, and tribulations, but the backdrop of history remained constant for most.

Clearly understand the difficult task of any slave seed's survival, readers must continue following history's uncertain course to find seeds, like the first Burl Lee, somewhere among the mass of millions of kidnapped Africans souls. I will share the circumstances of my family's journey to create me and other slave seeds as they struggled to reach ***"The 400th",*** once this circuitous journey reaches the first Burl Lee.

But, until then this narrative will follow the process, which transformed enslaved Africans into commodities that produced the wealth Europeans warred over for nearly two hundred years, which made the **Trans-Atlantic Slave Trade** the center of everything for Europe until 1807.

Discussing slavery with wealth accumulation has the overarching matrix, reduces all other ideas, theories, or conjecture of world economic development to secondary status. Money was all that matters to cash strapped Europeans, who were broke, until enslaving Africans gave them *"free enterprise."* The wealth of which I speak is not just having an abundance of valuable possessions and money, but having residual income streams to the degree, one never has to consider not obtain anything they desire, which can be possessed. Nations that got into the exploration business in the early to mid-1300 to 1400s laid the foundation for the power Europeans developed during the 18th and 19th Centuries.

The Trans-Atlantis Slave Trade

The *Age of Discovery* produced intense rivalries between European powers searching for, discovering, and claiming new lands. Europeans took possession of everything those lands contained, even people. Vying for control of newly discovered territories and the slave trade created wars that began with tensions between Portugal and Spain. Pope Alexander VI, in 1493, issued his famous Papal Bull, the *"Treaty of Tordesillas."* The Pope tried to preempt and end these wars with his Papal Bull. He drew a line on a map that ran down through the Atlantic Ocean and Brazil. The line divided the world between Castile (Spain) and (Lisbon) Portugal called the *"line of demarcation."*

Pope Alexander VI's *"Treaty of Tordesillas"* gave all newly discovered land east of that line to Portugal and all lands west of it to Spain, Brazil was the exception. The line trans-versed Brazil and made it Portuguese territory. Such "exclusivity" protected Portugal's newly discovered lands and natural resources from other Christian nations. Even though Spanish explorers were already trading with Africans for slaves, gold, ivory, spices, and other goods, Pope Alexander blocked all other countries from exploring and exploiting Portugal's discovery—Africa. Most European traders ignored this papal bull, especially English merchants, a nation desperately looking for a means to get into the lucrative slavery business.

The *"Treaty of Tordesillas,"* forced Spain (Castile) out of the slave trade. It required Spain to find alternative means of acquiring slaves for its Western Hemispheric colonies. Spain could purchase African slaves from other nations, but could no longer take them out of Africa. Consequently, Spain instituted the *Asiento system* to purchase slaves. This system gave Great Britain a-foot-in-the-door of the slave trade. Great Britain proved to be the only nation that met Spain's *Asiento system's* demands for slaves consistently.

On the way to becoming the world's largest slaver, Great Britain and Spain developed close historical ties. England got revenue from Spain, which it could not obtain other places. This relationship produced loads of revenue for English business investors, which they used for economic development, and expansion. The slave trade was like wildcatting for oil at this point, in the sense that slave traders were raiders, without a governmental sanction to cover their actions. Again, however, the crafty British developed and organized raiding Africa for slaves into the system that became the *Trans-Atlantic Slave Trade.*

King Charles II of England (1672) facilitated the growth of slavery by creating *the Royal African Company*. His charter formalized slave trading under a royal charter and gave the monopoly to the port of London. The ports of Bristol and Liverpool lobbied to change that charter and King Charles II ended the monopoly in 1698, opening the slave trade, and expanding the British system. ("The capture and sale of slaves," Liverpool: International Slavery Museum.)

A point about terminology needs to be made here. The term "capitalist," meaning an owner of capital, appears earlier than the term "capitalism," both words were derived from the root word *"capita"*—meaning assets owned or the equity of an owner. Also, the words *"chattel"* and *"cattle,"* have a similar origin. They signify movable property. *"Capita,"* as a term, emerged in the 12th to 13th centuries and referred to funds, stock of merchandise, sums of money, or money carrying interest. By 1283, capital applied to assets of a trading firm. It was frequently interchanged with several other terms—wealth, money, funds, goods, assets, stock, property, and cargo as well. All these terms were used, at some point, to refer to slaves, as free enterprise or property. Poor, except for Royals, before the advent of slavery, people in Europe had no use for such terms. Slavery put real money in the hands of people barely out of serfdom.

The **Trans-Atlantic Slave Trade** (also called the triangle trade route) worked this way. The first leg of the triangle exported goods from Europe to Africa. Trading with African rules, merchants sold or traded goods—textiles, metal tools, utensils, guns, ammunition, and other factory-made items—for slaves. However, as the slave trade grew, kidnapping Africans became the method of choice for white slavers.

The second leg of the triangle—***the Middle Passage***—was a horrifically brutal and deadly experience for kidnapped Africans. Exporting cargo across the Atlantic Ocean to the Americas, Mexico, and the Caribbean Islands, slaves that did not die en route were sold or traded for goods made in the islands, South, or Central America. Traders bought more slaves, took on goods and passengers headed to North America or Europe. Goods transported to North America, a British colony, were sold or traded. Again, taking on cargo and passengers bound for European ports. Traders closed the last leg of the triangle headed back to Europe.

Completing the third leg of the triangle, goods made in the Americas and the islands entered European markets. As slavery and colonialism grew, products from plantations, mines, and small factories, as well as raw materials, were regularly bound for European markets. Hence, all this commerce created the growing need for more and more slaves. The goal of the triangle trade route was providing slaves to the "New World" to produce cotton, sugar, tobacco, molasses, rum, gold, silver, and other products. With hundreds of slave ships on the seas daily, like oil tankers today, slaves became international capital. Father of the British slave trade, Sir John Hawkins, was the first to gain a profit on every leg of the triangle run (*The Atlantic Slave Trade*, Herbert S. Klein and Jacob Klein, 1999, Cambridge University Press).

Great Britain's history in the slave trade in North America began between the late 1500s to early 1600s. The date 1619 has been put forth by American historians as the date of the first slave arrival. However, that date is good only if one is talking about the United States. If one looks at the whole of North America, Canada, and Florida, some dates are as early as the 1520s.

While dates for other colonies in the US vary wildly—Massachusetts' first slaves arrived in 1624 with Samuel Maverick. New Netherland (New York) received a cargo of 11 Africans in 1626. The Isabella docked in 1684, with Pennsylvania's first slaves headed for the London Coffee House; there selling slaves became a routine business transaction.

Contrarily, South Carolina's first African slaves arrived in 1526 with a large Spanish expedition from the West Indies, and African slaves arrived in Florida with the Spanish in 1513. Slave arrivals elsewhere challenge the Jamestown, Virginia 1619 date for the earliest African slave arrivals in North America, those slaves came with the Virginia Company of London, and is disputed by many historians.

By 1700, wars to control land and people in central Europe were decreasing, but the battle for control of the slave trade was just heating up. Viewing this period, —1670 to 1807—through the lens of slavery is the most effective means of framing this period. Beginning in 1670, Monarchs that got into the exploration game early and invested wealth derived from the slave trade wisely, gained the opportunity to control the slave trade. What nations did with the wealth gained from the bloody trade in human beings became the deciding factor in this proposition.

A clearer picture of the geopolitical centers in Europe—France and England—during the 1700s, is best understood by viewing it like *the Line of Demarcation*, which divided the world between Spain and Portugal; except there was no one, like the Catholic Church to police the line. Looking at these two centers—Great Britain and France—one finds the most active players in the slave game, as events went forward. They serve as the best models, during the 1700s, especially from the 1750s until 1815, to understand the powers.

Classically, these two societies reflected the extremes of this proposition. First, France was most ostentatious in its use of slave revenues. France invested its wealth in pomp and ceremony, lavish parties, and outrageously opulent lifestyles. A great deal of French wealth went to outfit its land-based military. The French military, though very large, was designed to protect France against conquest not to take territory. One man would change all that just before the 1800s.

Nations that became involved in the slave trade in the late 1600 and early 1700s financed exploration voyages. They became dominant because they were able to gain possession of newly discovered territories, like Portugal and Spain. Their dominance was due to *"treasure," not "blood."* Once in power, Napoleon Bonaparte of France changed all that.

Napoleon's war strategy was based on conquer central Europe, as the means of controlling the slave trade. I surmised Napoleon assessed European

Monarchies and their armies as weak and inexperienced. Moreover, they were without real leadership and ignorant of the real use and cost of war. Capturing land and people was the key to Napoleon's strategy for gaining control of the slave trade. If successful, he would control the heart of Europe, thereby the slave trade (*The Napoleonic Wars: The Empires Fight Back 1808–1812*, Todd Fisher, 2001: Oshray Publishing.)

Across the channel stood Great Britain, a nation that had pushed its way into the slave trade. Britain, in my opinion, was seen as the new boy on the block, with newly discovered lands, but without revenue for development. Receiving the Spanish *Asiento* monopoly to supply slaves, and as part of the *Treaty of Utrecht*, between Spain, France, Portugal, Savoy, and the Dutch Republic in 1713, Great Britain also gained colonies, which provided the revenue it would use to become a real player in the slave game.

The polar opposite of France, the British invested their slave revenue in the Royal Navy and new industrial developments of the day—*the Industrial Revolution*. The main conduit, supplying lubricant (**black gold**) to oil the Spanish slavery machine, Britain was quick to learn the importance of having a fighting navy, opposed to one for show, as the French. Fighting off pirates and hunting them down to protect Great Britain's slave shipments to Spain, the British invested heavily in the Royal Navy.

During the **Trans-Atlantic Slave Trade**, triangle ships never sailed empty, which meant traders in places like London, Liverpool, Paris, the Netherlands, Savoy, Castile, and Lisbon reaped enormous profits. The slave trade was the richest part of British trade in the 18th century. James Houston, who worked for an 18th-century slave merchant, wrote, *"What a glorious and advantageous trade this is... It is the hinge on which all the trade of this globe moves."*

Between 1750 and 1780, about 70% of the government's (Great Britain) total income came from taxes on slave-produced goods from its colonies. The profits gained from chattel slavery helped finance Britain's industrial development, and the Caribbean islands became the slave trade hub for the British Empire. The Caribbean islands were called the sugar colonies and were Britain's most valuable possession. By the end of the eighteenth century, four million pounds came into Britain from its West Indian plantations, compared to one million from the rest of the world, (*The Atlantic Slave Trade*, David Northrup, 2002, Houghton Mifflin Co.).

Wealth gained from the **Trans-Atlantic Slave Trade's** triangle ships was vast. It poured wealth into Britain's and other European countries' coffers, like manna from heaven. Even countries not part of the slave trade reaped benefits from the general commerce slavery produced during the 1700/1800s. Whether a country was involved in the slave trade directly or not, slavery produced wealth for all. It changed Europe's geopolitical landscapes, making penniless former surfs into entrepreneurs of all types. I reiterate, in Britain, those who made their wealth from the slave trade built fine mansions, even establishing banks, such as the *Bank of England*, and funded new Industries, (*The Atlantic Slave Trade,* Herbert S. Klein, and Jacob Klein, 1999, Cambridge University Press).

The previous discussion was not a romance with European development. It was to frame wealth, as the premise of everything that happened during this period, in that, *"what nations did with their slavery revenues, not how much they gained, proved to be the determining factor regarding which nation emerged atop the power heap and in control of* **The Atlantic Slave Trade** *at the dawning of 1800."*

Nevertheless, an unthinkable event on the horizon just before 1800—*the American Revolution*—changed not only the course of colonialism in the Western Hemisphere but the dynamics in Britain's reliance on the slave trade as well. Also, an unintended consequence of that unthinkable event—*the American Revolutionary War*—was another harbinger that would draw America into war over slavery. But, while slaves across the world remained shackled, wars for control of the **Trans-Atlantic Slave Trade** brought revolution and freedom to some people in many parts of the world for the first time.

The question that must be asked, which most people think they know, but never really thought about is; why did slavery end? Pouring such revenues into coffers of European Nations; what would make them volunteer and give up slavery? The surprising answer, I will reveal in the following sections.

A Slave's Run Changed the Future of the World's Economic System

Slavery's economic potential outweighed any consideration of ending such a system—***The Trans-Atlantic Slave Trade***—which was producing enormous wealth for Europe. A continent just 100 years earlier that held tenaciously to its "flat earth" cosmology, and with people just learning to sail the oceans, was now vying to control the world. Ending the slave trade was not the slightest consideration in 1713 for England, at the signing of the *Treaty of Utrecht*. This agreement brought more colonial possessions to Great Britain than anyone ever imagined and a growing need for more and more slaves by the middle of the 1750s.

However, as 1769 dawned new and different considerations that affected those comfortable with human bondage. Those considerations pushed their way to the fore, as efforts to control ***The Trans-Atlantic Slave Trade*** brought wars to a world, drunk on economic prosperity, while other considerations fought to be acknowledged. The escape of one slave, ***James Somerset***, would have been of little consequence had it happened in 1713, at the signing of the Treaty of Utrecht. However, toward the end of 1769, a small and determined group of committed social change and social justice activists change the world's attitude toward slavery.

The prospect of ***James Somerset's*** escape in 1713 was like a gale far out at sea. However, Great Britain was fully involved in the slave business by 1769 and only beginning to reap the enormous profits pouring into its treasury. But again, once ***Somerset's*** gale blew onshore as ***Somerset v. Steward***, it kicked up one hell of a storm of controversy regarding slavery. The unexpected consequence of one slave's—***James Somerset***—escape, put the whole question of slavery on trial in Great Britain, with disastrous consequences for those slavery was making rich in England.

An escape enslaved African, ***James Somerset***, as time and events would have it, changed the prospects for slavery, in the British Empire, by bringing slavery before the bar of justice and the world, in a way no one imagined back in 1713. ***Somerset's*** run set off a chain of events that produced a counterweight to slavery, as anti-slavery forces began marshaling their strength. Notwithstanding, Somerset was eventually recaptured (1771), but while on the run, he was befriended by John Marlow, Thomas Walkin, and Elizabeth Cade. Still further, ***Somerset*** was baptized, as an Anglican Christian in England, posing a real dilemma for slavery supporters.

After his capture, ***Somerset's*** benefactors made an application before the Court of King's Bench, for a writ of habeas corpus to release ***Somerset*** from all obligations, as a slave. ***Somerset*** appeared before Chief Justice Lord Mansfield, whose opinion held that *"Chattel slavery was unsupported by the common law in England and Wales."* His ruling not only freed ***Somerset*** but gave the fight to abolish the slave trade new life in England and North America *("The Black Must Be Discharged - The Abolitionists' Debt to Lord Mansfield"* Stephen Usherwood, 1981, History Today Volume: 31 Issue: 3).

Somerset's victory and the controversy, his freedom, energized abolitionists fighting to end the slave trade in England and provided hope to those fighting slavery around the world, particularly in the United States. According to some writers, the battle to end slavery began with *the Quakers—a little known religious sect.* Following protests on Barbados in the 1670s, Quakers became a major faction in the abolitionist movement. Also, their counterparts began openly opposing slavery in both the United Kingdom and North America, by the early 1700s. The *Society of Friends (Quakers)* was the first organization to take a collective stand against both the slave trade and slavery. Supporting **Somerset,** they became the tip of the spear in the international and ecumenical thrush to end slavery.

Quakers had long viewed slavery as an abomination and an immoral blight. Evangelical English Protestants joined them to form **The Committee for the Abolition of the Slave Trade** in 1787. Allied with Quakers, William Wilberforce and Thomas Clarkson amassed indisputable evidence that exposed the horrors of slavery, which was an embarrassment to the rich class in England.

The Committee for the Abolition of the Slave Trade fought many long and brutal battles against the wealthy class that grew rich on the blood money from the bloody trade in black bodies. The power the slave trade lobby exercised in Parliament was second only to that of the United States Congress, after 1789. For example, Clarkson was attacked and nearly killed by a gang of Liverpool sailors, a major base and home port for slave ships of the notorious Gregson slave-trading syndicates (1787). Clarkson said he believed, *"They were paid to assassinate me."*

William Wilberforce, a Member of Parliament (MP), began the abolitionists' protracted battle in Parliament over slavery, by introducing the first Bill for the abolition of the slave trade in 1791. Slavery's supporters in Parliament easily defeated that Bill by a vote of 163 to 88. Nevertheless, Wilberforce would introduce similar measures for the abolition of the slave trade every year until abolition.

Clarkson, Wilberforce, and the **Committee for the Abolition of the Slave Trade** generated and sustained a national movement, which mobilized public opinion against slavery, as never before. However, Parliament refused to consider and debate any Bill abolishing the slave trade. Moreover, the outbreak of war with France (1801) effectively prevented serious prospects of passing a bill to abolish the slave trade, as Britain warred with France. Beaten back yearly, Wilberforce, Clarkson and **The Committee for the Abolition of the Slave Trade** could not break the grip slavery's supporters had on Parliament. However, war and revolution in France (1789) began to change that situation.

The seminal event for abolitionists in Britain came with the ***Somerset*** verdict. ***Somerset*** brought the disparate groups working separately against slavery into one major force to support **An Act for the Abolition of the Slave Trade**. Discussing the blood and lives lost, fighting over control of the slave trade, will give readers a greater appreciation for the enormous wealth gained from enslaving free Africans and the impact slave revenues had on Europe, as well as why those nations were determined to keep slave revenues flowing to their nations.

Researching abolitionists' efforts to outlaw the slave trade, I reviewed, *Amazing Grace: The Story of William Wilberforce*, a documentary on Wilberforce life. It provided a fascinating account of slavery and the battle to end it in England. More importantly, it made a very convoluted story—the battle to end slavery—as presented in America history books, far clearer. *Amazing Grace* showed why and how ending the bloody trade in black bodies had more to do with war and treasure, than liberating those black wretches trapped in the slave trade.

War for Control of the Trans-Atlantic Slave Trade

The Trans-Atlantic Slave Trade, by the beginning of the 1700s, made slavery the greatest producer of economic wealth Europeans ever witnessed. No one could imagine the level of economic prosperity enslaving free Africans would bring Europeans to enjoy. Compared to just fifty years earlier, Europeans were enjoying enormous wealth, which ushered in the 1700s, the century of war. Fighting raged among European powers on land and at sea. Historians tell the story of France and Great Britain's battles from the viewpoint of monarchs and military engagement, which consumed everything and everybody in Europe and the Western Hemisphere, but not from the point of view of effort to control of the ***Trans-Atlantic Slave Trade***.

Now *"The 400th"* narrative embarks on a very convoluted course that will put the century of wars over slavery into perspective. Understanding the economic dominance of the ***Trans-Atlantic Slave Trade*** requires a couple of hard U-turns and some back and forth. Historians describe this period in terms of power games, intrigue, and rivalries between monarchs. These wars were rivalries for power true enough, but popular historians never mention the rivalries were to control the slave trade's wealth.

The mid-1700s through the early 1800s, as mentioned earlier, was a period that pitted France against Great Britain in most of these wars, but Napoleon Bonaparte was not in control of France until 1799. Napoleon saw controlling the ***Trans-Atlantic Slave Trade*** as no other French leaders, even those in Great Britain. The conflicts between France and England began with the Seven Years' War, also called the French and Indian War (1755-1763) in North America. Then came the American Revolution (1776-1783), followed by the French Revolution (1792-1802), which spanned a decade. The world was gripped by several major events simultaneously, but war and slavery connected everything.

Historians offer several dates for the formal beginning of the Napoleonic Wars, and see these conflicts as separate wars, but I have a different opinion. However, whether individually or through proxies France and England were in opposition in these wars; while vying for control of the ***Trans-Atlantic Slave Trade,*** the prize that hang in the balance. Consequently, I see the situation, as one long war that extended from the 1750s through 1815, with breaks in between. And most importantly, Napoleon was not the leader of France through the entire 65 years of those wars.

The French Revolution 1789–1799 intervened in this protracted series of wars but did not reduce hostilities between the two nations. Although the British and French changed partners several times, their war dance kept them nose to nose, even when they were not fighting each other. Both nations vied for the same prize—control of the ***Trans-Atlantic Slave Trade***—and slave revenues made the difference.

However, the underlying factors for victory in these wars were what happened within each country, more so than actions on battlefields. Moreover, unintended consequences, in many cases, decided which nation came out atop the heap of nations, with dollars signs for eyes, beginning the mid-1700s. Slavery and how the destiny of enslaved Africans controlled the destiny of European nations is the purpose of the following length look back and discussion.

These wars and their disastrous consequences for French produced several major events, which sent France spiraling into chaos, and as a result, help bring Napoleon Bonaparte to power, following the French Revolution (1789-1799). Beginning his rise to power, Napoleon was appointed First Consul of France in 1799 and by 1800 revolution allowed Napoleon to take power and complete control in France.

More importantly, slave revenues were the key to Napoleon's success at the beginning of the 1800s. Pouring into the French treasury, slavery's revenues allowed Napoleon to stabilize France's finances and economy, as well as build a strong bureaucracy. Napoleon then trained and provisioned the army, but the French navy was his stepchild, which became his Achilles heel in more ways than one.

Looking at France geographically, it has two large sections of coastline separated by the Iberian Peninsula (Spain and Portugal). A split coast required two naval forces, one in the Mediterranean Sea and the other in the Atlantic Ocean to protect the French coast. But, politically and strategically, Napoleon was not concerned with invasion from the sea. His interest was the conquest of central Europe, not defending the French coast. He built a strong army rather than investing in the French navy.

Effective navies, like Great Britain's, require infrastructure—ports, dockyards, and foundries—which must be maintained during peacetime, as well as during wars. Moreover, officers and crews need experience at sea. I believe, Napoleon was shortsighted, showing little interest in the navy, while investing heavily in his army of conquest. As such, shortages of resources and political infighting repeatedly damaged the French navy and created a series of disastrous defeats, mainly against Great Britain.

The classic battle for control of the high seas came early in the Napoleonic Wars. One name, Vice-Admiral Horatio Nelson (1758-1805), stands out in the annals of the Royal Navy. He made all Britain's investments in a water war pay dividends. Severely tested in battle, Nelson provided The Royal Navy with decisive strategies, as well as effective decisions, while devising unconventional tactics to gain victories. Although wounded in combat several times—loss of one arm, sight in one eye, and was killed during his final victory at the *Battle of Trafalgar* in 1805—Nelson's inspirational leadership enabled The Royal Navy to gain decisive naval victories, ending the Napoleonic water war.

Defeating the joint Franco-Spanish navy at Trafalgar secured Britain's control of the seas, which gave the English control of the slave trade, the Western Hemisphere, as well as colonies in Africa gained through the *Treaty of Utrecht 1713*. Nelson's victory not only prevented Napoleon from dominating the high seas, it killed his hope of launching a full invasion of England itself. Following the *Battle at Trafalgar* (1805), the Royal Navy, as Lord of the seas, exhibited great pride over the fact few ships on the high seas were flying the French flags, *("The Royal Navy,"* Britannica Online; Encyclopedia Britannica).

The defeat—*Battle of Trafalgar*—continued dogging Napoleon's conquest plans. It limited his choices, as well as his ability to maneuver on land from that point forward. Also, Napoleon's early successes in his land war made the loss at sea seem insignificant. Various coalitions of European powers opposed Napoleon starting out, but they were weak and inexperienced. Therefore, Napoleon's land war went far better than expected, as he enjoyed a brilliant victory against the Russo-Austrian army (1805). But unexpectedly, Napoleon's bid to run the world sparked revolutions in Europe, as well as in the Western Hemisphere.

Amazing Grace

    Beginning in 1800, Napoleon's wars heaped destruction on Europe, while a war of a different sort was taking place, in the shadows, so to speak, as far as popular historians were concerned. Although deeply involved, America's history books do not provide the full context of this period, regarding America's role in these wars. I believe this is because no one wanted to admit the power America's desire for slave labor exerted over United States decision making.

    On the other hand, *Amazing Grace: The Story of William Wilberforce* is far more forthcoming in this regard. The back story of this entire period—1755/1815—according to *Amazing Grace* was all about the power and blood money slavery poured on Europe, as a result of its disregard for the humanity of enslaved Africans. The accounts in *Amazing Grace* revealed the brilliant strategy of how the **Committee for the Abolition of the Slave Trade,** pushed Parliament to end the **Trans-Atlantic Slave Trade**, while illustrating and highlighting America's efforts to keep the slaves coming into America, even after 1807.

    The point of this very circuitous and convoluted look backward is to learn exactly "how and why slavery ended?" Most people think slavery ended because governments realized it was wrong and ended it. But no, researching this story, I learned nothing could be farther from the truth. *Amazing Grace* is a statement about the resolve of humanity and shows the impact a group of dedicated people can have on history, even in the face of overwhelming odds.

    Amazing Grace revealed some startling facts regarding why slavery ended. It exposed the awesome power slaveholders in the US wielded, even up to and including the War of 1812, as slaveholders in the US fought to maintain slavery. The surprising turning point in the wacked saga was the information the **Committee for the Abolition of the Slave Trade** unexpectedly received, which proved to be the missing piece in the slavery/war puzzle. This information gave the **Committee** the advantage it needed, but how they used it became the key to ending the **Trans-Atlantic Slave Trade**. Pulling off this gambit, the **Committee** not only ended the slave trade, but helped bring Napoleon down as well. This fascinating and amazing saga, with its twists and turns is like a roller coaster ride, during a windstorm.

    Putting this puzzle together requires several looping turnabouts, beginning with the outcome of **James Somerset's** trial in 1769. Supporters for the abolition of the slave trade were very optimistic about ending the slave trade following **Somerset's** victory, but slavery forces in Parliament were unmoved by Lord Mansfield's ruling. They fought Wilberforce, Clarkson, and their coalition to a standstill. The **Committee** went on to build a groundswell of public support for ending the **Trans-Atlantic Slave Trade.** However, even after all their work the slave trade lobby in Parliament, like Republicans in America's Congress today, remained firmly against any measure that would end revenues slavery brought to the British Empire.

Recapitulating this drama, at the beginning of 1800, abolishing the **Trans-Atlantic Slave Trade** looked pretty bleak for the Committee. The Napoleonic Wars were raging across Europe and it seemed France had the upper hand. Everyone was depressed; even Wilberforce was downhearted. James Phillips, secretary and recorder of slave narratives for the Committee, left England on sabbatical. While on hiatus, Phillips documented every aspect of the slave trade he encountered, while traveling.

Disembarking in France, after several months of travel, Phillips noticed that even though cargos of slaves were being loaded and unloaded by French crews, the ships were flying American flags. Phillips' investigation paid enormous dividends. He learned the key information, which broke the impasse and brought Parliament on board ending the slave trade.

For readers to clearly understand the importance of Phillips' discovery, this very convoluted story begins an upside down long hard U-turn, ending up back at the *American Revolutionary War* (1776-1783). Fighting Great Britain, the most powerful nation in the world, for its independence, England's rebellious colony in North America was outmanned and outgunned. Fighting France's natural enemy—Great Britain—the Colonials appealed to the French Crown for support.

Agreeing to support the colonials, France entered the *American Revolutionary War* in 1778. Emerging victorious, America owed the French Crown a huge war debt. But, by the time the *Treaty of Paris* (1783) officially ended the American Revolutionary War and the United States Constitution was signed (1789), France was embroiled in revolution.

Over the intervening ten-years (1789-1799), chaos and fighting in France brought Napoleon to power (1799). Needing revenue, Napoleon called in America's *Revolutionary War* debt owed France. However, the Americans reneged, refusing to pay up, claiming it owed the debt to the Monarchy of France, not Napoleon. America's refusal to pay, drew the two nations into a little know conflict called the *Quasi-War (French: Quasi-Guerre), the Undeclared War with France, the Pirate Wars, or the Half-War in 1798 to 1800.*

The fighting was over the debt owed France that America refused to pay. The fighting took place mostly at sea and the affair lasted just over a year. The war itself is of little consequence, but what matters here is the agreement ending that conflict. That agreement is what justified this long eyeball twisting looks back through the rear-window, while trying to look straight ahead in order to put the War of 1812 into perspective.

With the French navy fighting Great Britain, Napoleon needed ships on the high seas to keep slave revenues coming to France. This meant France would need ocean transport for slaves, not war ships; the French ended the *Quasi-war* with a secret agreement with the United States. The French used the Convention of 1800 ending that war, with a deal that *allowed "French cargo vessels—slaves ships—to sail under the American flag."* Specifically, this provision allowed *"French slave ship to fly the American flag on the high seas."*

This *"slave ship"* agreement and maneuver is the devil in the details for the US. America helped disguised the nationality of French slave ship, which eluded British attack. Even though America was supposed to be a neutral nation in that war, it sided with France because its ships kept slaves flowing into America. This flag provision became the devil in the details for America. Simultaneously, The Royal Navy was being snookered, believing their water war has chased France off the high seas, because they saw very few ships flying French flags.

Other than the French and America's Congress, only the **Committee for the Abolition of the Slave Trade** knew that thousands of French slaves were aboard those ships, flying the American flag. The *flag deception* deal kept slave revenues flowing into France, feeding Napoleon war machine. While simultaneously, the *flag deception* scheme kept Napoleon in the war game, and slaves aboard French ships, flying American flags, flowing into America. Unbeknown to the rest of the world, James Phillips had discovered Napoleon's Achilles heel—learning the secret of the *flag deception* agreement.

The secret Phillips discovered—*the flag deception*—was huge. The vital knowledge of the *flag deception* scheme presented the **Committee for the Abolition of the Slave Trade**, with an intriguing proposition. With Europe fully engulfed in the Napoleonic Wars, the question was not whether or when to make the *flag deception* known, but how? After previous battles against the slave lobby in Parliament, following one disastrous defeat after another, the **Committee** knew it could not simply put the information out. If not done correctly, release of the information would have little or no affect and would not bring those opposed to ending the slave trade in parliament to their side.

James Phillips' gem of information provided the **Committee** with what it had been hoping for—a strategic advantage. The **Committee** needed to disguised maneuver to hide the intent of why the critical information was being introduced. The **Committee** knew the slave lobby in Parliament had to respond, but it need their response to come only after it was too late to stop their measure from passing. If used properly, the **Committee for the Abolition of the Slave Trade** had what it needed, but it needed a foolproof scheme.

Simultaneously, on the continent, the other U-turn this narrative took back at the beginning of 1800, with Napoleon's defeated of the Russian and Austrian coalition to open the Napoleonic Wars' unforeseen consequences were unleased in Europe. With that victory, Napoleon's war exploded all across Europe, prompting the implosion of the Holy Roman Empire (1806). *(The Holy Roman Empire was the multi-ethnic complex of territories in central Europe that developed during the early Middle Age and continued until its dissolution in 1806. The largest territory of the empire* was the Kingdom of Germany. It also included the Kingdom of Bohemia, the Kingdom of Burgundy, the Kingdom of Italy, and numerous other territories. The pressures of war broke all such ancient bonds).

Sowing seeds of nationalism, the Napoleonic Wars spread to Portugal, Spain, Belgium, and other nation-states in central Europe. The Napoleonic Wars eventually redrew Europe's political map. Napoleon's quick defeat of the Prussian and Russian coalition in 1807, allowed Napoleon to establish an uneasy peace on the continent for the rest of that year.

Concurrently, the **Committee for the Abolition of the Slave Trade** devised a different strategy and disguised their gambit behind a different tactic. MPs (Members of Parliament) on the **Committee for the Abolition of the Slave Trade** introduced **An Act for the Abolition of the Slave Trade** as a *"war measure."* Phipps' information was a game-changer for those fighting to end slavery. Previously, Wilberforce had presented measures to end the slave trade as humanitarian or social welfare measures. Their humanitarian appeals had moved the British public, but not those in Parliament opposed to ending the slave trade. However, the **Committee's** new tactic, introducing **An Act for the Abolition of the Slave Trade,** as a *"war measure,"* changed everything for the **Committee**.

The **Committee's** maneuver allowed MPs to explain that Napoleon's major source of war revenue was the slave trade. Hence, slavery was paying Napoleon's war bills. MPs explained the *"flag deception"* scheme to Parliament, while making the point that without slave revenues, Napoleon would not be able to pay his army. More importantly, Napoleon could not resupply his army or entice other nations to join him.

Changing their strategy, The **Committee for the Abolition of the Slave Trade** caught slavery's supporters in Parliament completely off guard. Putting a different spin on ending slavery, they flipped the need to abolish the trade in human beings. Flipping the issue of slavery as they did, The **Committee's** strategy made supporting slavery a different issue. Moreover, this isolated America with France, drawing the US even closer to war with England over slavery.

With that gambit, introducing slavery as *a "war measure,"* **An Act for the Abolition of the Slave Trade (1807)**, made supporting efforts to end the slave trade a patriotic gesture. While, on the other hand, supporting slavery became tantamount to supporting Great Britain's archenemy, Napoleon. Here is where how a nation used its slavery revenues determined, which nations ended up dominating the 1800s.

With its revenues from slavery, France financed a lavishly opulent lifestyle of pomp and ceremony, parties, and *Grande* estates. Whereas Great Britain built a fighting Navy, with its blood money, but more importantly at that juncture, its investments in new industrial technology (*the Industrial Revolution*), gave British investors a huge advantage. Great Britain's industrial base gave investors a way of getting out of the slave business and into other lucrative industrial investment ventures with gains rather than losses, as Frenchmen.

A Change for Slaves Changed the World

James Phillips and the **Committee for the Abolition of Slave Trade**, use the *"flag deception"* scheme between the US and France to pulled Parliament fully on board, ending the **Trans-Atlantic Slave Trade**. Parliament's change of attitude towards abolishing slavery began with **James Somerset's** run back in 1769. His court victory drew the splintered abolitionist movement together as one coalition.

Organizing this new coalition allowed them to broaden their efforts, bringing new MPs to join the **Committee for the Abolition of the Slave Trade**. Leading their effort for getting their measure before Parliament, new faces made their diversionary tactic seamless. It allowed high profile MPs, like William Wilberforce, to serve as decoys, while lesser-known MPs lay the gin, deploying their new strategy. A slave's run—***James Somerset***—started it all.

After passage of **An Act for the Abolition of the Slave Trade (1807)**, Parliament began passing measures designed to cut off Napoleon's only real source of war revenue—slavery. They tightened the noose around Napoleon's neck, by outlawing slavery, and enforcing their will at sea. Great Britain's strategy was designed to corner Napoleon and leave him no place to run. Without an industrial base, as England, France had no place to go to gain more wealth. Britain's industrial base made shifting investments out of slavery into England's developing industries, and other trade a big boost to its economy. It strengthened their economy in ways no one had considered. Rather than experiencing losses from ending slavery, England experienced an economic boom, while enjoying an increase in patriotic fervor.

Having gain control of colonies in Africa through the *Treaty of Utrecht* (1713), after losing its North American colony—the United States—in 1789, Britain no longer had any vital interest in the Western Hemisphere, regarding slavery. Parliament responded quickly to shift its interest from North America to its new colonial possessions in Africa. Once the *"flag deception"* scheme between France and the US was exposed, Parliament realized those black bodies, being taken out of Africa by smugglers and shipped across the ocean, was fueling the economies of other nations. Those nations, namely France and America, were gaining revenues, smuggling slaves that belonged to the British Empire. More importantly, France was vying for control of the slave trade, using British property to pay for wars against it. Parliament quickly reevaluated its strategy regarding slavery.

Defeating France made ending the **Trans-Atlantic Slave Trade** a strategic necessity to Parliament. Next, the battle to outlaw the slave trade through **An Act for the Abolition of the Slave Trade (1807)** pulled America's Congress on board abolition efforts. Bowing to anti-slavery forces in the UK, America's

Congress joined Parliament in March 1807, passing ***An Act Prohibiting the Importation of Slaves (1807)***.

This US federal law made it illegal to import slaves into the United States after 1807. The 1807 law did not outlaw slavery in the US. Also, slaveholders and supporters in Congress had no intention of enforcing the 1807 Law; it was to placate Great Britain. Moreover, the US Constitution granted slaveholders *"a 20 years grace period,"* until 1833, which was the earliest date permitted to end slavery in the US.

Consequently, America's law was a curveball in the dirt to see if Great Britain would go for its public charade of ending slavery, which it did. This law, ***An Act Prohibiting the Importation of Slaves***, ended the importation of slaves but did not outlaw slavery itself. Thus, smuggling slaves became a new technology and a new industry, to augment the loss of slaves from the *"flag deception"* scheme with France. America's slave lobby controlled Congress and prevented the US navy from enforcing the 1807 Act, abolishing the "importation" of slaves. But simultaneously, it brought the US even closer to conflict with Great Britain, because America continued smuggling African slaves into the US.

Following this convolution saga, may read like a fictional account or novel, at this point, rather than real history. However, it reflects what those refusing to end slavery did in order to continue reaping slavery's revenues. Nevertheless, even with Great Britain ended slavery, as a legal enterprise, Napoleon continued his hasty bid to take control of the very lucrative slavery enterprise through war in Europe.

A step too late however, I surmise, Napoleon, realized he thought he could kill two birds with one stone, if his plan worked. First, invading Iberia (Spain and Portugal), he hoped would eliminate France's double coastline, which was separated by Spain and Portugal. Simultaneously, he could gain the slave revenues coming into Spain and Portugal, two of the largest slavers in 1808. Hoping to cover his backside, at that point, Napoleon also was trying to crush two of Britain's biggest allies, while simultaneously, trying to isolate Great Britain economically.

Unexpectedly, the Spanish and Portuguese supported by Great British revolted. Not coincidentally, Napoleon occupied Spain's colonies in the Western Hemisphere, taking control of those slave revenues, which was the source of Spain's wealth. Napoleon's invasion of Spain prompted the Spanish Empire to unravel, as revolutions spread, like wildfire in the Americas—Central and South, as well as the Caribbean.

Napoleon's desperate grab, trying to control the slave trade continued pulling nations across the globe into his wars. Following his attack on Spain and Portugal, people desiring freedom among their colonial possessions launched popular revolts, especially in countries with large slave populations in South and Central America, as well as islands in the West Indies. Joining the fight to defeat

Napoleon, slave revolts swept the Western Hemisphere, as people made their desperate bids for freedom.

Under both British and American laws, the importation of slaves was a crime. Some in Parliament argued that slaves taken out of Africa were *"stolen property"* (contraband) of the Crown. MPs demanded the seizure of such cargos and the ships' crews imprisoned, as pirates and thieves. Privateers *(pirates employed by France or England to attack their enemy's ships)* were based mostly in the Southern US (in port like Tampa Bay, Florida; Mobile, Alabama, New Orleans, Louisiana) and the Caribbean. They began attacking slave ships, seizing them, and selling their cargos as prizes.

Finally, this discussion has returned to the place where it began the hard U-turn. Passing **The Act Prohibiting the Importation of Slaves of 1807** America hoped to head off further hostilities with Great British by making it seem slavery was ending in the US. Designed to appease Great Britain, America's calculated charade was to buy time to get as many slaves as possible into the South.

Even President Thomas Jefferson, a slaveholder, denounced the South's delaying tactics over slavery as a *"violations of human rights."* He called for its criminalization on the first day that was possible, during his annual message to Congress (1806).

Signing **The Act Prohibiting the Importation of Slaves of 1807,** President Jefferson and many in Congress believed that act would doom slavery in the South. Unlike the US, the British Parliament went after smugglers by establishing The Royal Navy's West Africa Squadron to suppress the **Trans-Atlantic Slave Trade,** after 1807 and stop smugglers, taking British property out of Africa. The West Africa Squadron patrolled the West African coastline and the **"Middle Passage."** Undisputed *"Lord of the seas,"* the Royal Navy interdicted the slave trade, but could not stop it entirely. The records show that after passing **An Act for the Abolition of the Slave Trade (1807),** the Royal Navy on parliament's command began boarding ships on the high seas, including ships flying the American flag (they were aware of the *flag deception* scheme).

Between 1808 and 1860—the year the American Civil War began—the West Africa Squadron captured 1,600 slave ships and freed upwards of 150,000 Africans. Those ships were in violation of **An Act for the Abolition of the Slave Trade (1807),** as well as **The Act Prohibiting the Importation of Slaves of 1807.** I repeat many of the ships the Royal Navy boarded were flying the American flag and carrying slave "cargos." Slavery, at this point, created a confusing picture for those not steeped its history. It is very difficult to follow the twist and turns of the game southern slaveholders played trying to hang on to slavery, the oil that greased the southern economy's wheels.

Rather than stopping hostilities between Britain and the US, **An Act Prohibiting the Importation of Slaves of 1807** increased them. The demands for slaves in the Deep South and out West increased, continuing to grow almost exponentially. Concurrently, during the Iberian stalemate in 1812, Napoleon became convinced slave revenues would continue flowing into French coffers. Consequently, he made the colossal strategic blunder of attempting to fight wars on two different fronts. While occupying Iberia and warring with Portugal and Spain, Napoleon launched an even larger and more daring plan with a massive invasion of Russia.

However, repulsed more by the very, very harsh Russian winter, more so than its army, Napoleon in his hasty retreat left behind a huge chunk of French slave revenue—cannons, munitions, other equipment, and the French *Grande Armée* in disarray. Things continued breaking bad for Napoleon. The six-year war with Spain and Portugal ended with the expulsion of the French army from Iberia. Great Britain ending the **Trans-Atlantic Slave Trade** combined with **An Act for the Abolition of the Slave Trade (1807)** began to bite Napoleon in the backside.

Briefly, returning to the trap the British set for Napoleon, back in 1807, Parliament recognized the critical condition of Napoleon's army. After being chased out of Russia and his inability to resupply his troops, Napoleon suffered another disastrous defeat at the hands of the Austria, Prussia, and Russia coalition. Great Britain read the handwriting on the wall for Napoleon and moved swiftly to tighten the noose around his neck. The Royal Navy cut off access to slave revenues by blockading slave ports across the Western Hemisphere.

It became obvious Napoleon was desperate and unable to address the critical needs and condition of his army; time had run out for him. Napoleon could not pay his army nor resupply it, which was being chased across Europe by Austria, Prussia, and Russia backed up by the British. The counterattack of Austria, Prussia, and Russia decisively defeated Napoleon at Leipzig in October 1813.

Great Britain prepared for the kill. Rallying European monarchs, Great Britain led the Allies in an invasion of France. They captured Paris at the end of March 1814. The Allies exiled Napoleon on the island of Elba, but he escaped in February 1815. Napoleon regained control of France before the coalition could move against him. Nevertheless, the allies cornered him at Waterloo. The British led coalition defeated Napoleon for his *Grande Finale* in 1815.

Although people in Europe, South America, and the West Indies, after Napoleon's defeat, tasted freedom, many for the first time, but their freedom did not end slavery. There was little to no concern among most new governments, over the horrible conditions and treatment enslaved Africans endured. It was clear governments were unconcerned about the pain and degradation slaves suffered. All the world cared about was the wealth slavery generated.

Great Britain, as *Lord of the Sea*, put an *Order-in-Council* (1805) in force, restricting the importation of slaves into colonies captured from France and the Netherlands and pressed other nations to do the same. Britain, after 1807 begun pushing other nations to end their slave trade and gained a series of treaties: the

Anglo-Portuguese Treaty (1810) whereby Portugal agreed to restrict its slave trade into its colonies; the *Anglo-Swedish Treaty* (1813) whereby Sweden outlawed its slave trade altogether; while Napoleon was in jail, France agreed with Britain that the slave trade was "repugnant to the principles of natural justice" in their 1814 *Treaty of Paris*. France agreed to abolish the slave trade in five years. The 1814 *Anglo-Dutch Treaty* with The Netherlands outlawed its slave trade also. Lastly, the *Anglo-Spanish Treaty* (1817), where Spain agreed to suppress its trade by 1820.

The Little Understood War of 1812

Now that you understand the critical question of how and why the **Trans-Atlanta Slave Trade** end I put into perspective the slave economy that developed after passage of **An Act Prohibiting the Importation of Slaves of 1807.** This act was predicated on not only keep slavery as the economic foundation of America, as it was enshrined in the US Constitution, the act was worded to permit struggled slaves to continue entering the US. Politicians never considered their scheme was a harbinger of dread and woe for the nation. They only saw the revenues they would gain, never considering the jeopardy they place on freedom for those that were not slaves. Explaining the previous statements and how the total commitment to keeping slavery, as the economic foundation of America, now becomes the goal of this narrative.

Over the last 400 plus years, the western world used slavery to build Europe and North America. The opulent mansions, grand estates, and entrepreneurial successes made Europe the leader of the world and Great Britain the master of Europe. Reaching the socioeconomic and political power Europe attained by 1800, Europeans adjusted to not having bond slaves, as part of their economy, but not America.

Providing the previous look back at that world development, I wanted to show the difference between American and European divergence on the issue of degradation, and subjugation of enslaved Africans. Americans refused to give up the means that had enabled slaveholders to continue the glorious life they enjoyed and would hold to at any cost. Simultaneously, the same transformation took place in Europe, in terms of opulence, which happening in America, although to a lesser degree. However, opulence points out the difference between the two nation and is best explained and clarified by the War of 1812.

Americans developed a die-hard attitude about maintaining slavery's domination, degradation, and subjugation of black skin for economic gain. Reading American history books, one gets an entirely different picture of this period, particularly the War of 1812. One gets the idea that war was all about, being a backdrop for writing *The Star-Spangled Banner*. On the other hand, reading or viewing *Amazing Grace*, one realizes that war was an extension of the *flag deception* scheme, without France as a partner.

Reading American history, I never understood, why American leaders allowed the nation to be drawn onto such a precarious perch, even risking subjection to Great Britain a second time, with how American historians presented the War of 1812. American historians never mentioned slavery, as an antecedent to the War of 1812, at least in the books sent to black schools. Those books made no mention of slavery as a causal factor. What historians wrote about the War of 1812 blamed Great Britain for aggressively trying to force America to concede several sections of land along the Canadian border, which were in dispute following the *Revolutionary War*. Those books went on to talk about The Royal Navy's hostile attitude and behavior, especially at sea toward America vessels, after losing its North American colony, mainly through help from France.

These books state that Great Britain wanted to goad the US into another fight. That perspective claimed this was why The Royal Navy began illegally boarding American ships. They accused Great Britain of harassing its sailors, impressing them into the British navy, illegally seizing American ships and cargos, while putting American sailors in prison.

First and foremost, the only "cargos" seized were slaves. These books failed to mention this fact or any of the discussion mentioned above, and definitely not the *"flag deception"* scheme between France and America. They left out entirely the fact that ships' invoices listed slaves simply as cargo.

Only after researching this subject and mostly watching and reading *Amazing Grace*, did I learn the truth of this matter. For those who need further explanation, I will now deal with how the actions of the slave lobby in the US Congress and the rest of America played Russian roulette with war in the chamber to keep slaves coming into the American South. Embracing smuggling to keep slaves flowing into the South, while blaming Great Britain for what happened—the War of 1812—shows the callous disregard for freedom and safety of American for profits from slavery.

The powerful slave-owning class in America, particularly in the South (Northerners owned slaves also), refused to accept any alternative to slavery, as the South's economic engine. The same as to day, and similar to Great Britain before ending the **Trans-Atlanta Slave Trade**, it was as though southerners valued slaves more than security. Moreover, they threw America in as the anti in their desperate gamble.

Frist and foremost, Southerners gained extra voting power at the signing of the US Constitution (1789) because of slaves. Founding Fathers added *Article I Section 2* to the US Constitution to gain the approval of the new United States Constitution by Southern representatives. Northerners agreed (many were slaveholders or investors) to count slaves for tax purposes and apportionment of legislatures. *Article I Section 2*, in today's terminology, was a tax cut for slaveholders.

Specifically, it said, *"Add 3/5 of the value to the whole, of others"* (add slaves to the numbers of slave masters). Secondly, the Constitution through the 3/5 Compromise put more white southerners in Congress than was justified if counting only white votes in the South. This is where through the Electoral College, slaveholders gain control in Congress, and smaller southern states control national election for US presidents. The Electoral College is why Donald Trump became president. Unlike in northern or so-called free-states, *one man one vote* determined representation. Therefore, each Southern white voter because of the 3/5 Compromise counted for 3/5 more than each Northern white voter, when it comes to the number of representatives in Congress and who occupies the White House.

Lastly, counting slaves in this manner was crucial to southerners controlling the US government and forcing the South's will—*the Fugitive Slave Act 1850*—upon the nation. Slaveholders, through the seniority system, were able to amass power in Congress and control budgetary matters, as well as legislation. Not only did the Electoral College give southerners power in Congress, but slaveholders also dominated the White House. The protections provided slavery coupled with the power gained by southern members of Congress, the 3/5 Compromise gave southerners control the of government in the US. The additional political power, through the 3/5 Compromise expanded links to the southern economy nationwide. Historian James Oliver Horton explains:

"*Slaveholders and the commodity crops of the South had a strong influence on United States politics and economy; New York City's economy was closely tied to the South through shipping, finance, and manufacturing. By 1822 half of New York's exports were related to cotton. Slavery allowed slaveholders through the southern Congressional delegations to dominate the United States presidency. Over the 72 years between the election of George Washington and the election of Abraham Lincoln, 50 of those years there was a slaveholder in the White House as president of the United States, and, for that whole period, there was never a President re-elected to a second term which was not a slaveholder.*" (<u>Slavery and the Making of America</u>, James Oliver Horton 2004, Oxford University Press),

Looking through the lens of history with the idea of slavery as the source of world wealth, during the 1700 and 1800s, the southern slave-owning class wielded enormous power. The 3/5 Compromise is why abolitionists in America, unlike the slave lobby in England before the passage of **An Act for the Abolition of the Slave Trade (1807)**, could not pressure congress to allow the US Navy to enforce the 1807 band on importing slaves. Southerners began to rely even more on smugglers that ran the Royal Navy's blockade patrolling the "**Middle Passage.**" The US Navy's blockade of southern ports was a sieve to allow slaves to continue entering America.

Southerners, after 1807, were in a mad rush to smuggle as many slaves as possible into the US to feed the ravenous appetite of farms, factories, fields, mills, and mines. With the price of slaves increasing daily, the demand for slave labor grew insatiably, as Southerners search for black skin reached into the North. Kidnapping free black became part of speculators and slave catchers' game for getting slaves into the South—*the Fugitive Slave Law 1850*—any way they could *(Solomon Northup biography, <u>Twelve Years A Slave</u> is an exemplary example)*. As the slave trade was ending around the world, at Great Britain's insistence, anyone in America with black skin could be kidnapped and smuggled across the Ohio River into legal slavery.

History reflects that southern states were determined to maintain slavery as their source of wealth at all costs. They saw slaves, as the engine of the South's economy and the only way of supporting their way of life; their proud heritage. Slaves, coming to America aboard French ships, were far more important to slaveholders, than possible hostilities with Great Britain.

Without France, as an ally, during the American Revolution and the agreement—the *flag deception*—ending the Quasi-War (1798-1800), there would not have been American flags on French ships, bringing slaves into the South. Ships flying French flags were sitting ducks for the Royal Navy and pirates.

The reality that broke through the lust and addiction in the South for smuggled slaves was increasing battles with the British at sea. These battles at sea became known as the *War of 1812*. Moreover, the British invaded the US along the northeastern seaboard, producing havoc and panic. They attacked Washington D. C., sacking and burning a vacated White House and other buildings in the capitol.

Fear ran rampant throughout the nation, finally forcing Southern slave-holders in Congress to capitulate and relent on allowing the US Navy to enforce **An Act Prohibiting the Importation of Slaves of 1807**. Refusing to acknowledge these facts, I believe American history books offered fictitious claims to avoid admitting America stuck its neck in the nose against Great British over slavery, causing the War of 1812. Also, no American historian wanted to admit the fact that the *War of 1812* was the first war America fought over maintaining slavery, and the Civil War was number two.

Concluding this discussion the **Committee for the Abolition of the Slave Trade's** strategy force Congress to introduce **An Act Prohibiting the Importation of Slaves of 1807** to keep secret its deal with the devil—*the flag deception*—scheme. Nevertheless, it validates my premise, *"It was what a nation did with its slave revenues, more so than how much it gained from slavery, which determined the nation that emerged as the dominant economic, political and military power throughout the 1800s."* This point is critical because France gains far more revenue than Britain from the slave trade, but it was Britain's investments that made it *"Lord of the Seas"* until World War I.

Amazing Grace has come to represents far more than a heartfelt and deeply religious standard. It reflects a level of humanity, uncommon to most. Some people move from a base of love, which extends to all without regard for their conditions in life, economic status, racial or national origins, as well as gender characteristics, to which such people respond to as human conditions rather than threats or problems. Their circumstances in life may place them beyond where such issues or aspects of their environment affect them personally, but they take on such issues that confront other human beings, as though such problems are their own.

In the battle to end the slave trade and slavery, William Wilberforce, Thomas Clarkton, James Phillips, and the Quakers sentiments and values are what moved them. Without such loving people, slavery may still be a physical presence in the lives of descendants of American slavery. Ending slavery with **An Act for the Abolition of the Slave Trade 1807,** showed ending slavery had less to do with slaves or freedom, than it did war, for Great Britain's Parliament. For Parliament, it was all about becoming the most powerful nation in the world. Above all, the *Amazing Grace* aspect in this long, convoluted saga shows in the case of human beings, even against the most powerful evil; love can find ways to keep hope alive when victims cannot see any hope!!!!

American Slavery: Entering the Valley of Dry Bones

Napoleon was defeated and driven into obscurity after 1815. Abolition ended the **Trans-Atlantic Slave Trade,** rescuing black skin from the 455-year reign of that murderous international economic system. Pouring slave revenues upon Europe, this economic monster that had gobbled up millions of African people for nearly five centuries, now thanks to Great Britain, it no longer terrorized Africans like Godzilla, but the hydra—slavery—would not die easily, especially in the US.

These two acts—***An Act for the Abolition of the Slave Trade 1807*** and ***An Act Prohibiting the Importation of Slaves of 1807***—were envisioned as killing blows that would end the life of the monster slavery, but not only were they not killing blows in America, they proved to be accelerants. These laws caused an explosive growth and development of the internal slave trade industry within America. It seemed to spring up like an overgrown child of the **Trans-Atlantic Slave Trade**, without the world even knowing it was pregnant.

As such, before the corpus of the **Trans-Atlanta Slave Trade** hit the ground, or the ink was dry on the paper, the child popped out of its mother fully grown in America. Slaveholders and supporters began enlarging the American internal slave trade system immediately, which had existed unnoticed by the world, since the early 1730s. This system had grown up as competition to the **Trans-Atlanta Slave Trade**. Its major function was breeding slaves within America, as a system, to provide a replacement workforce within the US.

The US government did far more than give lip service to the continuation of slavery as a major part of the American economy. It enacted policies, implemented procedures, and pass laws that made the internal slavery trade a border to border industry. Readers must understand that slavery was still an openly legal system all over the nation. Even if a state had abolished slavery, the ownership of slaves was still recognized. Clarifying this situation is this narrative's next topic.

Although floating coffins no longer legally flowed across the **"Middle Passage"** loaded with enslaved Africans, after 1807, smuggling slaves became a very lucrative enterprise for those willing to brave the hazards of dodging the Royal Navy's West African Squadron. Getting slaves into the South was such an important undertaking, smugglers became folk heroes—*Rhett Butler* in **"Gone with the Wind"** was reflective of such characters.

My family believed our ancestors approaching this point were already shackled slaves in the South, but maybe they arrived as part of early smuggled cargos. There is no exact number that accounts for the population of smuggled slaves. Documents show smuggled slaves landed, as late as 1861 in America, with the last known slave ship, *the Clotilda*, which landed in Mobile, Alabama. The internal slave trade ran nonstop, until Civil War ended, approximately 55 years after ***An Act Prohibiting the Importation of Slaves of 1807***, during which time smugglers brought tens of thousands of kidnapped African slaves into the South.

America and Brazil remained the only nations in the civilized world, still refusing to recognize black skin bore a human soul. Looking out at their new world, any enslaved African that walked off a slave ship into America in 1806, joined the millions who remained shackled slaves in the valley of dry bones, after 1807. Trying to find the seed that became Burl Lee, when slavery reached 1820, slaves everywhere in the world were freed, except slaves in America and Brazil.

My great-great-great-grandparents, Burl Lee's mother and father, were among them. While enslaved Africans around the world became free, Burl Lee's parents would still be chattel slaves when they conceived Burl in the early to mid-1840s. We know his mother was a slave because a child took the status of the mother. He would still be locked in the internal slave trade when he reached puberty in the late 1850s.

Burl Lee's parents, gazed upon a world where human beings, like themselves, were still lock in perpetual servitude. They were like people in epic stories, living under the domination of some terrible monster and awaiting a hero to slay it and give them freedom. However, slavery was a real monster for enslaved Africans, not some imaginary fairytale. It was a two-headed Hydra impossible to kill by ordinary means.

Those who fought to abolish slavery, and supporters of ***The Act Prohibiting the Importation of Slaves of 1807,*** believed that measure was the sword that would decapitate that monster—slavery—ending the life of a horrific economic system. Contrarily, however, those measures did not slay this Hydra and end the life of the child of ***The Trans-Atlantic Slave Trade's*** impact on kidnapped Africans. Rather than die, that blow caused it to grow another head, if not two. Supporters of abolition had believed slavery would wither and die a natural death, with the end of importation. And, slavery everywhere, except in the USA and Brazil, did die. It prevailed in the US, growing enormously, not simply because of the socioeconomics and political society in the South, but it grew tentacles that stretched well into the North.

What must be understood, first and foremost, is that the internal slave trade and breeding of slaves in America was about one thing and one thing only, wealth. Building wealth through slavery started with the ***Trans-Atlantic Slave Trade,*** which grew into an international wealth-generating mechanism for nations. Ending slavery around the world, with ***An Act for the Abolition of the Slave Trade 1807*** and ***The Act Prohibiting the Importation of Slaves of 1807,*** made slavery an individual dominated wealth-building enterprise in America.

The slavery system, within the US, had no socioeconomic or political restraints. It was government supported and facilitated. In contrast, when slavery developed as an economic system in Europe, those who grew rich from the blood money gained milking this monster, saw slaves as assets, investments that they enhanced, not only as property. The economic value of a slave was something investors and owners established conventions, which protected their investment. They tried to avoid needless damage and loss.

The concept of enhancement did not come to the internal slave trade in America. Primarily, poor whites entering the picture, as slave owners. I believe the internal slave trade and breeding brought in many that had not owned anything of real value. Poor whites in America, unlike most slave owners in Europe, were without business or basic education to any substantial degree, especially value enhancement. However, with the growth and development of the internal slave trade and breeding, ownership of property by poor whites made it possible for people without any real knowledge of anything, through ownership, became all-powerful over slaves.

With ownership, poor whites gained the right to dominate and do whatever they pleased with or to their property, without regard for enhancement or loss. This attitude unleased a viciousness that fed perverseness, which encouraged merciless brutality and total disregard for the lives of slaves. Such arbitrary and capricious attitudes made slavery a living hell for those in bondage. The movie *Twelve Years a Slave* serves as a graphic example of my statement.

Maintaining slavery, as the South's economic engine, allowed that Hydra to grow tentacles, which reached out of the Deep South and into the Upper South on into Northern States, gathering support for maintaining slavery. This narrative will show that monster—slavery—drew slaves southward through a regular system that aided the development of the internal slave trade and breeding. States supplying slaves were in the Upper South and developed the system of breeding and selling slaves going back to the 1730s. Southerners tied into the system in Upper South states, Virginia, Maryland, and Delaware. They created the infrastructure, as they supplied slaves to the Lower South, even before the 1807 law abolishing the importation of slaves. The internal slave trade in the North made this Hydra a many-headed monster. It gobbled up slaves faster than transporters brought them into the Deep South.

Ely Whitney's new invention—the cotton gin (1793)—changed everything for slaves. The cotton gin became the single greatest complication for throttling the demise of slavery, after the passage of the 1807 **Act Prohibiting the Importation of Slaves** into the US. The cotton gin and its economic impacts were not limited to the South. It truly made slavery a many-headed national monster. Whitney's cotton gin introduced several factors that counteracted the effects of the 1807 Act, ending the importation of slaves.

First, this narrative's course will follow how Southerners banked everything on slavery and were determined to hold on to it at all costs. Secondly, Northerners, like the slave lobby in Great Britain during the 1700s, did not want to give up the huge profits slavery generated. A third essential element was the availability of a ready supply of enslaved Africans, already in North American, at the passage of **The Act Prohibiting the Importation of Slaves of 1807.**

America's ballooning slave population was made possible by what slaver masters called *"natural increase"* (that is when the numbers of births exceeded the numbers of deaths). A replacement work population is why breeding was seen as essential and is a point I will return later. However, at this point, suffice it to say, the thing that would not allow slavery to die was the increase in cotton production caused by Whitney's gin and the profits derived from it.

Whitney's invention created a world no one, especially my ancestors, could never have imagined in 1807. By the time the 200th arrived (1819), the cotton gin had changed almost everything about the South. Southern planters saw the huge economic advantages that the cotton gin gave cotton production, as smuggling became a dying art. Before Whitney's invention, the South was handicapped, building wealth. Everything connected to wealth depended on cotton and slaves. The South had only a small industrial base, with its only commercial products, cotton, and land—its chief natural resource—the cotton gin made rapid economic development possible.

Previously, before the gin arrived, only one variety of cotton could be grown successfully in the South—*long stable*—which only grew in low coastal areas. Secondly, the vast majority of southern land was covered with forest, leaving little room for growing crops of any kind. Whitney's gin changed all that by processing a new variety—*short-staple,* which could be grown almost any place. Short-staple revolutionized the cotton industry, making the South's dry, forest-covered land prime real estate. Coupled with the cotton gin, cotton production increased in quantity tenfold in a day.

States like Alabama, Arkansas, Georgia, Mississippi, South Carolina, and Tennessee, with their forest-covered land, hot and dry climate, reaped the greatest benefits. Their land values soared. Once the cotton gin came online, land in the Deep South and out West gave the region even greater economic potential. Southerners quickly recognized the advantage and unlimited potential for cotton cultivation and production. But, southerners were just as quick to acknowledge the South's major drawback—they could no longer imported slaves. The **1807 Act** abolishing the importation of slaves presented the South with its most challenging obstacle—its growing need for labor, which smuggling could not satisfy.

The Internal Slave Trade and Breeding Slaves

"The 400th" discussion now returns to the little business in the Upper South, the internal slave trade. Similar to a Hydra, slavery did not only grow more heads, but it also increased in size as the internal slave trade and breeding became a full-blown industrial monster. While slavery in the rest of the world died a sure death, as a result of the ***1807 Acts***, the cotton gin caused an explosive demand for slave labor in the South. The Hydra—slavery—grew another's head, with eyes looking northward, as the only source for slaves, since smuggling had vanished as a real option. The need for slaves drove everything related to socio-economic and political needs and demands for a replacement population of slaves in the Deep South, until and up to Civil War.

Although very little is said by American historians about the Upper South States' *"exporting or internal slave trade,"* the facts of its existence bears repeating. Breeding and the internal slave trade systems were very well established, by the 1780s. The internal slave trade and breeding slaves enterprise was variously called the *"domestic slave trade,"* the *"Second Middle Passage,"* and the *"interregional slave trade,"* by American historians. It is my opinion this was to minimize stating actually what it was, a system for breeding and supplying slaves to the Deep South.

The domestic slave trade within the United States bred slaves, during the antebellum period—*time before rebellion*. Historians estimate that slavers transported over one million slaves in a forced migration from the Upper South: Virginia, Maryland, Delaware, Tennessee, Kentucky, North Carolina, and Washington D. C. Their slave went to the newly admitted states and territories in the Deep South and Western Territories: Georgia, Alabama, Arkansas, Louisiana, Mississippi, and Texas.

The internal slave trade and breeding industry, as shown above, had been growing continuously since the 1730s in Upper South states, principally Virginia, Maryland, and Delaware. The domestic slave trade within the United States did not begin, as is often assumed, with the demise of the **Trans-Atlantic Slave Trade** in 1807. It originated over a half century earlier in the 1730s and overlapped the end of the **Trans-Atlantic Slave Trade** from Africa. During the 33 year grace period provided in the ***1807 Act***, ending the importation of slaves into America, many land-hungry settlers were attracted to the South's new lands. Moreover, planters brought tens of thousands of slaves into the Deep South, more than during the previous two decades, hoping to import sufficient numbers, (*Some Economic Aspects of the Domestic Slave Trade, 1830–1860"*: Robert Evans, Jr., 1961; Southern Economic Journal.)

Historians like Ira Berlin, Peter Kolchin , Michael Tidman, James Oliver Horton, Ned, and Constance Sublette, as well as others, provide some very penetrating and provocative research on the subject of the internal slave trade and breeding. Their works serves as a major resource for anyone desiring in-depth knowledge on this subject. Northern states passed legislation, only incrementally ending slavery. Therefore, abolition was an ever-present possibility for slaveholders in the North.

As a result of this gradualist approach, New York did not free its last slaves until 1829. Rhode Island had five slaves still listed in the 1840 census. Pennsylvania (the Quaker State) freed its last slaves in 1847, and Connecticut did not completely abolish slavery until 1848. New Hampshire (Vermont was still part of New Hampshire until 1791) still had slaves in 1848. It was not until 1846 that New Jersey did what it called emancipating slaves, but qualified it by redefining slaves as apprentices, who were "apprenticed for life" to their masters. In 1830, of the 3,568 northern blacks, who remained slaves, more than two-thirds were in New Jersey, (*Slaves Without Masters: The Free Negro in the Antebellum South*, Ira Berlin, 1992).

North America imported approximately 427,000 Africans, but by emancipation, in 1863, the US slave population had grown to more than ten times that number. During the antebellum period, slaves in the US showed a natural population growth of some 25 percent per decade *("The Demographic Cost of Sugar: Debates on Slave Societies and Natural Increase in the Americas,"* Michael Tadman, 2000; The American Historical Review.) So far, as history reveals, no other slave society, whether of antiquity or modern times, has sustained, much less greatly multiplied, its slave population by relying on *"natural increase"* only, (*American Counterpoint: Slavery and Racism in the North/South Dialogue,* C. Vann Woodward, (Oxford, 1983).

Much of the wealth along the northeastern seaboard was tied to ocean commerce, most prominently transporting cotton and slaves. Many northern politicians and businesspeople were not eager to end the importation of slaves. Pressure from Great Britain, during the War of 1812, pushed the US and Southerners particularly, to allow the US Navy to enforce the slave blockade around southern ports along the East and Southern coasts, as well as apprehend smugglers. (There is no statement as to what happened to slaves the US navy captures from smugglers).

Slaveholders were desperately looking for ways to keep slaves coming into the South in 1808, a year after passage of **The Act Prohibiting the Importation of Slaves of 1807**. Even though businesspeople may have disagreed with slavery, they were unwilling to relinquish slavery's huge profits. Southerners had allies in the North, who were looking to sell slaves southward, particularly facing the prospect of losing money to abolition.

Although slavery was ending elsewhere in the world, the Southern US doubled down on slavery. They hoped to take advantage of the opportunities the cotton gin offered. Many slaveholders, after trying other methods to obtain sufficient numbers of slaves for cotton production, readily accepted breeding a replacement workforce of slaves, as the South's only option.

There was a large interregional slave migration (i.e., migration not due to the slave trade). Planters relocated their entire slave populations to the Deep South to develop new plantations or take over existing ones. The internal slave trade, in the Upper South and the Border States of the North, was based on breeding and supplying slaves to the Deep South. This system brought huge economic and social changes to America, (*American Slave Coast: A History of the Slave-Breeding Industry*, Ned and Constance Sublette 2016; Chicago Review Press Chicago IL.)

Moving slaves through the internal slave trade system had two elements. The substantial majority—from 60 to 70 percent (or 1.2 million people)—of slaves went by the long-distance domestic slave route, while the rest were part of planter migrations. Planters looking for new opportunities moved all or most of their slaves together to work new western land.

The Indian Removal Act by President Andrew Jackson (1830) robbed at least a million Native People of their lands, which were given to whites for "pennies on the dollar." The US government displaced Native People to make their lands available to whites. The availability of land pushed up demands for workers to clear land, cultivate cotton, rice and sugar cane crops.

The extensive development of cotton plantations created the highest demand for labor in the Deep South. Settlers moving southward demanded the land belonging to the *Five Civilized Tribes* and other Native People. The cotton gin, coupled with the labor-intensive nature of cotton, made slave labor an insatiable need in the Deep South. Southerners believed that demand could only be satisfied by breeding a replacement workforce.

To be *"sold down river"* was a dreaded fate for slave populations. Some destinations, particularly the sugar cane fields and plantations of Louisiana, were reputed to be horrific. The resulting movement destroyed families and was the reason slaves looked upon the domestic slave trade with such dread. Francis Fedric, who was born in Virginia and sold away to Kentucky, was part of such a terrifying force march and described its separation:

"Men and women down on their knees, begging to be purchased to go with their wives or husbands... children crying and imploring not to have their parents sent away from them, but all their beseeching and tears were of no avail. They were ruthlessly separated, most of them forever."

Speculators—slave buyers—preferred what they termed *"young and likely Negroes,"* mainly teenagers and young adults. This market developed its own terminology with such terms as, *"prime-aged slaves,"* ages 15–30, which accounted for 70 percent of the slave population relocated to the Deep South. Speculators wanted *"prime bucks"* to perform hard labor and the potential for lasting years. They also looked for young *"breeding wenches"* with many years of childbearing ahead. The great majority of slaves forced to migrate, trekked southward chained together in *"cofflers."* Sella Martin made "that dreaded and despairing journey from North Carolina to Georgia." He described such a convoy in which he and his mother were a part:

A long row of men chained two-and-two together, called a "cofflers" and num-bering about thirty persons, was the first to march forth from the "pen," then came the quiet slaves - that is, those who were tame and degraded—then came the unmarried women or those without children; after these came the children who were able to walk; and following them came mothers with their infants and young children in their arms."

Charles Ball was marched from Maryland to South Carolina, across three states, in a fifty-person coffle:

"The women were tied together with a rope, about the size of a bed cord, which was tied like a halter around the neck of each; but the men . . . were very differently caparisoned. A strong iron collar was closely fitted by means of a padlock round each of our necks. A chain of iron about a hundred feet long was passed through the hasp of each padlock, except at the two ends, where the hasps of the padlocks passed through a link of the chain. In addition to this, we were handcuffed in pairs."

Major traders moved south in what was called *"droves"* of up to three hundred people. These terrible journeys usually took seven to eight weeks and covered upwards of six hundred miles. En route, enslave Africans would sleep in tents or other rough accommodations. Once traders reached their destinations, they wielding guns and whips to keep of control slaves, after removing chains, preparing their "product" for market.

Though *"coffles"* were the primary means of transport, however as railroad routes became more extensive, by the late 1830s and early 1840s, rails also were used. In 1856, Lyman Abbot, a Northern visitor to the South, found that *"every train south has slaves on board . . . twenty or more, and [has] a 'nigger car,' which is generally also the smokers' car, and sometimes the baggage car."* Sometimes buyers, once they made purchases in ones or twos, sent people to collect them. Traders also moved gangs of people along waterways—the Mississippi River from St. Louis to Natchez and New Orleans. Also, the Alabama River from Montgomery to Mobile was used to get to New Orleans by sea.

The vast majority of slave owners relied on the *"domestic or internal"* slave trade. According to Ned Sublette, co-author of <u>The American Slave Coast</u>, states, *"The reproductive worth of 'breeding women' was essential to the South's prosperity, not just for labor but as merchandise and collateral stemming from a shortage of silver, gold, or sound paper tender."* He concluded that *"In a market premised on the continual expansion of slavery, slaves and their descendants were used as human savings accounts. They functioned as the basis of money and credit with newborns serving as interest."*

David Brion Davis said in <u>*"Slavery, Sex, and Dehumanization,"*</u> slave breeding included *"any practices of slave ownership, which were designed to systematically influence the reproduction of slaves to increase the wealth of slaveholders. Slave breeding included coerced sexual relations between male and female slaves and promoting pregnancies of slave women while favoring female slaves that produce relatively large numbers of children."* During this time, terms like *"breeding slaves," "childbearing women," "breeding period,"* and *"too old to breed"* became familiar terms, (*Slavery and Rice Culture in Low Country Georgia, 1750-1860*, Julia Floyd Smith, 1991; University of Tennessee Press). The purpose of *"breeding slaves"* was to acquire new slaves without incurring the cost of purchase and to fill labor shortages caused by the termination of the **Trans-Atlantic Slave Trade,** (*Sex, Power, and Slavery*: Gwyn Campbell and Elizabeth Elbourne, 2014; Ohio University Press, Athens, OH.)

Sex, Power, and Slavery is a collection of writings by 26 authors from diverse scholarly backgrounds who looked at the vexing and traumatic intersections of the history of slavery and sexuality. They argue that such intersections mattered profoundly and, indeed, understanding slavery is difficult without adequate attention to sexuality. *Sex, Power, and Slavery* bring into the conversation historians of the slave trade, art historians, and scholars of childhood and contemporary sex trafficking. It merges work on the slavery worlds of the Atlantic and Indian Ocean enabling rich comparisons and parallels between these diverse areas by such outstanding writers as David Brion Davis, Martin Klein, Richard Hellie, Abdul Sheriff, E. Ann McDougall, Marie Rodet, Ulrike Schmieder, Tara Iniss, Mariana Candido, James Francis Warren, Johanna Ransmeier, Roseline Uyanga, Marie-Luise Ermisch, Francesca Ann Louise Mitchell, and Salah Trabel are excellent examples.

Looking back to the beginning of breeding, during the 1760s, Pennsylvania, New York, New Jersey, and Massachusetts were also exporting slaves southwards. Slave traders also called *"speculators,"* regularly advertised in the Boston Gazette for *"healthy slaves, . . . Male or Female who have been some years in the Country, of twenty Years of Age or under."* Advertisements in the South Carolina Gazette verify this trend. Stories of numerous men and women who bought from Northern colonies appeared regularly. The slave trader Austin Moses advertised in Richmond, Virginia, for: *"One hundred Negroes from 20 to 30 years old for which a good price will be given. They are to be sent out of state; therefore we shall not be particular respecting character of any of them, hearty and well-made is all that is necessary,"* (*American Slave Coast: A History of the Slave-Breeding Industry*, Ned and Constance Sublette, 2016; Chicago Review Press, Chicago IL.)

According to the Sublettes, the American *"slave-breeding industry"* worked like this. *"Some states (most importantly, Virginia) produced slaves as their main "domestic crop."* Industries in states that consumed slaves in the production of cotton, rice and sugar, and constant territorial expansion anchored slave prices. Breeders could literally bank on future demand increasing prices, as the demand for slave continued growing.

Rising prices made slaves not just a commodity, but the closest thing to money that white breeders had. It's hard to quantify just how valuable slaves were as commodities, but the Sublettes calculated it this way: *"By a conservative* *estimate, in 1860 of the total value of American slaves was $4 billion, far more than the nations gold and silver supply, circulated then nationally ($228.3 million, "most of it in the North,"), total currency ($435.4 million), and even the value of the South's total farmland ($1.92 billion). Slaves were, to slaver masters, worth more than everything they could imagine combined."*

By the 1790s, Virginia, Maryland, and Delaware were the main slave exporting areas, the bulk of their *"slave shipments"* went to Georgia, Tennessee, Kentucky, the Carolinas, and the sugar-planting regions of Louisiana. Between 1790 and 1859, slaveholders in Virginia sold more than half a million slaves Southward. Maryland's slave dealers sold upwards of 185,000 slaves. Kentucky slaveholders sold more than 71,000 individuals. Most slave traders carried their slaves further south to Alabama, Louisiana, and Mississippi.

Moreover, by the 1820s, the Carolinas and Kentucky were exporting more slaves than they imported. For example, in South Carolina during the 1850s, transported 65,000 African Americans out of state, but still, the state's cotton production rose by 50,000 bales and its enslaved population increased by 17,000; *"breeding slaves was really big business"* (*American Slave Coast: A History of the Slave-Breeding Industry*, Ned and Constance Sublette, 2016; Chicago Review Press, Chicago IL.)

The total number of African Americans in the USA increased to 4.4 million, and of that number, 3.95 million were held in bondage until 1863, (*When Cotton Was King*, Gene Dattel, 2011; Opinionator New York Times). The dry bones in the valley of slavery continued growing, as the internal slave trade began to pull poor whites, bottom rung, into the internal slave trade and out of poverty. They became grave diggers in the valley of dry bones, which was swallowing slaves like a giant Hydra, toward the end of the 1820s.

The Making of the Middle Class in the South

In 1787, there was virtually no cotton grown in America. Two things, however, quickly changed that. Eli Whitney's cotton gin allowed cotton production to go from a process limited by manual labor to an industrial machine, allowing a person to "clean" 50 pounds, rather than one pound, of cotton a day. And of course, the cotton gin didn't remove manual labor from the process; it just shifted it. In fact, this labor-saving device extended slavery by creating a labor shortage in the cotton fields. (When Cotton Was King, Gene Dattel, 2011; Opinionator: New York Times)

Slavery, after 1807, became a three or four maybe even five-headed Hydra. Supporters of **The Act Prohibiting the Importation of Slaves of (1807)** believed with legislation; they had cut off the head and killed the single-headed monster. However, unlike the epic heroes in England that fought the monster—slavery—to the death, those in America found themselves confronting a very different Hydra. Decapitating it did not cause it to wither and die a natural death, as most thought. Rather than die, with government help, slavery in America produced whatever it needed to survive. The Southern Hydra grew heads that began spitting out little Hydra—minions—that defended it against attack. The economic system—the internal slave trade—produced myriad opportunities for poor whites, which made them allies in the fight to preserve slavery as the South's economic engine.

Why slavery did not die in the US, as elsewhere, is a proposition that requires intimate knowledge of the South's socioeconomic and political society? Southerners' attitudes gave them a sense of entitlement and white superiority. The death of slavery would have run counter to the southern socioeconomic and political order. Their mindset was supported by what southerners saw as "self-preservation."

Also, Ely Whitney's cotton gin created ready access to wealth for whites, whether already rich or poor. I repeat, the cotton gin created a world no one imagined in 1807. By the time the 200th (1819) rolls around, the gin had changed the South in ways, even ignorant bottom rung penniless whites had access to wealth.

Prior to Whitney's invention, Southern society was static, with rich planters/slaveholders at the top and slaves on the very bottom. Those in-between mattered very little to the socioeconomic structure of white society. The cotton gin changed the foundation of *"the Southern way of life."* Due to changing socioeconomic status and political power, white people with money were forced to accommodate the demands of the internal slave trade and breeding. This new structure had to respond to the need to produce a constant and sufficient workforce of slaves. Completely undercutting those that thought they had struck a killing blow against slavery with the **1807 Act**, Whitney's 1793 invention made

"Cotton King." Slave masters were convinced the South's only means of satisfying the need for increased cotton production was slavery.

Daily, the explosive need for slaves to clear land and turn that land into cotton cultivation increased the price of slaves. Satisfying the need for workers to clear the South's forest-covered land, brought more and more black bodies into the Deep South to satiate that ravenous and exploding demand. The process of clearing land became an unexpected bonanza for some. Southern lumber became a competitive commercial product, adding another source of wealth and jobs, with the need for more and more land.

Once cleared, the hot dry, formerly forest-covered low-quality soil throughout the Deep South and out West fetched top dollar. Breeding slaves became the chief source of securing labor, not only to clear land and work the fields of the South, but a whole new livelihood for poor whites came with the internal slave trade. Breeding slaves created all kinds of new and unimagined opportunities for poor whites.

The new internal slave system required a new infrastructure to deliver more and more slaves to clear and work fields far away from the ocean. It created a demand for overseers, guards, transporters, and way stations to house and attend slaves in transit. While in transit, getting slaves from the Upper South to markets in the Deep South and West required regular attendants.

The *"slave breeding industry"* gave poor whites regular jobs transporting, guarding, attending, and protecting slaves in transit. Poor whites became vendors, serving migration routes, as slaves moved from North to South or from the upper South into the Deep South, as well as out West. Slaves moved through networks of pens, yards, warehouses, and temporary billets. Poor whites found niches, providing all sought of goods—clothing, food, shackles, chains, repairs, and other supplies, as well as services. Slaves demanded attendants like horses in transit, (<u>Branches without Roots, Genesis of the Black Working Class in the American South 1862-1882,</u> Gerald D. Jaynes 1986; Oxford University Press, New York).

Most poor whites in the South, before the internal slave trade and breeding slaves, had no way to make a regular living, other than as overseers on plantations and other small industries. These jobs served a very limited labor pool. Considered *"poor white trash, bottom rung,"* most whites were too poor to ever hope of own a slave. But, the advent of this new economy, *"breeding slaves"* in the *"internal slave trade"* made them stakeholders. With this change, maintaining slavery, as a way of life, became a fixture in the mindset of poor whites. These minions became the South's middle class.

Similar to slave masters, poor whites, for the first time, began developing attitudes that slaves—black people—were a commodity, products that gave them a stake in the southern economy. Once able to make a living in this new industry, poor whites began viewing all black people as property, which belonged in the South. Southerners' mindset created the concept of blacks being the property of the South specifically. Therefore, black people other places were "runaways," that needed to be brought back to their rightful owners the South. Consequently, the concept developed that blacks had to be captured and returned, wherever they were found.

Transporting slaves overland and maintaining them through the internal slave trade's labyrinth became an industry unto itself. The dramatic increase in demands for slaves across the Deep South by 1810, drew whites on all levels of society into the effort to preserve the South's economic engine—slavery. Rather than diminishing, the 1807 **Act prohibiting the Importation of Slaves** caused that monster—slavery—to grow another head and produce minions to serve its needs. This five-headed monster gobbled up black skin anywhere it could be found. Southerners found it impossible to satiate the ravenous appetite for black bodies in fields, factories mills, and mines.

Fewer than 300,000 bales of cotton were produced nationally in the US in 1820. Over the next few years (1830), the amount doubled to 600,000 bales. Production reached into the millions, during the rising tide of breeding slaves in the internal slave trade of the 1840s. Once the 1850s arrived, production levels had ballooned. As a result, American cotton production exploded from almost nothing in 1787 to over 4.5 million bales, at 500 lbs., a bale by 1860.

On the eve of the Civil War, cotton comprised almost 60 percent of America's exports. The mass production of cotton produced a dramatic 90 percent drop in the price of a cotton textile garment. The consumer revolutions of raw material were slave-produced—cotton—80 percent produced in the South. (_"When Cotton Was King,"_ Gene Dattel, 2011; Opinionator: New York Times)

Such volumes required at least a tripling, if not quadrupling of the South's slave labor force to attain such production levels. Where would they have come from if not the internal slave trade's breeding operations? White men did not work in fields. That was beneath a white man. That was *"nigger"* work. Many slaveholders saw maintaining the South's economic power through the internal slave trade based on breeding a replacement workforce of slaves, as the South's only answer to its labor demands.

Many southerners deny slave breeding and claim it was never anything more than slave masters and overseers having fun in slave pens. Similar to the War of 1812, American historians try to avoid admitting that slavery controlled everything about southern culture and America's economy.

However, if one looks at the growth of cotton production in early 1800, compared to production levels beginning in 1830, the bodies working fields had to come from someplace to offset attrition.

Historian Ira Berlin saw the impact of the internal slave trade and breeding on slaves writing in _Many Thousands Gone: The First Two Centuries of Slavery in North America_:

The 400th: From Slavery to Hip Hop

"Forced migration was the 'Second Middle Passage' because it reproduced many of the same horrors as the Triangular Trade's Middle Passage during the transportation of slaves from Africa to North America. This large migration of slaves broke up many families and caused many hardships."

Peter Kolchin in <u>American Slavery: 1619-1877</u> (2008) wrote, *"By breaking up existing families and forcing slaves to relocate far away from everyone and everything they knew, replicated (if on a reduced level) many of [the] horrors of the Atlantic slave trade."* As a group tragedy, the forced migration of so many, along with breeding replacement workers, had to be horrific on an individual level as well. Historians estimate that during the decades between 1810 thru 1860, slave holders forced over one million slaves to leave their state of origin as part of forced migration, as they became part of this new Middle Passage. Conservatively, by 1860, the "slave population" in the US increased to over 4 million.

Michael Tadman, who wrote in <u>Speculators and Slaves: Masters, Traders, and Slaves in the Old South (1989)</u>, that *"60–70% of interregional migrations were the result of the sale of slaves. A child slave in the Upper South in 1820 had a 30% chance of being sold southward by 1860."* Again, with such volumes of slaves constantly on the move across the South, similar to the impact of slavery in Europe during the 1700s, its commerce benefitted those not directly involved in the internal slave trade. Hundreds of thousands of whites benefitted from this new land-based slave trade.

Historian Ira Berlin speculates that *"internal slave routes transported two-thirds of the slaves carried west."* Traders created regular migration routes served by networks of slave pens, yards, and warehouses. Moving slave to market required the same level of organization and a similar level of efficiency, as moving cotton to market. Again, as shown above, poor whites could become vendors providing all sought of goods and services. Traders had to ensure their property arrived in top condition, the same as livestock in transit.

Needing temporary housing, guards to attend and protect slaves in transit, as well as bounty hunters to track down slave raiders, also created opportunities for poor whites to make livings. The movie *"Django Unchained"* starring Jamie Foxx and Samul L Jackson is a graphic depiction of this period. Although fictional, it portrays enslaved African's reality.

Any poor white man, looking for a way to make a living, had only to be willing to go on the road. Enterprising bottom rung whites found opportunities to build a life on the backs of slaves. Slavery entrapped Africans in a dehumanizing death grip. Poor white southerners gained more than profits from slavery because it changed their living conditions, which were just above slave status.

Poor whites did not want to give up the respectability and prosperity that *"breeding slaves and the internal slave trade"* brought them. For instance, New Jersey passed a law in 1812, increasing the penalties for exporting slaves to the booming slave markets in the South. By 1820 there were reports slaves in New Jersey selling for $300 were bringing as much as 800 dollars in New Orleans (*The Planter "Aristocracy,"* Regan Miller 2014). Ira Berlin concluded, *"In all, the slave trade, with its hubs and regional centers, its spurs and circuits, reached into every cranny of southern society. Few southerners, black or white, were untouched by this new system."*

In Their Own Words Slave Narratives

Having detailed the world whites forced upon enslaved Africans, and their treatment, even as slavery was ebbing, it was clear, the US was not changing. Now, I present how slaves saw that world. The unchanging mindset of slave masters reflect a totally different mindset on the part of enslaved Africans. There is a record of slaves' attitudes revealed through the folk history of slavery in the United States. This history exists as a result of interviews of former slaves by the Federal Writers' Project of the Works Progress Administration (WPA) from the 1930s. Slave narratives were compiled as records, after the fact, to establish and document enslaved Africans' lives in southern states. Slave narratives are literary accounts of enslaved Africans.

The practice of collecting slave narratives began in Great Britain and its colonies, which later extended to the United States, Canada, and Caribbean nations in later years. Some six thousand former slaves from North America and the Caribbean gave accounts of their lives in the 18th and 19th centuries. One hundred fifty of these narratives are published accounts, as separate books or pamphlets. During the 1930s in the United States, as part of the Great Depression projects followed Great Britain's example once again. More than 2300, but an overall total of 10,000 of additional oral histories on slave lives from American slavery were collected by writers sponsored and published by the Works Progress Administration (WPA) of President Franklin D. Roosevelt's administration.

Introducing slave narratives, as part of ***"The 400th"*** gives voice to those the commemoration is all about. It is one thing, to be told slaves' stories concerning their survival and endurance, but to hear or read their stories in their own words, removes any thoughts of interpretations, filters, or characterizations. Moreover, I believe, through the very few slave narratives I present, readers will gain a realistic connection to what and how slaves felt and thought about their treatment, condition, mental state, fears, believes, and the sense of commonality that developed over the centuries. Their common connection they forged is the reason enslaved Africans today identify as one people. These narratives are all that is left of real live human beings. The factual stories they tell are from the last generation of slaves. Today, in hindsight, I wish I had been able to record the stories my great-grandfather, Burl Lee, shared with me, but I did not have that ability.

Wash Anderson

A frail, sickly man dressed neatly in white pajamas, lay patiently in a clean bed, awaiting the end, which did not seem far away. Although we protested against his talking, because of his weakened condition, he told a brief story of his life in whispers, his breath very short, and every word spoken came with great effort. His light skin and bald head denote no characteristic of his race. Graying around the crown and a slight growth of gray whiskers about his face was the only telltale signs of his years. Wash Anderson, although born in Charleston, S.C., had spent most of his life in Texas

"*Mos' folks call me Wash Anderson, but dey uster call me George. My whole name's George Washington Anderson. I was bo'n in Charleston, Sou'f Ca'lina in 1855. Bill Anderson was my ol' marster. Dey was two boy' and two gal' in his family. We all lef' Charleston and come to Orange, Texas, befo' freedom come. I was fo' year' ol' when dey mek dat trip. I don' 'member nuttin' 'bout Charleston. You see where I was bo'n was 'bout two mile' from de city. I went back one time in 1917, but I didn' stay dere long.*

My pa was Irvin' Anderson and my mommer was name' Eliza. Ol' marster was pretty rough on his niggers. Dey tell me he had my gran'daddy beat to death. Dey never did beat me. Dey made de trip from Charleston 'cross de country and settle' in Duncan's Wood' down here in Orange county. Dey had a big plantation dere. I dunno if ol' marster had money back in Charleston, but I t'ink he must have. He had 'bout 25 or 30 slaves on de place."

Ol' man Anderson he had a big two-story house. It was buil' out of logs but it was a big fine house. De slaves jis' had little log huts. Dere warn't no flo's to 'em, nuthin' but de groun'. Dem little huts jis' had one room in 'em. Dey was one family to de house, 'cep'n' sometime dey put two or t'ree family' to a house. Dey jis' herd de slaves in dere like a bunch of pigs.

Dey uster raise cotton, and co'n, and sugar cane, and sich like, but dey didn' uster raise no rice. Dey uster sen' stuff to Terry on a railroad to sen' it to market. Sometime dey hitch up dey teams and sen' it to Orange and Beaumont in wagons. De ol' marster he had a boat, too, and sometime he sen' a boatload of his stuff to Beaumont.

My work was to drive de surrey for de family and look atter de hosses and de harness and sich. I jis' have de bes' hosses on de place to see atter. I saw lots of sojers durin' de war. I see 'em marchin' by, goin' to Sabine Pass 'bout de time of dat battle. Back in slavery time dey uster have a white preacher to come 'roun' and preach to de cullud folks. Dey had plenty of hosses and mules and cows on de ol' plantation. I had to look atter some of de hosses, but dem what I hatter look atter was s'pose to be de bes' hosses in de bunch. Dey had a log stable. Dey kep' de harness in dere, too.

Atter freedom come I went 'roun' doin' dif'rent kind of work. I uster work on steamboats, and on de railroad and at sawmillin'. I was a sawyer for a long, long time. I work 'roun' in Lou'sana and Arkansas, and Oklahoma, as well as in Texas. When I was 'bout 36 year' ol' I git marry. I been married twice. My fus' wife was name' Hannah and Reverend George Childress was de preacher dat marry us. He was a cullud preacher. Atter Hannah been dead some time I marry my secon' wife. Her name was Tempie Perkins. Later on, us sep'rate on 'count of money matters."

Sarah Ashley on the Slave Block

Sarah Ashley, 93, was born in Mississippi. She recalls her experiences when sold on the block in New Orleans, and a cotton plantation in Texas. She now lives at Goodrich, Texas.

"I ain't able to do nothin' no more. I's jus' plumb give out and I stays here by myself. My daughter, Georgia Grime, she used to live with me but she's been dead four year. I was born in Miss'ippi and Massa Henry Thomas buy us and bring us here. He a spec'lator and buys up lots of niggers and sells 'em. Us family was sep'rated. My two sisters and my papa was sold to a man in Georgia. Den dey put me on a block and bid me off. Dat in New Orleans and I scairt and cry, but dey put me up dere anyway. First dey takes me to Georgia and dey didn't sell me for a long spell. Massa Thomas he travel round and buy and sell niggers. Us stay in de spec'lators long time.

After 'while Massa Mose Davis come from Cold Spring, in Texas, and buys us. He was buyin' up little chillen for he chillen. Dat 'bout four year befo' da first war. I was 19 year old when de burst of freedom come in June and I git turn loose. I was workin' in de field den. Jus' befo' dat de old Massa he go off and buy more niggers. He go east. He on a boat what git stove up and he die and never come back no more.

I used to have to pick cotton and sometime I pick 300 pound and tote it a mile to de cotton house. Some pick 300 to 800 pound cotton and have to tote de bag de whole mile to de gin. Iffen dey didn't do dey work dey git whip till dey have blister on 'em. Den iffen dey didn't do it, de man on a hoss goes down de rows and whip with a paddle make with holes in it and bus' de blisters. I never git whip, 'cause I allus git my 300 pound. Us have to go early to do dat, when de horn goes early, befo' daylight. Us have to take de victuals in de bucket to de field.

Massa have de log house and us live in little houses, strowed in long rows. Dere wasn't no meetin's 'lowed in de quarters and iffen dey have prayer meetin' de boss man whip dem. Sometime us run off at night and go to camp meetin'. I takes de white chillen to church sometime, but dey couldn't larn me to sing no songs 'cause I didn' have no spirit.

Us never got 'nough to eat, so us keeps stealin' stuff. Dey give us de peck of meal to last de week and two, three pound bacon in chunk. Us never have flour or sugar, jus' cornmeal and de meat and 'taters. De niggers has de big box under de fireplace, where dey kep' all de pig and chickens what dey steal, down in salt. De way dey whip de niggers was to strip 'em off naked and whip 'em till dey make blisters and bus' de blisters. Den dey take de salt and red pepper and put in de wounds. When de boss man told us freedom was come he didn't like it, but he give all us de bale of cotton and some corn. He ask us to stay and he'p with de crop but we'uns so glad to git 'way dat nobody stays."

Slavery Days of Mandy Cooper

Frank Cooper, an aged colored man of Franklin, relates some very interesting conditions that existed in slavery days as handed down to him by his mother. Mandy Cooper, the mother of Frank Cooper, was 115 years old when she died; she was owned by three different families: the Good's, the Burton's, and the Cooper's, all of Lincoln Co. Kentucky.

"Well, Ah reckon Ah am one of the oldest colored men hereabouts," confessed aged Frank Cooper. "What did you all want to see me about?" My mission being stated, he related one of the strangest categories alluding to his mother's slave life that I have ever heard."

"One day while mah mammy was washing her back my sistah noticed ugly disfiguring scars on it. Inquiring about them, we found, much to our amazement, that they were mammy's relics of the now gone, if not forgotten, slave days. This was her first reference to her "misery days" that she had evah made in my presence. Of course we all thought she was tellin' us a big story and we made fun of her. With eyes flashin', she stopped bathing, dried her back and reached for the smelly ole black whip that hung behind the kitchen door. Biddin' us to strip down to our waists, my little mammy with the boney bent-ovah back, struck each of us as hard as evah she could with that black-snake whip, each stroke of the whip drew blood from our backs. "Now", she said to us, "you have a taste of slavery days." With three of her children now having tasted of some of her "misery days" she was in the mood to tell us more of her sufferings; still indelibly impressed in my mind.

'My ole back is bent ovah from the quick-tempered blows feld by the red-headed Miss Burton. At dinner time one day when the churnin' wasn't finished for the noonday meal, she said with an angry look that must have been reborn in mah mammy's eyes—eyes that were dimmed by years and hard livin", 'Three white women beat me from anger because they had no butter for their biscuits and cornbread. Miss Burton used a heavy board while the missus used a whip. While I was on my knees beggin' them to quit, Miss Burton hit the small of mah back with the heavy board. Ah knew no more until kind Mr. Hamilton, who was staying with the white folks, brought me inside the cabin and brought me around with the camphor bottle. Ah'll always thank him—God bless him—he picked me up where they had left me like a dog to die in the blazin' noonday sun.

After mah back was broken it was doubted whether ah would evah be able to work again or not. Ah was placed on the auction block to be bidded for so mah owner could see if ah was worth anything or not. One man bid $1700 after puttin' two dirty fingahs in my mouth to see my teeth. Ah bit him and his face showed angah. He then wanted to own me so he could punish me.

'Thinkin' his bid of $1700 was official he unstrapped his buggy whip to beat me, but my mastah saved me. My master declared the bid unofficial. "At this auction my sister was sold for $1900 and was never seen by us again.

My mother related some experiences she had with the Paddy-Rollers, later called the "Kuklux", These Paddy-Rollers were a constant dread to the Negroes. They would whip the *poor darkeys unmercifully without any cause. One night while the Negroes were gathering for a big party and dance they got wind of the approaching Paddy-Rollers in large numbers on horseback. The Negro men did not know what to do for protection, they became desperate and decided to gather a quantity of grapevines and tied them fast at a dark place in the road. When the Paddy-Rollers came thundering down the road bent on deviltry and unaware of the trap set for them, plunged head-on into these strong grapevines and three of their numbers were killed and a score was badly injured. Several horses had to be shot following injuries. When the news of this happening spread it was many months before the Paddy-Rollers were again heard of."*

Mary Reynolds Slave Narrative

Mary Reynolds claims to be more than a hundred years old. She was born in slavery to the Kilpatrick family, in Black River, Louisiana. Mary now lives at the Dallas County Convalescent Home. She has been blind for five years and is very feeble.

"My paw's name was Tom Vaughn and he was from the north, born free man and lived and died free to the end of his days. He wasn't no eddicated man, but he was what he calls himself a piano man. He told me once he lived in New York and Chicago and he built the insides of pianos and knew how to make them play in tune. He said some white folks from the south told he if he'd come with them to the south he'd find a lot of work to do with pianos in them parts, and he come off with them.

We prays for the end of Trib'lation and the end of beatin's and for shoes that fit our feet. We prayed that us niggers could have all we wanted to eat and special for fresh meat. Some the old ones say we have to bear all, cause that all we can do. Some say they was glad to the time they's dead, cause they'd rather rot in the ground than have the beatin's. What I hated most was when they'd beat me and I didn't know what they beat me for, and I hated they strippin' me naked as the day I was born.

When we's comin' back from that prayin', I thunk I heared the nigger dogs and somebody on horseback. I say, Maw, its them nigger hounds and they'll eat us up.' You could hear them old hounds and sluts abayin'. Maw listens and say, Sho nough, them dogs am running' and Gawd help us!' Then she and paw talk and they take us to a fence corner and stands us up gainst the rails and say don't move and if anyone comes near, don't breathe loud. They went to the woods, so the hounds chase them and not git us. Me and Katherine stand there, holdin' hands, shakin' so we can hardly stand. We hears the hounds come nearer, but we don't move. They goes after paw and maw, but they circles round to the cabins and gits in. Maw say its the power of Gawd.

In them days I weared shirts, like all the young'uns. They had collars and come below the knees and was split up the sides. That's all we weared in hot weather. The men weared jeans and women gingham. Shoes was the worstes' trouble. We weared rough russets when it got cold, and it seem powerful strange they'd never git them to fit. Once when I was a young gal, they got me a new pair and all brass studs in the toes. They was too li'l for me, but I had to wear them. The trimmin's cut into my ankles and them places got mis'ble bad. I rubs tallow in them sore places and wrops rags around them and my sores got worser and worser. The scars are there to this day.

Sallie Carder Oklahoma Narrative

"I was born in Jackson, Tennessee, and I'm going on 83 years. My mother was Harriett Neel and father Jeff Bills, both of them named after their masters. I has one brother, J. B. Bills, but all de rest of my brothers and sisters is dead. No sir, we never had no money while I was a slave. We jest didn't have nothing a-tall! We ate greens, corn bread, and ash cake. De only time I ever got a biscuit would be when a misdemeanor was did, and my Mistress would give a buttered biscuit to de one who could tell her who done it.

In hot weather and cold weather dere was no difference as to what we wore. We wore dresses my mother wove for us and no shoes a-tall. I never wore any shoes till I was grown and den dey was old brogans wid only two holes to lace, one on each side. During my wedding I wore a blue calico dress, a man's shirt tail as a head rag, and a pair of brogan shoes. My Master lived in a three-story frame house painted white. My Mistress was very mean. Sometimes she would make de overseer whip negroes for looking too hard at her when she was talking to dem. Dey had four children, three girls and one boy. I was a servant to my Master, and as he had de palsy I had to care for him, feed him and push him around. I don't know how many slaves, but he had a good deal of 'em. About four o' clock mornings de overseer or negro carriage driver who stayed at the Big House would ring de bell to git up and git to work. De slaves would pick a heap of cotton and work till late on moonshining nights.

Dere was a white post in front of my door with ropes to tie the slaves to whip dem. Dey used a plain strap, another one with holes in it, and one dey call de cat wid nine tails which was a number of straps plated and de ends unplated. Dey would whip de slaves wid a wide strap wid holes in it and de holes would make blisters. Den dey would take de cat wid nine tails and burst de blisters and den rub de sores wid turpentine and red pepper.

I never saw any slaves auctioned off but I seen dem pass our house chained together on de way to be sold, including both men and women wid babies all chained to each other. Dere was no churches for slaves, but at nights dey would slip off and git in ditches and sing and pray, and when dey would sometimes be caught at it dey would be whipped. Some of de slaves would turn down big pots and put dere heads in dem and pray. My Mistress would tell me to be a good obedient slave and I would go to heaven. When slaves would attempt to run off dey would catch dem and chain dem and fetch 'em back and whip dem before dey was turned loose again.

De patrollers would go about in de quarters at nights to see if any of de slaves was out or slipped off. As we sleep on de dirt floors on pallets, de patrollers would walk all over and on us and if we even grunt dey would whip us. De only trouble between de whites and blacks on our plantation was when de overseer tied my mother to whip her and my father untied her and de overseer shot and killed him.

Negroes never was allowed to git sick, and when dey would look somewhat sick, de overseer would give dem some blue-mass pills and oil of some sort and make dem continue to work. During de War de Yankees would pass through and kill up de chickens, and hogs, and cattle, and eat up all dey could find. De day of freedom de overseer went into de field and told de slaves dat dey was free, and de slaves replied, "free how?" and he told dem: "free to work and *live for demselves." And dey said dey didn't know what to do, and so some of dem stayed on. I married Josh Forch. I am mother of four children and 35 grand children.*

I like Abraham Lincoln. I think he was a good man and president. Now dat slavery is over, I don't want to be in nary 'nother slavery, and if ever nary 'nothern come up I wouldn't stay here.

Willie Adams: A True Believer

William Adams, 93, was born in slavery, with no opportunity for an education, except three months in a public school. He has taught himself to read and to write. His lifelong ambition has been to become master of the supernatural powers which he believes to exist. He is now well-known among southwestern Negroes for his faith in the occult.

"Yous want to know and talk about de power de people tells you I has. Well, sit down here, right there in dat chair, befo' we'uns starts. I gits some ice water and den we'uns can discuss de subject. I wants to 'splain it clearly, so yous can understand. I's born a slave, 93 years ago, so of course I 'members de war period. Like all de other slaves I has no chance for edumacation. Three months am de total time I's spent going to school. I teached myself to read and write. I's anxious to larn to read so I could study and find out about many things. Dat, I has done.

There am lots of folks, and edumacated ones, too, what says we'uns believes in superstition. Well, its 'cause dey don't understand. 'Member de Lawd, in some of His ways, can be mysterious. De Bible says so. There am some things de Lawd wants all folks to know, some things jus' de chosen few to know, and some things no one should know. Now, jus' 'cause yous don't know 'bout some of de Lawd's laws, 'taint superstition if some other person understands and believes in sich.

There is some born to sing, some born to preach, and some born to know de signs. There is some born under de power of de devil and have de power to put injury and misery on people, and some born under de power of de Lawd for to do good and overcome de evil power. Now, dat produces two forces, like fire and water. De evil forces starts de fire and I has de water force to put de fire out.

How I larnt sich? Well, I's done larn it. It come to me. When de Lawd gives sich power to a person, it jus' comes to 'em. It am 40 years ago now when I's fust fully realize' dat I has de power. However, I's allus int'rested in de workin's of de signs. When I's a little piccaninny, my mammy and other folks used to talk about de signs. I hears dem talk about what happens to folks 'cause a spell was put on 'em. De old folks in dem days knows more about de signs dat de Lawd uses to reveal His laws den de folks of today. It am also true of de cullud folks in Africa, dey native land. Some of de folks laughs at their beliefs and says it am superstition, but it am knowin' how de Lawd reveals His laws.

Now, let me tell yous of something I's seen. What am seen, can't be doubted. It happens when I's a young man and befo' I's realize' dat I's one dat am chosen for to show de power. A mule had cut his leg so bad dat him am bleedin' to death and dey couldn't stop it. An old cullud man live near there dat dey turns to. He comes over and passes his hand over de cut. Befo' long de bleedin' stop and dat's de power of de Lawd workin' through dat nigger, dat's all it am.

I knows about a woman dat had lost her mind. De doctor say it was caused from a tumor in de head. Dey took an ex-ray picture, but dere's no tumor. Dey gives up and says its a *peculiar case. Dat woman was took to one with de power of de good spirit and he say its a peculiar case for dem dat don't understand. Dis am a case of de evil spell. Two days after, de woman have her mind back.*

Dey's lots of dose kind of cases de ord'nary person never hear about. Yous hear of de case de doctors can't understand, nor will dey 'spond to treatment. Dat am 'cause of de evil spell dat am on de persons. 'Bout special persons bein' chosen for to show de power, read yous Bible. It says in de book of Mark, third chapter, 'and He ordained twelve, dat dey should be with Him, dat He might send them forth to preach and to have de power to heal de sick and to cast out devils. If it wasn't no evil in people, why does de Lawd say, 'cast out sich?' And in de fifth chapter of James, it further say, 'If any am sick, let him call de elders. Let dem pray over him. De prayers of faith shall save him.' There 'tis again, Faith, dat am what counts.

When I tells dat I seen many persons given up to die, and den a man with de power comes and saves sich person, den its not for people to say it am superstition to believe in de power. Don't forgit—de agents of de devil have de power of evil. Dey can put misery of every kind on people. Dey can make trouble with de work and with de business, with de fam'ly and with de health. So folks mus' be on de watch all de time.

I says, 'Its de evil power dat have you control and we'uns shall cause it to be cast out.' Its done and he has no more trouble. You wants to know if persons with de power for good can be successful in castin' out devils in all cases? Well, I answers dat, yes and no. Dey can in every case if de affected person have de faith. If de party not have enough faith, den it am a failure.

Wearin' de coin for protection 'gainst de evil power? Dat am simple. Lots of folks wears sich and dey uses mixtures dat am sprinkled in de house, and sich. Dat am a question of faith. If dey has de true faith in sich, it works. Otherwise, it won't. Some folks won't think for a minute of goin' without lodestone or de salt and pepper mixture in de little sack, tied round dey neck. Some wears de silver coin tied round dey neck. All sich am for to keep away de effect of de evil power.

David Walker's Appeal

This narrative traced the development of the institution of slavery from before the ***Trans-Atlantic Slave Trade,*** through the wars to control it, which ended with slavery's abolition in 1807. Once abolished around the world, slavery lived on in America and Brazil. These were the only countries in the civilized world that allowed the horrid practice to continue. America's version of slavery became an individually base enterprise, not sponsored by the government, but supported and facilitated by it.

Looking at America, where my ancestors were captives, this narrative revealed the machine-like precision of the internal slave trade and breeding. This new enterprise replaced the international slavery system of the Western World. Following the litany of ***"The 400th"***, it highlights the evolution of slavery in America, and details the rise and growth of the *"internal slave trade and breeding industry"* major benefactors, and the socioeconomic practices it spawned.

"The 400th" points out the impact of slavery on poor whites, as individuals, and as a group. During that circuitous ride, through the valley of dry bones, readers were immersed in the commoditization of enslaved Africans, and the system that made them into ***"black gold."*** Enslaved Africans were the oil that lubricated, first the international slave trade then they became wheels as well as lubricant for the southern economy and product of the *"internal slave trade and breeding"* industry.

Now, this epic journey turns to look at the impact slavery had on enslaved Africans from their perspective. Slaves' narratives which I just presented, offered a small sample of how slaves saw their enslavement and their thoughts regarding it. Slaves had only their thoughts or some other individual's description of the uncaring world in which they were entrapped. For their perspective on their situation and conditions to change, slaves needed a new and different mindset about their bondage. They needed a view of the world that confronted them and the reality slavery represented regarding their survival prospects.

The first person to provide such a view was a swashbuckling, devil-may-care, lone rider, David Walker. He was the first descendant of American slavery to present a group perspective of enslaved Africans present and future. Arriving at this point, readers now begin to view the world through the eyes of slaves to learn what they saw as a life and what that perspective meant for them.

Reading slave narratives serves as the doorway into their world; the thing is that door opens in only one direction. Entering, one cannot reverse the flow of information as though they never entered. That view gives readers access to this world, as though trapped there, like one of its victims. Having seen the light, one has to choose to live in darkness.

Once the light of knowledge has entered, one has to pretend ignorance, to avoid acknowledging the light this narrative brings. Enslaved Africans' real life words and world shared in slave narratives penetrated readers' minds, leaving the truth behind that readers now carry forward, as part of their life experience. One can choose to live in darkness, if they wish, but they will never be ignorant of the light truth brought.

David Walker is the first writer of note that tried to give slaves an updated picture of their circumstances. Following the end of slavery around the world, the American internal slave trade and breeding industry made enslavement just a different kind of monster, giving them the worse possible future—perpetual bondage. The reality of unending bondage did not elude free blacks. They were involved in abolition efforts before it became a move.

Historians designate the 1820s until 1860, the antebellum era, meaning the time before the South's rebellion and Civil War. However, for descendants of slavery and far more importantly, it began the time slaves seriously turned to looking for alternatives to slavery even before a strong abolitionist movement development. The major problem for enslaved Africans was they could not envision the scope and breadth of the system that entrapped them or how to think about escaping it.

I believe these times were distinct from previous periods, during slavery, because it marks the first major turning points in the evolution of slaves' thinking, regarding their bondage. For this reason, many African Americans historians call this period the time of David Walker. He more than any black man, of that period, saw the events of this period clearest and penned his reflections in a scathing attack upon slavery: ***Appeal in Four Articles; Together with a Preamble, to the Coloured Citizens of the World, but in Particular and Very Expressly to Those of the United States of America.***

Walker was the first to talk directly to slaves and describe their circumstances in words and ways slaves understood. He explained that slave masters did not consider them human beings and did not care about their survival. Slave masters had converted them from free people into dependent wretches. Walker played a crucial role in slaves' mental evolution, presenting their circumstances in words with which they identified.

Walker left no doubt slaves had to change their thinking. They had to develop a new self-concept and thought process, regarding their prospects for surviving slavery. The key here is slaves had never had their situation explained from the perspective that even though it was a group tragedy, they had to respond to it as individuals. They had to see freedom as a slave's individual responsibility. No hero was going to ride to their rescue!!

Walker said, *"Every black person should obtain a copy of this **Appeal** and read it. If they cannot read, they should find someone who can and get them to read it to them."*

Make no mistake about it the economic system in America was slavery. Southern and northern political leaders supported slavery. They dug in and doubled down with government actions, which reinforced the socio-economic structures of slavery. The internal slave trade and breeding system submersed slaves in an oppressive system without end. Most importantly, from Walker's perspective, the critical reality slaves faced was how they saw themselves, as they reached 1810, three years after slavery ended around the world.

Communication between slaves and slave masters had always been one way—slaves were expected to only acknowledge demands for service. Statements from slave masters to slaves were demands for service. David Walker was the first descendant of American slavery, who addressed his statement directly to slaves, rather than slave masters. Walker's statements created a new perspective and dynamic, he explained enslaved Africans circumstances directly to them. Walker's approach was a major difference in communication and may seem small to some readers today, but back in the 1830s, from an ignorant slaves' perspective, it was huge. I present the following example to clarify the critical difference in the change in communication.

I encountered Olaudah Equiano's (c.1745/3-31-1797) statement about his life as a slave, while digging back through the dry bones in the early graveyard of slavery. I was looking for background information to support my point regarding communications. Stumbling across Olaudah Equiano, a slave who purchased his freedom, and wrote his story, _The Interesting Narrative of the Life of Olaudah Equiano, or Gustavus Vassa, the African (1789)_ was a perfect reflect.

Around age eleven, Equiano and his sister were kidnapped and sold to slave traders. Robert King, a merchant, bought Equiano to work on his shipping routes and manage his stores. King promised Equiano when he was about 20 years old (1765), he could purchase his freedom for 40 pounds (£6000 today). King taught Equiano to read, write, and calculate. He guided him along the path of religion, and Equiano was allowed to engage in profitable trading on his owner's accounts, as well as on his own behalf. Buying his freedom (1780), Equiano felt settling in London would be safer than in the US; because awaiting a ship, he was nearly kidnapped by slave catchers.

Early in 1783, Equiano became associated with abolitionists in Great Britain and MP Granville Sharp. He informed Sharp about the massacre of 133 enslaved Africans by the crew aboard the **Zong** (11-29-1781). The slave ship Zong was owned by the infamous Gregson slave-trading syndicate based in Liverpool. Running low on potable water, the crew threw the 133 slaves overboard into the sea to conserve water.

The crew of the Zong drowned the cargo of slaves, allowed owners to cash in on the insurance, thus avoiding losses on the cargo—slaves. The **Zong** tragedy helped abolitionists in Parliament bring the horrors of slavery before the public and those enjoying the blood money derived from the savage business.

Strongly influenced by Quakers, Equiano joined the *Society for Effecting the Abolition of the Slave Trade*, founded in 1787, 18 years after *James Somerset's* victory. He became a forceful advocate, describing the horrors of the bloody trade. Equiano's narrative recounted his journey and travails in slavery. It provides a powerful and interesting account of what slaves endured. Most importantly, Equiano hoped his writings would affect the conscience of white people and enlist their aid fighting to abolish the monstrous business. Equiano's narrative described the psychological and philosophical impact on slaves, being made into a commodity.

His book fueled a growing trend of publishing slave narratives and excited the anti-slavery movement in Great Britain, on the European continent, and in the New World (Western Hemisphere). Although, not as gruesome and horrific as the process many slaves endured, accounts of Equiano's life, after being captured as a boy, provides insightful details regarding slaves' journey to *The Door of No Return*. Characteristically, it described his treatment and told of communities and people he saw on his trek to the *Slave House on Goreé Island, Dakar, Senegal*. His autobiography details his voyage on a slave ship, after leaving *The Door of No Return*.

Equiano's story takes readers through the desperate condition endured in the hole of a slave ship. His account provided horrible imagery of the pain and toil of a slave's daily drudgery. He reveals further that the brutality of slavery in the colonies of the West Indies was as bad as in Virginia and Georgia in the US.

Equiano's engrossing descriptive narrative evoked shame among many white readers. His firsthand account of the suffering he and other slaves endured drew rich white people, who grew rich on the blood money from slavery into that world. Rummaging among the dry bones in the graveyard of slavery, Olaudah Equiano's story grabbed my attention and I embraced, even more, my great grandfather's lamented, *"Can these dry bones live again?"*

Brought to this point by Equiano, it was still impossible to identify for sure where and who my ancestors were. Slave breeding was growing into a full-blown industry, but I could not locate my ancestors. This narrative showed in the previous sections that the internal slave trade and breeding ripped families apart, even sometimes before the child passes through the breach.

Often, white slavers wanted their child to grow up with a personal slave, and bought babies before birth. The monster—slavery—during the internal slave trade, gobbled up human beings on one side of its mouth, while spitting dry bones out the other side. Slaves in America endured a different kind of bondage; they were only commodities, the same as cattle or horses, but their bondage was even more degrading.

Although it is tremendously important and had very serious consequences for those it touched, breeding slaves had its greatest impact on individual children. It denied many descendants of American slavery any personal family bonds, not even with their mothers. Here we may be talking about millions of orphans.

The definition says an orphan is a child deprived by death of one or both parents. Then, it goes on to specify young animals that lose their mothers, as orphans. I will admit there are other definitions, but the interesting thing in the context of this discussion, if a child's mother and/or father is alive, but the child never knew them, are they not considered orphans, because some children ever laid eyes on their mother or father. In such cases, millions of enslaved babies born during breeding; if not orphans, how should they be described?

Such children, in many cases, were taken from their mothers at birth or shortly thereafter, leaving the child without any knowledge of or any ability to know their mothers. Many of these human beings, depending on their age when emancipated, were without any familial or communal experience in a real sense. Slavery produced an orphan population that reached into the millions, and from that perspective, they were treated like wild animals.

Before the internal slave trade and breeding, life for poor whites was hard. It was described as *"root hog or die."* The *"new slavery"* gave them a living. This new slavery brought opportunities that created wealth for even the poorest of whites, if they fully bought into the internal slave trade industry. Slaves bought or sold of all types and varied purposes; many times, transaction records proved untrustworthy, or simply incomplete. Nonetheless, somewhere among the millions of slaves born, sold, or traded, my great-great-great-grandfather and mother were brought or came together long enough to produce the first Burl Lee.

The clearest vision of this time is reflected best, through the eyes and writings of David Walker. Although millions of enslaved Africans were kidnapped and brought to the United States, starting in the late 1500s, the attitudes of slaves toward their bondage was a matter of individual perspective. Captured, the same as Equiano and his sister, enslaved Africans were kidnapped from many different places up and down the West African coast. Not only did they come from many different tribes or nations, they also came from different areas in Africa. They did not speak the same language or share similar cultures. Skin color was their only commonality. Unlike Europeans/slave masters, it took enslaved Africans centuries to develop a common frame of reference.

David Walker was critical to slaves' mental development through his writings in many respects. His words offered the first common vision for slaves and those fighting to free them from bondage. Publishing his incendiary thesis just after the 200th in 1828 entitled, **_Appeal in Four Articles; Together with a Preamble, to the Coloured Citizens of the World, but in Particular and Very Expressly to Those of the United States of America_**, David Walker changed the arc of slavery.

Before Walker, writers like Equiano described the conditions slaves endured, but and still, these writers talked to slave masters and those who were benefitting from slavery's wealth, as well as those trying to free them. These writers offered a vision of the suffering slaves endured to draw sympathy from whites that grew wealthy from the degradation of slaves. Contrarily, Walker wrote his explosive narrative for slaves. Talking directly to slaves, he told them what to do about their circumstances and bondage.

The critical issue here regarding the arc of slavery is Walker's mindset. ***The Appeal*** was the first scathing attack upon slavery by a black person. Walker may have seen slavery, as the same kind of five-headed monster I describe, compared to the one headed Hydra most people saw. Reading ***The Appeal***, it seems, Walker sought to paint slavery as not diminishing but growing over slaves, submerging them even deeper in a hideous system with one goal—never-ending bondage for kidnapped Africans and descendants. He spoke to slaves through their commonality of being black kidnapped souls imprisoned and trapped in American slavery.

Following Walker's ***Appeal,*** slaves became more aggressive and defiant toward their condition. Many researchers believe Walker's insistence that *"slaves must fight to liberate themselves,"* changed slaves' attitudes during this period. Walker demanded, *"Slaves must rise up against their masters and defend themselves. It is no more harm for you to kill a man who is trying to kill you than it is for you to take a drink of water when thirsty."* Walker's combativeness pushed abolitionists toward extreme militancy—John Brown's raid at Harper's Ferry 1859 is an incisive example, (*African American Religious History: A Documentary Witness,* C. Eric Lincoln, 2000; Duke University Press).

Walker's ***Appeal*** made it clear why the tenor of the discussion about and description of slavery had to be more than just push back it forced the abolitionist movement to become more assertive in their opposition to slavery. Prior to Walker's ***Appeal*** opposition to slavery was a talking or writing affair in America. ***The Appeal*** brought a sense of urgency to the fight and quest for freedom through ending slavery in America. ***The Appeal*** transferred Walker's aggressiveness to the struggles for slave descendants, prompting many historians, especially blacks, to cite ***The Appeal,*** as one of the most influential political and social documents of the 19th century. They also feel Walker was the first outspoken African American and anti-slavery activist who try and carry the fight to slaveholders.

Black historians of Walker's day believed ***The Appeal*** exerted a radicalizing influence on the abolitionist movements, more so than all the speeches and writings by Fredrick Douglas or William Lloyd Garrison combined. Walker's thesis not only changed abolitionists' attitudes, but they became more defiant in their words and action. The best example of their change is the growth of the *Underground Railroad.*

Although the *Underground Railroad* had existed beginning in the late 1700s, it was haphazardly maintained and used. Walker's ***Appeal*** made it obvious abolitionists could not talk slavery to death or wait on a hoped-for general emancipation. They had to help slaves rise up or escape from slavery in the South. Again, John Brown's raid on Harper's Ferry in 1859 exemplified the sense of desperation and urgency some abolitionists felt, as slavery's economic impact continued expanding as its existence spread into the Western United States.

Outrage over **_The Appeal,_** in the South from states like Georgia, which offered a $10,000 reward to anyone, _"who handed Walker over alive or dead."_ Was tipical. Walker condemned "The 3/5 Compromise"—Article I Section II of the US Constitution. He felt, "_It gave, white voters in the South power in electoral office much greater than their numbers justified._" It resulted in Southern politicians having enormous power and to the election of Southerners, from George Washington to Woodrow Wilson. (_Thousands Gone: The First Two Centuries of Slavery in North America_, Ira Berlin (1998)

More than anything, Walker's **_Appeal_** caused a drastic change in attitudes of slaves, similar in magnitude to whites, regarding economic benefits brought by the cotton gin. Although legal slavery ended around the world, in America, it did not diminish, it expanded, reaching 1833. Growing daily, breeding and the internal slave trade, dramatically brought slaves and abolitionists to identify with David Walker's vision of slavery. Giving _VOICE_ to their undeniable degradation and hopelessness, Walker communicated a common vision of slaves' wretch existence.

The South's many-headed Hydra continued filling graves in the valley of dry bones to where there seemed no end to slavery. Enslaved Africans were faced with the dilemma, _"What does freedom really mean?"_ Simultaneous, poor whites in the South looked forward to the explosive demands for slaves. The internal slave trade and breeding made poor white stakeholders in the bondage of enslaved Africans.

Christianity's Role in Slavery

When Pope Nicholas V issued the *Dum Diversas* in 1452, the Christian Church set the stage for the longest-running instant of genocide—slavery—in the history of humanity. It is true; the Catholic Church blessed slavery at its beginning. However, Church has not openly repented and atoned for is sin, even though it was a major force helping to end the **Trans-Atlantic Slave Trade. The 400th** now turns to look not at Christianity per se; this look is about the use of religion in America to justify slavery and white supremacy.

More particularly, religious leaders in the American South have clung tenaciously to their biblical defense of slavery, as **"GOD's Will!"** White preachers in the South claimed and re-enforced the idea, **"God"** *ordained the white man to rule over slaves.* Slave masters tried to drive that point home in the minds of slaves in every way possible. **"Niggers are a cursed people! God created niggers to serve their betters. And, for a slave to rebel against slavery is to oppose 'God's Will!'"** was their subtext.

Slaves that showed real commitment to **"God's Will"** were taught to read the Bible. Any slave that could read was viewed by those slaves that could not, as possessing special powers given by God. Seen, as possessing magical powers, those slaves that could read were viewed, as spokesmen for God by other slaves, and commanded fealty *("Nat Turner" in African American Religious Leaders*, Jim Haskins (2008).

Discussing David Walker and his incendiary thesis: **Appeal in Four Articles; Together with a Preamble, to the Coloured Citizens of the World, but in Particular and Very Expressly to Those of the United States of America,** bring this narrative to slave revolts. The topic of slave revolts in America is difficult to appraise and properly place along the arc of **"The 400th"** to effectively highlight their significance. Historians talk about only three slave revolts, as major events in US history.

Historians list Gabriel Prosser in Virginia, as the first of note (1800). Denmark Vesey, in Charleston, South Carolina, led the second major attempt at a slave insurrection in 1822. Both were attempts; neither moved beyond the talking stage; other slaves betrayed those efforts.

However, Nat Turner's bloody slave rebellion, in Southampton County, Virginia in 1831, left no doubt slaves' attitudes toward their bondage had changed dramatically. Turner's deadly rampage, through the Virginia countryside, was not betrayed. It came on the heel of David Walker's **Appeal** (1828). Turner's act frightened whites and signaled a change in how slaves view their bondage.

Florida, on the Eastern Seaboard, was Spanish territory until late 1821, but until then, it was a refuge from slavery. It was home to many communities of Native Peoples, who were in rebellion against white invaders from Europe. They gave runaway slaves refuge. Some escaped slaves married and became members of tribes—Seminoles—were notable in that regard. Also, there were informal networks of sympathizers beyond Native People that helped thousands of escaping slaves.

The Florida sanctuary lasted even after the founding of the Carolina Colony by the English in 1670 and, even after the American Revolution, declares Jane Landers, a Vanderbilt University historian, who has researched the subject extensively. According to Landers, *"The first mention of escaped slaves in North America in Spanish records was in 1687 when eight slaves, including a nursing baby, showed up in St. Augustine. Spain refused to return escaped slaves and instead gave them religious sanctuary. Spain formalized that policy in 1693. The only condition was that those seeking sanctuary had to convert to Catholicism. Spanish policy in Florida was a total shift from the geopolitics of the Caribbean."*

The Spanish policy is important here because of The *Stono River Rebellion*. This little known uprising was the first and largest slave rebellion in colonial America, and later US history. But, like most Americans, I knew nothing about it until researching this narrative. *The Stono Rebellion* took place near the Stono River in South Carolina *(The Stono River or Creek is a tidal channel in southeast South Carolina, just southwest of Charleston).*

The details of the 1739 event are unclear, at best. Documentation for the incident comes from very limited and even suspect sources in turns of details—only one firsthand report and several secondhand accounts survived history. White Carolinians wrote these reports, and later historians have reconstructed the events of the *Stono River Rebellion* best they could. The point is the *Stono River Rebellion* could have been far greater than what those reporting the incident wanted known.

Early on Sunday morning, September 9, 1739, about 20 slaves gathered at a spot near the Stono River. They had pre-planned their rebellion for this day, and no one informed whites of their plan. Stopping first at a firearms shop, they killed the owner and obtained weapons. Mark Smith, a historian at the University of South Carolina, describes the situation, *"The slave leaders were from what is now Angola in Africa. They were Catholic because their homeland was at the time a Portuguese outpost. And they are thought to have been soldiers in their native land. They would have known about the rumor of freedom in Spanish Florida and decided to start the revolt on Sept. 9, the Feast of the Nativity of the Blessed Virgin Mary. They carried a white flag, which is not a flag of surrender. It's a flag to celebrate Mary's purity, and they shouted, "Liberty." They were not revolting only as just slaves, but as Catholic slaves."*

Well-armed, the group marched down the main road in St. Paul's Parish, located nearly 20 miles from Charlestown (today Charleston). Beating drums and singing, the group gathered other slaves as they headed in a southward direction toward Florida. After attacking farms and killing occupants over a 10 miles stretch, there is no count of those killed. The group of roughly 60 to 100 slaves stopped to rest. The white militia in pursuit ambushed the party, opening fire without warning. Some slaves escaped, leaving 21 whites and 44 slaves dead. The militia rounded up some of the escapees, decapitating them, and placed their heads on poles.

However, some who escaped made it safely to Florida, because there are reports of slaves arriving in St. Augustine in the ensuing days, according to Landers. The *"Stono River Rebellion" is a fascinating story, and it explains, at least in part, why the culture of slave descendants—known as Gullah in South Carolina and Geechee in Florida and Georgia—exists along the northeastern Florida coast."* Derek Hankerson, who is a Gullah descendant and a small business owner in St. Augustine, Fla. said, *"We have been hankering to share these stories, slaves escaped not only to the South but to Mexico, the Caribbean, and the American West."* Landers said *"Gullah creole is still spoken in churches in northeastern Florida."*

Jane Landers was also part of establishing the *"Fort Mose story"* of the *"first free black settlement"* in what is now the United States (1738). It was located just north of St. Augustine, Florida. The "Fort Mose" story played an important role in the development of colonial North America. Great Britain, France, Spain, and other European nations were competing for control of the New World and its wealth. All, in varying ways, rely on African slave labor to develop their overseas colonial possessions. British colonies located close to Florida in North America and the West Indies posed a threat to Florida a Spanish colony.

King Charles II of Spain gave slaves sanctuary in Florida. He issued an edict in 1693, which stated, *"Any male slave on an English plantation who escaped to Spanish Florida would be granted freedom provided he joined the Militia and became a Catholic."* This edict became one of the New World's earliest emancipation proclamations. By 1738 there were 100 blacks, mostly runaways from the Carolinas, living in what became *Fort Mose.* Many were skilled workers, blacksmiths, carpenters, cattlemen, boatmen, and farmers. With accompanying women and children, they created a colony of freed maroon people that ultimately attracted other fugitive slaves.

When war broke out in 1740 between England and Spain, the people of St. Augustine and nearby Fort Mose found themselves involved in a conflict that stretched across three continents. The English sent thousands of soldiers and dozens of ships to destroy St. Augustine and bring back any runaways. They set up a blockade and bombarded the town for 27 consecutive days.

Hopelessly outnumbered, the diverse population of blacks, Native People, and whites pulled together. Fort Mose was one of the first places attacked. Lead by Captain Francisco Menendez, the Fort Mose Militia briefly lost the fort but eventually recaptured it, repelling the English invasion force.

Florida remained Spanish territory for the next 80 years and remained a haven for fugitive slaves, *(Sources: Kathleen Deagan and Darcie MacMahon, Fort Mose: Colonial America's Black Fortress of Freedom ,Gainesville: University Press of Florida,*

1995: Jane Landers, *"Gracia Real de Santa Teresa de Mose: A Free Black Town in Spanish Colonial Florida," American Historical Review 95:1 (Fall 1990);* Jane Landers, *"Spanish Sanctuary: Fugitives in Florida, 1687-1790," The Florida Historical Quarterly 62:3 (1984).* Deborah Huso, *"Fort Mose," American Legacy: The Magazine of African American History and Culture (Fall 2006).* James Bullock, *Independent Historian, Fort Mose (Florida) | The Black Past: Remembered and Reclaimed)*

The *Stono River Rebellion* and *Fort Mose* are slave rebellions that are barely known. And, there may have been other battles for survival and other rebellions white people have kept hidden, even today. However, the one that could not be hidden was *Nat Turner's Rebellion* in Virginia, in terms of the effect on slaves and slave masters. Turner's uprising took place only miles from the Nation's Capital. News of Nat Turner's rampage shocked writes all along the Eastern Seaboard; fear spread wildly.

Literate and a preacher, Turner declared— *"God told me to rise up against slavery!* Turner's rebellion sent shivers through even stout-hearted defender of slavery. It made biblical sayings, coming out of the mouths of preachers, like Nat Turner, swords of vengeance. Turner and his band of followers killed over 60 whites. Slave masters hanged Turner and 17 other slaves, fighting for their freedom.

Turner's raid was like "shock and awe, producing real fear, as whites experienced slaves' changing mindset. Turner's dramatic spectacle not only shocked slave masters, they responded to the unanticipated level of noxious anger displayed towards whites with extreme measures. Slaveholders rose up across the South, trying to instill fear in slaves and free blacks across America again. Whites began to fear slaves as killers, rather than *"happy darkies singing and dancing the day away."*

Turner's attack struck terror in the hearts of slaveholders for the first time. It was clear slaves were no longer content to accept their lot on plantations. Slaveholders went on a frenzied retaliation, killing hundreds of slaves, (<u>The Fires of Jubilee: Nat Turner's Fierce Rebellion,</u> Stephen Oates, 1975; Harper Perennial). I have tried in this section to reflect the changing mindset and attitudes that developed among slaves following Walker's ***Appeal***. Slaves changing attitude showed glimpse of what was possible and many, perhaps began to see slaves as a threat among them, like the growing monster David Walker described for the first time. The incredible odds of surviving, rising up against slavery, pushed not only slaves but whites also began to look for alternatives.

Comparing and contrasting Olaudah Equiano's writings and mindset with that of David Walker was the point of comparing the two, which has more than symbolic significance. Although Equiano presented a different visions, Walker brings the two together. Walker gave slaves a harrowing picture of their bondage, which was so gruesome slaves not only believe him but accepted his solution—resistance. Walker produced a vision only slaves could truly understand

and identify with, because no one other than slaves were enduring its horrors, therefore would recognize the total beastly character of that monster—slavery.

The essential difference between Equiano's and Walker's communication is Equiano talked to slave masters, while David Walker spoke only to slaves. Put as simply as possible, Walker gave slaves a personal reason to fight slavery. Walker's words painted a picture of unending bondage, brutality, degradation, and death for slaves, which was so horrifying to them, many slaves accepted not only his vision but his solution. His image was such a clear reflection most slaves became convinced they could not make an accommodation with the monster—slavery—without betraying themselves.

Some slaves, as Nat Turner, and even white abolitionists, like John Brown, choose to fight to the death of slavery or themselves. On the other hand, some slaves took an independent approach and decided to run alone or on the *Underground Railroad*. Others decided to run, but took a communal approach. They carried everyone they cared about with them, including children and old folks. **The Undergrown Railroad**, at this juncture, became a real system for getting escaping slaves out of the South.

The Underground Railroad

"When my feet first touched the Canadian shore, I threw myself on the ground, rolled in the sand, seized handfuls of it, and kissed them."—Josiah Henson

Those are the words of Josiah Henson runaway slave, as he recalled in his memoir—*"The Life of Josiah Henson: Formerly a Slave"*—of his first moments as a free man. Henson had just escaped, following the course along the American borders with Canada. He traced the steps of many unnumbered escapees that became Canadian immigrants, after riding the *"Underground Railroad."* Henson's run put him beyond the brutality and oppression of American slavery. During the years from 1840 to 1862, more than 30,000 American slaves surreptitiously fled to Canada in search of freedom, which most found (*"Settling Canada Underground Railroad,"* Historical Minutes 1- 6-2010).

There is no way to know the total number of slaves that made the run to reach *"O Canada." "O Canada," French." "Ô Canada"* is the national anthem of Canada, and although the vast majority of runaway slaves never heard its words before arriving, Canada was seen as the *"Promised Land"* by slaves in the US. Lying directly beneath the North Star, *Polaris* was like a beacon in the minds of slaves', guiding thousands of runaways to their long-sought destination and safety. Canada was the answer to their yearning prayers for freedom, which slaves woke up with, and was the last thought just before sleep took them.

Imprisoned in the land of the free and home of the brave, America today, remains a nation without mercy for those with black skin. Graciously Canada took in all that made it to its shores. Although it treated Native People similar to America in its beginnings, Canada did not slaughter Native People and rob them of their land to the degree America has. Canada found a much-needed measure of compassion for runaway slaves, who saw Canada as their destination and vision of freedom. Yet and still, millions tried, but all were unable to see *"Dawn."*

The Underground Railroad made Canada an angel of mercy to thousands of slaves like Josiah Henson. Thousands of desperate souls sought freedom and found it there. The *"Railroad"* actually began operating sometime around the 1780s, but only became known as the *"Underground Railroad"* in the 1830s. Its organizers used railroad terminology as codes.

Those who helped runaway slaves move from place to place were called *"conductors,"* and the fleeing slaves were *"passengers"* or *"cargo."* Safe places where slaves could stop, and rest were called *"stations."* Conductors were mostly abolitionists working to help slaves escape bondage and reach Canada, after miles of travel.

Abolitionists were a varied group—Quakers, Methodists, farmers, businesspeople, politicians, blacks and whites, men and women to name the most

The 400th: From Slavery to Hip Hop 75

numerous fearless souls—that dared to help runaway slaves. The Underground Railroad's tracks ran up the East coast to places, like New York and on into New England, they also ran out West through Iowa and Illinois as well. But most of its tracks ran to the Ohio River and crisis-crossed Indiana and Ohio. The Ohio River was the closest point to cross onto free soil for most slaves, especially those in the Deep South.

Ohio, Indiana, and Michigan's coastlines along Lakes Erie, Michigan and Ontario were the nearest points to the Canadian border for those riding the *Underground Railroad*. The Underground Railroad was established haphazardly. It was made up of a network of secret routes, paths, hiding places, tunnels, and safe houses. But it became a reliable system of ordinary people, known as "friendlies" in the 1840s. Its web of waystations helped runaway slaves get to freedom, wherever whenever and however they could. *Underground Railroad* stretched into the *Deep South*—Alabama, Arkansas, Georgia, Mississippi, South Carolina, and Louisiana—a long way from the Ohio River. Thousands of African Americans escaping slaves took this metaphorical ride, trying to get to free states North of the Mason-Dixon Line or Ohio River, then on to Canada.

Many slaves tried, but few made it to Canada, compared to the number of slaves that tried. The lurid journeys forded dangerous rivers, stretches of wilderness, and through foothills and mountains, as well as treacherous swamps to reach the *"Promised Land."* Sometimes escaping slaves had to elude slave catchers, and lives were lost, getting to free soil north of the Ohio River.

Bryan Walls, University of Toronto, described his ancestors' harrowing escape on the *Underground Railroad* in his book <u>Up From Slavery</u>. He provides a vivid account of John Freeman Walls and Jane's, escaped from slavery and oppression. They fled by way of Detroit, Michigan, in 1845. The Walls family crossed Lake Erie in a steamboat *"the Pearl"* and arrived in Amherstburg in 1846.

Icons, such as Harriett Tubman, a famous *"conductor,"* aided hundreds like the Walls. She made over 40 trips into the South to lead slaves out. Legend has it; she carried a pistol and vowed to shoot anyone that tried to turn back. *"You can want to turn back, and you can even think about turning back, but if you say one word or make one step, I will shoot you dead, in your tracks,"* was said to be her words starting their journey, (*Be Free or Die* starring Cynthia Erivo tells the story of Harriet Tubman released 11-12-2019).

For slaves in the Deep South, fortunately, there was a back door for a while. This escape route ran South into Florida when it was a Spanish possession (1300–1821). It existed from the late 16th century until Florida became United States territory in 1821. There was also another on the other side of the US that led to the South that was just as important, if not more so, Texas, and I will address it later.

The US government purchased Florida from Span to eliminate that haven and escape route of slaves to safety and freedom. A few historians even believe obtaining the Louisiana Purchase in 1803 by the US was to close off the slaves escape routes to Mexico across the Mississippi River. Louisiana belonged to France and was a haven for runaway slaves. It also fought a war to gain Texas and close the US' backdoor to Mexico, once Louisiana became the US border with Mexico, (*"Fort Mose's Call To Freedom. Florida's Little-known Underground Railroad Was the Escape Route Taken by Slaves Who Fled to the area in the 1700s and "Established America's First Black Town," Sun-Sentinel 2018*).

Traveling north aboard the *Underground Railroad*, mostly at night, escaping slaves used *Polaris*, as their guide. It is unclear today whether some statements about the *Underground Railroad* are urban legends or facts. For example, there are claims that the *Underground Railroad* had secret codes and signs. The legend even says 'quilts were part of the conductors' messaging system.

Legend has it, there were ten quilt patterns used to direct conductors and slaves to take particular actions. Quilt designs, the legend says, signaled and direct conductors to certain routes, as well as escaping slaves, to places for assistance. The quilts were part of their nonverbal communication system. They were placed one at a time on a fence to alert those helping escaping slaves at particular points. This system of codes had a dual purpose: first to signal slaves to prepare to escape, and secondly, they provided clues and directions along the journey. Other objects, like the statue of the little black boy dressed like a jockey was also another. His placement, whether on the porch or at the gate, and the position of his hand, directed conductors and runaways to stop or continue on their way, (*"Unravelling the Myth of Quilts and the Underground Railroad,"* Stacie attempt (2007-04-03), TIME).

Similarly, some popular nonacademic sources claim that spirituals and other songs, such as *"Steal Away"* or *"Follow the Drinking Gourd,"* contained coded information and helped individuals navigate the *Underground Railroad*. Scholars, however, believe that while, *"slave songs may have certainly expressed hope for deliverance from the sorrows of this world, these songs did not present literal help for runaway slaves,"* in their opinion. The *Underground Railroad* did inspire cultural works, however. For example, *"Song of the Free,"* was written in 1860 about a man fleeing slavery in Tennessee by escaping to Canada. The song was composed to the tune of *"Oh! Susanna"* and each stanza reference to Canada, as the land *"where colored men are free."*

The Fugitive Slave Act 1850 was another big effort by the US government to help entrench slavery in America.

The new law allowed slave hunters to pursue and capture escaped slaves even in places like Canada, where they were legally free. It resulted in several attempts to kidnap escapees in Canada and return them to owners in the South.

Slavery in Upper Canada (now Ontario) became illegal in 1793. John Robinson, the Attorney General of Upper Canada, declared that by residing in Canada, black residents were set free and that Canadian courts would protect their freedom (1819), ("Black History-From Slavery to Settlement," Archives.gov.on.ca.). Slavery in Canada, as a whole, had been in rapid decline, after an 1803 court ruling. That court decision ushered in full abolition in 1834, (*Visualizing Slavery: Art Across the African Diaspora, Celeste-Marie Bernier;* Hannah Durkin, 2016, Oxford University Press.).

Fort Malden in Amherstburg, Ontario, was deemed the *"chief place of entry"* for slaves escaping to Canada. The abolitionist Levi Coffin supported this assessment, describing Fort Malden as *"the great landing place, the principle terminus of the Underground Railroad of the west."* After 1850 *(passage of the Fugitive Slave Act)*, approximately thirty fugitive slaves a day were crossing over to Fort Malden by steamboat. The Sultana was one such ship. It made *"frequent round trips"* between Great Lakes ports. Its captain, C.W. Appleby, a celebrated mariner, facilitated the conveyance of several fugitive slaves from various Lake Erie ports to Fort Malden regularly.

Estimates vary widely, but at least 30,000 slaves, most claim more than 100,000, escaped to Canada via the *Underground Railroad*. The largest group of slaves settled in Upper Canada (Ontario), called Canada West (1841). Numerous black Canadian communities developed in Southern Ontario. These were generally in the triangular region bounded by Niagara Falls, Toronto, and Windsor. Several rural villages made up mostly of ex-slaves were established in Kent and Essex counties.

Canada: A Haven for Runners

Canada became known throughout the US as a haven for slaves that decided to become runners in search of freedom. Canada opened its arms and accepted all, without question, able to reach its shores. British Columbia on Canada's West coast received its first large wave of black settlers in 1858. The group came to investigate an invitation from Governor James Douglas of Vancouver Island. Douglas was the son of an African Creole mother from the Caribbean and a European father. He was sensitive to the concerns of African-Americans in California, due to growing legal restrictions on their ability to live and work as equals. Black Californians became alarmed when a runaway slave was arrested in California (*Fugitive Slave Law 1850*) and given to slave catchers. Following that incident, all blacks in California had to register.

Concerned over this legal discrimination, the group set out to examine Canada's west coast as a haven and returned with a favorable report on Vancouver. About 400 black Californian families moved primarily to Victoria or Salt Spring Island. Their presence helped to increase the number of those who could be counted upon to support this British territory. It was part of the border territory America claimed and which came under dispute at the end of the American Revolutionary War in 1776-1789. It became a contentious issue approaching the War of 1812 and later in the 1830s with the slogan "54 40 or fight."

Another important center of population for runaway slaves in Canada was Nova Scotia. The first recorded free black person in Canada was a translator, Mathieu de Costa, for French explorer Samuel de Champlain (1600). Little is known of de Costa, and even less is documented, but he was a freeman favored by explorers for his multilingual talents. His portfolio of languages was said to include Dutch, English, French, Portuguese, Mi'kmaq, and pidgin Basque, the dialect many Aboriginals used for trading purposes.

The first wave of slaves came to Nova Scotia in the early 1600s. The founding of Port Royal in 1605, almost 15 years before the first so-called official recording of slaves arriving in the US (1619), black settlers of both French and English backgrounds, began settling in towns like Annapolis Royal (1604). Following their arrival, during the founding of Louisbourg and Halifax, blacks were brought to Nova Scotia, as slaves.

The first major migration of blacks occurred more than a century later, over 3,000 black loyalists fled to Nova Scotia, during the aftermath of the American War of Independence.

For example, Africville and other villages near Halifax became slave havens. Black loyalists built these settlements, after the American Revolutionary War (1776). They had been promised freedom for fighting with the colonials against Great Britain but fled to Canada once the US went back on that promise. The next major migration of blacks happened during the War of 1812 (*Racism's long history in quiet East Coast towns*, The Globe and Mail.)

In the decades that followed, Maroons—a group of freed slaves deported from Jamaica—joined refugees from America, who escaped to Canada on the Underground Railroad. These Jamaican Maroons' amazing story began on June 26, 1796. Their original destination was Lower Canada, but on July 21 and 23, 543 men, women, and children aboard three ships, the Anne, Dover, and Mary arrived in Halifax, Nova Scotia. They had been defeated in an uprising against the British colonial government.

Halifax was in the midst of a major construction boom, modernizing the city's defenses. Prince Edward, Duke of Kent and Strathearn's, immediately put the Maroons to work at the Citadel, Government House, and other defense works throughout the city of Halifax, easing the labor shortage. Edward was impressed by the Maroons work. British Lieutenant-Governor Sir John Wentworth, procured an annual stipend of £240 for support of a school and religious education, for Maroons from monies provided by Jamaica's Government. After four years in Halifax, the Maroons requested passage to Sierra Leone, which Canada granted on 8-6, 1800. The Maroons arrived in Freetown, Sierra Leone on October 1, 1800, ("*Black Immigrants into Nova Scotia, 1776–1815*", The Journal of Negro History. Vol. 58, No. 3 (July 1973).

Important black settlements also developed in other parts of British North America, including Lower Canada (present-day Quebec). Black Nova Scotians are black Canadians, and as such, the 2011 Census of Canada showed 20,790 black people live in Nova Scotia, mostly in Halifax. A large number of black Nova Scotians have migrated to Toronto, Ontario, since the 1950s. Before the immigration reforms during the 1960s, black Nova Scotians formed 37% of the total black Canadian population, *("Halifax's Black Loyalists – Halifax Nova Scotia."* highway7.com).

The Black Cultural Centre for Nova Scotia at the Africville Museum in Halifax tells the universal story of resilience and spirit of determination reflective of black Canadians. Through exhibits and presentations there, one can learn about the challenges African Nova Scotians faced as well as celebrate the triumphs of these proud African communities. *("Black Immigrants into Nova Scotia, 1776–1815"*, John N. Grant, 1973, "*The Journal of Negro History*" Vol. 58, No. 3).

Take the Railroad from Midnight to Dawn

The Fugitive Slave Act of 1850 ensured that even if slaves reached free soil in the North, they could still be captured, and returned to their slave masters in the South. The *Fugitive Slave Act* (1850) showed the US government's commitment to keeping slavery as the economic engine of America. Moreover, it forced freed slaves, to have on their person, manumission papers when slave catchers accused them of being slaves.

The law put any free black persons at risk of being kidnapped, as a slave and shanghaied back to the South. There was no protection against slave catchers destroying a slave's manumission papers, once they produced them. My example again is the story of Solomon Northup who was just such a victim, *"Twelve Years a Slave."* However, Canada, which lay only one mile across the Detroit River from the US, prohibited the return of runaway slaves, with or without papers, thus offering slaves full liberty and safety.

A very important stop on the *Underground Railroad*, Detroit, Michigan, was a major exit to enter Canada. Detroit was the terminal point of the *Underground Railroad*, leaving the United States, and its code name was *"Midnight."* Most slaves trying to escape the US on the *Underground Railroad* learned, if they made it to Detroit, sometimes after traveling a thousand miles, freedom was just a mile away in Canada.

The Detroit River's code name was *"Jordan."* Less than a mile of water separated Canada and the US. Metaphorically, it symbolized the river the *"Children of Israel"* crossed, getting to the *"Promised Land."* Canada's code-named became *"Dawn"* and was the end of a slave's journey. Such code names allowed people to communicate without being specific: *"Ride the railroad from Midnight to Dawn."* Although fleeing slaves arrived in Canada all along its border with the US, from Nova Scotia to British Columbia, most came to what is now southwestern Ontario. They settled in places like Windsor, Fort Erie, Chatham, and Owen Sound.

Secrecy was essential, even in Northern states, under the *Fugitive Slave Act (1850)* individuals found collaborating with runaway slaves could be fined heavily and sometimes imprisoned. Therefore, beyond verbal codes, nonverbal codes like flags and lanterns were clandestine signals. Such codes were placed on handbills and in newspapers to provide directions to conductors and escaping slaves. These embedded signals eliminated the need to verbalize information. Encryption allowed abolitionists to use symbols to help *Underground Railroad* conductors and others communicate and avoid detection.

The *Underground Railroad* was also a secret network of financial, spiritual, and material aid for runaways. Fugitive slaves generally made their way on foot, often at night, from one station to the next. They needed subsistence en route, and sometimes they had to lay low for weeks at a time, if slave catchers were known to be in an area. Conductors or stockholders received runaway and sent them on their way.

Conductors of all backgrounds risked their livelihood and freedom, helping those trying to get to freedom. They hid slaves in their homes, barns, attics, cellars, churches, shops, and sheds, among other places. Directly defying the *Fugitive Slave Act 1850*, these intrepid individuals provided runaways with food, places to rest and sleep. They also facilitated slaves' transference to the next stop or *Underground Railroad "station."*

A Detroiter named Seymour Finney was an important Railroad conductor. He owned the Finney Hotel in downtown Detroit. Finney aided fugitive slaves by housing them in his establishment. Outside Detroit, Michigan abolitionists, included a Quaker feminist writer, Elizabeth Chandler of Lenawee County. Chandler convinced members of her church to establish one of the state's earlier anti-slavery societies.

Dr. Nathan Thomas was extremely active in the *Underground Railroad*. He founded the Michigan Republican Party. His wife Pamela's memoirs, recorded they assisted 1,000 to 1,500 runaways. Dr. Thomas transported slaves to Battle Creek, where Quaker Erastus Hussey received them. Hussey was also active in abolitionist politics and started an anti-slavery newspaper called the *Michigan Liberty Press*.

One of the most notorious abolitionists in Detroit's *Underground Railroad* network was George de Baptiste. Born a free man in Virginia in 1814, he relocated to Detroit as an adult. A respected entrepreneur and business leader, he owned a barbershop and a bakery in Detroit before purchasing a steamship, the T. Whitney.

A clever man and a very active abolitionist, Baptiste used the boat to ferry slaves from *"Midnight to Dawn."* George de Baptiste also formed a secret organization known as *African-American Mysteries or Order of the Men of Oppression*, which worked in tandem with the *Underground Railroad* in Detroit. Baptiste's group took on the very dangerous tasks, like rescuing captured runaways from slave catchers headed back South.

George de Baptiste's church also played a monumental role in the city's *Underground Railroad* network. Detroit's *Second Baptist Church*, Michigan's first black congregation was established in 1836 by thirteen freed slaves, who split from the First Baptist Church. The church moved to its current location in Greektown in 1857. An estimated 5,000 fugitive slaves hid in the church during its 30-year history, serving as a station on the *Underground Railroad*.

Texas: Backdoor Underground Railroad

Historians, educators/researchers, genealogists, *Underground Railroad* state associations, historical associations, museum personnel, librarians, and county historians held a conference at the Walker Education Center at the Sam Houston Memorial Museum complex (3-21-2000). Attendees aimed to shining light on the little-known history of the Texas Underground Railroad. Today that subject has become a real interest and some are exploring and developing that history.

This narrative highlights the work of those involved in researching and reviving the Texas *Underground Railroad* story. Naomi and Allen Grundy, creators of the *Talking Back Living History Association*, along with the National Park Service and Sam Houston Memorial Museum, sponsored the two-day conference at Sam Houston State University entitled *"Blazing Trails to Freedom; The Underground Railroad in Texas."* Former teachers, the couple is now involved full time in researching, and presenting aspects of Texas history related to African-Americans and other minorities.

Their efforts are a growing movement in Texas to uncover the history of the *Underground Railroad* there. They are telling the story of Texans, who helped slaves from nearby states—Arkansas, Louisiana, Oklahoma, and Texas—to reach freedom in Mexico, which is an untold story. There is an estimate that upwards of 5,000 slaves fled southwest America to Mexico by way of Texas. Little is known of the people who were part of this network, which helped runners. Most Americans are very aware slaves took the *Underground Railroad* North to Canada, but very little is known about a similar path South into Mexico.

The story begins when Texas was part of Mexico up until 1845, which meant its border began at the Arkansas, Louisiana, and Oklahoma state lines. Mexico abolished slavery in 1829. Primarily that decision was pushed by President Vicente Guerrero. He was of African heritage and offered runaway slaves freedom in Mexico.

Roseann Bacha-Garza has worked for years, hoping to explain this story, which is why on this cloudy winter afternoon she is searched through an overgrown cemetery. Trying desperately not to step on tombstones that date back to the mid-1800s, Bacha-Garza is another historian threading the *Underground Railroad* story together from bits of history, found in all kinds of places. This day she is searching through the Jackson Ranch cemetery in San Juan, Texas. Texas became US territory in 1845, when the border between Mexico and the US move to the Rio Grande River.

Bacha-Garza manages the *Community Historical Archeology Projects* at the University Texas Rio Grande Valley. She says, *"The Jackson family played an instrumental role in south Texas, smuggling slaves into Mexico. After the 1850 Fugitive Slave Act, which allowed slave catchers to seize slaves in the north, but like Canada, Mexico adamantly refused* to sign any fugitive slave agreement with the US. So, once a slave made it to Mexico, which Texas was, they really were safer, in ways, not possible in the northern United States."

Bacha-Garza says also, "Through my research; I became acquainted with Nathaniel Jackson, who was the son of a plantation owner in Alabama. He and his family-owned slaves, but Nathaniel eventually emancipated his. He married Matilda Hicks, who was once a slave, owned by his family. They migrated to the Rio Grande Valley with their children and five other families in covered wagons in 1857. Nathaniel and Matilda was a mixed-race couple and needed a different environment. They probably felt the Rio Grande Valley would be a better place to re-establish their lives, far away from the long arm of the law (the Fugitive Slave Act 1850) than in Alabama. They wanted to live in peace, I believe, and as such, it seems they found that here in south Texas. The Rio Grande Valley was a place where people worked side-by-side. I think it seemed to them, a place where you could come and have a new beginning."

Roseann, who examines the genealogy of families who originally settled here, said, "Much of my research comes from oral histories of descendants of families that originally settled on the border during this time. Through my conversations and historical documents, I was led to believe, the Jackson family became known for offering slaves refuge and a safe-haven on their paths to freedom." Bacha-Garza believes, because the Jackson Ranch was so close to the Rio Grande, they helped smuggle slaves into Mexico. "The Jacksons were religious people trying to do the right thing and did not believe in the Confederate cause." She went on. "During the 1850s, it is reported that approximately 3,000 slaves escaped over the Rio Grande River."

Bacha-Garza says, "Some communities along the border in the US, historically, were empathetic to helping slaves because of events that took place in the past. Back at the beginning, Native American tribes thrived in the region; they lost their land when the Spaniards came and claimed it as their own. People who owned land north of the Rio Grande before the end of the Mexican-American War were Mexican citizens." (Following the Mexican–American War, by 1845 the US annexed the so-called independent Republic of Texas. Mexico considered its northeastern province part of its territory).

Texas seceded from Mexico in 1836, which was followed by the so-called Texas Revolution. The armed conflict between the United States and the United Mexican States lasted from 1846 to 1848. After the war, the US annexation the region making it part of the US. Bacha-Garza pointed out, "That's when Mexicans had to learn new government rules, while they were often cheated out of their lands. You have a region where people are feeling they were living here all copacetic and nobody was bothering them, but all of a sudden somebody came in and took everything away. They were sympathetic to slaves because they were feeling their pain. They were being mistreated and that's not fair. The Jacksons became subsistence farmers and cattle ranchers. They planted crops and traded their surplus with people in Mexico."

Looking back through time, Roseann says studies indicate, "There were many ferries set up in the 1850s, so people could easily trade across the Rio Grande. This also served as a opportunity for slaves to fit in among them and slip across the border into Mexico, and so border families assist in the smuggling of slaves."

However, not everything was entirely peaceful on the border. Military forts were also present along the river, remnants of the Mexican-American War of the 1840s. Bacha-Garza says, *"Officials at these forts were instructed to capture and return any slaves to their owners. But forts were far apart from each other, which made enforcement ineffective."*

Lupe Flores is a 27 years-old graduate student at the University Texas Rio Grande Valley. Lupe is studying Anthropology and Mexican American Studies; he is a descendant of the Jacksons and the Webbers. Along with the Jacksons, the Webbers, like other families on this side of the border, were so important to the *Underground Railroad* to the South. Lupe says, *"There's still a lot we don't know about these families and their histories."* Flores continued, *"I grew up hearing stories about my family's past, but at the time, I didn't think too much of them."*

I can identify with Lupe's statement regarding his family's history growing up. He commented, *"I was in undergrad school when I began systematically researching my grandmother and her family's history here in Hidalgo County. So, I always had a sense of, you know, there was something about the ranch, or whatever, but I just never really internalized it."* Speaking today, Lupe says, *"That's changed. I reflect on my family's history pretty frequently now. One thing I think and write about is what I call the "permutations of resistance —especially on the border. Through different times in history and the present, I mean, there's been people resisting policies of the state, the borders of the state."* Flores goes on, *"Back then it was helping slaves cross into Mexico. In the 1900s, you had prohibition, and this area was also a place of cross border movement."*

Lupe says for him, this all means, *"Today the border is much more militarized by the state, but resistance still occurs. Usually, in the form of helping undocumented people get into this country. Even with walls on the border, there's still always going to be a way to subvert the state, and it's machinations to control the border."*

After learning about his family's role in this story, Flores concluded, *"I look at the Valley's history differently. It's a story I want to magnify. Because, up until now, the story of the Underground Railroad that took slaves to the North, has been told. But the Texas story—the one where slaves found freedom by fleeing South—continues to be a local hidden tale. Mexico's role in the Underground Railroad to the South was very important to those who sought freedom by running southward."*

Mexico: Haven to the South

The *Underground Railroad* story is a major part of kidnapped enslaved Africans first organized effort to escape bondage. The story also details how the United States government tried to pull escaped slaves back into bondage, once they became runners. Even after slaves gained freedom where and however, they could, they became refuges where slavery was forbidden, after passage of *The Fugitive Slave Act 1850*. The US sent slave catchers to bring them back, and based on slave-catchers' word alone, a black person went from free to slave. That law made slavery a threat to any black person, whether in the United States or elsewhere, who became targets of slave catchers, like Olaudah Equiano. *The Fugitive Slave Act 1850* made the actions of nations, like Canada and Mexico, crucial to runaway slaves' freedom and survival.

The *Underground Railroad* to the South, as for as, freedom was concerned, getting to Mexico was a much easier road for runaway slaves. The Louisiana, Oklahoma, and Arkansas borders, before 1845, were the goal of black runaways escaping slavery. However, there was no established system like the *Underground Railroad* to the North.

The most interesting aspect of slaves in Mexico is they faced a different cultural matrix, rather than the Euro/American culture in Canada. Mexico, for fugitive slaves, leading up to emancipation and until the end of the Civil War, was more than a backdoor to freedom. For those who were able to survive that trek, Mexico was an open door of inclusion.

Mexico steadfastly refused to return runaway slaves to the US. The story of escaped slaves in Mexico reflects the reason the US purchased Florida and the Louisiana Purchase. The US acted as it did against Mexico because it would not deny runaway slaves a safe haven. Texas, becoming a breakaway colony of Mexico, was part of an American plot. American political leaders desired to close off Mexican territory, as a haven for escaping slaves, especially those from sugar plantations of Louisiana. First, America tried treaty negations. Readers must remember and understand whites in the South saw no end to slavery. The US was determined to make its territory a huge prison for slaves. Slaveholders banked on continuing slavery in perpetuity.

The US government was in league with slave-owners who saw war with Mexico, as the only way to push that nation aside. They saw Mexico as just another bump in the road of perpetual slavery, once Mexico refused its treaties. The Mexican American War was the second war America fought over slavery—with the Civil War number 3.

Similar to what happened during the run-up to the War of 1812, the US government blamed Mexico for slaves escaping across the Mississippi River to Texas. Sam Houston, Stephen F. Austin, Jim Bowie, William Travis, and Davy

Crockett were politicians and plantation owners, as well as part of the secret deals and collusion the US fermented to take Texas.

During the 37 years between 1807 and 1845, escaping slaves to Mexico faced only the Mississippi River. The US scam began with trying to persuade Mexico to accept slavery in Texas, and if it had, there probably would not have been a war. However, Mexico adamantly refused to allow slavery in its territory. Then those mentioned above, these so-called Texas heroes, fermented the so-called Texas Revolution with US backing. They were in league with the US government's efforts to eliminate safe havens to runaway slaves.

Although there was no *Underground Railroad* running southward, the US government was determined to stim the flow of escaping slaves next door to Mexico. In 1826 the Committee of Foreign Relations of the Mexican Chamber of Deputies refused to compromise on the issue of fugitive slaves. They defended the right of enslaved Africans to liberate themselves.

Mexican government officials cited *"the inalienable right which the Author (God) of nature has conceded to him (meaning enslaved persons)."* Congress member Erasmo Seguin from Texas commented that the US Congress was *"resolved to decree the perpetual extension in the Republic, the commerce and traffic in slaves and that their introduction into our territory should not be permitted under any pretext."* Again, in October 1828, the Mexican Senate rejected 14 articles of a newly-proposed treaty and harshly criticized Article 33, *stating "it would be most extraordinary that in a treaty between two free republics, slavery should be encouraged by obliging ours to deliver up fugitive slaves to their merciless and barbarous masters of North America."* Reporting on the growing number of Anglo settlers in Texas, Mexican Gen. Teran said, *"Most of them have slaves, and these slaves are beginning to learn the favorable intent of Mexican law to their unfortunate condition and are becoming restless under their yokes ..."* Gen. Teran went on to describe the cruelty meted out by masters to slaves.

By 1831, some Mexican officials reasoned as Vancouver Island would in 1858, which feared US military intervention. Mexican officials began encouraging the development of runaway slave colonies along the Northern border at the Mississippi, Arkansas and Oklahoma, as a way to lessen the threat posed by the US. Historian Rosalie Schwartz said, *"Mexican officials, reasoned these fugitives, choosing between liberty under the Mexican government and bondage in the United States, would fight to protect their Mexican freedom more vigorously than any mercenaries."*

In 1836, after the fall of the Alamo and losing slave-owning or pro-slavery leaders—William Travis, Jim Bowie, and Davy Crockett—the US government increased support for the Texas rebels. Mexican forces were defeated, and the US quickly annexed Texas, supposedly an independent state. However, the US annexed all Mexican territory north of the Rio Grande, not just Texas, the breakaway colony.

Before the expulsion of Mexican forces from Texas, Brig. Gen. Jose Urrea evicted scores of illegally-settled plantation owners, liberated slaves, and, in many instances, granted on-the-spot titles to them of the land they had worked. In 1850, facing a new treaty accord with the US, Mexico again refused to return fugitive slaves. Moreover, the institution of slavery in Texas was continuously undermined by defiant *Tejanos* (Mexicans in Texas), who took great risks and invested enormous resources toward facilitating the escape of enslaved Africans.

Whites suspected and accused *Tejanos* of *"tampering with slave property," "consorting with blacks," "stirring up trouble among the slave population,"* and *"a spirit of insubordination."* (*Tejano are residents of Texas who are culturally descendants of the original Spanish-speaking settlers of Texas and northern Mexico. They are variously Criollo Spaniard, Mestizo American, or Mexican American origin.*) Plantation owners in Central Texas adopted various resolutions aimed at preventing Mexicans from aiding the Texas slave population.

Whites in Guadalupe County prohibited Mexican *"peons"* from entering the county and anyone from conducting business or interacting with enslaved Africans without authorization from the owners. Bexar County whites suggested that *"Mexican strangers entering from San Antonio register at the mayor's office and give an account of themselves and their business."* Delegates to a convention in Gonzales resolved that *"counties should organize vigilance committees (the KKK) to prosecute persons tampering with slaves"* and that *"all citizens and slaveholders were to endeavor to prevent Mexicans from communicating with blacks."* These actions are a clear reflection of the southern slave master mentality.

Slaveholders in Austin decreed, *"All transient Mexicans should leave within ten days, and any remaining should be forcibly expelled unless their good character and good behavior were substantiated by responsible American (white) citizens."* And *"Mexicans should no longer be employed, and their presence in the area should be discouraged."* In Matagorda County, *all Mexicans were driven out under (banishment and ethnic cleansing) the bogus claim that they were wandering, indigent sub-humans who "have no fixed domicile but hang around the plantations, taking the likeliest negro girls for wives ... they often steal horses, and these girls too, and endeavor to run them to Mexico."* By the year 1855, estimates were that as many as 6,000 to 8,000 enslaved Africans escaped to Mexico.

Slave masters became so alarmed at Mexicans helping runaway slaves, they requested and received approximately one-fifth of the standing US Army, along the Texas-Mexico border in a vain effort to stem the flow of runaways. (This is like today, only it's going the other way).

The border battle shows that even though slavery was only legal in the South, the US federal government pursued its establishment, as if it was a national policy, in effect, it was and still is. Defiant Mexicans stood their ground, refused to return runaways, and continued supporting slave uprisings and providing assistance to escaping slaves. In the words of Felix Haywood, a Texas slave, whose experience is recalled in The *Slave Narratives of Texas*, *"Sometimes someone would come along and try to get us to run up north and be free. We used to laugh at* that. There was no reason to run up north. All we had to do was walk but walk south, and we'd be free as soon as we crossed the Rio Grande."

What a difference a border made (1857) because that year, the U.S. Supreme Court ruled in **Dred Scott v. Sanford,** an enslaved African who sued his master for his freedom. Scott's owner had forfeited any claim to him after taking him into a free state. Ironically, 1857 was the same year that the Mexican Congress adopted Article 13, declaring that an enslaved person was free the moment he set foot on Mexican soil. Mexico was a provider of job opportunities for African Americans during the 1890s. Hundreds of black migrants fed up with slave-like conditions and segregation left Alabama for Mexico and established ten large colonies.

After the Mexican Revolution in 1910-1924, large numbers of black people migrated from New Orleans to Tampico, Mexico, as the oil industry prospered. These Africans in Mexico established branches of *Marcus Garvey's Universal Negro Improvement Association.* One black oil worker, who came to Tampico, stated, *"There is no race prejudice; everyone is treated according to his abilities."* Black heavyweight champion Jack Johnson in 1924 said that Mexico was *"willing not only to give us the privileges of Mexican citizenship but was also willing to champion our cause."*

Juan Uribe, a major Mexican official, visiting Los Angeles in 1919 (300th) was quoted as saying during **Red Summer (1919),** *"My only regret is that it is not physically possible to immediately transport several million African Americans to my beloved Mexico. The north yields riches as nowhere else and where people are not disturbed by artificial standards of race or color."*

Similarly, African American immigrant Theodore Troy said, *"I am going to a land where freedom and opportunity beckon me as well as every other man, woman, and child of dark skin. In this land, there are no Jim Crow laws to fetter me; I am not denied opportunity because of the color of my skin, and wonderful undeveloped resources of a country smiled upon by God beckon my genius on to their development."*

Blacks established colony in Baja, California, in the Santa Clara and Vallecitos Valleys between Ensenada and Tecate, approximately 30 miles south of San Diego. Fifty families developed fruit orchards and engaged in cattle ranching; this community lasted into the 1960s. Not to be overlooked is the enormous success of the Negro Baseball Leagues in Mexico during the 1930s and 1940s. Black ballplayers, together with 500 family members, seeking relief from racism in the US and segregated institutions all over, were hosted in Mexico by generally respectful competitors and admiring fans. One competitor, in particular, Ray Dandridge, played for 18 years in Mexico before Jackie Robinson gained admission into US major league baseball.

Also, from the 1930s to the 1960s, major Mexican muralists, such as Diego Rivera, David Siqueiros, and Jose Clemente Orozco, invited prominent African American artists such as Hale Woodruff, John Biggers, Elizabeth Catlett and Charles White to the Mexican Art School. These Mexican muralists helped them developed their expressiveness, and effective artistic styles to connect images to the ethnic and class struggle. Of course, there are many more historical intersections where Mexican and African people cooperated.

A few examples of cooperation and solidarity between US and Mexicans are reflected by the Student Nonviolent Coordinating Committee (SNCC)/ Black Panther Party, Brown Berets, and the Alianza Federal de Pueblos Libres and also, El Movimiento Estudiantil Chicano de Atzlan (MECHA) and the Black Student Union (BSU). Mack Lyons, a Black member of the United Farmworkers Union's National Executive, negotiated a contract with Coca Cola, which owns Minute-maid and sizeable Florida orange groves. In Los Angeles during the '90s, Black and Brown students recognizing the common history and mutual interests formed the African and Latino Youth Summit (ALYS).

Bringing things up to date, descendants of American slavery can show their solidarity with Mexican and other Hispanic people trying to do as our ancestors, who found freedom from slavery across the Rio Grande. Black people owe a debt of gratitude to Mexico and its people today for what they did for runaway slaves when we were trying to get across the border for life and safety. Today the shoes are on another people's feet, but Hispanics are walking in our tracks, coming the other way to America. They are exhibiting the same need for help, as runaway slaves in the 1800s, but today the slave master attitude and mindset is building walls. Having been there, descendants of American slavery should empathize wholeheartedly with Hispanics that have human needs today, as did slaves during slavery.

Prelude to War: The Final Strategy to Preserve Slavery

Rage against slavery continued to grow and express itself in many ways. However, I believe many of the acts were individual attempts prompted by former slaves and individuals that desired to break the grip of slaveholders on everyone and everything in America. They saw how human bondage had wrapped every institution in the nation and made everyone party to the dehumanizing and merciless system of the internal slave trade and breeding creating an enslaved workforce.

This statement is offered to acknowledge and recognize that many individuals and groups struck out against a system so huge it had neither beginning nor end. Their acts were desperate statements to declare they were not part of anything akin to slavery. Slave revolts to me were such acts, whether large or small, desperation drove participants. Most were not inspired by any organized group, like John Brown, or giving help when they assisted those attempting to escape slavery, like the *Undergrown Railroad*. Other slaves joined Nat Turner, but his escapade was a one-man enterprise in terms of planning.

Turner's disregard for killing white people served notice on slave masters, regarding slaves' determination to be free. His rebellion declared holding enslaved Africans in perpetual bondage would be far more costly for slave masters than in the past. The slave narratives presented earlier provided a glimpse into the day-to-day drudgery, suffocating degradation, and total brutality slaves endured, as fixtures in their lives.

Following Turner's rampage through the Virginia countryside, whites in the South responded with laws that curtailed the already limited mobility and liberties of slaves. Black preachers were barred from the pulpit in Virginia for one hundred thirty years. Slave masters enforced laws against teaching slaves to read with jail time. Slaves were locked up and guarded during the night in many areas.

The 1860 Presidential Election brought everything to a head pitting forces for slavery against emancipation. They fought before and after the election to decide the question once and for all. Slavery supporters faced a crucial decision regarding the way of life they had embraced, and defied all moral justifications for ending it.

The internal slave trade in the North and Upper South was well entrenched. Wealth from the internal slave trade and breeding created a new system. A whole new way of life evolved for poor whites, a group that never had any money to speak about. By 1850, the internal slave trade had produced such wealth that these same poor whites had become plantation owners, merchants, bankers, politicians, and speculators. These were the beneficiaries of this new system, in terms of the magnitude of change. Poor whites, more so than any other white people in the South, reaped the rewards of the internal slave trade's breeding a replacement workforce in the South. It's new wealth created Southern society's middle class.

Looking at this new class, most were ignorant of economic principles, especially the enhancement of an investment, as they rode the backs of slaves to ownership and wealth. Poor whites only saw money on the front end and tried to squeeze every penny possible out of slaves; even at the risk of losing their entire investment—death or escape—altogether.

Poor whites gloried in the power of life and death over slaves. Never having power over anything more than a dog or cow, maybe a mule, they gouged slaves for every penny they could squeeze out of them. Again, I point out the movie *"Twelves Years A Slave,"* as an excellent reflection of this attitude toward slaves and slavery, which poor white exhibited.

This class had become the South's socioeconomic and political leadership. Unlike Southerners with "old money," this new crop of leaders had become rich over the last decade or two, only because of the internal slave trade and breeding. For them, slavery was everything, and without it, they were nothing; back to *root hog or die*.

These were the diehard supporters of slavery, and they were unwilling to give it up under any conditions. They became the force behind secession. They preferred to go all-in on slavery, trying to hold on to the one chance they had to be somebody. Secession became their threat. Southerners believed secession would push the North back from talk of emancipation, heading into the election of 1860.

Abraham Lincoln's election made emancipation a foregone conclusion for Southerners. Their threat of secession became the prelude to war and the final strategy to save bond slavery, as their way of life. The Confederacy opened fire on Fort Sumter on April 12, 1861, and war was no longer a threat. The Confederacy was similar to Napoleon Bonaparte in how he saw leaders in Europe, compared to how southern leaders saw the US federal government and Abraham Lincoln.

Southerners did not believe the Union had the stomach or heart for a real fight to end slavery. Similar to Napoleon and his slave revenues, the South's wealth was in cotton and slaves. However, cotton in fields across the South without slaves to pick it was like weeds in the field. Moreover, neither side took time to consider what would happen to millions of slaves caught up in a crossfire, once real fighting began.

Carrying the fight to the North, as its basic strategy for defending the Confederacy, the South's offense was its defense. Again, like Napoleon, the Confederacy seemed to have the upper hand, at first out of the gate. On the other hand, the debate over war and losing battles early on brought Lincoln to where Great Britain was deciding to end the **Trans-Atlantic Slave Trade** or face the harsh reality of defeat.

Desperately scrambling trying to find a fighting general, as losses mounted, Lincoln realized he could not allow the South to continue to benefit from holding enslaved Africans in bondage. This was like slave revenues to Napoleon, slavery was financing the South's war of session and unchecked the Union would lose.

Leaving slavery intact was giving the South the upper hand. The South not only continued gaining revenue from slavery to pay for its war of secession, but slavery and its revenues were supporting the people. Fighting the war on Northern territory put the pains of war too far away to cause real concern to the Deep South. Leaving slavery intact was providing food and other necessities of life for civilians and the army. They were enduring war without real cost or pain since all the fighting was taking place in the North or its border states. The deep South was where cotton was grown, the piggy bank for the South and it bread basket, unlike the slave breeding states, the South could afford to destroy, then rebuild.

The Confederacy's ability to keep slaves locked up on plantations gave it advantages the Union could not match. The South's ability to use slave-labor to build fortifications and other battle works was another advantage. Rather than use regular troops to perform such task, gave the South flexibility the Union did not have.

Based on his performance in battles, during the Mexican American War, the South believed Robert E. Lee gave the Confederate Army the best military strategist the US Army had produced, on its side. The outcome of battles, like the *Seven Days War, the Second Bull Run,* as well as Lee had chased Union Army Commanding General George B. McClellan off the Virginia peninsula, convinced southerners Robert E. Lee had the Union Army on the run.

Contrarily, Northerners were screaming for Lincoln's scalp, as they looked at an embolden Confederate Army guided by Lee, poised to invade the North. With Union Army losses mounting and few victories, Lincoln's back was against the wall. The battle of Antietam, even though it was considered a northern win, the tremendous loss of life did not give the North a sense of victory. The Union's mounting casualties and losing battles to the rebels made signing the Emancipation Proclamation, on the first of January 1863, a necessity for the Union in more ways than one. Lincoln resembled Britain's Parliament learning about the *flag deception scheme* and ending the **Trans-Atlantic Slave Trade,** contemplating signing the **Emancipation Proclamation.**

Looking at what Pres. Abraham Lincoln was up against, I believe he approached freeing slaves not just as his moral Christian duty and signing the Emancipation Proclamation was about far more than saving the Union. I believe from studying the matter, it seems to me, Lincoln figured out with one move, he could do two, maybe three critical things simultaneously. First, by freeing slaves, he would deny the Confederacy revenues that having slavery intact was providing the South. The southern economy in the Deep South, though at a reduced level, had continued functioning. Slaves were still working fields, in factories and in armories producing ammunition, which strengthen the South's war effort. Whereas, emancipated slaves, free roaming about would not be producing commodities for the South. Slaves wandering all over the countryside would create confusion behind Confederate lines.

Freed slaves on the move, running about uncontrollably, would be like a counterforce operating behind enemy lines. Emancipated slaves would force the Confederacy to put men in the field to try and keep slaves in place working. The Confederate Army, unlike the Union army, which used soldiers to perform many task, used slaves instead. Lincoln's move would strike at the heart of the whole Confederate system and strategy by causing instability among the civilian population and bring the cost of war home to Confederate civilians.

The second part of Lincoln's strategy most historians missed is even more subtle. The confusion emancipated slaves would cause behind confederate lines, would force the Confederate Army to make adjustments to its supply lines. It had to come up with a way to keep slavery intact, while invading the North, but that would spread the Confederate army too thin, which would be like fighting on senral fronts, again like Napoleon's invasion of Russia. Lincoln emancipating slaves make fighting on the move was far more than what the Confederate Army could compensated for, without changing its whole strategy. Emancipation was not something the Confederacy could ignore, because emancipation robbed the South of the one thing it had taken for granted.

More than anything, The Emancipation Proclamation brought Lincoln time to do the one thing he needed most, while the South was trying to come up with a new strategy, Pres. Lincoln was able find a real fighting general. Swinging back South, Southern slave owners would find it impossible to keep slaves working on plantations, in armories and munition works, which the Confederate Army desperately needed to avoid running out of ammunition and other supplies in the middle of battles. Politicians had to keep a slave economy going without slaves.

Emancipating slaves was like introducing **An Act for the Abolition of the Slave Trade (1807),** as a "war measure," which changed the dynamics of Great Britain's war strategy. Emancipation not only appeased abolitionists, but the true gambit was former slaves entering the fight. Moreover, it also forced the South to develop a new war strategy, similar to how France's *"flag deception game"* forced Parliament to change its strategy.

Thirdly, American history books present emancipation as thought it was a dreaded decision forced upon Lincoln and a country not ready to support and care for slaves unable or unwilling to care for their selves. I see the situation totally differently. Emancipation rescued the Union's sagging fortunes in the war, which it was unprepared to fight.

Although it was an experiment, using real live subjects, emancipation was like the *war measure strategy*, in that it caught the Confederacy completely by surprise, in terms of the impact, because neither side was prepared for mobile slaves running free. I say this in recognition that neither side had considered slaves impact and developed contingency plans to keep slaves locked up on plantations, roaming the countryside or jamming roads, interfering with troop movements.

Simultaneously, slaves' uncontrolled flight in search of safety and freedom bought time for the Union Army, even though it had no contingency, the confusion aided just the same. While all of this was going on, Lincoln desperately searched for a general, without sympathy for the slave-holding South, as Winfield Scott, George McClellan, and Henry Halleck. These generals led the Union Army into debacle after debacle. Even though individually, they won a few battles, the South had the Union fighting on its terms and on its territory for the most part. Lincoln needed a general willing to take the fight to the South. Finally, he settled on the best the Union had Ulysses S. Grant.

Lincoln's emancipation drew free blacks and freed slaves to the side of the union. Although it was slow in coming, for black men desperately wanting to get into the fight for their freedom, finally they hit the battlefield. They gave the Union one thing money could not buy, and the South couldn't get, even if it had money. Emancipation gave Lincoln access to thousands of black men—black fighters—as potential recruits. His move reflects how Vancouver and Mexico felt about slaves willing to fight to be free in their country rather than slaves in America.

Slaves, on the other hand, did not understand the nuances of emancipation, neither did they care. All they knew was they were no longer the property of slave masters. With emancipation came a new kind of survival struggle for former slaves. They entered this new world where, for the first time, their survival depended on what was in the heads and hearts.

Without direction or destination, leaving plantations, slaves faced obstacles impossible to clear without help. Desperation, scarcity and death were all that was immediately before them.

Lincoln's penniless emancipation unshackled descendants of American slavery, but the lack of resources, after 243 years of bondage, left them imprisoned by their poverty and ignorance.

Having arrived at a point, where Lincoln was determined to break the will of the South, I have tried to put his decision to emancipate slaves and end forced bondage in perspective, so it is clear it was not a desperate roll of the dies, a gamble trying to save the Union. Emancipation was very much a move of conscience but based on a sound strategy. Pres. Lincoln still had to find a means of dealing with the aftermath of his action, which he had not thought completely through. Signing the Emancipation Proclamation, though sorely needed, Lincoln created a level of chaos; neither waring side had taken time to consider, so both were unprepared for what transpired, following emancipation. However, since the fighting was in the Upper South starting out, but slaves abandoned plantations in the Deep South as well, emancipation created a far larger problem for the South than for the North.

Simply turning slaves out, without consideration for the task of surviving in a hostile war-torn environment, was an issue I believe Lincoln felt was worth the risk, if his gamble paid off. First, emancipated slaves without any basic knowledge of where they were in the world, had no idea which way to go to avoid the war raging all around them. No matter where they were in the South, all slaves had the same immediate problem. Although most slaves were in the same condition, they were not all the same.

There were few alternatives and even fewer choices; survival for slaves was not a day-to-day proposition, but a moment-to-moment survival act. Most slaves were without any basic knowledge of the challenges of surviving as Freedmen, let alone trying to survive under such unanticipated circumstances that war produced.

A Reality Between Slavery and Freedom

The next discussion is not about the events and battles of the Civil War; moving forward, the conditions Civil War produced for newly freed slaves to contend become the focus of **"The 400th"**. Looking through the eyes of slaves before the Civil War, at the world that entrapped them, readers saw the world slave masters created for themselves at the expense of slaves. Enslaved Africans were told everything in that world. Now, as former slaves, with emancipation and the Civil War swirling in their heads, with fighting and dying all around them at times, newly Freedmen were trying to take control of their lives, in a situation that was completely out of control. Pushed about by both sides, waring conditions made them like straws blown by the wind. For the first time, former slaves faced survival as an individual responsibility.

The concept of family for slaves had been destroyed by the internal slave trade and breeding, if not before. Even among those who came together, their relationships were functions of slavery, and many of those relationships disappeared with emancipation and choice. Emancipation was a greater challenge for women with children, who had, for whatever reason, been allowed to remain close to one another.

Survival was more of an individual undertaking for men, especially those used as breeders in the internal slave trade system. For the most part, it taught many black men, *"It is easier to walk away than to care."* All offsprings belonged to master, and for far too many, the lesson stuck. Yet, for others, caring about what happened to others around them began during slavery. These enslaved Africans looked after others, as best they could, even at their peril at times.

Leaving plantations did not mean slavery could be left behind: it was all they knew. Enduring to survive, former slaves had to learn to *make something out of nothing.* That lesson they would be taught and have to learn again and again, as their penniless emancipation opened a door, leading to a world unimaginable for former slaves. The story of my family began in slavery, as I've stated repeatedly.

Listening to stories and reading slaves' narratives and other materials about those terrible times, seemed to me, freedom was like a journey through a wilderness, not over a road or even a footpath that had been traveled and trodden down. My family, following slavery, like millions of others, tried to follow the path Burl Lee treaded. Following his path, those who came after him encountered gaps, where it seemed no one had gone before. If someone had, the path was so arduous, rugged or obscure in places there were no visible signs one could follow with confidence.

Each generation of slave descendants had to make paths for those who came after them. Similar to Burl Lee's offsprings, they had only indications of where those signs led. Without education, resources, and real knowledge of the world outside the plantation, the best former slaves could hope for was to keep moving forward, in hopes of reach a better place than where they were at the time.

Most historians address slaves' desperate conditions, as though they should have known or had some idea of what to do. With emancipation, their trek began with lots of back and forth steps, sometimes circling, trying to find a way forward. Historian Ira Berlin writes of slaves new world *(The Long Emancipation: The Demise of Slavery in the United States; 2015, Harvard University Press).*

"The Long Emancipation" emphasizes that freedom's arrival was the product not of a moment or a man, but of a process in which many participated—in the case of the United States, a near-century-long process. Moreover, the demise of slavery was not so much an occasion or a proclamation, as a movement that characterized the complex arrival of freedom, which created a history with multiple players and narratives. Reaching emancipation's long awaited arrival, slaves were not shed of the universality of violence, powerful clashes, confrontations and ceaseless carnage, manifested by material interests and deeply held beliefs of slave masters. Slaveholders and their numerous allies did not give way easily, even though they faced a movement for universal freedom, they responded with violent bloody conflicts that left a trail littered with destroyed property, broken bones, traumatized men and women, as well as numerous bodies. Emancipation manifested confrontations, kidnappings, pogroms, riots, insurrections, and finally open warfare."

"The 400th" narrative is an effort to look back at the convoluted saga life threw at newly Freedmen following slavery beginning with views through the eyes of two freed slaves, Robert Reed Church, Sr. (6-18-1839/8-29-1912), and Burl Lee, Sr. (sic. 1843-1915). Robert Reed Church was born a slave in Holly Springs, Mississippi, just down the road from Memphis, Tennessee. Beginning life, my great-great-great-grandparent came together long enough to produce the first Burl Lee, also in Mississippi. These two men, for me, dramatically illustrate the importance of family and community in determining one's level of success in later life. Although both were born in slavery, Church and my great-great-grandfather Burl Lee were born into two different worlds. Burl Lee was what was called a "field nigger." Cotton fields were all that lay before him, as a life's endeavor. Degradation and hard work were the legacy emancipation bequeathed him, and he passed that legacy to his progeny.

The major difference here is Robert R. Church, Sr., unlike Burl Lee, could trace his linage back to his European ancestors through his father. The son of Captain Charles B. Church, a white steamboat owner from Virginia, that built his wealth on slavery. His father belived as President Thomas Jefferson. Jefferson, who sired several children born to his slave Sally Hemmings, continued to hold his children in servitude until his death.

It's unknown whether Robert Reed Church was given his freedom, bought it, or was emancipated? But, we do know he grew up working as a slave. Captain

Church operated his boat along the Mississippi River from St. Louis to New Orleans. Robert Reed worked as a steward in the dining hall aboard his father's riverboat. Although he kept his son in slavery, Captain Charles B. Church taught his son to run the business. Robert Began as a dishwasher, then cook and finally steward; his father did not teach him to navigate his boat.

Church, Jr. purchased groceries wholesale, kept accounts and managing the provision of food, drinks, and gambling on his father's boat. While waiting tables, young Robert listened to passengers, and picked up business acumen and contacts. He saved whatever money he earned and, in 1863, bought a bar in Memphis, Tennessee, which he then traded for a saloon with a billiard parlor. Church established himself as a Beale Street entrepreneur (*American National Biography Online*, David Tucker, 2000; American National Biography).

Burl Lee may have been one of millions of orphans born during the internal slave trade and breeding, for all we know. Our family line could be the product of one or two orphans. Thinking about it, millions of descendants of American slavery had begun life without any possibility of knowing beyond themselves. If the internal slave trade ran nonstop until slavery's end, there were babies born right up to war's end.

The Civil War was a special hell for newly freed slaves. Often during battles, the land changed possession several times, going from one army's possession to the other then back again, with slaves caught in between, in "no man's land." Trapped in the fighting, sometimes they were caught on the wrong side. But under any circumstances, slaves dared not stay put long in any one place, since they were being hunted by southern slave catchers, who believed that slaves belonged to white folks in the South and all were runaways.

Once war came to their state, slaves became emancipated. Many slaves followed the Union army, as government contraband. Whether slaves were free at any given moment depended upon which warring party occupied the land they were on at the time. Caught up in battles, running for their lives, while trying to keep together, slaves died during the fighting the same as soldiers. However, neither side bothered to count these dead. They became more dry bones in the unmarked graves of slavery.

Presenting these two individuals, Robert R. Church, Sr. and Burl Lee, Sr., as I do, is to highlight the importance of making families and building communities for former slaves. Families and communities were the major forces behind newly Freedmen's ability to endure to survive. Robert Church and Burl Lee, my great-great-grandfather, though born slaves, they entered life on two totally different levels in two totally different worlds, regarding circumstances. Church's slavery was vastly different from that endured by my great-great-grandfather.

Life in Blackface

Totally unknown to slaves in the South, a very different course of survival was developing in the North that would give some slave and their descendants a sense of direction and access to wealth. This enterprise would become the most consistent, productive, and lucrative activity, as well as a major economic vehicle for some slaves and descendants. It would become the exit many former slaves and descendants would use to move beyond poverty.

Just the other side of the Mason-Dixon Line, an American phenomenon was taking place. It grew out of the total domination of slave masters over enslaved Africans. Slavery reduced those trapped in it to doing whatever they could to make surviving easier. Most slaves brought from Africa to the United States retained memories of life and culture in Africa. All Africans slaves, as they arrived in the US, brought knowledge, costumes, activities, and folkways, with them in their heads. The very smart ones concealed such things from master particularly, and white people in general.

Slave masters ruthlessly rooted out anything about enslaved Africans, they understood, as related to Africa. Master took away things they thought would help enslaved African preserve their heritage and communicate with each other, primarily drums. Slaves were only able to keep things master did not understand. Slaves worked diligently to learn slave masters' mindsets about slaves.

They learned to disguise or hide the skills and things they brought from Africa in their heads or learned what other Africans kept in their heads. Such knowledge gave enslaved Africans a sense of their African-ness. Slaves watched master's reactions to everything slaves did. Quick-witted slaves picked up on the delight master experienced, watching slaves clown around or doing things that tickled his fancy. Their antics drew favorable reactions from master when he had guests and wanted to entertain them and his family. *"Boy show me something you can do!!!"*

On such occasions, when master was pleased, he showed generosity toward his slaves in general, but to those that did the clowning around, he was even more generous. The master's reaction gave some slaves new ideas. Back in Africa, celebrations were communal affairs, during such events everyone felt inspired, or when there was a need to demonstrate their culture, those with special gifts or talent became involved. But, entertaining master introduced the idea of performing.

Slaves began making a calculated effort to please viewers. Once they realized the advantage in this, slaves work at being creative. They developed specific routines, movements, and actions while paying particular attention to what master laughed at and reacted to or told them he wanted to see. Using their bodies in unusual ways to white people or adding musical and rhythmic sounds, entertained master even more.

Slaves learned to use such things that started as impromptu actions, but over time they worked out specific routines. Although slaves did not see, what they did as anything more than a way to make things easier on them, and get rewards from master, slaves did not think of what they did as art. Although it seemed nothing, at the time, making master laugh, doing things he thought were funny or entertaining to him and his guest, no matter how humiliating or ridiculous it may have seemed to other slaves, those slaves became special. When other plantation owners had affairs, they would request these slaves for entertainment.

White men from the North that were guess saw what slaves did to entertain master, while enjoying slave antics. They also noticed the response slaves got from other white guests, which gave northern whites ideas too. They took what they saw and learned watching slaves back home up North. They began imitating what they saw slaves doing and were able to get a similar response from white people in the North, as slaves got from masters. But, the important difference here is they got paid.

The phenomenon slaves created gave birth to what would become American entertainment, beginning in the 1820s. Working-class white men (usually Irish) tried to look and act as authentic, as possible, imitating slaves. White men in the North developed routines to capitalize on what was a beginning technology created by slaves without them knowing it. These white men blackened their faces with burnt cork and dressed in rags, like enslaved Africans on plantations to ensure their audience understood they were imitating slaves.

White men imitated slaves' musical sounds and dance routines, as best they could. Trying to look, act, and sound like slaves, they even tried to speak in slaves' "broken plantation" dialect. They expropriated songs and dance materials by watching, whenever possible, slaves entertaining their master's family and friends. These white men became known as Minstrels.

Today, most people assume Minstrelsy, because of its blackface and degradation of enslaved Africans began in the South. Surprisingly, Minstrelsy was born and evolved in the North. Northerners did not have day-to-day contact with plantation slave culture; they assumed what they saw white men doing on stage, was the way slaves behave all the time. White men imitating slaves became pioneers developing Minstrel shows. These shows featured a variety of jokes, songs, dances, and skits based on the ugliest stereotypes of enslaved Africans, which white people came to know and love.

William Henry Lane was born a free black man in Rhode Island, where his career performing in minstrel shows began in 1825. Playing the banjo and the tambourine, Lane created a character that became known as Master Juba. Lane flipped the script and imitated what whites were imitating slaves doing, as well as the moves of the best white dancers of his time. Over time, he created his own innovative style and danced his way to international fame. Charles Dickens, the celebrated great English novelist, while touring the US in 1842, wrote a book about his travels called "*American Notes*." He described a visit to Almack's, a dance hall in Manhattan's notorious Five Points. He detailed the performance of a dancer called Master Juba:

> *"The corpulent black fiddler, and his friend who plays the tambourine, stamp upon the boarding of the small raised orchestra pit in which they sit, and play a lively measure. Five or six couple came upon the floor, marshalled by a lively young negro, who is the wit of the assembly, and the greatest dancer known."*

Even though most Africans were from cultures that relied on drumming for communicating, personal expression, and entertainment, slave masters did not allow slaves to have or play drums. So, slaves, with "nothing," began using their bodies as instruments—*making something out of nothing!* Over time, the hand-clapping, foot-stomping, body thumping and thigh-slapping evolved into a dance called *"patting juba."*

Lane combined *patting juba* with the jig and reel dances he learned watching poor Irish, trying to imitate slaves. He also added many other ethnic dance steps, such as the shuffle, the slide, buck dance, pigeon wing, and clog to create a new dance he called *"tap dancing."* As his reputation grew, promoters began calling him Master Juba; the *"Dancinest fellow ever was!"* American and European writers alike proclaimed Master Juba "the greatest dancer of all time."

Master Juba was the first black performer to get top billing over a white performer in a minstrel show in 1845. Lane competed in dance contests and defeated all comers, including an Irishman, considered the best white dancer in America named Jack Diamond. Master Juba and Diamond were matched, like boxers, in a series of staged tap dance competitions throughout the United States. Minstrelsy, as a genre, shaped the nation's views of blacks, poor blacks in particular, even until today. Reinforcing white supremacy well after the abolition of slavery, Minstrelsy's blackface, caricatures, and attitudes, reinforced the socioeconomic and political system of segregation that began in the 1880s.

Slaves, Struggles and the Civil War

On many occasions, talking with me during childhood, Rev. Burl Lee, Jr. described different aspects of my family's journey from slavery into freedom. It seems today he wanted me to understand and appreciate the hardships and struggles of our family. Although my memories of those conversations diminished over the years, researching and reading slaves' narratives revived many of those conversations, as I retold stories, he relayed to me of their efforts. I encountered many similar accounts, sometimes they connecting things for me, reawakening memories I thought were lost. Sharing his stories now gives my research real context.

Listening to his stories, it seemed, slaves, woke up on the road in the middle of nowhere. Seeing emancipation through the eyes of his father, Burl Lee, Sr., made survival for newly Freedmen seemed an individual struggle as emancipation began. However, over time, it seems his stories became more concerned with the fate of all former slaves, as though he saw former slaves as one family.

Before bondage ended, slaves had what they called marriages and families; freedom broke bonds on everything if that was what the individual wanted. People without attachment to anything beyond themselves had it easier, as slaves left plantations. The most basic structures of life, family, and community bonds developed during slavery were not binding, once some individuals had choices.

Looking back at those times to try and tell the story descendants of American slavery endured, struggling to get from one day to the next, was like trying to see through a fog. I believed their efforts during this period determined whether or not descendants of American slavery survived as a people. Former slaves' greatest challenge was establishing a stable existence. Though not done formally, newly freed slaves' decision to make families and build communities made all the difference, during their odyssey, from slavery to freedom. Their course was not an arc or a straight line. Their epic saga, at times, may seem we have passed this way before, but then a turn will take this narrative, where historians have never gone.

For instance, many individuals, black and white, were born during the same or different periods and in different places along the road from slavery to freedom. Once emancipated, slaves' lives in some way intersected and set in motion events or created effects, especially the lives of some white people, which reached out over decades to advance or hinder the hopes of slavery's descendants at later times.

Freed slaves followed the signs others left behind, if there were any marker at all. On most occasions, they could not anticipate or imagine their next steps and even less those consequences. Hard work during slavery was difficult true enough, according to Burl Lee, Jr. it was tolerable for people without choices.

The 400th: From Slavery to Hip Hop

Reading slave narratives in the previous section indicated that with the end of slavery, their prayers for no more beatings, enough food to fill their bellies, clothes for their backs, and shoes for their feet would answer the prayers for most. Slaves trying to survive these vicious and treacherous times in America, faced events and conditions that played out in many different ways, as survival needs took control. Consequently, my point is, in many cases, telling one story is to tell the story of many other enslaved people and places.

Memphis: The Home of the Blues

The most important story on the road to freedom for slave descendants was that everything grew out of their struggle to set down roots, make families, and build communities. Leaving plantations slaves' struggles were heart-wrenching, especially those, in the Mississippi delta, the Mid-South, Memphis, and on Beale Street. However, their travails on Beale Street were bound up with the origin, development, propagation, and perpetuation of the *"Blues"* culture they developed. Also, the *"Blues"* culture on and around Beale Street grew out of individual expressions, and survival strategies developed back during slavery, in many cases.

The *"Blues"* developed as slaves tried to anesthesia the pain, degradation, drudgery and brutality, during the tenebrous times of slavery. Their **Blues** grew out of trying to express their innermost, but unspoken desires. One of these expressions developed into a way of making master laugh when it seemed he might be displeased with them or some other slave. When slave masters were not feeling well and wanted a distraction or entertainment for his family and guests, he got slaves to do things he liked to see.

Again, slaves' moans, groans, and wails, giving voice to their misery, became their inner sanctum, and over time, they took on harmonic and musical characteristics. These slave expressions gained them an unexpected audience, as slave masters saw their expressions as entertainment. Even though white people did not understand the source of these rhythmic utterances, they were strangely affected by them. Somehow these tantalizing expressions developed into particular rhythmic patterns, which had a soothing and enthralling effect on some white people. Memphis is where all of this came together for many former slaves, my family in particular, and is why I tell about this saga as I do.

Officially began in 1826, Memphis' development was all about the river—traffic, workers, and commerce. Whitney's cotton gin, by 1840, had produced an economy that turned Memphis into a boomtown. Growing from a river landing, created by Native People along America's greatest waterway—Mississippi River—Memphis was incorporated as a city in 1841. It became the largest inland cotton market in the world because of "white gold" or "King Cotton," grown all around it. Cotton cultivation made slaves essential to industries in and around Memphis, since production, storage, and sale of cotton, was the base of the economic system of the South.

Called the "Big Muddy" by locals, the Mississippi River spurred the growth of Memphis in countless ways, as it became the transportation hub of the Mid-South. The Mississippi River was a water highway that ran from Minnesota to New Orleans, and like a major artery supplying blood, it gave life to Native People's communities for centuries before the white man ever arrived. White people used the river like Native People to ferried people and goods through the Mississippi Delta. Commerce flowed like blood through arteries, giving life to the heart of America.

Providing the major bridge across the Mississippi River, connecting highways, running in all four directions into and out of the city, made Memphis the crossroad of the South. Converging in Memphis, railroads made it a hub for trains crossing the Mississippi River, which aided the city's growth, as it became the banking center for the Mid-South. Continuing it growth, the clearing of land for cotton cultivation gave Memphis another title, the major hardwood lumber markets between St. Louis and New Orleans. A river town, railroad hub, connecting bridge, Mid-South cotton market, and the largest city between New Orleans and St. Louis, brought people to Memphis from all directions.

With its dock lying at the foot of Beale Street commerce from the river was funneled into the center of Memphis. River transportation brought travelers, black and white, from all over, which also made Beale Street a real business opportunity as well. Docks at the head of Beale Street, dumped travelers and drew locals with pockets filled with money and needing lodging, food, entertainment, and other goods, it seemed a magical melting pot. The Mississippi River made Beale Street the gateway to the city and the Mid-South, as it distributed commerce, as well as people throughout the region. Money flowed into the city, like water down the Mississippi.

Memphis was firmly part of the rebellious Confederate South, before and during the beginning of the Civil War. The city supplied more than 70 Confederate companies of recruits for the war effort in 1861. Tennessee was one of 11 Confederate states that declared war on the United States of America. A major crossing of the Mississippi River in the West, Memphis was considered the backdoor to the South.

Apparently, in terms of attack, the Confederacy saw Memphis as securely locked into the solid South. With Arkansas, Tennessee, North Carolina, and Kentucky sitting atop Tennessee, stretching from the Mississippi River to the Atlantic Ocean, the Confederate Army believed these states locked the Yankees out, like a "northern wall." However, General U. S. Grant understood that all too well, and made it his major objective, beginning the Union Army's Western campaign.

Grant, like a sneak thief, picked the lock on the gate to the South's "northern wall" by invading from the river. Steaming down the Ohio River, and invading Kentucky, Gen. Grant divided his forces. He took half of his army and continued to the Mississippi Rivers headed to Memphis from where he launched an invasion of West Tennessee. Grant's Union forces were a juggernaut, smashing through rebel lines, leaving the Confederate's "northern wall" in tatters.

Grant forces met up at what became known as *"Bloody Shiloh"* (4-6-1862). The battle at *"Shiloh"* was the first major victory for the Union in the West. The loss of Memphis cost the Confederacy far more than it realize, until fighting ended, and Memphis was in Yankees hands. The South's water highway—Mississippi River—was like a driveway, delivering Grant the victory over the South in the West.

The Battle of Memphis amounted to only a 90-minute scuffle, and after twenty minutes, Confederate gunboats that did not high tailed it downriver to Vicksburg, Mississippi, lay on the bottom of the river. Jubilantly, Union Naval forces struck the Confederate bars and stars, replaced them with the Union's stars and stripes. Gen. Grant made the city a hospital post for more than 5,000 injured Union soldiers; most were from the battle at Shiloh. Rebounding from the battle, Memphis merchants realized that Yankee dollars were worth far more than Confederate script.

Finally, locating my great-great-grandfather, who began life at the mercy of the internal slave trade and breeding industry in the Mississippi Delta? However up North, Minstrelsy had whites jamming it up, as a way of poking fun at the South. As another key element in the saga of enslaved Africans surviving slavery, while building lives and communities, their prospects seemed to be improving, but nothing was guaranteed.

By 1850, Robert Reed Church, Sr. had grown up a child slave and moved up from washing dishes to steward on his father's riverboat. Simultaneously, Burl Lee, Sr. while struggling to survive learned to work the cotton fields of Mississippi as a slave. Again, unlike Burl Lee, Robert Church was not part of the internal slave trade neither was he a product of breeding. Burl Lee, on the other hand, was a commodity in both, as far as we know. Robert's and Burl's philosophical and psychological environmental influences impacted them in ways that are not quantifiable. Those factors impacted their lives in innumerable ways, and the economic differences in their circumstances had corresponding effects on them throughout their lives.

During his apprenticeship on his father's boat, Church came to know Memphis (1852) from riding up and down the river and trading to restock his father's boat. Situated in a bend of the Mississippi, Memphis became a required stop for goods and passengers traveling up and down the river. Robert Reed Church, Sr. had a bird's eye view of his possible future, while still a slave. Time and events cast Memphis and the Mississippi River into a central role in the legacy of both Robert R. Church and Burl Lee, at different times and in different ways.

By 1863, newly freed slaves and anyone with money, looking for a place to set down roots, saw opportunity and prosperity in Memphis on Beale Street. Again, the gateway to the Mississippi Delta basin, Memphis' river/road/train connection was essential to surrounding communities for a hundred miles in all directions. Beale Street, as Civil War raged, drew contraband to the city, looking for safety and a place to settle.

The 400th: From Slavery to Hip Hop

Memphis became a post-battle command and control center of operation for the Union Army. It was as far down river union supplies could travel by water. The city became a major supply depot for Union forces in the Mid-South. War created an environment which had frightened contrabands running for their lives, trying to escape destruction and death. Memphis became a melting pot, drawing newly Freedmen into a new world of urban living. Many former enslaved Africans had never seen a city, let alone lived in one. But, similar to a catch basin, frightened refugees of war poured into Memphis, overflowing the city's meager resources.

The Mississippi River was the lifeline of the city, with its dock at the head of Beale Street, river commerce, put money in black dockworkers' pockets for the first time. Now, Freedmen were getting paid to do what they did for free, as slaves, found food and fun a short walk away on Beale Street. Roustabouts, railroad gangs, drivers of all sorts, and those trying to manage such activities took to free enterprise, like ducks to water. Even without a stable business location, enterprising ladies of the evening set up shop on Beale Street and worked out of its back alleys.

Robert Church departed his father's boat for life on his own and arrived in Memphis in 1863 and with his entrance prospects for former slaves changed forever. He brought the one thing into this mix slave descendants did not have and were totally unable to secure—wealth. How much, no one knows, but it is as one of this narrative's major themes points out regarding slavery—*It did not matter how much wealth he had, what he did with it made all the difference for descendants of American slavery in Memphis.*

Evolution of the Happy Slaves

"If I could have the nigger show back again in its pristine purity, I should have little use for opera."

-- Mark Twain

"Blackface performers are, ...the filthy scum of white society, who have stolen from us a complexion denied them by nature, in which to make money, and pander to the corrupt taste of their white fellow citizens."

-- Frederick Douglass

    One of the first independent money-making opportunities for emancipated slaves and a major development in America came through Minstrelsy. Initially, only a few blacks were allowed to participate in minstrel shows, before the mid-1840s, and only then by declaring they were the *"real coons."* Although they didn't need it, even black minstrels had to don charcoal or bootblack on their faces to perform in minstrel shows. They had to follow the same comedic routines, even though they confirmed the racist stereotypes of slavery.

    Minstrel routines allowed former slaves to develop real artistic flair and competence on stage. The "blackface" facade met whites' expectations for blacks. Donning a "blackface" gained acceptance of white audiences for blacks on stage. Former slaves learned rudimentary stills and the rigors of show business. Although the structure of minstrel shows changed and varied over time, its images—blackface and caricatures of dimwitted, inarticulate, and lazy blacks—remained fixtures of American entertainment, as well as everyday life, even with some people today.

    Before the Civil War (1861-1865), pro-slavers used these racist stereotypes to counter the abolitionist movement. Slave owners claimed denigrating stereotypes reflected the need to civilize barbaric African heathen slaves. Minstrelsy's fictitious images portrayed slaves as *"happy darkies, content with their lot in life, singing, and dancing, while fearful of life outside the plantation."* The Mammy and Ole Black Joe images of slaves, as well as buffoonery, during Minstrelsy was used to helped justify America's socioeconomic and political placement of blacks on the bottom of American society.

    Following emancipation and the Civil War, black performers were unable to alter the traditional racist stereotypes presented by Minstrelsy. By the beginning of Civil War (1861), these stereotypes were deeply ingrained in both theater and American society. Whites held tenaciously to their 18th-century views of blacks as not only inferior, but demanded blacks remain subservience and cater to the whims and excesses of white people. Nevertheless, by the 1880s, African Americans were able to use Minstrelsy and become established in all phases of show business. Former slaves became performers and composers. They moved into management and ownership of minstrel shows, as well.

As time and events would have it, Minstrelsy's success came at the expense of black performers' pride, personalities, and originality. African Americans faced discrimination daily. Personally, as artists, their performances did not receive the notice and credit deserved. Creatively, their roles were restricted. Whites saw blacks, as naturally talented entertainers, so their image as untrained took precedent during critiques. "White defined" roles forced black performers and those on the business side to conform to negative stereotypes of "Old Black Joe and Mammy." For decades there were no real choices or opportunities for blacks in show business that aided them in changing the stereotypes that controlled their success and lives.

Contrabands of War

Most students and readers of American history have encountered the word *contraband*, but an understanding of how and why exactly emancipated slaves received that designation, most cannot say. Once Confederate troops invaded the North and fighting became a reality for everyone in the South, slaves being the most prominent among them, everything changed. Lincoln declared with the **Emancipation Proclamation** (1863), all enslaved Africans in states fighting in rebellion against the United States were free. Although his act was expected by some in the North, and hoped for by slaves in South, nevertheless, and as Pres. Lincoln planned it caused dislocation and confusion behind enemy lines for all.

Once fighting began in the Upper South, slaves began abandoning plantations across the South and new prospects for former slaves began unfolding. Lincoln counted on slaves' masters would be unable to keep slaves on lockdown amid war, looking after them and their families. Whites in the South could only watch, as slave masters found it impossible to hold slaves on plantations that wanted to escape. Becoming fugitive slaves or runaways to Confederates, escaping slaves overwhelmed any effort to keep the old system intact.

Former slaves were on the move, whether they were considered emancipated or runaways. Most took advantage of circumstances and made their desperate dash for freedom and life. Without any idea what would happen once they reached them, most runaway slaves headed straight for protection behind Union Army lines, when they found them. Another subject, historians do not realistically visit, but I believe confusion is what Pres. Lincoln counted on when he proposed emancipating slaves.

Unprepared for the confusion escaping slaves caused, Confederate forces, along with the Union Army, were dumbfounded, once slaves began abandoning plantations en mass. Southerners never thought slaves would abandon them and their plantations like a jailbreak. They believed their propaganda about *"happy slaves, dancing and singing the day away."* No one considered the impact millions of slaves' on the move at one time across the South would cause before shots were fired at Fort Sumter (1861). Militarily, slaves sheer mass was like a third army in the field that both Confederate and Union forces had to contend, while fighting each other. Saves running about was a problem neither side had considered, except maybe Lincoln, as the South gloriously and pompously marched to war.

Civil War proved a blessing and a curse for slaves during this period. Neither the federal government nor the Confederacy had policies to deal with slaves under wartime conditions, let alone what to do with runaways. Union military commanders were no better off, than rebels.

The confederates were forced to use their discretion even though they could not enforce anything. According to circumstances faced, when dealing with emancipated or runaway slaves, everyone was a first timer. While trying to subdue a tenacious enemy that had mortgaged everything, including their privies to finance the war, Union generals, when it came to newly freed slaves were at wit's end also. Although, the war was desired by many in the South, one could not prepare for the reality that developed once the shooting started.

Trapped in what seemed, no-man's-land, trying to stay alive, slaves had no protection from death and destruction all around them. Moreover, both warring sides looked to the two presidents—Abraham Lincoln and Jefferson Davis—for policies and direction. However, the war came too suddenly for the Union to prepare, and the Confederacy was too busy marching off to war to bother with such minor details, as what would happen to slaves.

Union Gen. Benjamin F. Butler was the first to take matters into his own hands. He was first to applied the term *"contraband of war"* to three fugitive slaves that showed up at Fort Monroe. Learning that the Confederate Army had used them to build fortifications, Butler refused to return them, as non-combatants. Frank Baker, James Townsend, and Sheppard Mallory, three escaped slaves sought asylum, at Fort Monroe, after rowing a skiff to Old Point Comfort. They had been leased by their masters to the Confederate Army to help construct defense batteries at Sewell's Point.

Gen. Butler put them to work for the Union Army, but did not pay the escaped slaves for working at Fort Monroe. Butler claimed them as *"contraband of war,"* and continued to refer to them as slaves. Gideon Welles, the Secretary of the Navy, issued a directive to give "persons of color, commonly known as "contrabands," in the employment of the Union Navy pay at the rate of $10 per month and a full day's ration" on September 25, 1861. Three weeks later, the Union Army followed suit, paying male "contrabands" at Fort Monroe $8 a month and females $4.

The word and term—contraband—spread quickly among southeastern Virginia's slave communities. Readers should remember Virginia was a major exporter of slaves in the internal slave trade and breeding, so there were thousands of slaves on the move. Becoming "contraband" did not matter to slaves, even though "contrabands" were not fully free. Former slaves, I believe, considered it put them closer to what they wanted than staying on plantations as slaves. Former slaves had been prisoners on plantations for 243 years in the American South and had been praying for such an occasion to escape bondage, so they jumped aboard the freedom train at the first opportunity.

For days after Gen. Butler's decision, hordes of escaping slaves began finding their way to the gates of Fort Monroe and appealing for contraband status. The number of former slaves grew too large to house inside the Fort; so, contrabands erected a make-shift camp on the burned-out ruins of the City of Hampton. Contrabands massing outside the crowded fort moved into their new settlement called Grand Contraband Camp, which former slaves nicknamed "*Slabtown.*"

By the end of the war in April 1865, less than four years later, an estimated 10,000 escaped slaves had applied to gain "contraband" status in Virginia, with many living nearby. Across the South, Union forces managed more than 100 contraband camps by the end of Civil War, although they were not all the same size. Horace James developed a Freedmen's Colony on Roanoke Island (1863–1867) in 1862. James was a Congregational chaplain appointed by the Union Army. He led a group of Freedmen, trying to create a self-sustaining colony on the island. ("The Roanoke Island Freedmen's Colony," National Park Service, North Carolina Digital History: LEARN NC, 2010).

Near Fort Monroe, but outside of its protective walls, Mary S. Peake, a pioneering African American teacher (1861), formerly began the process that would become the major determinant of Freedmen's success—education. She was the first black teacher hired by the American Missionary Association (AMA). Peake set up a school to teach reading and writing to both children and adult contrabands. The AMA sent numerous Northern white teachers into the South.

This area of Elizabeth City County later became part of the campus of Hampton University, a historically black college (HBCU). Defying a Virginia law against educating slaves, Peake and other teachers held classes outdoors under a certain large oak tree. Contrabands and free blacks gathered beneath this tree to hear President Abraham Lincoln's Emancipation Proclamation read. The tree became known as the ***"Emancipation Oak."*** For most contrabands full emancipation did not take effect until the Thirteenth Amendment to the United States Constitution, which redefined *"who could be held in slavery,"* was ratified in late 1865.

Trying to get a handle on the problem contrabands created for the Union Army (1861), several officers recommended returning all fugitives to their owners because they had no system of caring for them. The House of Representatives (7-9-1861) passed a resolution absolving the army of any responsibility to capture and return fugitive slaves. Lincoln interceded on behalf of some Virginia slave owners seeking to cross the Potomac River to recover their property, a few weeks later. Congress passed the *Confiscation Act in August 1861*. It established the first official policy regarding contrabands: *any fugitive slave used with his master's knowledge to advance Confederate victory was to be considered a prize of war and set free,* which officially established the designation. Based on this criteria several commanders set up contraband camps where they provided, as best they could for fugitive slaves' welfare.

The army created a make-shift procedure for provisioning contrabands and their camps because it lacked funds to carry out extensive relief programs. The Union Army began leasing ex-slaves to loyal planters or hiring them as laborers for the army. Finally, in December 1862, Brig. Gen. Rufus Saxton, then commander of the Army's Department of the South, ordered the refugees under his jurisdiction settled on abandoned lands. Saxton issued each laborer 2 acres of land. He also gave former slaves tools and seeds to plant crops for their consumption; in exchange, they had to produce cotton for government use on portions of the land. Some commanders appointed superintendents to oversee contrabands' welfare, and private relief associations quickly organized to provide additional supplies, supervision, and education for Freemen.

Despite efforts to care for contrabands, part of the curse of emancipation and contraband life were un-thought-out or unintended consequences. Again, not realizing the mass of humanity that war would release upon the land, there was no way to control or disburse contrabands among camps equally, overcrowding in some camps, resulted in unhealthy conditions. Overcrowding brought death and disease and occasionally starvation. One camp reported a 25% mortality rate over two years.

Such statistics must be accepted with a grain of salt, as the overwhelming number of contraband crowding into camps for protection and provisions made good record keeping impossible. For instance, the 25% quantity is significant depending on the number in camps, which some camps housed only a couple hundred. Overcrowding was a serious problem, and the previous statement was not to devalue the lives loses. However, deaths came to contrabands that also died at the hands of both armies.

After the Emancipation Proclamation, Pres. Lincoln authorized the army to establish black military units. While some contraband returned voluntarily to former masters and many black men joined the Union army in 1863, the contraband problem continued mushrooming. Contraband camps developed around many Union-held forts and encampments. Thousands of former slaves and free blacks began enlisting in the United States Colored Troops (USCT). The Army allowed USCT units' families to live in refugee camps near their encampment. Black troops ultimately comprised nearly 10 percent of all the troops in the Union Army.

Regardless of relief efforts, commanders complained of the problem caused by hordes of contrabands following the army. Congress finally established the Freedmen's Bureau in March of 1865. The first formal effort enacted especially to help former slaves adapt to their new status by the US government, (*"Illustrated Encyclopedia of the Civil War,"* Historical Times Edited by Patricia L. Faust; 07/18/04). At war's end, over 100 contraband camps, including the Freedmen's Colony of Roanoke Island, where 3500 former slaves worked to develop a self-sufficient community.

The American Missionary Association and other groups, together with free blacks and Freedmen, assisted missionary efforts to help contrabands. Many teachers recruited from the North agreed that efforts to educate former slaves were of the highest priority. These teachers said they were impressed with the desire of former slaves, both adults, and children, for education.

Civil War: A New World for Slaves

Civil War (1860-1865) changed everything for Robert R. Church and Beale Street. During the years just after emancipation and Grant's victory (1862), Memphis and Beale Street became a gathering point for contrabands. Once Beale Street began to look like a squatters' camp, the Union Army set up settlements in several places in the Memphis area. The black population of Memphis at the beginning of the Civil War was 3,000. Once Union General Ulysses S. Grant invaded West Tennessee and captured Memphis, slaves began escaping plantations all over the Mid-South heading for Union lines. Thousands of West Tennessee's 275,000 slaves abandoned farms and towns anticipating freedom with the advance of approaching Union armies.

General Grant entered the heavely slaveholding territory of West Tennessee during the summer of 1862, and the population of Memphis exploded with former slaves. Contrabands clogged docks, turned railroad tracks into roads, and packed regular roads with an ocean of wondering humanity, trying to get to safety. Fleeing plantations all over the Mid-South, they converged on Gen. Grant's Union headquarters in Memphis. Hordes of hungry, poorly clad runaways surrounded and nearly overwhelmed the Yankees. Considered contraband under the *Confiscation Act (1861)*, former slaves had become property again, but now they were US government property, giving the title "Contraband" real meaning.

Grant ordered Chaplain John Eaton to requisition surplus tents, blankets, rations, and tools. Eaton began establishing contraband camps, first in West Tennessee and then in other areas. Fleeing Confederate army units, which used slave labor as teamsters, construction laborers, and body servants, escaping slaves headed for Grant's lines, as their only protection. Just after the passage of the *Confiscation Act*, Eaton established the first contraband camp at Grand Junction, Tennessee, in August 1862. By March 1863, three months after emancipation, contrabands numbered 1,713 there. Two years later, contraband camps stretched throughout the Mississippi Valley. Aiding freed slaves (1862), northern missionaries and church leaders began establishing schools, medical services, even providing political education for contrabands. The army put able-bodied freedmen to work at fifty cents per day, on abandoned farms, government-supervised plantations, and military projects.

By 1866 Tennessee had contraband camps in the three grand divisions. The largest camps were in urban areas: Memphis had four and Nashville three. Approximately 20,000 contrabands joined USCT units in Tennessee, comprising 40 percent of troops.

African American troops and contraband camps gave the Union Army a decided edge sustaining occupation in Tennessee. Fugitive slaves from the Arkansas delta, western Kentucky, northern Mississippi, and rural West Tennessee flooded Memphis until freedmen outnumbered whites by 1865. Missionaries, Freedmen's Bureau agents, and ministers performed and recorded the first legal marriages for former slaves in these camps. Families became the base of the emerging former slave society.

Contraband camps became so large, missionaries and local newspapers began calling them "New Africa." The largest Camps Shiloh, Camp Fiske, and Camp Dixie were on Memphis' southern boundary. Camp Chelsea was in north Memphis. Camp Shiloh, the first contraband camp, was located where Riverside Subdivision is today and where I grew up. Shiloh had log cabins, frame buildings, and tents with dirt floors. Camp Shiloh housed spouses of USCT units stationed at nearby Ft. Pickering. Camp Shiloh had over three hundred houses and 2,000 residents, as well as churches, schools, saloons, lunchrooms, and barbershops. Contrabands embraced free enterprise and self-sufficiency immediately. For instance, Camp Dixie's contrabands cultivated three hundred acres of cotton, built a sawmill, and a school by 1863.

Nashville's contraband camps were Edgehill to the south, the Northwest Camp, and Edgefield on the eastside. Between December 1863 and December 1864, the Union army temporarily lost control of Confederates in some areas. Over 1,600 contrabands were transferred from Holly Springs and Corinth, Mississippi to Memphis's Camp Chelsea. Once the smoke of war cleared, the Memphis' exploding population jumped to over 20,000 black residences by 1865. Robert R. Church, Sr., had begun building a business empire and directing the development of Memphis' black community.

Reconstruction

The Reconstruction Act lasted from 1865 to 1877. During this time, the 13th, 14th, and 15th Amendments became the law. Reconstruction hastened the end of the old Confederacy and bond slavery. Congress under the Republican Party tried to make the Freedmen citizenship a reality with the 13th, 14th, and 15th Amendments. Although they were supposed to guarantee civil rights, neither the federal government nor the US Supreme Court stood behind those Amendments. Confederate states reentering the union came under the control of the U.S. Army. President Lincoln set up reconstructed governments in Tennessee, Arkansas, and Louisiana, during the Civil War. He gave land to former slaves in South Carolina, as an experiment.

After Lincoln's assassination (4-14-1865), new considerations, or desires to reestablish slavery surfaced. I believe this was why Lincoln took as long mulling over emancipation. He decided on emancipation, I believe, once he considered the deaths and blood already spilled, and not to put an end to slavery once and for all would have been a waste of lives. I think he wanted to make an end to human bondage in America forever. He felt, I believe, emancipation, even if Congress did not give slaves all the assistance needed, or even if former slaves did not receive all the benefits of freedom, through emancipation, they could not be forced into legal bondage, as chattel slaves—property.

Although incomplete in many ways, emancipation, thanks to Mr. Lincoln, was far better than waiting for war's end and then fighting over the status of war contrabands. Although Mr. Lincoln closed the book on bond slavery forever, after his assassination, the forces dedicated to slavery, as America's economic engine, had a friend—Andrew Johnson—in the White House. Johnson was from Tennessee and very sympathetic to the South. He aided efforts to reestablish slavery.

The new President, Andrew Johnson, declared the goals Civil War, national unity and ending slavery had been achieved, therefore reconstruction was complete. Republicans in Congress refused to accept Johnson's lenient terms offered the secessionist states to reenter the union. Republicans rejected new members of Congress from the South because many had been high-ranking Confederate government officials. Johnson vetoed two key bills that supported the Freedmen's Bureau and the ***Civil Rights Bill of 1866,*** which provided federal civil rights to the newly Freedmen. Even though a Republican, Johnson was a southerner first, and broke with his party.

Reconstruction determined the outcome of Congressional elections in 1866. It produced a sweeping Republican victory in the North, which gave Republicans control of Congress. Overriding Johnson's vetoes, Congress passed the ***"Civil Rights Bill of 1866,"*** removed civilian governments in the South and put the U.S. Army in charge of the former Confederate States. The army conducted new elections, allowing freed slaves to vote. Congress denied the right to vote to leaders of the Confederacy, neither could they run for office, in ten states ("Reconstruction: America's Unfinished Revolution, 1863–1877," Eric Foner, (1988).

Contrabands on the Move: Life Goes On

The difficult thing, listening to my great-grandfather tell me stories, was understanding the outdated terms he used sometimes. I knew things my great-great-grandfather told his son and my grate-granddaddy told me were important, but family histories for a young child, are only entertaining tales. Sometimes I would sit and watch Papa, as he prepared sermons, he was so animated. His mannerisms and expressiveness were like he was actually preaching. A kid, watching him, I compare it to watching a movie. Back when I was a kid in the late 1940s to mid-1950s in Mississippi, movie screens were bedsheets hung on a wall. For me, great granddaddy was far more entertaining; he was live.

I believe the thing that posed the most difficulty for contrabands, during that period was getting through those very frightening and confusing times, while trying to figure out what it took to survive as individuals. Emerging from a system that provided very little, contrabands had to do without even more than during slavery, staring out as Freedmen. Those slaves that learned to scrounge for what they could find, while trying to catch master looking the other way, found life on their own less frightening. I learned about my great-great-grandfather times listening to his son tell about his father days,

'It wus new for us'ens tryin to live, strugglin long, but it wus jes some'em else ta do. We'ens had no bosses.'

Those not so fortunate—children, old folks, the sick and infirm—were at the mercy of events. Lost in the sea of contraband humanity, Burl Lee, Sr. was just another straw blown by the winds of change. Carried along by the influence of those struggling to survive, after the birth of freedom and during the contraband period, it took a moment for the idea that you were master now to sink in fully. Now, you were responsible for surviving, no matter what happened. I remember my great-grandfather telling me about his father, finding the will to hold on during these times.

"My father said,"

'Folk wus all over, dey wus on de road wonderin wit no place ta go. Lookin all tried and beat down. Some carried or drag bundles of who knows what. I see'em sittin on side de road, ready ta give up. Dat made me go over ta'em. I tell'em, you'ens got ta keep goin. Movin is de only way you'ens gon'a find food and maybe a place ta res. Sittin here, nothin good gona come ta ya. I reach down and pull on dey arm, while tellin'em, come on, leave dat stuff, it slowin ya down. Pullin on'em, dey look back, some pull away and run back and dig some'em out dey bundle. Waitin on'em, dey say some'en lake,'

"Dis b'lon ta my mammy. I can't leave it."

'It seem some folks had ta have some'em clos dey knowed. I guess it give'em comfort ta have. Helpin'em long, give me some'em to do and think about, other than dyin. Ya see some of'em again aftu a while, round a fire may be, eatin some'em. God only knows what? Dey smile and offer ya some. I believe dat wus dey way of sayin thanks.'

"Daddy Burl said,

'I found yo Mama Sarah wonderin the countryside around Jackson Miss-sippi. It wus good she wus in Miss-sippi, a rebel state, so dey wus free already. De battle over Vicksburg took up most of de middle of Miss-sippi where we'ens wus. Fightin put slaves a movin, dey wus scared runnin lookin fo a safe place. I wus no contraband cause I run off from de plantation a'fo de shootin start.'

"He would smile broadly, and straightening himself, with that statement. Then my daddy would say something like,"

'Contrabands ha'ta be told dey wus free. I been lookin fo a good chance ta run off since I wus a boy, but somethin always happen ta stop me. White folks talk of war so much, I saw my chance ta run and tuk it. I wus free, livin on my own, I believe two years, a'fo the fightin come to Vicksburg. Dat turn everybody loose dat want ta be free. De fightin had contraband hidin in woods, tryin ta dodge de bombs and slaughta. War cause trouble for everbody tryin ta stay out de way of battles, no matter which way we'ens went, fightin flared up without warnin. People dyin all round, contraband survived on grace and mercy. Fightin broke up folks you knowed and scattered chullins to the wen. Young'ens, mammays and pappyas may never knowed one'tter. Some babies got tuk soon as born. Wit war all round, ya learnt one lesson, if nothin else, death comes without reason or reprieve.'

My great-grand-father mentioned that his father talked about all the children on the move.

'Sometimes I see'em on side de road huddled in bunches. Der wus so many youn'ens. Dat's what struck me so powerfully. What could a body do, I knowed nothin bout carin for chullins.'

"The period just after the end of slavery was a very crucial time for my daddy and other contrabands, trying to learn to live as free people and develop a sense of community. Civil War scattered families and those you grew up around. Surviving for most was getting food, anything you could eat that didn't make you sick. For most, it was betta to keep on the move and look after yo' self. Being on your own was better than to care about what happened to others, for some."

Rev. Lee talked of the joy his father expressed when he spoke of seeing someone he recognized, during, and after fighting came to Mississippi.

'Ya hung on ta people ya seed more dan once, if ya wus goin de same way or iffin somethin cause ya ta go de way dey went. Stickin together, lookin out fo one'tter, keepin up wit chullins and makin sho old folks and chulluns git food wus somethin only special folk did. It took everbody lookin out, learnin ta stay alive.'

Rev. Lee said, "My father's face would always light up with a huge smile when he said,

'I never fo'git dat day I fiust seed yo' mama Sarah fo de furst time. I hurr' up and said we'ens kin make a family.'

Civil War ended legal slavery for millions of enslaved Africans; however, it did not end forced bondage in America. Emancipation by President Abraham Lincoln in 1863, freed only slaves in the rebellious states of the Confederacy. Once the fighting ended (1865), Republicans passed the 13th, 14th, and 15th Amendments. These Amendments were supposed to bring freedom to former slaves but as Pres. Lincoln feared southerners and northern capitalists refused to accept those Amendments. Rev. Lee talked of how his father looked forward to freedom, even though they had no idea what it was.

"My father showed such pride and joy whenever he declared,"

'I vote for Gen. Ulysses S. Grant fo president in 1868.'

Just being able to register and, vote was more than slaves ever thought would happen during their lifetime.

'Some contraband wus put up on land tuk from slave masters; some even got land from de govment fo dey own.'

My great-grandfather talked of those years during and following the Civil War as mixed blessings for contraband. He said his father told him.

'Movin round lookin fo a plac ta settle, hopin ta find somebody ta make a family wit, wus all dat kept some folk movin. White gangs of soldiers roam de countryside, tryin ta forc us'ens back to plantations. Dey made life so bad fo folk. De only contraband camp in Miss-

sippi wus in Corinth, I guess some 150 miles ta the North, so contraband round Jackson, had no help. Us'ens wus on our own. Findin safety in Union Army camps wus contrabands only hope ta get started wit freedom.'

Union Battled Confederates with Slaves in Between

The secession of fighting and armies facing each other across battlefields did not end the war over slavery; only the uniforms came off. Confederates decided they had enough and started dressing in civilian clothes again, those that had them. Command structures remained in place, as the rebs fought for control of state and local governments. Contrabands caught between the two warring factions did not have safe heavens on either side. Rebels produced the most deadly middle ground in this so-called peace. Courts and Union troops could not stop every act of terror. Local white governments would not protect former slaves. Local governments supported mob actions, while instigating acts of terror.

Civil War created a brutal and desperate time for former slaves. The contraband period proved to be more confusing and deadlier than war itself. Memphis was just such a place for contrabands. The first white mob action, after the war ended, occurred in Memphis (1866). This riot became a harbinger of disaster for former slaves. Similar events would be repeated, with similar results, as the government sided with mobs. Foreshadowing the dark times of the next one hundred years, governments would protect white culprits against their black victims.

Anger over the Civil War's outcome had former confederate soldiers up in arms all over the South. Desperately trying to push former slaves back into a status closely resembling slavery, as possible, the Union Army's pacification of the South was slow and ineffective. Most importantly, the federal government implemented Reconstruction piece mill. Some confederate units remanded intact for months after hostilities ceased. Confederates soldiers, in parts of the South, became gangs, robbing anyone, even southerners. Some gangs push their way into local government and waged a stealth campaign against the union army. Opposing Republican-run state and local governments, they fought newly Freedmen gaining political rights.

White opposition ignited a riot in Memphis in 1866. Many of the ex-confederate soldiers in this riot were part of the Fort Pillow Massacre, north of Memphis, about 40 miles. The Battle for Fort Pillow on April 12, 1864, ended in the massacre of almost the entire USCT garrison. Located above a bluff on the Tennessee River, Fort Pillow's white commander of the black USCT unit consisting of 600 Union soldiers attempted to surrender, as they were hopelessly outnumbered by over 3,000 rebels commanded by General Nathan Bedford Forrest.

While under a flag of truce, union troops laid down their arms and came out of the fort with their hands up in surrender. Rebel soldiers opened fire on the defenseless USCT unit. The overwhelmed garrison fled down the bluff and was trapped by the river in a deadly crossfire. Only about 65 out of 600 black soldiers survived the massacre. Rebels even shot union soldiers in their hospital beds. They continued shooting even though wounded soldiers in beds begged for mercy; the Union Army reported, *("River Run Red: The Fort Pillow Massacre in the American Civil War, Andrew Ward," Viking Press: New York 2005).*

Whites in Memphis were seething with anger and hatred against emancipated slaves, as well as losing the Civil War. The white mobsters went on a week of rioting because they were upset over the dramatic demographic shift in the black population (which jumped from 3,000 before the war to over 20,000 by 1865). Competition from mobile former slaves enraged former confederate soldiers, which had poured into Memphis, like contrabands, desperately looking for survival help.

Whites went on the attack and were joined by poor Irish, who dominated the police force and fire departments. Whites wanted to force blacks to flee Memphis so they could regain their population advantage. Whites attacked black areas of town, pillaging, and burning whole communities. Hoping to drive blacks out of Memphis with their mob action, terror, and intimidation, whites reacted, like rebel at Fort Pillow.

Police and firefighters joined rioters in the streets, but black Union soldiers and other African Americans fought the huge mob. Their heroic actions kept the mob at bay and prevented it from driving all blacks out of town. Memphis experienced the first riot by whites against blacks following the Civil War. The rioting and destruction killed 45 blacks, while thousands were injured. Whites destroyed houses, churches, schools, and businesses across the black section of South Memphis. Robert Church was shot and nearly died, defending his saloon, during the riot. Only two whites were reported killed, during the week-long rioting.

Pres. Grant's administration instituted Reconstruction, hoping to block resurgent Confederate forces, trying to re-enslave newly Freedmen. Grant, during the brief life of Reconstruction, tried to make the hopes of freedom former slaves had nestled for centuries a reality. Grant used federal troops to protect former slaves and improve their prospects as Freedmen.

Capitalists in the South and North fought Pres. Grant and Reconstruction; they made helping contrabands very difficult. Whites opposed to educating former slaves, also blocked land acquisitions and political participation by former slaves. The US Supreme Court acquiesced refused to enforce the Civil Rights Act of 1866 and reneged on Pres. Lincoln's promise of forty acres and a mule, as well. The Court returned land given former slave by Pres. Lincoln to slave masters. Lincoln believed former slaves deserved compensation for the 243 years of free labor extracted from slaves to build America. ("*Slavery in the Northwest Territory*," Library of Congress).

Although it had its problems, Reconstruction did several very important things for Freedmen, trying to learn to live on their own. Reconstruction provided an opportunity for them to price their labor. Secondarily, Reconstruction stationed federal troops in the South to protect former slaves and those supporting them. Thirdly, the federal government began educating Freedmen as a priority, ("<u>Reunion and Reaction: The Compromise of 1877 and the End of Reconstruction</u>"*,* Comer Vann Woodward(1951).

Rev. Lee said of his father, "He told me how much he looked forward to freedom and education."

'Gittin out of slavery and gittin some learnin wus what we'uns all prayed fo.'

"The ability, to read, write and count, was looked upon by slaves, as gifts from God," Rev. Lee would always repeat after such statements.

'Without learnin,' "he said," *'votin didn't matter. An ignorant man would make his X. Movin around we'uns wus not jes lookin fo a plac ta res and food ta eat, we'uns wus lookin fo one of dem schools dey talk about. I knowed if I got some learnin, I could help make things better fo us folk.'*

Even on the Supreme Court, there were slave owners. Judges, who refused to accept emancipation. The **13th, 14th,** and **15th Amendments** were supposed to bring freedom to former slaves, but white men in the South and North refused to accept emancipation. Immediately following the Civil War, they began pressuring politicians to compel newly freed black citizens to serve as unpaid labor.

What may not be clear here is slaves possessed most of the skills in the South. White men did not do work; work was beneath a white man. White men gave orders, and slaves did the work. Slaves were the craftsmen and artisans. Slaver masters never conceived of the time; they would not have slaves. Emancipation is why they put all their eggs into the Civil War basket, trying to keep blacks in slavery.

U. S. Grant became President (1869-1877) of a very divided nation when he took office. Facing confederates, Grant used federal troops against slave masters, state, and local governments that refused to accept emancipation. They tried to force slaves to work as unpaid labor. Democrats defied Republican-led governments, while white supremacists conducted reigns of terror throughout the South, during Grant's term in office.

Known as "paddy rollers," during slavery, the Ku Klux Klan was organized by six Confederate veterans in Pulaski, Tennessee, in 1865. Among its founders was the commander of the "Fort Pillow Massacre," Confederate General Nathan Bedford Forrest. He became the Grand Wizard (1866). The Ku Klux Klan violently intimidated and suppressed former slaves, while chasing Republicans back North.

William L. Sharkey Governor of Mississippi's Reconstruction government reported, *"Disorder, a lack of control, and lawlessness were widespread; in some states, armed bands of Confederate soldiers roamed at will. Dressed up in bedsheets and masks or hoods, while wearing KKK initials across their chest, they terrorize blacks while taking total control in the South."*

When Pres. Grant took office, the national divide, which existed, was even wider when he left. During this time, life took a turn for the worst for former slaves. Trapped in Mississippi, my family was in "the belly of the beast." Rev. Lee was born just as hard times got harder. Voters could not decide between Democrat Rutherford B. Hayes and Republican Samuel J. Tilden in 1876. Hayes cut a deal with Electoral College delegates to remove federal troops from the South and became president. He gave whites a free hand dealing with the so-called *Negro problem*, (*Reunion and Reaction: The Compromise of 1877 and the End of Reconstruction*, Comer Vann Woodward 1991; Oxford University Press).

Ignorance was not Bliss for Slaves

Education was mentioned third in the list of advantages Reconstruction provided former slaves, but in reality, from new freed slaves perspective knowledge was first. Gaining access to the ability to read, write and count were skills extremely critical to Freedmen's ability to live on their own. Such knowledge was a prayer answered for former slaves with the arrival of the Freedmen Bureau. Arriving at the end of bondage, access to knowledge was as important as food to some Freedmen.

Ignorance of the world around them had not been bliss for slaves. Providing slave narratives, beyond giving readers a firsthand perspective on what and how slaves thought about slavery, I want readers to understand the difficulty slave had surviving unable to speak and understand the words white people used to victimize them. Speaking and reading are problems that still dogs descendants of American slavery, even though their descendants have reached the 21st century.

Denying enslaved Africans knowledge was part of the master plan to keep slaves dependent on white people's generosity and goodwill, even after the civil rights revolution of the 1960s and 70s. Lack of knowledge made former slaves' victims in ways they still did not understand on most occasions. In that regard, during slavery, some risked limb—slave masters cut off toes and ears of slaves caught trying to learn to read—and life—slaves were hung for repeated violations, as examples to other slaves for attempting to learn to read. During Reconstruction, Freedmen were willing to struggle to become educated anyway, any place and anytime they could get it.

Finally, after centuries and countless prayers, Freedmen were able to gain their most cherished dream—real learning. Not only would this help former slaves develop a means to survive on their own, but it would also give them the knowledge needed to rise out of poverty. But, the task of educating Freedmen would prove far more difficult than simply setting up schools and providing books. The key to turning free Africans into slaves was making them fearful of knowledge itself.

This problem went beyond slaves, not desiring knowledge but slave masters trained enslaved Africans to avoid the thought of knowledge altogether. Knowing anything, beyond what master said, was a threat to a slave's life. This threat resided, in a slave, not knowing the level of intelligence of the white person a slave was responding. Solomon Northup (*Twelve Years a Slave*) illustrates this threat in his autobiography. His trials and struggles show clearly why a slave had to disguise what he knew, not doing so, nearly cost Northup's life.

Any white man could impose himself upon any slave, and that slave was bound by law to accommodate and indulge that white person no matters their demand. On that basis alone, a white person could take the life of that slave and give any story that entered their head to justify taking that life, as today in 2020 when police murder a black person. Killing a slave was not a crime, any more than killing a cow or pig. Keeping slaves ignorant was part of the capricious and autocratic power any white person could exercise over slaves. Consequently, a slave's first rule was playing dumb and stupid; the dumber, the better.

Making slaves obedient was the next goal. Slave masters determined how much knowledge slaves needed. For the vast majority of slave masters, minimal access to information was the rule. Keeping slaves ignorant meant demonstrating was preferred. Such tasks made limited word usage ideal and made most words unnecessary.

Whites expected slaves' responses to be approximations of words, as shown by slave narratives. Slaves' speech could not be fluent expressions. Garbled mumbles to acknowledge commands was the anticipated response. Hence, slaves developed a short, disjointed chopped up dialect. Fluency of speech by slaves was tantamount to being uppity or sassying—trying to act white or talking back—a flagrant violation of station, for a slave. Regardless of how well a black person could articulate words, in the South, fluency could cost a slave's life.

Along with being ignorant emerging from slavery, Freedmen were without any references to a former life, beyond slavery. Enslaved African could not return to a former country; nothing tied them to the land on which they stood. Knowledge of the US, concerning where they were and where they could go from there, did not exist for most slaves. Those slaves that had never gone more than a few miles from the plantation had no reference to anything beyond their immediate confines.

Former slaves, without resources, best hope, was to band together in small groups and survive communally. Communal living was not a new universe for former slaves. The universe newly freed slaves inhabited, after awakening in the world of emancipation made them contraband. No longer slaves, just contrabands, Freedmen had no value, like a wild horse, unbroken. Their immediate challenge was *"making something out of nothing?"* That statement may sound counterintuitive, but this was the reality slave descendants faced and had to contend. They had to demonstrate this ability—*"making something out of nothing?"* —time and again by surviving on their own.

The Miracle of Knowledge: Freedmen's Bureau Schools

Newly Freedmen's lack of resources and access to anything of value shaped their every consideration, as free people. This deficiency controlled every aspect of their lives. Contrabands' only hope following emancipation was help from the federal government. Slaves' penniless emancipation created a dependency on the federal government, which was responsible for contraband, and could not be changed by them. Pres. Lincoln freed slaves without providing for their survival.

I want readers to remember that I am describing people, who had been kept completely ignorant of rudimentary concepts of knowledge, under the threat of punishment, even death in some cases. But, then, out of the pain and death of the Civil War, like "Divine Intervention," Congress created the Bureau of Refugees, Freedmen, and Abandoned Lands in March 1865. Popularly known as the Freedmen's Bureau, this federal agency aided slaves starving for knowledge. The Freedmen's Bureau became the difference between avoiding permanent dependence on white people or struggle daily to survive on their own, in a world bent on their destruction.

Although its existence was short, just under ten years, like Reconstruction, the Freedmen's Bureau schools for many descendants of American slavery became a gateway out of the graveyard of poverty in the valley of dry bones. Its role was crucial for slaves who desperately needed survival knowledge and skills. For the first time, during slaves' entire existence in America, through the Freedmen's Bureau, enslaved Africans were given the means to fashion the thoughts and ideas in their heads into concepts that could benefit them.

Again, I cite Solomon Northup (*Twelve Years A Slave*), someone who learned to survive by disguising his intelligence from whites. Former slaves could begin openly expressing their imagination in ways never considered by most Freedmen. On the other hand, it was an opportunity to do as Robert R. Church, Sr., such former slaves, could use knowledge picked up listening and watching white people and do as whites that observed slaves to create Minstrelsy. They could flip the script and use the only thing they had—their bodies to—*make something out of nothing.*

Books were the greatest need for slaves in the South. Before emancipation, the possession of a book by a slave could cost a slave's life. Consequently, the Freedmen Bureau published Freedmen's textbooks. They emphasized a bootstrap philosophy, pulling one's self up by their own efforts to achieve a better life (again *"making something out of nothing"*). These books stressed the theme, "each person could work hard and achieve." They included traditional literacy lessons, as well as selections on the life and works of Abraham Lincoln. Also, they focused on forgiveness, with excerpts from the Bible. They contained biographies of famous African Americans that emphasized their piety, humbleness, and industriousness. Bureau books contained essays on humility, a good work ethic, loving one's enemies, avoiding bitterness, and temperance as well.

The Bureau's education benefitted former slaves immensely. Educating slaves that slave masters taught to fear knowledge and avoid learning, using terror, threats of punishment, and death, was a mammoth task. Slave masters taught enslaved Africans to think only about what they wanted and behave in ways that reflected their willingness to serve white people in general. Nothing about slaves' behaviors or their thought processes was naturally theirs. All things they said or did were learned behaviors, forced upon them for the convenience and economic benefit of white people. Freedmen were not given any adjustment or reprogramming period following slavery in which to assimilate the new status of freedom.

Newly Freedmen entered an environment that reinforced their ignorance. Nat Turner's bloody rebellion (1831), beginning the Antebellum period (1830), frightened slaves masters to the degree, southern legislatures passed laws against teaching slaves to read. Teaching slaves to read, even during and after the Civil War, was still illegal.

The first post-emancipation schools were clandestine. These schools were operated by blacks and whites that saw ignorance as former slaves' greatest challenge to maintaining their freedom; they organized secretive schools. Some schools were rolling affairs, according to Rev. Lee. He spoke about his father's efforts learning to read in one of these schools.

'We'ens couldn't wait ta git in a school ta git learnin. The first school moved round ta keep white folks from knowin the git together spot. We'ens be in de swamp, under big trees, and even under churches built up off de ground. We'ens had ta run out ta de woods when we'ens git word white folks about.'

That scenario began changing by early January 1865. The outcome of the Civil War was no longer in doubt when schools began operating openly. Schools for black people opened across the South, and former slaves crowded into them wherever they could find one. Freedmen crowding into schools, overflowing their capacity; the onslaught of students stretched teachers' ability to accommodate those seeking knowledge. At least 8,000 former slaves were attending schools in Georgia alone; eight years later (1873). Schools for former slaves struggled to accommodate nearly 20,000 students, their commitment to learning push everyone to try and accommodate them.

The Freedmen's Bureau was an arm of the US Department of War, and Union Army General Oliver O. Howard was its commander. Gen. Howard quickly learned his tasks would be very difficult, and it would require real innovation, accomplishing his mission. The US Army provided the Bureau with an existing organization across the South, as it pacified southern rebels. Operating against state officials oppose to helping former slaves make the transition to freedom, the Freedmen's Bureau used the army's resources to accomplish its goals.

The Bureau helped newly freed slaves get food, someplace to settle, medical assistance, decent clothes, and locate family members lost or dead. It helped provide facilities and made arrangements to educate Freedmen. The Bureau was the federal government's first efforts to address the needs of kidnapped enslaved Africans to overcome their tragic existence in the United States. Although its effort was very meager, Freedmen's Bureau assistance was crucial to helping former slaves make the transition to living on their own.

Educating Freedmen would prove to be a real challenge for Gen. Howard. He would have to disguise his real intentions, which was to educate Freedmen. Howard claimed his efforts were *"war measures"* that supported the War Department's goal of pacifying the secessionist south. The Freeman's Bureau made the Union Army a partner in educating former slaves.

Howard's major problem was southern legislatures. They passed laws—Black Codes—restricting movement, labor arrangements, and work conditions, as well as blocked the civil rights of former slaves. Southern legislatures created conditions, as close to bond slavery as possible, nearly duplicating 1840s conditions for Freedmen. The Bureau's first plan encouraged planters to rebuild their plantations and urged Freedmen to return to work for them. The Bureau kept an eye on contracts between the freed laborers and planters. It pushed whites and blacks to work together as employers and employees, rather than as masters and slaves.

Howard set up three grand departments: Government-Controlled Lands, Records, Financial Affairs, and Medical Affairs within the Bureau. Education was part of the Records division. Howard gave schools confiscated property, which included planters' mansions, former Confederate government buildings, books, and furniture for schools educating Freedmen. It provided transportation, room, and board for teachers from the North. Congress appropriated some funds for Freedmen's schools. It gave the Bureau the power to seize Confederate property for education through the *Confiscation Act (1861)*. Howard argued that "The Freedmen's Bureau was still a military necessity." He continued, *"The Bureau is needed to properly carry out the mandate of the Thirteenth Amendment, and is a work of sheer justice for ex-slaves, at a trifling cost to the government."*

Adult Freedmen sought the benefits of literacy for themselves, as avidly as they sought schools for their children. Rev. Lee remembered his daddy saying,

'Everbody wus dead set on gettin learnin. In winter and the slack time between plantin and harvest we'ens said our numbers and alphabets with youn'ems in schools. Dey had school

fo old folk, dat got to school when dey could. Schools in church wus call Sabbath-day schools. Teachers had night schools fo folk dat work day time.'

Rev. Lee said great-great-granddaddy Burl pushed him to read the Bible. *"It was the only book black folks had, before the books from the Bureau."*

Throughout Reconstruction, teachers reported adults often constituted one-third of their students. Formal secondary, higher education institutions, and normal schools for training teachers served adult students. For instance, in Georgia—Macon, Columbus, Savannah, and elsewhere—preparatory schools attached to colleges, and the colleges themselves: Atlanta University, Clark College (later Clark Atlanta University), and the Augusta Institute (later Morehouse College) were among the first to provide higher education for former slaves.

Teachers came from all over, more than half the black teachers worked within their state, while other black teachers hailed from the seaboard South, along with Pennsylvania, New Jersey, New York, Massachusetts, and Ohio. Many white teachers from the South had barely completed high school, many of the northern teachers graduated from post-secondary institutions, including Dartmouth College in New Hampshire, Yale University in Connecticut, Oberlin College in Ohio, and Mount Holyoke College in Massachusetts. Black teachers attended such colleges as Oberlin, Wilberforce University (named after William Wilberforce) in Ohio, and Lincoln University in Pennsylvania.

Other research shows that half the teachers were southern whites; one-third were blacks (mostly southern), and one-sixth were northern whites. Few were abolitionists, and fewer came from New England. Reflective of the times, men outnumbered women. Salaries were the strongest motivation, except for northerners, typically funded by northern organizations and had a humanitarian motivation. As a group, the black cohort showed the greatest commitment to racial equality; and they were most likely to remain teachers. The curriculum resembled that of schools in the north.

Literate black men and women opened self-sustaining schools. Aid organizations sponsored by northern Freedmen also established schools (mid-1865). Fifty aid societies were working to educate Freedmen after 1865. These benevolent organizations raised funds, recruited teachers, and attempted to keep the need for educating Freedmen before the public in northern states.

Though it did not hire teachers or operate schools itself, the Freedmen's Bureau assisted aid societies in meeting the burgeoning demand to educate African Americans. It rented buildings for school rooms, provided books, and transportation for teachers, superintended schools and offered military protection for students and teachers against the Ku Klux Klan. More importantly, Freedmen themselves provided substantial amounts of support for schools. They paid monthly tuition and raised funds for teachers' room and board. They purchased lots on which to construct schools and donated material and labor to build them. They supported schools that were independent of northern efforts as well.

The American Missionary Association, along with other northern missionary and aid societies, worked with the Freedmen's Bureau providing education. The AMA established eleven colleges in southern states to educate Freedmen. Missionary and aid societies were essential to former slaves acquiring knowledge. They helped make education a bedrock concern among Freedmen to improve their future. Aid Societies focused on raising funds to pay teachers and manage schools. But, improving the day-to-day operation of individual schools was a difficult task. More than 90,000 former slaves were students after the first two years schools operated in Georgia.

Hampton Normal and Agricultural Institute (Hampton University) in Virginia (1868) was created and led by Brigadier General Samuel Chapman Armstrong. Attendance rates for Freedmen in over 1,000 southern schools were between 79 and 82 percent in 1870. The Bureau spent $5 million setting up schools of all kinds in the South. J. W. Alvord, an inspector for the Bureau, wrote that *"the Freedmen have the natural thirst for knowledge. They aspire to have 'power and influence … coupled with learning,' and are excited by 'the special study of books.*

Whites opposed to educating former slaves refuse to fund education for Freedmen. They adopted new state constitutions, disenfranchising blacks, which prevented freedmen from fighting such decisions. They created literacy tests, grandfather clauses, and added pole taxes to restrict voter registration. Where they had to fund black schools, they reduced funds available for public education for blacks. White violence against schools and teachers exploded after the closure of the Freedmen's Bureau. Without federal support and protection, some of the Bureau's achievements fell apart.

White southerners considered teachers "carpetbaggers." The KKK "tarred and feathered," Republican politicians, then ran them out of the South.
Terror was a standard treatment for anyone trying to help former slaves. I reiterate keeping slaves ignorant was the top goal of whites in the South. Freedmen had developed a foundation for education by Reconstruction's end. Native and northern teachers taught thousands of former slaves to read and write. Former slaves were too poor and federal government and northern agencies assistance to paltry to fully address the massive problem of educating 4 million former slaves.

From 1880 into the twentieth century, southerners limited funds for educating blacks and refused to support secondary education for African Americans. Southerners did everything possible to discourage blacks from obtaining education. Teachers' salaries in black schools were kept lower than in white schools, regardless of race. School boards and legislatures neglected the construction and maintenance of black schools.

Determined to kill the Freedmen Bureau, Democrats hatched a plan to get around General Howard, who was very popular. Democrats send General Howard on an assignment out West. Then Democrats pushed legislation through Congress, which killed the Freedmen's Bureau. Learning of the Democrats scheme too late, Howard was unable to save federal education efforts. Congress effectively shut down the Bureau by refusing to approve new legislation funding it (1872). Congress officially killed the Bureau and terminated all of its activities by 1877.

Robert R. Church: The Savior of Memphis

Focusing on Robert R. Church, Sr. and my great-great-grandfather Burl Lee, Sr.'s adventures and accomplishments, during the contraband period, was to provide real context, not only for their lives but to reflect on important events of their times. Robert R. Church, Sr. was able to establish himself as an entrepreneur, in large part because of his birth, level of affluence, and community-based business psychology. Born without any of these advantages compared to Robert R. Church, Sr., Burl Lee, Sr. was born a commodity in the internal slave trade and breeding system. However, they shared a similar community-based concern and Burl Lee's limited resources would have been a tremendous disadvantage, if born in Church's environment.

The reality is that in an environment of scarcity and desperation, Burl Lee's skill set may have been as good as money. Essentially this contrast is about their day-to-day challenges, as they interacted with those around them, the way they impacted their lives, and were impacted by them. Developing survival strategies for themselves and people around them, they helped other Freedmen, without knowledge of life beyond the plantation, to understand the priority of setting down roots establishing stability lives, making families, and building communities. Setting down roots is the phrase they used to describe this process.

For Robert Church, Sr., his assent began following the Memphis riot in 1866. He stepped into the leadership vacuum in Memphis, especially in the black community. He rebuilt devastated sections in the black area of town, including contraband camps. His effort, along with that of the federal government, helped put money in the hands of former slaves, which kept the community rebuilding process going and encouraged contrabands to *"set down roots"* in Memphis. Money in the hands of destitute freedmen was a magnet, drawing even more destitute Freedmen to Memphis. Church's philanthropy could not save Memphis from the disaster headed its way in 1878.

Memphis developed a reputation as a sleepy backwater town. Such descriptions made it a target and laughingstock for newspaper reporters. They published statements such as, *"Memphis is regarded as the 'filthiest and most foul-smelling' city in the country."* The United States Surgeon General called Memphis *"shameful and a disgrace."* He explained, *"Bodies of maimed and euthanized animals littered the sides of roadways for days sometimes. The city lacks any kind of sewage removal system, relying on outhouses (privies) and private services to haul off human and animal waste."*

It is little wonder, after reading such descriptions, the yellow fever epidemic that hit Memphis in 1878/79 nearly swiped it out. The yellow fever epidemics depopulated Memphis almost overnight. Those who were afraid abandon the city for surrounding forests and fields. Church did as other wealthy Memphians, who moved their families to safety, (*"The Robert R. Churches of Memphis: A Father and Son Who Achieved in Spite of Race*," Annette E. Church, and Roberta Church, Memphis: A.E. Church, 1974). Death and mayhem stalked those that sought refuge outside the city in woods. Gangs of whites robbed and raped blacks running from the fever. Life hiding out in the bush was just as dangerous, if not more so than, taking a chance with yellow fever by remaining in the city.

Over 25,000 residences fled Memphis, as the death toll reached more than 5,000. News stories described the scene of death wagons rolling day and night, carting victims to cemeteries. Resembling covered wagon trains crossing the American frontier, cemetery attendants could hardly find space for arriving corpora. When they found space, they dumped wagonloads of bodies in mass graves.

The morbid tasks of digging graves and collecting bodies fell largely on former slaves that were either too poor or afraid to leave the city. Former slaves were the only able-bodied laborers. Funeral pyres of corpora, which could not be collected fast enough, dotted the city's skyline with their reddish glows. Similar to watch fires, nightly, the glow of funeral pyres on the horizon was visible for miles *(historic-memphis.com)*.

Creating perimeters, hoping to prevent yellow fever carriers from slipping into the city, officials used "shotgun quarantines"—official and vigilante—to protect the city. "Safety patrols" scoured the forests and fields looking for yellow fever refugees trying to slip into town to get food. Were it not for real leadership on the part of men with money, like Robert Church, Memphis may not have gotten up off its death bed.

Robert Church was the first African-American "millionaire" in the South. Once the plague eased and the quarantines was lifted, Church recognized the great opportunities in Memphis real estate, awaiting the opportunistic, as property values plumbed. He snapped up the great bargains. Church bought everything he could—commercial buildings, residential housing, undeveloped land, even bars in the red-light district. Although his motivation was not philanthropic, nevertheless, Church was considered the savior of Memphis. Following the yellow fever epidemic, the State of Tennessee declared Memphis bankrupt and revoked the city's charter. The State reduced Memphis to a tax district. Church was the first citizen to purchase $1,000 bonds, which encouraging other men with money to buy bonds. Church's leadership help Memphis earn its charter back.

Making Something Out of Nothing

Although it was a caricature, blackface began in white Americans' minds but became a reality in black Americans' world. Buffoonery was what white people wanted to see when a black person appeared. Blackface embodied all the emptiness bequeathed slaves at emancipation. The hollowness of freedom was not obvious in 1865, as the Civil War ended with slaves leaving plantations. Comparable to gypsies, former slaves walking off plantations were turned out across the South without resources and directions. Newly Freedmen walked into a world filled with death and confusion. For the first time their survival depended upon them rather than master. Their 243 years of chattel slavery in America yielded them nothing. So, the overarching challenge for contrabands was, *"How to make a life out of nothing?"* Nothing is all black people ever had that white people didn't take away. Left with nothing, black people had time to work with their nothing until they figured something to do with it.

Trapped in the belly of the beast, Burl Lee was just one among many penniless former slaves trying to figure out his next step beyond wondering the countryside. Rev. Lee talked of this time seen through his father's eyes.

'De roads wus pack wit folk on de move when I came out the swamp. Dey wondered not knowin where dey wus headed. I just followed along behind de folk in front of me, until I saw Sarah. She had a bunch of young'ens herdin'em round. Like a mother hen, tryin to keep'em together, none had folk dat dey knowed of. When I saw Sarah, and hur gaggle of youn'ens, I knowed dey wus't hurs, she wus too young hurself, and dey wus too many. She'd see little ones just sittin and hollerin on side de road, flies bout to eat'em alive, cause dey wus full of mess and some had sores and scabs on'em. She'd tak'em, clean'em up best she could, if dey wus near water or a creek, she'd wash'em. If not, she do de best she could. Dey follow hur round under foot. Sometime other folk see one of'em dey knowed and want'em to come with dem and cause Sarah had so many, she'd let'em go. You knowed, in a day or two, she'd have even mo. Dat wus the way it wus back den, folk had ta care bout one'tter.'

Der wus some big boys helpin hur scroung fo food. She wus just tryin ta make sho dey got som-tee. I watched her fo a couple of days, as she gathered in a few more. Dat mother hen gave safety ta all dat run under hur wings. I got de big boys and show'em a thang or two bout scroungin, but told'em not ta say nothin ta Sarah. She must'a knowed somethin, cause I noticed, after a few days uf dat, a big smile on hur face, whenever she looked my way. Den one evenin she brought me some of what she fed de young'ens and said,'

"You outta eat some too, after workin so hard ta git it."

'We laugh together for de furst time. It felt so good ta laugh. Until dat, I had fo'got hi. Dey came to be my family. Dis wus hi things wus in dem days. Takin care of dem, help me take care fo me. Folks, wus dependin on me.'

Readers must remember there was never much, if any, family structure for slaves, definitely not after breeding, going back to the 1730s for some. Even though that was the case, former slaves try to build families any way they could, even during slavery.

"Contrabands had to make things up as they went along; families were not any different. One could not count on anything from day-to-day. You accepted what was there when you opened your eyes that morning," Rev. Lee would say.

He said one time, "My father talked to me about those times, he wanted me to understand how important having a good woman was to help make a man."

'I never had folk, some uf de old women always kinda look after me. I run off from de plantation and hid out in de swamp, a long time fo all de fightin come. So, I wus on my own. It felt good fo folks to be round. You know, slaves just took up wit anybody dat treated'em kindly, especially chullins. Real families wus what white folks had. People took up wit who let'em. Being part of a group made stayin live not so hard and not so lonely. Sarah wus like me, no folks to speak of. She growed up around the old women too. Dey wus mammy ta hur. So I guss dat wus all she knowed. Havin hur and watchin hur do stuff fo chullins and old folk made me work hard to try and please her. When thangs got real bad, she would look at me and say, "Burl, what we gon do?" Dat made me think and work real hard. She made me fell lake a man when she said somethin lak dat.'

After breeding and emancipation, slaves lost the made-up family structure they had created, living together in slave pins. Many children had no idea who their parents were, and even if they did, where they were, or if they were alive, how to find them.

Rev. Lee said, "My daddy Burl seemed to draw real pride from talking about those times. I always felt they must have been like courting Sarah to him."

'Movin bout, tryin ta find a place ta settle fo a bit wus hard. Der wus so many folk tryin to do de same thang. We'ens had ta give de young'ens chance ta rest and eat. I learnt it wus good fo a small group ta try and make it on dey own, while dey wus on de move. Out scroungin one day, I stumbled on dis farm dat still had corn in de field. It wus way back off de road in de woods. De farm had two old white folk livin on de place. Dey thought I wus gonna raid it. Dey wus so afeared of me. But, I promised, iffin dey let us rest up der a while, we'ens a git de

corn out de field and do some work round de place, iffin dey let us stay. Dat wus how we'ens settled down fo a bit.

We'ens stayed on through de winter, but come spring, de three big boys left to join de Union Army. Dey talked bout de sound of cannons in de distance and play soljerin, practicin what I showed'em bout shootin. I run off from the plantation way fo de shootin start. I hid out in de swamps, where I got wit an old timer, who lived der ever since he wus a boy. He been a slave, but run off lak me. He sho me all bout shootin, huntin, scroungin for food and how ta tell what ta eat and what make ya sick.

De mornin our boys left, Sarah made'em a bit ta eat, corn pon and stuff lake dat, fo de road. Sarah fussed over'em, fixin on dey clothes and brushin dey hair with her hands and kissin and hugin'em. We'ens stood together wit de other young'ens, watchin dem as dey went out of sight in de woods. Of course Sarah cried, she just stood and watched de woods, long after dey gone. We'ems never saw our boys again.

We'ens stay on there thru winter and come sprang' the old white folk sa iffin we made a crop, da shar it with us'ens. Da wus the furst time we'en's got t rest fo a spel'.

Most readers probably have never considered or tried to imagine what it was like, coming out of slavery, living on your own for the first time. Trying to *make something out of nothing,* slaves did not have a pattern for anything. While, in the midst of it all, death stalking your every step, as war raged all around you. What does one do, caught up in such a tragedy? How does one keep it together, as life unfolds, trapping you, no matter which way you go in the South? You meet people desperately running from death and destruction, only to meet it head-on.

Fun Up North with Death and War Down South

Up North whites lived in a different world. War was an industrial boom for northern development. With money and lots of goods to spend it on, the booming economy increased prosperity in ways even northerners had not expected before Civil War. For many, it was like the boom times down South before the war, during the internal slave trade and breeding. Northerners grew rich, and the prospects continued long after the shooting and cannon fire ceased. With so much money floating around in the hands of working-class people, entertainment gave them, even more, to spend it on.

Minstrel shows were just the distraction, whites were looking for. Minstrelsy provided lots of fun, while anticipating the imminent defeat of the South. Blackface minstrels traveled the North, playing in large cities and small towns. They pitched tents and constructed makeshift stages in open fields and outback of saloons.

Newly Freedmen realized, after 243 years of bondage, they had nothing, but that was all they had, and something had to come out of that. Nothing more than a very slim hope for a slave, but northern whites had grown very fond of laughing at slaves portrayed by white men on stage. Minstrelsy had turned that nothing of slavery into something, not only whites wanted to see, they were willing to pay money to see it.

I believe many former slaves thought, if they were willing to pay to see white folks act like "niggers," they might as well have the real thing. Slaves' realization was a whole new deal for those that had entertained master, his family, and friends for free. No matter what others thought of former slaves, they saw it as a godsend. Getting paid to act like their selves, creating the same foolishness—singing, dancing and clowning around—the same as entertaining master, this had to be the work of God.

If slavery turned free Africans into a commodity—**black gold**—Minstrelsy made acting like, what white people imaged or thoughts was authentic black behavior—clowning, singing, and dancing—gave a slave a profession. Far more attempted than succeeded, but the opportunity to try something with nothing to lose was a new experience for slaves. Venturing beyond what they knew, many former slaves learned there was far more to life than what happened on plantations.

The fact that minstrel shows were exaggerated depictions, images that dehumanized blacks and were very inaccurate, meant very little to someone who'd never had anything. As a matter of fact, former slaves saw Minstrelsy, identical to how poor whites saw the internal slave trade and breeding slaves. Through Minstrelsy, former slaves were getting paid to be clowns, which they did for nothing, every time master looked their way. Former slaves had been trained for over 243 years to think as individuals to survive, instead of seeing what they did as representing other slaves. Performing as minstrels, those lucky enough to get the chance, Minstrelsy was similar to plantation life.

Surviving at any cost was the idea former slaves understood; black art and culture or reinforcing white stereotypes, former slaves had no concept. I think former slaves saw being blackface minstrels, as being something, which was far better than being the nothing, which slaves were walking off plantations. For them, blackface was a doorway to having and doing something, which was better than having or doing nothing.

After emancipation (1863), black performers, including former slaves, saw Minstrelsy as an opportunity for advancement. Some blacks wanted to introduce a humanizing element to Minstrelsy's portrayal of blacks. But performing in blackface, they found prosperity, so they did what they could with what they knew.

Life on the move, for contrabands, by 1870 had ended. The South was returning to a farm economy. For instance, Gen. Howard, through the Freedmen's Bureau, promoted the idea of contracts between Freedmen and former slave owners for working the land. The Bureau's arrangement gave newly Freedmen a way to set down roots and learn to live on their own. Under this arrangement, former slaves worked the land, while landowners supply the land, tools, a place to live, food to get through the winter, and seeds for crops. Freedmen planted, worked, and harvested crops for a set share of the harvest, hence "sharecropping."

I will say, in all honesty, all landowners were not tyrannical evil people. Some did not gouge sharecroppers for all but blood. Some white landowners were descent. However, they were, as former slaves, trapped in a government created system of laws designed to keep former slaves living on the same level as during slavery. The government system of segregation forced white people to conform to the new conditions, just as former slaves.

Fortunately, for my family, Burl Lee, Sr. contracted with a descent landowner. Although that may not seem like much on its face, but that allowed my family to acquire land, remain literate and increase their knowledge. Rev. Burl Lee, Jr. went to a Freedmen's Bureau school, became a preacher, built a family, joined a lodge, and became a leader among those not as fortunate as he.

Building Community

Trying to emulate my great-great-grandfather dialogue, along with slave narratives presented here and the actual historical record was to augment what I remember from Rev. Burl Lee, Jr.'s speech and stories as he talks with me. Those examples are models to give readers actual examples of the made-up vocabulary slaves' came up with in their desperate effort to express the thoughts in their heads. People today have no idea of the real-life challenges that slaves faced. Presenting the world of slavery and the struggles slave endured during bondage and after emancipation gives authenticity to the stories, I relay. I have presented everyday situations and circumstances former slaves faced as they try to advance culturally, while at the same time shed their ignorance.

Former slaves' inability to speak or write real words was a hurdle I present as a subtle indication of progress by former slaves from one generation to the next. They had to overcome their slave programming, based on their inner will to better themselves. With schooling, learning to read, children slowly developed better speech patterns than their parents.

Using slaves' made-up dialect, I showed how far former slaves had to come to be literate. I wanted to expose readers to that struggle so they would accept the idea that it took generations for descendants of slavery to change their speaking, thinking, and behavior patterns. After hundreds of years of slave masters demanding and reinforcing those patterns, slaves could not wish such problems away. They could not simply go there; they had to grow there.

Building lives from where they were, leaving plantations, slave descendants stepped out on their own. Their trepidation leaving plantations is understandable, but very difficult to imagine and explain today. A people, who had never imagined facing such challenges, as freedom offered, confronted these and challenged their formative years for developing their decision-making processes. Two concepts—making families and build communities—were their basic strategy for surviving in a hostile world, filled with whites unsympathetic to their situation, even though they created it.

Walking off plantations, former slaves' commonalities were part of their servitude, but skin color was what the world saw. Former slaves, though free of chains and shackles, remained tethered to their legacy of ignorance. Having originated from different places along the West coast of Africa, slaves were taught not to trust their kind. Once emancipated, most slaves understood that making families and building communities were keys to their survival. Their existence, as contrabands, was like a crash course in survival skills, because former slaves had to build trust and commitment towards one another.

I see the process of making family and community building, more like their first investment in their new enterprise of life. Newly freed slaves collateralized their investment with their lives, in my opinion. They saw their children as dividends they could cash in, through educating them, and as more help to work their land. Some even sent one child out of the South so that the family could follow. Former slaves saw the goals of the community and their lives as getting the next generation to a better place than where they started.

"Making something out of nothing" is a metaphor reflecting the process slaves engaged, leaving plantation life. I believe former slaves saw making families like starting bank accounts and building communities as the banks that maintained those accounts. I developed this metaphor thinking about how Rev. Lee described the life they built.

But even more importantly, this concept obliged each community member to support and protected their investments in the community, which justifies the metaphor. Former slaves did not work this out, say like the *"Mayflower Compact,"* but it was just as binding because most were in a hostile and isolated wilderness. They were nothing leaving plantations, and if their nothings were ever going to amount to anything, they had to figure out how to make their *"nothing into something."*

Surviving in the wilderness of America, after years of total ignorance and chattel slavery, was a life enslaved Africans had no way of contemplating, let alone anticipate. Emancipation was an audacious undertaking forced upon them also, the same as slavery. Regardless of fortune or misfortune, they faced circumstances no other people in modern times faced and/or attempted to overcome.

Former slaves were without reference, learning to live on their own. As such, one idea was as good as another, in terms of responses to their unique circumstances. Consequently, any information former slave received was suspect, in that, everyone was a first-timer, trying to figure out which way to go, what to do, and why?

Great-granddaddy Burl talked about these early times, and his words provided insight into great-great granddaddy Burl's perspective, as he faced day-to-day struggles and that of former slaves around him. Very little was recorded about black people by anyone, and slave narratives came after the fact. The history of this period is very unclear and hard evidence of why some things happened as they did, leaving researchers, like me, filling in the blanks? Also, how and what former slaves thought of their circumstances is unclear, which makes slave narratives even more after the fact.

Although lost in that sea of terror and death, somehow descendants of American slavery found ways to hold on to their humanity. The key to why so many slave descendants survived mentally intact, I believe, was due to their decision to make families and built communities. Their decisions gave them something greater than themselves to identify with and draw on for support. They were their only safety net and all they would ever have, which explains why they dedicated their lives, enduring to survive for their children.

What I discuss now are memories. They are supplemented by history and family discussions, with a young child (until age 11) and during Lee-Walker family reunion in the 1970s and 80s. These memories helped me visualize history through the eyes and words of my great-granddaddy and his father. How and why descendants of American slavery developed the concept of family and community they did, probably will never be known exactly? Hopefully, my recalling the brief engrams of memories I was given, listening so excitedly to what was said, must suffice.

The visions Rev. Lee conveyed of his time evoked such imagery, I cannot swear the overpowering emotions felt back then, I hope are words that conform to that time and the descriptions I provide today are the same. However, any untoward account suspected by readers may be due to the fact that my great-granddaddy was such a dynamic and powerful man in my eyes my imagination always took flight. So, what I give now may be more reflections saturated with imagination, more so than actual facts. Nevertheless, what I relay now maybe more visions and impressions than hard reality, but these are the images my family has as our word of mouth legacy.

Observing and listening to my great-granddaddy talk about how Papa met great-great-granny Sarah, I wanted to know how he met Mama Laura. He began;

"Well, I guess I was starting to come into manhood, and if Daddy Burl hadn't sent me to work with the missionaries at the crossroads, it wouldn't have happened at all. Once the family got settled on some land, we began making a crop every year. Daddy Burl began buying land for the family when the old white man passed on, and the old white widow woman didn't want to be alone in the woods. She offered to sell Daddy Burl her land. They had one boy, but he was killed early in the war.

After I grew into a big boy, and during the slack season between planting and harvest time, and after harvesting before planting time again, Daddy Burl started working with the missionaries at the crossroads. He helped out at the mission with folk trying to find family members or others they knowed, getting supplies into the backwoods for settlement folk, and counting them when new settlements were learned about.

Daddy Burl began taking me along going round, checking on communities of contrabands when I was about ten. He made sure every community had a Bible. There would always be a meeting every time we stop someplace. Daddy Burl let me read to them from the Bible; sometimes, he would, but he always led the gatherings in prayer. He even gave talks on the Lord sometimes. He never thought of himself as a preacher; he always said,"

The 400th: From Slavery to Hip Hop

'I ain't got the call. I ain't good enough to be no preacher. I'm too ignorant of God's plan and I did things I can't talk about. Now, you can be one. I know what kind of life y'all live and the kind of person y'all is. Y'all know right from wrong. Y'all care about folks and the community, like me. Y'all try to help out any way y'all can. Y'all watch things and learn quick, listen to old folks and watch out for young'ens'.

"After taking me with him, I guess almost three years or so; he said,"

'Son, I want y'all to start going over to the mission house on y'all own. Y'all can learn a lot just being rin God's folk. They like the way y'all is bout sponsibility at y'all young age. They kin learn y'all to be a preacher.'

"So, I started going over to the mission almost every day. I knew that was what he really wanted. So, I helped out for about a year and a bit, going on trips with the Old Reverend and the Sisters, taking supplies—Bibles and other stuff to folks in the backwoods. Cold weather in the winter, hot and boiling in summer, getting caught in rainstorms, and getting sick for weeks was hard on the Old Reverend and the Sisters. So, they gave me a horse and two pack mules a year or so after I started going out with them. They paid me $5.00 a trip starting out. I did things the way Daddy Burl showed me when we went out together. I tried to be just like him.

That part was easy; it was stuff that happened that had nothing to do with things you expect, which gave me a hard time. You know Mama sick and needs caring for a couple of days during planting or harvest season. Young'ens didn't eat in a day or so I became the cook. Baby just come and the midwife went back home, and mama still poorly. I be the wet-nurse for a week: hog-killing time and nobody to help. The cow just about to calf, the husband off working for the white folks and nobody knows what to do? The mule died, and a field needed plowing, while they try to git another. My pack mule and me went back behind the plow again. The worst was gitten sick on the road after gitten caught in a storm and trying to keep from dying of pneumonia. I learned being wet was just uncomfortable. Once you git soaked, its best to stay wet til you can stripe down, cover up with something dry and warm up."

Finding a Life

"So, that was the way it was for me, for about three or so years and a bit. I was nearin my 18th birthday, and I was doin all the traveling, specially in the winter and the hottest part of the summer, cept on special occasions. There was nothin I wanted to do, other than travel around, meetin folks talkin and helpin'em learn words and numbers. All the girls wanted to get married and start havin young'ens, so they could get out of working the field for a spell.

All that changed for me on a boilin hot July day. I was goin down this road; I never went down before. I turned on it, without really noticin. It crossed over a bridge, and just as you get cross, it turned into a big clearing. I saw a bunch of places with fields on both sides of the road and houses sittin way back off the road, near the woods. That's how they built'em in the backwoods, so folks kin run into the woods and hid iffin the paddy rollers ride through.

The place opened up where trees on the outer edge rounded off the sky, where it looked like I was in a bowl. One house, I could see from the road, had a well. I wanted a cool drink of water real bad, and I knowed my animals needed one more than me. Then off to on the side, I saw somebody plowin in a field, and the rows were pretty fair too.

When I rach the well, on that scotchin hot Mississippi day, before I could wet my whistle, a voice from the house hollowed.

"What y'all want? I got my shot gun sittin right here by de doo. We'ens don't 'llow no drummus or Bible thumpurs on dis land."

A woman stood on de porch seem like she want me to git. She stood lookin uninvitin. But, before I could say a word, a voice behind me said,

"He alright mama. He jes a young boy. He jes want ta water his hose and git some his self too."

"Lookin around, it was the person that was plowin the field. And liftin the big straw hat shadin the sun, to my surprise, even wit the big shirt and baggy trousers, I could see, it was a gal!! Two of the biggest and brightest eyes I ever did see wus rounded off by a pretty face, eye-ballin me. A big country smile beamed at me, and all I could say wus, 'Hey!'

"What y'all doing rin here, I hope y'all ain't no preacher? And, iffin y'all is, y'all bet not tell her dat, cause she'll shoot y'all. Mama Betsy hates preachers."

"The young gal said as she drew water for my hose and mule then some for me. We turned and walked to the house, once me and my animals got water. Reachin the porch, I could see a old woman sittin in a rocker, puffin on a corncob pipe. The woman doin du talkin squared up on me, wit hu hands on hu hips. She looked at me, tiltin hu head ta one side, givin me a kind of sideways look, den said,"

"*I ask y'all what y'all doin rin hun?*"

"Again fore I say somethin, du gal spoke up,"

"*All mama, he ain't sellin nothin. He jes want ta rest a spell afta gittin water and maybe a bit to eat. From de looks of him, he been on de road since day break.*"

"*I ain't got no food for no no-count or preacher. I don't care for preachers you know. Never met one dat wus worth a day's work. But, now, dey all kin eat dey way ta heaven and back.*"

I spoke up den, '*Yes'mam, I know what you mean. But now, I know what it is ta put my hands ta a plow, and I never set down ta de table til all de young'ens eat. And side dat I can pay, if you would be so kind as ta fix me some vittles.*'

"*Betsy let de boy lon….. and git his som'tee.*" The ol'woman said tween puffs. Mama Betsy went into de house, den the gal said,

"*Y'all show told hur. People rin here don't talk ta hur lak dat. What y'all do? Y'all don't live rin here, cause I know all de boys and most ain't wolff nothin. How y'all come ta be rin here?*"

'*I work wit du missionary folks over de other side de swamp.*'

"*Knowedddd you wus a preacher!!! I kin smell'em a mile away.*"

De woman wus back, she wus listenin, as she stood holdin de door open, comin out de house.

'*I ain't no preacher. I just work fo de preacher. I take stuff ta folks for de mission,*' I said hopin she wusn't reachin fo her shot gun.

'*Here,*' she hand me a plate wit beams and okra, wit a bit of fatback and cornbread. Takin it, hur hand stayed out, she said,

'Fore y'all give de Lord thanks, giv' me my due. And, I don't work fo no penny, neither."

So, lack a big shot, I flip hur, a nickel. She caught it wit'out takin hur eyes off me.

"Now, Betsy let de boy eat what he pay fo," Granny said still puffing.

"Dat's mama Dora. Come on over here," the gal said beckin at me ta follow hur, *"Come on!! You kin sit out under de tree and eat in de cool. Der's water in de pitcher by de wash pan iffin y'all want."* She said pointin.

After washin, I sat under du big Oak, as du breeze blo cool on me down. While I ate, du gal said in a askin kind of way, *"Y'all never said y'all name? Mins is Luara. What's yo's?"*
"Burl Lee, Jr. Umm name after my daddy," I said proudly.

"Y'all look too nice a boy ta be a preacher?" She said in a askin kinda way again.

I fill my mouth, so as ta have time to think den said, *'All preachers ain't good and all ain't bad, I thank, a preacher show how real God is ta him.'*

Full, I didn't want to over stay my welcome. Wit Mama Betsy hawkin me from du porch, still squared up and granny Dora puffin away; after sayin thanks, I got on my hose, den tip my hat and gallop off. Laura ran afta' me. So I slow down. She got up on a big stump, as I turn on de road. She hollow at me.

"Iffin y'all come back by dis way again, y'all gonna stop?"
I slow down and stop, turn my hose ta look at hur and ask, *'Y'all want me ta?'*

'Oh ya. Y'all kin be my furst friend,' she holla'.
Wit dat, I gave my hose a boot.

Staking a Claim on Life

My great-grandfather seemed to enjoy telling me about his young days, but when he spoke about meeting and getting to know Mama Laura, his demeanor change. First, a big smile would ease across his face, like sunrise slowly breaking over the landscape. His big pearly white teeth would reveal themselves in the same slow, easy manner. Most times when sitting, he would stand and walk a few paces, while pulling on his beard, before turning and facing me. Then he would begin something like this,

"Life wus bout helpin take care of others. Everybody wus in need at one time or otter; even when dey won't say. So, I let my eyes tell me. Askin sometime is a insult, so I always try to act on what I saw not what I heard. De missionaries wus happy when I told'em bout de settlement I stumbled cross. Dey wanted me to keep in touch wit it and git a count on de number of folk rin dar. Dis wus fine wit me cause dos big pretty bright eyes and smilin face found a place in my mind. Thankin bout Laura fill my lonely hours, whether workin round de mission or ridin by myself in de back country. So, I put Laura's area, call, Turtle Back Lake on de end of my next run. I really wanted ta see her again. I packed a special package and put it on my hose, not on de pack mules. I didn't wot ta git it mix-up wit de stuff for settlement folks.

It wus evenin when I got ta de farm. Everbody wus sittin on de porch as I rode up. Laura saw me and jump ta de ground and ran down de path, wavin as she came to meet me. I stop my hose fo she got ta me. She stop, bent over wit both hands on hur knees, but still had a big smile fo me. She said,

"Hey Burl, mama said yo won't be comin back rin dis way no mo. I sho didn't thank I be seein y'all again. I look fo y'all up and down de road everyday hopin you be comin. Where you headin?"

Luara asked wit out lettin me git a word in edge wise. I lack hearin her talk. So, I jes let hur rama on til she stop. Then fo I could say, she ask,

"Kin I ride up ta de house, on your hose, hind y'all?"

"Sho kin" I gave hur a hand up and she grab me tight rin my waist.

"Don't wanna fall," she said kinda gigglin.

I could feel her heart in her chest bet'in up again my back, ridin ta de house.

"*Gal, git down off dat hose fo it buck and y'all fall and break somethin.*" Mama Betsy said givin me her usual stern scowl. "*What y'all doin back out here so soon, y'all jes left here last week or so.*"

Steppin on de porch off my hose, Laura spoke up quickly, "*Mama dat wus almost four weeks ago.*"

Well de missionaries didn't know bout dis place. So, dey want me ta count folks and see iffin dey got stuff at de mission dey need," I said real quick. And den fo Mrs. Betsy could say somethin, I said pointin at de barn, '*I thought maybe I could put my hose and mules up der and sleep in de barn fo a night or two, while I count. Iffin you don't mind. I pay Laura a quarter a day to help out count de folks rin here, since she said she knowed where folks lives.*'

"*Oh, yes Mama, y'all know I know all de folks rin here.*" Laura said jumpin up and down a couple of times, while pattin her hands a little. She look so happy.

Mama Betsy's face kinda got tight and her eyes too, but I spoke first. Reachin for my saddlebag I said, '*I brong des ta cover my food and I pay a dollar fo de barn.*'

Mama Betsy took de sack and while she looked in it, I said, '*It flour, meal, coffee, sugar, grits, a side of bacon and stuff lak dat. Even, some tobacco fo granny's pipe.*'

Granny Dora spoke up, "*Coffee and sugar, I kin use a cup of dat rat now. And I ain't had no baca fo a month. I's been smokin dry corn silk, mix wit chicerky root.*"

Thinkin bout dat and hi dat taste made me wanna gag. I looked at Laura and she wus snicgulin with hur hand over hur mouth.

Handin de bag ta Laura, Mama Betsy said, "*Take dis in de house.*" den lookin at me, she said in a mumble, "*Don't start thinkin this is home,*" as she turn and followed Laura in de house.

De next monin Laura wok me up early fo ta eat, holdin a pan of grits, butter biscuits, bacon and peach preserves. She wus still excited.

"*What we gonna do Burl? How yo'all count folk?*" she asked.

'*It ain't nothin. We go ta a place, tell'em we work with de missionaries and dey want ta know how many folk live rin here. What kind of supplies dey need. I take dat back ta de mission and see what dey can do ta get what dey need.*'

Laura rattled on fo two days. She told me all bout every thang der wus ta know bout hur, mama Betsy, granny Dora and Turtle Back Lake. She wanted ta know as much bout me, what I did and de folk I met. What my family wus lack? What it wus lack where I live? She thought goin rin de way I did, doin somethin diff'ent all de time wus so excitin. She talk bout hur dull life on Turtle Back Lake. She ask bout everthang dat pop in hur head. Frankly, I never met a gal dat had so much to say bout nothin, as dat one. It wus nice bein rin abody, I didn't have ta do all de talkin. I could jes lis'en and watch hur. Laura really made my heart feel good jes bein rin hur. She seemed so serious bout life.

Ready to hit the road, after giving Laura a dollar, I gave Mrs. Betsy two dollars for the stabble. Lookin at it, she said,

"*Y'all wa'en in du barn but two nights?*" givin me a squint-eyed look, like she wau looking for a string.

So I said, '*Well I might be throu des parts someday and I wan have a dollar, so y'all jes hold on ta dat one til den and den we be even.*'

Leavin headin back to de mission, dis time, Laura stood on de porch wit de otter women, only sayin, "*We see y'all win y'all throu des parts a'gin Burl,*" as she waved by-by.

Belmead (St. Emma's Military Academy) Alternative Schools

The transition Freedmen made coming out of slavery amidst war into the contraband period was a time of danger, terror, and traumatic adjustments. It took commitment while suffering through the pain and humiliation of ignorance. Struggling to survive this strange and confusing world, former slaves were total victims. Based on the ignorance forced upon them, it would have been truly difficult for well-adjusted individuals, trying to make such a difficult transition without survival knowledge, immediately following 243 years of bondage. Why did slaves not suffer mental breakdowns or massive sensory overload, trying to compete for survivor resources, build lives and become educated jointly, while suffering violence and government repression is a quandary American historian and psychologists have avoided studying and researching. Why is the question?

First, the inability to read imposes limitations on one's ability to learn other things. The major limitation is learning based on the written word is undebatable. Reading is the doorway to written knowledge. That limitation is completely overlooked by historians when assessing former slaves' efforts and progress following emancipation. The inability to read extends beyond understanding the meaning of words, how to use them, and, most importantly, their contextual setting. Those born in a typical culture will picks up quite a bite, learning to speak languages. Unlike slaves, who were not included in the extended society and even allowed to speak properly. Their ignorance of words was government enforced and re-enforced by all social institutions with sanctions and threats including extra-judicial punishment.

Imagining the difficulty former slaves faced, will not simulate that reality today. A major aim of forcing slaves to speak non-standard made-up words, whites did not speak, was to keep slaves ignorant of whites' intentions. Words for slaves were to acknowledge commands for service. Manuals are written for adults and not written on an elementary level. So, while trying to learn a trade or profession, a slave had to learn to read on an adult level. Most slaves were exposed to alphabets for the first time during the contraband period. Survival demanded Freedmen balance all these negative events and circumstances, as part of their victimization, which swirled around them, as they tried to stay alive, while being targets of KKK terror.

The previous statements reflect the type of hurdles Freedmen had to surmount, building a floor of knowledge amidst their struggles. Former slaves advanced from concerns over individual survival needs and making families to concerns of communities. Some of these family structures defy description. Families joined together sometime two or three women shared one man. These arrangements were like confederations. They were formed based on mutual survival needs and agreements.

Just the same, whatever structure former slaves came up with, proved to be resilient enough that small groups of families became communities, aiding contrabands survival. Deciding to build communities, rather than dispersing among other or existing as individuals were slave saving grace, I believe. Their decision to build communities allowed what they learned, as individuals surviving in slave pens, to become group knowledge, underpinning their common experiences made all their other experiences a part of their communal strategies.

The success of these communities made the accumulation of resources possible, during these troubling and confusing times. Such communities either held onto surplus resources or traded them with other communities based on their projected needs. As Reconstruction ended, it was clear former slaves could not depend on government any more than they could master, for welfare and survival needs.

Beginning in the 1880s, former slave families had existed long enough to develop family networks. These networks sought supplies for exchange and helped locate family members and bring them together. Their networks became a full-blown system for transferring information to other communities, mostly using circuit riders through churches. The church played a major role in these networks. It was the only organized structure they could depend on beyond local communities and themselves. All families did not have a literate person in their households; other families filled that gap. People communicated all kinds of needs, including prospects for relocating, attending school, inquiring about work, and even finding mates.

Freedmen were no longer the confused desperate rabble that wandered off plantations, beginning in early 1863. Most had been free for 20 years. They had children who were born free, as Burl Lee, Jr. These children knew of slavery only through their parents' and grandparents' stories. They were the first generation that had no personal knowledge of bondage. Developing stable communities and lifestyles, these children knew only stability. Moving around was something one did at their pleasure. The growth in skills, among former slaves, brought wealth to communities, creating even greater opportunities.

The Reconstruction Era created great expectations and hopes for advancement among Freedmen. Blacks men were elected to political office, and many individuals, churches, and philanthropic societies established schools and several colleges. Again the church was a major force in establishing schools and colleges.

The amount of property owned by African Americans (1890) had tripled since the late 1860s, and literacy increased greatly over these years. More blacks were voting, and the new generation rejected old patterns of deference and subservience towards whites. Struggling to throw off ignorance, the "American dream" appeared to be a reality for a growing number of former slaves and their descendants, ("*Politics Reform and Expansion: 1890–1900,*" Harold U. Faulkner (1959).

The discussion on education presented earlier may have made it seem, black schools and welfare institutions, helping Freedmen after the Civil War, were founded only by white missionaries. However, the need for education was so critical it overshadowed other major problems and need. Orphans, as products of slavery were just such a major subject. Slavery and war left many children without family structures. Products of the internal slave trade and breeding, many children were without parents, families or guardians, emerging from slavery. Women with children, but no man, necessitated patchwork structures that brought broken families together with other broken ones. Orphans were another story; many were adolescences (10 years or so).

Just to reiterate Rev. Lee said his father would almost be in tears sometimes when he spoke of this,

'Der wus so many chullin wit no folk. At times, on de road, it look ta me, it wus more young'ens dan grown'folk. Dey jes follow up behind any folk dat gave'em food and didn't run'em off. Sarah wus always takin'em in. She'd see'em sittin or walkin the road, all nasty, little ones dat had no water on'em in days, cept rain. Flys bout ta eat'em alive. She'd tak'em and wash'em, find some clean rags ta put on'em and we'ed have a other mouth ta feed.'

Many black men and women build church schools and homes for black orphans in cities, large and small, by pooling their pennies, organizing fish fries, and church suppers. Large numbers of children were taken in by intact black families. Numerous African American churches and lodges raised thousands of dollars for the effort to find, care for, and educate former slave children that were without families and living any way they could on their own.

The effort continued into the 1880s through the 1890s. Virginia, for instance, had no home for orphan black boys and girls. The state refused to build one. However, black women of Virginia created their own home. Alabama had no institution for black children either, so again black women funded an institution for black children.

Colored women clubs, ministers, lodges, and fraternal organizations of former slaves championed and established a tradition of self-help and communal support. They became the real floor beneath struggling contrabands trying to stabilize their shaky beginnings of freedom. Men and women in communities in the South and North began the tradition, going from house to house collecting pennies and dimes to bury indigents and care for the sick and orphans.

Many Americans, white and black, mistakenly believe former slaves did not have skills coming out of slavery. They think slaves had no skills and needed teaching everything. They believe Freedmen were all dumb, lazy field hands. That was not true during slavery and certainly not true once it ended. I recapitulate, slaves possessed the skills during slavery; they were the craftsmen and artisans in the South, even though most could not read. White men were proud to say, *"I didn't do work. Work is for niggers; that's what we got slaves for."* Work was degrading for whites. Therefore slaves emerged after the Civil War, with most of the skill.

The black side of this coin began once Pres. Lincoln signed the Emancipation Proclamation (1863). Missionary groups (black and white), wealthy individuals, and other benevolence societies began exploring ways to help educate and train former slaves. Many different approached and techniques were developed in the 1880s to helped prepare former slaves for a life of freedom. Some developed wholistic approaches to educating Freedmen. These schools care for all their student's needs.

Such groups and individuals created different types of educational institutions. One type was the boarding school. Many of these schools were only for descendants of America slavery. They began appearing in the 1880s, and over one hundred schools flourished until the late 1930s. Boarding schools functioned like colleges with dormitories but had no tuition. The best example of such schools was *St. Emma's Industrial and Agricultural Institute.*

Began by Colonel and Mrs. Edward de Vaux Morrell of Philadelphia, they purchased Belmead a plantation in Virginia to implement their ideas on what they thought would help Freedmen. Impressed with Booker T. Washington's model, they changed the Gothic-style mansion, built amidst 2,265 acres of rolling hills, turning it into a school for male Freedmen (1895). Although Colonel Morrell's approach to educating former slaves, emphasized practical skills, like Washington's, St. Emma was in a class unto itself.

The Philadelphia Institute of Technology (Drexel University) instituted the curriculum at St. Emma. It included canning, farming, equipment repair, engineering, accounting, and management. An in-state agricultural school, St. Emma was second only to Virginia Polytechnic Institute and State University (Virginia Tech University). It opened its doors to "poor former slaves and descendants from the South" in 1895. Its first graduate, John Paul Scott, received his diploma in 1899. Over its seventy-seven year history St. Emma's curriculum changed and expanded to fit the times but maintained its entrance requirements.

Next, changing over time, St. Emma constructed a trade school in 1933. It was the largest trade school in the South, containing 35,000 square feet of floor space.

It offered technical and mechanical training such as blacksmith, iron-working, printing, woodwork, carpentry, masonry, plastering, plumbing, steam-fitting, shoe repair, auto mechanics, upholstery, and electrical training.

Changing again St. Emma became a Military Academy, which graduated 10,000 black men. The military academy had a nationally honored Rifle Team and received the Military Honor Star, awarded by the Department of the Army for high military achievement. St. Emma's peak enrollment was 370 cadets in the 1960s. Father Egbert J. Figaro served as Commandant of Cadets from 1958 until the school closed (1975).

St. Francis de Sales High School was created for African-American girls, and it was built by St. Katharine Drexel. It opened in 1899 just across the James River from St. Emma. St. Francis became affiliated with Catholic University, Washington, D.C., and offered courses that included homemaking, award-winning needlework, sewing/lace-making, laundering, nursing as well as marketing. In the 1940s, St. Francis boasted a championship girls basketball teams. They also had a nationally acclaimed choir.

During the 1920s and 1930s, many boarding schools became two or four-year colleges. These schools played huge roles in helping former slaves make the transition to freedom as professionals. Boarding school students taught others in their families, as well as communities, the skills and knowledge they acquired. Some even started schools themselves, extending their knowledge abroad even more. Freedmen were not dumb lazy field hands, who did not want to work, as whites claimed. Many had skills, while many more attempted to acquire them. Former slaves were working jobs that allowed them to develop real wealth by 1900.

The 1880s were a time of great prosperity. However, many white people wanted to maintain the old source of their wealth—the misery and degradation of others. Slavery had produced riches for white people for six hundred years. Their slave wealth allowed them to build great mansions, mighty estates and become moguls of huge industries. However, some were like Colonel and Mrs. Edward de Vaux Morrell or St. Katharine Drexel. They used their wealth to improve life for others locked in poverty by those that accumulated enormous fortune and lived opulent lifestyles with their slave wealth.

St. Katharine was truly a special person for former slaves and Native People. She made, caring for the poor, her life's work, as Jesus Christ commanded. She spent her entire inherited fortune, (over 2 million dollars) giving back to those robbed by slavery and "manifest destiny" of their lives and lands. She is a model for today super-rich, who, rather than giving back, continues scheming and grubbing for more money.

I compare attitudes of the rich to plantation/slave owners and their obsession with gaining wealth through increased cotton production. Optimizing this process, *"They produced more cotton to sell to buy more slaves, to make more cotton to buy more slaves, to make more cotton to buy more slaves, 'ad infinitum.'"* Today, this is called leveraging. This example is offered to highlight this period when Freedmen were optimistic about their hopes for real freedom. They needed only one push, which would make the promise of freedom a reality with good-paying jobs in America's booming economy.

The 400th: From Slavery to Hip Hop

Newly Freedmen look upon the 1880s with renewed hope, following the premature and aborted end of Reconstruction and the Freemen Buearu. Just twenty years out of slavery, most Freedmen worked relentlessly, establishing a solid footing with stable families and strong supportive communities. Turning its back on Freedmen, the US government and powerful captains of industry began structuring the Nation's economy to deprive former slaves of opportunities. During the 1880s, government actions set a course to control former slaves' ability to build wealth, while denying former slaves opportunities to improve the stable lives they were building.

The Gilded Age

"The Gilded Age," a time fueled by excesses of all types, was paid for by a booming post-Civil War economy. White Americans created a world built on pretense and outrageously opulent lifestyles. This booming economy created a huge wealth bubble that blew the rich class in America up so fast; no one knew what to do with all the wealth? Similar to the French in the 17th and 18th Centuries, gorging on wealth produced by the **Trans-Atlantic Slave Trade,** rich Americans went on a binge of; *"Spending more to have more because I can afford more!!"*

On the downside of this rich man's glory ride, former slaves' prospects for survival continually improved, coming into the 1880s. However, they needed access to America's booming economy to sustain their impressive advancements, considering they had come out of slavery an ignorant people less than twenty years earlier. Former slaves had adjusted to the demands of freedom and were building futures for themselves and their families.

Out of this fog of gaiety, pretense, and affluence, which began at the end of the 1870s, stepped Mark Twain to expose the excesses of the moneyed class. Twain ridiculed the pretentiousness of the late 19th Century, lampooning the rich for their greediness in his novel *The Gilded Age: A Tale of Today* (1873). He exhibited his usual homespun, but deadly serious witticisms, excoriating the rich for this time of extravagant self-indulgence.

Dubbing this period, *"The Gilded Age,"* Twain colored it green for the envy that drove the rich to consume more and more to showcase their wealth. Synonymous to the practice of gilding, "layering gold upon gold," he characterized them as "decorating the decorations." Twain was not content to simply poke fun at the super-rich, for amassing enormous wealth and power at the expense of the poor; he laid the blame for America's serious social problems at their feet. Twain said, "The very rich accumulated their excessive wealth by gouging poor people to the detriment of the whole society."

Pointing his finger at those he considered crass, Mark Twain satirized the era with biting commentary, gilding the supper-rich with blame. Twain characterized attitudes of the moneyed class in America, during *"The Gilded Age,"* like no other. It is uncanny how much, America's rich class then and today, resembled the French before and during the time of Napoleon I. Creating a 1880s caricature of burlesque, Mark Twain chided money-grubbing moguls, as they used their riches, to cover over their endless pretense of happiness. Twain's critique underscored how the rich showcased their obscene self-importance, with displays of their meaningless and wasteful lifestyles. Their endless pretense points up a major theme of this narrative, *'It's not how much wealth one gains, but what one does with wealth that matters."*

The 400th: From Slavery to Hip Hop

Partying it up, during *"The Gilded Age,"* the emptiness and wastefulness of the rich class were like chickens at sundown, toward the end of their exultant glory ride. Their luxurious living came home to roost, as *The Panic of 1893*. That panic changed everything for everybody, rich and poor, but especially for former slaves. The very rich portfolios were ravished, as the panic bit Wall Street's robber barons in the back pocket.

The Panic struck like a phantom in the night, although it did not come out of nowhere. The fat cats of greedy and extravagance ignored the signs of the times. These signs indicated their outlandish exorbitance, and meant ruin for those unable to sustain that wasteful lifestyle. Their *Gilded Age* pretense of happiness was a grotesque minuet, trampling down the poor, while masking the serious socioeconomic and political inequalities, their festival of sumptuousness spawned.

Lying just below the surface, the full-blown *Panic of 1893* sprang forth to ravish America and the world. Jacob Riis, three years earlier, partially uncovered it with his eye-opening exposé, <u>How the Other Half Lives: Studies among the Tenements of New York</u> (1890). Riis, a news reporter, popularized photo journalism. His exposé documented the squalid living conditions of the poor in New York City's slums of the1880s. Riis' study showed, as this narrative, poverty in America was unlike poverty in Europe and other parts of the world; it was government produced.

After the Civil War, industrial production transformed the US into an industrial superpower. The US government began importing waves of unskilled southern and eastern Europeans, as well as Asian and Jewish immigrants into America, as cheap labor. America's government refused to give those opportunities to newly freed slaves, its own *"cheap labor"* force. The US government brought over 5.2 million immigrants to the US (1.2 more than its 4 million former slaves). This government policy increased the population of New York City by 25%. Riis, as Mark Twain, became part of the effort to educate America about poverty.

Riis blamed the problems of tenement housing in New York City on tenement owners. Also, Twain pointedly blame greed and neglect by the wealthy for poverty. Charging the masters of *The Gilded Age* with gouging the poor, Riis tied the high crime rate, drunkenness, overcrowding and deprivation produced by slum living conditions to their greed. Riis's photographic exposé showcased the desperate circumstances poor whites endured. His photographs spoke directly to the conscience of white Americans. Unfortunately, Riis fail to see and connect what was happening to white European immigrants to the desperate lot of former slaves.

Slavery produced wealth in the US came as a result of 262 years of free labor. Not providing former slaved with good-paying jobs during the *"Gilded Age,"* hampered their efforts to progress. Instead, America brought European immigrants to the US to fill those jobs, while burying former slaves in the graveyard of poverty. America created employment patterns that structured and lock African Americans on the bottom of the American capitalistic economic system. More will be said later about this topic.

But for now, I look in-depth and providing numbers to give concreteness to how America created and attenuated poverty among former slaves with numbers; because numbers never lie. America's gross domestic product and industrial production, by the 20th century led the world. Rapidly expanding economic growth pushed American wages beyond those in Europe, especially for "skilled workers." Drawn to America by high wages, millions of European immigrants flooded the US.

Discrimination and overt racism became fixtures in the lives of African Americans and **"The Gilded Age"** reflects the early stage of segregation in the US. I want to be clear; there was not a shortage of jobs, which prompted America's government to implement segregation. There were more jobs than applicants, which is why America went to Europe for more white people. But, the aim was to preserving the southern slave master's mindset, by keeping slave descendants on the bottom, and white people on top of America's economy and society.

Giving more concreteness to that verbal description, P. J. Kennedy, American economist (1858–1929), supplies the numbers that put the previous statement in perspective. He said, *"U.S. national income, in absolute figures per capita, was far above everybody else's by 1914."* Per capita income in the United States by 1914 was $377 compared to Britain in second place at $244, Germany at $184, France at $153, and Italy at $108, while Russia and Japan trailing far behind at $41 and $36, *(Economic History of the United States § Late 19th Century, Robert Baron Industrialist).*

Wealthy industrialists and financiers such as John D. Rockefeller, Jay Gould, Henry Clay Frick, Andrew W. Mellon, Andrew Carnegie, Henry Flagler, Henry H. Rogers, J. P. Morgan, Leland Stanford, Meyer Guggenhein, Jacob Schiff, Charles Crocker and Cornlius Vanderbilt were labeled *"robber barons"* by Mark Twain and others. They argued their fortunes were made at the expense of the working class. Through chicanery and betraying America democracy they amassed riches, *(American Politics in the Gilded Age, 1868-1900),* Robert W. Chany, (1997) Wheeling, Illinois: Harlan Davidson).

Approaching the end of the decade (1890s), the US was experiencing economic growth and expansion, as wealth increased from high international commodity prices, especially in the North and West. Rapid industrialization and expansion led to real wage growth of 60%, which spread across an ever-increasing labor force, during the boom days of the 1860s and 1890s, especially for workers from Europe. However, after working for free for over 246 years (1619-1865) descendants of American slavery struggled, coming out of slavery in the late 1860s through 1890s, trying to get beyond their penniless emancipation (1863).

The average annual wage per industrial worker (including men, women, and children) rose from $380 in 1880 to $564 by 1890, a gain of 48% in ten years. However, *The Gilded Age* was also an era of abject poverty and inequality for former slaves because US imported poverty by bringing 5.2 million impoverished European to America. But, new immigrants from Europe were moved ahead of newly freed slaves.

More directly, America created even greater poverty for its population of slave descendants by denying them any real opportunity to advance through higher-wage jobs. These higher-wade jobs were restricted and held for Europeans immigrants or other poor whites, mainly from the South. They became a barrier, blocking newly freed slaves from entering the job market altogether in some industries. Other industries gave only the most menial, dirty, hazardous, dead-end jobs whites didn't want for the wages paid to former slaves. Whites had choices; former slaves did not.

Historians present poverty among African Americans, as their fault. They justified their conclusion by describing African America as lazy, uneducated, unskilled with poor work ethics, but numbers tell a different story. Government actions and directives structured the American economy, with built-in discrimination. It blocked former slaves' access to economic opportunities, while poor foreigners poured into the US and were given high paying jobs, as today. But, hard times were not only reserved for blacks, as the hand of Providence swung like a double-edged sword, cutting into families enjoying the high concentration of wealth among whites. The sumptuous living of the rich became more visible, producing contentious rhetoric, as the bottom fell out on everyone in 1893, when wheat prices crashed.

The Panic Struck Terror in the Hearts of Americans

The *Panic of 1893* solidified everything that structured former slaves on the bottom of American's economy that began in 1876 with the election of Rutherford B. Hayes. Hayes cosigned southerners' effort segregating former slave. I pointed out earlier, Hayes pulled federal troops out of the South, which allowed the South, through "interposition and nullification" to ignore the "Civil Rights Bill of 1866" entirely. What happened to descendants of American slavery was not the result of the blind will of chance or accidental caprice of events.

Segregation was a calculated and willful plot by America's government and capitalists dedicated to re-enslaving the newly Freedmen. *The Gilded Age* opened the door to the full implementation of segregation, convict leasing, sharecropping, and white supremacy. It set the edge for the legal denial of all socioeconomic, political, and human rights of African Americans throughout the 20th Century, which continues today.

In the larger American society, everyone was so busy making so much money, when the signs of trouble appeared, everyone ignored them. Investors had lost money in the market before but always recovered. America was the land of *"Manifest Destiny."*

But, European investors became concerned when the wheat crop failed (1890), and a coup in Buenos Aires ended the Baring Brothers Argentine bank interest. Baring Brothers, a financial house in London, defaulted on 21 million English pounds (about 27,000,000 pounds today) of debt. The Bank of England collateralized Baring Brothers' debt and investment in Argentina. Covering the default, the Bank of England borrowed from the Bank of France, which borrowed from the Bank of Imperial Russia. Numerous bank failures and runs on currency in Europe (1890) resulted. England had nowhere to go to make up the shortfall but to the United States.

Fears of a spreading crisis started runs on US gold. It was comparatively simple to cash in dollar investments for exportable gold. Next, the Philadelphia and Reading Railroad went belly up (1893) and brought the state of America's economy home to roost, like chickens at sundown. A credit crunch rippled through the American economy, as Americans depositors rush to withdraw funds, once Europeans bailed out of American investments.

Bank runs sent the financial crisis back to London. The panic caused a drop in continental European trade, putting the ball back in America's court. Similar to Great Britain, the US had nowhere to go. Panicky foreign investors began selling American stocks to obtain funds backed by gold. The bottom fell out of *The Gilded Age*, as a double whammy hit America, stocks plumed, when America loss gold reserves.

But however, the straw that broke the dollar's back was skyrocketing bank failures. Those failures caused a huge drop in stock prices; 158 national banks went under in 1893, the contagion was fatal to 172 state banks. All total 500 banks closed, 177 private banks, 47 savings banks, 16 mortgage companies, and 13 loan and trust companies fail. Numerous farms ceased operation, and 15,000 businesses failed. Banks reported declines in gold reserves; the United States debt increased as money and gold flowed out of the country. This is like America today, with the coronavirus, had the Federal Reserve Bank—government—not poured trillions of dollar into businesses.

Unemployment among factory workers became severe; wage reductions were widespread. Over 125 railroads went into receivership (1894). Unemployment hit 25% in Pennsylvania, 35% in New York, and 43% in Michigan. The depression reached its lowest point in July of 1894 but did not abate.

The very rich were unscathed by the panic, as now. The unequal distribution of wealth remained high. For instance, the wealthiest 2% of Americans owned over a third of the nation's wealth, while the top 10% owned 3/4. The bottom 40% had no wealth at all. The wealthiest 1% owned 51% of the property, while the bottom 44% claimed only 1.1%, *(The Age of Acquiescence: The Life and Death of American Resistance to Organized Wealth and Power*, Steve Fraser, Little, Brown, and Company (2015).

American history books did not report the other side of this coin. The story on the downside again was, *"it is not how much wealth is gained, but what is done with wealth that matters.* Former slaves were making families and building communities. They were not having parties, they were working, not traveling to Europe. Also, they were building small businesses, buying land for family farms and homes.

This invisible wealth became real economic power once prices for everything started falling. Slave descendants all over America did as Robert Church, after the "yellow fever" epidemic in Memphis in 1878. They began snapping up bargains in land, businesses, homes, furniture, horses, and buggies; it was a bargain-basement sale. Rich folks liquidated everything, trying to hold on to status, as the panic deepened.

The new reality, once the panic ended, was that black people owned a lot of stuff. Whites started looking at people, they once owned, as slaves, and saw they now had more than many of them. White people began questioning how penniless former slaves had wealth when white people were losing theirs. Black People did not jump into the stock market; they were saving for a rainy day.

White people that were working to re-enslave black American, now point the finger at the federal government.

They published the "Big Lie" that former slaves were on the federal dole. Newspapers picked up this line, many in the news business had lost everything, including their jobs. Politicians harmonized the chorus, blaming the government; many had lost positions in government and money in the market.

White supremacists began crafting a very deceptive scenario, claiming former slaves were *"an undeserving lot."* Their spill was, *"The government was supporting Niggers with white people's tax dollars,"* or *"Lazy niggers that don't want to work are living on white people's tax money."* White folks lying claiming, *"Freed slaves are why white people no longer have what they did before the end of slavery."* Their illogic became known as *"The White Man's Burden."* White people were paying for the good life "niggers" were enjoying.

"It was early spring, and things had started growing. You saw a few new foals and calves gallivanting about in pastures, and folks were in fields planting. Every time I saw a woman working in the field, I thought about Laura. You know, to be honest, every time I saw a woman, I thought about Laura."

We both laughed, as great-granddaddy Burl talked on about how he and Mama Laura got together.

"I kept hoping something would happen that would make me somebody she wanted as I wanted her," he said.

Then he reached over and picked up his Bible, opened it, and took out a letter. He didn't open it. He just waved it about, while saying,

"This letter made all the difference in the world, and it all began the day I went by the mission to start gathering supplies for my next ride. The Old Reverend said,"

"The Bishop of the CME Denomination (Colored Methodist Church) would be stopping through these parts today or tomorrow. We got word by messenger yesterday, and I want you to meet him. So don't plan to ride your circuit until he passes through. Do you remember our talk about a month or so ago? We talk about you possibly getting training for ordination, as a preacher. Meeting the Bishop could go a long way in bringing that about. So, stay close and help out around here."

"I only listen, not saying anything. We had talked about me getting some real education in a real school. I thought that might help me get to be somebody. If I did that, I would be what my daddy wanted. I would be respectable, maybe even get a government job, and become a real leader. I thought that would be something to help me with Laura. While he talked, I kept seeing Laura's bright, flashing eyes and her big smile. Maybe if that happened, she would have something to think about me, as a choice. We had known one another for about a year or so. We had seen one another six or eight good times, but I thought she just likes talking to me cause I was somebody she didn't see all the time. I worked hard, so my route took me by the farm as much as I could. This ride would take me by there.

The Bishop got to the mission in mid-afternoon before the sun started down. He rode in a buggy with a driver; they wore suits. The Bishop was a kind of large man, and shorter than I had imagined him. The Old Reverend introduced us,"

"This is Bishop William H. Miles from Jackson, Tennessee. Bishop Miles, this is Burl Lee, Jr. He is a very bright fellow and has been helping out here at the mission for some years now. I don't know what we would do if he was not helping out with outreach. He does all our traveling, never complains and is so obedient. Well, I'll leave you to talk while I attend to some things inside."

We took seats in the courtyard, in the warm spring sun. Bishop Miles began,

"That's a great report. How is it you have taken on such heavy responsibilities at such a young age?"

'Well, Sir, it was my daddy. He sent me to work with the missionaries when I was about 14 years old.'

"You weren't good at farm work?" The Bishop asked.

'Oh no sir, I mean, yes sir. I was very good at farm work, but my daddy said he wanted me to learn to be a preacher and that the people here at the mission could help me learn what I needed to know to make a good one.'

Bishop Miles asked.

"And have you learned?"

'I can't say for sure, Sir. But, I think I learned the most important things. First, I believe in God Almighty, as my Lord and Savior. Then, I try to live a righteous life. I love people and treat everybody fair, I lookout and help take care of people, especially, chullins, sick and old folks. And, of course, I believe in the Bible. Iffin it's more than that, Sir, I still have things to learn.'

The Bishop didn't say anything for a minute or two. He just looked straight at me then he said,

"Let me tell you a little about the Colored Methodist Church. We started up about ten years ago. Most of us did a little preaching on plantations around us. Sometimes, we did things like what you're doing now. Our masters let us go to meeting, white Methodists held. When the birth of freedom came, we just kept doing what we were doing, all through the war and after. Our white brothers helped us organize our church in Jackson, Tennessee. We started ordaining ministers and Bishops almost from the very beginning. We are looking for smart young men *like you to become ministers. That is why Rev. Honeysuckle told me about you. He thinks you would make a very fine minister, and so do I. I might add."*

I would like to recommend you to our board. If you are accepted, we will bring you to our boarding school in Jackson for training. I believe in about two or three years you would have your own church, maybe in a big city like Memphis, Birmingham or Atlanta. Our ministers earn thirty dollars a month, and if you are, as good as we believe, you may end up preaching in Washington DC, or Philadelphia, maybe even New York City."

He stopped, kinda sudden like. It may have been the look on my face that caused his pause. I had to be looking real funny because I sure felt funny. Then he said,

"Well, you don't have to make up your mind this minute. Think about it." He got to his feet and started inside.

I had been thinking all the time as he talked. He was saying all the things I dreamed about. It was what my daddy hoped would happen all along. But, as he talked about me living in Jackson, Tennessee, I started feeling funny in my belly. I kept seeing Laura's face and me telling her about all this, but she wa'en smiling. Then, as the Bishop got up to go inside, words just started coming out of my mouth, and I couldn't stop'em. I said,

'Bishop Sir, I don't want to sound ungrateful or anything like that for what the Reverend and you are trying to do for me. And, I really want to be a preacher in your church real bad. But, if I go with you Sir, who is gonna take my place here? If I leave, what's gonna happen to people rin here? Who's going to look after the folks I look after now? They live in the backwoods. Most don't even have a church and the ones that do, it's just a little shack. I help them build most of them. They don't have schools. It's only when I come through that they can have Sabbath Day school to learn their alphabets and number, so nobody can cheat'em. Most are just learning to write they names. Who's gonna do that Sir? Like I said Sir, I appreciate everything you and the good Reverend are doing, and I wanna be a preacher in your church real bad. But Sir, the people in Jackson, Memphis, Atlanta, even New York City, they don't need me. There are lots of preachers who want to do that. Nobody wants to do what I do. These people need me. They don't have nothing. If I leave, they won't have that.'

The Bishop left the next day. I couldn't bring myself to tell Daddy Burl what I did. I just said I would hear something in a while from them about it. I didn't think he believed me, but he never said nothing. I told myself I did the right thing, even if Laura didn't choose me. But that was when I learned; God has a plan for us all. Two months later, I got this letter from Bishop Miles. He said a lot of stuff, but this is what mattered," *"Going to school is very important, but it's something you may consider doing later. The most important thing is I agree you have already learned the most important things about being a CME minister; service to others. That is why I welcome you to our congregation."*

Life Begins Life Anew

I loved hearing Papa talk about his young days, so every time I saw Papa and he had time I would sak him something to get him to start talking. This time I asked Papa did he think Mama Laura wanted to get together with him, like Mama Sarah and great-great-granddaddy Burl. He pulled on his beard a few times, stood up, walked a few paces, still stroking his beard, before looking up at the heavens, then turning to face me. He said,

"Well, I thought Laura was de prettiest and sweetest girl I ever met. But, I didn't thank she really thought much about me at all. As she said, she knew all the fellows round where they live, and the two days we work together, I could tell by the way they looked and smile at her, they all wanted her. Their families had land, and they were growing crops, so she had choices.

I couldn't thank of anything that would make her chose me. Don't get me wrong; I was like all those followers, I show like her too. I was so afraid of asking her to thank about being with me; if she said no, then all my fun would be gone. As it was, I could come around and be around her, if I said something and she said no, I would be by myself. I was so scared of that, I could never get up the courage to say nothing. I wanted her any way I could be with her. But I did not dare ask, I lose all my happiness.

Things didn't go good trying to get back over by Tuttle Back Lake. First, folks over near Jackson west of us had a cholera outbreak. The missionaries went over there and carried a load of medicine and stuff. I drove the buggy with two mules hitch to it, loaded with stuff. One hauled supplies, and the other carried water. I was there three weeks, cause the only way some folks got clean water was the wagon and mules. The creek was bad, and folk wus scared to drank boil water from wells.

When I got back to the mission, folks up north got washed out when de Yazoo River covered de low land. Some folks lost everything. I made, Lord knows, don't know how many trips back and forth trying to get food and water to'em. Then the Union army sent word dey had food, blankets, medicine, and other stuff, but somebody had to come get it. So the mission gave me the wagon and a team of mules to go get what they had. That took three more weeks hauling for them. After that, it was time to make my circuit run to the East. That run went okay, as I hoped, so I had a little time to swing by to see Laura on the way back in. I packed a big sack for Mama Betsy and Granny Dora. As I rode up Granny Dora said,

"Honey child beta come on out."

Laura came out followed by a grim-faced Mama Betsy. Laura said,

"*I thought y'all fo'got bout us Burl.*"

'*I had lots of stuff ta do. I tell y'all bout it.* Handing the bag ta Mrs. Betsy, I said, *I cain't fo'git bout y'all and granny Mrs. Betsy. Der is coffee and sugar, and other stuff and another tin of bacco for granny Dora.*'

"*Dat's a good boy,*" granny Dora said, smiling, showing her one tooth in front.

"*Y'all brangin dat sugar to de wrong one.*" Mama Betsy said givin de bag to Laura. "*Take dis inside,*" she said.

Squarin up on me again, wit dat sideways glance, she said,

"*Y'all better git all de sugar y'all kin dis trip, cause dat one ain't gonna be rin har when y'all come back through. Watchin thangs rin har since y'all been comin by, dat gal is ready fo a man. I gonna find a man ta put hur wit. She need a man dat gonna take care hur.*"

Laura came through de door, pushin it wide open wit such force, it slammed a'gain de wall, comin out on de porch. Hur eyes bucked and face twisted, she screamed, "*MAMA!!!!*"

Before I could stop dem, words flu out my mouth. '*Umm a man! I want hur! I take hur!*'

Lookin even more stern and tight eyed, Mama Betsy, tiltin her head even more to du side said,

"*Preacher boy, y'all can't even take care of y'all self.*"

'*Kin to! I got a place, right next ta my daddy's place. I got land and it's got a house on it too.*' I said tryin to square up on hur, still sittin on my hose.

Granny Dora spoke up, "*Now Betsy, let de gal go wit him. I done got tid of 'em moon eyein one'tter rin here anyhi.*"

Mama Betsy looked at Laura, who had one of hur scowls on hur face all tight eyed. Den Mama Betsy looked back at me. She did dat back and forth looking at us, a couple au three or fou times.

Fin'ly Granny Dora, said "*BETSY!!!*" again.

Slow as molasses in de wintertime she said, *"Wellll, I-I-I-I guessss y'all can git y'all thangs,"* Mama Betsy finally said.

Lookin back at hur, as she ran pass and jumped from de porch onto de back of my hose, Laura said all in one breath.

"Don't want'em. Dey got flour sacks where I'm goin. Give'em ta cusin Mary. She be next."

Grabbin me tight rin de waist and pushin wit her body, she said, *'Let's go. Let's go.'*

I gave my hose a boot, it bolted forward and trotted off to de road. Laura held on, not lookin back. She pressed her head against my back. But I did in a quick glance, and I thought I saw a bit of a smile on Mama Betsy's usually grim face. Laura hollowed,

"Burl, I thought y'all wus never gonna open y'all mouth! I don got plum tired of battin my eyes at y'all!!" She said, holding on even tighter, as we rode away.

I just smiled, as I slowed my hose to a walk. We rode double some, but mostly, I walked, leadin the hose and mules, headed back to de mission. Sometime Laura walked wit me. I thank it wus easy fo hur to talk, walkin long side me. When we made it ta de mission, we both ran inside. De missionaries, two old women and de preacher, wus surprise to see me wit a gal.

"Who's that you have with you Burl?" Sister Mary Ann asked.

But, before I could answer, Laura added another surprise, *"Kin y'all marry us?"*

"Well, sure." Looking confused, the Old Reverend asked, *"Sunday alright?"*

"No!" Laura shouted, *"Now!"*

Looking from one to the other, Sisters Margaret asked, *"What are your parents going to say?"*

Laura answered, *"I mean rat now!!!. We can't spend de night in de same bed and not be married. My mama a' take a plow line to me."*

"Everybody was happy that I found such a lovely wife. That Sunday, everybody came over to my daddy's place to see us 'jump de broom.' That made it official. We were husband and wife. We had such a great time, eatin, singin and dancin to the music some of du boys made. Me and Laura comin ta gether, gettin married by the preacher, was so the missionaries knew I was serious bout building a family. I wanted to show them I was committed to Christian values.

On the other hand, jumpin the broom was for community acceptance. Jumpin du broom started back in slavery times. It said two slaves wanted all du other slaves to respect their commitment to one another. You see there wau no way to keep up community unity if folks don't respect other folks' families. This kept down trouble and built-up trust. My daddy said, *"Trust is de foundation of a community."*

Dance, Religion and Music Without Drums

necessary to the safety of this Province, that all due care be taken to restrain Negroes from using or keeping of drums, which may call together or give sign or notice to one another of their wicked designs and purposes."

The term *"black dance"* describes a range of styles of movements that originate among African tribes as dances. African slave dances came to the West Indies and the Americas, particularly the Deep South, which spread among slave populations, beginning in the 1500s. African dance and the slave dances from the plantations, both in the West Indies and North America, are the two main origins of *black dances*. Tribes or ethnic groups from every African country maintained their dances. Dance has a ceremonial and social function, celebrating and marking rites of passage, sex, seasons, recreation, and weddings. Everybody danced, but those that transferred dance traditions were dancers, teachers, commentators, spiritual mediums, healers, or story-tellers—Griots.

In the Caribbean, each island had its traditions linked to their African roots of the dances on those islands. The nature and characteristics of dance were affected by the colonial past, particularly—British, French, Spanish, or Dutch. The *Calenda*, an 18th-century black dance, along with the *Chica* are examples of slave dances based on African traditions and rhythms. They were the most popular slave dances in the Caribbean. They were banned by many plantation owners who feared it would encourage social unrest and uprisings.

Dancing the *Calenda*, men and women face each other in two lines. They move towards each other then, away, then towards each other again to make contact - slapping thighs and even kissing. The dance gets faster and faster and the movement more and more sexual and frenetic. The *Calenda* and the *Chica* originated with the courtship dances of the Congo.

Africans danced, before enslavement, for special occasions, such as a birth or a marriage, or as a part of their daily activities. Dance affirmed life and the outlook for a better future. Africans brought their dances to North and South America, and the Caribbean Islands as slavery advanced. The dance styles of hundreds of African ethnic groups merged with European dances, extending the African aesthetic in the Americas.

Dance has always been an integral part of daily life among Africans. In the Americas, it helped enslaved Africans connect with their African roots, keeping their cultural traditions alive. Many dances began on plantations in the Carolinas and Georgia and spread across Alabama to Mississippi. Slaves used whatever was available to make beats: spoons, washboards, furniture, and their bodies with hand-clapping, drumming on various surfaces of the body (Patting Juba), with foot-stomping and shuffling (Ring Shout), once drums were forbidden. These earlier practices are also the origin of modern forms such as tap dancing, which was created by Master Juba. *("From juba to jitterbug to jookin: Black dance in America,"* Denise Oliver Velez for Daily Kos 10-05-2014).

Dancing became an activity that gave slaves release and relief. One of the earliest slave dances in the new world was juba *("Juba—dance*—Britannica Online Encyclopedia," Britannica.com. 2007). Though, the name has not been traced back to *Mo'juba,* which is said in Yoruba, during a series of prayers, and means *"I give reverence to."* Some etymologists say the word *mojo* is a derivative of the word *Mo'juba.* West African traditions connected prayer and dance. The *Juba* dance was originally brought from the Congo to Charleston, South Carolina by slaves, *("Juba Dance - Streetswings Dance History archives,* Main Page," Streetswing.com. 2006).

Juba became an African-American plantation dance that was performed by slaves during their gatherings when no rhythm instruments were allowed, due to fear of secret codes hidden in drumming. The sounds were also used as Yoruba and Haitian talking drums to communicate. The dance—*Juba*—was performed in Dutch Guiana, the Caribbean, and the southern United States.

The ring shout developed from uniting West African spiritual practices with the Protestantism of the British colonies, essentially slave masters forced slaves to observe their religion. But slaves did not identify with the dry, motionless worship practices of that cultural. However, the songs of the ring shout are styles distinct from the more familiar American "spirituals." Lydia Parrish of the Georgia Sea Islands in 1942, says, *"spirituals" always roused my imagination,"* proclaimed *"to see how the McIntosh County 'shouters' tap their heels on the resonant floor to imitate the beat of the drum their forebears were not allowed to have."*

Dances that became dominant through the 18th century included the ring *shout or ring dance,* the *calenda,* the *chica,* and the *juba.* African-Americans sang and danced while working as slaves; they continued singing and dancing after slave masters forced their religions upon them. Enslaved Africans incorporated their traditions into these religions. Blacks, enslaved in the colonies of Spain, Portugal, the Caribbean and South America, were allowed more freedom to dance than enslaved Africans in North America. Many North American slave masters barred Africans from most forms of dance. Africans found ways of getting around these prohibitions. For example, lifting the feet was considered dancing, slave dances included foot shuffling and hip and torso movement.

The *cake walk* was the first slave dance that became a national craze. The *cakewalk* or *cake walk* was a dance developed from the *"prize walks"* held in the mid-19th century, generally at get-togethers by black slaves on plantations before emancipation and after emancipation. Alternative names for the original form of the dance were *"chalkline-walk,"* and the *"walk-around."*

After the conclusion of a performance of the original form of the dance in an exhibit at the 1876 Centennial Exposition in Philadelphia, the winning couple received an enormous cake. As a result, it was performed in minstrel shows by men until the 1890s, when women became performers. This *"made possible all sorts of improvisations in the cakewalk, and the original dance changed over time,"* and became very popular across the country, *("History of Black Dance: The Origins of Black Dance,"* Victoria and Albert Museum The world's leading museum of art and design). The *Creole Show*, a Broadway staged revue, was the first all-black musical that premiered in New York in 1889. The show starred 16 black women as chorus girls. The black leads were Dora Dean and Charles Johnson, who performed the *Cakewalk*, as the finale. It introduced The *Cakewalk*, which became the first dance created by descendants of American slavery that became popular with white people.

The Harlem social dances of the 1920s, the jazz dance of Broadway musicals, and other African dance are associated with social and civil rights issues. Researchers trace black-influenced dance trends, like the *Charleston, Lindy Hop, Jitterbug,* and *boogie-woogie*, to particular periods. Clarence Smith (6-11-1904 – 3-15-1929), better known as Pinetop Smith, was an American *boogie-woogie* style blues pianist. His hit *Pinetop Boogie-Woogie* featured rhythmic "breaks" that were an essential ingredient of ragtime music, but also a fundamental foreshadowing of Soul and rock & roll. The song was also the first known use of the term *"boogie-woogie"* on a record and cemented that term as the moniker for the genre *("Clarence Pinetop Smith," The Blues Trail, undated).*

The 1920s and 1930s were an especially fruitful time for black dance in the United States. During the Harlem Renaissance, similar innovations in theater, music, literature, and other arts accompanied African-American developments in dance. Black musical theater, derived from minstrel shows which derived from slaves entertaining master on plantations, helped continued popularizing and legitimizing black dance traditions and black performers, as it had in the 19th century. According to author Katrina Hazzard Donald, *"Without the African contribution, we would not have American dance as we know it."*

In three one-hour programs, *"FREE TO DANCE,"* which chronicles the crucial role African-American dancers and choreographers played in the development of modern dance as an American art form. Through first-person accounts by dancers and witnesses, the series documents how African-derived movement and other forms of dance were fused to make modern dance so distinctively African American. Landmark dance masterpieces by African American choreographers were filmed expressly for the series and woven throughout the historical narrative. They include the work of Katherine Dunham ("Barrelhouse Blues"), Pearl Primus ("Strange Fruit"), Donald McKayle ("Rainbow 'Round My Shoulder"), Talley Beatty ("Mourner's Bench"), Bill T. Jones ("D-Man in the Water"), Alvin Ailey ("Revelations"), and many others. *"Do something with your body."*

A New Time: Ragtime

Enslaved Africans, reaching *The Gilded Age*, had braved the disasters of their penniless emancipation and Civil War, with real determination. Surviving those terrible times, total uncertainty, and death during their contraband struggles, slavery's descendants continued trying to *make something out of nothing*. Former slaves had arrived where they were learning to develop the thoughts and concepts in their heads, which began with making families and building communities.

The US government refused to open good-paying jobs to former slaves; instead, the US brought Europeans to America to fill those jobs, depriving former slaves of opportunities. America's policy sealed former slaves' fate with discrimination. It blocked their access to jobs they deserved, after 243 years of working for free. Nevertheless, former slaves continued pulling themselves up by their bootstraps, as they made *something out of nothing* to advance. They use skills and knowledge, gained as craftsmen and artisans benefitted whites during slavery, but now to help themselves.

Entertainment, African Americans first technology, emerged as the most productive and successful path for black Americans' progress. The story of former slaves' became a fascinating and amazing saga, as their survival struggle continued. Facing many challenges and huddles descendants of slavery arrived at the 300th (1919), claiming to be "the new Negro." And to cement this belief, as time and events would have it, *Divine Intervention* created ways out of no way, pushing them towards ***"The 400th."*** Slaves' inadvertent creation of music, during their enslavement, even though whites stole what slaves produced and created, beginning with Minstrelsy, their theft I see as part of *Divine Intervention*.

Although, Minstrelsy (also called "Nigger Show") created an image of former slaves that fit the stereotypes white people carried around in their heads and wanted to believe, was part and parcel to Africa Americans overall progress. The stereotypes of Minstrelsy were more powerful to white people than the reality before their eyes. Minstrelsy's "blackface" gave vision to the denigrating stereotypes of former slaves, as an *"undeserving lot"*—stupid, dimwitted and lazy buffoons. That stereotype, more than any other, gave substance to white people's efforts to lock descendants of American slavery on the bottom of America's capitalistic system.

Minstrelsy's story began changing in 1895, the day a slender, handsome and engaging young man, strolled on stage, took a seat at a piano and began playing music most white people never heard. Caught up in the growing entertainment crave, they never notice the revolution taking place before their eyes. Like a bolt of lightning out of a clear blue sky, Scott Joplin (sic.1868–1917), with an original downbeat, became a revolution in and of himself. This revolutionary launched ragtime, which created a new time, like no time before for black people, as he changed time in music and entertainment.

Ragtime pierced the oppressive and deadly racist atmosphere of Minstrelsy. Joplin with an original syncopated beat shot black music into the stratosphere of new opportunities. He put African American music on a trajectory that made black entertainment the baseline of musical greatness. His new rhythm changed prospects for black people in entertainment forever. Rocketing pass "blackface," he flashed a "bird," as ragtime danced passed Minstrelsy, streaking in the opposite direction. Joplin's new art form made music far more portable and exciting.

Scott Joplin pushed aside Minstrel shows, as white people became enthralled and caught up in his lively rhythms. Joplin threw off the "blackface" that had been demanded over the previous eighty years, sitting at the piano, and nobody noticed. The sight of Joplin banging out his notes, without big white lips and smut on his face, was revolutionary for blacks, if not whites.

No black man had appeared on stage, not even the acclaimed *Master Juba*, without *"blacking up."* Yet, totally unnoticed, Joplin had figured out how to turn his black *"nothing into something,"* messing around on the piano. That something was "ragtime." His new music changed times, not only giving music a new time, but his time change made entertainment the art of black people for all times. Joplin's music was so new and exciting, the perception of black performers changed before anyone could say, *"Stop, let's lynched that nigger!!!"*

Ragtime became the music of the time— *"The Gilded Age"* (1880/1918). Though short-lived, as a genre, compared to music trends that proceeded or following ragtime, chased the straight European classical symphonic music white Americans loved, out of town with a beat. While driving Minstrelsy into obscurity by the late 1930s, ragtime rose to prominence almost overnight. Sliding in under Minstrelsy, ragtime became the music of the time.

Ragtime's basic trait was syncopation (a shift in accent in a composition that stressed the weak beat). Its "ragged" rhythm or ragged beat originated in African American communities in and around St. Louis, Missouri. Ernest Hogan (1865–1909) pioneered this musical form; he composed and published the first ragtime sheet music. His tune was called "LA Pas Ma LA."

Ragtime was sheet music for pianos. Some claim ragtime was a modification of the marching band-style of John Philip Sousa, but raggers say no. They protested, *"Ragtime is the addition of polyrhythms from African music."* Joplin began performing and composing ragtime very early as a teen.

He became hugely popular, after publishing the rag, *"The Entertainer"* in 1902 (The Entertainer, for those unaware, 71 years later was the theme and soundtrack for *"The Sting,"* a 1973 Oscar-winning film).

Joplin's *"Maple Leaf Rag"* (1906) heavily influenced subsequent ragtime composers with its melodic lines, harmonic progressions, and metric patterns. Some say the jazz crave, that began in New Orleans and came to Harlem around 1910, was ushered in by ragtime. Although its reign was short, but while it reined, Ragtime changed time with a new musical technology and made black music and those composing it, the artistic expression and leading entertainers of that day while influencing coming generations. It became the main track leading to what became America's music industry. There are no dissenters in saying, after Joplin, there was no going back.

A Sign that Became the Times

Ragtime was an event so divergent, unprecedented, and unexpected it changed the reality for black people before white people realized what was happening. Scott Joplin, with ragtime, exposed the absurdity of Minstrelsy's "blackface." Black performers, during the early beginnings of Jim Crow, hoped to change Minstrelsy's *"blackface"* stereotypes, but *"blacking up"* expanded into the newly popular genre *"Vaudeville."*

Derived from the French expression *voix de ville* "voice of the city," Vaudeville not only had a different audience, it had a different purpose. Whereas Minstrelsy was a spoof on slavery that white people embraced wholeheartedly, Vaudeville was a variety show. Unlike Minstrelsy, its audience was more urban, middle class, and heavily immigrant, as opposed to Minstrelsy's appealed to the "redneck" mentality of poor white America. Vaudevillians' reflected a different attitude toward performers and performances. It allowed newly Freedmen to bring a political agenda to stage performances.

Juxtaposing Vaudeville's audiences against Minstrelsy "blackface" audiences, they were an insightful contrast illustrating why "blackface" patrons held tightly to the traditional stereotypes projected onto black people resonated is the point here. For "blackface" audiences, it was all about race. Any deviation from the traditional role of *"down-home darkies,"* drew harsh and deadly rebukes from whites loyal to minstrel shows. The angry white-mob-mentality that seize America in the 1890s came out of Minstrelsy, to a large extent.

Mobs would form over the slightest provocation and would lynch black men—shoot, burn, hang and mutilate them—if they stepped out of the *"blackface caricature"* of black people whites loved, whether on stage or off. Writers cited how angry mobs of white men formed because a black performer did not *"black up,"* donning a *"blackface,"* was desecration by black entertainers. They also claim such acts were responsible for Minstrelsy's demise.

The following example makes my point regarding the typical reaction of angry white men mob madness that took over America, following the election of Woodrow Wilson (1912-1918). Mob rule became acceptable because local political and societal leaders—sheriffs, mayor, educators, preachers, and even presidents led and inspired these lynch mobs. Spectacle lynchings, like Minstrelsy, became entertainment for white people on all levels of society, not just "poor white trash."

Louis Wright, a minstrel, is my case in point. His situation exemplifies the advent and character of the angry white men mob mentality that became the hallmark of Minstrelsy, and a sign of the time. Wright, 22, was lynched in New Madrid, Missouri, in 1902. He was a trombone player, touring with a black minstrel troupe, Richard & Pringle's Georgia Minstrels. His lynching happened the same year Joplin introduced "The Entertainer." William "W. C." Handy gave this account of Wright's tragic death in his book *"Father of the Blues: An Autobiography,"* (1941). Handy was a member of the troupe and wrote;

"Louis and a lady friend were parading with the troupe, headed to our show. A group of local drunken white rabble-rousers attacked them with snowballs. Wright retaliated swiftly with snowballs and a blast of obscenities. An unusually talented musician, the slim sensitive boy resented insult with every fiber of his being. He would fight anyone, anytime, and with any weapon within reach. In our company, we understood his fierce pride; we knew how best to treat him.

During the Jammed packed performance, it became obvious; whites were aware of the earlier incident when the show didn't go as usual. Spectators at the opera house gave catcalls, jeered, and hissed while performers were on stage. Tear-jerking" ballads drew laughter, while funny gags and joke brought groans. Someone in the audience shouted, 'Let's do up the showmen,' at the close of the show. Shots cleared the building as members of the audience rushed the stage.

We had reassembled at our special railroad car when a mob arrived looking for Louis later that evening. Everyone went to jail. The mob found Louis during their interrogation and carried him outside. We never heard him cry aloud. But that morning, we learned they lynched him and cutting out his tongue before hanging him. The mob cut him down, chopped off his fingers, and kept them and his rings for souvenirs. On Monday morning, they placed his body in a box sent it to his mother in Chicago. His accusers said, "Cursing at white men, during the parade, is a fitting punishment for a nigger to have his tongue cut out and lynched."

Up from Slavery to a Renaissance of Freedom

The Harlem Renaissance in New York City pulled black Art and entertainers together, like a new technology. It became the first cultural developmental era for slavery's descendants and the most prolific art production periods for blacks in American history before the 21st Century. Many things and events contributed to making this period one of the more successful economic times, again, for blacks before 2000.

Beginning just after the turn of the new millennium (1900) and the 300th, Harlem drew black people from around the world to America's melting pot. Harlem was the incubator for many developing trends among former slaves. Blacks running north to escape racism, lynching, disenfranchisement, and other degradations saw Harlem as a refuge. Even before the mass exodus of WWI thousands of blacks out of the South sought a better place in Harlem's bustling metropolis for former slaves. It was a crucible, helping to transform the aggregation of ex-slaves, even those from around the world, trying to *make nothing into something.*

Harlem was a place of new everything. New speech, new thoughts, new ideas, new fashion, new music, and new dances, to name a few changes that produced what Harlemikes called the *"new Negro."* This term was popularized by *"The Niagara Movement,"* the first major black civil rights group founded in 1905 at Niagara Falls, New York. This group evolved into the National Association for the Advancement of Colored People (NAACP).

Ridgely Torrence, a white playwright, premiered the first stage production <u>Three Plays for a Negro Theatre</u> in Harlem (1917). Torrence's plays rejected "blacking up" and coon antics of Minstrelsy. For the first time, African-American actors on stage conveyed complex human emotions and yearnings, not clowning it up. James Weldon Johnson, a writer, called their premieres, *"The most important single event in the entire history of the Negro in the American Theater."*

Claude McKay, a poet, at the 300th (1919), published his militant sonnet **"If We Must Die."** It gave voice to African American's political, socioeconomic, and cultural desires in dramatic fashion, following the white riots and murder during the **"Red Summer of 1919".** This period gave formal recognition to black Arts production and allowed former slaves to create a new dimension of modern urban creativity. Although, **"If We Must Die"** never alluded to race, African-Americans interpreted its sentiments to be a statement of defiance. McKay's poem gave voice to the fears and frustrations of black Americans, as they recovered from the deadly destructive **Red Summer** riots.

By WWI's end, Harlem's prosperity made it a Mecca for slave descendants. Playing a key role in its international embrace, *the Liberty League* and *The Voice*, respectively, were the first organization and newspaper in Harlem to fully express hopes for the *"New Negro Movement."* Founded by Hubert Harrison, they became a megaphone for the *"New Negro Movement"* (1917)." Harrison's organization and newspaper emphasized the Arts (his newspaper had *"Poetry for the People"* and a book review section). Dubbed *The Father of Harlem Radicalism*, Harrison challenged the renaissance notion, as the beginning of the *"Negro Literary Renaissance."* He felt, *"it overlooked the stream of literary and artistic products that flowed uninterrupted from Negro writers,"* like David Walker's incendiary **Appeal** in 1828. Harrison said in the *Pittsburgh Courier* (1927) newspaper, *"The term Harlem Renaissance is a misconception and a misnomer, a white American invention."*

Industrialization during WWI brought money to urban areas, but much less to black people in the South. The war attracted rural black to Northern cities, giving rise to the new mass cultural movement of former slaves. Black people that dared to chance life on the road brought families, flooding Harlem en mass, like a tsunami, fighting for space. Taking advantage of the new mobility of modern transportation southern blacks invaded northern cities, as the war economy of WWI ramped up. Hitting the road all over the South, African Americans, looking for self-improvement, fueled the *Great Migration* (1910-1950s). Their mobility following emancipation and WWI ushered in tremendous cultural changes in northern cities.

Southern blacks brought their music, food, and general perspective to Harlem. Claiming space in Harlem and other cities, mobile African Americans escaping sharecropping plots in the grave of poverty, piled into urban centers throughout the North and Mid-West. Mobility was the magic that created the major exit for blacks out of the South's valley of dry bones. Ambitious blacks joined tens of thousands with talent, crowding into Harlem from 1910 into the 1930s. Entertainment made Harlem an artistic melting pot for former slaves.

Music became the signature product Harlem exported to the rest of the world. Introducing a new style of playing piano, like Scott Joplin's ragtime, the *Harlem Stride* brought young blacks and whites uptown to Harlem to experience the new phenomenon. Looking for places to learn all the new dances—the jitterbug, Charleston, lindy hop, boogie woogie, and camel walk, were just a few dancing craves of that period. Whites and blacks filled ballrooms, dance halls and lounges, hoping for new and different encounters. Young devil-make-care white and black adventurous fun seekers assaulted the color line, crossing into this no man's land and began jumping across it with reckless abandon. They blurred the social lines between young whites, poor and socially elite Negroes.

The popularity of jazz, with its liveliness, innovation, and instrumental modifications, gave wealthy blacks access to a new kind of music. Jazz was not a genre for the wealthy elite associated with, what they saw as the backwardness of southern blacks. Coming out of New Orleans, jazz musicians like Louis Armstrong, "Fats" Waller and Jelly Roll Morton showed masters like Duke Ellington, Count Bases, and Willie "The Lion" Smith, how it was done!

This very competitive and talented atmosphere created reputations and popularity overnight for some. Drawing musicians to Harlem, for experience and exposure, novice came to worship at the feet of masters, hoping and dreaming of replicating their success. The noted commentator Charles Garrett wrote, *"The portrait of Ellington reveals him to be not only the gifted composer, bandleader, and musician we have come to know, but also an earthy person with basic desires, weaknesses, and eccentricities. He shared his knowledge with newcomers, and challenged old-timer to keep up, as he lives on the edge of innovation."*

The nightlife in Harlem rocked. One could go out every night for a month and "never darken the same door" twice. The Alhambra Ballroom, a former Vaudeville venue, opened an upstairs ballroom in 1926. It hosted legends like Bessie Smith, Jelly Roll Morton, and a singing waitress named Billie Holiday. Patrons packed the place to see Cab Calloway, Duke Ellington, and Count Base, among many others.

The major venue for black performers in America was the Apollo Theater (1913). It is one of Harlem's, New York City's and America's most iconic and enduring venues. No matter your status and popularity or how big a star you became, until you played the Apollo, you were a "nobody." Harlem's unique flair and atmosphere jumped every night. Hot spots like Club Harlem, Lenox Lounge, Minton's Playhouse, Clark Monroe's Uptown House, Showman's Jazz Club, Small's Paradise, The Sugar Cane Club, and The Cotton Club, to name just a few of the hottest and most popular spots, that kept the party going all night.

The musical and artistic productions of blacks were viewed by whites, like Minstrelsy. White novelists, dramatists, and composers expropriate the work of African Americans, commandeering their works. Black artistic creations held such an attractive allure, whites grabbed them up, but black artists did not benefit. A book could be written exposing the whites across the entertainment genre that stole material from blacks. White composers used poems written by African American poets in their songs. They created rhythms, harmonies, and melodies taken from black musicians. They were like "sneak thieves" hijacking blues, spiritual blues, spirituals, and jazz—in their concert pieces. Centered in Harlem, its Renaissance is considered the birth of African-American Arts, so much so, many Francophones (French-speaking) black writers, musicians, dancers, painters, actors from Africa and the Caribbean, even from Paris, flooded into Harlem.

The Perfect Scapegoat

The **Trans-Atlantic Slave Trade** and slavery gave the white world a foolproof economy. Before the Panic of 1893, whites could always kidnap more slaves, buy more, sell more, or trade more to cover or avoid a national economic crisis. Following the 1893 Panic and without slaves, the American government embarked on a course to restore slavery's wealth by re-enslaving African Americans. Researching the times following emancipation, Civil War, and the early transition of Freedmen trying to live on their own, it became very clear descendants of American slavery proved to be a sturdy bunch.

Regardless of their lack of knowledge—the inability to read, write and calculate—in this new world, they were still quick to understand the necessity of setting down roots, making families and building stable communities, as keys to their future. Not just content to survive, as individuals, former slaves constructed group living situations, which increased their chances for survival. Leaving the contraband period (1863-1880), they began establishing communities in large cities and the countryside as well, setting down permanent roots they hoped. Former slaves wanted to have control over community membership, development, and resources, so they went with what they knew. Whereas, communal living was part of life in Africa, however, during slavery their group living was forced upon them. Freedom created choices, yet and still they opted for communal situations.

The *"Gilded Age"* represents a major turn for former slaves from the relative calm of the contraband period to the beginning of a more hostile and deadly time. This dark time began slowly, 1876 laid the foundation for what came next—the full disenfranchisement of former slaves. Rutherford B. Hayes made the deal that eventually allowed southerners state government, through nullification and interposition to ignore the **Civil Rights Bill of 1866,** and the full rights it granted former slaves. The fact cannot be expressed forcefully enough that **Civil Rights Bill of 1866** was never repealed by Congress nor was it overturned by the US Supreme Court.

The US Government and the US Supreme Court turned it back on descendants of American slavery and allowed southern states to re-enslave black Americans. It began with white politicians, academicians, religious leaders, and the press lined up behind scapegoating former slaves with false accusations to paint them as an *"undeserving lot."* The election of 2020 has created the same attempt by Republicans on behalf of Donald Trump. This time around, they began with trying to throw out votes by blacks with the trump up charge of "voter fraud."

Although descendants of enslaved Africans were very industrious, and only concerned with things that contributed to their survival, white people saw something entirely different. They saw opportunities to gain wealth again at the expense of former slaves, if they could turn the federal government's attitude and actions from Reconstruction efforts toward oppression and repression. But, they need a President that would go along with disenfranchising black people.

Communal living during slavery, taught former slaves important lessons regarding the need for centralized authority. Such experiences gave them the ability to create and control the growth, as well as direction of particular community institutions—schools, businesses, and churches. These new situations prompted a voluntary commitment to a cooperative existence. Communal agreements allowed allocation of responsibility and established order among people that face a common foe—poverty and racism.

Slave owning families and those that reaped great economic benefits from slavery were and still are, among the richest people in America. After Civil War, this class became leaders of the effort to re-enslave Freedmen. Before the ink was dry on the Civil Rights Bill of 1866, 13th, 14th, and 15th Amendments, slave owners on the US Supreme Court and in Congress began working to nullify legislation that gave Freedmen independence, freedom, and justice. Their first goal was countering Pres. U. S. Grant *Reconstruction* efforts. Grant began the one effort that mattered most too former slaves—education. He also established some Freedmen on land of their own.

White leaders demanded a system, reminiscent of the internal slave trade and breeding, when the South's economy was booming. They demanded a means of forcing former slaves to work but not get paid. Freedmen's amazing progress in less than twenty years, after walking off plantations ignorant and penniless, after 243 years of working for free, was belitted by whites, who pointed at the federal government as the culprit to explain former slaves wealth and the *Panic of 1893*. They ignored *The Gilded Age* restrictions blocking good-paying jobs for blacks. Governments and industry leaders disparaged Freedmen's progress, offering farcical, made-up claims and concepts. Key to this strategy was the *"white man's burden."* "Niggers living off white people's taxes" was used to portray Freemen as an *"undeserving lot."*

Freedmen, following slavery made crucial decisions that aided their successful efforts, setting down roots, making families and building communities. Contrarily, whites thought, slaves would grow tired of struggling to feed themselves and would come crawling back to the plantation; but no! Not only were they surviving, they were thriving. Although most were uneducated, they were able to "put a little away for a rainy day."

The following discussion is to present what happened in America to former slaves after 1890 through 1940 and is similar to what happened to Jews, during the 19th and 20th century in Russia. I view this period (from 1990 -1940), as a cold blooded plot by white leaders of government, along with the US Supreme Court's decision in **Plessy v. Ferguson** (1897) as the beginning of the dark times. The only fitting description for the deadly times African Americans endured, reaching 1950 is "pogrom."

A pogrom is a violent riot and political process aimed at the massacre or persecution of an ethnic or religious group. This narrative points to what happened to Jews in Russia, during the 19th and 20th Centuries, as a parallel and where the term originated. The Russian government's genocidal effort was an attempt to wipe out Jews in the Russian Empire and is why this designation.

That effort was repeated by the Germany governments, during Adolf Hitler's 1930s attacks against Jews. Today pogrom also describes publicly sanctioned and purgative attacks against Palestinian people. The definition in part came about after The Armenian Genocide (also known as the Armenian Holocaust) orchestrated by the Ottoman government between 1914 and 1923. Following a systematic act of mass murder, the Turks, banished 1.5 million ethnic Armenians. The characteristics of pogroms vary widely, the specific incidents may vary, but the circumstances culminate in massacres.

I describe what happened to black people in America beginning in 1900 as a pogrom based on the definition. The US government helped design a system to re-enslave black Americans with a calculated, deliberate, well thought out plan of destruction, a similar to the pogrom conducted by Russia, Germany, Turkey and other governments. America's genocide killed hundreds of thousands of former slaves, many in plain view of cheering thousands. The aim was to subjugate, imprison and force African American to serve as a slave workforce in the southern US. This narrative now explains the process the United States of America used to accomplish this end.

White politicians and businessmen in America used government to set up a system that reduced black people, as a class, back to a status closely resembling slavery as possible without calling it that. This system was called segregation *"separate but equal,"* white supremacy or any other name that describes that system. The aim of that system was to rob black people of their labor, possession, wealth and lives. The tragedy is it worked exactly as it was designed. If readers do not learn another fact from reading **"The 400th"**, this one proposition is this narrative's goal.

That system "was not" the result of circumstances of life, historical necessity or something that naturally occurred in the course of human events. The murder, robbery and hatred whites heaped upon black people were fermented in the White House, the halls of Congress, state capitols and it began at the bar of justice in US Supreme Court of the United States of America.

News publications, politicians, educators, and religious institutions weaponized concepts like—*the white man's burden, "an undeserving lot" and lazy, dimwitted niggerss unwilling to work are living off of white people's taxes.* They physically, politically and economically declared war on descendants of American slavery and this war continues today. These statements became the psychological and philosophical justification that made former slaves the *"perfect scapegoats."* White leaders championed America's slave masters' mindset, as they denied Freedmen were industrious, thrifty, and productive. America's leaders used Minstrelsy's *blackface* to embed the idea former slaves were—lazy, dimwitted and perfidious buffoons.

Magnates of industry, captains of politics, prophets of the pulpit, overlords of finance, and gurus of education all deluged the public with fictitious and outlandish claims against Freedmen. Their pronouncements blamed black people for the troubles white people suffered, following the *Panic of 1893*. White people made blacks, targets of hatred, and toward which white people should vent their rage. American slave descendants, based solely on stereotypes, allegations, and downright lies, were scapegoated with every negative charge white leaders, the press, and any other white person launched against them. Projected as pariahs by whites Americans, descendants of American slavery had no defenders beyond themselves.

The point of keep slaves ignorant and afraid of knowledge, without real understanding of words, is made clear, during this period. The average black person could not formulate and articulate a proper response without the ability to use words effectively. Those who could respond or mount a defense were muzzled, and denied *VOICE* in the press. The chorus of blame left newly former slaves defenseless and unprotected from what came next.

Lacking knowledge of "words," Freedmen heard white people talk openly, voicing their plans in publications, without concern for responses. Former slaves had no way of present counter-arguments on a national level. Whites created a common vision of black people based on claims, such as the *"white man's burden, undeserving lot, and niggers were living off of white people's taxes."* Black people's knowledge gap would last into the 1950s, as the US government and US Supreme Court supported scapegoating black people with laws and regulations—segregation.

Black people were defenseless against national persecution and open to the scurrilous attacks of white racists. The sheer volume of the national clamor that blamed emancipation, Civil War, 13th, 14th, and 15th Amendments and Reconstruction for all the bad economic times' white people were experiencing. The clamor shouted down, while drowning out, even the bravest vociferous and stout-hearted defenders of Freedmen's productiveness. The *Panic of 1893*, like the coronavirus pandemic of 2020, brought out the worst in America, but some say it only revealed what white Americans were thinking and wanted to say and do all along. Discussing what happened in America and the desire of southern white people, following their lost in the Civil War and the pogrom launched by white people to recover from the Panic of 1893, during "The Gilded Age," is to set the stage for the election of Woodrow Wilson.

Absurdity in Place of Justice

The question is how did white Americans go from emancipation and the **Civil Rights Bill of 1866** to Woodrow Wilson, who helped create the political process that re-enslaved descendants of American slavery and their descendants? Their change was no presso-change-o magic act, where former slaves awoke one day and were slaves again. The re-enslavement process was a long protracted period extending over 50 yearys.

The US Supreme Court began the process in 1857 with **Scott v. Sanford**, the first ever case involving a slave to reach the US Supreme Court, as a plaintiff. The Court's decision in that case sprang the trap on slaves and descendants, with the trap door built into the US Constitution (1789) at its signing. The US Supreme Court used the law to deny slaves and descendants access to courts, while allowing government to strip former slaves and descendants of all constitutional rights.

Even though America claims to be a law bidding country, the US Supreme Court violated every legal principle it was supposed to represent, if constitutional law was actually what the Court and governments in America stood for. The Supreme Court weaponized the law, preventing Freedmen from defending themselves in court, while the US Supreme Court became a defender of white culprits against their black victims. The courts would not allow blacks to defend themselves against individual white people and sent a message to state courts "not to entertain complaints against white culprits from their black victims at the local level. So the vast majority of cases brought by black plaintiffs never got beyond local courts to the Supreme Court.

Consequently, enslaved Africans and descendants were unable to change their status, in American as a result of the US Supreme Court's commitment to protecting white culprits, by denying black Americans justice. It reinforced discrimination, disparate treatment, and the hostile environment former slaves endured. The Court prevented enslaved Africans from changing their second class status through its judicial edits and rulings. The Court's first major decision, after the Civil War (1865) and the **Civil Rights Act of 1866** was **Plessy v. Ferguson** (1897).

The Civil Rights Act of 1866 was enacted April 9, 1866. It was the first United States federal law to define citizenship and affirm that all citizens are equally protected by the law. It was mainly intended to protect the civil rights of newly freed slaves and descendants born in or brought into the US, as slaves. **The Civil Rights Bill of 1866** was a law Congress passed in 1865 and US President Andrew Johnson of Tennessee vetoed twice, before a two-thirds majority overrode his veto in each chamber after Johnson's veto, following Congress' override, it become law without presidential signature. "The Act, while protecting the Civil Rights of all Persons in the United States, furnished the means for their vindication" as citizens, by declaring that all people born in the United States who are not subject to any foreign power are entitled to be citizens, without regard to race, color, or previous condition of slavery or involuntary servitude. A similar provision (called the Citizenship Clause) was written a few months later into the proposed Fourteenth Amendment to the United States Constitution.

The Civil Rights Act of 1866 also states that *"Any citizen has the same right that a white citizen has to make and enforce contracts, sue and be sued, give evidence in court, and inherit, purchase, lease, sell, hold, and convey real and personal property."* Additionally, the act guaranteed to all citizens the *"full and equal benefit of all laws and proceedings for the security of person and property, as is enjoyed by white citizens, and ... like punishment, pains, and penalties..."* Also, *"Persons who denied these rights on account of race or previous enslavement were guilty of a misdemeanor and upon conviction faced a fine not exceeding $1,000, or imprisonment not exceeding one year, or both."*

The acts language is very similar to that of the **Equal Protection Clause** in the newly proposed Fourteenth Amendment. In particular, the act discussed the need to provide "reasonable protection to all persons in their constitutional rights of equality before the law, without distinction of race or color, or previous condition of slavery or involuntary servitude, except as a punishment for crime, whereof the party shall have been duly convicted." This statement is the "devil in the details" for black Americans.

The text of the **Civil Rights Bill of 1866** is presented here so readers have a clear understand that the law actually gave former slaves the same rights white people have. These are the facts I want readers to carry forward, as they follow this section all the way to the 1954 Civil Rights Act. The following section is an explanation of what and how white used the Supreme Court to create the conditions, where governments—federal, state, and local—nullified this law and the US Supreme Court supported southern states "interposition" argument, permitting re-enslavement of descendants of American slavery until the 1960s.

How did this happen? That question drove my efforts to understand why descendants of American slavery were unable to rise out of the grave of poverty in the valley of dry bones. Research shows that legal jargon and judicial interpretation lie at the heart of my dilemma. Proving this point requires I give another technical explanation that is far longer than I desire. However, Supreme Court judges must be disrobed, as imposters, to show they are—tricksters—not judges. Supreme Court justices play games with the law to achieve what white people in America desire.

Since 1866 "it has been illegal in the U.S. to discriminate in employment and housing on the basis of race." However, even though federal penalties were provided for enforcement, remedies were not enforced by government, courts, or individuals. The US Supreme Court through its decisions, as well as non-decisions, prevented civil rights laws from being enforced based solely on skin color. Everything white people needed fell in place when Woodrow Wilson was elected president.

Throughout the 20th century, the US federal government refused to enforce the US Constitution and laws that flowed from them against white people, even after passage of related civil rights legislation. Landmark decisions that were supposed to remedies discrimination, like *Jones v. Mayer* (392 U.S. 409 (1968), which held that *"Congress could regulate the sale of private property to prevent racial discrimination: "[42 U.S.C. § 1982] bars all racial discrimination, private as well as public, in the sale or rental of property."* That statute, properly construed, *"is a valid exercise of the power of Congress to enforce the Thirteenth Amendment."*

US Supreme Court judges were able to support racism, lynching and robbery, while hiding behind the title of being august men, as they supported implementing draconian, capricious, despotic and totalitarian regimes to justify discrimination and segregation for 60 years. I cannot withhold or hide my disdain, loathing, and revulsion regarding the deceit, mayhem, and murder these so-called august men caused slave descendants beginning in 1857. With its ruling in **Dred Scott v. Sanford,** the US Supreme Court became the bastion of American racism and white supremacy. **Dred Scott v. Sanford** marked the beginning of the court's role of protecting white culprits against their black victims, and entrenched it with **Plessy v. Ferguson.**

With those two rulings—**Scott v. Sanford** and **Plessy v. Ferguson**—the Court became the stronghold of injustice, discrimination, and disparate treatment against descendants of American slavery. Historians have disguised the US Supreme Court's role in maintaining American slave descendants in a second class status, remember the Civil Rights Bill of 1866 was never repealed by Congress or declared unconstitutional by the US Supreme Court, so how and why did the court helped create the system that resembled slavery as closely as possible? The court used esoteric jargon—words—to give racism and white supremacy the force of law in America.

This statement is without dispute because the Court was the lead actor perpetrating the fraud and charade of freedom, which descendants of American slavery endured from 1857 until the 1970s. The court's rulings, during that period, allowed it to disguise its intent behind esoteric jargon. It interpreted laws, so their rulings supported the political will and desires of white people in general and those with power and money particularly. **Scott v. Sanford** was the ruling US Supreme Courts used to entrenched white supremacy and white privilege.

There are two concepts or groups of words—**"absurdity doctrine"** and **"scrivener's error exception"**—which I was completely ignorant until this research. Moreover, I believe most white people and the vast majority of blacks are also ignorant of them. Examining these two concepts is essential to understand my point, regarding the court. What is absurd is all the classes I've taken and information presented, these concepts never came up. Even the Supreme Court's decisions I've read and discussed never mentioned these terms.

First, the *"absurdity doctrine"* is a legal theory, which allows American judges to *"interpret statutes contrary to their plain meaning"* to avoid what "**judges feel**" at the time *"are absurd legal conclusions or results."* Secondly, the *"scrivener's error exception"* says that a map-drafting or typographical error in a written contract may be corrected by oral evidence *if the evidence is clear, convincing, and precise*. Taken as a statements; all this sounds very reasonable, but in actuality, the fact is, when slavery came before the Supreme Court for the first time, it became the devil in the details for black people, as I said, because everything changed about this logic.

I have stated this before and now I reiterated, slavery is an issue that entered the US Constitution at its writing (1789). The Founding Fathers made a deal to gain southern states support for the new constitution. It added what is known as the 3/5 Compromise. This statement designated slaves (others) as 3/5 of a white man, reducing the human capital of slaves to less than one (3/5) of a whole human being (a white man). The 3/5 Compromise gave Southern slave owners a tax break (slaves were property). Slaved were counted for tax purposes and apportionment of legislative bodies. Moreover, slaves 3/5 status was used in apportioning legislative bodies, even though slaves could not vote. Black people's power was given to white people, which gave them more political power than counting only white people in the South.

US Supreme Court's first occasion to invoke Article I Section II (3/5 Compromise) beyond its stated purpose in the US Constitution (taxes and apportionment) arrived in 1857. A very straight forward and simple case, **Scott v Sanford** arrived at the US Supreme Court, with a very straight forward, simple, and clear request. Dred Scott (1795–1858), the plaintiff, a slave, sued Dr. John Emerson, a white slave owner for the release of his wife, two daughters, and himself from slavery. Emerson had violated the law in Ohio and the *Northwest Ordinance of 1787* (a federal law), which made slavery illegal in Ohio. These laws are why runaway slaves tried to make it across the Ohio River; it was free-territory. Scott had partitioned the court, asking simply that the Court *"enforce the law."*

Scott and his family had lived with Emerson in states and territories, including Ohio, where slavery was against the law. According to both laws—state of Ohio and the *Northwest Ordinance of 1787* (a federal law), they should have been freed but were still being held against their will, illegally as slaves in Ohio. For most, fair-minded individuals, there was nothing ambiguous or absurd that judges should have *"felt was an absurd legal conclusions or results by enforcing the law as written,"* unless judges were slaveholders and therefore refuse to enforce the law against themselves, as they did.

However, this is where terms and concepts like the *"absurdity doctrine"* and *"scrivener's error exception"* became a disguise for judges' real intent. It allows judges to impose their personal philosophies and other agendas in the place of law. Their ability to use the *absurdity* doctrine to **"interpret statutes contrary to their plain meaning**" *to avoid,"* what they feel will be, *"absurd legal conclusions or consequences."* The opinion in **Scott v Sanford** makes it abundantly clear that judges' ability to interpret laws can create *"absurdity."*

The *Northwest Ordinance of 1787* (a federal law)—under which Scott sued for released from *illegal* bondage, as well as his family, which also was being held against their will, as slaves, were in keeping with the **"scrivener's error exception."** To wit, the evidence and situation was **"clear, convincing, and precise."** The whole institution and legal structure of slavery in America would have changed, if the court had enforced the law and ruled in Scott's favor. Such a ruling would have allowed a slave to change his status through court action. Slaveholders on the Taney Court took refuge behind the 3/5 Compromise, which was not added to the US Constitution for that purpose. There were slaveholders on the court, Taney was one and they refused to follow the law. The 3/5 Compromise was not intended to address a slave's effort to change his status but was brought into Scott's hearing to deny this slave justice and serve the purposes of slaveholders, not justice.

The **"absurdity doctrine"** gave slaveholders the means to avoid enforcing the law, as it was intended, which was their only purpose. The Taney controlled Supreme Court's aim became, *"How to refuse to enforce the law by not granting Scott's just right to change his status based on his slave master violation of Ohio law and the United States law?"* Slaveholders believed granting Scott justice would be **"absurd,"** because it would set a slave free without compensation. The Taney court believed, freeing Scott based on such a **"legal technicality"** would be absurd, but that was the whole purpose of the law. Moreover, if that was an opinion that could be sustained, they would have declared those laws unconstitutional. However that would have impacted more that slaves. The Court took refuge behind a "made up absurdity. The Court found a means to avoid enforcing the law in Scott's case. It ruled Scott had no right to come into court in the first place to challenge his master's violation of the law.

The Supreme Court became *"a protector of white culprits against their black victims."* It stood justice and equality on its head. Chief Justice Roger B. Taney's opinion is why I speak of the Supreme Court with such revulsion, disdain, and loathing. Taney's opinion had nothing to do with law but was a diatribe of personal views and insinuations based on how white people saw Africans. Denying Scott's claim, Taney said, *"Neither he [Scott] nor <u>any other person of African ancestry could claim citizenship in the United States</u>, and therefore Scott could not bring suit in federal court under diversity of citizenship rules, (a slave being in a state, where slavery was illegal). They <u>(person of African ancestry)</u> had for more than a century before been regarded as beings of an inferior order, and altogether unfit to associate with the white race, either in social or* *political relations and <u>so far unfit that they had no rights which the white man was bound to respect</u>."*

The court's opinion flies in the face of the **absurdity doctrine** and **scrivener's error exception concepts**, because they were used erroneously to support the contention—American judges (courts) have the right to interpret statutes contrary to their plain *"meaning."* This ruling, like everything involved with it, applies only to descendants of American slavery and is only invoked when the situation involves slaves and their descendants. This is why the Court did not address the law and declared it unconstitutional. If the matter had ended there, the problem would have been solved by emancipation, Civil War, the Civil Rights Bill of 1866, 13th, 14th, and 15th Amendments because this ruling came before the Civil War. But no, it did not end there.

As time and events would have it, 32 years after emancipation, Civil War, the Civil Rights Bill of 1866, the 13th, 14th and 15th Amendments became the law of the land, Homer Plessy (1896), a black man, purchased a train ticket. A white conductor refused to allow Plessy to select a seat and sit in any empty seats in a train car designated for white only. The conductor forced Plessy to sit in a car reserved for "colored" only.

Plessy challenged his treatment in Court. According to the Civil Rights Bill of 1866 and 14th Amendment, he was denial choice; not allowed to select a seat. Plessy claimed the same right as anyone who purchased a ticket, which was to choose where they sit. Plessy went to Court demanding his 14th Amendment right of equal protection. He claimed *14th Amendment guarantees* right of due process. **Plessy v. Ferguson** was the first major challenge to segregation that reached the Supreme Court (1897).

The Court rejected **Plessy's** arguments that the law violated his *14th Amendment right of equal protection*. US Supreme Court Justices stated **Plessy's** claim of discrimination and disparate treatment was in his head and not in the law. Summarizing, Justice Brown declared, *"We consider the underlying fallacy of the plaintiff's argument to consist in the assumption that the enforced separation of the two races stamps the colored race with a badge of inferiority. If this is so, it is not by reason of anything found in the act, but solely because the colored race chooses to put that construction upon it."* Now that's an absurdity! Another judge's beliefs made its way into law, without any legal bases in the Constitution.

Based solely on the ability of judges to use the **"absurdity doctrine,"** which allowed the Court, to supersede a plaintiff's legal rights stood in the place of law. The **"absurdity doctrine"** protected white culprits from black victims.

The Court's invoking the *"absurdity doctrine"* and *"scrivener's error exception,"* created an *"absurdity,"* which was based on what white people wanted. Supreme Court judges claimed they *"saw no reasonable way in which the Louisiana statute violated Plessy's right to do as white people,"* select where he wanted to sit. The decision rejected the view that the Louisiana law implied any inferiority of blacks, in violation of the *14th Amendment*. The whole idea of *"separate but equal,"* was "black inferiority." Why else maintain separation?" This narrative shows that white people will come together and agree to say and do anything to justify, keeping black people on the bottom of American society. But more than that, this decision was based on **Scott v. Sanford**, as Chief Justice Taney claimed: *"for more than a century before had been regarded as beings of an inferior order."*

Scott was the first and only precedent involving blacks' civil rights claims the Supreme Court had ruled on before **Plessy v. Ferguson**, if **Scott,** was not the precedent **Plessy** was made up law. **Plessy v. Ferguson** is the same miscarriage of justice as **Scott** and is what is meant by "interposition," where the state of Louisiana, placed itself between federal law and black people. The point of segregation relates to the first and only statement of inequality in the US Constitution—the 3/5 Compromise.

Again, Judge Brown and his colleagues were guilty of strictly constructing *"separate but equal."* The **Plessy** decision was a "made-up concept," without constitutional basis, something designed to fit what white people wanted. White people will agree to do whatever, no matter how absurd it is when the situation involves maintaining descendants of American slavery in second class status. **Scott v. Sanford** and **Plessy v. Ferguson** showed the situation black people faced time and again, before the Supreme Court. White people and black people can see or experience the exact same situation from the same position at the same precise moment, yet arrive at totally different scenarios.

This decision legalized *"separate but equal,"* which is a legal absurdity on its face. I must reiterate, when it comes to descendants of American slavery, legal is what white people want. They bend or even break the law, as in **Scott v Sanford**, then make up absurd rulings in situations involving black people, while everyone, especially lawyers, wink and nod, allowing *"wrong to trump right,"* as in **Plessy v Ferguson.**

Dissenting in **Plessy v. Ferguson,** Justice John Marshall Harlan was in the minority, but on the side of justice, as its only voice. Marshall predicted the court's decision would become as infamous as **Scott v. Sanford** (1857). Justice Harlan rail against *"separate but equal"* saying:

"The white race deems itself to be the dominant race in this country. And so it is in prestige, in achievements, in education, in wealth and in power. So, I doubt not, it will continue to be for all time if it remains true to its great heritage and holds fast to the principles of constitutional liberty. But in view of the constitution, in the eye of the law, there is in this country no superior, dominant, ruling class of citizens. There is no caste here. Our constitution is colorblind, and neither knows nor tolerates classes among citizens. In respect of civil rights, all citizens are equal before the law. The humblest is the peer of the most powerful. The law regards man as man, and takes no account of his surroundings or of his color when his civil rights as guaranteed by the supreme law of the land are involved. It is therefore to be regretted that this

high tribunal, the final expositor of the fundamental law of the land, has reached the conclusion that it is competent for a state to regulate the enjoyment by citizens of their civil rights solely upon the basis of race."

Pryor to **Plessy v. Ferguson**, Congress passed the Civil Rights Act of 1875, which entitled everyone to accommodation, public transport, and theaters regardless of race or color. Justice Joseph P. Bradley gave the majority opinion struck down the Civil Rights Act of 1875, holding that the Thirteenth Amendment "merely abolishes slavery" and that the Fourteenth Amendment did not give Congress the power to outlaw private acts of racial discrimination. Associate Justice John Marshall Harlan, the lone dissenter again, wrote, *"Substance and spirit of the recent amendments of the constitution have been sacrificed by a subtle and ingenious verbal criticism."* The decision ushered in the widespread segregation of blacks in housing, employment, and public life that confined them to second-class citizenship throughout much of the United States.

The US Supreme Court legitimized state laws establishing racial segregation in the South and in states that desired separation. It proved to be the impetus for further segregation laws. Laws passed at the end of the Reconstruction Era—the Civil Rights Bill of 1866, 13th, 14th, and 15th Amendments—were erased from the law and in the minds of white people instituting "separate but equal." The Supreme Court decision limited the federal government's ability to intervene in state affairs. The Supreme Court strengthened states' rights and power by guaranteeing that Congress could only "restrain states from acts of racial discrimination and segregation;" another absurdity!! The Supreme of today is following in the tradition of the Taney court in 1857, Plessy v. Feruson 1897 and continues to deny descendants of American slavery Constitutional rights by upholding voter suppression in 2021.

Entering the Dark Age in America

Following the previous discussion, it should be very clear, ***Plessy v. Ferguson (1897)*** and ***"separate but equal"*** (1896) were design to put black people beyond the aegis of law, by eliminating access to fair courts for black people in America. How ***Plessy v. Ferguson*** changed the US justice system, as well as created a blood lust state of mind for many white people, becomes the next focus of this narrative. The tool or technology white politicians, religious leaders, educators and business people created was a lynch mob or lynch law culture in America.

Lynching by the 1900s had become a scourge. Watching a black man die was similar to attending a tailgate party for an NFL football game today for some white people. The point of the following section is to communicate that 1900 through the 1950s was a lawless period in the US, where lynching was a pogrom used by white people to re-enslaved black people in America. Their pogrom was suborned by federal, state, and local governments and lead by the US Supreme Court. This pogrom allowed white people to rob, rape, murder, and banish slave descendants from their homes and land, as a means of gaining wealth they did not work to gain.

Plessy v. Ferguson exposed former enslaved Africans to the most deadly and terroristic environment any people faced in the history of the world. This genocidal period began with the ***Trans-Atlantic Slave Trade*** (1452), and was reinforced in the 1880s, which continues today in America. It is enforced on the streets by police murders supporting "wage slavery." Similar to the harsh and brutal treatment of slaves, workers are modern day "wage slaves," which is the basis of corporations' wealth today. Once freed, enslaved Africans had no value to white people.

Former slaves became something whites never imagined, competition for resources. Preventing competition from former slaves was the whole idea of keeping slave ignorant—unable to read, write and calculate. From white people's perspective, emancipation of slaves robbed whites of their superior status. Whites readily help and support any white person's effort to gain advantages over blacks. The fact is once emancipated, white people felt former slaves were worthless—nothing. However, competing against blacks and losing, psychologically whites' transfer the worthlessness they attribute to blacks to the losing white person, anytime a black person came out on top. Whites were in league and did whatever it took to force former slaves to accept the second class re-enslaved status white people demand.

White people's scapegoating former slaves before and after ***Plessy v. Ferguson,*** which was to make former slaves appear responsible for the desperate straits white people found themselves, as a result of the *Panic of 1893*, during *the*

Gilded Age. They needed someone to blame other than themselves. Unlike Mark Twain who charged that their lavish excesses and spending of the rich and near rich caused their losses, during the *Panic of 1893*. Consequently, after their losses, white leaders double down blaming former slaves, with the "Big Lie." They painted Freedmen, as despicable wretches *"that didn't want to work and were living off white people taxes."* White people claimed "Reconstruction," along with efforts to educate former slaves and give them first-class rights, caused white people to lose their wealth and their place in society.

Further, politicians, and business leaders claimed, helping Freedmen after Civil War debased US currency. Those bent on re-enslaving blacks described the situation as *"the white man's burden."* They claimed further that the Civil War made white people responsible for taking care of former slaves, who were unable to care for themselves. These deceptive propositions posited that former slaves were enjoying the wealth they caused white people to lose, during the *Panic of 1893*. Not any of these claims made sense, but they fit the desires of those hell-bent on re-enslaving Freedmen. The important thing here is this illogic gave white people a target at which to vent their rage. Any statement that blamed black people for the financial losses whites suffered became part of the "big lie." Irrationality fed on even more irrationality, creating more and more assertions of blame for black people.

The US Supreme Court set the stage for a time in America when a black man could not resist what white people did in any way. If they did, they forfeited their lives. The US Supreme Court engineered this time with **Plessy v. Ferguson** and launched this deadly period of terror, which I called the **"Dark Age"** *angry white men mob madness era*. It was a time unlike any other in America or world history. The Supreme Court stripped blacks of all rights gained through legal actions, like emancipation, the Civil Rights Bill of 1866, 13th, 14th, and 15th Amendments by barring the courthouse door to them.

Displaying a willingness to disregard the dictates of justice, the highest court in the land became *"the protector of white culprits from their black victims."* Rendering former slaves defenseless with its absurd and ridiculous ruling in **Plessy v. Ferguson,** the Court *"stood justice on its head."* It took the lead, depriving black people of legal standing by eliminating fair courts in America for black people as plaintiffs. Their obtuse statement, *"separate but equal"* and *"white supremacy,"* the Court left black people without any defense. It made blacks prisoners in America and a new kind of slave in the South.

Introducing the metaphor—**"Dark Age" angry white men mob madness**—here does not attempt to explain this period. It simply describes and emphasizes what occurred, as unexplained in rational terms, beyond being a wealth gathering pogrom by white people. The ability to communicate the horror, terror and gruesome inhumanity heaped upon African Americans, during this period, for the most baseborn reasons, I needed a very powerful figure of speech to convey the impact of this terroristic period for black people. As with slavery, I went back to the first *"Dark Age"* as the very edge of current knowledge for a model, regarding such mass societal derangement.

Looking back at the Middle Age, historians describe it as a time of demographic, cultural, and economic deterioration, following the withdrawal the Roman Empire. The decline in Western Europe had an impact similar to the *Panic of 1893 or COVID-19* today. Diseases, like chorea, tuberculosis, bubonic plague devastated Europe, and the 1918 flu pandemic or coronavirus of 2020 are the only examples comparable to that time in America. That period in Europe was also a time of persecution, torture, and death. There were mass witch-hunts, where people were stretched upon the rack, hanged or burning at stake, as witches. But, the most important comparison and contrast between the *"Dark Age"* in Europe and the 1900s in America is rejection of knowledge. Europeans held tightly to their flat-earth cosmology.

Most scientists agree, the *"Dark Age"* in Europe, developed out of ignorance, but America's case, was as if it was teleported back to that pre-knowledge period for guidance. Scientists also agree that diseases—chorea, tuberculosis, and bubonic plague—had a major impact on life in Mid-Evil Europe. However, America had the equivalent of what Europe didn't have—penicillin, anti-biotics, and other medicines—to protect itself from such plagues. However, America could not protect itself from itself, once the *"Dark Age"* *angry white men mob madness* struck, like a plague.

America had government and an enlightened citizenry, as well as courts and law enforcement, but amazingly those institutions were like malaria or yellow fever carrying mosquito. Not only were these institutions agents of the *"Dark Age"* *angry white men mob madness* plague, they were the plague's chief carriers. They help spread a virulent strain that infected only white people.

Although the *"Dark Age"* *angry white men mob madness* is a metaphor, it describes what actually happened to real live people, right here in America (1900-1960). Given the imagery and symbolism, the effect of the metaphor, I hope will help identify similarities between the two *"Dark Ages."* I will not speculate on why historians said it happened but know that the few examples cited here happened to real black people upwards of 5,000 times.

There isn't a precedent in the annals of world history that explain what occurred only in America from 1900 through the 1960s. The lack of stability in the Roman Empire caused a withdrawal, which is blamed for precipitated the *"Dark Age"* in Europe. However, slavery in America is the only precursor for white people's actions. Slavery is all one has to look back on as a precursor, but it produced the victims, not the perpetrators.

Never the less, in America, there are no factual antecedents that explain the government engineered and supported pogrom of hatred. The viciousness, and brutality heaped upon black people during those times, leaves only greed and madness, as a possible explanation. My efforts are to guarantee America's ***"Dark Age"*** *angry white men mob madness* period will not slip into the recesses of people's minds. My effort is to guard against the ***"Dark Age"*** *angry white men mob madness* will not be reduced to insignificance, the way the internal slave trade and breeding of slaves has, and viewed today, as nothing more than slave master and overseers having fun in slave pens.

Compared to the huge numbers of cases in the historical record of lynchings, I present a very few actual incidents that occurred in America. These incidents are like slave narratives, which offer an accurate illustration of how federal, state, and local governments conspired to generate terror and subordinated a murderous environment of racial hatred against black people for 90 years. Moreover, these incidents were not spontaneous occurrences by over-exuberance white men. The ***"Dark Age,"*** *angry white men mob madness* metaphor, makes it very clear this period was not a natural outgrowth of human activity.

Lynching: Backdoor to Wealth for Whites

The next section may seem like an anomaly, but it is only one example of a process that occurred upwards of five thousand times to thousands of black people not only in the South but across America. Lynching was far more than the rapes, robberies, mayhem, and murders black people endured, it was a process that masked the methods whites used to gain wealth by victimizing black people.

One may ask, what does wealth have to do with lynchings? It may seem presenting the **"Dark Age"** *angry white men mob madness* as a metaphor, makes it a spoof, parody, or even humorous. Considering the events that started in the 1880s and extended ninety or so years, following this gruesome period in America, everyone can judge for themselves, whether to laugh or cry.

Beale Street was essential to the development and survival of black communities, large and small, in the Mid-South at the end of the 19th Century. Having survived the madness of the Civil War, the riot of 1866, the contraband period, and the yellow fever epidemic (1878), newly Freedmen established stable communities in and around Memphis by the 1890s. Some areas were producing wealth that became the envy of white men. Freedmen opened schools, built churches, and started businesses. Their theme was, *"Git yourself a job or some land, a wife, start a family, help out in the community and you will have something in life."*

The downside on this coin shows that poor whites men were still very angry over their loss in the Civil War, well as the internal slave trade and breeding. That period had provided more than they ever dreamed of having. They would not accept—their loss of status and economic opportunities—competing for resources against mobile Freedmen. White people all over the South felt the emancipation of slaves took away their natural-born rights as white people to make a living.

They saw competition from people they once owned, as thievery, and watching them doing and gaining thing whites believed was rightfully their province, generated real hostility among white men. They were unified in their effort to take from black people what they felt, rightfully, belong to white folks. White men in government were in league in a cult of revenge and murder. Government officials engineered and coordinated white people efforts to rob black people with impunity.

The system of segregation mandated by the Supreme Court gave white people the legal means to accomplish their thievery and murder by barring the courthouse doors to black people. Simultaneously whites used these same courts as a weapon against former slaves. White politicians created the means to reclaim what whites saw as their natural superiority and heritage to dominate blacks. White community leaders believed former slaves had gotten out of their place and were acting like, *"they were as good as white folks."* White supremacy justified their actions against former slaves. Whites felt it was their right to block former slaves' access to the province white people controlled.

Segregation made the government a defender of white people against former slaves. Whites felt blacks were encroaching on rights and prerogatives of "their betters." Similar to former slaves during the contraband period, poor whites poured into Memphis in search of the means to survive. This scenario set the stage for a period of grisly revenge, death seeking, and blood lust rituals that grew into a confrontational atmosphere of whites against blacks all over the South.

The example I selected to open this brutal period of robbery and murder by whites occurred in Memphis in 1892. It demonstrates the role governments played, aiding whites' efforts to rob and murder African Americans for their possessions. A white grocery store owner, William Barrett, had a business in a predominately black community called *"The curve."* Similar to white landowners in the South, Barrett's store used credit to rob black people. He sold bootleg whiskey and had a "gambling room" in the back; in other words, he was a gangster. Supported by the white power structure in Memphis, whites like Barrett were given virtual monopolies in black areas.

A group of Memphis black businessmen Thomas Moss, Calvin McDowell, and Henry Stewart opened the *"People's Grocery Store"* in *The Curve*. It was a cooperative venture, which put their store in direct competition to Barrett. The white man was enraged that black men, dared put a store in *"my area."* He felt *"these are my niggers"* and argued daily with the blacks store owners. The situation escalated to where fights among supporters on both sides occurred almost daily.

Increased racial tensions in the neighborhood led to threats against the *People's Grocery Store* cooperative owners. The police refuse to intervene on their behalf. They said *The Curve* and the store were outside city limits, and they could not interfere in private business matters. Thus, this gave Barrett, the white store owner, a free hand dealing with his black competition.

One night (3-5-1892), three white men broke through the back door of the *People's Grocery Store*. The store owners defended themselves and their business, which was their right. Fearing they were being robbed or raided, they open fire on the intruders. Once the shooting was over, two Deputies lay on the floor, wounded.

Reports in the white newspapers described the shooting as a *"cold-blooded and calculated ambush by the black store owners,"* even though the so-called ambush took place inside the black owners' property. Besides, the store owners had no way of knowing the intruders were Deputes; they thought robbers had broken in on them. Neither of the deputies died, however, the *Appeal-Avalanche* newspaper predicted the face and neck wounds of one of the white men would *"prove fatal."* Notwithstanding, the store was outside city limits, where police said they had no jurisdiction, white newspapers claimed: *"deputies were only doing their jobs by making inquiries, in search of a suspect."*

The *St. Paul Appeal*, a black newspaper, reported an entirely different story. *"As soon as the black store owners realized the intruders were law officers, they dropped their weapons and submitted to arrest."* Judge Julius DuBose, a former Confederate soldier, ignored the fact that police had no right to be there, let along make arrests, said to the *Appeal-Avalanche* newspaper he wanted to *"form a posse to get rid of the 'high-handed rowdies' in the Curve."*

The *St. Paul Appeal* said, *"The deputies arrived with a rout in mind, even though they did not have jurisdiction in The Curve. They went first to talk with Barrett at his store. Deputies then divided into two groups, arriving surreptitiously, without a warrant or announcing their intentions in any way, posted men at the front and rear entrances to the Peoples Grocery Store. The men inside had been prepared for a mob attack for a week. Once Deputies, who were not in uniform and armed, broke in on the black men unannounced, they attempted to surround. But, the black men defended themselves, once the deputies opened fire."*

Learning that the deputies were the ones, who got shot, Judge DuBose ordered the Sheriff to send re-enforcement and *"shoot on sight any nigger causing trouble."* The result was the random shooting of blacks by whites. The Tennessee Rifles, a group of black men, took up position guarding the jail to prevent a lynching. Learning through the newspaper that the injured deputies were not going to die, they decided that since the Shelby County Jail was said to be impenetrable, they felt their presence was no longer need; so, they withdrew.

However, early that morning, about 2:30 a.m., seventy-five men in black masks surrounded the Shelby County Jail, and nine entered. They did not storm the jail or break down the door; they were allowed in. The mobsters took Tommie Moss, Will Stewart, and Calvin McDowell from their cells. They carried them to a Chesapeake & Ohio railroad yard a mile outside of Memphis.

What followed was described in gruesome details in white newspapers. It was clear the reporters were at the scene and had been called in advance to witness the lynching. The report said,

> *"Once at the railroad yard, McDowell 'struggled mightily,' and at one point, he managed to grab a shotgun from one of his abductors. After the mob wrested it from him they shot at his hands and fingers 'inch by inch' until they were shot to pieces. Replicating the wounds the white deputies suffered they shot four holes into McDowell's face, each large enough for a fist to enter. His left eye was shot out and the 'ball hung over his cheek in shreds.' His jaw was torn out by buckshot. Where 'his right eye had been, there was a big hole, where his brains oozed out.' The Appeal-Avalanche added his injuries were in accord with his 'vicious and unyielding nature.'*
>
> *Will Stewart was described as the most stoic of the three, 'obdurate and unyielding to the last.' He was also shot with a shotgun, and a pistol on the right side of the neck and left eye. Moss was also shot in the neck. His dying words were reported in the papers, 'Tell my people to go west. There is no justice for them here.'*

The story made the *New York Times'* front page. It said, *"This lynching on March 10 counters the image of the "New South" that Memphis had tried to promote."* The lynching sparked national outrage, and in an editorial in the *Free Speech and Headlight* newspaper in Memphis, Ida B. Wells' embraced Moss' dying words. She encouraged blacks to strike out for the West and *"leave a town which will neither protect our lives and property, nor give us a fair trial in the courts, but takes us out and murders us in cold blood when accused by white persons."*

The Peoples Grocery Store sparked an emigration movement that eventually saw 6,000 blacks leave Memphis for the Western Territories. She also indicated from her investigation, Barrett and DeBose had engineered the lynching to kill his competitors from the *People's Grocery Store.* Judge DuBose ordered the sheriff to take possession of the swords and guns belonging to the Tennessee Rifles and to dispatch a hundred men to the *Peoples Grocery Store* where they should *"shoot down, on sight, any Negro who appears to be making trouble."* Gangs of armed white men rushed to *the Curve*, shooting wildly into groups of blacks and looted the grocery store, once the shooting ended.

Subsequently, DuBose sold William Barrett, the grocery store, for one-eighth of its value. It is not clear what gave the court the right to sell private property not involved in a court action. Such assaults, as this and the riot in 1866, became wealth-building strategies for whites in America, which continued into the 1970s in Memphis.

One Hundred Years of Lynching

It may seem to some this discussion of lynching is overblown. For those readers, I offer Ralph Ginzburg's book <u>One Hundred Years of Lynching</u> to make it clear, I present only a very very few lynching events in this narrative. The following comments are by two readers concerning <u>One Hundred Years of Lynching</u>: *"This book took me months to read (a lot longer than a book normally takes me)—It is one thing to know about this aspect of American history and the magnitude of the atrocities committed at that time.... but it is another, to peel through so many accounts one by one in detail... It was painful, but I believe necessary to go through. I did not expect to grow, and crumble, and grow... in the ways I have with this book. Keep your eyes open, and look around you."* And then there is this, *"This book moved me to tears. It's a compilation of local newspaper articles detailing thousands of public murders committed right here in the United States, mainly in the southern part of the country. This is what happens when hatred is accepted in American society. A perverted bloodlust by those in power, documented word for word, article by article from newspapers of that day."*

Without Sanctuary: American Lynching Photographs

For those who cannot muster the courage to read page after page of the monstrous lynchings from this period in America, there is James Allen's pictorial exposé. The Tuskegee Institute recorded established there were 3,436 lynchings of blacks in 1882 to 1950. Many times professional photographers, that attended lynchings, carried cameras to record the gruesome business. Many lynching photographs became postcards, which vendors sold as souvenirs to participants and others in attendance. These horrific images were peddled to the general public as cherished mementos.

Lynching photographs are physical records of these brutal murders and survive today, as reminders of the terrorism unleashed against America's descendants of slavery and their communities. James Allen tells this shocking and hideous pictorial story in his book *"Without Sanctuary: Lynching Photography in America.*" Allen exhibit presents nearly one hundred such images of original pictures preserved from that time. They remind the world what supposedly enlightened America did to thousands (well over 5,000) of black human beings for over one hundred years for entertainment.

Lynchings are part of a mindset that is still very much alive in America today. Many white people wish or choose not to acknowledge, while claiming not to remember their history of hatred for black skin. Consequently, such public memories regarding this period of atrocities are repressed. Some even pretend what happened, even though Allen's exhibit of lynching photos exists, insist lynchings are an exaggeration. Most pretend lynching is a grotesque abstraction, and a disturbing effort to deny America is a law bidding and justice-loving society.

James Allen's book introduces the truth about lynching with factual images left behind from that period. Such sights make many whites want to disgorge in disgust today, but back during the **Dark Age angry white men mob madness** were part of the reveling. Photos of the racialized, grotesque, and violent spectacles from the lynching period, are not only preserve in books like Allen's but are being revived in spaces, like the Levine Museum of the New South.

President Emily Zimmern said "Levine's exhibits recognize the humanity of those that were executed, and acknowledges that these atrocities took place. It promotes cross-cultural discussion that can bring healing and vigilance against future acts of bigotry and violence, which must be remembered." Otherwise lynching will be like the internal slave trade and breeding today, only remembered as *"slave masters and overseers having fund in the slave pens."*

Importantly, the Levine Museum recognizes the necessity of exploring and preserving such horrific chapters in our nation's history. *"Without Sanctuary"* explores lynching in the United States and particularly the South through the disturbing photographs, postcards, and memorabilia from these horrific events. James Allen, an antique collector, after gathered these artifacts, courageously presents his postcards and photographs collection to recognize what happened across America, during the lynching era (1880s through 1940). These artifacts can help society remember and hopefully openly discuss the brutal violence and murder black people endured without sanctuary or mercy.

Lynchings of the owners of the *"People's Grocery Store"* and that of *"Louis Wright"* began the effort to reverse all gains Freedmen made through emancipation, the Civil Rights Bill of 1866, the 13th, 14th, and 15th Amendments. Lynching or *"lynch law"* occurred only in America (1880-1950). It was the **"Dark Age"** *angry white men mob madness* era, a time when social enlightenment was rejected, even by educated white people. They rejected logic and knowledge, replacing it with superstitions and stereotypes regarding black people, much like today (2020) under Donald Trump.

The **"Dark Age"** *angry white men mob madness* was an embrace of blood lust rituals, which the President of the United States Woodrow Wilson inspired from the White House. This fact may have been very difficult to believe and accept years ago, but with Trump in the White House, such a time is more than believable but it is what we had to live with for 4 years. Were it not for his defeat by Joe Biden, Americans could have experienced that period again. Lynching was white Americans' response to the end of forced bondage for enslaved Africans.

After lynching began during *"The Gilded Age,"* Hoagy Carmichael and Stuart Gorrell wrote the song *"Georgia on My Mind."* (1930). Ray Charles, an iconic **"Blues"** man, re-recorded it 30 years later, with such feeling, the State of Georgia designated it the official state song. Most people are unaware and have never thought when they hear the melody of that heartfelt ballad; it was not the music playing in the ears of the 586 lynch victims in Georgia from the 1890s through 1948.

The 1890s began a very dark time for black men across America, but in Georgia, the threat was greater than any place. There was no relief if a black man displeased a white man for any reason, even without reason. When an individual white man or group of white men desired a black man's life, it was forfeited. If he defended himself, the result was still a death sentence; there was no reprieve.

The scourge of lynching was well underway in 1899 when Sam Hose, (c. 1875/4-23-1899), an African American farm laborer, wanted time off to visit his sick mother. Alfred Cranford, a white man, his boss, pointed his gun at Hose and threatened to shot him, if he didn't get back to work. Believing Cranford was going to shoot him, Hose in fear of his life, while chopping wood, swung an ax in his defense, killing Cranford.

Hose fled the scene. During the ensuing ten-day manhunt, rival newspapers in Atlanta broke sells records competing to provide the most lurid details of Cranford's death. Stories mushroomed, claiming Hose raped Cranford's wife. Other stories accused Hose of committing infanticide and other "unnatural acts," during the sexual assault on Cranford's young daughter.

After his capture, Hose was being transported by train, when a mob boarded at gunpoint and took him from the train. They carried Hose to Newnan, Georgia, the scene of the incident. Meanwhile, in Atlanta, excursion trains were arranged to transport hundreds of Georgians to the site of Hose's pre-planned lynching. The pre-announcement—date, place and time—of the lynching appeared in Atlanta newspapers days before the actual murder of Hose. Hysteria abounded among whites, trying to buy tickets on trains, ferrying whites to the lynching.

On Sunday morning (4-23-1899), Hose was brought to the Newman town square, where over 2,000 excited onlookers reveled, as vendors sold whiskey and food before the big attraction—Hose's murder. The crowd marched Hose to the Cranford home. Once there, Hose was stripped bare, his ears, fingers, and genitals were cut off. A mobster skinned his face. He was then burned alive on a pyre. Souvenir hunters fought over his body parts, organs and bones.

Activist Ida B. Wells-Barnett hired detective Louis P. Le Vin to investigate the Hose lynching. He concluded Hose acted in self-defense, and rape was added to incite his lynching. Mr. Le Vin stated, *"Hose killed Cranford without a doubt, but under what circumstances can never be proven. I was thoroughly convinced that a Negro's life is a very cheap thing in Georgia."* In the book <u>Lynch Law in Georgia,</u> he stated:

> *"The real purpose of these savage demonstrations is to teach the Negro that in the South he has no rights that the law will enforce. Samuel Hose was burned to teach the Negroes that no matter what a white man does to them, they must not resist."*

Historian Leon Litwack states in, <u>*Trouble In Mind: Black Southerners in the Age of Jim Crow*</u> that during an investigation by a white detective, *"Cranford's wife, Mattie, revealed that Hose had never entered the house, and had acted in self-defense."*

According to the Tuskegee Institute, Florida led the nation in lynchings per capita from 1900-1930. Georgia led the nation in overall lynchings from 1900-1931 with 302 incidents. The *Equal Justice Initiative (EJI)* published a study in 2015, which found over 4,075 black men, women, and children were lynched in the 12 southern states.

African American newspapers denounced lynching. Ida B. Wells, a crusader against lynching, documented and condemned those heinous events. After Wells wrote on May 21, 1892, that no one believes *"the old thread-bare lie"* that black men assault white women. The Memphis Daily Commercial Appeal (formerly *The Avalanche Appeal Newspaper*) called her a *"black scoundrel"* for her story. White businessmen threatened to lynch the owners of her newspaper *(Free Speech and Headlight newspaper)*, while a mob raided and ransacked the newspaper's offices then sold the equipment

Chattanooga Choo Choo Hanging Around

The 400th: From Slavery to Hip Hop

As lynching was sweet music to white supremacists' ears, I add a sour discordant note, which is incongruent with those harmonious and glory times for mobsters. *"Chattanooga Choo Choo"* is a 1941 hit song written by Mack Gordon and composed by Harry Warren. It was originally recorded as a big-band/swing tune by Glenn Miller and His Orchestra. The 1941 movie *Sun Valley Serenade* featured *"Chattanooga Choo Choo,"* and it became the first-ever song declared a gold record. RCA Victor made the designation in 1942 for sales of 1.2 million copies. However, the train tussle over which the *Chattanooga Choo Choo* traveled, crossing the Tennessee River, was involved in several lynchings over the years. Today the song prompts the question, is *"The Chattanooga Choo Choo a racist song?"* The following example cries out for answers.

Just after the turn of the 20th Century, a lynching in Chattanooga, Tennessee (1906) exposed the horrors of the socioeconomic and political system across the South, but particularly in Chattanooga. Its disregard and contempt for law and order are unparalleled. The lynching history of Chattanooga, if not the music of the *"Chattanooga Choo Choo,"* is truly a dissonant note for supporters of law and fairness in America. The disregard for law and justice shown by authorities and white citizens in Chattanooga was a baseline that sounded the death knell for justice in America's legal system. Replacing justice with "lynch law"—***Dark Age" angry white men mob madness***—white supremacists poisoned America's entire socio-economic, political, and legal environment with hatred, racism, and murder.

The merciless death of Ed Johnson and the tragic circumstances surrounding it may have disappeared from memory all together were it not for Mark Curriden, a Dallas reporter, and Leroy Phillips, Jr., a Chattanooga attorney, who published their clarion call for remembrance in, *"Contempt of Court: The-of-the-Century Lynching that Launched a Hundred Years of Federalism."* Only once in its history has the US Supreme Court conducted a criminal trial. Outraged over the lynching of a black man convicted of raping a white woman, after issuing a stay of execution for the accused, Justice John Marshall Harlan ordered the trial of the sheriff, his deputy and four members of a Chattanooga lynch mob, for causing the death of an almost certain innocent black man—Ed Johnson.

The tragedy began when white men in Chattanooga became outraged over Justice John Marshall Harlan's stay of execution for Ed Johnson. A mob had murdered Johnson on March 19, 1906, in his hometown of Chattanooga, Tennessee. The lynching prompted the only criminal trial ever conducted by the US Supreme Court. Johnson received the death penalty for the murder and rape of Nevada Taylor, a white woman. His murder exemplifies the *"Dark Age"* angry white men mob madness era.

Unfolding like a sick grade B horror movie, lynch mania enveloped America, rapping it in bloodlust rituals that left a bloody trail that led to the White House. The stage was set for this tragedy when Sheriff Joseph F. Shipp, who normally had multiple deputies on duty, guarding the jail each night, sent all law enforcement officials home, except for an elderly nighttime jailer. Earlier that day, Shipp's chief deputy recommended he keep extra guards posted to prevent mob violence, but Shipp refused. Additionally, deputies moved all prisoners except Ed Johnson and Ellen Baker, a white woman, from the third floor.

Between 8:30 and 9:00 pm, an uncovered mod entered the jail; they broke through three sets of third-floor doors to get Johnson. It took the mob nearly three hours using an ax and a sledgehammer, to reach Johnson. Shipp showed up at the jail but was neither outraged nor did he draw his weapon in an attempt to stop the mob. He pleaded with them, *"Please cease your violence and allow the rule of law to remain in effect."* Annoyed with Shipp perhaps, several mobsters walked him to a restroom, where he remained unguarded, cooperatively sitting on the stool until the lynch mob carried Johnson from the jail. Even then, he did nothing to intervene and stop the murder.

The mob took Johnson to the nearby tussle over the Tennessee River, "Walnut Street Bridge," and hanged him from a beam with a rope. Hanging for only minutes, several mobsters began shooting Johnson. The mob shot him over fifty times. One bullet severed the rope, and Johnson's body fell to the ground. When it moved, one mobster, later identified as a deputy sheriff, placed his revolver against Johnson's head and fired five additional shots.

Following that, another mobster pinned a note to Johnson, which read *"To Justice Harlan. Come get your nigger now."* The large mob had gathered around the jail and followed those carrying Johnson to the bridge. They acted as a defensive perimeter to deter members of the city's black community that resided just across the bridge from interfering. Many blacks in Chattanooga walk across the Walnut Street Bridge daily, going to and from work.

The public was outraged and protested during Johnson's incarceration. They showed great interest in the case. The day after his murder, there were widespread strikes among black residence in Chattanooga. Two thousand people attended Johnson's funeral the next day,

Noah Parden and Styles Hutchens, the two African American attorneys from Chattanooga showed tremendous courage successfully defending Johnson. Disregarding death threats, they proceeded with his defense, even after the members of Johnson's legal team believed an appeal would be fruitless. Following their successful appeal, the two attorneys and their families fled Chattanooga.

Beale Street: Rise of the Negro Politicians

Before 1900 former slaves were not politicians. They participated in politics but had no real role in determining policy. White politicians told blacks the issues and how to interpret them in a political context. Black politicians spoke for former slaves and tried to give *VOICE* to their needs. More of a cynical fact than a sinister reality, newly Freedmen were up against college-educated adversaries, with family histories of political involvement. If most black politicians could read, it was barely. Plus, in reality, the political system was closed to blacks, whether former slaves or free black.

So, now this narrative comes to the one issue that had eluded descendants of American slavery—political power. One would think it would have been the first system or technologies former slaves would have attempted. Without segregation and white supremacy dominating their lives, they would have. White supremacy was the real strategy behind **Plessy v. Ferguson,** which denied former slaves any power, not even control over their own lives. Terrorizing black people was to force them to accept the second-class status white people demanded. Black people were denied access to the vote and fair courts, which foreclosed all avenues to change their status.

Terror forced former slaves to bide their time, and they could not take that monster on directly. Nevertheless, enduring the straight jacket of segregation was not a one size fits all situations. My case in point Memphis, Tennessee, where my family resided, and I grew up, as well as where I learned what I know of politics, was a different type of monster than most places in the South. Memphis reflected several prominent realities which best illustrates my point of why politics was the last area Freedmen invested real effort, while trying to survive and better themselves.

The rise of black politicians in Memphis, as well as other places in the US, was not a predetermined or predestine proposition. Many different individuals and events played crucial roles, planned and unplanned, prompting former slaves to move or act as they did. Some political actions made the road to **"The 400th"**, a very rocky journey. There were trouble areas, lynching is one, which were not slight cavities, but major craters, deep curves with narrows so tight former slaves barely squeezed through in single file, trying to access or exercise the franchise offered by the 14th and 15th Amendments, while having to fight segregation and white supremacy to get to polls and ballot boxes.

Memphis is this narrative's model, not simply because it is where my family resided, and I cut my teeth in politics, but major events developed and transpired there on the way to **"The 400th"**. Consequently, the story I tell could not have happened any other place. It was the location, as I said, of some major events, some known and some not so much, but as this narrative will show, they determined the progress of black people in America.

The history of black people in Memphis and the Mid-South I have developed from black people's word-of-mouth culture or stories passed around, in most cases. They exist today almost entirely, as result word-of-mouth account, which influenced how I tell this story. The amount of hard evidence available for detailing this story was scant compared to those kept alive by black people who passionately lived, observed, and enjoyed the excitement and entertainment of life on and around Beale Street and in most cases are all that is left. Their efforts were not about making history but making Memphis a place where black families could live in decent communities.

Robert R. Church Sr. (1839-1912) was a major player in this drama. This narrative has pointed out that, as a Freedman he migrated to Memphis (1862), during the Civil War. Following his arrival, Church became a unique benefactor of not only former slaves but the city as well. Church bought a bar and began a business career that spanned fifty years on Beale Street. He rescued the black community after the riot in 1866, then the city, after the yellow fever epidemic in 1878.

Buying property, while rebuilding burned out areas, Church put money in the hands of destitute contrabands, during this period. Rebuilding destroyed homes, churches, and schools, after the 1866 riot; he invests in property heavily, following the yellow epidemic (1878). Church was more of a savior for former slaves, even though he did not pose as a philanthropist; rather he was a great entrepreneur.

With the official beginning of segregation in Memphis, the 1880s, European-American families that lived in the Beale Street area began their flight to all-white communities across town. Once their exit was complete, Church began transforming Beale Street from an upper-middle-class European Americans neighborhood into a commercial area for Negroes. This point cannot be overstated and should become part of the mental baggage readers carry forward, regarding what it took to maintain a viable commercial area for descendants of American slavery.

The changeover, from the late 1870s to the 1880s, was aided by the Freedman's Bank, which financed black-owned businesses on Beale Street. It supported entrepreneurial opportunities and prosperity for Freedmen, trying to learn about business and become entrepreneurs on Beale. For instance, Joseph Clouston, an African American barber, invested in Beale Street real estate, buying several buildings in the area. African Americans controlled the barbering, local taxi (hack) and freight (dray) businesses, during the contraband period.

However, by the 1880s, white politicians began using segregation to control the development and progress of former slaves, as blacks tried to build wealth. The city started a streetcar system, whether designed or an accident of fate, it killed the black taxi business. The next move was the design of white leaders, preempting the black dray business. Whites began using segregation laws to mandate where black drivers could pick up and deliver freight. These restrictions helped white immigrants take over the freight (dray) business. Segregation put many black drivers out of business in the 1890s and reduced others to struggling to survive.

Robert R. Church, Sr. opened the Solvent Savings Bank and Trust Company on Beale in 1899. Church was on the way to becoming the richest black businessman in the South, maybe in the country at that time. He looked for ways to use his wealth to strengthen the black community. Church realized for prosperity among black people to grow, the black community needed an economic engine, especially in the face of segregation.

Responding to the challenge of the city's segregation policies, Robert Church anchored his Beale Street transformation around a premiere venue for black people in Memphis. Segregation barred or restricted Negros' access to theaters, meeting halls, and entertainment venues in the downtown area. On land he purchased, after the yellow fever epidemic, he built Church's Park and Auditorium on six acres.

Church's Park and Auditorium was a splendid two-story structure that seated 2,000 people a huge capacity in 1899. It included a stage, floor space, a parlor, meeting rooms, and a refreshment stand. It was one of the largest, if not the largest venue of its type strictly for black people, in the South. Church's Park and Auditorium hosted cultural, recreational, civic, and entertainment events.

A political leader as well, Church gave black politicians an important link to Republican Party leaders. He brought Pres. Theodore Roosevelt to Memphis in 1902. Pres. Roosevelt, who usually spoke from the rear of his train car, addressed over 10,000 black people from the steps of Church's Park Auditorium.

George W. Lee, author of **Beale Street: Where the Blues Began** was a resident historian of Beale Street, along with numerous others. The difference between, Lee and the others was he put his thoughts in writing. He was fond of extolling the virtues of Beale Street.

"All night Halloween Balls," big "Jitterbug Contests," and weekend concerts at Church's Park Auditorium, even free dinners for the poor on Thanksgiving were events black people crowded onto Beale Street to experience. Friday nights were for folks that worked and lived in the city. Saturday nights belonged to the field hands, who poured into the city for fun and relief from a week of toiling in the hot sun. While on Sunday, church folks filled the famed thoroughfare.

Tennessee's oldest surviving African American church edifice was built on Beale Street. Beale Street Baptist Church began as a frame structure erected in 1864. The congregation, which numbered over 2,500 (1866), purchased a lot and began constructing the brick and stone building, which was located next door to Church's Park and Auditorium. Beale Street

Baptist Church still stands on that spot, former president of the United States Ulysses S. Grant visited the church on April 14, 1880, escorted by Edward Shaw, Memphis's leading Negro politician.

A delightful eye-catching scene was provided by dark town stutters in their daily fashion show, promenading down Beale Street. Mac Harris, "King of the Gamblers," stutted down Beale in a cutaway coat, striped trousers, a wide brimmed felt hat, sporting a twisted mustache, beard, and a cane. Jimmy Turpin, who ran the Old Monarch gambling joint, wore knickerbockers, an argyle pull over vest, with matching socks and a Tam Ó Shanter. Lymus Wallace operated a saloon at 117 Beale Street, sported a waist coat, vest, bowtie and a top hat daily.

However, Beale Street was about business, while fashion was for fun. George Jackson opened the first black drugstore on Beale (1893). Around 1903 Mrs. Lucie E. Campbell (1885-1963), a nationally known composer, publisher, artist, educator and African American leader, who wrote over 100 songs, was also Tennessee's most famous gospel song writer. Organizing musical pageants on Beale Street, she gathered a group of Beale Street musicians and formed the Beale Street Music Club. Bert Roddy (1886-1963) and Robert Lewis Jr. opened the Iroquois Cafe across from Church Park. Roddy was the first president of the Memphis branch of the NAACP. In 1917 Beale Street's Negro businessmen included William Burrows (contractor), George R. Jackson (pharmacist), L. J. Searcy (real estate broker), Paul Sneed (bookkeeper), A. F. Ward (cashier), and C. A. Terrell (physician). During the depression, following the Panic of 1893, owners of the secondhand clothing stores on Beale stood on the sidewalks, trying to enticed customers inside to buy coats for $1.95 and dresses for a quarter.

Even with its stereotypes, Minstrelsy was the entry-level to entertainment for newly freed slaves. Giving those looking for opportunities and desperate to make money, as well as willing to do anything to earn it, Minstrelsy gave them a chance to perform on stage. Regardless of its humiliating *"blackface"* image, for penniless former slaves, it was something to do, which was better than nothing. Minstrel shows provided a doorway to entertainment for black performers—dancers, vocalists, instrumentalists, and entrepreneurs—even though they had to accept the *"blackface"* of humiliation.

Looking for a way to get into business doing something they knew, entertainment was the perfect vehicle for former slaves to develop the one Art that flowed naturally from them. Going back to before *Pattin Juba* during slavery, slaves began using their bodies as instruments entertaining but did not get paid. Whether on the sidewalk out front or on stage inside on Beale Street, entertainment became a way for black people to not only make *something out of nothing* but build wealth doing it.

W. C. Handy built a reputation playing and writing music, which gave him special status. Minstrelsy was a crazy ride that was nearing its peak when W. C. Handy (11-16-1873/3-28-1958) toured with *Mahara's Minstrels*. They performed at the 1893 Chicago World's Fair. Later, they toured Cuba, where Handy learned the styles, variations, rhythms, and other techniques of Latin music. Handy's education while there was essential, building his musical knowledge, especially creating the tango rhythm for *"St. Louis Blues."*

Performing with *Mahara's Minstrels* and getting entangled with the lynching of Louis Wright in New Midrid, Missouri (1902), W. C. Handy, like Olaudah Equiano, came to believe life in larger cities was just that, life. Handy organized a band *the Black Knights of Pyhtias*, before arriving in Memphis in late 1902. A river town, railroad center, and highway crossroads on the Mississippi River, with several large industries, Memphis provided black workers with pocket money for entertainment. Beale Street provided places to spend it, Handy became part of what they spent it on.

Born in a log cabin in Florence, Alabama, Handy was searching for a place to set down roots when he arrived in Memphis (1902). The excitement of playing in clubs and juke joints nightly, coupled with the bright lights and gaiety on Beale Street, brought Handy to the end of his search. Lying at the foot of Beale Street, the Mississippi River gave him quick and easy access to popularity.

Performing on riverboats traveled up and down the river from St. Louis to New Orleans, Handy found regular work. Entertaining at all kinds of venues in towns along the river where riverboats stopped, Handy got real exposure to the river culture. Trains running out of Memphis gave him even easier access to towns that were not close to the river. Playing little towns in Mississippi like Clarksdale, Tutwiler, Leland, Tunica, Grenada, Indianola, Greenwood, Mound Bayou, McComb, Columbus, and Meridian, Handy became immersed in the delta music culture of field hands.

Fascinated by the music local field hands made, which captured white people's attention so completely, Handy's interest grew every time he witnessed field hands' music's mesmerizing effect on whites. Observing the enthralling power of the music played by "field niggers" on white people, Handy could not help but notice a less hateful and abusive nature than was displayed in Minstrel Shows toward black performers. He began to study this strange phenomenon.

Drawn by the emotional impact and genius required to produce this music, Handy once regarded as "primitive," launched him on a quest to understand delta music. Understanding the **"Blues"** became a lifelong love affair, as he studied the music, habits, and attitudes of dealt musicians. The sounds that grew out of the very soul and roots of black people's misery during slavery, became their music. Handy drew real pride from this music, as he learned about what slaves and their descendants created without guidance or instruments, (*pattin Juba*) in many cases.

Handy rode riverboats up and down the river; trains got him to communities that could not be reached by water, and roads carried him deep into the backwashes of the Mississippi delta. Chasing the story of the **Blues** was like dining at a smorgasbord for Handy. He devoured the variety of music and varying styles served up in these out of the way places and backwashes of humanity.

This music began long before emancipation, even before slaves began entertaining master, which gave them a reason to continue its development. Their efforts playing and developing their unique sounds was not spurred on by thoughts of heritage, but survival and love. Handy was engaged in the same process he employed in Cuba, learning from Latin musicians.

Captivated by the originality and sophistication of the music he heard, Handy recanted one such encounter, in his memoir, <u>Father of the Blues: An Autobiography.</u> He shared the impact of his education just listening, "*Setting in a train station in Tutwiler, I listened to a slide guitarist, bluesman, sitting beside me. The lean, loose-jointed Negro, pluck on a guitar and as he played, he pressed a knife on the strings of the guitar. This was a style popularized by Hawaiian guitarists, who used steel bars. He called it 'weirdest music,' something I'd never heard, but the tune did stay in my mind.*" Sharing his story, Handy said he realized "*The music I was studying had many stories. And, those stories were as varied as the people who made it.*"

Another epiphany for Handy came while performing at a dance. He said, "*During my orchestra's break, I listened to a string band playing a mix of country, ragtime and blues. That band was making more money from the audience tossing coins to them, than my band under contract.*" Handy began arranging tunes for his band. The first tune was "*Make Me a Pallet on the Floor,*" an old tune by the immortal John Hurt.

Handy never claimed to have created the *"Blues"* genre and was not the first to record music in the *"Blues"* form. What he did was take the *"Blues,"* which was just a regional style of music, local un-standardized folk favorites, with a limited audience, and apply his knowledge of music. He created a structure that made those tunes something people not born and bred in the delta could understand and play.

No, Handy didn't create the *"Blues,"* rather he made the *"Blues"* more accessible to the world. As such, Handy took African Americans' music and made it the first and only original American musical creation. An educated man that taught music at the Agricultural and Mechanical College in Normal, Alabama, Handy, like a wizard, developing the music of *delta folk singers, bluesmen* and *blues predecessors,* who were around long before he ever picked up his first cornet. Even though their names have faded into history, not laying claim to it, Handy honored them as creators.

I see Handy tapping into these undefined sounds. African slaves first uttered those sounds in slave pins at **"The Door of No Return,"** Goreé Island, Dakar, Senegal. No doubt, they were fearful of being forced aboard ships, headed who knows where. These sounds flowed from and through Africans touched by and trapped in the **Trans-Atlantic Slave Trade** cultures. These were sounds firmly rooted in the innermost being of slaves. These sounds began to emerge while in the dark and deathly holes of slave ships, bringing them to North America.

Slaves held tightly to the only thing they had, love for self. Their self-love was all slaves would never have, because slavery took everything else, leaving them nothing. Those sounds became the songs of the poorest of the poor, even among slaves, and it belonged to the most illiterate and forgotten wretches of the earth, the so-called *"cotton or sugar cane field niggers."*

They were the *"folk music"* singers among American slaves. Again Handy wrote that *"Southern Negroes sang about everything....They accompany themselves on anything from which they can extract a musical sound or rhythmical effect..."* He later reflected, *"In this way, and from these materials, they set the mood for what we now call* **'Blues.'"**

"Blues "was a deeply emotional and personal response to the brutality, desperation, and scarcity of their lives. These sounds rose out of a place that had no notes, regular rhythm, or name. These sounds oozed up from the bowels of slaves' into their hearts, then out through their nose and mouth. Moaning, groaning, wailing, and even crying, slaves sang the *"Blues"* all the time.

Slaves sang it when they went to sleep on a cold night, in a cold house, alone on a cold floor, which was their bed. The *"Blues"* is what rocked them to sleep at night and woke them up the next morning. If it wasn't the white man wanting something, it was their mate wanting what they could not give. They sang the *"**Blues"*** while on field gangs, chain gangs, for back pain, and when they could not do anything, they sang the "***Blues"*** just the same.

Writing in his memoirs about his adventures, Handy said, *"Whether in the cotton fields of the delta or on the levees up St. Louis way, it was always the same, Negro roustabouts, honky-tonk piano players, wanderers and others of the underprivileged, the undaunted class from Missouri to the Gulf, these themes were a common medium through which any such individual might express his or her personal feeling in a sort of musical soliloquy."*

Blues: More than Just a Sad Song

Handy rescued those *"Blues soliloquies"* from anonymity and raised them to the level of Shakespearian sonnets. Seeing W. C. Handy, as just another black man that gave the world another kind of music, does him a grave disservice. **Blues** was and is more than just another sad song of the poor and downtrodden. It is high art at its finest.

First, such individuals are missing the entire point of what slave masters did turning free Africans into slaves. For one to survive slavery, it had to become a state of mind. Slavery was a caricature, and slaves always had to be in character. Caught outside of that personage by the wrong white person, anything from a sharp rebuke to the ultimate penalty—death—could be a slave's final scene.

Secondly, slave masters, along with servitude, imposed a continuing need for slaves to perform. Those slaves that entertained master understood and embraced that role. Their performances placed them among the greatest role players that ever lived. It was their impact, Handy recognized, while watching the reactions of white people, who thoroughly enjoy seeing black people in the delta exorcise their pain and deprivation. Slaves gave words like acting, pretending, and performing a whole new meaning.

For white people, slaves were entertaining, but to slaves and Handy, who recognized their **Blues,** knew they were doing a dance for life. One wrong statement, gesture, or action, and the curtain could ring down in a final Louis Wright performance. This dance put a slave's life on the line, filled with total seriousness, forever playing a death scene. With this reality hanging over them, like the "Sword of Damocles," the motivation to perform was a true life and death scenario on or off stage.

My last statement is not about those who did not grasp the significance of W. C. Handy's momentous discovery. The importance of notating the music of slaves cannot be overstated, in terms of magnitude for their descendants, who followed in their **Blues** tradition. For me, it was every bit as important to black people in the South, as Ely Whitney's cotton gin was for Southern plantation owners in the early 1800s.

Arranging and notating the ***"Blues,"*** Handy opened the door to a world of possibilities for African American slave descendants they would walk through, as developers of a kind of magic that no one truly understood but them. This magic flowed out of slaves based solely on their everyday experiences. Handy's discovery, in a very real way, supports the claim slaves' bodies were instruments *(pattin Juba).* Their bodies, during slavery, became tools, a force and/or an expressive work of live art at the same time. The effects their bodies produced change the world's view of what entertainment was and could be, beginning with their music.

Doing things with their bodies, descendants of American slavery became an Art form. I know this is a very strange statement and difficult to believe for some and may make them want to laugh, but before Handy notated and arranged the sounds black people were making with and through their bodies, it was just something black folks did. Most people did not see anything special, neither was it marketable and compelling, nor did they believe it contained sufficient energy to lift a whole race of people, as sounds and movements poured out of them. Descendants of American slavery, through their Art, gave the world a new kind of fun and entertainment.

Probably another strange statement for some people, but growing up in Memphis and the Mid-South, a "field hand," gave me a unique perspective on this subject in several ways. This narrative, as it plays out, will explore the major twist and turns of how and why music/entertainment had such a powerful impact on people like me. Music, the **Blues**, its presence, and economic impact on the lives of people in the Mid-South, both black and white, change the trajectory of ***"The 400th".***

W. C. Handy discovered how to bring the magic of Beale Street alive, and that gave it a special existence. Before the **Blues**, Beale Street was like a slave pin, in that, it was the place white folks allowed former slaves to have to keep them out of sight and out of mind, until they were needed. White people saw Beale Street, as just another place black people could be crowded together and ignored. Handy's arrival added a dynamic no one ever imagined. Not only did he figure out how to make *"something out of nothing,"* he captured the magic of the **Blues** in doing so, but he made it the possession of all descendants of slavery.

Capturing the magic of the **Blues** was not the first-time slave descendants created *something out of nothing*; clowning it up to entertain master created Minstrelsy. This *"nothing"* slaves created became the foundation of American entertainment. Before Minstrelsy, European based music, dance, and theater entertained whites. **Blues** was the first-time black people had something they created claimed in their name.

My point here is that Handy was not the first to write a **Blues**, but he was the first to notate or give an arrangement to the desperation and pain of black people's survival struggles. His ideas opened up the magic of **Blues** to the world, so anyone who appreciated and loved music could understand and play it. His creation became the first, and thus far, the only original music developed by any Americans. An educated musician, researching **Blues**, Handy became connected to his slave roots. The **Blues** with its mysterious utterances and sounds created by "field niggers" lured Handy into its magic.

Fascinated by the way listeners were enthralled by the magical way the music of old **Blues** masters affected listeners, Handy's search was to discover a way to translate what they had created into compositional form. Driven by a magic he did not understand, Handy rode with and talked to old masters. He picked up the characteristics of African American folk music. Handy, trying to understand, what seemed, melancholy sounding, but cast joyful spells on those it touched, was captivated.

During his travels, Handy set about trying to figure out its melodic sequences and patterns. He found the secret to codifying and notating its mysterious and melodic rhythm. Handy's genius was hearing and understanding a standard note structure that allowed anyone who could read music to play and sing his 12-bar style.

Handy comprehended the unique style and role of what's called the *"blue"* note or slightly flattened seventh tone of the scale. The *"blue"* note gave Handy's expression the same magic conjured by black field hands' **Blues.** No one ever envisioned or imagined the sounds coming out of black people and their instruments, some they made, and others they just played, would produce music that would inspire the world. Performing frequently in Beale Street clubs, Handy and his band rose to real popularity in and around Memphis. Handy's music brought him to the attention of Robert R. Church, who hired his band as Church's Park Auditorium's orchestra.

For Beale Streeters, Handy's **Blues** was like hoodoo, because he took something that resided within black people's hearts, heads and minds but emerged from them as sounds and emotions. They knew it existed, but could not see or touch it, yet it moved people in such a way, it was a force that affected them with real power. *Making something out of nothing*, Handy's **Blues** on Beale Street was folk magic, and the spirituality of hoodoo blacks had relied on back in slavery. Handy created a whole new dimension of life for black people that offset their pain and degradation with the sounds that emanated from them. Those musical sounds, for people who'd known only suffering, provided entertainment and fun.

Again like hoodoo, the effect of his notation was, as if he cast a spell when he played. Handy drew black people into Church's Park Auditorium by the thousands. Standing room only crowds, allowed other businesses to benefit from Handy's magic.

Fortune continued smiling on Handy, as the election for mayor of Memphis arrived.

An aspiring young white politician, E. H. Crump, sought him out. Crump recognized Handy's popularity and what seemed magical drawing power; he brought him on board his campaign for mayor. Handy wrote a campaign jingle called *"Mr. Crump don't llow that Round Here,"* and it had black and white folks dancing and singing along every time he performed it. Crump became Mayor of Memphis, and the rest is history. Handy, on the other hand, reworked the tune into what many consider the first **Blues** song ever published— *"Memphis Blues."*

After its publication as sheet music, *"Memphis Blues"* became the first commercial success of a **Blues** song. Beale Street magic began to touch the world, once it flowed out of Handy's horn. A pioneering black bandleader, James Reese Europe, adapted the *"Memphis Blues"* to accompany the headline dance team of Vernon and Irene Castle. Inspired, dancing to Handy's arrangement, they invented the dance called the **Fox Trot**. They gave credit to Europe for their success. However, he deferred to Handy, saying, *"The* **Fox Trot** *was created by a young negro from Memphis, Tennessee, Mr. W.C. Handy."* Now, that was magic and how to *"make something out of nothing!!!!"*

After the turn of the 20th Century (1900), segregation, convict leasing, and sharecropping dominated black people living in and outside Memphis. However, black people in Memphis had something no other southern city had—"Boss" Crump, its Mayor. It may seem strange for a white man to reflect hope for former slaves, but it was not that "Boss" Crump, liked black people, he was the same as other "red neck" whites. Diverging, Crump saw a different way of using black people to gain and maintain power; and he was all about power.

Segregation made former slaves bare down to survive. Conditions in urban areas were different for blacks, but surviving wasn't a whole lot easier than for field workers. Having done both, I consider myself a pretty good judge of that. Living in the city was a different game. Although Memphis was an urban area, some of the most brutally vicious and truculent white men the plantations system in the Mississippi Delta produced populated the city. Every slave overseer in Arkansas, Mississippi, and West Tennessee that believed he could *"make niggers work"* came to Memphis, running from the poverty spawned by the Civil War and its aftermath, especially after the *Panic of 1893*. One of these refugees was E. H. Crump.

A sharecropper from Holly Springs, Mississippi, Edward Hull Crump (10-2-1874/10-16-1954), was not "Boss," when he arrived in town. He married well and used his wife's family's political connections to get into politics. He flipped the script, rather than keeping blacks from voting, Crump made sure blacks could vote, but only for him. Crump, in his way, made sure black had an area to let off steam on weekends—Beale Street—but he wanted it run his way.

E. H. "Boss" Crump and Robert R. Church, Sr. both were born in Holly Springs, Mississippi. He and Rev. Burl Lee, Jr. were born about the same decade. I make this point because being a white man made all the difference in the world for Crump compared to the other two men. Again, this reflects one of this narrative's themes; *one's circumstances, at birth, are very reliable indicators of success in life*, but not always. Sometime especially, back during segregation, skin color trumped everything.

During one of the worst recessions in United States history—*the Panic of 1893*—Crump arrived in Memphis at age 19. Finding work during this period was all but impossible for black people in Memphis, but Crump obtained a clerical position with Walter Goodman Cotton Company on "Cotton Row" in downtown Memphis. Crump's schooling—his level of education and training—was not mentioned, but at 19 from Mississippi, he couldn't have had much. His position on *"Cotton Row,"* allowed him to begin a successful business career, as a broker and trader of cotton. Segregation prevented a black man with a college degree, from even applying for that position.

A dirt poor white boy when he arrived in town, Crump's position on *"Cotton Row"* gave him access to the bounty of Memphis, as well as America. Barred from even attempting what Crump did, based solely on skin color, black people were not allowed in the building where Crump worked without permission. Crump married Bessie Byrd McLean, daughter of Robert McLean, vice president of the William R. Moore Dry Goods Company, the largest in Memphis. Crump's position put him in the center of deal makers on *"Cotton Row,"* home of the business elite that dominated the cotton industry. Wheeling and dealing among the cotton row crowd, Crump wrangled his way to becoming a delegate to the Tennessee Democratic State Convention in 1902 and 1904. Pulling that off was something a black man could not get in either political party.

Memphis had a Commission Government. The Commissioners ran for election but appointed most other government officials. Crump maneuvered to get an appointment to the municipal Board of Public Works (1905), and later, he was appointed Commissioner of Fire and Police in 1907. Yet to put his name on the ballot for anything, in just ten years, Crump was one step from Mayor of Memphis.

Crump built his political power like a typical big-city boss, similar to Luke Lea, head of the political machine in Nashville. He used all the familiar techniques—ballot manipulation, patronage for friends, and erecting bureaucratic obstacles to frustrate his opposition—on his way to gaining and maintaining control of Memphis politics. He also silenced or made sure dissenters had little or no voice. Crump built a complex alliance with established power figures at the local, state, and national levels.

Maneuvering as he became "Boss," he was Tennessee's leading supporter of Pres. Franklin D. Roosevelt and the *New Deal* (1933). He controlled political largess, coming to Memphis from federal or state government. The *New Deal* provided ample relief programs and jobs for the unemployed, during the *Great Depression*. These jobs, Crump's machine lieutenants filled. The city also got major federal building projects, which Crump gave to his cronies in the business community. Secondly, his circle included the modernizers: business-oriented progressives, who were mostly concerned with upgrading the city's waterfront, parks, highways, and building skyscrapers, as well as a moderately good school system, for white kids. Working-class whites got their share of jobs, but labor unions were of marginal influence.

Crump incorporated blacks in his outer circle, dispensing patronage in return for black votes. Memphis was one of the largest southern cities in which blacks could vote, but segregation was as rigid as any place. Unlike most Southern Democrats of his era, Crump was not opposed to blacks voting, as long as they voted his way. And, this was one reason blacks in Memphis became reliable Crump machine voters, it put them in the game.

Crump power in the black community had three levels, preachers, insurance and funnel homeowners. Then came thugs in the black community, follow by the police. "Boss" Crump power began with preachers/insurance/funnel homeowners; they controlled the business, professional, and intellectual class of blacks. They were the lieutenants that told blacks what to think and do. They also passed out jobs and assistance that came to the black community. Thugs/henchmen were enforcers in the black community. They kept everyone else in line. They rounded up black voters on election days to make sure they voted "right." They passed out whiskey, watermelon, and barbecue to celebrate the "Boss'" victory.

Thugs also handled bootlegging, gambling, and prostitution for the Crump machine. This operation had the impact of major industries, like Firestone, Plough, Inc., or the Ford Motor plant, on survival in some black communities. These operations were the economy in some neighborhoods. Although Crump preferred to working behind the scenes before and after serving only three two-year terms as Mayor of Memphis (1910–1915) early in his career, he was not popular in Nashville.

Segregation: Slavery Without Chains

The socioeconomic and political reality under which slave descendants developed was determined by where they were in the United States of America. Here we're not talking about the usual North/South dichotomy or state and city, but sections in the black communities. Segregation produced a kind of stratification that was part of whites' efforts to control black people's economic development.

The position of a black person reflected not only their status but their acceptance by whites. Stratification was physical, as well as psychological, based on an upper, middle, and lower-class mindset of blacks status expressed itself by the neighborhood in which slave descendants lived. Even more importantly, this reflected similar stratifications, as in the larger society, within classes and communities nationally.

This stratification had real implications and played out as everyday situations of life, no matter where one was in America. The thing that made Memphis different, was within these subdivisions, subtly individuals loomed large at particular points and during particular events. My point here is that from his entrance into Memphis politics E. H. "Boss" Crump worked to make the city "one big plantation." If one understands the plantation system, you know what it was like to live in Memphis. If not, you are exactly like blacks that lived under that system. So going forward readers' understanding of this fact—Memphis was a big plantation—will make it easier to keep the situation in perspective.

Segregation was designed to push or crowd black people together, into places across the tracks, on the backside of towns or in areas that had no value to white people. Segregation amounted to slavery without chains for descendants of American slavery. The idea was to make sure black people understood they had a place and not to get out of it. Their place was outside American society. Whites in government used *"separate but equal"* to provide only the barest minimum of what black people received.

Denying Freedmen resources, coming out of slavery, white people tethered them to poverty, using scarcity to promote desperation. Whites believed, without any real experience outside the plantation, after a few months, struggling on their own, trying to feed themselves, slaves would gladly come crawling back to the plantation, begging master to take them back, and some did. However, for the vast majority, once Reconstruction ended and newly freed slaves were not only surviving but thriving, whites designed segregation (1900) to lock them on the bottom in poverty.

Surviving the confusion of contraband life, freedmen learned a thing or two about what it took to build lives on their own. Rev. Lee's conversations about these times provided great insight.

"My daddy said, '*Seeing how Sarah wus always showin folk what she knowed bout thangs, I start showin de big boys and men dat looked lake dey want ta live, thangs I knowed bout scroungin and stayin alive. I member, master and overseers, showed us'ens what dey want till we'ens figure out hi ta do it. I tell'em, show folks what you knowed and try ta learn what folk knowed. So, I start tellin folks, show'em hi ta do what you'ens knowed and they will learn it. Dat way we'ens all knowed de same thangs. We'ens got to help one'tter, I tell'em. We'ens can make it together. Soon, dey start learnin dat freedom wus lack slavery, hard but we'ens learnt. Ta have somethin we'ens got to git it ourself.*'

Even though the chains came off, segregation kept most Freedmen's minds on lockdown. Having survived in Memphis through the contraband period, and the white power structure seemed happy with the result, they let black people have Beale Street. Crowding black people together fits their strategy of keeping them in one area, until they needed them. The one thing they had not counted on, in Memphis, was Robert R. Church, Sr. really caring about what happened to other black folks.

Headquartered on Beale Street, Church gave black people a benefactor that had saved not only Beale Street on several occasions, but the whole city as well. With Church's Park and Auditorium, he made Beale Street the anchor of African American culture. He was very active with civil rights, political, religious, and other community activities. Church's plan made it easy for blacks to do business with each other and stay out of white people's sight doing it.

However, the most important thing about Beale Street for black people's survival was the Solvent Saving Bank and Trust Company. Black people were able to hide the amount of money they made, and keep it circulating in the black community. Blacks were able to build wealth, right under white people's noses, without them knowing black people had two nickels to rub together.

I submit again, *the most reliable indicator of success throughout life is an individual circumstance at birth.* Robert Reed Church, Jr. and Burl Lee, Jr. were born after the end of the Civil War, and neither had been slaves. The second generation, but first-generation free, they reflect their fathers' legacies. Burl Lee, Jr. was not quiet in his teens when Robert, Jr. was born. Although neither was born a slave, freedom for Church began on a totally different level than my great-grandfather, Burl Lee, Jr.

Burl was born in Mississippi, and attended a Freedmen's Bureau school. He received the equivalent of a 6th-grade education, became a preacher with the CME Church. Following in the footprints of his father, Burl while making a family, dedicated his life to helping build his community.

Church, Jr., on the other hand, was born in Memphis (10-26-1885), at the family home. Beginning his education, he attended private schools. First, Mrs. Julia Hooks tutored him in kindergarten. Church attended parochial schools in

Memphis. He attended Morgan Park Military Academy, Morgan Park, Illinois. He earned a B.A. from Oberlin College in Ohio and received an M.B.A. from the Packard School of Business in New York City. Returning to Memphis, his father taught him the banking business, as his father taught him the steamboat business. Beginning his training, Robert Jr. started as a cashier at the Solvent Savings Bank and Trust Company (1906). He married Sara P. Johnson of Washington, D. C. (1911). *(A Colored Woman in a White World*, Mary C. Terrell, Amherst, NY: Humanity Books, 2006)

After the death of his father Robert R. Church, Sr. in 1912, young Robert took over the bank his father founded. He became an important businessman, politician, activist, and philanthropist in his own right. He managed and presided over the family's extensive real estate holdings and other family businesses, particularly, Church's Park and Auditorium on Beale Street.

Church's Park became the cultural center and local headquarters for civil rights, politics, and religious activities for African Americans. Beale was a street on which one could not inherit a place; they had to earn it. Similar to his father, after the 1866 riot and yellow fever epidemic (1878), young Robert used the Solvent Savings Bank and Trust Company to support black entrepreneurs and the community during the 1920s. Building a solid reputation, as a result of his education, Church, Jr. became an astute businessman. He dealt with white people on an equal footing, in most cases. I say, also, a family's tradition also indicates an offspring's possible mindset in life.

Robert Church, Jr.'s exemplified an aggressive leadership style, which is why whites saw former slaves, as such formidable competition. Church's stalwart support, innovative solutions, and business acumen enable Beale Street entrepreneurs to stay ahead of whites, trying to control their efforts. Memphis' white leaders responded with threats of violence when they could not counter Church's leadership. Beale Streeters came to feel he was the man to direct their progress.

Robert Church, Jr. continued his father's legacy of involvement in politics, as well. Also, he followed the tradition of political leaders of Beale Streeters, like Pastor Taylor Nightingale, who ran for a position on the Memphis Board of Education in 1886. Building his power base, Church Jr. founded the Lincoln League (1916). Through the Lincoln League, he worked to counter the segregationist policies of Woodrow Wilson and democrats in Memphis, mainly "Boss" Crump. Many Memphians consider Church, Jr. *"father of black political organization in Memphis."* He felt, *"The most effective ways for Negros to gain political, social, and economic equality was actively participating in the political process."*

The Lincoln League gain power through voter registration drives (registering over 10,000 voters, a large political base in 1916. It held voting schools, while paying poll taxes for black voters. The Lincoln League organized political campaigns, held fundraising drives, and fielded candidates for public office. The

League even ran the first Negro candidate for Congress. Such aggressive political tactics were unheard of in the 1920s and 30s. Although unsuccessful in most of those campaigns, Church and the Lincoln League created an organization that evenly expanded statewide.

Republican Party officials acknowledged Church's leadership by consulting him on federal patronage in the region, which made him a perennial delegate to the Republican National Conventions from 1912 to 1940. His Lincoln League provided the swing votes that propelled Republicans to victory in several Memphis and Shelby County elections. The rise of Pres. Franklin D. Roosevelt's New Deal, in the 1930s, began African American defections to the democrats.

Georgia On My Mind: Anti-Semitism Laid Bare

Three events that occurred in 1914/1915, although widely dispersed, were closely related in more than their temporal connection. Release of the film ***The Birth of a Nation*** (1914), the reorganization of the Ku Klux Klan (1915) with a new emphasis on violence against immigrants, Jews, and Catholics, and the lynching of Leo Frank (1915) was a prelude to one of the darkest times for justice in America for such groups.

During the early to mid-1900s, black writers characterized the period of the **"Dark Age"** *angry white men mob madness"* in America, as the most violent and murderous times for slavery's descendants in American. These three events reflected an open disregard for legal authority, justice, and life, if one was not white. The consensus among white was America was a nation for only white people, as the federal government indorsed white supremacy as its philosophical and psychological goal. America's political atmosphere was identical as today, except blacks were the only opposition.

During this period, "lynch mobs or lynch law" became the legal system for anyone whose death, whether black or white, served the purposes of white supremacy. These hate-filled years demonstrated how virulent, humiliating, and painful white people could make dying for a black person. Striped of all legal protection, by the US Supreme Court, blacks lived at the mercy of white people.

Life was a complete hell for blacks in the South, but worse for lynching victims. Lynchings became a spectator sport. Huge crowds with a craving for blood gathered to watch, while feeding their appetite for a black men's life. The lustful craving for black blood grew wildly among whites, like an epidemic. White men, women, and children flocked to participate or simply watch such grotesquely loathsome events.

Thousands of black people died without justice or mercy, during this period. A postcard industry, selling pictures showing the invidious cruelty of hanging, burning and mutilating a human body sprang up. James Allen's <u>*Without Sanctuary: Lynching Photography in America,*</u> exhibits many lynch scenes. Surreally, everything happened amidst a carnival atmosphere. America stood alone in the civilized world, as government, educational, business, and religious leaders endorsed and espoused lynch law to "protect white women." However, lynchings occurred on this level in no other industrialized nations.

Even though they had similar last names, Ann Frank and Leo Frank were not related; however, their deaths had similarities. Leo faced a similar environment in America in 1915, as Ann faced in Nazi Germany (1930s). True, their circumstances were vastly different, but the terroristic mob controlling society in America was similar for Leo, as Nazi Germany for Ann. Both terror events resulted from government's refusal to exercise power.

Leo, a factory superintendent, was convicted of murdering 13-year-old Mary Phagan, a worker at the National Pencil Company in Atlanta, Georgia (1913). Leo's trial and lynching (1915) attracted national and international attention. His murder was a social, political, and racial focus around the world regarding anti-Semitism.

Frank's attorneys sought commutation from Gov. John M. Slaton. Thomas E. Watson, a populist published of *The Jeffersonian*, stirred up lynching fever. He led a bitter campaign against Frank, a Jew. Watson increased his paper's sales, soliciting letters to the editor. The enormous number of responses made him a lynching superstar. Watson fueled public outrage daily, urged his readership toward mob violence. While Gov. Slaton reviewed the case, Watson's readership grew tremendously, pressuring Slaton to "let the courts' verdicts stand.

Slaton reviewed over 10,000 documents, before commuting Frank's sentence to life in prison. But Georgians wanted blood, not justice, and rioted throughout Atlanta. Slaton declared martial law and called out the National Guard. His term, as governor, ended a few days later; he and his wife left Georgia never to return.

A group of *"prominent citizens of Marietta, Georgia,"* appeared at the gate of Milledgeville prison farm and identified themselves as the Knights of Mary Phagan. Frank was given over and driven back to Marietta, where they lynched the next morning. Many Georgians denounced Leo Frank and Jews in general, for using their money to undermine justice in Georgia. Later, evidence proved Frank' was innocence!!!

Leo Frank and Ed Johnson, as well as many others were victims of a bloodlust culture that captured the minds and hearts of white people not only in Georgia but throughout America. Whites imbued with hatred and a desire to satisfy bloodlust, in mobs by the thousands, exacted vengeance, in defiance of legal authority. They nullified justice anytime verdicts were disliked, a if they waited that long. This attitude was preached and glorified from the bully pulpit of the White House by Pres. Woodrow Wilson.

This period (1880-1940s) created an atmosphere of terror for anyone or any group, white people disdained. America's leaders—politicians, preachers, and teachers—on all levels of society championed the culture of bloodlust, terror and murder. Many may ask, "How could such an outrageous and hideous mindset take control of such a peaceful, freedom, and justice-loving nation?" My great-grandfather said when I asked him, *"Such rot, starts at the top."* I say look at America today with Trump in charge.

The Spread of Bloodlust: Lynching a National Past Time

Lynching's bloodlust grew, as though lynch mobs were practicing one-upmanship. Lynchings became more vicious and larger, thousands of deliriously frenetic supporters flocked to shed black men's and woman's blood. Lynchings no longer occurred in the dead of night, isolated forest, or secluded swamp (1917). Lynchings became very public and publicized events. Memphis' exhilarating zeal for lynch law and shedding innocent blood mimicked the rest of America. Whites in Memphis were eager to lynch and observe the horrific events of a black man suffering and dying, as whites any place in America. Unlike the *People's Grocery Story* lynching (1892), only one black man died on May 22, 1917. The Memphis Commercial Appeal Newspapers announced Ell Persons' lynching days in advance. The gruesome spectacle was not a common garden variety lynching in the dead of night among friends. Dying, for a black man was entertainment for white people that attended lynchings, as though going on vacation.

Bloodlust drew whites from miles in all directions, if not to participate, simply to witness and celebrate the festive occasion. Lynchings were "happening events" and white men planned and found ways to create lynchings. Those that produced these appallingly hideous spectaculars claimed credit and build reputations for such mega-events. Producing these mega-events, which took place in plain view of the public brought promoter's glamour, similar to *"rock stars."* The murder of Ell Persons became the model for spectacle lynchings, which dominated these madding times.

Ell Persons' murder was the featured attraction for one of the most gruesome and diabolical demonstrations of **"Dark Age"** *angry white men mob madness*, as it swept through America from 1900 to 1950. An African American man, Persons, was accused of raping and murdering a 16-year-old white girl, Antoinette Rappel. She was found in woods near Macon Road, half a mile from Persons' home, a fifty-year-old woodcutter. Ax dents, at the scene of Rappel's bludgeoning connected Persons to the murder.

Mike Tate, Shelby County sheriff, ordered Persons to stand trial on May 25 4 days after the murder. On May 21, Persons was being transported by train to Memphis, after being held at the Tennessee State Prison in Nashville, awaitig arraignment and trial. Typically, the mob waylaid the train, adducting Persons. Reports said, *"David J. Mays,"* one of the lynching organizers howled with excitement, when he heard the mob had taken Persons from the train.

The Commercial Appeal's headline on the day of the lynching, May 22 read: *Mob captures slayer of the Rappel girl: Ell Persons to be lynched near murder scene; May resort to burning.*

The press reported the time and place of the lynching; 9.00 and 9.30 a.m. near the bridge at Wolf River. It also reported this will be first time a lynch mob operated in broad daylight and in plain view of the public without masks. The scene at Macon Road near the bridge was like a "holiday." According to one newspaper, *"many people waited at the spot raveling overnight,"* like a tailgate party for a football game.

Thousands of men, women, and children gathered; automobiles packed the road. The crowd estimated at over 5,000 created a *"fanatic and celebratory carnival-like"* atmosphere. Spectators bought soft drinks, sandwiches, whiskey, and beer. Women wore their best clothes, and parents excused children from school. One teacher said, *"50 boys were absent."* Some Shelby County schools didn't open, so school principals, teachers, and children could attend the lynching. Trucks of drinks sold out, sandwiches and beer were high, but whiskey flowed like water down Wolf River.

Orchestrated like another gruesomely perverse grade B horror film, where the supposed grief-stricken mother was not too distraught to attend the festivities and entered on cue to give a speech. Reading from "prepared" remarks: *"I want to thank all my friends who have worked so hard on my behalf ... Let the Negro suffer as my little girl suffered, only ten times worse."*

Bloodlust desires flowed through the crowd, mimicking the anticipation before a football game by home team fans at kickoff. After chaining Persons to a 10-foot high scaffold, mobsters doused him with a large quantity of gasoline. A roar went up as the flames, and smoke from Persons' body rose from the platform. Reports said Persons was *"calm and casual,"* emitting only a *"faint squeal,"* when set alight.

Mays said, *"I stood close to Persons head, in spite of the African odor and watched the whole performance."* While Persons burned, spectators tried to snatched pieces of souvenirs; clothes, rope and even body parts from the flames. A news story described the moment of the lighting: *"A crowd of some 5,000 men, women and children cheered gloatingly as the match was applied and a moment later the flames and smoke leaped high in the air and snuffed out the life of the black fiend."*

After burning Parsons alive, Mobsters decapitated and dismembered his remains. They scattered them around Memphis. The mob targeted African American communities, as places to display pieces of Persons remains to intimidate black people. One newspaper reported mobsters threw Persons head from a car at a group of African Americans on Beale Street.

Although a huge crowd, well over 5,000 whites, attended the lynching, amidst the carnival atmosphere, with community leaders prominently and personally visible, no one went to jail. Their faces were recognizable, clearly visible on photographs, but no arrest in connection with Persons' murder happened. Photographs of people that attended the lynching appeared in newspapers along with the story describing one of the most vicious in American history; nothing happened to any of the murderers.

The lynching and its aftermath prompted blacks led by Robert Church, Jr., to organize the Memphis chapter of the National Association for the Advancement of Colored People (NAACP), one of the first in the South. Robert R. Church, Jr., Bert M. Roddy, and other black businessmen, at a meeting on June 11, 1917, began the chapter with 53 members. Although they began with mostly businessmen and professionals, over the next few months, membership grew with the support of hundreds of ordinary people. Roddy was elected president of the branch, and Church became a member of the national board of directors. By 1919 (the 300th), the branch was the largest in the South.

The Beginning of an Anomaly

The ***"Dark Age"*** *angry white men mob madness* developed, like new technology—a way of doing something—but with an old methodology. Lynchings grew in magnitude, becoming more frequent with time. By 1920, lynchings moved from dark, isolated backwoods to very public viewings, in the heart of communities. Growing in complexity, with promoters, MCs, marketers, and support vendors, lynchings became MAGA-spectacles. Lynching was big business, drawing upwards of 10,000 white people, on many occasions. Motivated by hatred and bloodlust, historians never mentioned the economic benefits lynchings produced for some. This hidden aspect of the lynchings business was comparable to big sporting events or rock concerts today.

Americans and people around the world have no real idea of what this period was like for African Americans. Family stories or historical records do not convey the terror experienced by defenseless communities. Some people struggle to understand and explain the politics behind what happened in America during this period. Very few, if any, followed the money produced for publishers, magazines, newspapers, authors, and books to understand the phenomenon. One only needs to look at Donald Trump's rise and his time in the White House, especially raising money on the way out the door, for an understanding of my point.

The hidden aspect of the lynchings business, one only need look at publications, which earned advertising dollars promoting lynching. White men built MAGA-reputations as politicians, judges, reporters, photographers, and other public figures. Lynchings should be viewed, from the perspective of the "People's Grocery Story lynchings; a wealth-building enterprise. The number of lives loss did not matter; it was the wealth gained and the business generated that drove the bloodlust culture.

Most people believe there is no precedent or model for what is happening in American government today. They look at the rise of Donald Trump and white nationalism, and fail to understand the current nationalistic fervor and see it as totally out of character for America's leaders. They are upset and feel an alien philosophy, and psychology has gripped the nation, especially with America's history of free speech, tolerance, and democracy.

These white people see white nationalism as an anomaly. However, I say this happened before and is being orchestrated by the same class that created the last rise of white nationalism and bloodlust culture in America, that is what MAGA—*Make America Great Again*, really means. It is a repeat of what happened to bring Woodrow Wilson to the White House in 1912. This class had worked fifty years, creating the right conditions to maximize their desires to enshrine white supremacy in America and lock descendants of American slavery in a second-class status of poverty perpetually.

This narrative presented the previous discussion of lynching, as the prelude to discussing the full-blown period of racial terror of which Woodrow Wilson became the figurehead. He created the philosophical and psychological atmosphere of American terror and white supremacy. The goal was to subjugate black people in second-class status, using a mindset that took charge of America in 1912, like lynching, it began subtly.

Wilson laid the foundation for white supremacy and segregation, as he entering the White House. Few, if any, black people suspected Wilson's plan, similar to the one presently in power in America (2016). Some blacks voted for Woodrow Wilson, the same as some blacks support Trump today. The turn toward fascism is being led from the White House, as Woodrow Wilson led the drive toward white supremacy. Many rose to join his clarion call, which he claimed would save America and make it great.

Wilson made those that rallied around him feel comfortable expressing their hatred. They were encouraged to engage in revenge and bloodlust against those whose deaths served the purposes of white supremacy. Wilson made disparaging statements or undertook despicable actions from the White House. He demeaned black people but claimed people misunderstood his statements or took them out of context, while his statements were harmless thoughts, he said out loud. White Americans that became imbued with bloodlust excused his statements. Glorying in the murders of innocent people, like Sam Hose, Ed Johnson, Leo Franks, Ell Persons, and many others, lynchings were no longer anomalies.

Spectacular lynchings did not happen in some faraway Eastern European petite dictatorship, far eastern den of despotism, or even some banana republic dominated by a colonial master; it happened in America, the land of the free and the home of the brave. These God-fearing, righteous, flag-waving, and standing up for the national anthem Americans came to see lynching black men, as entertainment, like a big, big tailgate party. These Americans did not spring up out of nowhere, like phantoms in the night. Hooded red necks, plotting in dark and desolate marshes didn't instigated these horrific events.

The most powerful white American leaders in government, education, business, and religious communities championed and fully supported the **"Dark Age"** *angry white men mob madness*, the same as slavery. Woodrow Wilson from the White House led bloodlust and lynching as a national craving in the United States of America.

The Birth of a Nation

This section began the effort to explain how government made America a white nation. That efforts imbused America with the **"Dark Age"** *angry white men mob madness*, the major weapon for terrorizing black people, who were it target. Their aim was forcing descendants of American slavery to accept second class as white people demanded. Many Americans saw lynching, as an anomaly that sprang out of nowhere to ravish black people and sustained itself of its own volition, not as part of white American culture.

The previous discussion foreshadowed what 1912 would bring, once Woodrow Wilson moved into the White House. Wilson was a southern boy from Virginia, a state in the forefront, providing bodies for the internal slave trade, by breeding a black workforce. He was steeped in the myths of slavery and white supremacy—*the lost cause*. Selling slaves—exporting black bodies to the Deep South—was Virginia's number one domestic money crop. Wilson was a progeny of a family that sold slave, as a business. He did whatever he could to re-establish "the family business." He supported re-enslaving African Americans as a goal while in the White House and after he departed.

Another invention at the dawn of the 20th Century was not only similar in effect to the impact of the cotton gin on life in the South, but it changed the landscape of America, as well as the rest of the world. This invention changed communications, not only in the US, but around the world. It brought everything together for Wilson and his supporters. Only in its infancy in the 1890s, this world-changing invention was the motion picture machine. The motion picture machine made visual images the currency of political speech.

Although controversy surrounded the two men that invented it (1885)—American Thomas Edison or Frenchman Louis Lumiere—neither man realized the impact their invention would have, in my opinion. Motion picture production was only beginning to tweak Americans' psyche, as the 20th century peeped over the horizon. The motion picture machine gave those searching for ways to influence public opinion, an image-making machine that did the trick. The movie **The Birth of a Nation** began motion picture production's inexorable trek to becoming the most formidable weapon in the battle to control public opinion, especially the image of black people.

The Birth of a Nation had real-life implications for African Americans. Far more effective than Minstrelsy, **The Birth of a Nation** rekindled southern outrage over the outcome of the Civil War. Its images depicted black people as *"despicable wretches"* and *"an undeserving lot."* **The Birth of a Nation** produced whites rage, racist hatred, and outright viciousness against black Americans, especially among southerners.

The movie was designed to illicit strong resentment againstFreedmen exercising freedoms gained through emancipation, the Civil War (1865), the Civil Rights Bill of 1866, the 13th, 14th, and 15th Amendments. Contrarily, former slaves saw those events giving them a clearer vision of their future. **The Birth of A Nation** changed the socioeconomic and political landscape for former slaves and the vision of freedom, they envisioned walking away from plantations after emancipation.

Setting the edge for whites dedicated to driving former slaves and descendants back into conditions resembling bond slavery, D. W. Griffith turned back the clock. Producer and director of **The Birth of a Nation,** Griffith flipped the script on the South's disastrous gamble, going to war over slavery. Through **The Birth of a Nation,** with the motion picture camera, Griffith glorified whites' vision of slavery, particularly poor whites. Fully embracing the *"white man's burden,"* **The Birth of a Nation** was a romance of the splendid life southerners believed slavery gave them.

The South was eager to believe emancipation, the Civil Right Bill of 1866 and Reconstruction victimized them. Griffith's storyline made former slaves and Pres. Abraham Lincoln the bad guys in his absurd dramatization. The motion picture camera in Griffith hands allowed him to celebrate the defeated rebels, as the hero. Through the lens of the motion picture camera, he seeded his grotesque drama, with an elaborate role reversal of the KKK.

Anointing the Klan *"saviors of the South,"* Griffith used very positive and deceptive brush strokes, painting the KKK, as the only redeemers of the South, determined to avenge *Reconstruction*. He portrayed lynching, burning, torture, terror, and other inhumane sanctions against black people, as heroic acts, defending the glorious South. Continuing to extoll virtues of the KKK, as redeemers, Griffith gave cover to white men's allegation, lynching protected white women from black men. Portraying mob terror and bloodlust madness against black people, as an honorable undertaking and heroic acts of patriotism, proudly defending the South against blacks, Griffith justified the **"Dark Age"** *angry white men mob madness*.

Exploding off movie screens across America, **The Birth of a Nation** incited hostility and vengeance among white people, who blamed former slaves for their losses in economic power and social standing (*Panic of 1893*). It gave the *"big lie"* physical form, drawing whites into nickelodeons—movie theaters—like a siren's song. It portrayed black people as objects of scorn, hatred, and ridicule.

Embittered over the South loss of the Civil War, Griffith embedded themes that exemplified the *white man's burden* and *the lost cause of the Confederacy*, to make the Civil War a righteous fight to save the South's glorious way of life. Crafting a very unsympathetic image of slavery's descendants, Griffith projected them as an *"undeserving lot,"* and contemptable *"wretches,"* deserving only abhorrence. Although a complete fantasy, white people saw in **The Birth of a Nation** what they truly wanted to believe, like Minstrelsy. This completely fictionalized dramatization allowed whites to anesthetize their pain, while satiating their cherished belief in *"the lost cause of the Confederacy"* myth.

The novel, <u>THE CLANSMAN</u> by Thomas Dixon, a lifelong friend of President Woodrow Wilson, became *The Birth of a Nation*. Dixon and Wilson saw the events of the Civil War and Reconstruction identically. Both saw it through the eyes, emotions, and experiences of Southern whites, which they were. Dixon vehemently opposed educating former slaves. He fought desperately against political and social changes that Freedmen received at the end of Civil War. Dixon was all in, throughout his entire writing career, arguing for white supremacy and racial superiority of whites. His book, <u>THE CLANSMAN</u> became **The Birth of a Nation.**

Writing with Lightning: Birth of White Nationalism

If **The Birth of a Nation** had remained just a movie in theaters, its impact would have been far less and probably not became the instrument I described above. Moreover, Woodrow Wilson would not have used it as an organizing vision for whites. But it did not, so in this discussion, I show how and why it became a major tool for those hell-bent on re-enslaving Africa Americans.

Woodrow Wilson biographers, Ray S. Baker and William E. Dodd (eds.) in **The Public Papers of Woodrow Wilson,** described Wilson as follows, "*Wilson never presented his racist face to the world, but Pres. Woodrow Wilson's first act, after his election in 1912, began with segregating the US federal government*". Wilson justified his actions this way, **"Self-preservation [forced whites] to rid themselves, by fair means or foul, of the intolerable burden of governments sustained by the votes of ignorant Negroes."**

Wilson was from Virginia, a state that continued to deny black people education, even during Reconstruction. Consequently calling black voters ignorant was complimenting their handy work. Wilson talked as though he was not part of denying black children education as a politician. Virginia kept former slaves ignorant because slave masters, like Wilson, wanted them ignorant. The thing is, they never thought they would face them as voters, like Donald Trump.

Wilson's statement reflects his intent throughout his time in the White House. It reveals Wilson's racist attitude toward black people. It marks the point at which the US Government became an instrument for the darkest force in America. The **"Dark Age" angry white men mob madness** flourished because it was Wilson's instrument.

Wilson's political pitch was a curveball in the dirt to see what Americans would go for. The adage, **as the President leads, the nation follows,** truly exemplifies Woodrow Wilson's leadership, as Donald Trump's today. A member of the slave owning class, born in Staunton, Virginia, Wilson was a true son of Robert E. Lee. He personified leadership for aspiring southern politicians. Wilson publicly endorsed Jim Crow segregation and mob rule before and after entering the White House. He brought his very provincial views of black people into government, like an old suitcase he'd never unpacked, until entering the oval office.

Embracing the themes expressed in **The Birth of a Nation,** Wilson implemented his racist views through government policies and edits. He mandated segregation throughout the federal government. Wilson pushed thousands of black workers off federal jobs, particularly in the US postal service. Some had held their positions since the contraband period (1865 to 1880s).

Wilson spread segregation throughout the federal government, and denied black Americans access to America's socioeconomic and political benefits based solely on skin color. His policies prevented black workers from competing in America's free-market economy. He expanded *The Gilded Age* policies and formalized his discriminatory actions to blocked former slaves from getting "good-paying jobs" the US gave European immigrants, making discrimination official government policy.

Wilson's policies interrupted the progress descendants of American slavery made after emancipation. He didn't only reverse the result of emancipation, Civil War, the Civil Rights Act of 1866, 13th, 14th, and 15th Amendments; Wilson presided over segregation from the White House. He entrenched white supremacy, as a national policy. He doubled down, denying black people the slightest sense of humanity. Wilson inspired the use of coercion, intimidation, subjugation, suppression, and terror to force blacks acceptance of white supremacy and the second-class status demanded.

Wilson was a full partner with the US Supreme Court's use of **Plessy v. Ferguson,** making segregation and white supremacy fixtures in the lives of black people in America. Segregation placed every black American at the mercy of any and every white person they encountered. Exacerbating the problems black people faced, he enjoined the US Justice Department to fight attempts by former slaves to gain access to courts, as they tried to fight segregation.

As Commander-in-Chief, Woodrow Wilson's career is tethered clearly to the movie **The Birth of A Nation,** more so than to WWI. Wilson was so overcome by the film, after his first viewing, he said, *"It is like writing with lightning, and my only regret is that it is all so terribly true."* A disingenuous platitude, Wilson's fascination with **The Birth of a Nation,** was so empowering, he screened it in the White House over thirty times. He invited his staff, cabinet, Supreme Court judges, Members of Congress, business leaders, captains of industry, clergy, and press to his White House soirées to view the film. Donald Trump adopted Wilson's tactic but use Camp David for his confabs, rather than the White House like Wilson.

Black writers saw Wilson's soirées as focus groups, where he raved and extolled the truth he swore **The Birth of A Nation** told. Biting on Wilson's curveball in the dirt, White House guest went after his spitball every time he threw it. Attendees at his White House soirées went abroad singing his song of white supremacy and segregation to America, like the national anthem.

East St. Louis: Foreshadowing Red Summer

"Writing with lightning" was an amazing statement by Pres. Woodrow Wilson, supposedly an educated man. Viewing **The Birth of A Nation,** the first time, Wilson accepted lies in the face of the truth his education should have taught him. Denial of truth was a major characteristic of the **"Dark Age"** in Europe in the 5th to 12th Centuries. Embracing **"Dark Age"** *angry white men mob madness* in America, "intellectuals," rejected known and accepted knowledge, enticing thousands of highly educated white Americans bit on Wilson's spitball, as Donald Trump today with COVID-19.

Wholeheartedly, they embraced lies and fantasies, rejecting facts. They went after Wilson spitball—**The Birth of A Nation**—and set everything in motion, like a shot from a starters' pistol to begin a race. Wilson made lies, the philosophy, and the psychology of America. **The Birth of A Nation,** which premiered in 1915, brought everything together into a unified vision of blacks in America.

Wilson began pointing his finger at black people, as the source of all of America's problems. During his speeches, he insinuated white workers need to press the point with their employers; *Negros are taking good jobs away from white Americans who needed them more than blacks.* Putting that statement in context, this was the time when America was bringing millions of European immigrants to America to fill jobs; American employers would not allow blacks to fill.

Many black writers believed the following events were a test case to gauge how the public would respond to Wilson and the federal government when faced with wholesale rioting and burning of black communities. For many Americans, the labor/race riot in East St. Louis, Illinois, raised a red flag of real concern about the role the government, during and following this tragedy. The federal government did not act with a sense of urgency; neither did it assist black victims, nor did the murder and mayhem prompt an investigation into its causes. There was no hue and cry that went up to punish culprits, other than from black people.

East St. Louis, Illinois, is an industrial city on the east bank of the Mississippi River across from St. Louis, Missouri. It became embroiled in labor unrest in 1915. Southern black workers began arriving, as labor recruiters filled jobs replacing European immigrants no longer able to travel to the US. Fighting raged in Europe and at sea during WWI (1914-1918), which created labor shortages in the US. The labor crunch forced labor recruiters to go into the South, looking for black workers. White workers resented the presence of blacks on jobs next to them.

The labor problem originated during the economic boom times of the *"Gilded Age."* The federal government brought millions of European immigrants to the US, as industrial workers, rather than allowing black workers to fill those jobs. War prevented Europeans from coming to America to fill the growing need for workers in the war economy. Blacks were the only workers available to fill jobs, when Europeans couldn't travel, with fighting at sea. Even though this was the case, American leaders continued Wilson's labor policy, refused to give Freedmen those jobs.

The Central Labor Council in East St. Louis requested the State Council on Defense investigate their complaint that *"southern Negroes had been misled by false advertisements and unscrupulous employment agents that recruited them to come to East St. Louis".* They insisted' *"This was done to take white men jobs,"* even though there were lots of vacancies. They claimed, as Wilson advised, *"black men had been recruited under false pretenses, promising blacks would get 'good-paying jobs' and decent living quarters."*

Even if mislead by such claims, whatever black workers got in East St. Louis was far better than their lot sharecropping in the South. Even more important to southern blacks, labor recruiters had gotten them out of the South, at their expense and put them on a job, no matter the circumstances. Following a meeting on May 28, 1917, some 3,000 white men marched into downtown East St. Louis, and for all the world knew they could have been an army unit the way they attacked African Americans.

These mobs destroyed buildings and beat black people on the street. The governor called in the National Guard to prevent further rioting. Following the May disorders, tensions continued smothering, as white workers remained resentful of black workers. White workers' anger grew because of the increasing numbers of blacks that came to town, encroached on their spaces—living, eating, and entertainment places.

On July 2, a car occupied by white males drove through a black area of the city and fired several shots from their car, at a group of black workers. Police would not investigate or attempt to apprehend culprits. Later, as tempers frayed in the black community, another car, containing four white people, drove through the same area. Black residents opened fire on the car. They were unsure of the intent of those in the car or whether black residents were under attack again. The shots into the car, killing one officer and wounded another mortally, neither was in uniform.

Later that day, thousands of whites stormed the black section of town shooting and looting. They torched buildings, and when fire trucks arrived, the white mob cut water hoses, allowing entire sections of the city to burn. Mobsters shot inhabitants, trying to escape flaming buildings. Rioters chanted, *"Southern Niggers deserved a genuine lynching,"* and actually lynched several blacks in plain view of police and firemen. Once the National Guard arrived, they joined the mobs.

After the riot, the *St. Louis Argus* newspaper said, *"The entire country has been aroused to a sense of shame and pity by the magnitude of the national disgrace enacted by the blood-thirsty rioters in East St. Louis Monday, July 2."* According to the *St. Louis Post-Dispatch*, *"All impartial witnesses agree that police were either indifferent or encouraged the barbarities, and that the major part of the National Guard were the same. No organized effort was made to protect black citizens or disperse the murdering groups. The lack of frenzy or a large infuriated mob made the task of stopping the riot easy. Ten determined officers could have prevented most of the outrages. One hundred men acting with authority and vigor might have prevented any outrage."* This opinion came from the St. Louis Post-Dispatch.

Black writers and newspapers called it the **East St. Louis Massacres**. The death toll of black people was unclear and over $400,000 in property damage occurred. After the riots, there were varying estimates of the death toll. The police chief estimated that 100 African Americans died. The renowned journalist Ida B. Wells reported in *The Chicago Defender* said deaths were over 350 African Americans, while NAACP estimated deaths toll was 500. Six thousand African Americans were left homeless after the burning, and at least that many were injured.

The riot in **East St. Louis** was another curveball in the dirt, a test case for Woodrow Wilson to gauge the attitude of white Americans, in general, regarding the treatment of black Americans. That riot showed working-class white men enthusiastically attack black people without mercy, lynching an untold number, as the riot unfolded. Considered the worst labor-related violence and among the worst race riots in 20th-century American history, while most white newspapers did more to justify the riotous behavior of white men than condemning their burning of black communities and killing innocent people.

In New York City, on July 28, amidst a record heatwave on July 28, African American held a silent protest estimated at 10,000 to 15,000 marched against lynchings in Memphis, Waco, Texas, and especially East St. Louis. Black people marched down Fifth Avenue in a Silent Parade. The NAACP and groups in Harlem organized the march. Women and children were dressed in white, while men dressed in black; they carried signs highlighting their outrage over those riots.

Prelude to Red Summer: The First Red Scare

The work of three men—D. W. Griffith's ***The Birth of A Nation***, Thomas Dixon's ***The Clansman*** and Pres. Woodrow Wilson framed the period 1890-1950. These three men—Griffith, Dixon, and Wilson—more than any other Americans, bare responsible for the deaths and destruction in East St. Louis, and even more for those that occurred in 1919. Wilson established Jim Crow segregation—white supremacy—as the underlying philosophical and psychological premise of government in America.

Wilson boldly took the US where no President had gone before. He used the images and scenes in ***The Birth of A Nation,*** like incantations, casting his evil spill of racism over America. Most black historians view Wilson as the first openly racist President to occupy the White House. As part of this trio, Griffith not only reflected Dixon's storyline; he used the very words of his friend, President Woodrow Wilson, for emphasis. A silent movie, Griffith used prose from Pres. Wilson's book ***A History of the American People***, as title cards to introduce scenes related to Reconstruction.

The ***Red Scare of 1917*** and ***Red Summer of 1919,*** although separated by two years, both are intimately related. I was ignorant of both before researching ***The Birth of A Nation***. Researching the ***Red Scare of 1917*** showed the Russian Revolution became part of ***"The Red Scare" of 1917***. The federal government, under Wilson, viewed union workers as communists, especially the International Workers of the World (IWW). Having brought European immigrants to America, during *"The Gilded Age,"* America imported a different kind of worker. These workers were more anti-management and anti-capitalistic than Americans, white or black. Ardently anti-communist, the Wilson administration created the ***"The Red Scare"*** of 1917 to deal with what it described as the *"communist threat."* Viewing left-wing radicals as subversives, Wilson and US Attorney General, A. Mitchell Palmer, claimed the IWW was fermenting discontent and dissent among American workers.

Woodrow Wilson made union activists a target of the federal government. Secondly, those in the White House presented the Russian Revolution, which took place during WWI, as the wellspring of communism. Also, Wilson saw the Russians, after their revolution, as trying to spread communism around the world, as America was pushing so-called democracy. Wilson also claimed Russian Communists were the source of a plot to take over America. Finally, those fighting the Russian Revolution loyal to Tzar, ruler of Russia, were called "white" Russians. Those fighting to overthrow Tzar were communist— Bolsheviks— were called "red" Russians. Hence, the Bolsheviks were ***"Reds."***

I thought ***"Red Summer,"*** was like the East St. Louis riot, in which hundreds of black people die. So, ***"Red,"*** I thought indicated the blood black people shed and the deaths that resulted, during the East St. Louis riots. Further research showed not only was I absolutely wrong about *"Red,"* I was totally ignorant of the entire affair. So, understanding the critical importance of the three events—the Russian Revolution (1917-1918), the **Red Scare of 1917** and **Red Summer of 1919**—helped me understand how Wilson established white supremacy in America.

First, Pres. Wilson stirred up anti-Bolshevik sentiments among whites Americans (1917) to make black Americans a hated group. The KKK and ***The Birth of A Nation*** became keys to Wilson's plan. He painted blacks' demands for social change—equality, justice in courts, and an end to racial terror—as part of the communist plot to take over America.

Wilson ordered the US Justice Department to round up *"the Reds." "Red baiting"* became the job of J. Edgar Hoover, who was beginning his 60 years of service in government. Setting black people up, as **Reds**, Wilson scapegoated black people by telling newspapers, **"The American Negro returning from abroad (WW I) would be our greatest medium in conveying "Bolshevism" to America,"** (*Young J. Edgar Hoover, The Red Scare and the Assault on Civil Liberties*, Kenneth D. Acherman (2007).

Wilson identified black Americans as a threat to the nation. Without offering any evidence or allowing African Americans to respond, his statements made white people feel threatened by black people's demands for equality and justice. Wilson gave a free hand to those working to re-enslave black people, which was his real aim. Again, the adage, **As the President leads, the nation follows,** was truly reflective of Woodrow Wilson's impact on black people.

Following his statement, **"The American Negro returning from abroad (WW I) would be our greatest medium in conveying "Bolshevism" to America,"** Wilson made black Americans a hated group, helping the *"Red"* take over America. Wilson ordered Attorney General Palmer to *"rounded up the Reds"* to save America from the enemy within. Calling black communities, *"havens of the Reds,"* Wilson painted bull's eyes on them, as part of his plot to *"round up the Red."*

Talking to the press, he continued, not only scapegoating African Americans but made them the target of government surveillance and harassment. Wilson insinuated black people were *"Reds."* He made it seem they were allies in the communist plot by calling them *"tools of the Red."* He pointed to their support for rent strikes in Harlem, in which other groups also participated along with communists. This was the time Jacob Riis with his book *How the Other Half Lives"* was exposing the robber barons of New York tenements, which many groups were protesting.

Pres. Wilson created an atmosphere of alarm anytime African Americans advocated social changes—racial equality, labor rights, voting rights, and the rights of self-defense for black that fought white mobs attacks. Civil rights demands by black Americans were labeled *"plots to aid communists to overthrow America's capitalistic system"* (<u>Racism in the Nation's Service: Government Workers and the Color Line in Woodrow Wilson's America</u>, Eric S. Yellin; UNC Press 2013).

Continuing to scapegoat black people, Wilson fanned rumors he started that *"there was an imminent attempt to overthrow the US government by the communist"* and *"Communists are supporting Negro demands."* Talking to the press, Wilson said, *"The colored people are being helped by communist groups, the Bolshevik, while the federal government is under threat from the Red."* Wilson insisted that *"black Americans want to create a regime like the Soviets."* His statements were repeated by politicians and government officials, together with much of the press and whites on the street. Wilson projected black Americans as the enemy of America, even though they were the ones being attack.

Engineering Red Summer: The Face of Racism in America

The statement that Woodrow Wilson, the President of the United States of America, engineered **Red Summer** is probably very hard for most Americans to believe about any American President; that is before Donald Trump. I accept their skepticism, but I address such doubters next. Supporting my proposition requires a lengthier historical discussion than I desire; nevertheless, I will digress and began with my great grandfather's very far away view (in Mississippi) of the President. I remember his statement about Wilson when I asked him about the worst times for him and Mama Laura? It took a few tugs and strokes of his beard, standing and walking a few steps, before turning and saying,

"I think the election of Woodrow Wilson, as President, changed everything for colored folks. He took back all the freedom everybody thought they had. For a lot of folks, it was like they got put back in slavery, if you lived on the wrong white man's land. Then the paddy rollers were hard; they were on the roads to lock you up iffin you were out after dark without a pass. I was too old to go to war, besides me and Laura had four young'uns. Your grandmamma, Ada was just trying to set up house. Everybody member them bad times! The war got lots of black men and their families out the South. White folks couldn't stop black boys going to the army. And, once a labor agent signed you up, as a hand, for a company that made stuff for the war, they had to let you go. Sometimes there was a whole train loaded of colored boys headed north to work. White folks didn't like that neither, but they couldn't do nothing bout it. A lot of them boys, once they got out of the South, never came back. If they didn't send for they family, they never saw them for years, iffin at all."

WW I was an unforeseen adjustment that interfered with Wilson's real plan to make black people scapegoats for white supremacy, according to his biographies. WWI was more of a hindrance and distraction than an obstacle. Wilson was not excited about the war in Europe. It was not part of his plan and not the war he wanted to fight. Preventing immigrants from coming to America, the war overseas made it very dangerous, traveling on the high seas for Europeans, with German U-boats sinking anything afloat. This created labor shortages in industrial cities of the North and Midwest (East St. Louis is a prime example).

Another unforeseen situation was black Americans demanded they be among those going to fight in Europe hindered Wilson's plans of scapegoating African Americans. The Espionage Act (1917) and the Alien and Sedition Act (1918), made critics of the war effort or anything Wilson did subject to fines and jail time. Also, with northern factories needing another source of cheap labor, and the army needed men, for more than fighting—cooks, orderlies, trench diggers, men for loading and unloading ships, and so forth. These were jobs most blacks did in the military, during those times.

Black men going off to fight in Europe put Wilson's real plans on hold. However, fighting in France gave black boys a chance to show white folks in Europe, something other than the racist propaganda American newspapers offered. Plus, they introduced Europeans to *JAZZ*. Even though whites remembered the Civil War, they did not remember black men as fighters. Thousands volunteered, and exalted the army 10% quota for black men, which was usually filled the first week at most draft board calls.

America had an Expeditionary Force that fought under French Commanders, during WWI. Several black units showed conspicuous gallantry, and the French decorated these black units for heroism. Frenchmen nicknamed these US Army units with monikers like Black Rattlers, Men of Bronze, and Harlem Hellfighters. The fighting 369th, "Hellfighters," spent 191 days in frontline trenches, sustaining 1,400, casualties, tops among American unit.

All eyes turned toward the South as America's need for men became acute. Desperate for laborers in factories, stockyards, and mills, as well as soldiers for the battlefield, the country's demand for men for WWI, like emancipation, brought unintended social changes and other consequences to Dixie. WWI was the beginning of the greatest movement of black Americans from the South ever. Black men answered the call for workers in northern industries and viewed it as their chance to escape sharecropping and violence in the South. Their mass exodus became known as the *Great Migration* (1912 through 1960).

WWI opened the floodgates, washing blacks out of the South and into Northern cities, like a tsunami. Already desperately trying to escape hard times, those who dared took their chances on the road. Trying to make their way northward and into cities in the Mid-West and up along the eastern seaboard was like a jailbreak, as blacks escaped northward. Black workers replaced white workers that became soldiers or those no longer able to travel to the US from Europe. Over a million African Americans made their getaway (1910-1920) north. They dared to dodge white games of paddy rollers patrolling roads, bus and train stations, trying to keep black families down on the farm.

Leaving behind lynching, Jim Crow laws, lack of protected franchise, and the poor economy of the rural South, blacks escaped just ahead of the boll weevil devastation (cotton farmers in Mississippi lost 75 percent of their crops beginning 1908 to the boll weevil), as well as vicious white people. By 1919 large areas in the North—Harlem in New York City, Cleveland, Chicago, Philadelphia, Washington D. C. and Detroit, among others—became cultural centers for black Americans. (*World War I in U.S. Popular Culture*: Hana Layson and Patricia Scanlan).

The end of WWI brought rapid demobilization of veterans' black and white of WW I. Their discharge put a large number of unemployed men back in the job market. Such a large number of unemployed men dumped back on a job market unprepared to receive them, created hard economic times for veterans.

Competition for jobs increased resentment against black workers among working-class whites, immigrants, and first-generation white-Americans. These were the people who flocked to the polls to re-elect Woodrow Wilson (1916), basically due to WWI.

Social conditions in America resembled a pressure cooker. A volatile mixture of competing economic interests and social needs combined with the sentiments conveyed by **The Birth of a Nation**, **Red Scare 1917**, few economic opportunities and competition for jobs from more mobile blacks, started this pot of white hostilities and resentment against black people started this kittle boiling, ("*The Negro Holocaust: Lynching and Race Riots in the United States, 1880–1950,*" Robert A. Gibson, New Haven: Yale University, 1979.)

Wilson's **Birth of a Nation** rhetoric was like a poker, stoking coals beneath the caldron of white anger, resentment and desires to retaliate, as well as express their rage and hatred for blacks. This pressure cooker began boiling, as Wilson continued spewing his **Birth of a Nation** fiery rhetoric, during his White House soirées. Similar to a fuse in a powder keg, Wilson's strident **Red Scare** rhetoric turned the smothering pot of socioeconomic fears and racial tensions into a bomb. Igniting in early 1919, as rioting exploded, blowing the lid off America, with African Americans in the crosshairs. This tinderbox of resentment, anger, and desire for revenge against blacks, because white people believed they were responsible for their loss of socioeconomic power, igniting the **Red Summer of 1919** across America.

Many writers believe the image Wilson projected from the White House encouraged lawlessness and mob rule across America. According to the noted writer James Weldon Johnson (6/17/1871—6/26/1938), "**Red Summer** *ushered in the greatest period of interracial violence the nation had ever witnessed.*" During the summer and early autumn of 1919, white mobs attacked black communities across America with military precision. These military-style attacks swept the nation, occurring in more than fifty cities over the following months. Other writers from this period, Cameron McWhirter, David Kruger, Ida B. Wells, and many others, published statements to the effect that "*Wilson fed the racial hatred among whites for blacks, than any individual, as the leader of that period. Wilson openly pushed racism, publicizing the movie* **The Birth of a Nation.** *Making statements in the press, he unleashed a wave of terror upon black people, the likes of which blacks or the world had never seen.*"

Many researchers—Claude McKay, Zora Neale Hurston, Wallace Thurman, Amaud Jamaul Johnson among them—did not see **Red Summer** as a series of spontaneous, sporadic and isolated emotional explosions of outraged whites. Instead, they saw armed attacks on black communities, as the plan hatch by Wilson at his **The Birth of a Nation** White House soirées.

Attacking the Reds

The year 1919 was the 300th year since the ***Trans-Atlantic Slave Trade*** began bringing enslaved African to North America, and that year would prove to be the most destructive and deadly period ever in American history, for descendants of that mournful journey. After the ***East St. Louis Massacres*** (1917), Pres. Woodrow Wilson spent his time scapegoating and blaming descendants of slavery for everything bad that happened to white people, going back to emancipation (1863). Beginning 1919, fear, dread, and trepidation gripped black Americans, as news stories gave vent to all the blame Wilson heaped on black people. Their dread became a reality, as black communities large and small, suffered unbelievable terror and mayhem.

All over America, black communities became bull's eye, as lynch mobs targeted prosperous urban areas, with East St Louis kind of lynchings. Call the ***"Red Summer of 1919"*** by black Americans because white rioters stretched whole communities upon gallows. My aim in this section is to show what happened to real people, not caricatures in ***The Birth of a Nation*** and Woodrow Wilson, made them and their communities' victims of a pogrom. These were simple, honest, hardworking, mostly poorly educated men, women, and children, who were only trying to keep families together and build strong communities when tragedy struck out of nowhere. The previous section described the environment black Americans woke up each day and lay down with each night. Prayers invoked by such earthy people were to be let alone!

The atmosphere in the US for black people turned caustic and deadly by mid-1919. Dr. George E. Haynes, an educator, and director of Negro Economics for the US Department of Labor, described this atmosphere. *"The return of the Negro soldier to civil life is one of the most delicate and difficult questions confronting the Nation, north and south."* Dr. Haynes reported to the US Senate Committee of the Judiciary on ***Red Summer.*** He identified 38 separate riots, where whites attacked blacks in widely scattered cities:

"Lynching is a major problem within the United States. Between January 1 and September 14, 1919, white mobs lynched at least forty-three Negros, with sixteen hangings, eight burned at the stake and others shot. States have shown themselves, unable or unwilling to put a stop to lynching, and seldom prosecuted the murderers. The fact that white men have been lynched in the North as well, demonstrate the national nature of the overall problem. It is idle to suppose that murder can be confined to one section of the country or to one race."

With the end of WWI, former slaves and descendants had built on their prosperity, since emancipation. Simultaneously, the actual scheme many believe Woodrow Wilson hatched, during his White House screenings of ***Birth of A***

Nation, unfolded, like a dress rehearsal in Charleston, South Carolina on May 10, 1919. Reminiscent of the day the first shots was fired at Fort Sumter to begin Civil War (12-18-1861), **Red Summer** exploded across America. The fear of riots, which had been building, during the first part of the year, became a reality for African Americans. Erupting without warning, the riotous period that followed, sent black people running for their lives, in large cities and small towns, all over America.

Newspapers gave lynching extensive coverage during the attacks throughout **Red Summer.** They did not condemn the outrages, the same as with lynching; they were cheerleaders. No major white publication condemned the attacks. Most praised the mobs. White historians wrote as though mob rule was justified. Faulting black people's demands for "equality and justice," unlike the present, where reports conflate **"Black Lives Matter"** protest with "violence and destruction," newspapers justified white attacks. Cynically, news stories said, "*White people were fearful, uncomfortable or outraged, at demands for social change and justice in America's courts, may have overreacted, but with good reason.*"

Wilson's motivation, as a politician was the *"lost cause"* myth of the South. A true son of the Confederacy, Wilson's policies reversed Civil War gains made by former slaves. Symbolically, Charleston, South Carolina's riot (5-5-1919), in the same place where the first Civil War began, made **Red Summer** seem a "Civil War" reenactment. This time the South would not lose, similar to Abraham Lincoln to the North, because a "native son" held White House.

Rioting began when Four US Navy sailors and one civilian attacked and killed three black men, Isaac Doctor, William Brown, and James Talbot. They led a mob through the black community, attacking and burning stores, homes, and other buildings. The fact that it began without provocation and no legal authorities did anything to stop the mob is totally unbelievable, unless the authorities were the mob. US Navy investigators established the previous facts. However, neither the Navy nor civilian authorities did anything to stop the mayhem and murder or apprehend, arrested and prosecuted culprits, is even more unbelievable (*Encyclopedia of American Race Riots: Greenwood Milestones in African American History,* Vol. 1, Walter C. Rucker and James Nathaniel Upton: 2007 Westport).

Spreading like wildfire, a riot in Washington, D.C. (July 19 to 23) grabbed headlines across America. Newspapers documented that *"White men, many in military uniforms and in the shadow of the White House, went on a four-day rampage of mob violence."* Newspapers said, *"Whites became enraged over 'rumors' a black man 'raped a white woman.' Military personnel randomly attacked black people and destroyed property in black sections of town,"* (*Race Riots & Resistance: The Red Summer of 1919:* Jan Voogd, (New York: Peter Lang, 2008).

Washington D.C. police ignored cries for help from blacks while joining mobs. Pres. Wilson acted the same as he did during the East St. Louis riot. He did not order intervention by federal troops or police. Black veterans of WWI, along with other black men, fought mobs, providing the only protection. The violence ended with 15 dead, ten whites and five blacks. The rampage destroyed over a million dollars in property in black communities.

Pleading for protection for black citizens from white mobs, the NAACP sent Pres. Woodrow Wilson a telegram:

"...the shame put upon the country by the mobs, including United States soldiers, sailors, and marines, which have assaulted innocent and unoffending Negroes in the national capital. Men in uniform have attacked Negroes on the streets and pulled them from streetcars to beat them. Crowds are reported ...to have directed attacks against any passing Negro....The effect of such riots in the national capital upon race antagonism will be to increase bitterness and danger of outbreaks elsewhere. The National Association for the Advancement of Colored People calls upon you as President and Command-in-Chief of the Armed Forces of the United States of America to make statements condemning mob violence and to enforce such military law as situations demand."

Putting the magnitude of **Red Summer's** violence in perspective, by July, several other major riots occurred in—Bisbee, AZ, Longview, TX, Norfolk, VA, and other small towns in the US. Again, Wilson did not do or say anything to stop attacks, (http://en.wikipedia.org/wiki/Red_Summer_(1919) - cite_note-young-14). Eight days after Washington DC, and even more notorious riot struck Chicago, Illinois (July 27).

Chicago's beaches, on the north side of Lake Michigan, were segregated. A black youth swimming there drowned when whites attacked him with stones. Chicago's police refused to act against the rock throwers. Enraged at blacks' demanding justice, white mobs and Irish gangs began attacking black neighborhoods without provocation. Fighting across the city raged for thirteen days. White mobs violence caused 250 deaths and destroyed hundreds of black homes, as well as businesses on Chicago's South Side. Destructive mobs left several thousand black families homeless, while 537 were injuries.

The Northeastern Federation of Colored Women's Clubs, during their annual convention, denounced the burning of homes and murder of Negros. They urged Pres. Wilson, in a plea, *"...to use every means within your power to stop the rioting in Chicago, and the propaganda used to incite such."* Following in August, the NAACP protested to Pres. Wilson again, *"How long, the Federal Government under your administration intends to tolerate anarchy in the United States?"* Wilson sat in the Oval Office, refusing to stop the violence or apprehend killers. It wasn't that Wilson didn't provide leadership; he was the leader. Wilson was in charge of the mobs and was using lawlessness to rule the nation.

Even Omaha, Nebraska serves as another deplorable example of **Red Summer.** A mob of 10,000 white people attacked and burned the county courthouse to get Will Brown, a black man "suspected" of "raping a white woman." The mob hanged him and burned his body. Mobsters fought over Brown's remains, before attacking black areas of Omaha. They burned stores, homes, and murdered black residences.

If these attacks were spontaneous occurrences, as newspapers claimed, imagine the terror that seized black people when such a mob suddenly descended upon their community. Amidst screaming, burning, raping, and killing, frantic, helpless residents took refuge in schools and churches praying for deliverance and safety. Women, children, elderly, sick and infirm, fled for their lives, looking for shelter, but found no refuge, as buildings were burned down upon them.

Again, no one went to jail. No compensation for victims of mob violence ever came up. Black people did not receive consideration from authorities, and they did not answer complaints. No court opened its doors to victims. Although pleas went out, Wilson didn't act, for one reason and one reason only, these were black people, the object of **Red Summer.**

Finally, the dreadful scene in Elaine, Phillips County, Arkansas (9-30-/2-1919) was by far the most brutal and tragic incident of **Red Summer's** madness. After the Supreme Court signaled with **Plessy v. Ferguson** it would not entertain complaints from blacks and Wilson implementing both segregation and white supremacy, white people were free to display their raw hatred and political power, like a reenactment of ***The Birth of A Nation.*** The Supreme Court's ***Plessy v. Ferguson*** ruling, creating a time in America when there was absolutely no respect for law and justice regarding black people in America.

Local blacks in Elaine were trying to organize a sharecropper's union. They met with the Progressive Farmers and Household Union of America at a church in Hoop Spur, a small community in Phillips County, Arkansas. They gathered because black sharecroppers in the Elaine area wanted better payments (shares) for their crops from white plantation owners. White owners used segregation to dominate black sharecroppers. White landowners refused to accept black sharecroppers, right to demand agreed upon payments, and they could not get into court against landowners, because of the Supreme Court ruling.

Local whites claimed sharecroppers were socialists, **Reds,** plotting to kill whites and overthrow the government. A mob surrounded the church, declaring they were *"Going coon hunting?"* Gunfire erupted from the white mob of over a 1,000-armed men that came from surrounding counties and as far away as Mississippi and Tennessee.

They killed blacks, ransacked and burned homes. This is the type of reaction Donald is "dog whistling" white nationalists for today with his re-election appeal. Word spread throughout African American communities, some blacks fled, while others armed themselves in defense. When the authorities intervened, they went about disarming and arrested blacks, who fought back.

U.S. Army arrived (10-2-1920), and the mobs disperse. Federal troops rounded up and placed several hundred blacks in temporary stockades, where they were tortured and beaten. No blacks were released unless their white employers vouched for them. There was also considerable evidence that many soldiers sent to quell violence engaged in systematic killings of black residents.

In the end, 122 blacks but no whites were charged by the Phillips County grand jury with crimes related to the riots. Blacks farmers went before all-white juries and all were convicted, and 12 received the death penalty. The U.S. Supreme Court, on appeals, overturned their convictions. The state of Arkansas showed no concern for the deaths of farmers in their homes. The land that belonged to blacks was claimed by whites. There were reports by writers like Ida B. Wells and Zora Neale Hurston of murdered farmers going as high as 600 causalities.

The press played a crucial role in publicizing accusations regarding **"Reds"** in Elaine. Newspapers blamed the introduction of *Bolshevism* for inciting violence. The Dallas Morning News headline: *"Negroes Seized in Arkansas Riots, Confess to Widespread Plot; Planned Massacre of Whites Today,"* drew several US Justice Department agents from the Bureau of Investigation (BOI) to Elaine. They filed nine reports stating, *"There is no evidence of a conspiracy of any kind, for sharecroppers to murder anyone."* Their superiors in Washington ignored their analysis. (*Young J. Edgar Hoover: the Red Scare and the Assault on Civil Liberties* (2007 by Kenneth D. Ackerman).

The Wall Street Journal wrote: *"Race riots seem to have for their genesis a Bolshevist, a Negro, and a gun."* The *New York Times* reported *"Bloodshed amounting to local insurrections, indicate 'a new negro problem.' Communist influences are now working to drive a wedge of bitterness and hatred between the two races. Black leaders, until recently, showed a sense of appreciation for what whites suffered on their behalf in fighting a Civil War that bestowed on the black man opportunities far in advance of those he had in any other part of the* **white man's world.***"*

Attorney General A. Mitchell Palmer brought J. Edgar Hoover, who was beginning his career in government, in to set up the Radical Division of the BOI. He analyzed **Red Summer's** riots for Palmer. Hoover blamed the Washington, D.C. mob attacks on *"numerous assaults committed by Negroes upon white women."* For the October massacre in Elaine, Arkansas, Hoover blamed *"propaganda and agitation of a radical nature in a certain local Negro lodge."*

Disregarding the death toll for **Red Summer,** Hoover charged that socialists were feeding propaganda to black-owned magazines such as *The Messenger,* which in turn aroused their black readers. One BOI report cited the NAACP *"urging colored people to insist on equality with white people and to resort to force,"* (*Young J. Edgar Hoover: the Red Scare and the Assault on Civil Liberties* (2007 by Kenneth D. Ackerman).

Hoover began investigating "Negro activities" and targeted Marcus Garvey, as part of **Red Summer**. He claimed Garvey's newspaper *"Negro World"* preached *"Bolshevism."* He authorized hiring black informants to spy on Garvey and infiltrate Garvey's *Universal Negro Improvement Association (UNIA)*, even though no one had launched a complaint suggesting Garvey or accused him of wrongdoing. Hoover investigated black organizations and publications in Harlem as communist fronts, (http://pacificaradioarchives.org; *World War I; red scare; Harlem renaissance; lynchings in the South; Depression, urban family life in a packing-house town.*)

The Irony of Woodrow Wilson's Legacy

The irony of Woodrow Wilson for non-racists, if I can make that statement, is that America's leaders and those at the top echelon of society still support his racist legacy today. Their continued support is comparable to the thousands of confederate statues and monuments that still dot the American landscape, as well as the legal celebration of confederate holidays. Wilson's hatred and racist attitude are very clear and unmistakable, so what is there to honor, if there are non-racists white Americans?

Woodrow Wilson was the first openly racist President of America. Before Wilson, some presidents held racist views, like Andrew Jackson, with his *Indian Removal Act 1830*. But, even Jackson did not mandate racism as a practice of the government. Wilson implemented policies and edits that made white supremacy the underlying philosophical and psychological motive of government. It doesn't take an exhaustive survey of history to see Woodrow Wilson accomplished his white supremacy goal of pushing black people back close to slavery, as possible.

Sponsoring and facilitating segregation in government, Wilson's racist legacy left descendants of American slavery, trying to recover lives, his policies destroyed. During his time in office, Wilson's policies reduced descendants of American slavery to struggling to recoup their loss progress resulting from the devastation of **Red Summer of 1919**. Former slaves were victims of Wilson's plan hatched during those White House *The Birth of A Nation* screenings.

Slavery's descendants had no significant defenders, beyond themselves. They were defenseless victims against attacks by the government, as courts—federal, state, and local—lock their doors to black plaintiffs. Woodrow Wilson used mob violence to force black Americans to accept segregation and submit to white supremacy. The **Red Summer of 1919** was not produced by uncontrollable circumstances of human events. It was the willful design of white people in control of government policies and judicial edits that mastermind that plot.

The US Supreme Court was Wilson's full partner and ally in generating the hostile environment descendants of American slavery endured during the **"Dark Age"** *angry white men mob madness*. Wilson's diabolical pogrom went beyond a travesty. He inspired and leading the verbal assault that culminated in bloody attacks on innocent descendants of American slavery. Those attachs resulted in thousands of deaths and millions of dollars in destruction by **Red Summer** wrought.

Wilson entrenched white supremacy by implementing policies and edits that supported white only practices, reinforcing discrimination and justifying disparate treatment. His legacy of terror that began at the 300th, allowed whites to continue creating havoc for black American, while gaining wealth they did not earn.

For doubters, who cannot accept that a President of America, particularly Wilson, would engineer such attacks as **Red Summer,** I recapitulate my case in a different manner.

First and foremost, Woodrow Wilson almost singled handily, established white supremacy, reversing the progress Freedmen began after emancipation (1862). Secondly, Wilson encouraged southern legislatures to utilize the wording in the 13th Amendment—*except as a punishment for a crime, whereas the party has been duly convicted*—to create convict leasing. It was a vicious irony, Wilson's using the 13th Amendment, which supposedly freed slaves, as the trapdoor, through which newly freed slaves fell into re-enslavement.

The Supreme Court's decision in **Plessy v. Ferguson** establishing "*separate but equal*," which allowed Wilson when he entered office in 1912 to establish segregation and white supremacy, as a national policy. Those two decision, allowed southerners to use "interposition" to "nullify" the Civil Rights Bill of 1866, giving them the ability to *"force blacks to serve as unpaid labor*—convict leasing. The US Supreme Court barred the courthouse door to black people preventing African Americans from challenging what was happening to them under convict leasing and sharecropping.

Thirdly, former slaves and descendants were disenfranchised and based on Wilson's admission, **"Self-preservation [forced whites] to rid themselves, by fair means or foul, of the intolerable burden of governments sustained by the votes of ignorant Negroes,"** they had no rights. Slave descendants were locked completely out of the political process on all levels of the electoral process, particularly in the South. The federal government was the major culprit because it refused to enforce voting rights for former slaves.

Courts and legislatures in the South became instruments for forcing blacks to serve as unpaid/free labor. Millions of poor blacks unable to pay fines in cash, for petty crimes and trumped-up charges were sold to large industries, mines, lumber mills and plantations.

Finally, the system of sharecropping, which began with contracts Gen. Howard encouraged contraband to sign at the end of Reconstruction 1860s, became *"slavery without chains"* in 1912s. Living under a constant state of lynch law and mob rule in America, sharecroppers were peons, without mobility. Families inherited debt from year to year and generation to generation.

Truth Eventually Shines Through

Truth eventually finds the light is not an absolute! However, in the case of Woodrow Wilson, truth, if not justice, finally tracked the blackguard down. Trying to learn the truth, as well as understand **Red Summer,** I stumbled across some amazing facts about Woodrow Wilson. One source, the **Black Justice League at Princeton University (BJL),** uncovered and posted this amazing fact about Woodrow Wilson, the honored president of Princeton University. Following the BJL's lead, I learned of Woodrow Wilson huge deception. While US President, he perpetrated a hoax as a hero and major force behind establishing the *League of Nation*s (1920). Yes, he was involved in its creation, but pretending to be a great humanitarian was his fraud.

Wilson dedicated his life to racism, terror, murder, and white supremacy, and in that regard he was definitely a hero to white people imbued with the blood lust ritual and lynching in America, especially during his time in the White House. Wilson's true record of inspiring racism and segregation through the **"Dark Age"** *angry white men mob madness* pogrom against African Americans, as well as masterminning **Red Summer 1919,** Wilson was a changeling not a great humanitarian.

However, 95 years later, the **BJL** unearthed the truth about Wilson's racism and exposed his true legacy of racial hatred, detailed here. After the **BJL's** disclosure, Wilson's family has agreed, he was a racist. Wilson's great-grandson said, *"His racism did some harm,"* but he had no apology.

In 2015, the **BJL at Princeton University,** a bi-racial student group, protested Wilson's legacy by camping out in President Christopher L. Eisgruber's office. They refused to leave unless he signed a pledge to remove Woodrow Wilson's name from the college and school of international affairs. Also, they demanded his mural in a dining hall be demolished. Saying, *'No one should eat under the hateful stare of a former President of the United States that gloried in his 'racist legacy'* as a *'proud Klansman."* Student demonstrators demanded mandatory classes on the *'history of marginalized peoples'* to create a better learning environment for minority students and 'cultural competency training' for Princeton's staff, (Wills Robinson and Ollie Gillman www.dailymail.co.uk).

Albeit admissions, regarding Wilson's racism, have been acknowledged, popular historians insist, *"He was a man of his time."* No! Wilson was a man in leadership, who created his time of racism and white supremacy. Wilson led, not followed, establishing racism as president of the United States of America, and was very very successful!

He was not a victim of circumstances. Black people were his victims. They suffered the circumstances Wilson created. Where is the contrition for his atrocityies? There were American men who stood up and acted against Wilson's prevailing mindset of white supremacy.

Status quo opinions refuse to hold Wilson responsible and accountable for damage and death he inspired, which continues today against millions of black families. Black families are still living with the hatefulness and injustice Wilson fermented, and entrenched, establishing white supremacy. His dreadful decisions set in motion policies that drove black Americans into re-enslavement for another 60 years. Most emphatically, the point of **BJL** students is, *"Wilson's hateful and demeaning legacy did not die with him; it continues to hurt today."* His legacy—fermenting hatred and death—while standing at the podium receiving the ***1919 Nobel Peace Prize***, <u>was his fraud</u>.

Yes, Woodrow Wilson received the ***1919 Nobel Peace Prize***. Can you believe that? How could such a sardonic turn of fate be, I asked? I could not believe what I read. Even if he was given the *"Nobel Peace Prize"* by mistake back then, today, it is clear that simultaneously, while he was receiving the *"Nobel Peace Prize,"* Wilson was planning and executing the riots and massacres of ***Red Summer in 1919.*** Wilson's heinous past—reputation and legacy—is clearly known today, so how is it such a vicious travesty—listing him alongside such noted "peace activists" as Mother Teresa, Albert Einstein, Nelson Mandela, Dr. Martin Luther King, Jr. and others—goes unnoticed still? The world should be outraged!!!!!

The sensibilities of all human beings should be offended, especially those on the Nobel Committee. Only if one is a supporter of such madness, the irony should make one vomit, knowing a fiend with Wilson's legacy was accord such honor by the Nobel Committee. That would be like giving Donald Trump a Nobel Prize for science because of his COVID-19 leadership.

Rather than being universally denounced and condemned as a genocidal murdering pariah, the Nobel Committee has underwritten Wilson's pogrom—***Red Summer 1919*** against America slavery's descendants. While Wilson was in the White House, he spent his eight years as president, laying the foundation for and executing ***Red Summer's*** madness, which was far worse than I could detail here in this narrative.

I feel all human beings should join with the ***BJL,*** demanding that the Nobel Committee rescind Wilson's Nobel Award. The truth of Wilson's real legacy of hatred, racism, terror, and lynch law murders before and after 1919 may have gone unnoticed, but today, only true racists continue to honor him. Removing Wilson's name will not cleanse and disinfect well enough to remove the stain and stench from the Nobel Peace Prize because Wilson's name is attached to it. Wilson received the ***Nobel Peace Prize*** under false pretenses, demeans it international standing for all time. The world's real shame is it took 100 years for the truth to track the scoundrel Wilson down.

The 400th: From Slavery to Hip Hop

This particular award is not like the Nobel Award in economics, science, biology, mathematics, or physics, where one's knowledge is a bridge that extends a field of study. The peace prize is symbolic. It reflects qualities that are non-quantifiable and are validated by what one does during their life, which is the point with Wilson. This narrative has shown what Wilson spent his life doing. Nobel Peace Prize winners are individuals, who during their lifetime, help establish peace and justice among human beings. That was definitely not Woodrow Wilson's role. He did just the opposite!!!!!!!

There is no way under God's heaven; facing that true, such a humanitarian symbol should glorify Wilson's ghoulish mindset and legacy. The sheer absurdity of esteeming someone with Wilson's heinous, gory and appalling activities is a travesty in and of itself. Such venerable designation and recognition as the Nobel Peace Prize are supposed to reflect the values and virtuous characteristics of love, respect for life, all kinds, and a willingness to sacrifice for the good of others. If that is so, there could be no way, the same values and characteristics as those Wilson displayed, planning and executing, as well as standing by not intervening, doing nothing to helpless defenseless people that were dying during **Red Summer** reflects peace.

The idea behind *"The 400th"* is to recognize the suffering and pain of slaves while exposing the horrific genocidal actions of Americans like Wilson. Extending such honor, as the Nobel Peace Prize to Wilson is an affront to humanity. The world should demand Wilson's name be stricken from the record, like his mural in the dining hall at Princeton—*No one should eat under the hateful stare of a former President that gloried in his 'racist legacy' of a 'proud Klansman.*

Until then, the Nobel Committee continues to honor one of the world's more despicable human beings, which should be identified among "mass murders," like Idi Amin Dada or Pol Pot. The only thing that could compare to this travesty and vicious irony—including Wilson in the same category of peace-loving people like Mother Teresa and Dr. Martin Luther King, Jr.—would have been to award Adolf Hitler, the Nobel Peace Prize in 1939. Shame on the Nobel Peace Prize Committee!!!!!!!!!!!

Truth forever on the scaffold, Wrong forever on the throne,—Yet that scaffold sways the future, and, behind the dim unknown, Standeth God within the shadow, keeping watch above his own. James Russell Lowell

Spectacle Lynching: An American Phenomenon

The following section reflects Woodrow Wilson's handiwork, building his legacy of pain, mayhem, and murder, as well as his fraudulent **Nobel Peace Prize.** This narrative looked at the impact of that legacy on slavery's descendants as his presidential goal. Lynching—extra-judicial punishment—was the instrument of choice for those dedicated to keeping American descendants of slavery locked on the bottom of America's cheap labor capitalistic system. It blunted black Americans' demands for social changes and social justice until the 1960s. the vast majority of white people wholeheartedly embraced the **"Dark Age"** *angry white men mob madness* (the 1890s-1940s) as it rolled across America, like the COVID-19 pandemic. Their aim was forcing descendants of American slavery to accept the *cheap labor* second class status in the graveyard of poverty.

During the 19th century in the US, lynching became almost an exclusive means to murdering black men, usually by hanging, shooting, burning, or other horrific acts. The years from 1889 to 1923, saw 50-100 recorded lynching a year, many went unrecorded and do not show up in any record. Although lynching began in western America, during the 1700 to early 1800s, it came east after slavery ended. Lynching became Woodrow Wilson's chief weapon, pushing the newly Freedmen into re-enslavement after 1912, (*The betrayal of the Negro: From Rutherford B. Hayes to Woodrow Wilson*. Logan, R.W. New York: Macmillan (1965).

African Americans mounted resistance to lynching, with intellectuals and journalists leading public educational debates, arousing attention to the horrors of blood lust in America. They encouraged black people to protest and actively lobby against lynch mob violence. Black citizens held massive protests against government complicity and inaction against lynch mobs, much like Black Lives Matter protest to stop police murders. Artists produced anti-lynching plays and literary works. The NAACP and related groups, organized support among both white and black Americans that publicize injustice, investigated lynching incidents, and worked for passage of federal laws against lynching. Amazingly, although lynching was outright murder, it is not illegal today. If considered a lynching, no one went to jail; white people revered these murderers as heroes.

Not all racially motivated lynchings in the United States took place in the South, but its victims were black, in most cases. One such incident occurred in Duluth, Minnesota. Three young black travelers (6-15-1920), accused of raping *"a white woman,"* were dragged from their jail cells and lynched by over two thousand whites. One lynching but three deaths, which is why it is difficult to come up with the exact number of black people lynched. The event became the subject of a non-fiction book, *The Lynchings in Duluth*, 2000, by Michael Fedo.

Lynch mobs put thousands of African Americans to death. The *Equal Justice Initiative (EJI)* has officially documented lynching's death toll at 4,075 in the

South. Deaths by lynch mobs no longer occurred in the dead of night or in some dark and deathly swamp after 1890; they were no longer anomalies or unusual shocking events. They became huge celebratory occasions. One account (1882-1968), showed approximately 4,742 individuals lynched; 3,445 or 73 percent were black. During lynching's heyday (1889-1918), 3,224 individuals were lynched; 2,522 or 78 percent were black. These statistics highlight the variance in lynching statistics. Typically, the victims died at the hands of white vigilantes led by civic leaders frequently in front of thousands of spectators, like Ell Persons. Many spectators took pieces of the dead person's body, as cherished mementos from the spectacular event (<u>Lynching in the new South: Georgia and Virginia, 1880-1930:</u> W. F. Brundage, 1993, University of Illinois Urbana Press).

Far from suppressing news about lynchings, newspapers embraced them, providing abundant, even graphic details, covering vigilante violence. A write up on the *"southern country editor"* states, *"Many editors did not spare their readers' sensibilities. Whatever their motives, editors wrote full, detailed accounts. Reading through many volumes of the period from 1875 to 1920 is somewhat like walking through a chamber of horrors"*

Major newspapers or metropolitan dailies sometimes described lynchings that occurred outside their geographical area. For example, the February 2, 1893 issue of *The New York Times'* headline *"ANOTHER NEGRO BURNED,"* described the grisly lynching of Henry Smith in Paris, Texas. Smith was placed on a ten feet-high scaffold and tortured with red hot branding irons for 50 minutes to cheers of thousands. He was set on fire, then mobsters fought over his charred remained.

Newspapers identified victims, as a Negro most times. There was no restraint against anonouncing victims' guilty and deserved to be lynched. The *New Orleans Picayune* described an African American lynched in Hammond, Louisiana, as a *"big burly negro"* and a *"Black wretch."* It may seem newspapers treated all lynch mob victims, with equal ferocity. Newspaper stories identified the race of black lynch victims with a special vitriolic quality, editors, and readers assumed without question victims were guilty. News articles used several dehumanizing terms for black victims, "wretch," "fiend," and "desperado." They assumed black victims' race predisposed him to commit violent crimes, particularly rape; they self-righteously defended lynchings of black individuals.

R.W. Logan's book <u>The betrayal of the Negro: From Rutherford B. Hayes to Woodrow Wilson</u> looked at the experiences of African Americans between Reconstruction in 1877 to the end of WWI. It provides a full-scale account of this neglected phase in American history by most white historians. The author examines every aspect of America's post-Reconstruction retreat from equality: the economic factors, the Supreme Court decisions, Booker T. Washington, and his "Era of Compromise." Logan presents a unique and disturbing survey reflecting the racist caricatures that dominated the most liberal newspapers and magazines of the day. Dispassionate and insightful, Logan unfolds a narrative of national betrayal as harrowing as it is heartbreaking.

Lynchings became even more widespread reaching the 1890s and would remain common in the South until the late 1940s. During the period (1880-1940), one estimated accounted for 4,400 black men, women, and children lynched. A partial list of "crimes" that prompted lynch mob actions, underscores a chilling disregard for black life: quarreling, arguing with a white man, gambling, attempting to vote, unruly remarks, demanding respect, and "acting suspiciously." It is no exaggeration to state that any black man, woman, or child in the South, during these years, was in danger of getting lynched for any real or imagined improper behavior in the view of whites.

Local citizens composed lynch mobs; a core group would actually carry out the dirty deed, while many of the town's residents would watch. Spectacle lynchings often included "respectable" men and women, who often brought their children to lynchings. The word "picnic," "pick a nic (nig-ger)," came into vogue with lynching. White writers did not discuss the fact that in cases of successful lynchings of black farmers or immigrant merchants, their property was claimed by white Americans.

It may not be clear that those that wrote the vast majority of stories about lynchings spoke from personal experience and knowledge. They participated in the gruesome events. They gave very detail descriptions because, as it was, they became imbued with blood lust and savored the skinning, roasting, castrating, fighting for body parts and the whole party atmosphere of the lynch culture, like NFL tailgate parties. Descriptions flow not from outraged bleeding hearts crusaders fighting these heinous act; writers were advertising the fun and gaiety, like "gender reveal" parties today.

The first politician to take a visible stand against lynching was President Harry S. Truman in 1946. Shocked by a lynching in Moore's Ford (Monroe, Georgia), in which four people—one a WWII veteran and hero, George Dorsey, his pregnant wife, May Murray, a friend Robert Malcolm and his wife, Dorothy—were brought by the sheriff to a mob, they were shot dozens of times and the baby was cut out of the mother.

Pres. Truman launched a campaign to guarantee civil rights for blacks. Truman pushed for federal anti-lynching laws, but Dixiecrats killed his effort with the "filibuster." The US Congress supported lynching and refused to outlaw lynching. Although unsuccessful, for the first time since Abraham Lincoln, a President spoke up against the injustice and terror black Americans endured.

Often Jim Crow tensions went hand in hand with economic oppression. In 1887, ten thousand workers at a sugar plantation in Louisiana, organized by the *Knights of Labor*, went on strike for <u>an increase in pay to $1.25 a day.</u> Only convict leasing could supply 10, 000 workers for one planation. Most of the workers were black, but a few were white. The strike infuriated Governor Samuel

Douglas. He ranted, *"God Almighty has himself drawn the color line."* Douglas called in the militia but withdrawn it to give free reins to a lynch mob in Thibodaux. The mob killed over 300 people. A black newspaper described the scene: *"Six killed and five wounded" is what the daily papers here say, but from an eye witness to the whole transaction we learn that no less than thirty-five Negroes were killed outright. Lame men and blind women were shot; children and hoary-headed grandsires ruthlessly cut down! The Negroes offered no resistance; they could not, as the killing was unexpected. Those of them not killed took to the woods, a majority of them finding refuge in this city."*

Lynchings became massive spectacles, taking on a circus atmosphere. Children often attended public lynchings, which anti-lynching advocates saw as a form of indoctrination. A large lynching was announced beforehand in the newspaper, and in some cases, lynchings began early so a newspaper reporter could make his deadline. Postcards depicting lynchings allowed newspaper photographers to make extra money, peddling their photos like drummers. These postcards were popular enough to be an embarrassment to the postmaster, who officially banned them from the mail in 1908. However, lynching postcards continued as a cottage industry through the 1930s.

The Black Press: Our Only Voice

Kidnapped and shanghaied across the *"Middle Passage"* to North America, from the moment of their capture, slavers denied enslaved Africans *VOICE*. Slaves had no defenders, then or after they arrived in the land of servitude. They were without words to tell their story; neither did they have a common language nor drums to create a rhythmic connection to one another. Enslaved Africans had to create words they understood, and that white overseers and masters did not. Emancipation offered education or at least words others understood, as standard speech. Most people today cannot understand the difficulty descendants of American slavery had overcoming this word deficit, while trapped in a society bent on keeping them ignorant.

Trying to become literate, gaining the ability to comprehend socio-economic rules and intercourse, slaves had to master the political language, which controls their lives. Their word deficit was more than understanding what words meant, but how to use them so that others comprehended their intent. Although eventually, there were systems that attempted to address this deficiency, the major aid for black people, in general, were writings of authors and journalist. Black writers understood the need to address the commonalities among black people.

Former slaves' most pressing need was addressing their ignorance regarding how the larger society victimized them. These writers learned how to translate the confusing political speech between former slaves and white people. Black writers deciphered white's coded socioeconomic and political language, which controlled the systems, dominating black people, which kept them locked on the bottom of America's cheap labor economy. This system's demands changed the word of mouth culture and learning process enslaved Africans relied upon, during, and after slavery. Those able to read and write peeled away the confusion, like the skin of an onion, revealing the mysteries of American speech.

During the very dark and desperate times of the middle 1900s in the South, white people locked black people behind what they called the *"cotton curtain."* This was their way of describing their isolation from the rest of the world and from other parts of the US, even including other black people. Denied *VOICE*, imprisoned in the South, black Americans' only connection to the outside world was the church and the black press, both began developing during slavery.

Not a household name today, but back during the dark and dreadful days of the **"Dark Age"** *angry white man mob madness*, one man was a beckon, shinning the light of knowledge that guided black people through their dark and ignorance present. When one speaks of impactful black historical figures that provided leadership, helping slavery's descendants learn to survive these treacherous and deadly times, John Herman Henry Sengstacke (11/25/1912–5/28/1997) stands head and shoulders above all others, as a model. He is an excellent example from those times, especially when speaking out or opposing segregation, and when white supremacy could cost one, not only their business but their life.

Mr. Sengstacke stood tall, as a devil-may-care, swashbuckling, lone rider, during this draconian period in American history. It was a time when the lives of blacks hung on the whim of any white person; for whatever reason, desired a black person's life. Defending the dignity and rights of descendants of slavery, John H. Sengstacke for more than 60 years, displayed the kind of quiet power that reached into the White House, Congress, Statehouses and Mayors' offices to represent descendants of American slavery. Though not identified among the riches black entrepreneurs, as Robert R. Church, Sr. and Jr., but as they, he used his resources to aid the black community in any way he could.

Beginning his professional career a newspaperman, John Sengstacke began working for his uncle Robert Sengstacke Abbott, owner of an African-American newspaper, *The Chicago Defender*. John took over the paper after the death of his uncle (1940). John Henry eventually became the publisher and owner of the largest chain of black newspapers in America. The *Chicago Defender* anchored, what became the most dominant black newspaper empire in American history, serving African Americans. Also, a civil rights activist, Sengstacke, worked tirelessly building a strong black press. His greatest legacy is founding the *Nation Negro Publishers Association (NNPA)* in 1940. He believed that organization could unify and strengthen African-American owned newspapers. Sengstacke served seven terms as president of the association, which by the early 21st century had 200 members.

Taking over the Chicago Defender, Sengstacke became publisher of the Michigan Chronicle in Detroit; Tri-State Defender in Memphis and Pittsburgh Courier. During the years of World War II, Sengstacke acted as a national spokesman for African American journalists and publishers. He worked with President Franklin D. Roosevelt to ensure that African American reporters attended presidential press conferences.

Sengstacke was a major force pressing to get opportunities for African Americans in the United States Postal Service, which Woodrow Wilson ended. One of Sengstacke's major political goals was desegregating the US Armed Forces. President Harry Truman supported his goal and named Sengstacke to the commission he formed in 1948 to integrate the military.

The *Chicago Defender* was the base of Sengstacke's reach and power. During these times, it was the most storied and historically successful black newspaper in America. Sengstacke was an amazing innovator, educator and organizer of black people through his business enterprises. Beginning with only the *Chicago Defender*, Sengstacke saw the black press, as a means of building unity among black people. He championed their causes and defended their right of access to America's bountiful resources.

John Sengstacke took a page out of David Walker's book, getting the word out in the late 1930s into the 1970s. One hundred years before John Henry, Walker used black sailors to distribute his **_Appeal_**. Flipping his script, Sengstacke was just as clever and innovative, getting the *Chicago Defender* and later, his other papers into the South. Forming coalitions with groups and organizations like *"the Pullman Porters"*—the Brotherhood of Sleeping Car Porter—to distributed the *DEFENDER* from their trains, as they traveled throughout the South.

This particular coalition became an essential part of *The Defender's* great success. Southern Jim Crow authorities were known to search trains, even passengers at times, hoping to stop *The DEFENDER* from reaching black people in the South. *The Defender* was the "pied piper," inspired millions of blacks to take their lives in their own hands on the road, as they hope for better lives. Their mass exodus was called *"The Great Migration,"* and it filled Northern and Midwestern cities with over 2 million African Americans out of the South from 1910 into the 1950s.

Mr. Sengstacke was courted, not only, as a clever businessman, but even more, as a very savvy politician. A New York Times article: *The Lives They Lived: John H. Sengstacke; Citizen Sengstacke* by Brent Staples (1-4-1998) tells a very revealing story about John Sengstacke's world. Distributing his newspapers, he believed, was about more than selling papers, the information they carried linked black people to progress.

Getting the word out through his newspapers, filled a need so great, even newspaper boys shared the hazards. If caught selling the Defender, they risked being jailed and sentenced to convict leasing or even lynched. The *Defenders*, Chicago, and Tri-State, editorials urged Negroes to abandon the Jim Crow South for better lives north of the Mason-Dixon Line or out West. The *Defenders* were read aloud in churches, treated like textbooks in schools, and held on reserve at barbershops for personal pick up.

Delivered on Thursdays, the Defender was the center of conversations on Friday evening and Saturday barbershop gatherings. Barbershop philosophers read and expounded on the news of the week, as others followed along. These reading sessions ensured the correct words and interpretation went out to the community, for those who didn't attend church. When The Defender came out, it was like a Joe Louis fight was on the radio; every ear listened if they had a radio. Those without radios got reports hollowed out of windows, round by round. During the tail end of the deadly **Dark Age angry white men mob madness** years from the 1940s and into the 1950s, the *Defenders* reached a million readers a week at the peak of its influence.

Mr. Sengstacke expanded his concept of unity, including others in the black press. Hoping to bring real professionalism to black journalism, he founded the National Negro Publishers Association (1940), which became the Nation

Newspaper Publishers Association (1956). Mr. Sengstacke said at the organizational meeting with other African-American publishers; I desire to *"harmonize our energies in a common purpose for the benefit of Negro journalism."* Serving as its president for seven terms, he brought the organization to where the NNPA today has over 200 members in major cities and smaller ones throughout America. Establishing unify among Africa American newspaper publishers through the NNPA, Mr. Sengstacke insisted, *"The power of the black press could be magnified through a strong joint association."* Throughout his life as head of NNPA, Mr. Sengstacke served the black community fatefully and his guidance is a major reason descendant of American slavery reached **"The 400th"** as one people.

Ocoee Massacre: Banishment and Ethnic Cleansing

The *"Ocoee Massacre"* was a race riot that occurred the year after **Red Summer 1919** in Orange County, Florida near Orlando on November 2, 1920. Death and destruction erupted following the US quadrennial presidential election, as blacks citizens tried to vote. African-Americans in Ocoee owned farms, buildings and residences that were the envy of white Floridians for miles around. On Election Day, Moses Norman, a prosperous black landowner, attempt to vote but was driven from the poll several times by whites guarding the poles to prevent black people from voting. Norman returned several times hoping to vote, but whites continued denying him access. Complaints to authorities drew a Woodrow Wilson reaction and gained no assistance for black voters.

Orange County, like the rest of Florida, was dominated by white Democrats. The weeks leading to the presidential election, blacks, as the rest of America, were registering in record numbers. Black voters responded to Pres. Wilson's **Red Summer** madness by supporting the Republican Warren G. Harding. They held mass voter registrations, opposing the resurgent of the Ku Klux Klan under Woodrow Wilson's eight years.

Judge John Moses Cheney, Florida's Republican senatorial hopeful, started a voter registration campaign. Moses Norman and Julius "July" Perry led the local voter registration in Orange County. They paid poll taxes for those who could not afford it. The KKK held "marches in full regalia" in Jacksonville, Daytona, and Orlando. Hoping to preserve "white supremacy and one-party rule," they threaten black voters before the election. Three weeks before Election Day, the KKK vowed that *"Not a single Nigger will be permitted to vote,"* (<u>Emancipation Betrayed: The Hidden History of Black Organizing and White Violence in Florida From Reconstruction to the Bloody Election of 1920</u>, Paul Ortiz, (2006), University of California Press).

Voter fraud was rampant; white poll workers challenge African American voters' and refuse to allow newly registered black access to vote, unless the notary public R. C. Biegelow substantiated their registration. However, Biegelow was on a fishing trip and could not be located. Black voters, including Norman, were prevented from voting, although they had been previously registered.

A mob of outraged white formed and paraded through the streets of Ocoee, spoiling for a fight. African Americans gave up on voting and left polls. Later during the evening, Colonel Sam Salisbury, a white leader of the town, who was a native-New Yorker, as well as former police chief of Orlando, led a lynch mob to "find and punish Norman."

The KKK mob, over one-hundred men, marched to Julius "July" Perry's house; they surrounded his home and demanded Moses Norman surrender. Perry another prosperous local black farmer and contractor was armed and fortified his dwelling. He did not respond to their demand for Norman. Receiving no answer, the mobsters attempted to break down the front door. Perry opened fire on the intruders, wounding several and driving the white mob back. During the battle, Sam Salisbury, leader of the mob, knocked in the back door, producing the first white casualty. Perry killed two other whites attempting to enter the back door.

The white mob called for backup, then withdrew awaiting reinforcements from Orlando, Apopka and Orange County. Once the shooting stopped, July Perry, his wife and daughter, attempted to flee but were captured. Mobsters lynched Perry, "riddled his body with bullets," and flagged it from a utility pole. A sign reading *"This is what we do to niggers that vote"* was left with his body.

A local photographer sold photos of Perry's body for 25 cents each; several store owners placed the photo, in their windows, as an exhibit of white power. Although the identity of Perry's killed could be obtained from photographers at his lynching, no one went to jail. Perry's wife, Estelle and their daughter received injuries during the assault on their home, but survived and received treatment in Tampa.

The mob began rioting in the African American community. They set home afire and shot those fleeing the flames. Mobsters burned African-American churches, schools, and a lodge. African American residents fought back from their burning dwellings. Eventually, whites drove the residents into the nearby orange groves and swamp.

The reinforced mob destroyed the black community. Norman disappeared; but relocated to New York. African American residents in southern Ocoee were driven out (racial cleansing or banishment), following the massacre. They escaped to neighboring towns, leaving behind their homes and possessions. Whites killed nearly 100 African Americans; their body count is uncertain because many were driven into the swamp and may have died there. Whites mobs droved survivors out of town with threats. Ocoee became "an all-white town until 1981," like Forsyth, County Georgia, another banishment and ethnic cleansing site" *("Kill Two Whites and Six Negroes in Florida Riot,"* 11-4-1920, New York Times). Along with East St. Louis, this riot was considered *"one of the bloodiest days in modern American political history;"* that is until "Black Wall Street!!!"

Ethnic Cleansing: The Destruction of Black Wall Street

Getting the word out promptly to black people in the US, about what happened in places like Ocoee was all but impossible. Black journalists and authors were crucial to informing former slaves. The role of writers became lifelines, keeping black Americans informed about what life was truly like for other blacks living in far-flung communities, backwoods huddles, isolated glades, and desolate stretches of nowhere.

Former slaves after surviving the terror and desperation of slavery; progressed through the contraband period. However, only the renewed efforts to re-enslave them with the coming of *"Gilded Age,"* stopped their progress. This became a time when the actions of whites could not anticipated, let alone trusted. Peering into the darkness surrounding them, after massacres during the riots of **Red Summer**, spectacle lynchings, banishments, and ethnic cleansing in in places like Ocoee—former enslaved Africans refused to be cowed. Reading such heart-wrenching episodes and accounts described by black writers of this disastrous and devastating time, descendants of slavery resolved to endure to survive.

Readers looking with today's eyes have a difficult time envisioning this period. Also, it is mind-boggling, trying to understand the madness white people heaped upon former slaves from the 1880s through the 1940s. Imagining the destructive hatred and deadly forces whites leaders unleashed upon a helpless people, not quite 25 years out of bond slavery without defenders or access to fair courts. Black people during this period held on to life any way they could.

Legally prevented from defending one's self, how does one survive? Knowing that the government was not going to intervene and do anything to stop such attacks or help once such incidents occurred, had to be totally disheartening. Hoping against hope, prayers appealing to the wellspring of grace continued going up, as black journalists and authors tried to offered hope with their writings.

The next example is a rebuttal to those writers that believed such an atrocious situations and incidents only occurred in the South and were convinced, leaving that vicious place would be the answer. This example shows that enslaved Africans in America had no refuge any place. The hatred, bloodlust, and downright vicious mindset of white people were national in scope, as it is today. This deplorable and horrific act is another example of ethnic cleansing and banishment.

The following example reflects the level of enmity white people's showed black people. Even though whites had everything, "envy" was at the heart of lynchings. Whites destroyed an entire black community based on their outrage over competition for resources, after witnessing what blacks were able to accomplish despite discrimination, disparate treatment, and the hostile environment enforced against them. This outrageous pogrom stands alone, as the most devastating and heartless event, during the ***"Dark Age"*** *angry white men mob madness* period. It is known as the ***"Black Wall Street Massacre."***

Once oil began flowing from the first successful well in the U.S. (1859), extracting crude developed into the American oil and gas industry. It claims it has transformed the US into the world's largest oil and gas producer. A driver, not only of industrial innovation but a path to financial security for almost anyone, regardless of background, who is willing to put in the work, is how the industry promotes itself. It claims the American Petroleum industry is the egalitarian engine of the US economy.

Even with its egalitarian claims, black oil workers have remained on the bottom of the crude oil business over the years, similar to black workers in other industries. With the advent of new technologies, such as fracking and horizontal drilling, black oil workers remain marginalized as bottom-rung workers. Industry executives overlook this trend, which is similar to other industries.

Jack Gerard, former president and CEO of the American Petroleum Institute (API), while seeking support for a US House of Representatives bill, he claimed the industry would encourage hiring more women and people of color, way back in February 2016. *"Our energy renaissance has created unprecedented opportunities for Americans of all backgrounds."* Nevertheless, the American Petroleum Industry, for African-Americans, as a path to upward mobility, has proven to be a dry hold.

Still filled with hurdles and potholes, in spite of well-publicized diversity campaigns and claimed outreach, by the industry's largest companies and trade groups, African-American workers remain only 9 percent of the workforce in oil and gas extraction, according to the US Labor Department. Blacks have never broken the 10% ceiling in the US oil and gas industry, following oil booms of past decades, also as in other industries. Further analysis showed black workers continue to be paid, on average 23 percent less than their white workers.

Although the oil and gas industry made such statements in recent years, life for blacks reflects the same conditions they faced following the Tulsa riot—***Black Wall Street Massacre***—of 1921, in Oklahoma and other oil producing states. Attempts to increase black workers, in the oilfields, became one of the contributing factors to the Tulsa riot. For half a century, the Tulsa race riot went unacknowledged and overlooked entirely in official history. Also, newspapers of that time and even today, especially in Tulsa, continued obfuscating, not even bothering to deny the riot.

Tulsa was like many western towns that benefitted from black newspaper stories, like the *Chicago Defender's* and writers, like Zora Neale Hurston and Ida B. Wells that encouraged immigration to the West, before this tragedy. It was Wells appeal, after *the People's Grocery Store* lynching that drew 6,000 blacks out of Memphis to Tulsa and other towns out West. However, this was before 10,000 whites in Omaha, Nebraska (1919) stormed a jail to lynch a black man, then raided and burned the black community there.

Over the years, the story of ***"Black Wall Street"*** was passed around in the black community, like an urban legend. The advent of the civil rights movement, including increased awareness of black history and black power in the 1960s, pushed the Tulsa riot story, which kept finding its way into various publications, exposing the tragedy anew. Finally, the Oklahoma state legislature set up the *1921 Tulsa Race Riot Commission* to unearth the facts of that infamous time and incident. A government commission was set up to investigate the 1921 riot, and it released the results on 3-28-1997.

Over 50 family members and other volunteers, spread out like an army of scavengers, searching for riot evidence everywhere. Digging for the truth, volunteers were reminiscent of prospectors hoping to unearth gold. They dug through newspapers, government files, and National Guard records, as well as historical society archives. Unpaid researchers made hundreds of calls. Volunteers interviewed survivors and found photographs. They solicited secondhand accounts, and using sophisticated equipment to locate unmarked burial sites of victims from the riot.

The commission's report provides a glimpse into the social dynamics in Tulsa before the riot. It found institutional racism existed in Oklahoma, leading up to the riot and during its aftermath. Local history showed the oil business spurred Tulsa's population growth from 10,000 in 1910 to over 100,000 by 1920. The rapid influx was due to whites and blacks seeking jobs in the booming oil industry in the late 1800s. However, all the people that ended up in Oklahoma were not volunteers.

Thousands were part of the *Trail of Tears* outrage perpetrated by Pres. Andrew Jackson. Known as an "Indian fighter," Jackson was openly hostile toward Native People. He sponsored the *Indian Removal Act of 1830*, which evicted Native People from millions of acres of their lands in Georgia, Tennessee, Alabama, Florida, North and South Carolina. The Cherokee, Muscogee, Seminole, Chickasaw, Choctaw, Ponca, and Ho-Chunk/Winnebago nations were part of Jackson's forced removal and relocation to reservations in Oklahoma.

The forced march from their lands in the South to Oklahoma began during the winter of 1838. The Cherokee began the 1,000-mile (1,600 km) walk wearing scant clothing and most on foot without shoes or moccasins. Their march began in Red Clay, Tennessee the last Eastern capital of the Cherokee Nation. En route, many suffered exposure, disease, and starvation. Many died before reaching Oklahoma. The forced march included runaway slaves that lived in "the Indian territories" also.

The majority of Tulsa's 10,000 blacks living in the Greenwood district near downtown suffered discrimination. Whites barred blacks from high-level jobs in the oil industry and most manufacturing jobs in the area. Black workers labored under harsh conditions, as janitors, ditch diggers, porters, day laborers, maids, and other domestics. Nevertheless, blacks were able to mount and foster entrepreneurial efforts.

A small group of black businessmen successfully created an echelon of prosperity that grew into the commercial district known as **"Black Wall Street."** Buying and selling to black in their community, they kept the little money blacks made, compared to whites, circulating in the black community. Low paying jobs, allowed them to finance a political, social and cultural nitches, with a library, two newspapers, two large theaters, a funeral home, several business associations, fraternal orders, and colored women clubs.

Oklahoma lynched law breakers however by 1900 lynching was reserved exclusively for blacks. Only one lynching victim after 1911 was not African Americans. Over the next decade, 23 black Oklahomans—including two women—were lynched by whites. It was common, the *1921 Tulsa Race Riot Commission* reported for, *"White politicians and the local media promoted and perpetuated racist attitudes and tried to build resentment among whites against blacks, especially by pointing to the prosperity of the Greenwood district."* White complained blacks did not spend money in white businesses, even though whites didn't buy from blacks and displayed signs saying "white only."

The riot lasted from May 31 through June 1, 1921. The *Riot Commission* called it a **_"pogrom"_** that took place with the support of city authorities and state government, supported by the National Guard. During the 16 hours of terror, white mobs shot black people, looted and torched black homes and businesses. They forced thousands of survivors to flee the Reports said, *"They bombed us from the air using 'Sinclair Oil Company' planes,"* the *1921 Commission* agreed.

A false accusation in a local newspaper accusing Dick Rowland, a young black worker, of assaulting a white girl, was the excuse whites and historians gave for the riot. Incited by the inflammatory stories, a white mob gathered at the Tulsa County Courthouse. African American WWI veterans armed themselves and offered their services to defend the courthouse, *the 1921 Commission* reported. A mob of whites, estimated at more than 1,000, grew even more unruly at the sight of black men with guns at the courthouse. After authorities refused the first group's help, a second group of 75 black men arrived and offered to defend the county building.

The *Commission* reported the crowd at the courthouse grew to over 2,000 whites. It described what happened when a shot went off, as a white man tried to take a black man's gun. The white mob and some law enforcement officers opened fire on the black men, as they walked back to Greenwood. According to the *Commission*, many whites joined the assault on the retreating black men.

The commission said further, when the National Guard intervened typically of other such pograms, the mob assaulted black citizens, instead of disarming the racist mob. The Guard unit concentrated on disarming and arresting nearly all of Greenwood's residents, putting them in holding pens. The city's official policy was to release a black person, only if a white person vouched for them, like in Elaine, Arkansas.

The report contains a chilling account of how "civil officials" deputized and armed those who perpetrated the violence, while *"failing to take actions to calm or contain the situation. People, some were agents of the government, also deliberately burned 1,256 homes, along with virtually every other structure in the Greenwood district. No government at any level, offered adequate resistance to residents, if any at all,"* or *"assisted those being assaulted."* Finally, *"the restoration of Greenwood, after its systematic destruction, was left to the victims,"* the report said.

The Daily Tribune, according to the report, played a big role in inciting the riot, like southern newspapers, it fanned the flames of the lynching. The headline on May 31, 1921, *"Nab Negro for Attacking Girl in Elevator,"* stirred anger among whites. The local paper ran an editorial, *"To Lynch Negro Tonight."* The paper destroyed all copies of the pages with these two articles.

Describing the assault, *The Commission* began at the National Guard Armory, where the mob got machine guns and sprayed Greenwood with automatic fire. But the truly killing blow came from the air. At daybreak, six biplanes belonging to *Sinclair Oil Company*, according to *The Commission,* spotted action on the ground for the mob. In the first hours, home and the business district were beyond the reach of the advancing mob, which faced stiff resistance from African-American residents.

The fighting was house-to-house, as black defenders battled block by block. The National Guardsmen loaded planes with dynamite and balls of fabric soaked in turpentine for airdrop on the commercial buildings and homes in Greenwood. Their bombing assault commenced at 6:00 AM and continued throughout the day. Returning and refueling, planes flew additional missions from late morning into evening.

Whites rained "firebombs" down on the African-American business district. The incendiary started fires raging in the center of *"Black Wall Street."* The worst was over by sundown. Greenwood was ablaze. *The Commission* report said local whites said, *"The uppity Niggers got what they deserved."* Hospitals admitted over 800 people. Over 6,000 Greenwood men, women, and children were arrested and placed in concentration camps, where they were required to carry 'passes.' Whites detained residents illegally at three facilities, but arrest no whites, even though bombs and fire destroyed thirty-five city blocks, containing 1,256 residences. The estimated property loss reached above $2.3 million (over 300 million in today's US dollars). The Oklahoma Department of Vital Statistics officially listed the death toll at 36; other, more plausible estimates range from a reasonable 75 to the Red Cross' high estimate of about 400 dead.

The commission recommended the state and city pay $33 million in reparations. Oklahoma governor Frank Keating did not welcome the proposal. What

The 400th: From Slavery to Hip Hop

Keating and other officials refuse to admit is that government was not a bystander, an unwilling participant. Government was the leader, fasciliating and directing some actions. It incarcerated the majority of Greenwood's residences and made no effort to save any part of the community.

Some legislators said they were supported the suggestion of building a memorial site for the victims and providing some economic development funds to the Greenwood district where the rampage took place. A memorial will not compensate families who wealth was taken, which white people have been living good lives on since 1921.

However, even after that nothing suggestion, today nothing has been done either way. Talk is all black victims have gotten from the government, which caused the tragedy. The 200-page *1921 Tulsa Race Riot Commission* report, which includes several pictures, can be found on the web at www.ok-history.mus.ok.us/trrc.htm

Granddaddy's Run

I compared getting religion to a bolt of lightning out of a clear blue sky, as a metaphor to highlight the total unlikelihood of one lone riding devil-may-care swashbuckling white woman could bring about such a startling and amazing outcome. Jessie Daniel Ames would not only shake the very foundation of the **Dark Age** *angry white men mob madness* lynching culture, when there was no end in sight. Even more powerful was her action, with white men in total control of southern politics and society, as with *Lysistrata*. Under such conditions it is totally unbelievable to me, a lone woman could put the force of love behind her statement, so much so, she brought the entire lynching technology down.

That is what real religion does. If one has it, they make a profession of their faith and go to work. That is my point; it changes one so much that what they believe is what they live, again as William Wilberforce. That is how it is in the fight for social change and social justice regarding slave descendants in American.

If I could weigh the infinitesimal odds that a surviving seed, from those desperate times, would be a Lee family seed, I never imagined the scale of life would tip in my direction to tell **"The 400th"** story. There was not any way, beginning life in a Mississippi cotton field, as I did, to cognize such a thought or outcome. How could I formulate such an event in my head, where time and fate would come together to favor me, as that messenger?

But, the amazing part of this audacious saga is that I would be the one that Divine Providence selected, like Jessie Daniel Ames, to give voice to all those long departed souls and those still surviving. Nothing in my past prepared me for such a daunting task. There is nothing special about me or my experiences, especially during my early days, which prepared me for such an awesome challenge.

Born into a family with only sharecropping as its major legacy, which meant, down through the years, it was as though desperation and scarcity was bequeathed, like a birthright. Not knowing the real circumstances of my family's true origin, before and after slavery and sharecropping, all I can say is poverty produced a family of runners. The need for mobility was also a legacy bequeathed to descendants of American slavery like DNA. Mobility was the first thing slavery took, and we have been trying to reclaim it ever since. Our struggle, as a people, even before emancipation, was to reclaim mobility, as a personal and communal need such that it motivated enslaved Africans longing to be free, and dared to take the *Underground Railroad*.

Burl Lee, Sr., the first runner in my family that we know, was also the last slave. Born (sic, 1843-1905) during slavery, a decade before the confusing and deadly times of the Civil War, emancipation and slaves contraband existence,

Burl survived the internal slave trade and breeding industry. During that time, the birth of some slaves brought milk to their mothers' breast, for masters' newborns to suck. Those unfortunate souls were second on their mother's tit, behind young master; they got what was left.

There, they would remain for the duration of life, second behind some master's offspring. There were no sentiments or concerns for a slave's family. Yet, against such daunting odds, after becoming a runner, Burl Lee found Sarah and increased the prospects that I, his descendants, would survive not only to see but write ***"The 400th"***. Their son, Burl Lee, Jr. was Sarah firstborn in a family of 9, only six were Sarah's.

History books make it seen former slaves were *"lazy no counts because slavery was just a short ease walk in the park, where slaves sang and danced the day away."* Not emerging from slavery to become successful farmers or whatever, most whites believed because slavery was so easy, slaves did not deserve better. Burl brought my family out of slavery into what the US federal government said was freedom. Never having experienced such a state, freedom was something that existed only in slaves' heads. It was clear to many former slaves before the 300th (1919) America had gone back on every promise made to them at the signing of the Emancipation Proclamation and passage of the Civil Rights Bill of 1866, the 13th, 14th, and 15th Amendments.

White supremacy replaced America's promises to former slaves, making them scapegoats for every negative thought and impulse white people had, after losing the Civil War, as well as their slave master heritage. White supremacy flew in the face of equality and justice, like the flag of freedom that flies on the White House lawn today. Unapologetically, Woodrow Wilson, set himself the task of reversing all political gains made by former slaves, while making them scapegoats for white supremacy.

Convict leasing and sharecropping became the killing blows that felled the majority of American descendants of slavery. Those two monstrous technologies ended former slaves bid for prosperity and pushed most into the grave of poverty. Convict leasing and sharecropping became fixtures in my family's life. They were the impetus for my grandfather and grandmother, Eddie and Ada Wilson to begin life together as runners before they joined in marriage in 1919. Their run extended my family's survival, with the birth of Willie May (1920), my mother. The circumstances of just how Ada, my grandmama, and granddaddy got together always depended upon who was telling the story. I always like granddaddy's story best; it was more exciting.

On cold winter nights, gathered around the potbelly stove, eating popcorn, roasted peanuts, or breaking hickory nuts, granddaddy regaled me with stories of his young days. He told me stories about becoming our family's second runner, after Burl Lee, Sr. His stories made my hair stand on ends sometimes, as goosebumps rose all over my body; his stories were better than a movie.

Bud Drain (a.k.a. Eddie Wilson his name after his encounter with the law) talked of his times:

"I had no family ta speak of. I wus on my own when I come ta know myself. I scrounged around, livin hi ever I could, livin wit who-sen-ever I could, ta get what I could, til I wus a young buck. I had no schooling. I wus too busy tryin ta live ta sit in a school. Yo grandma Ada learnt me what I come ta know bout readin and writtin. She always tuck care of dat suff. I was strong. I could pick 3 or 400 pounds of cotton, and on a good day, in high cotton I could git 500. Dat was hi it wus in dem days, women did da learin and teachin. Men took care of da farm and work da field. Das hi come I made show yo ma, Willie May and Charlene, got schooling. Yo mama was a teacher."

Telling me how he became our family's next runner, granddaddy began the episode this way.

"I wus just a young buck, on de way ta church to meet yo grandma Ada and I wus lookin pretty good I thought. It rain all de night before, so when I saw des white folks comin, I got ta de side up'genst de wall. But dis ol'red neck peckerwood and his woman stop and he said 'Nigger git out my way.' Nin I knowed I wus pose ta git off the sidewalk ta let'em by and I thought since he saw I wus dress fo Church, and a mud hole long side the sidewalk, he would pass, cause he had lots of room."

Then granddaddy would straighten his posture and puff up his chest while pulling back his shoulder, he would say,

"I ain't gonna step in mud in my Sunday shoes fo nobody! The ol' white man start hollin at me ta get off de sidewalk. A young lawman took me to the lockup".

Granddaddy was arrested and convicted of *"smart mouthing,"* a white man plus not yielding the sidewalk. (Charges during convict leasing fit the incident as a white person described it). They fined him and sold his time to a prison work farm in 1919, the 300th. I cringed, as granddaddy told how he escaped that work farm with a posse and dogs on his trail. He hid out in a swamp, after running away from that prison farm. I shivered, hanging onto his every word, as he described, barely avoiding the bites of poisonous snakes or the jaws of huge alligators, wading through that bog. He said,

"Wit Gators in front and white folks hind me, I tuk the gators every time."

Granddaddy hid out in that marsh for over a month. Running as he did, granddaddy made his mad dash for freedom and life, escaping that convict leasing chain gang, with bloodhounds on his trail. He survived in that creature

The 400th: From Slavery to Hip Hop

infested swamp, sleeping in trees at nights and moving carefully in the day. With white folks hotly dogged his trail, he evaded his captors, just the same. Gathering up my grandma, while still on the run, the two became runners together, like slaves on the *Underground Railroad*. Hiding during the day, and walking mostly at night, they stayed off main roads, and used the North Star, when it was visible, to stay on a northerly course. They covered over one hundred fifty miles to reached northwest Mississippi, where they found relatives and safety. They began lives as sharecroppers. My mother was born on that farm.

My grandfather's encounter with the law introduced me to both parts of the South's new slavery economy—convict leasing and sharecropping. Although I became very familiar with sharecropping, I had no idea what convict leasing was at that time. I would learn years later that this system turned black folks into criminals then sold them to industries, businesses, framers, lumber camps, mines, and mills. It denied an entire race *VOICE* for over 90 years.

Assimilation: A Failed Strategy

This next section changes the focus of *"The 400th"* discussion once again. It marks a very important change in the philosophical and psychological approach of slave descendants' toward their survival. This turn reflects their efforts to create a new mindset and thought pattern regarding freedom, as promised by emancipation, the Civil Rights Bill of 1866, 13th, 14th, and 15th Amendments. It is the second major mental adjustment by Freedmen trying to develop a definition of freedom to fit their reality and their role in America. This definition began with trying to change the second class status of "cheap labor" in America's capitalistic economic system.

The American capitalistic economic system denied former slaves access to America's bounty, fair courts and the vote. Similar to the place slaves arrived in 1828 when David Walker pinned his caustic **Appeal**, which prompted the first real change in slaves' thinking and attitude toward servitude. That change in thought pattern inspired more aggressive actions against slavery. Slaves began fighting to break the chains of bondage or escaping its grip on the *Undergrown Railroad*.

Entering the 20th century, facing **Plessy v. Ferguson**, white supremacy, segregation and "**Dark Age** *angry white men mob madness*," former slaves encountered a new and different hydra—the monster slavery changed again. Although its nature was the same, it continued disguising its appearance, as the American economy evolved. It developed new ways to keep black people locked on the bottom as cheap labor—wage slaves.

Events during the 1890s through 1920 showed former slaves that the federal government was not their friend. Freedom became a façade, as the federal government changed from emancipation and Reconstruction concerns under Pres. Grant to surviving segregation under Woodrow Wilson. Facing white supremacy, segregation, convict leasing and sharecropping became re-enslavement under the Supreme Court.

"The 400th" narrative established earlier that the US government turned its back on former slaves and took the led locking them in the new plantation system. Abolitionists and others fighting to end slavery believed with emancipation, former slaves would develop as free people. As such, former slaves began building independent lives, after gaining the ability to price their labor, gaining the promises of wealth. Freedmen develop real families and communities, like new technologies. They began acquiring education, aiding their acquisition of survival knowledge and improving their communications. They gained entrepreneurial experience participating in entertainment and other business endeavors. They believed mobility made progress possible and allow them to escape poverty.

However, former slaves faced a political system dominated by whites determined to keep them locked on the bottom of America's socioeconomic system, as *cheap labor*. The government gave the ability to vote in writing, but the ability to exercise the franchise in the South was a life or death matter. The vote was the way former slavers could change their status. No one considers freedom for slaves would require a new mental adjustment by not only slaves but whites as well. The fact is, after nearly 413 years of forced bondage, former slaves are still trying to begin life anew without any guarantees, except pain, terror and death.

Their desperate days during contrabands life taught them, in most cases, they were the only real help they would have, learning to live on their own. My family, along with millions of others, struggled through the 1860s and into the 1880s, based on one guiding principle—making families and building communities, as their means of creating stable lives. The saving grace for descendants of American slavery during this period was always was black women! In the face of such a doubtful and daunting future, black women decided to keep having babies, even against those incredible odds of surviving. It was as though they decided to throw babies at the problem until black men figured out a better strategy for *making their nothings into somethings.*

Events and circumstances turned against even that strategy when the US Supreme Courts through **Plessy v. Ferguson** wiped away all gains supposedly guaranteed through emancipation, Civil War, the Civil Rights Bill of 1866, the 13th, 14th, and 15th Amendments. Stripping away all legal protection, and access to courts, former slaves were defenseless against a ravishing reality produced by those working to re-enslave them in a system of *free or cheap labor.*

Abolitionists talked as though, during the struggle for freedom, once emancipated, former slaves would be allowed to assimilate into the larger American society, as free citizens. Historians wrote of the period following emancipation, Civil War, and the contraband period, as though former slaves sat around waiting for white people to save them from their laziness. They ignored the effort government, the US Supreme Court, and white men in tandem organized to block former slaves from changing their status as products of the 3/5 Compromise.

For descendants of American slavery, this is what the 13th, 14th, and 15th Amendments were supposed to eliminate. But following all the events discussed above, enslaved Africans remain, in the eyes of white Americans, despicable people without benefactors. White people's disparaging attitude rendered former slaves' survival a very doubtful proposition, no matter what they attempted.

Following their attempts to assimilate into American society, after fifty years (1865-1919), former slaves began looking for alternatives strategies that would aid their survival. Although they had shown their productive capacity gaining education, starting businesses, making families, and building communities, efforts to degrade and subjugate them continued. Reprisals against blacks by white people in general and government—federal, state, and local—specifically to re-enslaving them, African Americans remained without redeemers.

Assailed on all sides, as this narrative has shown, attacks against them were justified on all levels of society—government, educational, and economic institutions led such attacks. Descendants of American slavery saw no indications assimilation was possible, let alone profitable. African American thinkers and writers began developing the concept of **Black Nationalism,** as a strategy to serve the interest of former slaves.

Beginning this section, I reviewed what descendants of American slavery faced as a backdrop after David Walker introduced *Black Nationalism*. It became the other side of the divide between *assimilation* and Walker's statements in his **Appeal**. Walker was the first to call on slaves to aggressively defy slave masters and slavery, as their right as human beings. Rather than accepting such disparate treatment, as discussed above, Walker offered his sentiments as an alternative to the oppression slaves endured. Walker's prescription became the cornerstone of *Black Nationalism*.

Coming amidst a time when such expressions could cost his life, regarding his thought about slavery, Walker condemned America. A devil-may-care swashbuckling lone rider, David Walker was a beckon for future thinkers on this subject. His statement was so provocative the state of Georgia placed a bounty on Walker's head of "$10,000 dead or alive." America's leaders had no intention of changing their response to former slaves' efforts to change their status. They continued implementing policies that lock them on the very bottom of its capitalistic *cheap labor* economy.

Assimilation gave former slaves only false hopes, a "carrot and stick" strategy to keep former slaves, trying to climb out of the grave of poverty through America's capitalistic "free enterprise" cheap labor system. Keeping descendants of American slavery chasing the capitalistic "free enterprise" system's illusion, as the way to freedom, denied former slaves *VOICE*. Giving *VOICE* to any thoughts contrary to assimilation drew the federal and state government's ire. Whites gave lip service to assimilation, even though access to America's bounty was denied by whites with a rope.

Nevertheless, other intrepid lone riders defied the hazards by working to develop alternatives to assimilation, as David Walker. They ventured into those shark-infested waters at their peril. Now, this narrative explores their efforts to provide a way forward for descendants of American slavery beyond assimilation.

Black Nationalism became more than words for former slaves reaching the 1920s. Developing *Black Nationalism* as a strategy was only recommendations, when Woodrow Wilson took office in 1912, rather than well thought out philosophical principals to guide individuals and groups. These intrepid lone riders developed and voiced political and socioeconomic hopes for the African Diaspora. Prince Hall, Henry Highland Garnet, Sojourner Truth, Frederick Douglass, and others offered glimpses of possibilities for former slaves. These writers grouped in darkness, hoping to develop a strategy that allowed the promise of freedom for blacks in America to shine through. Early thinkers, like abolitionists, express a shared vision of collective desires for former slaves, but most of these ideas had assimilation as the centerpiece. They voiced common demands based on the hope America would welcome former slaves as new citizens.

Black Nationalism: A Strategy of Survival

After 242 years in American bondage, newly Freedmen no longer had countries or any idea of their place of origin. Even if they did, they had no means of returning. Reaching the time of David Walker's **_Appeal_** (1828), Nat Turner's desperate rampage through the Virginia countryside, in 1831, frighten but enraged whites during this period. Turners' revolt served notice and left no doubt enslaved Africans' thinking had changed drastically.

Slave's thinking diverged from the past, signaling a real change in thoughts of how and what they were willing to do about their bondage in America. Two concepts—emigration and assimilation—became the point of this divergence in former slave's visions of their future. These concepts became either side of the fault line of the questions—*Do I leave or do I stay in America?*—separating the two camps in the late 1920s. Those two questions drove the philosophical and psychological strategies African Americans developed and employed trying to survive in America.

"*Returning or not returning to Africa*" began the major debate, which is best exemplified in the writings of Martin Delany on the side of e*migration* and Frederick Douglass' assimilationism and Booker T. Washington's accommodationism on the other. Douglass, Washington, W. E. B. DuBois, and others are the best-known writings for assimilation/accommodation. Newly Freedmen attempted and experimented with the concept of assimilation following emancipation, Civil War, 13th, 14th, and 15th Amendments, the contraband period, and into the *Gilded Age*. They tried to build lives by becoming part of America's mainstream, but found no entry level, but were relegated to the very bottom of America's capitalistic system, as wage slaves.

On the other hand, history books disparaged the ideas and impact of emigration (*Black Nationalism*), if mentioned at all. Yet, Martin Robison Delany (5-6-1812/1-24-1885) saw the challenge for African Americans through the eyes of a *Black Nationalist*. His thinking and writings served as the jumping-off point for those that looked for alternatives to *"assimilation."* This narrative now takes up the ideas of *emigration,* beginning with Delaney's thesis.

For an understanding of the challenge before *emigrationists,* returning to Africa as free citizens, we begin with Paul Cuffe. The first to make a real effort to return emancipated slaves to Africa, Cuffe sought the support of The African Institute (United Kingdom). It showed real interest in working with Paul Cuffe, an African American entrepreneur. In 1810, three years after the end of the **Trans-Atlanta Slave Trade** (1807), the Institute approached the British government, on Cuffe's behalf.

The African Institute requested a land grant in Sierra Leone for Cuffe's *emigration* project. They identified with and facilitated Cuffe's desire to organize a colony for freed slaves in Sierra Leone, Africa (1787). His effort was the first attempt by an American to repatriate freed slaves back to Africa, but it was unsuccessful. Cuffe's project was unrealized due to opposition from white merchants in Freetown, Sierra Leone. They had an absolute monopoly over trade, granted by the British government in Sierra Leone. They saw Cuffe's effort as competition and block his project. Nevertheless, his attempt became the model for even more ambitious attempts in the future.

Martin Robison Delany made the next serious attempt to develop a colony in Africa for freed slaves through *emigration* by a descendant of slavery. Delany was a free black man who rose up through the tremendous disadvantages of being a slave descendant in America. His family became runners, fleeing Virginia to the free state of Pennsylvania. His mother, a literate free woman, demanded education for her children. Martin became an abolitionist, journalist, physician, writer, and international statesman, as well. Attending the first-ever National Negro Convention in 1831 in Philadelphia, Delany encountered David Walker's ***Appeal***. Upon returning to Pittsburg, after hearing abolitionists and other conventioneers' discussions of Nat Turner's rebellion, Delany became an activist. He published *The Mystery*, a black-controlled newspaper (1843) in Pittsburg.

Delany was one of the first four blacks admitted to Harvard Medical School in 1850. He had been trained locally and applied to Harvard, at the same time as three other black men. Harvard expelled the four when white students refused to accept them as equals and would not attend classes with them. Many scholars believe this episode ignited an infernal that burned away Delany's illusions about assimilation and enslaved Africans' ability to achieve equality within America's racist system.

Returning to Pittsburg, Delany was outraged over *The Fugitive Slave Act (1850)*. He gave an impassioned condemnation of slave catchers. "*This law exposes many free blacks to being conscripted into slavery by the law. With courts willing to accept just the word of whites, while requiring a black person, at the time of arrest, to have on his or her person papers of manumission, which allowed slave catchers to cherry-pick through black populations until they find a victim.*" Again, Solomon Northups' *Twelve Years A Slave*, exemplifies how free people were victimized.

Completely over on the side of *emigration—returning to Africa*—Delany left the US to investigate starting a colony in Liberia (1859), a new black nation began by the *American Colonization Society*. But, his dream and trip were cut short by Civil War in America. His thoughts of freedom for all enslaved Africans in America lit Delany's fire. He returned to America and became part of the United States Colored Troops (USCT). Delaney actively recruited blacks, slaves and free, to join the USCT. Delany was commissioned a major in the USCT, becoming the first African American field grade officer in the history of the US Army. Working with the Freedmen's Bureau, after the war, Delany appealed to former slaves to emigration to Africa, Central or South America, as a way of achieving equality.

He said, *"Blacks must leave America to achieve their rights. I feel for that to happen, they must be able to reach majority status in society. I never see that happening within America's racist system."*

Delany railed against the dominant assimilationist theme, *"America is a great land, and the story of your life is how well you fit into that great story."* Delany countered, *"To hell with this place. I want out; it's not heaven, it's hell."* His efforts earned him the respect of most scholars, who proclaim him the *Father of Black Nationalism.* Reading this statement caused me to wonder, how is it possible to write about *Black Nationalism* and not even mention thinkers like David Walker and Martin Delany, as American historians have done in most cases, at least in the books I read?

The next towering figure on the side of *emigration/Black Nationalism* was Edward Wilmot Blyden (8/3/1832-2/7/1912). Blyden immigrated to America from St Thomas, Danish West Indies, to be trained as a minster but was refused entrance into Rutgers Theological College. Following Delany's example of searching for a home outside America, Blyden immigrated to Liberia. He became editor of the *Liberia Herald* and wrote a column, *A Voice From Bleeding Africa.* Traveling over West Africa, particularly Nigeria and Sierra Leone, Blyden edited *The Negro* and *The African World.* He sought every opportunity to build philosophical and psychological support for the struggles of African people against colonialism, which he saw as a twin of American slavery. Taking on David Hume, who popularized and exemplified the prevailing view of *Caucasian superiority*, Blyden declared:

An African is a man like any other and not an inherently inferior being. Those who either refused to learn about the true nature of Africa or distort it to fit into an ignorant mindset are the product of the crudest and most ancient xenophobia..."

Blyden's major work, <u>Christianity, Islam and the Negro Race</u> (1887), was controversial in Great Britain, both for its subject and because whites did not <u>believe a black African was capable of such scholarship.</u> He believed *emigration* was the answer for former slaves, *"Black Americans could eliminate the racial discrimination they suffered in America by returning to Africa and helping to develop it."* This view clashed with African American *assimilationists/accommodationists.* For Blyden, it was a question of blood—*"which does one favor"*—their African ancestors or the handouts received as children of slave masters? For Blyden, *assimilationists* were seeking to attain access to opportunity and equality within the American system, by refusing to leave the plantation, even though slave masters had turned them out.

Let us do away with the sentiment of Race. Let us do away with our African personality and be lost, if possible, in another Race. This is as wise or as philosophical as to say, let us do away with gravitation, with heat and cold and sunshine and rain. Of course, the Race in which these persons would be assimilated is the dominant race, before which, in cringing self-surrender and ignoble self-suppression they lie in prostrate admiration.

Most scholars and researchers regard Blyden as the father of *Pan-Africanism*. His political ideas became a resource for African independence movements and leaders of the 1950s and 60s who followed him—Kwame Nkrumah, Julius Nyerere, Ahmed Sekou Toure and his grandson, Edward W. Blyden III, whose *Sierra Leone Independence Movement (SLIM)* played a key role in winning Sierra Leone's independence from Great Britain (4-27-61).

Blyden believed that exploitation and greed made slave **"black gold."** He seemed to agree with the sentiment that their free labor made them the anchor of the world's economy. Descendants of slavery's *"cheap labor"* continue to underpin the prosperity whites enjoy; simultaneously, it is the source of poverty among Africans the world over. Locked in by the 3/5 Compromise, on the very bottom of America's *cheap-labor* strategy, slave descendants have remained mired in the grave of poverty in the valley of dry bones, as a result of working for free.

Black Nationalism and Garveyism: Building the UNIA

The most noted, yet maligned writer, thinker, strategist, exponent, and proponent of emigration was Marcus Mosiah Garvey. The one word that best describes Marcus Garvey is audacious. He was the first black man who offered hope to millions of former slaves still trapped in America's graveyard of poverty in the valley of dry bones, sixty years after the birth of freedom. His daring scheme of *emigration* spread hope beyond the shores of America to the millions of slavery's descendants around the world. Mr. Marcus Garvey made getting back "home"—back to Africa—a real possibility for slave descendants everywhere. Garvey used emigration, a thought enslaved Africans held close to their hearts, and breathed life into the hopeless dreams of desperate confused African souls across the globe. These were the helpless souls buried in the valley of dry bones Rev. Lee prayed over continually.

Garvey's attempt at *Emigration* gave slave descendants' efforts real focus, trying to establish an independent existence in Africa or in the world elsewhere. Enslaved Africans were brought to America, as individual kidnapped African souls, which came from all along the West coast of Africa, were given unity of purpose. They could not claim citizenship any particular place, even if they knew their progenitors former country. The line of many had spent roughly 300 years in America, or some other slave culture, but America refused to claim them as citizens.

The valley of dry bones is a metaphor, describing the penniless and leaderless vacuum Pres. Abraham Lincoln's emancipation created for enslaved Africans in America (1863). Albeit, emancipation was desperately needed and was a very good thing to do, however, not providing any means of survival for slaves, Lincoln created a confused leaderless people. Hanging on the brink of disaster from that point forward, they remained tethered to poverty, struggling to survive. Consequently, Garvey sought to give former enslaved Africans, a way back home!!!!

David Walker, Martin Delany, and Edward Blyden's thoughts and writings were major guides that help lay a psychological and philosophical foundation to support former slaves' hopes of true freedom. Twenty-two years after the emancipation of slaves around the world, Marcus Garvey was born in Jamaica (4-17-1887). There he struggled, trying to provide leadership, while becoming a journalist, publisher, orator, staunch proponent of *Black Nationalism* and *Pan-Africanism* as well. He left Jamaica looking for the best environment to build an economic movement among descendants of enslaved Africans. He looked first at England but settling on America. Garvey felt New York City offer a conducive and supportive climate for his project.

Stepping into the leadership vacuum Lincoln created, Marcus Garvey set out to build his business model—***The Universal Negro Improvement Association (UNIA)*** in America. His goal was to lift former slaves out of poverty through education, business training, community organization, and self-reliance. Garvey believed the **UNIA** would change the socioeconomic and political prospects for descendants of slavery the world over. He created the first and only socioeconomic revolution for descendants of slavery around the globe.

This Jamaican born entrepreneur entered the leadership vacuum in America, facing the backdrop of white supremacy, segregation, the ***"Dark Age"*** *angry white men mob madness*, convict leasing and sharecropping in the South. Garvey looked at former slaves and saw millions working individually, trying to escape poverty. Through the **UNIA**, he envisioned uniting them into one force, big enough and strong enough to lift millions of former slaves out of poverty. His goal was to teach them how to build wealth, while offer a plan to repatriate of millions back to Africa.

Garvey believed *The-Back-to-Africa Movement* would draw descendants of slavery around the world to his cause. It addressed the two things they could identify with wholeheartedly. Today the idea of going home (back to Africa) may not be palatable to super-modern educated slave descendants. However, in the 1920s, following burning, carnage, disenfranchisement, and deaths, during, before and after **"Red Summer,"** there seemed to be no place for slave descendants to live in peace, except Africa. Along with the lack of access to a fair court system in America, also in other parts of the world, former enslaved Africans, even with the less than modern conditions in Africa, could help create true freedom. Trapped in environments of scarcity and desperation the world over, millions of descendants of slavery looked upon going home to Africa, as true liberation. That sentiment would intrigue and inspire millions of former slaves with hope, as Garvey offered the chance to build wealth by investing in the **UNIA.**

Garvey's decision to come to America was a strategy based on several factors. First, Garvey understood that America had the largest pool of industrially trained black workers in the world. Next, he realized that, even though they were discriminated against and prevented from getting good-paying jobs, black people still had more disposable income than workers in any industrialized nation. Thirdly, most people were not aware, as Garvey, that during bondage, slaves did the work in the South and North, no matter what it was. For Garvey, that meant slaves had lots of skills. He believed, if he could get former slaves to trust him and invest in his plan, his business model could take advantage of their skills, and simultaneously, companies he organized would prosper.

Garvey opened the first **UNIA** division in New York City in 1917. He envisioned the **UNIA,** as a multi-national corporation, anchored by the *Black Star Ship Line*. *The Black Star Line* was the centerpiece of the *Back-to-Africa Movement*.

It provided passage for those in the African Diaspora's return to their ancestral home—Africa *(emigration)*. The **UNIA** reached around the world with divisions such as the *Universal African Legion*, a paramilitary group; the *African Black Cross Nurses*; *African Black Cross Society*; *the Universal African Motor Corps*; *the Black Eagle Flying Corps*; *the Black Cross Trading and Navigation Corporation*; as well as the *Negro Factories Corporation*. The **UNIA** had over 1,100 divisions in more than 40 countries by 1920, one year after **Red Summer.** There were divisions outside America—Mexico, Panama, Costa Rica, Ecuador, Venezuela, Ghana, Sierra Leone, Liberia, India, Australia, Nigeria, Namibia, and Azania/South Africa—to name some countries. Cuba had the most divisions among Caribbean nations. (*Marcus Garvey: Look for Me in the Whirlwind* from Season 13 at TVGuide.com).

Mr. Garvey realized that former slaves could manufacture merchandise whites were selling black people. His intention was to eliminate dependence on white people for survival. Garvey envisioned millions of black workers manufacturing merchandise blacks bought from whites, allowing that money to circulate in black communities. Garvey's changed slave descendants condition as wage slaves working for less, being degraded, and treated as second class Americans making whites richer.

Producing merchandise former enslaved Africans needed would make black people rich instead of whites. Black people, as producers, represented a real threat to American's capitalistic *"cheap labor"* strategy. America opposed the **UNIA** and worked to prevent black Americans from developing, as entrepreneurial competition. Garvey made clear what the expression *"competing with white business"* or *"supporting the American capitalistic system"* meant for black people.

What Made Garvey Successful

Arriving in New York City in 1914, Marcus Garvey recognized, the valuable of the skills Freedmen gained during slavery would be crucial to his plan. Maybe not penniless, but Garvey certainly was not capable of competing with American capitalists, and definitely not able to bankroll the **UNIA** by any stretch of the imagination. His challenge was building trust in his business model, a concept no one had tried any place in the world. Garvey used his self-confidence and persuasiveness, like a checking account, to establish the **UNIA**.

First and foremost, no descendant of slavery had ever established any functioning business on the scale Garvey proposed. He told descendants of American slavery he was going to build the **UNIA** and built it. He preached, *"If I can do it, you can do it too!!"*

Before Garvey, black men were salesmen, shopkeepers, and the sort. Garvey's bold vision made him the quintessential entrepreneur to a people without a prototype. He shared his knowledge with young aspiring industrious black men, as he gained it. Garvey was the first "self-made black man" to help other black men gain experience and confidence in business on an international level.

Garvey believed he could not be a man in the shadows, like assimilationists Douglas and Washington and succeed. Assimilationists insisted former slaves had to be patient and work for *"the acceptance of whites to progress."* Garvey believed just the opposite! He believed he not only had to exemplify what he was saying, but had to demonstrate what that meant for black people.

The text of his sermon was *"If I can do it, you can do it too."* He preached this constantly to build former slaves' confidence. Garvey counted on vicarious learning and visualization to capture former slaves' attention. He unleashed his unrestrained enthusiasm, presenting ostentatious demonstrations to convince descendants of slavery they had untapped potential and economic productivity, while encouraging them to support his movement. Put another way; he displayed real showmanship.

Garvey selected the perfect place to set up—New York City. Harlem had become a magnet, drawing African people from around the world to the *Harlem Renaissance*. **Look for Me in the Whirlwind,** a documentary of Garvey's life, the same as *Amazing Grace' The Story of William Wilberforce*, educated me. Synonymous to David Walker, once established in Harlem, Garvey spoke only to former enslaved Africans descendants about his project. He took his plan straight to the masses, who were starving for leadership. Garvey roared his credo, *"One GOD! One Aim! One Destiny!"*, to huge crowds, eager to hear his message. Taking to the streets of Harlem, Garvey drew admiring crowds wherever he appeared and to whatever he presented.

Garvey sold-out Madison Square Garden, something no individual black man had ever done. He held gigantic full-dress parades through Harlem's street for **UNIA** followers and events in places that demonstrated his appeal. Again, this was a first for a black man in America. No one had ever seen the likes of Garvey. His ability to reach and excite descendants of slavery around the world was unprecedented, for established black leaders, let alone, an almost penniless immigrant from the islands.

The Negro World, Garvey's newspaper, was the key to his success. Once Garvey began speaking to the Diaspora through his newspaper, enslaved Africans responded to his message. Garvey developed a unique distribution system with black seamen. They delivered **The Negro World** as they docked, traveling the globe. He used a similar system developed by David Walker with his **Appeal,** and John Sengstacke would emulate with the **Chicago Defender. The Negro World** gave all former slaves the same vision of their plight.

Building his model, Garvey was the first black man to speak beyond America's ghetto continuously. **The Negro World** allowed him to pitch the **UNIA's** multi-dimensional approach, which offered several different programs. Garvey built an image of a very fluent, aggressive, and powerful spokesman for the African Diaspora.

Garvey's newspaper carried his words and dreams to millions, who saw him as an honest idealist. **The Negro World's** circulation grew by leaps and bounds, as more and more blacks around the world identified with his dream and bought into his vision. Through **The Negro World,** Garvey's words gave descendants of slavery a common vision of their place in the world. Black people began to believe they could do whatever Mr. Garvey said; he convinced them, it was possible to become whatever they imagined.

The Negro World allowed Garvey to build upon Delany's *Black Nationalism* and Blyden's *Pan-African* philosophies. His words inspired millions around the world; he captivated black people that flocked to join his global movement. Garvey's image as an honest idealist, create real devotion between millions of slave descendants that lined up shoulder to shoulder with him.

After only a few months, the **UNIA** ballooned. It gained over 2 million members across the US and twice as many across the world. Seeing the **UNIA** as their future was so alluring, descendants of slavery began pooling their pennies to invest in Garvey's magical vision. Black people came to believe they could build something for their families—their children—by buying into his dream. He promised independence for blacks through the **UNIA,** something former slaves truly desired. Black people in larger and small communities began investing their pennies, buying stock in **UNIA** divisions weekly.

Even though the individuals in these communities were impoverished, the communities had wealth. That fact brings this narrative back to its major theme, *"It did not matter to former slaves, how much money Garvey made, what matters to poor black folks was what he did with that money."* Descendants of slavery were not concerned with how much they were making on their investment with the ***UNIA***. What mattered most was they were making something, whereas, before Garvey, they had nothing. Their investments were making their heap of nothing into something that was changing the future for theirs and other families. For the first time a black man had answered black women's decision to "throw babies at the problem until black men developed a better strategy."

Why the Federal Government Plotted to Destroy the UNIA

The problem I encountered writing about Mr. Marcus Garvey was finding the words. There were plenty of them available, but I needed to find the rhythm of his **Blues,** because what happened to him is a very sad, sad song. His basso profundo was so far below the legato I wanted readers to hear. Moreover, it was of such exceptionally low and uneven range, its jagged quality and vibrations should have shaken and awakened the dead in the valy of dry bones that Rev. Lee prayed over.

Unjustly stretched upon the gallows, before the world, as a fraud, by the US government, no number of shrill cries or crescendos from bleeding hearts could drown out that one long lonely gravelly groan, his steamship's horn made, leaving the United States Harbor. It is as though, the ship's horn, understood what that low, long and deathly sound really meant, as it rattled the dry bones in the graveyard of poverty, trying to live again for Mr. Garvey.

My inadequacy expressing the deep sorrow and pain descendants of slavery felt, as the US government drove Mr. Garvey into exile was beyond words. His grievous lost was something only slavery's descendants felt and understood what losing Mr. Garvey truly meant. The lynching of Mr. Garvey made what follows a deeply regretful ode and the best I could compose for such an audacious, devil-may-care, swashbuckling, lone rider.

The US government destroyed the truth of his written story, once they completed their dirty deed. And, that which they did not destroy has been distorted, making the truth impossible to know. Although reminiscent of the trump up charges my granddaddy was sent to that convict leasing prison farm, the impact of Mr. Garvey's lost was far more egregious. *"The 400th"* narrative now looks at how Mr. Marcus Garvey was railroaded out of America because of his powerful impact on descendant of American slavery. This look back began with his Mr. Garvey's legacy. It is not an assessment from the perspective of successes or failure, but from the new perspective, he brought to former slaves' survival battles, as penniless emancipated slaves.

Mr. Garvey's self-improvement strategy for slave descendants across the world is why they supported his business model and the technology he developed. Why the federal government responded with such hostility towards the **UNIA,** most people have no idea, but it is comparable to *"the People's Grocery Store"* lynching just 12 years earlier. Mr. Garvey's business model addressed the things slave descendants desired most—educational opportunities, business training, and political involvement. He was one man, up against the white business socioeconomic and political structure in America and Great Britain. These two super power—the US and Great Britain—worked in tandem to destroy Mr. Garvey and his UNIA because he gave them unity.

The **UNIA** was trying to counter the political forces, economic power, and wealth slavery produced in the western world for white people, and the US federal government stepped in to protect the wealth white people gained from "wage slavery."

For descendants of American slavery, David Walker's ***Appeal***, Martin Delany's ***Black Nationalism,*** and Edward Blyden's ***Pan-Africanism*** laid the foundation upon which Mr. Garvey stood. He gave status and meaning to the term *"black businessman."* Former slaves and descendants believed he was trying to build an economic floor beneath them, as well as a stairway out of the valley of dry bones. They saw escaping poverty through the ***UNIA's*** self-help collective enterprises, like an escalator, elevating former slaves, up out of the grave of poverty.

Never before had anyone presented such programs to benefit descendants of slavery, as Mr. Garvey's ***UNIA***. Mr. Garvey inspired millions of former slaves and descendants across the world to believe they had a way out of poverty, if they threw in with the ***UNIA***. Mr. Garvey believed that the knowledge and opportunities provided by ***UNIA*** were keys to empowering those that bought into his model. Providing jobs and opportunities for former slave and descendants made his ***UNIA*** opposition to America's capitalistic *"cheap labor"* strategy. (<u>The Marcus Garvey And Universal Negro Improvement Association Papers</u>: Robert A. Hill).

I also offer another perspective on the US government's plot to destroy the ***UNIA*** because it was imperiling America's *"cheap labor"* strategy. Woodrow Wilson and J. Edgar Hoover's ***Red Summer*** attacks were developed during Wilson's White House screenings of *The Birth of Nation*. The fact that the ***UNIA*** had its headquarters in the US became Mr. Garvey's Achilles' heel and the weakness in his brilliant plan. Resembling a modern-day *"Othello,"* Mr. Garvey had no way to defend himself against the federal government, which is what makes what happened to him such a tragedy.

The US government had one thing Mr. Garvey could not counter, *"no fair courts in America for black people."* Without fair courts, the federal government tied both of Mr. Garvey's hands behind his back. Simultaneously, J. Edgar Hoover had both hands free, plus all the hands of the informants he hired. All these free hands went to work digging the grave in which the government's lynch mob buried Mr. Garvey. But, this mob was not in the street; it was in a US courtroom. And, the government plot illustrates why America's slave descendants have never been able to escape poverty.

The federal government built a fallacious case against Mr. Garvey based on trumped-up charges, concocted by Hoover's agents and informants. First, the attacks of ***Red Summer of 1919***, in large part, in my view, were designed to cut off Mr. Garvey's revenue stream, by attacking prosperous black communities in America. These attacks allowed Wilson and Hoover to kill two bird with one stone. The US Supreme Court as protector of whites with ***Plessy v. Ferguson***—

separate but equal, left former slaves vulnerable, as lynch mobs attacked and robbed blacks during the **"Dark Age"** *angry white men mob madness era.*

Along with another government plot, during *"The Gilded Age,"* bringing millions (5.2) Europeans immigrants to America to fill jobs, it would not allow former slaves to fill. The government's plan was to keep blacks on the bottom of America's *cheap-labor* strategy, by structuring discrimination against black Americans into America's economy. The federal government, through segregation and white supremacy, restricted access to economic opportunities for former slaves. Without fair courts in America, slave descendants could not challenge their unjust treatment.

Woodrow Wilson's instituted segregation and white supremacy to create scarcity and desperation among descendants of American slavery. J. Edgar Hoover's job, as the point man against radicals, was to identify and neutralize any individual or group, trying to change the environment of scarcity and desperation the federal government created for African Americans.

There is no doubt this was Wilson's goal of maintaining black people as the foundation of America's *"cheap labor strategy."* In essence, Woodrow Wilson's statement coming into office, **"Self-preservation [forced whites] to rid themselves, by fair means or foul, of the intolerable burden of governments sustained by the votes of ignorant Negroes,"** said it all. Making an even sharper point regarding the federal government's plot, in 1917, Pres. Woodrow Wilson tasked Hoover to "round up **the Reds,"** painting bull's eyes on black communities calling them *"havens of the Reds,"* and *"tools of the communists,"* created alarm when descendants of slavery made demand for equality and justice. Wilson created an atmosphere that made African Americans demands for social changes—racial equality, access to education, labor rights, voting rights, justice in America's courts and the rights of self-defense for black that fought white mobs attacks, (*Racism in the Nation's Service: Government Workers and the Color Line in Woodrow Wilson's America,* Eric S. Yellin, 2013 UNC Press.)

Woodrow Wilson laid the foundation for the attacks of **Red Summer 1919,** during his White House screening of **The Birth of A Nation.** Wilson's strategy was to kill the **UNIA**, a successful black business model. Again, killing two birds with one stone, the federal government's plot against Garvey hinged on trumped-up charges. Those charges create the illusion that Mr. Garvey and the **UNIA** engaged in criminal activity, which nothing was farther from the truth.

Hoover focused on Garvey, as a radical when he began publishing **The Negro World** newspaper in Harlem in 1917. **The Negro World** allowed Garvey to speak beyond the ghetto to slave descendants around the world. Author, Robert Hill, in his eye-opening treaties *Marcus Garvey, Universal Negro Improvement Association,* 1983 presents complete documentation of the first official surveillance of the **UNIA** by Hoover's Radical Division of the BOI. My research shows

The 400th: From Slavery to Hip Hop

Hoover used the **Red Scare 1917** to cover up searching for a reason to deport Garvey.

The record shows in a conversation between Hoover and an agent, code name Riddly where Hoover said, *"As of yet, you do not have anything we can use to proceed against him (Garvey), to deport him, but keep looking."* Hoover had nothing illegal when he began investigating both the **UNIA** and Garvey. Hoover set out to make it appear the **UNIA** was a criminal enterprise. The criminal and civil prosecution efforts, arose because Garvey was seriously affecting Pres. Wilson's efforts to keep former slaves in America locked on the bottom of *"America's capitalistic cheap labor strategy,"* the goal of white supremacy.

Preserving white supremacy and *"American Capitalism,"* were the bottom line for Wilson and Hoover's plot against Marcus Garvey and was design to stop black people from building wealth. Hoover left telltale signs behind, trying to entrap Garvey. He hired informants and used black leaders to undermine the trust poor blacks had in Garvey. Prior to finding any evidence of probable cause, Hoover used so-called African American leaders, like W.E.B. DuBois and James Weldon Johnson of the NAACP, Chandler Owen and A. Philip Randolph of the Messenger Magazine, in his plot. These Negro leaders were tremendously jealous of Mr. Garvey's success. They could not understand Mr. Garvey's success neither could they emulate what he was accomplishing among descendants of slavery, nor could they appeal to poor black as Garvey. They envied the way black people rally to his side. Whether hired by Hoover or just trying to make points with white people, they joined Hoover's attack on Garvey's credibility. (<u>Racism in the Nation's Service: Government Workers and the Color Line in Woodrow Wilson's America:</u> Eric S. Yellin, 2013 UNC Press.)

Aiding Hoover's plot, DuBois (1924) echoed assimilationists claim, *"Marcus Garvey is the most dangerous enemy of the Negro race in America and the world."* Owen and Randolph reflected integrationists' sentiments speaking about Mr. Garvey in their magazine. They wrote as though the race issue was more about class than skin color. They called Mr. Garvey the *"messenger boy of the Klan"* and a *"Supreme Negro Jamaican jackass,"* while using the initials of the **UNIA** as a derogatory slur, the *"Uninformed Negroes Infamous Association."* (<u>Marcus Garvey Universal Negro Improvement Association:</u> Robert Hill, Univ. of California Press (1983),

Following his White House screenings, Wilson projected the **UNIA** as a threat to *"American Capitalism."* I believe capitalists and politicians, at those White House gatherings, saw the plan for the attacks of **Red Summer**, as a way to "interdict" Garvey's revenue streams coming from prosperous black communities. Mob attacks, during **Red Summer**, struck cities where over 2 million black people were investing pennies to fund **UNIA** activities. Although on a much higher level, this is not any different from what Judge DuBois and Barratt concocted against the owners of the *People's Grocery Store* to kill them as competition.

Pres. Wilson and Hoover thought by interdicting (destroy) Garvey's source of investment from the US; the **UNIA** would wither and fall apart. The point here is that white mobs during **Red Summer** sacked and pillaged particular black communities. They stripped them of valuables, carrying off what they could, while burned what was left (**Black Wall Street** is another example; mobsters destroy the community wealth of people supporting the **UNIA**). These attacks brought desperation and scarcity back, as fixtures in many prosperous black communities, which were left trying to recover, after **Red Summer** and other mob attacks. Many were buying stock in the **UNIA** weekly.

Hoover's plan interrupted Mr. Garvey's revenue stream, coming from black communities in the United States, by destroying them. However, those attacks did not destroy the **UNIA**. Garvey proved to be far more resourceful and resilient than either Wilson or Hoover imagined. Using the special magic that got him where he was, Mr. Garvey shifted resources around, because he had investments coming to the **UNIA** from other parts of the world. The **UNIA**, though not a Hydra, had more than one head. Enslaved Africans people truly believed the **UNIA** belong to them, so they invested even more in the **UNIA** to help Mr. Garvey fight off the US Government.

Again I say, the one thing Mr. Garvey could not counter or protect against was *"no fair courts in America,"* for black people. Similar to sharecroppers and those trapped in convict leasing, Hoover's plan became *"Getting Garvey into court any way possible to face an all-white jury!"* The charge did not matter because Garvey was not an American citizen. The federal government could deport him, as an undesirable, for getting arrested. As I said earlier, with Hoover's own words, *"As of yet, you do not have anything we can use to proceed against him (Garvey), to deport him, but keep looking."* Hoover's informants searched for any reason to deport Garvey from the US. That is why he hired hundreds of black informants to infiltrate the **UNIA**.

Hoover's informants' job was to make Garvey appear to be a scoundrel. So, not only would he be discredited, but his business model would be repudiated as well. Following Mr. Garvey's conviction, the US and British governments destroyed thousands of documents related to the prosecution of Marcus Garvey. Consequently, there is no way of knowing today, with any degree of certainty, what Hoover did, getting Mr. Garvey into court. But, we do know, he used black leaders like Chandler Owen to float accusation that *"Garvey is a con man, who in the name of black pride is perpetrating one of history's greatest swindles," (Marcus Garvey, Universal Negro Improvement Association* (1983) Robert Hill).

Garvey's message of *Black Nationalism* and a free black Africa met considerable resistance from prominent leaders in America and Great Britain (United Kingdom). Taking advantage of this dissension among so-called black leaders, Hoover's informants, after infiltrating the **UNIA**, circulated lies claiming Garvey was wasteful, incompetent, and motivated by greed. Informants sabotaged the

UNIA, along with jealous black leaders like DuBois and A. Philip Randolph, creating further dissension within the ***UNIA*** <u>(Black Power and the Garvey Movement;</u> 1971 Theodore Vincent). They spoke at times, as though they believed poor blacks were holding educated Negros back from gaining greater acceptance from whites because of Garvey.

Unable to find any illegality with which to charge Garvey and get him into court, to face all white prosecutors, judges, and juries, Hoover used a black man, one of his informants, to create a spurious and frivolous trump-up charge that did the dirty deed. Hoover's informant claimed he sent Garvey a twenty-five dollar ($25.00) check through the mail. Charging that the twenty-five dollar ($25.00) check constituted mail fraud, the US Government sentenced Garvey to 5 years in prison. They deported him to England, where the British exiled Mr. Garvey to Jamaica.

The US government, in a world with fair courts, would have had to prove Garvey/UNIA actual received the check through the mail and was not planted, while the BOI agents rummaged through ***UNIA files***, looking for evidence that they never found. As far as the world knows, Hoover could have written that $25.00 check, sitting at his desk. The bottom line in Garvey's sad, sad ***Blues*** is a chorus of groans from the valley of dry bones, as they rattled, trying to live again for Mr. Garvey.

Everything America did after emancipation was to maintain black people in poverty, as the foundation of its *"cheap labor"* capitalistic workforce. If Mr. Garvey's success had continued, America's *"cheap labor"* strategy would have gone down the drain. The deportation of Mr. Marcus Garvey and the destruction of the ***UNIA*** said to me; the US Government did not want descendants of American slavery getting out of poverty or leaving the country, going *"Back-to-Africa."*

Garvey Through the Eyes of Rev. Burl Lee

I say again, this narrative is not about the lives of those that inspired changes, but the impact those changes had and how they affected conditions and circumstances slave descendants faced from an international perspective. My great-grandfather, Rev. Burl Lee, Jr., told me stories of attended lodge meetings, conventions, ceremonies, and other large gatherings, and Marcus Garvey was the only conversation.

Rev. Lee said, *"Me and the rest of the colored folks prayed that God send us somebody to help us. And, I believe he sent us Mr. Marcus Garvey. He wus the best thang ta happen fo colored folk since God sent the birth of freedom. At meetins many spoke bout Black Nationalism. Although, I wus not sho of the real meanin of the words at the time, as some folks, but I knew what wus being said, when they mentioned Mr. Garvey's leadership. They had long talks, and some got pretty hot under the collar, concerning Mr. Garvey's business program. I feel he spoke as a man of God. He was not talking bout life in the hereafter. He talked bout success in this life; achieving economic, cultural, social, and political success, these were the things that would help poo Negros."*

Speaking of Garvey's religious message, Rev. Lee declared,

"He was a man of God like me. He tried ta look out for folks that couldn't do that for they self. Mr. Garvey was a great man because he made ignorant poo penniless colored folks into folks with respect."

I believe descendants of slavery saw Marcus Garvey, as bigger than life. Rev. Lee said,

"He was a lone rider, fighting white folks on behalf of us poo colored folks, who really needed a hero. Folks trusted Mr. Garvey to learn'em how to live by them self."

Garvey: A New Model of Leadership

The following statements may seem vague or even cryptic to some degree, but it reflects what J. Edgar Hoover had at the beginning of his witch hunt, in terms of authority and evidence as proof at its conclusion. It was Marcus Garvey's blackness that prompted the government's dedication to bringing him down. Hoover used government resources, and his position to make his suspicion a legal matter, without any evidence of wrongdoing. Understanding what Freedmen faced, walking off plantations by the millions, without any knowledge of the world awaiting them and fifty years later, for Mr. Marcus Garvey, someone they never heard of before he showed up, to produce the successful existence of the ***UNIA,*** with him being a penniless immigrant from the Islands, I consider the man a miracle worker.

The major dilemma driving white people of J. Edgar Hoover's ilk is their overpowering need to know the what, how and why of black people. This breed is very suspicious when it comes to black Americans. They desired to know and verify a black person's veracity, presence, actions, and statements, at all times. Whenever or wherever a black person shows up unexpectedly someplace, at an unexpected time, during an unexpected venue, even though such a black person has a right to do or act as they are, and that knowledge may be beyond a Hooverike's available knowledge regarding such persons, they will act on their desire to satisfy their curiosity or overpowering need to know all about that black person. This fact is verified continually today, in regards to police murders, where black people are accosted, without probable cause, and demands are made to satisfy a policeman curiosity. A many a black man end up dead because they refuse to satisfy that white man's demands, which violate their rights of self-incrimination.

Such a white person will investigate any black person that comes under their perusal. Whether the actions of Hooverikes are legal or illegal is of no consequence. That person is black, and in their mind, they are up to something, why else would they be there? The best example comes from a movie, although it really happened, *"American Gangster,"* when Frank Lucas (played by Denzel Washington) enters the scene wearing a matching fur coat and hat. Unknown to an undercover cop (Russell Crowe), based on his appearance alone, he becomes a suspect, of what is not clear.

Marcus Garvey's problem began with a suspicious white man. Garvey was doing something white people disproved. He was trying to give former slaves hope through the ***UNIA.*** But, a suspicious white man—Hoover—looked and saw something totally different. His job was to quash anything that might give black people hope. White people see hope as a dangerous thing when it comes to black people. Hope is a threat because it can grow into real possibilities. If it does, then "niggers" might start acting and thinking like white folks. These types of suspicious attitudes or actions by white men, black men encountered on all levels of interaction in America's socioeconomic and political environment, and they spell trouble for black entrepreneurs, based solely on a white man's suspension. No other situations, actions, and individuals exemplify the previous statements, as did Marcus Garvey.

Unlike any other slave descendant before him, Mr. Marcus Garvey's leadership united former enslaved Africans, around the world, behind a vision only he saw. That vision was the **UNIA**. Mr. Garvey preached *"One GOD! One Aim! One Destiny!"* He gave former slaves a common vision for the first time since David Walker. Garvey's genius was the ability to make that vision come alive in the minds of poor black laborers and farmers, so much so, they pooled pennies into millions of dollars on his words alone.

Mr. Garvey taught poor blacks what it truly meant to *"make something out of nothing."* He showed poor black laborers and farmers that *"making something out of nothing means making something out of yourself because white folks see you as nothing."* Former slaves had never seen, and neither had white people, an individual black man rise from nothing, to become an international leader and entrepreneur in the face of government opposition. Under such conditions, whites, like Hoover, were convinced something is amiss. *"The nigger is during something wrong!!!!"*

Based on Mr. Garvey's words alone, his business model became so inspiring and impressive it brought former slaves thinking out of the 1600s into the 20th century. Garvey had a different magic from Robert Church, Jr. Mr. Garvey built his model on faith alone. Penniless former slaves were awed by the vision that came through Mr. Garvey's eyes. His words made them believe in something they could see only through Mr. Garvey's eyes.

More so than David Walker, Martin Delaney, and Edward Blyden, Garvey actualized the concept of *VOICE*, addressing slave descendants worldwide. However, Garvey spoke to the African Diaspora as his only audience. He made entrepreneurial success a real possibility for African Americans. Through his newspaper—**The Negro World**—he educated blacks across the globe, with messages of self-respect, being productive, the need for unity and cooperation. Mr. Garvey reversed the subservient and dependent mindset slave masters created during bondage.

Mr. Garvey was the archetype for *making something out of nothing*, which deserves repeating *"making something out of nothing means to make something out of one's self."* Emancipation made former slaves something to themselves, but freedom made them worthless to white people. Slaves had economic value for whites, but free black men were worthless to white capitalists. Garvey was teaching former slaves how to become a real value to them. Garvey was lining up African nations that wanted **UNIA** members to come to their countries. His *Back-to-*

Africa Movement gave those that wanted to return to Africa the possibility of doing so.

These countries saw how they could benefit from their skills and commitment former American slaves would bring to their nations as citizens. Without any investment, they saw gains, because former slaves would pay the cost to emigrate. Moreover, such countries would also gain people that could train their people. Similar to Vancouver's and Mexico's desire for runaway slaves to settle on their borders because slaves would fight to stay free, African nations, wholeheartedly supported Mr. Garvey's *"Back to Africa Movement."* For the first time, after 300 years, hundreds of thousands of disaffected blacks would reverse the **"Middle Passage,"** going back home.

Garvey is the brightest star of black business along the arc of social change leading to the 21st Century, as black people approached ***"The 400th".*** More than just a man in the eyes and imagination of slave descendants worldwide, they saw Mr. Garvey as a phenomenon. Most assuredly, Rev. Lee echoed Mr. Garvey's concerns for the fate of enslaved African descendants when he sermonized, *"Will these dry bones live again?"*

Traditional Slaves Belief in Magic and Hoodoo

Deporting Marcus Garvey and destroying the ***UNIA*** were devastating blows to descendants of American slavery. Hoping to build an independent existence in America, after emancipation, they faced efforts dedicated to maintaining their dependency. Exiling Mr. Garvey allowed the US to sever connections he established between Africans and former slaves in different parts of the world. Africans knew Garvey's people in Africa, but not in America and other places.

Chandler Owen, A. Philip Randolph, W.E.B. DuBois, and James Weldon Johnson helped J. Edgar Hoover, and the US government destroyed the ***UNIA*** and depot, Mr. Garvey. Africans witnessed black leaders helping whites destroy the ***UNIA***, an organization that helped black people. Consequently, Africans did not know who to trust. Not coincidentally, US slave descendants could not leave the US without government permission. Going back to Africa looked like a jail break to white people. White people considered "niggers" that wanted to leave America as renegades or desperado. Those who did were labeled communists. Hence, the whole African American population was on lockdown. Maintaining communications Mr. Garvey established was impossible for black Americans.

Moving from Mr. Marcus Garvey to my next topic may seem to break the continuity of this storyline, but this section looks at enslaved Africans efforts maintain self-knowledge and intelligence. Primarily following emancipation, Freemen were unable to speak, write, or clearly understand language written or spoken. Pushed out into a world where death came at the hands of whites with or without reason, Freedmen's survival teetered on the brink of disaster. Without guidance and very little support to aid their survival, but with words alone, Marcus Garvey taught former slaves to believe they were far more than what white people said and were willing to allow them to be.

Enslaved Africans were isolated in America, which prevented or made it very difficult for them to communicate with those in other parts of the world. Unable to communicate across the Diaspora, blacks in the South described their isolation, as being locked behind the *"cotton curtain."* Former slaves were hampered by the random and haphazard manner they had for acquiring language, which was not incidental to education being critical to their survival. Their difficulty understanding information communicated in Standard English created needs for interpreters, who could be trusted? Black Americans were defenseless, isolated and disconnected from the rest of humanity, as the government on all levels—federal, state, and local—sponsored and supported massacres of entire communities.

Consequently, it seemed all the dark forces in the universe were actively preying on them. Their cries to government for help to move beyond their *free or cheap labor* status fell on deaf ears. Former slaves probably felt all the wicked forces in America had the government under a spell cast by "the dark of the moon." Evil spells seemed to blind politicians to the degradation and death former slaves faced and endured.

Without help or sympathy, all they could depend on were their beliefs and practices that brought them to that point. Former slaves depended on the beliefs and practices they believed were tied to Africa. During slavery, they used things they remembered or picked up from other slaves that seemed to be knowledge brought from Africa. Anything that connected them to Africa gave them comfort and was cherished. Such things or knowledge, they believed held magical significance and powers. Slaves had nothing that connected them to a past beyond slavery. African beliefs connected them to a past that said there is something other than slavery.

These memories became a system of thoughts that guided many slaves in this alien world that could not be trusted. Many called such things and thoughts or beliefs superstition—a belief or trust in magic, chance, or a notion contrary to evidence—and considered ignorant on the part of slaves. This opinion is shared by today's super-educated and sophisticated upwardly mobile blacks who look back at such times through their education and religion. They reject any information from the past and trust what their education says about everything.

Educated people have something they believe they can trust and depend on to work a particular way, in most cases. Slaves, on the other hand, looked upon a murky and confusing reality, where nothing was certain from one moment to the next except terror, pain and death. For all intent and purposes, white men stood in "God's" place. Whatever they said affected them as "God" speaking from on high. For slaves in that world, the only sure things were toil, pain, degradation, terror and death.

I wanted to understand, as much as I could, about whether folk magic had real significance to enslaved Africans, coming out of slavery. Moreover, whether folk magic played any real role or had any basis in former slaves' survival, once they faced life on their own. Whether what they believed, aided newly Freedmen in any way, was my dilemma. The following segment is an investigation into the subject of traditional African American folk magic and healing. I introduce this topic here to give background to the question— *"Why black people think and behave as they do?"* That question motivated my research which looked into the impact of slavery on Freedmen's mindset once free.

The first thing I learned was the answer is not straight forward or clearly stated. Denied the most basic knowledge of themselves—how, why, and what made them slaves—left former slaves wondering how the real world worked. In a world without context, former slaves had to fill in the blanks best they could. Memories of the past before bondage or what others said were all they could rely. Enslaved Africans' thoughts may not have fit their situation, but what they had they trusted to worked in a life where the only guarantees beyond toil, terror, pain, and punishment was death.

My intention is not to influence readers' beliefs on this subject or convince them of anything. I provided this retrospective for those who did not grow up as I did. This discussion is a very quick glimpse backward at a world many believe slaves left behind, if they were aware of it at all. Leaving slavery did not mean it was left behind and was not part of the everyday thinking and living habits after surviving slavery.

One of the strongest influences on slaves' psychological and philosophical development was Christianity. There is a lot said about Christianity's influences on slaves. However, today very little is said about former slaves' influences on Christianity. Before enslaved Africans arrived in the Western Hemisphere, they had spiritual beliefs and customs. This narrative has shown that slave masters considered those spiritual beliefs and customs heathen, ignorance, or idolatry. The same as drums, which were very important to Africans' rituals and worship, consequently, slave masters ruthlessly suppressed anything slaves believed about their world before bondage.

Slave masters forced their beliefs upon slaves and compelled them to accept or pretend to accept their beliefs. Slaves accepted their master's religion but held on to the spirituality that they remembered or was passed to them by older slaves. Those past beliefs shaped what and how completely slaves accepted those new beliefs forced on them. Slave master's religions worked well for white folks, but slaves could not trust it to answer their prayers of deliverance from bondage and the brutality, which these same white Christian who supposedly believe in the same God.

Slaves' basic beliefs and spirituality were a kind of magic they understood. It was the only thing that gave them a sense of self. Old habits and beliefs die hard, if at all. So, out of sight of master, slaves learned to disguise, how they spoke to their African Gods, with what master wanted to see and hear, like Minsterlsy. Slaves pass their thoughts and beliefs to other slaves, which was the nature of their spoken word culture. Their religious practices became entrenched; it reflected their African-ness. Deeply recessed in their psyche, African folklore and beliefs were part of their adaptations to life in America.

These rites, spells, amulets, curses, and recipes were all part of the magic of their belief system. This magic worked in the culture from which they came and formed the bases of enslaved Africans medicinal and protective belief systems in America as well. Without doctors or restraints on slave masters' brutality and viciousness, slaves utilized anything or any thoughts that aided their medicinal and protective needs. They used rites, spells, amulets, curses, and recipes, trying to deal with the harshness, cruelty, and caprice of slave masters. Such beliefs seem nonsensical or stupid, in black people's present-day sophisticated and educated context. However, slaves were not the only ones affected by such beliefs; whites accepted them, as slaves accepted Christianity.

While during this research, I became familiar with slaves' rationale for many things I thought were ridiculous, in my educated mind. After reading slave narratives, just a few ideas out of the mouths of slaves aided my understanding. Slaves had to weave mental and cultural matrices to sustain their survival through all the arbitrary changes and deathly outcomes around them. Slaves weaved mental and cultural matrices to sustain their survival through all the arbitrary changes and deathly outcomes around them. Most importantly, they brought that mindset with them, as emancipation gave them what white people said was "freedom."

Much has been said and written about black churches and the African religious traditions across the slave Diaspora. African American spirituality developed similar diversity over the centuries. Today less information is available on the subject of blacks' spirituality and the role of magic in it than was available in previous times. Hoodoo, Conjure, root work, and candle burning exemplify the very superficial look I take at these concepts and may seem to some these concepts have nothing to do with an intelligent look at slave descendants' mental development in America.

African-American Hoodoo: more than magic was a topic posted by Ed Moorhouse of Rutgers University (1-4-2013). It is a discussion of traditional forms of herbal healing known as **Hoodoo**. Just one form of several herbal healing beliefs, hoodoo is about more than using hex-breaking oils and candles to ward off bad vibes. According to a new book by scholar Katrina Hazzard-Donald, who says, *"Some of the material on African culture and tradition presents inaccurate premises. This has happened a lot with Hoodoo."* Explaining the rationale for her statement in her book, *Mojo Workin': The Old African-American Hoodoo System* (2012), " *Hoodoo is a form of African-American folk magic, (Hoodoo, Voodoo, Oeah, Palo Mayobe, Santeria and Quimband) that developed from a combination of belief from a number of separate African cultures, after Africans were kidnapped and brought to America, during the slave trade."*

Although Hoodoo began as a religion among African people, it took on secular status after the 1880s, when former slaves introduced their cultural perspectives into the churches they organized—Colored "Christian" Methodist Episcopal (CME), Zion African Methodist Episcopal, (AME) and African Methodist Episcopal Church (AME)—to name a few. Hoodoo first emerged in the South when people from West African tribes—Congo, Sierra Leone, and Ghana, which is the region my family is believed originated—began arriving in America as slaves. Hoodoo beliefs are purely naturalistic and use herbs, minerals, and even animals in its practices to achieved healing. According to Dr. Hazzard-Donald:

"Chewing the root" was done to release the sap of a plant to conjure its spiritual power. A tremendous amount of exploitation began right around World War I (1912), when white merchants started viewing Hoodoo as a commercial enterprise. Such merchants were not believers or practitioners but simply sold Hoodoo products for money." Hazzard-Donald went on, *"What many people started to see is something that I call commercialized or tourist Hoodoo. It has been presented as the 'real authentic' Hoodoo, but is just a sham."*

Whites took advantage of black people spiritual beliefs commercializing hoodoo. In support of Dr. Hazzard-Donald description of commercial products as gimmicks, I offer the following information published by Time Magazine (1939). The article gives a partial list of products sold nationwide by the white owners of Keystone Laboratories (1920). Keystone was located in Memphis, Tennessee. It was one of the largest mail-order suppliers of Hoodoo and Conjure products, as well as cosmetics for the African American market.

Keystone Laboratories, Inc., 491 South Third St., Memphis, was a Mail Order House, Curio Products Company, and White Line. It represented Poreen Ointment, La Jac Lovin' Pink Cream for Dark Skins, or La Jac Orange Beauty Glow Cream skin foods or skin whiteners. Another of its products—La Jac Brite Skin Bleach—was said to eliminate wrinkles overnight or in any stated time to make skin five shades lighter. *Lucky Mojo, Good Luck Incense, Hindoo Mystic Love Perfume, Holy Oil with Live Loadstone or High John the Conqueror Root,* and other similar products that bring good luck, love, romance, power, life, inspiration, easy money or irresistibility."

According to Carolyn Morrow Long, in *"Spiritual Merchants: Religion, Magic, and Commerce"* (2001), *"The Keystone Chemical Company, later called Keystone Laboratories, was established in 1925 by Joseph Menke and Morris Shapiro ... and ... combined the sale of ethnic [i.e. African American] cosmetics with spiritual products.... Product development and marketing strategy were shared by Menke; his wife, Hilda; Morris Shapiro; and two vice presidents, Lista Wayman and Connie Clark. The products were formulated by a staff of chemists, one of whom, Jackson Green, was African American. The principles in the company were all Jewish Americans."*

Folk Beliefs, Spells, Amulets, and Signs

Emerging from bondage, the topic of magic, and how it was thought of and used, as slaves tried to take advantage of anything that help them psychologically was a full time effort. I believe entering emancipation unshackled slaves' subconscious spirituality, as it related to Africa, even though master tried to make slave into what he called Christians. There may be confusion on the part of some regarding the role of folk magic in slaves' lives is a subject that needs clarifying, as much as possible.

The role and meaning of the word magic (traditional African American folk practices), when used by slave descendants has a different meaning for slaves than for others. I hope to give the reader an authentic context for the use of the word magic (or other substitute words) and the thought pattern it triggered among slave descendants. Slavery required slave to develop double meanings for many words master used when they responded to master than when they talked to one another.

I begin with the following entries from *The Southern Spirits Collection of 19th Century Texts on African-American Magic and Spirituality*, and these excerpts are part of their *Southern Spirits: Ghostly Voices from Dixie Land* page. *Southern Spirits* brings the ghost-voices of our magical past into the modern age. These are our spiritual ancestors speaking—both as others heard them and as they told the world about themselves.

This series begins with an excerpt from **"*Seership!*"** by the great 19th century African American magician and Rosicrucian, Paschal Beverly Randolph (1825-1875). Born in New York State (of parents from Virginia), Randolph traveled the world widely as a "free man of color." He was a world-renowned Spiritualist and Clairvoyant Reader. He wrote extensively on Sex-Magic and the art of Mirror Scrying. (Scrying mirror or black mirror is a surface used for divination. One focus on a particular intention and stare into the mirror to get visions related to your query.) He also worked for abolition before the Civil War and helped to raise money for the *Black Militias of Louisiana* during the war. Immediately after the war, he taught literacy courses to newly freed slaves in New Orleans under the auspices of the Freedmen's Bureau until its end (1877). He returned to his former career as a Spiritualist author, publishing **"*Seership!*"** in 1870.

"I beg leave to introduce the following article concerning "Voudooism—African Fetich Worship Among the Memphis Negroes," from the Memphis Appeal. The word Hoodoo, or Voudoo, is one of the names used in the different African dialects for the practice of the mysteries of the Obi (an African word signifying a species of sorcery and witchcraft common among the worshippers of the fetich). In the West Indies the word 'Obi' is universally used to designate the priests or practices of this art, which are called 'Obi' men and 'Obi' women.' It may not be generally known to the public, but it is nevertheless a fact, that these barbarous African

superstitions and practices prevail, and are increasing among the 'freedmen' not only of Memphis and Tennessee, but of all the southern States."

Randolph describes the various heavenly spirits who watch over human affairs:

'Not all invisible onlookers, however, are to be counted in along with seraphs and angels, nor do they always take a subject away from the mesmerist for that subject's good; but it may happen that obsessing forces of the "Voodoo" grades step in to serve their own peculiar ends. People may laugh as much as they please at the idea of wicked, mean, obsessing, tantalizing, tempting beings, or at the old notions of the alchemists and others of that ilk; my researches and experience tell a far different story. When it is asserted that there is no mysterious means whereby ends both good and ill can be wrought at any distance; that the so called "spells," "charms" and "projects" are mere notions, having no firmer foundation than superstition or empty air alone; -- then I flatly deny all such assertions, and affirm that the conclusions arrived at are so reached by persons wholly ignorant of the invisible world about us, and of the inner powers of the human mind."

This excerpt is from <u>*"Slave Narratives: A Folk History of Slavery in the United States from Interviews with Former Slaves."*</u> The Federal Writers' Project of the Works Progress Administration for the State of Georgia was prepared and published first in 1941. Only a small number of the FWP/WPA Slave narratives mention hoodoo or conjure, and those are the only interviews collected in this archive.

I selected Mrs. Celestia Avery's interview conducted for "Slave Narratives" on 2-30-1936. Her account is about conjuring among slaves. She lived in a small house at 173 Phoenix Alley, N.E. Atlanta, GA. A small elderly woman about 5 ft. 2 inches tall and was an ex-slave. She was interviewed on slavery previously; this interview was to gather facts concerning superstitions, conjure, signs, etc. She began,

'When you see a dog lay on his stomach and slide, it is a true sign of death. This is show true cause it happened to me. Years ago when I lived on Pine Street, I was sitting on my steps playing with my nine-months old baby. A friend of mine came by and sat down; and as we set there a dog that followed her began to slide on his stomach. It scared me; and I said to her, did you see that dog?'

"Yes, I show did," 'she said.

That night my baby died and it wasn't sick at all that day. That's the truth and a show sign of death.

Another sign of death is to dream of a new-born baby. One night not so long ago I dreamt about a new-born baby and you know I went to the door and called Miss Mary next door and told her I dreamed about a new-born baby, and she said,'

"Oh! that's a show sign of death."
'

The same week that gal's baby over there died. It didn't surprise me when I heard it, cause I knowed somebody round here was gonna die.

She continued, *'Listen, child! If ever you clean your bed, don't you never sweep off your springs with a broom. Always wipe 'em with a rag, or use a brush. Jest as show as you do, you see or experience death around you. I took my bed down and swept off my springs, and I jest happened to tell old Mrs. Smith; and she jumped up and said,'*

"Child, you ought not done that cause it's a sign of death."

'Sho nuff the same night I lost another child that was eight years old. The child had heart trouble, I think.'

Mrs. Avery believes in luck (a kind of superstition) to a certain extent. The following are examples of how to get luck.

'I believe you can change your luck by throwing a teaspoonful of sulphur in the fire at zackly 12 o'clock in the day. I know last week I was sitting here without a bit of fire, but I wasn't thinking bout doing that till a woman came by and told me to scrape up a stick fire and put a spoonful of sulphur on it; and show nuff in a hour's time a coal man came by and gave me a tub of coal. Long time ago I used to work fer some white women and every day at 12 o'clock I was told to put a teaspoonful of sulphur in the fire.

Another thing, I show ain't going to let a woman come in my house on Monday morning unless a man done come in there first. No, surree, if it seem like one ain't coming soon, I'll call one of the boy chilluns, jest so it is a male. The reason fer this is cause women is bad luck.

The following are a few of the luck charms as described by Mrs. Avery:

'Black cat bone is taken from a cat. First, the cat is killed and boiled, after which the meat is scraped from the bones. The bones are then taken to the creek and thrown in. The bone that goes up stream is the lucky bone and is the one that should be kept. There is a boy in this neighborhood that sells liquor and I know they done locked him up ten or twelve times but he always git out. They say he carries a black cat bone,' related Mrs. Avery.

The black cat bone rite is notorious. Two uses are generally ascribed to the bone: invisibility with respect to the law and the power to force a straying lover to return.

'The Devil's shoestring looks jest like a fern with a lot of roots. My mother used to grow them in the corner of our garden. They are lucky'.

The Devil's Shoe String Root is as popular in conjure today as it was during Mrs. Avery's lifetime.

'Majres (?) are always carried tied in the corner of a handkerchief. I don't know how they make 'em.

"Majres" is probably a mis-hearing for mojo or mojo hands. In parts of Africa such as Tanzania, magical packets of this sort are still tied up in the corner of a cloth garment rather than placed in a drawstring bag.

'I bought a lucky stick from a man once. It looked jest like a candle, only it was small; but he did have some sticks as large as candles and he called them lucky sticks, too, but you had to burn them all night in your room. He also had some that looked jest like buttons, small and round.'

I suspect these tactics Mullein stalks, which are also called "Witches' candles." The stalks are pithy and can be dried, dipped in oil, and will burn as long as any candle. Mullein has a number of uses in hoodoo in addition to its use as a source of light.

The following are two stories of conjure told by Mrs. Avery.

'I knowed a man once long ago and he stayed sick all der time. He had the headache from morning till night. One day he went to a old man that wuz called a conjurer; this old man told him that somebody had stole the sweat-band out of his cap and less he got it back, something terrible would happen. They say this man had been going with a woman and she had stole his sweat-band. Well, he never did get it, so he died.'

This headache trick is an old and common spell. Compare it with the several sweat band tricks for coercive love referenced in <u>Hoodoo Herb and Root Magic</u> page 149 under *"Personal Concerns"* and the spell to run a man stark crazy with his hat on page 174 under "Salt.

'I had a cousin named Alec Heard, and he had a wife named Anna Heard. Anna stayed sick all der time almost; fer two years she complained. One day a old conjurer came to der house and told Alec that Anna wuz poisoned, but if he would give him $5.00 he would come back Sunday morning and find the conjure. Alec wuz wise, so he bored a hole in the kitchen floor so that he could jest peep through there to der back steps. Sho nuff Sunday morning the nigger come back and as Alec watched him. He dug down in the ground a piece, then he took a

ground puppy, threw it in the hole and covered it up. All right, he started digging again and all at once he jumped up and cried:'

"*Here 'tis! I got it.*"

"*Got what?*"

'*Alec said, running to the door with a piece of board.*

"*I got the ground puppy dat wuz buried fer her.*"

'*Alec wuz so mad he jumped on that man and beat him most to death. They say he did that all the time and kept a lot of ground puppies fer that purpose.*'

Continuing, she explained that

'*A ground puppy was a worm with two small horns. They are dug up out of the ground, and there is a belief that you will die if one barks at you.*"

<u>A Ground Puppy</u> -- also called Mud Puppy, Ground Dog, or Water Dog -- is usually a kind of salamander. In parts of the South, however, the common Mole-Cricket, Jerusalem Cricket, or Potato Bug is also called a Ground Puppy. (And note that this so-called Potato Bug Cricket is not the same as the Colorado Potato Beetle that also bears the name Potato Bug.

Mrs. Avery related two ways in which you can keep from being conjured by anyone.

'*One thing I do every morning is ter sprinkle chamber-lye [HW: (urine)] with salt and then throw it all around my door. They sho can't fix you if you do this.*'

The use of both urine and salt for protection is very common in hoodoo and other forms of folk magic.

'*Anudder thang, if you wear a silver dime around your leg they can't fix you. The woman live next door says she done wore two silver dimes around her leg for 18 years.*'

For more early accounts of the use of a silver dime for protection, see these other southern-spirits pages: <u>*"Voodooism in Tennessee"*</u> *by Sallie M. Park (1889) and Sam Jordan: Silver Dime For Protection from the "Oklahoma Slave Narratives" (1930s)*

Closing the interview, Mrs. Avery remarked:

'That's bout all I know; but come back some time and maybe I'll think of something else.'

A very small glossary of terms, I believe, will help the uninitiated understand what I'm trying to accomplish with this section.

The word <u>Hoodoo</u>, or <u>Voodoo</u>, is one of the names used in the different African dialects for the practice of the mysteries of the Obi (an African word signifying a species of sorcery and witchcraft common among the worshippers of the fetich). In the West Indies, the word 'Obi' is universally used to designate the priests or practices of this art, who are called 'Obi' men and 'Obi' women. [The word Obi is more commonly spelled Obeah today. It is the Jamaican equivalent of hoodoo, root work, and conjure.]

Practitioners of the art, who are always native Africans, are called hoodoo men or women, and are held in high regard and great dread by Negroes, who apply to them for the cure of diseases, to obtain revenge for injuries, and to discover and punish their enemies. The mode of operations is to prepare a *"fetich,"* which being placed near or in the dwelling of the person to be worked upon (under the doorstep, or in any snug portion of the furniture) is supposed to produce the direst and terrible effects upon the victim, both physically and mentally.

The word fetich—more commonly spelled fetish—is of Portuguese origin and signifies an idol or magical object of worship, particularly a small one. Also, it is often used in English to refer to any spell that is worked within a bag or packet, such as a mojo hand, toby, conjure bag, jack ball, or nation sack.

A **"tricker bag"**—more often called a "trick bag—is a <u>mojo bag or toby</u>. <u>Tricking or conjuring</u> people through their food or drink is a common practice. Biscuits, dumplings, and other amorphous dough products are always suspect, as are dark-coloured drinks like coffee, tea, or soda.

A **"jack ball"** is to be carried for luck after the manner of a <u>mojo hand or conjure bag</u>, but it could also be used for divination, a trait common to jacks.

"Guffer Dust" <u>(usually spelled "Goofer Dust")</u> is usually graveyard dirt which is an essential component in the mixture and/or the compounding of the finished product is accomplished by a practitioner who worked according to <u>magical moon phases</u>. The New Moon, also known as <u>"the dark of the moon,"</u> generally symbolizes getting rid of the old and embarking on a new phase. Since <u>Goofer Dust</u> is used to harm people or kill them, the idea would be that "dark works are done at <u>"the dark of the moon."</u>

Then there is **"Tie-Them-Down Powder,"** which slyly slipped into tea, coffee or other beverage is guaranteed to fill the husband with an intense desire to spend his evenings at home. Other titles for similar products include <u>Stay at Home, Stay With Me and I Have You</u>

<u>Tied and Nailed.</u>] *If, having been given Tie-Them-Down, the husband still shows no signs of curtailing his cruising radius, he becomes an "Aggravated Case" and the situation calls for <u>Bring-Back Powder,</u> similar in nature but greater in potency than <u>Tie-Them-Down</u>. <u>The Bring-Back</u> retails at $50 for 25 powders; <u>Tie-Them-Down</u> at $25 for 25 powders. They are sold by the West African Remedy Co., Pearce Health Institute, Oriental Institute of Science and Africa-American Institute of Science.*

Magic was a very big part of the psyche of former slaves all over the South, especially in Memphis. There were several companies, besides Keystone Laboratories that masqueraded as authentic hoodoo merchants. Lucky Heart Labs was another, also in Memphis. My mother worked there for several years in their cosmetics branch. Moreover, hoodoo practitioners were numerous and shops to purchase items as well. Many people believed the prosperity on and around Beale Street had to do with the impact of hoodoo and the merchants located on and near Beale Street. Old-timers believed hoodoo gave Beale Street the ability to survive segregation and other efforts of white people to keep black people from making money. Old-timers called it *"the magic or luck of Beale Street."* For them and many others, Beale Street was a magical place, like a *"Never Neverland."*

This statement is the basis of how and why I present Beale Street and life on and around it as I do. Beliefs are the bases of the psychology that motivates people and determines how they approach life. They form the basis of how and why they see the world as they do. Walled off by segregation, Boss Crump and most white people in general, saw no problem with "niggers" getting together, as long as they stayed in what white people defined as "their place." So, Memphis and Beale Street developed a unique character. Not coincidentally, there were no white people running things and making money off of black people on Beale Street, they considered it a magical place.

Old-timers declared, Beale Street was a place unlike any other, because it had hoodoo protecting it, which kept white people away. Of course, they were convinced hoodoo and conjure made it a place for only black people. Beale Streeters believed hoodoo merchants controlled all such things, which was why white people could not take over or destroy Beale Street and their businesses, as they did Greenwood—*Black Wall Street* in Tulsa, OK, and other prosperous black communities.

Black people running everything that mattered to black folks made Beale Street a place like no other in the South, if not America. Whether this belief was true or not, did not matter to Beale Streeters, they believed in hoodoo's power. They felt conjure and hoodoo protected Beale Street and every black person connected to it. Their special magic helped people get their businesses going and protected their loved ones, made them lucky gamblers, as well as helped some find lovers. Many, many blacks truly believed the rites, spells, amulets, curses, and recipes they acquired from Hoodoo or conjure men kept the magic of Beale Street alive.

Although segregation restricted black people's movements in the rest of downtown, they felt conjure, and hoodoo powders kept white people away from Beale Street. There are stories that particular Hoodoo men had a daily ritual of spreading protective powers around Beale Street to keep white people away from the area. They were convinced because of Hoodoo they did not have to worry about white people.

Today this may sound like a bunch of mumbo jumbo, but one must remember, back then black people had only recently emerged from under the total domination of any white person during slavery. Once free, they still had to be on guard at all times, when white people were around, anything bad could happen. Now, they had hoodoo and conjure, so they did not have to be concerned about them. Their experience taught them; they needed whatever protection they could get against the devil (white folks). Beale Street freed them of that constant state of fear, now no white people lurked.

Education Made All the Difference

Freedmen's Bureau schools made education more than a mysterious gift from God for newly freed slaves. Even though these schools operated haphazardly getting started, they made education something ***"God"*** did not have to bestow. These schools helped former slaves understand there was nothing magical about slaves learning to read, write and calculate. Nevertheless, the impact of bureau schools, compared to the number of former slaves they did not serve, when looking at the benefits of education, was minuscule.

Education was a major part of former slaves struggles to begin life anew. Their struggles convinced them God had answered their prayers. They accepted the challenges of education while getting over the fear of knowledge. Slave masters used terror to instill fear of learning, so schooling was a huge change for contrabands, yet and still they prayed to receive that magic. Knowledge gained by those that were able to find a Freedmen's school helped end their lack of knowledge.

Although Freedmen's Bureau Schools' offered only rudimentary educational skills, however, their greatest accomplishment was creating an expectation for learning. They helped dispel the belief that education took mystical powers to obtain. Showing former slaves education had a structure for the learning process was its most powerful impact. It went beyond teaching those who found schools, because those who found them taught those they knew what learned that were unable to attend school. Former slaves teaching former slaves became part of their survival patterns. Newly freed slaves regarded knowledge as essential and were willing to meet wherever and under any condition to gain knowledge from whomever they could.

The Freedmen's Bureau in Memphis, Tennessee, was far more than just a magic act in a tent show. It provided public schools for "contraband children," before the Memphis City School System was forced to incorporate them into its system in 1865. However, more like sleight of hand, hordes of white rioters appeared suddenly and touched the whole educational enterprise for former slaves, during the 1866 riot. Disappearing like a puff of smoke in a magic act, all Freedmen Bureau schools went up in a blaze of terror. Rioters were not magicians or sorcerers; they were common garden variety white haters, trying to maintain slavery's ignorance among newly Freedmen. Whites burned black schools and churches, forcing newly Freedmen to start over from scratch with new building. But they were unable to burn away what former slaves had already gained. Freedmen went back to learning by any means, any place, any time, and from anyone they could.

Reconstruction forced southern governments to provide former slaves a chance to learn. Consequently, the Freedmen's Bureau forced, with the Union

Army backing them up, white governments to set up schools and accept the idea, educating former slaves as their obligation. The Bureau insisted that all black children have the opportunity to become educated, coincidentally this helped former slaves realize there was nothing magical about knowledge, it only had to be obtained. The Freedmen's Bureau solidified a knowledge base among former slaves.

After Congress shut down the Freedmen's Bureau (1875), contrabands were on their own again, trying to become educated. Prior to its dissolution, the Bureau forced the Memphis School Board to incorporate Bureau schools in its system (1866), which allowed contraband to keep getting an education. Even though it was never the same as the education white children got, it was better than no education at all, which was the case in many parts of the South.

Bureau schools used visiting missionaries or itinerate teachers, who wanted to help the newly Freedmen succeed. Along with former slaves teaching one another, their learning process continued. Trying to guard against tragic events of the past—riots and burning—to prevent the community's drive to acquire education, Freedmen suffered through whatever, building a community reservoir of knowledge.

The Clay Street School (1867-70) evolved from a Freedmen's Bureau school. It was the first Freedmen's Bureau school folded into the Memphis Board of Education schools system for "Colored children." H. J. Barnum, a white man, was the first superintendent of "colored" schools. The first teachers were all white, but by 1872, there were six white and five black teachers. Continuing to build a framework for education, 11 woman and nine men all black were teaching contraband children by the late 1870s. The first teachers were Virginia E. Walker Broughton, America W. Robinson, James Dallas Burrus, and his brother John Houston Burrus. Broughton was the first black woman and among the first four blacks to receive a college degree in the South. The first former slaves graduates (1880) from the "colored school" in Memphis were Fannie Thompson, and Green P. Hamilton, who returned as teachers.

Kortrecht Grammar School replaced the Clay School in 1873 before the Freedmen's Bureau closed. Virtually every black child, for the next 75 years, could trace their education to the Clay School or Kortrecht Grammar School. Kortrecht High School, built in1891, became Booker T. Washington High School. And, this is when the magic of Beale Street reached out several blocks to bring the poorest of poor black children under its wing. Booker T. Washington is in a unique class unto itself, and Green P. Hamilton became its first principal. Booker T. Washington's first class graduated in 1891. It is among the last, if not the last Freedmen's Bureau affiliated school in the nation, still actively educating black children. Pres. Barak H. Obama gave Booker T. Washington's commencement address on May 16, 2011.

The 400th: From Slavery to Hip Hop

Blair T. Hunt (10-1-1888/7-26-1978), a legend in black education, not only in Memphis but the Mid-South, became the principal of Booker T. Washington High School in 1932. The son of former slaves, he graduated from LeMoyne College, Morehouse College, Roger Williams College, and Tennessee State A&I College. According to biographical information, as principal of Booker T. Washington, Prof. Hunt established a long and storied career, *"educating the poorest of the poor in the roughest most poverty enveloped part of Memphis."* The community environment in which "BTW" delivers knowledge is what makes its history such a compelling story in the development of black professionalism in Memphis. Many of its facility and students continued popping up throughout this narrative, as leading figures in Memphis and the nation, especially in entertainment. My brother Tommy, sisters Willie May, Molly and Bernice all graduated from BTW.

Manassas High School is the next magical place that educated black students in Memphis. Booker T is located on the Southside of town, whereas Manassas is on the Northside, and it is seen as the little brother by those partial to Booker T. These biases created the strongest rivalry in the bluff city, whether it was sports, academics, talent or the neighborhood brawls following such events. Manassas fateful always puff their chests up while saying, *"Manassas was the first four-year accredited black high school in Shelby County (1899)."* They boost talents like Jimmie Lunceford, who taught band at Manassas in the 1920s, and Hank Crawford, a legendary saxophonist, were students there. Washingtonians claimed Mrs. Lucie Campbell (4-30-1885/1-3-1963), the *"Grande Dame"* of Memphis music, graduating from Kortrecht High School in 1899 (renamed Booker T. Washington) was valedictorian of her class.

Judging talent, whether music, dance, sports, or oratory, everyone from teachers, preachers to the guy on the corner pushed black children to learn to *do something with their bodies. "You gotta make something out of nothing."* Echoing Marcus Garvey's admonition, they would say, *"That's the way you can make something out of yourself. Your body is all you got. That's your magic. You got to learn to do something with it. That can't be taken from you. If you learn to do something with your body, you can always make money on your own. That's something no white man can stop or take away."* And, that brings this narrative to where the magic of Beale Street made believers out of thousand, as life expressed itself on the magical street.

Beale Street: A Bronzeville

Although segregation was a tremendous disadvantage for black people, it had its benefits. Areas like Beale Street across the South were called "Bronzevilles." The term "Bronzeville" is most relevant in cities or towns where white people concentrated or segregated black populations in particular areas, served by mostly black-owned businesses as in Memphis. "Bronzevilles," were areas white people designed to make segregation work by crowding blacks together in particular areas to keep them in poverty. Whites controlled black people's prosperity with scarcity and desperation, as a weapon. However, segregation created business opportunities for the stout of heart.

"Bronzevilles," like Beale Street, provided more than music and entertainment for black folks, especially in Memphis. It filled their needs, whether looking for fun or frolicking, gambling or liquor, fashion or furniture, and everything in between. Robert Church, Sr.'s leadership, made Beale Street, not just a "Bronzeville," but one of the more successful. He was the most prominent philanthropist in the city, giving liberally to local schools, private and public, social, as well as civic and charitable organizations.

Whites controlled the lives of blacks with poverty and segregation. Hanging on the rim of poverty, most struggled constantly trying to keep from sliding back down to the bottom of the valley of dry bones. Always hungry, the grave of poverty's viciously snapped at their heels, pulling many over the edge, particularly families like mine. It was that way for the poor in Memphis.

The late 1930s brought the last thing people concerned about peace and tranquility in the world dared think—war again all across Europe. Coming amidst massive economic dislocation that began in 1930, the Great Depression grip America, similar to the Panic of 1893. Depression was hard on everyone; white people could not escape its vicious bite any more than blacks. But, white people had the "Dark Age" angry white men mob madness bloodlust lynchings, banishment and ethnic cleansing ear (1890- 1950) going that soften the economic blow on them, while it was total hell for blacks.

Cotton prices dropped through the floor and everyone spent their timing trying to step around the huge hold it made in everything. Even though it spoiled the peace and tranquility of the world, Pres. Franklin D. Roosevelt got the economy moving helping out in Europe with lend-lease. (The Lend-Lease Act (1941) was the principal means of providing military aid to foreign nations during WW II.)

Most white people were against allowing black men to fight and kill white folks in Europe, even though Hitler and the Nazis were making a bid to rule the world. Again WWII, like WWI, was about nothing but killing, and dying, Europeans deeply embroiled in the dying did not care about color. They welcomed anyone willing to try and pull their fat out the fire. They were in deep trouble, as Hitler's Nazi blitzkrieg gobbled up countries, like sausage and sauerkraut, while making bratwurst out of the rest. Not a coincident, white families with boys headed for the front line did not want, dying in Europe to be just a "white boy thing." So, the debate was on.

Before the Japanese bombed Pearl Harbor, the American press made a big deal of the fact; black men would be killing white people. For them, this meant, once back home, they might continue what they learned in Europe. The thing was, the ones doing all the talking, about not allowing black men to fight, were not going to the front line no matter what happened in Europe.

The fear of black soldiers fighting and killing local whites was justified, especially when most whites still treated blacks as slaves. The press alluded to a similar incident during WWI when blacks soldiers fought whites. They reminded America of The Houston Massacre, which whites called The Houston Mutiny, where white civilians and black soldiers in Houston fought a real battle. Verying estimates said over fifty whites died, and one hundred fifty black soldiers were court marshaled. No whites went to jail, but the army executed sixty black soldiers. The Houston Massacre, as black people called it, is a very good example of what whites feared, and the press waved like a flag.

WWII brought the party life back to Memphis, beginning around 1939. The War Department pumped up the US economy, and Memphis benefitted, as it put money in the pockets of everybody, especially black workers and farmhands. The army needed lots of uniforms, tent, packs, bandages, sheets, blankets, and everything else made of fabrics. The war started cotton prices moving up, which took a swan dive into the toilet, along with other businesses during the "Great Depression."

"Boss" Crump got things moving in Memphis for whites as a result of his ties to FDR's New Deal. Black workers got the crumbs that fell off the table, which allowed them to make a little money again. But a little was better than nothing, even though that was not "the Boss" intention. What black field hands got was more than they had and they made the best of that to get things moving for them.

Beale Street had not become a "raisin in the sun" during the "Great Depression," which meant the magic of the Blues kept black businesses from withering on the vine. Beale Street's survival was tethered to Robert Church's grand vision, Church's Park and Auditorium. It may not have been magic, but it sufficed to keep things going through economic hard times. Church's Park was the political and cultural center for blacks in Memphis; it kept things moving with its 2,000 seats. A magnet, it drew black people to Beale Street, it kept hope alive.

Old-timers saw Church's Park, as the center of everything. They talked of opportunities created for everyone on Beale that found a way to become part of the party. Street hawkers peddling food, clothing, jewelry, and sex, awaited anyone looking for a good time. Bar and club owners presented special events that accompanied shows at Church's Park. Many of those that came out were street-strollers, taking in the view. Nevertheless, they added to the carnival atmosphere and night life, making people want to join the festivities. Other business-minded blacks found locations on or near Beale Street, which took advantage of the overflow from Church's Park.

Commerce and gaiety developed as a direct result of the Church family's use of the Solvent Savings Bank and Trust Company supporting black business. They bankrolled much of the entrepreneurial development on Beale Street. The Solvent Savings Bank and Trust Company did not only loan blacks money to finance businesses; it helped them buy homes also.

Church, Sr. showed tremendous courage during the 1907 financial Panic. It was also known as the Knickerbocker Crisis or Bankers' Panic—in the US. The 1907 Panic resulted from the New York Stock Exchange 50% loss of value. The subsequent economic recession caused numerous banks runs and trust company failures). As white banks went under, Church, Sr. stacked bags of money in the windows of The Solvent Savings Bank and Trust Company for black people to see. The confidence-building measure was enough to allay fears. Although it sounds fantastic, newspapers reported the story nationwide. It was a sign the bank had adequate reserves.

Headed for battles in Europe, black soldiers by the hundreds came to Beale Street on weekend furloughs to experience its special magic. Enterprising merchants of fun on Beale Street believed entertainment was at the top of a soldier boy's list and sought to provide whatever they wanted. Cash-hunger businessmen on Beale Street saw black men in uniform, with pockets stuffed with dollars, like walking cash registers. The trick for Beale Streeters was getting it out of their pockets and into their registers.

Going off to fight Adolf Hitler, young men wanted a few things they never had, before leaving, just in case they didn't make it back. Soldiers flocked to Beale Street from several Military installations around Memphis. The major base was the Millington Naval Air Station, about twenty miles north of Memphis.

Getting to town and back to base before curfew was difficult for black recruits. An enterprising black man, Preston Hayes, who ferried cotton field hands to Arkansas, as day laborers, during the week, saw an opportunity in war and Beale Street, once the fighting heated up. Hayes began transporting soldiers from Millington to Beale Street and back for fifty cents ahead. By war's end, he had three buses.

If a soldier was looking for fun and entertainment, during the massive military buildup, all he needed do was follow "the yellow brick road" to Emerald city's magical world on Beale Street. And, if Beale Street merchants didn't have it, one of its cash-hungry entrepreneurs would make it appear, like waving a wand. With black soldiers pouring into town on furloughs, by early 1939, the mystical street was jumping again.

A magical place of glitz and glitter, Beale Street's bright lights, fancy women, gambling and liquor, made it a good timing sporting man's paradise. This world of juke joints, dance clubs, speakeasies, honky-tonks, and houses of ill-repute, enchantingly beckoned the novice, curious, and profane. The times were ripe for new musical sounds and new energy. After W. C. Handy conjured the Blues, jazz, bebop, swing, and the big band era blew into town, one after the other like whirlwinds. The Blues mojo brought soldiers and cotton field "niggers" together for hoodoo magic in smoke-filled dens of gambling, drinking, sex, and mayhem.

Thriving alongside nightclubs, theaters, restaurants, stores, pawnshops, and hot music, conjure curios coexisted like they were in New Orleans' French Quarter. There were urban hoodoo and conjure readers using astrology or "Gypsy fortune-telling." Some read tea leaves, while others read palms or cards—52 card decks or tarot cards, it didn't matter to luck starved gambler. A few conjure men even did West African "bone casting," which was the oldest type of conjure divination. But, most wanted the familiar hoodoo, where a specially prepared mojo hand or Jack-ball for luck with women and gambling did the trick.

Known, as a "bucket of blood," the Monarch Club was called, "The Castle of Missing Men." Men were seen going in but never came out. Their epitaphs didn't mention the gun, knife, or razor fight to which they fell victims. Their bodies were hustled out the backdoor quickly to the alley where undertakers waited on standby.

Nightly on weekends, expensively dressed patrons mingled with those in overalls from cotton fields. Advertising their wares, young ladies of the evening promenaded around bars and gamblers, giving prospects an eye full. Awaiting wide-eyed country boys fresh from cotton fields or new recruits' first time in town, bright lights and big city fun, camouflaged city slickers and easy marks, trying to play it cool.

If a mark wasn't cleaned out in a back alley crap shoot or sidewalk three-card-molly, they might get mesmerized watching the ladies from behind, as they sashayed, only to fall victim to "the best pickpockets in the South." Then again, 'homeboy' might get snookered in Pee Wee's Saloon playing pool. But, if he was a sporting man, he might visit one of the local mystics, hoping to secure a bewitching hoodoo portion to hit the jackpot gambling or for luck catching his dream date for the night or both.

Clubs like the Flamingo Room, Club Ebony, and Club Handy, offered soldier boys or regular patrons' music, drinks, dancing, or an intimate conversation followed by a close encounter with a lady to set the mood. With W. C. Handy on the bandstand, partygoers packed Church's Park, stretching its 2,000-capacity beyond standing room only for "dance-o-rama."

However, the Hippodrome (formerly a skating rink), with its block-long dance floor and a raised double bandstand (modeled on the Savoy Ballroom in Harlem), drew dancers of all types, especially those from big cities. Jamming the joint, trying to show off the latest steps of the Jitterbug, Charleston, boogie-woogie, or Lindy Hop, these dance aficionados came for the weekly dance contest. Contestants laid down all the local favorites but stepped out with foreign dances such as the Argentine Tango, Spanish Paso Doblé, Brazilian Samba, Puerto Rican Merengue, Cuban Mambo, and Cha Cha. Sometimes they even threw down with an English Quickstep, Austrian Waltz, or an occasional American Fox-trot and Peabody.

By the Dark of the Moon: Mother's Run

WWII was no different from WWI, in that it pulled men out of factories and fields as well as off farms all over America to help defend the world from a scourge, like the *"Dark Age" angry white men mob madness*. But, since it was killing white Europe, the world cared; of course, it cared, so white nations rose up to stop it.

Adolf Hitler killing Jews got their attention much quicker, than Americans, who had been massacring black people, like voracious carnivores to cheers and revelry since 1880. Unlike in America, where President Woodrow Wilson's *"Dark Age"* angry white men mob madness was doing to black Americans what Hitler was doing to Jews, the world rush to Europe's rescue, while watching Wilson mercilessly slaughter black people—shooting, skinned alive, and burned them at the stake. Black men were killed in the most horrific ways to entertain white people, but nobody cared.

Again, for most, there is nothing magical about war. But, for millions of black men and their families, who were prisoners on the land, locked behind America's *cotton curtain*, letters appeared in mailboxes, bringing hope, like magic, with their arrival. Those letters changed lives, in ways, minutes before their opening, there was no way of imagining, the new lives they brought, once read.

Draft notices coming to thousands of families were like get out of jail free cards! The funny thing about draft boards was they had a 10% quota for black men. Once filled, Draft Boards closed the books on black recruits for that call-up. They sent the overage back home. The overage was due to whites not knowing how many blacks would answer their draft notice, so they overloaded each call-up.

If a black man did not answer the draft letter, the board sent the secret service or FBI after "no shows," as if *"they'd raped a white woman."* US Draft Boards sent almost as many black men to jail for dodging the draft, as they did to the war. The trick, for a black man to avoid getting killed fighting or not going to jail, as a "no show," required some real magic. But strange as it may seem, believe it or not, my father was able to do both, even though he knew absolutely nothing about magic.

The war in Europe brought a different kind of magic to those trapped in convict leasing and sharecropping. Singing halleluiah jubilee draft notices had black families dancing in cotton rows, after draft notices arrived. Adolf Hitler's Nazi blitzkrieg trickery in Europe became abracadabra in America for black men that began disappearing out the South back door. Headed off to war, it was if the Army opened an escape hatch for black families, without waving a wand.

Even more magical and amazing than that for my family, the draft turned the trick that got us out of Mississippi and sharecropping forever. A draft noticed, turning a trick, arriving at our farmhouse in Mississippi, bringing the magic of WWII to my father. For him, that draft noticed was like incantations of a sorcerers' apprentice had gone haywire, as the bright lights of Emerald City began flashing in his head.

"It was early summer, but it was hot enough to fry an egg on your head, and I had to go to the mailbox up on the gravel road. It seemed the mailman always ran during the hottest part of the day in summer and coldest in winter. I saw the car stop, so when grandma hollowed, "Junior!!" I knew that meant, get the mail, right now!!! I always tried to wait until the dust on the dirt road cooled off a bit. I hated tiptoeing barefoot through hot dust, and gravel got even hotter. Plus, gravel hot or cold, is hard on the feet. So, I decided to run, maybe the air blowing over my feet would cool them down just a little. A letter addressed to Daddy Cal was in the mailbox. It was from the War Department, which meant it was very important."

Tommy was the oldest, and the one everybody called if something important needed doing. He was proud of his named Tommy Cal, and being named after our daddy even though everybody called him "Junior." Unlike me, I hated my first name John; it was a joke name. Everyone laughed when they said, "Old John did this or did that. Everyone had a favorite old John joke. The worst thing about the name John was he always did stupid stuff. Mostly, I never like being name for a man I never met, my daddy's granddaddy, John Smith. Everybody said he was a white man. Unlike my middle name Burl, my mother's granddaddy, I knew him because we talked.

"I knew daddy wanted to see any letter for him that looked important, so I took off."

Tommy would always stop to laugh, and then continue,

"I ran on pass the house into the field where Daddy Cal was working. He took the letter and opened it. Reading it, daddy started shouting, 'I'm going to the city. I'm going to the city.' He screamed, jumping up and down. I never saw Daddy Cal so happy about nothing."

Sitting around the dinner table talking, after all these years, my mother and sibling (Tommy, Willie May, Molly, and Bernice) always talked about times before they left the farm. Everybody had their favorite part of any family story. Willie May, the oldest girl, would pick this one up.

"I was the first one to see Daddy Cal and Junior running to the house. Daddy was hollowing something while waving the letter in his hand. So, I ran in the house to get Mudear; she was in the kitchen. I said, 'Mudear come quick, something happened, cause Daddy and Junior are running to the house hollowing.'"

Mother would start,

"I didn't know what was going on. I almost fell over, trying to get to the front door. I thought somebody had gotten hurt or something. Tommy ran up, shouting, jumping up and down saying, 'I'm going to the city! I'm going to the city!' I didn't know what he was talking about. So, I took the letter from his hand and read it. It said, "He had been drafted and had to report to the induction center in Memphis in two weeks."

When we talked in this manner, I always wanted to know how Mudear felt or what she thought. I would ask something like, *"Mudear, did you want to go to the city?"* She would pause, tilting her head slightly to one side before answering,

"Well, I was tired of hard work. Mama didn't have no boys, just Charlene and me. I was the oldest so I had to work like a boy. I could hoe and pick a hundred pounds of cotton, drive a team of mules, behind a plow or driving a wagon. I could herd cows or slaughter hogs by the time I got married (age 16). Anything I didn't know, by the time Junior was born, I'd learned that.

I'd graduated 8th grade and was teaching at the school in between seasons. That was pretty good for a girl who wanted to make a life of farming. But, I felt I had a nice voice and everybody seemed to like it. Singing in the choir at Pilgrim Rest CME Church, they called on me for all the special occasions, wedding, funerals, convocations and things like that. I would listen at women and men singing on the radio and I thought I could do as good as most of them. I thought, in the city, I might get a chance to sing, like them. I was hoping Tommy do good on everything."

I could tell she loved talking about her dreams and how she hoped to get an opportunity to just try. Then my sister Molly would say,

"I was so hurt when the army didn't keep Daddy Cal. His letter said that since the war was almost over and the army had a quota, they already had too many black boys by the time they got to him. Once in the city though, there was no way Daddy Cal was coming back to the farm. He hated chopping and picking cotton. He spent more time leaning on his hoe than chopping and not to mention plowing mules. I'm so glad he stayed in Memphis. But, I'm even happier that he came back to get us because I hated farm life too."

These were their memories of those times. I didn't have those memories. I was so little then, but my siblings and mother talked a lot about those times, so most of what I know from those days, are their memories, but listening to them tell stories about those days, they became my memories also.

My Dark of the Moon Memory

Those were great times, listening to family stories and exchanging fond memories. However, there is one memory the family does not have of those times I have. I never shared it with them; it is all mines. Sometimes when we shared memories, I thought about my memory but never said anything. Like millions before, Mudear and Daddy Cal, after the Army didn't keep him, they staked their claim on life beyond the farm.

The foliage was green and very thick by late summer. That was when mother and daddy decided, by letters, to take their chances and make their run, during *"the dark of the moon."* Daddy Cal had been in Memphis 3 months and Mudear didn't tell us what they were planning; nothing was certain. When granddaddy came through the back door that night, I could hardly see him. The darkness covered him; there was no moon. I heard the screen door close behind him, and as he entered the front room, he gave us his usual admonition.

"It's time you youn'ens start fixin y'all's beds," on the way to their room.

We lived in a four-room house. Granny and granddaddy slept in the big front room. Behind that room was what we called the dining room. It was the only room big enough for a table, which is where we ate during the warm months. During the winter, everybody ate around the heater in the front room. It had canned food on shelves for winter and anything else without a place we put in that back room. The kitchen was next to that, behind the other front room, where we slept. Mudear and daddy slept in the big bed while we had pallets on the floor, next to the heater, in the front room.

Soundly asleep, I suppose, noise and voices awakened me. My sisters were dressing, and daddy was there. When he came through the room, he said, *"I told you young'uns not to wake him up."* He said, passing through, grabbing arms of stuff. He didn't stop to pick me up or hug me, like always. He just kept grabbing boxes of stuff, throwing them in the back of a truck at the edge of the front porch.

I didn't understand what they were talking about then, but over the years, it seemed to come back. I'd listened while Granny and mother talked, mother said,

"The last letter Tommy sent me from Memphis," she told Granny, *"he said he was coming back on the third night of the dark of the moon, and he wanted us to be ready when he got here."*

That made me happy, the thought of seeing my daddy again. It seemed he had been in the city so long, Granny said,

The 400th: From Slavery to Hip Hop

"Well, you know that's a real good sign. The "dark of the moon" is the best time to start something like a new life, moving or doing something you not sho bout?"

That was when they started putting stuff into boxes. Wiping the sleep from my eyes, I just watched as everyone ran around, like the house was afire, picking up boxes of stuff. Nobody was saying anything to me until Mudear came over. She picked me up and kissed my face. She hugged me really tightly, while she kept saying, *"I'm coming back to see you real soon. I want you to be a big boy and not to cry. I'm coming back for you cause I loved you so very much."* Granddaddy took me from her arms, as she hurried to the truck, waving and throwing kisses.

Granddaddy let me down to the floor, still holding my hand. The truck pulled away, and I watched the taillights fade into the darkness. My only thought was, *"What did I do wrong?"* This scene became my constant companion, during lonely times when Granddaddy and Granny were in the field working. The problem why everybody said, *"you were too little!"* wasn't so much my size; I was about four years old. I understand now, *"Too little"* meant, I couldn't go to school in the city, unlike down in Mississippi, where all five of us went to school every day in the offseason. Granny wouldn't be in the city to keep me. So, I remained behind with Grandma and Granddaddy. And that is a memory no one has but me!

I don't know the impact on other children left behind, as their families made their desperate dash to get out of sharecropping. Now, I know, like my family, they joined millions who became runners, as part of the *"Great Migration."* Today, I know there were millions of children, just like me, all over the South. Although I was very lonely at times, I know today I was not alone. I don't remember the tears I know I shed, being without my family. It felt like a punishment to me. I remember the loneliness more than anything. But I would learn in a couple of years, times were even harder for my family once they got to Memphis than times ever were for me back on the farm.

Jazz Around the Horn

W. C. Handy built a national reputation for Beale Street with his magical hit *"Memphis Blues."* He commercialized the heartbeat of black people, putting the **"Blues"** to music. The **Blues** was not the only beat moving black feet, nor was Beale the only street in the South, where music had people jumping. Basin Street in New Orleans, at the mouth of the Mississippi River, had its style and favor of music—Jazz. Anchored by French classical notation, spiced up with Cajuns/bayou rhythms, all stirred together and colored by slave music from the cane fields, made it a real party.

All these influences found their way into the music of the Crescent City. Bands played it all—marching and in clubs—which gave New Orleans its unique sound. Jazz, unlike the originality of **Blues'** un-notated structure, developed form standard musical notations. But jazz was still black people giving *Voice* to their pain, degradation, and even enjoyment, while celebrating their survival.

Developing American music, slaves made *"something out of nothing."* New Orleans' musical tradition grew out of Second-line marching bands, club bands jamming, and riverboats cruising up and down the Mississippi River. *"Proud Mary, rolling on the river,"* took New Orleans' musical tradition into the Mid-West—St, Louis, Chicago, and over to Detroit. But, the big change came when it traveled around the horn of Florida. Jazz skirted up the East coast, aboard steamships headed for New York City. They docked for layovers, and bands played cities like Richmond, Virginia, Washington D. C., and Philadelphia, PA, before reaching the *"Big Apple."* Hitting New York City, jazz landed with a big blast, and before the world knew what was happening, that *"nothing"* from the *"Big Easy"* was the biggest musical *"something,"* to ever hit the *"Big Apple."*

Jazz, once it hit New York City, the world started jumping and hasn't stopped. Harlem musicians treated jazz, as everything blacks did once in the *"Big Apple;* they blew it up." Band leaders, like Duke Ellington, Willie "the Lion" Smith, Count Basie, and others, took jazz one step further. Adding their special favor and magic, they made its sound bigger!!! Adding musicians and instruments the *"Big Apple"* blew up the *"Big Easy's,"* musical style. Harlem bigger sound made the swing era hit "big time."

Most blacks never think of Harlem as a *"Bronzeville"* because it was not design by segregation, but like down South, blacks turned it into an area that fit their special needs. In a society that wanted their music but not their presence, as part of the deal, black musicians made money entertaining; like *"blackface"* and laughed on the inside. Nevertheless, Harlem's black music and dance crave swept the nation, and the world.

Jazz was quickly picked up by white musicians, and it left the **Blues** behind, for a while, that is. Although Jazz had lots of improvisation, it evolved from standard musical notation. It was the first indigenous American musical style accepted by the world. Jazz contained the beat and syncopation of ragtime, the driving brass of second-line bands, as well as the soaring inspiration of gospel choirs, then came the deep-down growl of the **Blues**. Jazz had it all. Combining these roots in a celebration of African American creativity and originality, like American GIs, jazz took Europe by storm.

So, white boys got into the game, taking jazz to wider audiences. Since it was music, Memphis got into the game also. Early jazz men and bands in Memphis took their lead from other places and never develop a unique Memphis sound, as did bluesmen. Yet and still, bebop, swing, and the big band craze found enthusiastic adherers on Beale Street. Memphis had its share of great jazz on Beale Street and in America.

A Manassas High School athletic instructor organized a student band called the *Chickasaw Syncopators* in 1927. They became such good musicians he quit his day job teaching, and took to the road, after changing the band's name to the Jimmie Lunceford Orchestra. Born James Melvin Lunceford, he was the first public high school band director in Memphis.

Lunceford started his professional band career in 1929 and developed his special style by 1930. His orchestra toured the country, debuting at iconic venues like The Cotton Club in Harlem in 1934. Lunceford's band made several appearances during the famous *"Cotton Club Parade,"* starring Adelaide Hall (She's in the Guinness Book of World Records 2003, as the world's most enduring recording artist, having released material over eight consecutive decades). They displayed their tight musicology while maintaining their reputation of outrageous humor in their music and lyrics, Lunceford's orchestra gave the *"Cotton Club's all-white"* patrons some performances to remember.

An alto saxophonist, known for his two-beat rhythm, called the "Lunceford two-beat," the new rhythm propelled his band, during the swing era. Lunceford's Orchestra was considered the equal of Duke Ellington, Earl "Fatha" Hines or Count Basie. His orchestra often performed in Memphis clubs and Church's Park. Jimmie Lunceford's built a legacy of popularity other musicians sought to duplicate or emulate.

Phineas Newborn, Jr., a horn man also, Father Phineas Sr. drummer, and younger brother, Calvin, a guitarist, was Memphis' next offering to the music world. A young musician, Phineas Jr., began studying piano, then trumpet, before moving to tenor and baritone saxophone. His first gig was with an R&B band led by his father on drums, brother Calvin on guitar, Tuff Green on bass, Ben Branch on saxophone, and Willie "Papa" Mitchell on trumpet, while he played the piano. They first recorded with B. B. King, in 1949 and did a follow-up session in 1950. Ike Turner with Jackie Brenston on vocals also showcased Newborn's band as the "Delta Cats." While touring, they produced what many considered the first-ever rock & roll recording "Rocket 88," recorded at Sam Phillips' Sun Records Studio in Memphis (1951).

Most Memphis musicians, who became big-time jazz artists, started out playing in R&B bands. Hank Crawford was no exception. Born Bennie Ross Crawford, Jr. (12-21-1934/1-29-2009), Hank became a R&B, hard bop, jazz-funk, soul jazz, alto saxophonist, arranger, and songwriter. Hank began formal piano studies at age nine and played for his church choir. Similar to Manassas High School band icon Jimmie Lunceford, and the Newborn family, Hank desired to follow in their footsteps and achieve fame. Hank Crawford picked up his father's alto saxophone and joined the Manassas High School band.

Hank credits Charlie Parker, Louis Jordan, Earl Bostic, and Johnny Hodges as early influences. Ray Charles hired Crawford to play baritone saxophone, but Hank switched to alto in 1959. He became Ray's musical director in 1963. While musical director for Ray Charles, Crawford embarked on a solo career. He formed a septet, an already established with several well-regarded record labels—Atlantic, CTI, and Milestone—Hank recorded twelve LPs. Among his biggest hits, were "Misty," "The Peeper," "Skunky Green," and "Whispering Grass."

The Fight for Power: Loss of a Benefactor

Pres. Franklin D. Roosevelt's *"New Deal"* and WWII strengthened "Boss" Crump's hand through segregation. More importantly, white folks hammer hard, trying to terrorize black people, with the **"Dark Age"** *angry white men mob madness.* They tried to force black people to accept the second-class status white supremacy demanded. Backed by Democrats in Washington D. C., during the 1930s, Crump began efforts to push Robert Church, Jr. out of political power. Although black people in Memphis were surviving, "Boss" Crump desperately tried to control how well; he was truly "the wicked witch of the South."

A supreme egotist, "Boss" Crump ran everything in a way everyone knew he was in charge. Watching prosperity grow among black people in Memphis, without white people having control over money coming into the black community, did not sit well with the "Boss." Segregation served black people's interest, even though they were convinced hoodoo turning the trick.

Although segregation dictated separation by laws, also it did not allow whites to open a business in the black area of Beale Street, where money flowed. They could not come down to *"Nigger Town"* and mess around in the mud, having fun with black folk. Segregation kept white folks uptown, which left black people running downtown, which is why hoodoo got the credit.

These circumstances gave Church Jr. a free hand, wheeling and dealing on Beale Street. However, Crump set out to bring Church down, even though he was a Memphis benefactor and like Marcus Garvey, had not broken any laws. The truth is, through the Churches generosity, but with "Boss" Crump in control, again like Marcus Garvey, little people were powerless against the government. The Churches used their wealth to fight segregation and white supremacy, which softened its blow on African Americans and allowed them make money. But, "Boss" Crump continued hovering, like a buzzard waiting for eyes to close.

Crump had a long and impactful career in Tennessee politics. It depended on your bread—burned black or white—and which side it was buttered on, whether Crump's power was good or evil. Crump's rise to power began as a delegate to the Tennessee Democratic State Convention in 1902 and 1904.

A short recapitulation shows Crump's rise began on the municipal Board of Public Works (1905); from there, he was appointed Commissioner of Fire and Police (1907), then mayor of Memphis from 1910 to 1915.

Continuing to rise as though he had a *"mojo hand"* or *"black cat bone"* in his pocket, Crump was appointed treasurer of Shelby County from 1917 to 1923. Crump amassed his real power in that position.

Roger Biles, a reporter for the *Commercial Appeal* newspaper, argues that Memphis politics was virtually unchanged for 40 years—1910 into 1950. He explained beginning in 1930; Crump became the leading Democrat supporting

Pres. Franklin D. Roosevelt and his *"New Deal."* Crump's support brought *New Deal* relief programs to Memphis. Those programs provided jobs for the unemployed and who got those jobs depended on Crump's machine lieutenants. That was his power, no *"jack ball"* or *"mojo hand."* Black leaders hooked up with Crump's machine had the inside track, but not as part of his inner circle. They were not magicians either. They got the crumbs, job from federal projects white people considered "nigger" work.

Robert R. Church Jr., on the other hand, was a countervailing force against Crump. Money gave him the power to work his magic opposing "Boss" Crump's efforts to run Beale Street his way, which burned his bread with Crump. Church organized a Republican political club, the Lincoln League (1916), named for President Abraham Lincoln to do battle with the Boss' machine and white supremacy.

Church wanted the Republican Party's national office to recognize and appreciate the support African American voters gave the party. Looking back, Pres. U. S. Grant, a Republican in the 1870s, brought former slaves' Republican support. But, their participation did not produce political patronage, like Crump got from FDR. Building the League, Church brought in several black businessmen and professionals such as T. H. Hayes, J. B. Martin, Levoy McCoy, J.J. Stotts, Bert M. Roddy, and J. T. Settle.

From its inception, the league had an impact on Republican politics in West Tennessee. They held mass meetings at Church's Park and rallies against lynching (especially Ell Peason's lynching in 1917). I noted Peason's lynching earlier as the start of spectacle lynching, which prompted Church to form a NAACP chapter in Memphis. The first chapter in the South, it began with 53 members in 1917 but became the largest branch in the South (1919).

Bert M. Roddy was elected president, and Church became a member of the national board of directors. The NAACP gave Church real political clout nationally, as black people in Memphis rallied to his side and supported his political agenda. The league organized block clubs and collected money to pay poll taxes for poor blacks. Also, it established night schools to educate African Americans about voting. The League nominated candidates for local, state and national political offices.

Heading into the 1916 election, sixteen hundred African Americans from Hardeman, Tipton, and Fayette Counties joined with the Memphis-Shelby County contingent to nominate candidates for the November elections. The Lincoln League quickly gained the attention of the national Republican Party. Church convinced Republicans to support a national Lincoln League and became a key black politician in the South.

Robert Church, Jr. became a perennial delegate to the Republican Party National Conventions from 1912 to 1940. Republicans acknowledged Church's leadership, after the league provided swing votes in several Republican victories.

They began consulting him on federal patronage. But, the *New Deal* was like "Boss" Crump hired a conjure man to sprinkle *"goofer dust"* on Robert Church's trail.

First, the *New Deal* caused a shift in loyalty among black voters in the 1930s. Black voters began moving away from Church's alliance with Republicans because of benefit "Boss" Crump brought Memphis from the *"New Deal."* African American defections to the Democratic Party increased from a slow talk to a stampede, as FDR won a second term in 1938. Under such defections, Church's political influence waned.

During the 1920s and early 30s, "Boss" Crump recognized Church's political influence, with Republicans in the White House. He cultivated an uneasy relationship with Church, while playing "footsy" with other African American Republicans in Memphis under the table. So, "Boss" Crump and Church never became allies. With FDR and the *New Deal,* Crump grew stronger under, as Church grew weaker.

Tasting blood in the political waters, following FDR's landslide in 1938, Crump ready his machine for the kill. Even when Republicans were in the White House, Democrats had J. Edgar Hoover as FBI Director, so the "Boss" had friends in high places. He believed Church's "Ruby Red slippers" would be his with help from the wicked witches in Washington. As Pres. Franklin Roosevelt got ready for an unprecedented third term, Crump believed he could run Church out of his shoes.

Laying his trick, Crump did not need hoodoo. He had his own *"Dark Overlords,"* J. Edgar Hoover, and the US Justice Department to do the *"Marcus Garvey"* thing on Robert Church, Jr. The Justice Department orchestrated several tax evasion charges against Church. The "Boss" believed like Woodrow Wilson *"By fair means or foul white people were force to rid themselves of the intolerable position of government sustained by ignorant nigger."* Democrats in Washington gave the "Boss" the inside track, with unfair courts, *no jack ball.* Unlike Marcus Garvey, fortunately, Church had something Marcus Garvey did not. Some say it was the mojo people in Memphis called upon to protect Church. Others say Church got the best white lawyers money could buy. Either way, Church walked!!!! He was able to beat both evil spirits and wicked witches, J. Edgar Hoover and "Boss" Crump. That trick, for me, took real magic. So, like many Beale Streeters, I lay my money on hoodoo. Church read the handwriting on the wall; he was done in Memphis. Run out of town, like W. C. Handy; Church moved to Chicago.

The Stuff of Legends

With the passage of the Church family from the Beale Street scene, particularly regarding an economic and political counterweight to segregation and white supremacy, the socioeconomic and political development of descendants of American slavery made another important turn. This period required not only new tactics but new technologies, as well as continuation of the **Blues** magic. For people in places other than Memphis, it may seem this narrative gives more importance to the story of Beale Street and the **Blues** than they deserve. Their concerns are legitimate. Yet and still, Memphis is where I spent my formative years and where events as well as people gave real socioeconomic and political relevance to my family's struggles and provided my perspective on the world.

Moreover, the major problem I faced presenting this history is knowledge of stories other places are like the story of Beale Street, unwritten. Even more importantly, enslaved Africans' story the world over is shrouded in "word of mouth" cultures. The vast majority of these cultural sagas exist, as stories passed around, like urban legends and were kept alive by word of mouth.

Historians, the vast majority I believe, feel the story of enslaved Africans is not worth noting, at least the way they have presented black people's legacy. It has taken years of listening to conversations old-timers conveyed to reconstruct and record details and events from the lives they lived. Moreover, those with training and skills among enslaved Africans seem to feel there are not sufficient rewards to dedicate one's life to such a pursuit.

Over the years, I have pieced together much of the story of enslaved Africans I tell here, which came to me as stories passed around by those who passionately lived the adventures I detail. History tells us what happened, but in many cases, it is unable to explain why things happened as they did. Black people's "word of mouth history bears out the occurrences of what I discussed here, but the dilemma history creates, left me trying to explain how and why black people have the history they do. Spoken word narratives, as a result, are the arbiters of my efforts when historical facts are absent.

A major piece of this story is the impact of Marcus Garvey. Although most people in Memphis, during his time, never saw anything more than a picture of him, but never heard him speak. Reading about him is how he came to loom so large, in their minds. But even this was passed around and came to most slavery descendants, as something they heard discussed. So most did not read his words themselves; most did not realize they were echoing his thoughts or were trying to mimic his behavior.

Consequently, word of mouth filled black people's heads with expectations that demanded a different type of mental approach than that they developed after emerging from bondage. Even during the *"Dark Age"* *angry white men mob madness* of the 1920s through the 1930s, and the *Great Depression* (1930-1940), those expectations Mr. Garvey created did not die. If anything those word of mouth stories gained in power.

Research changed my perspective on Mr. Garvey, form what black children were told and read about him in school, which picture him as a ridiculous dressed buffoon and con man, swindling black people out of their pennies. Nevertheless, after all that word of mouth still made him seemed a magician to blacks that read or heard his story. He showed former slaves how to make themselves into something more than what they imagined they could ever be—which is his greatest trick, and why I call what he did magic.

Former slaves began aggressively pursuing the imagined image Garvey put in their heads. Watching him or hearing about Mr. Garvey legendary creation—the **UNIA,** former slaves were motivated to attempt things spontaneously, whereas, before him, such attempts would have been an impossible dream. Former slaves had no way to envision doing such things before Mr. Marcus Garvey told and showed them, *"If I can do it, you can do it too!!"*

Such actions were taboo for former slaves to think, let alone do; they were what white men did. Mr. Garvey model such positive and aggressive entrepreneurial actions before the world, it was like former slaves were witnessing a new magic act. Creating the **UNIA,** something that had never existed before, for former slaves, was tantamount to making something appear out of nowhere. Mr. Garvey's actions gave real meaning to his demand to *"make something out of nothing."* Much like Handy's **Blues** *magic,* when he first conjured it on paper, it didn't look like much, but hearing, black people got his message.

Reading about Mr. Garvey and watching his documentary **"Look for Me in the Whirlwind,"** I felt writing about his exploits, I could not feel his **Blues.** Something was missing, at first, I seem only to be mumming along, rather than singing his praises. However, then I realized he was modeling a totally new and different kind of leadership style, not what I had been trained to expect from Black leaders. Understanding he was single handedly overcoming segregation and white supremacy, removed the veil covering my mind. More than anything, I realized Mr. Marcus Garvey was marketing hope! Something poor black people needed most. They needed something to truly believe in, so Mr. Garvey gave them what they had all alone, themselves. Garvey's act giving former slaves confidence in their ability was truly a magician's trick, after enduring slavery and Wilson and J. Edgra Hoover tried hardest to kill.

Mr. Garvey gave them hope, because former slaves could never emulate the well-educated and highly financed white man's image of leadership Robert Church, Sr. and Jr. modeled. Former slaves, before Mr. Garvey visualized the world through the subservient eyes slave masters forced upon them and they transferred that vision to other, like Chandler Owen, A. Philip Randolph and others. Mr. Garvey reflected behaviors black people never witnessed by someone who looked like them. Without Garvey putting such images and ideas in their heads, former slaves had no way of creating that mind-set.

I suggest, the difference is, in Jamaica, Garvey's home, slaves endured a different kind of bondage, which ended with the abolition of the **Trans-Atlantic Slave Trade** (1807). Slavery there was not as vicious and virulent, as in America. Their slavery did not expose them to the internal slave trade and breeding system, as was enslaved Africans in the US. Mr. Garvey was born in 1887, 80 years after slavery ended in Jamaica, and 25 years after it ended in America. Truly a descendant of slavery, but he was never a slave. His persona, especially to blacks in the South, was inspiring, an image to emulate.

After beginning their penniless emancipation in America, without education and no structure, former slaves needed instructions and a new reality. Mr. Garvey was among the first generation fully free of the physical reality of slavery. He saw the world through eyes that knew only freedom, as Burl Lee Jr. Even if a black people in America had not experienced slavery personally, they experienced its acculturated in America's slave society. That environment limited expectations for black skin in America's *cheap labor* structure. Consequently, blacks in America did not have the vision Mr. Garvey brought to America when he stepped off the boat in New York City.

The reality of the **UNIA** changed how descendants of American slavery saw themselves and the world. This drama played out in many ways in different places around the world. In Memphis, and on Beale Street, this reality resembled a *"soap opera"* or a fairy tale like **"The Wizard of Oz,"** and to describe what I was told about Beale Street by old-timers, I visualized it as a metaphor, because the actual story, as it happened, was not written. Many of these events prompted actions and responses that were unrecorded, although they happened, I was left without verification. Most events or happenings were memories passed around until they became fantastic back slapping big fish stories, which is why they lived on in the memories of these great storytellers.

Memphis politics is a perfect example of a whirlwind of a story like **The Wizard of Oz**, but it depends on which end of the spectrum or continuum one is on, as to whether the whirlwind blew good or ill. I offer the following two metaphors, **The Wizard of Oz** juxtapose against **The WIZ** to illustrate my point. Their dichotomy reflects how white people and black people can look at the same situation, event, and place and see two totally different realities. Using these two fairytales, I endeavored to capture the drama and surreal character of Beale Street and Memphis politics, as orchestrated by the "Boss." Most old-timers talked about the "Boss" as if he was truly the *"wicked witch of the South."* Most fairytales, like these two, are symbolic and reflect a real struggle for power and these stories—**The Wizard of Oz** and **The WIZ**—fulfill the same purpose.

My point that white and black people can observe or experience the same event, yet come away with two entirely different scenarios, reflect the contrast and comparison of life on Beale Street, is a point, counter-point reality using **The WIZ.** Moreover, I use **The Wizard of Oz** to reflect "Boss" Crump's effort to make Beale Street match the story for black people in his head. Symbolically, the world I describe, which former slaves inhabited on a daily bases, reflects the world the "Boss" tried to create from observing life on Beale Street, like a play.

The world in which black people live and deal with is a world, like **"The WIZ."** It reflects the world Marcus Garvey tried to change, as described in **"Look for Me in the Whirlwind",** which is the story of his life. I present these metaphors as the diverging and diverse vision white people had and tried to force upon black people, compared to the world black people tried to create and live, and which black people believed only magic could change.

The difference in these two views can, in a real way, only be communicated through some fairytale or another literary device. The difficulty here is events that effected life on Beale Street must be presented from two totally different directions. White people consider their view of the life they create for black people, better for them than the life black people saw for themselves.

Even though white people are continually affecting by factual evidence from the other end of the spectrum, whites still insist and consider their view, the only thing that matters. So, whites hold tenaciously to their imaginary world view and continually try to force that world view on black people. Their imaginary life for black people reflects the fantasy in white people's heads, like **"The Wizard of Oz."**

Considering this dichotomy and trying to illustrate the difference, one has to envision both as satires. First, **"The Wizard of Oz"** *("The Wonderful Wizard of Oz")* is well-known as a powerful symbol of monetary reform by economists and academicians. It is a reflection of the socioeconomic and political storm that blew across America during the *populist and free silver* movements in 1896-1900 (During the Panic of 1893) when **"The Wizard of Oz"** was written by L. Frank Baum. It reflects William Jennings Bryan's run for president as a Democrat.

"Oz" is a weight measure associated with gold. The yellow brick road was a reflection of economic stability in America, the gold standard, which leads to the American dream—Emerald City. The *"wicked witch of the West"* was Cleveland banker J.D. Rockefeller, and the *"wicked witch of the East"* was NY banker J.P. Morgan. The Emerald City of Oz also symbolized the medium of commerce—greenback money. Even Dorothy's slippers were changed, for the movie, from silver slippers to ruby red.

Originally, the slippers symbolized L. Frank Baum, and William Jennings Bryan's belief *"adding silver coinage to gold would provide much-needed money (liquidity) to a Depression-strapped 1890s America (The Gilded Age) economy".* Of course, Dorothy represents the American value *"purity."* The Munchkins are the little people, or the common folk, who believe in Dorothy *(purity and virtues)*. The Tin Man reflects industrial workers. They were dehumanized and treated like machines. Scarecrow is the Western farmers, who had been devastated by the fall of commodity prices, which caused *the Panic of 1893*. Devastated and deceived farmer were confused and mentally unable to fight back. Cowardly Lion symbolized William Jennings Bryan, a politician from the late 1800s who supported the *free silver movement* (the slippers ruby or silver). Everything was set in motion by the cyclone or tornado, which represented trouble and disaster wrought by the *"Panic of 1893,"* and the political upheaval from the free silver movement, like Donald Trump's impact on America from 2016-2020.

Juxtapose against **The Wiz** (1978), directed by Sidney Lumet, on the other hand, like the downside of the cone discussed previously, the characters, from my perspective, reflected aspects of black people's personality, based on their slave acculturation. Dorothy (Diana Ross) is a super-modern courageous multi-tasking and quick-witted young black woman of the 80s to 90s, who experienced the black power movement.

Dorothy is an intelligent and empathetic sister, during a time of change and activism (forerunner to Black Lives Matter) is swept up by the whirlwind of life and carried to a new world without context. She teams up with a group of confused psyched-out misfits, and has to find a way to get the best out of the team she has drawn to her, if she is to succeed—a return to the days of black power. However, in this new world, she is inhabited and trapped by the unrealized success of that bygone revolution and longs to return to that time.

The Scarecrow (Michael Jackson) reflects black people's sense of inferiority. African Americans are victimized by inadequate information, which leaves them unable to compete successfully in the white world, which is reflected by his lack of a brain. Cowardly lion (Ted Ross) reflects another character trait, black people's perceived impotence; what to do. His inadequacy symbolizes black people's lack of confidence in their abilities, hence no courage. He has to be told and have agreement—mental support—before he acts.

The Tim Man (Nipsey Russell) reflects black people's inner terror of acting independently or against the will of slave masters (white Folks), a leftover trait instilled during slavery. Tim Man reflects black people's victimization and reticence. This trait causes black people to freeze up when they must act independently or confront white people. It is very hard for him to go against his machine-like programming.

The Emerald City is a gated community. It is the world outside the ghetto, strange and mysterious to black people who only see it from the outside, but where everything of value happens and exists. One must have permission to enter and has to pay a high personal cost to hang around. If one accepts offers, they will get messed around. The wicked witches are white people, whether from the East, West, North, or South.

The would-be-good-witch from the West (Lena Horne) could help, but only if Dorothy's team learns to *make something out of nothing*, will they have a chance to succeed. White people—wicked witches—are in charge, and they are the ones messing black people around. The yellow brick road is the illusion of success at the end of the rainbow—*the American dream*. **"The Wiz"** is what life is for black people in America.

The **Wiz** (Richard Pryor) reflects a classic character in every black community. He is a guy with lots of ideas but without financing to get them up and running. His problem is getting people to trust him. When he gets things moving, they blows up so fast, it sucking him into a world he could never imagine existed. Appearing out of nowhere, suddenly, everyone believes he is a wizard. Although he knows he isn't, everyone wants him to do magic for them, which he knows he cannot. Rather than tricking them, he figures out how to convince them they can do for themselves whatever they are asking him to do. The trick is everyone is happy because the outcome is what the wizard predicted for them.

White people looking at **The Wiz** do not understand why anyone would create such a hideous imitation of life when they have created, in their heads, this wonderful imagined life—**The Wizard of Oz**—for black people to live. White people have a life in their heads for black people, which is the world of *Evillene*. She is the wicked witch of the East and does the **Boss'** dirty work. She enforces the life forced upon the powerless little people by the **"Boss"** and is a totally different story than the life the "little people" are trying to live on their own. There is only one good witch (Lena Horne) but even she has to work within the **Wiz's** plan to be able to help Dorothy.

The problem is white people run and control everything, and their vision of life is the only view that matters. That reality means black people's lives seen by white people is an imagined and fantasized life. Simultaneously, white people forced black people to try and live out white people's made-up ideas or fantasy about black life. Nonetheless, and at the same time, black people must cope with the real-life situations and consequences white people's fantasizing create for them but become real-life conditions black people must endure to survive.

Trapped in this fictitious world of white people's fantasies about black life, where suspicion becomes law for a black man, and a death sentence, whereas a guilty white man gets a free pass for murdering a black man or gets paid to walk away, so the government will not have to press charges, the story is always the same. These two views are reflective of life in Memphis, but it matches the fantasized view of white history, at the same time. With the two metaphors—The Wizard of OZ and The WIZ, I add some color to an otherwise totally black and white story.

Here Comes the "Boss"

"Boss" Crump's shenanigans gave him what he coveted before running Robert Church, Jr. out of town. Following his trick, as the *"Wicked Witch of the South,"* Crump tried to play the role he imagined and schemed to acquire in real life. Crump's fantasy created only drama for black people on Beale Street. Powerful enough to take over Beale Street, but once in possession of it, Crump tried to play the role; he imagined Church filled. Similar to a sorcerer's apprentice to black folks living in terror of his next move, like munchkins, Crump created doubt and confusion, since hoodoo seemed to have vanished with Church. Once rid of Church, the "Boss" entered from stage right, which was like the house fell on a good witch, rather than a bad one. Left to struggle on their own, like a shepherd-less flock, without a leader to compete with the "Boss," even hoodoo and conjure masters were chased out of town.

Stories passed around by old timers from those days are the only remaining record from this bygone time. Other than word of mouth, virtually no hard evidence survived that period. So all I had to rely on was the perspectives and stories of Beale Street old-timers. The few written accounts that remain makes "Boss" Crump the hero? Most Writers from those times did not tell the story of Beale Street from the perspective of the man that would replace both paragons—Crump and Church—even after the whirlwind of life blew him to town.

Robert Church's departure left Beale Streeters looking for a new kind of leader and image. They no longer saw men like "Boss" Crump, as leaders. Arriving on the scene, like a "Tin Man" with a heart, Sunbeam Mitchell cut and chopped his way from the outer edge of obscurity, learning to be a devil-may-care swashbuckling lone rider just making it to Memphis.

Once on the scene, the name Sunbeam Mitchell rose like the evening star over Beale Street, lighting the way out of the darkness, once Church became a shooting star. Beale Street old-timers that witnessed Sunbeam's legerdemain, which returned the street to a magical place, speak glowingly of his arrival. Today, such flamboyant gentlemen still talk exultantly of Sunbeam's efforts and how he brought the party life back to the fabulous thoroughfare. A mystical character once he began laying down tricks, old timers during interviews, talked about his exploits, as though Beale Street's magic passed directly from Handy to Sunbeam.

Reaching this point, most of what I have written about Beale Street came from the historical record. The story of Beale Street that black people lived, I repeat, is unwritten, so I had only antidotal information and stories Beale Streeters passed around to rely. These are stories told during old-timers Saturday morning barbershop conversations or under big walnut trees around checkerboards. These stories come out during "big fish" storytelling sessions and are all that remain of those grand times.

Readers must remember these old-timers were storytellers, not historians. They claimed to be eyewitnesses to the accounts I retell here of people and places from this bygone period. Although these stories may sound fantastic or doubtful, they comport with the little history that made it into the historical record in some way. So, as faithfully as the stories I received from old-timers and the writing on Beale Street, I convey these stories and scenarios, which made a quick left turn away from Robert R. Church, Jr.'s leadership. The man who filled Church's shoes did not buy them in a second-hand store or pawn shop on Beale Street. He made them to fit only him. Cutting, chopping and stitching pieces he picked up, in the wake of the mess "Boss" Crump made, forcing his big over-size feet into Church's tiny "red slippers." That fit is why Church's undersized Beale Street "kickers" fit Sunbeam so well,

Listening to tales of old-timers, they seem to think "Boss" Crump, trying to run Beale Street, was a similar tale, as *"The Sorcerer's Apprentice,"* with a different beginning, but an identical ending. True to that tale, the "Boss" got things moving but his inability to control the speed and size of the effects his actions created cause chaos. Without knowing the rotation pattern that determined success, Crump's attempts at magic were like "a bull in a china shop." How, things developed or the way things went, once they started moving, was similar to trying to forecast a tornados' path from the basement!

Back then, hoodoo and conjure masters were big parts of how and what black people believed. Moreover, to them, after Crump descended on Beale Street and chased hoodoo and conjure men out of town, everyone had to bowed down to Crump, the evil spirit or *"wicked witch"* of the South. The "Boss" believed once he forced his big feet into Church's tiny "red slippers," his role would flow naturally, allowing him to simply *"ease on down"* Beale Street, as though no one knew they were not made for him. However, just because Crump wanted the same power as Church, his oversized feet left no room for magic in Church's shoes. "Boss" Crump could not see Church's wizardry, which took place out of sight, behind the Beale Street magic curtain and not out front with smoke and mirrors.

Unlike Church, who was part of the action on Beale Street, but like Donald Trump today, the Boss' needed to know and control what was happening on Beale, but never wanted to listen to anyone, who was actually part of making thing happen, chaos resulted. The "Boss" nerve wanted advice, which made the fit of Church's shoes, more like a straightjacket, than spiffy dress kickers or comfy house slippers for the "Boss." The result, according old-timers, Crump's rather large footprint, smashed some little munchkin underfoot, every time he moved, no matter what he did or how he moved.

Having worked overtime getting Church's boots to strut around Beale Street, even though they hurt his feet to wear them, Crump couldn't gloat over them hanging on his wall. The reality from black folk's perspective, in no time at all, Crump made such a mess of things for people on Beale Street; they were like munchkins before the whirlwind blew Dorothy to town. Daily they sprinkled *goof dust* everywhere, trying to ward off what everyone was convinced was a "buja whammy" cast by the *"wicked witch of the South."*

Contrarily, leaving Beale Streeters operating on their own made Church's shoes too small for the foot prints the "Boss" loved to make. The tight grip he loved to feel when running thing, had Beale Streeters, squirming trying to conjure someone with, not only a new vision of how and what to do to keep business going on Beale but a different way of thinking, with Church gone and the "Boss" in charge. Crump's dilemma, trying to run Beale Street, illustrate the major point of comparing and contrasting these two fairytales; *white people can look at or experience the identical situation as black people, but see or approach the situation in totally different ways.*

The trick to making money for people on Beale Street was getting around the limited view Crump's segregation minded minions had running things. The problem facing the black community was producing new and different leadership or knuckle under to the "Boss," while accepting his second-class segregation type fun. Those conditions left Beale Streeters two alternatives, with segregation in Memphis and across the South, having denied African Americans *VOICE*. Under Crump's legerdemain, Beale Street's "yellow brick road" led back to the plantation or was the road Church took leaving town.

A Tin Man with a Heart

Since Robert Church, Sr. arrived in Memphis (1862), as an emancipated slave, his money had rescued contrabands running from death and destruction in the wake of Civil War. Following Church's community development strategy, provided the impetus for blacks in Memphis to build Beale Street into a successful *Bronzeville*. As a result, many in Memphis saw Beale Street, like the "Harlem of the South." Beale Street's magical story, I repeat, points up the profound difference in what white people and black people saw, looking at the same place. As with everything connected to black people, the value depends on who made the assessment. White people did not see or experience the unseen magical character of Beale Street, during the 1930s through the 1960s. Looking at Beale Street, white people saw *"just a place where niggers did what niggers do"* nothing of value. However, that story and vision changed, once the 1940s arrived.

Once Andrew "Sunbeam" Mitchell's blew into town a new vision of Beale Street began to emerge. He changed the character of the famed thoroughfare forever. A small-town country boy, who ran the backwoods, haunting whiskey houses, chicken shacks, and juke joints, learning to cut and chop his way through deals, Sunbeam was a man with a plan. His developed his plan not only living on a farm, but in Detroit, where he joined the army. After discharge in Detroit, he worked in the automobile industry before coming back south.

Arriving in town, he saw bright lights, lots of clubs and heard blaring music, and decided to hang around. The real trick for Sunbeam was black people spending money on entertainment all week, not just on weekends. An eye-opening sight for a poor country boy, like Sunbeam, if Beale Street was not a magical place in the early 1940s, it would do, until a stronger wind blew him there.

The magic of Beale Street disappeared once Church departed and with his loss, African Americans in Memphis lost a true benefactor. Blacks in Memphis did not only lose a voice, white people could not dismiss because the city might need Church again, as during the yellow fever epidemic, but blacks also lost leadership. After Marcus Garvey's show, African Americans learned their prosperity depended on their adaptability and faith in their ability to work together, no matter what white people threw at them. They were also learning to emulate Mr. Garvey's audacity and cunning, dealing with white folks. When circumstances, events, and personalities came together like a whirlwind and blew Sunbeam Mitchell to town, Beale Streeter believed hoodoo brought him around.

Sunbeam Mitchell entered the Beale Street story in the early 1940s, while segregation and white supremacy added more layers to the oppression of black people. White's new technology that began dominating black people across the South at the turn of the 20th century—***Plessy v. Ferguson***—white believed they had the ability to control money coming into the black community. The key to that strategy was denying enslaved Africans human rights, real mobility, and access to fair courts.

White people thought they had control of every penny black people got and spent when they created sharecropping. Totally in control of laws, courts and the economic system, sharecropping was a bookkeeping economy. The term "bookkeeping economy" describes the power government gave white people to control black sharecroppers with credit. Segregation made white men's words law; whatever they said was all that mattered. The legal system gave them control of the books and all other resources that came to black sharecroppers, they thought. Blacks signed or made their X, for whatever credit white people gave in most cases.

Woodrow Wilson a southerner from Virginia made this system work by implementing segregation, and using the ***"Dark Age"*** white men mob madness to force black people to accept the second class status white's demanded. Segregation was designed to keep cash out of black people's hands. Prisoners on the land, sharecroppers were trapped by segregation, in a system designed to created scarcity and desperation. Struggling to survive without relief or hope, black people endured to survive.

Settling up time was the next big event in the sharecropping system. Without fair courts sharecroppers were locked up working white people's land for next ninety years. Settling up time occurred after the harvest was sold and when the landowner was supposed to divide up the money from the harvested based on the agreed upon percentages. Settling up usually happened in late winter into early spring. However, the sharecropping economy did not yield cash to sharecroppers, except to blacks working regular jobs or those who filled some niche white people could not or would not fill.

White landowners did not deal fairly with sharecroppers. The hand dealt blacks, always came from the bottom of the deck. Holding all the cards that mattered, landowners also owned the store, so sharecroppers were given credit, and the landowners kept the records. His tally, no matter what share croppers' records showed, was the only tally that counted. Black families survived on credit for most of the year, signing the lander owners' book. Most times black sharecroppers always came up short of clearing the books, leaving them in the hold another year. Credit mandated another year on the same land, which kept sharecroppers on lockdown.

Sharecroppers could get cash for things the lander did not sell in his store, but it came as an advance against the next harvest. Black people could only change goods where they sharecropped, without the agreement of the landowner on whose land they presently lived. Sharecroppers that moved without permission committed a crime, and if caught, judges sold their fine to the business that paid it, usually the same landowner.

This is when convict leasing became the backup. The families usually ended up sharecropping the same land for the same landowner for free, paying the find.

Also based of the sharecropping system it seemed white people held all the cards, but however, black people had gotten pretty good at making something out of nothing. After its beginning, one would not call the *"Chitlin Circuit's"* existence clandestine, because it operated out in the open. Its appearance did not disturb any establish stereotypes; consequently, it seemed, *"niggers were just during what niggers do."* As far as white people were concerned, *"Niggers were always getting together, getting drunk, and clowning around."* That was all white people saw. The trick here was even during the work season—planting, chopping, and cotton picking times—black folks in the delta had money. Relatives that escape sharecropping, going up North, out West or to the military, sent money back home. Many children in the South were like me, left behind with grandmas and granddaddies that needed help keeping things together.

The trick was getting money to them, without white people knowing. Black families could not use the postal service for that, because it was run by whites, who could not be trusted. Whites were known to open black people's mail. Code words could not disguise money, so getting around white folks, was like hoodoo, black folks went through the Church.

Circuit riders played that very important role. They delivered messages and other things, mostly money and important papers. These were things black people could not afford to allow white people to see or know. Such items came to the circuit rider in the area where that family lived. Rev. Burl Lee, my great-granddaddy, played this role. My granddaddy had a favorite saying, *"Showin white folks ya got something, git it took!!"*

Sunbeam Mitchell was more than a legend. But his name is not found among the official **Blues** archives of Memphis, like Robert Church, senior and junior, W. C. Handy, Ida B. Wells, or George W. Lee, to name a few. His presence on Beale Street came at a most critical point in the development of black people, not only in Memphis but throughout the Mississippi Delta.

Few people come alone during a period when their unique skill set is demanded, in ways they seemed totally unprepared to deliver, looking at their résumé. Similar to Marcus Garvey, who did not light up the pages of history, when he stepped off the boat, in New York City in 1914, Andrew "Sunbeam" Mitchell did not raise an eyebrow with his ignoble entrance. A fugitive from justice, when he hit town, he had to keep a low profile, so all most people knew was "Sumbeam."

According to Beale Street old-timers, Sunbeam was a desperado, and definitely not a businessman went he blew into Memphis. Sunbeam's story, like so many others, was not written down. Beale Street historians say he was running from a shootout with the sheriff in Fayette County, Tennessee. (Some old-timers even claim Sunbeam was really Burton Dodson, who was accused of murder related to the killing of a Fayette County deputy sheriff in a shootout outside the home of a black man in 1940. Dodson fled Tennessee after the incident).

Just a step ahead of the law, they say Sunbeam had lived the life of a gambler, card shark, hustler, and devil-may-care lone rider. Setting up in Memphis on Beale Street, he would bring its special magic alive once again. W. C. Handy had conjured the **Blues**, giving Beale Street its special magic, changing the scenarios for black people, and staked those depending on it to a possible future. Sunbeam became the man, once he figured out how to use its special powers.

The **Blues** magic did not flow just anyplace or to anyone. Its presence was an emotional effect, which Sunbeam Mitchell seemed to draw like a special attraction. Old-timers say Sunbeam received the special touch of the **Blues**, like a *"black cat bone,"* that gave him all the power of hoodoo. However, I say, one does not have to believe any of this to appreciate the impact of Sunbeam's extraordinary vision.

The sort of magical power Beale Street old-timers attributes to Sunbeam came with **Blues** magic on Beale Street, not card tricks, disappearing objects, or pulling rabbits out of hats. This magic is the ability of some black people to persevere in the face of overwhelming odds. What I offer are not just statements about a man, but they are reflections of eyewitness accounts that verify some of the innovative solutions Sunbeam provided for intractable problems, which seemed to them impossible to solve, like dealing with the "Boss." Facing the most daunting task, which the most courageous among them refused to attempt, Sunbeam made look easy, once done. Those are the qualities that Sunbeam unveiled once the whirlwind of life blew him to Beale Street.

Ode to Sunbeam Mitchell: Cutting and Chopping with a Beat

Arriving in Memphis, looking for a game, he was new, and without fame. Sunbeam didn't know tricks from tricksters, but unmasked them, like a jester, just the same. A step behind in the game, when he met Ernestine, though she was not a queen, they became a thing. She had a plan for her man and knew Beale Street like the palm of her hand.

Ernestine found a house with a basement and two floors, so Sunbeam spread his net when they opened the doors. Drawing everyone into his lair, Sunbeam had a place for those who thought they were player. With Ernestine up top folks knew what it meant, Sunbeam was in the basement taking care of the rent.

His games drew sporting men into his liar, and in no time at all, Sunbeam's was a player. With a quick move they were part of the flow, as Sunbeam hobnobbed with those in the know. Some old-timers said Ernestine had the magic that made things go, while others saw Sunbeam behind the curtain, running their show. But, what was out in the open, for all to see, was a new dynamic duo making magic, but not for free.

Ernestine rented rooms on the top floor; her game was this, for all to know, two bucks all night was the go. In came working girl at night, that lick for them was just right. Then for girls who couldn't afford that slice, a quickie on Sunbeam's back seat was half the price. While cooking and selling food out the back door, Ernestine hustled drinks for dancers on the first floor.

Cutting and chopping his shady games—bootlegging, loan sharking and fronting merchandise, Sunbeam had the deal, if you had the price. Some said he was just lucky, a new face in town. Opening a policy bank the "Boss's" enforcers came round. Everyone was shocked when they didn't shut them down. Old-timers said he had conjure, <u>*Aunt Sally's Policy Players Dream Book,*</u> although he wasn't Ernestine, Sunbeam knew how to cook.

High roller or slow stroller, it didn't matter to the "Boss." It was all like black people on Election Day, as long as they voted his way, the "Boss" was okay. Crump didn't care what your game was or not, as long as you kept it off the street, and he got his off the top. If his money didn't drop, his goons showed up, not the cops. No one in the know could say for sho' how Sunbeam and the "Boss" made it a go. That wasn't in the open to be seen, how Sunbeam hooked up with "Boss" Crump's machine. Everyone knew he was cool and not just a fling, cause chopping and cutting deals; he stayed on the scene.

I know this all sounds fishy old-timers said, debating Sunbeam capers while scratching their heads.

Beale Streeters have lots of big fish stories, and all had their favorite of Sunbeam's glory. Beale Streeters couldn't say if Sunbeam magic was a *"black cat bone"* in his deck or the "mojo hand" Ernestine kept tied around her neck. But all jaws dropped when Abe Plough did a flop, fronting Sunbeam two floors above his shop. Pantaze Drug Store was Abe's spot. He was a wheeler-dealer, avoiding the "Boss'" and his cops. With segregation ruling with an iron fist upside your head, if the "Boss" didn't get his, both you and your game were dead. Pantaze on the corner of Beale and Hernando was the spot to be; Sunbeam put a club up top so all could see. When the doors open on the fabled Street, old-timers packed the Domino Lounge ten deep.

 The top floors over Pantaze Drug Store became the Mitchell Hotel. This deal made everything Sunbeam did work so well. Like rabbits jumping out of his hat before he put another one in, the Mitchell Hotel gave black folks a "do drop inn." Travelers within 200 miles by boat or road, the Mitchell Hotel was known as a good abode. The best "Colored hotel," black travelers couldn't pass; it was where colored folks could eat and sleep in first class. The second floor became *The Domino Lounge*, for cool smooth people, not for clowns. Sunbeam and Ernestine's first spot became "The No Name Club," high rollers flooded in no matter how it was dubbed. With a hotel, clubs, and restaurants, Sunbeam had clout, all high rollers could say was "well shut my mouth!" *The Domino Lounge* became *Club Handy*; Sunbeam was the MAN and a real dandy. With the Mitchell Hotel and Club Handy, Sunbeam spread *"Chitlin Circuit's"* magic like it was candy.

Legend of the Chitlin Circuit

Sunbeam Mitchell's deal cutting brought the real magic back to Beale Street. He conjured a way to share the prosperity up and down the Mississippi River and out into Texas. Adding to his mystique, old-timers' backslapping big fish tales, still float around, and everyone has their favorite Sunbeam Mitchell whooper. First, he hooked up with some black businessmen from across the South and up North, who rejected the whole idea of segregation. These self-made men were hard nose, down for anything to make a dollar from any business. They refused to give white folks the inside track on making money. They were a breed of black men that believed, *"When money hits the table, it belonged to the one who picked it up."* They refused to be regulated by white folks to get money; these men didn't feel segregation prevented black people from making a living; it just made living harder.

For a black man to make a dollar, in the 1930s and 40s, put him out on the road at night, taking care of business. So, people he dealt with knew he could cover his back in a fight. Despite Jim Crow and paddy rollers on the road, money was out there, and a black man had to roll. Many a night, out under southern skies, traveling treacherous roads in Jim Crow land, the stout of hearted had a plan. They had to be ready to do whatever it took, to stay alive and make book. A black man, whether preacher or entertainer, caught in such predicaments, was up against the viciousness of the KKK, looking to decorate southern trees with **strange fruit.**

There are legendary stories of Sunbeam, shooting his way into and out of roadhouses, backroom dives, juke joints, lean-to eateries, fried chicken shacks, greasy-spoons, and gambling holes to come away with what he was owed. On the road chopping and cutting deals, like a Tin Man with a heart, sunbeam was surveying the route and laying the foundation for the *"yellow brick road"* and the *Chitlin Circuit* he saw as a dream. While Sunbeam was out putting together his ring, Ernestine was back in Emerald City doing her Dorothy thing. She held down the Mitchell Hotel, while Sunbeam was on the road trying to stay alive.

Not getting their hands dirty or keeping them clean, during these times, a black man had to be hard and mean. Making money in their businesses came down to what life demanded at the time. The first rule of life and the trick to surviving that game was knowing, how much skin to give up or keep to stay in the game; with very little, if any control, when you can't win, you fold.

Hustlers, numbers men, bootleggers, whiskey-runners, con artists, gangsters, and gamblers pick a suit, these descriptions and more to boot, fit men that traveling this route. Sunbeam and his crew were not mobsters with back up waiting in the wings, if trouble came their way, they did their own thing. They were not salesmen, pushing burial policies, furniture, dry goods, or foodstuffs. Early in life, they saw the world through their own eyes, and in their favor, things did not add up.

These men enrolled in Marcus Garvey's school of hard knocks and learned the business by doing and taking stock. You received your MBA if you avoided ruin and stayed alive while doing it. They lived in the real world of Jim Crow white supremacy, where whites controlled everything worth doing. This meant white hands always held the dices. The best black men could expect in that world I was told was to cut craps on a losing roll.

Old-timers claimed Sunbeam had nine lives; his world was hard to break into but even harder to break out alive. His crew had shady enterprises to give their legitimate businesses' cash flow. The fact was, *"Banks did not deal with 'hard cut' black men."* Moreover, loan sharks in the South felt, *"Niggers came a dime a dozen, so a nigger wasn't worth a bullet, costing ten cents each."* Many a young novice, who dared to tread such treacherous shark-infested waters, and thought they could move faster than the lessons taught, paid with their lives for this grievous fault.

Trying to build something out of nothing, Sunbeam and his group of astute hard-driving businessmen were not to be trifled with. Once they hooked up, they took black entertainment to a new level, as an enterprise. These were men historians overlooked, as not even worthy of footnotes in black, let alone American history books. However, in black communities, where poverty swallowed everyone at birth, such men were legends in their own time. They did not just eat well; they also fed others catching hell. More than that, if you wanted to catch your own dinner, they taught you to fish, as well. I speak of them, as wizards and mystics, because feeding others was their biggest and best trick.

Sunbeam and Marcus Garvey were like men, who inherited a bankrupt company; it wasn't worth anything, but it was all they had. Garvey's history is clearly known, but Sunbeam's story is shrouded in mystery, at least that which is known. The word is he started in Mason, Tennessee, a sharecropping community. Sharecropping is identical to a bankrupt company, you are broke and in debt, before you spend time or a dime. On one's own, the task is daunting, but managing for a family, leaves you in a hold too deep to climb out. However, black sharecropping families did it and survived.

As a young man, steeped in sharecropping, Sunbeam Mitchell had to learn to measure and manage everything that had to be done, against what one could actually do, in a world controlled by segregation and white supremacy too.

Dealing with and getting around white people became a way of thinking and living for black men. Coming to Memphis, Sunbeam was like a man that recused his bankrupt company from ruin; he brought the business savvy of sharecropping to Beale Street, as part of his magic act, trying to bring the famed thoroughfare back.

The 400th: From Slavery to Hip Hop

Starting the *Chitlin Circuit*, Sunbeam lined up his crew of astute businessmen who knew what to do. First, there was Denver Ferguson up in Indianapolis, Indiana. Denver had been out there butting heads with white men since 1919 (the 300th). He owned the *Cotton Club* at the South end of The Avenue. Sunset Terrace was on the North end, and Denver Ferguson provided all the fun in between. His big move up was getting into the numbers game, printing policy slips for an out-of-state lottery, the kind that was prominent in Harlem and on the south side of Chicago.

Down South, Don Robey, another devil-may-care lone rider, owned the *Harlem Grill* on W. Dallas Avenue in the middle of the Houston stroll. He also owned the *Bronze Peacock* and *Duke-Peacock Records* in Houston. He was the traffic cop along the Houston stroll.

Swinging over to New Orleans, Frank Painia's *Do Drop Inn* was the spot on LaSalle Street near Sixth Avenue. Painia built a hotel, restaurant, and nightclub around his tonsorial parlor. He rested easy in the "Big Easy" although he was slippery, he wasn't greasy.

Moving East toward Atlanta's, *The Royal Peacock* on Auburn Avenue packed them in all week long. But between Atlanta and New Orleans, everybody for miles around wanted to layover in Prichard, Alabama. Tom Couch had a great stopover, *The Harlem Duke Social Club*. With the *Harlem Hotel* and *Eddie's Diner*, a neighborhood eatery nearby, bands kept the party going all night. These were just some of the clubs these men owned and pulled together for Sunbeam, as he brought the *"Chitlin' Circuit"* alive.

Performers had always traveled the road entertaining, as far back as minstrel shows. The thing Sunbeam and his group brought to their game, just out of white folks watchful eyes, they made entertaining black people a real enterprise. The phrase was, *"If white people can't see, they don't know what niggers are doing. So, they think niggers are doing what niggers always do, nothing for white folks to get excited about."* That was how the logic of black people deduced the situation. So, the *"Chitlin' Circuit"* grew up right under white people's noses, and they never had a clue. The beauty of the whole game was white folks thought black folks in the Delta didn't have any money. They thought they'd sucked up every dime with convict leasing and sharecropping.

However, when one talks about the *"Chitlin' Circuit"* (*the yellow brick road of black entertainment,*) we are talking about a story that began in the early 1940s. Back then, names like Sunbeam Mitchell, Don Robey, Denver Ferguson, Frank Painia, and Tom Couch had a magical ring for black people.

These guys developed the idea of booking entertainers in "nowhere backwoods nothing *"hole-in-the-wall"* places," for poor nothing cotton field black folks. Along the way, they created something that made millions of dollars for black people before white businessmen ever noticed.

Many people probably are unaware of the term *"Chitlin' Circuit,"* if that's the case, Preston Lauterbach's book, <u>The Chitlin' Circuit: And the Road to Rock 'N' Roll</u> does a very good job presenting a subject that has been completely overlooked by historians. His book will be a major source for those who want more information than is presented here. Sunbeam's alchemy conjured the notion of rotating entertainers through their system of clubs, and Memphis made it work. Whether entertainers were going North or South, Memphis was the key, and Sunbeam Mitchell locked it down.

W. C. Handy and the **Blues** gave Memphis a reputation as a music hotspot or Mecca. This reputation made black people want to experience Beale Street and the **Blues** firsthand. While at the same time entertainers, looking for regular work, heard about the clubs on and around Beale Street that partied all week. Owning Club Handy, most entertainers (bands and vocalists), came to Memphis looking for Sunbeam. He became the man to see if you wanted work.

Memphis was the destination for hard up, hard luck, down and out of luck bands and singers that had nowhere else to go. During the early 1940s, down and out, entertainers made Beale Street a place that had more entertainers than places to entertain. For a couple of years, Sunbeam had sent bands on the road to perform in clubs he owned, but now he added the men in his group to his lineup. They were all in the same kinds of businesses and could be trusted to take care of artists on the road.

Anybody could put acts together and send them out on the road, but who was going to be responsible for them getting paid. Yes, there was trouble at times. So, someone had to guarantee entertainers would show up and give a good show. Without someone taking responsibility, while making sure everyone understood the cost of not holding up their end of the deal, things fall apart. For a businessman like Sunbeam Mitchell, the South was filled with roads; one could not just **"Ease on Down,"** and you definitely **"carried a load,"** looking out for the black community.

Another major reason the *"Chitlin' Circuit"* worked was the Mitchell Hotel. It was known in the trade back then that, *"If you had a decent act and a reputation of putting on a good show, playing in what were called 'a bucket of blood,'"* Sunbeam was the man to see. On any given night, in such places, there may be a knife fight, shoot out, or women fighting over a man that *"just got paid,"* like *"Little Richard"* said in *"Rip it Up."* For most patrons, this was all part of the entertainment, so the show had to go on, and the band had to keep playing. The rumor is Sunbeam had to shoot his way out of a few such spots. It seems he and those owners had words over door receipts. Although people talked about the dangers of the *"Chitlin' Circuit,"* during the early days, Sunbeam always said, *"It was just business."*

Entertainers knew Sunbeam and Ernestine would give them a meal and a bed at their hotel if they made it to Memphis. So, hard-luck, down on their luck, and those having a hard time finding work or hoping to break into show business headed for Memphis. Sunbeam gave many hard-luck acts, time to get it together. With the Mitchell Hotel and Club Handy, Sunbeam's spot grew into a sort of rescue mission for acts on the road looking for work and would work for food.

Beale Street was also the crossroads for entertainers moving either North to South or East to West. No matter, either way, Sunbeam's spot became the stopover for black entertainers in Jim Crow land. Sunbeam's joint was the only good place, between St. Lois and New Orleans, where entertainers could rest up if they were working or lay up until they got work.

Traveling in America was very dangerous in certain places during the time of Jim Crow for black people. Victor Hugo Green (11/9/1892 –10/16/1960) was an African American postal employee from Harlem, New York City. He is known best for developing, writing, and first publishing *The Negro Motorist Green Book*, then it became *The Negro Travelers' Green Book*. *The Green Book* was a travel guide for African Americans in the United States.

During the time of Jim Crow laws and racial segregation, choices for black travelers finding lodging, restaurants, and even gas stations were very limited in many areas, both in the South and North. The Green book reviewed and recommended hotels and restaurants that did business with African Americans, even where to go if you had car trouble. It also had places where black people could find a telephone. It was great helped for black travelers, avoiding business establishment, towns, highways, and roads where police and white people were known to mistreat blacks. Sunbeam's Mitchell Hotel was listed in the 15,000 copies of The Green Book printed each year.

As I stated earlier, segregation was designed to crowd black folks into particular areas of towns to limit opportunities and keep them in poverty, which created *"Bronzevilles."* These mini-metropolises were big business opportunities for the stout of heart. And, if Beale Street was a *"Bronzeville,"* Andrew "Sunbeam" Mitchell was its Mayor. The center of Sunbeam's universe was Abe Plough's corner building at Beale and Hernando. Sunbeam also owned *The Grill* on S. Third Street, *Club Ebony*, and the *Hippodrome* on Beale, but the flagship of his armada was the Mitchell Hotel.

Sitting atop Pantaze Drug Store, directing his nightclubs, eateries, numbers racket, and whiskey-running businesses, Sunbeam was the "Man" in Memphis. Ensconced on the pentacle of business on Beale Street, during the late 1940s into the early 1960s, Sunbeam played both sides of the line between the law and lawbreakers. *Lattimore*, a longtime R&B man said, and many agreed, *"Sunbeam was a saint because he would give you room and board if you had a halfway decent story and had a halfway decent voice. Sunbeam loved music and cared about the people who made it."* Sunbeam was recognized, as a power broker, and the man to see, by both black and white folks, when they needed something done. True, he came to town on the run and was no Robert Church, but before he finished, he became the man on Beale Street, if you had trouble or looking for fun.

Even though a colorful character, flamboyant and bigger than life, Sunbeam was a *Tin Man* with a heart, which played a very important part. Holding court above Pantaze Drug Store amidst prominent Beale Street figures, like promoter Robert Henry, photo-documentarian Ernest Withers, bandleader Jimmie Lunceford, horn man/producer Willie "Papa" Mitchell, radio personalities Nat D. Williams, Rufus "the Dog" Thomas, A. C. "Moohah" Williams and many others, Sunbeam's band of tricksters, made real magic in the *Emerald City* on Beale Street. With the *"Chitlin Circuit,"* blowing up the countryside, Sunbeam extended Beale Street's *"Yellow Brick Road,"* throughout the South and into the North. Once he gave entertainers a magical ride on it, they thought the bricks on the road were yellow, because Sunbeam paved it with gold.

Legendary all-night jam sessions and "head-cutting" contests, between some of the best musicians in the land, drew patrons from all over the Mid-South to witness their virtuosity. On any given night, patrons at Sunbeam's clubs might see Ike and Tina Turner, Muddy Waters, Howlin' Wolf, Fred Ford, Stan Kenton, John Lee Hooker, Lou Rawls, Ruth Brown, Little Richard, Denise LaSalle, James Brown, Joe Simon, LaVern Baker, Little Milton, Count Basie, Albert King, Percy Sledge, Bobby Rush and Tyrone Davis. Several artists starts at his clubs, including Bobby 'Blue' Bland, B.B. King, Little Junior Parker and Johnny Ace to name a few (*The Chitlin' Circuit: And the Road to Rock 'N' Roll;* Preston Lauterbach, 2011, New York: W. W. Norton).

Pride Comes Before a Fall

Proverbs 16: 18 actually say *Pride goeth before destruction and a haughty spirit before a fall*. Similar to most lessons from the Bible, their understanding slowly unfolds in the text. "Boss" Crump's legacy followed a similar course. Memphis was one of the largest southern cities in which blacks could vote, but segregation was as rigid as any place. Crump had allowed Robert Church, Jr. a freehand on Beale Street, because of black voters, until he was sure he could drive him from power. Crump, like a fox in the woodpile, played a waiting game, until he believed Democrats were in control of Tennessee politics.

A trickster par excellent, Crump did a very cozy dance with Republicans, especially blacks, in West Tennessee. It is true Crump was a "red neck" politician, like most whites in the South, but he was a power broker first. As such, he danced with anyone who stepped the right way to give him an advantage, whether he like the music or not.

Illustrating the deviousness of the *"wicked witch of the South,"* Crump had more than one *Evillene* as witch apprentices and many minions spreading his evil magic, while he tried to play a *"good witch"* before the public. Longtime Crump apprentices Beulah Georgia Tann, illustrates the role of his many apprentices. Tann, a notorious black-market trafficker in babies, operated the *Tennessee Children's Home Society*. The movie *Stolen Babies* (1993), starring Mary Tyler Moore, chronicles one episode of Tann's criminal activities and reveals how her illegal adoption agency in Memphis, enjoyed Crump's powerful protection for thirty years (1920-1950).

Tann's unlicensed home was a front for her black-market baby adoption racket. The state began investigating her closed institution, based on numerous complaints of adoption fraud. Tann died before reports showed she stole hundreds of babies and illegally placed them in adoptive homes. However, there is no public record of the actual number of stolen babies; the count could reach into the thousands.

Tann is one of many examples of why Crump was called "Boss." Essentially, he was Memphis mayor from 1910 to 1950, even though he only served three two-year terms (1910-1915). Republicans in East Tennessee were angered, during the 1930s, when Crump, with Franklin D. Roosevelt's *New Deal* support, extended his influence to the state capitol in Nashville. His rise to political prominence disturbed many in Nashville. They felt Crump was out of his league, exercising power in Nashville.

Setting a gin, Republicans used an "Ouster Law," pushed through the legislature to ensnare Crump. Political leaders in Nashville felt their power threaten, by the power Crump wield. The "Boss" used blacks to counter Republicans, particularly in West Tennessee. He skillfully manipulated Republicans, which were weak in the western two-thirds of the state, but dominated in East

Tennessee. Frequently, West Tennessee Republicans found it necessary to align with Crump to accomplish some goals.

The *"Ouster Law"* removed officials that refused to enforce state blue laws (prohibition), but Crump evaded Republicans for years. Republicans attempts to drive him from power developed slowly. They had removed officials in other localities that refused to enforce "Blue Laws." Crump grew rich and powerful, repeatedly refusing to enforce state laws against gambling, bootlegging, and prostitution.

However, Republicans worked patiently for years, bating their trap. Crump's illegal activities were the base of his power. Lax enforcement of state laws enabled Crump to control politics in the black community. The "Boss" was Shelby County Treasurer from 1917 to 1923. He cover his tracks by controlling taxes revenues.

Being white in America allow Crump to avoid Marcus Garvey's fate. Mr. Garvey built a legitimate business and operated it within the law, but could not *"stop the government from violating his rights, destroying his business, unjustly put him in jail, and then deport him."* Whereas *a white scoundrel, everyone knew was a crook, like Donald Trump, the government could not touch.* When it did, it took a special law to put him out of business. Outrageously, he did not go to jail or lose any of his ill-gotten gains. The government did not confiscate his wealth. *"He suffers no loss,"* unlike Mr. Garvey, the government confiscated every asset linked to his **UNIA** and sold it to whites for penny on the dollar.

After working behind the scenes for many years to run Church out of town, in the early 1940s, Crump's fortunes waned. His machine struggled during the elections of 1944. Approaching the 1948 presidential election, Crump developed a new strategy to pull even more black voters away from Republicans. Crump, in desperation, hatched a scheme that left even shocked Republicans, stretching their heads.

Pres. Harry S. Truman was facing a very formidable challenger, in Thomas E. Dewey, Governor of New York. Dewey had the Democrats in deep trouble heading for the 1948 election presidential election. Truman became President in 1945 with the death of Franklin D. Roosevelt and had never stood for national office. Crump's machine had lured many blacks away from the Republicans, but was watching them go back the other way in 1948. Dewey and police brutality against blacks in Memphis put Crump's back against the wall, again like Trump in 2020.

Police brutality was a very serious problem for black people. Several blacks died in police custody, and a black man died when pushed from a moving police car. Blacks were up in arms and out in the street holding demonstrations over the problems. Also, the community was outraged because while answering a domestic disturbance, police killed a black WWII hero. "Boss" Crump resisted recognizing independent political actions by black people, but to quiet the political storm he relented headed into the presidential election. The "Boss" did the unthinkable to placate the black community.

Crump named eight black men to the Memphis police department. With that gambit, a dead silence fell across the white community, while cheers went up from black Democrats and Republicans. It was one of the "Boss'" classic "sleight of hand" moves. Although soundly cheered by blacks, it changed nothing. The fairness or justice in how "Boss" Crump dealt with the problem of police brutality was not debated in either community. Besides, what could they do?

White folks hated the idea of deputizing "niggers" and giving them guns. Even though it did not sit well with most white folks, neither did "niggers" out in the streets protesting, as they had for months. The consensus seemed to be; if they kept other "niggers" in line and not bother white folks, they would live with the change.

On the other hand, it points out how a situation can appear totally and completely different in the eyes of whites and blacks, even though they are viewing the same incident. Black men in police uniforms amounted to progress to most blacks. For them, integration had finally come to Memphis. It became the first city in the South to have Negros among its uniform police. The only change was the job of brutalizing blacks went from whites to blacks. Yet and still blacks believed things had gotten better. The black community looked upon the whole thing with pride and as progress, but ironically, black police patrolled only on Beale Street and did not drive cars.

Pictures of the eight black officers were bought by blacks, like pictures of lynchings by whites. My mother bought one and hung it in the living room, on the wall opposite the picture of Jesus Christ. And, this was the pattern across the black community, which should tell readers how black people saw the event's importance.

Although Truman won the election by the smallest of margins, the "Boss'" fortunes did not improve. East Tennessee Republicans went after him with a vengeance. The fact that Democrats won big elections in Tennessee, from the governor's house in Nashville, down to the Mayor's office in Memphis, did not help the "Boss."

They were not the "Boss'" Democrats. The "Boss'" situation resembled Church at his end except, he didn't have to leave town. Driven from power, the scoundrel Crump passed from the scene in 1954.

An Unintended Consequence of Change

One unintended consequence of slavery was the auditory utterances of slaves and their unique vocalizations, though filled with pain, they took on harmonic resonance, magically affecting slaves' persona. As those guttural moans, groans, and wails flowed out of them, their **Blues** anesthetize their agony, giving mental relief to slave descendants' desperate existence in the Mississippi Delta. Black people's history and their day-to-day struggles contending with tremendous challenges surviving, segregation and white supremacy was unabated, as its effects were unnoticed by popular historians.

As a result, the world misses the amazing balancing act descendants of American slavery performed daily, with their lives teetered on the brink of disaster. *Divine Intervention* on many levels, delivered black people from the scourge of segregation and the clutches of white supremacy, as they reached the mid-1940s. Rescued many times, while adrift in the sea of humanity, washed about by what seemed a dastardly flood of insufferable events, unintended consequences like a lifeline, extricated blacks from their desperate fortunes. Repeatedly retrieving their failing hopes by thrusting individuals into roles, both desired and undesired, and only by grace were they delivered.

Photographs of the first eight black policemen hung on thousands of living room walls for years in Memphis. The photograph my mother hung in the living room had turned yellow when she took it down. The faces of the men in that picture, whether they realized it or not, gave them a public persona. Although Crump was gone, the unintended consequences of his shenanigan create a world that those men in the police photograph probably had not considered the day it was taken.

Then again, Marcus Garvey and the **UNIA** had instilled many desires in the heads of black people. The desire that had the greatest impact on black people was to own a business. Mr. Garvey inspired millions of blacks all over America to chase their dream to be entrepreneurs. Many held tightly to the hope of making their nothing into something through becoming businessmen. One of those faces in the photograph of the first eight black policemen, Ernest C. Withers (8-7-1922/8-15- 2007) is my case in point.

Returning to Memphis, after serving in WWII, Ernest harbored Mr. Garvey's dream and was one of those wannabe black businessmen. While in the army, he received training as a photographer and fell in love with what he saw through the lens of a camera. Mr. Withers told me, *"I took the job not because I wanted to be a cop, but I hoped it would do what it did, helped me open my shop."* After a few years, as a policeman, Ernast's ambition to become an entrepreneur, superceeded his other survival concerns. Supported by his wife Dorothy and their children, Ernest opened his family business.

The 400th: From Slavery to Hip Hop

The most significant aspect here is that unintended consequences made him one of the first eight black men on the Memphis Police Department. Ernest was in the picture, only because another black man was left out. A replacement for the original selection, another veteran that was unavailable for the photo-opt "Boss" Crump desired, put him out the picture, as well as history, and Ernest Withers in. Mr. Withers reflects how one unintended consequence of "Boss" Crump's action benefitted slave descendants in ways no one imagined at the time, especially "Boss" Crump.

The unintended consequence part of this picture is incidental regarding Crump and had nothing to do with Beale Street per se. It reflects how *VOICE* for black people is exemplary of the reality that sometimes *"a picture is worth more than a thousand words."* Such results most black people call magic because they seem to come out of nowhere just when there seems there is nothing one can do to alter the situation. The unintended part of Mr. Withers amazing role in the lives of countless poor black people are the crucial stories that would have gone unnoticed and untold, if men and women like Mr. Withers had not found ways to *make something out of nothing*, giving *VOICE* to descendants of American slavery, while telling stories from their lives.

Again, the nothing aspect of Mr. Withers' work is his subjects; people society cared nothing about—black people. The impact of one lone rider, like Mr. Withers, not only in preserving slave descendants' stories, but his pictures made a thousand words unnecessary, telling the tragic story and preserving the history of thousands of voiceless black Americans. Without the insight and candid view of black life, seen through the lens of his camera, so much of the story we know today of black people in the Mississippi River Delta, would not exist, had he not recorded them.

Dr. Withers told the story of ordinary people alongside that of notables. Baby pictures, weddings, graduations, anniversaries, sports events, parties, parades, entertainers, protest marches, politicians, demonstrations, Civil rights, black power leaders and funerals were all his staples. The thing that made his eye so special, he always looked for those pictures and stories that no one cared about at the time, except him.

One classic example of his impact and his pictures came as a result of being the only photographer on the scene to document the heart-wrenching story of sharecroppers in West Tennessee (1959-64). He not only informed people in the mid-South but the rest of America of *"Tent City"* in Fayette County, Tennessee. Dr. Withers' caught on film the devastating evictions of more than 400 families, as the demise of sharecropping produced *"Tent Cities"* across the South. These evictions told stories most people were unaware. However, an Ernest Withers picture showed the misfortune blacks families suffered. White landowners in Fayette County and many other counties in Tennessee pushed thousands of black families off farms, after they tried to register to vote in 1959.

Mr. Withers tracked down stories about black people in backwoods and other isolated bachwashes that people in Memphis only heard about, but an Ernest Withers' photograph told their stories. Along at night, he ventured into strongholds of segregation to verify reports about sharecroppers and civil rights workers that were victims of harassment or disappeared without a trace. These were stories that would not have been known, beyond the victims and families in many cases. The gruesomeness and brutality of their deaths, many times, would have slipped into anonymity, like Emmett Till, if not for the fact Mr. Withers' lens captured the hard evidence of a tragedy.

For so many families and the world, his pictures made a thousand words superfluous. However, I believe the thing most people miss when viewing Dr. Withers' work, is the personal danger he faced, getting many of the images he preserved. Many stories occurred in the "dirty South," that appeared in the *Chicago Defender, Pittsburg Currier, Tri-State Defender, New York Amsterdam News*, and other black newspapers, would have gone unnoticed, as well as undocumented were it not for Dr. Withers' camera. Deaths and other atrocious racist acts, like cross burning, murders, police brutality and protest he captured would have fallen through the cracks of history into obscurity, except the lens of Dr. Withers camera was there to catch and rescuing them for posterity.

Dr. Withers, for over 60 years, captured the cavalcade of history in iconic images, as well as dreaded results on African Americans in the segregated South, like the Montgomery Bus Boycott, Sanitation Workers Strike, the Invaders, Memphis music, Negro league baseball, not to mention murders like Emmett Till, Medgar Evers and Dr. Martin Luther King, Jr. Dr. Withers' dedication and devotion preserved the desperate times and ever-changing deadly world of African Americans, mostly in the South. He produced over 1.8 million images froze in time by his camera's lens. Dr. Withers was part of documenting descendants of American slavery's amazing trek reaching **"The 400th"**. The "Invaders" the documentary, are extremely indebted to The Withers Collection Museum and Gallery for providing many stills of the Invaders efforts from 1967, 1968 sanitation strike and the desperate times of the 1970s..

The Library of Congress is presently archiving Dr. Ernest C. Withers' work. Also, the Smithsonian Institution's National Museum of African American History and Culture in Washington, D.C. plans a permanent collection supplied by The Withers Collection Museum and Gallery located at 333 Beale Street in Memphis. Rosalind Wither is Director/Conservator. A visit will provide a view of history in its most pristine and authentic preservation.

Knowledge was His Stock and Trade

The arrival of "Sunbeam" Mitchell, after losing W.C. Handy and Robert Church, Jr. was like the finale of **The Wiz**. Trapped by the *"wicked witch, Evillene,"* it seemed the desperate band of misfits had come to their end. But, just in the nick of time, our heroes realized that world was a toilet, and all they needed do was flush *Evillene* to end "Boss" Crump's wicked reign and their revolution would be complete. *"Everybody Rejoice"* (Can't You See A Brand New Day).

The munchkins on Beale Street's joyous reaction to "Boss" Crump's loss of power, truly was a brand new day. Coming alive, they shaded the covering from that old world, and revealed the new time that was dawning. Beale Street began to live again. His departure foreshadowed the coming of a new wizard that stepped forth, like a troubadour to sing the praises of self-love for black people and Beale Street.

Some people, because of their presence, knowledge, and generosity, graced humanity with their touch; they change not only people they meet but some who are unaware they lived. Some of those who are touched by them are unaware; such a dynamic individual has influenced their lives. Nathanial Dowd Gaston Williams (10-19-1907/10-27-1983) was just such a person. He was affectionately known as "Nat D" by those who loved and cherished life and memory.

Knowledge was his stock and trade. Rather short in stature, but a giant in the hearts and minds of many he touched. Nat D's bespectacled eyes and penetrating gaze unmasked the disguise of ignorance that clouded the minds of young and old in Memphis and beyond. A demure and retiring persona belied the skills of an adroit wizard, which left old-timers that once haunted Beale Street, still benefitting from and marveling at his wisdom.

Nat D was among the thousands of slave descendants educated at the Freedmen Bureau Clay and Kortrecht Grammar schools and Booker T. Washington High Schools. He gained the magic of knowledge, pursuing education as a lifelong endeavor. Most who knew him would say, Nat was generous to a fault, but like a wizard, with a bag of tricks, he shared his lore with anyone who would listen. With humility and grace, he advanced the dreams of others, exemplary of the *"good witch of the West."*

Born on Beale Street and nurtured as one of its children, Beale Streeters watched him develop into its most vociferous exponent and enthusiastic historian emeritus. He earned degrees in history from Columbia and Northwestern Universities and increased his extensive knowledge as a reporter for and editor of the *New York State Contender.*

Returning to Memphis in the late 1920s, he became a reporter for the *Memphis World* and *Tri-State Defender.* A student and graduate of Freedmen Bureau schools, Nat D jumped at the opportunity to teach the children from the poorest communities in Memphis, at his alma mater Booker T. Washington High School. Even though black history teachers were not allowed to teach the truth of

American slavery before the 1970s, Nat D emerged his students in their slave heritage, during 42 years at Booker T.

The most successful historians in Memphis for more than 40 years, all black students, can trace their knowledge of history back to Nat D or one of his students. Nat D edited BTW's student newspaper and taught them about the newspaper business. A Sunday school teacher and a member of his church's choir, Nat also led a Boy Scout troop. He was involved in the creation of and coordinator for the annual *Cotton Makers Jubilee*, a big deal in black segregated Memphis. Nat D also emceed amateur night at the Palace Theater on Beale Street (Memphis' answer to the Apollo Theater in Harlem). With all that going, he managed to trained icons like Rufus Thomas (one of his students) as stand-in for amateur night. Amazingly, while riding that wild whirlwind and balancing his many activities, Nat still had time to be a devoted and loving husband and father to two girls.

Segregation rigidly controlled almost every aspect of black people's lives outside of their homes, shackling them to poverty into the 1950s. White supremacy limited black people's progress and kill their dreams. That system created unmet aspirations and arrested the development of millions of blacks in America with economic restrictions, like *"Wicked Witch, Evillene,"* casting diabolical incantations.

Segregation's major limitation on black people was their access to open communications with the general public—*VOICE*. Miraculously, unintended consequences and the magic of Beale Street played tricks unmasking these disadvantages as imposters. Open communication created opportunities for black communities in Memphis and eventually throughout the Mississippi Delta and America. The change that happened next did not blow into Memphis in a whirlwind, but it made Nat D the *"wizard of Emerald City"* just the same.

Beale Streeters tell Nat's story, as though it was truly a magical fairy tale. They have Nat D behind the curtain engineering *Emerald City's* enchanting and bewitching return to the cultural center for black people in Memphis and throughout the Mid-South. A new day dawned according to old-time Beale Streeters, once Nat D began casting spells. They revealed what they swore were events they witnessed. Most Nat D. stories of his emergence as the *"wizard of Emerald City"* begin or open something like this.

"There were these two hard-luck white boys, whose backs were against the wall. John Pepper and Burt Ferguson were owners of a radio station about to go bankrupt. With its finances going up in smoke, they heard about the wizard of Beale Street and came looking for Nat D. They wondered if he had a trick or two up his sleeves that could pull a radio station owned by some broke and desperate white boys "fat out of the fire?"

The 400th: From Slavery to Hip Hop

At this point, stories about Nat D's wizardry diverge. So, what follows is a synopsis of Nat's magic act for a bankrupt radio station and a community in dire need of *VOICE*. John Pepper and Burt Ferguson had banked on pop/country and western music, as a spellbinder for white folks in Memphis. Blasting white Memphians with their country format made their ears pucker from the sour notes. Pepper and Ferguson needed a potion, which would make their music sound, as sweet as a cash register's jingle in white people ears. They needed a real necromancer's magic to get their *"fat out of the fire"* and back into the frying pan before their whole enterprise burn down around them. Similar to "Boss" Crump, when he put eight black men on Memphis' police force just a few months earlier in 1948, Pepper and Ferguson had to come up with some real magic.

Neither Pepper nor Ferguson believed in sorcery. However, they had tried their hot idea of sprinkled *"goofer dust"* around their station, but the result had their station about to go dead silent. Their radio station had continued blasting "B" flats when they needed crescendos of legatos to break the evil spell country and western music cast on their bank accounts. Banking on country and western, as their magical whirlwind ride to financial success, instead had their station about to blow away in a puff of smoke.

Desperate, while preparing to close their business down, Pepper and Ferguson came to Beale Street, hoping Nat D's magic bag had a trick that provided two broke and desperate white boys one last change. They hoped the *wizard* of Beale Street could make *"something out of nothing"* for them. So, as "Boss" Crump, they did the unthinkable in Memphis in late 1948. Ferguson defied segregation and hired Nat D. Williams, as the first black on-air radio personality across the South, possibly in the USA. Nat D began casting his **BLACK magic** spell over the Mid-South on October 25, 1948.

Nat D tried one more trick with strange things happening. He convinced Peeper and Ferguson to change their call letters to **WDIA**, so black people knew where to find him. The word went out, across the Mid-South, as a new day dawned, that Nat D had magically put **Blues** on radio at 1070 on the dial. No fairy tale wizard, Nat did not hide behind a curtain, using gimmickry to make things happen. A magic man like Marcus Garvey, Nat took center stage in a full-throated celebration of the **Blues**. Debuting the **Tan-Town Jamboree** at 3:00 p.m., Nat D began spreading his enchanting web over the Mississippi Delta, like a magician's cape.

Signing on that first day, with W. C. Handy's classic horn blasting its lonesome wail, Nat D and **Memphis Blues** woke up the dead. Beale Streeters still asleep; after Handy's first blast, Nat let out his iconic laugh, shocking them awake. It boomed out across the black South, as a new era dawned for black people in the Mississippi Delta. It was the beginning of radio becoming a big deal for descendants of American slaves!!!

"Ha Ha Ha Haaaaaaaaaaaaaaaaa!!!!!!!!!!!!!!! Well, yes-siree, it's Nat D on the Jamboree, coming at thee on seventy-three (on the dial), WDIA. Now, what-chu-bet."

Nat D opened with his full-bellied iconic laugh and followed with another huge classic roar, and then, 60 minutes of the best R&B on the planet poured out of radios like a cornucopia. Nat D did more than spin records; as I said earlier, he was a history professor par excellent. So, between Ruth Brown, LaVern Baker, the Five Royals, Sarah Vaughan, Dinah Washington, Nat King Cole, the Moon Glows, Ray Charles, "Big" Joe Turner, Sam Cook, TNT Braggs and Ike and Tina Turner as well as many others, Nat dropped bits of knowledge on his fateful.

Pepper and Ferguson were unaware of the untapped potential—underserved talent and advertising dollar power—in the black community. Once cash registers started playing music, white folks loved; they thought those two white boys were the wizards, rather than Nat D. **WDIA** skyrocketed in popularity. That year, only partially using the power of blackness in its programming, **WDIA** went to number two in the Memphis market. Nat D's wizardry started publicity-starved entertainers and desperate promoters lining up to be apprentices.

Outrage is a mild description of the response among the *wicked witches in Memphis*. They held *pow-wows* trying to hex **WDIA**. "Boss" Crump, like other wicked witches, could only send out his minions to threaten, while gritting his teeth. Weakened by his fight with the State of Tennessee, the "Boss" could only howl at the moon, hoping to drown out Nat D's iconic laugher. Bomb threats and a cross burning at **WDIA** only gave more power to Nat D's great wizardry. Bringing in more apprentices, some of which were women, Nat stacked the deck at **DIA** with a montage of thaumaturgic party people that had Memphis boogieing with a new beat. Even the first black policemen became part of Nat's magic act. They volunteered to serve as his bodyguards until he made the trouble vanish.

Nat D stacked America's first black radio station with sorcerer's apprentices, and they pumped black music all day, with an all African-American on-air staff. **WDIA** became Memphis' top radio station and the first to gross a million dollars in a single year. Nat's wizardry boosted **WDIA's** signal's power from 250 to 50,000 watts. Even white people saw that as magic, for such a nothing radio station. The **Blues,** screaming over the airwaves, from the boot heel of Missouri to the Mississippi Gulf Coast, put **WDIA** among the top radio stations in the nation at the time.

WDIA became the model for black radio stations that would come online over the next ten years nationwide. Other radio station owners across the nation came to the *Emerald City*, like sorcerer's apprentices wanting to study at the feet of the master. They were awed by what seemed like supernatural power over the natural forces in a segregated universe. Nat D's bewitching power over **WDIA** reached Atlanta, which bought into the magic and started its first black-owned radio station **WERD** one year later (10-1949).

Nat D. Williams was not a one-man show. He brought to radio a cast of character, that while apprentices, had developed their own brand of mysticism. First, he brought in Rufus Thomas, as a backup MC for amateur night at the Palace Theater, before moving him to radio. Blowing up the airwaves, Rufus made listeners feel like they were on Beale Street, jamming with him in a club.

Nat D's band of wizards brought live talent such as **B.B. King** to perform on air. Through his close association with Sunbeam Mitchell, the *Tin Man with a heart*, who had a connection with Abe Plough, Nat got B. B. a 15-minute spot. B. B., "Blue Boy," took a page from W.C. Handy's jingle book, he wrote and sang a promotional ditty advertising a cure-all elixir Pep-t-Con—*"Pep-t-Con show is good, (repeat several times) you can get it anywhere in your neighborhood!"* followed by several cords on *Lucille*. The promotion went over so well; black people did not only sing along; they bought Pep-t-Con, like soft drinks. Although they seemed like "snake oil" salesmen, B.B. recorded his first single at WDIA, during off-hours, *"You Upset Me, Baby."* It reached number one on Billboard's ***"Black Singles"*** chart as the highest charted ***Blues*** single.

B.B.'s gave other hard-luck bluesmen the idea they could *"make something out of nothing,"* at *WDIA*. B.B. brought his friends, **Little Milton, Little Junior Parker, Rosco Gordon, Bobby "Blue" Bland** and **Johnny Ace** to the station, as live guesses. Those sessions at **WDIA**, for some, became their first recordings, like B.B. **WDIA** was the first real exposure for gospel groups like the **Spirit of Memphis,** the **Southern Wonders, Mighty Clouds of Joy, Rev. "Gatemouth" Moore, Clara Ward Singers, Dixie Humming Birds, Brother Cleophas Robinson, Sister Rosetta Tharpe** and many many more. Gospel filled up WDIA's Sunday spiritual programming all-day.

Nat D brought A. C. "Moohah" Williams, a biology teacher at Manassas High School, who moonlighted as a blues singer, to the station as a disc-jockey. Nat continued staffing WDIA with his apprentices. Early evening Rev. Dwight "Gatemouth" Moore, Theo "Bless My Bones" Wade, Willa Monroe, and Ford Nelson became familiar voices throughout the gospel community over the Mid-South. *"The Queen,"* Martha Jean Steinberg added her smooth, sensuous voice on the *"Swing Shift,"* bringing in the guys for early night listening. Then Maurice *"Hot Rod"* Hulbert woke them up, got them on their feet and out in the streets with his beat. Robert *"Honeyboy"* Thomas cooled them down and closed things out aboard the *"Night Train."*

Working with artists that came to **WDIA** to record segments, program directors David Mattis started his recording studio—***Duke records.*** Duke Records started in Memphis in 1952 by David J. Mattis and Bill Fitzgerald, owner of

Tri-State Recording Company. Their first release was Roscoe Gordon, *"Hey Fat Girl."* Later, Mattis sold Duke to *Chitlin Circuit"* pioneer, Don Robey out of Houston, Texas.

"Moohah": A New Kind of Magus

Nat's wizardry became evident as a new day dawning. He held back the waters of segregation that washed over black people, flooding their world with scarcity and desperation. Casting lifelines to would-be apprentices drowning in a community awash in entertainers, Nat opened the floodgates at WDIA. "Moohah" followed the legend, Nat D., in more ways than one. Andrew Charles "Moohah" Williams, Jr. (no relation) became a trailblazer and left an enduring legacy, which coincided with **WDIA** and a group of Memphis teenagers he took under his wings. "Moohah" was a confidant of Nat D, but lacked confidence before coming to radio. Nat brought "Moohah" on board the **DIA** team to help shape the careers of others, which made him vital to **WDIA's** trajectory toward greatness. "Moohah" spread his wings, like a giant eagle and soared once he found his confidence.

However, getting started, "Moohah" resembled the *"cowardly lion."* Although he possessed tremendous talent and abilities, he felt his ideas would get shot down, so "Moohah" flew low out of sight, close to the ground. Convinced by Nat D, he needed help at **WDIA** developing community programming, especially for young people, "Moohah's" courage came slowly. Although "Moohah" was reluctant, Nat D pushed him to pitch his idea for a Saturday morning program that showcased the talents of African American high school students through a singing group. Bert Ferguson, co-owner, and station manager at **WDIA,** bought the idea. Ferguson spotted "Moohah" a live thirty minutes show on Saturday morning called the ***"Teen Town Singers."***

The high school singing group was truly magic for teens, who thought they had real talent but had no way to develop their gifts. Nat D's desired to provide opportunities for young people beyond singing in church choirs, high school Glee Clubs, and trying to get on stage at the Palace Amateur Night, or simply do-woopping on street corners, became a hit and was truly needed, especially for teens from poor family. Even more important than those outlets, the *Teen Town Singers* offered young aspirants a way to develop their talent and confidence singing but their other abilities, which many never imagined they possessed. *"Moohah,"* like Nat D, *"saw more in young people than what was on the surface. I believe he saw young people like seeds, which one never knows what they have until they put them into fertile soil, water them and allow for growth,* according to Mark Stansbury.

One such seed, Stansbury, who was on staff at WDIA for 57 years, began as a *Teen Town Singer.* He went on to become an assistant to the president at the University of Memphis. Stansbury said, *"I couldn't sing, but Mr. Williams saw something else in me, I didn't know was there. He saw other qualities in his young people beyond vocal talent, even the ones, like me, who didn't have a voice, he welcomed in the group."* Stansbury credits Williams and other WDIA luminaries—such as Nat. D. and Theo

"Bless My Bones" Wade—with helping to create a pathway for him and many other young blacks in radio. *"I thought Mr. Williams (Moohah) always showed lots of courage. But it was just that; his ideas were so far ahead of what other people were thinking at the time, they would get rejected because they were so new. People needed time to catch up to where he was. That was the way it was with the Goodwill Review. It got rejected, but Nat D and the rest of us kept after him; once accepted, it was a tremendous success."*

During his tenure, *Moohah* developed and promoted other community programs as well, including *"Feature for A Wonderful Teacher," "Soul of School Award," "Top Scholar Program," "Saturday Night Fish Fry," "Delta Melodies"* and *"Wheelin' on Beale."* The first show of its kind, Williams found ways to increase the success of **WDIA's** *"Goodwill Revue."* He pitched it as a show during the Christmas season. The catch for **WDIA** was the show's proceeds provided toys for poor children.

WDIA became known as the *"Goodwill"* station after the *"Goodwill Review"* debuted. **WDIA's** *"Goodwill Review"* featured the best gospel, blues, R&B, and soul performers in the nation. Moohah followed with the *"Starlight Revue."* It was an outdoor show at Rustwood Park scheduled around the 4th of July. Moohah's influence made **WDIA** an integral part of the Memphis black community with the *Goodwill* and *Starlight Revues*. He helped develop both as charitable events that raised funds for needy children and little league sports programs, a first in Memphis as well.

The "DOG" Rufus Thomas

After performing on the street, as a kid, Rufus C. Thomas, Jr. became a rhythm-and-blues, funk, soul and blues singer, songwriter, dancer, DJ, and comedic entertainer. Born (3-26-1917/12-15-2001) in Cayce, Mississippi, just south of Memphis, his family made their run as my family to escape sharecropping. Trying to become an entertainer, after learning to tap dance at age 10, Rufus began performing on Beale Streets sidewalks. He performed on talent shoes at Booker T. Washington High School.

Nat D., his high-school history teacher, thought Rufus had the drive to be an entertainer. Nat made him a regular on his weekly talent shows at the Palace Theater on Beale Street. With Nat D the reigning *Wizard of Emerald City* guiding, Rufus became one of his apprentices, while in high school. Much smarter than he looked, Rufus always reminded me of the *"scarecrow."* Most of all, Rufus wasn't afraid of challenges. Very daring, Rufus tried anything that seemed it would advance his chances for success. He was the jester in Nat D's cast of characters that entertained on Beale Street and radio. Similar to many other black youngsters, after performing at the Palace, Rufus left Tennessee State A&I University for life on the road entertaining.

Still, a very young man, Rufus, performed on the traveling tent show circuit. He joined the *Rabbit Foot Minstrels,* in 1936. *Rabbit Foot* was an all-black revue that toured the South (1930-40s). Rufus became a tap-dancing comedian, as part of a duo, Rufus and Johnny, as Minstrelsy ended. Teaming up with Robert "Bones" Couch, they were a traveling tap dance/scat singing act called "Rufus and Bones," that toured Vaudeville.

Returning to Memphis in the mid-1940s, Nat D brought Rufus and Bones on board to MC the Palace Theater amateur hour. The largest venue in Memphis for beginning artists, winners like B. B. King, Bobby "Blue" Bland, Mal Rainey, and Johnny Ace, went on to successful entertainment careers. After playing Minstrelsy and Vaudeville singing, scatting, and dancing, Nat D got Rufus in at **WDIA** and he embraced the opportunities, as Nat D's back up on the *Tan-Town Jamboree.*

Rufus responded to his brand new days, taking to the airwaves, and showed patients pays. Like a fateful apprentice, he moved from radio to STAX Records, trading in his *scarecrow* persona for his trademark *"The Dog,"* then *"Walking the Dog.* Breaking onto the top-ten R&B chart (1963), he dropped *"Do the Funky Chicken"* (1970), *"Do the Push and Pull"* (1970) and *"The Breakdown"* (1971). Touring and performing on Beale Street, well into his 80s, Rufus earned the title of the *"World's Oldest Living Teenager."*

Desperation and Scarcity: Motivation or Curse?

Following emancipation, former slaves began making socioeconomic and political advances, even though desperation and scarcity regimented their progress by keeping them dependent on white people for survival. Desperation and scarcity were more than episodic distractions for black people in Memphis. Poverty exaggerated life's circumstances and these events became themes dominating black Americans existence, without regard to their location in America.

Particularly in Memphis, these two variables—desperation and scarcity—dictated almost every decision regarding survival most black people made. The great hand of desperation, if not scarcity, reached out without regard to race and condition many times with the same force and power to impact whites, but less dramatically. Intervening in local politics, the great hand of fate brought desperation to "Boss" Crump's doorstep. Crump integrated the Memphis Police Department, as unintended consequences forced him to act against his segregationists' policies.

Similarly, owning a business headed for bankruptcy, desperation put two white guys' backs against the wall and pushed them beyond the laws of segregation and customs of white supremacy. Unintended consequences held out one forlorn gamble for these white guys, like fish out of water, whose enterprise teetered on the blink of disaster. Hoping to save their dream, their roll of the dice meant snake eyes if they held tight to tradition, or they could break the bank and benefit millions, who never knew their names or what they did. Such acts during different times and under different circumstances would yield different results, and left the status quo intact.

These acts, taken as isolated incidents, would probably seem small but loomed large from the perspective of black communities all over the South. This time around under these particular circumstances, white and black people, viewing the same situations, from the same perspective and made decisions that impacted black people's survival positively. Consequently, these two white men helped uproot the socioeconomic structure, not only in the Mississippi Delta but across the South and the US.

The desperate efforts of two southern white men hoping to save their business opened a hole in the very thick and high wall of white supremacy and segregation. These two men hired a very dynamic and persuasive black man Nat D. Williams. Nat proceeded to force open the door of opportunities in radio for black people, who at the time, had no idea such hopes existed.

Nat D popped through the hold in a dike that had stood decades; he flooded broadcasting with hundreds of African Americans. A successful Nat D made blacks in radio a winning proposition for African Americans, the black community, and the broadcast industry. Nat D. Williams was a master mason, laying bricks on what became the *yellow brick road of entertainment success* for black Americans. He paved the way for black radio to become a major route to careers in American entertainment for thousands of blacks, who didn't even know his name.

The previous discussion brings together what began as separate threads or trends—Minstrelsy, black music, entrepreneur acumen, the *Chitlin Circuit*, and radio—to advance the development of American entertainment. It became the major route black Americans created getting to ***"The 400th"***. Former slaves' expressions of talent became entry-level skills during Minstrelsy. Slaves and descendants learn to—*do something with their bodies*—dance, sing, play instruments, play sports, clown it up as comedians, and made these endeavors individual entertainment professions.

These endeavors became the most productive enterprises on the glory road of entertainment. Segregation and white supremacy restricted and controlled the success of black entertainers, dictating where, when, what, and how they performed, even though black people created American entertainment. Nevertheless, slave descendants endured it all, *making something out of nothing*, turning their chances into opportunities for themselves and others that followed.

Unintended consequences forced change upon white people, which opened doors Robert Church, Sr. and Jr., W. C. Handy, Sunbeam Mitchell, Nat D. Williams, and many others in Memphis and across America walked through to find opportunities and create success. These swashbuckling, devil-may-care, lone riders saw opportunities and made the sacrifices necessary to change the course of human events, while developing and changing the business of American entertainment.

Reaching the 1950s, fighting segregation, white supremacy, discrimination, and disparate treatment in their efforts to succeed in American entertainment, former slaves' mindsets toward their conditions changed. Their understanding of the power of social changes evolved, bringing even greater knowledge of how to use their bodies through entertainment to create even more changes in entertainment. African Americans used their demand for socio-economic and political change to expose the US as a hypocrite. Descendants of slavery standing on the precipice of this new horizon are reminiscent of the finale of ***"The Wiz," Everybody Rejoice" (Can't You See A Brand New Day)***, with black power waiting in the wings.

Communist Party - USA

Former slaves learned to live on their own, after leaving plantations all over the South in 1862. Emancipation launched slaves on a very dynamic journey. Surviving Civil War began efforts to drive them back onto plantations. Then slavery supporters re-enslaved blacks in the South with convict leasing and sharecropping for over eighty years. Former slaves faced mob rule, lynch law and unfair courts, along with the **"Dark Age" angry white men mob madness** *era*, which victimized and terrorized them. Black people had to bide their time, endure to survive, as they made families, and built communities. They suffered through their second-class status in America. Most importantly, they kept their heads down, sending up prayed, hoping for better days.

African Americans reached a less deadly time in the 1940s following 60 years of white men pillaging and burning whole black communities. African Americans suffered through pogroms and massacres—ethnic cleansing, banishment, and terror attacks—on their communities in places like *Black Wall Street* Greenwood, Tulsa OK, Forsythe County, Georgia, Ocoee, and Rosewood, Florida and other places, but they continued holding on, enduring to survive. The goal of white people in general and governments specifically was to intimidate former slaves, and force them to accept second class citizenship, as their rightful lot in American.

Such deadly time began to recede after reaching 1950. This narrative now begins a look back at why and how Black Arts and politics developed hand-in-hand for black entertainment and entrepreneurship, and other black Americans. Understanding the critical beginnings of Black Arts, requires another hard u-turn, which takes this retrospective on a convoluted ride with back and forth, as it has covering the past 600 years.

Again, I begin and lean on *Divine Intervention* as the impetus for black Americans getting help from a group that was hated almost as much as black people. The Communist Party-USA (CP-USA) before you slam this book and close your mind at the mention of that word—communist—at least stay with me long enough for the introduction of the subject, while keeping an open mind. If you do you will learn, as I did, CP-USA's role providing guidance, instructions, and financial assistance without which African Americans would not have made it to 1950 with a clear vision of their future.

This narrative now explores one of the major contributors to slavery's descendants' efforts to develop an artistic and cultural perspective. It traces the CP-USA's story, which provides a look at its essential role helping to develop Black Arts. CP-USA also played a key role in black Americans developed the political mindset, especially social justice, grassroots and street protest organizing, which went hand and glove with art becoming the leading expression of their efforts to be recognized as human beings. Art produced a face to face confrontation with the political forces that dominated America's government. This struggle began just after the **Red Summer of 1919** in 1920s and it made the 1950s a battle ground and the gateway to *"The 400th"*.

Growing up in Memphis, white people denigrated the CP-USA as the dreaded enemy of all freedom-loving people, especially African Americans. "Boss" Crump's view and it was like a law, which I and other blacks in Memphis obeyed religiously, as a means of gaining white people's acceptance. Before undertaking this research, I had no real idea about the relationship of the Communist Party-USA to African Americans' efforts to develop an artistic foundation. I didn't have an understanding of CP-USA's crucial connection to black American's struggle against racism, white supremacy, and segregation in America. It was only through research for *"The 400th"* that I learned they joined the fight and stood shoulder to shoulder with black people when no other group dared.

What I thought I knew about the Communist Party-USA but never thought about came as a result of propaganda disseminated by J. Edgar Hoover's FBI. Researching subjects, like lynching and entertainment, I learned a much different story than that communicated by American media. The life and death story of what happened to the CP-USA is not only very different than popular myths, history books, newspapers, novels, and movies portrayed, but it turned out to be very complicated and far more dangerous for black people than history indicates.

My beliefs were no different from most Americans. I saw communists as loudmouthed, sign-carrying, troublemakers out to destroy America, and *"our capitalistic way of life."* Over the past 10 years investigating the beginning of CP-USA, after the turn of the century (1900), I was not interested in the philosophical and ideological underpinnings of communism. I wanted to know the psychological and physical impact it had on the development of black people in general, but Black Arts and politics in particular. Organizing in black communities, CP-USA generally, began helping black people create an organizational approach to their problems in America in Harlem in the 1920s. CP-USA helped develop ideas and principles slave descendants applied to their everyday existence and struggles for liberty.

Black Americans began their most dangerous times in America, following **Plessy v. Ferguson** in 1897, and their struggles intensified after **Red Summer 1919**. No fair courts and the **"Dark Age"** *angry white men mob madness* rolled across America rampaging like an epidemic. Against this plague black people had neither defenders nor refuge. Former slaves faced a society and political system without sanctuary. The US government was determined to force black people to accept second class status on the bottom of American society, as *cheap labor*. After 355 years of the **Trans-Atlantic Slave Trade,** plus 58 years in America's internal slave trade and breeding system, former slaves' penniless emancipation left them uneducated, prisoners in America's *"cheap labor"* economic system and without hope of economic advancement.

During slavery and after emancipation, some newly freed slaves cast their lots with Minstrelsy as the first real opportunity to gain wealth through entertainment. But its stereotypes of blackface, buffoonery, and degradation disgusted most blacks with talent. They felt they would be sacrificing themselves and their talents on the altar of white supremacy to participate in Minstrelsy. So, they looked for something more reflective of Art. They hoped for something that would allow them to *do something with their bodies*, other than clowning it up for money. Black artists may not have arrived at their decision in the manner I outlined here, but their choice made the Communist Party-USA gleam, as a real opportunity in the black community. Approaching black Americans just after **"Red Summer"** *(1919),* CP-USA brought more than rhetoric to the party.

Europeans brought communism to America. They came from cultures that developed during feudalism. Along with other cultural knowledge, the Roman Empire's occupation introduced art to serfs in Europe. Serfs were bound to the land and subject to the will of their feudal lords. Similarly to former slaves, they also understood the desperation and scarcity that resulted from being dominated by overlords.

Their lot in life was no different from slaves, except for skin color, everyone was white, and they were not chattel property. Nevertheless, they came from countries where the rich class developed cultures based on the Arts. Although they were serfs, the Arts in such countries exposed them to writing, printing, sculpture, painting, theater, and so forth. Former slaves had no exposure to the Arts, as a class, not even language.

Europeans, unlike slaves who had to speak a made-up language of broken words that did not give them access to standard knowledge of most things. Again, serfs spoke the same language as their Europeans lords. They understood how knowledge and crafts could help their class gain rights. They were able to organize and protests to gain rights. The writings of Carl Marx and Friedrich Engels allowed them to develop and broaden their sense of culture and its role in society.

There had been a communist presence in America with those early beginnings of Marxism, and CP-USA began organizing in America before the Russian Revolution (1917). Bolsheviks were communist, and after their successful revolution, they created the Communist International (the Comintern). Inviting all socialists to join their International, Bolsheviks raised their red banner atop the palace in Leningrad (formerly St. Petersburg). Rejecting white supremacy and the whole idea of white privilege, the CP-USA brought a new and different approach to the struggle for freedom, justice, and equality for black people.

For the first time, since the abolitionist movement, such thoughts came from the white side of the equation. During its first few years of existence, the

The 400th: From Slavery to Hip Hop

CP-USA functioned clandestinely. Woodrow Wilson and J. Edgar Hoover launched the first *"Red Scare"* in 1917 to drive communist and socialist out of America. The socialist and communism movements went underground. They tried to avoid the surge of anti-radical and anti-immigrant hysteria, investigations, deportations, and raids by the BOI (Bureau of Investigation) at the beginning and during World War I.

Making Communism Mainstream CP-USA Aid of Black People

That introduction was to set a clear pattern of how communism came to America and before any real activity or organizing on a major scale in America. Once CP-USA began working with blacks in Harlem, the federal government began attacking CP-USA, as part of scapegoating black people to justify white supremacy. The federal government began its effort to drive communism out of America once black people became part of their strategy to make communism mainstream. Helping former enslaved Africans interfered with America's *"cheap labor"* capitalistic economic strategy. Pres. Wilson, as part of the *"First Red Scare of 1917,"* began attacking the CP-USA. He claimed communists were planning to overthrow America's government and were using former slaves in their plan.

The socialists and communists split under pressure from the *"First Red Scare,"* which ended in 1920 when Woodrow Wilson left office. However, Wilson pass the job of keeping black people on lockdown, as the foundation of America's *"cheap labor"* capitalistic economy to his "dark overlord" J. Edgar Hoover. After Wilson and the democrats departed the White House in 1921, making communism mainstream became the new approach of CP-USA.

The change in strategy of CP-USA brought communism to black people in large cities, like New York, Boston, Chicago, Philadelphia, Los Angeles, and elsewhere. Communists believed American black communities offered greater success for their ideas based on numbers and needs. They believed other leftists and white liberals, who saw the Soviet Union as a symbol of hope amidst the attacks on dissidents in America, would join them. CP-USA launched its effort to make communism mainstream by creating a *"Popular Front"* and adapting it to the US.

Seeking members in black communities in the 1920s, CP-USA found real acceptance among black people, who were more than happy to attend events that supported their fight against racism in America. Communists not only pushed social change, but they also provided financial and legal assistance for blacks who challenged segregation and racism. Communists were the first group to provide desperately needed support to black men on trial for their lives, after accusations of *"raping white women."* Black Americans desperately needed CP-USA's help in America without fair courts, especially in the South, with mob rule running rampant, as thousands of whites attended **"Dark Age"** *angry white men mob madness* spectacle lynchings. Before the CP-USA, no groups championed black people's causes.

Communists, in most cases, were the only group willing to step into the breach to aid African Americans. CP-USA became a voice, where members initiated and led many struggles against discrimination and disparate treatment, as well as poor housing and evictions. Communists also spoke openly against the use of terror and lynching. They demanded unemployment relief for black people and organized mass campaigns for the defense of victims of racial injustice, (*Old Negro, New Left: African-American Writing and Communism Between the Wars*, William J. Maxwell, New York: Columbia University Press, 1999).

The Popular Front era saw communists integrated into mainstream political institutions through alliances with progressives in the Republican and Democratic Parties. The CP-USA enjoyed influence and popularity among workers, as a result of their link to the newly formed Congress of Industrial Organizations (CIO), which they helped organize. Communists, in these organizations, were in the forefront, as strong opponents of "Jim Crow" segregation and white supremacy. CP-USA had a presence in both the NAACP and the American Civil Liberties Union (ACLU). Moreover, CP-USA established "front" groups, such as the League of American Writers, in which some intellectuals participated even with knowledge of its ties to Communism.

The CP-USA organized the "Upper Harlem Council of the Unemployed." They followed with a nationwide day of action to point out unemployment among blacks, which brought 500,000 to street protests. Mass protests in New York's Union Square and direct actions to stop evictions helped build up a core of Harlem communists. When a black activist was arrested and sentenced to six months in jail, hundreds—black and white—demonstrated in front of the judge's house. The Young Communist League—the CP's youth organization—and the African American group known as the Young Liberators initiated those demonstrations.

For example, in May of 1935, Howard University held a conference to discussed concerns for the status of the Negro. The National Negro Congress (NNC) came to signify the growing alliance between the Communists and black intellectuals during *The Popular Front Era*. The National Negro Congress was a newly formed group. The NNC participated in organized labor strikes, resistance to fascism, and used mass protest tactics against racism. CP-USA fought blacks' disenfranchisement in the South, as well as fought for employment of blacks through job campaigns. CP-USA held rallies, meetings, and discussion groups while highlighting concerns and problems of African Americans. Their actions put African American issues before the press and general public, while other groups were fearful of J. Edgar Hoover's *Red Scare* tactics.

The disastrous impact of Joseph Stalin's non-aggression pact with Adolf Hitler was a jolting setback for CP-USA (1939). It gave those fighting African American advancement, J. Edgar Hoover and the FBI, an advantage launching its divide and conquer strategy waged against black communities. Many black intellectuals fled the Party for left-liberal anti-communists alliances organized by Hoover and the FBI. Hoover also targeted communists, pushing them out of organized labor, liberal think tanks, and groups that gave legal support to black activists. FBI pressured groups that had communist members to purge them. The *Popular Front* collapsed in 1940.

The African Blood Brotherhood (ABB) was founded in 1918 by Cyril Briggs and they joined the CP-USA en masse, during the early 1920s. Formed as a secret, underground organization of radical "*black nationalists*," the ABB supported collective working-class action. It advocated armed defense against lynching, as well as racial equality and self-determination for Africans and peoples of African descent.

The ABB was absorbed into the CP-USA, and ceased to exist as an independent group. But, the party created the American Negro Labor Congress (ANLC) in 1925 as an independent labor force for black issues. It built interracial unity and support for the black labor movement. The ANLC evolved into the League of Struggle for Negro Rights (LSNR) in 1930.

The LSNR proved successful because of the popularity of its newspaper, *the Liberator*. Under the editorship of Cyril Briggs, *the Liberator* became a journal of black news highlighting issues like fighting evictions, confronting social workers, and opposing utility shutoffs. The merger with CP-USA brought in many talented black activists and leaders like Hubert Harrison, Jack O'Dell, Abner Berry, James W. Ford, Hosea Hudson, Benjamin Davis, Harry Haywood and others individuals joined the party.

The American Communist movement during the next three decades included a significant group of black women leaders during the Great Depression and World War II such as Mae Mallory, Audley "Queen Mother" Moore, Louise Thompson Patterson, Bonita Williams, Claudia Jones, Dorothy Burnham, Moranda Smith, and Esther Cooper Jackson. They participated in and produced various civil rights organizations, antiwar movements, labor unions, and black nationalistic struggles. The CP-USA maintained a significant black constituency among Black Arts groups.

In the meantime, the federal government worked to create legal grounds to abolish the CP-USA. FBI joined public officials to create the impression that CP-USA members were a threat to *American Capitalism* and economic stability—America's *"cheap labor"* strategy. Congress established the House Un-American Activities Committee (HUAC) in 1938. This committee became the Communist Party watchdog. Still not content, anti-communists worked to eliminate remaining CP-USA influence from progressive institutions, including the NAACP and the CIO. Passage of *The Taft-Hartley Act* (1947) gave anti-communists an instrument to pressure union officials to purge communists from the labor movement.

The National Negro Congress (NNC), the International Labor Defense (ILD), and the National Federation for Constitutional Liberties (NFCL) merged in 1945. These three organizations came together to create the Civil Rights Congress (CRC) lead by Att. William L. Patterson. The Civil Rights Congress fought for civil rights and defended anti-communist prosecutions targets of the

McCarthy era's *"Second Red Scare"* (1947-1957). The FBI targeted these groups before they merged and zeroed in on the one group, after their merger. CP-USA thought becoming one organization would broaden their appeal and attract young white radicals to join the fight for civil rights for black Americans, (<u>The Communist Position On The Negro Question,</u> William Z. Foster, Benjamin J. Davis, Jr., Eugene Dennis, Alexander Bittelman, James E. Jackson, James S. Allen, Et Al. NY: New Century, 1947).

CP-USA sponsored interracial meetings and dances, in the North and South, to encourage racial harmony. Their objective was to use social gatherings to demonstrate equality among the races. But, their most important effort was helping black victims of racist prosecutions, beginning with the **Scottsboro Boys** (Nine African-American teenagers accused of raping two white women on a train in Alabama in 1931).

Facing all-white juries in unfair courts, black men finally had a group willing to make a public stand on their behalf. CP-USA supported hundreds of penniless blacks, fighting for their lives, during the height of the **"Dark Age"** *angry white men mob madness* era of the 1920s and 30s. Communists were critical to demonstrating that black people had a group on their side that was not afraid of *"Jim Crow."*

(http://www.isreview.org/issues/01/cp_blacks_1930s.shtml).

The Cold War

The 1940s brought new faces and personalities into the struggle for and against social justice. The US *"Cold War"* became the lead technology for the right-wing bipartisan anti-communist consensus against a left-liberals alliance. It included politicians, policymakers, journalists, scientists, educators, entertainers, business and civic/religious leaders, the same forces that fought for white supremacy and that fought against CP-USA under the banner of *"The Cold War."* Moreover, *"The Cold War"* was a code name for the battle to stop social change, which energized these old enemies that always opposed African Americans' demands for freedom, justice, and equality. It also brought new initiatives from the left that advanced the struggle against the wretched conditions black people endured.

Reaching 1945, a new and different world of possibilities literally exploded, changing the balance of power in the realm of global politics. America dropped two atomic bombs (8-29-1945) on Hiroshima and Nagasaki, Japan (the two bombings killed 129,000–226,000 people). Those bombs gave America a "big stick," which it used to club other nations into accepting its new claim *"leader of the free world."* However, almost as suddenly, the USSR in just four years (8-29-1949), like lightning out of a clear blue sky to Americans, exploded a similar bomb, creating a bipolar world.

The Russian bomb although it struck terror in the minds of white people, Americans, and Europeans alike, but nobody died. Similar to the terror enslaved Africans endured under slavery, and the **"Dark Age" angry white men mob madness,** but to a much lesser degree, white Americans saw "doomsday" in the Russian blast. It was the type of threat they could not lynch or legislate against, to regain the advantage, as they did black people after emancipation.

The nuclear conflagration sent shivers that griped whites with fears they could not escape or dismiss, especially if it materialized. The blast that devastated Hiroshima and Nagasaki was not a cause for alarm or regret among white Americans; they were not white people. Contrarily, however, the Russian blast (which didn't kill anyone) made white people cringed at the thought of the world the Russian bomb created.

The USSR's explosion produced a world nobody outside of Russia was even considering. This bi-polar world of the bomb placed the Soviet Union at one end of a continuum of fear and America at the other. It made "brinksmanship" a viable option for many Americans, especially those in power. Each side became deeply involved in intrigue—spying, plotting, and even murder—US and USSR's trigger men kept a finger on the button at all times.

The equator on this global chessboard was called the *"Iron Curtain."* A metaphor, not a physical structure, it was the same as the *"cotton curtain"* in America.

The 400th: From Slavery to Hip Hop

The *"cotton curtain"* was also a metaphor southern black used to point out being on lockdown in America. The *"iron curtain"* and *"cotton curtain"* comports to the *"line of demarcation"* Pope Alexander VI drew, dividing the world between Portugal and Spain (1493).

The *"Cold War"* confrontation, following WWII, is framed as a "war," even though neither, the USSR nor the US fired a shot at one another across a battlefield. However, black people of that day thought the name—*cold war*—described the frigid treatment they endured from the US government, during and after the *"Gilded Age."* The US blocked access to its bountiful resources and jobs, during the "Gilded Age," which felt harsher than an arctic blast to former slaves. America's frigid treatment pushed millions of blacks into a deep freeze of unemployment. A metaphor, the graveyard of poverty—sharecropping and convict leasing—is to identify how black people were frozen on the bottom of America's economy, like pons, with *"Cold War"* propaganda. Unbeknownst to them and the rest of the world, American Pres. Woodrow Wilson and his number one henchman J. Edgar Hoover began this chess game just after the first **"Red Scare of 1917"** with **"Red Summer 1919."**

The *"iron curtain"* divided the world into spheres of influence. The USSR led the *"communist bloc"* in Eastern Europe, while the US, as *"leader of the free world"* claimed everywhere else. The idea was to maintain a nose to nose confrontational presence anywhere the Russians set up in the world, much like the anti-communist opposition of the US to CP-UAS working to help black in America. However, America had to avoid any direct contact, which might trigger World War III. *Ice Station Zebra* starring Jim Brown exemplifies the cold war mentality and atmosphere of these times.

The struggle for world dominance by the US and Russia is reminiscent of the battles for control of the **Trans-Atlantic Slade Trade** in the 17 and 1800s, when the enslavement of Africans, made them pons in that fight also. This statement reflects how America and Russia use client states and proxy wars to try and gain an advantage over the other side. The *"Cold War"* was fought on this make-believe chess board.

Deception—lies and counter-lies—in the *"Cold War"* were comparable to bullets in a hot war. America built *"Radio Free Europe"* and beamed propaganda into Eastern Europe continuously. America shot off barrages of accusations, like long-range artillery or missiles, lambasting Russia and the communist bloc, with "Radio Free Europe." Those propaganda attacks encouraged Eastern Europeans to escape the *"communist bloc"* for freedom in the West. America offered Eastern Europeans freedom, something it was denying black Americans, keeping them locked behind the *"cotton curtain"* in America. Each side concocted scenarios to make the other side sound like the *"evil empire,"* both were. While at the same time, each side tried to make it appear, it was the savor of the world; neither side was. The two governments—US and USSR—claimed to represent freedom and justice, truthfully; neither did.

The 1950s found black Americans still locked behind the *"cotton curtain."* It was like the world David Walker described to slaves, during the internal slave trade and breeding period, in the1820s. A dome of white supremacy and segregation covered black people in a suffocating prison without hopes of justice, freedom, and equality. White supremacy and segregation was synonymous to the Russian regime trapping Eastern Europeans as prisoners behind the "iron curtain," the same as black people were trapped behind the *cotton curtain* in the USA. The new world created by the bomb made life far more dangerous for everyone.

Although white supremacy and segregation were old fixtures and major components, in terms of concern of black people, nuclear Holocaust reduced survival struggle to secondary considerations. Consequently, America's charade of freedom and justice for black Americans became hostage of cold war politics and intrigue. White Americans considered whatever negatives that happened to blacks, as a result of the threat of nuclear holocaust and the propaganda war, as usual, would be acceptable collateral damage for African Americans. Trying to gain acceptance from white people, African Americans muted their demands for social change and justice, as during WWI, to avoid being painted **"Red"** by Hoover and the FBI.

Then another event happened similar to a bolt of lightning, not out of the blue, but it was just such an unexpected occurrence. The United Nations (UN) birth in 1946 was just as powerful an occurrance and game changer for African American, as America's and Russia's A-bombs. For the first time something blew a hole in America's *cotton curtain strategy.*

The birth of the UN created an opening in the total isolation surrounding African Americans. That opening not only allowed African Americans to look out, but allowed the world to see or at lease know what was happening to black people in America. A few black leaders, with the birth of the UN, looking through that hold saw the false and deceptive world America's bomb created. This new view of the world revealed what could be a chess game-changer for black American in the UN. African Americans saw and believed through the creation of the UN, they would be allowed to address a world body and expose America's discrimination, disparate treatment, and scarcity and desperation blacks have endured since slavery and after emancipation.

Then Russia built the "Berlin Wall" to duplicate the efficiency of America's *"cotton curtain."* The "Berlin Wall" was a physical structure, not a metaphor, mostly in and around Berlin. It made the old *"iron curtain"* idea, a physical barrier that ran from the Barents Sea at the Arctic to Ukraine on the Black Sea (not a solid wall all the way). The *"Berlin Wall"* was a *"cold war"* structure that emulated America's thirty-year-old *"cotton curtain strategy."* History tells a much harsher story regarding the Russian wall than it does America's *cotton curtain.* The *cotton curtain* was a metaphor blacks used to describe how America hid the truth of its lies regarding white supremacy, and the **"Dark Age" angry white men mob madness.** It—the *cotton curtain*—was America's continuing denial of freedom, justice, and equality to black people since emancipation.

America's government railed self-righteously against the USSR's treatment and control over Eastern Europeans; they were white people. The US verbally assaulted Russia, as a totalitarian state for denying Eastern Europeans what it was denying African Americans—*VOICE*—as well as mobility with lynching, while Russia was only keeping Europeans locked behind the *"iron curtain."* Simultaneously, the US government was doing everything possible to hide the fact that America was doing even worst—a pogrom of **Dark Age** *angry white men mob madness*—to black Americans. The previous discussion was not a defense of Russia, but a total condemnation of America's hypocrisy claiming to be *"leader of the free world,"* as it kept African Americans isolated prisoners behind its *"cotton curtain,"* on lockdown, denying them *VOICE*.

The Beat Goes On

The dichotomy of the USA and the USSR created the *"Cold War"* rhetoric that drew a line the two sides fought the propaganda war across. The US and USSR governments became confrontational foes, in the bi-polar world spawn by their bombs. The Communist Party and the *"Cold War"* were the first two major ingredients added to the crucible known as the *"Second Red Scare."* The next ingredients added to this volatile mixture were *social change* and American *radicalism*. Activists in America began applying heat to a pressure cooker filled with repression, oppression, socioeconomic, and political tyranny, which was smothering in black communities. Black American hopes simmered on a low flame of social pressure with denial of *VOICE* approaching critical mass.

The sparks from those flames were so insignificant their embers were barely felt by those they touched in the 1940s. Some young people touched by and caught in the radiation of those embers, burst into flames before realizing they had gotten burned. The next ingredient was the *"color line."*

The *"color line"* was another relic from slavery. A metaphorical non-physical barrier, as the *"Cold War,"* its anomalous occurrence was a fixture in white American's psyche. Internalizing the mental racial divide, which existed only in the heads of white people, and projected onto the larger society, it made skin color a warning sign.

Those not party to this mindset sought alternative environments where they could follow their natural inclinations. Such areas began popping up and offering new environments for different kinds of experiences, and those searching for such unusual and secluded places found them in big cities. The *"color line"* had continued as a basic social construct in Americans' mindset regarding race, since the beginning of slavery. It defied emancipation, as a barrier to freedom, equality, and justice for former slaves, but it became a legal construct with **"Plessy v. Ferguson"** and segregation.

I believe, and some psychologists agree, social interactions take place not only between people but other entities as well. Enter-personal relationships are processes not very well understood, but what is known indicates that during such interfaces, communications take place on many different levels simultaneously. And, many believe far more than words are involved in these exchanges. People, in particular, develop a sense of commonality, through such exchanges and draw clues from one another regarding their place and acceptance in socially bindery situations. Social interactions, as young blacks and whites reached the 1940s, began taking place across the *"color line."*

This mental construct—*the color line*—originated with the footprints made by the first African slave dragged aboard a slave ship in chains. That line stretched from Africa across the *"Middle Passage"* to North America. It became the Mason-

Dixon Line, separating North from South and freedom from slavery. Stretched across America by **Plessy v. Ferguson,** that mental construct was erected, as a legal divide to regulate all social, economic, and political intercourse. It was the operative concept, whether in employment or in the bedrooms, even accommodations in restrooms were regulated.

Although the *"color line"* began as a mental construct, it gained concrete physical impacts, like the *iron curtain*, once **Plessy v. Ferguson** became the law of the land. Symbolizing whites' sense of superiority and entitlement, the *"color line"* ruled interracial contact in American society, like a border without guards. Blacks, on the other hand, had been conditioned to accepting denial of rights, as a reality controlling their world.

Changing the *"color line"* from a mental construct to a legal barrier, **Plessy v. Ferguson** reinforced white supremacy and white privilege. Unlike the *"cotton or iron curtains,"* **Plessy v. Ferguson** was more like the *Berlin Wall*. Over time this arcane and dubious construct created a logical fallacy for young whites, as their relationships extended across this once imaginary, but now legal line dictating separation. I want to be clear and this narrative has shown; white people have been part of enslaved Africans' struggle for freedom even before the abolition of the **Trans-Atlantic Slave Trade**. However, this slow burn brought blacks and whites together on a personal and social level publically, in a new and different manner.

Government policies and actions produced two different mindsets in America. The upside of this coin was how white people saw blacks. The downside was the impact of how that legal construct created a divide that controlled former slaves' lives. Individuals elaborated on how they saw and what they thought of America's social concepts. The federal government victimized blacks through white supremacy and segregation, while ostracizing whites that ventured across the *"color line."*

The low slow-burn continued sucked fuel from the logical fallacy of racism, white supremacy and segregation. This friction caused sparks, while its embers ignited small brush fires among young whites. Through their daily contact and interactions, whether personal or through some medium, attitudes, habits, perspectives and work situations where individuals on opposite sides of the *"color line"* began to meld, congealed and solidified into group concepts.

These barely noticed or ignored happenings reflected the fact that likeminded individuals began gathering in small private out-of-the-way urban settings. They began gathering in large cities like New York City and San Francisco, where they ventured beyond seclusion and secrecy in places that became cultural melting pots. These enclaves were magnets that drew young adults together, who shared their hopes for a different world from the one they saw looking at their lives.

The modern "American dream" that enveloped young people just after the turn of the 20th century was the world of the parents of young people who gathered in such out-of-the-way places. Their parents had envisioned a "white only" world, without any former slaves spoiling their view or their children. They expected their children to take up life with secure jobs, happy marriages, nice families, well-deserved retirements, and markets offering a wide variety of consumer goods.

Parents of children from that generation paid for their education and expected them to get jobs and live moral lives. Again, parents of these younger people expected they would get married and have children. Virtually, follow in their footsteps as parents in thoughts and actions. The younger generation was also expected to take the torch of leadership their parents' world offered, embrace their prepackaged-lives, and pass them on to their progeny.

Conformity was safe, and the *"Establishment's"* prerequisite for being a good citizen. Out of this silent racist and "escapist" society, the low slow-burn that began with sparks now had become a flame. Young progressives regrets were like the smoke released by flames from that slow-burn. The illusionary visions of their parents' world became the fuel, which burned away the old world, revealing the vision of a possible new future young people envisioned, gleaming through the smog.

Tugged on by the demands of one world and the magnetism from the other side of the *"color line,"* released strong emotions that became the traffic cop at the intersection. How does one anticipate an emotion, they never had before? How does one learn to relate to situations without real context?

Instead of buying into what young progressives saw as madness—chasing America's new found affluence and materialism—young white progressives made a hard left turn. Breaking through the *"color line,"* like the new supersonic jets that were breaking the sound barrier and speed records at that time; their inner voice screamed "NO." They made a hard left turn smashing through the *"color line"* leaving it in tatters.

Young nonconformists came together in out-of-the-way niches in *The Village* in New York City. They rejected the unauthentic, prepackaged lives of their parents and began seeking alternatives to what they saw as the insanity of their parents' world. Debating and discussing questions, like *"What does freedom mean, if Americans are truly free?",* young progressives began formulating new ideas about life, relationships, sex, social roles, religion, race, gender and many other issues as well.

Thess young people became the *"Beat Generation!"* They responded to that low slow-burn, whivh became a flame in the early1940s. It was another major ingredient contributed to what became America's *Counter-Culture Movement.* Young progressives of the *"Beat Generation,"* were also called *"beatniks or beatsters."* They were as unprecedented as they were unanticipated. Beatsters sowed seeds of social changes and nonconformity while seeking spirituality and authenticity, as fruit to nourish the restoration of the human community. Some even sought spiritual enlightenment through Buddhism.

The beat scene germinated without iconic leaders. It brought together dropouts like Allen Ginsberg, Jack Kerouac, and William F. Burroughs, along with hundreds of others, who saw Greenwich Village as a refuge from the world of their parents. "Beatniks," also called beatsters revered such dropouts as innovators, whom the outside world considered weird and out of step with the mainstream. Throughout the 1940s and into the 1950s, these young progressives explored life, wrote poetry and novels, examined various philosophies, and contemplated their role in a new world. Beatsters rejected the *"Establishment"* and expressed their revulsion for it through their art (music, poetry, theater, books, and movies), as well as various types of visual and audio productions.

Blacks came down to the Village from Harlem, bringing their own unique cultural experiences—styles of language, music, dance, and behavior. These young people aspired to be writers, philosophers, dancers, actors, musicians, and all searched for authenticity in their expressions. Some were jazz aficionados, community activists, and ardently anti-racists. Experimentation was demand, as part of this emerging scene. Some tried drugs—usually marijuana and Benzedrine; sometimes heroin. Some became bohemians, sharing alternative lifestyles, enjoyed sex liberally, and all without steady jobs. Mainstream conservative considered beatniks' lifestyles scandalous and felt they were dangerous radicals and bums. Beatsters, like Allen Ginsberg and Jack Kerouac, believed they were the in-crowd, relegating themselves to the fringe of the mainstream.

A flourishing art scene—music, poetry, literary discussion, and experimentation—was viewed as ideal. Young progressives viewed their community as a place to begin building social change. Their minds were fertile ground, and communists showed up like farmers to plant seeds for thought. Communists saw Harlem, during the Depression years, like a garden overgrown with weeds, in needing constant gardening.

The fact that most communists had flexible perspectives and held sophisticated sets of aesthetic values made the Communist Party an attractive alternative to many black artists. The CP-USA helped fund such cultural organizations as the *Federal Negro Theatre*, which employed 350 people and gave black playwrights a chance and a place to develop material. *The Federal Writers Project* got into the act by aiding black artists, as they documented the history and role of blacks on the New York artistic scene. Communists even funded the *Harlem Community Arts Center*, which gave free space and a stage for many aspiring artists in Harlem. These projects gave a tremendous boost to the morale of black artists in Harlem, following the painful and deceitful government purge of Marcus Garvey and the demise of the **UNIA**.

The CP-USA's artistic values struck a chord with black intellectuals and the middle class, but not working class Harlemikes. Addressing that shortcoming, communists set out to help improve schools in Harlem. CP-USA helped African Americans create an organization called the *Harlem Committee for Better Schools (HCBS)*, which lasted, form 1935-1950, when the CP-USA was chased out of America.

The HCBS included parents, teachers, church leaders, and community groups, which helped form alliances with schools in the area. Communists were very much part of a vibrant art scene in Harlem. While looking for recruits, communists cultivated the vital avant-garde collection of progressive-minded young black and white students, beatsters and those living alternative lifestyles in the beat scene of large cities. CP-USA members were also instrumental, pulling together the coalition that organized around **_We Charge Genocide_**. This coalition helped change the culture in America for blacks and whites alike.

Prelude to the Second Red Scare

The CA-USA, *"Cold War"* and the *"Beat Generation,"* were not planned as such, but became major forces that helped lay a cultural floor beneath descendants of American slavery. Struggling to rise out of the graveyard of poverty in the valley of dry bones, blacks in Harlem began using the Arts as a major expression in the early 1900s. After the "First Red Scare" (1917) the federal government became concerned regarding the help the black communities in Harlem was receiving from CP-USA. Woodrow Wilson put J. Edgar Hoover in charge of organizing the Radical Division of the Bureau of Investigation (BOI) (1912) and he zeroed in on CP-USA's work in Harlem.

Hoover worked throughout 1920 and into the 1930s, trying to drive communists out of America concentrating his efforts in black communities. CP-USA centered its organizing in Harlem among artists, writers and entertainers who responded with enthusiasm to their support. The federal government followed CP-USA looking for a program to sabotage communist efforts. The previous discussion shows Hoover, and the BOI began in the 1920s into the 1940s, specifically trying to undermine CP-USA's efforts to help African Americans develop artistically.

In January 1947, FBI records indicate it began putting together a liberal-lead anti-communist coalition made up of the Americans for Democratic Action (ADA), and NAACP. Labor leader Walter Reuther (UAW), Walter White (NAACP), as well as historian Arthur Schlesinger Jr., theologian Reinhold Niebuhr, and former First Lady Eleanor Roosevelt led this liberal-anti-communist coalition. They worked feverishly to defeat the popular front-backed candidacy of former vice-president Henry Wallace's run for President.

They developed an appeal that combined social and economic reforms with staunch anti-communism to supported Pres. Harry S. Truman. Black Americans supported the ADA's and NAACP's appeal on Truman's behalf for two reasons beyond being a Democrat. First, they wanted a president that spoke out against white supremacy. Secondly, they support Truman's presidential bid as a way of avoiding being painted **"Red"** by the FBI. The FBI publically characterized supporters of Wallace, as communists. FBI claimed Wallace was soft on "communism," and a client of the USSR. So, blacks deserted Wallace for Truman to avoid FBI's "red baiting".

Scholar Mary Helen Washington, in her book *The Other Blacklist: The African American Literary and Cultural Left of the 1950s,* does not gloss over the role of the Communist Party in fostering, facilitating, and supporting a black 'Popular Front' of literary and cultural figures. She writes, *"...it is clear why the CP attracted blacks, especially during the depression. For, it was the Party's leadership in the Unemployed Councils, the National Negro Congress, the Sharecroppers' Union, the Civil Rights Congress and the Council on African Affairs, among others that fought for equality, which is what led thousands of African Americans to join the Communist Party, and form a Red-Black alliance."* These organizations were groups CP-USA help organize and financed. They were the only groups that were working to help African Americans overcome racism, segregation, and white supremacy in America.

The low slow-burn I alluded to earlier, by the end of the first five years (1946- 1951) of the *"Cold War,"* had become a flame. Opposition to America's claim of—*leader of the free world*—was only a bud on the rose and had not flowered in UN debates. The *"Cold War"* made the UN the point of America's juggernaut against international communism. It shoved its title—*leader of the free world*—down the world's throat.

Controlling debate in the UN, America isolated Russia, calling it capitalism's enemy. America's new world, but like the old world of white supremacy, segregation, and the **"Dark Age"** *angry white men mob madness* of the past, it locked African America in the grave of poverty without *VOICE*. The new world that dawned, with the birth of the United Nations (UN), offered a ray of hope to slave descendants. However, *"Cold War"* considerations kept black people still locked behind a tattered *"cotton curtain."* However, the big deal that changed things for everyone, most particularly African Americans, was *"getting caught dealing with the CP-USA, which now in 1948 could get you thrown in jail."*

The birth of the UN became a refuge for oppressed and exploited people, victims of colonialism and slavery across the globe. Oppressed and exploited people were petitioning the UN for the right to tell their stories in their own words, and were being granted hearings. African Americans hoped to gain the same recognition for themselves. America, as *"leader of the free world,"* demanded exploited and oppressed people be allowed to speak for themselves, and their petitions were being given full hearings.

Descendants of American slavery identified themselves in the same way as other oppressed and exploited people of the world before the UN. They got in line with others filing human rights petition for relief from the crime of genocide in America. Everything changed for America's oppressed and exploited slave descendants, once its petition reached the UN.

African Americans were placed in a special category unto themselves, like *"separate but equal."* Unfortunately, African Americans occupy a position no other people occupied. Apparently, black Americans are not considered human beings, like other oppressed and exploited people by the UN. Why the UN refused to recognize the isolation imposed on black people by America with its *"cotton curtain"* strategy, still in place today, yet the UN has never clarified why.

The UN's actions are very difficult to understand because the UN was accepting petitions from other black people. Nothing like the UN's denial of America's slave descenteands happened to others, during this process. The UN's actions against black people could not be anticipated by leaders pushing the petition. I offer a visual metaphor to exemplify the magnitude of change black people's petition made in the UN. Reading about this time and trying to visualize the spectacle, I liken it to watching basketball in the 1970s and 80s. One basketball player convinced the world, *"a man could fly."* Yes, *fly!!!* Once "Dr. J," Julius Ervin, began making house calls, basketball changed forever.

Before fans saw "Dr. J's" basketball aeronautical fantastic flights of fancy, sometimes seeming to float, even hover, as he soared to the basketball goal, no one could envision such physical airborne acrobatic spectacles with a basketball. "Dr. J's" visual human highlights, during his spectacular incredible basketball moves, gave future players, like Michael Jordan, Kobe Bryant, and now LeBron James, visual fantastic flights of fanciful spectacles to fill theirdreams with possibilities. Dr. J flights were like Marcus Garvey for former slaves, something must happen for other to realize certain possibilities exist. Seeing "Dr. J" they went on to soar through the stratosphere of basketball fame. "Dr. J's" amazing aerial spectacles have become legendary moves. Although I never saw his wings, I believed a man could fly!

The thing is American descendants of slavery, dreamed of being able to rise above the rim of America's *cotton curtain,* figuratively like "Dr. J," soaring to the basket. Similarly, blacks saw themselves elevating their argument and rising above America's discrimination, hatred, degradation, and isolation, through the new game, the birth of the UN created. Driving toward the goal of telling the world of their plight, as other exploited and oppressed human beings, would have gain American descendants of slavery, consideration as human beings for the first time.

However, employing a *"double standard,"* the UN's refusal to give *VOICE* to African Americans was a devastating foul call. Stepping in against slavery's descendant, as they drove to the basket for the biggest score in America's slave game, the UN call a technical foul to end the game. Unfortunately, the Communist Party-USA was the only source of political and financial support for African Americans struggling to gain freedom, justice, and equality. Consequently, black communities, during the repression of the *"Second Red Scare,"* had not only lost a friend after the CP-USA was force out of the US, but regained an even more powerful and determined enemy in J. Edgar Hoover.

African Americans' hopes of rising above oppression in America by appealing to an international body went nowhere. The UN refused to recognize former enslaved Africans' right of *VOICE,* as it did for other oppressed and exploited people. The UN called a technical foul as African Americans drove for the goal, taking the ball and giving it back to US. Moreover, once CP-USA, the only ally of slave descendants, was forced out of America, African Americans slavery descendants were left without any leverage against America's geo-political economic power and exploitation.

Then again, the seeds planted by beatniks began growing in the mid-1940s. They budded into the baby boom generation. Young progressives of the *"Beat Generation"* coalesced with the remnants of CP-USA. Beatniks fanned the tiny sparks that touch beatsters, who busted into flames, which started raging infernal in their minds. Those flames fired the *"counterculture movement,"* and beatsters developed real political ideologies in the early 1950s.

Many of these young people became researchers, writers, and strategists for **We Charge Genocide.** Their efforts brought a new perspective to African Americans' fight for recognition as human beings. Again, the previous topics may have seemed nothing more than a romance and smooch party with America's communist past. However, it was necessary background information that allows me to layout the full foundation for what came next.

"Dr. J's" fantastic flights of fancy are important as a metaphor to give visual contexts to black people's desperate efforts to rise above America's *"cotton curtain"* with **"We Charge Genocide,"** as a slam punk. I wanted readers to visualize the mental agility and political dexterity demanded and the Herculean effort required to get **"We Charge Genocide"** in UN hands. That move—getting **"We Charge Genocide"** into UN hands—highlights the most pivotal and amazing event of the 20th Century for descendants of American slavery, after Marcus Garvey.

The previous discussion provides an understanding of why and what it took for slave descendants to make it to the 1950 at this point in history. The hard left turn African Americans began in the 1920s brought them into the 1950s, where they close the door on the past, but opened a new future only a few saw, whether reading tea leaves, bones, books, or stars. No matter how they did it, none of this was predictable.

Thinking back to my state of mind before beginning this research, I agreed with the US government's fight to destroy the "evil" communist threat. Today, I admit with deep shame and regret that I fell totally for J. Edgar Hoover's propaganda. If what I have presented thus far has not persuaded readers to adopt the same mindset, hopefully, what I offer now will turn the trick.

The Civil Rights Congress (CRC) led the effort to build a case against America's more than one hundred years of inequality and injustice it began heaping upon former slaves following emancipation. That group—Civil Rights Congress—like "Dr. J's" totally unexpected and unstoppable moves—developed a brilliant strategy to bring the problems of black Americans before the world. The CRC was the first African American organization to challenge America and charge it with genocide on appeal before an international forum. The CRC led American slavery's descendants' demand for recognition with its petitioned to the UN. The CRC demanded the same rights the UN was granting other oppressed and exploited people, which allowed them to speak on their own behalf. The CRC's request put the spotlight on America, as an international hypocrite for the first time. Such a challenge from former enslaved Africans had never been attempted and was like "shock and awe" to the world community.

Paul Robeson and William L. Patterson, two giants in the battle for social change, equality, and justice, took the struggle to gain recognition as *"human beings"* for African Americans to the UN. They presented **_We Charge Genocide: The Historic Petition to the United Nations for Relief from a Crime of Genocide by the United States Government against the Negro People_** to UN Secretary-General **Trygve Halvdan Lie**. The UN's charter mandates it represents the interest of *"human beings."* The CRC's petition highlighted the fact that America was the last industrial nation in the world to end forced bondage—chattel slavery—in 1865, but with the end of bond servitude, Americans did not end slavery.

America isolated black Americans behind what black people in the South called the *"cotton curtain"* to hide its genocide from the world. The US imposed isolation, denying black people *VOICE*. The CRC felt, if the UN and the world saw black Americans as *"human beings,"* they would grant slave descendants' the same right of *VOICE,* it granted other oppressed and exploited people. Instead, America doubled down, refusing to fold in the face of **_We Charge Genocide._** It deployed a full-court press on the UN to keep former enslaved Africans bottle up on their end of the court.

An artist, athlete, concert singer, and actor, Paul Robeson (4-9-1898/1-23-1976), was very well known as an activist on behalf of black people. However, J. Edgar Hoover labeled Robeson, as he did Marcus Garvey, a communist, hoping to isolate him, as well as mute his voice in other parts of the world. Hoover moved to prevent Robeson from speaking beyond the black community to world audiences, about US genocide against black Americans. His name atop the **_We Charge Genocide_** petition gave it real credibility and prestige.

William L. Patterson (8-27-1891/3-5-1980), on the other hand, was a different story. Patterson was an outspoken leader in the Communist Party-USA **(the Reds)** and headed the International Labor Defense (ILD). The ILD was a crusading force for black people. Without fair courts in America, Patterson, through the ILD, provided legal representation for African Americans, who had political or racial persecution issues and could not afford legal counsel.

Patterson's autobiography, **_The Man Who Cried Genocide_**, published in 1971, is a very exciting and forcefully dynamic picture of the man that made crucial contributions to former enslaved Africans' struggle for justice in America. Helping to develop the solid intellectual, yet aggressive arguments that *Black Nationalists* advanced during the 1960s, Patterson's impact was enormous. His exploits and image, as a freedom fighter, motivated young communists and other progressives to join his **_We Charge Genocide_** effort, as researchers and supporters.

Patterson was in the forefront supporting the CP-USA, as the only organization willing to take the burning issues of *"Jim Crow"* segregation and white supremacy in the US from the streets into the courtroom and onto the world. Showing great courage in the late 1920s, early in his organizing career, Patterson traveled to Moscow, along with other US radicals, black and white. These were rancorous times, during very intense days, pitting Patterson against seasoned communist, in a very different environment from the US. Sometimes there were rough and tumble political debates over **_the Negro question_**—a topic that commanded much attention in the USSR in the 1920s and 30s. Patterson came to view blacks living under racism in the USA and blacks under European colonial rule, as united allies-in-the-struggle for freedom.

Author, Gerald Horne, Patterson's biographer; **_Black Revolutionary: William L. Patterson and the Globalization of the African American Freedom Struggle_** wrote,

> *Patterson built a life as a well-to-do New York lawyer, but was drawn into the fight for justice and equality. He was not trained to be an activist, but became a revolutionary and international leader in the struggled against Jim Crow, South African apartheid, colonialism, and red-baiting, regarding his relationship with the Soviet Union. Patterson led the fight to save the Scottsboro defendants—nine African American youth falsely accused of raping two white women.*
>
> *Patterson was also the director of the Civil Rights Congress, which was widely viewed as the legal defense arm of the broader African American freedom struggle. An emerging and prominent African American leader affiliated with the Communist Party-USA, Patterson traveled widely, going to Moscow several times. He met dozens of future leaders of the African liberation movement and forged the international contacts that proved to be so important in the battle against Jim Crow in America and colonialism in Africa.*

In advance of talking about Willian Patterson and Paul Robeson's fight to get **_We Charge Genocide_** before the world, I will say, I think they are two of the unsung heroes in the real battle black Americans waged during the 1940s and 50s that provided black Americans with a solid psychological and philosophical bases for the rhetoric needed to supported black radicalism—*Black Nationalism*—coming into the 1960 and 70s. David Walker and Marcus Garvey were the first black men that laid the foundation of knowledge black people truly needed to understand their real political situation, which aided this move on the UN. It is well established that after **_Plessy v. Ferguson_** the US government closed courthouse doors to black people then unleashed the **_"Dark Age"_** *angry white men mob madness*, a pogrom of genocide against defenseless black people. **_We Charge Genocide_** was the first statement, after those spokesmen—Walker and

Garvey—to address black liberation of descendants of American slavery to open the 1950.

We Charge Genocide required Robeson and Patterson to be very deceptive, getting around the US State Department's *"cotton curtain,"* which had a full-court press in place, trying to prevent them from delivering their petition directly to UN delegation in Paris. The State Department was on alert and poised to block distribution and discussion of **_We Charge Genocide_** by UN authorities. US State Department officials put a blackout on press coverage of **_We Charge Genocide_** in the US. Working behind the scenes to prevent **_We Charge Genocide_** from being presented to or recognized by international leaders, US agents censored mail leaving the US.

The US State Department confiscated Robeson's passport to prevent him from leaving the country. Next, it blocked his efforts to speak on behalf of **_We Charge Genocide_** to the press and on other public forums in the US. When Robeson was granted interviews, he charged *"The US government is muzzling black people."* Robeson and Patterson faced the same problems David Walker encountered in the 1830s distributing his **_Appeal_**, or editor and publisher John H. Sengstacke of the *Chicago Defender*, getting his paper into the South.

Getting **_We Charge Genocide_** into UN hands required the kind of razzle-dazzle, getting around the State Departments' blockade of the UN, for Dr. "J" to get to the basketball goal. It was as though Robeson and Patterson used hoodoo to disguise their two-pronged approach of *"now you see me, now you don't,"* disappearing act to eluding American agents and escape the *cotton curtain*. First, Robeson was accompanied to the UN by over 1,000 signees of their petition. Robeson and supporters, with fanfare, marched to UN Headquarters at Dag Hammarskjöld Plaza in New York City (12-17-1951), where he presented **_We Charge Genocide_** to Secretary-General **Trygve Halvdan Lie,** capturing the US State Department's undivided attention.

Then as now, blacks needed some real stand up heroes, a different type of leader, like Marcus Garvey, to teach slave descendants how to fight under the new conditions they faced. I present **_We Charge Genocide_** as I do because William L. Patterson put his life on the line for black people standing up to the US government. Presenting **_We Charge Genocide,_** Patterson got the truth out about the day-to-day conditions black people faced in America. Those conditions were similar in many ways to the tragedy Adolf Hitler and the Nazis imposed on Jews. The difference is, the world held them accountable. Presenting **_We Charge Genocide_** to the UN, Patterson hoped the UN would do the same to America. He asked the question, *"What is the difference between American slave descendants and other oppressed and exploited people?"* As of yet, no one has answered!!!!!!!!!!!

Anticipating the 125 copies of **_We Charge Genocide_** mailed to Paris would be intercepted by the US government, Patterson shipped smaller packages from

Canada to homes of communist friends in Paris. Paul Roberson captured the US government's attention hand-delivering **_We Charge Genocide_** to Secretary-General Trygve Halvdan Lie at UN Headquarters in New York City. With a behind the back crossover dribble "Dr. J," Patterson going backdoor. Simultaneously, with another classic "Dr. J" spin move before leaving the floor, on a fantastic flight of fancy and slam dunks, Patterson made his way unnoticed to Paris, by way of Canada. When his big shipment did not arrive, as he suspected, Patterson distributed his backup copies sent to friends.

Putting **_We Charge Genocide's_** 237-pages in the hands of UN Delegates meeting in Paris, who were accepting petitions from oppressed and exploited people, requesting recognition for their right of *VOICE,* Paterson closed the circle began by David Walker with his **_Appeal._** The game was afoot for William Patterson, as he was on his own in Paris. He knew getting back to the US would require even more innovation and creativity than getting to Paris.

The US government had shown disinterest concerning statements by black people inside the US about its treatment of them. However, during the *"Cold War,"* when African Americans made similar statements abroad, American politicians went berserk. Once **_We Charge Genocide_** taught the world the truth about convict leasing, sharecropping, and **"Dark Age"** *angry white men mob madness,* the State Department sends Walter White (NAACP) and other high profile Negros to Europe to speak in opposition to it. Their speeches made it seem life in America for black people was improving.

Pulling the hooded off US' white supremacy head, **_We Charge Genocide_** exposed America's racist face to world officials. **_We Charge Genocide_** demanded the UN grant slave descendants right of *VOICE,* he claimed the human rights of descendants of American slavery to *"speak on their behalf and tell their story in their own words."* Again, **_We Charge Genocide's_** demands were no different than other oppressed and exploited human beings, which the UN granted the right of *VOICE.*

A bold statement to a world body regarding American racism had never been given such exposure nor had it been laid out so embarrassingly bare. Having exposed America, as a hypocrite, before world leaders for muzzling black Americans, while simultaneously demanding other oppressed and exploited people have voices. **_We Charge Genocide_** made America's denial of *VOICE* to black people obvious.

Getting **_We Charge Genocide_** to UN Delegates in Paris so smoothly, Patterson caught US State Department officials with their pants down. Exposing America's bare backside, denying charges contained in **_We Charge Genocide_** amounted to burlesque, before the world body. Disrobed by **_We Charge Genocide_** before the UN, US State Department officials could not hide its barefaced hypocrisy supporting *VOICE* for other oppressed people, but blocking it for black Americans. Nevertheless, America's *"Dark Overlord,"* J. Edgar Hoover, had tricks up his sleeves as well.

First, he declared Patterson a fugitive from justice, making him a wanted man. Secondly, he and the State Department sent agents to apprehend Patterson in Europe and return him in chains to the US. Like a fugitive slave on an *Underground Railroad* wanted poster, Patterson became number one on America's hit list of radicals. Any bounty hunter could collect on Patterson, like David Walker, after Georgia posted its $10,000 reward.

Supposedly, J. Edgar Hoover's manhunt, scouring Europe, looking for Patterson, was only to bring him back to the US to answer questions. But, Patterson audaciously flew the coop, going on the lam in Europe. Making it up, as he went along, Patterson escaped the first trap set by US agents or hit squads, poised to waylay him at his hotels. Barely eluding that trap and several others, Patterson had to duck in and out of back doors or side entrances, just ahead of America's modern-day *"slave catchers."*

Unfolding like a World War II spy novel, agents stalked hotels and bars, as Patterson became a *will-ó-the-wisp*. Disappearing, then popping up totally unexpected to agents on his trail, *"now you see me, and now you don't,"* Patterson's vanishing act, left America's army of killers, chasing their tails. Patterson's intrepid run across Europe was a desperate gamble trying to evade the US posse.

Communist supporters in Europe aided Patterson's escape. They covered his tracks, as he hopped from country to country, avoiding capture or death, but he was unable to get out of Europe. While US agents tracked him, dispatches flew between capitols, with the American government claiming Patterson was a spy, desperately trying to get sensitive information to Moscow. The US State Department demanded European government agents intercept Patterson in Western Europe any way they could. The US Government claimed Patterson was headed for Moscow and had to be prevented from disappearing behind the *"iron curtain"* with sensitive documents. They posted standing orders to apprehend Patterson with extreme prejudice, without regard for circumstances before he reached Russia.

With a target on his back, Patterson vanished suddenly, like a puff of smoke, as his cloak and dagger chase across Europe became a cliffhanger, the second week. Disappearing off everyone's radar without a trace, ***We Charge Genocide*** faithful in the US feared the worst for Patterson. Speculation on his whereabouts, capture, and possible death, filled the airwaves and press in Europe, but silence covered the US. Calls, dispatches, and cables ceased, leaving those rooting for Patterson's successful escape, holding their breaths.

Through their communist contacts, Robeson and his ***We Charge Genocide*** colleagues in the states tried frantically to locate Patterson. European supporters sent groups searching for information on his whereabouts, but there was nothing. The second week ended with dire scenarios, which flew wildly back and forth across the ocean. The silence had everyone feeling maybe, Patterson had met the fate he tried so desperately to elude.

Entering the third week, feelings of gloom gave way to scenarios of doom, among **_We Charge Genocide_** faithful. Everyone braced themselves for tragic news. Suddenly, a news flash came across the wire from Szabad Nép in Budapest, Hungary, of all places. Patterson had surfaced. Telling a hair-raising tale of avoiding capture by eluding several ambushes while hiding out, Patterson praised farmers and workers who hid and transported him.

His dispatch to the Hungarian newspaper began with a scathing attack on the US. Patterson charged the American government was *"muzzling black people."* He said the US *"kept black Americans in isolation to stop social change in America."* During Patterson's escapade, **_We Charge Genocide_** was big news in communist dailies in Europe, as he avoided the State Department's death hunt. Receiving international media attention, **_We Charge Genocide_** exposed many shocking examples and conditions African Americans were enduring under white supremacy in America. **_We Charge Genocide_** accused the US government of hundreds of wrongful executions and lynchings. It documented 10,000 cases of discrimination, disparate treatment in employment, education, and public accommodations. Charging that the US had disenfranchised black people, preventing them from voting by using suppression, intimidation, poll taxes, grandfather clauses, and literacy tests, all of which are commonly used today, by Republicans, as they continue denying black voters access to the poll in 2022.

We Charge Genocide cited thousands of police brutality cases. It cited convict leasing to show there were no fair courts in the US, as well as its criminal justice system was rigged against black people. Southern judicial systems legitimize using trumped-up charges to imprison millions of African Americans. Courts used black's inability to pay finds to sell them to private industries that paid their fines but gave them nothing. Slave descendants in the South were an unpaid labor force for American industries, businesses, and plantations, making them millions of dollars for 90 years after emancipation.

We Charge Genocide made the critical argument that the US government was both complicit with and explicitly responsible for the genocidal situation in the US black people faced, based on the UN's *Genocide Convention adopted by the UN General Assembly in December 1948*—**Any intent to destroy, in whole or in part, a national, racial, or religious group is genocide!!!** Seeking to make comparisons between American genocide and Nazi genocide explicit, **_We Charge Genocide_** focused on incidents occurring after 1945. Ultimately, **_We Charge Genocide_** charged *"US government sponsored the longest-running genocide against human beings, through its endorsement and support of racism, white supremacy, convict leasing, sharecropping, and 'monopoly capitalism,' without which the persistent, continuous, widespread institutionalized commission of the crime of genocide would be impossible."*

The 400th: From Slavery to Hip Hop

The *National Black United Front* petitioned the United Nations again in 1996–1997, directly citing **We Charge Genocide**" restating discrimination, disparate treatment, and genocide against African Americans by the US government. Nevertheless, even after **We Charge Genocide,** the US continued denying descendants of American slavery *VOICE*. Again, like Woodrow Wilson during **Red Summer,** the UN did not say or do anything to recognize slave descendants' right of *VOICE*.

So, the Second Red Scare Began

If there are still some diehard readers that are unconvinced by the previous descriptions and discussion, I'm positive America's response to ***We Charge Genocide*** will carry the day. The *"Cold War"* produced unintended consequences that forced America to show a *"false face"* to the world. America's *"false face"* gave the impression the US was moving in the direction of social change—equal justice, freedom of choice, fair courts and opportunities to advance economically for slavery's descendants.

Most white Americans had not even considered liberalizing America's socioeconomic and political structures when ***We Charge Genocide*** hit the UN. America's unchanging behavior over the seven decades (1920s into the 1950s) following **Plessy v Ferguson** (1897) segregation and white supremacy continued to be the law of the land. The international community through the UN refused to honor its commitment to its own charter and challenge America's government's political and socioeconomic "isolation" ***We Charge Genocide*** revealed black people in America were enduring. The US deployed white supremacy, segregation, convict leasing, and sharecropping to dominate the lives of black people, and the UN turned its back on its mandate to represent and serve humanity, even though, America has never lived up to any promises made, regarding equality, justice, discrimination, disparate treatment and the right of *VOICE* for its descendants of slavery.

America's containment policy toward communism in general and the USSR, in particular, gave America confidence it could continue that strategy. However, ***We Charge Genocide*** threw a monkey wrench into America's *"leader of the free world,"* strategy. America aimed its communist propaganda at Europe and Africa hoping to gain adheres. After ***We Charge Genocide*** reached the UN, communist countered US charges by calling it the world's biggest hypocrite. ***We Charge Genocide*** was an unexpected challenge to America's policies, because it reflected America's false and hypocritical face, which ***We Charge Genocide*** exposed. It was like a pie in the racist face of America in Europe and Africa, which was unable to lie about its treatment of its slave descendants.

Moreover, reaching the 1950s, J. Edgar Hoover had served frothy years, as FBI Director, under six presidents, four different Supreme Court Chief Justices, and a bandwagon of Attorney Generals. Over that extended period, Hoover collected dossiers on everyone—friends and foes—on the way to becoming one of, if not the most, powerful man in government, including presidents. Hoover was the **Grand Dragon** of white supremacy, which he inherited directly from Pres. Woodrow Wilson its creator. Hoover opposed social change for black Americans at any level and fought to protect his legacy of segregation and white supremacy, throughout his years of government service. Fighting the *"Cold War"* was just an extension of Hoover's lifelong fight to stop social changes for African Americans.

For instance, winning a seat on the City Council in New York City in 1945, Benjamin Davis Jr. was an active member in the Communist Party, which drew both black and white support. However, his astonishing victory, during the *"Cold War"* era, drew a vengeful reaction from the FBI. They went after him and encouraged local governments to keep communists off ballots and out of power by any means they could. New York City gerrymandered City Council districts, after Davis' election. Consequently the FBI's interfered in America's electoral politics, and blocked the will of the people, Davis lost the next race in 1949 by a landslide because of government action.

Then the FBI went after Davis. The US Justice Department indicted Davis for a statement "advocating overthrowing of the US government." Their catch-all charge, like disorderly conduct in the South, although he escaped prison, the charge and media attacks, ended Davis' political career.

Next in 1946, communists tried to adjust to Hoover and the FBI's constant attacks and changed tactics. As stated earlier, they merged the NNC, NFCL, and ILD into the Civil Rights Congress (CRC). They thought becoming known as a group dedicated to defending the constitutional rights of American citizens would shield them from the *"Cold War"* ambushes Hoover set for communists. However, Gerald Horne, William Patterson's biographer, to his credit, makes it clear that even though things didn't work out quite as they planned, Patterson and the CRC continued fighting for black people, during the *"Second Red Scare."* They refused to retreat or abandon the Communist Party during the height of the *"Cold War"* attacks.

We Charge Genocide became the point of the spear of social change for those involved with CP-USA. Hoover went to Congress, and it retaliated against CP-USA by passing the *Communist Control Act (8-19-54)*. This law effectively criminalized the Communist Party. Following that law, Attorney General Herbert Brownell Jr. declaring the CRC a subversive organization, the CRC received especially hostile attention from state authorities in both the North and South. Southern law enforcement agencies raided CP-USA offices, regularly destroying equipment and carrying off files.

Cowed by the threat of nuclear annihilation and global "totalitarianism," an intolerant and skeptical political world, sprang up and embraced the *"Cold War."* It inspired liberal Arthur Schlesinger to write *The Vital Center (1949)*. He dubbed this period the *"age of anxiety."* The CRC became increasingly isolated in that *"Cold War"* climate, as Hoover and anti-communist pressure had CP-USA's former allies running away. Enraged that agents let William Patterson slip through FBI's fingers when they had him where Hoover wanted, in Europe, Hoover continued his vendetta.

Hoover targeted both Patterson and Robeson once **_We Charge Genocide_** derailed the US' *"Cold War"* strategy of *leader of the free world*. Paul Robeson received a summons to appear before the *House on Un-American Activities Committee* in 1956. (U-tube: Afrikan MANhood! Paul Robeson in his address to the Devils in the House Un-American Activity inquiry.!) Robeson chided his *HUAC* inquisitors, for putting him on trial, not for his politics, but because he spent his life *"fighting for the rights"* of his people. *"You are the un-Americans,"* he told them, *"and you ought to be ashamed of yourselves."* But, having no shame, they rolled out *McCarthyism* to claim other black victims, showing first-hand the irrationality and dedication of those behind the *"Second Red Scare."*

Hoover used the *Alien Registration Act* to do Patterson, as he did Marcus Garvey. Even though Patterson was a lawyer, in America's unfair court system, legality was not the issue. With all white prosecutors, judges, and juries, verdicts depended upon what white people wanted. And in Patterson case, Hoover wanted revenge because Patterson had beaten him in Europe. Hoover used the *Smith Act* to create a trumped-up charge against Patterson, sending him to prison for a year. Reading the *Smith Act*, it is easy to see why the Act created legal problems for anyone the government desired to put in jail, as a communist:

Congress legislated the Alien Registration Act (aka the Smith Act, 18 USC § 2385) making it a crime to "knowingly or willfully advocate, abet, advise or teach the duty, necessity, desirability or propriety of overthrowing the Government of the United States or of any State by force or violence, or for anyone to organize any association which teaches, advises or encourages such an overthrow, or for anyone to become a member of or to affiliate with any such association"—and required Federal registration of all foreign nationals.

Anxiety caused by the *Communist Control Act (8-19-54)* pressured the CRC until it dissolved in 1956, just as the civil rights movement in the South became a mass movement. This also shows how white people can use government to create the circumstances to destroy any group it desires, but groups like the KKK, government claims they are protected by the constitution. CP-USA renegades continued exposing and denouncing discrimination in America's judicial system, segregated housing, unemployment, and other forms of disparate treatment blacks faced in both the North and South. The CP-USA hoped to continue fighting racisn in American, but was only able to unmask racism, which was **_We Charge Genocide's_** greatest contribution.

After years, as a devil-may-care swashbuckling lone rider, fighting investigations, surveillance, harassment, imprisonment, and approaching the age of 80, William Patterson remained on the frontline fighting racism, segregation, and white supremacy. He supported the Black Panther Party and played a key role building and organizing the defense of Professor Angela Davis (Angela Yvonne Davis (1-26-1944) an American political activist, academic, and author. Davis, a prominent counterculture activist in the 1960s supported the Communist Party USA, became a targeted and charged with "aggravated kidnapping and first-degree murder," for a shootout at the Marin County courthouse, which resulted in the death of Judge Harold Haley. Davis had no involvement in the crime. But in California during the radical purge, *"all persons connected to the commission of a crime, whether directly involved in committing the act or not, constituted a principal in any crime committed."* Davis was acquitted).

Patterson drew support from prominent personalities, such as Ossie Davis, Ruby Dee, Rev. Ralph Abernathy, and Dick Gregory among others, during the turbulent period throughout the 1960s and 70s. Patterson remained a black leader of great stature and influence in the broader *Black Nationalists/Black Liberation Movement*. Walter Howard's *We Shall Be Free,* an annotated collection of original documents by seven leading African American Communists, including Patterson, is a worthy complement to those Gerald Horne considered the most valuable Black Revolutionaries of that day. Howard includes a section of **_We Charge Genocide_** (1951) in his book. He reiterated,

"That petition, presented to the UN, charged the US Government with genocide against the 'Negro people.' Supported by documentary evidence and based on the Genocide Convention adopted by the UN General Assembly in December 1948. Together these two books make a most welcome contribution to the literature on the CP-USA, the American left, and the struggle for racial progress during the twentieth century."

The Other Blacklist: An Alternative View to the Second Red Scare

All the Communist Party's work in the black community was missing from my education, in or out of school. Believing Hoover's propaganda, I could not have formed an accurate opinion about communism or communists, even if they had been organizing in Memphis. Nevertheless, though I held deeply negative attitudes about them, as people and an organization, nothing I believed about them was good or true. My thoughts on the subject were drawn directly from Hoover's "good American" propaganda playbook. Thinking about it now, it seems, "mental closure," filled in the blanks with his rhetoric, anytime the subject came up.

However, once I became an Invader and involved in social change, I still did not have an understanding of communism that cleared up my confusion. My lack of knowledge left me assuming things without any real evidence. The results were in between what happened and what I imagined and guessed about, regarding what the story truly was and why. Without knowing the actual circumstances, what I thought I knew, but never really thought about, regarding communists, left me ignorant, even if my speculation was correct, at a particular point.

The problem for me, and anyone who can identify with my previous scenario, arose when I needed to act on what I thought I knew, but never thought about. How does one know whether they are acting on real or imagined information in such situations? I offer my experiences with communism, as my case in point. More than communism, my dilemma was more about the cultural development of African Americans. I had no idea how Black Arts developed, let alone the role communists played in its origin. Especially important here is, without real knowledge of communism's impact on black culture, I could not answer the questions that began this whole discussion, which was "How did Black Arts develop?"

My first assumption was the society—meaning white people, who were in control of everything—paid for both. That assumption led me to take a whole range of things for granted related to black culture. A second assumption, related to this subject, occurred when I became a black power activist in 1967. A community organizer, again, I assumed, but for different reasons, society funded such activities, as it had funded the development of Black Arts. These erroneous assumptions, I believe, were shared by most activists in the black liberation struggle. I make this statement because we knew black people had not funded them, besides activists were not saying anything to the contrary to my knowledge.

Our whole vision of the future going forward was driven by the belief, *"When the money comes from white folks, we will be able to develop and implement the changes that we planned."* We acted on that misconceptions, but we also had no idea what white people would provide the money.

The 400th: From Slavery to Hip Hop

Of course, *"no money ever came"* from any place, and the social changes we envisioned never happened on the level we imagined. My point in this scenario is to highlights my eventual question, *"If the society paid for the black community's artistic and cultural developments, in the 1920s (the Harlem Renaissance), why were they not doing so in the 1960s?"* The other part of my dilemma was not as much an assumption as ignorance.

Growing up under "Boss" Crump's despotism in Memphis, as the original title *"Mr. Crump Don't 'llow that Round Here,"* which became W.C. Handy's *"Memphis Blues"* reflects my problem. There were three things, among others, the "Boss" did not allow in Memphis. First, Unions that did not strictly enforce segregation were out. Next, no *Marcus Garvey's UNIA*, because that would get you tarred and feathered then run out of town, if not lynched. Lastly, followed second place closely, but it was the most severely sanctioned was communism or communists, who definitely deserved lynching.

So, like the **UNIA,** all I knew about communism came straight out of J. Edgar Hoover's propaganda playbook, newspapers, movies, and TV. Most assuredly, the brainwashing I received, while in the US Air Force, locked the door on that subject. Readers must understand that in black communities, like Memphis, with *"Cold War"* investigations, the *Red Scare/McCarthyism* witch hunts, and fear of losing jobs on everyone's mind all the time, communist or ism were words black people did not want coming out of anyone's mouth in their presence. The mere mention of the word could draw unwanted attention from white folks, and only bad things happened in that case.

Now that I have provided proper context for my questions, the following discussion will clear up why I was confused about communism, once I became a black power activist. Through black power, I learn about communism, but the answers to my question did not come until I began researching **"The 400th"**. Going through books, articles, blogs, videos, and other sources, I encountered several very enlightening accounts on the Communist Party's role in the development of black Arts—artists, writers, dancers, and other types of performers—beginning in the 1920s. Unknown to me, but I learned communists provided the black community much-needed support—financial and instructional—and other assistance that continued into the late 1950s. These accounts told a very different story than the one I imagined and truly explained why *"the money ever came."*

The history of the CP-USA is intimately involved with the black cultural movement, which came to life in the 1920s and began expressing itself again most profoundly in the 1960s. Coming to understand the impact of the US Communist Party at that point, I realized the tremendous influence it had on the growth and overall development of black people. CP-USA did not lecture black people about what they needed to do, as most white Americans of Hoover's ilk. They jumped in with training and financial support for black Arts productions.

Black art and culture was not something explained during my education or that other black student received from school books or regular college textbooks.

The history of the CP-USA reflects a radically different story than American education provided. So, I will establish first that the Communist Party was a real "political" party in the United States, not a "storefront operation or organization." The federal government's refusal to accept the Communist Party as a real "political" party became the source of its problems. The US government promulgated rules to keep communist off ballots or worked surreptitiously to defeat any candidate that espoused communist views. The idea was to make CP-USA appear a threat because it was help black people.

Nevertheless, CP-USA had candidates, who campaigned and won elections, as did Benjamin J. Davis Jr. in New York City (1945). Regardless of what one may think of communists, the Communist Party represented the interest of millions of people in the US, as the Democrat and Republican Parties, just not as many. It was only in America; the government made communism appear to be a plague that needed stamping out, while the ***"Dark Age"*** *angry white men mob madness* was pushed from the White House by Wilson and Hoover.

CP-USA was the first and only political party in America to take a formal stand against racial discrimination and devote itself—through its resources—to anti-discrimination campaigns in defense of black people. The federal government devoted its resources to fighting against anything that would advance black people and change their status as the foundation of America's *"cheap labor"* workforce. It attacked communists because they made such a commitment to black people, and more than anything that brought about their demise.

And, therein lay the problem for the CP-USA. Similar to Marcus Garvey and the **UNIA**, CP-USA was in America. Had CP-USA remained concerned only with issues that affected the white working class, it would have avoided the ire of J. Edgar Hoover and the FBI. Today, the role of that the communist Leftists played, helping black communities develop culturally—has been distorted, and its contributions were swiped out of US history altogether in many cases, according to black scholars today.

The work communists did helping black people develop the cultural and literary foundation that is now an immensely interesting and richly insightful body of research that is growing because of Mary Helen Washington's research. Mary Helen is at the forefront of research efforts to recover the lost treasures from this period, which I am investigating through this narrative.

She has provided insight that allows African Americans to rediscover this period of black history. African American history rarely contains the information Washington presents. Black history, as related to the communist party's history, has been erased from social memory and any permanent record from the 1920s through the 1970s.

I stumbled upon Mary Helen Washington's book, **_The Other Blacklist_**, published in 2015. I was looking for information about William L. Patterson, when I came across Washington's book and her research caught my eyes, like a diamond in the rough. It provided a treasure trove of knowledge with the eye-opening discovery of her book, which helped me confirm my belief, *"There is far more to the story of black culture than what the public has been allowed to know."* Learning the real story made it clear; my assumption about the American Arts community's involvement in establishing Black Arts was not only "wrong," but "misguided."

Research shows the American Arts community holds the same attitudes about Black Arts held by the rest of American society. And, that is the real point about my assumptions and questions. My assumptions were wrong, but the assumptions of white people, right or wrong, always have real consequences for black people right or wrong. For instance, during the *"Second Red Scare,"* careers were destroyed based solely on the assumptions of J. Edgar Hoover. Based on those assumptions, he destroyed the careers and lives of many black artists.

Addressing that dilemma for white people, I offer the confession (my word) of Peter Clothier. Peter describes himself as *"a nice, left-leaning, transplanted Englishman, entirely without racial prejudice."* His admission came in an article about graphic artist Charles White, written for Huffington Post entitled *'The Other Blacklist': A Very Personal Book Review*. Clothier was discussing his tribulations, getting information for his article. His statement gives credence to my earlier remarks regarding assumptions. He said;

"I made two important discoveries in the course of that work: first, that the art world, as I knew it, was fraught with systemic prejudice against African-American artists and the work they produced; and second, that I unknowingly—and shamefully—shared that prejudice.... My work, then, was not only to research my subject, but to develop a whole new mind-set about values, traditions, and aesthetic conventions I had never previously questioned. And not only that, I very soon came to realize that I'd need a new approach to the work I had set myself.

Clothier, like me and communism, is a victim of *"what he thought he knew, but never thought about,"* and this is the way it is with the story of descendants of American slavery over the last 400 years for white people and black. Clothier goes on;

As a well-schooled academic, I had learned that the first place to go, when embarking on a research project, is the library. Not much use there," in Charles White's case, *the published material was surprisingly scant. I discovered that there were only two ways to get the information that I needed. One was to go to the ultimate source himself. I did this in a series of extended interviews with both Charlie and his wife. And the second was to go directly to every other living source I could find, which meant a great deal of travel, from New York to Seattle, Washington, from Chicago to Jackson, Mississippi.*

Getting material for his story, Clothier paints a very clear picture of his difficulty obtaining information on Charles White, a very important black artist, during this time. Clothier's hunt was similar to my scavenger hunt, trying to piece together background info on the **Blues,** Beale Street, and Sunbeam Mitchell. The difficulty finding written information on black icons to satisfy skeptical white "gatekeepers" with demands they already know in most cases cannot be satisfied, due to the word of mouth culture of descendants of American slavery. And, this was the whole point of keeping slaves ignorant, and requires true persistence to overcome getting a story. More importantly, it points to the critical nature and importance of Mary Helen Washington's CP-USA's contribution to black writers who tried to tell the story of black people during the 1920s, but were shut out of the market, specifically if they were communist. Clothier went on;

It was quite a journey. To be embarrassingly honest, it was often difficult, even a scary one. Laugh at me if you will, but such was my prejudice and ignorance that the prospect of a trip north of Central Park into the depths of Harlem or down to the South Side of Chicago left this nice white guy fearful for life and limb!

Until I ventured forth, that is and encountered nothing but goodwill, generosity, and warm welcomes. I met with artists and scholars, writers and curators, and began to tap into a vital, genuinely American culture virtually unknown—except for its music and perhaps, by that time, a handful of writers—to the vast majority of American intelligentsia."

I presented Clothier's remarks and admission, because his ignorance and regret are palatable to mine, but are different at the same time. The CP-USA gift to black cultural development was huge, but the majority of white Americans have neither the courage nor honesty to make such a public acknowledgment, as Clothier.

The famous Hollywood blacklist of the 1950s was, but the tip of the iceberg of fear that gripped America, during the communist phobia or *Second Red Scare.* Even today, some black people still avoid reading about anything that mentions the word communist. Their fear is like the Old Uncle Remus fable, *"The Tar Baby,"* something might stick to them. Mary Helen Washington says of that time,

"The other blacklist"— resulted in the suppression or mis-hearing of many African American voices," **<u>"The Other Blacklist"</u>** *features six authors and artists from the Black Popular Front. It showcases the range of political views and influences that were hugely popular with black people during its time, but because of the "Second Red Scare and McCarthyism," many black artists were pushed into relative obscurity and never allowed to rehabilitate their careers, as some white artists were. Although obscure today, novelists like Lloyd L. Brown, Frank London Brown and Julian Mayfield; graphic artist Charles White; and playwright*

Alice Childress, as well as many others, who faced the fire that burned white hot against the Left, are getting a belated second look."

Drawing on a plethora of sources that included extensive FBI investigation files, first-person interviews, and archival material writing **_The Other Blacklist,_** Washington showed a real need to uncover and restore the rich history of the radical *"Black Left."* Moreover, the contributions made not only to black culture but American Art and entertainment, before and during the *"Cold War"* era, has tragically been whitewashed. During the *Blacklisting* and the *"Cold War"* period, black writers and artists played a pivotal role in advancing black cultural development. But their efforts were swiped out or swept under America's white supremacy's rug by the FBI and the CIA.

The *Red Scare* hid the essential role of Marxism, and CP-USA played bringing Art to the black community. Deleting and omitting all relevant accounts of the role CP-USA played helping to develop black American culture is a travesty. It also gives support to assumptions like mine that "white people" are responsible for the development of Black Arts. But, more importantly, this resulted in African Americans and the public in general, confused as to the real story of Black Arts, as I was.

It may seem I have applied a scattergun approach at times, presenting the history of black people, but there is a method to my madness. Without help provided by CP-USA, black Americans would not have developed culturally, as they did, during the 1920s and 30s— **"Dark Age"** *angry white men mob madness.* That story, without CP-USA's contributions, black history before the 1950s would seem only about slavery.

The real history is not presented in books. It has been supplanted with caricatures like a *"White only Left"* that existed entirely separate from civil rights activism. During the *"Cold War"* era, artists on the *"Black List,"* struggled to develop a black aesthetic, while playing major roles in other profound cultural changes. Washington's **_The Other Blacklist_** debunks the thesis of a *white-only Left*, arguing instead that the Left was *"the most racially integrated movement of that period."*

The Other Blacklist shines light on the whitewash of communist aid to black cultural development, during the *"Second Red Scare."* Washington offers an illuminating perspective, which mainstream history bastardized. She addresses specific historical omissions of particular black artists, performers, and writers, chased out of their particular professions during the *"Second Red Scare."* The government attacked many black artists as anti-American. It used stereotypes to justify discrimination. Washington posits that *"nearly every major black writer of the 1940s and 1950s in some way came under or influenced by the Communist Party or other leftist organizations."*

The CP-USA functioned more like a cultural beacon, lighting the way for black writers and artists, as it guided them through the dangerous and deadly shoals of the *"Cold War."* CP-USA was a harbor to "weather in" at the start of the coming anti-communist storm. According to Washington, the *New Left* provided not only the political inspiration for some of these artists but spaces that nurtured their talent and creativity. Providing examples, like *the South Side Community Art Center* in Chicago.

Then there was the progressive *American Negro Theatre* in Harlem, and many others, which Washington shows that communists offered the institutional structure and support necessary for the dissemination of their work. Newspapers and left-wing presses—including Paul Robeson's Harlem-based radical newspaper *Freedom* and the Marxist journal *Masses & Mainstream*—were very powerful voices. They provided forums for the publication of black leftist writers and reviews of their work.

Washington's work is an acutely needed examination of the true roots of black cultural development in America. It is needed as a major supplement that contributes immensely to the story of black survival in the throes of poverty—desperation and scarcity. **The Other Blacklist** is a body of research that illuminates the cultural struggles for slave descendants, which began in the dark times of Minstrelsy. The efforts of slaves are the earliest example of what became American entertainment.

Picking up on the ideas of the Communist Party's Popular Front strategy of the late 1930s, Washington argues that the continued influence of a *"Black literary, cultural, and political Left throughout the 1950s constituted a 'Black Popular Front'"* or a *"Black Cultural Front." "During the Cold War,"* she argues, *"when blacks were not even a blip on white Americans' cultural radar, it was in these leftist spaces of the Black Popular Front that African-American literary culture was debated, critiqued, encouraged, performed, published, produced, and preserved."* She also preaches that *"Black writers and activists who created and resisted during the height of McCarthyite repression is of vital importance."*

Washington insists through her research, *"This is the missing link in a long history of black political activism, which inextricably links to the history of the "radical Left' in America."*

The Gift that Keeps on Giving

"Why Communist help mattered?" is a question Mary Helen Washington's insightful analysis elaborates and clarifies in great detail, from both the black left and government perspectives. Beginning her analysis, which starts before the 1920s, when African American culture was in its anlage, she paints a very detail picture of black culture. It shows only Minstrelsy, as the major outlet for black performers, after emancipation. The development of black music, singing, and dancing was begun by slaves as a therapeutic release but became entertainment for slave masters.

Their folk songs and the makeshift instruments they created during slavery, led to the creation of **Blues**. These rudimentary developments began long before white saw slaves entertaining master and carried what they learned back North to start Minstrelsy. What the communist brought to the party was a broader perspective of Art. They also brought organized approaches for expressing black talent and culture. However, their most significant contribution was the expertise and financial assistance they gave that underpinned black artists fledgling artistic efforts which was unassisted in slavery.

The unfortunate truth is there was no significant effort in the American Arts community to aid African American art development move beyond plantation lifestyles. The federal government and whites in general, viewed communists' helping the black community, as a grave threat to the nation. The federal government attacked CP-USA, as though they had invaded and were helping "black men rape white women." The government did everything possible to blunt their effort eventually driving CP-USA out of America. Although it may seem America feared the communist ideology would take over, but the federal government was not concerned with communism per se. The whole game was design to deny black Americans access to anything that could help change their status as *cheap labor*. Hiding black artistic successes from the public was also a companion activity of FBI attacks.

Mary Helen Washington's thesis posits that the historical distortions and efforts to sabotage communists' help to blacks trying to develop a cultural base were engineered by J. Edgar Hoover's FBI and the CIA. Her research points out how the work communists did to kick start the artistic, and cultural advancements of black Americans were gifts that *"keeps on giving"* even today. Especially and very expressly, when one looks at their impact beyond individual artists to the tradition of art and politics, they helped develop. It becomes even more important when one looks at their help in tandem with blacks elevating the struggle for equality, justice, and socio-economic independence, as a community, CP-USA gave far more than it received.

The training and other experiences black artists of all types passed on to their children and other young people were the result of what was learned from communists. Their efforts tapped into the tradition of slaves teaching slave, during the contraband era. Sharing knowledge became a community possession and reservoir, as those who learned from communists, shared their knowledge with friends and others who did the same. Sharing and teaching one another what blacks learned from communists, has provided generations of black artists a cultural legacy that under pens **"The 400th"** party today.

Mary Helen Washington points to the real cultural and literary legacy African Americans debated during the *American Society of African Culture (AMSAC)*, at its 1959 conference. Washington charges as part of the government's sabotage and eraser of the Communist Left; the government created front groups and organizations. Supporting her charge, she points to the *AMSAC* conference in New York City as a sham.

With **The Other Blacklist,** Washington exposes federal government efforts to stop the cultural advancement of black artists and covered over the help received from communists. She charges that the federal government sabotaging Black Arts was a fact no one took seriously back in the 1950s, other than those on *the Left*. However, the public learned the truth after the *"Second Red Scare"* when courts ordered the government to release its files on radicals. Similar to **We Charge Genocide,** all charges of sabotage made by black leftists, regarding the FBI and the CIA, were true.

Those files showed, *"That the American Society of African Culture (AMSAC) was a CIA front group funded and organized to undermine communists' efforts, thereby black people's efforts, to build art and culture in the black community."* The CIA's heavy-hand influenced everything about *AMSAC*. Washington offers the black writers' conference held in 1959 as an example. That conference the—*"First Conference of Negro Writers"*—included among its participants all artists featured in Washington's book **The Other Blacklist** and many others from *the Left* and *Right*. The conference became embroiled in several fairly contentious debates between leftist radicals and rightist anti-communist liberals.

Washington went on to give examples of the CIA's heavy-hand to supports her thesis, *"The US government erased all evidence of leftist presence at the conference. There is no record of the debates or papers submitted in the official narrative of the conference published the following year. AMSAC President John A. Davis edited the conference official narrative* <u>The American Negro Writer and His Roots</u>.*"* A chauvinistic title compared to conference participants if there ever was one. Davis undercut or cut out the efforts of black women in general while obliterating any role or impact the *Left* had at the conference. He excluded panels on social protest, specifically the papers by Alice Childress and Frank London Brown.

Likewise, the closing address by Lorraine Hansberry, perhaps the most radical speech of the conference, was unceremoniously scuttled. Simultaneously, capitalizing on Hansberry's presence, popularity, and success as a writer, Davis included her photograph under the caption, *"The Conference Closes with a Note of Success."* These photographs serve as a stark reminder of the CIA's clean erasure of the *Left*. It also highlights why word of mouth is virtually the only record of black people's achievements that has endured.

The valiant and determined struggles of some black people to develop and advance was aided tremendously by communist. Keeping that story alive without a permanent record has been all but impossible. Considering what the government did to not only stop communists from helping black people but it wiped out any record of what CP-USA did to help establish black arts is known only because of the work of some very courageous researchers, like Washington. Denying black people a record of their real history of struggle has always been the goal of white America.

Presently the work of one such determined and dedicated academician—Mary Helen Washington—which I used to illustrate the US government's actions underscores Washington's very critical research. Alvin Ailey made the point this way, *"Typically throughout the 1950 and 60s, the US Department of State sponsored tours of black artists overseas. The first overseas tour of the Alvin Ailey Dance Company (1962), I was suspicious of the government's motives. I suspected we were being used as propaganda to advertise a false tolerance by showcasing a modern Negro dance group."*

Without the *VOICE* given African Americans by the *Communist Left*, descendants of American slavery may have remained caricatures, *"happy darkies singing and dancing in Minstrelsy's 'blackface.'"* Washington's thesis dovetails mine. However, we come at the problem from different environments. She saw the efforts of government repression of the Communists Left as the key. On the other hand, I got my perspective looking directly at Minstrelsy, as the beginning of American entertainment and what former slaves taught white people, just being themselves. For me, Minstrelsy is the taproot of American entertainment. Even though it was inspired by what slaves did entertaining master, they had to fight an uphill battle to get into what they invented.

I wholeheartedly embrace Washington's efforts to correct misconceptions about Black Arts. She exposed the government's campaign to destroy the record of African American culture development. Deleting the impact of the Communist Left's aid was not to hid communists presence, but to cover up any black accomplishments. Moreover, it also explains why I was so confused about the beginnings of Black Arts and why I agree with Mary Helen's thesis and assessment. Washington's research more than proves her charge of deletions and distortions were the design of J. Edgar Hoover, FBI and CIA. They used a fierce attack led by a hoard of anti-communists of all stripes to accomplish their dirty deed.

Washington not only raised the issue of America's vicious destruction of the only organization that helped black people received, unless you count

Minstrelsy's *"blackface"* caricature. She went on to point out that by distorting and destroying what communists did in the black community, and how FBI attacks deprived black American communities of a *"gift that keeps on giving."* Successfully destroying the Communist Party, then walking away from black artists in desperate need of assistance was similar to America's penniless emancipation and not providing survival resources after slavery. Former slaves penniless beginning, as Freedmen, forced them to *make something out of nothing.*

The FBI's scheme destroyed the only group willing to help the black community. Hoover's vicious trap caught hundreds of black artists, of all types, in the *Second Red Scare,* which was like a dragnet. It destroyed careers and reduced many black artists back to struggling to avoid desperation and scarcity in the graveyard of poverty in the valley of dry bones, which Rev. Lee prayed over.

Moving out of the 1950s into the 1960s, the importance of this fact will become abundantly clearer for artists, writers, performers, and those who learned to develop, organize, produce and present their works. Undoubtedly during the 1920s into the 1940s, the CP-USA taught slave descendants to stand on their own cultural feet. Mary Helen Washington's work, ***The Other Blacklist*** may not clearly and entirely delineate the legacy of the *Black Left*, in all respects, but descendants of American slavery have an opportunity through ***"The 400th"*** to demonstrate, commemorate and celebrate the CP-USA's *"gift that keeps on giving"* and establish a written record of the critical help CP-USA gave black people on the road to ***"The 400th".***

Things are Never as Imagined

The taxi stopped in front of 1038 W. Greens Alley. That was the address Granny wrote on the paper she pinned on me, putting me on the train in Darling, Mississippi. Leaving Mississippi for the first time, I was stepping into a world built on fantasies, given me by my sisters, Molly and Bernice, when they visited the farm, once school was out for summer vacation. Looking at the line of row houses, Greens Alley did not match the fairy tale image in my head. Their fantasied stories of Memphis were what I expected, but thing are never as they are imagined!!!

Everyone knew I was coming but didn't know exactly what time I would arrive. It was late evening when I walked through the door, so even Mudear was home from work. Everybody was so glad to see me. Bernice, Molly, and Willie May all hurried to greet me. Mudear picked me up and hugged me so tightly, I could hardly breathe, but it felt so good, I never wanted her to let me go.

Junior was at work, but he was not the only one not there. So, I asked, *"Where is daddy?"* Silence fell over the room, as Mudear let me down to the floor. She looked at me with blurry eyes. There was a kind of crackle in her voice as she said, *"Hmmm, your daddy doesn't live here anymore. He'll come by to see you tomorrow."* I would learn, with Daddy, it was always tomorrow. Later, Willie May, the oldest girl, told me, *"Daddy left us, and he's not coming back. So, don't ask mother anything about him; it always makes her cry."* I didn't understand, but Willie May always look out for me, so I always did what she asked.

Greens Alley appeared grim and dilapidated, even to a country boy. It was the place my father brought the family, following their late-night *"dark of the moon run,"* escaping the dreary and constant toil of life as sharecroppers. The place was certainly different from what I thought—things are never as imagined. Describing Greens Alley today is not difficult. I see the place now in my mind, almost as clearly as during those days. Psychologically, its image is etched indelibly upon my brain.

That image is of a dingy, woebegone bustling community of the downtrodden, poorest among the poor. Although I didn't see the place or the rather large families residing there in that way at the time, scarcity and desperation were permanent residents. The well-to-do would call children like us, ragamuffins, or pickaninnies.

Greens Alley was situated on a slag heap created before the strip of row houses were built, which is why it was without vegetation. So, being covered with dirt and needing washing several times a day was the kind of attention we could not get.

The ash mound belonged to Illinois Central Railroad (ICR) switching yard and roundhouse before houses came, and it grew from years of dumping coal and ash residue there. Looking out the front door, we saw the IC railyard, which buttressed Greens Alley on the Westside.

The strip of row houses dead-ended like a blind alley on the North end, where foot traffic was the only way in and out of that end. A fence on the East side separated us from the white people who lived on the next street. The street on the South end was the opening to Greens Alley and the major entrance into our little boxed-in world. Were it not for the fence that ran the length of Greens Alley; it would have been, as though we lived in white people's backyards that lived on the next street. The thing was transgressing that fence was a major violation of segregation etiquette. Today, I understand clearly the fence I saw, looking out our back door, represented a physical color line, segregation enforced, keeping blacks separated from whites.

The slag heap had double slopes, and during rainstorms, these slopes turned into sluices, channeling rain runoff from the street, right passed our front and back doors. If the rain was heavy, the slag blackened runoff collected in a pool at the North end of Greens Alley, while waiting to seep into the only culvert in the area. Even more disgusting, if the downpour was particularly heavy, houses built close to the ground at the bottom of the little hill flooded on such occasions.

Compounding that problem, pluming—water faucets and toilets—were out of doors in Greens Alley. So, along with the houses at the bottom of the second slope, toilets flooded, creating a cesspool on the lower end of the alley for several days. The scum collected, waiting to seep into the one culvert, which clogged sometimes. Blessed that we lived between the double slopes on the slag heap, we escaped the indignity of the blacken runoff containing human waste, flooding our house. Every time this disaster occurred, at least twice maybe three times a year, sometimes worse than others, which means everything at the bottom of the little hill, smelled like toilets for days.

Similar to steel mill towns, smoke from the railyard hovered over the area unless a stiff breeze blew constantly. Soot in the blacken smoke, belching from exhaust piles atop coal-burning train engines, rained down, like snow. The soot from the heavy black smoke covered everything. It collected in corners and saturated the air with a sulfur stench. Saturday was wash day because the railyard was closed on weekends. Those were the only days' everyone breathed clear fresh air and washed. Everybody looked forward to weekends.

A slum is the only word that describes this area. Nevertheless, after sharecropping, the rat-infested backwash of Greens Alley still represented a big move up from cotton fields for us. Strangely, with all its downsides, the railyard had its advantages, beyond providing jobs for those lucky enough to get one. Its greatest advantage was access to coal, which was appreciated most dearly during the cold bone-chilling months of winter.

The 400th: From Slavery to Hip Hop

The houses in Greens Alley were constructed in the late 19th century and without insulation. So, once the temperature dropped, in late fall, the cold moved in, like a relative, staying until spring. The hawk exploited every crack, as wind seeped through the thin shingled covering the outer walls of those two-room duplexes. Molly, the middle girl, always said of those times, *"After late September or early October, I never warmed up again until July!"*

Every house had wood-burning shoves. Wood was a luxury in terms of cost, but a necessity when cooking. We hated the taste of food cooked with coal. We couldn't smell any aromas, just coal. Food cooked using coal made wood, a fuel of necessity, more so than choice.

However, we use coal to warm the living room. Coal kept the potbelly shove glowing pink, warming everyone. We gathered around it daily, reading or telling stories and talking about our day. Firing train engines with coal gave the rail yard the aforementioned advantage. A huge towering coal shoot stood in the center of the switching yard, loading car after car with coal. Heavily laden coal cars spilled excess lumps, speeding along tracks. The railyard was off limited to anyone that did not work for IC.

As temperatures dropped, black men that worked in the yard and lived in the area became angels of mercy, during the bone-chilling days of winter. When the wind whistled, and shingles flapped from winter's breath, Illinois Central Railroad (ICR) coal was the cavalry for those in dire need of heat in Greens Alley. Black railyard workers signal from the top window of the coal shoot, as night yard detectives changed shifts or went to lunch. Their signal called forth small armies of scavengers that curried into the yard, scouring tracks for the much-needed bounty. Gathering up sacks, tubs, and baskets of as much coal, as one could carry, scavengers made off into the night before detectives returned. My mother and brother Tommy were among those scavengers.

Coal gathered in this manner was an especially important ritual for my family once my father walked away, leaving Mudear to struggle alone. Enduring the throes of poverty, at times, we barely stayed afloat, as the hardships of life stalked my family, like hyenas looking for a kill. I shudder to think, the sacrifices mothers, like mine, made to keep their families together.

Mudear struggled to clothe and feed five young ones; while our father moved into a house with indoor plumbing and gas heat near downtown. He worked at a bakery shop near there. When things got particularly difficult for us, Mudear would send me by the shop to ask him for help. Most times, he gave none, not even doughnuts. His usual words were, *"Tell Willie May I'll come by tomorrow."* With my father, it was always tomorrow.

Tommy, the oldest, we all called him Junior, had not become a teenager when he took an after-school job at a grocery store around the corner from the house. Like a little man, he did what he could to help the family. His job may have been the only way we had food some days.

My greatest regret for Tommy is our father stole his childhood. Junior never had a chance to be a kid. He never had a childhood, like me. He was the reason I had one. Though not tall, he seemed a giant to me. Despite being a child, Tommy carried the load of a full-grown man, before becoming a teenager. Admittedly, I may not have fully emulated his example growing up. Nevertheless, Tommy's image, helping to support the family, provided the greatest role model, the kid that I was could have. I'm so very proud and blessed to have had him as my "swashbuckling lone rider."

Arriving in Memphis in January, beginning the second semester, meant I started school a half year in the hold. I, nevertheless, was promoted to the second grade, which meant I missed most rudimentary principles upon which one's educational foundation rest. This disadvantage revealed itself most profoundly the following year when I was held back a full year in the second grade. Repeating the second grade put me behind a full year. Although I tried mightily to make up that deficit, I truly believe I was never able to fully catch up.

One day, for the first time, this big guy, with very broad shoulders, showed up at our house. Beaming a big bright smile, mother introduced him, *"This is my friend from work, Mr. Otis Gray."* Very muscular, but quiet and unassuming, Mr. Otis had a presence about him that said, *trifle at your own risk*. Even though we didn't know him, we were so glad to see him, because he made Mudear smile. After he became part of Mudear's life, things got better for the family. Mainly, not too long after Mr. Otis showed up, we moved out of the smoke-filled environment of Greens Alley and the railyard forever. He was like Jesse in the movie **"Romancing the Stone,"** he showed up and pulled us out!!!!

Readers have slogged through the *First Red Scare, CP-USA, the Beat Generation*, **We Charge Genocide**, **The Other Black List,** and *Second Red Scare* to finally arrive where the hard left turn I made beginning this discussion. Historians consider **Brown v. Board of Education of Topeka, Kansas** the greatest change for black people after emancipation. They heralded it as the second birth of freedom, and most black people agreed, but old folks said *the proof is in the pudding*. I was one of those who believed the "new birth" thesis for most of my early life, and long before beginning researching **"The 400th"**, I had learned the difference along the way.

Brown v. Board is another convoluted explanation but very necessary to put the events of the late 1940s, 50s, and 60s into a proper perspective about why descendants of slavery are still trying to make that statement a reality. Dominating those decades, **Plessy v. Ferguson**—segregation and white supremacy—has denied black Americans equal rights and access to America's bounty, while barring the door to fair courts and relegated them on the bottom of society as *"cheap labor"* in the US economic system with scarcity and desperation. All of that is a mouth full but that again is what you have read getting here, only to make another hard u-turn. However, this u-turn is because **Brown** was not the change African Americans were told or believed it was.

Newspapers predicted **Brown** would be the fulfillment of emancipation; rather, the life blacks have endured since **Brown** tells a very different story altogether. I remind readers of this narrative's thesis that *white and black people can observe or experience the same event at the same time from the same position, yet come away with two entirely different scenarios*. And, that is the point here; the **_"definition of freedom."_** White people when thinking and looking at a black man, and juxtaposed against that definition never think the same thoughts when they look in the mirror.

The previous point became even sharper, after black people began their thrust to live out the promise of **Brown** and demanded recognition as **human beings** received an entirely different response. My case in point is the UN when **We Charge Genocide** was presented. That petition—**We Charge Genocide**—became a wild card in the US' marked deck. Clarifying that statement, as I said, requires another tortuous recapitulation of the many unforeseen, unexpected, and unintended consequences which flowed from **Brown v. Board of Education.** It was supposed to be the answer to descendants of American slavery's denial of equality, justice, and freedom. Having endured their penniless emancipation, segregation, white supremacy, discrimination and the **_"Dark Age"_** *angry white men mob madness* in the US, over the previous 89 years, descendants of

American slavery, thought the promises of **Brown,** would finally be the fulfillment of their long-awaited reprieve from oppression, desperation and scarcity.

The previous discussions, though centered on the CP-USA, including J. Edgar Hoover and the FBI's efforts to shut it down, were really about America's claim of being *"leader of the free world."* America used that claim or slogan to establish hegemony, building its powerful geopolitical coalition against the Soviet Union. Without this claim, America would not have been unable to isolate the USSR, with its charge of being a totalitarian system, characterized by absolutism.

With that charge, the US projected Russia as the *"evil empire."* America spent 1945 through 1953, including the Korean War, bullying the world with its *"leader of the free world"* rhetoric. **We Charge Genocide** gave Russia and other communists a powerful counter-charge against America, which called its hand with, *"America is the world's biggest hypocrite."* The key here is the unexpected, unforeseen, and unintended consequence that developed at the end of WWII when this whole game started at the birth of the United Nations (UN).

At the UN's birth, American made it an instrument of its foreign policy and because of America's huge bankroll. It took control of political issues and debates in the UN through what became known as the *"Cold War."* Although the UN did not come out in support of William Patterson and Paul Robeson's petition, **We Charge Genocide,** nevertheless, the fact that Robeson and Patterson got it into the hands of UN delegates, whether the world acknowledged it or not, America could not deny it, without admitting its existence and answering its charges.

That debate was something the US definitely did not want in public. **We Charge Genocide** was not a "word of mouth accusation." It was a written statement that gave black people's argument more power than ordinary pawns on the US' international chessboard. It gave the USSR control of the middle of America's *"leader of the free world"* international chessboard. America, which was trying to rule the world, had to get around Russia's charge before the UN of *"the world's biggest hypocrite,"* which it was because of what the **We Charge Genocide** petition showed.

So, **We Charge Genocide** became a game changer this time around for the USSR, in America's international chess game. Though un-heralded, **We Charge Genocide** because of Russia occupied a strategic position. The fact it was submitted to officials of the UN, an international body, as well as circulated across Europe, during William Patterson's death run, the US could not ignore it and pretend it did not exist. Every time Russia voiced the charge, *"America is the world biggest hypocrite"* before the international body everyone knew to what the Russians were alluding.

There is still one more small but vital complication in this convoluted scenario for America, which added more drama to America's *"Cold War"* charade. On June 25, 1950, the *"Cold War"* became a "hot war," as North Korea invaded

South Korea, following a series of clashes along their border. America, as *"leader of the free world,"* brought the United Nations into the "hot war" as an ally of South Korea, but the UN did not have an army. So the US supplied the bulk of the troops and tried to get other nations to ante up with troops.

The *"Cold War"* drastically changed the geopolitical world black people faced, even though they were not players. America's *"Cold War"* strategy made proxy wars a real option for the US, but very dangerous for the world. America claimed to be defending freedom-loving South Korea against an attempt by communists to dominate it. The US waved it flag *"leader of the free world"* in everyone's face, especially the USSR. But of course, the Soviet Union also entered the fray between South and North Korea, along with China. They gave North Korea assistance, as part of the *communist bloc*. That's when things got really hot.

America was the principal force aiding South Korea in terms of troops and material. The upshot of all this was the UN became the talking battlefield of that war. While the *communist bloc*, led by the USSR, became the "mouthpiece" for North Korea, America was the ventriloquist for the *free world*. A year after the Korean War heating up, **_We Charge Genocide_** hit the UN (1951). America's blood pressure shot up, as though Russia had developed a new kind of A-bomb.

Every time the USSR charged America with being a *"hypocrite,"* before the world forum, it was as though a huge mushroom cloud formed in the ventriloquist's throat, choking off America's vociferous response. Once the *communist bloc* began impeaching America with the charge of being a *hypocrite*, the game changed for the Russians. The USSR scored with that move every time, like a "Dr. J" crossover between the legs and behind the back dribble move, before making a house call from the free-throw line. Communist fans went wild on the sidelines every time the ball was in Russia's hands.

Russia, with the charge of *hypocrite*, kept the ball on the US's end of the court. It forced America to play defense, which was not its forte. Unable to call offensive fouls, heads of governments, supporting America in UN debates, were only able to move their lips, while America's words came out their mouths. Once William Patterson made his death run across Europe, **_We Charge Genocide_** had European leaders choking on America's words. Those supporting US claims of representing freedom and justice around the world drew howls and catcalls because everyone knew America had re-enslaved black people, holding them prisoners on the land in the South, while denying them access to a fair court system. **_We Charge Genocide_** detailed how America had deployed convict leasing and sharecropping, which made black Americans *"cheap labor"* in its capitalistic economic system of slavery without chains. America's claim, *"leader of the free world,"* rang hollow, making other world leaders backing America, *hypocrites* also.

Caught between yielding Russia's point of *hypocrisy*, which was **_We Charge Genocide's_** point, the US had to either concede the game or come up with a game-changing defense. Thus enter **_Brown v. Board of Education of Topeka_**.

Brown became the player to be named later on America's outmanned team without a lockdown defense against the USSR *hypocrisy* fast break. Thus ***Brown v. Board of Education of Topeka*** was like Kareem Abdul-Jabbar began playing center, as the US' player to be named later against the Russians *hypocrisy* fast break. The USSR was driving their point up the middle for scores as America's *"leader of the free world"* offense, fumbled the ball without a score every time down court. ***Brown v. Board*** was like feeding the ball to Kareem Abdul-Jabbar for slam dunks each time up the floor, reestablishing America's geopolitical game of monopoly.

Brown was a very sophisticated scheme, but a move only intended to save face. It required cooperation, from even the racists on it foreign policy team. This was like white boys that hated playing with black guys on integrated basketball teams in the 50s and 60s, because they would never be stars, but went along to stay on the team. America was exposed by <u>**We Charge Genocide,**</u> which made ***Brown*** the only counter to the USSR's charge of *"the world's biggest hypocrite"* against America.

Brown became America's cover defense to answer the USSR's *hypocrisy* charge, rather than changing its racist white supremacy policies. For millions of blacks Americans and me as well, it seemed ***Brown v. Board of Education of Topeka*** was pulled from beneath America's racist hood like a rabbit out of a hat. Brown was identical to "Boss" Crump appointing black men to Memphis' police force, not like WDIA's owners hiring Nat D, defying segregation policies.

The thing is ***Brown*** was not an act of Congress; neither was it an executive order from the President. Southern white racists Democrats controlled Congress, as the Republicans now, and nothing was happing there. The president would have had to issue an executive order to give the appearance real change was occurring. But, that would have made federal agents or troops available to enforce ***Brown***, as Pres. U. S. Grant did against the KKK to enforce Reconstruction. A Supreme Court decision, on the other hand, bought time for America's politicians to disguise ***Brown v. Board,*** as a real social change measure, not a *"war measure."* This is very relevant, in that, the Court had no enforcement apparatus, so its decision had no bite. It depended on the Chief Executive to enforce its edits and Pres. Eisenhower, a Republican, was not about to mount up and lead the charge on that fast break. Moreover, neither the President, the State Department, nor Congress, publically acknowledged <u>**We Charge Genocide**</u>. So the public debated ***Brown*** while nothing changed.

The US Supreme Court's decision gave the appearance the US was making changes to address the charges in "<u>**We Charge Genocide,**</u>" while nothing happened that changed white supremacy and segregation in America. ***Brown's*** hocus-pocus sleight of hand was only smoke and mirrors, a charade to counter

Russia's charge of *"America is the world's biggest hypocrite,"* which is obvious and clear today.

Nothing significant happened to change the fact that African Americas still do not have the same rights as white people. The Supreme Court found the magic that fooled the world. The rabbit, the Supreme Court, pulled from under its racist hood, was dead on arrival. The Supreme Court's hollow statement, *"State-sanctioned segregation of public schools was a violation of the 14th amendment and was therefore unconstitutional,"* struck down *"separate but equal,"* but the ruling did nothing to change the racist culture and status quo of white supremacy in America, which remains today.

The Court did not offer any implementation or enforcement procedures; it gave only statements. The Court's, **Brown v. Board of Education,** ruling turned its back on descendants of American slavery, again as the federal government did to newly freed slaves, with it penniless emancipation (1863). Nevertheless, it accomplished the US' goal; it placated Europe. Europeans wanted to believe America was making changes in its racist regime of white supremacy and was extending freedom, justice, and equality to African Americans on all levels of society.

Chief Justice Earl Warren (1953-1969) took over a very conservative Supreme Court, which is why I feel **Brown v. Board of Education** was a hat trick with smoke and mirror. It made it appear Warren had pulled out some real magic, being Chief Justice for less than a year (1953). **Brown** was his first big opinion for the new court under new leadership. Warren's actions said more about why he was selected Chief Justice than about his desire to provide justice for black people in America. Without a real track record, doing what America needed to help mask its racist **Plessy v. Ferguson** face was easy. **Brown** was a pageant of pretense to disguise segregation and give the appearance of real change, while keeping its practices, as the law of the land and that has not changed.

The Court, in rendering its decision made it seem, it turned its back on *separate but equal*—**Plessy v. Ferguson**—segregation. The Supreme Court had backed **Plessy v. Ferguson** almost unanimously for 58 years, and most of those judges were still sitting on the court. The Warren Court made very very narrow rulings that involved interstate commerce, which did not address *separate-but-equal* in America. Up against the Soviet Union and world communism, the United States needed a face-saver. America needed to fool the world. More than anything, the US wanted Europeans to believe it had committed itself to serious social changes to justify its *"cold war"* claim *"leader of the free world."* **Brown v. Board** was supposed to reflect this change but was just a charade.

Brown v. Board of Education was "only" a political stunt and not intended to change the status quo of white supremacy. Brown was never intended to *"giving black people the same freedom white people enjoyed."* And, today, black people still do not have that. **Brown** was more of a public talk-O-thon, like the *Cold War* in the

UN. ***Brown*** was a stunt to placate white people in Europe that were embarrassed by what **_We Charge Genocide_** showed the world. Reading **_We Charge Genocide_**, Europeans saw a repeat of what America had condemned the Nazis and Adolf Hitler for doing to Jews in concentration camps, during the 1930 and 40s. Reading what America's media said about ***Brown v. Board of Education,*** they covered up America's legal sleight of hand. Then Europeans had no way of knowing, like black Americans, the USA never intended to deliver on the promises made in ***Brown***.

The simple fact is there was nothing new in ***Brown*** that had not been presented to the Supreme Court previously, in challenges to *separate but equal*—***Plessy v. Fergusons*** for 58 years. The court had litigated all issues in ***Brown***. Courts from Chief Justice Melville Fuller (1896) to Fred M. Vinson (1953) had sustained ***Plessy v. Fergusons*** since 1897. Many of these same "august" white men were the judges that voted to sustained ***Plessy v. Ferguson***—*separate but equal*—almost without descent, except John Marshall Harlan, and were still on the Warren Court. If those judges had recused themselves from this case, based on their past racism, there would not have been anyone to hear the case, but Warren, maybe not even him?

So, with ***Brown***, the world was lead to believe Warren, a newcomer, with only the force of his personality, because the legal arguments had failed to persuade them for 58 years, swayed these same racist individuals to strike down J. Edgar Hoover's and their legacy of white supremacy and segregation. Not only is this highly unlikely, but it is also preposterous, as an outcome. ***Brown v. Board of Education*** was only smoke and mirrors, and history has born my assessment out. Previous Courts had consistently refused to give slave descendants relief from racial discrimination and disparate treatment. They refused to allow descendants of American slavery to change their status going back to 1897. Only communists in America had seen black people as ***human beings*** and tried to address their inequality and J. Edgar Hoover and Congress ran them out of the country. Again, for me, as it was for most Americans, ***Brown v. Board of Education*** came out of nowhere.

More than anything, the record of ***Brown v. Board of Education*** clearly shows the decision was not about benefiting black people or helping them achieve equality and justice. Had that been the case the Warren Court could have done as US Supreme Court Justice John Marshall Harlan, after the lynching of Ed Johnson in Chattanooga, Tennessee. The US Supreme Court, at the behest of Justice John Marshall Harlan did something no other Court did. It put a sheriff and his deputies on trial and in jail for their part in Johnson's lynching. Contrarily, the Warren Court did as Woodrow Wilson, it simply refused to use its power to back up it's ruling on behalf of black people.

Brown was part of America's *"Cold War"* strategy against the Soviet Union. Similar to the federal government's *"Second Red Scare,"* once the court decided

Brown, it had accomplished its mission. The federal government had finished its job and walked away. The whole charade was not an effort to provide black people with first-class citizenship and access to America's bountiful resources, like all other Americans. The Supreme Court had no intention of "disturbing the undisturbed," "status quo," segregation and white supremacy in America. Black people were prisoners on farms and in factories across the South. They were virtually locked up in the South, without mobility, access to fair courts, or the right to vote and the Supreme Court knew this. They followed Woodrow Wilson who accomplished all of that as president.

We Charge Genocide seriously undercut America's claim of *"leader of the free world."* Conservative leaders expected black people to continue waiting on the Supreme Court and the federal government to act on their behalf, as most had done since the end of Reconstruction (1877). However, the example of William Patterson and Paul Robeson, like Marcus Garvey, gave black Americans new ideas. Regardless of whether one agrees with this analysis or not, they have to agree that African Americans in 2020 still do not have or cannot exercise the same rights as white people, only black men and women are being murdered by police with impunity. If ***Brown*** had done its job, and politicians fought as hard to end Woodrow Wilson program of segregation and white supremacy, as he did establishing them, the US would not still be a racist nation!!!

The US was unable to prevent Paul Robeson and William L. Patterson's petition—***We Charge Genocide***—from reaching UN delegates. Consequently, America could not keep the world from reading about racism, segregation, white supremacy, convict leasing, sharecropping, and the *"Dark Age" angry white men mob madness* in the US. ***We Charge Genocide*** exposed America, as the liar and hypocrite it truly is. The world accepted Nazi genocide against Jews in Germany, but after WWII ended and on America's insistence, it condemned Germany. However, there was no one willing to step up and condemn America for it genocide, not even Germany.

When America's pogrom was revealed—***We Charge Genocide***— against African Americans in 1951, the UN refused to hear or speak out about the oppression, segregation, *"Dark Age" angry white men mob madness* and white supremacy in America it revealed and today still has not acknowledged receiving it. ***We Charge Genocide*** was such an embarrassment to the international community it muted the UN and European's leaders support for America. This threatened America's charge and sleight of hand of ***Brown v. Board of Education.*** The US threatened to withdraw its financial support from the UN and walk away from the UN and Europe, as Trump today with the World Health Organization (WHO). The US threatened to allow Russia to run the world, if the UN recognized ***We Charge Genocide*** publically, in any way. America's threats left descendants of American slavery with only the CP-USA, as a defender, which at the same time the US was chasing it out of the country with the *Second Red Scare*.

Relegated to second class status below even other black human beings across the world, the UN was recognizing and allowing them to speak on their own behave, and they would not speak up when the UN refused to recognize African Americans. The UN was totally afraid and consumed with losing US dollars than what was happening to poor black people in the South. The fact that black people in the South were locked on the bottom of America's capitalistic *"cheap labor,"* economy, and without an economic base, suffering discrimination, oppression, no fair courts and denied VOICE, the UN continued supported America's hypocrisy, mading Europeans and the UN hypocrites.

Germany was financially bankrupt and defeated, charging it with genocide was easy and did not cost the UN anything; it was what America wanted. But on the other hand, losing America's money, which the US was gaining and accumulating via its continued re-enslavement of African Americans since 1900, was all that matter to the UN and Europe.

US dollars were the "big stick" America used to beat the UN and Europe over the head until it accepted US genocide. Europe always cowed and knuckled under to America. So the world and the UN agreed to allow US genocide to continue against America's slavery descendants.

African Americans, especially **_We Charge Genocide_** supporters, believed by exposing that the US re-enslaved black people in the 1890s, would move the UN to speak up for slave descendants. Instead, the UN, like Great Britain's Parliament, during the extended debate over ending the **Trans-Atlantic Slave Trade**, before *"Amazing Grace"* and the *"flag deception scheme,"* racist in America continued benefitting from racism. Slave descendants believed the UN would condemn the US, as it condemned Nazi Germany for its genocide against Jews, once it learned the truth that supposedly free human beings in America were locked in convict leasing and sharecropping by the millions, as free labor—slavery without chains.

The UN's refused to act according to its own charter on behalf of black Americans for fear of losing American dollars that is what the UN's denial was all about. Its decision to keep silent, regarding **_We Charge Genocide_** left black Americans, still outside the human community. African Americans remained locked on the bottom of America's economy of *free labor*, sharecropping, and convict leasing most until death. The UN's decision not to accept oppressed and exploitation of people, freed around the world from legal human bondage rased hopes. But the UN's decision left America's descendants of slavery in 1950 and even today in 2020, still locked on the bottom of America's cheap labor economy as *"wage slaves."*

Even though the UN turned its back on black people in America, **_We Charge Genocide_** created a small bit of relevance for African Americans. Black people affected America's geopolitical standing in the world. **Brown** was supposed to change racism and white supremacy in America's society, but it only went underground. Slowly, the major impact of **Brown v. Board of Education** began unfolding. After a long protracted fight, black and white signs came down, but in reality, white supremacy and segregation only changed its look, like Confederate soldiers, after the Civil War changed clothes.

Brown on the ground *"left black people without the same freedom as that white people enjoy."* Similar to emancipation, Civil War, Civil Rights Bill of 1866, 13th, 14th, and 15th Amendments, the freedom **Brown** gave black people was still tether to the 3/5 Compromise and discrimination. **Brown** left descendants of American slavery trapped in a state or condition created only for them. White people were happy with this description of freedom for black people, crafted by the Supreme Court to fit the 1950s, and they are even happier today in 2020.

I can remember, after **Brown v. Board of Education** came down, looking for changes that never came to Memphis, Tennessee, or the rest of America. The legal sleight of hand in **Brown v. Board of Education** exposed America's hypocrisy and pretended "about-face" on *"separate but equal."* The US Supreme Court never mandated American restructure its society with freedom and justice for all. Without restructuring America's segregated white supremacists society, the status of descendants of American slavery will not change. Segregated and white supremacy excluded black Americans from enjoying America's bounty, as white people.

Brown did a mind wipe on Europeans; they gave America a pass, falling for and swallowing its *leader of the free world* "*Cold War*" bull. The reason America was able to conduct a similar genocide against descendants of American slavery, as Adolf Hitler's Nazi reign of terror against Jews, was the world does not care about black skin. American dollars were what matter to the world. Europeans gladly knuckled under to America, because its victims were not white. Europeans didn't see black people as human beings or cared enough to stand up to America over black people. We're not talking about 1819, not even 1919, but 1954 and, more importantly, 2020.

The thing here is, during this time in America, there was a big debate about reducing or eliminating US contributions to the UN. A "Dixiecrat," US Sen. Strom Thurmond of South Carolina, an earlier version of Sen. Joe Manchin, led this debate. He was making threats to run for president in 1952. Withdrawing from the UN was his big issue for the 1952 presidential campaign. Thurmond, Truman nor Eisenhower mentioned **_We Charge Genocide,_** which I, like most Americans were unaware. I realize today, after researching **_We Charge Genocide,_** that "withdrawing from the UN" was a code, like preserving *America's capitalistic economic system*, to disguise what white people were really talking about from black people. Brown was the compromise not only to fool Europe but keep southern democrats—Dixiecrats—in the fold on America's *"Cold War" "leader of the free world"* smoke and mirrors charade.

All the legal sleight of hand, around ***Brown*** on the ground, is best understood from the perspective of an elementary school kid back then. I'm talking about the world of segregation in America, as I joined my family in Memphis and began school in 1949. Segregated schools re-enforced the sense of second class that black children endured becoming educated. Besides being relegated to inferior buildings and other facilities, the books issued black students told our whole second-class story.

The Memphis Board of Education sent any new books it purchased to white schools. Black schools got the old outdated books white kids wore out. The previous owners had torn covers lose on these books. If they were still attached, the edges were frayed and worn. The worn covers and pages said what the board thought of educating black students. Pages were torn or missing altogether. White students underlined passages and scribbled throughout these books. But, the most humiliating part of this fiasco was the dates and names of white children assigned these books were still legible. Having their books told us who the idiots were that scribbled all over them. When teachers passed them out, they called them "new" books, and if you lost one, your parents paid for the new book you never received.

Everyone hoped to get a book; the previous owner understood the purpose of books. Everything was this way regarding what the Memphis Board of Education supplied black students. They got hand-me-down, secondhand books to match their second-class education and status. I feel the knowledge we received would have been the same were it not for the very dedicated black teachers, who were determination to educate black children, whether they wanted education or not.

The **Brown** on the ground resulted in court battle to support the excuses Southern Boards of Education gave for not educating black children. On May 17, 1954, the day the decision in **Brown v. Board of Education** came down, I was a 4th grader. That day I remember teachers scurrying around, all excited, saying, *"Jim Crow is dead."* When they explained **Brown**, today it is clear to me, they really wanted to believe what they told us, *"segregation is over and white people cannot deny black people rights anymore."*

I still have salient memories of euphoric teachers, making predictions, as school ended. Their rosy scenarios sounded as if black and white kids would be attending the same schools in the fall as classes began. I recall how **Brown** created great expectations for the coming school year. Black students anticipated real changes as school began. However, nothing changed and rosy scenarios planted in black children's heads about segregation's demise grew to become more flowers on the open grave of poverty.

My mother was cautiously optimistic about **Brown.** Having grown up in Mississippi, she had never completely embraced integrationist rhetoric. She identified with that mindset and appropriated some of its socio-political ideals, but she always said, *"Well, we'll see?"* Like religion, I accept her perspective as my own. Politically aware but not an activist, I remember Mudear as a vocal supporter of President Harry S. Truman.

Mother's first real involvement with politics was the 1952 presidential campaign, as a volunteer for Adlai Stevenson. Although only nine, I remember walking door to door with her soliciting votes. We were living in Riverside when John F. Kennedy ran for president, and I was attending George Washing Carver High School. We were all in during that campaign. I had no real idea who Kennedy was, beyond a face on the cover of *Look* or *Life* Magazine.

Nevertheless, we canvassed the community without reservations, and his victory gave everybody hope that **Brown** would finally redeem black people's faith. Following that election, I began viewing the needs of black people in political terms. Kennedy's run for the White House changed the way I viewed white people, as maybe not all the same and government as the means to lift oppression off the backs of black families. Black people accept Kennedy's rhetoric, making him seem a different kind of white man. I believe that perceptions change the way I thought about America.

Isolated in the southwest corner of Memphis, and especially in Riverside, we accepted what leaders like the NAACP told us. Their "New Negro" ideals had not produced any real changes, yet everyone accepted its leadership. Its rationale/rhetoric had not changed since the 1920s. Basically "black people needed to gain the acceptance of white people, if they wanted to progress." Very Booker T. Washingtonian in their integrationist/assimilationists emphasis, but in reality, it said black people needed to *"pull themselves up by their bootstraps;"* and *"make something out of nothing,"* as always.

So, teachers' visions of **Brown** on the ground was, *"little black boys and little white girls,"* joining hands together in school. Identical to this narrative's theme *"white people can observe or experience the same exact situation from the same position and time, but develop entirely two different scenarios."* The same dreamy vision in white women heads created the desire to pick up the **"Dark Age"** *angry white men mob madness,* where they convinced white men to leave it in the 1940s. Although there were not any physical lynchings, but the vitriolic outrage white women expressed had the same mental effect and impact on little black children, trying to get educated. Daily, wild, angry mobs of white women surrounded elementary schools each morning, taunting and terrorizing black children. They drew federal troops into the field, beginning with Little Rock, Arkansas (1957), igniting a forth Civil War in America. Battles over busing raged from El Paso to Boston, from 1950s well into the late 1980s.

Facing litigation, as southern "red necks" filed lawsuit after lawsuit, the US Supreme Court back-peddled on **Brown**, retreating toward **Plessy v. Ferguson** with every decision. **Brown,** on the ground, became a charade of equality. Segregationists, anti-busing/state's rights advocates, had the Supreme Court on their side, as slave master in 1857 **Scott v Sanford**. Supreme Court justices could no longer hide their hand, around black people throats, as they choked the life out of their hopes.

The Court continued playing Woodrow Wilson's hand dealt black people. The Court did nothing to change the situation or defend its decision for black people. Anti-busing forces ran wild like "red neck mobs" in the 1920s or far-right "Proud Boys" in 2020, cheered on by Donald Trump. Fighting equal education for black children from Dallas to Boston, the federal government stood calmly by and let white people express their outrage, while police used billy clubs, dogs or water hoses against black children at schools and in the streets.

Again, the practical effect of **Brown** on the ground for black people was black kids in school getting the same education white kids never happened. Those visions produced angry mobs that terrorized black children, evoking images like **Red Summer** and the **Dark Age** *angry white men mob madness* days of lynching, in their parents' minds. Fueling a white backlash that rekindled racial fires, which blazed across America, the resulting impact on black people was similar to Woodrow Wilson's do-nothing policies in 1919.

Today, thinking back to the way my great-great-grandfather and other former slaves felt at the end of the Civil War and their expectations for emancipation, black teachers sounded similar. I know today, in reality the results were the same. Neither Reconstruction (1866) nor ***Brown v. Board of Education*** (1954) produced fundamental changes in America for descendants of slavery. Readers need to remember and understand those two attempts were American's only actions ever taken supposedly aimed at addressing the debt owed former slaves, after working for free since 1619 and the ninety or so years of convict leasing and sharecropping as well.

The Awakening of the Counterculture

The US Supreme Court's decision in **Brown v. Board of Education** in 1954 was another disappointing outcome for descendants of American slavery's drive to get first-class status. It is not that **Brown** did not have some needed positive effects for African Americans; it did not live up to its pronouncements regarding freedom, justice, and equality for black people, compared to other Americans. Most of all, **Brown** did not provide access to fair courts, which was the major problem in the US. White people expect African Americans to be happy with some less-than-status they defined. The Supreme Court created expectations it had no intention of fulfilling regarding the Constitution's promise to all Americans. **Brown v. Board of Education's** impact on inequality, injustice, white privilege, discrimination, and disparate treatment against African Americans was negligible; then only because of young progressives stand.

The thing everyone, particularly politicians, lawyers, Judges and Supreme Court justices continued pretending that **Brown** was needed when the Civil Rights Bill of 1866 was still on the book as current law. That is the charade of Brown; it was unnecessary, except for the UN game to cover over **We Charge Genocide.** the proof is Bryon Allen's recent suit (2020) against Comcast, which he filed under the **Civil Rights Bill of 1866** was not rejected but sent back to the 9th Circuit Court of Appeal. If the **Civil Rights Bill of 1866** was not current law his case would have been thrown out of court. My question is, with that logic what was the purpose of Brown v Board?

Previously, most of this discussion has been about the impact of the US government and white people on descendants of American slavery. Now, this narrative, like the change in slaves' behavior after David Walker' **Appeal**, follows African Americans hard left turn that began in the 1940s to look at black Americans impact on America. The real power of young people in the US began to emerge during the 1950s, as their disregard for the restrictions of the *color line*, segregation, and white supremacy continued impacting their lives .

CP-USA, during the 1940s, brought young progressives into the marshaling years of the 1950s. Words like methodize, muster, organize, and mobilize described the frenzied activities they engaged, while readying themselves to attack inequality in the South. The strategy they implemented against the South in the mid-to-late 1950s, followed years of soul searching. Young progressives sought to redefine themselves and their world, as the *Beat Generation* offered direction.

The *"Beat"* scene of the mid-1940s repeated itself in many places and in many ways, but on different levels. However, the results were very similar. The magnitude of the physical signs may have been less in some places than in others, but their psychological development brought new behaviors that reflected real changes. I call it a marshaling time because the counterculture seemed to be poised, gathering strength for years, as it probed for weaknesses in a system that had proven impervious to attack.

This time around, however, **_We Charge Genocide_** had exposed what seemed a real vulnerability in the heart of the South, as the citadel of American racism. Young people came to understand the South's soft underbelly was it could not keep the world blind, deaf, and dumb to what was happening to black people behind the *"cotton curtain"* any longer. **_We Charge Genocide_** had created a hole through which young progressives' could see how to deployed their strategy and break the grip of white supremacy on America, using and attacking with a force far smaller than the opposition in the South.

Young progressives wanted to create a sympathetic link with people around the world by staging events or situations that drew the world's attention toward the South. Readying themselves for what they knew were going to be brutal and bloody battles, yet and still, they drew courage and strength from **_"We Charge Genocide"_** and William L. Patterson's run for his life across Europe. They, like Patterson, believed the fight was worth it. Young progressives developed a new organizing technology for this new time with new tactics. The *counterculture* planned to attack the American South's soft underbelly of racism, segregation, and white supremacy in its stronghold.

Woodrow Wilson's strategy had reigned supreme since his election in 1912. Now, with the Supreme Court's unexpected decision in **Brown v. Board of Education,** young progressives believed they should strike while the iron was hot. They were determined to test their power, as well as their tactics for social change. They want to answer the question *beatsters* asked themselves, *"What does freedom mean if Americans are truly free?"* However, now they added a caveat, *"If black people are not free, neither are we?"* This caveat was not an open question asked aloud. Their commitment reflected their determination to change America, with their new vision.

The *cotton curtain* had hidden the terror, mayhem, and murder white people in the South committed against blacks, who were virtually defenseless without fair court to challenge their treatment. **_We Charge Genocide_** blew a hole in America's lies of freedom, justice, and equality. America was telling the world with **Brown** freedom for black people did not matter. So progressives wanted to create a way for the world to see through the lies and learn the truth. Looking at news reports, photographs, and films, through that hold, they would see what **_We Charge Genocide_** described was happening in the South.

A new world vision dawned, as young progressives readied their attack. Their attack woke up a sleeping world, bringing alive the horrors of segregation and white supremacy black people endured. Young progressives wanted people in Europe and across the globe to see and know what America's UN blood money was buying. That blood money bought the hateful truth in the US for black people to Europeans cowed by America's dollar power to them in newspapers at their breakfast tables.

I single out Europeans here because they were the enablers and backbone of America's *"leader of the free world"* facade. Young leftists wanted to expose America as the liar and hypocrite it truly is. After **_We Charge Genocide_** described the reality of life for black people so graphically, they were willing to throw their bodies at the problem to validate their anger and vindicate their purpose.

Emmett Till

The event that brought all of what young progressives wanted the world to know about what was happening to black people unfold in August of 1957. The following hideous example of the lack of justice in American courts reflected in previous discussions, while the virulent hateful acts of white people against black people in America all came together in this one act. Also, young progressives wanted the world to witness what was happening that created the reality for many black people in the US, and know that nothing happened to those whites that commit such heinous acts. Preceding young progressives' charge at the South, one of the most haunting and tragic events unfolded in Mississippi that affected me profoundly.

Just the tip of the iceberg of hatred and viciousness hidden behind America's *cotton curtain* under American racism, the dastardly act seared my psyche. Scotching the brains of other young blacks and white kids, as well as robbed us of contentment and any comfort derived, accommodating **Brown v. Board's** sell-out to segregation and racism. The lynching of Emmett Till touched me like a personal tragedy. Emmitt's death shattered any sense of hopefulness I had, while putting my existence into perspective, as a black man in America. His awful death was unimagined and definitely I could not forget it.

Emmett was a handsome, outgoing 14-year-old black kid from Chicago, just a couple years older than me. He was visiting his grandmother in Mississippi, as I had every summer. Roy Bryant and J.W. Milam (8-28-55) accused Emmett of flirting with a white woman twice his age, Bryant's wife. These two fully grown white men took Emmett a child to their farm, and once there they tied, bound, and beat him unmercifully several hours. They shot him in his head and threw his lifeless body into a river. This atrocity sent shivers through black families across America, but if you lived in the South, it was particularly frightening.

Although I was born in Mississippi and went back to visit my grandparents often, I never personally experienced or was made aware of the barbaric hatred some white people held for black skin. The area where my grandparents lived, and I grew up was inhabited by black sharecroppers mostly. Even though white men ran Quitman County, I never witnessed or was told of any incidents involving the Ku Klux Klan. As such, in our area, there were stories of "paddy rollers," but I never saw any.

More importantly, my folks had explained segregation and given me a strategy that enabled me to avoid trouble with white people in Mississippi and Memphis. The murder of Emmett Till made me afraid of Mississippi for the first time. That fear was not petrifying; it produced a wariness related to the viciousness of some whites, especially when they know they have the ups on you, like Emmitt.

So, I knew I had to guard my life when I was caught in a vulnerable position by more than one white man.

Only, after learning the truth of Emmitt's murder, did I realize the depth of hatred and racism some white people harbored for black skin. White people did whatever they please to blacks, and no one asked questions, even if there were complaints, nothing happened. Emmitt's murder was not like the movie *"In Heat of the Night,"* the reality was more like, *"The Liberation of L. B. Jones."* Memphis police, as all over the South, were notorious for doing dastardly things to blacks in general and prisoners in particular. Black men were found beaten to death or hanging in jail cells, frequently. Other times, black men were found on the street or in dark alleys dead, after being stopped by police, especially if the person was known to oppose the status quo.

In our minds, death lurked around every corner or behind every tree, so a black person had to be ready to run because if the police stopped you the encounter could be deadly. The outcome depended upon how whites felt at the time. Although there were many such scenes, like Emmett Till's murder, his death, seemed to magnify the danger for me a thousand times. Death came to black men at the hands of white men on account of white women—real and imagined—in many different ways.

The factors involved in a black man's death, like Emmett, depended on what was going on inside some white man's head at that moment. It may or may not have anything to do with the current situation, but if it did, their responses, on most occasions, are totally out of proportion to the incident, as with Emmitt. The metaphors **The Wizard of Oz** compared to **The Wiz** illustrate how white and black people can see or experience the same incident but develop two totally different scenarios for its occurrence.

Reading about the trial of Emmitt's murderers and its aftermath, I learned what it truly meant for black people not to have access to fair courts in America on any level. Rewarded for their cowardly act in two ways, these two dastardly scoundrels would never pay for their dirty deed. In, Tim Tyson, author of *The Blood of Emmett Till* (2017) revealed that Carolyn Bryant, recanting her testimony, admitting Emmett Till had never touched, flirted, threatened, or harassed her. *"Nothing that boy did could ever justify what happened to him,"* she said after the fact. But back in September 1955, Bryant and Milam were acquitted by an all-white jury of kidnapping and murdering Emmett Till. Protected against double jeopardy, the two cowards publicly admitted in a 1956 interview with *Look Magazine* that they were indeed the murderers of Emmett. Reports said that *Look* rewarded the murderers with $10,000 for their story. No justice no peace!!!!!

From the Ridiculous to the Absurd: The Kiss that Shamed the World

Far more ridiculous and arcane than the murder of Emmitt Till, the following incident still reflected the same societal madness and actions of white people in the South when black skin is involved. Yet and still, this atrocity, in 1958, illustrated the lack of proportionality on some white people's part when responding to contact between white women and black men, even when they are children. Though not as egregious an outcome as the murder trial of Emmitt Till, it supports my belief there have never been fair courts on any level in America for black people.

Notoriously called **"The Kissing Case,"** this horrific travesty, and absurd outcome began with the arrest, followed by the conviction and lengthy sentence given two young African-American boys. These young men lived in Monroe, North Carolina and were charged with rape. Ostensibly, these two boys were sent to prison for **"being kissed by a white girl their age on their cheeks."**

This madness started in late October 1958, when Sissy Marcus, a 7-year-old white girl, told her mother she had kissed 9-year-old James "Hanover" Thompson, and 7-year-old David "Fuzzy" Simpson, on their cheeks. The boys were African Americans. Sissy saw them playing with other children and recognized James as her friend from earlier childhood. Sissy and James had played together when James accompanied his mother to work. His mother was a domestic for the Marcus family, so they had money and standing in the white community. When Sissy proudly told her mother, Bernice, about the incident, she became enraged. Totally out of proportion to the situation, Sissy's mother called the police and accused the boys of **"raping her daughter,"** ("*The Kissing Case' And The Lives It Shattered,*" National Public Radio (NPR), April 29, 2011).

Robert Williams, a civil rights activist and head of the NAACP at the time, was deeply involved in attempting to provide the young men with some degree of representation on behalf of their families, who were not allowed to see them. He tried desperately to see and talk with the boys, but the judge granted no requests. The families could not see their sons for over a week. They were not allowed legal representation the entire time, and while they awaited arrangement, the boys were beaten and threatened by investigators, hoping to extract confessions. Their case illustrates the unfair operation of courts in America for descendants of American slavery. Their treatment also reflects the lack of proportionality southern courts viewed contact between white and black skin (*"Remembering Southern Black freedom fighter Mabel Williams,"* Sue Sturgis (4-25-2014), Facing South, Institute of Southern Studies).

Local officials unlawfully arrested and detained the two juveniles. They refused to allow their parents or legal counsel to visits them. Police, while beating up on the little boys (9 and 7 years old), threatened them with more serious injuries, if they did not confess. After three months in jail, the boys were charged and convicted of molestation by Juvenile Judge Hampton Price. Price sentenced them to reform school, possibly until age 21 (that would amount to 12 years for James and 14 years for David). Readers must remember these two children did nothing, accept allow a white girl to express her emotions, they had no control over that. ("*Championing Civil Rights,*" Allida M. Black, (1996), (*Casting Her Own Shadow: Eleanor Roosevelt and the Shaping of Postwar Liberalism,* Columbia University Press).

National leaders and members of the local NAACP, Eleanor Roosevelt, President Eisenhower, and other civil rights organizations, such as the New-York-based *Committee to Combat Racial Injustice (CCRI)*, protested the charges, trial, and sentencing. The United States was embarrassed by protests from other governments around the world, plus this underscored the charges in **_We Charge Genocide._**

Demonstrations occurred in major cities, and there was strong criticism in the international press. Southerners in North Carolina reacted to the negative press from around the world, like a punch in the belly. North Carolina Governor Luther H. Hodges finally granted clemency to the boys. They were released from the reformatory in early 1959, after serving three months. Neither Hodges nor authorities in Monroe ever officially apologized to the boys or their families.

Sit Ins to Freedom Rides: The Counter Culture Rises Up

The Kissing Case is a very clear instance of the unreasonableness and blind hatred that can boil up within white people and yield a reaction totally out of proportion to situations involving white women and black men. During or as a result of contact between the two, hatred can explode in the minds of white people with disastrous results when black skin is involved. Had these three children all been white or black, responses would have been altogether different.

Sissy's mother and other white people involved probably would have thought it was cute. Everyone would have had a good laugh at kids trying to act like grownups. But, this was the American South in 1958, unlike today, back then there were no restraints on white people, who desired to openly express their hatred for black skin. However, since 2016, white nationalists are again boldly, acting out attitudes, and scenes from the **"Dark Age"** *angry white men mob madness era.*

On the heels of **We Charge Genocide,** the fledgling Civil Rights Movement developed slowly. When beatsters, communists and leftist thinking young people committed to social change in America, came together it was a game-changer in the South. Young leftists developed their coalition away from the eyes of the general public. They reflected the beginning of the civil rights movement. The nascent growth of the new movement became a refuge for CP-USA faithful, after it was outlawed. Young leftists and beatsters found a home among the new social change organizations that sprang up to replace groups destroyed by J. Edgar Hoover's **Second Red Scare**. All these new and different groups and gatherings coalesced around the new ideas of those who research and wrote **We Charge Genocide.**

Following the decision in **Brown v. Board of Education,** young progressives stepped up to challenge America's oppression and suppression of African Americans' human rights. They had picked up valuable skills to test America's commitment to **Brown.** Survivors of J. Edgar Hoover's attack on the CP-USA with the *Second Red Scare,* they ready themselves for the coming battle over segregation and white supremacy.

Young progressive—whites and blacks—had become very comfortable working together. Many young white leftists hated segregation and white supremacy, as affronts to humanity. They witnessed the FBI's merciless attacks on good people, not un-Americans, as the FBI portrayed them. They began to emulate the nonviolent measures espoused by Rev. Martin Luther King Jr. (the 1955 Montgomery bus boycott). They began adopted some of the tactics to help African American activism gain acceptance and support across the US and around the world.

On February 1, 1960, young progressives began deploying their new technology and tactics, peaceful activism. On a cold February day (2-1-1960), four African American freshmen students, Ezell Blair, Jr. (Jibreel Khazan), Franklin McCain, Joseph McNeil & David Richmond from North Carolina A&T (HBCU) walked up to a whites-only lunch counter, took seats, and ordered coffee at the local Woolworth in Greensboro, North Carolina. Refused service as expected, they unveiled their new strategy—sit-ins. The North Carolina A&T students continued sitting patiently, waiting for service. Despite threats and efforts to intimidate them, they continued sitting silently and peacefully. These students became the point of the sit-in movement and signaled the dawning of the civil rights era.

No one was allowed to participate in a sit-in demonstration unless they were seriously committed to the tactic of nonviolence. Young leftists showed how essential their skills and courage were to the black and white coalition that became the foot soldiers the sit-in movement in early 1960. The training young progressives received working with the CP-USA had accustomed them to taking unpopular stands. They faced violent confrontations from counter-protestors and police.

Their instructions were simple: sit quietly and wait to be served. Often participants were jeered and threatened by local customers. Sometimes they were pelted with food or ketchup, sodas or ice cream poured on their heads, but they sat quietly. Angry onlookers tried to provoke fights by spitting on them and using profanity toward them, again they continued sitting.

Most times they stayed focused giving no response. But, when physically attacked, sit-iners were instructed to curl up in a ball, on the floor, cover their heads and take the punishment. Any violent reprisal from them, was believed, would undermine their cause and spirit of the sit-in tactic. When local police arrested demonstrators, another line of students took their vacated seats.

Sit-in organizers believed if violent acts were only on the part of angry white onlookers, the world would see the righteousness of their cause. Over 1500 arrested of sit-in demonstrators occurred by the end of school in 1960. But, over the next year or so their sacrifice brought the desired results.

Although the first lunch-counter sit-in had only four students, they drew the attention of HBCU students across the South. They motivated black college student to join the sit-in movement. Throughout 1960 into 1961 upwards of 70,000 black and white students in 20 states join the movement. Slowly, lunch counters and restaurants abandoned white only policies.

In April 1960, black activists included Ella Baker, Fannie Lou Hamer, Stokely Carmichael, H. Rap Brown, Cleveland Sellers, and others joined Rev. Martin Luther King Jr., who sponsored a conference to discuss strategy. Out of that gathering, the *Student Nonviolent Coordinating Committee (SNCC)* was organized. The *Congress on Racial Equality (CORE)*, a northern student group organized by James Farmer, joined with SNCC. CORE was a key member of this coalition. It organized grassroots sit-ins at lunch counters, swim-ins, and wade-ins at segregated swimming pools or beaches, even pray-ins at white-only churches.

Bolstered by the success of direct action, CORE activists planned the first freedom ride in 1961. CORE modeled the 1961 freedom rides after the organization's 1947 *Journey of Reconciliation*. During the 1947 action, African-American and white bus riders tested the 1946 US Supreme Court decision in **Morgan v. Virginia,** which found segregated bus seating was unconstitutional. The 1961 freedom ride tested a 1960 Supreme Court decision that segregation of interstate transportation facilities, including bus terminals, was unconstitutional (**Boynton v. Virginia)** as well. It challenged laws mandating segregated interstate transportation and facilities, but not **Plessy v. Ferguson**—*separate but equal*—segregation policies.

The first group of freedom riders left Washington, D.C., in May 1961 en route to New Orleans. A big difference between the 1947 *Journey of Reconciliation* and the 1961 freedom rides was the inclusion of women. In both actions, however, black and white riders traveled to the South—where segregation continued unabated. They attempted to use whites-only restrooms, lunch counters, and waiting rooms.

The original group of 13 Freedom Riders—seven African Americans and six whites—boarded a Greyhound bus on May 4, 1961. The group traveled through Virginia and North Carolina, drawing little public notice. The first violent incident occurred on May 12 in Rock Hill, South Carolina. When John Lewis, an African-American seminary student and founding member of SNCC, and white freedom rider, World War II veteran Albert Bigelow, as well as other riders attempted to enter a whites-only waiting area, and were viciously attacked by a mob.

After reaching Atlanta, Georgia, some riders split off and boarded a Trailways bus headed to Birmingham, Alabama. The diversionary move did not elude the white mob hot on their trail. Arriving in Anniston, Alabama (5-14-1961), an angry mob of 200 white people waited; afraid, the driver continued past the bus station. The mob gave chase in automobiles and some believe the mob shot the tires on the bus to stop it. Immediately, a mobster threw a firebomb into the bus, they attacked escaping freedom riders as the bus burst into flames.

Freedom riders that split off in Atlanta arrived in Birmingham and the mob of angry whites, they thought they eluded was waiting. Arch-segregationist Bull Connor, Birmingham Police Chief boasted facetiously, *"I knew the freedom riders were arriving and violence awaited them, but I didn't post no police at the station because it was Mother's Day."* Following the widespread violence, CORE officials could not find a driver and abandoned the effort.

However, Diane Nash, an activist with SNCC in Nashville, Tennessee, organized a group of 10 students to continue the rides. US Attorney General Robert F. Kennedy, brother of President John F. Kennedy, negotiated with Alabama Governor John Patterson, and the bus company to secure a driver. They resumed their ride, departing Birmingham under police escort, on May 20.

The next morning photographs of the burning bus in Anniston and the bloodied riders greeted readers at breakfast, on front pages of newspapers throughout the nation and around the world. For Europeans, those pictures confirmed the charges in **_We Charge Genocide._** Drawing international attention to the freedom riders,' put the spotlight on the state of race relations in the US. It was like, the CP-USA reached out from the grave to continue impacting America through its leftist children.

Authorities did not quell the violence; mobs chased freedom riders across the South. Rather than stim violence, it escalated, as angry white mob attacked riders with baseball bats and clubs, as they disembarked in Montgomery. Attorney General Kennedy sent 600 federal marshals to stop the violence.

Thronged by a thousand supporters of freedom riders the next night, Rev. Martin Luther King Jr. led a service at First Baptist Church in Montgomery, while angry whites thronged the church. Outside black supporters and white mobsters fought, while Rev. King preached inside. Rev. King called Robert Kennedy, requesting more protection.

Federal marshals used teargas to disperse the white mob. Gov. Patterson declared martial law and dispatched the National Guard to restore order. Freedom riders departed Montgomery for Jackson, Mississippi, the next morning. Hundreds of supporters greeted riders in Jackson. However, police arrested any entering whites-only facilities. The judge sentenced riders to the notorious Parchman penitentiary. American racists baptized young progressives—black and white—in blood, as the civil rights movement came of age. The US Supreme Court looked on without response, emulating Woodrow Wilson following the East St. Loius Riot.

The *1963 March on Washington* began a water shade period, while sit-in and freedom riders officially christening direct action against segregation and white supremacy. Foreshadowed by Paul Robeson and William L. Patterson's work with **_We Charge Genocide_**, a social activist cohort of young progressive began organizing around *Black Nationalism* to the chagrin of integrationists.

Integration—assimilation—became the theme of most "Negro" leaders during the 1930 and continued as their strategy well into the 1960s. Negros dedicated to assimilation took the leadership and control of the civil rights movement. They had helped J. Edgar Hoover and FBI destroy the **UNIA** and deport Marcus Garvey. They also helped Hoover outlaw the CP-USA. These same civil rights leaders also circled the wagons around leadership in the black community and helped Hoover isolated William Patterson and Paul Robeson.

Accommodationist of segregation fought *Black Nationalism* as a threat to their position as go-betweens. Nevertheless, Patterson and Robeson's voluminous report—***We Charge Genocide***—would bring those who supported integration and assimilation into confrontations with the new heirs of *Black Nationalism*—black power activists. This confrontation projected poor blacks, as the central focus of the battle for power in the black community in 1968.

The End of an Era and the Beginning of Another

One era ended as another peeped over the horizon, as the 1950s began a time for slavery's descendants that produce new leaders and new technologies to cope with the new demands. One of these amazing devil-may-care, swashbuckling, lone riders for the new era was Robert Franklin Williams (2/26/1925–10/15-1996). The defining moment for Williams occurred when he returned home to Monroe, North Carolina—after his discharge from military service—to witnessed Jesse Helms, Sr., police chief, publicly beating a black woman. The local NAACP recognized Williams' forceful activism and elected him president. Under his leadership, they successfully integrated public facilities in Monroe. During a time of high racial tension and official abuses, he intervened in the *"Kissing Case"* and helped bring the incident before the world.

Williams is best known for promoting armed self-defense for blacks in the US. The FBI began investigating Williams for advocating armed self-reliance for migrant laborers and victims of civil rights abuses. His views were uncommon to say the lease, at the time among civil rights activists. The Ku Klux Klan and other white gangs attacked and terrorizing black communities with impunity in North Carolina. Williams obtained a charter from the National Rifle Association and he set up a rifle club to defend blacks in Jonesboro Crossing, a black community in Monroe.

NAACP supported freedom riders, as they traveled the South (August 1961), testing the integration of interstate buses and facilities. Freedom riders also demonstrated against segregation, while registering black voters. When freedom riders arrived in Monroe, a mob assaulted them. Williams gave them sanctuary in the black section of town, as he battled Monroe officials and the KKK over the line of defense he established on the border between the white and black sections of town.

A white couple driving through this very tense black neighborhood was stopped and detained by people in the community. Residents brought the white couple to Williams. The white couple took refuge in Williams' home hoping he would protect them, until they could leave. Later Williams learned the city police and FBI filed kidnapping charges, claiming he held the couple against their will. Facing unfair courts in America, Williams and his wife Mabel left Monroe, and like William Patterson in Europe, after delivering **_We Charge Genocide_**, they went on the lam, later leaving the US for several years.

The FBI knew Williams was a *Black Nationalist* and sought an excuse to arrest him. Becoming an international runner, Williams was given asylum in both Cuba and The People's Republic of China. During his self-imposed 'exile' (1961 until 1969), Williams avoided kidnapping charges and jail time. These charges were dropped by North Carolina in 1975, after the white couple repeatedly and adamantly refused to press charges saying, *"He protected us."*

Williams wrote **_Negroes with Guns_** (1962), while in Cuba. It details his experiences with violent racists and his disagreement with the non-violent wing of the Civil Rights Movement. For diehard *Black Nationalists*, like the Black Panther Party, Williams' book ranked alongside **_The Autobiography of Malcolm X_**. The documentary about the Black Power movement (LET IT BURN - The Coming Destruction of the USA? 1968) (2005) used Williams' book to tell a unique story about him. During his exile and after his return to the U.S., he and Mabel published the militant journal Crusader and broadcast radio messages on Radio Free Dixie, as they continued fighting racism. His book **_Negroes with Guns_** (1962) has been reprinted many times, most recently in 2013. Huey P. Newton, a founding member of the Black Panther Party, said: *"Williams' book was a big influenced on me and was a major inspiration."*

Tent City: The End of a Technology

"We Charge Genocide" made poor black people the center of the fight for freedom from scarcity, and desperation, also gaining equal access to compete in America's economic system, and justice in America's courts. These monumental problems began stalking former slaves' as they walked off plantations into their penniless emancipation. The US denial of African Americans' human rights lay at the heart of their case for reparations against the US government. The case for convict leasing I will present later, but for now, I present the case of sharecroppers' claims against America.

Two machines, changed slave descendants' lives innumerably, after the end of ***The Trans-Atlantic Slave Trade***. Eli Whitney's cotton gin was the first technology, and it had a devastating impact on enslaved African, reinforcing their place on the bottom of America's *"cheap labor"* capitalistic economic strategy, as the base of the South's economy. The cotton gin's need for labor imprisoned the majority of the American black population on the land in the south for a century and a half. Whitney's cotton gin gave cotton production a capacity, limited only by the potential and availability of labor, as slavery in America entered the 1800s. Whites in the South saw slaves and their descendants as indispensable once this new technology came online. Black bodies were purchased, corralled, or shanghaied and dragged into the South, if they were not born there. The government implemented *The Fugitive Slave Act 1857* in an effort to maintain sufficient labor in the fields of the South.

This new technology for cotton production created another new technology—the internal slave trade and breeding. The new system created new horrors for millions of enslaved Africans. Civil War destroyed slavery, a growing monster that refused to die of its own volition, but war snuffed it out, the world thought.

However, in less than a decade, after emancipation, the US government found a way to resuscitate this monster, with an even more monstrous technology. That technology was sharecropping. It imprisoned millions of free black human beings on the land once again, after emancipation. The potential of cotton production demanded the South maintained sufficient quantities of labor in place to maximized production. This system reduced black skin back to a commodity. That commodity had to be stable, durable, and interchangeable. Slaves had satisfied that need before emancipation, and production was limited only by cost and slaves availability.

Availability of labor would remain a problem, even more so after emancipation. But, government intervention into the supposedly free market, creating a system to handle the complications of mobile former slaves by imprisoning them on the land in a system of slavery without chains and shackles. In that system freed slaves became *cheap or free* labor by the millions once again.

The 400th: From Slavery to Hip Hop

The US Supreme Court locked the courthouse door to former slaves with **Plessy v. Ferguson.** Unfair courts were the mechanisms that became the doorway for drawing free black people into this new system. Courts sustained this new technology and made the system go, which made it something slaves and descendants could not resist in any way. This government—**Plessy v. Ferguson**—produced unfair courts, denying black people access to fair courts, as plaintiffs.

Courts prevented black people from challenging their victimization. Simultaneously, these same courts used trumped-up charges to create free labor for cotton fields, factories, mills and mines. Legislatures passed law that allowed courts to draw African Americans into this system to provide an unlimited flow of free labor.

Trapped in this government-created technology, even though emancipation ended "chattel" bond slavery, black families became locked in bondage and dreary once again. The government created a system to support cotton production technology, making sharecropping a new type of slavery and a fixture of life for black families. Similarly to how the cotton gin rescued slavery and the plantation system, this new government-created technology was a return to the plantation for former slaves, but without ownership or responsibility for the human beings trapped in it.

White landowners had the best of both worlds. They were not responsible for the lives of sharecroppers, which were now throw-away commodities, like beer cans or plastic containers. Also, like the old system, it continued pouring wealth into the coffers of America and "former" slave owners. Exposing this dreadful system is what made **_We Charge Genocide_** such a powerful statement

The new system, as well as the old slavery system, needed constant replacement workers for fields, farms, factories, mines, and mills. However, dreary and daily toil wore workers out. Their life expectancy was short, like overworked, outdated equipment. Convict leasing and sharecropping kept millions of black families, prisoners on the land. Similar to a revolving door, courts kept rotating black workers as a permanent free replacement workforce.

Always hungry for more, courts kept black people trapped in the revolving door of this new system of slavery without chains. Sharecropping required the availability of millions of workers to clear land and work fields—plant, chop, and pick cotton at harvest time. Until my mother and father made their *"dark of the moon"* desperate dash for freedom and life, this was my family's legacy.

Being in the South and West Tennessee, I saw the advent of the second machine as it changed cotton production in ways black people trapped in it never imagined, like slaves in 1862 watched the monster of bond slavery died. The cotton-picking machine made its debut in the early 1900s and began its ascent to become the dominate technology by the early 1950s. It changed life for black people in the South forever.

The cotton-picking machine produced a different kind of survival battle for descendants of American slavery across the South, much like emancipation and the contraband period for former slaves. Out of sight of the world, locked behind America's *cotton curtain*, in the *belly of the beast*, black people had endured hell and total domination for centuries, now faced a new kind of survival threat. Without organizations, like the CP-USA, black sharecroppers had always been on their own. No group had helped them learn to fight to free themselves, and without real education, they could not learn to fight on their own. Now, they were in a new fight against government-engineered schemes, which kept them locked on the bottom of America's *cheap labor capitalistic system.*

However, as time, events, and Divine Intervention would have it, the new cotton-picking machine brought another profound change to the South's economic system in the 1950s. This machine did something over one hundred years of struggling, trying to escape by night, and two world wars had allowed only a few to break free, like my family. Although that system left millions of black families still locked up on farms, like peons, unable to change their lives, the new cotton-picking machine became an escape mechanism. Albeit the path it opened was tremendously difficult, but like former slaves at emancipation, it taught sharecroppers to stand on their feet, while fighting for a real life.

So, like the preverbal bolt of lightning out of the blue, the cotton-picking machine reduced the sharecropping system to an obsolete technology. However, not only had the cotton-picking machine, make sharecroppers obsolete, for workers, it made them obsolete, as human beings. No one needed poor black, barely educated people that sharecropping had trapped like slaves since 1900. Their education, those that had one, was just as obsolete as cotton sacks, hoes, and mules as equipment.

Cotton production brought in herbicides, as part of the new technology to augment the cotton-picking machine. Sharecroppers became tantamount to emancipated slaves a century earlier without any place to go. In the span of history, five or ten years seemed like overnight, and this is how it was with the cotton picking machine and herbicides to sharecroppers. Suddenly, millions of black families, whites locked up on the land in the South, in a system that kept them ignorant and dependent, now no longer needed or wanted them.

The end of sharecropping threw human beings it had made prisoners, but now obsolete, onto the scrap heap of humanity. No better off than the tools—hoes, cotton sacks, and weighing scales they used, millions of black people now faced a reality no one considered over the last 83 years. Landowners began throwing black families off land many had worked since just after emancipation and felt they owned. Sharecroppers were only marginally better off, than slaves, walking off plantations 95 years ago; the difference is the technology ending sharecroppers did not allow them to apply for contraband status.

The 400th: From Slavery to Hip Hop

After keeping sharecroppers locked up on their land, under the threat of prison or death, just a few years earlier, white landowners began, turning black field hands out, ridding themselves of people they no longer needed, and definitely never saw them as competition. Now, like Civil War, internal slave trade and breeding at their end, except the situation was going the other way. Unwanted "niggers" were pushed off land, as whites ridded themselves of the past.

My case in point happened just a few miles up the road from Memphis in Fayette, Hardman, Haywood and Tipton Counties in West Tennessee. (There were hundreds of other counties identical to these, whether in Tennessee or other southern states.) I will concentrate on Fayette County because that story is very familiar.

Turning back the clock to before the cotton-picking machine showed up in cotton fields, this area was a striving community of white cotton-growing landowners, who were out-numbered by thousands of sharecroppers. Landowners kept sharecroppers locked on the land, denying them basic rights, as human beings, particularly education and voting rights. Many black men, like Preston Hayes, who ferried cotton field hands from Memphis to Arkansas, as day laborers, developed businesses transporting day laborers to Fayette County. But the coming of cotton picking machines and herbicides killed that old economy overnight.

Black people in Tennessee caught hell more so in rural areas than in cities. The laws and socioeconomic practices in urban areas, namely Davidson (Nashville) and Shelby (Memphis) counties, were tolerable. However, blacks in rural areas were isolated and easier to intimidate with acts of terror to prevent them from establishing stable communities, getting education, buying land, and voting. White peoples used intimidation tactics to preserve their economic and political advantages.

The state of Tennessee and the U.S. government, going back to the 1890s, did not intervene on behalf of African Americans any place, especially in places like Fayette County. The government supported the sharecropping system every way it could all the way to the White House. Government refused to help black farm hands, during their transition from sharecropping to nothing, like emancipated slaves. Sharecroppers had to *make something out of nothing*; with nothing to start with; no longer trapped in the new system controlled by mechanization and herbicides, they had even less than that. Fayette County and places like it across the South became ground zero for the upheavals blacks families experienced in the late 1950s and 60s, as sharecropping finally died.

They had no CP-USA or civil rights movement to draw the world's attention to their plight; that world was still a decade away. Black people willing to make a stand were on their own, the same as slaves leaving plantations in 1863. The world changed a lot between 1890 and 1959, that is, everywhere but between the ears of white people. In that barren space—the minds of white people—they felt no obligation to black sharecropper than they did for the mules they owned to plow their fields. Those tools—mules and other equipment—they traded in for tractors, but like former slaves, sharecroppers had no value.

On the downside of this coin, many black Americans communities were demanding fair treatment, and former slaves in Fayette County were not any different. By the late 1950s, having needed all the field hands that could be corralled and locked down, over the years, Fayette County's population was approximately 70 percent African-American. The power white people exercised, over black folks, came as a result of the ***"Dark Age"*** *angry white men mob madness* period and unfair courts in America—**_WE Charge Genocide_**.

First and foremost, even though black were in the majority, whites in Fayette County controlled the socioeconomic and political system and deprived African-Americans of the ability to own land, in most cases. The system forced sharecroppers to live in small homes (shacks) on white farmers' land. Across the South, many white landowners began evicting, what they called *"tenant farmers,"* especially those that tried to exercise the right to vote.

Such actions—trying to vote—created a homeless population of families and individuals without any places to go or means to leave. The *Great Migration* was no longer an option, northern factories had a glut of employees, and war was not on the horizon. Many white business/land owners refused to give blacks credit for food and fuel, as the way of forcing evicted families to move on. Local governments did not allow black families to receive basic welfare services. It was that way in Memphis until late 1968. So, hundreds of families were pushed out on the road, like contrabands without subsistence. Just a few years earlier, "patty rollers" were driving black people back to farms; now they were driving them out of their area, if not out of the South.

There were several WW II African American veteran landowners and prominent members of Fayette County's black community. Harpman Jameson, along with local merchant John McFerren and Attorney John Estes before evictions began, helped local blacks organize and register to vote. The system changed for African-Americans in Fayette County once the primary arrived in 1959. Registered blacks voters were turned away from the polls and told the *primary* was *"all-white."* The black community created an organization, the *Fayette County Civic and Welfare League*. The league filed lawsuit contesting the legitimacy of the election. The White Citizens Council (local KKK) of white landowners retaliated, evicting black sharecroppers in the county.

Shephard Towles, a black landowner, and farmer secured surplus Army tents and set them up on his land near Somerville, Tennessee. He allowed evicted families to live there, and like contraband camps, within a week, there were hundreds of families living in what became the first *"Tent City."* Eventually, other landowners, like Mrs. Gertrude Beasley, erected *"Tent Cities"* to help destitute sharecroppers. The evictions continued, as the number of homeless families rose, and anonymous donors gave more tents. According to an estimate, well over 600 families (upwards of 3,000 people) lived in the first *"Tent Cities."* The numbers continued changing as families move out, and others moved into *"Tent Cities."*

According to Early B. Williams, who was evicted by his landlord in the fall of 1959, *"Tent City was a miserable life. The tent was sixteen by fourteen ... my wife and four kids livin' there. We had to cook in there; we had to sleep in there; we had to eat in there. And mud — when it rained in Tent City, it got so bad on Tent City ground, you had mud almost up to your knees. We'd sit around outside, nothin' else to do. But I was never sorry I registered. I figured we'd overcome someday."* There were many such accounts; it is like reading slave narratives. This situation, I believe, foreshadowed Dr. Martin Luther King, Jr.'s *"Resurrection City"* in Washington, D.C., during the **"Poor People's Campaign"** in 1968.

Fayette County's black population endured many negative impacts, during these times. The most severe was living in *"Tent Cities"* for over five years (1959-64). Although *"Tent city"* farmers' made incremental progress every year (1960), some families remained in tents longer than five years. Avoiding *"Tent City,"* many families moved in with relatives, sometimes, as many as three families lived in one dwelling, with only one bathroom. Living with the hardships in *"Tent City",* their stories received some national publicity, thanks to dedicated black activists, which brought attention to their plight. The world learned of the tragedy through the *Tri-State Defender* newspaper, because the New York Times picking up many of its stories.

Classically and iconic fashion, Dr. Ernest C. Withers began capturing *"Tent City"* activities almost from its very beginnings. From the early stages, when evicted sharecroppers were holding organizational meetings for the *Fayette County Civic and Welfare League* he was on the scene. Dr. Withers photographed the beginning evictions in Fayette County. Dr. Withers supplied many photographs of the *"Tent City"* tragedy that appeared in newspapers, as he camped out in *"Tent City,"* at times, helping to bring the tragic images before the eyes of the world.

I continually point out how unintended consequences precipitated improvements in slave descendants' lives, even though the situations may have seemed hopeless at the beginning. Things are difficult or maybe even tragic starting out, like emancipation or my family while living in Greens Alley, however self-love made surviving such circumstances seem impossible, as lives fall apart. But life has a way of improving situations when families are willing to struggle together, as former slaves entering the contraband period. Most times, as with *"Tent City,"* over time, as life unfolds, people learn new ways of surviving, education becomes a major priority, new and different lifestyles evolved. Children learn hard lessons of life, as they grow up, and their lives improve, changing their struggles.

But most importantly, the misery and hardship white people caused black people, trying to make life easier for theirselves turn back upon them, when hard times unexpectedly track them down. Those struggles descendants of American slavery did not ask for any of the horrible circumstances endured in America as slaves, and sharecroppers. But because of the sacrifices families made, enduring to survive the hatred and diabolical effort of white people, they grow stronger. White people in no way deserve thanks for their devilishness, but the people we have become, make us better human being than we would have ever become.

For instance, another positive impact of Dr. Withers' presence for black people, his work enabled them to move beyond a "spoken word history and culture." His photographs told their stories to an unaware world. Documenting *"Tent City"* with his photographs gave physical and permanent existence to stories of human beings struggling to survive the impact of government on their lives. With such evidence, voices from the grave, like unwritten stories, found expression through the lens of Dr. Withers' camera.

And following that, the publicity generated by Dr. Withers pictures and news stories, brought young white progressive activists from colleges such as Oberlin, Dartmouth, and the University of Chicago into the South to help register black voters in Fayette County and other places. A radio station in Pennsylvania picked up WDIA's newscasts and used them to raised money and send supplies to *"Tent City."* National labor unions picked up the story and sent donations, tents, and other supplies to desperate people in need, but government was like Donald Trump today, did nothing.

Beyond individual tragedies, perhaps a major point of the *"Tent City Movement"* is it was far-reaching. It opened the 1960s civil rights activism with a clear vision of what was to come. As I said in the opening paragraph, **_We Charge Genocide_** put poor black people in the center of the struggle for human rights. Several organizations began championing the cause of poor people. Eventually, Dr. Martin Luther King, Jr. organized the *"Poor People's Campaign."* He picked up the challenge of helping the poor, even though other civil rights leaders did not stand with him.

Events in Fayette County made it obvious that in parts of the South, African-Americans still could not exercise their basic rights to vote and that the elimination of poll taxes and grandfather clauses did not give black people open access to voting. Today in 2020, black voters are fighting Donald Trump for access to ballot boxes through mail in voting. Even without lynchings and other violent acts, whites have many other ways—eviction, economic retaliation, voter suppression and reprisals of all kinds—to intimidate black people and deter them from their desire to vote.

Many researchers believe the Fayette County *"Tent City"* movement was a major part of promoting the two landmark Bills the *Civil Rights Act of 1964* and the *Voting Rights Act of 1965*. But like "poll taxes" and "grandfather clauses," those two pieces of legislation have not eliminated discrimination, voter suppression or disparate treatment and the hostile environment slave descendants endure.

This topic still has not died. Today black American voters still have to fight white people for the Right to Vote. I will take this discussion on a quick u-turn to 2016 to make a personal point. Although I have been on the voting rolls since arriving in Georgia in 1982 and have remained at the same address in DeKalb County, however, in 2016, I was purged. During early voting, I was told at the pole I had never been on DeKalb County's voting rolls. All though I voted for Barak H. Obama in 2008 and 2012, I was told there was no record of my ever having registered. I had to vote provisionally in 2016, but the county still disallowed my vote. It has taken three years of protesting and investigating to learn why someone violated my voting rights.

I was told, unbeknownst to anyone in authority why, my voter registration and residents were transferred from DeKalb to Fulton County, by some unknown person. In other words, my Constitutional right was taken away without any notice to me, even though the county took no action to notify me or verify change in my voting status. No one talked with me during this hold process, not even during the provisional voting process. Had they tried, I could have established my residence by showing my precinct card, as it is presently. But, no one inquired to see if I moved or remained at my present address.

The Right to vote should be a federally protected right. Anyone who make changes or anything that changes a voter's status without notification should be a violation of federal law. A voter should be notified through registered mail at least 60 days before any change is made and should be a violation of federal law. Congress should make it a federal offense with jail time to tamper with a voter's ability to cast a ballot.

Election officials should be required by law to notify an individual voter at least 60 days before any change is made that will result in preventing them from casting their vote and no purges should be allowed, during regular elections years. To date the state Georgia has purged over 400,000 voters from the rolls for the convenience of the state. There is no way to know how many voters are like me in 2016 caught up in that purge and they will not know until, like me, when they show up at the poles. Voting is the only legal way citizens have of changing government and its actions. That is why voting by mail with same day registration is so important. A voter's access should be a federally protected right so that what happened to me does not happen to citizens in the future without penalties.

Bill Carey, researcher, writer, and reporter from Nashville, the co-founder of *Tennessee History for Kids*, posted information about *"Tent City"* for today's kids. Learn more detailed from stories of the *"Tent City"* movement through *"Our Portion of Hell,"* a book by a civil rights activist Robert Hamburger. The website www.memphis.edu/tentcity of the Institute for Social Change at the University of Memphis provides first-person accounts from people such as John and Viola McFerren and many others.

More importantly, the *"Tent City"* movement was the death throes of a system—***The Trans-Atlantic Slave Trade***—that had ravaged lives of slave descendants for 568 years. Government in the United States has been a major partner in this enterprise for 156 years from its very beginnings (1600), and the US government supported and facilitated it until its technological death in America in the 1960s, then it walked away. It felt no obligation to do anything to help or pay the debt it owes descendants of American slavery for the wealth their lives created for white people that engineered it.

Lorraine Hansberry: Calm Before the Storm

The United States, for most of its existence, claimed to be a relatively egalitarian, liberal middle-class democracy, with structures in place that supported the aspirations of ordinary people. The illusion, on the part of its people, was that a basic deal existed between America's government and the people. The belief was that if you worked hard, follow the rules, and educated your children, you would be rewarded, not just with a decent life, but with prospects of a better future for those children. Also, you would be recognized by society, with a place at the table. Southern racists and Northern conservatives over the years added a series of riders and clauses to this unwritten contract that excluded large numbers of Americans, black people in particular and other minorities—women, Hispanics, Native People, the gay community (LGBT)—leaving them without even a backdoor to enter into this rest.

Brown v. Board of Education was supposed to be the correction or adjustment that opened the door to America's bounty for all Americans, while closing the door on racism and white supremacy in America. **Brown's** was intended to influence young, well educated, professionally motivated, altruistic black and white social activists. The CP-USA had gathered up young people, and they took to the streets, demanding equality for all Americans.

Young progressives saw America through the eyes of **<u>We Charge Genocide</u>**. They saw through America's pretense of **Brown** as the correction for racism, segregation, and white supremacy. **Brown** was supposed to be the means of keeping these young people in the fold, but they rejected the facade.

America did not aim **Brown** at influencing radicals, like William L. Patterson, a devil make-care swashbuckling lone rider, willing to run across Europe, eluding government agents, while making headlines as his life hung in the balance. **Brown** was definitely, not aimed at *Black Nationalists*, like Robert Williams, who escaped America's *cotton curtain* to become an international runner. Globetrotting across the communist world, as a black revolutionary, Williams called for the destruction of America's *"cheap labor"* capitalistic system, which did not put him in a unique class by any means.

So, contrary to those images, the American government wanted young radicals that believed, through **Brown,** it offered a seat at the table of "responsible" leadership. Properly reared and educated Americans, they were the best society had to offer, as a bulwark against the William Pattersons and Robert Williams of America. All they had to do was, buy into and join America's status quo, which they had resoundingly rejected. The current American administration is offering the same warmed-over deal. It wants todays' young progressives to join MAGA ("make America great again") and support their renewed efforts to reinvigorate

Woodrow Wilson's vision of America—hatred, violence, white supremacy and racism.

One young radical that fell within the demographic targeted by the US government was Lorraine Hansberry. The quintessential recruit, in the government's bullseye, Hansberry came from middle-class surroundings in every respect. Lorraine Hansberry reflected the ideals of assimilation. She was educated at the best schools (University of Wisconsin–Madison) and exemplified America's values, like no other. The American government looked upon young progressives, like Hansberry, with real hope. She was at the top of this class the US government calculated that ***Brown*** would attract.

The game was to convince them that real social change would come through US Supreme Court action, changing laws. Giving *VOICE* to Hansberry's generation, the government wanted to attract young idealistic Americans from that demographic bullseye, after it projecting them as America's future leaders.

Even more to the point, one cannot view ***Brown v. Board of Education*** like looking in a mirror; one has to try and visualize ***Brown*** through the eyes of young people, coming into the 1960s. One has to remember the last few discussions of this narrative, beginning with the 34 years (1920 to 1954) of CP-USA's activities, all the way to ***Brown***. I offer the following view, through the lens, I believe, Lorraine Hansberry saw her life and the impact she hoped that vision would have on those that would stand on her shoulders to view the future of black people.

Hansberry came along at the end of one era—the end of sharecropping, hatred, denial, degradation, and death for black people—while entering at the beginning of a new time of access and mobility for blacks. During discussions in this narrative, I've tried to recreate the environment that dominated descendants of American slavery's existence. Now, arriving at the beginning of the new world of the 1960s, I present what they contended with trying to change the world using social change and social justice.

A black woman, facing this new world, I believe, Lorraine envisioned a future few were concerned about or even aware. She was the fruit from generations of black families struggling to educate and develop their daughters. Educating girls was a family tradition that began in slavery, even though it was not referred to as education. While black boys worked fields and tried to find ways to provide for made-up families. Black girls were the depositor of what it took to care for everybody. The brightest and most attentive the ones slave women were seen, others cooked and cleaned but all shared what they learned.

Entering emancipation and the contraband period girls were the ones that could be spared from working the fields; they were the hope for gaining knowledge and education to advance African American families. Whether that meant being sent to work in white peoples' house or to school or both, girls were the choice. Boys were chosen only if white folks needed a driver, someone to work outside, or had no girls.

Coming along when she did, Hansberry's seed was a hybrid that became a model for not only black women but all women, trying to break into male-dominated endeavors. A very motivated, highly intelligent, and self-directed individual, definitely Hansberry came out of the demographic **Brown** was designed to influence. But, Lorraine did just the opposite of what the government hoped. Hansberry, like hundreds of young radicals, was on the precipice of change, and out in the streets, pushing social justice issues. I see her, much like a soothsayer, creating her allegorical and satirical metaphors **A Raisin in the Sun** (1959). Through her play, she reflected the pretend side of America, rather than the reality **Brown v. Board of Education** tried to cover over. Subtly through **A Raisin in the Sun**, play and film version (1961), Hansberry pointed out the fallacy of assimilation—the American dream—offered African Americans as a substitute.

Young people during the 1950s did not have a voice in what was done or said to create the world in which they awoke. Opening their eyes, they recognized, the older generation expected them to ask permission to speak then say what their parents would say, even though their parents would never think the thoughts germinating in their minds. With open eyes, they could see they were already pigeonholed, as Hansberry's protagonist Walter Lee, in **A Raisin in the Sun**. Walter Lee, like millions of young people in the US, especially black, was trapped by a reality so large it had neither beginning nor end; its dominion was total and complete. Young blacks and many young whites of that day could only do as Walter Lee, watch their flowering dreams of a different and better life and world, bud-like grapes, then dry, shrivel and die, like raisins in the sun.

Who was Lorraine Hansberry (5-19-1930/1-12-1965) anyway? I compare Lorraine's effect or impact on America's sociopolitical environment to a spoon of sugar in a very strong cup of coffee. She didn't change the color or strength of it but very subtly mellowed its savor. Although charming and very attractive, Hansberry, seemed to me, like a dormant volcano in her seemly sequestered emotions. Given my perspective, she didn't seem to be volatile or explosive, but on the inside, Hansberry seemed to churn with intense energy.

I say this because of her play **A Raisin in the Sun** *(3-11-1959)*, which seems rather calm, tame, and without much explosive action from her characters. However, they reflected a kind of quiet rage, most blacks possess, that boiled just beneath the surface, poised to erupt under sufficient pressure, like a volcano. Cleverly seeding her characters' personalities with deep and controlled emotions, only hinted at, during most scenes. However, at other times, when facing ordeals or battles for relevance, their passion is released. Sometimes oozing out slowly, but at other times they are channeled, like a carefully aimed force.

With the success of **_A Raisin in the Sun,_** Hansberry attained several first. She was the youngest and first black dramatist, as well as only the fifth woman to receive the coveted New York Drama Critics' Circle Award. Growing up, based on her family surroundings and social backdrop, it seems to me; her environment should have produced an unobtrusive and arrested development. Through experiencing Hansberry's work, I came to feel that beneath the surface of what seemed a very demure, calm, and placid exterior, raged a tiger, roaring and clawing to get free. Studying her many involvements and accomplishments, one finds the same fiery spirit displayed by activists like Pauli Murray, Ella Baker, Dorothy M. Smith, and Fannie Lou Hamer. Those women were all very passionate social change activists, but were not drawn to the spotlight, like moths.

Hansberry, like those icons, cared deeply about people and worked tirelessly against things that affected them or their communities negatively. She not only worked relentlessly in the civil rights movement, but Lorraine was also involved with CP-USA's social change projects. Hansberry not only spoke out in support of the global struggle against colonialism and imperialism; she also took stands while seasoned leaders ran for cover. Unknown in the larger political world, and out of the blue to some, Hansberry wrote impassioned articles in support of the *Mau Mau Movement* (MMM) upraising in Kenya (1952-1960), while notable international leaders ducked the issue altogether.

Hansberry openly attacked mainstream media for their biased coverage of African uprisings against colonialism. She represented the modern views held by African Americans. Identical to William Patterson and Paul Robeson, regarding oppression, colonialism and imperialism, Hansberry gave *VOICE* to their efforts, while African American luminaries distanced themselves from the *Mau Mau Movement*.

Satirically portraying the conditions and spirit of the 1950s, **_A Raisin in the Sun,_** poignantly captured the subtle nuances of segregation in the North. **Raisin** cleverly exposed residential segregation in areas where there were no white only signs. She showed how whites close ranks to support white supremacy and keep blacks out.

Hansberry illuminated how former enslaved Africans, tried to adapt to the demands of white people since slavery, and went from being former slaves (contraband) to colored people and then Negros. But, their socioeconomic and political situation or status did not change substantially. Although, Hansberry was in the middle of popular cultural happenings, she took positions on the edge, arguing that black people had been contortionists changing and shaping themselves, then reshaping themselves, again and again, to fit how and what white people considered a good Negro. But, no matter how often or well they changed to fit and adjusted to the demands whites placed on them, Negros ended up where they start, in poverty's grave—the valley of dry bones.

Displaying her sassiness, on the night before her wedding, Hansberry, with her husband to be, attended a rally protesting the execution of Julius and Ethel Rosenberg in New York City. (Julius and Ethel Rosenberg were US citizens targeted by the FBI. Accused of being communist spies, like William L. Patterson, but additionally, the government accused them of selling US nuclear technology to the Russians. Patterson may have shared a similar fate had he been caught in Europe. The US government executed them on June 19, 1953. Leftists believed they were casualties of the *"Cold War,"* scapegoats to cover up, why no one could explain how Russia got the bomb.)

The communist label did not deter Hansberry. She appeared at a peace conference in Montevideo, Uruguay, as a stand in for Paul Robeson. The US Department of State refused to allow Robeson to leave the USA. They kept him and his passport locked behind the *"cotton curtain."* They tried to keep him from speaking about **WE Charge Genocide**. Hansberry, more than lived up to her billing as the inspiration for Nina Simone's anthem **To Be Young, Gifted, and Black,** through her human rights and civil rights activism.

Lorraine Hansberry is the ideal example of what denial of *VOICE* means in America. Although tremendously successful with **A Raisin in the Sun,** Hansberry struggled to get her work before the public. Similar to CP-USA, J. Edgar Hoover and the FBI made every effort to destroy her career. They used the communist allegation to hamper her getting her work accepted in the American market.

For instance, Hansberry wrote two screenplays of **Raisin** for Columbia Pictures, but they rejected both, as "too controversial." It was not that the screenplays were too controversial, Hansberry was. Lorraine based the screenplays of **Raisin**, the same play that won the New York Drama Critics' Circle Award for Columbia Pictures. But, with her views expressed and projected through her play, the world is asked to believe her screenplays for the movies were "too controversial."

Following that fiasco, she was commissioned by NBC (1960) to create a television program about slavery. Hansberry wrote **The Drinking Gourd**. NBC praised her script, calling it "superb," yet refused to produce it. White people can find money to produce any story they wish. But, similar to finding advertisers to save Nat "King" Cole's TV show, black writers and producers must still shape their stories' content and characters to fit white people's *"in blackface"* images of *"blackness."* This statement reflects how white and black people can look at the same event or situation and see entirely different scenarios.

Hansberry impacted the women's movement before people began speaking of it as a separate entity from the civil rights movement. I believe that separation was a divide and conquer strategy to weaken the impact of black women's *VOICE*. Hansberry gave voice to the frustrated dreams and desires of professional upwardly mobile American descendants of slavery.

Identifying with women who were unable to find political expression, after beating their heads against the "glass ceiling," Hansberry, through her trials, gave voice to all women. She serves as an archetype for the latter-day quick-witted, rapidly responding, and multi-tasking women of today. They, like Hansberry, exude a quiet confidence that allows them to thrive in male-dominated environments, like sugar in a strong cup of coffee. Through social change, women activists today exemplify Hansberry's strategy of confronting men and pulling them and their yesteryear thinking toward progressive ideals and issues.

Mudear's Raisin

After moving out of Greens Alley and two years before moving to Riverside in South Memphis, Mudear married Mr. Otis. A rock of stability in the quicksand of poverty, Mr. Otis pulled us out of dire straits. His quiet presence and patient love gradually won us over. But, Tommy, the oldest, gathered us one day and put words to our sentiments. He said, "We can't ask for anyone better for Mudear, and he has always treated us like his children, better than our own daddy, so I think it is time we start giving him the respect he deserves." So Mr. Otis became Daddy Otis. He bought the family's first car; used, of course, but it was first class to us. We settled in Riverside (1955), a working-class community built in the early 1940s.

Primarily, Riverside was a subdivision built for whites that worked at the Ford Motor plant, on the North end of the Community. When Ford moved its operation to Texas, whites moved with it or out of the community, as black families moved in. A car and our "new" house gave us the feeling we had made a real move up to middle-class status—assimilation in action. The house was actually new. We were the first family to live there. The move put us a long way from our first rat-infested dwelling, situated on that slag heap in Greens Alley.

Daddy Otis coming into our lives created hope for better times. The move also made another earlier family decision among us kids very important. This one was prompted by Willie May, the oldest girl (whom we called Suster), after leaving Green's Alley, she told Molly (who was called Bay Bay), Bernice (Baby Sister) me and I was Bay Brother, "We are no longer in the country, where everybody got nick-names. We need to start calling everybody by their real names. That way new people we meet will know what to call us and other people will know who they are talking about." If you have never had a nick-name you may not understand the importance of this decision but imagine hearing your name only in school or being asked , "what's your real name boy?"

Daddy Otis was a piece of granite, he was always there, unlike my father whom I saw, but never got to know. We talked when I visited him; he always had lots of words but never said anything. Daddy Otis, on the other hand, was a man of few words, I called him a "three word man;" when laying down the law you never wanted him to go beyond that; if he did he was fussing. And nobody wanted Daddy Otis to fuss. Mother took care of discipline. I don't mean Daddy Otis and I never talked, he was a great listener. The most profound statement I remember him making came after I engaged him about my confusion as a kid about something I did not understand. He said with a broad smile, *"Well, John, if you ain't willing to do any more about it than what you just said to understand, knowing for you is always going to be, a lost ball in high weeds."* After thinking about his comment, I realized his few words said if all I was going to do is talk about my confusion, knowledge would continue eluding me and understanding would always be lost to me. That was more than three words, I know, but for the wealth of knowledge departed, I believe make my math comparable!

Often I talked with Mudear about things before I joined the family in Memphis and other times in her life. This particular time, I wanted to know if she was disappointed that she didn't have a big career singing, once she got to the city. Like a kid, I asked, "Mudear, do you regret not becoming a popular singer in the city, not getting your big chance?" She smiled, while tilting her head to the side slightly, then said,

"Well, I will say, I definitely got my chance to sing. I sang every Sunday at Pilgrim Rest Baptist Church. But to your point," she said after another slight pause, *"Everybody needs a dream, something to shoot for to keep them going. I had a chance for a career singing after we got here. Pilgrim Rest had a very good choir, that's why I joined. Rev. C.M. Lee (no relation) was very active in the community. He pushed his members to get involved in politics and so I became a member, even though I was raised a Methodist. I joined a singing group at Pilgrim Rest. We were the 'M&N Junior Girls.' It was Mildred Gage, Elizabeth Kelly, Cleo Satterfield, Virgy Kelly, Jesse Ruth Williams, and me. You remember these women, don't you?"*

"Yes!" I agreed.

"There was a men's 'M&N' group also. We travel together to programs all around the city. We competed in singing battles and gospel group competition against some great quartets, like the Gooden Girls, Harps of Melody, The Evening Doves, and The Song Birds of The South. All these groups were pretty good too. We went all around to different churches, and we were on **WDIA** *lots of times. Everybody knew the "M&N Jr. Girls"; we were pretty good ourselves. But, I learned, good in the country is one thing, then good in the city is something else altogether. There are lots of good voices just like yours. You have to have something special to stand out.*

The women in our group were married with families, so we couldn't travel across the country, like men groups, and some women's group, which became very popular across the South. The big thing for me was Tommy moved out and left me, which changed everything. Some of the women in our groups had family situations, too; that's why we broke up.

I never thought about being by myself. I really didn't know what to do. I nearly fell apart. I had y'all, but I really wanted to sing, I could feel it in my heart. It was really hard without Tommy, being in Memphis, where I didn't know anybody, hardly. Trying to pay bills, keep a roof over our heads, food on the table, the lights on and all that, what's a body to do? There was no place to go for help but to the church. And, I didn't want to go from church to church, like some women, asking for handouts. The only way I could make it as a singer was to take y'all back to the country and leave you with mama and daddy. Losing Tommy was bad enough. I didn't want the rest of my family broken up.

The 400th: From Slavery to Hip Hop

I tried really hard to get Tommy back. I would go over to his place, hoping to see him. Sometime we would talk, but other times he wouldn't come to the door. I could see him peek out the window. I would sit on the porch sometimes, waiting for him to come to the door or come home. One day the lady that owned the house finally told me,

'Child you may as well find you somebody else, he don't want you no more.'

Oh! That hurt so bad!! Although, I had cried before, this time I just broke down. Walking home with tears running all down my face, I prayed real hard, and I said, God, if you just take this pain and hurt off me, I will go in whatever direction you show me. Even though I had that little piece a job at Bemis Bag Company, it wasn't enough, but it was all I could get.

Junior, God, bless his little heart, got that job at Mr. Jimmy's store. He was such a little man helping out, even though I never asked him to. As young as he was, he understood what I was going through. With a big smile, every week, he brought his little money home and gave it to me. I felt so bad taking it. No matter how tough things were, I tried not to take more than half; he needed something for himself. He was the only man I had in the house.

Then one day, while I was at work, this big guy walked up to me and picked me up over his head, and said,"

'Little girl, I'm gonna marry you!!' He put me down and just walked off.

"*I was so shocked; I didn't know what to think or say when he put me down? He just walked away before I could say anything. I didn't even know his name. I had seen him standing back, looking at me. But, you know how it is on the job. Men are always looking and saying stuff. All the other girls said,"*

Girl!! He's a real bad guy. He's always getting into fights and getting locked up for being drunk on weekends. He's a real fighter. You bet not mess with him.'

"*He started coming over at lunchtime, I started not to talk to him, because of what all the other girls said, but I thought about my prayer too. And, since I didn't know God's mind, I let him talk. He told me all about himself and stuff he found out about me asking around. He said he even came to a few of the programs to hear us sing, but never stayed around to talk.*

So, I said, anything you want to know about me, you ask me. I told him some of what I heard about him, and I told him; I'm a Church woman. I got five children and no husband. I don't have time for a man who's always fighting, getting drunk, and going to jail. If you want to be anything to me, you got to stop all that foolishness and join the church. He looked at me for a moment before saying,"

'Then, you'll marry me?'

"*I said, well, we'll see!"*

She looked at me for a long moment, while tilting her head slightly to the side, as though she was allowing her statement to sink in, and then said.

"Life is not about loss; it's about gain. Am I disappointed I didn't become a big gospel singer? No, not at all! A dream is just that, a dream. Life is what you have when you wake up. Life is what you can make out of it. It doesn't come dressed up, looking like an angel. Most of the people you meet that try to make you think they're angels are real devils. They come at you trying to look and sound like God folks to fool you. I trust in doing right cause God ain't going to help you do wrong.

So, if you're like me and need God's help, the only way to get it is to do right. Knowing that, I asked myself What will I have chasing my dream? If I don't catch it when I wake up, what will I have? God answered my prayer. And, along the way, he gave me seven children, 19 grandchildren, and I lose count on my great-grands and great-great-grands. God has blessed me with 100 years of life to this point. But even more than that, God gave me a man that loved me until his last breath and beyond, if that's possible."

Lorraine Hansberry's magic was the way she satirized American society, while subtly using the nuances and emotions involved in keeping a family together, as her message. Most importantly, she cleverly showed ways family love is difficult, but the hard circumstances of life can hold black people together when it's easier to walk away. Lost dreams that fall apart, deferring one family member's hopes, so that the whole family does better is how we made it to **"The 400th"**. These aspects of life have always been part of black families' survival patterns. "Family is everything!!!!"

With scarcity and desperation dominating slave descendants every waking minute, success and failure have different meanings to black people, like magic or freedom than they do for white people. If you've never lived through things like slavery, lynching, unfair courts, discrimination, disparate treatment, and the hostile environment they generate, as a way of life, trying to survive makes life a glass "half full," so you expect more. Though not pessimistic, but living through and enduring such thing, black people learned, life is a glass "half empty," so you know that's all you will ever get, so you can never waste a drop.

Mother's raisins didn't shrivel up and die. If one puts a juice fill grape in the ground, it rots. Luscious grapes have to lose all that juiciness before it can gather strength for growth. Mother had to find fertile ground for her raisins to create her magic. Describing her life, it is obvious her bowl is overflowing with her bounty.

The Magic Continued at WDIA

The best time in life for me began as the 1960s rolled in, and with black people in Memphis jamming to **WDIA**. Nat D blasted black people over the airwaves, serenading and dropping announcements on them about actives—gospel shows in churches, talent contests on Beale Street, high school productions, and weekly dance contest— **WDIA** kept things jumping. The Wizard of Beale Street kept the beat going at a very high level. Nat D brought more of his history-making magic to radio, with *Brown America Speaks*, *Black Montage*, *Voices in Black*, and *Dark Town Review*. These programs gave the black community current news, perspectives on Negro progress, coming events, and future attractions.

Casting spells and dropping knowledge on the community through talk shows, the lineup began on Saturday morning with the *Teen Town Singers*, followed by *Future Tan American Talent* and *Young Black America Speaks*. These programs showcased the pride of the Negros community—their children. Sunday was God's day, and black people listened to WDIA get the word about gospel shows, church pageants, and other activities in and around Memphis.

Those churches that could afford it broadcasted their services over **WDIA**. That was really "big time." Nat D gave community leaders and activists *VOICE*, on his Saturday and Sunday shows, *Voices in Black*, *Tan Town Business Review* and *Politics Black or White*. He played devil's advocates to draw out the relevant points in discussions with his guess. Nat's level of knowledge and skill in the classroom allowed him to take his audience to school.

Nat D spotted his apprentices, like Rufus Thomas on **Tan-Town Jamboree,** as well as MC during the Amateur Hour at the Palace Theater. After releasing his first recording, *"Bear Cat"* produced at Sun Studio, Nat D did his magic at **WDIA,** and got Rufus an R&B show of his own; a star was born. Featuring a total African-American appeal, **WDIA** became known as the *"mother station of Negroes."* It was the source of Delta Blues and R&B music for several generations. Rufus began with a spot called *Sepia Swing Club*, then *Heebie Jeebies*, and finally his iconic *Hoot and Holler.*

"I'm young, I'm loose, I'm full of juice, I got the goose so what's the use. We're feeling gay though we ain't got a dollar, Old Rufus is here, so let's hoot and hollerrrrr!!!!!!!!!!!!!"

The late 1950s was a coming of age time for me. I had survived elementary school and escaped junior high, but it wasn't until my second semester in the tenth grade of high school that it occurred to me, I was wasting my life, clowning for my classmate. I had to really buckle down quickly if I was going to graduate.

I declare that graduating from George Washington Carver High School (1962), in the top 10% of my class, was a victory over mediocrity.

But my coming out time was 1959, because that was when I became old enough to leave my neighborhood of Riverside. I began to see Memphis as never before. There was a neighborhood crew of guys that I grew up with, Richard Rice, R.C. Mangum, Oscar Landcaster, Frank Hall, the brothers Allen and Eddie Franklin, as well as the brothers Williams, Victor, Dicky, and John Gary. Friends since elementary school, we played sports and "Tarzan" in Riverside Park; we were truly rambunctious kids, proud to be from Riverside.

Riverside Park, although it was in our neighborhood, it was for white people, but we didn't care about segregation, under those circumstances. We knew the park, like the palms of our hands, and the police couldn't catch us, even when they tried. Dodging the police was part of the fun. We didn't have a gangs in Riverside, but when other neighborhoods tried to push us around, guys like Albert Jackson, William Boggin, Harold "Iron Jaw" Adams, Mose Marr, and a few others step up for the hood.

Dancing was a new kind of fun we found by 1960. The big thing for my crew was sock hops in high school gyms all over town. Also, house parties in winter, and back yard dances in the summertime were the rave for teenagers. Everyone had to have a 45 record collection. Swopping or trading the latest hit record was the popular thing. We spent the whole summer looking for parties.

Sometime there would be two or three parties on the same night. The biggest dilemma for my crew was which backyard party to try first? But, the real party was always going downtown to Beale Street for the early evening *"Summertime Get Downs"* at Club Handy. Kids from all over the city came to exhibit the latest dance moves or crave, with neighborhood pride on the line. The Nikki Hokkie, Boogaloo, Shemmy, Hully-gully, Shing-a-ling, Hulk-a-buck, Mash Potatoes, and the Twist were just some of the more popular dance craves my sister Bernice taught me.

Bern attending Booker T. Washington High School, and was a cheerleader. BTW was located just a few blocks from Beale Street, so any new dance that came to town went there first. And, Bernice brought them home and taught me all the new moves and dances. The first one on the dance floor, with my cousin Juanita, made me popular in certain groups, as I passed my friends dance moves, Bern taught me.

During the *"Summertime Get Downs,"* many a reputations were gained and lost on Club Handy's dance floor. Among the best, Lance "Sweet Willie Wine" Watson was a legendary character. Paralyzed in one arm, so "Wine" danced with that hand in his pocket. One of the more innovative dancers and flamboyant characters in town, looking so cool, as he moved, kids began imitating his style. He created a dance crave called, you guessed it, the "Willie Wine." The late 1950s and early 1960s were my time and a great time.

The Counter Culture Comes of Age: Fire Next Time

The 1963 March on Washington (8-28-1963) brought black Americans over to the side of integrationists/civil rights leaders. Malcolm X describes that march, as a charade in his book, *Autobiography of Malcolm X*. So, I will only say the event led black people away from freedom, justice, and equality, because some leaders wanted a big image in the eyes of white people. White leaders ignored the screaming headlines, detailing the hatred, murder, injustice, and inhumanity some white Americans heaped upon those willing to stand for right—freedom, equality, and justice/fair courts in America. The words of **"We Charge Genocide"** never come out of anyone's mouth, if they were even aware of it.

Leaving the 1950s, African American enters a new time symbolized by the caustic but honest rhetoric of Malcolm X. His words, declaring *Black Nationalism*, and were like a shot in a dark room; everyone broke for the exits. Malcolm's word were a wakeup call, entering the 1960s, he described the desperation, scarcity, and oppression black people endured, as no other observer or activist.

Having fought alongside blacks, during sit-ins and freedom rides, young progressives saw the real enemy as **Brown v. Board of Education's** failure to change white people. Even though school buses had picked up and dropped off white children for years before **Brown,** after that decision school buses became a hated symbol to whites. Once they began bringing black children to white schools, screaming white women became monsters that terrorized black children, like their husbands and fathers during the **Dark Age** *angry white men mob madness era*.

The third civil war was on big time!!! White people showed they were unwilling to accept equality of blacks even at the lowest level of society. State and local governments, in the South and North on all levels, were in open rebellion against conceding any socioeconomic or political advances to black people, especially in education.

Sitting astride this changeover, Lorraine Hansberry used **A Raisin in the Sun** to reflect the end of one era and the beginning of another. It was a time Americans had not considered, as black people fought to make it their time. Hansberry's plotline subtly arrayed events, changing social roles and attitudes, as well as the evolving psychology of black people in her storyline. She portrayed the importance of the black family, surviving this volatile period in iconic fashion. Lynching, burning, and lawlessness of the **"Dark Age"** *angry white men mob madness era* had subsided, but the attitudes behind it remained the bedrock of white hatred for blacks in America.

The *Great Migration* brought 6 million southern blacks to northern cities during 1920 through the 1950s. But, the *"Tent City Movement"* dumped even more southern blacks into Northern ghettos, after the demise of sharecropping.

Brown supposedly expanded opportunities, freedom, and equality for slavery's descendants, but Hansberry's ***A Raisin in the Sun,*** showed even the North segregation was the law.

However, as this narrative has pointed out, similar to Hansberry's plotline, the lack of progress for black families in the North mimicked what was happening in the South. Amidst southerners pushing black sharecroppers off farms, some formerly imprisoned families headed out West, as well as North, trying to find living space. Hansberry used her play to satirize America's promise of freedom and equality while painting a dimming fresco of the unfulfilled opportunities for ***Brown's*** christening.

So, the early 1960s open to a continuation of denials enslaved Africans faced since the first kidnapped souls began arriving in North America (1530s). Those behind the terror that kept black families on lockdown refused to relent. Instead, they doubled down, demonstrating their commitment to white supremacy and segregation with an act that sent chills through peace-loving people around the world. They brutally and blatantly showed their total disregard for life with their resolve to spread hatred in a monstrous demonstration on the Sunday morning of September 15, 1963 in Birmingham, Alabama. On a bright sunshiny autumn morning, just one month after the *1963 March on Washington*, four white men—KKK—placed 15 sticks of dynamite, with timer, beneath the 16th Street Baptist Church. The bomb killed four little girls Addie Mae Collins, Cynthia Wesley, Carole Robertson, and Carol Denise McNair.

Had CP-USA perpetrated such a dastardly act, as the Ku Klux Klan, the US Government wouldn't have stopped short of declaring WAR on Russia! Not only was there nothing done to the KKK, it was learned later the FBI was aware of the plot. That act of terror—deaths of those little girls—by white supremacists, Dr. Martin Luther King, Jr. described as *"one of the most vicious and tragic crimes ever perpetrated against humanity."* The death of those little girls was a message, like the egregious murder of Emmitt Till's in 1955 both said: *"Whites still believe racial terror is an acceptable weapon against black people and could strike anyone at any time, anywhere without warning."*

Prophetically, that same year (1963), James Baldwin seared the pages of history with these immortal words, ***"No more water, fire next time."*** Baldwin's aphorism was an essay to his 14-year-old nephew. His sizzling assessment of conditions in America for black people, following the bombing in Birmingham, which still griped America, and left no doubt, the centrality of racism was alive and well in America.

Baldwin's words foreshadowed the most tumultuous periods of urban disorders like a fuse to an explosive reaction of black youth in America's cities. Baldwin's stinging commentary pointed to the insidiousness of racism and white supremacy, which ignited the most explosive period ever initiated by slave descendants in US history. He gave his nephew similar advice; my parents and grandparents gave me to help guard my life.

The deaths of thousands, during lynching and throughout American history, even today (Trayvon Martin to Amaud Arbery, Brennia Taylor, George Floyd and many others), bear witness to the need for such warnings. However, Baldwin posed a question, *"How do slave descendants rise out of poverty, progress in America's system, which is designed to keep them on the bottom?"* Laying his intriguing proposition on the table, Baldwin challenged America to offer solutions.

Ignoring America's history presented here in previous pages, white Americans castigated Baldwin, "as a trouble maker, trying to incite violence between the races." This is such a preposterous statement and reaction from whites looking at the same events but not seeing the **Dark Age** *angry white men mob madness* as violence between the races, which make all white people culprit. They offered excuses to justify the **"Dark Age"** *angry white men mob madness* in order to deny black people's demands for justice and equality, as well as access to fair courts.

I belabor this point because obviously, white people did not consider what they did to black Americans—lynching, burning, bombing, and lawlessness, during the **"Dark Age"** *angry white men mob madness era*—violence against black people. White Americans minimize conditions government created by viewing their denials of rights for black people, through the big end of the telescope. That view reduces their perception of racism, discrimination, and disparate treatment heap upon black people.

Whites' narrowed vision allows them to focus on isolated problems, while ignoring the environment and context surrounding their view. Narrowing white people's scope, given their circumscribed view of discrimination, disparate treatment, racism, and the hostile environment whites enforced against blacks—police murders—less importance. Their view exemplifies the point white and black people can look at or experience the exact same situation or event but develop two totally different scenarios. This view gives them a tiny view of the huge impact of whites' discrimination on black life in America. Whites are very comfortable with their treatment of slavery's descendants. They make the self-righteous claim that such government policies *'will end when black people 'prove' to white people they are ready for the 'responsibilities' of equality.'* Not quite four years after, Baldwin's prophetic precognition exploded, echoing through the streets of America's ghettos in 1967. Those riots warned of coming disaster, echoing like antediluvian wails through American cities.

These rebellions occurred in over 159 communities, large and small across the US, frightened by black rebellions whites ran for the exits. Urban rebellions became alternative speech for black youth. Their only *VOICE*—street demonstrations—further clarified the proposition Baldwin laid on the table. Many white Americans refused to accept an alternative vision of US society, included black people as first class citizens. Whites also refused to admit their mindset deny black people are human beings and deserving of all human rights, which the ***Civil Rights Bill of 1866*** granted whites, which refused to recognize and accept.

Progressive white Americans joined African Americans on the front lines, fighting for social change and social justice, and died at the hands of racist standing with black people. However, the media gave ***Brown v. Board of Education*** credit for the changes their deaths produced. The media however did not give the US Supreme Court credit for the bloodshed and lives loss across America. During the 1950s, the Supreme Court stood idly by, and watched, as peaceful young black and white sit-in demonstrators and freedom riders, continually mounted lunch counter stools and piling aboard buses headed down South, where police aided KKK attacks. The US Supreme Court did, as Woodrow Wilson during ***Red Summer 1919***, nothing to support its ruling in the fight for freedom against segregation and white supremacy.

Riding through the South, facing perils from police, mobs, and local racist groups, freedom riders braved terror sponsored by "state governments." Freedom riders were not only up against individually enraged white citizens but state government agencies. There was no difference between government agencies and the KKK, they were one and the same people. The *Mississippi State Sovereignty Commission,* coordinated attacks on freedom riders and played a role in the kidnapping and murders of Andrew Goodman, Michael "Mickey" Schwerner, and James Chaney, three civil rights workers killed in Mississippi. *(The Mississippi State Sovereignty Commission (MSSC) was a state agency that preserved white supremacy and segregation during the 1950s and 60s. The Commission was directed by the Governor of Mississippi, covered up violence and murder to preserve white supremacy in Mississippi. The MSSC employed a huge network of informants that spy on over 87,000 Americans).* The MSSC was involved in the deaths of—Medgar Evers, George Winston Lee, Viola Liuzzo, Jimmie Lee Jackson, Andrew Goodman, Michael "Mickey" Schwerner, and James Chaney, as well as many many others— their bodies littered the landscape across the South. States governments allowed known murderers to go free, as with Emmett Till's killers, to preserve white supremacy and segregation in the South.

Fire Comes to Cities Across America

The federal court ruling on December 5, 1955, in *Browder v. Gayle* declared the Alabama and Montgomery laws that segregated public buses were unconstitutional. The Monday after Rosa Parks, an African-American woman, was arrested for refusing to surrender her seat to a white person, the Montgomery bus boycott began. One of the first major mass protests and political campaigns against the policies of racial segregation; blacks refused to ride the public transit system of Montgomery. The campaign was a seminal event in the civil rights movement. Revs. Martin Luther King, Jr. and Ralph D. Abernathy were among many in the civil rights movement that supported the boycott. One year later the boycott ended on December 20, 1956.

Over the next eight years, Rev. King built a solid reputation and following as a civil rights leader. Based on his leadership and on the heels of *The 1963 March on Washington,* new black leaders began to eclipse those who'd held sway since the early 1930s. During that march, Rev. King delivered his powerful and iconic speech; *I Have a Dream*. His speech, more than the march itself, gave the world renewed hope that **Brown v. Board of Education** (1954) would be fulfill and mimic his speech.

Rev. Martin Luther King, Jr.'s speech brought international exposure and the attention of the world to the current lack of justice in the US. He gained further prominence and recognition as the Nobel Peace Prize recipient in 1964. That acknowledgment allowed him to do, as Marcus Garvey, Paul Robeson, William L. Patterson, and Malcolm X, speak beyond the American ghettos. His prestige created a schism within the civil rights movement regarding image, popularity, goals, direction, and leading personalities. The civil rights movement had become wedded to integration/assimilation, but young radicals grew more and more concerned about the plight of poor black Americans.

Suddenly, like lightning out of a clear blue sky, James Meredith (1966), an unknown civil rights activist, at least outside of the South, was gunned down on a Mississippi highway just outside of Memphis. Meredith believed a lone black man could walk from Memphis to Jackson, Mississippi without fearing for his life or help from civil rights leaders. Once Meredith took to the highway on his solo 220-mile *March against Fear,* a white man sprang from the weeds in ambush, shot gunning him just across the Mississippi/Tennessee state line. Following the unforeseen sneak attack civil rights leaders and social change activists descended on Mississippi declaring, "the prospect of murder would not intimidate black people."

Fortunately, Meredith survived the ambush, and although he declared before his march, *"I didn't need help from civil rights leaders,"* they flooded the state, vowing to finish his march following the ambush. Dr. King became the leader of the march, and other civil rights leaders converged on Jackson, like it was the end of the rainbow for civil rights. After that white man shot Meredith, civil rights leaders vowed they would liberate black people from bushwhackers, racism and white supremacy. However, not interested in rainbows or the gold at their end, young black radicals enjoyed an even richer find, gaining the ability to push their way out of the shadows of civil rights leaders.

More significant than the march itself, while on the way to Jackson, Stokely Carmichael uttered the immortal words **"BLACK POWER!"** With those two words, activism in the US changed forever and the black liberation struggle has never been the same since around the world. When those words began coming out of other young activists' mouths, the vision of black activists changed in ways no one could have anticipated let along predicted, before James Meredith was gunned down. Those two words produced new personalities who made a hard left turn from the radical fringe of activism straight for the heart of the civil rights movement. Leaders of the black liberation struggle claimed a place at the table of leader ship in black communities.

Following the birth of black power, activists made a B-line straight for the center of black politics, but civil rights leaders circled their wagons around black communities and politics, denying black power activists a seat at the leadership table. Civil rights leaders took a defensive stand against young black radicals denying their legitimacy. Similar to the 1920s, the same the "new Negro" movement leaders that opposed Marcus Garvey, were at it again, causing dissension within the ranks of the black liberation struggle. Differences over tactics fighting the struggle widened from a schism into a chasm. The split created a huge divide, as Dr. King's star, as the *"number one civil rights leader"* continued rising.

Civil rights leaders pressured Dr. King, trying to force him to focus less on the poor and more on middle-class gains. They also wanted him to condemn black power. With each speech, march and demonstration, as the 1960s progressed, the chasm grew, pushing Dr. King into a "no man's land" between civil rights and black power.

Most assuredly and clearly, Carmichael's words created an even larger crack in the civil rights coalition, than Dr. King giving *VOICE* to the plight of poor people. Those words **"black power"** changed many young activists' mindset regarding life in the US, and their defiance would eventually reach around the world, like William Patterson's run across Europe, after **<u>We Charge Genocide</u>**. Those two words—***black power***—uttered by Stokely Carmichael, created a philosophical and psychological impact that raised a black fist, *"blackinizing"* young activists even though they had no idea what black power actually meant, coming out of Stokely's mouth.

Rebellions, in urban ghettos, also began flaring up, as young blacks grew impatient with the slow pace of change. HBCU campuses were ablaze with new energy and the only thing coming out of black activist the mouths was black power. It was the burning issues on campuses and black empowerment won the hearts and minds of students. Black power was a growing schism on HBCU campuses and black students took the lead from the left, pushing middle-class civil rights ideas to the curb.

On one side of the huge developing gulf of poverty, stood black power activists while on the other, were civil rights leaders' refusing to even talk to black power activists. This left Dr. King stretched out across the middle, trying to hold the two sides together in the black struggle. Unknown to the general public, civil rights leaders began undercutting Dr. King's efforts because he would not retreat form supporting the needs of the poor, as well as building a new coalition between civil rights and black power activists.

Leadership among black people has a short history; prior to the 1920s, there was no black leadership class. During that time, particular black individuals served as spokespersons, mostly preachers. A few individual rose to prominence as leaders of local groups, unions or lodges mostly in Harlem. Others became early leaders with the Niagara Movement, which became the NAACP. Most civil rights leaders rode the coattails of the new Negro movement from the 1920s, as NAACP leaders or as part of the unionization movement, like A. Philip Randolph with the Pullman Porters.

The concept of a "black leadership class" began with the *"talented tenth,"* a concept developed by northern philanthropists, which said, *"Only 10% of the black population had leadership potential."* W.E.B. DuBois publicized this theory and was one of the *"talented tenth."* Although some will disagree, the old guard in the 1960s inherited leadership and power, doing J. Edgar Hoover's dirty work.

Black leaders that helped Hoover deport Marcus Garvey and destroyed the *UNIA*, while joining Hoover's effort to drive the CP-USA out of America, were promoted by Hoover in the press as "the kind of leaders black people should follow." Hoover's promotion made them official spokesperson, replacing the unofficial preachers and abolitionists as people like Fredrick Douglas faded with age.

These leaders, according to Malcolm X, made an accommodation with segregation working with J. Edgar Hoover and they became even more prominent, as leaders through *The 1963 March on Washington*. Segregation created a role for blacks willing to continue playing the role Hoover created as go-betweens as their claim to leadership. They grew comfortable with maintaining the status quo, pushing middle class goals. These leaders did not want to end the role or relationships they had established through their accommodation with segregation; hence, Malcolm X's description of them as "accommodationists." Their rhetoric indicated they felt they had gotten on the inside and had been accepted by white people, as leaders of *"the Negro."*

Reflecting Malcolm's assessment, even more, they had established themselves as go-betweens, the ones to talk with white folks, regarding the needs of

Negros. They became arbiters of black people's demands, as well as managers of black people's progress, as white people determined. Their behavior indicated they felt they were the only ones qualified to talk with whites *(the Talented Tenth)*, which gave them something to protect or lose to black power activists.

Poised on the other side of this growing divide, between civil rights and black power, young black activists stood ready to claim a place at the leadership table. They had come of age with groups like SNCC, CORE, CP-USA, and other left-leaning groups that had no allegiance to the status quo. In other words, they had earned their place as activists. Some of these young blacks had studied at the feet of established black leaders or were beginners with CP-USA, not journeymen like Bayard Rustin, Paul Robeson or William Patterson.

These young activists saw themselves as the next wave to inherit leadership among black people. Lorraine Hansberry and her generation are reflective of the first wave. Although they accepted integration, they were not "accommodationists." However, status quo leaders of civil rights refused to concede leadership or make room for the new generation that were developing in the streets of ghettos across America.

The civil rights schism created a three-legged stool of leadership—old-line leaders, preachers, business people; next civil rights movement leaders, and last black radicals. The third leg of that stool had been shaped by *Black Nationalists*, like Malcolm X, Robert Williams, Ron Karenga, Imamu Baraka, and others. Then an even more aggressive breed of young radicals came to the fore, putting a black fist in the face of white people. Their black fist became the symbol of the age.

The first wave of radicals came out of the *Student Non-violence Coordinating Committee (SNCC)*, led by Stokley Carmichael and H. Rap Brown, who gave voice to demands for **"Black Power."** These black power radicals rejected everything about the past in terms of black politics and culture. Much like the demands for *"new"* at the beginning of the *Harlem Renascence* and the new *"Negro Movement,"* not only did they demand new leadership, they demanded new everything—new hairstyles, dress, ideas, customs, traditions, even names. No more waiting for what black people were supposed to have received with emancipation, they demanded it now, *I mean right now!*

Out of the first wave, came a second, which was for more aggressive than the first. The second wave of black activists to rise, exhibited complete irreverence reflecting their demands of *Black Nationalists*. These radicals took their lead from Malcolm X and Robert Williams; both believed in *by any means necessary* and guns to back it up. But unlike Malcolm X, they had no religious leaning. They picked up on Robert Williams' armed self-defense model, which he outlined in **Negros with Guns**, as their credo. These radicals were the *Black Panther Party*, organized by Huey P. Newton, Bobby Seale, and David Hilliard. Firing hard cored black revolutionary rhetoric, like bullets, they personified the most radical form of *Black Nationalism*, ever to be advocated by descendants of American slavery.

Civil rights leaders, from their rhetoric, actions, and perspective, saw the *Black Panthers Party*, as the worst possible outcome for black people and said so. Similar to W. E. B. DuBois, A Philip Randolph and other Negro leaders' perspective on Marcus Garvey, they went on the attack against *black power*, particularly the *Black Panthers Party*. They called the Black Panthers, *"a destructive force trying to destroy the black community."*

Civil rights leaders castigated and excoriated young black radicals, and joined J. Edgar Hoover's campaign to destroy the black power movement, as they did Marcus Garvey. I don't mean to make the *Black Panthers* the cause of riotous conflagrations that followed their demonstration and declaration before the California Legislature. I am simply pointing out that the *Black Panthers* radicalizing influence on young blacks had an affect, similarly to how *Students for a Democratic Society (SDS)* and the rise of the *Weather Underground*, affected white youths.

The Black Panthers' confrontational image increased the likelihood that black youth would respond violently during encounters with whites in general and police in particular. Racial incidents put black pride on the line at all times. Consequently, young blacks saw confrontations with white people, as affronts to the black communities. Confrontations with white people were seen, as affronts to the black communities. Young black power activists' demands respect stuck a black fist in white people's face and did not retreat. Their reaction was unlike blacks' response to lynching, and white attacks on black communities in the past (1900-1950).

The rebellion in Cleveland, Ohio (7-18-66) was a classic example of heightened sensitivity from blacks to whites' insensitivity. The first large scale urban disturbance since Harlem, New York City (1964) and Watts, Los Angeles (1965), Cleveland seemed to come out of nowhere to people in other parts of America. But in Cleveland, a sign reading, *"No Water for Niggers,"* hung outside the 79'ers Bar at E.79th Street and Hough Avenue for years without comment. However, that sign during the supercharged racial atmosphere of 1966, prompted an emotional incendiary response. The bar's sign was like a spark in gun power to a black community on edge. Outraged blacks that had grown tired of insults, and broken promises became angry crowds. Incidents that had not drawn any serious response, on this day (7-23-1966), brought Ahmed Evens and his followers into an urban guerrilla confrontation with police, sitting Cleveland ablaze.

During the spring (1967) other cities like Omaha, NA; Louisville, KY; Chicago, IL; San Francisco, CA; Wichita, KS; Nashville, TN; and Houston, TX experiences racial disturbances, not as deadly or destructive, but they were signs of the times. As such, one cannot simply throw a few numbers and words at readers and expect them to grasp the magnitude of pinned up frustrations smothering in the black community at the beginning of 1967. Much like today in cities across America, this narrative echoes James Baldwin's words, like a shot in a dark theater (1963) *"No more water, fire next time."*

Black communities across America, by mid-summer were seething with anger, disappointment, resentment, and hostility, resulting from the grandiose promises made after ***Brown v. Board of Education*** and the ***1963 March on Washington,*** as well as the ***1964 Civil Rights Bill*** and ***1965 Voting Right Act***, which had only produced meager cosmetic changes, whereas black people were demanding and looking for real change. As it was suspected then but has become evident today, government programs produced only superficial changes for blacks. A disturbance in Roxbury, Boston (6/2/67), exploded into another rebellion while igniting the most destructive summer of urban American disorders ever.

At the most southern tip of the US in Tampa, FL (1967), city leaders believed they had weathered the long hot summer's storm of riots of the previous years. Unaware of the threatening storm hovering on the horizon, like the outer bands of a hurricane, a Tropical depression far out at sea put Tampa in the eye, as it came ashore. After not experiencing trouble during previous summers—racial violence elsewhere in large urban centers such as Los Angeles, San Francisco, Chicago, and Cleveland—Tampa's community leaders breathed a collective sigh of relief. They were confident that racial harmony was the norm in Tampa, as all along Florida's Gulf Coast.

Tampa's politicians, as most white leaders, were complacent. They dismissed the undercurrent of anger in Tampa's black neighborhoods. Another incident, which went unnoticed, during previous years by blacks, like a tropical wave coming ashore (6-11-1967), finally made landfall. It unleashed a wave of violence that changed the racial climate in Tampa forever. Yet, events in Tampa were no more than a campfire compared to the blaze that erupted in Newark, NJ, a day later. Newark (6/12/67) was the most devastating urban rebellion since Watts (1965). It resulted in 25 deaths, 1,200 injured, and over 1,300 arrest, while costing over $100 million in overall damage.

An even greater show of outrage followed the conflagration in Newark. In less than a month, the most destructive urban rebellion of the decade exploded in Detroit, MI (6/23/67). The riot, which lasted almost two weeks, left 43 dead, over 2,000 injured and more than 4,000 arrests. Conservative estimates of damage climbed to nearly one billion dollars. Following that destructive episode, Detroit spiraled into a slow downward tailspin of neglect, as the black community asserted political control. Long-time white investors and corporate America, in general, vacated the city, and new ones avoid Detroit like COVID-19.

There were riots around the country, with outbreaks in Buffalo, NY, Phoenix, AZ, Washington, D.C., and New Haven, CT, among other cities. According to the report of the Senate Permanent Committee on Investigations released in November 1967, 75 major riots occurred in that year alone, with 21 rebellions in which 83 people died, compared with 11 in 1966 and 36 in 1965. During 1967's long hot summer, racial disturbances, not only swept through large urban areas like Detroit and Newark but also exploded in smaller ones in such places as Minneapolis, MN; Dayton, FL and Cincinnati OH, as well as other cities unaccustomed to racial violence.

The Counter Culture Becomes the Spirit of the Age

Back on April 17, 1965, an antiwar gathering in Washington, D.C., was the first organized by a small unknown group of campus radical called *Students for a Democratic Society (SDS)*. Much to the surprise of organizers, over 15,000, mostly college students, which was considered a huge turnout by prevailing standards, showed up to protest the draft. Dramatically, they gave voice to demands to end the war in Vietnam.

Most Americans were unaware of the great convergence that was occurring among social change forces in America, in the late 1950s and early 1960s. Disaffected young white activist of the *Beat Generation—Beatniks*—came together with the hippie counterculture to form one movement. The peace-loving flower children were swallowed up by the anti-war movement, which gave them a political edge. They joined the rampaging civil rights movement, which engulfed most college campuses.

Moreover, the convergence of black activists with young white progressives, like *Students for a Democratic Society (SDS)*, began another hard left turn. This convergence pulled the rampaging anti-war movement together with the once very irenic communal flower children, who lost their petals, facing the harsh breath of American racism. They followed SDS into the battle for freedom in America. Disaffected progressives radicals came together like a gathering storm that mushroomed into the peace movement. That explosion of political activism of young progressive wrote their story upon the winds of change, blowing across the US in the mid-1960s.

Developing new technologies for social change and social justice, as during their attacks on segregation in the South, the counterculture rolled out **Human Be-Ins and Teach-ins,** as their new technology. (Human Be-In began in San Francisco's Golden Gate Park Polo Fields (1-14-1967). It was a prelude to San Francisco's Amazing Summer of Love, which made Haight-Ashbury a symbol of the American counterculture. It introduced the word "psychedelic" to suburbia. Called a "Gathering of the Tribes," it drew more than 20,000 young people to Golden Gate Park, as the vanguard of the counterculture movement.) Human Be-Ins formulated the key ideas of the counterculture, and like crusaders they spread the counter-culture's message.

These confabs—*Human Be-ins*—brought young progressives together much like beatsters developed their movement or the sit-ins and freedom rides. Inspiring hundreds of young white kids across America to think differently, about their world, the *Human Be-in* and *Teach-in* movement became classrooms against the war. The first *Human Be-in* and *Teach-in* were held at the University of Michigan, bringing anti-war groups and the new counterculture together. They form the point of the movement that became the thrust against the Vietnam War.

The hippie culture joined anti-war demonstrations, spreading the word against the Vietnam War. Starting with small protest, on college campuses across the nation, SDS organized the first massive march against the war in Washington, D.C. This time 25,000 anti-war protesters attended. A mammoth response at that point; SDS became the leading edge of the anti-war movement.

The media projected SDS as the leading "new left" student group against the war on college campuses. Anti-war sentiment and government betrayal drew more and more hippies into the fray against the war like a magnet. Beatsters' distrust of authority became the *spirit of the age*. No longer a "stand-a-lone" movement, hippies became amalgamated in the massive antiwar coalition sweeping the nation. *Human Be-Ins* became the organizing technology, as young progressives moved from focusing on personal growth to political empowerment.

Young radicals no longer viewed the government simply with great suspicion; it became the **"Establishment,"** with J. Edgar Hoover as its *"dark overlord."* Hippies not only closed the door on the racist mindset of their parents, but made an even hard left turn then dropped off the edge of mainstream society altogether. Dropping out and turning on, hippies rejected consumerism, while stressing ecological awareness and achieving higher states of consciousness through psychedelics drugs. Also, they pursued a radical liberal political agenda, opposing the War and racism in America.

By the thousands, counterculture radicals moved away from war and racism. San Francisco and then New York City became ground zero for hippies, starting with the legendary amazing **"Summer of Love."** Frisco hosted the iconic happening in 1967. It reflected the *sign of the times* for radicals. They serve notice on America that things had changed. The **"Summer of Love"** was the counterculture's shot across the *Establishment's bow*. Like the *"pied piper of Hamelin"* and loader than the shot heard around the world, blaring guitars drew over one hundred thousand young people to Haight-Ashbury from all over America. The counterculture threw a party, and it seemed most young people in the country showed up to *"get stoned,"* while getting down at rock concerts, wild parties, and love-ins all summer. These were great times!!!

Throughout 1967 and into 1968, progressives white kids held several *Human Be-Ins* in New York City's Central Park, included an Easter Sunday march (3-26-67). That *Human Be-in* included Hispanic families from the Easter Parade, poets from the Bronx, beatsters from the Village, interior decorators from the East Side, teachers from the West Side, and teeny boppers from Long Island (*The New York Times: 1967*). A month later, the **Spring Mobilization to End the War in Vietnam** threw another huge anti-war *Human Be-In*, producing estimates of 400 thousand in Central Park. It drew Native American (Sioux) from South Dakota with a sign—*Do Not Do to the Vietnamese What You Did to Us."* African Americans from uptown Harlem came to march for civil rights and ending the war. Those parading were adorned in flowering bed sheets, buttons, tights, carnation petals, paper stars, tiny mirrors on their foreheads, paint around their mouths and on their cheeks, and all spoke with one voice, fighting for one cause—peace. Also, folk singers and rock bands held a peace concrete.

A march led by Dr. Martin Luther King, Harry Belafonte, Dr. Benjamin Spock, and others marched to the United Nations. Gathering momentum before giving his "***Why I am Opposed to the War in Vietnam***" sermon, Dr. King declared he opposed the war in Vietnam because he loved America. *"Vietnam is an unjust war, a conflict against a colored people. I speak out against it not in anger but with anxiety and sorrow in my heart, and above all, with a passionate desire to see our beloved country stand as the moral example of the world,"* (Village Voice: 1967).

The Drum Major Instinct

Black people in America, during the 1960s, struggle with many challenges—injustice, discrimination, and poverty—lack of access to America's bounty. Dr. Martin Luther King Jr. confronted the schism between civil rights and black power by trying to bring the two sides together. In his speech, ***"Why I Am Opposed to the Vietnam War"*** (4-30-67), at the Riverside Church in New York City, he outlined his opposition. His remarks upset many civil rights leaders, who kept one eye on J. Edgar Hoover' reaction, stepped away from Dr. King's position. The civil rights chasm widened, as war and protest against poverty lead by Dr. King continued developing. He believed his strategy would bring the two sides—civil rights and black power—together. Dr. King's efforts and legacy around the plight of the poor, became the defining moments of his life.

Dr. King charged America with responsibility for slavery's descendants' penniless emancipation, which produced desperation and scarcity—poverty—and demanded America address it's legacy of slavery. But few black leaders were interested in a fight over poverty, pitting them head-on against segregationists and the federal government over the needs of the poor. Their recoiling questioned *"Whether there would be gains for the middle class, even if they won such a battle?"*, showed where their real alliance was regarding Dr. King's commitment.

Civil rights leaders upset with Dr. King over his new strategy to help the poor claim *"he had abandoned the middle-class."* Black leaders complained that *"by taking the spotlight off middle-class goals and putting it on the poor, was a selling out of his class."* Leaders of the old guard exhibited an unwavering commitment to making gains for the middle class first, *even if they came at the expense of the poor.* The poor fell outside of the *"talented tenth"* and could not claim the loyalty of old-guard leaders, who had used the poor as a bargaining chip. Malcolm X said *"they used the poor to justify their positions."*

Dr. King offered a blueprint to hold the fracturing civil rights coalition together. He thought it would seal the breach while addressing America's denial of freedom, justice, and equality for black Americans. Symbolizing his commitment to Jesus Christ's and his commandment to care for the poor, Dr. King designed his new strategy to *"take the fight against poverty into the streets of America."*

Although other civil rights leaders may have understood Dr. King's motivation, only a few stood with him. Offering his plan for the poor on December 4, 1967, Dr. King held a press conference in Atlanta to announced the ***"Poor People's Campaign"*** to the nation. He immediately went on the road, preaching in churches, stumping for the ***"Poor People's Campaign"*** across the nation, following that announcement. But, as December 1968 drew to a close, Dr. King was virtually alone among civil rights leaders, concerned with helping the poor.

Civil rights leaders who had been at Dr. King's side, during his other campaigns, were conspicuously absent from his poor people's effort. Watching from the sideline, and according to Dr. King, *"they were not helping to raise money or get volunteers for the '**Poor People's Campaign.**'"* Two months after his announcement (2-4-1968), Dr. King preached his famous ***"Drum Major Instinct"*** sermon from the pulpit of Ebenezer Baptist Church. His message to civil rights leaders was, *no matter the outcome, I will move to help the poor, whether I have the two sides—civil rights and black power to help me or not.*

Dr. King wanted to make his unwavering commitment to the ***"Poor People's Campaign"*** clear. He left no doubt he would go forward if he had to go alone. During his prepared remarks that Sunday, he emphasized Christ's challenge to service the poor. His sermon spoke of Christ's response to a question from his disciples, James and John, the sons of Zebedee, who asked Jesus *"that we may sit, one on thy right hand, and the other on thy left hand, in thy glory."* However, Jesus answered with a question, *"Can ye drink of the cup that I drink of? And be baptized with the baptism that I am baptized with?"* Elaborating further, Dr. King said among other things:

"If any of you are around when I have to meet my day, I don't want a long funeral. And if you get somebody to deliver the eulogy, tell them not to talk too long. And every now and then I wonder what I want them to say. Tell them not to mention that I have a Nobel Peace Prize—that isn't important. Tell them not to mention that I have over three or four hundred other awards—that's not important. Tell them not to mention where I went to school.

I'd like somebody to mention that day that Martin Luther King, Jr., tried to give his life serving others. I'd like for somebody to say that day that Martin Luther King, Jr., tried to love somebody. I want you to say that day that I tried to be right on the war question (Vietnam War). I want you to be able to say that day that I did try to feed the hungry. And I want you to be able to say that day that I did try in my life to clothe those who were naked. I want you to say on that day that I did try in my life to visit those who were in prison. I want you to say that I tried to love and serve humanity.

Yes, if you want to say that I was a drum major, say that I was a drum major for justice. Say that I was a drum major for peace. I was a drum major for righteousness. And all of the other shallow things will not matter. I won't have any money to leave behind. I won't have the fine and luxurious things of life to leave behind. But I just want to leave a committed life behind. And that's all I want to say."

Dr. King's sermon reflected his commitment to serve humanity, especially in his last days. Although he entered a time filled with intrigue, treachery, and betrayal, Dr. King challenged America to get on the right side of the fight for freedom, justice, and equality for slavery's descendants. After pointing his finger at the federal government, as a hypocrite and the culprit responsible for slavery's descendants still residing in poverty, J. Edgar Hoover became his arch-nemesis.

Hoover saw Dr. King as he saw Marcus Garvey, Paul Robeson, William Patterson, and Malcolm X. Hoover had dedicated himself to thwarting any effort by African Americans to change their status as *"cheap labor"* in America. Dr. King, like those men, had been in Hoover's bull's eye, since the *1963 March on Washington*, but when he came out against the Vietnam War, he drew Hoover's ire as he said, *"Martin Luther King is the most dangerous man in America."*

When Dr. King announced the **Poor People's Campaign** he made newspaper headlines around the world. Hoover reacted as though Dr. King's statement was declaration of war on America's *"cheap labor"* strategy. Dr. King went to the top of Hoover's social change hit list. Most people are unaware of the deadly environment Dr. King entered after announcing the **Poor People's Campaign**. Taking on the federal government, Dr. King staked himself out as a sacrificial lamb to force America to change.

The real issue Dr. King faced was twofold. First, he desperately wanted to help the poor but was being hamstrung by the lack of support he was getting from civil rights leaders, after he mounted the **Poor People's Campaign**. The divide between civil rights and black power leaders was seriously challenging his plan to help the poor. During his last days, working with the striking Memphis sanitation workers (2-13-68), Dr. King was also trying to establish an independent *VOICE* for black Americans, so they could, *"tell their story to the world in their own word,"* which is what Paul Robeson and William L. Patterson had attempted with **"We Charge Genocide**.*"*

The second part of Dr. King's dilemma was how to close the schism between civil rights leaders and himself, as well as between civil rights and black power. After the *1963 March on Washington*, the media anointed Dr. King, *"the number one black leader in America."* This anointing seemed to create distance between civil rights leaders and Dr. King. Then following the awarding of the Nobel Peace Prize, some black leaders grumbled and complained, *"All our work in the past, the media is crediting to Dr. King, while we are being overlooked by the press."*

I feel this is an issue American media has glossed over and continue to overlook, so have all who wrote about this period. The implications of my statement I will fully explain in the following pages, but for now surfice it to say, the role of the federal government in the deaths of Dr. King and Malcolm X should have received new looks. Marcus Garvey, Malcolm X, and Dr. Martin Luther King, Jr. shared a common connection with America's *"Dark Overload,"* FBI Director J. Edgar Hoover.

These three men were all victims of Hoover, as black leaders. Hoover's job was to stop any movement, group, or individual who sought to change the *"cheap labor"* role of slavery's descendants in America. Also, Hoover managed the cover-up of the government's denial of *VOICE* for descendants of American slavery.

Hoover's job was to prevent black people from speaking to the world about discrimination and disparate treatment, which they continued enduring. As I showed earlier, Hoover weaved the web that entrapped Marcus Garvey. Although he did not physically kill Garvey, he drove him into exile and killed the *UNIA*, his real target.

Next, once Malcolm X became the voice of African Americans in 1960, he was targeted by Hoover and labeled a communist, as Hoover tried to prevent Malcolm from speaking beyond the *cotton curtain*. A very astute individual, Malcolm traveled to Mecca, as a religious pilgrim, which blocked Hoover's effort to keep him from leaving America, as he did Paul Robeson, or declare him "an undesirable" and prevent him from returning a free man. But upon his return Malcolm was like William Patterson, a marked man because of **We Charge Genocide.** While in Mecca Malcolm made contacts that were helping him prepare a petition to file with the **World Court in The Hague.** Malcolm X was going to charge America with genocide against black people in a legal forum not the UN, in that forum America's dollar power had no weight.

Malcolm's move would have renewed and extended the charges made by **We Charge Genocide** before a legal body. His petition in 1965 would have renewed the charge of hypocrite and genocide against America before world leaders, as did **We Charge Genocide.** It is the opinion of many researchers and investigators that Hoover instigated the animosity between Malcolm X and the Nation of Islam to cover-up, putting the trigger man in the Audubon Ballroom that cold February night (2-21-65). (https://www.nytimes.com/2020/02/06/nyregion/malcolm-x-assassination-case-reopened.html?referringSource=articleShare)

Malcolm X gave black commentary such a sharp edge; it sliced through the textbook history taught black children. He laid bare the racist underpinnings of that history, which I have detailed throughout this narrative. Thankfully, along with Malcolm and the work of writers like Dr. Lerone Bennett, Jr., **Before the Mayflower: A History of Black America** *(1964)* and Dr. Chancellor Williams' thesis, **The Destruction of Black Civilization: Great Issues of a Race Between 4500 B.C. and 2000 A.D.** (1971) became just some of the sources that opened the world of black history for me. They provided answers to questions white historians said were unanswerable. Their views help me understand the forces that worked to keep black people confused and in poverty. The knowledge they imparted helped bring Malcolm X into sharper focus.

Although he knew it was not true, Hoover insisted Malcolm and other black activists and leaders, were part of the communist plot to destroy America. Targeting Dr. King, after the *1963 March on Washington*, Hoover renewed his charge that black leaders were all working with communists. I had no idea, at that time, Hoover used the same accusation to taint black leaders during the Harlem Renaissance, *"blacks are helping the Bolshevists who are trying to overthrow the US government"* back in 1917, during the **First Red Scare.** The tragedy is that even though Hoover knew there was no communist threat in 1963, because he destroyed CP-

USA, during the *Second Red Scare* (the 1950s) and drove them out of America. The media allowed him to continue making the charge to justify using the federal government's resources to attack black leaders and never called Hoover's hand by demanding he produce proof.

Hoover remained a formidable foe of the black liberation struggle throughout his 60-year tenure in the FBI (1912-1972). Hoover was just as determined in 1967, as he was in 1917 to use any charge to stop black people from changing their status and gaining access to America's bountiful resources. Accomplishing this, Hoover organized the infamous Counter-Intelligence Program (Co-Intel-Pro) to destroy any organization fighting for black liberation, as well as break the grip of segregation and white supremacy in America.

The Poor People's Campaign and the Sanitation Worker Strike

The Invaders were very active, as street organizers, during the Memphis sanitation strike, before Dr. Martin Luther King, Jr. arrived to aid the sanitation workers (3-28-1968). But it was not until the march on the 28th that the Invaders came to the attention of Dr. King. The Invaders were virtually unknown outside of the Memphis and Mid-South. They were and still are a community organization dedicated to social change and social justice.

A black power group—Invaders—were organized by Charles "Cab" Cabbage, Coby Smith, and me in July 1967. Charles "Cab" Cabbage brought black power to Memphis, when he returned home, after graduating from Morehouse University in May 1967. We began organizing in our community of Riverside in July 1967, and were joined by Cob Smith. The Invaders faced the brutal police of Memphis, which along with Birmingham, Alabama was a hot bed of racism.

The Invaders joined the Memphis Sanitation workers' strike once community leaders organized a support committee, called the *Community On the Move for Equality (C.O.M.E.)* to manage the strike for sanitation workers. Memphis' all-black sanitation workers tried several times previously to organize a union. However, the City of Memphis refused to talk with workers about their grievances and used intimidation to break those strikes.

The City's recalcitrance in dealing with black workers demands—increase in pay—allowed it to keep wages low, avoid paying overtime, sick pay, paid vacation and other time off. More importantly, it would not improve work conditions or repair worn-out and faulty equipment. Sanitation workers were the lowest-paid workers of the city. Workers continuously complained about unsafe working conditions.

The event that prompted the strike occurred on a rainy afternoon (2-1-1968) when two workers were crushed to death in the back of a compactor garbage truck. Echoles Cole, 35 and Robert Walker 29, took shelter, from a sudden storm, in the back of the sanitation truck. Black sanitation workers, like Cole and Walker, took cover in the back of the truck to avoid the city's policy of sending black workers home, without pay, during inclement weather.

Contrarily, the City allowed white workers to return to the locker room to await better conditions or for the remainder of the day with pay. Under the city's segregation policies, black workers could not ride in the cab portion of a garbage truck under any circumstances. Only white workers could ride in front. The city said Cole and Walker died when the truck's compactor malfunctioned and started up without warning.

The City of Memphis denied any responsibility for the loss of life, even though it's poorly maintained equipment malfunctioned, killing these men while on the job. The city, following Mayor Henry Loeb's instructions, and gave each family only $500, equivalent to a month's pay. Mayor Henry Loeb said the money was to help with funeral expenses. Loeb dismissed any thought that the City had any responsibility or obligation to provide a safe work environment. Neither did it accept any responsibility for the deaths of these city employees that died on the job.

Loeb's attitude went far beyond simply supporting segregation; he believed in subjugating blacks to white men. He talked to blacks workers as though they were less than whites. His behavior indicated he felt blacks had a place and should be kept in it.

Loeb was a reflection of the segregationist leadership established by "Boss" Crump, and Loeb inherited leadership, as part of the remnant of the old Crump machine. As a disciple of Crump, who believed like Woodrow Wilson and J. Edgar Hoover, Loeb took a very hardline against black workers. More importantly, the sanitation strike also reflected the last of the three things "Boss" Crump did not allow in Memphis. Hoover had destroyed the first two already— "No Marcus Garvey's UNIA or CP-USA—but the third, unions that refused to enforce segregation," was staring him in his face.

The City maintained a belligerent attitude towards unions in general, but when the all-black sanitation workforce went out on strike, after the deaths of Cole and Walker, the City's attitude and policy toward black people became even more aggressive. Sanitation workers tried to organize a union by striking a few years earlier, but the city fired all workers, as a result of that strike. T. O. Jones, who became president of the local 1733 *American Federation of State, County, and Municipal Employees (AFSCME)*, but the city was still refusing to recognize their union in 1968. On February 13, 1968, P. J. Champa, International Field Staff Director of *AFSCME*, presented the City of Memphis with ten (10) grievances from Sanitation Workers;

1. That Local 1733, AFSCME, be the representative of the workers.
2. That workers should have a grievance procedure plan.
3. The City should have a dues-check-off plan for the workers (where-in
The City would automatically take out Union dues before they get their (paychecks.)
4. Some recourse for the workers in regard to suspensions.
5. The city should pay for workers Life Insurance& Health benefits.
b. There should be some uniformity in promotions.
7. There should be sick leave benefits.
8. Vacations.
9. Pay for working on holidays.
10. Overtime pay.

Simultaneously, Mayor Loeb counterattacked, trying as in the past to break the strike, before it began. Loeb obtained an injunction from Chancery Court that declared the strike illegal (no fair courts in America). Also, following Loeb's lead, the court outlawed the strike any strike activity by union officials, ruling it was a threat to public health and safety. The injunction prevented *AFSCME* union officials from participating in demonstrations or acts of civil disobedience in support of the strike.

The injunction made their participation in strike activities very costly for *AFSCME,* because the union was unrecognized as the legal representative of sanitation workers. Ipso facto, the Chancery Court's injunction made activity by the union illegal. This is very important to how strike activities against the city were organized. The injunction gave City officials the right to seek contempt of court citations and damages against any union officials that engaged in marches or other demonstrations. They could only talk to the City, but Loeb refused to listen.

The court's action brought black community leaders into the fight, trying to organize the strike. Black leaders—NAACP, preachers, and other politically minded blacks, joined the effort to help the leaderless sanitation workers fight the city. The Invaders also joined the community support effort. Community leaders created the *Community On the Move for Equality C.O.M.E.,* which allowed the organization to avoid violating the court injunction. *C.O.M.E.* developed the strategy and led the community's nonviolent effort.

I will say upfront, these were very conservative, accommodationists and status quo minded individuals. With nonviolence as a goal, they wanted no part of black power, as part of the strike, especially in its leadership. They were against involving any black power activists in their strategy. Consequently, C.O.M.E. shut the Invaders out of any leadership role connected to the strike.

Meanwhile, Stokely Carmichael's cry of *black power* had galvanized young radicals in urban areas across America. Black power activists were confronting civil rights and old line black leaders, as we were in Memphis, demanding *black power* advocates share leadership and power. Their opposition to black power created the divide, which was hampering Dr. King's strategy mounting the **"Poor People's Campaign"** to help the poor. Also, it divided his attention helping the poor, while trying to bring the two sides together to fight poverty. Dr. King was trying to head off the confrontation, which the Memphis sanitation workers strike would become ground zero and threatened to erupt into a feud within the civil rights movement.

The impact of this confrontation became the impetus for confusion and outright hostility that play out, during the last days of Dr. King's life. Old-line and civil rights leaders saw *black power* as an effort by young activists to supplant them and take over leadership of the civil rights movement. They saw black power advocates, as the ones that would takeover talking to white leaders in their stead, which would cut them out. In a phrase, *"they circled their wagons around black community leadership,"* as if black power activists were attacking marauders. Civil rights leaders fought to keep *black power* advocates out of any real role, especially those resembling leadership in the black community across the nation. They claimed black power activists were troublemakers, left them without any legitimate role in the black community.

The Invaders joined the sanitation strike effort, before this became apparent. We had been attending community meetings and participating in other community efforts. Primarily, the Invaders helped black students at Memphis State University organize a Black Student Association. So, it was not like we were an out of town or unknown group, trying to horn in on or takeover the strike.

The following is a lengthy discussion designed to help readers understand the dynamics at work, which brought the Invaders to not only the attention of people in the South but help expose the divide Dr. King was trying to seal. He hoped his efforts would rescue the sagging fortunes of the **"Poor People's Campaign,"** which civil rights leaders were not wholeheartedly backing. The sanitation workers strike came to symbolize and focus the issues that Dr. King was trying to address, if he could bring the new coalition between civil rights and black power together.

This narrative presents his Memphis effort as a water shade to highlight how and why Dr. King entered the Memphis strike, the legacy it created and culminated in his assassination. This perspective and events of this period have never been present before from the Invaders' perspective and their struggles during and after the sanitation strike has remained shrouded in rumors and suspicion. Much of the story about what actually happened became known during the 1978 Congressional investigation into the assassination of Dr. King. However, Congress sealed the report, evidence and conclusion of those hearings, before its findings were made public. Locking down Dr. Kings' assassination file created confusion, and left many questions unanswered. With that being, the case this narrative presents is a far more detail look at the strike and many unknown facts about the Invaders' history most of which continue to be covered over.

Memphis' middle-class accommodationists black leadership built their role helping white leaders manage segregation in Memphis, and leading C.O.M.E. was part of their role. They could not, from their perspective, afford to endanger their relationship with white leaders, pressing sanitation workers grievances, even though they were the go-betweens negotiating with Mayor Henry Loeb.

Loeb refused to talk to union representatives, so *C.O.M.E.* leaders played that role but treaded lightly. They developed a very weak strategy, only proposing daily marches, sit-ins at the city council chambers, while discussing of boycotts of downtown merchants in the press and talking with white people they had political relations. These were tactics used during previous strikes, which the City always broken.

On the other hand, the Invaders were not unknown among these people but had no standing in their eyes. Nevertheless, the Invaders brought a different strategy and new tactics to the fight against the City. The Invaders became a new dynamic compared to the history of strikes in Memphis. We had nothing to protect and had only sanitation workers' interest as concerns. We took a different approach to the strike, once we understood what was truly at stake, even though we were not strike leaders. C.O.M.E. held nightly rallies and mass meetings, while the Invaders talked directly to sanitation workers about their grievances, hopes, and goals for the strike at rallies.

Talking with workers in small groups outside before and after meetings, we listened to them tell about previous strike efforts. They desired more aggressive tactics this time around to get Loeb's attention early. They expressed fears Loeb would break their strike, with the same type of black leaders in charge, as before.

Taking a different tact, we gave workers our ideas about how to put real pressure on Loeb. Sanitation workers like what we suggested and carried those suggestions to the steering committee. However, C.O.M.E was set against black power activists becoming involved in the strike and did not accept our ideas.

The major problem for striking workers was their union was unofficial, at lease, the city refused to recognize it. The City refused to take union dues out of their checks—dues checkoff. Dues check-off meant the City recognized *AFSCME* as the official bargaining agent for sanitation workers. Dues check-off was really what the fight was all about—representation. Dues check-off would also mean City officials—the Mayor—recognized workers had rights the City had to respect.

Loeb knew as long as sanitation workers had to talk to him themselves, he could fire anyone he wanted to keep control of negotiations. That was T. O. Jones' fate; he was fired during the last strike because he would not yield to the City's demands. So, Loeb fired all sanitation workers that did not report to work the morning after he issued his ultimatum to return to work or be fired, as in the past. This tactic had worked previously to divide workers and eventually break their resistance.

Loeb hired scab replacement workers, and the city continued picking up garbage. Loeb simply closed his door in the union's face, refusing to talk to union representatives and only talk with C.O.M.E on workers behalf. The strike became a stalemate for the union and C.O.M.E., but for Loeb, it was business as usual.

The Invaders saw an opportunity and stepped into the leadership void. Here is where an even more detail discussion is necessary for readers to understand what sanitation workers were up against with C.O.M.E in charge. I saw the strike as a fight for power and striking workers as insurgents. I developed tactics based on what I learned in the Air Force, as part of counter-insurgence training, before heading to Vietnam.

The 400th: From Slavery to Hip Hop 495

The main idea of insurgency is to create havoc for your opposition, doing things to keep the opposition from relaxing or getting rest, especially at night, since all first responders were on unlimited overtime. The tactics I designed were to keep first responders on their toes and on the move during the night and day. We were not in a Vietnam jungle, but like Riverside Park when we were kids, I knew the ghetto, like VC, knew jungles.

The Invaders developed as a neighborhood club of kids in Riverside. They were high school students that grew up together, and Donny Delaney brought them together as the *"Invaders."* Some members were Cab's sister Shela, brothers Richard and Van, Rose and Barbara Briggs, Larry, Jewell, and LaMorris Davis, Nadean Montgomery, Womack "Speedy" Stevenson, "Big" Doc and others. These high school teenagers impressed me because they were trying to organize black students at Carver High School, in order to have black history classes, black books in the library, ware Afros and Afrocentric outfit to school. The Board of Education outlawed these demands and banded anything Afrocentric, and students that protested were expelled.

Impressed, I adopted their name—Invaders—in solidarity and put it on the back of my army field jacket, making them part of our black power organization The *Black Organizing Project* (BOP). The BOP was an umbrella group with 7 other units (1967). Working with the Invaders gave me the idea of bringing kids that came to the nightly sanitation strike rallies into my strategy. A large group of high school students, children of sanitation workers and their friends, attended rallies nightly, so I recruited them.

These high schoolers and their friends wanted to help their families and neighbors. Without knowing what to expect, I employed an urban guerrilla-style campaign. I organized them into roving patrols for both day and night action. I told teams to use their neighborhood as their cover. They knew the places to hide and how to use back alleys and drainage canals to avoid police getting around.

Doing the day, they attack the scab garbage crews and trucks with bricks and bottles, and disappeared into the neighborhood. They held hit and run marches to clog and impeded traffic at busy intersections creating gridlock, and vanishing before police arrived. Traffic jams during drive time, caused whites to complain to newspapers and Loeb. The idea was to make motorists complain, as they did. They also turn out schools by pulling fire alarms, drawing fire trucks to schools, which became a favorite tactic.

The night operations made sure first responders, stayed on the move, not resting. They filled tries with gasoline lit them and rolled them into grassy fields, wooded areas, and empty lots starting grass fires. Kids all over town turned in false alarms. I taught teams to make Molotov cocktails, and they firebombed vacant buildings, as well as white businesses and vacant houses belonged to white realtors. Night patrols blocked streets with metal garbage cans and dumpsters and set them afire. Night fires kept everybody on their toes.

These tactics had *C.O.M.E.* up in arms, and when they met with Loeb, he breathed fire over community hotspots, demanding they cool things down. Striking workers were emboldened and began to feel they could win if they stayed out on strike, while *C.O.M.E.* leaders tried to talk them into going back to work to allow things to cool down. This return-to-work ploy is how the city always broke previous strikes.

Dr. King Comes to Town

The Invaders involving students and other young people in the striking sanitation workers strike gave it a very radical edge. Workers responses to the Invaders radical protest put real pressure on C.O.M.E. Leaders were between trying to calm things down, while supporting sanitation workers demands for more pressure on Loeb to come to the negotiating table with the union.

During meetings, C.O.M.E. tried to convince sanitation workers to trust Loeb and return to work to give things time to cool down. Each time I confronted them during mask meetings, urging workers not to trust Loeb. Each time I shouted from the floor, "You are selling striking workers out to Loeb, asking them to return to work before Loeb addressed their grievances." Each time workers voted to continue their strike.

C.O.M.E. leaders invited Dr. King to Memphis, as a strike mediator. I believe they thought Dr. King would be a counterweight for them against the Invaders, as a civil rights leader. Moreover, they thought Dr. King would join their status quo effort, at the expense of poor sanitation workers. Arriving in Memphis amidst a celebratory atmosphere, it was like Palm Sunday, as Dr. King entered Mason Temple, the location of the rally. Black people responded to the announcement that Dr. King would speak in Memphis on his first visit to sanitation workers.

Entering Mason Temper the night of March 16th, Dr. King saw an overflow crowd of cheering strikers and supporters that exceeded its 2,500 capacity. There was pandemonium, from the cheering crowd eagerly awaited Dr. King's every word. The church could not accommodate the throng of people. Scores stood outside in the street, enthusiastically listening to speakers to hear Dr. King. Crammed together, like four sleeping in one bed, two at the foot, and two at the head, people were everywhere. They sat on the floor, on stairs, along the walls, in aisles and doorways.

After entering through a side door, Dr. King was swept along to the podium by a human wedge of burly volunteers. The sound of applause and stamping feet increased to a deafening roar, as Dr. King took the podium. Near the end of his speech, he talked of things the overflow crowd wanted to hear, *"You should consider a work stoppage if your demands are not met. I'm going to return to Memphis in a few days, and I will lead a March in support of your strike demands. If you want me to, I will lead that march to City Hall."*

Predictably, the crowd responded uproariously with applause. While the overflow crowd roared, Dr. King took his seat. Once the cheering died, he came back to the mic; the crowd roared once more. Waiting for calm, Dr. King said, *"And anyone in sympathy with the striking workers should stay away from work that day, and students should stay away from school also."* After Dr. King advocated a general work stoppage in Memphis, their clamorous response shook the rafters. Following his promise to lead a march to City Hall and calling for a general strike, Dr. King took his seat again amidst tumultuous applause and stumping feet. Just as the cheers died once more, he returned to the podium with his final remarks and declared, *"The Poor People's Campaign will begin here in Memphis."*

Mason Temple exploded in deafening cheers, once again. They roared and stamped their feet until Dr. King left the building. C.O.M.E. had worked tirelessly, trying to chill the Invaders momentum and bringing Dr. King to town was their coup de grace that was supposed to freeze the Invaders out, but their gambit backfired, blowing up in their collect face. The blowback, rather than icing thing for Loeb, Dr. King's presence lit a blaze hotter than the Invaders nightly street activities. C.O.M.E. became victims of it own strategy.

A clear example of the increased pressure on C.O.M.E. from Dr. King declaring a general strike came from his closest aides Reverends Ralph Abernathy, Hosea Williams, and James Orange. Stoking the fire of radicalism, Dr. King's SCLC aides' actions and words add gasoline to the out-of-control fire that C.O.M.E. had tried to douse. Dr. King's aides began advocating tactics that diverged from the pure nonviolent approach SCLC had employed in past demonstrations. Their aggressive civil disobedience tactics had C.O.M.E. sweating bullets from the heat they produced on C.O.M.E when they met Loeb. Instead of decelerating pressure on Loeb and cooling things down, Dr. King's presence became an accelerant. SCLC fanned the sparks the Invaders caused into a blazing inferno on Loeb, and in the hearts and minds of striking workers.

Immediately following that speech, Dr. King's staff took over the job the Invaders had been doing intensifying heat on Loeb. Rev. Abernathy gave another incendiary speech, again at Mason Temple (3-26-68). He called for a *"Black Man's" holiday in Memphis on March 28 to support the sanitation workers march".* He implored strike supporters, *"If the march doesn't force the Mayor to meet the garbage collector's demands, you should lie in front of the garbage trucks to stop them from leaving the barn or use any other means necessary."*

Rev. Abernathy's incendiary remarks added more fuel to the volatile mixture. His statement was far more radical than any ingredient the Invaders added to the volatile mixture. Rev. Abernathy's statement increased the heat on C.O.M.E. and ratcheted up the pressure on Loeb until no one knew what would happen next?

The Big March

The Dr. King's big march was the only thing on everyone's lips and minds; it was the only conversation. The Invaders had no role in planning the march's activities. Completely sidelined by C.O.M.E., without a role in the march, everybody wondered what the Invaders would do and with C.O.M.E. calling the shots what would happen?

There had never been such an event in Memphis ever. Black people had never been in open defiance of white people, the city, and the law. Even during the long hot summers' riots of 1966 and 67, Memphis was one of the few large cities without a riot. The Invaders street activities had sanitation workers almost giddy about the way the strike was going. They never thought Dr. King would lead a march for them.

With the big parade approaching (3-28-1968), the Invaders were like the rest of Memphis, and the march conversation was all coming out of our mouths also. On the eve of the big show, the Invaders met at my apartment, which served as the Invaders headquarters. The leadership, Cab, Coby, Edwina Harrell, Clifford Taylor, Hellen Bridges, Charles "Izzy" Harrington, Verdell "Gee" Brooks, Oree McKenize, Charles Ballard and a few others gethered one last time. Having received information and heard rumors, as well as warnings, regarding our safety, everyone was unsure how to proceed. For instance, tips came to us from several sources that the Invaders would be blamed if any trouble happened, during the march; everyone expressed opinions.

Coby Smith learned through a friend, he and Cab's safety would be at risk, they decided not to attend the march. Coby's friend was dating a policeman. She told him, *"I saw a picture of you and Cab in my boyfriend's wallet and asked why he had them."* The boyfriend responded, *"We have orders to keep eyes on the Invaders at the march, and if any disorder erupt during the march, we are to shoot these men on sight."* She advised Coby not to attend the march.

Similarly, I received information from Mrs. Cornelia Crenshaw, an old-timer in politics, from back in the days of "Boss" Crump, who still had reliable connections. She relayed that, *"If a disturbance happened during the march, the Invaders will get blamed for any trouble. You and your people should stay away."* After considering these and other warnings, the leadership advised Invaders could attend as individually.

Originally, I decided not to attend, but waking up that morning, the suspense and my interest increased during the intervening hours. Consequently, there was no way I was going to sit it out. I had to be there to see for myself what happened. I didn't want to hear or read about it, I needed to see with my eyes and know. If we were right in our assessment of C.O.M.E.'s ability to control the number of marchers we believed would show up, C.O.M.E. would have their hands full, trying to keep things together.

C.O.M.E. kept the Invaders out of the loop on their strategy, as well as march information. We were not at any meetings, so the Invaders couldn't help even if we wanted. Consequently, Invaders felt, if we did anything, C.O.M.E. would see it as mischief. We decided to concentrate on impressing Dr. King by turning people out for the march. What he and his aides did after coming to town assured us, unlike C.O.M.E., they were trying to help striking workers.

Invaders concentrated on producing a larger turnout for Dr. King's march than C.O.M.E. expected. Again, we believed such a turnout would overwhelm them, because they believe we were only talking. We wanted to show everyone we knew how to turn people out. So I didn't want to imagine or hear about what went down; I wanted to know. My thoughts were not a desire for anything bad, it was that, C.O.M.E. had shown it was concerned only with it public image, as white people saw them.

Our perspective was, these were our people and anything e could do to help striking sanitation workers we would do. But, knowing the people in charge of C.O.M.E.—they had already tried to sell workers out several times, so it was just a feeling we had. Invaders didn't want to be seen as working against the community. C.O.M.E.'s leaders were preachers, not street organizers. They showed a lack of confidence in the Invaders' ability, as black power activists and organizers. C.O.M.E. said, *"All the Invaders ever do, is talk! Invaders are a street gang, thugs, out to extort money from people. All they've done, doing the strike, is cause destruction in the black community".* C.O.M.E. downplayed the Invaders' strike role and continually disparaged our involvement, while taking credit for our work in the press, they kept us on the fringe of their plans.

Inviting Dr. King to Memphis, C.O.M.E. had taken credit for all strike-related activities, even street, community, and school organizing. Dr. King's demand, *"Workers should stay home from work and students not attend school on the day of the march,"* was far more than C.O.M.E. leaders expected from Dr. King. It was certainly far more radical than what the Invaders had proposed to the strategy committee. Although Dr. King's words may have been more than C.O.M.E. expected, it was definitely what striking sanitation workers and supporters wanted. As such, we believed C.O.M.E. anticipated about 3,000 people, a thousand more than their largest marches to City Hall, on March 28th. Invaders had not tried to turned people out for such activities. We suspected C.O.M.E. leaders had never handled a crowd of mostly young people, as large as the ones we had worked to turn out and would be coming their way later that day.

C.O.M.E. was unaware of the Invaders' organizing effort. Inviting Dr. King to Memphis, and after his call for a general strike, during his speech at Mason Temple, C.O.M.E. acted as though the strike was all but over. With Dr. King at the head of the march, C.O.M.E felt empowered. We believed, they thought they could handle everything, even street activities. It was as though they thought the march would be on "auto-pilot!"

Dr. King's speech, not only emboldened C.O.M.E. leaders, but it was also a huge boost to the Invaders recruiting efforts among young people in the mid-South. The Invaders leadership felt it was very important to show our ability to produce a very large turnout for Dr. King. we wanted it to be far larger than C.O.M.E.'s biggest march to City Hall. Invaders put teams of organizers in the field, sending them down into Mississippi, over into Arkansas and up into West Tennessee recruiting young people, students—College and high school—mostly, to come to Memphis for Dr. King's march. Young Invaders had responsibility to turning out schools, so we believe they would be eager to come to hear *"the number one black leader in America"* speak in Memphis. Again, I repeat, this was the first time ever Dr. King made a speech in the Mid-South and we believe most young blacks would not want to miss this once in a lifetime opportunity.

Beginning the morning of March 28th, black people across the city were on the move early. The first instances of strike-related harassment, fires, and vandalism began coming into police headquarters at 12:45 AM, according to police. Probably, with images of black people finally getting revenge for outrages at the hands of whites, dancing in their heads, their dreamland visions began with a bang that morning.

The rising sun found high school students, up and ready for a day no one could anticipate. According to breaking news, trouble was afoot long before snoozing marchers' feet hit the floor. Students that joined the Invaders' felt Dr. King had given them license, with his speech at Mason Temple, declaring a general strike and asking them not to attend school, but join him for the march. Young people were talking about changing their world as a generation. Many felt Dr. King had made a personal appeal to them for help.

Bells opening school doors at 7:50 AM were like a shots from a starter's pistol, setting things in motion. The school day at Lester, Northside, Manassas, Douglas, and Booker T. Washington High Schools began with students blocking entrances to prevent their classmates from entering school. They implored their classmates to join them as they head downtown for the big march. Shortly after the bell sounded, the lid blew off completely at Green P. Hamilton High School, where more than 250 students were massed on campus, blocking entrances.

Anticipating the arrival of police, students opened up with barrages of bricks, bottles, and rocks, as police cruisers came to a halt, like targets, in front of the school. A police helicopter gave a blow-by-blow description of the donnybrook, as rocks and bottles smashed windows of squad cars and hit officers, trying to dodged missiles. Even the press, which accompanied the scrambling police, was pelted. Students' projectiles rained down on police for over 10 minutes before they charged students.

Resembling a bizarre game of cat and mouse, students fled down side streets or took refuge behind the school, when officers charged, giving chase. Quickly regrouping, as though they planned a retaliatory strike, students launched another barrage of bottles and stones that sent chasing police, scurrying back to their cars for the cover. Similar to boxing matches on an undercard, after several preliminary melees, students began walking towards downtown heading to the main event downtown.

A police radio log (3/28/68) from another helicopter reported a crowd of 200 students marching westward from LeMoyne College toward Clayborn Temple at 9:29 AM. Then at 10:00 AM, a police helicopter reported that over 9,000 people packed Vance Street and Hernando Avenue in front of Clayborn Temple, as well as other side streets. A police radio log indicated at 10:03 AM the Q & S Liquor Store at 346 Vance, around the corner from Clayborn Temple, was being raided, and black men were walking away carrying cases of liquor. A police helicopter reported a group of 150 students moving from Booker T. Washington High School toward Clayborn Temple at 10:14 AM. Southside and George Washington Carver High Schools (10:20 AM), reported disturbances, students were walking out of class, if they bothered to enter.

Police Chief Henry Lux announced 19,000 students were absent from schools that morning. A further indication of high school students' response to the day came from Booker T. Washington's principal, J. D. Springer, who reported approximately 1,200 absences out of 2,200 students. These observations do not include African Americans coming into the City from areas surrounding Memphis from down in Mississippi, over in Arkansas, and up in West Tennessee, who wanted to march with Dr. King. The Memphis Arkansas Bridge was shut down by gridlock; people believed coming to the march from Arkansas caused the shutdown.

The march was scheduled to begin at 11:AM, but like estimates it continued growing, waiting for Dr. King, as the count reached over 20,000, according to police estimates. Looking like ants, zeroing in on a picnic, TV cameras onboard helicopters showed streams of people converging on Clayborn Temple at 10:30 AM. Police observers estimated that the crowd's swell was due to young people at least half were school age. It was obvious the Invaders organizing program was a huge success. The throng of people, once I saw it, I knew C.O.M.E. could never innovate and compensate fast enough to control a crowd far larger than anyone imagined.

Charles Ballard, "Gee" Brooks, "Izzy" Harrington and Oree McKenzie, decide individually to attend the march, during the meeting, while I had agreed with Cab and Coby that night not to attend the parade. However, that morning when they came by the crib on the way downtown, I joined them. We decided to keep low profiles. We rode a bus packed with people headed to the march. The area around the march's route was cordoned off by police. Disembarking, we walk several blocks to Clayborn Temple. Obviously, like C.O.M.E. leaders and most people, we felt, on such a bright sunshiny day, the march would be a walk in the park.

The 400th: From Slavery to Hip Hop

People coming to the march were very celebratory, some had children, and a few were on crutches or in wheelchairs, converging from all directions on Clayborn Temple. They were chitchatting and waving to acknowledge one another; the mood could not have been more festive. Contrarily, however, turning onto Hernando at Beale Street, things were already getting out of control. A group of men stood rounded the shattered hulk of another looted liquor store, consuming their booty on the scene, as police calmly observed.

Marchers had been lining up in the street in front of the church for at least two hours, awaiting Dr. King's arrival. We hadn't planned to get into the march, so we took up positions on the base platforms that supported columns on either side of the entrance to the church. It seemed things were becoming chaotic, as several events were occurring that aided the confusion.

Parade marshals tried to keep participants in ranks and files. Others struggled to prevent people from jumping in at the front of the march, while still others marshals handed out hundreds of clubs dressed as cardboard "signs" that read, "I AM A MAN." I say this because they were mounted on stout 4 ft. pine sticks. While that transpired, the sidewalks on both sides of the street, overflowed with on-lookers.

Dr. King still hadn't arrived by the time the march was scheduled to begin and the atmosphere took on an anxious restive mood. The march was originally planned to begin at 11:00 AM in front of Clayborn Temple, but inched forward, as it grew. A security buffer between Dr. King and other marchers was supposed to be ranks of sanitation workers just behind him, at the very front of the march. However, people continued jumping into the march ahead of striking workers, which pushed the line beyond its original starting point in front of Clayborn Temple. That activity pushed the starting point forward two blocks and onto Beale Street.

The march finally moved out sometime after 11:30 AM, even though Dr. King still had not arrived. The line of marchers was moving up Beale Street when Dr. King arrived from the airport and took his place at its head. Not bedlam, but confusion seemed to have taken charge already, as the massive gathering, without real form moved forward, after Dr. King was in place.

Meanwhile, a growing contingent of Invaders collected around us on the steps, as we remained at Clayborn Temple. We were simply observing the throng of marchers file pass. Standing on the column platform and steps, observing the massive gathering of marchers was a breathtaking sight for me. Looking out over the largest gathering of black people I had never been associated. I could not help but marvel at our accomplishment. I was proud to have been partly responsible for their appearance.

Watching marchers filed by our position, many waved or threw up a black power fist, which we acknowledged. Also, looking at the young Invaders surrounding me, my thoughts wandered back to just over six weeks earlier, when I began recruiting them. Back then, looking into their very young faces, bright eyes, and questioning gazes, I debated the wisdom of entrusting such young minds with such heavy responsibilities. Most had nothing to say; they listened; then walked away.

Now, on this day, I recognized them as war-worn and battle-scarred heroes, exhibiting pride not seen back when I recruited them. Watching marchers, they produced filing pass but led by men that had no idea how and why so many people showed up; their maturity was evident. Young Invaders did not exhibit the anxiety C.O.M.E. volunteers showed struggling with the massive crowd, as marshals scrambled, trying desperately to deal with a crowd far larger than anyone had projected. These intrepid young people understood why so many people were there; their work had produced them, and they were taking pride in their handy work.

C.O.M.E.'s marshals were no longer able to maintain orderly lines or well-defined ranks. The procession was more like an ocean of humanity, flowing in one direction, with the person in front carried along by the one behind them. For all practical purposes, the march had become perpetual forward motion.

Realizing at that point, in such a huge crowd, if we were going to get close enough to City Hall to see and hear Dr. King ourselves, we needed to start moving in that direction. I started towards Beale Street, walking on the sidewalk. I was able to move faster than the march itself. The group of about twenty or so young Invaders that stood with me on the steps followed. Turning onto Beale and crossing Third Street, marching in the street began leaving the march and joining us on the sidewalk. Simultaneously, some people on the sidewalk joined marchers. This act of trading places broke down the little orderliness of the formal march, merging it with sidewalk bystanders.

Walking up Beale, one could see police sharpshooters with weapons clearly visible, wringing the roofs of buildings. Each intersection was cordoned off with barricades and manned by thirty or more police officers. Such a heavy police presence made me feel; we were under the guns of an occupation force. This atmosphere replaced the festive feeling I had getting off the bus after arriving downtown.

Then All Hell Broke Loose

Talking as they walked, marchers moved forward, like an ocean of people. Suddenly, the perpetual forward motion halted. Its abruptness was like marchers up ahead, went into a blind alley, or encountered a stone wall, maybe some immovable object or force. People halting at the front of the march cascaded backward, sending a wave that flowed around the corner from Main Street onto Beale Street and on back through marchers as they crashed into the person ahead of them. Forward motion ceased completely. People crashed and piled up, like truncating railroad cars in a train wreck.

Suddenly, a loud "BOOM" sound came from Main Street. The sound was like an explosion. Then, without notice, even more suddenly, it was as if the march turned back upon itself. Convulsively, marchers came rushing back around the corner from Main Street onto Beale. They crashed into and pushed passed marchers, still trying to go forward. Those coming back around the corner ran frantically, as though being chased. Screaming marchers rushing wildly onto Beale Street, seemly in terror, crashed into marchers still trying to get onto Main Street. The rampaging crowd, rounding the corner, was followed by the sounds of breaking glass, exploding in their wake.

Dashing headlong back onto Beale Street, Rev. James Lawson, the leader of C.O.M.E., appeared in the sea of pandemonium, carrying a bullhorn. Marchers had no idea who he was. As he ran, he shouted to the confused marchers, *"Go back! Go back! Go back to Clayborn Temple! The march has been stopped on Main Street! Go back to Clayborn Temple! The march has been stopped by police!"* Shouting return to Clayborn Temple by a galloping Rev. Lawson, at that point, was not reminiscent of "Paul Revere."

Abruptly, amidst people rushing about in dismay, police that were guarding intersections began wading into the crowd, in an all-out attack on marchers up and down Beale Street. It was as though police received orders to assault marchers. Without provocation, police charged the march, clubbing people indiscriminately, as they ran. Marchers trying to get out of harm's way were being chased and beaten as they tried to get to safety. Some, who from their perspective, were running for their lives, became victims, as police turned the march into a stampede. Rather than a source of safety and protection, police became assailants.

Exploding breaking glass had the sound of bombs as the scene went from a festive celebratory walk into total choas in less than a heartbeat. The march erupted in discombobulation, as police igniting panic in our midst. Instantaneously, children, relatives, friends, and people part of groups they accompanied to the march became separated; most ran before thinking.

Obviously, during such times one's ability to keep one's wits about them is a key to surviving. If one has never experienced utter panic—where one moment everything is tranquil and festive, then in an instant there is total confusion and panic all about—it is difficult to imagine the emotions that can grip one. Such emotions can unleash the most primal responses, as the world goes mad all around you. While people rushed about incoherently, reacting calmly to trepidation can be canceled by survival instincts.

The prudent response, for most, is to try and escape the mayhem, rather than facing it. During such disarray, fear, dread, and hysteria, the natural reaction or response, is not to charge police. But, that is what some black men did, who carried signs mounted on sticks that read "I AM A MAN!", seconds earlier.

Facing attacking police, these valiant black men did just that!!! They tore off the cardboard disguises, turning signs into what they actually were—clubs. Young Invaders around me began picking up discarded signs and anything else within reach, with which they could defend themselves against the police attack. Some had two sticks, flailing at the ensuing police. The clash became a battle, rather than a frantic retreat. Facing attacking police, up and down Beale Street, black men fought courageously, covering escaping woman and children.

During those days, there were thoughts ever-present in all our minds, *"we are targets of the police,"* and the warnings Invaders received, made every move we made at that point, a survival effort. Life took on a sense of urgency and real desperation. I joined other black men, fighting their way out of the police trap. We fought, as the police pushed us back to Clayborn Temple. Though nearly surrounded and with our backs against Clayborn Temple, black men continued battling police with sticks, throwing bricks, and bottles, trying to hold them at bay. Standing, as we did allowed the huge crowd of women and children huddled in the shadow of Clayborn Temple to seek cover inside, though it was a church, it was not a refuge. Re-enforcements arrived, as police pressed their attack. They tear-gassed the church, before crashing the doors attacking those inside—women, children and old folks.

Ballard, Gee, and I became separated from Izzy, as more police re-enforcements arrived and poured into the church. A young man, driving a somewhat beat-up car, stopped and screamed to us, *"Get in quickly!"* Once in the car, he sped away. He explained frantically, *"I was at the march, so when I saw the Invaders jacket, I pulled over."* Simultaneously, we gave him a quick, *"Thanks, man for picking us up!"* He went on talking,

> *"I was at the head of the march. You see, I thought if I followed Dr. King, I would get a good place to hear him speak. So, I was up front when the whole thing started. Those damn police started everything. Can you believe that? I was right there when it all started.*
>
> *The police stopped the march, dead in its tract. They had triple lines of police across Main Street. It looked to be about fifty of them. They wouldn't let Dr. King any further, but the marchers kept coming around the corner at Beale Street, pushing him forward down Main Street towards City Hall. There was a policeman that grabbed a young black guy and, while*

wrestling with him, threw him against a plate glass window. The cop tried to hit the guy with his billy club, but as he swung, the young guy quickly ducked, and the cop hit the huge plate glass window behind him, shattering it. The exploding window sounded like a bomb. Everybody jumped and ducked down; then, it was like all hell broke loose. People started running back around the corner down Beale Street. Where were you guys when everything jumped off?"

Passing police car with lights flashing and sirens blaring headed downtown, as he raced South, I gave him a quick rundown on where we were and what happened there. He dropped us off at the crib and disappeared around the corner. As his image faded, I realized I never asked his name. This scene happened almost fifty-three years ago, but only as I wrote was I reminded with such clarity of the terror that accompanied those few fleeting fear-filled fragments, although, at the time, they seemed like hours.

Shortly after the four of us entered the apartment and turned on the TV, a newscast was reporting a young black man had been shot and killed by police. All the warnings we'd received came flashing back. We feared that he could be an Invader not present. No sooner than the thought crossed my mind, it seemed, Izzy, Cliff Taylor, and Cab walked through the door to our relief.

By late afternoon, Mrs. Crenshaw's admonition rang in my head, as media reports came, like a toiling bell. I felt the Invaders were being stretched upon the scaffold of ridicule, and lynched before the world. Our wishful dream of glowing praise and recognition that came with the sunrise, turned into recriminations by late afternoon. The fact that we turned out the largest gathering of demonstrators ever in the history of Memphis was now a dagger aimed straight at the Invaders back, and it did not miss.

Coming off my TV screen was a story totally unlike anything I witnessed, during the day's madness. Pictures of scenes and words describing them were completely different from what witnesses at the march encountered. The most prominent image, from newscasts of that day, was a frightened-looking Dr. King, being pushed toward City Hall by the momentum of marchers behind him. However, there were no images of the triple lines of police, like a wall across Main Street halting Dr. King's forward progress.

Unable to stop instantly, as police arrayed across the street opposing him, with one outstretched hand and the other holding a raised billy club, was the source of Dr. King's fearful look. This scene had to revive memories and images from *"Bloody Sunday"* on the Edmond/Pettus Bridge (3-7-65) for Dr. King, and the beating waiting if the crowd continued pushing him from behind, toward City Hall.

Following that scene, TV news reporters began describing police waded into the crowd, as an attempt to *"halt the unruly demonstration and restore order down on Beale Street."* According to reports, *"Without provocation, young black youth began breaking windows on Beale Street."* Then newscasters identified the young people as

Invaders. This image sent an overarching message that *"the Invaders started all the trouble,"* as Mrs. Cornelia Crenshaw's warning kept ringing in my head, like a telephone no one would answer.

However, the wakeup call meant it didn't matter that the Invaders didn't do anything. It didn't matter whether or not the Invaders were at the march, they got blamed, as Mrs. Crenshaw advised. There wasn't any evidence to support any claims that the Invaders did anything. No Invaders were arrested nor were there pictures that identified Invaders in any way, there was not even a picture of me or anyone else to show we were at the march. But, the chorus continued building to a crescendo, until there was no one saying anything to the contrary.

Scenes of rampaging youth, being chased by police, became the paint J. Edgar Hoover's used to color the portrait of the Invaders, as culprits. Covering the Invaders with blame, Hoover's image of the Invaders became etched inin history, like in stone. Police, reporters, and C.O.M.E. leaders picked up brushes, and joining the FBI's Invaders' paint party. Anyone could become Picasso or Michelangelo if they were willing to paint the Invaders with blame.

Insidiously, reporters repeated C.O.M.E. insinuation, *"The Invaders were bent on destroying Dr. King's reputation as the leader of the nonviolence civil rights movement."* There was universal condemnation from the FBI, City police and C.O.M.E. We knew that meant we had targets on our backs for sure, and no amount of explaining would change that.

Miraculously, while tossed about, in what seemed a sea of condemnation, like a ship in tempest-tossed waters, Dr. King threw the Invaders a lifeline late that evening. The ray of hope offered by Dr. King came as a message delivered through Calvin Taylor. Calvin was a young black man, trying to become the first black reporter for the Commercial Appeal Newspaper, he was also an Invader. Dr. King had contacted Calvin through the newspaper and wanted him to tell us, *"C.O.M.E. kept me in the dark about the Invaders organizing when I came to town. That was why I hadn't reached out to the Invaders earlier. Had they been upfront with me, I would have gotten with the Invaders before the march. C.O.M.E. had claimed it was responsible for all strike activities."*

Calvin's message brought a real ray of hope and proved to be the connection we had hoped for when we mounted our recruitment effort for the big march. While arranging the meeting Dr. King requested, Calvin explained to him, the Invaders had planned to work with him all along. He pointed out that following the police riot and all the confusion surrounding the march, as well as the blame now, being heaped upon Invaders, were unsure he would talk to the Invaders or be like everyone else. Cab and other Invaders headed for the Rivermont Hotel, where Dr. King and his entourage had rooms.

During that meeting with Dr. King, Cab helped him understand that *the Invaders had been the tip of the thrust trying to break Mayor Henry Loeb's truculent and adamant resolve and refusal not to talk with striking workers until,* as he put it, *"they get back* to work." Unable to bring the sanitation workers into the negotiations, C.O.M.E. leader asked you to come to Memphis as a counterweight because striking workers were following the Invaders' advice and voted to remain out on strike. The Invaders were trying to keep Loeb from breaking their strike, as the City had in the past. The City tricked sanitation workers to return to work before an agreement, in the past. And as you said, C.O.M.E. had deceived you once you got to Memphis, which put you in the middle of the riot, they lied to sanitation workers.

Although not planned, the riot brought everything out into the open. Beneath the public show of the strike, there was a battle for power and control of politics in the black community, where C.O.M.E. leaders were determined to keep the Invaders on the sideline, as foot soldiers. The details of everything discussed during the meeting with Dr. King are unimportant; what mattered was Dr. King's statement to the Invaders and during his press conference.

After first offering his regrets for recriminations and false impressions given by the city and police officials, blaming the Invaders for the riot, Dr. King explained that C.O.M.E. had misrepresented the Invaders as *"a street gang, thugs that extorted money from whomever they could. C.O.M.E. kept me in the dark about the Invaders organizing, and if I had known about them, they would have been the first we would have gotten with when we came to town had I known the real story."* After the press conference, he told the Invaders,

"I'm going back to Atlanta but will return to Memphis to lead another march, and I want to meet with the Invaders about being marshals for that march."

The Fights to Keep the Invaders Out and Dr. King's Last Strategy Meeting

Dr. King returned to Memphis on April 3, but did not meet with the Invaders until the next day, the 4th. The meeting with the Invaders took place against the advice of some of Dr. King's top aides and C.O.M.E. leaders. Both groups continued blaming Invaders for the riot. Irate, they fought to keep black power activists on the sideline and out of any real role in Dr. King's coalition. This group declared they would not work with Invaders no matter what Dr. King did to make Invaders part of the ***"Poor People's Campaign"*** coalition.

C.O.M.E. and SCLC (Southern Christian Leadership Conference) staffers had gone ballistic, following the riot, when Dr. King proposed meeting with the Invaders. Dr. King's insistence on the meeting created a very caustic environment for Invaders. SCLC staffers supported by C.O.M.E. had spent the week before Dr. King returned to Memphis, castigating the Invaders in the media. They met all week at the Rivermont, then continued at the Lorraine Motel after learning Invaders were lodged there.

SCLC and C.O.M.E. frantically held marathon meetings on how to stop Dr. King's plan to not only talking with Invaders but bring us on as staffers. They were unanimously opposed to Dr. King acknowledging or recognizing the Invaders' work with the sanitation workers in any way. Recognizing the Invaders would give black power national status and undercut their fight against sharing power.

The chaotic backdrop and the series of meetings after Dr. King left town created an atmosphere of urgency surrounding everything that happened, during the last four days of Dr. King's life. Local leaders and SCLC met continuously developing plans to sabotage Dr. King's peacemaking efforts to bring civil rights and black power activists together under the ***"Poor People's Campaign"*** banner. Here readers must remember, this fight pitting integrationists/accommodationists against *Black Nationalists*/black power activists was to maintain the status quo civil rights leaders inherited when the integrationists/accommodationists strategy was created back in the 1920s.

C.O.M.E. opposition to the Invaders was to protect their middleman's status in American politics. They felt their position, I believe, placed them at the pentacle of leadership in the black community, which they believed was the best a black man could aspire. In their view, if they lost that position, they had no future. They met all week at the Rivermont, and after learning Invaders were lodged at the Lorraine Motel; they move and and the meets continued. The Invaders were not included in these meets and when Dr. stayed returned, he lodged there also.

On the other hand, the Invaders were nobodies. Invaders, as other black power activists, were not trying to push black leaders out; we were pursuing a different role or power relationship for young blacks, as well as having to depend on handouts from white people. Black power activists insisted *"to hell with the status quo,"* which was a sellout to the past, as well as an acceptance of the second class status white people demanded. Status quo meant accepting white leaders, like Mayor Henry Loeb's handouts, which would come through them. Furthermore, the community would get the leftovers after middle-class leaders divvied up everything worth having.

However, the real problem was the turnout the Invaders produced for the march. If civil rights leaders could keep Dr. King from acknowledging the Invaders' work, C.O.M.E. could use the turn out and the poor, as a "bargaining chip," with white leaders. They could continue claiming the Invaders work, as their own, which they did to Dr. King when he came to town. Today, turning out 50,000 people for an event (Black Lives Matter protest) isn't too difficult, but back in 1968, such a turn out for a poor people's protest march by only black people was historic. The number of black people that turned out for Dr. King's big march was the source of all the meetings and tension.

Getting black people to show up in such numbers for a poor people's demonstration in defiance of white people in the South had never happened and showed black power activists had developed a different relationship with the poor than civil rights leaders. If black power advocates could get that kind of response from poor people, civil rights leaders would be out of jobs, as middlemen. However for Dr. King and his **"Poor People Campaign"** that would be a game-changer and allow him to break out of the box in which J. Edgar Hoover had Dr. King trapped.

Dr. King gathered with about fifteen Invaders in the lunchroom at the Lorraine Motel about 1:PM. That meeting went well, but some Invaders still had questions, based on SCLC staffers and C.O.M.E.'s adamant refusal to work with the Invaders or any other black power group. Following a couple of hours, trying to hash out those problems among ourselves in our room, there still remained one outstanding issue, involving civil rights leaders refusal to work with black power activist and where Dr. King would come down, once SCLC town.

The problem was Invaders wanted Dr. King's "personal" assurances that he would not abandon the Invaders once SCLC moved on. Cab and I went to Dr. King's room to resolve the issue. It was approaching late afternoon, about 3:30 or 4 PM, as Charles and I left room 316 and walked down the balcony to 306, Dr. King's room. His accommodations on the first floor, which is what he usually received had been switched, someone wanted him to have an upper room. So, he was given the second-floor accommodation down the balcony from our room.

Charles knocked, and the door opened slowly, as a haggard-looking Dr. King invited us in. Barely smiling, he poked his head out the door, as though he thought others were behind us. Entering the room and looking around, I thought it very strange he was alone. The empty room, except for him, made it seem, he was isolated, even though SCLC staffers and C.O.M.E. members were all over the Lorraine. I thought he, his staff, and C.O.M.E. would be deeply involved, planning for the upcoming march, since the previous one ended in a riot.

The dimly lit room, with the draperies drawn, a table lamp was the only illumination. His room was a double, and Dr. King offered us seats on either of the two beds. Cab and I sat on one together, while he sat across from us on the other. After Cab gave him a preliminary explanation of why we needed a second meeting, Dr. King said he needed to explain, in more detail, why he felt an alliance between he and the Invaders was so important, *"I was amazed by the massive turnout for the march"* (Art Gilliam of WLOK radio station estimated march attendance, before the riot and people were still coming at 50,000 people). *"After my brief talk with you Charles, the night following the riot, I began rethinking my strategy for the Poor People's Campaign, because I was not getting the response and support I usually got when I called marches in the past. I proposed meeting with you to discuss my new approach, which includes the Invaders."*

Dr. King insisted, *"After speaking with Charles a new strategy began to develop. It began with the Invaders and other black power activists, as I thought about what could be done on the local level, and how that could help* **"The Poor People' Campaign.'"** Dr. King, like me, was truly surprised and impressed with the Invaders' organizing effort, which produced the huge turnout, I knew it would be big, but nothing like it was. The march turnout seemed to have become the key to Dr. King's new strategy. Surprised also, Cab asked *"What did I say? What do you means?"*

First, Dr. King said *"I'll say a few word about the other big problem I have, J. Edgar Hoover. After meeting with Mr. Hoover, he held a press conference where he said,"* "Martin Luther King is the most dangerous man in America. Once I announced the Poor People's Campaign, *he threatened to stop it from reaching Washington D.C. any way he could. Mr. Hoover told me when we met, 'your mouth is going to get you in trouble.' I thought those who had supported me in the pass would be behind my effort as they had in the past, but they were not coming to meeting I called or raising money or offering their churches to help with marchers. But the thing that mattered most at that stage was volunteers and they were not recruiting them. The Memphis sanitation workers and their strike along with the march turnout have given me a new approach to the Poor People's Campaign, and I will proceed no matter what Mr. Hoover says or does."*

Announcing the **"Poor People's Campaign"** (12-4-1967), Dr. King had proposed carrying a million poor people to Washington, D.C. The thought of a million black people descending on the Nation Capitol over poverty frightened white leaders. Gravely concerned, leaders on Capitol Hill began sharing Hoover's desire to stop Dr. King. During this meeting, Dr. King continued elaborating on his change in strategy.

> *"I feel an alliance with the Invaders will energize the 'Poor People's Campaign' and I hope will gain the interest and attention of other black power groups. There are black power groups across America, definitely in the top 16 larger cities. If I can get them to trust and work with me, this will broaden the base of the Poor People's Campaign. If I get your help and you undertake the task, you will be a major part of my strategy.*
>
> *I want the Invaders to recruit other black power groups to join the effort to bring the plight of America's poor to the attention of the nation and the world. I will be able to coordinate my demonstrations in Washington D.C. with demonstrations black power groups mount in their cities simultaneously. If the Invaders are successful, that will make the Poor People's Campaign the VOICE of Negros in those cities and other cities as well. Going forward Negros will be speaking with one VOICE at the same time, and their VOICE, in this manner will demonstrate the political power we have."*

Dr. King talked at length about his concept of *VOICE* and his new strategy.

> *"I see the 'Poor People's Campaign' as our ultimate expression of VOICE.*

His concept of *VOICE* seemed to be evolving as his strategy for the **"Poor People's Campaign."** Elaborating on it, he referred back to the last march,

> *"I believe the police riot was a denial of Negro's right of VOICE. That march was a reflection of their right to express their attitudes about their condition as a people. Negros ability to tell their story, in their own words, as they live it, is a human right all people have and is a basic right to life. If Negros cannot tell the story of what is happening to them to the world, they are denied the most basic right of human beings."*

I understood his words at the time, but it took years (1982) for me to understand why that concept of *VOICE*, for Dr. King, was the major reason he took his life in his hands, launching the **"Poor People's Campaign"** in direct defiance of Hoover threats. I believe Dr. King's concept of *VOICE*—*the ability of Negros to tell their story, in their own words*—led him to denounce the federal government as the culprit responsible for the continued impoverishment of slavery's descendants. It led him to stake himself out like a "sacrificial lamb" to expose the wretched existence slavery's descendants endured at the hands of the US federal government and men like J. Edgar Hoover.

Desperate Times for Dr. King

The disastrous week seemed to have changed back to the rosy scenarios we imagined earlier, before talking with Dr. King. Cab and I believed prospects had returned to the bright future we hoped for before the riot. Leaving his room, we began planning our futures working with Dr. Martin Luther King, Jr.—the number one civil rights leader in the world. Cab and I were the last two people to meet with Dr. King in a strategy session less than an hour before his assassination. No one had the slightest inkling the desperate time he faced. We certainly did not, while we spent the last minutes of his life with him, talking about ***"Poor People's Campaign"*** and the future he painted in such vividly bright colors. Not even his SCLC staffers seemed to have a clue, before his life came to such an abrupt and tragic end. So very shortsighted, they busied themselves spatting over Dr. King's plan to make the Invaders staffers of his ***"Poor People's Campaign."***

If Dr. King, as some people believe, in giving his *"Mountain Top"* speech, expressed a premonition of his fate, it is truly amazing, he gave us no indication, as we talked just less than an hour before, our world changed again, this time forever. My dilemma over the years 53 something years, if such thoughts have any validity, why did he spend his last desperate hours of life, talking with the Invaders, of all people. Why? That thought or question has always made me feel Dr. King gave Cab and me something; he truly felt the world needed to know. One thing he told us, during those last minutes was that he had become dispirited in late January before his ***"Drum Major"*** sermon.

"After preaching to people I'd counted on for support, but they were not responded with help, as they had in the past when I called boycotts, demonstrations, and marches. That left me without any place to go for support. I had counted on them to have mass rallies, and funding support for the people making the trek to Washington D. C. Instead they were not stock piling food and erecting camp sites for marchers on the road. Without volunteers for marshals to help keep things organized along the way, there would be chaos people would suffer and the whole thing would fall apart. And most of all, I was disappointed when I called meetings and they did not come.

But, once the sanitation workers came out on strike, I thought by helping the sanitation workers, who were among the poorest of the poor, would not only help them but the Poor People's Campaign as well. But, the turnout of people—poor black workers and others—that came to the last march convinced me something new and different was happening here in Memphis. Talking to the young reporter (Calvin Taylor), *I learned about all the work the Invaders had contributed to the strike effort and how young people respond, told me the real story of why so many people came out. That is when I realized the Invaders and other black power groups and the young people who were listening to them would be the way forward for the Poor People Campaign."*

I understood after his statement, the numbers of people that turned out for the march on the 28th, not only had impressed the Invaders, Dr. King saw us as his hold card in the biggest gamble of his life. However, Hoover had put plans in motion to stop Dr. King, and he was not a one-man-band. As with Marcus Garvey and Malcolm X, Hoover had the power of the entire federal government at his disposal to help him, bring Dr. King down, and end the **"Poor People's Campaign,"** no matter Dr. King's new vision. Hoover's plan reduced Dr. King from a man who had always had lots of help, down to a *"lone rider."* According to his words, in my opinion, he was alone and on his own, except for the Invaders although hundreds claimed they were standing with him at the end.

It may seem to some I have given far too long an explanation for something that happened over fifty years ago, which most people have forgotten, and even if they have not, there is no way to change the outcome. I agree the outcome cannot be changed. However, the amount we know about what happened can be changed. My aim here is to set the record straight regarding the lies in the record.

Those lies have controlled events and outcomes in the lives of many people, like the *Second Red Scare* and CP-USA, regarding Woodrow Wilson's legacy. Specifically, the Invaders were painted as culprits that started the riot by J. Edgar Hoover and supported by SCLC and C.O.M.E. leaders, which gave cover and respectability to Hoover's lies, as well as help cover up the truth of Dr. King's death. It is also like the story of the CP-USA, which was also covered over, similar to Hoover's death hunt against black power activists. Civil rights leaders help make Hoover's association—CP-USA—of communism with the Invaders a targets of blame.

Hoover's FBI claims resulted in police harassment, false imprisonment, destroyed careers, and denials of opportunities throughout our lives, even today for me. Many of these individuals were dear friends and comrades and have passed on from this world, as unsung heroes, but not unremembered. The unintended circumstances of **"The 400th"**, can help establish the truth and clear their record for those left behind.

My comrades were victims of "truth crushed to the ground, still waiting to rise again." and the US House of Representatives (1978) have become part of holding down the truth of Dr. Martin Luther King, Jr.'s assassination, by refusing to open up its investigation file of his death. That file contains the truth, and with Rep. John Lewis gone, only a few are left, who know the real story.

With the Democratic Party majority in the House of Representatives, it is pass time for America to know a truth that has been hidden for over fifty years. My comrade will finally have *VOICE* J. Egar Hoover denied, but even he has passed on, so what is there to hide. The truth is an epitaph for Charles "Cab" Cabbage, John Gary Williams, Charles "Izzy Harrington, Juanita Thornton, Charles Ballard, Verdell "Gee" Brooks, Jewell Davis, Janice Lewis, Maurice Lewis, Big John Smith, and others.

On the other hand, as a result of several lawsuits and court rulings in the 1970s, the FBI was ordered to release some of its surveillance files on Dr. King. Reading files, the federal court ordered released, made it possible to identify some of what J. Edgar Hoover did to kill the **"Poor People's Campaign,"** as he did the **UNIA,** and undercut Dr. King's organizing efforts. One of those FBI surveillance files contained the *Arkin Report (April 1968).* The *Arkin Report* informs the world of what J. Edgar Hoover's surveillance networks did to stop the **"Poor People's Campaign"** and Dr. King from reaching Washington, D.C.

It begins with FBI LHM *dated 5-6-68 [TO: DIRECTOR, FBI (157-8460) FROM: SAC, MEMPHIS (157-1067*), shows clearly FBI Director, J. Edgar Hoover's plot to prevent the **"Poor People's Campaign"** from reaching Washington D.C. was very substantial. Hoover deployed four different spy operations—POCAM (an acronym for Poor People's Campaign), Co-Intel-Pro (Counter-intelligence Program), GIP (Ghetto Informant Program), and a Rabble Rouser Index—all these spy networks were deployed to stop Dr. King. Pres. Johnson even got into the game, with his *Trouble Maker* information gathering network he ran from the White House. It seems Woodrow Wilson reached out from the grave and continued destroying the hopes of black people through his handyman J. Edgar Hoover's dark hand of death. Wilson brought Hoover into government to head the Radical Division of the BOI in 1912. The federal government used every trick in the BOI/FBI playbook—legal and illegal, (**fair or foul**) to use Wilson's own words—that was developed going back to 1917 and the *"First Red Scare"* to stop Dr. King and the **"Poor People's Campaign,"** as he told the press.

The *Arkin Report* shows one month after Dr. King announced the **"Poor People's Campaign,"** and three months before his assassination, Hoover launched the FBI's full-court press against Dr. King on January 4, 1968. Hoover sent a directive to FBI offices in twenty-one cities, outlining his plan to destroy the **"Poor People's Campaign."** Hoover's surveillance enterprises began with the FBI's counter intelligence program began just after the *1963 March on Washington (The Arkin Report: 5/1968)* aimed at destroying Dr. King as a political leader.

Five years later *The Arkin Report* shows with FBI LHM *(5-6-68),* the FBI began a new surveillance drive with a *"racial conference"* in Washington D.C. in early March of 1968, one month before Dr. King's assassination. Disrupting the activities of the **"Poor People's Campaign"** and techniques from Co-Intel-Pro were adopted and deployed by Hoover's directive creating. Tactics included, but were not limited to, spreading *"lies, rumors, innuendoes and other misinformation efforts* *that discouraged people from joining or contributing money to the* ***"Poor People's Campaign."***

Again information from the *Arkin Report* shows Hoover still operated on the theory if he, *"Cut off the head, the body will die!"* First he isolated Dr. King, as he did Marcus Garvey and Malcolm X, even though there were lots of people around them. Hoover through his spy programs discredited Dr. King's, as he did Marcus Garvey efforts. Having witnessed Dr. King's offensive with his *"Letter from the Birmingham Jail,"* locking D. King up would have only promoted the ***"Poor People's Campaign,"*** and as a US citizen, Hoover could not deported Dr. King, as Marcus Garvey. So, what was left?

The assassination of Dr. King rob the Invaders of the opportunity to work with the most dynamic black leader of our times, but the world lost much more. Yet and still, it intensified our commitment to the ***"Poor People's Campaign."*** Hoover did not anticipate the Invaders' would exhibit the same motivation and overarching concerns for the poor, as Dr. King, even though we did not possess his political clout and stature. The Invaders kept his dream alive. Hoover had no way of knowing the Invaders would continue working on the ***"Poor People's Campaign,"*** without Dr. King's physical leadership. Hoover miscalculated the Invaders' resolve to help slavery's descendants escape the open grave of poverty in the valley of dry bones.

The FBI victimized the Invaders, but they were not victims. Slavery's descendants were victims due to their lack of knowledge as to what happened to them and why. Dr. King pointing his accusatory finger at the federal government giving black people their first real clue or piece of the puzzle about why they remained locked in poverty since their penniless emancipation. That question— *why were descendants of American slavery still residing in poverty, after 105 years of so-called freedom?*—Dr. King believed black Americans were no better off economically in 1968 than former slaves walking off plantations in 1863, in terms of freedom, justice and equality.

Descendants of slavery have always been up against government on all levels, which managed their re-enslavement since emancipation. Dr. King's statement was my first real clue, learning the truth of why African Americans still resided in poverty. Dr. King was my first professor, during his last intrepid hours. I believe, Dr. King figured out that, if there was a way out of the desperate straits he found himself, an alliance with black power was his best exit strategy. Turning to the Invaders, Dr. King tried to set the stage for a full-frontal assault on segregation and white supremacy in America. He planned to use the ***"Poor People's Campaign"*** like a juggernaut. Later thinkers, who research the questions discussed here, followed Dr. King's accusatory finger, as it pointed to the federal government, as the culprit, which maintained descendants of American slavery in poverty.

Dr. King described it this way, *"The federal government has written Negroes a check that has come back stamped 'insufficient funds.'"* The debt to which he referred was swept under the federal government's white supremacy rug when Woodrow Wilson instituted segregation, paving the way for convict leasing and sharecropping. Dr. King clearly showed racism was a tool of the federal government, which spread racism throughout the nation, protecting and supporting it. Racism, discrimination, and disparate treatment against descendants of American slavery became the base of the federal government's *"cheap labor"* capitalistic economic strategy. It locked slave descendants in the grave of poverty in the valley of dry bones.

Aiming his **"Poor People's Campaign"** strategy at the federal government, Dr. King dramatically staked himself out as a "sacrificial lamb." He pointed out that the federal government used Article I Section II of the US Constitutional—the 3/5 Compromise—which is the foundation of American discrimination and disparate treatment. The 3/5 Compromise was also used as the basis to justify **Plessy v. Ferguson**—segregation, all of which, constitute the ultimate denial of black people's right of VOICE!!!!!!!!!!!!!

Trying to Seal the Breach and Fight Poverty

Dr. King's actual dream the—***Poor people's Campaign***—never equaled his imagined manifestation; things never develop as they are imagined. Dreams are particular hoped-for outcomes. Materializing, as a fact of life, they never completely resemble what was imagined or drawn up as a planned. I believe Dr. Martin Luther King, Jr's "Poor people's Campaign" was just such an outcome.

Dr. King's monumental effort, as a leader, was undercut by civil rights leaders in 1968, as he tried to seal the breach between civil rights leaders and black power activists, while simultaneously mounting the *"Poor People's Campaign."* However, hundreds of pages of reports, like the Arkin File, attest to J. Edgar Hoovers master plan was the killing blow that fell Dr. Kill's and his *"Poor People's Campaign."* The US House of Representatives investigation file, which it locked up to keep Hoovers' and the US Government's role in his assassination, verify all charges made by this narrative.

During his last strategy meeting with Cab and me, at the Lorraine Motel, he shared the wisdom gained from a life fighting for poor people and others still trapped in poverty. It seems Dr. King had no personal concern for his place in history. He outlined what he thought of himself in his *"Drum Major Instinct"* sermon. Elaborating on his commitment to bring the Invaders on board the *"Poor people's Campaign,"* Dr. King detailed his hopes, facing J. Edgar Hoover and the all-powerful federal government, if the Invaders stood with him.

Dr. King, having shared with us his hopes for the poor, during his last desperate hours, affected me profoundly through his unwavering commitment to poor people over the years. It was only after years of digging back through the graveyard of poverty in the valley of dry bones that I learned about the massive surveillance operations arrayed against him, by the federal government, to prevent the ***Poor People's Campaign*** from ever getting off the ground. I struggled over the years, trying to remember every word of his conversation with Cab and me that last day. As the years passed, I realized he didn't see the poor, like other civil rights leaders. Why his commitment to poor downtrodden people of the world extended to staking himself out, as a "sacrificial lamb," became a vexing question for me.

Dr. King's life was nothing like mine. I was a child of desperate times, economic scarcity, hardships, and lack of access to society's bounty. Dr. King's life, growing up, resembled most civil rights leaders, such as Whitney Young of the *Urban League*, James Farmer of the *Congress of Racial Equality (CORE)*, and *NAACP* leaders like Walter White, Charles H. Houston and maybe Roy Wilkins.

Dr. King was born into an upper-middle-class black family, like Lorraine Hansberry, raised to identify with middle-class values. Unlike me, Dr. King did not experience up-close personal encounters with poverty. Hence, life did not give him cultural and psychological ties to the harsher realities of life, as it did me. Poverty did not oblige him to develop instinctual opposition to the wretchedness of black life.

My brother-in-law, Willian Brandon has a maxim, *"Given a choice, choose, always choose!"* I believe his maxim reflects Dr. King's attitude regarding his commitment to those in need; he chose poor people over the middle class as a commitment, which isolated him, except for the Invaders and a few of his close aides, during his last days.

Dr. King's life was filled with things he said *"not to mention"* in his—*Drum Major Instinct Sermon*. He went to the best schools, Morehouse College and Boston University (where he obtained his Ph. D). He preached at prestigious churches all over the world, even in Germany, under the communists. His road carried him to places where he received hundreds of accolades, even the Nobel Peace Prize. Dr. King's success was not a journey that required him to fight his way from the outer edges of obscurity to the back door of opportunity, as my life has been. Middle-class leaders accepted Dr. King as a leader.

Not having been one of his civil rights disciples, I came to believe, from our brief encounter and research, that civil rights introduced Dr. King to a broader slice of humanity's pie. Figuratively, it was as though he got down in the nitty-gritty mire of life's grungier aspects, fighting for the poor. Meeting and talking with people like me on his journey, he came to feel, I believe, there were no differences in our humanity. Metaphorically, I think, he found that the American pie poor people got, the crust was charred and filled with maggots.

On the other hand, Dr. King knew the taste of life sliced off the top, rather than having to scrape the bottom of the barrel, and eat guts—*Chitlins*—not as a delicacy, but to survive. Leading the Montgomery bus boycott, his letter from the Birmingham jail and the *1963 March on Washington*, brought him to the attention of not only people in the United States but around the world. Such exposure prompted his selection as *the 1964 Nobel Peace Prize* winner. Given such recognition, his class saw him as a superstar, and above the nitty-gritty aspects of life, that his marches and protests exposed.

Dr. King said during our conversation on his last day that, civil rights leaders felt by launching The **"Poor People's Campaign,"** he was taking the focus off middle-class goals—accommodations, better jobs, buying homes in white communities and attend school with whites—was a betrayal of his class. For them, it was all about class; these were the aims or goals of their civil rights efforts. But, for the poor, it was all about color. Civil rights leaders felt if they benefitted first, this would help the poor, a "trickle-down effect." He said, *"Civil rights leaders did not want to mortgage the political clout they gained, joining a fight that even if such a battle could be won, it would not advance the middle class."* For them, I say, the values of freedom, justice, and equality were not streams that flow uphill. They had to drink first, and the poor got what was left.

The 400th: From Slavery to Hip Hop

Dr. King, in my opinion, was truly slave descendants' Sir Lancelot; even more, he was the poor's, King Arthur. I say this now because if his efforts to bring civil rights and black power together at the table had been successful, he would have sealed the breach. Yet and still, I believe he thought those at the table would become his *"round table of knights,"* which could attack the federal government and poverty behind the **"Poor People's Campaign."**

During our talk, Dr. King reached over and placed his hand upon my knee, as he continued imploring us to join his team against poverty. That touch, as he reached out, seemed to grab my mind, and pull me into his consciousness, which made everything he said palatable. I felt his plea for the poor was genuine, and I bought into his dream.

I have come to believe his fight to end poverty was a righteous one in all respects. Echoing his *Drum Major Instinct sermon,* he belabored the point that his fight was not about wealth, *"I won't have any money to leave behind. I won't have the fine and luxurious things of life to leave behind. But I just want to leave a committed life behind.* Listening, I came to truly believe he saw working with the poor, as an expression of his faith and commitment to Jesus Christ.

His statements about poverty showed he understood why the wealth slave descendants produced for America did not trickle down. America's *cheap-labor* economic strategy left the vast majority of black Americans still trapped in poverty, while the white middle class continually advanced and expanded. The wealth gap between the haves and have-nots doubled, by the time slavery's descendants reached the 1960s. Denied *VOICE*, black people, were still hidden behind America's *cotton curtain*, even after **We Charge Genocide**.

As a recipient of the *Nobel Peace Prize*, Dr. King became a megaphone for the poor, so he spoke beyond black America's isolation. Dr. King's ability to speak beyond the ghetto was the power middle class civil rights leaders felt, he was wasting on the poor. Dr. King's death did not keep black middle-class leaders from moving into white middle-class communities, their children from attending school with white kids, or access to better jobs, hotels, and other accommodations, but it robbed the poor of their champion. The success of civil rights left the poor still trapped in poverty's valley of dry bones, which Rev. Lee prayed over, as Dr. King was a prayer answered, giving his all to the last.

After almost fifty-two years, this 400th narrative is finally giving *VOICE* to the truth and reality Dr. King shared with the *Invaders*. Through my family's narrative, I tell the story of the terror and hardships of slavery, convict leasing, sharecropping, segregation, and white supremacy in America. Cab and I spent those last fleeting hours listening to Dr. King and his conversation reinforced why he pointed an accusatory finger at government—federal, state, and local— as the culprits maintaining descendants of American slavery in poverty. I continue reiterating this point because it is the baseline in all descendants of American slavery's **"Blues."**

Walking into Dr. King's room, just a couple of hours before his assassination, my thoughts were that although there were many people around him at the end, he was virtually alone in his desire to expose the federal government, as the culprit maintaining black people in poverty, and is a fact time has sustained. His strategy to seal the breach between black power and civil rights, and bring the two sides together, as one force, under the ***Poor People's Campaign,*** J. Edgar Hoover viewed as the most serious threat to America's *cheap labor* strategy, since Marcus Garvey and the UNIA. Hoover doubled down stating that Dr. King " was the most dangerous man in America." And, I believe he dealt with Dr. King from that perspective, because of his move—***The Poor People's Campaign***— would have demonstrated to black people, the political power they can bring to bear when they work together.

The Invaders have kept their commitment, which Cab, and I gave Dr. King to fight poverty by supporting the ***"Poor People's Campaign."*** I sent a contingent of Invaders to Washington D. C. lead by Lance "Sweet Willie Wine" Watson (today he is known as Minister Yahweh). But the commitment of civil rights leaders to work with black power groups Dr. King made with us was never kept. There were turf battles, confrontations over status, some leaders flat out refused to work with the Invader because rumors related to the riot in Memphis, as well as lies spread by the FBI. The poor people's effort fell far short of Dr. King's vision and expectations, mainly because of J. Edgar Hoover's spy programs. But the proof was placed on lockdown by the US House of Representatives; only they can set the truth free!!!!!!!

While Art Imitated Life, the Counter Culture Became An Easy Rider

The desperate times of Dr. King put the circumstances, commitment, and legacy of his dedication to the poor in perspective for people of goodwill. Throughout America, following the assassination of Dr. King, the FBI had plans that did not include goodwill. J. Edgar Hoover began his mop-up operations against black power. Through his spy operations, he began stalking black power activists, like slave catchers enforcing the *Fugitive Slave Act of 1850*. J. Edgar Hoover planned to wipe out black power advocates with his Co-Intel-Pro's death hunt. Hoover's pogrom put black power activists on the run, trying to stay alive, all across America. The most blatant example of Hoover's Co-Intel-Pro death hunt was the assassination of Fred Hampton and Mark Clark in Chicago (12-4-1969). The black power revolution was being driven underground or out of business altogether, like CP-USA, without bothering with courts.

Between, April of 1968 to June of 1970, police across America began locking up black power activists or killing them, like the Constitution was on vacation. Memphis was at the head of the line and known Invaders were in the bullseye. All the original leaders of the Invaders, like other black power groups were either on the run, went underground, left the country, in jail, or dead. Cab went on the run, while Coby went underground for a few years. I, on the other hand, was one of those they jailed. Most, like me, without fair courts in America, were hauled before white prosecutors, white judges, and all-white juries to face trump up charges. It was like convict leasing, but no fines, jail time was the only outcome.

Sitting in the Shelby County Jail, I followed the efforts of the Invaders, as new leadership emerged. These new leaders evolved out of the contingent I sent with "Willie Wine," today Minister Yahweh to Washington D. C., in support of the ***"Poor People's Campaign."*** Minister Yahweh, along with Roy Turks, "Big" Janice Lewis, her brother Maurice, Cacheatuh Smith, Juanita "mule train" Thornton, Willie Henry, "Big" John Smith and others moved in the direction of the Black Panther Party.

Two very iconic images came out of 1968, other than the assassination of Dr. King. First young progressives, mostly young white radicals invaded Chicago for the 1968 Democratic Presidential Nomination Convention. Trying to push ending the Vietnam War to the top of America's political agenda, it became a blood bath for young radicals. Mayor Richard Daily, a diehard war hawk, followed the lead of Mayor Henry Loeb, during Dr. King's last march for Memphis garbage workers, turned his club swinging cops loose on demonstrators. The blood baths and general mayhem made front pages of newspapers and the top stories on TV news around the world for the entire convention.

Bidding my time in jail, it seemed things were going downhill for the counterculture and black power. The 1968 Summer Olympics Games in Mexico City became ground zero for black power, as Chicago was for the counterculture. Two black athletes dropped a flash bomb on the Olympics that lite up America's hypocrisy while blowing up its claim and pretense of freedom for African Americans. Sprinters Tommie Smith and John Carlos mounted a demonstration that gave *VOICE* and presented black power's vision of this new world. Making history, they finish first and third in the 200-meter race, a first for blacks. After their stunning victory, they mounted their award pedestals and turned to face the American flag. With the national anthem—the Star-Spangled Banner—blaring in the background, they raised clinched black-gloved fist—the black power salute—shocking the world.

These intrepid devil-may-care African American lone riders—Tommie Smith and John Carlos—showed the kind of courage no African American athletes has shown until Colin Kaepernick. Creating an international furor in general, but in the US, alarm bells went off as if a Russian nuclear attack was imminent. Even though we were in jail, the day room erupted uproariously, every time the news clip flashed. Black inmates cheered and gave hi-fives, while performing their best dance moves, like they were back on the street in a night club.

With their black clinched fist, even though they were silent, Smith and Carlos became megaphones, expressing the denial of *VOICE* slavery's descendants endured since **The Trans-Atlantic Slave Trade** began in 1452. Their raised clinched black clove fist became known as the Olympic Human Rights Salute, even though black people in America still do not have the human rights the UN refused to recognize when **"WE Charge Genocide"** was presented.

Further, driving home the point, Smith, Carlos, and Australian silver medalist Peter Norman all wore human rights badges on their jackets. The event is considered one of the most overtly political statements in the history of the modern Olympics Games. Their act—Smith, and Carlos—replaced Jesse Owens, as black Americans swashbuckling devil-may-care lone riding Olympic heros.

Slave descendants in America, reaching 1969, developed new thoughts, images, and perspectives, trying to design a strategy to fit the new times. After black people broke the back of physical segregation, they were unleashing for a second time, similar to slaves after emancipation and Civil War. Blacks had to learn to think differently about almost everything. *VOICE,* although not consciously worked out as a personal expression, slavery's descendants, on all levels of society, openly stated what was on their minds.

The fear of what white people might think, say, or do, if certain words came out of black people's mouths, were no longer being swallowed and choked down. Instead, at the slightest provocation, they spit them out all over white people, in ways that made even Stokley Carmichael duck for cover. America's slavery's descendants, without consideration for the response of whites, like shackles, threw off concerns for whites' reactions. Almost every black person had an opinion about what black people needed to do to improve the wretch state they endured.

Responding to the impact of black power, whites saw something entirely different in black people's demand for equality and justice. The two incidents just presented, one bloody in Mayor Richard Daily's Chicago, and the other, Smith and Carlos' black-gloved fist salute in Mexico City, were viewed in totally different ways by whites and blacks. The two groups gave totally different responses. The acts and demands for equality and justice conveyed by black and white progressives terrified white people, like screaming fire in a dark theater for the majority, and they totally rejected any demands for equality and justices.

Whites running for the exits heading for suburbia, with their tax dollars, burned rubber abandoning inner cities. Whites left smog in their wake, sucking up wealth, escaping hollowed-out inner cities. The acts and demands for equality and justice conveyed by black and progressives, terrified white Americans and those demanding change were like screams of fire in dark theaters for the majority of white people, as their reaction was a total rejection of equality and justice. Called ghettos, a euphemism for slave pens, whites left dying and decaying hulks, boarded-up storefronts and empty promises behind, getting away from black people. Inner cities became *"Raisins in the Sun."*

However, today, whites are back, leaving suburbia running from skyrocketing gas prices, but they are supported by government and banks again, they are facilitating their return. Whites are reclaiming neighborhoods black people stayed behind and saved. Banks with low-interest rates and government with regulations are helping whites take back neighborhoods they abandoned in the 1970s and 80s.

Today, governments and banks have a new term, for whites' displacement of blacks. Instead of "white flight," their return is called *"gentrification."* This is the "new" racism for the same old reason. Black people know Trump is not going to do anything; the question is what will Mr. Biden do?

"This is the same "old" red neck, red lining mentality" Woodrow Wilson's **Birth of a Nation** pogrom used to entrench racism, segregation, and white privilege in the 1920s, has become the dominant theme in Trump's America. And as such, America's government pretends it is doing black people a favor saving inner cities. They claim the returning of whites to inner cities, is bringing money back. But, in reality, whites are sucking up tax dollars black people paid to keep cities solvent, after "white flight."

And, as during white flight, blacks could not get any money for anything. Government, black or white, claims the tax money black people paid before, during, and after whites abandoned inner cities, is now being given returning whites for *"revitalization."* However, the same city governments refused to spend any tax money to improve these cities, while they built up suburbia, once white ran to the "burbs."

White people always have a term for what they do, when they screw black people around. When blacks stayed in inner cities, they were the only tax money cities got. Now the government is bringing back the children of whites that ran to suburbs, is called "saving urban life." Again, black people are in the back of the bus, even when black Mayors are in the drivers' seat, like Atlanta.

Back when whites were running scared in the1960s and 70s, the hippie counterculture flipped America a bird, while flipping the scrip on America's hypocrisy. Back then, the counterculture tried to teach their parents what racism and hatred would yield. Progressives had an answer in theaters for young people desperately hoping and looking for life beyond consumerism, chasing dollars, war, racism, and hatred which presented a new and different vision—***Easy Rider***.

Bringing a new spirit of defiance to the counterculture's fight, the film ***Easy Rider*** roared off movie screens in 1969. It captured the hearts and minds of young white and black Americans, giving new hopes that the ideals of the counterculture might yet prevail. Like no film before it, ***Easy Rider*** reflected the changing socio-economic dynamics and views among and between young white progressive Americans. ***Easy Rider,*** like COVID-19 today, blew blinders off the eyes of millions of young white kids but didn't require masks. Believing there was an alternative to their parents' racist world of war, the *Baby Boom Generation* threw a new psychology at the world. ***Easy Rider*** screeched across America's psyche, like a phonograph needle knocked out of a record's groove—scratching.

Almost totally recasting the ***old West,*** with modern-day desperadoes, rolling across America's new frontier, director Dennis Hopper and producer Peter Fonda gave urban cowboys outlaw wheels. Prizing freedom, love, and self-expression above all other ideals, Hopper and Fonda were two outlaw bikers on an iconic road trip across America. Although it was an epic drama, ***Easy Rider, for*** some, was a wink and nod at Jack Kerouac's, *On the Road*.

Laden with avant-garde imagery, ***Easy Rider*** spoke a language young urban dwellers, and those imprisoned by customs and tradition understood so very well. It said, *"There is a different world out here. Real things are happening, and to experience them, you better get out there now and see and do them before they disappear."* Emblematically the beauty of America, ***Easy Rider*** contrasted the ugliness young white, and black Americans were fighting in streets across the nation.

Oscar Micheaux: A Self-Made Man

The Judge sentenced me to 1 to 5 years in the penitentiary in Nashville, my conviction was on several expose-facto trumped-up riot charges, that were not even laws when the incident occurred. Do not let the 1 fool you. When I left the streets in 1968, black power activists, as I said earlier, either went on the run, undercover, left the country, in jail, or were dead. Life didn't seem fair when I went to jail, as part of J. Edgar Hoover's plan to kill black power. However, before I hit the streets again, I realized jail had saved my life, in more ways than one. Jail gave me time to reflect on the life thrust upon me as a result of the infamous *"gas cap incident."*

A long story made short, a white gas station attendant stole my gas cap and tried to sell it back to me. Incensed, I called the police. Once they arrived, I went to jail, while the guilty white thief walked away with a smile. Life really wasn't fair. The incident and its ramifications were like that *gas cap* jumped me into black power, and I became an activist.

Believing I could get justice, as a true American Vietnam War veteran, I called the police on a thief. But, white men in the South would never be arrested on the word of a black man, even if he was a war veteran. That was the lesson I learned, which changed my life for all times. This time around however, as my brother-in-law William Brandon's maxim urged, *"Given a choice, choose, always choose,"* I needed to learn what I was choosing. So, I chose to become educated about my choice, whatever I did.

Having survived Hoover's Co-Intel-Pro death hunt for black power activists, I knew I could not go back to the life I left. Compared to the possibilities the future offered, I had real potential. Without a doubt, the Invaders had developed new leadership, while I was locked up. They seemed happy with the transition and playing that role, so I chose to leave well enough alone. The interesting thing about all the new changes black people had gone through, and some were huge, by far the biggest change was black and white activists had come together in America and broken the back of segregation. Black power activists and young white radicals ended that 90-year system of terror, suffering, injustice, and government-sponsored tyranny over black people.

Coming back to my old hood in 1971, I had already found a new life while in jail. The riot charge had a misdemeanor attached to it, which the judge refused to run concurrently with the 1 to 5-year prison sentence just serviced. They wanted to keep me off the street, as long as possible; as I said, life really was not fair. Nevertheless, as time and events would have it, while locked up, Divine Intervention smiled on me.

Serving the eleven months and 29 days in the Shelby County Penal Farm, which was outside of Memphis, Providence smiled on me, turning dread into good fortune. I believe only God can engineer such convoluted outcomes, as that I encountered while serving time. Locked away from the real world, I had to learn to be a man among men. While looking for a way to go back to the world with options, I got involved in a rehabilitation program developed by a white psychologist Martin Kindig. But, the thing that made everything happen for me was a black State Representative from Riverside, I knew from childhood, Harold E. Ford. He was an up and coming black politician with a doubtful future.

Harold's misfortune became my exit strategy and good fortune. His fortunes were fading fast for future success in Nashville. His re-election bid was headed South but the legislature met North of Memphis in Nashville. Headed in the wrong direction Harold needed to show he was doing things for the Riverside community, now that black power was a political force.

I sent Harold word that I needed help with the rehabilitation program. We needed help getting state funding for the post-release part of the program. The idea was to provide transitional services for parolee after release. They needed support to find jobs, places to live, drug counseling, and other services. Harold came through, and I hit the streets with a job. The gig was coordinating released inmate services while becoming one of Harold Ford's reelection campaign co-ordinators.

Almost seamlessly, I was back on the streets with a new life. New, as I said earlier, was the operative term. There was even a new saying, **"I'm black and I'm proud."** James Brown took that saying, ditched his process, grew an Afro, and became *"soul brother number one."* Isaac Hayes donned gold chains like a slave, went to "WATTS STAX, and became *"black Moses."* Recording artists were dueling to come up with the next black hit record. Marvin Gaye gave black power a love song "What's Going On!"

Amazingly, white people had begun changing also, at lease superficially. They were wearing hairstyles that looked like Afros. And, if one saw only their dress and hair, not their skin color, one wouldn't know whether they were black or white. None of this was even remotely evident when I left the streets in September 1968. The changes white people made in lifestyle gave what black people did a different edge.

The 1960s and early 1970s brought political changes that reflected the growth of a people that tried to redefine themselves since emancipation. Psychologically, their growth produced cultural changes that drove political changes. Such cultural do-overs prompted actions and ideas only few of slavery's descendants had ever contemplated before black power, but none had tried. So, many of the actions black people initiated seemed like revolutionary statements. Such changes became ***the new spirit of the age***.

Although a new age had dawned, black artists still had to fight the same old battles, getting from the outer edge of obscurity into the mainstream of

The 400th: From Slavery to Hip Hop

conscious American thought. Whether looking back at former slaves, trying to get into Minstrelsy or new visionaries like Lorraine Hansberry, the battle was the same. That is the downside of the entertainment coin, where the black side is always down. So, one never knows what's up or actually happening, until the deal is done, and for black people, the script gets flipped again. Then it's too late; blacks got the short end of the stick again, if they got anything at all.

Black people, since their enslavement began, have fought desperate battles against incredible odds, always having to *"make something out of nothing."* Once emancipated, doors descendants of America slavery were supposed to enter to access freedom, justice, and equality were locked and bolted on the inside. Then some really smart white guy crawled through a window and nailed the door shut from the outside to be sure no blackface would spoil their view of white fun, on the inside.

Black entertainers died, as Minstrelsy performers, trying to make a place for former slaves, during "blackface," Louis Wright became a classic example. "Blackface" was not just make-up. It was an attitude and a statement reflective of a black person's willingness to submit to humiliation to express their talents, as a result of white domination. Accepting "blackface" surrendered a black person's right of *VOICE*. Blackface became a permanent scowl, as white faces reflective the opinion most white America's hold regarding African American Art and artists. Shuffled off the main stage into anterooms, so as not to be seen in polite company, black entertainers before the 1960s were "Old Black Joe and Mammy."

A major part of the entertainment industry that evolved from Minstrelsy, which evolved from slaves entertaining master, history books made it seem there were no blacks involved in entertainment, especially making movies. During the early years before motion picture production developed into the industry it is today, history books pretended it was not until Hattie McDaniel, blacks were allowed in movies.

Two movies became huge statements that reflected white people's world vision. The first **"*The Birth of A Nation*"** became the model for the world Woodrow Wilson forced upon black people. Then fifty-four years later, **"*Easy Rider*"** reflected a counter vision and hope for young white people in America for escaping the world Woodrow Wilson created. Then on the downside of the movie-making coin, which is the black side, two movies also reflect a counter vision of what black people thought of the vision whites forced on them as a world.

Looking back, it is like a visit to an amusement park, where Jimmy Crow is behind the curtain playing tricks with all the rides. The Amusement park in this particular case was Hollywood. This was no Disneyland or anything like that; this was J. Edgar Hoover's playground. This was the time he entered government in 1912, and Woodrow Wilson extended segregation and white supremacy throughout America. The motion picture industry was in its infancy. Jim Crow ran all the shops in and outside Hollywood. Gatekeeping gave Jim Crow, who was played by enforcer J. Edgar Hoover, a starring role in everything the movie industry produced. Playing Jim Crow, Hoover was honcho in charge of keeping blacks out of the movie business.

But, regardless of Jim Crow's determined effort, there was one black man even more determined to make a statement with film once he saw **Birth of A Nation.** That man is Oscar Micheaux, a self-made man. If Oscar Micheaux had never made movies, many stories detailing the struggles of black people's survival would not be known.

Oscar was a Pullman porter (sleeping car attendants) on trains. Then in 1904, at the beginning of **Plessy v. Ferguson,** convict leasing and sharecropping, Oscar began homesteading nearly 500 acres of land near the Rosebud Sioux Reservation in South Dakota. Micheaux became an author, he published his novels, while homesteading. First, in Nebraska, then New York City, and later made movies in Chicago and Los Angeles. His first three novels, <u>The Conquest</u> (1913), <u>The Forged Note</u> *(1915), and* <u>The Homesteader</u> *(1917),* were "autobiographical."

Oscar's novels featured him as a young black man in rural, white South Dakota. He sold his books door-to-door to his white neighbors. Once he watched D.W. Griffith's powerful and vitriolic anti-black production **The Birth of a Nation,** Micheaux experienced "the captivating power of film." Through this new technology, he found a new kind of power. Oscar came to believe motion pictures could give him *"the ability to tell a complex, multi-character story, every bit as compelling, as in the words of a novel."*

He moved to Chicago, where his filmmaking career began during the **"Dark Age"** *angry white men mob madness era.* He made a movie version of his novel—*The Homesteader.* With his first film, Micheaux became the first African American to write, produce and direct a full-length feature film. It was also a commercial success, grossing over $5,000. There were other black filmmakers, and some may have been, as good as Oscar, but they did not make full-length feature films, and their work is lost to posterity.

Micheaux's control production and distribution of his films to protect his legacy. Some say that limited his success, but that may have been what saved his work for posterity. Micheaux persuaded the best black actors, women and men, of his time to work in forty-four films he produced between 1919 and 1948.

Oscar's work held great appeal for the rapidly growing black urban audiences of post-World War I America. Most of Micheaux's films were detective stories, he wrote, filmed, edited, and released. His African American audiences were starved to see people who looked, talked, and acted like them on the silver screen. Desiring to make a statement that answered **The Birth of a Nation,** Micheaux used his first productions to gain experience he felt necessary to present and portray racism in film.

Micheaux wrote, directed, and produced **Within Our Gates,** a 1920 silent movie. The *Great Migration* brought millions of southern blacks to cities of the North and Midwest, which fueled the emergence of the *"New Negro."* This movement gave Micheaux a very receptive audience for **Within Our Gates.** However, the whites press described **Within Our Gates** as a ***"race film."***

"Within Our Gates" featured an African-American woman in the lead role. She travels to a northern city to raise money for a rural school in the Deep South for poor black children. **"Within Our Gates"** though a movie was not a fantasy. It reflected the times in which it was made and was an accurate depiction of what happened to black people, during those days, unlike ***"The Birth of A Nation."***

The heroin's romance with a black doctor eventually leads to revelations about her family's past and mixed-race, European ancestry. The film portrays racial violence under white supremacy and the lynching of a black man. "**Within Our Gates"** is the oldest known surviving film made by an African-American director and filmmaker.

There are two excellent sources for biographical information on Oscar Micheaux. Rap Mogul Bayer L. Mack made a documentary on the early 20th-century black filmmaker. Mr. Mack said he was, *"especially unhappy that no one had produced a major documentary about such a towering figure in black history. It is amazing to me, that the first black man to break into film making, no one, not even a black film make, saw Micheaux as worthy of a film about his Herculean efforts."* Mr. Mack set out to remedy the situation. Mack added a television dimension to his independent record label, *Block Starz Music,* and created an hour-long production (2014). Biography.com has a lengthy story on Oscar Micheaux.

Most importantly, Oscar Micheaux's films in the 1920s and 1930s contrasted sharply with the Hollywood *"in blackface"* image of black people as lazy, ignorant, and sexually aggressive toward white women. Micheaux's genius was playing a crucial role opening opportunities for African Americans in front of and behind the camera. Today Oscar has gained some posthumous recognized. In 1987 Oscar Micheaux was memorialized with a Hollywood Walk of Fame "Star."

Also, he was honored by the Black Filmmakers Hall of Fame with an award (1989) and the Director's Guild of America honored him (1989) as well. But the **"Oscars"** have continued to give Oscar an in *"blackface"* response. Each year Gregory, South Dakota, Micheaux's adopted hometown, presents the Oscar Micheaux Film Festival (*Writing Himself Into History: Oscar Micheaux, His Silent Films and His Audiences:* Pearl Bowser and Louise Spence: Rutgers University Press, Piscataway, N.J. 2000).

Jim Crow: Battles in the Shadows

Oscar Micheaux's career and life demonstrated the fallacy of white supremacist government—federal, state, and local. The Supreme Court edits—***Plessy v. Ferguson***—demanded American slavery's descendants accept second class, as their rightful place in life. The Court supported white people that refuse to accept they were not superior, especially to African Americans. Slavery's descendants survived every effort whites mounted to prevent them from developing as competition. White Americans today (2020), like Mitch McConnell, stack the Supreme Court with racist dedicated to keeping white supremacy and white privilege alive and well in America.

Allegorically, as well as actually, Jim Crow continued to live long after Oscar Micheaux successfully competed from the 1920s until 1948. J. Edgar Hoover disguised as the *"Dark Overload"* of Hollywood blocked opportunities for blacks in filmmaking. He played Jim Crow enforcing segregation and white supremacy, along with the *Second Red Scare* and *McCarthyism*. These operations were real life dramas for hundreds of blacks trying to break into the movies. His efforts bloomed like ragweed all over Hollywood. Serving as the backdraft to racism, Hoover gave everyone hay fever, sneezing racism all over Hollywood, like COVID-19, when a black person showed up.

Hoover declared black filmmakers were a plague and he was stamping out their contagion of communists. He was relentless, using that charge to quarantine and lock blacks out of Hollywood. Hoover used government power personally enforcing segregation in *"Tinsel Town."* He denied black entertainers and filmmakers, as well as anyone who supported them, access to opportunities in the movie business.

The historical record reflects that after Oscar Micheaux, the most noted black filmmaker of the 1950s and 60s was Gordon Park. "Gordon's war," like Ossie Davis' movie by the same name, reflects Parks was an intrepid lone rider in Hollywood, surviving Jim Crow's effort to keep him out. Gordon Parks should have enjoyed even greater success, but Jim Crow took up residence and bird dog him, like Marcus Garvey, Malcolm X and Dr. Martin Luther King, Jr.

I repeat, Jim Crow played a big role in every production in and outside Hollywood, but he was very difficult to identify on the scene, because central casting kept changing his role and wardrobe to disguise his presence on sets. My description may sound like a satire or spoof, but the fact is, J. Edgar Hoover/Jim Crow was judge and jury anytime blacks, whether filmmakers, actors, or grips, voiced complaints. Jim Crow was a "heavy" enforcer in Hollywood, and would show up looking like any white person known or unknown for keeping blacks out. So, only black entertainers that learned to play and beat Jim at his own game successfully broke through.

The 400th: From Slavery to Hip Hop

Jim Crow always entered from stage right; that way, he could make sure only a very few blacks made it into Hollywood productions. Studios said this was to ensure not too many blacks got in and clutter up the place with their "ghetto-ism." Whenever there was a need to assure white people were comfortable regarding whether black actors ("actresses") were safe and noncontroversial before an offer, Jim Crow show up. Continually changing Jim's role and costume insured he did not resemble the character he played previously. This made it very difficult for a black actor to prove Jim Crow was on the set determining decisions about black actors.

The battles, behind the camera for black grips or stagehands in entertainment, were even bloodier than in front of the camera. Behind scenes in the shadows, out of public view, Jim Crow didn't care what he did or how he looked doing it. Jim Crow left black stagehands and grips battered, bruised and scarred after squeezing through loop holds, and under barriers, Jim erected to keep them from getting backstage, during the 1950s and 60s. For black women, getting rough up or felt up was an expectation, if one got in the door, whether in front or behind the camera; asked Harvey Weinstein. Even though Jim was easily recognized, after such bloody encounters, studio executives, as the Supreme Court, always blame the victims, rather than the culprit.

The point of that introduction is to show that Hollywood Studio executives were just as committed to white supremacy and segregation, as Gov. George Wallace or NFL owners today. Even after Minstrelsy blackface was no longer acceptable in general society, Hoover, through executives in Hollywood, continued enforcing white superiority, like in 1920. So after blacks in studios gained some leverage, once social change and social justice forces intervened, studio executives had to deal with Jim Crow's antics. Hoping to get around demands from unions, protesting the lack of opportunities for black actors and grips, again like the US Supreme Court, executives tried a little sleight of hand.

Events and protests continued until studios concluded they had to put Jim Crow on a tight leash to relieve the pressure from demonstrations by unions. Studio executives tried subterfuge to buy time. Knowing their hearts were not in fighting white supremacy, unions pressed their demands. Studio executives gave directors and other production types, authority to check Jim Crow's impact. Executives were allowed to bring a few nonaggressive and unobtrusive blacks into studio crafts.

One such individual considered was Will Yarbrough. I met Will through one of his relatives, a lifelong friend, Vincent Taylor. Their family was from Mason, Tennessee (Sunbeam Mitchell's hometown). Will moved to LA as a very young man. He got into a studio as a "gopher and pick up man" (you know, go for this or go get that, while pick up this or pick up that). Union protests pitted workers like Will against studio executives where they worked, trying recruit black grips, like Will to walk out and join their protest. Coveting the few blacks that survived Jim Crow, a studios executive approached Will.

While talking with Will, he recanted his encounters, *"They were looking for a black person for sound (audio) engineering and asked me, 'Will, how much do you know about sound mixing?'"* Will said he thought a moment and while thinking, he remembered his father's words leaving Mason, Tennessee, *"White folks don't like niggers that think they know something."* So Will responded, *"Well, Sir, I think I know how to plug in an extension cord without shocking myself or blowing out power all over the set."*

Listening, as Will told of his experiences, reminded me when I broke into show production, as a stagehand in Atlanta in 1996. Everyone knew Jim Crow ran everything down South, so white guys dominating crafts was no surprise. When I broke into the stagehand business, there were only a few black stagehands who did has Will to get in and learn the ropes. I depended on them for help, recognizing and getting around Jim Crow's antics. One such stagehand was Moses Williams. Moe, as we call him, was a pioneer. He broke in, with Turner Broadcasting in Atlanta, during the very early days of cable TV. I know it was tough for Moe, because for me (1996), it was like things had not changed much since Minstrelsy's "blackface."

On many occasions, Moses did battle with management to get move-up opportunities for young brothers and sisters. We tried to encourage younger black stagehands to think about starting a black stage production company. Now, today, Moses has partnered with his son Korry, and they've opened a stage production company—Tech Hands Production LLC of Atlanta. Also, Moe has continued sharing his business knowledge and expertise with young black entrepreneurs, hoping for a future in show production, as he did me.

Will Yarbrough never thought of himself, as a pioneer or trailblazer either, he was trying to make a living and take care of his family. Will began as a cable page for the TV show "Room 222." Most people have no idea what that fight in the shadows and in the trenches for blacks, trying to break into Hollywood crafts in the 1960s and 70s, was like. When Will came along, it was harder to make it behind the camera than in front of it.

First, getting in a studio seemed to require a *"black cat bone"* to evade Jim Crow, who may disguise himself as anyone on the set, except you. It took some special magic, playing stupid and doing your job, without making it look not too easy. Today, grips and stagehands owe a great deal too black men, like Will and Moses. They were willing to do all the stupid stuff demanded of them until studios realized they knew and could do their jobs, without someone looking over their shoulders.

Today, Will is an award-winning icon. He moved up from cable page to become a sound mixer and spent nine years with *"MASH"* on TV. He also worked *"Thirty-something"* and a host of other productions. Will has five Emmy nominations and was recognized by Primetime Emmy Awards for Outstanding

Sound Mixing for a Drama Series *"Thirty-something"* (1987), *"ER"* (1994), and *"The Watcher"* (1995). He won *Outstanding Achievement in Sound Mixing for the Television Series—"ER"* (1994) awarded by the Cinema Audio Society, USA.

What I am stressing in this narrative is not the daily details in the lives of black actors in front or grips behind the camera but the impact of people like Will and Moses. Similar to Nat D. Williams with *WDIA,* they opened doors through their successes for other blacks, who today don't know their names. Their stories are part of the arc of ***"The 400th"*** because they are survivors of America's genocide. Their stories are lessons for young slave descendants who don't understand what it took to get to ***"The 400th".*** I know, when Will's father gave him that advice, he never thought it would change his life. But, it's as I said about dreams, *"They never resemble what one imagined or drew up as a plan once the reality materializes."* Nonetheless, because he had that warning, Will was able to use the information, and that is all that matters.

Another Self-Made Man

The previous discussion may have seemed weird or bizarre, but satirizing African Americans' efforts to get into the movie business and stage production was to show the difficulties black Americans faced, as a side note to all their other struggles to survive racism and white supremacy in America. That interlude was to open the discussion of the second filmmaker and movie that made big changes for black Americas, similar to *"Easy Rider"* for whites. It reflects the barriers in Hollywood during 1960 into the late 1980s which made black filmmakers seem like magicians, making a film. This filmmaker was an extremely audacious individual. His film required a very confident mindset, attempting an even more ambitious and spectacular effort than Oscar Micheaux, who wrote, directed, and produced movies to become a swashbuckling, devil-may-care lone rider.

Venturing into such shark-infested waters, after the first splash, one has to be willing to risk all for success. Whether in front, behind the camera or the one directing those in front of it, one court's disaster with every decision. Such an ambitious individual, without regard to which hat they wear, falls in the bullseye of Jim Crow with their first decision.

Opening this section, as I did, was to create a proper entrance for just such a modern-day devil-may-care swashbuckling lone rider in a business with very few models. I wanted readers to know the real risk based on the historical circumstances a black person, man or woman, was up against, skinny dipping in Hollywood's treacherous waters. Hollywood feeds such ambitious black men and women to the sharks, as smacks between breakfast, lunch, and dinner.

Most descendants of American slavery identified with Dr. Martin Luther King, Jr.'s view of poverty—the federal government was the culprit underpinning America's *"cheap labor"* capitalistic strategy. The fight for change towards the end of the 1960s required new efforts, ideas, and personalities. Black power advocates, rather than evolving out of the counterculture, as young white progressives, came straight out of mainstream civil rights.

The difference between the two groups, beyond skin color or because of it, white kids went to jail on misdemeanors, if they went to jail at all, whereas most black actives, like me, if they lived, were charged with felonies. There was no question, once they got you into court, before all-white prosecutors, judges, and juries; going to prison was the idea unless one had backing like Angela Davis. Getting out of jail in 1971 put me back on the streets after 3 years and seven months. I definitely saw things differently.

While incarcerated, I study the problems of black people for the first time. I wanted to learn the what, why, and how black people became trapped in poverty. Unlike other races, black people seemed unable to get out, and Dr. King's words, regarding poverty, kept bouncing around in my head. I came to believe something unforeseen or unexplained had occurred, in regards to the education slave descendants received.

Entering this new environment created by black power, after almost four years off the street, I was looking forward to a different kind of life. I was still committed to the black liberation struggle, but I was looking for a new technology to fight for it. Everybody, especially black power activists, were giddy with excitement and raving about Melvin Van Peebles' powerful drama **Sweet Sweetback's Baadasssss Song.** They felt he had brought the struggle of black people to the silver screen. Since I was not there in 1915, I can't say if black people reacted similarly to it, as white people watching *The Birth of A Nation.* What I will say is, I believe, their reactions were very similar to black people, who watched Oscar Micheaux's "**Within Our Gates.**"

Watching **Sweet Sweetback's** run, I saw black people over the centuries making the same run. Born into a family of runners, I could identify with **Sweet Sweetback's** struggle, running to get to a place where he no longer needed to run. Slaves in the Deep South made their run Northward. They were trying to get across the Ohio River, some with the *Underground Railroad*, while others on their own, maybe headed south to Mexico. Six million black families, including mine, made similar runs getting out of the South or maybe just out of sharecropping, as part of the *Great Migration* (1910-1960). My grandparents made a similar run, getting to the farm where my mother was born. My mother and father extended my grandparents' run (1919), getting out of Mississippi and reaching Memphis in 1946. My family's run from Jackson, Mississippi to Memphis, Tennessee (202 miles) took three generations.

Melvin Van Peebles was not the first black filmmaker to use cinematic images to tell our story, as I have shown. But he not only told their story in their own words; he had those words coming out of their mouths, without any concern for what white people thought when they heard them. He gave *VOICE* to millions whose words or their stories would never be told. An iconic point along the arc to **"The 400th", Sweet Sweetback's Baadasssss Song** was released in 1971 to cheers from blacks and boos from whites. Here we have another example of how white people and black people can observe and experience the very same event or reality, at the exact same moment, under the same conditions, yet come away with totally different scenarios.

Sweet Sweetback had a very powerful impact, something akin to a religious experience for some black moviegoers. Van Peebles spoke to black people in ways preachers never did. Seeing their world come alive before their eyes **Sweet Sweetback's Baadasssss Song** brought their ghetto world to the silver screen. **Sweet Sweetback's Baadasssss Song** exploded in black people's heads and minds, shattering the calm ghetto mindset of contentment blacks settled into, hoping **Brown v. Board of Education** would bring changes white people refused to grant after emancipation (1863), Civil War (1865) and including ***Brown v. Board of Education.***

Amazingly, Melvin Van Peebles was more of a one-man band than Oscar Micheaux. He wrote, directed, produced, edited, starred and composed the soundtrack for his powerful epic. First, Melvin was a fish out of water, trying to make a movie. Before shooting a frame, Jim Crow chased Melvin out of the US in order to get access to knowledge of filmmaking. Not quite a runner, fleeing the US into the waiting arms of France, Melvin sojourned in Europe for several years. After learning the craft of motion picture production, he returned to the US and rejoined the battle he escaped, going to Europe. Yet and still, he had to fight his way from the very edge of obscurity, breaking into the filmmaking business.

Melvin's production was made possible, not only because of actors in front of the camera but grips behind it as well. Secondly, he could not get financing for his project from any place. Banks in America are like courts; there is no fairness or justice to be had. So getting a business loan is still not a consideration for a black start-up of any kind in America. Economically, starting his project, Melvin was like Sunbeam Mitchell, trying to get money from a white bank, in the South, to start the *Chitlins Circuit.* Getting money for a project is still a *"going to family and friends proposition"* for black entrepreneurs. Getting money in this fashion is problematic because funds may get called in at any time, or unforeseen life circumstances or crisis can intervene and shut the whole enterprise down.

I foreshadowed Van Peebles' adventure in this way so that readers understood Melvin's need for the kind of special magic required to *make something out of nothing* getting started. Without a *"mojo hand"* or *"jack ball,"* the magic for Van Peebles' abracadabra was plastic—the almighty credit cards. Maxing out credit cards and nickel and diming it from friends was just enough to get Melvin into the deep end of the pool, in water over his head, wearing boots too large; Melvin was underwater and drowning before he knew it.

Trying to avoid sharks, before he was halfway, creditors at this point were even more vicious to elude than sharks. Reaching this very crucial point, while still underwater, trying to keep from drowning, as he went down for the fourth time, Bill Cosby threw him a lifeline. Mr. Cosby stepped up like an angel of mercy, rescuing Melvin with a critical 50,000 dollar package of financial help. Operating on a shoestring budget, made craftsmen like Will and Moses indispensable to Melvin's success. Most actors and crafts worked on promises based on the finished film.

The real fun started for Melvin once his movie hitting the screen. **Sweet Sweetback's Baadasssss Song** fed into and energized black people's desire for change. It foreshadowed a new political consciousness, in ways Van Peebles could not have foreseen, definitely when his idea was only a gleam in the eye of chance. The first major independently produced feature film by an African

American since Oscar Micheaux, ***Sweet Sweetback's Baadasssss Song,*** placed Van Peebles in a class unto himself. Succeeding in Hollywood against incredible odds, Van Peebles' ascent was like a dandelion struggling for life, pushing its way up through a concrete sidewalk in an inner-city ghetto.

Van Peebles propelled creative excitement with ***Sweet Sweetback's Baadasssss Song,*** while projecting the urge to excel among other blacks, trying to *make something out of nothing*. Disregarding Hollywood's efforts to lock doors and keep them closed, Van Peebles gave descendants of American slavery a sense of empowerment. Similar to Oscar Micheaux's production—***Within Our Gates***—which was labeled a *"race film," Sweet Sweetback's Baadasssss Song* was labeled a ***"blaxploitation films."*** Although not intended, Van Peebles' is credited with creating a whole new genre. The intend was not to praise *"Caesar but to bury him"*; it was a *"blackball,"* not a *"jack ball."* More than anything, it was a curveball in the dirt, trying to make sure Van Peebles would not get a hit.

Make no mistake about it; the intention or designation was to single out the successful black production in a way that made it seem of lesser value or quality than a white production. I have never heard of a *"Whiteploitation"* film, even though white filmmakers have made all kinds of outrageous films about white people, doing all kinds of outrageous things. Singling out black productions is a typical Jim Crow tactic in Hollywood and the rest of America. Jim Crow's job is limiting the impact of Black Arts with signals that say in some way whites can ignore it. Typically, Hollywood will create or makeup some special category, which is like placing an asterisk before the name to signify devaluation or relegate it to a lesser status for black artists' works.

Whether films, novels, music, paintings, plays, or dance, black productions are stigmatized and placed on a different level to reduce head-on competition against white productions. I believe Lorraine Hansberry's work faced similar treatment, following her success with ***A Raisin in the Sun***. Whites accepted ***Raisin's*** greatness because they could not deny it, but they did not want to accept Hansberry, as great. Black artists are maintained in some second-class status or *"separate but equal"* category to signal that things connected to black people are never as good as that produced by white people—***the white man's ice is always colder!!!*** Such descriptions like ***"blaxploitation,"*** are made-up black categories, like *"separate but equal"* by the US Supreme Court.

Whether black filmmakers, playwrights, novelists, or other artistics efforts that proves their worth at the box office, whits place in special categories, not standard, like white productions. Exemplary of this practice, "***Sweet Sweetback"*** ignited a new psyche and self-image among black people, especially black men. Van Peebles, with ***Sweet Sweetback's Baadasssss Song,*** broke through the *"black funk"* enveloping black people following the devastating loss of Dr. Martin Luther King, Jr. Projecting a sense of defiance, ***Sweetback*** laid claim to blackness in ways no colored man dared think, let alone attempt. ***Sweetback*** made an individual black man a source of strength in the ghetto.

Making *something out of nothing*, Van Peebles' magic made ***Sweet Sweetback*** a folk hero to black people. Creating a black hero probably seemed like hoodoo and conjure to white folks. If not hoodoo, Van Peebles definitely seemed a sorcerer to white folks, when ***Sweet Sweetback's Baadasssss Song*** hit the movies. It was as if, Van Peebles threw a *"chitlin party"* in the heart of Hollywood for the hood, but didn't invite anyone who lived there. With the release of ***Sweet Sweetback's Baadasssss Song,*** black people responded with pride in the cultural, economic, and psychological vindication and affirmation Melvin gained. Descendants of American slavery came out of the woodwork to be part of the ***Sweetback*** experience.

Hungry to see real black faces with no "in black-face" bamboozle to please whites and dull the edge of seeing almost nothing but black faces, acting like black people on the silver screen, Melvin Van Peebles stated, *"At first,* **only two theaters in the entire United States of America** *would show my film: one in, Detroit and one in Atlanta. The first showing in Detroit was a disaster. But by the second day, people brought their lunches and sat through it three times. I knew that I was finally talking to the audience; I wanted to reach."*

However, 27 years later Melvin took on the whole Hollywood/movie making establishment with an excoriating criticism in a documentary underscoring his true feelings—***Classified X.*** The 1998 documentary was directed by Mark Daniels and narrated by Van Peebles. His walk back down memory lane was not a romance with the past, it details the portrayal and history of black people in American cinema throughout the 20th century.

Melvin Van Peebles, after directing the breakthrough ***movie "Sweet Sweetback's Baadasssss Song,"*** turns his acerbic insights and homespun humor on Hollywood's degradation of its sepia citizens. ***Classified X*** examines the treatment of black characters throughout the history of American cinema. Van Peebles documentary presents classic examples of white films, beginning with footage by Thomas Edison in 1903 to show and trace how Hollywood has aided and abetted the derogatory public perception of African-Americans down through the years. From its earliest days, Van Peebles says, *"Hollywood reflected society's fear of blacks and has encouraged public acceptance of the ugliest stereotypical images of African Americans, as servile, ignorant, superstitious, or untrustworthy."* With candor and wit, he explores the institutionalization of racism before his groundbreaking film ***Sweetback*** and afterwards. Melvin Van Peebles said,

"...the very first thing we must do is to reconquer our own minds. The biggest obstacle to the Black revolution in America is our conditioned susceptibility to the white man's program. In short, the fact is that the white man has colonized our minds. We've been violated, confused and drained by this colonization and from this brutal, calculated genocide, the most effective

and vicious racism has grown, and it is with this starting point in mind and the intention to reverse the process that I went into cinema in the first f***ing place."

Finally, Melvin Van Peebles made ***Sweet Sweetback*** the embodiment of black power's rejection of the quiet rage and doleful subservience of slavery's subjugation, which blacks had never fully throw off. Although ***Sweetback*** is on the run for almost the entire drama, his run is about what happens when a black man makes a stand. ***Sweetback's*** run symbolized black people's historical need for mobility, which extended descendants of American slavery's never-ending struggle to escape the grave of poverty in the valley of dry bones. I feel ***Sweet Sweetback's Baadasssss Song*** underscores black people's growing aggressiveness reaching 1971. ***Sweet Sweetback's Baadasssss Song's*** overall effect was similar to David Walker's ***Appeal's*** on slaves in the 1830s.

Sunbeam: A Stand-Up Tin Man

Entertainers traveled roads to make a living before Minstrelsy and certainly long before Sunbeam Mitchell was even born, let alone set up shop in Memphis. Even more importantly, slaves created the **Blues** decades before W. C. Handy's arrival on Beale Street. **Blues'** special magic was more than something to entertain master. The **Blues** developed new opportunities for slave descendants that grew into what became their **Blues** lifestyle, and black people used it to learn to make more than music.

Robert R. Church, senior, and junior used their wealth to expand economic potential and opportunities for former slaves and help them development entrepreneurial, entertainment, and other cultural activities. The foundation they laid drew even more former slaves into Memphis from all over the Mid-South. Some brought their special brand of magic and added it to the melting pot of Beale Street. Andrew "Sunbeam" Mitchell was one such individual. He was what upper-class Negros called a "field nigger."

Sunbeam was considered a low-class hustler, gambler, and uneducated thug the kind of Negro socially prominent blacks believe made it harder for them to gain the acceptance of white folks. Simultaneously, so-called black leaders went to Sunbeam when they needed him to work his special magic with white people for them. However, they never acknowledged the critical role he played on Beale Street and in the black community. Their refusal to acknowledge his leadership created a dual image of Sunbeam that remains unclear, even today.

My research revealed Sunbeam was a major developer of black entertainment in Memphis and across the South. He established businesses—Club Handy, Club Ebony, the Hippodrome, the Mitchell Hotel, several eateries, as well as the *"Chitlin Circuit."* Sunbeam's enterprises gave him the type of relevance and clout, middle-class Negros long to possess, but did not have the "drive" to step away from white people and take their success in their own hands. After the benefactor for the middle-class Robert Church, Jr. got chased out of town in 1942, Sunbeam's businesses became the key for poor black people access to economic benefits and prosperity.

Having heard many stories about Sunbeam and his times, I was able to find only a few written facts about him. I had to be very creative in getting and developing information that helped assess Sunbeam's true role and impact on the arc of *"The 400th"* for slavery's descendants in the Mid-South and other areas of America.

Researching background information on the importance of Beale Street and the role played by some of its eccentric characters that helped build the legacy of the noted thoroughfare, I talked with many *"old-timers."* They verified stories, information, and antidotal tit-bites about the man known as Sunbeam Mitchell.

The 400th: From Slavery to Hip Hop

These legendary characters established most of what is known and cherished around the black community, like heirlooms. Stories relayed by these flamboyant gentlemen were my only library, piecing Sunbeam's incredible and amazing story together. These word of mouth archives offer big fish, back-slapping stories that have taken on lives of their own over the year. For certain, these whoopers have been told and retold but are not found in libraries.

I was in Memphis for the Invaders 40th get together (2008), so I asked my friend, Vincent Taylor, who knew some Sunbeam stories pretty well, to serve as an intermediary and arrange a conversation with Mr. Walter Brooks, a proven authority on Beale Street. Mr. Brooks was a friend of Nat D. Williams, and before Nat passed, they often held sessions where *"old timers"* traded stories from their times. Residing in Memphis since 1914, and like a Beale Street cat, Mr. Brooks lived eight of his nine lives roasting, toasting and boasting the virtues of Beale Street. The ninth life ended this year (7-28-2020), he was 105 years young at his passing.

However back in 2008, I hoped through my friend Vincent's close connection—his mother and Mr. Brooks were friends—would give me an inside track, getting an interview with the then 92-year-old icon and historian emeritus. I asked Vince to arrange an afternoon lunch with Mr. Brooks to discuss Sunbeam. Mr. Brooks, I believed, would be the best source of any of Beale Street's classic *"old-timers"* I'd spoken with about Sunbeam. I felt Mr. Brooks could help clarify the duality Sunbeam's legacy reflects, since he was no longer with us (8-22-89). I talked with Nat D about Sunbeam while Nat was still with us, so I had good information, but Mr. Brooks also knew all the saints and sinners. He not only knew where the bodies are buried, he knew who buried them, in *God's little acre*.

Vincent arranged our confab at *Four Way Grill* at Mississippi Boulevard and Walker Avenue," a traditional meet and greet spot on the Southside of town. *Four Way Grill* is a great stop-in where *old-timers*, who love great soul food, still gathered. It has served the best Memphis cuisine to classic flamboyant characters, as well as the top echelon of the black middle class for 72 years (1946). I knew Mr. Brooks would feel at home, talking about the past in such iconic surroundings, while we ate a late lunch. We waited outside on a bright sunny afternoon until Mr. Brooks arrived.

A very cool and colorful gentleman, we could only marble and admire his style as he walked up. Decked out from head to toe in classic Memphis duds, he wore a black tailor-made two-button double-breasted jacket, and tan slacks, topped off with a badge Dobbs fifty. Coordinated, with a shirt that matched his Dobbs, a black, brown and tan striped tie, and brown British Walkers, accompaniedby a couple of big rings on each hand and a gold diamond-studded watch on his right wrist, he was sooo fly!!!! Greeting Mr. Brooks, he gave us a businessman's handshake and a big smile. Vincent did the introductions,

"Mr. Brooks, this is Mike Hampton, a friend and business associate from Nashville, and John Burl Smith. John wanted the interview for his project on Sunbeam." Mr. Brooks said quickly,

"Oh, yes! It's nice to meet you, young man; Mike is it?" He checked, shaking his hand then saying, *"Now I know of John, from his Invader days, and I also know his mother, we go way back."*

Entering *Four Way Grill*, the front area as always was crowded, so we got a table in the back dining room. While eating, the back area makes conversations more enjoyable and intimate. Mr. Brooks pull an extra chair over to the table we selected. Removing his hat, he carefully rested his Dobbs on it. Patiently, while we selected a table and took seats, the waitress said,

"I'll get menus."

As we got comfortable, after taking seats, Mr. Brooks asked,

"What did I do for you young men to waste such a beautiful afternoon like this, talking with an old man like me?" While banishing his biggest smile, then asking,

"And by the way, John, how's your mama? Fine, I hope. You know, she's such a wonderful lady."

Surprised, I asked, "So, you know my mother, Mr. Brooks?"

"Of course, I do!" He said, still smiling. "We met years ago, not long after she moved the family to Memphis from Mississippi, back in the late 40s. Now, those were some good times."

"That's the way she describes them also when we talk about *'the good old days,'* as she called them. Tell me about them, please, I requested."

"Well, back in the late 1940s and early 50s, gospel singing was really big in Memphis. It was almost as big as **Blues**. The preachers and churches were all behind it. We had really big personalities like Mrs. Lucie Campbell, Rev. Herbert Brewster, and others leading everything. Folks would really come out to see those shows. Radio announcers from **WDIA,** like Ford Nelson, Theo "Bless My Bones" Wade, Willa Monroe, Cornell Wells, and "Gatemouth" Moore, put on gospel shows around the city, and I traveled that circuit.

They did lots of things to promote what they called *"Gospel Battles."* Your mother was in a group with four other women from Pilgrim Rest Baptist Church. They were pretty good too. Their gospel group was the "M & N Junior Girls." They talk about them in this book, "Happy in the Service of the Load." It goes way back talking about all kinds of gospel groups. There were the Pattersonaires, the Brewsteraires, Clara Ward Singers, Mighty Clouds of Joy, The Five Blind Boys, and The Dixie Hummingbirds. I could go on naming them all day and talking about all those wonderful singers. Your mama's group had a chance to be big; she even wrote a song that became a favorite of some groups, *"I Got Two Wings,"* but you know how things go. There was a male group, the M & N Quartet; they traveled together. Your mother loved singing gospel."

"Yes Sir, I know!" Mr. Brooks looked over at Vincent and said,

"She was like your mama Ernestine, with the 'Golden Girls.' There was always a big singing contest almost every Sunday at some church, and people would pack the house. That was really good entertainment and lots of fun."

The waitress returned with menus, Mr. Brooks said,

"Honey, I don't need that sweetheart."

He motioned in our direction.

"They might need one. You know what I want!"

Mr. Brooks said as he leaned back in his chair, smiling, like watching an audition after his statement.

The young lady took a deep breath then said like reciting a poem,

"A big pork chop, collard greens, macaroni and cheese, sweet potatoes, okra on the side, cornbread, and a big glass of sweet ice tea with a slice of lemon, right,"

She checked while flashing her biggest smile.

"You got it," he said, smiling back.

"And you,"

She looked in my direction. After reeling off Mr. Brooks' menu from memory, I figured it had to be pretty good, since he ate it often enough for her to remember, so I said, "I'll have the same." I looked at Mike, then at Vincent. They must have felt the same because they echoed in agreement. A jukebox stood silently in the corner until Mr. Brooks said,

"I always like music with my food."

He went over, dropped in some coins, and pushed several selections, with a blast on his iconic horn, Junior Walker's *Road Runner* jumped out the Jukebox. Mr. Brooks did a little quickstep with a spin move as he returned to the table. Taking his seat, he said,

"Young men, when I was your ages,"

Looking more at Mike and Vincent than at me, I'm obviously, twenty years older than Vince, but Mike I'm not sure. Mr. Brook continued,

"Back in the day, I use to run'em just like that."

Mike leaned back in his chair and said,

"Well, I don't know Mr. Brooks, as sharp as you are today, looks like you would still blow up the stroll this evening, if you went there."

Everybody had a good laugh. The waitress returned, bringing our food, and after setting it out Mr. Brooks began eating, as I opened,

"Well, Mr. Brooks, I'm writing about Beale Street and Sunbeam Mitchell's role and his impact on the fabled street as well as on people in the Mid-South. Everyone tells me you're the man to talk with about some of the stories floating around about him. Also, I have an idea which ones are true, I talked with your buddy Nat D. when he was still with us, so I know some stories are just legends. But there are some I need to separate out. I wanted to know how much of what I've heard are facts and which are fiction, so I want to know, as much as possible, who was the man everyone called Sunbeam."

Mr. Brooks sat back in his chair after a few more bites, looked at me for a long moment, as he chewed and swallowed. His eyes tightened, as though he was gauging my intent. Then he flashed them from one to the other of us before speaking. He said,

The 400th: From Slavery to Hip Hop

"Well I don't know about all of that, people say a lot of things. I'm not sure I can help you much with what you want to know about Sunbeam? You know we weren't close, we knew each other, true enough, and we did some business, but I was not in his close circle. When I was around, I didn't get into many of the conversations. Mostly, I just listened, and if I did, I always learned something."

"That what I mean, what did you learn? I agree that just being around Sunbeam taught me a thing or two. I went to his clubs and saw him sitting on his stool. I heard people talk about him, but it wasn't until 1968 that I actually met him. That was back during the sanitation workers strike. He gave several benefits for the striking sanitation workers. He also threw a couple of benefits for the Invaders at the Hippodrome and Club Paradise, when we were trying to get our people out of jail. Those benefits gave me a chance to be in his presence. So I know he was a good guy. I'm trying to establish that for those who never met him. I'm interested in stories about the *Chitlin Circuit*, why people, white and black, speak of him with such respect, things like that. And, then there is the famous one, the story about Tina Turner when she was just first getting started, and they first met. Do you know about Tina?"

He took a few more bits before speaking.

"What I know, I heard from Sunbeam's lips, other than that I can't add anything."

"If you don't mind, Sir, please, could you share that with us?"

"Well, I heard Sunbeam tell this story on many occasions, and it was always the same. I think he loved talking about that memory. You know how it is when some things happen or with some people you meet, sometimes things have a special effect on them or meaning to one more than the other, where for other people, it doesn't really matter, even to the people involved. Sunbeam always began,"

'I was sitting in my usual place at the bar. It was one of those nights, slightly rain and kind of cold for early fall.'

"He would always kind of shiver, shaking his shoulders before continuing."

'The door opened, and this skinny litter young girl, without a coat, came through it. She was wet and shivering as she came to the bar. I just looked at her, kind of sizing her up, you know. She asked.'

"Mister, can you tell me where I might find Mr. Sunbeam Mitchell?"

'I knew the story before she ever opened her mouth to say a word. I'd heard it a thousand times, and seen that look on a thousand faces. So, I asked, who wants to know? Not wanting to sound interested. Like she'd been rehearsing for this chance, a big smile pop on her face. Her smile was warmer enough to melt ice cream on a cold day. Then she said,'

"I'm Tina Turner. I'm the lead singer for Ike and Tina. That's my band. I heard that Mr. Sunbeam was a club owner and promoter. And that if you were pretty good, he might get you some work. I'm hoping if I could meet him, he might give us a chance."

'All the while she talked she was flashing those big pretty eyes and trying to keep smiling. So, I said, I'm Sunbeam. Now, what are you really trying to tell me? Her eyes doped, she looked down for a moment then her eyes came up slowly to meet mine. I just watched, saying nothing. I waited to see what was coming next. She said,'

"Mr. Sunbeam, I'll be honest, we're having a real hard time. We worked three gigs last week and got messed around on all three. The first one, the promoter ran out with all the money. Next, the man promised us three hundred dollars, but after the show, he said he didn't make any money. So, he gave us fifty bucks and two big basket of fried chicken and two loaves of bread. On the last gig, a storm came up that evening, and it rained most of the night, so we didn't make any money at all. We had to slip out the back door and leave most of our stuff at the rooming house. Mr. Sunbeam, we ain't had nothing to eat since those baskets of chicken two nights ago. If you can help us out a little, we'll work for food and maybe a place to sleep. I'll do anything, just name it."

'As she talked, and I was looking into those big watery eyes; Ice cream was run all down on the floor by the time she finished.'

"He always let out a big laugh and slapped his thigh when he said that."

Mr. Brooks laughed, as we did, after that remark. Then he continued. "Sunbeam said,"

'I turned to tell Ernestine to fix her something to eat, but Ernestine was coming out the kitchen with a big plate. I set it on the bar in front of her, and I was lucky to get my hand back with all my fingers.'

"Sunbeam would let out another big laugh, while shaking his right hand and looking at it, wiggling his fingers, like he was counting'em to make sure they were all still there. He continued."

The 400th: From Slavery to Hip Hop

'She was sucking on the last rib bone when she remembered and said,'

"Ho, Mr. Sunbeam, my backup girls and band are in the car, can I have a little food for them."

'I said bring'em on in. It took about a week for them to rest up. I believe Tina slept two days before I saw her again. I gave her some money to go and get their stuff from the rooming house. After they got some rest, they did three or four shows before I made a few calls and put them on the road again.'

With that, Mr. Brooks gulped some tea and settled back in his chair. He asked,

"Is that what you're talking about?"

"Yes sir!" I said excited. That story had me smiling too. "I heard it said that if you had a half-way decent story and a half-way decent voice, Sunbeam would feed you and give you a bed. That story makes what I heard very believable."

"Sunbeam said doing that episode; he realized after telling it a few times how the *Chitlin Circuit* might work."

Mr. Brooks said. So I asked, "What did he mean?" to get him to tell us about that. He continued eating. Then after a while, he began,

"Well,' Sunbeam said,"

There were plenty of entertainers and acts coming to Memphis, trying to make a name. And, most of them were just hanging around, trying to find work. You see, there were two problems. First, there were more entertainers in Memphis than places to entertain. Second, as Tina indicated, there were a bunch of shysters out there robbing hard-working people, giving black promoters a bad name. So, I talked to people I did business with running whiskey and numbers. We all had the muscle to make our word good and make it bad for anybody that didn't keep their word and hold up their end of the deal.'

Mr. Brooks would pause, after taking a few bites, and get a swig or two of tea, before continuing his inside info on Sunbeam.

'With WDIA going all up in the boot heel and down through the Mississippi dealt, I had a plan. During the cotton-picking season, black folk had money and on weekends, during the spring after settling up time and into late fall. After working in the field all week, come

Friday, Saturday or Sunday night, they wanted to get drunk, maybe get a woman and have a ball, at least one night. I knew and worked with Nat D, Moohah, Rufus, and all the other DJs at the station. With money on and under the table, they helped my promotions reach folk all in the backwoods through WDIA. They would read a list of what was happening and where all week. DJs I took care of pushed my shows when they were on the air. They kept the word going all week. The ones that really helped me like Rufus and Moohah, I paid to MC some of my show where we could really pack 'em in, and they would tell folk where they would be, all week long and to come out and see 'em.

Once people that owned a chicken shack, greasy spoons, roadhouse, corn liquor dive or home brew house, and any other place they could get thirty people in at one time, and had a corner for a band, wanted in the game. They didn't care how many could get inside; they were selling food, liquor, women were turning tricks on back seats, gambling outback, and they were getting a piece of all that. Man, carloads of women followed those shows, like it was their job. That was what brought the men out, knowing lots of women would be there. A woman could pick up fifteen or twenty dollars, while eating, getting drunk and have a good time, other folks were paying for. People saw how to make a little money, and they wanted in on the deal. But, now you know, you had to keep things straight, when people tried you.'

"Yea! That's why people said Sunbeam carried a pistol, at all times!"

Vincent said, answering what sounded like a question.

"No," Mr. Brooks said, "Sunbeam didn't carry a pistol, he carried two," correcting him.

'Knowing I carried two pistols,' "Sunbeam would say," *'folks understood I wasn't going to run out of bullets quickly. You see, firing two or three shots, most times, you weren't trying to hit or kill nobody. What you wanted was for everybody to duck, get down and scatter out the way. Then, you could see if somebody was coming after you. If there was, that was what the other pistol was for.'*

We all had a good laugh at that. Then I said, "You would think, getting in and out of such situations, gunfights and all, Sunbeam was a money-grubber." I asked, "What kind of man was he? What was his philosophy? We're not walking Plato here. I mean, he didn't seem to be concerned with accumulating a lot of personal wealth to me. He seemed very community orientated. As best you can, Mr. Brooks, tell us about how he saw what he did."

"Well, you're right, he wasn't about having a lot of money in his pocket or flashing a big roll, and he was a community man. Sunbeam said,"

'Money needs to stay in circulation. Money sitting somewhere doing nothing is really worthless.'

"Sunbeam believed,"

'Money only has value if it is producing growth in the community. I try to keep money in the hands of those who will spend it. Don't get me wrong, saving is good, but you don't save money to make money. So, I try to put it back out there through people who had needs. That's why I loan money to poor Negroes. Red neck crackers don't loan money to poor folks. Loaning them money, I put my money to work doing something. It may keep a family in someplace to live and off the street. I even help poor red necks, if somebody that knowed'em brought'em to me.

I created events that allow people to make money. Some folk trying to go into business or just want to work for the event. People always ask, what if your events don't make any money, you make no profit? I say the profit is in all the dollars that are changing hands. I get my profits because I have so many ways to make a return. Keeping money in a shoebox or under your mattress, that money can't grow.

For that to happen, money has to be like seeds. Seeds in a jar sitting on a shelf can't grow; to grow they have to be in the gound.'

"Most people don't think this way, but Sunbeam saw people in the same way as he saw money. He didn't think he had to make a nickel off every dollar that went out. He would help some people just because they needed help, sometimes. He would say,"

'If I didn't help'em, they wouldn't get help. When people are desperate, they do stupid things. Then they might try to take something from somebody, and somebody might get hurt really bad.'

"This didn't apply only to black people, but to whites as well, as I said. There's a white man here in Memphis today, who's deeply indebted to Sunbeam Mitchell. He has a very successful business on Beale Street today, and he will tell you,"

'If Sunbeam hadn't taken care of me at particular periods in my life, I wouldn't have gotten the opportunities I enjoy today. That why I got his star on Beale Street. He deserved the honor!!"

"I've heard that man say," Vincent cut in, "Sunbeam didn't have to help me when he did and in the way he did. He always treated me like a man. He taught me a lot about business. And he's Bud Chittom owner of Blues City Café on Beale Street."

"If Sunbeam had a philosophy," Mr. Brooks said, "It was the big dollar versus the little dollar. Sunbeam would say,"

Negros always look for the big dollars, not the little dollars. But you see there are more little dollars than big ones. The big dollars you might turn one, two maybe three times a month. But the little dollars you can get every night. You just have to have lots of ways of gettin' em.'

Mr. Brooks turned to Vincent and asked,

"What do you think of Sunbeam Vincent, he was your father?"

A surprised look came over Vincent's face. After appearing to think about the question a moment, Vince said,

"You know for most of my life I didn't know he was my father. He and my mother weren't married. In those days, nobody talked about those things. People knew things, but you had to get through life the best way you could. Other than Mama Rosie or Buddy Perry saying," 'Vincent, Sunbeam needs somebody to do some work at the Paradise.'

"With that, I knew to head for Club Paradise. I never understood why he needed me, since all I did was empty a few trash baskets, maybe sweep the floor and deliver a few packages. But, I was always glad to get the ten or fifteen dollars he gave me. A teenager with that much money in his pocket was pretty cool.

It wasn't until I became a man that people began pointing out my resemblance to Sunbeam. I thought it had to do with body type. We both were rotund about the middle. Then, people began sending me pictures of Sunbeam saying, "This can't be you back in the 1940s or 1950s?"

Things started to click once people, such as you, Mr. Brooks, began telling me stories they knew. I asked my mother, and she admitted the truth. But by then, he'd passed, so we never had the opportunity to develop a father-son relationship.

My mother didn't have any complaints about whatever or how things when down. My regret is not having a relationship with him, and I say he must have been one hell of a man to keep two Ernestine's content.

Most importantly, I'm proud to be part of his legacy and to say I'm Sunbeam Mitchell's son. I'm working with John trying to preserve his legacy. I feel preserving his legacy is important and can continue serving the Memphis community.

Presently, I've put together a team that is developing a proposal for a Beale Street Museum. I think there needs to be a place to keep and preserve some of the artifacts of people from all walks of life that have contributed to the true legacy of Beale Street.

For example, today, we've lost Ben Cauley of the Bar-Kays and Marvelle Thomas, not to mention his father Rufus. Then all the original "Mad Lads" John Gary Williams, Julius Green, William Brown, and Robert Phillips are all gone. Jabo of the Temprees is also gone. Here is no place to honor and display artifacts to preserve their stories. It would be great to tell Tina Turner's Memphis story in such a place. John and I have been working on this project for almost five years now.

There is great interest in this project for Beale Street. A place to preserve the memory of Beale Street icons is the very reason we're having this conversation today. We must establish a need to recognize Sunbeam as a real community leader. This conversation and my goal is to separating facts from myths, is really important. I want to establish the real legacy of the man called Sunbeam."

Mr. Brook looked over at Mike and posed a question,

"Young man you're very quiet, why aren't you saying anything."

Mike smiled, and like the cautious businessman he is, replied,

"Well, Mr. Brooks, I guess I'm like you about being in Sunbeam's presence when he was speaking; you just listened. That way, you never missed a lesson."

"Very well spoken, young man," Mr. Brooks returned his smile. He followed that with, "I have really enjoyed the afternoon, talking about the past, but this old man has other obligations. I do have time for one more question if you have one."

I know what you think about Sunbeam, Mr. Brooks, and Vincent has said what he thinks. Did Sunbeam ever said anything that indicated what he thought of himself?

"Yes, certainly," Mr. Brooks offered. "He had a kind of speech, so to speak, he would make when people were trying to back out of a deal or maybe, even though they wouldn't ever need Sunbeam again. He'd say,"

'I know what it is to be down and out, on the run, scuffling trying to keep it together, so I try to help anybody that's trying to help themselves get up. An entertainer, somebody trying to get into business, a woman that needed money to get out of jail or keep her family from getting thrown out on the street, I've listened to real stories and did what I could.

But, don't come crawling to me with your hand out, and then when you get up, and things look different, now you got a conscience or just join the church. So now, you don't want to go, or I don't do that stuff no more, but you still owe me. So, I tell them, I'm a provider of last

chances and a lender of last resort. If you have choices, go there. The people, who come begging to me, have tried everything else. Anything they had worth something been sold or pawned. Their pride is gone. Life has already put'em down on their knees, so crawling is easy. That's when they show up at my door, begging for help. Then there are some; when they get up, they start talking about what they can't do.

So, I tell'em. That's alright with me, cause you see, I'll get mine one way or another. It ain't no never mine to me. It's going to come out of your pocket or out of your hide. So, let me ask you this, do you think your ass can take the wear and tear? After that, I get my money.'

Ain't Got Nothing but the Blues

If I didn't use the word magic to make my points regarding slavery's descendants' survival and advancement, their survival would seem a normal and uneventful outcome without mysteries. Descendants of slavery survival and their continually need to make *something out of nothing*, by a people the world considered nothing, falls into a special category occupied by no other human beings. So, with history failing to establish in a real way, how and why a people, uneducated and powerless, who walked off plantations into their penniless emancipation 155 years ago, reached 2020 as creators of the world dominates culture?

Undeniably these facts are presented as a reality, the world should recognize and marvel, because there is very little accompanying written history to substantiate such a statement. Looking at the history record there are no accolades, testimonies and awards honoring such a story. This statement points out why on most occasions, situations, events, or circumstances that are viewed at the same time from the same place by white and black people, white people's view of that happening is totally differently than black observers. Illustrating this situation, I contrasted **The Wiz** juxtaposed against the **Wizard of Oz** to make this point. The difference is some white observers view such outcomes, explanations or scenarios from a black person's perspective as unsubstantiated superstition or pure speculation, even though black people were eyewitnesses. If white people are eyewitnesses, and without background information to understand the happening, they will substitute their opinion in place of a black person's "word of mouth" accounts. Even though, a black person was an eye witness, and provides the only historical evidence available.

Interviews, with those who claim to be eyewitnesses, concerning what is known, but unwritten, are all that exist to explain the physical evidence and facts left behind. So again, what remains in most cases, as far as black people are concerned, are considered legends, which have been told, interpreted and retold by storytellers, not historians. All these different sources—storytellers—have their versions by which they swear, constituting the reality that resulted, as the only historical record.

I continually make this point, because tracking down many stories, like the **Blues**, Beale Street, black entertainment, Sunbeam Mitchell and the *Chitlin Circuit*, I have encountered this duality trying to establish facts regarding these subjects, writing **"The 400th"**. As a result, I have come to trust such eyewitness accounts more so than the written word, in many cases, because what is provided comes based on those that did the dirty deeds of history.

With that as a premise, descendants of American slavery survived and developed in a spoken word culture, reflecting the previous statements. They were denied knowledge and education to tell their story in their own words.

Specifically, slave masters' adamantly denied slaves any education. They claimed benevolent intentions, God's will to justify their action, but the malevolent vicious ill will and spiteful results, left death and destroyed lives of black hinged on black people's "word of mouth" history. Their only intention was to leave slaves ignorant of the written word and most other knowledge.

Slaves' minds were their only depositaries in which to store their records of events of their survival, in most cases. Former slaves endure whatever whites did to make them into slaves. Not only denying slaves knowledge, white people imposed conditions on them to maintain slaves' subservient mindset, after bondage. Regardless of how or why white people treatment enslaved Africans as they did, everything had an economic value for white people, not enslaved Africans. The outcome was what white people wanted and why slaves and their descendants had to rely almost exclusively on a "word of mouth" history. More importantly, that is why magic is the explanation that best fits the "word of mouth" stories that remain of slaves' survival.

Slaves and their descendants did not see benevolence in white people's actions, they saw and felt evil demons or devilish witches casting wicked *"bujia whammies"* upon them. The God white people forced on them were not like their African Gods, which loved them. They provided bounty and mercy in Africa, not pain, brutality, scarcity, and desperation, as white Gods in America.

Consequently, I offered the dichotomy of **"*The Wizard of Oz*"** and **"*The Wiz*"** to reflect their difference in views, and to represent how slaves saw their survival, which requires words like mystical, magical, and miraculous to fit what black people called such evil wickedness—*Evillene*—Woodrow Wilson spread over America. Their miraculous survival has allowed them to endure the effort of white people to destroy them time and again since their penniless emancipation, as reflected by their "word of mouth" accounts. Their stories are the only record, from their view point, that explain why black people are still here.

Although the vast majority of white historians never bothered to provide terms, even educated white people agree that an "evil spells" is the only description for some events, like the **"*Dark Age*"** *angry white men mob madness*. Such descriptions make slave descendants survival too large and powerful for prosaic words, like determined, persistent and unbelievable too weak to communicate the heroism and audacity of their struggles. Those ordinary terms do not carry the explosive energy needed to communicate enslaved Africans miraculous efforts challenging the forces that threatened their survival. Somehow slave descendants summoned the fortitude, temerity and impetus that not only enabled them to survive but keep smiling, singing and dancing, like characters in ***The Wiz***—*Everybody Rejoice (Can't You See A Brand New Day)*.

After enduring that life of pain, anguish, and death enslaved Africans continued their painful and degrading trek that began in 1619 headed for **"*The 400th*"**. The wretchedness of their circumstances, during slavery produced the expression, *"We ain't got nothin but the **Blues**."* This reality inspired Don George and Duke Ellington to turn that emotional response of enslaved Africans to their history into the recording ***"I Ain't Got Nothin' but the Blues"*** (1937). Their creation, though a song, is not a metaphor. Their lyrics celebrate the magical reality of how black people used their emotional state and physical existence, like a magnet that drew other slave descendants into their psyche, connecting them to the same reality.

Had their lyrics reflected the true facts of black people's existence, they would have been moribundly downhearted and a melancholy people. Although, describing their lives sounds as though, they should have been disconsolate or heavyhearted, mentally they retreated into their inner sanctum. For this reason, they considered their survival a special kind of magic. Their magic allows only slave descendants to enter into that rest; no melancholy there! That is also why it is called the magic of the ***Blues!***

Their ***Blues*** was the reality for black people in Memphis on Beale Street and throughout the Mississippi Delta. During and after they developed it, the ***Blues*** inspired all manner of muse, celebrating their existence with gaiety in that place in their minds, but in their daily lives, their doldrums and struggles always produced a sad reflection. The ***Blues*** is the only musical expression that evolved and flowed out of the very misery of the people who endured the hellish conditions about which they sang.

The uniqueness of ***Blues*** magic is that even though it was born in pain and degradation, while its creators were treated like nothing, given nothing, not allowed to have, keep or do nothing, descendants of the ***Blues*** culture realized because they were alive, they had something; they had their ***"Blues."*** That is why black people held on to it so tenaciously and sang the ***"Blues"*** all the time. ***"I Ain't Got Nothin but the Blues"*** although lively sounding and made people want to dance, other people that love that nothing, do not want to live as nothing to enjoy that nothing—the ***Blues***.

Therapy, at best or at least, the ***Blues*** was a source of motivation for descendants of slavery in Memphis. The ***Blues*** offered solace to former slaves, which exemplify the previous statements about the birth of the ***Blues***. As a result of the ***Blues*** culture on Beale Street, it became known as the birthplace of the ***Blues*** the world over. However, even though white people despised the ***Blues*** and the people who made it and tried for year to control and even take the fun out of Beale Street because of their hatred of the ***Blues***, again as time and events would have it, whether for ***"fair or foul"***, unintended consequences brought about a change.

Although what follows may read like a fairy tale or novel, it describes what actually happened and shows why black people have only a "word of mouth" account of their history to reflect their past and present in America. Memphis City Government, which always loomed like the *"wicked witch of the South,"* finally had a change of mind about Beale Street, but definitely not a change of heart. With a history of doing things that made black people on Beale Street feel like munchkins, and considered nothing, these same munchkins created an international reputation for the **Blues** and Beale Street.

Although black people created the **Blues** and made Beale Street a point of international recognition of black people's creativity, without a change of heart, the Memphis City government hijacked Beale Street, and denigrated the **Blues** heritage of black people in the process. They created a project that made Beale Street a "white only" tourist attraction. Today, the Memphis City government is spending private and public funds promoting Beale Street, as a mega tourist creation of white people.

The distinction is they are promoting Beale Street, but not the **Blues.** They see no honor in the **Blues,** if they did, the **"Blues"** would not be a side note for the song white folks are singing on Beale Street today. Memphis City government has always seen the true history of Beale Street, as a bad reflection or sour note, white people saw or heard when it came to the **Blues**. (White and black people can observe or experience the exact same event at the exact same instance, but come away with two totally different scenarios.) The story of Beale Street is no different, so when that story is told and promoted today, it reflects the same white people attitudes, as those that engineered the riot of 1866 or 1968. Those riots destroyed the black community or what it depended on, reducing former slaves back to *"making something out od nothing."*

Memphis government cannot hide the fact that white people created the horror story of indifference and denial they heap upon black people, which forced them on to Beale Street and left them with only the **"Blues."** Now, as back then, it is their greed and willingness to take from black people what they create, produce or developed, without any regard for right or justice. They forced black people on to Beale Street as the only place they were willing to allowed them. White people's attitude today is why they have taken over Beale Street and rob black people to serve as their heritage. Their actions are identical to and a reflection of Pres. Woodrow Wilson's admission, **"white people have been force by means, fair or foul,** to take Beale Street for white people, and run it as their heritage.

This narrative has painstakingly, even at length and laboriously at times, detailed the creation and development of Beale Street. That circuitous and convoluted presentation acknowledges that both blacks and whites contributed to the history of Beale Street. But the Beale Street I now present is entirely a creation of "only" white people—the Beale Street Management Corporation (BSMC). Primarily, the BSMC is a creation of the City of Memphis Government, which pursued a white-only policy, not even a *"separate but equal"* project to take possession of Beale Street. They arrogantly froze black people out completely.

The 400th: From Slavery to Hip Hop

Cold as an Arctic blast, riding on the wings of an Alberta Clipper, they blew through Beale Street and froze it in a time that never existed. It is an ice castle and the exclusive domain of cold-blooded white people. Black people view the takeover of Beale Street by white people, as ***"the great street robbery."*** Unfortunately for Beale Street's legacy, the monstrosity existing today is pale in comparison to what black people created.

Beale Street, that impactful place no longer exists, except in the minds, hearts and "word of mouth" stories of the people who built it, which I presented in this narrative. Explaining how this happened will require another convoluted circuitous back tract, as I detail the ***Great Street Robbery***. Again as I have detailed, the real story began while black people toiled in slavery. Through their moans, wail, grunts, and groans, they found a way to give *VOICE* to their anguish and subconscious longings. Without instrumental accompaniments, their guttural groans and hollows evolved into rhythmic and musical chants. Psychologically, black people created a commonality that grew out of their communal misery. Immersed in their shared pain, slaves produced a unique emotional connection to their expressions and experiences, which gave solace to their combined degradation.

The Great Street Robbery: Timeline to Thievery

Melanie a broadside against the American music industry fired off **"Look What They've Done to My Song, Ma"**. Written and recorded for her album **Candles in the Rain**, the single made the Top 40 in the UK, France, and Norway. However, America never caught on. **"Look What They've Done to My Song, Ma"** makes what Memphis City Government did to Beale Street truly, a bleeding-heart parity. This horror story began with a *Memphis Commercial Appeal* headline (1966) *Beale Street was placed on the National Register of Historic Places.*

I remember the occasion and rejoiced that Beale Street had finally gained some long overdue recognition. It was the first-ever recognition for such a place in Memphis and it started wheels turning in the white community. Unlike in the past, when whites looked upon the nothing they viewed Beale Street as, following the *National Register of Historic Places* designation, however dollar signs popped into white people eyes, like sales on a cash register. For the first time, whites saw value in Beale Street that they could harvest, but didn't wanted any part of the **Blues** story, which they could not claim. The problem was how to get it away from black people, who had developed it and the ones that applied to the *National Register of Historic Places* for its designation.

Spearheaded by Andrew "Sunbeam" Mitchell and others, Beale Streeters had been trying to get federal assistance to revitalize Beale Street for a number of years. During that time, late 1950s, the groups from the black community developed an urban renewal proposal for redeveloping Beale Street. They applied to the Kennedy/Johnson administration for a *"black business redevelopment grant,"* in 1960. Black leaders felt, like Robert Church, Jr. in the 1930s, that their support for the Kennedy/Johnson ticket against Richard Nixon (1960) should be rewarded. The US Department of Housing and Urban Development (HUD) agreed to fund the urban renewal grant (with an initial $3.5 million study grant) and announced the award in the early 1960s which was part and parcel to the *National Register of Historic Places* designation.

White people through Memphis City Government fought the urban renewal grant application throughout the remainder of the Johnson Administration. But, in 1968 (two years after the *National Register of Historic Places* 1966 designation), Richard Nixon was elected, and the city under new Mayor Henry Loeb took control of grant funds for Beale Street, as a Revenue Sharing Block Grants from the Nixon Administration.

Block Grants eliminated categorical funding, which allowed Loeb to take control of funds for redevelopment on Beale Street. Taking over redevelopment funds, the City cut the black community completely out of Beale Street redevelopment.

The 400th: From Slavery to Hip Hop

The process of taking over Beale Street by the Loeb Administration was not simple or easy. The City could not drive black people off Beale Street and move in without some compelling need identified by City government. The justification Memphis City Government used to begin it takeover process happened on that warm sunny morning of March 28, 1968. That was the day an estimated 50,000 angry black people packed Beale and surrounding streets. They showed up in support of striking sanitation workers, and in defiance of Loeb's segregationist policies.

Police lines across Main Street that stopped Dr. Martin Luther King, Jr. from reaching City Hall was the pretext for the Memphis police to attacked protestors, after stopping the marchers on Main Street, but attacked marchers on Beale Street, producing panic, broken windows and sporadic sparatic looting, which Loeb used to declare it a riot. Attacking and assailing panicky marchers, the City produced the conditions it wanted to begin taking control of Beale Street. The City described the broken windows which happened during the police attack on demonstrators, a riot.

This narrative detailed earlier the police mayhem on Beale Street, where Dr. Martin Luther King, Jr., leader of the march, fled rampaging police. He was able to escape the police mayhem, in Mrs. Cornelia Crenshaw's car. Miraculously, she was parked exactly where the police stopped the March. Had she not been there, Dr. King would have gotten trapped by the club swinging police rampaging attack.

Nevertheless, I feel Loeb killed two birds with one stone, as City government, police, and media blamed young black militants (the Invaders) for the disturbance and damage that police caused. The City used the police attack, as the pretext to begin its takeover of Beale Street. It cited the damage, caused by the police attack, but was blamed on the Invaders, to justify closing down Beale Street. So, Loeb used that incident to not only stop Dr. King and the sanitation workers march, but to justify taking control of Beale Street redevelopment, which most black people were unaware.

Calling the Invaders a *"street game,"* while labeling them a lawless element, and using that description, justified by C.O.M.E. leaders' statements, *"a destructive force out to destroy the black community"* Loeb justified taking over Beale Street. Concocting that fictitious story, Mayor Loeb pointed to damage (broken windows), as a coming crime wave in the Beale Street area that the City had to stop. The same tactic Donald Trump is using today, to essentially declare "martial law" without calling it that. Loeb promised to clean up Beale Street and chase this lawless element from the area. He would create a management group, afterwards to revitalize Beale Street. He lied claiming, "urban renewal grant/revenue sharing funds would pay for the project."

The City rejected all proposals from the black community. After rejecting those proposals, Loeb, over the next several years, did several things to lock the black community out of Beale Street redevelopment. He used the urban renewal block Grant funds to purchase all property in the black business area on and around Beale Street, but allowed white owners on the West end, near Main street, to keep their property.

Loeb's plan began with evicting everyone in the black area that did not voluntarily move. The funds Mayor Loeb used came to the city as redevelopment funds for Beale Street and other black economic programs for black community business development. The Loeb Administration foreclosed on black businesses still on the street.

Next, Loeb implemented what he called, "Beale Street I and Beale Street II." These two programs spilled the death of Beale Street, as black people knew it. The loss was truly disastrous in terms of eradication of the only economic engine and cultural mecca for the black community. Loeb saw Beale Street, like striking sanitation workers, he bulldozed the area and wiping out area housing, evicting its population.

Driving out black people, Loeb demolished 474 structures. The vast majority were apartments or rooming houses of people that were the main customer, supporting Beale Street merchant. The demolition created an area of empty lots between African Americans and the Beale Street business area.

Finally, Loeb erected a ten-foot-high hurricane fence around the black commercial district on Beale Street. Loeb did to Beale Street, what police did to Invaders, during this period. Enclosing the entire black business area, Loeb put Beale Street in jail, like it caused the riot. Nothing like this happened to another black community in modern times. Beale Street redevelopment was a clear case of banishment or ethnic cleansing. The City dispossessed the black community, like the destruction of *"Black Wall Street"* or what happened during **Red Summer 1919.** City government However, not an angry white mobs in the street, the was the culprit, destroying and taking what black people developed and gave to white people.

Even though black businesses were still serving customers, the day before the fence went up, the city cut off access to everything in the black business area of Memphis with its fence. The Memphis government forced black entrepreneurs to relocate. Sunbeam Mitchell had to leave Club Handy and the Mitchell Hotel on Beale Street, even though the building belonged to Abe Plough and still stands today. Sunbeam closed had to close the Mitchell Hotel and relocated to a closed bowling alley, where he opened Club Paradise: the only business in that area. Dr. Ernest Withers moved his photography studio to South Memphis.

The real tragedy of the street robbery was that some black businesses, could not survive without the foot traffic along the centrally located area of Beale Street. The city did not provide relocation assistance or compensate for black entrepreneurs. Most fled with no place to go and later folded. This City created disaster did not have to happen, because redevelopment did not begin immediately. The area lay dormant for another ten years. Therefore the demolition and erecting the chain-link fence was aim at destroying the only economic engine in the black community.

The Memphis Press-Scimitar (June 10, 1979) declared that the city used "**_Urban renewal to destroyed Beale Street._**" The City forced African American businesses, which were doing business to leave Beale Street. That same year (1979), a preservation and neighborhood revitalization movement by black entrepreneurs gained real support from black residents, but the new City Mayor Wyeht Chandler declared it was *"too late to save Beale Street."* The City proceeded with its destructive plan.

The demised of Beale Street was an economic and cultural disaster for the African American community. Even today, the black community still has not received any compensation from the city of Memphis. Simultaneously, the city refused to allow any African Americans to become part of the Beale Street redevelopment project. To date, the City has not done anything to help replace what it took from the black community and gave to white people.

Government Steps In

Memphis Mayors Henry Loeb and Wyeth Chandler's Beale Street takeover was not to capitalize on its fame. Taking Beale Street was not a simple mugging; it was like gang rape. They ignored the history detailed in this narrative. The city government did what only government can do. It created a body to cover up its theft of the iconic street.

The city created the *Beale Street Management Corporation (BSMC)* in 1977. The mayor said at its birth, *"The City's grand plan will create an entertainment district to celebrate the unique history—music, traditions, and culture—of Beale Street* and a bigger lie was never told. That was the last time that statement was made by anyone involved in the project. Underscoring the hyperbole, not a single black person was part of it, so "Beale Street's music, traditions, and culture has been reduced to black bands playing music for white folks at clubs own by white people. There is no resemblance to black culture.

Using slogans the City claimed possession of Beale Street and took the legacy of black Memphians that extends back over 100 years to Robert R. Church, Sr. (1860s). None of that legacy is reflected any place in Beale Street Management Corporation's redevelopment thievery. The City never had a plan! Its only aim was to take over Beale Street. It totally disregarded the investments black entrepreneurs, like the Church family, W. C. Handy, T. S. Hayes, J. J. Stotts, Matthew Thornton, Robert Henry, Andrew "Sunbeam" Mitchell, and other icons made.

BSMC made revitalization about what "Boss" Crump wanted Beale Street to be, not what the *National Register of Historic Places* recognized. The City redirected the wealth coming from Beale Street away from the black community to the white community, depriving its rightful cultural owners of that revenue. The City redirect Beale Street's legacy to benefit white people, without investing a dime creating it.

Black entrepreneurs like Sunbeam Mitchell and his group, provided the reason the *"National Register of Historic Places"* recognition. They suffered through the indignities of segregation for their children benefit, only to see white people with the help of City Government through BSMC rape or reap that wealth. After 130 years of investing and developing an area of business for black people, the *Beale Street Management Corporation* reduced them back to *"making something out of nothing,"* in a city where white people will not allow black people to keep the "nothing" they develop. That's why black people, **<u>Ain't Got Nothing but the Blues</u>** reflecting Melanie's hit **<u>Look What They've Done To My Song, Ma</u>**!!!!!!!!!!!!!!

What Made White People Want Nothing

The question is, *"What would make racists like Henry Loeb and Wyeth Chandler see value and worth in a nothing place like Beale Street for white people?"* A vision of "white gold," prompted by a white rock 'n' roll star, put dollar signs in white people's eyes. That vision put even more and larger dollars sign in white Memphians eyes. Unlike Liverpool, the United Kingdom, which created the **Trans-Atlantic Slave Trade,** then created **The International Slave Museum** to preserve and commemorate its role in that horrid institution. However, the United States of America in general and Memphis specifically, are still dedicated to raping the heritage and wealth of African Americans, while hiding the evidence in government vaults. So now, I present another outrage perpetrated against black Americans, as another example of how and why two white Mayors—Henry Loeb and Wyeth Chandler—were willing to commit thievery to get their hands on black heritage—Beale Street—rather than making it a joint venture, where everyone shared in its black legacy.

The second and most powerful event, which changed Henry Loeb and Wyeth Chandler's perspective on Beale Street, after the *National Register of Historic Places*' designation, was a white entertainer, whom they hailed the *"King."* That entertainer was Elvis Presley. Unless you are a true Elvis fan, you probably are unaware of how enamored Presley was of Beale Street culture and is why white racist without "masks" robbed the black community. Once Elvis acknowledged Beale Street, as a major part of his development, as a Rock 'n' Roll star, the value of Beale Street to white Memphians, especially these two mayors, shot through the roof.

Overnight, white people saw Beale Street like "El Dorado." (According to the Spanish legend, *El Hombre Dorado "The Golden Man"* or *El Rey Dorado "The Golden King,"* both terms describe a mythical tribal chief (Zipa) of the Muisca native people of Colombia. Zipa, for his initiation ritual, covered himself with gold dust and submerged himself in Lake Guatavita. The *El Dorado* legend evolved from a man to a city, onto a kingdom, and then an empire).

Maybe an empire is what Loeb and Chandler saw Elvis creating for white people in Memphis on Beale Street, if so their dream never materialized as imagined. A point I have made previously regarding another black American icon Dr. Martin Luther King, Jr. But, in their dream, Memphis City Government crowned its white phenome the *"Golden King of Beale Street."* And, for me, this is the only reason Loeb took Beale Street out of the deep freeze, where he placed it, after his vengeful act of taking it then demolishing and fence it in.

Even though, Elvis did not have gold dust, not even plain cotton field dust he owned to cover himself and submerge himself in the Mississippi River, when he was on Beale Street, immersing himself in the *"golden magical traditions of the*

Blues," and black people's culture to simulate *"Zipa in Lake Guatavita,"* nevertheless, white people like Loeb and Chandler saw Elvis as a golden King just the same. They decided to mine the gold Elvis would bring to Beale Street; as I said *dreams are never as imagined.*

Once Elvis told the world he was proud of his relationship to what he saw as a glorious culture, but like Donald Trump, whites were ashamed to be seen hanging out with black people. Only white people would think of stealing black people's culture and trying to make it theirs to celebrate a big white "LIE." The city, after eye balling Beale Street, the El Dorado gold mine of black culture, "claim jumped."

The City of Memphis set about supplanting the **Blues** and it culture with the image of only rock n' roll. They used the government to "claim jump" what black people struggled to build to reap the grand vision of Elvis as the *"Golden King of Beale Street,"* as though the world cannot tell the difference between Elvis the king and B. B. King. Absurd, I know, but white people were really eager to believe that "a stolen legacy" with Elvis as *King of Beale Street*, was better than no music legacy at all.

I remember, during my young days, while partying on Beale Street, hearing the "word of mouth" stories passed around about Elvis, and seeing a young white boy hanging out on Beale Street. Most whites in Memphis never saw this. For them, they never saw anything black people did worth their attention, unlike Elvis, definitely not worth them stealing. Whites in Memphis definitely did not want to come down to "nigger town"—Beale Street—like Elvis and get down in the mud, and cover up in it, trying to soak up anything he could associating with black people. Elvis was just the opposite; he loved it. He covered himself with all the Beale Street mud he could smear over himself. A young, poor white boy wanting to be an entertainer, Elvis worship at the feet of black entertainers.

Drawn by adoration, Elvis drank up, as much of the magic elixir of the **Blues**, flowing from Beale Street entertainers. He not only copied the styles of black guys, Elvis also tried to look like them. He wore Levi jackets and jeans, Otis Redding's favorite outfit, trying to fit in and pick up on anything black entertainers put down. So, after becoming successful, he wanted the world to know black people embraced him, so he had real authentic soul roots.

Elvis claimed Beale Street, as a major part of his legacy, to let the world know from whence he came. But, his appreciation and gratitude for how black people took him in, like an orphan, would never allowed his name to be associated with anything so perverse, foul and underhanded, as stealing Beale Street in order to place his name there. Elvis was not a covetous liar, as most white people in Memphis.

Elvis would not become part of white people's *"claim jump"* or *"Great Street Robbery"* while he was alive. Naming Elvis king of Beale Street happened only after he passed (8-16-77), then white people in Memphis made Elvis part of their "Big Lie."

My point of the *Beale Street Management Corporation's (BSMC) "claim jump,"* was if they were interest in developing the culture and heritage, rather than destroying the **"Blues"** culture of Beale Street, as it relates to Elvis, it would have included Lauderdale Courts, a low-income housing project in its plans. Elvis Presley "lived" there in the 1950s. A young Elvis Presley walked from there to nearby Beale Street and hung around clubs, soaking up the very styles and essence of Beale Streeters, as I said.

Barred by segregation laws from being on that part of Beale Street, a young Elvis would stand at the doorway of clubs, while pleading with owners to let him inside. When he found one, like Sunbeam Mitchell, owner of Club Handy, Elvis found space, as close to the bandstand as he could. There, he would spend the night listening and watching black entertainers do their thing. He copied, as much as he could of the different styles of Beale Street entertainers.

Elvis even copied the flashy dress of black musicians and entertainers, even copied the way they talked. He shopped for clothes at Lansky Brothers and other men's shops on Beale Street, where black entertainers bought or had their clothes made. Later, Elvis used what he learned from his Beale Street experiences, even the mumbling speech and high pitch voice were Beale Street accents. Elvis used those accents when he recorded *"That's All Right Mama"* at Sam Phillips' Sun Studio located a few blocks north of Beale Street. Sun Studio supported rock n' roll in the early days, several then-unknown musicians in the 1950s, including Roy Orbison, Carl Perkins, Johnny Cash, Jerry Lee Lewis, Howlin' Wolf, Rufus Thomas, and Ike Turner recorded there. In fact, Ike Turner, before Tina, but with Jackie Brenston on vocals, is credited with recording the very first rock n' roll record *"Rocket 88"* there.

The Great Street Robbery: Prologue to the Theft

The thing that is most mystifying to African Americans in Memphis is not that the City undertook *"The Great Street Robbery,"* but it shut black people out of redevelopment and continued to prevent them from becoming entrepreneurs on the street they built. Black people created and established the history the *National Registry of Historic Places* recognized, which declared them the only legitimate developers of Beale Street, and the riot did not forfeit their claim or rights. So I ask, *"What gave white people the right to claim something they did not build, establish, maintain or even support, the power of white government?"*

Memphis City Government—Henry Loeb and Wyeth Chandler—forced Beale Street redevelopment down black Memphians throats. They were the white mob in the street. The City did not give any consideration to the historical and cultural legacy on Beale Street black Memphians created. It proceeded without involving a single black individual in the redevelopment plans. There was not one black person allowed to participate, represent, act or engage government on behalf of the black community.

Memphis government did the black people, like Henry Loeb did the sanitation workers, when he closed the door in their face and refused to talk to them face to face. They refuse to create a place at the table for any black participation to discuss protecting and preserving black heritage. There was total disregard for thing and places in the Beale Street area, like the first house *"The No Name Club"* Sunbeam and Ernestine opened. There was no one to point out which of the 474 demolished structures had cultural significance to Beale Street and the black community. The City did not conduct an environmental or historical study or impact statement to determine which of the buildings the *National Register of Historic Places* recognized was in Loeb's destructive path.

This narrative has shown that over the years, black entrepreneurs invested not only economic resources, but their sweat equity and blood nourishing the growth of the culture that developed on and around Beale Street. There were no outside investors, like the CP-USA in Harlem that aided its development. Local black people struggling to *make something out of nothing* is what made Beale Street such a point of social identification and historically relevance for black and American culture. That is what the *National Register of Historic Places* recognized in its designation, not the fact Elvis spent time there. Beale Street history is something particular to black people and the black community, which gave Memphis its **Blues** legacy. White people did not make any investment in Beale Street, and avoided Beale Street like COVID-19.

The first time I visited Beale Street, after Mayor Loeb's redevelopment was fully underway, looking at the 10 ft. chain-link fence that locked it in jail, it was like visiting the grave of a relative. I thought of the black people who struggled and endured, while surviving the oppression, degradation, lynching, segregation, and white supremacy imposed by the very white people who took it, which I have detailed here. Lusting for Beale Street, the city's plan after Elvis, emulated the **"Dark Age"** *angry white men mob madness.*

Only because Elvis hung out there for a very brief period compared to the length and breadth of its history, white people destroyed an entire culture, simply to put a white man's name there, stealing the wealth black people created. Elvis did not do anything to advance the culture of Beale Street, if anything he took far more from Beale Street, than he gave back, and walked away, like other white people. Elvis claimed Beale Street, Beale Street, did not claim Elvis. He never even entertained once on Beale Street. Elvis' little nothing made it worth everything to white people.

Once Elvis' love affair with Beale Street was over, like a white boy in love with a black girl, became known to whites, something black people knew all alone, white people decided to lie about the history to make the their stolen baby acceptable. That reality brings this narrative back to the theme that white and black people can look at the same place or situation from the same perspective and have or develop two totally different scenarios. Now, black people, **"Ain't Got nothing but the Blues"** left from the Beale Street the baby they raised and cared for, until it grew to be somebody, then the white family claimed it. It was no longer the bastard child they refused to acknowledge. White people in America took black people from Africa, robbing them of their freedom to gain the wealth they have. White people riding the backs of black people took the only thing they were able to produce for themselves in Memphis after slavery.

A Thief Among Thieves

The third event that drove white people's desire to possess Beale Street was the US Congress declared Beale Street the official *"Home of the Blues"* in 1977. Congress gave this designation before the City of Memphis spent one dime developing it. The wacked thing about all this thievery is Congress declared Beale Street *"The Home of the Blues,"* but BSMC has made it the home of rock n' roll, with Elvis as the King. BSMC' redevelopment scheme is just a wink and nod at *"Blues"* and its history, like a bad dream for white people in Memphis. The true history is nowhere to be found.

Immediately following the national recognition by the US Congress, the City of Memphis saw even more economic value in Beale Street for white people. Wyeth Chandler shifted the City's plan into high gear. He pushed those few remaining black people out of the cultural center they built. The City didn't offer the pretense that black people walked away, and left Beale Street unattended, so white people moved in.

Wyeth Chandler never came or sent representatives to the black community regarding Beale street redevelopment; he closed the door in the face of any that try to push their way into the process. He was not interested in plans the black community had for Beale Street redevelopment. During the intervening years, until its full-fledged takeover, black people in Memphis pressed the City government for a role in Beale Street redevelopment. The black community continually sought ways to protect the heritage and image of Beale Street, but that was a countered to what Memphis Government's all-white plan to make Elvis its legacy. The City turned its back on the black community and its efforts to have a *VOICE* in Beale Street redevelopment. Even today there are groups still trying to play a role in Beale Street development, one such individual is Sunbeam Mitchell's son Vincent Taylor, but the City refuses to talk with him or any other black entrepreneurs.

The City pushed the *Beale Street Management Corporation (BSMC)* down the black community's throat with a plunger, wreckeverything, "a bull in a china shop." It launched a white only economic redevelopment plan for Beale Street in late 1977. Wyeth Chandler searched high and low for the perfect white man and the City found John Elkington in 1982. A thief among thieves, he bulldozed Beale Street redevelopment over black people. John Elkington, was a white boy that did not do as Elvis; he never spent time learning Beale Street's history.

Elkington was given total control of redevelopment and his primary responsibility was marketing, leasing, and managing the property on Beale Street. He adhered to the City's pattern of not offering opportunities to African Americans. He pushed aside plans the black community developed before the city saw gold in Beale Steet.

The 400th: From Slavery to Hip Hop 571

Now, here's the curveball in the dirt. Elkington was responsible for developing the entertainment theme of Beale Street, which was the **Blues**. By keeping black entrepreneurs out, Elkington changed the culture of Beale Street through the "selection of tenants." Only whites were allowed in on the deal, and this made it easy to make Elvis the *"King"* of Beale Street. There was no one to point out that if Beale was going to have a King, it should be B. B. King. His name was King and he spent his young life singing on Beale Street sidewalks, before entertaining in clubs. The world knew where B. B. was from he did not need to say.

Elkington was not only part of the Beale Street "hijacking" and street robbery, he was the a thief among thieves. Elkington's perspective and community investment visions were white entrepreneurs developing new businesses—clubs, theater renovations, shops, and restaurants for Beale Street. He controlled everything through "selecting of tenants," this guaranteed black applications would not be approved.

However, it all came down to a double robbery. Elkington had his own *"Great Street Robbery"* going, as he perpetrated a different fraud. During his tenure, Elkington, through the BSMC, robbed both blacks and whites in Memphis of millions of dollars. The exact amount has never been determined or disclosed to the public. After getting caught with both hands and one foot in the cookie jar, the city, rather than put the thief in jail, paid the scoundrel to leave town, like "Boss" Crump, he kept all of his ill-gotten gains. If a white man is robbing black people, white people consider that smart business, but if a black man successfully competes against whites it is seen, as thievery, similar to "The People's Grocery Store!!!"

Consequently, had Elkington been a black man, the city would have demanded restitution of all missing funds and jail time for the culprit. Even more outrageous than Elkington, the City of Memphis retained control of Beale Street Management Corp and Beale Street. Elkington's thievery was permitted only because Beale Street had been the possession of black people. The city did not prosecute nor demand payback of stolen funds. I believe that the city wanted to avoid a court fight to recover stolen funds, because that would have exposed how the City got possession of Beale Street in the first place to create the *BSMC*. Also, the City would have put statements in the record that would have become the bases of lawsuits to challenge the city's actions establishing *BSMC*.

"The Great Street Robbery," was tantamount to a reenactment of banishment and racial cleansing, during the **"Dark Age"** *angry white men mobs madness era*, only in this case, City government was the mob vanquishing black people through the power of government and white politics. It was government political power that allowed white people in Memphis to do whatever to rob slavery's descendants, no matter how it looked. During racial cleansing, banishment, and lynching,

nothing ever happened to whites that robbed and killing black people to get their property and wealth, in Memphis nothing has changed.

The *Beale Street Management Corporation (BSMC)* is a symbol of white power and the ability of government to dominate black people. It is synonymous to confederate flags, segregation, and white supremacy; gentrification dressed up as progress. It reflects the agreement among whites to do what they see as necessary to keep descendants of American slavery, as the foundation of America's *"cheap labor"* capitalistic strategy. As Pres. Woodrow Wilson said, **"Self-preservation [forced whites] to rid themselves, by <u>fair means or foul</u>, of the intolerable burden of governments sustained by the votes of ignorant Negroes."**

This is the real basis of Donald Trump's efforts to throw out votes and remain president. White people still see black people as ignorant, which is why they undertook to rob them in such a blatant manner. After researching the history of *Beale Street Management Corp.*, I think *"The Great Street Robbery"* was the same as the *People's Grocery Store Lynch,* except this time white people lynch an entire community. I also believe a more appropriate headline would be; **Urban Renewal Replaces Red Summer and "Dark Age" Angry White Men Mob Madness as the means to Rob Blacks of Wealth.** According to those in charge now, *"Beale Street is a wonderful entertainment district, changing once again from its past of "sad old days" back to glory."* That's a white person talking, sounding like the slogan **"Make America Great Again!"** The image of white people, drinking and dance, filling Beale Street nightly, is exactly the place *BSMC* envisioned to replace the black culture this narrative has presented. The purpose of *"The Great Street Robbery"* metaphor is to show that whites can still rob blacks with impunity assisted by government.

A New Reason to Sing the Blues

Creating *Beale Street Management Corporation's* (1977) and its takeover of Beale Street, the City of Memphis ended opportunities on the fame thoroughfare as a place for developing black talent. Good times on Beale Street for black people faded along with opportunities. No more talent shows at the Palace Theater to develop young entertainers. Schools became embroiled in desegregation and busing, while the freedom for teachers, like Nat D. and Moohah to develop black students' talents in black schools, disappeared as integration took seats in classrooms. However, **WDIA** was still a force, and the *Teen Town Singers* were doing great. "Moohah" had begun with a group of junior and senior high school students from seven schools. Although young and inexperienced, the *Teen Towners* were the *Voice* of young black America in the Mississippi delta through **WDIA**.

Some became known throughout the Mid-South. Black schools, before integration, had the freedom to develop a kind of "mini-Chitlin Circuit." Schools put on talent shows to raise money for other school projects and activities. They presented a Vaudeville type variety show format with comedians, vocalists—individuals and groups—bands and dancers that traveled to perform at schools around the Mid-South, but mostly in Memphis. These shows were mostly at night, where the community could attend. Schools that hosted shows raised money and paid the expenses of performers. I was in a dance troupe that played that circuit, while in junior high.

"Moohah" launched the *Teen Town Singers,* and their Saturday 9:30 AM broadcast attracted listeners to **WDIA** in and around Memphis. Early on Saturday morning, ears all over town, up through the boot heel of Missouri and down through the Mississippi Delta, were glued to radios until early afternoon. Moohah brought Mrs. Cathryn Rivers Johnson, a teacher at Booker T. Washington, as his musical director. Collaborating, Moohah and Mrs. Johnson trained and produced some standouts young vocalists through the *Teen Town Singers*. Many went on to greatness, as recording artists include Carla Thomas and her brother Marvelle, both were among the earliest STAX recording stars. Many found success as recording artists, like Ed Townsend, Regina Bennett-West, Isaac Hayes, Frances Kelly, Percy Wiggins, Spencer Wiggins, Tina Bryant, Shirley Jones, and others found successful as *Teen Town Singers*.

Carla Thomas is the quintessential *Teen Town Singer,* who experienced success as a recording artist, but many more found success in other fields of endeavor, like Mark Stansbury. Carla was born into an entertainment family—Rufus Thomas was her father, and Marvelle played keyboard—which created great expectations for the young high schooler. Carla, like many other girls, enjoyed the direction and tutelage the *Teen Town Singers* provided, as they matured. I know the *Teen Towners'* routine and story well. My sisters, Molly and Bernice, sang with the group, and like Carla, they had our mother's love for singing, as a family legacy. I asked Carla about those days, a couple of years back when we talked, and she was still giddy, talking about all the fun they had before and after practice at the YMCA. Carla said,

> *"Those were the best days. We had so much fun, clowning around, playing little jokes on each other, or trying to teach each other new dances. Bernice was one of the best dancers. After practice, Molly, Bernice and I would walk four blocks to eat at the Harlem House (a favorite local burger place). We went to different schools (Carla attended Green P. Hamilton High, while Bernice and Molly went to Booker T. Washington), so we didn't see much of each other or spend time together, except on practice days and Saturdays after the show. We would eat, laugh, and talk about our plans. Those were such great times. The Teen Town Singers brought some really great people together."*

During the 1960s, Carla Thomas played an important role in the early success of STAX Records. Her duet with Rufus, *"Cause I Love You"* in 1960, was an international hit. Carla launched her solo career with *"Gee Whiz"* in 1961 and was billed as the *"Queen of the Memphis Sound."*

The list of young people trying to get on stage at talent shows at the Palace Theater, Club Handy, and other spots on and around Beale Street was tough. Many young vocalists like Carla, Isaac Hayes, David Porter, Al Green and groups like the Temprees—"Jabo" Phillips, Harold "Scotty" Scott, and Deljuan Calvin: The Mad Lads—John Gary Williams, Julius Green, William Brown and Robert Phillips, as well as The Ovations—Louis Williams Jr., Nathan "Pedro" Lewis, and Elvin Lee Jones were just a few trying to get into show business. Were it not for the opportunities Beale Street offered, these young show biz aspirants would have been do-wooping under street lights at night. More importantly, they would not have been stage-ready when opportunities came knocking. The question is—*why isn't the City of Memphis and the BSMC continuing this Beale Street cultural tradition to support the only original brand of Memphis—music?* The City's thievery robbed young talent—entertainers and entrepreneurs—of opportunities, only to give white people, who already had open access to everything, another place to wild-it-out and get stoned.

Creating a Brand Only to Watch It Die

I believe an overview of the desperate times, following the demise of Beale Street, as the major source of economic empowerment for black people is necessary, for those who are unfamiliar with Memphis. Beale Street was an incubator of black talent, especially during the 1950s to 1970s. Its demise was devastating to the economy of the black community. Beale Street was a launching path for some of soul music's greatest stars. I beg readers' indulgence once again, as I offer the following lament. It is necessary because, Beale Street's loss left young entertainers without opportunities older black entertainers relied upon for training, while getting started. Living in separate worldsAn unforeseen tragedy forced blacks and whites that relied on entertainment, unforeseen tragedy forced them to come together.

   Although they worked together on some occasions, building past successes, the loss of Beale Street meant they had to collaborate more than ever, if either was going to survive. The uncertainty caused by the demise of Beale Street created an environment that required not only new ideas, themes, and approaches, but it demanded new personalities to guide entertainers and producers, once the magic of Beale Street moved on. And, as fate, time, and events would have it, necessity forced the entertainment community to come together to create some of the most exciting and impactful music in American history.

   The *"Memphis Sound"* was the brand that emerged, and it made soul music a featured product of the *Emerald City*. It began with siblings Jim Stewart and Estelle Axton, white owners of Satellite Records Store. They were the "Bert Ferguson and John Pepper" of the Memphis Sound. Their business, Satellite Records Store, was going nowhere, similar to **WDIA**. However, they were not going bankrupt but this time around there was not a Nat D either. Amazingly though, Beale Street's **Blues** magic was strong enough to reach out and anoint some new slave descendants with greatness.

   The *"Memphis Sound's"* story developed without design. It was by happenstance that Jim Stewart and Estelle Axton got the magic, like *WDIA* with Nat D. Theirs—the Axtons—was a fate not in the hands of a magic man born on Beale Street. Their savior wasn't even an apprentice when he showed up. Just the same, he was born close enough to Beale Street to conjure success for these "fish out of water," flopping around in the backwash of country and western music in of all places, the middle of the black community. Even beach-loving white folks could not foresee a wave of success, washing up on their shore, especially in the Memphis ghetto, with their "honky-tonk."

   The unintended consequence in this magic act did not arrive in a whirlwind, like ***The Wiz*** or Sunbeam Mitchell; neither was it pulled out of a hat, like a rabbit. It came with a bag of grocery, delivered by the most unlikely wizard, who was not even aware he possessed magic at that point. A dreamer, imagining success and willing to try anything to obtain it, David Porter was just another high school grocery store sacker, when he became a sage.

David played Elvis Presley's game, as Elvis immersed himself in Beale Street culture. Delivering bags of grocery across the street to Satellite Record Store, Porter began hanging around; it had a recording studio in the back. So, he politicked or conjured his way into the recording studio and began learning the magic of making music and recording music. True to form, like Nat D, he got his friend Isaac Hayes into the recording room. Although Isaac was not his apprentice, he wanted to learn the magic of songwriting and production also.

The Blues magic even made Jim and Estelle magi of sorts. Their record store was a wing of an old movie theater, which became STAX. Their next trick was finding a group for their studio band. STAX's first big trick was not a hocus-pocus gimmick act, although the mix was like salt and pepper. This spicy setup mingled a duo of Booker T. Washington High School students Booker T. Jones, keyboardist and Al Jackson, Jr. drummer with white guitarist Steve Cropper and bass player Lewie Steinberg (later replaced by Donald "Duck" Dunn), though not well seasoned, the blend had a great flavor for STAX. The house band gave STAX a new kind of mysticism and a recipe that cooked up some flavorful soul music that made black and white work like a duke's mixture of success. Really well seasoned for the first time in Memphis, their interracial brew conjured a spicy sound that became a gourmet's delight with a mega-hit for STAX. Although their groove was funky, *"Green Onions,"* did not stink up the joint. It catapulted Booker T. & the M.G's to the top spot on Billboard's Hot R&B Sides.

Breaking segregation's taboos once again, Jim Stewart kept the magic going, bringing in another wannabe magic man, drowning in the backwash of obscurity. Throwing a lifeline to Al Bell, an African American, who loved cooking down-home stew, Bell became STAX national sales director. Blending Bell into STAX's duke's mixture, brought in a magical hash slinger that believed he could really cook up magic, like a soul food *chef de cuisine* at *Four Way Grill*. Even more, **Blues'** magic was stirred into the mix by David Porter and Isaac Hayes. Porter and Hayes became real necromancers, bringing in other wannabe sorcerers. First, they tapped Sam and Dave with their magic wand and sent the message to black people, *"Hold on I'm Comin"* (1966). The next year they cooked up what black people were really hungry for a *"Soul Man"* (1967) to lead the way. Those hit were rescue packages and far better than chicken soup to get an ailing STAX on its feet.

Those successes made Porter and Hayes STAX top songwriters. However, Isaac Hayes showed he was no flapjack flipper, but instead a real magic man in STAX's kitchen of hot hits in 1971. Ike mesmerized the world with *"Shaft,"* winning the Academy Award for Best Original Song (1972).

The 400th: From Slavery to Hip Hop

Believing, after the mega-success of *"Shaft,"* they had learned the magic of the **Blues** well enough, Al Bell and Jim Steward left school early. Very ambitious enchantresses in 1972, Bell and Steward conjured *The Watts/STAX Summer Festival. Watts/STAX* was an all-day concert by STAX recording artists, which sold-out the Los Angeles Coliseum. A teen sensation, John Gary Williams fronting The Mad Lads, brought the young crowd to Watts/STAX, following hits like *"I Want Someone," "Seeing Is Believing,"* and *"Make This Young Lady Mine."* Headlining the show, Isaac Hayes donned gold chains, like a slave, and presto-change-o, without smoke and mirrors, on stage before the world, Ike became **"Black Moses."** The Watts/STAX review and *"Shaft"* blew STAX up into an international record label, for many it seemed overnight. Al's magic made STAX the big thing in 1972.

Jim Stewart and Al Bell began learning the fate of sorcerer's apprentices that leave school early trying to carry the **Blues** magic too far, too fast, and in too many directions, creating a whirlwind of success. STAX successful spin swallowed up the whole enterprise. Getting the "Memphis Sound" going, like young inexperienced magicians, STAX magical whirlwind of success and fame grew faster than anyone imagined or could control. Similar to the real fairy tale *"The Sorcerer's Apprentice,"* by Johann Wolfgang von Goethe, they learned how to get it started, but left school before learning to control its speed and slow or stop the whirlwind, before they lost control.

STAX Records gave voice to the last generation of sharecroppers and the first generation that fought for black power to end segregation. Some may say nothing that happened at STAX was magic. But I say, if not magic, how can one explain, a man arriving at STAX chauffeuring a wannabe star that gets turned away, while the chauffeur gets the recording contract.

The unknown chauffeur became one of STAX biggest stars Otis Redding. Otis believed *"Try A Little Tenderness"* (1966), kept him from becoming a *"Tramp,"* he was sure *A Change is Gonna Come*, so *"Sittin' On The Dock Of The Bay*, was his last message to his faithful." Booker T and the MGs, Sam & Dave, Isaac Hayes, the Staple Singer, The Mad Lads, Wilson Pickett, the Bar-Kays, the Emotions, Soul Children, Eddie Floyd, Carla and Rufus Thomas along with many others were part of STAX legendary bill. They brought the world classic soul hits like *"Green Onions," "Soul Man," "Wait till the Midnight Hour," "Gee Whiz," "Soul Finger," "The Dog," "Respect Yourself," "I Don't Have to Shop Around," "By the Time I get to Phoenix," "Knock on Wood"* and *"The Best of My Love"* are just a few from STAX golden age.

Just a few blocks South of STAX, the other half of the *"Memphis Sound,"* where another Memphis music wizard Willie "Papa" Mitchell was conjuring a different kind of music magic. A horn man, bandleader, songwriter, music studio executive, and entrepreneur Willie "Papa" Mitchell was casting spells at Hi Records. Willie Mitchell played trumpet with Phineas Newborn, Sr. and Junior, as well as every other band of any note out of Memphis. He got his magic performing on Beale Street, going back to the 1940s. "Papa" dropped *"Soul Serenade"* in early 1968 and put himself in the class with all the great magic music men from the *"dirty South."* Hi Records was as instrumental as STAX Records, conjuring the brand *"Memphis Sound."* That brand brought prosperity back to the black community in the 1960s into the 1980s.

Willie Mitchell single-handedly produced Hi Records' greatest hits catalog. Gaining an international reputation, as one of the best soul musicians and producers in the business, Pops' incantations guided his primary artist Al Green, to a string of soul smash hits—*"Let's Stay Together"* and *"I'm So in Love With You"* in the 1970s into the 1980s. Signing with Pops, Al Green learned to conjure *"Love and Happiness"* like waving a wand to gained success.

Having served as an apprentice to most great magical music men on Beale Street, Papa Mitchell was the only sorcerer at Hi Records. Nevertheless, he drew other classic soul artists into his lair, like a soothsayer casting gifts. "Pop" Willie put some great soul singers in the spotlight, as Hi Studio artists, like Don Bryant, Ann Peebles, Tina Bryant, Sly Johnson, O. V. Wright, and Otis Clay. Willie Mitchell provided the world with great music like *"That's How Strong my Love Is," "Is It Because I'm Black," "I Can't Stand the Rain," "You Gonna Make Me Cry,"* and many others.

An Icon Down for the Count

This narrative has shown if anything, that white people in America have had descendants of slavery on the canvas, down for the count on many occasions. However, just before being counted out, slavery's descendants always found the courage and strength to get to their feet. Since leaving **"The Door of No Return," Goreé Island, Dakar, Senegal,** crossing the **"Middle Passage"** to reach the wildness of North America, which became the United States, there have been two historical questions, *"How did they do that? How did they survive?"* Beginning their horrid saga in the **Trans-Atlantic Slave Trade,** after reaching North America, enslaved Africans dreadful and perilous saga gave them the one thing that brought them through untold perils **"Blues magic."** Although millions of words have been spoken, written and sang about it, no one has been able to offer a better explanation for their endurance and survival story than magic.

Slave descendants survived the **"Dark Age"** *angry white men mob madness*, lynching, convict leasing, and sharecropping, which trapped them in the grave of poverty. And, during those dark and deathly times, their survival was a cliff-hanger, as they teetered on the brink of disaster. White people were throwing dirt over them, yet, miraculously, somehow, they found the will to rise up out of the grave of poverty and many escaped the valley of dry bones to live again. All but dead, they were stretched upon the scaffold of injustice; then buried beneath mountains of oppression and turmoil, but miraculously again like escape artists, they rose up to face the light of hope, beaming brightly, lighting those dark times, as slavery's descendants found the courage to continue standing before the world undaunted.

When leaders fail or were cut down in their prime, like a whirlwind foretelling disaster, unknown potential or unintended consequences blew away ominous clouds, while guiding the faithful to new beginnings. That is the way Beale Street and the magic of the **Blues** worked. It's called magic because, even condemned as wretches, unworthy of human considerations, descendants of American slavery defied the odds, rising up on their feet once more to state the answer to the opening question; "We are still here!!!"

Foreclosing on Beale Street took away the only area black people were allowed to develop businesses and a cultural center in Memphis for African Americans. Memphis City government foreclosed on black people's entrepreneurial hopes, pushing them out and shutting off what had been black Memphians' major economic engine. Entrepreneurial magic and Divine Intervention delivered new hope in the form of a grocery sacker, which made STAX Records another chance, as it picked up the slack, pumping resources back into the black community.

Pumping wealth into South Memphis, entertainment got a new start, thanks to Moses in black skin. A reflection of **"Blues"** men before him, Isaac Hayes, **"Black Moses,"** led the African American community out of the wildness of desperation and scarcity. No magic wand or bolt of lightning out of the blue, Isaac Hayes, **"Black Moses,"** created **Shaft,** parting the waters in the ocean of poverty, washing over slavery's descendants. A new inspiration gleaming brightly, like the "morning star" for a people without benefactors, following the devastating loss of Beale Street, black people, in response to the City of Memphis' knife in their backs, found the strength to rise up once more.

I tell the story of the *"Memphis Sound"* much like a fairytale because the real truth of surviving the harsh realities of life that black people in Memphis faced was a story almost as harsh as the ones some mothers endured keeping their families together. That story is not spoken of, as it truly happened in polite company. Memphis black entrepreneurs only had music and Beale Street beyond cotton fields and factory work.

Unlike success at "Motown," The Temptations, Mavelettes, Mary Wells, Four Tops, Stevie Wonder, Marvin Gay, Diana Ross, and the Supremes, Smokie Roberson and the Miracles, Jr. Walker and the All-Stars, and a host of others, the "Memphis Sound" didn't compare to the "Philadelphia Sound," Jerry Butler, The Delfonics, Patti LaBelle, Dionne Warwick, Teddy Pendergrass, The O'Jays, The Manhattans, Lou Rawls, Stylistics, the Spinners, Archie Bell & the Drells, Harold Melvin & The Blue Notes and others, it did not have a stronge economic and political base.

As far as black people were concerned, Memphis was a "one-horse town." For blacks, trying to build wealth independently, rather than following the example of civil rights leaders, who groveling before white people, and refused to fight the theft of Beale Street, the black community was down for the count again. Not having the convenience of a centrally located business district, entrepreneurs and entertainers found new ways to express the **"Blues"** magic. Black Memphians were back to *make something out of nothing* to survived that disaster.

Black entrepreneurs transitioned even deeper into the black community. Mimicking Sunbeam Mitchell's example with Club Paradise, they relied on stand-alone clubs, like *The Living Room, Hawaiian Isle, Malunda's, Log Cabin, Currie's Club Tropicana, Aunt Cora's Café* and many other spots to take the place of one area. White people would have to shut the entire black community down to kill their new survival strategy. Caught by something no one thought would ever happen—loss of Beale Street—black entrepreneurs were like white people in the South never imagined not having slaves; no one foresaw a time without Beale Street.

The problem for STAX began in the late 1970s and early 80s, its wizards Jim Stewart and Al Bell, after conjuring WATT/ STAX, lost control of the whirlwind of success that brought money pouring in to "Soulsville USA," like water. The

The 400th: From Slavery to Hip Hop

success of *"Shaft"* convinced everyone that the glory ride would match *"Motown's."* Even money men from New York City and LA, wanted in on what looked like a sure thing.

Deals coming to STAX were, like pails of water, conjured by the *"Sorcerer's Apprentice."* More money flowed in than could be reconciled with that flowing out. Awash in success, while drowning in red ink, STAX was broke and no one noticed. Before the hit makers knew what happened, STAX was going down for the third time. Jim Steward sought a lifeline of temporary financial assistance from Memphis City Government, because it aided other businesses, but the city saw STAX, like Beale Street—it was for "niggers."

By the late 1980s, all hopes for a revival of either Beale Street or STAX disappeared like a puff of smoke, in a magic act. An icon was down for the count, and the City of Memphis walked away. Everything seemed to be falling apart for the only business capable of driving the economy in the black community. The lost of Beale Street, meant no money bag like Robert Church and buyouts, downsizing, and a lack of concern for the black community by **WDIA** made it a shell of its former self. Old wizards like Sunbeam Mitchell, Nat D, Rufus, and Moohah were still around, but those icons had no rescue packages for the *"Memphis Sound."*

Blamed Everything on the Invaders

The horror show reflecting the loss of Beale Street and STAX—the "Memphis Sound"—was avoidable. There were young leaders, with a new and different mindset, fighting the white-only political leadership in Memphis, as today, but "civil rights leaders and preachers," like during the sanitation strike marches, refused to deal with or even listen to those voices. An icon was down and those leaders walked away to preserve their role, as "go-betweens," and to please white folks and stay in their good graces, while those whites kelp black people on their knees, like field hands still in cotton fields.

All bad outcomes after the police riot on Beale Street (3-28-68) engineered by Mayor Henry Loeb, especially the City's takeover of Beale Street and the demise of STAX were blamed on the *Invaders*. Piling on, many black leaders, who benefitted from segregation, joined the chorus of blame, while they worked to banish the *Invaders* and black power from Memphis. They still claimed the *Invaders* and black power were *"destructive forces in the black community."*

Everyone ignored the fact the Invaders were running youth programs in low income underserved communities in South Memphis. They started the first free breakfast program for school children, as well as an after school homework lab. The Invaders asked the City to help fund these programs, it refused to support them. Rather, they proceeded to make the Invaders persona non grata. Memphis' political community white and black leaders scapegoated the *Invaders*, supporting criminalization of the *Invaders*.

STAX, "Soulsville USA," folded, and of course that was blamed on the Invaders also. Its folding was just more collateral damage thrown into the pyre to fry the Invaders, along with the riot on Beale Street and its loss. My opinion is, the City allowed STAX to fold to further subjugate black people. Black Memphians siding with black power, and the boldness of the gathering of over 50,000 protestors that showed up in support of striking sanitation workers hit Henry Loeb, like a pie "in his face." Loeb had to put black folk in the place, he felt they belonged, subservient to whites.

The City government renewed its efforts to keep black people locked on the bottom of the socioeconomic and political structure in Memphis. Loeb's retaliation pushed blacks back to depending on the white community's generosity. Black people had to accept discrimination and disparate treatment once again. They return to working to gain the acceptance of white people, as during segregation. The theft of Beale Street spoke volumes about white people's intentions.

STAX had begun to change black people's dependency scenario, but Memphis needed a scapegoat, and the news media focused all its vitriolic condemnation on the *Invaders*. They made John Gary Williams, lead singer for *"The Mad Lads"* their focus and target. John Gary joined the Invader, after his discharge from the Army. He, more than any Invader, became the one person the police and media focused on, because of his celebrity status and rising entertainment career. He faced the brunt of the attacks on the Invaders.

John was a leader among entertainers in Memphis, during and after the sanitation workers strike. He was targeted during J. Edgar Hoover's black power death hunt and pursued as though he was public enemy number one. The news media kept him in the bullseye of condemnation, and Memphis police went after him, as though he was a fugitive on the *Underground Railroad*.

The FBI, Memphis police and News media, in tandem, did everything they could to not only destroy John Gary's music career but John as a man. The venomous attacks began when John intervened during a police shootout involving some Invaders. John tried to stop it, but like me and the riot charge at Carver High School that sent me to prison, John was on the scene, a known Invader, and was charged. Even though the police could not show any involvement by John, like Angela Davis and the Marin County courthouse shootout, but in the South there still are no fair courts, before all-white prosecutors, jury, and Judges, going to prison was the point.

The music and entertainment industry in Memphis were running scared in response to black power. Simultaneously, STAX management was fighting for its life and courting the City for money, it turned thumbs down on John Gary. They ran for the exit, like NFL owners today, regarding Colin Kaepernick, exercising his right of *VOICE*, STAX joined the lynch mob. John Gary Williams' music career was all but over, as it came to a dead standstill in the 1980s.

As I said beginning this Narrative, *"A slave's life amounts to a desperate voyage in treacherous tempest-tossed waters, chained and locked in the hold of a leaky ship."* Surviving, the only thing awaiting a slave was a life of servitude. The only word that describes what happened to the *Invaders* is "reprisals." However, John was always a man who looked within for strength. He kept his head up and looked to the future for inspiration. He continued writing and making music.

John Gary was encouraged by "Pop" Willie (Willie Mitchell) at Hi Records Studio, to stay with his music. Papa recorded some of John Gary's work, even though he did not have the cost of studio time. Through it all, John wore a big smile, as if he knew a secret, the rest of the world was unaware. Today after 50 years working to keep his life and family together, we all know now his smile was for the doubters, who do not believe in second chances.

John is being rediscovered today by a new generation of music lovers. Also, the re-release of his album "**John Gary Williams**" is giving his career new life and the world some great music, which was locked up along with John back in 1971. Locked away all these years, the lead song on his album, **"I Believe the whole Damn World is Going Crazy,"** was a prophetic reflection of today's madness, more so than in the 1970s. Those mad hectic times for the *Invaders* and the fall of an icon—STAX Records—put John and his music in a deep freeze, not a grave.

For me, ten or fifteen years ago, he wrote my favor, **"I See Hope!"** John was a prophet. It became a lullaby for my wife Dot, as she battled cancer in 2005. ***I See Hope*** is also the title of the documentary on John Gary's life. Six years ago, he teamed up with John Hubble, a filmmaker. Although he is a white guy, Hubble was extremely impressed with John Gary's life and struggles. Hubble committed himself to telling John's story in film. John said in our last meeting in 2019, *"Like sunshine at daybreak, the darkness parted, as the old world disappeared and the light of a new beginning shown through. I saw a new world before me; once I let the old world go. The crazy times were behind me, as I saw hope in the life I'd lived."* John is also a major character in *The Invaders* documentary (2016) by Pritchard Smith. The *Invaders'* story is currently touring the world as part of the **Black Power Tarot Card Exhibition** by Arish "King" Kahn, which commemorates the fifth years of the "***Poor People' Campaign.***"

I See Hope

John Gary Williams was not the only one whose life was in the midst of change, and his work is seeing a revival as things began turning around. John and I saw David Porter during a commemoration for Ben Cauley, original member of the Bar-Kays, in 2017. David told us then he was working on a big deal for "Memphis Music," but couldn't be specific.

Later, I read that the STAX icon (7-25-2018) had launched his new studio, *Made In Memphis Entertainment*. Enjoying renewed success, David has surrounded himself with a team of young professional talent—Tony Alexander, President & Managing Director, and Hamilton Hardin, Vice President of A&R—to help him build a new legacy for Memphis music. I was back in Memphis in November 2018, and I talked with some of the old gang. Everyone was very excited for David and hoped *Made In Memphis Entertainment* will fill some of the voids in the wake of STAX's demise and the *Great Street Robbery* of Beale Street.

John Gary, David, Isaac, Carla, Booker T., and others, as this narrative has pointed out, were teenagers still in high school, when they broke into entertainment. Everybody was fighting to get into the recording business. So, in that regard, Memphis was like *"the wild wild West,"* before Kool Moe Dee ever rapped a note. Anything could happen at any time. The smart ones kept their cards close to their chests. The way things went down sometimes, left hard feelings some people never let go. That's why it is good to know music entertainment people are happy for David Porter.

Talking with John at that time about' my hopeful feelings and how glad I was for someone from our side was *"making something out of nothing."* He told me about some advice David Porter offered him when he was just beginning with STAX, and I pass it on to young people hoping to make a success in entertainment. John said,

"David was one of the few guys who had been around a while that tried to give young entertainers a heads up about the recording industry. He pulled me to the side one day and said,"

'Show business is a tough game. And, even though there are people who are supposed to look out for you, you have to look out for yourself. Everybody has ideas and think their ideas are the best. They want theirs to be accepted, as you want yours. The reality is everyone is pushing for themselves. If the deal goes against you, don't get upset with the people who got their idea in. They may have been willing to fight harder for what they wanted and believed in their ideas more than you at the time. They may have been willing to put other things on hold, come in early, stay later, and even go along with something they really didn't think much of at the time. But, by going along, sometimes you may only get part of what you wanted. A piece of

something is better than all of nothing. That will keep you in the game. Next time around, if you're still around, you may have learned how to fight harder for your ideas than in the past.'

"As I said, I was young," John responded. "I didn't spend a lot of time thinking about what David said, but as time passed, I realized he was right about a lot of things he told me back then. But, you know the best thing of all? David takes his own advice. It took a lot of fighting and patience for a black man to pull something like his own recording studio off when nobody wants to see a black man get ahead and succeed at anything. I've learned you can't get upset because a decision goes against you, as David said. If you're around, there's going to be other decisions made, get ready for those. I wish David, GOD blessings; it couldn't have happened to a more deserving guy."

I agreed with John G. New things are happening in Memphis. It seems there may even be a new mindset developing. I see hope in this new mindset. It is far different than those that engineered *"the Great Street Robbery,"* and made *Beale Street Management Corporation* an all-white deal on Beale Street. There's a new inclusive mindset coming from young whites, like those that had the vision to see value in the two documentaries *The Invaders* and *I See Hope*. They talk in terms of projects that demonstrate there's room enough for both blacks and whites to be successful entrepreneurs in Memphis. That is why *"I See Hope!!!* Walking away after speaking with John G, my great grandfather's refrain came to mind, *"Can these dry bones live again?"* (My beloved brother John Gary Williams succumb, after an extended battle with cancer on 5-28-2019. He will be sorely missed).

Fighting for a Political Voice

Reviewing descendants of American slavery's sojourn in North America, beginning with **The Trans-Atlantic Slave Trade,** while struggling to reach the **"The 400th",** a reoccurring question remains, *"Why isn't there a plan to extend the same rights and freedom to descendants of American slavery, which white people presently enjoy?"* The downside of this warped coin is the same question asked another way. *"When will slave descendants be accorded the same rights, as people today, who come to America from other countries that arrive aboard ship, on airlines or in boat flotillas, maybe even those that trek across the desert, receive upon request for citizenship?"* The downside of that coin shows slave descendants since landed in chains in North America and have had to jump through hoops, kneel in protest, stand against incredible odds, and continually lay their lives on the line defending America in wars. But remain in a second class status, which Pres. Woodrow Wilson established within the federal government (1912) 80 years ago. He built on the racism from the 1880s, which was compounded by Plessy v Ferguson (1897).

Now that descendants of enslaved Africans have reached **"The 400th"**, such questions must be asked aloud. *"Why do descendants of American slavery still bear the 3/5 Compromise stigma, which legally made them less than white men, perpetually locked on the bottom of America's economic structure as cheap labor?"* No other Americans citizens bear this second class stigma. *Why is that? What does that mean today in 2020?* Will there ever come a time, when the US Government acknowledge that it maintains discrimination against black people, while not accepting the fact that America is violating their human right of *VOICE,* in violation of the Civil Rights Bill of 1866?

Descendants of American slavery have paid every price put before them to purchase all rights other Americans are accorded at birth or given through application. For example, I purchased my first ticket aboard the political bandwagon, walking door to door with my mother, canvassing for Adlai Stevenson, Democratic candidate for President in 1952. Entering the 1960 campaign, we were all in campaigning for John F. Kennedy, the first progressive to be elected President of the US, in my lifetime. Kennedy (1960) opened government service to thousands of young Americans, who wanted to change the world, and he gave them the *"Peace Corps."* He made it possible for even some blacks to rise above the 3/5 Compromise line—then called the colored line—blocking their progress. But, as the color line, discrimination, disparate treatment, and the hostile environment black people endure didn't disappear?

Finding fertile ground inside the head of generations of white Americans, discrimination, disparate treatment, and the hostile environment black people endure, grew like weeds on steroids. Crashing and trashing the color line forever, with the wild ride of the counter-culture and black power/**Poor People's**

Campaign, many young progressives joined US Rep. Shirley Chisholm's campaign for President of the United States of America in 1972.

The Chisholm campaign was unsuccessful in getting the 1972 Presidential Nomination, but it produced some tremendous changes that reshaped the Democratic Party's Presidential Nomination process. The importance of the previous remark is not an overstatement regarding African Americans political access. The changes her campaign produced paved the way for the solid progressive coalition that is currently vying for power within the Democratic Party.

Most Americans probably have no memory of US Rep. Shirley Chisholm's campaign for President. She is a mystery to most Americans today, even though her candidacy was one of the most impactful for black people and other minorities leading to 2008. Her candidacy, other than for Rev. Hosea Williams, was not the aim when he called the first National Black Political Convention since 1864. Backed by the remanets of Dr. Martin Luther King, Jr.'s last dream, the **Poor People's Campaign,** and, Mayor Richard Hatcher of Gary, Indiana, they hosted the **National Black Political Convention** (3-10/12-1972.)

The idea for holding a National Negro Convention first emerged among black leaders during the late 1820s. It was a response to events in Cincinnati, Ohio. White leaders in Cincinnati proposed ousting its black population, as their way of reducing white political and racial tensions that developed over several decades. The tension culminated in white riots against black Americans, which lasted several days. However, these riots were not as devastating as **Red Summer's** murderous rampages.

Nevertheless, they were an expression of white people's desire to maintain the 3/5 second class status of slavery to maintain their national domination, as today. After city officials abolished slavery in 1803, its free black community expanded rapidly throughout the 1820s. Concerns increased among whites over blacks' political potential, once the official state census counted 10% (1829) of its population as "blacks and mulatoes."

The conflict over jobs and other competition increased between black and white men. The same situation occurred in Memphis in 1866, which ignited the first post- Civil War riot against former slaves. Responding to the Cincinnati Riot (1829), black leaders across the Midwest and Northeast fought the violence and discrimination against former slaves. Their concerns brought blacks together for the first National Black Political Convention in Philadelphia (1831).

Similar concerns followed riots and conflict during the mid-1960s, as black power activists gave *VOICE* to the plight of blacks in ghettos across America. But this time, blacks took to the streets in riots pushing their demands. The 1972 gathering in Gary was stormy from the first gavel. Modern "Negroes" had not attempted anything this political since the assassination of Dr. Martin Luther King, Jr. (1968), even though they supported *"The Poor People's Campaign."*

Civil rights leaders led black people into a kind of "black funk" of resignation. They feared a backlash from whites if they supported black power; civil rights leaders were running away from black power and the head on confrontation with Pres. Richard Nixon, similar to how they are today, cozing up to Donald Trump. Rev. Rev. Williams had continued fighting to bring black power and civil rights activists together, after Dr. King's death. However, civil rights leaders had tried to isolate Rev. Williams, as they did Dr. King following his ***"Poor People's Campaign"*** announcement.

Black conventioneers had no expectations beyond integrationists' politics. Most civil rights leaders spent their time chasing after and taking over protest and demonstration local blacks mounted. That was their way of controlling political forces, direction and black progress. So, no one knew what to expect with civil rights leaders still on the attack against black power activists, as a *"destructive force out to destroy the black community,"* when Rev. Hosea Williams began using the ***"Poor People's Campaign"*** to continue Dr. King's efforts to unify civil rights and black power activists. The ***National Black Political Convention*** (1972) was part of his strategy.

The gathering started with a bang when the Convention voted to exclude whites from the gathering. That vote angered white progressives; some charged reversed discrimination. Blacks conventioneers felt they needed to get together first and develop a strategy, before including whites. Although it was not the aim when the convention convened, for most delegates in Gary, but behind Rev. Williams' leadership, the convention produced a very unlikely presidential candidate, US Rep. Shirley Chisholm. Her candidacy made her the first black person and the first woman to be nominated by a major political party for president of the United States, however that result was not easily to obtain.

Although George McGovern received the Democratic Nominating Convention's nod for president, Richard Nixon soundly trounced him that November. However, a major event for black people occurred at that convention, which was far more important than gaining the nomination for President, as a result of US Rep. Chisholm's candidacy. Just before the Democratic Nominating Convention in Miami (1972) adjoined black activists, delegates, and Rep. Chisholm's supporters, flying under the radar, organized the first Black Political Caucus within the Democratic Party. The press and most Democratic Party delegates missed the event altogether. Organizing a Black Political Caucus was something no one was even talking about before the convention convened, and definitely not thinking about when it ended.

Cab and I were there representing the Invaders, as well as supporting US Rep. Shirley Chisholm. Moreover, we were also part of a determined group of black power activists that had agreed to push the idea that at such gatherings, blacks needed to caucus independently and develop a common strategy to oppose *"Southern Dixiecrats."* McGovern supporters fought to pull Rep. Chisholm's

295 primary delegates away to prevent her from being officially nominated for President of the Democratic Party.

Rep. Chisholm needed at least 100 votes for her name to place in nomination for US President. Jessie Jackson led the effort to stop her and had peeled off some of her delegates, since the primary campaign ended. Trying to hold Rep. Chisholm's coalition together clearly showed the need for a black political caucus, where black delegates could come together and hash out such issues among themselves. Saving Rep. Chisholm's effort, holding the 100 delegates needed to put her name in nomination together, was a victory most American were unaware, and have no idea what that effort took. Black activists, black convention delegates, and representatives from the Chisholm

Campaign met almost continuously counting heads. The need to keep a moment to moment update, further pointed out the need for a black political caucus. Following Rep. Chisholm nomination vote, we voted to create the first black caucus. Rep. Chisholm conveyed to vote to Democratic Party leaders and they agreed to recognize the first black caucus within the Democratic Party. However, beyond a few convention delegates and black activists working for other candidates, almost no one, except party officials, knew the vote had taken place when the convention adjoined. Nevertheless, it changed American politics forever.

McGovern's defeat by Richard Nixon left Democrats in disarray, much like Republicans today, following Donald Trump's defeat by Joe Biden (2020). Bruised from the battering and humiliating loss to Nixon, Democrats call a Midterm convention in Kansas City, KS (12-5/7-74). They were hoping to develop a unified strategy for the 1976 presidential election. The idea of the mini-convention was to give party insiders an idea of what the real field would resemble.

Following the convention in Miami, I climbed aboard the political bandwagon of a young black Democrat, Dedrick "Teddy" Withers in July of 1974. Teddy was the son of Dr. Ernest C. Withers. I became "Teddy's" campaign manager. All seasoned black democrats had committed to the white incumbent democrat T. H. "Tommy" Powell. A 12-year legislative incumbent and Chairman of the Shelby County Legislative Delegation, Powell was the most powerful labor candidate in the House of Representatives.

When I joined Teddy's campaign, he had only a few novice campaign workers. His campaign was "outspent, out maned and outlandish" according to the media. Everyone said Teddy didn't have a chance against Powell. In fact, in some quarters, Teddy's campaign was a laughing stock, as he tried to get it off the ground.

My coordinator was Richard L. Kirksey, Jr., a friend I helped organize a community youth group called *"Big-Brothers Junior Achievers"* (1972). This group was my first community involvement, after getting out of prison. Richard and I were Teddy only seasoned organizers. We built our campaign effort on *"Big-Brothers Junior Achievers,"* which were junior and senior high school students and another group I organized at Lemoyne-Owen College, *"The Men of Progress,"* led by Teddy's brother "Andrew "Rome" Withers.

Although we were called a rag-tag-bunch of nobodies in the press, we handily defeated Powell, electing, not only a black man but the youngest legislator ever in Tennessee history, at 22 in 1974. The point here is during December, "Teddy" led a contingent of *"Big-Brothers Junior Achievers," "The Men of Progress,"* and the **"Poor People's Campaign"** from Memphis to the Mini-Convention in Kansas City, KS. Young progressives and the first Black Caucus arrived to arrive early for the mini-convention, hoping to make systemic changes within the Democratic Party.

Following the disarray from 1972's lost to Nixon, some Democrats—young progressive—saw the Mid-term (mini) Convention as an opportunity to realign and reorganize the party for the 1976 presidential campaign. Most Democrats were still unaware of the *Black Political Caucus*. Consequently, we caught Dixiecrats completely by surprise. Our aim was to break the stranglehold "Dixiecrats" (southern white conservatives) had on the Democratic Party.

Dixiecrats had a power lock on party machinery. They had used the Credentials and Rules Committee to lock women, Hispanics, Native Peoples, and poor whites out of power while banishing blacks to the fringes of party power. The *Black Political Caucus* believed the key to victory hinged on pulling those delegates—women, Hispanics, Native Peoples, poor whites, and blacks—into a coalition.

That coalition succeeded in changing the composition of state delegations for National Nominating Conventions. Progressives restructured the party regarding racial and gender representation. We also won battles before the Rules Committee. *The Black Political Caucus* coalition fought for the inclusion of more women, Hispanic, blacks, Native People, the poor, and physically impaired, as delegates during conventions. It also added members from the coalition to the Rules Committee, which was huge.

Another major battle was reducing the number of extra delegates party leaders could select for National Democratic Nominating Conventions—super delegates. These votes on delegation composition and extra delegates went before the whole convention, which were fought out on the convention floor, during regular session. The progressive coalition won those fights and changed the makeup of Democratic Nominating Convention delegations.

What's at Stake for Black Voters: Unemployment and Median Family Income

Although most Americans are unaware of the impact of the 1974 Democratic Mini-convention, it set the pattern for inclusion that brought African Americans into the 2000s. Descendants of American slavery did indeed enjoy more political success and power, after that point, than the previous 137 years of emancipation. However, descendants of American slavery still do not have access to the same level of equality and justice; all other groups enjoy in America, whether or not they are citizens.

Now, the gloves come off. This narrative has laid the foundation for today, beginning with the long circuitous and convoluted look back at the **Trans-Atlantic Slave Trade (1452)**. That nightmare began the longest-running instance of genocide in the history of humankind. White Americans do not accept what they have done to descendants of enslaved Africans as genocide. They assert their brutality, degradation, terror, and death heaped upon slaves and descendants was to civilize a heathen people.

Clarifying this rebutal I began by calling history, as the first witness to establish the what, why, and how the American government has maintained descendants of slavery in a second class, less than equal status. The federal government locked former slaves in the grave of poverty with scarcity and desperation. **"The 400th"** narrative offers sharecropping and convict leasing as the most outstanding instances of US governments genocide. Now, **"The 400th"** will use the government's data collected over that period, as witnesses against it, to support the charge the US government is the culprit, which Dr. Martin Luther King, Jr. identified as responsible for maintain slavery's descendants in poverty, through genocide.

Although the history presented here stands unopposed, I offer the government own statistics as witnesses against America to represent what it has done, even though readers are already aware of America's crime. But, many are still troubled by the lingering question why? Researchers today have shown the why—wealth disparity—also termed *"the wealth gap."* It reflects what and how the American government exploited enslaved African beginning with the first enslaved Africans dragged aboard a slave ship at **"The Door of No Return," Goreé Island, Dakar, Senegal."** I now offer the following summation, for those still unconvinced by my thesis or those struggling to reconcile that thesis with the present.

The following addendum answers the question before it is asked! It is like a cheat sheet for a test. I want readers to know the importance of my wife, Dorothy M. Smith's groundbreaking research published in 1982, which present day research supports. Back then, when Dot presented her work, it was dismissed as too farfetched and out of the realm of possibilities to be believable.

Academicians and government officials declared, *"There was no way black people could have been held in poverty, while white people advanced."*

Moreover, with her research (1982), she debunked their baseless charges that *"the wealth gap,"* that black people talked about, *"is their fault."* Academicians, economists, and government researchers claimed: *"the so-called wealth gap is the result of black people's poor work ethic, lack of education or laziness."* Dot Smith's research predates work of researchers today by 37 years. Their research, which is known clearly today, serves as the underpinning for her findings. Now, here is the pretest.

The Powerful Hand of Government Policy

Declining homeownership reflects dire consequences for African Americans as retirement looms. Today *"Black people are moving into homeownership at a much 'slower rate' than at any time in the past,"* says Laurie Goodman, co-director of the Urban Institute's Housing Finance Policy Center and the co-author of its May 2017 report, *"Are Gains in Black Home Ownership History?"* Homeownership among African Americans has declined to levels not seen since before the passage of the *Fair Housing Act of 1968*. The long-term impact is an ever-present concern of black economists, who paints a very grim picture, this looming crisis foretells.

Researchers see disaster for the retirement hopes of African Americans in terms of homeownership. Looking back to the passage of the *Fair Housing Act*, discrimination has erased black homeownership gains. According to the Urban Institute's report, the black homeownership rate in America rose by nearly six percentage points but the black homeownership rate dropped to roughly 41% from 2000 to 2015 erasing gains. By contrast, the homeownership rate among white Americans was virtually unchanged at 71%, a 30% bulge.

"Gains in black homeownership were hard-won, which amplifies the concern that over the last 15 years, black homeownership rates declined to levels not seen since the 1960s, when 'private race-based discrimination' was made illegal," the report states. The black community got hit hardest by the housing crisis—2008—compared to other groups. In general, *"African Americans that bought homes at the 'peak of the housing bubble,' paying higher rates than whites. They were offered costly subprime loans, even though they qualified for lower prime loans interest rates,"* black families did not benefit as much as white families, overall, from the post 9/11 recovery.

This huge homeownership declines for black households was for all age groups, especially young adults. The homeownership rate for blacks 35-to 44 year-olds fell from 45 percent in 1990 to 33 percent by 2015, half the level for whites of the same age. Moreover, it dropped lower than the black homeownership in 1960. Homeownership fell from 1990 to 2015 for whites, Hispanics, and others in this age group.

The following is an example of what happened with homeownership for blacks 35-to 44 year-olds. It is very telling, when one combines the drop with the hourly pay gap. It has widened to its worst disparity in 40 years, according to the *Economic Policy Institute (EPI)*. The picture has becomes dire, as the wage gap amounted to roughly a 27 percent difference in 2015.

Whites earned an average of $25.22 an hour vs. $18.49 for blacks; a difference of $6.73. at the end of the year for a regular job, the difference amounts to $96,912 and over 20 years it equals 2 million dollar. These numbers show clearly the impact of the wealth gap on racial disparities. Creating and maintaining this wage disparity is where the heavy hand of government takes its greatest toll. Failure to enforce anti-discrimination laws maintains current disparities, combined with not raising the minimum wage government maintains the growing black-white wage gap, according to the EPI. Rockeymoore says:

"Blacks are earning less than whites, and it is not a reflection of talents or skills. It is a reflection of discrimination in the labor market. We talk about the gender-pay gap, but we need to talk about the "racial-pay gap." We need to be having forums addressing labor-market discrimination and decisions."

The previous example shows why **the wealth gap is growing**. On average, white families' wealth in 2013 was more than $500,000 higher than African American families ($95,000). In 1963, the year of the **March on Washington** (1-28-1963), the average wealth of white families was $117,000 higher than that for black families. This difference is compounded by the fact that white families accumulate more wealth over their lives than African American families, as the wage-gap shows, which means the wealth gap is also a factor of age, in that it widens with age. Whites have an average of $140,000 more in wealth in their 30s than African Americans (three times as much). Obscenely, whites have over $1 million more in wealth than African Americans (11 times as much) by their 60s. The wealth gap is also a reflection of the years of banishment and ethnic cleansing, from 1900 through the 1940s. During that period, white took wealth from blacks to get what they have, while pushing black people deeper into the grave of poverty in the valley of dry bones.

Furthermore, the Federal Reserve report said that *"whites are five times more likely to receive large gifts and inheritances than blacks, and the amounts receive by whites tend to be much larger."* Nick Abrams of AJW Financial Partners in Columbia, Md., a financial planner, says, *"The wage-gap is one of the main issues. We [African Americans] are starting at ground zero every generation."* Rockeymoore agrees as she points to disparities between blacks and whites regarding employer-sponsored retirement plans. *"The wealth gap is serious. A significant number of us [blacks] are in jobs where we do not have access to pre-tax preferred retirement vehicles like 401(k) or 403(b) accounts."* Many blacks work in small businesses where such plans frequently are not available. If we do work in jobs that offer tax-preferred vehicles, we tend not to contribute at rates similar to whites (This also reflects the pay gap). And loans we take out are offered at the highest rate."

The use of credit scores and arrest records are to deny or push blacks into the highest interest rates, which is totally discriminatory. Blacks pay more for everything, which is like a "ghetto tax." The thing white will not admit is the use of interest rates and credit, in general, discriminates against blacks. Credit scores are manipulated specifically to push blacks toward "pay day loans," where they pay obscene interest.

Considered in tandem with the heavy hand of government, the previous examples answer questions regarding why whites and blacks pay different rates for everything. Banks, lenders, credit card issuers, and other financial instruments use the prime verse subprime game discriminately against black people, forcing them to pay more.

That point brings us back to Homeownership. It plays a big part in the wealth gap. The typical white household aged 47 to 64 has housing wealth $67,000; the typical household of color in this age group has zero home equity, according to the December 2016 report by the National Academy of Social Insurance which says "Social Security is also part of the racial gap in retirement wealth." Now, here comes the test, which is on the big question "WHY?"

The Why: Unemployment and Median Family Income

This section will complete the summation for ***"The 400th"***. It is imperative readers understand the what, why, and how of slavery's descendants' socioeconomic and political struggles, reaching ***"The 400th"***. These questions—what, why and how—regarding those struggles, I state again, began with **The Trans-Atlantic Slave Trade,** then through American slavery, emancipation, the contraband period, **Plessy v. Ferguson,** Marcus Garvey, the ***"Dark Age"*** *angry white men mob madness*, CP-USA, <u>**"We Charge Genocide,"**</u> **Brown v. Board of Education**, the battle for civil rights as *VOICE*, as black power brought enslaved African into today—Hip Hop Generation. White people did not face any of the obstacles they imposed on black Americans to limit their access, as they built wealth. Those periods were pogroms, called as witnesses to substantiate government's—federal, state, and local— instruments and political weapons to enforce desperation and scarcity on black people.

Their testimony bore witness to the fact that government created a system based on discrimination, disparate treatment, and racism, as the base of America's *cheap labor* capitalistic strategy. Former slaves struggled against desperation and scarcity, while making families and building communities following emancipation. Reaching the 1980s research showed the wealth gap between white and black families began in slavery and continued growing. Having read what it took getting here, the issues of <u>*why did America force descendants of slavery to endure such degradation, humiliation, denial, brutality, terror, and death.*</u> Dorothy M. Smith explored this question in her thesis entitled **Recession and Unemployment: A Retrospective Analysis of the Economic Welfare Loss.** Her research answers the lingering questions left by the history described in this narrative.

Dorothy M. Smith's thesis begins the summation for this lengthy explanation. Following Dr. Martin Luther King, Jr.'s accusatory finger, which he pointed at the US Government, as the culprit responsible for creating and maintaining the wealth gap that entrapped African Americans in the graveyard of poverty in the valley of dry bones, Smith's thesis establishes "Why." Synonymous to the dry bones God showed Ezekiel and Rev. Lee prayed over, she explains why descendants of American slavery have faced only wretchedness, scarcity, and desperation.

Smith created a key mathematical function, which she called the *"chasm of inequality"* analysis for her groundbreaking research, <u>**Recession and Unemployment: A Retrospective Analysis of the Economic Welfare Loss.**</u>

She postulated that the chasm is the result of external forces and pressures orchestrated by US Government policies and procedures. These policies and procedures produce particular outcomes for descendants of American slavery, which differed from whites. They generated negative outcomes for slavery's descendants but benefit whites.

Smith's search began after graduating from Southwestern College (now Rhodes University in Memphis). She entered the MBA Economics program at Memphis State University (now University of Memphis). A child of poverty, her interest became welfare economics. Her interest in poverty was prompted by the question, *"Why have black people remained trapped in the graveyard of poverty, unable to escape as others groups?"*

Dot Smith entered the fight against poverty as an economist. She was a complete departure from the historical mold of black leadership. Smith did not think of herself, as an activist or leader. She considered herself a pure scientist, *"I'm simply trying to say something useful about the human condition,"* is the way she described herself. She avoided trying to appear to have *"the answer"* or *"the plan"* for slavery's descendants. She would say, *"I believe black people are intelligent. If given good information, they will learn. The problem seems, from my research, no one is willing to admit the real origin of poverty among black people."*

Smith brought an entirely different perspective to a question, which some of the best minds over the last 156 years grappled with, but left unresolved. Even though not an activist, Smith came out of the Ella Baker mold. Ella suffered many harsh rebukes from SCLC and other civil rights leaders for her bottom-up approach to the problems of poverty. Smith advocated poverty among black people was not innate, but rather a function of their environment.

Even though an economist, Smith viewed the solution to poverty from a compassionate, empathic perspective of a sharecroppers' daughter. But Smith, astoundingly, maintained a detached non-doctrinaire perspective, in giving the numbers black people represent real physical meaning. She began graduate studies in 1979, researching the history of poverty among black people in America. After two years, she published her eye-popping study, **Recession and Unemployment: A Retrospective Analysis of the Economic Welfare Loss,** which was published in the **Mid-South Journal of Economics (Vol. 6 No 3).** Her thesis showed poverty among slavery's descendants was the result of how the government structured American's economy.

Readers learned this point earlier, as I discussed *"The Gilded Age."* Dot Smith challenged the prevailing view of poverty in America. Her work gave substance to Dr. Martin Luther King, Jr.'s speculation that *"the federal government is the root cause of poverty among Negros."* Smith presented her research in 1982, but economists and political leaders ignored her findings.

Everyone resisted reexamining the status quo assumptions about poverty among black people. No one wanted to examine her theory that *poverty in America is a function of how the government structured the American economy.* They were happy blaming black people for their impoverished existence.

The 400th: From Slavery to Hip Hop

Here, I will restate a few things about poverty in America to make this point. Poverty in America is a *"special case."* A nation just over two hundred years old, American poverty did not develop, as poverty in other parts of the world. Poverty in the old world—Europe, India, Russia, China, etc.—was built up over many centuries of families being poor (Europe was poor at the beginning of the **Trans-Atlanta Slave Trade**). In other words, poverty in Europe and other places are the result of historic structures and conditions arising out of serfdom or class—the *untouchables*.

However, poverty in America has a totally different origin. Large scale poverty among descendants of American slavery began during bondage and continued after emancipation (1863). Emerging penniless after emancipation at the end of the Civil War (1865), their socio-economic circumstances did not change. It is at this point; one can begin comparing the economic welfare loss between enslaved Africans and whites who had always been free.

During the entire period, 413 years of the **Trans-Atlantic Slave Trade** and 58 years of American slavery—the internal slave trade and breeding—enslaved Africans worked for free. Admittedly, there were pockets of poverty in large American cities. However, this narrative has presented ample evidence, showing that the massive poverty among black people in America today, continued for the 4 million penniless slaves turned loose, during and following the Civil War, who worked for free 471 years.

America's 4 million former slaves began their so-called freedom penniless, but their poverty was compounded during the **Gilded Age**. America added to former slaves' impoverishment by importing poor whites from Europe it moved ahead of its former slaves. The US government brought 5.2 million southern Europeans to America to fill jobs in its rapidly expanding economy. Simultaneously, the federal government structured discrimination into America's economy by denying former slaves good-paying jobs it reserved for white Europeans, Irish and Jews. Former slaves could get only the lowest paying jobs, if they were employed at all. Pres. Woodrow Wilson followed that with segregation, which pushed former slaves deeper into poverty. He implemented policies that denied black workers access to federal jobs and fired the existing black federal workers force, like those in the US Postal service.

Again, simultaneously, white employment was at its highest level, as the *Gilded Age* prospered. More importantly, for eighty years (the 1880s to the late 1960s) in the South, convict leasing and sharecropping imprisoned the vast major of the 4 million former slaves on farms and in jails, working for free once again and others on the lowest paying jobs, as *"cheap or free labor."* This period ended in early 1960 with *"the Tent City era,"* the terminal end of the internal slave trade and breeding 80 year run.

Those eighty years were tantamount to re-enslavement for African Americans. While slave descendants worked for free (convict leasing and sharecropping), white Americans had unfettered access to the bounty of America's wealth.

Dot Smith's research established that poverty among all poor Americans did not have the same origin. Economists and politicians, when discussing poverty, dumped all poor people—whites included—on top of descendants of American slavery, as they developed their notions to explain American poverty. They hid the facts Smith's research showed, pretending that descendants of American slavery had the same opportunity, as whites to avoid poverty, after slavery. Even though, slavery's descendants were the only people with a history, as former slaves of poverty, which resulted from 363 years of bondage in North America. Hence, the 4 million former slaves and descendants started life in the grave of poverty. Historians and governments dumped all poor people together to obscure the impact of slavery to ignore their special case—origin of poverty among descendants of American slavery. Hence, there is no debating the origin of poverty among slavery's descendants which result from government actions.

Smith used regression analysis to analyze government data on poverty. She isolated variables important to amassing wealth—education, age, sex, mobility, family history, etc. She zeroed in on poverty in the aggregate. Comparing black to white economic welfare loss or gain, she measured the trend of poverty among blacks and whites over time, like tracking the weather. Smith selected the two most reliable measures, median family income, and unemployment, which are the keys to families' building wealth.

Smith rendered poverty accessible to statistical analysis by developing a mathematical function she called the *"chasm of inequality"* analysis. She used the chasm analysis to study the effects of US Government policies and impact of its procedures on blacks relative to whites. Smith's research proved that the federal government orchestrated external forces and manipulated outcomes for black Americans through programs, like unemployment, level of income, homeownership, interest rates, credit, insurance, convict leasing, sharecropping etc.....which determined black people's level of general welfare compared to whites, who were not victims of these processes. The most important point here is white people did not suffer any of the situations or conditions pointed out here that blacks endured. US Government maintains poverty as an economic outcome for slave descendants by manipulating those external variables.

Dr. Martin Luther King, Jr. realized this in 1967, which is why he launched the *"Poor People's Champaign"* to make this point clear to black people. He pointed his finger at the federal government, as the culprit in America's capitalistic economy responsible for poverty among its descendants of slavery. White Americans, in general and the government specifically, claim that poverty among black people is due to laziness, poor work ethics, lack of education, and other such variables.

Dot Smith, traced the litany of events—*slavery, emancipation, Civil War, 13th, 14th, 15th Amendments, Brown v. Board of Education, 1964 Civil Rights and 1965 Voting Rights Acts*—which were supposed to leveled the playing field in America economically and create equality among slave descendants and whites, who had always been free. Smith showed that slavery's descendants reach the 1980s without ever rising out of poverty in any significant numbers. More importantly, when one looks back over the events explicated in this narrative for those periods, it is easy to understand why Smith's research is on target.

Smith's—*Recession and Unemployment: A Retrospective Analysis of the Economic Welfare Loss*—research revealed that the only times a significant number of whites fell into poverty was during the *Panic of 1893* and the *Great Depression (1930-1940)*. But during those periods, whites had the help of government, which aided them when they took wealth away from blacks with mob rule, the **"Dark Age"** *angry white men mob madness era,* and **Red Summer 1919**. Their thievery softened the blow of poverty on whites but increased it among former slaves. Consequently, poverty among slavery's descendants was compounded by mob rule, the eighty years of convict leasing, and sharecropping (the 1880s to 1960s), which were concomitants events to *The Panic of 1893* and *Great Depression (1930 to 1940s)* impacts on black people.

All the while, banishment, and ethnic cleansing pushed many blacks that had climbed out of poverty back in, as whites rob blacks of their wealth with impunity to avoid poverty. White thievery made blacks even poorer, while making whites richer. The impact of these events on black Americans' that lost wealth to whites cannot be calculated, they can only be transfer and added to events, like the destruction of *Marcus Garvey's* **UNIA**, Greenwood **"Black Wall Street"** Tulsa, OK, Ocoee, FL. many other places, based on losses by blacks and gains by whites. Consequently, slave descendants continued slipping deeper into poverty after **emancipation (1863), Civil War, 13th, 14th, 15th Amendments, Brown v. Board of Education (1954), 1964 Civil Rights and 1965 Voting Rights Acts.**

So, Smith's chasm analysis shows that wealth among white people increased over the same periods that blacks were robbed of wealth. Moreover, whites were getting paid for their work at the highest level, while slavery's descendants were being robbed and paid at the lowest level. White people were not locked in jail on trump up charges and constantly robbed by America's economic system.

Whites were not victims of higher interest rates, poor education, less pay, subjected to more and longer periods of unemployment, etc. Plus, whites acquired wealth they did not work for through events like **Red Summer, lynching, banishment, and racial cleansing**. Whites gained wealth through taking the wealth black people created—the *"Great Street Robbery"* of Beale Street in 1977—which is making whites richer today, while blacks' that invested wealth and their lives in Beale Street are made poorer today, while whites are getting richer. Following the period of convict leasing, sharecropping, banishment, and racial cleansing, I repeat slavery's descendants entered the 1980s, never having crawled out of the open grave of poverty in the valley of dry bones. Smith, as a result of her *chasm of inequality* analysis, concluded, *poverty among slave descendants was the result of the heavy hand of government actions*. She not only proved that her assumption was correct, but she also established conclusively why!

Economics for Dot was like the movie camera in the hands of D. W. Griffith, creating *The Birth of A Nation*. She showed that the socioeconomic disparities between blacks and whites are a function of Article I Section II of the US Constitution—the 3/5 Compromise. The relevant factor here is that the 3/5 Compromise is the statement in the US Constitution that legalized slavery while justifying discrimination and disparate treatment against slavery's descendants. The **13th, 14th, 15th Amendments, Brown v. Board of Education (1954), 1964 Civil Rights and 1965 Voting Rights Acts** are the legislation that was supposed to eliminate the effects and impact of the 3/5 Compromise. But just 35 years after slavery and emancipation, the US Supreme Court denied slavery's descendants any legal standing in courts and access to the same socioeconomic and political rights white people have. But even more than that, government was in violation of **the Civil Rights Bill of 1866**, a law that has always been on the book, and was never overturned, so **Plessy v. Ferguson**—*separate but equal* was illegal, yet the federal government allowed it to stand in the place of that law.

US Supreme Court Chief Justice Roger Taney's statement and opinion in **Scott v. Sanford** leaves no doubt that the 3/5 Compromise is not a bygone relic in the US Constitution. It established slaves as less than whole human beings, which the 3/5 Compromise designated, as the value of slaves and descendants human capital. It allowed whites to denied open access to courts to fight the discriminatory value of 3/5 or .6 for black human capital relative to white men, who had a value of 5/5=1.

Smiths' research—**Recession and Unemployment: A Retrospective Analysis of the Economic Welfare Loss**—had to withstand rigorous scrutiny to get published, and for her to receive her MBA. Smith showed that poverty in America for black people is a function of government's use of the 3/5 Compromise. She substantiated her thesis that—*Poverty is a function of how the government structured America's economy, combined with poverty following slaves' penniless emancipation.* It made slaves less than whole human beings, allowing government to justify and build institutionalized racism into America's socioeconomic and political system in defiance of the **Civil Rights Bill of 1866**.

Those government actions placed black Americans in their current second class status. This locked slaves and descendants on the bottom of America's socioeconomic structure. Slavery's descendants are the only American citizens covered by the 3/5 Compromise and who were subjected to pogroms like—the

"Dark Age" angry white men mob madness, **Red Summer 1919**, convict leasing, sharecropping, banishment, ethnic cleansing and denial of fair courts to fight what was happening to them.

So again, Smith showed clearly that *emancipation, Civil War, 13th, 14th, and 15th Amendments, Brown v. Board of Education (1954), 1964 Civil Rights* and *1965 Voting Rights Acts* did not change African Americans' actual conditions or status relative to white Americans. Emerging from slavery penniless continued the gap between the medium family income of black compared to white families, which has continually grown, as the previous discussion showed.

Smith did not only discuss the situation; she brought numbers to the party. Smith showed that there is a consistent, stable, and inverse relationship between the negative socioeconomic consequences blacks endured compared to the positive socioeconomic outcomes white Americans enjoy. Blacks are on top of every negative category and on the bottom of all positive statistic of welfare, while whites are the direct opposite.

She and other researchers have documented the historical trend of black unemployment resting consistently at twice that of whites or higher, across every business cycle. Furthermore, Smith's research indicated that changes in black to white unemployment ratios fluctuate between the narrow intervals of .5 to .65. If blacks and whites were equal, there would not be any variance; both would rest at zero. This gap in black to white unemployment is unbroken and extends from today back to slavery.

There is no debating that the impact of black to white unemployment currently exerts a greater negative socioeconomic impact on slavery's descendants' ability to accumulate wealth, than on whites. However, slavery can be laid aside in this discussion at this point. While at the same time, that does not mean slavery should be dismissed as a relevant casual factor when considering the gap in welfare loss. It simply means that the impact of convict leasing and sharecropping (1880-1960), as well as unemployment and income disparities, are more recent and relevant indicators of discrimination and disparate treatment, which are the bases of poverty among black Americans. Smith looks at the impact of these indicators over the last 80 years (1900 until 1982), which are closer to the wealth that has been accumulated by whites and blacks today.

Pointing out the 80 years of convict leasing, sharing cropping, banishments, racial cleansing, and working for free are better and clearer indicators when comparing the current socio-economic conditions of black families relative to whites based on discrimination and disparate treatment that continues to negatively impact black families today, as opposed to white families. This analysis shows that black Americans' ability to accumulated wealth today, compared to whites, is far less. And nothing is being done to address the fact that government—federal, state, and local—used convict leasing and sharecropping to make white people richer while robbing black people of opportunities to build wealth.

Economists completely ignore the fact whites' wealth accumulation benefitted from convict leasing, sharecropping, banishments, ethnic cleansing, and regular employment, even though such events dramatically increased poverty among slave descendants. The best indicator here is median family income. Data from the US Labor Department, which is where Smith obtained her data, allowed her to zeros in on the gap between blacks and whites median family income. Smith showed that median family income for these groups fluctuates within the narrow range of .35 to .5.

These percentages indicate that on average white median family incomes are consistently 40 percent greater than the median family incomes of black families. (The previous discussion provides the latest data and statistics on black/white income, pay levels, and wealth-building). Other researchers have consistently documented the same result. Remarkably, the 40 percent difference in medium family income mimics the 2/5 income blacks never receive because they are paid less than whites (the 3/5 Compromise) which did the same jobs. The 2/5 value blacks are not paid or received in any way, because of their second class—3/5 Compromise—status, extends back to the signing of the US Constitution (1789), which legalized slavery.

Defining slaves as less than whole human beings (3/5) meant the 2/5 residual blacks never receive (because of Article I Section II of the US Constitution) has always accrued to whites. Smith's statement is borne out by the fact that even when blacks were paid, their pay has never equaled whites. The "why" of descendants of American slavery's poverty is just that simple! This 2/5 goes to whites in the form of higher salaries, better school, gated communities, more recreation, street improvements, lower interest rates, political and economic access, you name it. As such, Smith labeled this gap in medium family income and unemployment *"the chasm of inequality"* to point out its relationship to poverty. It is the open grave in the valley of dry bones Rev. Lee prayed over.

Smith's research explains "why" black Americans continually face discrimination and endure disparate treatment. Poverty among slavery's descendants reflects *the way the American job market is structured*. Blacks are the last hired and the first fired. They endure more and longer intervals of unemployment, and it reduces their potential for obtaining benefits or retiring. Such discrimination shifts all their survival cost to social security (SS), during their later years. But, even this works against black people because their life expectancy is far less than whites. Shorter life spans are a variable of poverty. So, blacks draw fewer years of SS due to underlying health issues, which accrues to whites because of their longer life span. Their longer life is due to their affluent lifestyles, money for doctors, and other health maintenance options.

The 400th: From Slavery to Hip Hop

Smith's work clearly establishes the gap in black to white wealth began during slavery and has persisted through **emancipation, Civil War, passages of the 13th, 14th, 15th, Amendments, Brown v. Board of Education (1954), 1964 Civil Rights and 1965 Voting Rights Acts.** I repeat that these were the laws, which supposedly leveled the playing field for slave descendants, making them equal to whites. Supposedly again, this was the reason behind **Brown v. Board of Education**, but like the first **Civil Rights Act 1866**, which was nullified, and not declared unconstitutional, by the US Supreme Court, yet land given former slaves, court returned to slave masters.

Research by Smith and others have never found any evidence that the gap between black and white Americans in medium family income and unemployment have ever narrowed significantly at any time during **"The 400th"**. Statistics projects the same result in 2020, which is why I supplied the answer to "Why" before the test. I wanted readers to understand what they needed to know to pass with a perfect score.

As I said earlier, academicians claimed Smith did not identify a 3/5 Compromise mechanism, nor did she have a *"smoking gun."* They demanded she clearly show how it was possible for whites, in general, and the federal government specifically, to maintained slave descendants in poverty, while whites enjoyed unfettered access to wealth. They denied the possibility of whites accruing wealth from the 3/5 Compromise, while keeping blacks in poverty. They readily claimed Smith's results were pure speculation that is until Mr. Douglas A. Blackmon fired his *"smoking gun."*

The Shot that Woke Up the Dead

Dot M. Smith unimpeachable Research shows beyond any doubt that t*he powerful hand of government policy* in America has assisted white people in their accumulation of wealth, at the expense of African Americans, since they were kidnapped and shanghaied from Africa's ***"The Door of No Return," Goreé Island, Dakar, Senegal,"*** to North America. Dot Smith presented her *chasm of inequality analysis* research in 1982, 38 years ago, and subsequent research has consistently substantiated her finds presented here.

The previous discussion showed clearly, government rules supported and are responsible for discrimination, disparate treatment, and the hostile environment slave descendants endured and government has continued those policies, since Smith presented her thesis. America's job market and economic system have not opened up to black people. Moreover, governments—federal, state, and local—have not addressed Smith's research, even though subsequent research has substantiated all her findings.

The situation is not a case of white and black people looking at the same thing from the same view, yet seeing entirely different pictures. Numbers are not black or white; numbers only reflect a particular reality; everyone views the same quantity. With that being the case, it seems obvious that governments are admitting they are discriminating against blacks to give white people advantages at black people's expense.

Why else would governments not address the numbers that reflect what everybody see, but only governments can change—their discrimination and disparate policies. For me, denying Dot's research exists or insinuating it is not good science is like governments' climate change stance. Further, governments' position seems to say to black people, **"Yes we know we are discriminating because we are doing it and stopping would end the American capitalistic system that rests on the backs of black people. And we are not going to change that!"**

Evidence presented indicates this is governments' present attitude regarding African Americans, as human beings. Black Americans face governments—genocide—against slavery's descendants and refuse to change its discrimination. Descendants of American slavery are not going to accept second class, after fighting their way to ***"The 400th".*** There is no way African Americans will accept what is clearly a genocidal situation against them that governments in America have sponsored since African enslavement began ***"The 400th".*** Governments in the US are definitely aware of what they are doing, but have no intention of stopping, no matter what statistical evidence or analysis shows.

Benefitting white people is their goal and is why white people kidnapped Africans and brought them to America. They never planned for or thought slavery would ever end. Governments' job is maintaining black people, as second class, and that is the only condition or situation white people in America are willing to accept for its descendants of American slavery. However, enslaved Africans had no say, when they were brought here, but they dam well have a say now. One way or another slavery in America will end and *"The 400th"* generation will die to insure that happens.

So now the proposition is not a yes or no situation but only a question of how? How is the only question before America going forward, not when! This narrative— *"The 400th"*—has come full circle, bringing the situation back to **"We Charge Genocide"** without a "Cold War" for America to hide behind. The question for the world is, which side of genocide is it going to support this time, freedom and justice, or tyranny and oppression? Today the world stands in the shadow of Adolf Hitler and his Nazi concentration camps. No nation can claim unawareness this time around.

The missing piece in this puzzle is the inequality problem and the unjust results is the "How?" Turning the corner on the past is only a vexing question for those who want to continued discrimination, while dodging Dot Smith's *chasm of inequality analysis,* as the way to view the mechanism that makes it possible. Critics continued hiding behind alternative explanations to evade acknowledging the truth and conclusions Smith's analysis established. Dot's goal was to present facts that eliminated obfuscations.

Then like a prayer answered, another devil-may-care, swashbuckling, lone riding researcher fired *"The shot that woke up the dead."* Out of the smoke from that blast, stepped Mr. Douglas A. Blackmon, who single-handedly took on the entire system of white supremacy, segregation, convict leasing, sharecropping, and unfair courts in America. Mr. Blackmon presented indisputable evidence that substantiated Dot Smith's thesis. Cracking his book **Slavery by Another Name: The Re-enslavement of Black Americans from the Civil War to WWII (2008),** was such a shrill sound the *"shot woke up the dead."* Douglas Blackmon not only fired truth like bullets, which killed off all the South lies, his bullets came from the South's own guns. His new and different perspective exploded, like a new kind of atomic bomb, creating a new reality America's slavery descendants have brought to the fight.

Blackmon blew up myths historians offered to obscure the truth of American slavery and poverty lies. Zeroing in on the period—1865-1942—with words and visions of those who creating and maintaining the hellish conditions in the *chasm of inequality* in which black people were trapped, **Slavery by Another Name: The Re-enslavement of Black Americans from the Civil War to WWII (2008),** was like lightening out of the clear blue. Bringing such clarity, I call it *"the shot that woke up the dead,"* because he gave *VOICE* to souls long buried in the grave of poverty an opportunity to speak on their own behalf.

Digging in the graveyard of poverty in the valley of dry bones, Mr. Blackmon created a means for the dead to tell of their wretched existence and daily degradation, though they departed long ago. His shot made such a piercing sound it opened the ears of those long dead, both victims and culprits alike, as when **_Slavery by Another Name: The Re-enslavement of Black Americans from the Civil War to WWII_ (2008)** was first cracked by readers. Standing with the gun still smoking, Blackmon was reminiscent of Clint Eastwood, blasting away in *"Fist Full of Dollars."*

Similar to a repeating rifle, he blasted the South with descriptions of how southern states raked in millions of dollars robbed from black victims. Blackmon blew holes in the US government and southern politicians' textbook obfuscations for poverty among descendants of American slavery. His work was so explosive, it gave Dot M. Smith's work such power, even diehard academicians fled out windows and backdoors.

Blackmon's assault broke down the wall of lie historians built to hide details about the gap in socioeconomic and political status between black and white Americas. He turned Smith's thesis into bullets that ripped through cover stories southern apologists used to stonewall her theory and findings. His rapid-fire responses sent historians scurrying back to libraries for cover. Once Blackmon became the triggerman for the millions of voiceless blacks corpora once trapped in convict leasing, he was like a bounty hunter defending the voiceless dry bones Rev. Lee prayed over.

Never having been considered relevant, the dry bones of millions of voiceless corpora, long-buried, and forgotten stories reached out from beyond the grave through Mr. Blackmon's excellent thesis. Their words were indictments, pointing their accusatory fingers at governments across the South that did the dirty deed. **_Slavery by Another Name_** tells an amazing tale of forced human bondage long after slavery ended. It describes the gruesome world of convict leasing and sharecropping in which they were imprisoned by state and local governments.

Astonishingly Blackmon, like writing an epitaph, used the words of victims and those that victimized and entrapped them in a netherworld of pain, degradation, inhumanity, and death. He blasted away all doubts about what and how it happened. So, if one refuses to believe Dot's and my assessment of events from slavery through the 1940s, one must accept eyewitnesses to the dirty deed Mr. Blackmon called to the stand.

Douglas Blackmon found his ammunition in records of white southern politicians, judges, lawmen, plantation owners, and the federal government's archives, with which he riddled their self-serving explanations. His research is the final rebuttal to Southern whites, whose words establish what, why, and how they re-enslaved African Americans for eighty years. Convict leasing and sharecropping are the—what and how—of white Southerners crimes. Blackmon published confessions straight out of the mouths of thousands of public officials. Their writing and records show they committed genocide, a crimes whites in the South admit and are convicted by their own words. They described in vivid detail what they did for eighty years to keep slavery's descendants locked in poverty, as *free labor* behind the *cotton curtain*. Blacks in the South were shackled in a genocidal system of force bondage in twentieth century America, while the **"Dark Age"** *angry white men mob madness* was in full bloom. This system began after the official end of slavery and ran nonstop until its *"Tent Cities"* demise.

Douglas Blackmon's hellish ride into the valley of dry bones began while he was the bureau chief for the Wall Street Journal's Atlanta office. He was assigned to research and writing an article about U.S. Steel Corporation and described his catharsis this way, "*Stumbling upon a graveyard filled with thousands of unmarked graves on U. S. Steel's property, left me without words. I was astonished when I stumbled upon this huge necropolis. It was a boot hill in the middle of Birmingham, Alabama. Mystified, I set out to learn the truth of this unknown graveyard. After learning government officials had knowledge of the graveyard, I learned further, bodies in those graves were convicts, U.S. Steel purchased from the City of Birmingham and the State of Alabama. Those long buried there were slave laborers for Birmingham's U.S. Steel's foundry works.*" Blackmon went on, "*I asked myself, what if American corporations (1999) were examined through the same sharp lens of historical confrontation, as German corporations that relied on Jewish slave labor in World War II and Swiss banks that robbed Holocaust victims?*"

Blackmon compared this period in the South for black Americans to the Holocaust for Jews in Germany. He connection what the United Nations (UN) refused to connect in 1951 to draw the same conclusion, when William L. Patterson and Paul Robeson presented **_We Charge Genocide._** Patterson and Robeson were first to reveal the bodies Southern genocide produced. Black Americans died in the same extraordinarily high numbers, during convict leasing and sharecropping, as Jewish worked as slave laborers. Instead of incinerating blacks and gasing them in shoulders, while robbing them, southern whites worked slave descendants to death. These times were definitely not a simple matter of white only signs, being called "nigger" or humiliated going to back doors. It was about denying black people the slightest sense of dignity, while refusing to acknowledge they bore human souls. The UN joined the culprits and helped cover up and hide it all the same as US Courts.

Completely substantiating and validating Dot Smith's thesis, Blackmon blew away any challenges regarding the appropriateness and correctness of her finding. His relentless pursuit of the truth regarding the re-enslavement scheme Southern legislatures created and perpetrated against black people, established **"We Charge Genocide,"** like a falsely accused and exonerated victim. Intrepidly, exploring these deadly times, Blackmon embarked on this dreadful task to unearth the truth, as though he was on a treasure hunter.

Douglas Blackmon was like a bloodhound, searching through records of the ***"Dark Age"*** *angry white men mob madness, convict leasing, and sharecropping eras.* He <u>uncovered the secret of how whites in the South built wealth while keeping descendants of American slavery in poverty, working for free</u>. As though prospecting for rare earth minerals, he unearthed many literary relics that brought my family's stories of survival alive in my head once again. Reading **<u>Slavery by Another Name: The Re-enslavement of Black Americans from the Civil War to WWII (2008),</u>** I could see Blackmon holding the "smoking gun," southerners historians claimed did not exist. Facing them down, Blackmon shot holes in their conventional explanations that covered over the truth of what they did to re-enslave black people, during the period from the 1880s until WWII. Investigating convict leasing in the South, Blackmon gunned down all claims that denied Dot Smith's findings. He detailed the role of government in this dastardly plot, exposing a system totally devoid of human dignity and compassion for black skin.

Courageously, Blackmon searched through the wasteland of southern history. He found the story of "how" it all began just before the 300th, "*Southern legislatures robbed black people of even the market value they had as slaves and courts were the major instruments in this devilish plan, not a refuge from tyranny.*" Courts justified, imprisoning an entire race of people—4 million—for nearly a century against their will, in the South, after emancipation and Civil War.

Mr. Blackmon was not just a sharpshooter; he was also a dedicated prospector. He did not shoot from the hip, as he unearthed a period in American history covered over by myths about the 13th Amendment, freeing American slaves. His was not a shot in the dark presenting his analysis. Blackmon took careful aim at Southern states—Alabama, Arkansas, Florida, Georgia, Kentucky, Louisiana, Mississippi, Tennessee, Texas, North, and South Carolinas—after the Civil War, as his bullseye. Unlike Dot Smith, who relied on US Labor Department statistics, Blackmon blasted these states with incontrovertible evidence from their own files and archives.

During his seven-year odyssey, Blackmon learned how and why US Steel Corporation had such an enormous number of unmarked graves of dead people, buried in its backyard. He discovered, "*A vast treasure trove of original documents and personal narratives housed in attics and basements of courthouses, old county jails, storage sheds, and local historical societies.*" Rummaging through these cemeteries of horror, while digging in archival graveyards, Blackmon unearthed tons of files that read like diaries of governors, sheriffs, judges, prosecutors, politicians, and entrepreneurs.

I believe he was not simply trying to substantiate a thesis. His goal seemed to me, was establishing a foundation that explained how black people were "legally held against their will, as the property of southern states. While at the same time, white people used their entrapment to amassed wealth and opportunities, based solely on skin color." Blackmon explains the ***"how"*** this way.

The 400th: From Slavery to Hip Hop

"Eviscerating black citizenship to rebuild the South's broken economy, whites forced former slaves and descendants to work for free, as convict laborers. Southerners created a new kind of slavery. Politicians passed laws that courts and prosecutors used to reduce black people to a condition far worse than bond slavery. Superior socioeconomic and political power allowed whites to deny blacks access to education, voting rights, and other benefits of citizenship, thereby denying them opportunities to better themselves or even fight what was happening to them. This period amounted to "decades of re-enslavement that stripped blacks of wealth and opportunities, **which accrued to whites***. This must be taken into account when assessing the damage done to African-Americans, during centuries of involuntary servitude."*

Smoother than a quick draw artist, with the gun still smoking, Blackmon cornered the South. Loading up with evidence he uncovered from their files and archives. Blackmon fired away at explanations Southerners used to obfuscations and hide the truth of convict leasing and sharecropping; what they did to re-enslaving black people! He uncovered undeniable evidence of a fee-based system used to trapped descendants of American slavery and re-enslaved them for almost ninety years, after emancipation. Showing **"how"** whites were able to enjoy unfettered access to wealth, while using their legal systems to make it impossible for blacks to compete for wealth or escape poverty, Blackmon shot holds in their claims of justice and fairness.

Slavery by Another Name detailed the smoking gun this way:

"Emerging from the Civil War, the South's economy was in ruins. For 247 years, Southern states enjoyed free labor. Their love became an addiction. Prosecutors and judges used trump up charges against blacks that drew fines, which had to be pay in cash to get out of jail or be sold to companies or plantations that paid those fines. Blacks were entrapped in a new kind of slavery, where Southern states saw incarcerating and selling hundreds of thousands of former slaves, as their right. They leased prisoners to companies or private individuals that generated mountains of revenue for state governments and private individuals. Compensated from fees charged convicts for each step in their own arrest, conviction, and shipment to private companies, sheriffs, deputies, and court officials got rich. Sheriffs also pocketed any savings from feeding prisoners as little as possible."

Blackmon established the **why** this way. Whites that joined the middle class, during the internal slave trade and breeding industry, which was destroyed by the Civil War, *"saw re-enslaving blacks in this system, as their way to reclaim their slave master heritage."* That allowed whites to reestablish and maintain their wealth-building system. Whites, made penniless by the Civil War, saw denying black people any right to live their own lives, gave them back what they called their *"God given right to make a living."*

Resourcefully locating and excavating mountains of archival records, Blackmon pieced together this amazing story. *"Following the Civil War, Southern states reconfigured their judicial systems to make them instruments of coercion, suppression and intimidation for former slaves. Whites forced African Americans to comply with social customs and their labor demands, which set the stage for the full disenfranchisement of black people throughout the South."*

Mr. Blackmon exhibited an enormous amount of scholarship, obtaining truly insightful interviews from victims that survived their captivity. Interviewing black victims snared and entrapped in convict leasing, they told of their degradation as victims of black codes—*laws that criminalized, disfranchised, and re-enslaved blacks*. Investigating these interlocking systems of racial exploitation, Blackmon showed how, through convict leasing and sharecropping, **"whites were able to amass wealth, while keeping former slaves and descendants mired in poverty."**

"Blacks were helplessly trapped in this system of peonage or forced labor for decades, many for life, if they could not pay fines in cash for trumped-up charges or petty crimes. This fee-based judicial system manufactured criminals to meet the forced labor demand of corporations, mines, lumber camps, plantations, mills, small farms and the like."

Blacks sold, as convicts, told horror stories of endless punishment, torture, and death. These stories confirmed that southerners forced over a million blacks to serving time on bogus charges in this fee-based system. Blackmon's treatise flew in the face of conventional history. It proved slavery did not end in 1865 but was dressed up in the 13th Amendment to give actions by America's courts' constitutional legitimacy.

Slavery by Another Name reflects Blackmon's evolution from a white kid, who grew up in the Mississippi Delta—the belly of the beast—into a man, *"trying to understand the legacy of Southern slavery and how after more than a century of freedom such deep disparities between blacks and whites remained."* Blackmon illuminated the South's devilish plot of re-enslavement, with amazing excursions through the underbelly of the darkest graveyards of American history, and revealed a nightmarish hell for former slaves. Blackmon put a spotlight on this murky underworld of terror, injustice, torture, pain, and death of all descriptions.

"Not hatched in backrooms or some obscure dark swamp," Blackmon explains the plot this way, *"Whites systematically used the bright halls of justice to strip and rob former slaves and descendants of the barest sense of humanity."* Now, as a result of this author's unflinching honesty, powerful research, great storytelling, and keen insight, the world is finally and fully informed of how the South, beginning in 1880 until 1960, submerged former slaves and descendants in total terror in the land of the free and the home of the brave. Blackmon's work, also fully substantiate, not only Dot Smith's thesis, but **We Charge Genocide**, as well!!

The 400th: From Slavery to Hip Hop

The US Government suborned the unthinkable terror and denial of the barest sense of humanity for African Americans. Slavery's descendants were shut off from the outside world by the *"cotton curtain,"* while suffering through some of the grimmest, most despotic, inhumane, terroristic, and psychotic shades of Apartheid, ever perpetrated against human beings. The re-enslavement of black Americans is part of the longest-running genocidal pogrom ever painted over any people in the modern course of humanity.

Douglas Blackmon painstakingly provides the ***"how"*** that, when added to Dot Smith's ***"why,"*** clearly shows convict leasing and sharecropping entrenched "white supremacy's socioeconomic dominance." Blackmon provided incontrovertible proof, answering the *"no smoking gun"* demanded by academicians, historians and politicians. This charade was a *smokescreen* by economists and government officials, demanding a *smoking gun*, was only to obscure and dismiss Smith's *chasm of inequality analysis*. The *chasm of inequality analysis* showed that poverty is a functional part of American's economy, as well as why blacks are still trapped and have never had an opportunity to escape poverty.

Douglas Blackmon made the same point this way, *"Almost as soon as the Civil War ended, powerful white politicians, plantation owners, and industrialists began re-instituting slavery through laws that "criminalized" black life. White politicians created a system; they justified with language in the 13th Amendment*—**Neither slavery nor involuntary servitude, except as a punishment for a crime whereof the party shell have been duly convicted, shell exists within the United States**. The 13th Amendment did not free slaves. Instead, it gave constitutional legitimacy to whites dastardly scheme based on word in the US Constitution ***"duly convicted persons"*** can be held as slaves, which was the whole purpose of creating trumped-up charges and fines. Although it may be hard to believe, slavery, like lynching, is still not illegal in the United States of America, because they have served as mechanisms to re-enslave black people. The whole game was to create a system that made black people criminals, which allowed them to be sold as convicts to business and private individuals as *"free labor."*

Exclusively reserved for black men, women, and children, this system made violating laws, such as *vagrancy, changing employers without permission, disturbing white females in a railroad car, , selling cotton after sunset, talking back or loudly in the presence of white women, being in town after sundown, and using abusive, obscene language towards whites* or *failure to yield the sidewalk for whites to pass* drew fines of $5 to $10 cash. This system relied on the obvious fact white people made sure black did not have cash. My grandfather was a victim in this system 60 years after my Great great-grandfather escaped a plantation around 1854.

Black people signed or made their X for purchases, until harvest time. But once ensnared in this system, those without cash to pay fines, state and county officials leased or sold to corporations, small-time entrepreneurs, and provincial farmers. Also, thousands of convicts worked off their fines in "hundreds of forced labor camps run by states and counties across the South." Many of these work farms raised cotton, which was a cash crop for those running such camps.

Alabama is a prime example of a judicial system organized to *"supplied dirt-cheap labor"* to feed the ravenous appetite of plantations, sawmills, fields, steel mills, mines, and other industries. Probing like a surgeon, Blackmon opened up a cancerous malignancy that ate away any pretense of southern humanity,

> *"Thousands of convicts died as a result of living in squalid conditions, poor medical treatment, scant food, and frequent floggings. Entries on a typical page from a 1918 state report on causes of death among leased convicts included: killed by a convict, asphyxia from an explosion, tuberculosis, pneumonia, shot by a foreman, and gangrenous appendicitis. Annual mortality rates among prisoners ranged from 3% to 25%, and these percentages are indicative of the 4,000 fatalities reported by the Alabama convict-board in 1918 alone."*

With 13 southern states deeply involved in convict leasing, allows one to extrapolate an ungodly number, like 50,000 convicts died each year (from the 1880s to the 1940s), but over the 80 years the number would be in the range of 3.5 million died across the South. One can also consider convict leasing and sharecropping was a system for culling black populations, the case of descendants of American slavery. A mind-boggling number anyway one looks at it, but nobody cared, not even the UN. These statics do not include slave descendants who died in sharecropping. There is no way to number those worked to death in cotton fields. With such death totals, if not genocide, what does one called it?

The convict leasing and sharecropping systems robbed black individuals of any value or uniqueness. If a convict was hurt, damaged, killed, or died, one simply got another, while the black convict ended up in a place like US Steel's backdoor graveyard. There wasn't any concern for the health and safety of a convict. Blackmon's perspective on history clarifies why he pursued this story.

> *"According to many conventional histories, slaves were unable to handle the emotional complexities of freedom and had been conditioned by generations of bondage to become thieves. Sympathy of whites for such victims, however brutally abused, was tempered by the belief they were criminals. Moreover, most historians concluded that the details of what really happened could not be determined."*

Once and for all, Blackmon dispelled such lies. *"In Alabama alone, hundreds of thousands of pages of public documents attest to the arrests, subsequent sale, and delivery of hundreds of thousands of African Americans to mines, mills, lumber camps, quarries, fields, farms, and factories. More than thirty thousand pages related to debt slavery cases, sit in the files of the US Department of Justice at the National Archives."*

Again, Blackmon documented how whites were able to continually accumulate wealth, while forcing black families to provide free labor and endure poverty for almost one hundred years after slavery supposedly ended.

> *"Hundreds of forced labor camps were scattered throughout the South, operated by state and county governments, large corporations, small-time entrepreneurs, and provincial farmers. These bulging slave centers became the primary weapon in the suppression of black aspirations. The Ku Klux Klan terrorized black citizens with mob violence, while the return of forced labor, as a function of government, became a pervasive fixture of African American life. These were not unavoidable events, driven by invisible forces of tradition and history. The record is replete with episodes in which public leaders faced a true choice between a path toward complete racial repression or some degree of modest civil equality, and emphatically chose the former."*

State officials supplied large blocks of black men and women—often hundreds at a time, who were state prisoners unable to pay rigged fines. Companies entered into separate deals with county sheriffs to obtain thousands more, who had been convicted of misdemeanors and likewise could not pay fines. Of the 67 counties in Alabama, 51 actively leased convicts in this way."

Mr. Blackmon reviewed the convict board's records from 1900 to 1920 in Alabama. That investigation showed Alabama's forced-labor system generated nearly $17 million for state government alone—between $225 and $285 million in today's dollars." Convict leasing and sharecropping were not small enterprises; it gobbled up black people "like a giant destructive suction machine." Not only did this allow states like Alabama to keep taxes low on white people, as part of the 2/5 that accrued to whites, there is no way to know the benefits that accrued to private individuals in all types of enterprises. The total amount of money collected from selling black prisons by counties is also unknown.

A newspaper, in Birmingham, gives an idea of what small towns could have received. Blackmon reported (1908) that *"U.S. Steel's unit in Alabama paid Jefferson County about $60,000 ($1.1 million in today's dollars) for county convicts in that year alone (1908)."* Revenues from neo-slavery poured hundreds of millions of dollars into the treasuries of Alabama, Arkansas, Georgia, Florida, Kentucky, Louisiana, Mississippi, Tennessee, Texas, North and South Carolina, as individual states. More than 75 percent of the black population in the United States lived in these states."

Giving *VOICE* to these "dry bones," long buried in the graveyard of poverty in the valley of dry bones, I thank Mr. Douglas A. Blackmon for rescuing millions of voiceless corpora from anonymity with his grand eulogy.

An Ode to Hope

Douglas A. Blackmon's brilliant work and presentation of convict leasing made its ceaseless brutality, total violence, and unsung deaths seem gratuitous for those in charge of that monstrous system. Some readers may have desired to have that explanation of convict leasing in its entirety when I first mentioned the term. Contrarily, I felt compelled to present it at a time and place where the knowledge gain would bring clarity to more than the past, as well as illuminate and highlight an unimaginable reality, where no one cared or answered cries of pain, in a world of total darkness beyond inhumanity.

Moreover, I believe discussing convict leasing earlier in this narrative would have required knowledge of many enabling social and political structures, as well as support mechanisms, without that knowledge and understanding just received, would have made convict leasing seem like just another prison story. Introducing it earlier would not have conveyed the same significance to poverty, as the previous section on wealth disparity conveyed. My point was to present the structures that helped support convict leasing, which was a vital part of the South's wealth-building mechanism for whites.

Knowledge of those support mechanisms and attending systems required, I lay a solid and strong foundation for my attack on convict leasing. The southern legal system as well as the national courts worked hand in glove to make convict leasing appear a judicious function. It made imprisoned black people in the way it was done in the South seem normal, rather than a completely different legal system from that which white people were arraigned. This system of injustice placed African Americans upon a scaffold of tyranny, no different from lynch mobs of the **Dark Age** *angry white men mob madness era.*

Following the circuitous route through convict leasing, readers learned, rather than a bar of justice, slave descendants faced kangaroo courts, which functioned, like piggy banks for state governments. My point is, readers were given information in the previous section, that if given at other times and places in this narrative, would have made some of that information seemed incidental to the true purpose of convict leasing. That purpose was to create a system that had the appearance of legality, while disguising how southern states generated wealth for white people, as during slavery, without calling it slavery.

Mr. Douglas Blackmon's research exposed southern courts, as a major part of the wealth-building structure government in the South created, while pretending it represented justice. Specifically, the system was created to help white people gain back what they claimed, as their rightful heritage. Also, losing slavery, southerners convinced themselves they had been robbed. Their logic was devoid of justice, or ethics.

The 400th: From Slavery to Hip Hop

History showed clearly that the US Constitution is not the hallowed document that protects all of it citizens equally, nor is the US Supreme Court a place where august men gather in defense of the institution of justice. But rather, the US Supreme Court is a dungeon of thieves that stole the lives of millions of black Americans, while defending and justifying the 3/5 Compromise, as a bedrock principle of America.

The education black people receive said just the opposite. As such, even black teacher when I was in school did not understand what they were teaching black children when they say **emancipation, Civil War, passages of the 13th, 14th, 15th, Amendments, Brown v. Board of Education, 1964 Civil Rights and 1965 Voting Right Acts,** made descendants of American slavery free people in America. More importantly, nor do they understand today, they are teaching a lies, plain and simple! The fact is slavery's descendants have to fight just as hard today for justice, fair courts, the right to vote, equality and fairness, as slaves that walked off plantations, after their penniless emancipation in 1863. Moreover, I defy anyone to prove this statement is a lie.

Instead of teaching such lies, which cloud the minds of slavery's descendants', regarding their true status, teachers continue perpetuating the lies they were taught. Rather than being free equal citizens, descendants of American slavery are modern-day "wage slaves" without chains, because they are still without first-class rights. Colin Kaepernick's stand makes this even clearer in a real modern-day fashion. NFL owners have tried to kill his access to America's economic system, because he demanded his right of voice. NFL owners as a group tried to kill him economically by refuse to allow him to work.

After reading the *"400th"*, it should be obvious to American slave descendants that when it comes to black people, white people are still able to ignore the US Constitution when it comes to rights former slaves were supposedly gained through all the laws and decisions mentioned above, particularly the "Civil Rights Bill of 1866." It is that very document—US Constitution—that made convict leasing possible. The Constitution allowed southern courts to victimize black people by locking them in convict leasing and share-cropping until the appearance of the cotton picking machine in the 1960s. That machine liberated black people from their sharecropping prison, not the US Constitution.

So, I offer what follows, as an ode to the hope, Dot M. Smith's and Douglas A. Blackmon's indisputable research provides the modern-day context and reality American slavery's descendants needed to understand the power of *"The 400th"*. The US Constitution and the US Supreme Court's interpretation of laws—federal, state, and local—are what black people fought getting here. They are the major malediction, responsible for why descendants of American slavery reside in poverty's grave today.

I will say again that white and black people can view or experience the same exact incident, from the same exact perspective, at the same exact time, but white people will come away, with a, totally different scenarios. White people, who have total control of all America's systems sway the scale of justice, making it a scaffold upon which the socioeconomic and political system lynch slave descendants daily.

It is clear from Smith's and Blackmon's research, government collusion, discrimination, disparate treatment, and denial of *VOICE* are their aim. These government systems or programs produced desperation, scarcity, and the hostile environment, which buried black people in the socio-economic and political graveyard of poverty.

Now that American slavery's descendants have reached ***"The 400th",*** facing COVID-19 and police murders daily, the question must be asked aloud. *"Will, leaders in the White House and the US Congress ever see black people as first-class citizens, and if so, what are they going to do to address the issues* ***"The 400th"*** *laid on the table?"* Dot Smith's and Douglas Blackmon's work has pulled the hood off of the American government's racist white supremacist face.

America's government began racism with Pres. Woodrow Wilson and J. Edgar Hoover. Those two made collusion, discrimination, disparate treatment, coercion, terrorism, and denial of *VOICE* for African Americans a government functions. Once those two scoundrels entered government in 1912, lynching and killing black men and women became entertainment for white people, like tailgate parties at NFL games.

The hope of 2020 was that someone who is just as dedicated to establish freedom, justice, and equality for all, as those that encouraged white men to kill black men and women in the streets of America because they will not bow down and accept "second class," as their place in America will stand forth. My hope is just an idea, but ideas are the most powerful force in the university.

"I See Hope," the title song of John Gary Williams' new album and documentary, expresses how hope became my prayer for life, during Dot's battle with cancer that began in 1995. Drawing courage from her valiant struggle, I looked for something to give me "hope," once she transitioned to a different reality in 2013. Working on ***"The 400th",*** which was just an idea, at that point, not even clearly conceptualized back then, but that idea grew to consume me.

Reading and thinking about the battle my ancestors wage, no matter their losses, I drew strength from their stories, as I thought of the life I had. Trying to visualize and mentally conceptualize the historical retrospective on 400 years, gave me a mission. Presenting my perspective to a world that truly needs hope more than ever, I realized hope was the wings of prayer upon which descendants of American slavery's innermost desires rode getting to ***"The 400th".*** Hope became that vision which gave me a reason to open my eyes each morning, as I tried to live through another day without Dot.

Only a thought, hope is divinely inspired, I believe. Sometimes it can lift ordinary individuals to a level where only heroes reside. It is a reservoir from which devil-may-care swashbuckling lone riders draw strength. Hope is that tiny spark, though barely visible or maybe only barely perceived mentally that sustains, during times when all else fails. It is what black people in the South called the *"magic of the **Blues**."*

What it gives an individual can be felt throughout the body, once embraced wholeheartedly. It can motive, while inspiring individuals and groups, to hold on and keep the faith, as they suffer, trying to survive incredible odds, just one more day. Hope is the source of slavery descendants' magic and can explode into unimagined possibilities. For the true believer, it is the helmet of determination, the breastplate of courage, the shield of confidence, and the sword of defiance.

All these qualities or attributes were the magic that gave enslaved Africans the will to endure to survive their arc of struggle detailed in this narrative. Following the passage of the 13th, 14th, and 15th Amendments, the idea of a black president was one such thought. Just an idea, it meandered through slavery's descendants' heads, like a reoccurring dream, but never verbalized.

Nestling in black folks' minds, like morning fog in the low country, the idea just lingered. No more than a wistful longing or childish fantasy that never really goes away, other than Abraham Lincoln, Franklin Roosevelt, and the John Kennedy/Lyndon Johnson decade, there was not much else to do.

The idea that God cared about delivering American slavery's descendants from their hellish bondage, as he did the "Children of Israel" was just an idea also. Only an idea, true enough, but deeply nestled within every groans, moans, and screams of black folks, which was their ***Blues.*** Hope was all true believers had. Imbued with self-love, they kept their prayers going up on the wings of hope for a better day for their children.

Bewailing their bitter days, they put even great hopes in their children, as they beseeched the power of the Almighty for deliverance. Nonbelievers laughed at the idea that black people could pray up a Barak H. Obama, as the audacious answer to their cries. Some say a century is but a day in the flash of God's eyes. Cries for Divine deliverance slavery's descendants' began whaling back in the 1590s, as the first enslaved Africans touch terra farma in North America, after being drag aboard slave ships leaving ***"The Door of No Return," Goreé Island, Dakar, Senegal,"***.

Arriving on the wings of hope with the new millennium, Barak H. Obama was the morning star, shining brightly from the East. His ride to the White House in 2008 was not an accident, a chance happening, or blind luck. Progressives began in the 1940s, working and hoping for just such an unbelievable answer to their forlorn prayers. Barak H. Obama may not have been what black folks and progressives were asking for, but he is what God sent.

I was there freezing, along with thousands on that cold fateful January morning. Huddled together for warmth, almost with bated breathe we waited for our hero to stand before the world. Shivering as the sun peeked over the horizon, I moved around, chasing its warmth. Bathing the scene in a golden orange glow, the sun, although bright and warning to my face, the chilly winds nippy gusts frosted it over, as it kissed my skin. The moisture from our breaths condensed so rapidly, I could hardly see Irvin's or Mitchell's faces. High school classmates at George Washington Carver High School in Memphis, Tennessee, Mitchell Brown lived in Washington D. C. He invited Irvin Grice and me to President Barak H. Obama's inauguration celebration.

Looking out over the wind-swept reflection pool on the mall between the Capitol Building and Abraham Lincoln's monument, its waters also condensed rapidly. The pool released floating clouds that drifted into the crowd, casting shadows across the vista. The misty orange and black floating bellows enveloped the scene in its striped aurora.

The steamy condensation against the sun's rays, breaking through the trees, gave the scene a surreal reddish blush. Framed by trees lining the mall, the view reminded me of locomotives on cold mornings, waiting in line, at the Illinois Central Railroad (ICR) yard behind our house in Greens Alley, as a kid.

We came down early on the first train at 5 AM, for the inaugural and parade scheduled for noon, but had arrived too late to get a hoped-for place with a close-up view of the proceedings. Some true believers, on this very frigid January morning, had camped out overnight in temperatures that dropped to 14 below in the early morning hours, but they stayed on. Days in advance, some true believers staked out locations, trading places, like work shifts, trying to hold on to their hoped-for vantage point.

Estimates of the crowd went as high as a million adoring supporters, all prancing to keep warm, while waiting and watching for the unfolding of history in the making. People came from around the world to see and experience an event, I believed, no one, definitely not my 88-year-old mother, truly thought she would ever see.

During this surreal experience on that historic morning, my thoughts went back 556 years to the slave pens at ***"The Door of No Return," Goreé Island, Dakar, Senegal***, enslaved African left never to return. Once the proceeding began, watching president-to-be Barak Obama take the oath of office, I felt centuries of humiliation and degradation go down, as his hand went up.

Walking down Pennsylvania Avenue, each step The President took seemed to be an extension of the first footprints made by that first enslaved African coming off a slave ship on North America's shores. Those steps led to the nightmare of slavery in America for kidnapped Africans. As Pres. Obama and First Lady Michelle advanced toward the White House, at times it was as though a fleeting specter flashed, reminding me of that last day at the Lorraine Motel (4-4-68), as I listened to the hopes of Dr. Martin Luther King, Jr. for his ***Poor People's Campaign.*** Simultaneously, it was as if I heard Rev. Lee's words explaining why he took such changes with his life;

"The role of intrepid circuit riders wasn't only delivering spiritual consolation and guidance, but lifesaving information to far-flung communities in treacherous swamps, isolated glades and desolate stretches of nowhere. Circuit riders were lifelines, connecting marooned pockets of black families out of touch with the world in most cases. We delivered letters, messages and warnings when paddy roller rampaged through a state. I was armed with only my faith and guided by prayers. I trusted God to see me through."

I envisioned Pres. Obama, through his administration, daring to wage, such a one-man battles against conservatives, who were relentless in efforts to stop anything attempted, that advance slave descendants, while pushing their draconian measures. During such times, the hope was that Mr. Obama would believe, as Rev. Lee, *"I was armed with only my faith and guided by prayers. I trusted God to see me through."* For me, President Obama fulfilled David Walker's hope, as he penned his **_Appeal._** Mr. Obama also answered the called for the new kind of leadership Paul Roberson and William Patterson sent up delivering **_We Charge Genocide_** to the UN and the world.

The 2008 financial crisis put The President's back against the wall before he ever raised his hand, taking the oath of office. I saw in him as an intrepid lone rider fighting racism, discrimination, and disparate treatment leftover from American slavery. It would take the kind of resolve black people adored in Mohammed Ali, for Pres. Obama to keep the hard-won ground conservatives have fought to take back since **_Brown v. Board of Education (1954)._**

Shivering on that frozen morning, after hours exposed to the gelid gusts, however, the warm feeling on the inside, I gained looking out over the sea of humanity, stemmed the ache of my ears, hands, and feet. The massive gathering was of all types and colors, children and old folks, all standing shoulder to shoulder, smashed together, while being swept along by the massive parade. Some were even brave enough to face the wind's vicious bite high in the leafless trees. They had to see with their own eyes, if but only a glimpse of the first black man to be sworn in as President of the United States of America, beginning his tour. Unlike the morning in Memphis (3-28-1968) watching the throng of marchers in the huge turnout we produced, I was at a loss for words to explain how this one came together. Maybe back during the campaign something moved people, like the warm glow I felt on the inside at that freezing moment, like **_Blues_** magic, had gone out across the nation, thawing the frozen hopes, slave descendants had nursed nearly 389 years (1619-2008).

Possibly progressives standing up for right and trying to live out the true meaning and hope of America's creed—*freedom, justice, and equality for all*—became a real force that connected people of goodwill. And as such, we are bound by love across the centuries, which connected human beings with a line that bounded slave descendants and slave masters from 1619 to **_"The 400th"._**

Already under fire from conservatives plotting to block his every move, while planning his downfall, I heard a tongue as sharp as Malcolm X's and saw stands as audacious as Dr. Martin Luther King, Jr.'s in the 1960s, throughout the eight years Pres. Obama serviced America. He was progressives only champion—our Sir Lancelot. African Americans' audacity to continue hoping, even against hope, but on that frosty morn, we saw Barak H. Obama bloomed like a rose in winter. Flowering, he brought progressives to within sight of *"The 400th"* (2020), where now they can do more than hope, they can act.

"The 400th" will give everyone a look back down that dark and hideous road of pain and death of slavery, white supremacy, the *"Dark Age"* *white men mob madness,* which brought us here. It is clear that Pres. Obama's true impact and legacy will not be known for years. But, if this narrative has shown anything, as it presented the history of enslaved Africans, in most cases, actions and decisions taken at one point follow a society or nation into the future. A situation may be like slavery, even after 555 years passed, it continues to impact its descendants in ways that were impossible to calculate or imagine when Pope Nicholas V issued the **Dum Diversas**.

It is impossible to know what will grow from seeds plant today and what those seeds will yield tomorrow. On some distant sunrise, as this day, when decisions and actions called forth by time and events, as has happened, during my lifetime, who will step forth as a devil-may-care swashbuckling lone rider?

Again sometimes, as with slavery, my hope that, as times in the past, the self-love that made this narrative a love story, descendants of American slavery will re-affirm their decision to make families and build communities, as their best survival strategy. But, changes over time can make decision made keys to a new kind of survival, like the first Burl Lee was for my family. However, unimagined, as well as unintended consequences from actions and decisions can reverse fortunes and conditions that change hopelessness into hope, and little-noticed events or situations can become crucial to humanity's prosperity and survival. I think about how Divine intervention in the form of a stolen gas cap changed my life and gave me this ode I sing of hope for descendants of American slavery!!!!!!!!!!!!

LET US NOT FORGET
By Ray Moore

America at its very inception began with deception.
1787 a document of protection meant for
citizens of the fair complexion.
Wrote in Philly at a convention.

LET US NOT FORGET to Mention.

The 400th: From Slavery to Hip Hop

No black man helped write this constitution,
a document full
of amendments and institutional solutions.
A group excluded with No proper power distribution.
They tried with Reconstruction.
The Klan was started, and they stopped that resolution.
 A white resistance with no Feds another point in human
 hate.
Blacks wanted to live along side and not take their place.
The laws said change but hate wanted no part of it.

LET US NOT FORGET
The crack of the whip the screams and the pain as flesh it
slits.
Work harder nigger. Come here let me rape you bitch.
Whip crack whip, until more flesh splits.

LET US NOT FORGET
Harriet Tubman, Frederick Douglas and Nat Turner just to
name a few.
Revolted and fought against oppression to gain justice for
me and you.
Humanity continues on a shameful past.

LET US NOT FORGET
The Human pinnacle seems to be profit for the capital
class.
Ham called it a curse. I say it's a flaw to find justification for
the colonial enterprise that is still being upheld today by
modern law.

LET US NOT FORGET
Scottsboro, Emmit Till, Judge Edward Aaron, King
Johnson, The Rosewood massacre, William Burns, Hazel
Turner, Mary Turner, Jamar Clark, Mike Brown, Keith
Scott, Tamir Rice and hundreds more are on a death list
that should not even exist.

LET US NOT FORGET
We had a Silent Parade they have a silent crusade of
Genocide
through a racist institutional plague.

Why pledge allegiance to a piece of cloth and the law.
Pledge allegiance to humanity a cause for applaud.

LET US NOT FORGET
it's a shame that in 2020 we still have to protest this shit.
LET US NOT FORGET

The Past Became the Present

I've said before, leaving slavery did not mean slaves could leave it behind. That statement is as true for descendants of American slavery today as back then; leaving the fight to end legal racism, segregation, white supremacy, convict leasing, and sharecropping did not mean black Americans left them behind. Currently, these dreaded outcomes, in the person of Donald Trump, racism, segregation, discrimination and white supremacy are openly staring all Americans in the face, as a choice. They are like fish in water, it's everywhere, so many Americans do not know they're wet.

The previous sections showed all the problems of slavery are still with slavery's descendants today, as they are still trapped in the valley of dry bones in the grave of poverty, the only difference is, we do not have Rev. Lee to pray over us. America's *"cheap labor"* strategy has produced the wealth gap and continue denying enslaved Africans VOICE, which began with slavery—**The Trans-Atlantic Slave Trade** (sic1452)—which lasted, not only through emancipation (1863), but into the 20th century. Dot Smith's, Douglas Blackmon's and my research supports the fact that governments—federal, state, and local—are the culprits that maintained slavery's descendants in poverty as Dr. Martin Luther King, Jr pointed out with his accusatory finger—**"People's Campaign"** in 1968.

I became involved with Dr. King's thesis when the *Invaders* joined his last dream—the **"Poor People's Campaign."** Dr. King's talk, with Cab and me about his plans, during his last hours, opened my eyes to the role of government, as the source of poverty among black Americans, even today. Before I discuss what it means to be where we are, the role of government getting here needs to be clearified. Descendants of American slavery began with their penniless emancipation, which extended the poverty they endured during bondage into their supposed freedom, which government actions compounded even further. The US federal government brought millions of European immigrants to America, during *"The Gilded Age"* to fill good-paying job it would not allow its former slaves to fill. US Supreme Court compounded former slaves' penniless emancipation, adding institutional racism, discrimination and disparate treatment through **Plessy v Ferguson**. The US Supreme Court became the protector of white culprits from their black victims, while efforts to change their 3/5 second class status. It nullifying the **Civil Rights Act of 1866, 13th, 14th, and 15 Amendments** with **Plessy v. Ferguson**—*separate but equal* to enshrined former slaves' 3/5 less than human status.

It laid the foundation for Pres. Woodrow Wilson, who introduce "mob rule" with the **"Dark Age" angry white men mob madness.** Wilson used that terror-ridden era to entrench discrimination and disparate treatment to reinforce segregation and white supremacy as government policies.

William L. Patterson and Paul Robeson's took their desperate gamble **_We Charge Genocide,_** to the UN to challenge the US government's pogrom, which kept slavery's descendants locked on the bottom of America's *"cheap labor"* capitalistic economy. Coalitions of black radicals and young progressivists fought to make the promises of **Brown v. Board of Education** real change and reality in the lives of black people. Their fight ignited the civil rights and black power eras. Enter Dot Smith with her *chasm of inequality analysis* exposing America's pretense of freedom, justice, and equality, as a false face, hiding its genocide. However, it took Douglas A. Blackmon's thesis, **_Slavery by Another Name: The Re-enslavement of Black Americans from Civil War to WWII_**, as the final rebuttal in this lengthy summation to conclusively showthe past has become the future.

However, the fact that Douglas Blackmon is a white man makes his rebuttal as the final as the final witness, such a powerful statement. His statement indicates he saw poverty and responded to it much like Dr. King. Similarly, Blackmon had a good living, working for a prestigious publication—the Wall Street Journal. He enjoyed professional recognition and public acclaim. But what spoke loudest for me, reflected a white man, with nothing to gain, when he drew his "smoking gun" on the South, except knowing the truth existed. Blackmon took up a challenge that could have cost him all of his success, stability, and recognition.

Nevertheless, Blackmon pressed on with an investigation in which only he saw truth worthy of such a risk: *"Truth forever on the scaffold, wrong forever on the throne!"* Descendants of American slavery not only wanted but needed a crusader for right and truth, as his thesis revealed. I believe, if truth served as a guide for the US government, **_Slavery by Another Name: The Re-enslavement of Black Americans from Civil War to WWII (2008)_** would have convinced America's leaders to pave over the valley of dry bones, which would have made the grave of poverty an express lane to equality and justice for its descendants of American slavery. That action would have ended the longest-running instance of genocide in the history of the modern world. But it did not, which is what it means to be here in 2021.

Being here today means the long lengthy rebuttal I just rehearsed is not the past, but an ever present reality, facing the next generation of descendants of American slavery. This means my grandchildren are face the same prospects I faced, looking out my grandparents' backdoor at cotton fields, as "cheap labor"—wage slaves—in 2030 when the last one graduates from college. The question is where is the **HOPE???**

Learned Helplessness: The Why of American Terror

Although the physical reality I saw, looking out my grandparents backdoor, changed for me over time, my prospects in life remained a battle for relevance, trying to reflect my potential. This battle is to establish a consistency between what is on the inside with what is on the outside to the world black descendants of American slavery face in their moment to moment existence, which white people refuse to recognize, acknowledge and accept. This reality leaves me with the choice of pretending not to see what is before my eyes or teaching my grandchildren what I taught young Invaders, during the sanitation strike.

Learned Helplessness, make the past far more than a commentary, reflects the present, and makes "The 400th" the launching path of the future. Leaving slavery, I repeat once more, did not mean it could be left behind!!!! That statement makes my next discussion an imperative. Readers must keep in mind that slave masters forced enslaved Africans to think only about what they wanted and their behaveior reflect their willingness to serve white people.

Nothing about slaves' behaviors or their thought pattern was naturally theirs. Slave masters forced upon slaves everything they said or did openly, as the learned behaviors slave masters desired. White people re-enforced slave's mindset and behaviors for their convenience. Slaves were not afforded adjustment or reprogramming time following slavery's end, nor were they given time to assimilate new thoughts and behavior patterns, once emancipation gave them what white people called freedom.

Proposing to commemorate and celebrate **"The 400th"**, one may ask, after reading this far, *"What is there to commemorate and celebrate for a people, who were made into slaves and still mired in poverty?"* We celebrate not just the love story of slavery's descendants' survival—why we are still here—but we offer the following question, *"How did America's slavery descendants, a people who were kidnapped from all over the western coast of Africa, unknown to each other or maybe were enemies, before being forced aboard slave ships, become one people?* That journey for slaves began as, *"A desperate voyage in treacherous tempest-tossed waters, chained and locked in the hole of a leaky ship. With water pouring in upon them, slaves drowned even though the ship did not sink".* I reiterate this point because so many did not survive that horrific first challenge.

The tragedy of kidnapping traumatized slave before they were dragged aboard slaves ships. Kidnapped slaves had to survive that voyage only to encounter and endure an even greater horrifying existence. For those that survived the horrid journey, *only unending servitude awaited them and their descendants, as kidnapped souls*. Enduring and surviving desperation and scarcity, is a socio-economic and political reality mere words cannot describe. They faced, endured, and survived conditions no other people have ever been subjected. Surviving slavery's horrors, slaves created the amazing and inspiring love story I have presented here. Their epic love story is one for the ages and it engendered only greater love by those who got us here. Recognizing that it is a love story, in and of itself, is more than enough reason to commemorate and celebrate *"The 400th"*.

The self-love story slaves carried with them across the *"Middle Passage"* is the saga of people who fell in love with being themselves and were willing to brave the most incredible odds, holding on to their idea of who they are. That is what we commemorate. Their love was so powerful, even after being terrorized, traumatized and driven for four centuries; their love binded them to one another, creating a people that had not existed before the **Trans-Atlantic Slave Trade**.

Over the *"The 400th"*, white people in America witnessed the evolution of a new people being created before their very eyes, yet blinded by racism, they missed this natural phenomenon happening in real times. Enslaved Africans were forced to be the foundation of white people's survival and their road to wealth in America. Unlike white people, enslaved Africans learned to survive on their own.

Again, slave descendants did not ride the backs of another people, they learned to survive, as a result of their efforts. Instead, white people became dependent, addicted to slavery, discrimination, disparate treatment, torture and terrorizing slavery's descendants, as a way of life. Today, slave masters are still hopelessly tied to a mindset of dependency, depriving enslaved Africans of all humane considerations to maintain their affluent lifestyle, riding the backs of black people.

Kidnapped and shanghaied off to North America, enslaved Africans suffered through an excruciatingly painful and grueling indoctrination that made them into a commodity. For that to happen, slaves had to be made to accept be property, owned by another person. Slave masters used a horrific regime of terror, pain, anxiety, desperation, scarity and fear of death to control slaves' minds. The process of gaining control of slaves' minds required excruciating misery, painful and degrading regimentation that reinforcement the will and desires of slave masters. Slave masters produced a total dependence mindset, using a process so brutally, degrading and terroristic, I believe, some slaves literally trembled when thoughts of defying white people entered their heads.

The indoctrination regime of enslaved Africans is what readers have slogged through getting to this point in this narrative. What drove my research was the desire to learn and understand "why black people behave and think as they do?" I got on the right track accidentally when I encountered the subject or concept I believe most African Americans are unfamiliar or are completely ignorant. I will say even most white Americans are no better off, ever though it is their legacy. Here I refer to the concept of *"learned helplessness."* Have you ever heard a black person say, *"White folks know stuff about black people that they don't even know?"*

But, they never offer a representative example of what they are referring. Once I present the following discussion, you will understand why?

Readers may feel I should have explained this regime, at the very beginning of the internal slave trade and breeding, if not before. However, like convict leasing, I wanted readers to maintain all their skepticism, doubts, and maybe even outright reject my argument and bring their doubts with them to this point. Explaining the what, why, and how white people made free Africans, they kidnapped and shanghaied to North America into slaves that still generate wealth for them today, requires real patience.

Only after reaching this point, as a reader, do I feel you deserve the reward of your persistence and patience, continuing to read in order to learn what you will going forward. It is only after such a convoluted, tortuous, even laborious slog through some topic, are you able to truly appreciate your effort getting here. What you learned during that slog is why I've delayed introducing this topic. Had I introduced this topic before now, you would have received the answer to the question before it was asked. That knowledge may have even caused undue confusion. So, I ask it now without any concern for losing or confusing readers. Have you ever heard of the term *"learned helplessness"*?

I was, as most readers now, when I first encountered the term, totally ignorant of it. *"Learned helplessness"* was the indoctrination process white people used that create slaves' mindset. This circuitous journey began when I encountered a pamphlet entitled **How to Make a Slave,** by Willie Lynch in the 1970s. Admittedly, it could have been an urban legend passed around the ghetto. However, reading it, faint thoughts or images, like sparks, began flickering, so to speak, in my mind, as I read it. I understood that during the annals of slavery in the Western Hemisphere in general, but in America specifically, anything was possible when it came to slavery and white people, so I investigated. According to this pamphlet back in the 1700s, Lynch was a noted practitioner of what he claimed was *"the best way to break the spirit or will of defiant Africans and make them obedient slaves."* His sales pitch was, *"If you (slave masters) used this system fifty years, your slaves will be tame, obedient, and docile for <u>three hundred years</u>."*

The pamphlet contained a vivid example of Lynch's classic technique for breaking the will of human beings' and turning defiant slaves into loyal and subservient slaves. Lynch's regiment began with *"putting the fear of God into niggers."* The pamphlet described Lynch's method this way, *"Gather all your niggers together, making sure all women and children are present. Bring out the offending or most vocal and rambunctious slave. Tie him between two horses pointed in opposite directions. Then put the whip to the horses."*

With that example, Lynch created a very visually, ghastly, and traumatic spectacle that slaves could not forget. Terrified at the sight of a body being torn apart, as the horses try to run, was beyond shocking and frightful. Agonizing screams from the victim, as blood oozed, then gushed from the torn body was a scene that became etched, like a tapestry of terror and total gruesomeness, on the brains of slaves, witnessing Lynch's spectacle. All the while, white bystanders cheered and screamed with delight, as though being entertained.

The sight of cowing slaves empowered whites. Lynch continued, *"Bring out the next most defiant nigger. Strip him down, then beat him within an inch of his life. Never kill that slave,* Lynch admonished. *"Just make him plead and beg to die, to end his pain."* The screams and cracks of the whip against the skin on each stripe, exploded in the ears and minds of slaves, witnessing the horrible torture.

Those lashes, I believe, created impressions on the brains of slaves similar to stripes on that slave's body. Further, the experience became imbedded, like grooves that transported the fears and anxiety of slaves deep within their subconscious emotional being. The death of one slave, while the screams for mercy of the other, became memories, like master inside slaves heads, monitoring their every thought.

Psychologically, this experience became an outcome for any slave, if ever they dared transgress master's will. Those memories remain within their brains, like a spy, poised to spring forth, whenever thoughts of defying white people arose. Lynch allowed the second slave to live. *"Let him live, so he will be a living example and reminder of what happens to any nigger that thinks of rising up against white people."*

Willie Lynch's legend exemplifies the horrific and painful way slaves were trained and regimented, if slave masters used Lynch's demonstration. This process created a *"residual self-image"* for slaves, like a white man inside slaves' heads. Using Lynch in this manner to make my point drew criticism from those who felt such an "urban legend" cheapens the real-life horrors slaves endured. Critics, like former University of Georgia, Prof. Reginald L. Moss offer Josiah Henson, as the real slave's life, the Willie Lynch legend is based. Critics claimed, as Josiah did also, Harriet Beecher Stowe's novel **Uncle Tom's Cabin** *(1852),* plagiarized his life's story **The Life of Josiah Henson, Formerly a Slave, Now an Inhabitant of Canada, as Narrated by Himself.**

Henson's book was first published in 1849, four years before Harriet Beecher Stowe's novel, <u>Uncle Tom's Cabin</u> *(1852).* Josiah's father was a victim of such a horrible and terrifying punishment, and those thoughts prevented him from escaping slavery earlier in life. According to Henson, his fears motivated him to keep other slaves from running off when he was transporting a group of slaves through Ohio, a free state. Henson said, *"My feelings of loyalty were so powerful that when I was in Ohio, a free state, I convinced slaves, I was transporting, not to remain there, as free men, but return to bondage with me ."*

Josiah was a preacher; he confused loyalty with fear. His slave programming held such power over him; his fears restrained him from acting against his master, which was the point of Lynch's programing. Whether the controversy is true or not, regarding Willie Lynch, the important fact is Josiah's story is definitely real. Both stories center on the horrific torture and terror used to train slaves. This excruciating, beastly, and grisly training process was a living nightmare slaves endured. As such, it is easy for me to see the saga of Josiah Henson, as the basis of the Willie Lynch legend.

Lynch's version presents the story from a slave master's perspective, as Harriet Beecher Stowe's novel <u>Uncle Tom's Cabin</u> *(1852)*. On the other hand, Josiah Henson's narrative is the bottom-up view of a slave. It speaks not only of the physical pain, torture, and terror that consumed Africans once slave masters made them into slaves, but the psychological dilemma that their slave acculturation imposed on them.

There may not be any saving grace for Henson, who convinced people like him to remain, slaves while he escapes slavery later and reach Canada, following the *Underground Railroad*. However, there is no record detailing what happened to those Josiah convinced to remain slaves, similar to civil rights leaders today.

I became acquainted with such fear, moving from urban legend to my factual research. While in graduate school, reading research reports, I came to understand the power of the slave masters' indoctrination regime. I was a graduate student in the Department of Psychology at Memphis State University (now University of Memphis) when I was introduced to the concept of *"learned helplessness"* by Dr. Frank Leeming. I was ignorant of the concept, so here, I provide a quick and dirty explanation of *"learned helplessness"* for those unfamiliar with the term.

Psychologist Martin Seligman pioneered the concept. He was studying depression in humans when he developed the *learned helplessness* paradigm (1967). During *learned helplessness* training, researchers placed animals (basically rats) in cages with electrified grids, for floors. Researchers administer painful electric shocks, which the animal cannot avoid. Shocking subjects (rats) repeatedly, subjects attempt to escape the pain but learn their behavior has no control over shock occurrence or duration.

Convinced, nothing they do will terminate their agony (shock) rats eventually cease struggling against what they can not affect. At that point, rats helplessly endure shocks. They become immobile, excepting the pain of shock for whatever duration administered. The key here is **unavoidable pain** (shock). Researchers want to achieve a state called ***"total lack of control."*** Once ***"total lack of control"*** is achieved, researchers can train the submissive subjects (rat) to exhibit some bizarre behaviors. From that point forward subject's behavioral repertoire will include responses shaped by the researcher. A rat's response is called the subject's response sequence or ***"residual self-image."***

"Total lack of control" allowed researchers to use pain (shocks) to shape the animal's behavior. Researchers trained subjects to perform exotic behaviors, not normally part of an animal's behavioral repertoire. When first introduced to this concept by Prof. Leeming, I was very skeptical. Naively, like most people, I believed animals, especially humans, would continue struggling in such situations until death, trying free themselves from such pain and terror. Animals are adaptive.

My problem at that point was I felt I had not returned to school to spend my time running and training rats. This research had nothing to do with "why black people "think and act," as they do. I wanted to learn why humans behaved as they do, not rats or other creatures.

However, I must digress for a bit at this point. My wife, who returned to school, after extracting a promise that I would follow her, as soon as our son Yohannes was old enough to attend daycare. I had attended LeMoyne College in Memphis in 1971. Dot and I met during the height of the black power movement. Back then, I went back to school, not as a student but felt I was there to teach black student liberation philosophy and psychology. Black power activists at HBCU taught black student activism.

I returned to school at Dot's continued insistence, and because I never wanted to disappoint her, I transferred to Memphis State. Complying, she supported me, and helped me develop solid research techniques and habits. I graduated *Magna* cum laude (375 avg.), with honors in psychology and was a Milton C. Addington Award recipient as *"top student in psychology"* in 1980.

Over the summer, Dot encouraged me to apply and helped me write a grant application to the National Science Foundation. I was awarded a four-year grant based on my honor's thesis, which I will not discuss here. So, I felt greatness awaited me, but I had become disappointed with my training, as I said, "I did not return to school to run rats." Impatient with my regular studies and running rats in mazes seemed to be going any place.

I will admit today, choosing the field of psychology had been an emotional choice. I knew almost nothing about how the field worked. I had only a vague notion of what psychologists did. Once in graduate school, I was the only black student, so things did not improve. I selected psychology as my major because, while in prison, I worked with a psychologist, Dr. Martin Kindigg, who used behavior modification techniques, and cognitive psychology, as part of his rehabilitation regime with inmates. His research impressed me.

Although, I did not understand the theories behind any of these paradigms, intuitively I could see he believed what I hoped to do, which was to change black people's behaviors. Working with him is what hooked me on psychology. What I thought I knew about psychology but never thought about was laden with myths about mind control or manipulating the mind in some mystical way. Other than Dr. Kindigg, the only psychologists I met were instructors. I was unfamiliar with the esoteric knowledge, procedures, principles, and rituals that determined success in the field.

My hope in choosing psychology, as a field of study, was to find clues that explained why descendants of American slavery thought and behaved as they did. I thought if I dug deep enough and learned those mind tricks, I could help black people elude the open grave of poverty and escape the valley of dry bones. My dilemma was somewhat reminiscent of the scarecrow in the *"WIZ."*

Somehow, somewhere deep within the recesses of my mind, I was sure the answer to the dilemma concerning black people and poverty resided in their minds. I believed, without proof, but somehow, it had to do with their lack of knowledge about what happened to them, during slavery. Although I had no way to prove it, intuitively I believed, it had to do with what, how, and why slave descendants thought, as they did.

Working with Dr. Dr. Leeming on his "learned helplessness experiment, because he needed an assistant and I hoped to learn the magic of the mind. Getting up to speed and to prepare for his class, I began reading research reports in this area, which described research techniques for training subjects (rats). Basically, running rats in mazes and shocking them to get the correct responses. Sometimes subjects (rats), during training would stand not moving, trembling, simply shivering until they keel over. Sometimes their paws and fur caught fire. Involuntary muscle spasms cause their bodies to twitch and jump, while lying helplessly on the electric grid, sometimes before current was terminated. It was very difficult to read such reports. I imagined, at times, what that must have been like to watch and do daily.

After being introduced to *"learned helplessness"* in undergrad school, I also remembered the Willie Lynch's legend. The concept of *learned helplessness* took me in a totally different direction from the alcohol addiction paradigm of Dr. Leeming was trying to create. The intriguing thing about the *"learned helplessness"* paradigm, for me, was the reactions of subjects (rats) to extremely aversive stimuli, which modify the subject's behavior. Essentially, whether the Willie Lynch character existed or not is unimportant. The important fact is the technique attributed to him could very well have been the same as psychologist Martin Seligman's regime.

Lynch did not have the power of an electrified grid to create the level of pain, Seligman used to train rats, but he did have terror, and that was the key. Suddenly, the light came on and stayed on for me this time, no flickering sparks! This time I began thinking maybe, terror was why slaves and descendants act as they did. I know after all my explanation, this sounds fairly obvious today.

But back in 1981, this was ground breaking for me. I was not working in an environment, like Simi Valley California's computer hub. I was in the heart of the South, the only black student with a full ride through graduate school, in his own right. But however, I was dependent on white professors to open up the field to me or I would fall flat on my face. A note here, about what black teachers tell black children about slavery is very benign. If they know the real truth, they have bought into the slave survival strategy. They avoid the harsh and brutal aspects, like the terror that still controls black people's lives.

Terror has been a real factor in slaves' lives, since the first captive slavers was kidnapped and shanghaied off to America. They endured—merciless beatings, raped repeatedly (women, men, and children), tortured, degraded, and lynched; you name it. Seligman's electrified grid and techniques seemed to mimic and obtain the same effect, as Willie Lynch's horse demonstration. Seligman had to find a means of creating Lynch's system of pain.

Slaves were synonymous to rats on electrified grids. Shocks exposed rats to extreme pain, similar to Lynch's technique. Extremely aversive or punishing stimuli introduced **"unavoidable pain"** that produced **"total lack of control."** I remembered the novel ROOTS, and the slave Kunta Kinte's master beating him unmercifully to force him to accept the name he gave him. It was only after severe torture and punishment did Kunta submitted and repeated the name "Toby master Toby." Even today, that scene, more than any other, in the entire movie and book, has remained the most salient for me. ("*Roots: The Saga of an American Family.*" Alex Haley, 2016, Hachette Books)

However, one day, while reading and thinking about rats being shocked by researchers. Imagining one keeling over, as its body bounced on the grid, I had an epiphany. Vicariously, the whole concept of *learned helplessness* came to me, while thinking about a rats getting shocked, the torture sequence made a connection. I understood what happened to black people, like Kunta Kinte, extreme torture made him a compliant slave. I imagined the reaction of slaves watching the gruesome scene of one of their own being tortured, torn apart and killed. Suddenly, the tortured terrorized rat scene, I was imagining, changed, I no longer saw a rat bouncing around on the electric grid. I saw a black man, a slave.

The scene seemed to connect me in a very real way to the reality slaves endured. I realized slave masters were modifying slaves' behaviors using terror, pain, and torture. Behavior modification is how slave masters created obedient slaves.' They changed slaves' *"residual self-image."* A slave (he or she), trying to avoid or reduce pain, terror, and torture, became willing to do or say whatever whites demanded.

Slaves, after emancipation, were turned out, with their *"learned helplessness"* fully intact. Slaves did not receive an adjustment period of de-programming or time to throw off their slave acculturation. Their *"learned helplessness"* remained buried deep within their psyche, controlling their responses to white people, without them even knowing it, in most cases. This was my main purpose and idea behind including slave narrative, so readers could hear from slaves in their own words and learn what happened to them.

The historical arc of this narrative has established the fact that slaves experienced **"unavoidable pain"** and **"total lack of control."** Slaves were arbitrarily punished and had absolutely no control over any aspect of their lives. Slavery's terror, lynching, rape, convict leasing, and sharecropping became extensions of former slaves' *"learned helplessness"* regime.

The 400th: From Slavery to Hip Hop

For former slaves, even though they had no idea what was happening, white people's power over slavery's descendants, was the same as electric shocks. *"Learned helplessness"* is why slavery never ended. Moreover, Willie Lynch said, *"If you (slave masters) used this system for fifty years, your slaves would be servile, tame, obedient, and docile for <u>three hundred years</u>."*

Today, the brutal treatment by police has a real purpose. It helps to maintain and re-enforce *"learned helplessness"* among descendants of American slavery. *"Learned helplessness"* doest affect other people, who did not endure the residual impact of slavery. American slavery's descendants are the only people put through this horrifically painful process for 400 years. Even more pertinent, *"learned helplessness,"* is not mentioned in the education of black children. Black children are not taught in school what really happened to enslaved Africans during slavery.

Slavery, as a subject presented, as a massive topic, so code words and images permeate the topic, which helps gloss over its importance. Teachers are unaware how, what and why white people used *learned helplessness* to control black people. White people are continually trying to modified and manipulate black people fears in ways they do not realize or understand.

If one's learn helplessness is still firmly intact, you are convinced your responses to white people are your idea. Descendants of American slavery were continually shaped and manipulated by *"learned helplessness,"* so much so, such responses seem natural, they even fight to hold on to certain behaviors, without questioning why, they respond as they do. Decisions black people believe are choices; in many cases, are ideas planted deep within their subconscious and are triggered by statements, suggestions or actions of white people. Auto-suggestion is another form of conditioning or programming of the subconscious mind—behavior modification.

The *"learned helplessness"* paradigm and regimen trained black people to be the people they are today, unless they have consciously tried to reconstruct their mental processes. Black power happened for me and many other young black radicals that became activists. Black people are still fighting to free themselves of what they do not understand. Black power negated the involuntary responses to slaves masters suggestions, which were created with terror—anxiety, desperation, and scarcity.

Self-confidence and determination to show one's blackness in every way, awakens black people's defiant spirit. The legacy of slavery operates so subtly in the heads of descendants of American slavery, even after 154 years (Lynch predicted 300 years) of freedom, slaves and descendants still have not broken free of the terror of *learned helplessness*. Mainly black people are unaware of *"learned helplessness,"* so they continue their susceptibility and re-enforce their *learned helplessness* segregations from the larger society, totally unbeknownst to them, as black victim.

The trick of *learned helplessness* resides in the power and sequencing of punishment. The scientist turning on and off shocks is how subjects are led to the object of desire, as seen from the subject's perspective, but the scientist has a different objective in mind. The scientist wants to lead the horse (subject) to water, and the <u>horse drinks "willingly," as though it is its idea</u>. I believe familiarly *learned helplessness* is passed from generation to generation, like DNA. Why else would Lynch say "300" years, 5 lifetimes for a slave.

No different, in effect, from the electrified grid of *learned helplessness,* such re-enforcement, as police brutality and murder, haunt slave descendants today, the same way as Josiah Henson's ghosts terrorized him. He not only led slaves back into slavery but he gave up his chance for freedom also. Josiah returned voluntarily, submitting to his misguided sense of loyalty.

That dilemma reflects the power and trick of *"learned helplessness."* For instance, Negro leaders that were supposedly supporting Marcus Garvey, Malcolm X, and Dr. Martin Luther King, Jr. allowed J. Edgar Hoover to activate or trigger their *learned helplessness,* and they became his lackeys. They believed helping Hoover would free black people; instead, they were like Josiah Henson helping to keep slaves in bondage.

Today, the chains of slavery are on black people's minds—*learned helplessness.* The shackles of slavery are on the brains of slave descendants. The terroristic scene of Josiah's father and millions of other slaves became like an electrified grid to mothers, who vicariously experienced the agonizing punishment. Inwardly, I believe, such scenes have traveled through history until today and are part of descendants of American slavery's *"residual self-image."* Mothers terrorized by scenes in today's urban existence, vow to teach their children to be submissive and subservient for safety's sake. Think of mothers' and fathers' reactions to murders like Trayvon Martin, Michael Brown, George Floyd, Ahmaud Arbery, Breonna Taylor, the nine members of the Emanuel African Methodist Episcopal Church in Charleston, South Carolina and on and on, so many others. Murdered while praying, they serve as classic examples of the research I present, remember the aim of white people is to *"lead the horse to water and the <u>horse drinks "willingly," as though it is its idea</u>.*

Were such incidents shocking to you? Did the incident lead you to act and think aggressively about doing something, or were you resigned to your anxiety? Such instances are synonymous with *learned helplessness* experiments. *Learned helplessness* is the very idea that prompted James Baldwin to pen his letter of warning to his nephew in <u>*"Fire Next Time"*</u> and my grandparents' warnings to me.

Nothing happens to whites that killing blacks because whites share an understanding and know they are messengers of *learned helplessness.* It helps to keep black people in line and in their place. Today one can see older generation white people are united.

Considering slavery's descendants, as subjects in ongoing *learned helplessness* experiments, adds real credibility to the urban legend of *"Willie Lynch."* The Lynch theory was an attempt to explain slave descendants' *"residual self-image,"* which unknowingly and subconsciously constructs slave descendants' behavioral responses to white society.

Finally, remember the trick of the researcher *"is to lead the horse to water and the horse drinks willingly, as though it is its idea."* As rats during *"learned helplessness"* training, the only coping mechanism for some slaves was to accept their situation, to avoid an even worse fate, awaiting any slave that defy white people. Most slaves became stoic and endured the terror and horrors of their predicament, like some rat in *learned helplessness* experiments.

They did not expend energy getting worked up over aversive stimuli, which they had no control over. Resignation is the fate of millions of descendants of American slavery today. I believe commemorating and celebrating **"The 400th"** can be the very therapy, catharsis even, to help black people today counteract the effects of *learned helplessness.*

What was left off the question I asked starting this discussion, *"White people know stuff about black people they don't know,"* and this caveat *"about themselves,"* which is the point of how *learned helplessness* works.

EJI: A Light for the Future

Although I was aware of the general impact of slavery and studied *learned helplessness*, the syncretism of the two escaped me until I began researching **"The 400th".** Reinforcing the impact and effectiveness of *learned helplessness* became an ongoing pogrom, after slavery. First groups like the Ku Klux Klan, which were called *"paddy roller"* during slavery by slaves, became a societal activity of white people in general, similar to slave catchers, who became police. Woodrow Wilson after his election made reinforcing *"learned helplessness"* was a government function.

The **"Dark Age"** *angry white men mob madness era* was a campaigns America', where the South initiated to re-enforce *learned helplessness,* as a function of convict leasing and share cropping. Wilson directed inhumane scantions from the White House, and Donald Trump attempted to reintroduce them in 2020. During that time, lynching exemplified the *"electrified grid,"* used to modify subjects (rats) behavior in behavior medication experiments. The Klan burned huge crosses atop Stone Mountain in Georgia, had such a huge flame and glow against the night sky, could be seen hundred miles in all directions by black families. Such terror tactics invoke mass fear, and dread causing anxiety.

Terrorizing black families under those flames was such a powerful and affective tool and symbol of mass terror, like the noose. Black communities never knew in which direction Klansmen would ride. Just the sight of a noose evoked terror and anxiety among American slavery's descendants, even today. Poor whites were hostile regarding any effort that gave former slaves opportunities to escape poverty. They tried to regain their middle-class status gained during the internal slave trade and breeding, which they lost. Poor whites were foot soldiers re-enforcing *learned helplessness* in hate groups—Ku Klux Klan—during the terror-ridden **"Dark Age"** *angry white men mob madness* era.

Today a pioneering group, the **Equal Justice Initiative (EJI)** in Montgomery, Alabama, is during groundbreaking research, much like Dot M. Smith and Douglas A. Blackmon's research, to establish government's role and impact of lynching on the psyche of black people. *EJI* has located thousands of sites where whites lynched blacks, before and during the **"Dark Age"** *angry white men mob madness* period. *EJI* has established 4,075 lynchings that occurred across the 12 Confederate States. There are unverified counts of well over 6,000 lynchings when the US, as a whole, is included. The *Equal Justice Initiative* is a very bright light, showing the way to **"The 400th".**

EJI is the brainchild of Brian Stevenson, Professor of Law at NYU. Many *EJI* attorneys took Brian's courses on *Racial Justice and the Law* and *Eighth Amendment Law and Litigation*, before enrolling in his clinic course at EJI. The **Equal**

The 400th: From Slavery to Hip Hop

Justice Initiative was envisioned as a crusading force, establishing the truth about lynching.

Brian established a reputation as a fearless lone rider, defending death row inmates. Beginning as a young lawyer, Brain fought the practice of sentencing children, as young as ten years old, to "life in prison without parole" in the US. Shining light on the 4,075 places where lynchings occurred, *EJI* has established the *Community Remembrance Program*.

Ruth Hopkins, a journalist/activist from Sweden, worked in South African to producer the new groundbreaking documentarian **"Prison For Profit,"** about South Africa's horrific privatized prison system, introduced me to EJI. Ruth invited me to participate in EJI's *Community Remembrance Project*, while interning with EJI's in 2016. *EJI's* light came on for me when I joined Ruth to searching for lynching sites. I became a volunteer with *EJI* once I realized, many of the ideas and programs I was contemplating (like my slavery and lynching research presented in **"The 400th"**), Brian and *EJI* were developing.

The *Community Remembrance Project* give volunteers, like me, opportunities to help in their mission of locating and documenting actual lynch sites. For instance, *EJI* began by compiling information black community obtained from historical records, newspaper stories, and images on postcards or family stories. Their search was like chasing down rumors, passed around by word of mouth, like urban legends, and lynchings people heard about in many cases.

I have participated in 3 lynch site searches with EJI's *Community Remembrance Project*. Similar to other volunteers, I arrived at *EJI* on Saturday morning. I received an orientation, a gallon jar with three sheets of paper—an explanation of what to do, directions to a documented lynch site, and the story of the human beings murdered there—plus a small flower garden spade. The task of those who volunteer is to travel to the site and collect a full jar of soil from the area of the lynch site.

Ode to the Memorial of Peace and Justice
By King Khan (International president of Invaders Forever)

I was given but a piece of paper
with an address, a name and a jar
I drove from Atlanta, Georgia to Montgomery, Alabama
I followed my instructions and they led me to the hanging tree
I got on my knees and put my hands into the soil
I took the soil where his blood was spilled and dripped from his toes
I held the dirt that once swallowed his burned and beaten remains
I placed the soil into the jar and brought it to a special resting place
I brought his stolen body back to the people
I gave him a place to be remembered

I brought him to a house of all loss lynch souls
I bathed his body in the light of hope
his respect and dignity rose from the darkness
his soul was shown the glorious path of illumination
I gave him a place for all of his tears and for all of his loved ones
the ones who wondered where he had gone
I gave him a grave that will last for ever
an obelisk of immortality
I gave him a place to rest in power
to rest in peace
The light from above shown differently that day
the clouds parted and the hand of God reached out
I carried the burden of all the forgotten
I lifted his invisible body and carried it back home
For all of us to see
For all of us to bear witness
For all of us to cry, to shake, to scream and sing
I took him back to his home,
the place where he always belonged.

Traveling to those lynch site, Bryan's vision became truly profound for me. While en route, driving through "nowhere" Alabama, looking for my lynch sites, my emotions raced wildly. Alone with my thoughts, lynchings filled my head. Images of the **"Dark Age"** *angry white men mob madness* era were everywhere I looked, it seemed. As I rode, I wondered, *"Were there still people in Alabama bent on expressing their hatred for black people as they did during the 1920s into the 1960s?"*

This question popped into my mind, with every white face encountered. My thoughts seemed stuck in rewind on that question. But, I drove on searching for my destination. The hair-raising part of my search carried me into the backwoods in the middle of "nowhere" Alabama. I found myself digging at the edge of some white person's front yard, trying to fill my jar, which seemed as large as a bathtub, at the time. While digging I thought, *"They might have gotten this property through racial cleansing or banishment?"* I also thought, I could go knock at the door and introduce myself. Then tell the occupant a lynching took place in your front yard and I would like to collect soil from your yard to document that fact. Instead, I fill my jar under a big Oak tree, near the side of the road, as quickly as I could. Packing my jar, I made a hasty retreat. Fear truly gripped me, I was definitely afraid, while filling that jar.

Once volunteers fill their jars they return them to EJI. Although the lynching period lasted eighty years and *EJI* has documented near five thousand, the story of lynching in the South is still mostly incomplete. EJI researcher and lawyer, Jennifer Rae Taylor says of their work, *"Part of the challenge of doing this research is* that we are trying to document events that occurred many years ago, when standards of reporting and verification were different than they are now, and communication was far more difficult across distances, and many publications and individuals did not have much interest in collecting accurate information about lynchings."

For that reason, I believe there are far more lynching sights across America than has been located and counted thus far. Rev. Burl Lee, my Great-grandfather, the first free born Lee, his father was the last slave in my family, told stories and described times when black people died at the hands of white people for little or no reason, and nothing was done or said. Families dared not complain less they met the same faith. Fleeing, leaving everything behind was their only means to save the remaining family.

Nevertheless, like an angel of mercy for the victims of such horrific and gruesome tragedies, Brain's lynching monument make the horrors of their deaths and those times as a living memory for all to see. However, the most important thing is documenting these tragedies, will help black people move beyond their "word of mouth" culture, giving stories of their history permanence and will help them confront their *learned helplessness*, as well.

Returning to EJI, I thought, how through Brian's work I was helping to recognize and memorialize these long lost but not forgotten souls. I placed my full jars of Robert Mosley's soil with all the others displayed on the *Wall of Remembrance* at EJI. But, that's not the end of Brian's daring plan.

Brain purchased six acres of land a few miles away from EJI where he built a memorial for lynched victims. Brian plans to put a portion of the soil in the huge obelisks, which will hang throughout the memorial in remembrance of those who were victims of lynchings. That, more than anything, is why I had to get my jars full of soil from some very scary places, or I would have failed to help memorialize murdered but not forgotten of descendants slavery, like Robert Mosley and others, who died so horribly. The story of each lynched victim is etched onto their obelisks for visitors to read.

Brian's efforts to build such a prestigious shrine are tremendous. I believe it can bring closure, to a certain extent, for those souls murdered so long ago, and memories of many of these events have faded into anonymity. Finally, their tragic end will be fully acknowledged. This project is a perfect example of why commemorating and celebrating **"The 400th"** by slavery's descendants are so essential for me.

Everyone should rally around Bryan's efforts with contributions and energy now that he has completed this important statement for 2020. But, that is not all Brian is doing. The Alabama River, which flows past Montgomery, was a major water highway, during the internal slave trade and breeding era. Back then there were many slave warehouses in Montgomery. Brian purchased one for *EJI's* headquarters. Brian created an interactive museum in the basement to educate the public about slavery's horrors.

If descendants of American slavery want to do something big with lasting implications for *"The 400th"*, now that the museum is complete, they should make the pilgrimage to *EJI*. These two projects—lynching memorial and slavery museum—will stand as African Americans first holocaust monuments. Slave descendants should contribute mightily to Brian's efforts, because there is still so much to do. His dream has truly become a statement for descendants of American slavery as part of commemorating and celebrating *"The 400th"*.

EJI's Community Remembrance Project brought another issue into focus for me. *EJI* used a system created by NAACP established, to determine whether some murders of African Americans were lynchings. They developed a system I believe can help determine whether Dr. Martin Luther King's murder was a lynching. The NAACP's criteria were used by *EJI* to establish the 4,075 lynching victims across the South. Their are four criteria to distinguish lynchings from other murders: (1) there must be evidence a person was killed; (2) the person must have met death illegally; (3) a group of three or more persons conspired or participated in the killings; and (4) the group acted under the pretext of protecting tradition or justice. The first two criteria were easily satisfied in Dr. King's assassination, but the last two—how many persons were involved and protecting tradition or justice, are the two, I believe Congress has kept secret since 1978, after the US House of Representatives investigation of Dr. King's assassination end.

Only when Dr. King's assassination file is opened to the public by the US House of Representatives, which put it on lockdown to prevent the public from knowing the truth, is released, will the public know what really happened. The US House of Representatives sealed the investigation file on Dr. King's murder, after their investigation in 1978 but locked it down before the public was allowed to know what was learned. Consequently, the public still does not know who was involved and what role they played in Dr. King's death. The house of Representatives is faced with what to do about murders, like George Floyd, Breonna Taylor, Ahmud Arbery and many others, who were lynched before the world, no different than Dr. King's assassination.

Slavery and Lynching Never Ended

White NFL fans' controversy with Colin Kaepernick's refusal to stand during the "Star-Spangled Banner" drew attention to the unequal treatment black athletes and other people of color endure in America, especially regarding equal justice. White Americans get outraged when slavery's descendants' *VOICE* objection to disparate treatment. The vitriol white fans express is nothing new when black athletes are involved. Their actions are an effort to reinforce *learned helplessness*. Black Americans supposed to have the same equal rights as whites. However, there is a different reaction from the NFL when black players express outrage than when white players and fans can go to the front office and their statements are taken serious. The so-called Colin Kaepernick controversy points up and reflects a major theme of this narrative—white and black people can view or experience the identical situation from the same position at the same time, yet come away with two totally different scenarios. However, the fact is racism is alive and well in America, as it was during slavery.

The Colin Kaepernick controversy puts the NFL in the eye of a storm that threatens to engulf sports and America in due time. ***"The 400th"*** narrative now examines the controversy from several perspectives—NFL fans, owners, the national view, and finally young people. I review the controversy through the windows of social change and equal justice activism, as well as their impact 156 years after emancipation, while slave descendants prepare to experience ***"The 400th"***.

The annals of sports controversies, if one looks back, whether involving owners, coaches, players, or fans, one finds, there has not been a level of degradation or indignation white fans have not tried to subject black athletics. I reviewed different sports controversies over the years, starting with the NFL. Jim Brown stands out as its most noted social change lightning rod and "devil-may-care, lone rider." I reviewed Jim Brown's stands in the 1950s and 60s. White sports fans and the media labeled Jim "arrogant." Brown, who did not comment often, stood his ground, maintaining his right of voice, while stating his opinion. Jim demanded respect as a man and would not retreat an inch, no matter the people who confronted him. Fans said things like, *"his stands make it hard to accept him as a star,"* still Brown would not relent. Until Colin Kaepernick, Jim Brown was the most ardent social change advocate lone riding NFL trailblazer.

White fans' reactions to black athletes in boxing, goes back to Jack Johnson, then up to and beyond Joe Louis to Muhammad Ali. White fans did not miss a trick, hoping to degrade black athletes, especially since most were unbeatable. Black athletes' composure has been amazingly calm and reserved compared to white fans blew controversies completely out of proportion, similar to the Kaepernick carbuncle now. They always claimed, *"It's not about race or color,"* to justify their whites view and outrage.

No matter the controversy, white fans were vehemently determined to drive the black athlete from the field, court, or mat and damage their financial viability. Whites tried to disguise their racism against Jackie Robinson to cover their abuse they heaped upon him to block his efforts to play major league baseball. They claimed, *"Black men do not have the ability to compete with white players."* As old folks say, "the proof is in the pudding."

When Ferdinand Lewis Alcindor Jr. changed his name to Kareem Abdul-Jabbar, white fans hit the ceiling, and the press castigated him. It was truly a big deal with white people. Even though, Kareem's name change had nothing to do with white people or basketball. The hullabaloo drew whites vitriol and it impacted Kareem overall public perception even today, as a man and sports figure.

White people believe it is part of their heritage, as slave masters, to micromanage the opinions and actions of black people. Kareem has never been able to take full advantage of his stellar basketball career, as a result of the controversy white people created over his name change. Many players, especially whites, with less successful careers, received opportunities and enjoyed greater access to America's bounty than Kareem, simply because of white people's controversy with his name change. Kareem refused to beg, dismissing the name change bull; he threw off his *"learned helplessness."*

The classic demonstration of white power over black athletes came after another name change by a brash young black boxer that floated like a butterfly and stung like a bee. Standing up like a man for his believes, Muhammad Ali refused to go to war in Vietnam, like a sheep. Whites try to call down the wrath of God upon one of His chosen to make him crawl like a worm or be branded a coward and banned from boxing. Muhammad Ali, a man, loved universally, valiantly continued his stand. White people were enraged and tried to kill his career by preventing him from earning money, and used reprisals against him, but his adoring fans around the world counted that out, standing with him.

Finally, the hart courts of Compton, California for Venus and Serena Williams were more than comparable to the concrete sidewalks of New York City for Althea Gibson. These women had lots in common, even though their careers were more than three decades apart, yet the three had their share of fan controversies. Foul calls were common to the three, from the very first toss and serve. White officials and fans alike, claimed to be *"color-blind,"* when it came to players, but their blindness only extended to line calls.

Who can forget Serena's stand at Indian Wells, during the height of the women's movement, when none stood with her in support? White tennis fans tried to drive her from the court with boos and kill her promotional appeal, but this valiant devil-may-care, swashbuckling, lone riding "woman," Serena continued her stand, endearing herself to fans—black and white. A happy new mom today, Serena reigns supreme, "Queen of her Royal Court."

The 400th: From Slavery to Hip Hop

Black athletes/entertainers are the only people that can be held hostage by white fans pleasure or displeasure. Whites' exasperations have always had a financial bite. NFL owners have lined up together behind the same racism that kept black players out of baseball long after everyone knew that ban was to keep white players' jobs. Today the big issue is pensions. Jim Brown made millions for football at a time when he was one of only a few "superstars," but his NFL pension is so low, he is compensated like he was a "field nigger." Fear of fan reactions, if Colin Kaepernick is allowed to play, will go the way of all previous controversies, but NFL owners and managers will hold on to their personal racism, even after the controversies dies.

Slave Masters or Bosses?

I ask the question aloud, **"Are NFL owners slave masters or bosses?"** The best example of this question is the controversy involving Colin Kaepernick and the NFL's Baltimore Ravens. Ravers Management exemplified the way the NFL circled its wagons to put Kaepernick in a "no-touch" zone, even after admitting they closed their eyes to equality and justice. During the height of this controversy (2017), according to TMZ, the story behind the Ravens not signing Kaepernick, when starting QB Joe Flaco went down, unfolded this way. Head coach John Harbaugh sought advice from some "trusted friends" on the matter, after speaking very highly of Kaepernick. It seems a high-ranking military honcho, voiced opposition. He felt bringing the versatile QB to Baltimore, *"might not be such a good idea, it could be problematic."*

The unnamed military official did not flat-out tell Harbaugh not to sign Kaepernick but reportedly cautioned Harbaugh saying, *"Signing the free agent (Kaepernick) could present a difficult challenge if he continued to kneel."* The Ravens preferred to sign less talented, untested, and out of shape Thad Lewis, who had not thrown an NFL pass in four years. This "rap" is not about Thad Lewis; he was just another pawn on a crowded NFL chessboard.

Here comes the snap over the kickers' head, as NFL owners tried to punt their way out of a "tar baby" mess. Jerry Jones exemplifies NFL slave master management style regarding black players. A diehard, Jones said, "I'll bench any of *"my players"* for taking a knee," and it seems, Harbaugh's military buddy's admonition has created a *"Kaepernick team rule,"* "if a black player wants to keep a job," according to TMZ. The NFL's actions are similar to Kareem Abdul-Jabbar's domination of college basketball from 1966 until 1969. The rule banding the "slam dunk," was part of the *"hate Kareem Abdul-Jabbar"* effect.

Although NFL management scrambled trying to get its punt off, the very low kick barely cleared the line of controversy by late September. That was when Ravens legend, Ray Lewis, brought a "hearsay" element into the controversy, mixing apples and oranges, or plums and cherries, trying to support Raven's management. He said, *"The reason Kaepernick didn't have a job in Baltimore is that Kaepernick's **"girlfriend,"*** who will never play a down or throw a pass in the NFL, *"was critical of Ravens management."* "SO!!!!" She, which is her right to voice her opinion, posted a social media comment, *"Ravens owner Steve Bisciotti is a slave owner and Lewis, a slave."* No "black" player has a right to an opinion unless the NFL gives it to them, or it agrees with the status quo, like Lewis.

The denial of *VOICE* is very much a slave issue for black players. Considering NFL franchises and the power they exert over players and their contracts, it is totally asinine to suggest that a ***"girlfriend"*** has the power to alter their terms. If that is the case, NFL black players are the only employees whose girlfriends can preempt their employment. This controversy has "exposed Lewis as one of the biggest hypocrites in sports," according to TMZ. It cited how Lewis criticized Kaepernick for kneeling and advised him to ditch the protest, yet later in the season, "Lewis got down on two knees, during the anthem." He may have been praying for master Bisciotti (source TMZ). Kaepernick remains ostracized from football while "sub-par players like Thad Lewis have jobs. Kaepernick accused NFL owners of collusion last year, and his lawyers continue building their case against the NFL.

More importantly, the truth of the Colin Kaepernick matter was laid out in this narrative and has been stripped bare before the world. I reminded everyone of Tommie Smith and John Carlos at the 1968 Summer Olympics in Mexico City. Standing before the world with an extended black-gloved fist, they refused to honor the *Star-Spangled Banner* and the flag of the US. They refused to honor a country that refuses to acknowledge black people are human beings with human rights, while the US continues refusing to acknowledge that fact.

America has stood firmly against apologizing or acknowledging its racism, and the NFL has followed suit. Today, NFL teams and players have made a charade of "kneeling," because Colin Kaepernick is still "black balled." "Racism" in America is as H. "Rap" Brown said in 1967, **"Racism is as American, as apple pie!"** Rap's words created pandemonium, as did Kaepernick kneeling. White Americans screamed the same ill-tempered, *"He's disrespecting America."* Rap Brown's comment drew Vice President, Spiro T. Agnew into a rhetorical battle that began the federal government's crackdown on black power activists. With Donald Trump parachuting into the controversy, like a kamikaze tweeter, the NFL will have to sign a surrender at the 50 yardline to end the "kneeling war." The slave master mentality is alive and well, even preferred, in the NFL.

The World Outside of the NFL

Athletes are entertainers in the truest sense of the word. American entertainment going back to Minstrelsy's *"blackface"* and racism was there. Minstrelsy was born out of the desire to degrade black people, as fun and entertainment, like lynching during the **"Dark Age"** white *men mob madness era*. Entertainment has never been easy for descendants of American slavery; consider Louis Wright's lynching in New Madrid, Missouri, (1902) by white Minstrelsy fans. Minstrelsy and NFL fans are similar. Slavery's descendants endured humiliation to participate in Minstrelsy, like NFL players, to make money. Today is a different time, NFL fans and management lynched Colin Kaepernick just the same and the show goes on.

During Minstrelsy, African Americans had to put shoe polish on their faces, even though blacks did not need it, but it was about white audiences so they would not know *"who were the real coons!"* *"Blacking up,"* was the price demanded of blacks to appease white fans. NFL owners have lined up together behind the same *"blacking up"* racism with a rule, demanding African Americans stand like "Cigar store Indians" to play football. That is the "Colin Kaepernick rule." Owners claim they are fearful of fan reactions if Colin Kaepernick is allowed to play.

Now we know very clearly how NFL racist fans and owners feel and what the media thinks, but what about the rest of the world. Monitoring "Who's" doing what for causes other than themselves is an annual activity of *DoSomething.org*. This website keeps tabs on the social action activities of celebrities. It sponsors an annual award—*Celebs Gone Good*—to recognize those who use their influence to raise awareness of social justice causes and to affect social change in the world. The *Celebs Gone Good Awards* include both young activists and other individuals in entertainment, who dedicate their time to making social change through activism and altruism. The top four *Celebs Gone Good* nominees receive a $10,000 community grant, while the grand prize winner receives $100,000 to push their social change projects. According to its website, *DoSomething.org* is inspiring 5.5 million young people around the world to make positive changes, both online and off. The organization has members in every area code in the United States and over 131 countries.

Beyoncé was on top of the 2016's list. **Chance, The Rapper from Chicago,** captured the top spot for 2017. Chance raised over $2 million for charity in Chicago. Helping his hometown's Public Schools (2017), he co-founded SocialWorks to helps empower youth. This young "lone rider" launched the New Chance Arts & Literature Fund to support arts in public school. A young musician, 25-years old, Chance hopes to improve the educational system. Taking chances, Chance hopes to improve the chances of his people.

The 400th: From Slavery to Hip Hop 649

"First Lady," Michelle Obama, presented the 3-time Grammy winner The BET Humanitarian Award (2017). She also sent a video message to the young artist before presenting the award on BET. It said,

> *"With these passionate efforts, Chance is showing our young people that they matter, that they have something inside of them that is worthy of being expressed, and they have so much to contribute to their community and our country. I can think of no better legacy to leave, and I am thrilled to celebrate you here tonight and honored to call you my friend."*

Some past winners of *Celebs Gone Good Awards* are Van Jones founder of *the Ella Baker Center for Human Rights* (1996), Mark Levine founder of *Credit Where Credit Is Due and Neighborhood Trust Federal Credit Union* (1998), Jacob Komar: Created *"Computers for Communities"* (2007), Katia Gomez provides education to the youth of Honduras through her foundation *Educate2Envision* (2012) and Daniel Maree Founder of the *Million Hoodies Movement for Justice*, which helps combat the issues of racial profiling and *Florida's Stand Your Ground Law* following the death of 17-year-old Trayvon Martin (2013). This year's list also includes Ava DuVernay, Rihanna, Ariana Grande, Nicki Minaj, Zendaya, Yara Shahidi, and J. J. Watt.

Colin Kaepernick has made the *Celebs Gone Good Awards* two years in a row, finishing runner-up to Chance this year. He continued his fight against injustice and racism even after being barred from the NFL. This year he donated $1 million to various charitable organizations, including Meals on Wheels and 100 Suits. These contributions led to Kaepernick receiving the prestigious Sports Illustrated *Muhammad Ali Legacy Award.*

Beyoncé, after some very warm and supportive words for this "devil-may-care lone rider," presented Kaepernick's award. Beyoncé said;

> *"Thank you, Colin Kaepernick. Thank you for your selfless heart and your conviction...Thank you for your personal sacrifice. Colin took action with no fear of consequence or repercussion only hoping to change the world for the better. To change perception, to change the way we treat each other, especially people of color...We're still waiting for the world to catch up. It's been said that racism is so American, that when we protest racism, some assume we are protesting America. So, let's be very clear. Colin has always been very respectful of the individuals who selflessly serve and protect our country and our communities and our families. His message is solely focused on social injustice for historically disenfranchised people. Let's not get that mistaken."*

The Sports Illustrated presents the *Muhammad Ali Legacy Award* to *"individuals whose dedication to the ideals of sportsmanship has spanned decades or whose career in athletics has directly or indirectly impacted the world."* Michael Rosenberg of Sports Illustrated said, *"In the last 16 months, Kaepernick's truth has been twisted, distorted, and used for political gain. It has cost him at least a year of his NFL career and the income that should have come with it. But still, it is his truth. He has not wavered from it. He does not regret speaking out. He has caused millions of people to examine it."*

Kapernick: *"I say this as a person who receives credit for using my platform to protest systemic oppression, racialized injustice, and the dire consequences of anti-blackness in America...I accept this award not for myself, but on behalf of the people. Because, if it weren't for my love of the people, I would not have protested, and if it were not for the support from the people, I would not be on this stage today. With or without the NFL's platform, I will continue to work for the people because my platform is the people." With or without the NFL's platform, I will continue to work for the people'@Kaepernick7.*

And what do I say, NFL owns make themselves look ridiculous with every move. The NFL reminds me of George Wallace or Bull Connor, who showed the world they did not care about civil rights for black people. Similarly, the NFL denies players their First Amendment Rights. In classic slave master fashion, they are forcing players to stand against their will to horror the very flag that is supposed to protect them against such oppression.

Out of the Mouth of Babes

I offer this next response to the controversy involving Colin Kaepernick as an example of young people's voices. My assessment of young people today is they are far smarter, more motivated, and definitely more adventurous than my generation was during the 1960s. Older Americans regard young African Americans as rude and they long for a time when what elders said commanded acceptance.

So today, they view young people as offensive. The thing they fail to recognize is young progressives today have far more information at their disposal due to technology than my generation, which allows them to verify statements without regard to the source. Consequently, their opinion is what they respect, more so than the source of information, which makes them self-assured and fearless. This is why the older generation regards them as crude.

Baby boomers stood up and fought, but relied on the older generation for direction until black power. Young progressives' understanding and recognition are clearer and less attached to the racist vision of the past than their parents. Young people are far less concerned about white privilege for themselves, as a right, than baby boomers.

Young Americans do not understand why white people need an advantage; they already have access to everything. Today's progressives would be happy competing on a level playing field, like athletes, if level playing fields existed any place in America. But, America's system is always slanted to favor white people, no matter the circumstances. Older white people believe because the system has always favored them, they see it as a *"God-given right!"*

I was unsure whether young people, meaning teenagers, had an opinion on the Colin Kaepernick controversy. I was concerned that maybe I would need to intrude on their world before they express their thoughts regarding the issue? I offer the following discussion to support my previous statements. Young people reflect why I have truly hopeful feelings for the future of America.

When Colin kneeled rather than stand for the national anthem, and once the controversy began swirling about him in 2016, I joined his protest, as I had on many occasions since 1967. I watched news coverage of white NFL fans ranting and venting their outrage at Colin kneeling rather than standing for the *"Star-Spangled Banner."* I was so proud of him because I have not stood for the national anthem, since Dr. Martin Luther King, Jr.'s assassination.

On this particular day, while I ranted and raved watching TV news, as white fans went totally vitriolic at Colin, who had a Constitutional right to give *VOICE* to his outrage, I screamed, *"They're lynching that Kid!!"* My ten-year-old 5th-grade granddaughter, Tahlia, asked, *"Granddaddy, what do you mean, lynching him? Why do you say that; what do you mean by lynching?"* Surprised by her question, I thought for a moment, trying to formulate a simple response, but realized there was no simple response to her question. Then I said, *"Rather than granddaddy explaining what lynching means sweetheart, why don't you research the subject."* The fact that she's my grand-daughter has very little to do with my choice in this situation; I see her as indicative of young minds today.

A few days later, Tahlia returned after her research and said, *"Granddaddy, I agree with you; he has a right to stand or kneel. I want to do my social studies project for this semester about lynching."* Even more surprised, I said, I'll help if you need me. So, she was off. Although Tahlia is a very good student and attended Barak H. Obama Elementary Magnet School of Technology in DeKalb County, Georgia, which is viewed as very progressive, I never thought of Tahlia, as very precocious. On the other hand, Tahlia's black teaches were shocked and appalled by her choice.

Tahlia's teachers thought lynching was to gross a subject for young children to be exposed, *learned helplessness* abounds. They called Tahlia's mother, my daughter Laquitta, about her choice. They advised her that they believed "a better topic would be Ida B. Wells, Booker T. Washington or sit-ins during the 1950s". Laquitta promptly pointed out that, *"When viewing lynching photographs, there are children—alive and in person—sitting atop white lynchers' shoulders, getting a total view of the murderous act, taking place in real-time."* Meanwhile, Tahlia screamed, *"No!!!" "I've done all of those. That's all we do! I want to do something important, something about today that affects my life."*

The procedure or rubric called for a standard tri-fold board to display artwork, other material, and a one-hundred-fifty-word report. Tahlia's topic was *"How Lynching Changed Over the Years."* her design traced the history of lynching from the "Wild West" into today. Collecting pictures and stories of lynchings, even those who fought to stop it, she used her artwork to tell lynching's story. She ran a rope, with a hang man's noose at the end, up and down her board. Symbolically, the rope tied scenes from slavery, **Red Summer**, creation of the NAACP, the rise of the Ku Klux Klan, civil rights era, the 16th Street Baptist Church bombing, Meager Evers, black power, Jena Six, on to Trayvon Martin. Tahlia put Colin Kaepernick's picture in the noose, as the example of lynching today.

Tahlia's write-up pointed out the growth and development of lynching, which began with the rope in the west, then came South with slavery. Guns, fire, clubs, even rape became part of certain types of lynchings. Dynamite and other incendiary explosives became lynching tools in the 1960s.

Even an automobile was a lynch tool for James Byrd. He was dragged by two white men behind a pickup truck as a lynch victim, in Jasper, Texas (6-7-1998).

The news media, through stories done against black people, became a lynch tool, during Jena Six (12-6-06). Then the lynch mob moved to TV news, where

The 400th: From Slavery to Hip Hop   653

a picture was like a rope to hang unsuspecting black victims on the scaffold of public ridicule. As on Tahlia's board, today, a gang of irate white fans became a lynch mob at a sporting event. The purpose of lynching is to intimidate, while re-enforcing *learned helplessness* and prevent black people from exercising first-class rights, like white people. Tahlia made these observations in her report, as the point of lynching black people today. I was so impressed with how a 5th grader saw the racist way NFL fans and owners reacted to Colin Kaepernick expressing his Constitutional rights.

A few months later, I was invited to give several talks in Colorado Springs, during the celebration of Dr. Martin Luther King, Jr.'s birthday (2016). I used Tahlia's 5th Grade project, as a visual aid. I sat it on a table and invited students at the University of Colorado at Colorado Springs (UCCS) to come and view the tri-fold display for about 20 minutes. The exercise was entitled *"Are You as Informed as a Fifth Grader?"* Students at UCCS were amazed by the pictures and information, of which most were unaware. However, they were even more impressed with the fact it was the vision of a 5th grader.

Daisy McGowan, Curator for the Gallery of Contemporary Arts (GOCA) at UCCS, who mounted the **Black Power Tarot Card Exhibition** and ***Invaders Documentary*** screening, sponsored the events. She was also impressed, Daisy kept Tahlia's Project on display at Gallery of Contemporary Art (GOCA) for the three-month run of the show. She wrote Tahlia a very warm thank you message, encouraging her to *"continue fighting for your ideas."*

The question is, *"How far have descendants of American slavery come* in America *when the controversy surrounding Colin Kaepernick reflects that black people in America are still fighting for the same right of VOICE Paul Robeson and William L. Patterson fought for in 1951 with* **We Charge Genocide**?" African Americans remain tied to the **Trans-Atlantic Slave Trade, Goreé Island, Dakar, Senegal,** as the place where the madness began. *"The Door of No Return,"* sealed a loathsome and depraved fate that still denies black skin a place among humankind.

America's vision of enslaved Africans as exiles them from the human race and judge them by the 3/5 Compromise. The US Constitution designated enslaved Africans' value as 3/5 of a white man when signed in 1789. That fact has not changed, so what is there for black people to honor, other than a big "LIE" white people love because it allows them to dominate black people.

Colin Kaepernick's treatment shows that the slave master's mentality is still alive and well in the NFL. The fact that a ten-year-old fifth grader produced this particular vision of life in America for her and her people means my granddaughter's life, if those running America today have their way, will be a repeat of my life. Americans and other people around the world must ask themselves, *"How long will such a level of ignorance be allowed to 'trump' intelligence?"* With their response to COVOD-19 and mask mandates, Americans still have a long ways to go. This narrative has discussed the history of **"The 400th"**, and now I ask, *"Are there real* *and factual reasons why black people are still not recognized as human beings by Americans, after 400 years?"* I have found none!

The latest boomerang in the Colin Kaepernick saga with the NFL began when Donald Trump anted up. He joined the critics protesting Kaepernick's kneeling, during the national anthem. Tweeting, *"What was Nike thinking?"* Trump show what he thought of constitutional rights for black people. His tweet complained about Nike using Kaepernick in a TV spot recently (2-1-2019).

Tiger Woods has been a Nike athlete since turning pro in 1996. He responded to Trump's attack on Nike. Tiger rarely comments but said, *"I'm a fan of the apparel giant featuring the former San Francisco 49ers quarterback known for his social protests. I think Nike is trying to get out ahead of it and trying to do something special, and I think they've done that,"* Woods said at the BMW Championship. *"It's a beautiful spot and pretty powerful people (are) in the spot. They did not tell me it was coming."* Woods continued, *"When corporate does things that are outside of golf, and outside of my realm, that's what they do."* Tiger Woods endorsed Nike's latest *"Just Do It"* ad narrated by Colin Kaepernick with a message nearly as succinct. *"It's a beautiful spot."* He has been part of Nike Golf, and one of his 14 major championships moment was his great putt at the Masters on the 16th green. Golfers watch breathlessly, as his putt hung on the lip of the cup two seconds—with the swoosh facing the camera—before dropping. His "TW" logo has made him the embodiment of the Nike brand.

Serena Williams, who played her ninth U.S. Open final (2018), said, *"I'm proud of Kaepernick!"* He was in Flushing Meadows to watch her play. Serena continued, *"I think every athlete, every human, and definitely every African-American should be completely grateful and honored for Kaepernick."* The two-minute ad spot with Kaepernick narrating it, debuted during the NFL opener. Superstar athletes like LeBron James, Serena Williams, and others, high-fived Kaepernick's Nike spot, which touches on the knelling controversy involving NFL player protests, during the national anthem.

Tahlia was right!!!! If my granddaughter has to fight the same battle today, I fought, during black power, my mother fought in the 1940s, and her granddaddy fought in the early 1900s, how far has black people come in 138 years? Leaving slavery did not mean it was left behind, especially while NFL keeps black athletes in slave pens!!!

However, as time and events, with Divine intervention standing in the wing, Colin Kaepernick is becoming a pop culture world figure as the Nike commercial that features him won an Emmy for outstanding commercial at the 2019 Creative Arts Emmy Awards (via CNN).

Salute to Black Power

The previous section is important for two reasons. First, it reflects my pride in young black descendants of American slavery, like Serena Williams, LeBron James, Tiger Woods, and of course, Colin Kaepernick, my granddaughter, and many other young people fighting for a place in America that conservative whites do not want to yield. I love the "pride they are exhibiting and celebrate their blackness."

Next, they are celebrities, not including Tahlia, with wealth and prestige, which puts them beyond things that impact those still buried in the grave of poverty in the valley of dry bones. However, they are standing together and representing African American unity. ***"The 400"***, I said beginning this narrative *"is a love story, about a people that fell in love with being themselves."* The greatest need in the fight to gain access to fair courts, equality, and America's bounty for poor and middle-class African Americans is unity, which signals that we are all engaged in the battle as one people.

Unity among descendants of American slavery is the expression of self-love that held enslaved Africans together in slave pens. No longer forced to be together today, unity still depends on self-love, if we are to improve on our survival as one people. Rev. Burl Lee's generation put their hopes in their children has an extension of that self-love and passed that desire onto the next generation until it reached us today. I repeat ***"The 400th"*** is a love story that has been lived out by people who fell in love with being themselves.

Bringing black power into ***"The 400"*** celebration and commemoration maintains the continuity of struggle slavery's descendants brought with them leaving slavery, stepping into emancipation. Black power is no longer just about color because today, in the streets of America, white kids are there shoulder to shoulder with black people, some they know and some they have never seen before. They are trying to teach their parents and grandparents what it means to be human beings.

However, more than anything, white kids are hoping, it is not too late for mom and dad. Americans families today are composed of all colors, kinds, genders and cultures. No one is concerned with the myth of racial purity. Making families and building new kinds of communities are the philosophical and psychological challenge black and other people are facing, the challenges of trying to find a way to sustain their progress, not riding the backs of others to have a good life—that is the new normal.

Unity is why I began this section expressing pride in the children my generation and its children have produced. I say to this generation; you are doing what we fought to allow you to do. Commemorating and celebrating ***"The 400th"*** will be your way of doing the same for the next generation. Supporting and pushing black unity and solidarity with others engaged in the same struggle, **Commemorating and Celebrating *"The 400ᵗʰ"*** can be the doorway to not only preserving todays progress and create a legacy everyone can be proud. This generation has already advanced the new normal culture we are creating and has already advanced beyond what I imagined when I presented Talhia's project to the students at UCCS.

Those of us that stood on the front line in the 1960s are proud of the present generation, as leaders and we expect you to lead. For my generation, we feel it is a reward for those that stood, providing the shoulders on which you stand. Secondly, it is not because she is my grand-daughter; any grandparent would be proud of a ten-year-old that stood up for what she believed was important to her, then delivered on her confidence in herself. I am proud because her potential offers even more proof and hope for the generation that will stand on the rising generation's shoulders.

I present the following salute to black power in honor of what we, as generations, have been able to do, pushing social justice and social changes, black people and other people of color need. We hoped to make a better world for young people waiting in the wings, as leaders of *"The 400ᵗʰ"* generation. Truthfully, *"The 400th"* was conceived as the platform on which they can build their dreams, and further the hope that arrived with *"The 400ᵗʰ"*. My generations' challenge is to turn that platform into a launch path for the budding dreams of starry-eyed dreamers that see a tomorrow without racial or economic barriers. *"The 400ᵗʰ"* can open access to America's bounty, where they will receive the benefits of our fight against discrimination, disparate treatment and denial as a reward of American citizenship.

It is true most of my social change and social justice work concentrated on reducing problems descendants of Americans slavery faced, but the impact of projects I have undertaken today has spread abroad to touch people the world over. I had no idea people I would meet and work with on this amazing journey, whether they are descendants of slavery or descendants of slave masters, would embrace *"The 400ᵗʰ"*.

Growing up in poverty, during my life before adulthood, nothing I experienced indicated the importance of what I would do throughout my life to help change the world for the better. Everything important that happened in my life has been a result of my encounter with black power and helping organize the *Invaders*. That fortuitous event for me was like lightning out of a clear blue sky. It changed everything about me, and with those changes, a new world opened to me. Since encountering those two words—black power—which probably does not mean much to most people today, but for me back then, encountering the bear face of racism, hatred, and denial of *VOICE*, I experienced that July evening, I wouldn't have traveled that path.

The 400th: From Slavery to Hip Hop

Unprepared for what that event did, change, time and *Divine Intervention* made my *"stolen gas cap"* the doorway to my future. Sometime change seeks one out for their own good, although they would never embrace what it brings, if it came any other way. Such changes bring choices, whether one realize it or not. **"Black Power,"** because of that *"gas cap"* created a story through a chain of events, which gave me an opportunity to be part of the changes from the pre-1960s world of segregation, denial of voice and total degradation to the hopeful world black power engendered. Those events did not bring guarantees that those out in the streets could bank on to justify their efforts, but that is why the hope change brings becomes an act of faith and courage. One must trust and believe in what is going on in their heads, not what they are told or even see. One can not get a sneak peek behind the curtain, to learn how the magic works. This is why some people, even more unlikely than I, were drawn into black power and the production of the Invaders story, as characters.

A hushed-up story since 1968, the Invaders reached out across time and space to touch two very unlikely characters Prichard Smith and J. B. Horrell. Much like me before the "gas cap incident," these unlikely heroes were lured into this convoluted saga, by an even more unlikely character that never should have become part of their lives "Sweet Willie Wine." An event in Memphis they only heard about trapped these two white guys, as the hand of fate reached across 40 years to draw them into this story that would not die.

Prichard became a cutting edge documentarian after film school at the University of Memphis. J. B., somewhat like Douglas A. Blackmon, looking at the graveyard in US Steel's backyard, stumbled across this well buried story about the Invaders, through a friend that told him about "Sweet Willie Wine and the Invaders," which he shared with Prichard. They asked themselves, *"How could we grow up in Memphis and never hear about the Invaders. A black power group in Memphis that was the last to meet with Dr. Martin Luther King, Jr., minutes before his assassination? This is unbelievable. Why or how is it we never heard anything about them?"*

Drawn into an incredulous sounding story, at the beginning, they became consumed by it. Prichard and J.B. became enthralled, trying to piece together such an incredible story only a few people knew about, so they shared the story with another friend, Chad Schaffler. Again, like the way black power took over my life, they have spent the last seven years researching, developing, filming, and recreating the story of those heady days in 1968.

I detailed most of the *Invaders* story earlier in this narrative, but how the documentary came together is a story in itself. As I have said, this narrative is about the impact of people I present, not their lives. Researching the *Invaders*, Prichard and J. B. learned that black power was far more than just a catchy phrase.

JB was in Grad school at the time but the *Invaders* story stole him from a fate he had come to question, as it did me. Prichard brought new eyes that looked at that period—1968—including the last turbulent days of Dr. Martin Luther King's life, and saw a struggle for power against the forces of the old universe of segregation and the new world black power was creating in Memphis. The vision he and J. B. brought to this many sided story, they told from the perspective of the police and the FBI, then C.O.M.E, as complicated by civil rights leaders, coupled with the suffering of the sanitation workers and finally, the story of a powerless community. I believe not knowing anything about the story, left Pritchard, J.B. and Chad without filter, which allowed them to follow their instincts; that made the difference in how the story emerged.

Again though white guys, Prichard's team brought a different energy, pushing a desire for truth over the lies of segregation. That demand produced a powerful story, even though they began with very few artifacts on which to hang their beliefs about what really happened, during that very hectic 9 mount period in which the Invaders emerged from the Riverside ghetto in South Memphis.

They did something no one had tried, seeing the story through the eyes of the *Invaders* and telling it in their own words, as much as possible. Prichard, JB and Chad were like flies on the wall, given wings 44 years after the fact. They used archival footage to visually transport viewers back to, not only the founding and activities of the Invaders but gave a truer reflection of the police attack upon Dr. King's last march.

Seeing the police riot and battle today, which occurred as a result of police blocking Dr. King's advance toward City Hall, then they attacked marchers, causing the chaos that erupted, overwhelming and engulfing marchers. The dramatic footage had never been seen, except as news footage. Reviews get the Invaders reflective response to the chaos created by attacking police. Prichard Smith's perspective made it abundantly clear the police were the culprits. Instinctively he swung the camera to show the line of police, with clubs drawn awaiting Dr. King, as they sprang the trap on marchers. Using actual scenes from archival footage of that day, the action comes jumping off the screen, leaving no doubt of the story's authenticity. The mayhem exploding before viewers eyes, make them eyewitness to those anxious rancorous moments, as young black power activists battling police on Beale Street. Their heroic stand covered frighten, panicky and retreating marchers trying to escape the police trap.

The *Invaders* documentary, gives physical existence to a history that had existed only as part of black people's "word of mouth history." It was a legend that has been talked about for over fifty years only among black people in Memphis. Consequently, the *Invaders'* story has lived on thanks to flamboyant characters that cherished everything that happened on and around Beale Street. The assassination of Dr. Martin Luther King, Jr. was such a huge and devastating event it overshadowed the *Invaders'* involvement, so most people were unaware of their existence.

The 400th: From Slavery to Hip Hop

Thanks to Prichard, J. B. and Chad's presentation of *The Invaders* story, African Americans are able to visually mark a major turning point in our effort to reach **"The 400th"**. This fact is borne out by writers that contend the assassination of Dr. Martin Luther King, Jr. is the most prominent event of the late 20th century. Moreover, telling the *Invaders* story Prichard, J. B., and Chad provides a visual link to an event that allows descendants of slavery, America and the world to witness their completion of the transition from civil rights to black power in our drive to become one people.

The *Invaders* documentary becomes a globe trotter in the next section. An international runner, Arish "King" Khan, takes the salute to black power on the road. Using his international clout as a "punk rock" entertainer and artist, Arish takes black power to an entirely new audience.

Much like my efforts digging around in the graveyard of poverty in the valley of dry bone, Arish has breathed life into an international effort to bring hope to millions, looking for a way to give *VOICE* to their demands for social change and social justice. Hip hopping the world with "King" Khan, like runners on the *Underground Railroad*, we picked up icons like Floyd Tunson, who joined the party in 2016 and made **The Black Power Tarot Card Exhibition** and ***Invaders Documentary Screening*** part of his exhibition **"Floyd Tunson "REMIXED"** at Red Line Gallery in Denver, Colorado for a big party in July 2020 and the introduction of **"The 400th" From Slavery to Hip Hop** to the world. Unfortunately, COVID-19 has put the world on lockdown as well as **The Black Power Tarot Card Exhibition** and ***Invaders Documentary Screening***, so that party, like everything else is on hold, but to be continued in 2021 same place and same city.

Taking Black Power on the Road

This new black power revolution found other new advocates, like Prichard Smith (documentary filmmaker). They are finding new and different ways to tweak the minds of young progressives around the world. One of these devil-may-care, swashbuckling lone riders is Arish A. Khan (aka King Khan). I met "King" Khan just after I was introduced to his music by Prichard. Impressed, I suggested Prichard asked Arish to compose the soundtrack for the *Invaders* documentary. "King" Khan is a really popular, well known and highly regarded punk rock artist on the international music scene. He has lived in Berlin, Germany, for the past two decades.

The thing that brought us together, as brothers, was Arish's **Black Power Tarot Card Exhibition.** Arish created a deck of Tarot cards along with Irish artist Michael Eaton, under the tutorage of Tarot master Alejandro Jodorowsky, an avant-garde surrealist film director from the 1970s. Arish and Michael developed the **Black Power Tarot** deck from the original Tarot de Marseille deck, created in the 17th century. For those unfamiliar with tarot, the Tarot de Marseille deck is among the oldest decks in existence. Following Jodorowsky's guidance, tarot became Khan's creative muse.

The uniqueness of Arish's **Black Power Tarot** deck is he used images of 26 prominent African American entertainment legends, including two magicians, one civil rights activist, and one comedian, which serve as icons along the *"path of illumination."* The *"path of illumination"* begins with the "Fool's journey," which beginning with trying to gain an understanding of *"The World."* I will give just a little insight into why King's tarot deck reflects the importance of the new movement of black power. Today, as social change and social justice activists, we are using Arish's deck to bring people together around keeping the hopes of Dr. Martin Luther King's **"Poor People's Campaign"** alive.

Arish's real-life adventure began while still a very young man. *"My journey to enlightenment began when I fled the house of my tyrannical drug-addicted father. Leaving home at age seventeen, I felt like maybe, Sweet Sweetback's Baadasssss run to find freedom or maybe even like slaves trying to get to Canada on the Underground Railroad, my life was awful and that is no exaggeration. I know I'm not the same as a slave, because that had to be the worst experience of any human being. When you are in such a place and a kid your imagination takes over. Lucky for me I found refuge among Native People in Canada, and was able to find a real purpose in life. Living with the Mohawks, on their reservation, I learned to tap into their spirituality, searching for meaning for myself, in a world without a role model for people like me. I was not running from demons in my past, but running toward the freedom to be something I understood."*

That journey of spiritual growth enabled Arish to connect with the struggles of Native People, as well as, American descendants of slavery. He read the

The 400th: From Slavery to Hip Hop

<u>*Autobiography of Malcolm X*</u> at age 12 and continued studying black culture, as a maturing young man. Arish said, *"I became captivated by black power because it encouraged me to pursue free expression of new ideas."* Arish was also shaped by the early punk rock scene, which left an indelible mark on him, as most young progressive in the 1970s. Arish is not an anomaly. He resembles millions of young people that change took one way, while taking others in another direction; whatever the forces of the universe designed? Once on the *'path of illumination,'* I believe, those universal influences brought us together around his **Black Power Tarot** deck.

Arish's entertainment career was another wild ride from the edge of obscurity into the heart of "punk rock," as **"Black Snake."** Rather eclectic by nature Arish said, *"I dabbled in and was influenced by many musicians and musical styles that is how I became known as 'King' Khan. I was drawn into the world of R&B and free jazz, where I met and was tutored by some of R&B's most eccentric characters and iconic legends, like Andre Williams 'The Mighty Hannibal,' Jalacy 'Screamin' Jay' Hawkins and 'Sun Ra Arkestra.'*

These **Blues** *icons befriended and even mentored me, like a son. Many of black music's icons became the father I never had; they helped me learn to draw on the universal' energy through music. This is when music took charge of my development, as a maturing young man."*

I will say finding his path in music is why and how the two of us were brought together around the **Black Power Tarot Card Exhibition** project and the **Invaders Documentary**. Those projects became important quest for "King" Khan. He wanted to show the world that tarot is an ancient language that can help people find and follow their path to knowledge of self—*"illumination."*

Arish explained that, **"Black Power Tarot** *is not gimmickry and has nothing to do with fortune-telling. It is not fan worship or spook-ism. I believe using the likenesses of prominent black entertainers, infused my deck with the mythology of the archetypes from the timeless universe of tarot. Drawing on the spiritual power of black icons, like comedian Richard Pryor, soul music legends Nina Simone, 'Screaming Jay' Hawkins, Etta James, Sun Ra, James Brown, Little Richard, Tina Turner, Irma Thomas, Curtis Mayfield, as well as hip hopper icon Tupac Shakur, spiritualist Sister Rosetta Tharpe and others, tapped into the hoodoo roots of African American spirituality through the reflections of these archetypes. I followed the example of painter Kehinde Wiley, He flipped the script, on early renaissance "old master" painters, replacing Caucasian Arch Dukes, replacing the faces of contemporary young men of color. I applied a similar psychology and technique to infuse my* **Black Power Tarot** *deck with the essence of comedy, wizardry, priestesses, preachers, alchemists, revolutionaries and R&B icons."*

True to his nature, 'King' Khan went one step further, *"I hooked up with artist Michael Eaton to recreate my tarot cards. I was very impressed with Michael's work creating the charts and maps for 'Game of Thrones.' Mike helped me create an art exhibit of Black Power Tarot by painting and turning the 22 cards into giant 4x10 ft. high artistic renderings."*

Arish's genius was obvious to me when he created the art exhibit that allowed us to take **Black Power Tarot** into Art Galleries. Arish's exhibit flipped the script for social change and social justice, adding the **Invaders Documentary** screening to his **Black Power Tarot Card Exhibition.** This blew up **Black Power,** giving it new life. It allowed us to take it to new audiences without actual direct exposure to black power around the world. Arish created a roadshow for us to bring *"The 400th"* to the world.

So, Arish and I took to the road, hip-hopping the world raising awareness about the unmet goals of Dr. Martin Luther King, Jr.'s **"Poor People's Campaign."** But, the thing that makes "King" Khan's road show a hit with young people is he has also turning his art exhibition into a meet and greet tour. That allow us to introduce international audiences to the *Invaders'* story, as well as, connect with young people in ways I never dreamed. Through Arish's tour, I'm able to share my experiences, as a social change and social justice activist, with both older and younger audiences.

Together "King" Khan and I took on the goal of educating the world about the fact the investigation file into the assassination of Dr. Martin Luther King, Jr. is a prisoner in Washington, D.C. It was locked up by the US House of Representatives in 1978; **"Free Dr. King's File!!!"** as well as **"Help Get the Truth out of Jail in America!!"** are our slogan. The investigation file is on lockdown in jail in Washington, D.C., to keep the truth about the government's role in Dr. King's assassination hidden from the public. America is the only modern nation in the industrialized world where the truth can be locked up in jail indefinitely. Arish decided to use his **Black Power Tarot Card Exhibition** and the **Invaders Documentary Screening** to bail the "truth out of jail" in America. The fact that 2018 was the 50th year since the assassination of Dr. King and the truth is still on lockdown in jail in Washington D. C. "King" Khan and I think that is long enough for a lie to run free.

"Truth forever on the scaffold, wrong forever on the throne—yet that scaffold sways the future, and, behind the unknown, standeth God within the shadow, keeping watch above his own." (James Russell Lowell).

Black Power Heads for Europe

Taking black power on the road, "King" Khan and I kicked things off, at the University of Colorado at Colorado Springs (UCCS). Daisy McGowan, a very brave and forward-looking curator for the Gallery of Contemporary Arts (GOCA), truly believed in Arish's mission with the ***Black Power Tarot Card Exhibition and Invaders Screening Tour***. She recognized the positive force for good it is and insisted on being the first to present the tour, with a three-day weekend affair, back in 2016.

The tour allows me to speak about the relevance of social change and social justice with students. I used my granddaughter Tahlia's Social science project, as a visual aid. Arish presented ***The Black Power Tarot Cards Art Exhibition*** at GOCA and held readings while the ***Invaders documentary*** was debuted. The Q&A following the viewing was truly enjoyable, taking the audience back to a time that is very difficult to imagine now, but with Donald Trump madness dominating America, it is like living in a time warp. The audience responded enthusiastically to the film and the discussion on social change and social justice. "King" Khan was so impressed with young progressives' response to the tour he decided to take it on an international spin.

We hit the Autobahn, beginning in Berlin, Arish's home, with the ***Black Power Tarot Cards Exhibition and Invaders Screening***. Arish threw a three day (11-1/3-216) affair before we headed to Utrecht, The Netherlands (11-4/6-16) for *"Le Guess Who?"* Although this tour is built around music, as well as having a good time with young people, we were using entertainment for a very serious purpose. We were trying to get the word out to young progressives and interest them in the power of social change and social justice.

Germany, is a nation, which had its problems with human rights violations and battled back to earn its place among progressive nations again, unlike America which is headed in the opposite direction. Sooner or later, America will have to make a similar journey, as Germany, because it continues its' genocidal violations of descendants of American slavery's human rights. Berliners showed real support for our campaign to get the "truth out of jail" in America.

The Black Power Tarot Card Exhibition and ***Invaders Documentary*** is more than a talking tour; one can consider it a crusade, with music as a weapon. "King" Khan wanted his tour to really "rock" the world out of its sleep, which allowed fascism to rise again, not only in Europe but of all places, America where the "Trump era" is in full bloom. It is as though African Americans are afraid to let the words ***black power*** come out of their mouths. So, when Arish "King" Khan said we should do a tour, I said, "HELL YES"!!!!

The tour opened with a viewing of the Invaders documentary at Il Kino, an avant-garde theater/bar. An overflow crowd of young progressives maxed out the theater, eager to be part of the first *"Invaders take Europe."* Anastasia Lévy hosted the evening's event. Although they were unaware of the *Invaders*, before the screening, everyone identified with the archival footage of Dr. King. German's "punk rockers" are really big fans of "King" Khan. They enthusiastically wanted to kick his tour off in style.

Following the viewing the next evening, we rocked with *"Black Lips,"* as they headlined a fabulous concert at Festhalle Kreuzberg. Wilding it out with these "bad boy" punk rockers, trying to get the truth out of jail in America, was a real blast. However, before *"Black Lips,"* hit the stage to do their thing, the crowd treated me like a celeb or "MC," as I introduced the next generation of rockers, Saba Lou, Khan's daughter, and her band.

Opening the show, Saba Lou really pumped up the crowd for this classic rock throw down. Taking the stage with their usual wild antics and great music, *Black Lips* showed this stateside R&B boy, Berliners really know how to jam. Capping the night, the party moved to Alberto's famed *"Wowsville"* Bar/classic Record Collector's Emporium. Alberto served his internationally renowned "Paella" for late-night dining. I had a great time for my first Berlin. I had no idea what to expect, so I was the only one surprised by the truly great reception and send off to Utrecht for the internationally recognized *"LE GUESS WHO?"* music festival." I still get very warm feelings, thinking of all the fun and great times we had, jamming it up with new and old friends.

"Le Guess Who?" is one of the premier music throw downs in Europe. It has a long-standing reputation for presenting great music and special attractions like the **Black Power Tarot Card Exhibition** and **Invaders Screening**. Bob van Huer, director of *"Le Guess Who?"* showed tremendous courage, stepping out, as the first major international music festival to present the **Black Power Tarot Card Exhibition** and **Invaders Screening**, at a hugely prestigious venue, like *"Le Guess Who?"* **"The Black Power Tarot Card Exhibition and Invaders Screening"** was extremely fortunate to be included among such an outstanding lineup of international talents. For instance, Pharaoh Sanders, now in his eighties, was there, still jamming. Although it was very risky to present an unknown quantity, like our show, festival-goers responses justified Bob van Huer confidence, because we received a very warm and enthusiastic reception. Concert goers waited in line for each session "King" Khan held readings. It seemed everyone wanted a tarot reading by "King."

Although festival revelers were unfamiliar with the *Invaders*, like those in Berlin, being paired with "King" Khan and **Black Power Tarot** readings, the *Invaders* screening became part of the theme and magic of *"Le Guess Who?"* The *Invaders* documentary viewing went great, and while being on the international scene, as well as an unknown quantity, extended the Q&A. *"Le Guess Who-ers?"* were very interested in social change and social justice. They are serious in their search for knowledge, so the **Invaders Screening** filled in some of the blanks

The 400th: From Slavery to Hip Hop

about the importance of taking real stands in the world we have today, with the return of leaders like Donald Trump.

I was blown away when *Black Lips* strolled into the **Invaders Screening and Q&A** just before the documentary rolled. It was so great seeing Cole, Zumi, Oakley and Jared; they are truly helping get the word out about the tour. Running long, I continued the conversations and answering questions, while we hurried to catch "Moor Mother," a Philadelphia rapper that is making real waves on the international scene.

The whole venue was so stimulating and interesting, talking about social activism/social justice, while comparing the 1960s and Dr. King today, with serious young progressives looking for direction was awesome. I hung out with a different group of young people each day, while "King" Khan held **Black Power Tarot** readings for lines that did not end. Both events were big hits with concertgoers. The *Invaders* documentary created great interest among *"Le Guess Who-ers,"* wanting to help get the truth out of jail in America. Interest is growing among people on the international scene, who want to be part of pushing America to let the truth out of jail. The liar in Washington should be in jail; instead truth is. Locked up in America, truth is on the scaffold, and Arish and I are asking young progressives to help spring the truth in 2020!!!!!!!

Viva con Agua: Water is Life

During the Berlin tour, I met a young progressive, Maria Owczarz. Excited by the Invaders documentary, she proposed bringing it to students at Humboldt University in Berlin in 2017. Maria and her professors talked with the US Embassy about the project, which was initiated before Donald Trump took control. The US still represented a beckon of hope for many in Europe.

Moreover, the US Department of State was still trying to keep alive its past image, by fostering its cold war rhetoric that was pervaded by Radio Free Europe and its WWII propaganda. The Embassy jumped on board the social change and social justice tour. Envisioning the tour as a means of influencing young people in Germany through social change and social justice, the Embassy set up a four-city 15 days tour for the *Invaders Screening* and Q&A.

The four-city German tour was to commemorate Dr. Martin Luther King, Jr.'s 1964 visit to Berlin. It was not an arts presentation, so it did not include the **Black Tarot Card Exhibition**. Even though, "King" Khan was not part of the bill, thankfully he graciously consented to accompany me and be my envoy for the first three cities. The tour began in Leipzig on Monday. However, I arrived in Berlin on Friday to catch another *Black Lips* "bad boy" throw down that night at *Wild at Heart,* a classic rock venue Alberto is bringing back to popularity with groups like *"Black Lips."*

It was another wild night, no pun intended, with the Berlin gang from my first stop over, plus a growing family of social change and social justice activists, showed up and made it a great night. Catching my first Berlin sunrise, after the show, I met and talked with Berliners that wanted to get aboard the social change and social justice train ride. We partied with lots of great German beer, while I spent the early morning hours, hanging out at "King" Khan's place with his wife Lil while talking with *Black Lips*—Cole, Zumi, Oakley, Jared and Jeff, an excellent Canadian guitarist. There were other longtime family friends I became acquainted, while talking about ***"The 400th"*** and watched the movie *Cobra Verde* (1978) starring Klaus Kinski. *Cobra Verde* is about the end of the **Tran-Atlantic Slave Trade (1807);** it fit the occasion perfectly.

Monday afternoon, Arish and I boarded the train to Leipzig, where the tour began Tuesday morning. The US consulate invited me to commemorate not only Dr. Martin Luther King, Jr.'s visit to Berlin in September 1964 but his birthday as well. Berlin was a divided city, as well as the rest of Germany in 1964. It was great starting the tour speaking to a very enthusiastic group of high school students of advanced English at Evangelisches Schulzentrum, plus their teachers. I met a Libyan student, Almontaser Bujazia, with whom I talked at length. I was touched, as he talked of his desire to stay home and fight for a new Libya. His

The 400th: From Slavery to Hip Hop

family sent him to Europe to insure their family's story continued, somewhat like me, remaining behind in Mississippi.

I detected a note of shame on Almontaser's part, so I told him, "There is no shame in being the hope of your family. You should be honored that they had such confidence in you. The sacrifices your parents made, getting you to Europe, comes with real obligation. So, you must do well in school to justify their confidence."

Almontaser was also a reflection of his classmates, beyond being good students, they were all great kids. And of course, everyone wanted to take selfies for their Facebook page. Truthfully, I enjoyed the selfies also.

Our tour guide, Embassy Information Specialist, Anika Kreller, drove us to the Martin-Luther-King Zentrum Center, which is in of all places, a very small village out in the countryside Stadtgutstraße, Werdau. Its location was very surprising to me, in that Dr. King had such devotion among the German people. Although there was a language barrier, Anika did a marvelous job interpreting.

The screening was for members of the MLK Center, students and teachers from local high schools. They were unfamiliar with the *Invaders*, like everyone in other places, but the archival footage of Dr. King and the sanitation workers strike provided real context and a point of identification. Returning to Berlin, I got an extended look at Germany's lovely countryside. It was like being in a scene from old black and white movies of Europe; I watched as a child. The narrow roads, confusing road signs, and of course, driving on the wrong side of the road made the trip very personal.

Cultural Affairs Assistant Kerstin Reichert met us the next morning back in Berlin and accompanied by Cultural Attaché Michelle Logsdon; we toured all the sites Dr. King visited during his 1964 trip to Berlin. Students of two high schools (Ernst-Reuter-Schule from Wedding and Rosa-Luxemburg-Oberschule Berlin-Pankow) worked together to develop a multifaceted project and tour, which they called the "King Code." It retraces Dr. King's path from his 1964 visit.

Students and their teacher, Daniel Schmöcker from Rosa-Luxemburg-Oberschule Berlin-Pankow, guided us to each site along the "King Code." Together with students from the Ernst-Reuter-Schule from Wedding, they designed and completed the project in 2014. The "King Code" project tour, like my trip to Germany, was also in recognition of the 54th anniversary of Dr. King,'s legendary 1964 visit to East Berlin.

Riding on the way to the next stop, we passed the Holocaust Memorial just before the Brandenburg Gate. The Holocaust Memorial was the first place Arish showed me, during my first trip to Germany, on the way to *"Le Guess Who?"*

I feel a special connection to the Holocaust Memorial because both Jews and American slave descendants suffered genocide. Even more importantly, Germany recognized the horror of its actions and took responsibility. But

America, the last nation to end legal slavery, even after a bloody Civil War, still refuses even to acknowledge its crimes against humanity.

First, we visited Stallschreiberstrasse 42 in Kreuzberg, where, unlike Dr. King, we saw only remnants of the "Berlin Wall." This site memorializes hundreds of East Berliners that made their mad, desperate dash for freedom and life; many died in the process. Memories from watching old WWII and Cold War movies were refreshed on the way to visit Marienkirche, the oldest church in Berlin. We passed "Check Point Charlie," a major East/West Berlin Wall border crossing. Also, it was part of Arish's tour on my first trip to Berlin. Arriving at one of the most iconic sites—Marienkirche—which was in East Germany and why Dr. King went behind the "Iron Curtain." No one was sure Dr. King would be allowed into communist East Berlin. Nevertheless, hundreds of East Berliners were waiting in the packed church and outside when he arrived, even though there was no announcement. Based on "word of mouth," so many East Germens showed up, Dr. King preached a second sermon at Sophienkirche, which was our third stop.

The West German authorities were afraid of what the communist East Germans might do, so they didn't want Dr. King to go to East Berlin and took his passport. They were confident that would stop him from going to East Berlin. But, Dr. King was very determined, as well as very clever. When he reached "Check Point Charley," he gave the East German guards his *"American Express credit card."* They accepted it and allowed him to cross and go behind the *"Berlin Wall"* into East Berlin.

The last stop was Hotel Albrechtshof. There Dr. King met religious leaders of all faiths. They prayed and had a meal together. Just as amazing, as touring these sites, I learned these students designed an app for cell phones, which visitors to Berlin can down loud and follow Dr. King's steps, as we did. The app provides the information students gave at each stop along the *"King Code."* The tour was awesome, but more importantly to me, Germans students cared so much about Dr. King's legacy, they devoted their time, so others could experience what few people know. (Flickr photos of the King Code tour: https://flic.kr/s/aHskCQpUPh)

Leaving Cultural Attaché Michelle Logsdon at the Embassy, the tour continued to the screening of The *INVADERS* and Q&A with students and faculty at Humboldt University. Maria Owczarz hosted the events. Of course, the Q&A ran over because students attending the packed theater were so interested in the *Invaders*, a group they had never heard about, as well as their interest in social change, it seemed everyone had questions.

After the screening, Maria, Oskar, her supporters, and faculty members took me out for pizza, German beer, and more questions about social change and social justice.

The 400th: From Slavery to Hip Hop

Later that evening, the old Berlin gang got together at *WOWSVILLE* again, where Alberto and Arish threw a big welcome back to the Berlin party. Oskar, a member of Saba Lou's band, opened the show with a rocking set. Oskar was followed to the stage by *"King Khan and BBQ Show"* with Mark Sultan, even Jared Swilley of *Black Lips* showed up to do a couple of songs. We had a great time wilding it out again. I had a great night. The German tour continued providing surprising connections, as people really identified with **"The 400th"** and wanted to be part of it.

For instance, I met a friend of "King" Khan's, Nadia Buyse. A very cool activist, who writes for a London magazine called *Ragged Cult*. Our conversation was about collaborating on some interview ideas, but we ended up talking about **"The 400th"** also. Nadia offered, "*I would love to help promote it; however, I can when you get it going. It would be great for you to do something in Liverpool, like what you are doing here — bringing the Invaders and* **"The 400th"** *to Brighton and London around 2019 or 2020 that would be an awesome time. I so look forward to reading* **"The 400th"**. *I will be in the UK doing my Ph.D., maybe we could do that. I have a friend who was a curator at BFI, who would definitely know where and how to make that happen in London, and I could work on Brighton.*" Nadia has started the ball rolling. The tour of Germany began much the same way. Maria got the idea and went to work, bringing people into the project. Her success brought Nadia and me together.

The next morning Arish and I were on the train headed to Hamburg. Hamburg was a very special visit for two reasons. The first reason will take a little time. Hamburg is also the location of Viva con Agua de Sankt Pauli e.V. FC Sankt Pauli football Stadium, so bear with me. The second will come after I introduce Viva con Agua, which has a lot going on. Although millions of people around the world are very familiar with Viva con Agua, I was unacquainted with it and its nonprofit mission. Viva con Agua's mission is getting clean drinking water to people in some of the poorest nations around the globe. However, in January 2018, Arish told me he had submitted my name to Michael Fritz, head of Viva con Agua for special recognition.

Michael is the brains behind Viva con Agua's (VCA) international charity, and on "King" Khan's recommendation, Michael named me their *"Ambassador of Water."* I was totally astonished and proud that Viva con Agua confirmed Arish's suggestion (3-22-2018). I was elated VCA's wanted to honor me. Its proclamation said, *"For your vital contribution to the civil rights movement, as co-founder of the Invaders and for your service to Dr. Martin Luther King, Jr.'s* **"Poor People's Champaign."** Also, the award recognizes, *"People who have served humanity by engaging in the creation of positive social change activities as part of their life."* The award celebrates those who *"not only made change a possibility but made it a reality."* Viva con Agua hopes serving as Ambassador of Water, *"The recipient will fight to protect water and provide it to all those who are in dire need of potable water around the world."*

"Arish" explained the major reason he submitted my name was, *"VCA is a powerful advocate of corporate community responsibility and is very dedicated to getting clean drinking water to those who need it most."* Reading about VCA's mercy mission, I realized it is a story that could have come from my young life. Benjamin Adrion, former FC St. Pauli football player, while at winter training camp, experienced very serious problems, as a result of drinking contaminated water in Cuba.

Adrion called for the VCA initiative in 2005. His call began Viva con Agua's first project in Havana. VCA installed water dispenser (2006) in 153 kindergartens and four sports boarding schools to supply clean drinking water. The Cuban initiative was so impressive, Viva con Aqua replicated its new concept and mercy mission. It has expanded to 15 projects in other countries, especially several in East Africa.

Viva con Agua has groups working on the water problem in 55 cities across Germany. More importantly, since coming online in 2006, Viva con Agua De Sankt Pauli e. V. expanded to include independent clubs in Switzerland in 2009 and Spain in 2011. Growing faster than imagined, VCA accepted other spin-offs, in Austria (2014) and the Netherlands (2015), as partners in its mercy mission. Continuing to grow, Kampala, Uganda, brought Africa into the fold in 2016. "King" explained that *"Viva con Agua, which sold over 17million, bottles of water in 2016, sells toilet paper also.*

It is the *first socially relevant toilet paper* worldwide." The main idea behind VCA's use of toilet paper is to make it a social tool, similar to Arish, using his **Black Power Tarot Cards and Invaders Screening** for social change. The focus of VCA's use of toilet paper as a social tool is to raise awareness regarding the 2.5 million people across the world without access to sanitation and hygiene. Viva con Agua is a network of people and organizations committed to establishing access to basic sanitation and clean drinking water for human beings worldwide.

Again, VCA's humanitarian concerns and mercy mission—attacking the water problem—during its first six years have been very impressive. Michael has shown real commitment to his maxim, *"Water is life."* VCA's water projects used more than 2 million euros in donations to provide free access to fresh water. Michael's maxim is like giving life to over 2,000,000 people in Africa, Asia, and South America. While in Hamburg, Michael gave King and me a tour of FC St. Pauli's football club's home field Millerntor Stadium and Millerntor Gallery. It was being made ready for VCA's annual music festival held the week of July 4th. On that weekend, Millerntor Stadium and Millerntor Gallery become a canvas for artists from some of the most politically oppressed, as well as economically depressed nations.

FC Sankt Pauli football arena turns its walls, floors, support columns, and other surfaces into canvases for poor artists to recreate their work. Millerntor Gallery also provides space for poor artists to put their work on display for sale.

The 400th: From Slavery to Hip Hop

More than 20,000 people come to VCA's yearly 5-day art, music, and social festival.

What We Know About the Problem with Water

I accepted the honor "Ambassador of Water" presented by Viva con Agua, knowing I had to be a very quick study, trying to understand the myriad health problems contaminated water presents to the world. Contaminated water ranks as the number one culprits in VCA's battle to improve health for millions by giving them access to clean water. However, in the past, I approached the water problem, as a vocal critic of man-made pollution, because I thought that was the only issue. Man-made pollution is a very deadly threat to life true enough, but instead, in this case, it is not the culprit; VCA has another target. I learned first, this aspect of the problem is not so much, man-made pollution, as it is a fight against the naturally occurring cycle of life in poor underdeveloped nations.

The problem of access to clean water in such countries, in most cases, results from the way people live. For instance, visualize this scene of rural life. Typically there is a body of water—lake, river, or stream—as the sun glistens off the surface, women are washing, children are splashing about playing, while others are washing animals.

What is missing from this scene is someone, off-camera, dipping a cup in this same body of water, and takes a drink. Also missing, from this scene, are lines of women and children carrying buckets and other containers of this water home. There they not only wash their bodies with it, but their vegetables and also cook and drink this same water as well.

What am I complaining about, some may ask? These people have plenty of water to drink, they even have enough for washing, well as, some may say. However, the problem is not so much the quantity, as it is the quality of the water they have access that makes the situation a world health crisis. There are numbers of various disease-causing parasites that live, spawn, and incubated in such water. Poor water quality in many parts of the world is a major culprit, causing problems like gastrointestinal diseases, reproductive problems, neurological disorders, cancer, and even death results in many cases. Anyone can be negatively affected by these problems, but babies, young children, elderly individuals, and pregnant women are most susceptible, especially those predisposed to weakened immune systems. Much like COVID-19, such condition can worsen and become aggravated with continuously exposeure to bad water.

Lack of access to clean drinking water produces a litany of negative outcomes, which are usually accompanied by sanitation and hygiene problems. Looking at countries, like Ethiopia, Kenya, Nepal, Bangladesh, Rwanda, Uganda, Nigeria, Chad, Burkina Faso, Mali, Mauritania, Niger, Senegal and Ghana where people swim, wade, wash, bath, cook, drink and wash their animals in the same freshwater lakes, streams or rivers. Beside problems involving water quality, in such countries, one also finds the bulk of the world's other health problems.

Again, those countries mentioned above are a major source of the world's health issues and other problems related to human hygiene and sanitation as well.

People in those countries suffer from a cluster of water-wash diseases, including bacterial and protozoal diarrhea, Leptospirosis, and hepatitis A and E. For instance, Leptospirosis is a bacterial disease—genus Leptospira—that infects humans with a wide range of symptoms, including high fever, headache, abdominal pain, vomiting, diarrhea, jaundice, and joint pains. These common symptoms may be mistaken for other diseases.

Schistosomiasis, is also known as snail fever and bilharzia, is a disease caused by three species of parasitic flatworms and trematodes worms (flukes), called Schistosomes. These flatworms and trematodes lodge in the urinary tract or the intestines in humans and animals. Typhoid fever is a typical deadly infection cause by these parasites, which is marked by fever, diarrhea, and allergic reactions. Chronic effects are due to fibrosis around eggs deposited in the liver, lungs, and central nervous system.

The thing I learned which shocked me most is these diseases, though very prevalent and dangerous, are also very preventable. According to the Centers for Disease Control and Prevention (USA), *"Diarrheal diseases account for 1 in 9 child deaths worldwide, making diarrhea the second leading killer of children under age 5."* Think about that!!!! Contaminated water is a very serious problem that causes severe pain, disability, and even death. Parasites cause common water-related diseases such as Guinea worm, amebiasis, schistosomes, cryptosporidiosis (Crypto), and giardiasis. They are the source of major health crises in countries where people do not have access to clean drinking water. These waterborne diseases enter the picture most times during that placid scene of women washing and children splashing about in open water or even people work in places like rice paddies, a huge industry in many countries across Asia and some parts of Africa.

People become infected with previously mentioned diseases when they make contact with water contaminated with parasites. Sometimes they swallow such parasites because they are not visible to the necked eye. Also, swimming or wading in freshwater lakes, streams, and rivers or drinking water contaminated by fecal matter, expose individuals to Entamoeba histolytica (an anaerobic parasitic amoebozoan).

Amoebiasis, also known as amoebic dysentery, is an infection caused by any amebae of the Entamoeba group. It is a disease of the intestinal tract—an invasion of the intestinal lining results in bloody diarrhea. Common symptoms, during infection by Entamoeba Histolytica, include abdominal pain, diarrhea, or bloody diarrhea.

Complications can include inflammation and ulceration of the colon with tissue death or perforation. It may result in peritonitis (Peritonitis is bacterial infection following any rupture (perforation) in the abdomen, colon, and appendix or as a complication of other medical conditions. Symptoms include abdominal distension, bloating, fever, nausea, vomiting, and loss of appetite. People affected may develop anemia due to loss of blood.

Cysts of Entamoeba can survive for up to a month in soil or for up to 45 minutes under fingernails. If the parasite reaches the bloodstream, it can spread through the body, most frequently ending up in the liver, where it can cause amoebic liver abscesses. Liver abscesses can occur without previous diarrhea. Entamoeba is a genus of ameba parasites that lodge in the oral cavity, cecum, and large bowels of humans and other primates, in many domestic and wild mammals. It is estimated to infect about 50 million humans worldwide.

Water-based diseases are transmitted by organisms (parasites) that live in water used for human consumption or—drinking, cooking, bathing and washing. The problem is magnified when there is no other source of water. Water-based diseases are an acute problem, especially in the case of children who play and bathe in contaminated water. Such parasitic organisms, as shown above, cause a variety of serious infectious diseases that included trachoma—a bacterial infection of the eyes. Trachoma, "blindness," believe it or not, is caused by the inability to wash the face with clean water, and occurs most notably in Africa and Asia, where clean, freshwater is a major problem. It also results from poor hygiene and sanitation. Trachoma is the world's leading cause of <u>"preventable blindness."</u> Approximately 41 million people suffer from active trachoma, and nearly 10 million people are visually impaired or irreversibly blind. A process as simple as increased facial cleanliness with soap and clean water, and improved sanitation could prevent many of these 50 million cases of trachoma infections in these areas.

Another gem of knowledge I learned is Scabies—the "seven-year itch"—is a contagious skin infection caused by a female mite, Sarcoptes scabiei var. hominis, an ectoparasite that burrows into the skin to live and deposit eggs. The female mite causes an infection that is accompanied by severe itchiness and a pimple-like rash. Crowded living conditions, such as camps, group homes, childcare facilities, or prisons, are excellent examples. Huddled together, people increase the risk of spreading such infections. Also, Shigellosis is a common infectious group of bacteria that thrive in wet, damp environments. Shigella causes diarrhea, stomach cramps, and fever. Most cases get better with fluid replacement and rest; if fluid replacement is from the same contaminated water, the condition will become aggravated.

For those living in most industrialized nations, it is relatively easy to prevent most diseases mentioned here. One simply goes into the bathroom wash their hands, face, and body regularly. They drink water from bottles or tap, so they maintain good health and hygiene. However, such easy access to clean water and sanitation remains a major hurdle for 783 million people living in countries like Uganda, Nepal, Ethiopia, Kenya, Senegal, Ghana, and South Africa—the Slave

Coast. Also, they are among the "2.5 billion human beings" that have no access to sanitary facilities.

According to the World Health Organization (WHO), access to a clean water supply reduces diarrheal morbidity by 21%, improved sanitation reduces diarrheal morbidity by another 37.5 %, and additional improvement of drinking-water quality, such as point of use disinfection, could reduce diarrheal episodes 45 %. Think of the number of babies under age 5 years that would survive. Access to clean water may impact other water-borne diseases and parasitical infections similarly, as it does for diarrheal episodes.

The litany of negative effects presented here underscores the importance to me of Viva con Agua de Sankt Pauli e. V's appointment as "Ambassador of Water." For me, it is an undertaking I accept with anticipation, and I believe it recognizes my social change experience and activism, as an asset in the battle to improve world health. Together we can do battle physically and psychologically on this old battlefield but with modern technology. We can carry the fights of bringing clean water and better hygiene and sanitation to poor regions of the world.

Through VCA's aggressive program I have opportunities to have a positive impact on dire outcomes among many desperately poor human beings around the world. I can't say, this is what Dr. Martin Luther King, Jr. had in mind when he launched the ***"Poor People's Campaign"*** (12-4-67), but I do know he wanted to help the poor any way he could where ever they resided, VCA and I feel the same. Unfortunately, there are only a few nations and groups like Viva con Agua that are currently working diligently on such preventable health problems related to contaminated water worldwide. But joyfully, I will have an opportunity to get into the fight against waterborne diseases on Viva con Agua's side.

Back to the Second Reason

The second reason that made the trip to Hamburg special, as I said earlier, was seeing Viva con Agua prepare for its major event of the year. So, the US Embassy arranged tour to Hamburg, allowed me to make my social change and social justice advocacy truly rewarding in new ways, plus interact with others engaged in those processes, as well. The most interesting place we visited was once a battle ground, fought over space for homeless and others in Hamburg, similar to other urban communities in industrialized counties.

The area in Hamburg is called Fabrique im Gängeviertel. According to Nils Kasisk, a Viva con Agua specialist, the community was slated for gentrification. It is an area where artists, refugees, and the homeless made their community. Artists, social justice, and social change activists led the effort to arouse the community of refugees and homeless, who came together in a fight to preserve their space. They fought to preserve the natural charm, beauty, character and architecture of the community.

Along with keeping their community, they kept rent and other aspects of the community's economy affordable for those who live there. For me, what they have preserved is so impressive—coming from America, where anything older than yesterday is a throw-a-way piece of the past. Americans want new and modern everything, except with race and human relations, where they want the past!

The first thing we encountered that really caught Arish "King" Khan's eyes was a relic, which captured the essence of East Germany's past. A huge monster water-cannon tank, dominated the view, which was used for crowd control, back when the East German secret police ruled Hamburg. The water-cannon tank parked out front of Fabrique im Gängeviertel reflected another change in times. The scene brought back flashes from 1968, during the Memphis sanitation workers strike and the attacks by billy club swinging Memphis cops or water hoses and dogs in Birmingham, Alabama.

Looking up and down the street, I saw several huge murals painted on the exteriors of buildings, while others had individual paintings on their walls. Some paintings covered buildings almost entirely. There was an open garden area with sculptures made of natural and man-made materials. A couple of painter worked at easels, while groups of young people were hanging out, they seemed like fixtures in this peaceful setting. Some young people sat on windowsills, porches, in hall and doorways all around, giving the area character, blended into this avant-garde backdrop. The atmosphere really gave me a sense of continuity, as we headed for the *Invaders* screening and Q&A. I felt I could anticipate the conversation following the screening, after walking through such a naturalistic scene.

The 400th: From Slavery to Hip Hop

Fabrique im Gängeviertel is a community artist workshop, and to my surprise, the room overflowed with enthusiastic attendees. The community came out big time, and after viewing the *Invaders* documentary, they were very eager participants in the Q&A. Enthusiastically, the audience contributed stories of their battle to preserve their community, quickly bringing us together on social change and social justice. I knew I was talking with people I came to see, as they reveal their social change strategies to save their community. We came together as comrades for social change and justice.

Surprisingly there was a large contingent of Africans attendees, some were refugees, but all made an effort to make me feel welcome. They were very responsive to the story behind the *Invaders*, just as I identified with their fight for their community. I met Raoul Tacou, an activist leader with several African community organizations in Hamburg that works with refugees. He is from Cameroon and has lived in Germany ten years. Raoul works in the chemical industry, dealing with chemical safety. His specialty is environmental health issues. He is a qualified regulatory toxicologist.

Raoul believes in integrating Africans (refugees, workers, students, and children with African backgrounds) into Germany's communities. He promotes and defends their rights, as well as access to German society. He also helps African and Germans contribute to sustainable development in Africa through different projects that try to maintain political, educational, health, and environmental integrity. Currently, he is an active participant with several important round table projects. One project, *"Hamburger Runder Tisch Koloniales Erbe,"* reviews colonialism and discuss restitution of colonial heritage from Germany to Africa.

Nils Kasisk is a big supporter of Fabrique im Gängeviertel and gave a tour of a very special space—the art gallery. It provides a venue and opportunities for refugees and other artists unable to leave countries that are dominated by oppressive governments. The gallery displayed some very beautiful artwork of refugees. Some artists are not allowed to leave their countries and must smuggle their works out. This gallery helps artists earn money and get exposure. Many artists Michael brings to Millerntor Stadium and Millerntor Gallery, for the July 4 celebration, got their first exposure at this gallery, before Michael recruited them to the July 4 celebration.

After the *Invaders'* screening, the second big event for coming to Hamburg arrived. Michael presented me with a huge plaque, officially appointing me *"Ambassador of Water"* for Viva con Agua. The award is why I made a big deal out of my Hamburg trip. Hamburg was very special, for the international exposure for Arish and my efforts with the **Black Power Tarot Card Exhibition** and **Invaders Screening**.

Munich: A Fitting End to a Great Adventure

Leaving Hamburg headed for Munich, the guys—the Viva con Agua FC St. Pauli crew —Felix, Nils, Tobias, Big-F, "King" Khan, and Michael gave me a great German sendoff. Munich was the last stop on my Germany tour and very different for two reasons. First, Arish "King" Khan was unable to accompany me, so I was on my own in Munich, at least for a while. The second reason is I met some amazing people who made Munich a fitting end to a great adventure. Starting on Thursday, Public Affairs Officer (PAO) Stephen Ibelli, from the US Consulate in Munich, was my envoy. Stephen carried me to a 6:00 PM *Invaders* screening and Q&A with American Studies and History students at Ludwig-Maximillian University.

I had the pleasure of meeting another contingent of Africans; some were exchange students. Program Assistant Jasmin Araghi and Mathilda Legitimus led this group. But, amazingly, I met an ex-patriot homeboy from McComb, Mississippi, Ray Moore, who was in attendance. An artist from the early school of hip hop, Ray also works and dabbles in various genres on many levels to keep his magic strong. Ray is a very serious brother, especially when it comes to advancing the cause of oppressed people. His poem *"Let Us Not Forget"* conveys why he climbed aboard **"The 400th"** international ride to help get the word out in Germany and across Europe.

The Q&A was a very relaxed affair, where several in attendance, while asking questions, gave lengthy introductions, before their questions. Although a bit irregular, they added clarity to world situations, during discussions. The audience was very well informed, and they were interested in information pertaining to Dr. Martin Luther King, Jr.'s 1964 visit. No one wanted to end the conversation about the *Invaders* or **"The 400th"**. So, the excitement and interesting stories were put on hold, as we adjourned to a nearby student hangout, Ray's choice, called "Puck" for pizza and more great German beer. Along with Ray and the African exchange students, Kirsten Hirschberger, assistance for event management/customer care at the Munich Trade and Convention Center, joined us.

Kirsten has been providing the light of knowledge since she was a teen. Though she does not see herself as a social change or social justice activist, I think Kirsten's writings betray her real passion. She says, *"I try to impact the world through poetic, short stories, plays and fictional creations."* Strangely, Kirsten feels more comfortable writing in English more so than her native German. She says, *"I want to speak to the world in the language most people understand. I love writing fiction, but I'm more into screenplays, that's how it all actually started. I love creating characters and putting them in play. I believe my stories give hope and offer encouragement. I write my stories for all mankind no matter their age, gender, or ethnicity; we are all the same beneath the skin".*

The 400th: From Slavery to Hip Hop

I found Kirsten to be a very engaging, insightful, and wonderful human being. She helped make my Germany visit such a pleasure.

The African exchange students were in Germany with *"Change through Exchange: Training young Change Makers Through European African Exchange."* They were sponsored by the Farfina Institute, which organized their tour; it was founded in 2012. The term "Farafina" means "Africa" in the Bambara language of West Africa. Farfina is a think-tank and research institute developed by a group of African and European scholars. Among other things, the institute focuses on discussions and research into issues that affect development and governance in Africa. Outreach allows the institute to positions itself as an international platform for reflection, dialogue, and action on Africa. Exchange students were Moses Ngoni Musanhu from Zimbabwe, Akonobea Ophelia from Ghana, and Joyce Opare also from Ghana. They were spending two weeks with social change organizations in Munich and Berlin.

Tina Monkonjay Garway oversees the exchange project. She is also a member of both the *Pan-African Working-Group in Munich AKPM e.V. /NRDB e. V.* and *"Netzwerk Rassismus and Dikriminierungsfreies Bayern"* also *"Network for a Bavaria without Racism or Discriminations."* Mathilda's son Naim-Éric was there, although he is not an exchange student. A plea got him in on all the fun and education. At 18, he was very excited to be part of the whole affair.

Moses Musanhu immediately began talking with Mathilda's brother Samuel Legitimus (initiator of the "James Baldwin Collective" in Paris), about an *Invaders* tour. Everyone was very interested in the project after viewing the *Invaders* Documentary and hearing about Dr. Martin Luther King, Jr. Students said they were, *"Encouraged by the film and enjoyed it very much."* They also commented about how they were, *"Amazed learned all the new information it presented and seeing the archival footage from the actual time of Dr. King, while learning about the Invaders for the first time!"*

Mathilda, Tina, and the African exchange students talked of organizing an effort to bring the *"Invaders"* documentary screening to Ghana and Zimbabwe. They want to organize a festival around **"The 400th"**. Their idea was to included other documentaries like *"I Am Not Your Negro," "The Price of the Ticket," "I Heard it Through the Grapevine," "Sing Your Song"* and maybe a few other films about the struggles for civil rights from the same period as *"The Invaders."* Mathilda suggested adding subtitles for French-speaking (Francophone) countries. They spoke glowingly of my desire to make a huge world-wide special festival of **"The 400th"** because it will bring other enslaved people and those that were dominated by colonialism into the celebration.

Commemorating victims of the **Trans-Atlantic Slave Trade**, while celebrating the survival of all Africans that will see **"The 400th"**, will be a historic occasion. **"The 400th"** will be the first time both continents have been able to come together on such a splendid activity around the Diaspora and **"The 400"**. I definitely think the "James Baldwin Collectives" in Europe will be a very powerful and worthy partner for such a great project on the African continent, as my European Tour!

Learning all about the African students, how they came to be in Germany was so interesting. I was very impressed with how they all wanted to be part of spreading the word about the *Invaders* and joining *"The 400th"* effort. I took photos and selfies with students and members of the *James Baldwin Collective* (German wing). The party went late, but it was not as wild as Berlin; nevertheless, it was great fun!!

My day began early on Friday, after a late-night at "Puck." The next morning I had an early rise for Gisela-Gymnasium Arcisstrat of Munich with about 90 10th, 11th, and 12th-grade students. The school is also the headquarters of the *Intercultural Youth Magazine trait d'union*, which is a platform—https://traitdunion.online for intercultural communication and cooperation for and by young people, especially students and their teachers around the world. *Trait d'union* was founded by students and teachers of the German School of Toulouse (France) and the Lycée Polyvalent International Victor Hugo of Colomiers in 1999. Since its beginning, 27 schools from 14 countries on five continents have made contributions in 30 languages. They are now partnering with schools in India and Italy.

Students interviewed me for their next issue entitled *"Integration or separation: How do we want to live?"* Of course, the fight against racism is an important topic for this issue, and during the Q&A, their questions reflected these concerns. After meeting with students, the young journalists interviewed me for about half an hour. They videotaped the interview, which was to be shown later as a podcast on YouTube through *"trait d'union TV,"* and on their Soundcloud Channel *"trait d'union Radio."* Also, they will publish the text of the interview.

My only *Invaders* screening and Q&A left was at 6:30 PM with Amnesty International for University of Munich students and *the Initiative Schwarze Menschen in Deutschland* (Initiative of Black People in Germany) at EineWeltHaus, Schwanthalerstrasse. Most of those attending the screening were members of James Baldwin Collective. Their presence made this a very easy gig. They all had stories and other antidotal information that I was more than glad to hear. After talking almost nonstop for two and a half weeks, it felt really good to let others have their say.

The next day, Saturday, was the City of Munich's birthday. A Bavarian city was established by "monks," "Munichen"born in 1158. So, I had a full day off. My homeboy, Ray Moore, graciously became my envoy for the day. He gave me a tour of Munich in a way I totally did not expect.

On this full-day off, Ray and I began with a subway excursion to the center of the city, where we began with a walk through Ray's favorite garden park on the way to "The Frauenkirche" "Münchner Dom" or "Munich Cathedral." Benedictine monks, who settled the City, constructed the huge church. The church was a stop on the *"Salt Road,"* which was a historic trade route for transporting salt, which was essential, but many regions lacked.

While strolling through the City center, I collected information on many German notables, including Orlando di Lasso, W. A. Mozart, Richard Wagner, Gustav Mahler, Richard Strauss, and Max Reger. These individuals represent the Golden Age of culture for both Munich and Bavaria. Even for a short time, Vladimir Lenin lived in Schwabing, an avant-garde heaven. Other luminaries, such as Thomas Mann, Heinrich Mann, Paul Heyse, Fanny zu Reventlow, Oskar Panizza, and Erich Mühsam also hailed from Munich. While soaking up all this culture, I was also on a souvenir hunted for the grandkids.

I learned about social change, as well as social justice advocates, like *"Der Blaue Reiter"* (The Blue Rider). This group were artists united against the Neue Künstlervereinigung München authority, which was very authoritarian and traditional (1909). Then there was *"The White Rose"* society or movement.

"The White Rose" was the first group to openly oppose the Nazi regime. Internal dissent in Germany was quickly, brutally, and efficiently smashed by the Gestapo (like social justice and social change in the south for black Americans). These activists were led by siblings, Hans and Sophie Scholl, Christoph Probst, Willi Graf, Alexander Schmorell, and Professor Kurt Huber, at the University of Munich.

Most important, *"White Rose"* was a non-violent, intellectual resistance group that fought the Third Reich, beginning in June 1942. The group conducted an anonymous leaflet and graffiti campaign, which called for active opposition to the Nazi regime. Most were arrest and faced Gestapo show trials. They were paraded before so-called Nazi People's Courts, most received death sentences.

Ray also arranged lunch with Jonathan Fischer, an independent journalist who writes for some of Germany's top publications. Jonathan is an old school **Blues** guy, who has traveled to the US several times, learning about and immersing himself in **Blues** culture. We had lunch in a little tree cover beer garden owned by *Trikont Records*, a legend in the underground or now the social change community.

Jonathan wowed us with stories from interviews with the like of Bobby Seale, Jamal Joseph, and Kathleen Cleaver. *Trikont Records*, not only released two acclaimed German documentaries, *"Black & Proud - The Soul of the Black Panther Era"* and *"Public Enemy Number One,"* which were reviewed by the New York Times. But, *Trikont Records* amazingly also released Chuck Perkins' recorded work. I learned, as with Ray, even though we never met, we know some of the same people, like my man Charleston "Chuck Wagon" Perkins, New Orleans radio personality on WBOK 1230 AM.

After the little tree cover beer garden, Ray's guided tour of Munich took me to Koeniglicher Hirschgarten, the largest beer garden in the city, and it's a public park, overlooking a beautiful lake. You can bring all the food you wish, but one must purchase German beer, which comes in huge steins. Our day ended at a street festival for people with disabilities, held in a community park.

However, by the time we arrived, it had spilled into the street. The very popular "Express Brass Band" had the gathering jamming it up. The night was great and ended with another subway tour, guided by Patrick Clemens this time. A good friend and business associate of Ray's, Patrick is a cutting edge clothing designer in Sweden. He was home, back in Munich, celebrating the city's birthday.

It may seem I'm just throwing a lot of names that are unknown to most people. And, I agree, except I will add, some were unknown to me also, before this trip. I will say further that learning about Germany in the way it gave me a different view of the world. Maybe, I was like Quincy Jones, on his first trip to Europe. Quincy said, that trip, *"turned my world upside down."* Germany became a big part of my education, as I prepare to commemorating and celebrating **"The 400".** This realization came to me the first time, as we retraced the *"King Code."*

For example, Americans have grown up with Dr. King. They study his life in school. Moreover, some people are proud to say, *"I walked with Dr. King,"* but they cannot trace his steps to any place. Yet and still, there is nothing comparable to the *"King Code"* any place in America. I know, reading about me running around Germany, going to concerts and parties, sounds like social justice, and social change is only about having a lots of fun, and it was fun, but with a very serious purpose.

Before I began writing about my Germany tour, I hadn't thought of talking about such events or even about seeing places and the people I met, visiting and enjoying Germany. However, once I started writing, my thoughts continually focused on what impressed me most regarding the differences in cultures. Subtly, things that seem unimportant, as I experienced them, like the cordiality of the people, crept into my thoughts. Differences did not seem to frighten Deutschlanders. They were not reclusive, rather they were easily engaged. They seemed eager to create a sense of comfort for me, being in their country. Such thoughts crept into my head, pushing out disparaging statements and thoughts I heard foreigners make about Germany, now that I have been there.

The best example would be what I learned riding Germany's train system, which is huge compared to America's. It is great for Germans. It reduces the need for cars, and also reduces pollution. But that is not my point. For a foreigner, who doesn't speak or read the language, traveling by train can be a nightmarish experience, and that is my point. Even restricted by the language barrier, most Germans tried to be helpful, as I was without Arish trying to figure out what train to catch and where. Consequently, most of all, I wanted to communicate the interest and excitement I gained in Germany, meeting new people, and learning about them.

The 400th: From Slavery to Hip Hop

Returning to the US, I thought about the cities I visited, their ancient cultures, the architecture, cathedrals that have stood centuries, and when you see them, you understand why. During those thoughts, again very subtly, something else dawned on me. On the flight back to America, for the first time in my life, I truly understood what not being able to go back beyond my great-great-grandfather for a family history actually meant. Slavery took from descendants of enslaved Africans the ability to know a sense of continuity, which connects them to something permanent beyond one's self.

I began this narrative with history, as it developed in Europe because to understand the world the **Trans-Atlantic Slave Trade** created, one must have a real idea of the world it replaced. Germany wasn't even a country then, it was part of the Holy Roman Empire. My Germany tour, more than anything, gave me a visual image or exposed me to a reality, words alone can never describe, as when one experiences something for oneself. It provided clarity regarding all the unfulfilled dreams ex-patriots have and hope to capture living in Europe. The freedom they have acquired living in Europe becomes a continual reminder of the second-class status black people have been relegated to in America, which they left behind. Their lost, like mine, neither of us can ever recapture. That could-have-been life is never to be.

I have written this narrative as I have, so arriving at this point, Europeans and their descendants will see the world of slavery Europeans produced. Getting this far in this narrative, looking out their windows, Europeans see the world they gave enslaved Africans and descendants. The story you have just read getting here describes the world European gave enslavement descendant, while enslaved Africans read about the world Europeans gave enslaved Africans. That world for Europeans came to an end with the abolition of the **Trans-Atlantic Slave Trade in 1807,** and the world I visited is what has grown from the seeds of poverty Europe planted enslaving my ancestors, before and after 1807.

However, there is no world any place for the descendants of those whose blood watered those seeds. The fruit from that world is what Europeans gorge on today and was produced by the world after 1807. Simultaneously, while Europeans eat the lusciousness fruit, they feed descendants of slavery only the peels, from that world.

"The 400th" give those that have grown fat on the lusciousness between the seed and the peel, thinking about equity, now that you have read and know the injustice of the past you created for descendants of slavery is no longer shrouded in mystery; the peel no longer covers the what, how, why and where the obligation falls on the scale of justice.

As a result of America's slave culture, African American's knowledge of their past extends only to the next generation for most. White people in America, like Germans, can trace their lineage back centuries, but many white Americans take this fact for granted. My Germany tour made it clear why the Berlin Wall was unlike the *"Cotton Curtain,"* which was a physical structure and was dismantled.

Contrarily, the *"Cotton Curtain,"* like *"learned helplessness,"* neither were physical structures. They are mental barriers or covering over black Americans' minds. A leftover from slavery, its descendants are unable to get outside or beyond the racist environment of America inside their heads. No matter where they go, they carry that world with them. *"Learned helplessness"* re-enforces the chains on their brains.

America's slave descendants have a heritage that shackled them to a history they were given by white people. White people had no idea, nor did they care what their true history actually was. Essentially, I've presented this information from my German tour to reflect what slavery took from black people in America that can never be returned.

The Invaders Take TD Vancouver International Jazz Festival 2019

The following discussion was the first event of the inaugural year for **The Black Power Tarot Card Exhibition and Invaders Screening,** which kicked off (2019) **"The 400th" Commemoration and Celebration**. This event was also somewhat a reunion. It brought Arish, and I back together with Rainbow Robert, as a crew since *"Le Guess Who?"* Utrecht, The Netherlands (2017). *"Le Guess Who?"* was the first time Rainbow experienced **The Black Power Tarot Card Exhibition and Invaders Documentary Screening**. She came to check out the talent line up. Rainbow is the Managing Director of Artistic Programing at *"The TD Vancouver International JAZZ Festival."* Similar to Bob van Heur during *"Le Guess Who?"* and Daisy McGowan at GOCA, she showed amazing courage presenting our tour at their prestigious music festivals. Arish, as he did readings, Rainbow, not only checked us out, she joined Arish, as he did readings, providing natural vocalization that add to the atmospherics, as I said we all had a great time.

Rainbow decided, "I'm going to get you guys for my festival in Vancouver, because the world needs to experience your magic. She went to work on getting us there. It took two years of looking for the right fit to get us in, and as she promised, 2019 became the perfect year. Now today, looking back through the COVID-19 pandemic, her vision was like a premonition and was perfect timing. Bringing **The Black Power Tarot Card Exhibition and Invaders Documentary Screening** to Vancouver was truly spiritual, not only for our reunion, but with the lineup, we fit right in like a *"gathering of the tribes."*

The TD Vancouver International JAZZ Festival has as a mission—*connecting, transforming, inspiring, and nurturing artists and audiences in the joy, passion, and power of jazz*. It was founded in 1985 and incorporated in 1986, as a community-based, not-for-profit, charitable arts organization. Through determination, passion, idealism, and sense of community, the festival is creating the story of the Coastal Jazz and Blues Society with music. From the very beginning, the society has worked diligently to establish Vancouver, as a center for the creation and exchange of sounds and ideas between local, national, and international music communities.

Over the years, this story has grown to include far more than just music, which is why we were part of the venue. I cannot speak on the impact its many festivals have had since beginning in 2011, but its beginning was definitely a "big bang" for Vancouver music. That first festival boasted such talents as Christian McBride's *"Inside Straight."* A Grammy Award-winning bassist and composer, McBride was one of the most in-demand musicians, during that time, as a result of working with artists from Herbie Hancock, Sonny "Stitt" Rollins and "Sting" to Pat Metheny, Diana Krall and The Roots. Then there was the Dawn Pemberton Gospel Group, a Vancouver singer and former soloist.

Also, Fito Garcia, a Vancouver-based musician, who began his career at age 14. Fito Garcia debut album *"Mi Bajo Rumbero"* (My rumba bass) was nominated for the West Coast Music Awards 2009; it is an experimental work of Afro-Cuban rhythms performed on four basses, with Cuban percussion, and singers. His recording surprisingly makes use of the bass, playing the role of a melodic and harmonic instrument; the result is an innovative, interesting and daring concrete piece.

Even back in 2011, the festival brought cutting edge performers to the stage, like Group Doueh (pronounced "Doo-way"). If you think you've heard all the great electric guitar styles in the world, think again. This Saharan sand-blizzard of passion and virtuosity will blow your mind. Group Doueh played raw and unfiltered Saharawi music from the former colonial Spanish outpost of Western Sahara. Doueh is their leader and a master of the electric guitar. His music is the same mode and structure as Mauritanian music. He began as a child performing and playing in many groups before creating his own in the 1980s. Similar to Arish "King" Khan, Doueh says western pop and rock music, especially Jimi Hendrix and James Brown, influenced his music.

Today, the TD Vancouver International JAZZ Festival's mission is to not only increases the appreciation of music but strengthens the arts community by developing special projects, artistic exchanges, partnerships, educational initiatives, community programs, and collaborations that further the art form, which is why we fit their mission, so well. Its vision encompasses a wide spectrum of jazz, blues, world, creative, and improvised music, including evolving forms of jazz and technologies and media that influence jazz, as an art form. The Society ranks as BC's top presenter, as well as producing the annual *TD Vancouver International JAZZ Festival's* "*Bright Moments* series." Its year-round concerts bring local, national, and international artists, to Frankie's Jazz Club, five nights a week.

The society has a long-standing commitment to music education. It presents the TD High School Jazz Intensive Program exclusively for high school students. *"The Sounds of Youth"* performance stage is also a regular workshop by local and visiting international artists, along with music presentations, which includes the monthly *Cool School: Get Hip to Jazz* series, children's music programs, and more. The *TD Vancouver International Jazz Festival* has multiple locations across the beautiful city of Vancouver, framed by an idyllic setting surrounded by mountains and the ocean.

With 1,800 artists, 300 performances, 35 venues, and 150+ free shows for the 2019 annual Northwest "uptown throw down (6-21/7-1- 2019). The festival's description is what got us—**The Black Power Tarot Card Exhibition and Invaders Documentary Screening**—into the mix in Vancouver. Truly, social change and justice were risky for *"Le Guess Who?",* Rainbow insisted,

The 400th: From Slavery to Hip Hop

"because the Vancouver festival is designed to not only inspire a passion for a diversity of musical expressions, the desire is also to challenge, stimulate, and engage people of all ages in the many joys of learning, listening and experiencing how music impacts other genres, Vancouver needed the message and is ready for the experience."

The International Institute for Critical Studies in Improvisation and Coastal Jazz this year presented its eleventh colloquium—*Agile Futures: Approaching Improvisation*. The colloquium takes place at the *Western Front Theater*, during the opening weekend of the festival. The *Western Front* is one of Canada's leading artist-run centers for contemporary art and new music. The colloquium features keynote addresses and artist talks by world-renowned improvisers who are performing at the festival: Darius Jones, Mats Gustafsson, Meredith Bates, and Jing Xia, are examples. As part of this lineup, we—Arish "King" Kahn, creator of the soundtrack for *the Invaders* documentary was our ticket and the real attraction, talking about his music. I, on the other hand, a founding member of the *Invaders*, brought up the rear presenting and emceeing the free public screening of *The Invaders Documentary*.

The colloquium hopes presenters and performers will provocatively engage the audience by addressing such questions as: *In a world marked by social and cultural exhaustion, what can the improvising arts and activism, contribute to the realization of hopeful futures? How do theatrical, musical, and artistic practices of improvisation offer new and alternative forms of creative knowledge? How does improvisation enable responsive and responsible agility? What are the intersections of improvisation with speculative fiction or with Afro-futurism or with experimental art-forms? How can improvisation enliven or challenge various forms of composition and performance, and contribute to an enhanced sense of awareness? Can improvising help us engage with nascent communities or public initiatives or counter-publics? How can improvisers push back at injustice or advocate for human rights? How can better, transformative, and diverse futures be imagined from our immediate unruly present?*

These provocative questions can be very elusive if one's presentation is not well-grounded in humanitarian causes. My social change and social justice activism began amidst the 1960s culture of black power, so Arish and I are bringing a renewed radicalism to the hip hop generation of activists. That period (1960s) was ushered in by such luminaries and militant leaders as Malcolm X, Amiri Baraka, Dr. Rom Karinga, Stokely Carmichael, and H. Rap Brown. Young college students, Vietnam vets, musicians, and intellectuals led the black power movement from HBCU campuses across the South, while the Invaders were a Memphis group only began in 1967, they had real impact. I have detailed the *Invaders'* story in this narrative, so I fast forward to 2011.

The same year the *TD Vancouver International JAZZ Festival* began (2011) its rise to prominence, Prichard Smith, J. B. Horrell and Chad Schaffler discovered or uncovered the history and significance of our often-overlooked group—*the Invaders*. An avant-grade documentary filmmaker from Memphis, Prichard re-envisioned this period in black people's fight for *VOICE* in America, during those caliginous times. He uses archival footage to capture the reality and mood, as well as the inside story of the *Invaders* surprising behind-the-scenes reality of this historically overlooked group. The Invaders played a pivotal role in supporting Dr. Martin Luther King, Jr., helping to mount **The Poor People's Campaign**, during his last days, before his assassination.

Today, our mission is to engage the world by coughing the *Invaders* screenings in social change and social justice activism, using entertainment as a backdrop, which is the essence of improvisation. And, as such, **The Black Power Tarot Card Exhibition and Invaders Documentary Screening** tour is designed to open minds, not only regarding injustices of the past, but point out their continued impact today. I gave a pre-show talk and post-show Q&A. This presentation is an opportunities for "King" Khan and I to help audiences learn about how and why they should become agents of social change and social justice, which are very improvisational activities. In that regard, I say, *"Everyone is making it up as they go along!"* Social change and social justice cannot be pre-packaged in a one size fit all medium. I compare it to music, in that, there are soloists and groups; either way, the music created must harmonize for listeners, if the experience is to benefit them, which is the whole idea behind improvisation.

Following the delightful experience at the Western Front, we experienced *TD Vancouver International JAZZ Festival* fun and entertainment at its main outdoor stage. I, along with thousands of other festival-goers, enjoyed a free venue that showcased the new generation of up and coming artists. It was so refreshing to experience a festival with a free main stage that presented rising stars of quality in hip hop, as well as jazz. I will admit not being a hip hop aficionado, therefore, new or best is not the measure here. Rainbow Robert provided acts with unique styles and originality. She gave them the main stage and put them before a very enthusiastic audience.

One such group, "NYS" (New York Subway), gained notice playing on New York subway platforms, which lent itself more to an indigenous kind of sound. Their performance seemed geared toward their enjoyment in playing more so than pleasing an audience. These acts were really good and definitely deserved to be there.

Then a raiding party of Native People commandeered the stage. The first raid was by a duo *"DJ & the Bird,"* who brought indigenous rhythms mixed with a hip-hop flair and backdrop. They brought some really great sounds to the stage. Also, a young lady dressed in a colorful outfit with long fringes, which made her resemble an Egret or another large winged creature, as she danced and floated about the stage.

The main stage truly reflected an international character, when a young Ethiopian rapper *AVEX*, from Italy, whose rap style sounded as if he could have come from the Southside of Chicago, the Bronx, or Atlanta. He threw down some great raps giving *VOICE* to the struggle of descendants of slavery, victims

The 400th: From Slavery to Hip Hop

of colonialism, and other oppressed people. Ready for the big stage any place in the world, *AVEX*'s was stronger than Ethiopian coffee. *AVEX* brewed a pot of his java sweet enough to give America a shot and earn a spot atop hip hop dreamland ride to the to the top.

It seemed Native People were on the warpath on the big stage, as a really powerful duo hit the stage like a raid on Vancouver, but no scalping. *Snotty Nose Rez Kids* took the stage with total attitude. It was as though they came to pillage and burn away the vestiges of the white man's domination with rhymes and rhythms, while leaving their tomahawks in the car.

Their raps opened a whole new chapter in the mis-told white man's legends of the real wild wild West story. I rode their vibe like a mustang, as they galloped down the real "trail of tears" with tales of what Americans really did to possess their land, while trying to wipe them out. It's the same story, but with different characters being told in **"The 400th"**, as a continuing sequel to an unending genocide, that white people refuse to admit, let alone to atone. *Snotty Nose Rez Kids* describe their existence in their own words this way:

We are an indigenous hip-hop duo from the Haisla nation. We speak back to the stereotypes that present us as untamed, ill-mannered and vulgar savages, reclaiming ourselves as the 7th generation on the rise. We tell our stories to show that we may be a little rough around the edges but that roughness makes our lives interesting. We don't carry certain privileges afforded through colonialism-fenced in backyards, green grass suburbia- but we are privileged in other ways. We were privileged to be raised by the ocean with a forest in our back yard. We are rich through learning our traditional way of life while being raised on our ancestors' territory – there is a great deal of wealth in knowing who and where you come from. We were able to learn by doing, (DIY) to run around the reservation, get stung by devils nettle and not cry over it but wipe our snot on it and keep going. We learnt about the ocean's depth and the rivers' current. We learned how to survive without actually having to only survive. We ran in packs. We were raised by our parents; we were raised by our community. Our culture is strong and continues to shape us into who we are today. We are storytellers, dancers, singers and artists. We are survivors. Our ancestors live through us and as individuals we have a platform to communicate this with our community. With whatever lens you see us through, we will always be the snot nosed kids from the rez and that's what makes us beautiful.

The *TD Vancouver JAZZ Festival* was a blessing; I was able to experience Native People, bringing totally positive messages about who they are and what that means to them. Native People have the same mindset, as those of us working to bring **"The 400th"** forward, as a platform from which descendants of American slavery will give *VOICE* to their degradation and genocide. And most definitely, the second huge pleasure was just such an occasion for me when *Enter the Wu-Tang* blew up Vancouver from the stage later that night at the Queen Elizabeth Theater.

Wu-Tang Clan opened with all 36 Chambers blasting, and brought back real black power to the stage, like back in the day when they were the skateboard for New York City's hip hop ride to worldwide prominence. Wu-Tang symbolized the need to make a stand and represent the fight descendants of American slavery waged, since being kidnapped and shanghaied off to North America. *Enter the Wu-Tang* (36 Chambers) kick in the door of hip hop with its gritty, distinctive sound that became the blueprint for hardcore hip hop during the 1990s.

No less forceful, than back in 1993 when they first took the stage, today at the *TD Vancouver International JAZZ Festival,* Wu-Tang came packing and fully loaded. They opened up, blasting and emptied all 36 Chambers, leaving nothing standing but their pride, as fans grabbed space up in the rafters to be part of Wu-Tang's jam. Blowing up and maxing out the venue, like it was recess, as their old school throw down took elders and youngsters to school like back in the day, when Wu-Tang's raps controlled the day. Now, Wu-tang is kicking off the new era bringing a return to the East Coast conscious hip hop renaissance.

Hitting the stage with their yester-year explosiveness, Wu-Tang went to work chopping and cutting through the confusion young hip-hoppers display today. Unsure who they are and trying to figure out what they stand for, Wu-Tang stepped out of the smoke and shadows of yesterday, with the same game and ready to play. Without smoke and mirrors, their alchemy turned yesterday into a line in the sand, dropping old school hip hop like bombs, reclaiming the territory on which they made their stand.

Wu-Tang brought knowledge to a disbelieving world and showed a glorious return is not only possible; it's here. They took command of the stage with their persona, power, and lyrics. Their performance was reminiscent of when Wu-Tang served as a template for many "latter-day-come-afters" as Wu-Tang's magic flashed like a beckon for hip hop rappers, Nas, The Notorious B.I.G., Mobb Deep, and Jay-Z as cappers.

It was truly gratifying for me to see Wu-Tang raise slavery's descendant from the grave, demanding black men stand unafraid, as *Wu-Tang* commanded the battle of **"The 400th"** from the stage. Despite its raw, underground sound, *Enter the Wu-Tang* didn't live and die by success on the charts, peaking at #41 on the US Billboard 200 chart, while selling 30,000 copies its first week (11-9-1993) on the street. Chart makers had to throw in the towel by 1995, *36 Chambers* went Platinum, as the RIAA surrendered completely by October 2018, throwing in a triple platinum-certified towel. Initially receiving positive reviews from most music critics, *Enter the Wu-Tang (36 Chambers)* is regarded today as one of the most, if not the most, significant albums of the 1990s, as well as one of the greatest hip hop albums ever, featuring the "Ghost."

The *TD Vancouver International JAZZ Festival,* as I stated opening this discussion, has a mission—*to connect, transform, inspire and nurture artists and audiences through the enjoyment, passion, and power of jazz.* It is also an excellent example of why

The 400th: From Slavery to Hip Hop

"The 400th" organizing committee selected such an extended performance period to commemorate and celebrate black people's arrival as one people. Rainbow Robert worked for two years to bring the **Black Power Tarot Card Exhibition and Invaders Documentary Screening** to Vancouver, even though she was all in for presenting it back in 2017. But as time, events, and Divine intervention would have it, The *TD Vancouver International JAZZ Festival* became the initial opening event for the inaugural year of ***"The 400th"***. Many will come after, but none will ever come before; Vancouver will always be first.

This protracted process is "the nature of the beast," in the Art world where nothing happens overnight. And even with the eyes of Janus, overnight takes years. I watched the sun set over the mountain, leaving Vancouver, as it cast its orange glow on the Strait of Georgia. I realized the *TD Vancouver International JAZZ Festival* had flipped the script from the past, as it became the present reflecting a bright future for the **Black Power Tarot Card Exhibition and Invaders Documentary Screening**!!!!!!!!!!

Hopes for The 400th

"*The 400th*" is the hope of the present, which is where things happen. It is like a doorway, through which the past continually exits in real time. It remains part of the present as it lives in the minds of those with privilege. Standing on the threshold of the present one can look back and see, what has transpired to bring them to at place. Looking forward choices before one is the future, and the choice one selects becomes what happens in the present and where one is then it becomes the past. Those steps once taken, all the praying, wishing and regretting cannot recall decisions made.

Slavery was one such choice Europeans made and their decisions are what slavery's descendants' have as a present today. The good lives and legacy Europeans reaped are the benefits of that past, while enslaved African descendants suffered from that past and continue struggling, trying to overcome impacts of those decisions, even though they stand in the doorway of the present.

Participating, supporting and benefitting from the enslavement of free Africans and their descendants for economic gain continue hanging over western civilization, like the "Sword of Damocles." Their wealthy existence is fruit of the longest running instance of genocide in the history of humankind for enslaves Africans descendants. Simultaneously, for such instances of humanity to change, standing on the threshold of the present, for a different future, humanity must chose to make different choices and act differently in the present to create a different future. Continuing to perpetuate the present, Europeans dictated enslaved Africans future, which continues that past, not create a different future. That is why this narrative has shown descendants of American slaves have been unable to move beyond their penniless emancipation to having a different future.

Today that is the dilemma before the world, which is why I began this narrative with the parable God showed Ezekiel of the valley of dried boned, which has returned in real time, as COVID-19. And, combined Black Lives Matter and the demonstrations around the world they organized have created a present no one anticipated, and the rich and powerful in America refuse to accept this new present, as foreshadowing a new normal, as their future. COVID-19 is a harbinger of the kinds of disasters possible in a world devoid of compassion, rule by greed and racism. It matters not the intensions of the rich with self-serving charitable contributions, hoping to preserve their wealth and status in society teetering on the brink of collapse. With events like COVID-19 laying siege to their keeps, gated communities and motes will not save their wealth from the have-nots because the life styles the rich has forced upon them are incubators of the disasters they face.

Changing always takes place in the present; nothing ever happens in the past because it is the result of the old normal and what one is living with presently.

The 400th: From Slavery to Hip Hop

The future differs from the past, if the new normal is pushing the old normal aside. Consequently, this is why America is where it is today, facing massive protest around the world, following George Floyd's lynching, and COVID-19 scorecard has topped 390,000 death, and antidote not online. The social and economic threats this pandemic foretells are echoes from the past, like antediluvian voices calling back the old normal, those like Donald Trump are trying to reinforce the idea that a slaves life does not matter. This message to black people echoes back down through the past to **"The Door of No Return," Goreé Island, Dakar, Senegal** to where the first enslaved African was dragged aboard a slave ship is the future Trump offers.

The hope **"The 400th"** offers descendants of American slavery, colonialism, and other oppressive government systems—victims of that past—is a new normal of the present with opportunities to create a new present that will lead to a future world where social justice and social change are a reality. Commemorating and celebrating **"The 400th"** is how slavery's descendants can build a platform to support changes, where the present new normal will bring innovations for the future the present will determine. Young progressive will be able to plan and initiate programs and projects that produce the desired result. They will be able to increase access for slave descendants, as they build this platform of ideas that will become **"The 400th's"** new normal.

Changing the future is not simple. But, the fact that slave descendants have survived the last 156 years since their penniless emancipation shows they can use the knowledge gained from those hideously dark and deathly time to build a present that reflects the future they desire. Making things happen in the present will determine how descendants of enslaved Africans commemorate and celebrate **"The 400th"**. The question each descendant of American slavery must answer over the next years or so is what does becoming one people mean to them.

The **Trans-Atlantic Slave Trade** and its aftermath—the story of how enslaved Africans arrived in the Western Hemisphere—cannot be undone; it is the past. Not any of what has happened to us over the last 400 years—the outrages, pain and deaths—can be altered or made less salient. What **"The 400th"** does is brings everyone, no matter where or who they are, into the same present, at the same time. **"The 400th"** is what happened, and presents the task of creating a different future—a new normal—for not only descendants of American slavery, but a chance for change for slavery's descendants and descendants of slave masters, as well.

That day Arish "King" Khan first suggested I write **"The 400th"**, I cringed at the thought. He said, *"John B. you should write an invitation asking artists to produce works to commemorate the 400th". You're probably best able to tell the story of slavery so that they will understand the importance of* **"The 400th"**. *Since it is your idea, you see what it is all about and why they should care about commemorating and celebrating it."*

I cringed because I was unsure, I possessed the knowledge base and skill set required to produce a clear, succinct and unambiguous statement informative enough to do justice to the struggle slave descendants waged reaching *"The 400th"*. Well over 800 pages now, I have tried several times to close it out. But this story is so large, packed with so many essential individuals and events that continue, revealing themselves in ways that without them, "events like the lynching of George Floyd, means I would not dent the surface of such an important, powerful and fascinating saga of self-love.

Beginning "*The 400th*" saga, I made clear with my first words this is a love story; a living drama that sprang alive in my head eight years ago. Just an idea back then but talking about it with Arish Khan and others was like pouring water over seeds, the ideas grew. The seeds of slavery were planted over six centuries ago in the alien soil of the Western Hemisphere. Trapped in a hellish reality, those seeds sprang up in this harsh alien soil; but they grew misshapen.

Growing, those slave seeds had to break through levers of repression and oppression, similar to the rock hard sidewalks in concrete jungles in America's ghetto. Germinating in soil unplowed for centuries, yet these seeds grew and once they broken through, slaves had to dig out a life, surviving in the barren soil of their contraband penniless emancipation. Somehow after their burial in this harsh and barren soil, they grew a little, just enough to endure. Miraculously, enduring to survive, the magic of their *Blues* cast a spell, like fertilizer, which over the centuries energized their efforts, so much so, they not only survive they thrived.

Facing Arish's challenged, my cringing doubtful response—my ability to present slavery's descendants struggles, and there were many—in such a way that someone, who had no connection, in a real sense, to slavery or any ideas about those conditions, would understand the challenges slavery's descendants had to overcome to reach *"The 400th"*. Put another way, readers would not need to consume several libraries to comprehend the importance *"The 400th"* represents to a people without a clear historical record. Facts are known yes, but what do they really mean to people who have problems tracing their linage beyond their parents, at best grandparents.

Adding artifacts to illustrate and exhibit these stories would require an effort similar to that Great Britain's undertook, beginning in 1980. The United Kingdom was very courageous, showing a desire to atone for its role in the *Trans-Atlantic Slave Trade*. In a world where most descendants of slave masters were not concerned. The UK has created the *International Slavery Museum,* located in Liverpool, England. This museum focuses on the history of the *Trans-Atlantic Slave Trade* and its legacy. The *International Slavery Museum* has three main galleries, primarily concerned with the lives of West African people, their enslavement and their continued fight for freedom the world over. Originally, a part of the Merseyside Maritime Museum, which opened in 1980, it tells the story of the ***Trans-Atlantic Slave Trade*** (1452-1807). It also included Liverpool's maritime history, which was part of how the UK grew, to dominate the slave trade. A decision in 1994 to explore Liverpool's huge historic role in the slave trade, resulted in The ***Trans-Atlantic Slavery Trade Gallery***.

The period—8-23-1807 thru 8-23-2007—reflects 200 years marking and commemorates the annual *International Day for Remembrance of the Slave Trade's* abolition (1807). Also, it marks the slave uprising in Santo Domingo, Dominican Republic. The UK's bicentennial (2007) celebrated the passage of the ***Slave Trade Act of 1807,*** ending slavery in the British Empire. America passed its ***Act Prohibiting the Importation of Slaves (1807)*** that year also, but did not outlaw slavery. This word difference meant enslaved Africans in America endured 58 more year of the internal slave and breeding and US displayed no interest in commemorating anything related to slavery.

America's slavery story lies buried in private files, archives, and maybe even museum basements. Telling America's slavery story requires the kind of access and resources the ***International Slavery Museum*** had telling the UK's story. Without such resources at my disposal, telling America's slavery's descendants love story required a great deal of imagination—similes, allegories, and metaphors—to establish a story no one has tried to tell, especially those unfamiliar with the murky period I designated ***"The 400th"***.

Personally, retracing this saga, as a family narrative, was amazing. I was without words at times, trying to explain the what, why, and how of events to connect with the known history. The way things occurred, and black people's "word of mouth" legacy were the arbiter of these know fact, but unknown to history books.

Consequently, similes and metaphors were like expansion bridges get to the other side of the huge information gulfs encountered, stitching this story together. Spanning some information gulfs, which were wider and deeper than the Olduvai Gorge, another metaphor was all that enabled me to reach the other side. (*Olduvai Gorge or Oldupai Gorge is in Tanzania. It is one of the most important paleoanthropological sites in the world today. It has proven invaluable in furthering understanding of early human evolution. A steep-sided ravine in the Great Rift Valley that stretches across East Africa, Olduvai Gorge is about 48 km long, roughly 31.07 miles. It runs through the eastern Serengeti Plains across the Arusha Region, close to Laetoli, another important archaeological site of early human existence*). Yet some claim white people were the first human, not humanity's cradle Africans, to justify white superiority.

The hope and task of those of us committed to ***"The 400th"*** is to gain the world's attention and support in getting recognition for enslaved Africans as human beings, something most countries have refused to acknowledge. Even though descendants of enslaved Africans have shown, they have real value, serving as the world's economic engine for over 600 years, that fact has no value to most nations that reaped the greatest benefits from enslaving free Africans in chattel bondage.

Today descendants of enslaved Africans are still treated as nothing. The truth or fallacy of that statement will be reflected by America and European nations' willingness to help commemorate and celebrate ***"The 400th"***. Descendants of enslaved Africans invite all those that benefited from enslaving Africans in bondage and the degradation they suffered, to become part of healing the pain, terror, and death white people wrought and slavery's descendants' subjugation throughout ***"The 400th"***.

The Problem: Real or Imagined?

Finally, we are here. *"The 400th"* organizing committee of volunteers, is currently working to create an action plan of organization for commemorating and celebrating *"The 400th"*. We believe the major focus of *"The 400th"* should be supported by the Arts/Academic communities. Their support will allow the committee to reach out to those most prominently involved in designing, producing, managing, mounting, presenting, and communicating information about the importance of Arts and other cultural events. The committee has taken on the task of bringing major American Museums and art affiliated institutions and organizations on board commemorating and celebrating *"The 400th"*. The committee enthusiastically hopes and anticipates also that the Arts/Academic communities will wholeheartedly embracing our efforts and will give their full cooperation by offering black artists access to facilities and financial support. However, I realize manifesting this hope will not be easy.

I can say starting this effort has been very productive. Even with venues, like Gallery of Contemporary Art (GOCA), US Department of State's Germany Tour, *Le Guess Who?*, TD Vancouver International JAZZ Festival, the Stone Awards, Redline Gallery and other individuals, those organizations, have taking the lead recognizing and mounting shows, which indicates the uphill struggle the committee will face. However, these groups responses showed social change and social justice are very worthy and important undertakings, which will serve their organizations, constituents, and the world in good stead. So, they boarded *"The 400th"* train before tickets are available.

The concern of the committee, real or imagined, reflects one of the major themes of this narrative. *"White and black people can view a situation or event from the same position or perspective, at the precise same moment, yet come away with two entirely different scenarios.* Yet and still, as young progressives joined sit-ins and freedom rides, some are not waiting for others to lead. Next I offer an explanation for the committee's dilemma!

The following is a view by Duane McKinley, which I offer to open this discussion. McKinley's views were presented in an article posted by Afropunk.com., *"The Other Black History: Why is The Louvre Hiding African Art?"* McKinley's reflections illustrate the belief many African Americans hold, which is white Americans and Europeans have very negative views of *"Black Arts."* This article expresses beliefs and opinions many descendants of slavery share. Real or imagined, they feel white Americans and Europeans detest or disdain *"Black Arts,"* simply because black artists are the producers.

McKinley begins with the question, *"Why is Egyptian art located with the European art collections instead of with the African art collection?"* He points out that *The Louvre's Art of Africa, Asia, Oceania, and the Americas* collection is detached from other collections and relegated to a diminutive, windowless corner of arguably the world's most famous art museum. McKinley also points to how *Black Art* in most of the top museums in Europe and America follow this trend and treat art by African Americans and art by other people of color, as if it is *"second class"* and given a *"separate but equal"* location.

McKinley cites *The Metropolitan Museum of Art New York City (The Met)*, which shares similarities with *The Louvre*. The African art collection is rather small and combined with Oceania and the Americas section. The Egyptian collection has an area, which seems to be larger than the entire area for the other three combined. Moving westward McKinley visited the *Art Institute of Chicago*, which isn't any better. Their *African Art Collection* is displayed separately from other collections, at the end of a long, dead-end hallway, where the flow of visitors by-pass the exhibit altogether. Then there is the *Los Angeles County Museum of Art*, which is truly reflective of museums and Art galleries in America—there is no African Art collection.

Rather than just discussing the attitudes of white art connoisseurs, I defer to Peter Clothier to buttress my point. I presented his words earlier in this narrative; they are even more appropriate here. He makes the point about white people and *Black Art* better than I ever could. Peter, as I said earlier, described himself as *"a nice, left-leaning, transplanted Englishman, entirely without racial prejudice."* Clothier in his Huffington Post article entitled *"The Other Blacklist': A Very Personal Book Review"* makes the admission,

"I made two important discoveries in the course of that work: first, that the art world, as I knew it, was fraught with systemic prejudice against African-American artists and the work they produced; and second, that I unknowingly—and shamefully—shared that prejudice...."

I believe few white people, especially those connected to the art world, are courageous enough to make such a public admission, about whites but particularly about themselves. But, that is the attitude I also feel black artists and Black Arts faces. Nevertheless, as Peter said after his admission,

"My work, then, was not only to research my subject but to develop a whole new mind-set about values, traditions, and aesthetic conventions I had never previously questioned. And not only that, I very soon came to realize that I'd need a new approach to the work I had set myself. I ventured forth,"

And so, will I.

Clothier at that point reflected a statement I have repeated several times, *"Black Arts is something he thought he knew but never thought about."* What I admire about Peter is his willingness to take a second look without blinder to make sure he saw what he thought he saw through an unexamined mental state based on prejudice!

Not to lump every art Museum and gallery into the same pot, Denver, Colorado, in the middle of the United States of America, seems to be a very bright spot for black artists. Jordan Casteel had her first solo show *Returning The Gaze*, at the Denver Art Museum in February 2019. Following that show, Denver's Redline Gallery is presenting a major exhibition by Floyd D. Tunson entitled ***Floyd D. Tunson: Remixed*** in July 2020. Floyd D. Tunson was the first artist to volunteer his support for ***"The 400th"*** back in 2016. More importantly, he will create a piece commemorating ***"The 400th"***, sometime during **The 400th Performance Period.**

According to Daisy McGowan, Floyd's curator, the Executive-Director and show co-curator at Redline, Louise Martorano, is connecting the exhibitions to the theme ***"Afrofuturism"*** in 2020—and other galleries and museums in Denver are buying into that theme. Denver has becoming a very bright spot for Black Arts and ***"The 400th"***.

Speaking about himself, Floyd says, *"I have become a Janus."* (In Roman religion and myth, Janus is the god of beginnings, gates, transitions, time, doorways, and endings. With faces on both sides, he looks to the future and the past simultaneously.) Janus is the present.

As Aristotle said, *"Learning is the greatest of pleasures. My work reflects my journey to acquire knowledge. Along the way, I have become a Janus. Looking at life from one direction, I see the terror of chaos, man's inhumanity to man, mortality, and the vastness of the unknown. From another direction, the human condition seems like a magnificent, orderly evolution of extraordinary beauty. The totality of my work reflects my quest to comprehend and express these forces and their interconnectedness. Even my non-objective painting is based on this dialectic, where uninhibited strokes play against geometric order."*

I first encountered Floyd D. Tunson, not as an artist but as a friend of a friend. Daisy McGowan introduced us. Watching and talking with Floyd in his studio, as he gave Arish "King" Khan and me a look through, he reminded me of several old-timers that befriended me. They helped me understand that there is far more to life than what one perceives visually and auditorially. They talked about seeing and listening with my mind to comprehend an experience. Back then, I didn't understand the totality of their observation and statement. However, as Floyd drew me into his thinking, sharing his inspiration as a creator, I connect with him as an artist. Unfortunately, readers missed my introduction to Floyd, so I share a press statement describing Floyd's exhibition inaugurating the *Ent Center for the Arts* in Colorado Springs (2-1-2018).

For over four decades, Floyd Tunson has been among the most highly regarded and influential artists in the Rocky Mountain region. He has achieved a rich and diverse body of work via media such as painting, sculpture, photography, and printmaking—often combining the language of these various media in single works. The exhibition reflects the scope of Tunson's career and work.

Given the turbulence of the times, it's understandable that anyone familiar with Floyd D. Tunson's work might have assumed that the art in this exhibition would sting with social commentary. But Tunson seldom does what anyone expects. For this show, he chose not to be a political provocateur. He chose, as his subject, art itself. He chose the basics of visual experience — line, color, form, and light. As a Janus, he looked to the past, to his experience, with these essential elements, and to the future to purify and refine them.

The motivation for his decision reveals the depth of Tunson's mind. "The more horrifying this world becomes," said Paul Klee, "the more art becomes abstract." But Tunson is wise: He knows that a meaningful visual response to events requires time to contemplate, assimilate, and evaluate. His choice of abstraction is no mere retreat from reality; rather, it derives from the challenge of cutting through the chaos and rendering with clarity the most basic elements of the visual experience in a way that engages the viewer in the process.

Because the subject of abstract art is not identifiable figuration, the work asks the viewer to stand back and look at the whole piece, each small section, and the techniques and rhythms that unify all the parts. The work cannot be comprehended in a rush any more than it could have been painted in a rush, for Tunson had to make whatever effort was necessary to dig deep into his imagination and exercise his unforgiving editorial eye before allowing any piece to leave his studio.

In the spirit of Janus, he sees the Ent Arts Center as a physical and inspirational gateway to a new level of all the arts for the region, and he has often expressed his gratitude for the opportunity to initiate the Marie Walsh Sharpe Gallery. It is in this context that he chose an art genre that inspires a look back and a look ahead to the fundamental things, but never in a tired, simplistic way. "Of all the arts," said early abstractionist Wassily Kandinsky," abstract painting is the most difficult. It demands that you know how to draw well, that you have a heightened sensitivity for composition and for color, and that you are a true poet. This last is essential." Floyd D. Tunson is a true poet."

T.D. Mobley-Martinez, in an article *"Floyd D. Tunson Is Not Done Yet"* said, *"At 42-feet wide, Untitled 147 goes and goes and goes. Order nips at the heels of chaos as color and form swoop and drip, chug, and zip explode, bubble, breathe raspy, and smooth. It's musical if you can ever really call a painting that. Like the meaning of life, the cornerstone of Floyd D. Tunson: Janus — the UCCS Galleries of Contemporary Art's inaugural exhibition at the new Ent Center for the Arts — is almost too monumental to process. (It's actually 12 smaller canvases arranged in a grid.) Stepping back (and back) only compels you to step closer (and closer)".*

"Floyd's fearless," says GOCA director and Janus curator Daisy McGowan of Untitled 147, *"one of eight new works here and his largest to date. Haitian Dream Boats*

and Untitled 143 hang elsewhere in the building". McGowan calls Tunson, *"One of the most influential contemporary artists in Colorado. He's not interested in sitting back, doing what he's done in the past,"* she says. *"He reinvents the work he's making continually. I believe he has a bottomless curiosity about existence through the making of art."*

Floyd is definitely my kind of poet, I believe, all art lovers will become enamored as fans of his art, once they are exposed to his insightful and powerful creations. With that said and with Floyd in the middle, after the article by Duane McKinley, *The Other Black History: Why is The Louvre Hiding African Art?* I didn't want to leave the subject where it seems the whole Art world was one big plantation in 2019. I reviewed another article on this subject, *AFROPUNK INTERVIEW: REGGIE VAN LEE'S BLACK EXCELLENCE* by Emil Wilbekin (March 1, 2019). I present the following excerpts from Emil's article to add a little balance. Emil opens,

"Reggie Van Lee is what we call a legend, a status he achieved by breaking barriers, growing up in the Jim Crow South, attending MIT, receiving a Bachelors and a Masters, and becoming a painter. Van Lee defied the odds that most black males encounter; he refused to be relegated to stereotypes that come with being marginalized, and embody the racist tropes white America often try to place on our Black bodies. Reggie's story is not only interesting; it is a fascinating account of a black man who defied the odds to achieve success in education, business, and the cultured world of the Arts".

The highlights from Wilbekin's piece belie the grunt word Van Lee did getting business degrees and rising to the position of Executive Vice President at Booz Allen Hamilton, a global management and technology firm. Becoming a patron of the arts, Lee is one of the trustees for the storied *Studio Museum of Harlem* and sits on the Board of Trustees for the John F. Kennedy Center for the Performing Arts. He even danced with the *Alvin Ailey American Dance Theater* on his way to the top. Obviously, that introduction should indicate only a book of his own, could provide proper acclaim detailed Van Lee's many amazing accomplishments and circuitous journey to prominence. However, my purpose for selecting Reggie Van Lee for this narrative is to show there is great potential for getting major Arts facilities to support commemorating and celebrating **"The 400th",** rather than using the political arena, as a base.

Van Lee is a native of Houston with residences in New York, and like me in this narrative, uses his family history and his sense of self and community-worth to ensure that the broader Black community—and all marginalized communities—have access to the arts. A tribute to Van Lee and his work with the Arts was given on March 11, 2019, by Theater Development Fund (TDF). It honored Van Lee for his contributions, making the arts accessible to the community. He said during this interview with Emil Wilbekin,

"I like to support the arts, audience development and getting people who reflect our country and our city to see theater. What TDF does is not only the TKTS booths that sell discount tickets, which we all know about, but they also provide free tickets and discounted tickets for students and parents who could not otherwise afford the theater; they also have autism-friendly performances for kids and parents on the spectrum to come and enjoy the theater."

Talking with *AFROPUNK* about the importance of the performing arts, particularly to the black community, and why he thinks it is important that the performing arts be sustained, as a healing force in the black community, Van Lee said,

"This may sound a little trite, but I think performance and the arts are transformative for people, in general, and especially for Black people. The theater is a wholesome, safe way for us to express ourselves. Even our history and our culture, and things that are deeply ours, deeply rooted in our culture, can be expressed theatrically, in a comfortable way, to audiences. That perhaps couldn't be done the same way in a corporate context. So, all my life I've felt that the arts are transformative, and I think it brings out the creativity in kids and it is a healing balm for people in difficult situations. So for a lot of reasons I think it's a really good thing and I want to support it however I can."

How are the arts good for healing, and also for dealing with social injustice and issues that we face as Black people?

"I think the arts put you in touch with your humanity, almost by their very nature. And so, it allows you to understand humanity, your humanity and others', and how some other people that seem to be evil people doing evil things do that because there's a pain that they have as well. If you can identify with that, sometimes you can get them through their pain and get them to a better place that will benefit you as well. But, certainly when you are troubled, to have that artistic release, to get that out of you, to not feel embattled and encumbered by that, and to release that out of you is important as well. So you may go dancing and twirl, and twirl, and twirl. You may go to church and sing really loudly, but that sort of release really is important. So, whether it is healing others or understanding others to heal, or healing yourself I think the arts are very helpful."

When were you first introduced to the arts growing up?

"When I was three or four years old, I used to draw and paint, then at the age of five I told my mother I wanted to be an artist, and my mother said, "No, no — artists starve, you should be an architect. So at the age of five, I decided I would be an architect, and then in high school, my mother said, "Okay, you need to be an engineer, so maybe you can get into architectural engineering." I ended up being a civil engineer. That appreciation for the arts came as a kid, and my parents encouraged me to draw; they got me the paper and the pens and the paints

and the boards, and all these things, so I was able to express myself artistically from an early age."

So, how did you balance the left brain and right brain? If you're artistic, but then you went into science, how did that work for you?

"I was always encouraged to do whatever worked for me. Of course, my parents were very concerned that I'd create a career for myself, that I could earn a living, so the math and science stuff, they loved it, right? But, they were okay with the artistic stuff as well, and I had to make a decision at some point. Their hope was I would decide to go the direction of business and to make the arts an avocation, and that's what happened. I became an arts patron, and I think I was a better arts patron than I would've been an artist. So, it's never really been a conflict for me.

Over the years, I asked myself, can I study dance as well? And I danced for a while, and that precision and presence and stamina that one has to create as a performing artist, and connecting with audiences and all of those skills, I put into a business context. So as a consultant, the precision and stamina and accuracy, and engaging with people, and engaging with clients, were important. So I practiced it as a performer and then actually employed it as a consultant. And then to be a patron of the arts, and use those skills and those resources to help the arts; so I think I've advanced the arts much more in that way than if I had just been an artist."

I want to talk about your family legacy and how you discovered your great grandmother's 38 acres of land in Texas and made it your family's home again.

"Like many of us, as a kid, if you lived in the city, you would sometimes go to the country to visit your relatives. We had a great-aunt and uncle who lived in the country, in a town called Wharton, Texas, outside of Houston. When I was a kid, it was a two- or three-hour drive down dusty, rocky roads and backwoods, to this house on family land. And I remember my grandmother telling us, when she was a kid, as far as the eye could see was Jefferson land — that was her maiden name, Jefferson. To us, it was just dirt and cows and pigs, cotton and corn. It didn't really mean a lot to us.

As I became older, as a young adult, my mother made it clear that land is a thing that we have to hold on to the most that many of our ancestors struggled to get land. So, for us, to throw that away would just be a sin. So she paid the taxes on her little portion of this family land that was in Wharton, Texas, for many, many years. When she passed in 1998, she left me her land.

She had an aunt who never had children, and her aunt left her portion of this land to me, because I'm the only male child on that side of the family. When you put it together, it was a little over an acre. Flash forward to 1998, Wharton, Texas, is a one-hour drive from Houston because there are now highways to get there. There's a junior college in Wharton, Texas. On the TV morning news, when they talk about the weather in Houston, they also talk about the weather in Wharton. I was like, where did Wharton come from all of a sudden?

So I thought maybe I should go and check out this land, maybe build a little house and we could do some family gatherings out there. My family always spends major holidays together, a bunch of us, direct family, extended family. Maybe we could make that our summer getaway or our holiday getaway. I went out with my attorney and the land surveyor so I could see exactly where my land was, and as it ends up, my portion of the land was such a distance from the main road that, in order for me to reach my land, I basically would be trespassing on somebody else's land.

I tried to find out who owns that land, so I could just buy a driveway, basically, out to the property. After some research, my attorney said, "Well, you realize that this property has been in your family since 1899?"

I responded, "Excuse me?" She said, "Yes, it was 38 acres that your great-grandmother purchased in 1899, as a freed slave. My great-grandmother was born in 1862 in Louisiana. At the age of three, they were freed. Her family moved to Wharton, close to Houston, but where they could farm and make a living. Records there show that my great-grandmother's father, my great-great-grandfather, voted in Wharton in 1866. Can you imagine Black people, former slaves voting. Having the nerve to vote, right? Having the courage to vote?

Long story made short, the attorney told me, "I think you need to get back all this original land." So I thought, "Okay why not?" So, it took nine years for me to buy back all the land, it was like a jigsaw puzzle, and she was the front person making the purchase because if people had known I was buying it, perhaps they wouldn't have sold it, or they would have increased the price because I'm some person from New York. So, it took us nine years to get the land back, and then the question was, what do we do with the land?

Well, the second part of the story is, when I was a sophomore in college, in Boston, I had a friend who was friends with Caroline Kennedy at Harvard. And, one long weekend, Caroline invited my friend to the Kennedy Compound in Hyannis Port, and she invited me as her plus one. So here I am, this little black kid from Houston, Texas, in 1976, at the Kennedy Compound, meeting Rose Kennedy. And I said to myself, I'd like to have a family compound someday, just sort of said it, I don't think I mentioned it to anyone else, I said it to myself.

Flash now to 2007 or so, when I now have all this land back, and I said I think I'd like to build a compound. And I talked to my sisters and they said, "Let's go, we'll do it." So, it took us a number of years to design it and build it, but now that's where the family is, that's the story."

Each year AFROPUNK picks a different mantra for the year. Last year, it was THE PEOPLE RESIST. The year before it was WE, THE PEOPLE. This year, we're moving in a different direction with WE SEE YOU. What does WE SEE YOU mean to you?

"That you're not invisible, that you are a person, that you have value, that you have worth, that I can connect with you. In terms of community, especially the black community, you talked about how it's important to build your own community, but why is it important that we support the arts as a community? The majority of the population has a tendency to take anything of value from black people and make it their own. If we don't support our art forms, they will take them. And so, for example, the largest collectors of African-American art are Jewish people, not other African Americans. It's similar to what has happened in Harlem and in other gentrified communities. People take our communities from us, so they'll take our art forms from us, as well. I could go on and on about this."

So, how do we own our culture?

"Well, first, we have to invest in it. When you go to a show on Broadway and most of the people on the stage are Black, but most of the audiences are white people, that's a problem. Maybe it's because of the ticket price, but we've got to find a way to support each other, and I can understand why many black artists go to the white donors because the black folks didn't sufficiently support them. We can't have that happen. The worst case of that is not just in the arts, but it's in community service in general. In many of these organizations that support black kids and black people, the board is mostly white, the staff is mostly white, and the volunteers are mostly white. It's crazy. We need black mentors for black kids, not a bunch of well-intended, wonderful people who don't look like the kids they serve, and a kid that looks at them and says, 'Well, I can't do that. I know they're trying to be nice to me, but.' There's no role model there, so I think that we get our culture taken away from us if we don't invest in it and support it."

And then how can the arts for the black community be used, as a form of self-care and resistance?

"I think it's no surprise that so many people in the Civil Rights Movement were artists because they have that sense of humanity, and desire to make the world better for themselves and others. I think the arts are connected to things such as social injustice and advancement, equity and self-realization. I think it's all interconnected in that way, so I think we can use that as a tool to help with those issues."

I see Reggie Van Lee, through this interview, becomes a devil-may-care swashbuckling lone rider, which makes my case, for basing commemorating and celebrating **"The 400ᵗʰ"** in the Arts community rather than in politics, better than I ever could. Real or imagined, if **"The 400ᵗʰ"** is based in the political community, I feel, it will be mistaken for a demonstration or protest. Rather in reality, it is an expression of descendants of American slavery's efforts to establish for the first time, "WHO" we are as a people and "HOW" we see ourselves, as well as "WHAT" we want other people around the world to think of us.

"The 400ᵗʰ" was just an idea bouncing around in my head eight years ago (2012). Over the years as I thought about it, my dilemma was how can one conceptualize such a huge story that commemorate and celebrate ***"The 400th"***, something that has never been done by anyone? The task was not just finding words, but bringing those words together in such a way that the Arts community, artists and academicians would join this effort, as major partners and sponsors. Floyd D. Tunson helped me understand that for *"a meaningful visual response to events requires time to contemplate, assimilate, and evaluate."* For ***"The 400th"*** effort to be successful, the Arts and other entertainment communities need time. This realization also points up how these communities operate. First and foremost, museums, galleries, and other cultural venues operate two or three years out in planning their yearly activities.

Time has become the arbiter of what, when, where and how ***"The 400th" Commemoration and Celebration*** will be presented. Historians designated 2019, as the official arrival of the first enslaved Africans in North America. This narrative has pointed out alternative date to show the verity in such designations. Renewing this point, my research shows enslaved Africans began arriving as early the 1530s. Jane Landers of Vanderbilt University says runaway slaves from South Carolina were also part of the "Fort Mose story" where they established the "first free black settlement" in Florida in 1738, which is now the United States. Nova Scotia, Canada recorded enslaved Africans arriving as early as 1600s. During the founding of Port Royal in 1605, enslaved Africans help build fortifications almost 15 years before the first so-called official recorded slave arrival in the US in 1619. The point here is with the multiple dates of slaves arrivals, settling on a single date would force African Americans today to try and shoehorn such an important occasion into one year that has already passed before any preparation, for as such an occasion has passed and the celebration has not begun. Even more salient, COVID-19 locked the world down, putting everything on hold, not to mention NFL, NBA, MLB, Golf, Tennis, stage shows you name it. So ***"The 400th"*** simple must get in line behind COVID-19.

This is why I raise the issue of time for museums, galleries, entertainers and other cultural venues, which operate two or three years out in planning their yearly activities. That time would be good if the ***"The 400th" Committee*** was fully set up and functioning, which it is not. Consequently, the committee has designated ***The 400th Performance Period*** to adjust to conditions and give slavery's descendant's time to organize themselives fully and get projects, programs and other activities up and running. Plus, enslaved Africans were not only brought to North America and other parts of the Western Hemisphere, they were carried into the Indian Ocean's islands to places like Indonesia. Some enslaved Africans were carried to islands in the Pacific Ocean. These descendants of enslaved Africans will want to be part of such a commemoration and celebration of their heritage. ***"The 400th" Committee*** has designated 2020-2030 as a period to organize, and celebrate 2030 as the Quadricentennial year of ***"The 400th"***.

The 400th: From Slavery to Hip Hop

Finally, the Truth Can Be Told

Now, that you are here, I can finally admit the truth behind this narrative. Getting you, the readers, here was the real trick and idea of this narrative. The magic cast by the light and shadows, smoke, and mirrors of history enthralled you and lured you here. History weaved the web that ensnared you in this intriguing and fascinating epic love story. Readers must not forget the folk history relayed here is a love story for the ages, as I said in my opening remarks.

Self-love drives this narrative. Only someone who loves themselves will fight, struggle and endure a life filled with brutality, degradation, and unrewarding toil in a meaningless existence, filled with the desperate times' slavery presented. One had to have a deep and abiding love for self to suffer continually, while seeing only blackness, looking at the world of scarcity and desperation before them.

Slavery was such an existence, which made giving up or mass suicide, seems a reprieve from heaven, but was never considered by most. Holding on to themselves through self-love, slaves found love in other slaves, even more despicable than themselves. Self-love is what allows one to love another, which made making families and building communities group acts of love. Families and communities struggling together are why this narrative played out as it did getting you here. The same love that brought me here brought you.

Truly an epic, as large as history itself, ***"The 400th"***, stretches across millenniums, revealing the unbelievable, yet the amazing mysteries of slave descendants' survival and journey endured reaching ***"The 400th"***. Having read this heart-wrenching story of their day to day challenges, as they held families together makes you no different from me. Its enchantresses, wizards, and spell casters produced the alluring special effects in the words of this story that drew you in and would not allow you to turn away.

A fantastic epic, that almost no one wanted to take time to hear, let alone put aside their day, long enough to read, began mysteriously popping into my head, and I became its instrument. ***"The 400th"*** through its reflective thoughts and words jumped into my mind without summons in 2012. Those haunting spirits overcame my disinterest, and lack of confidence to enthrall me in this love story. ***"The 400th"*** created an emotional desire to invest the time required to tell a love story so incredibly difficult, yet sublimely enlightening, and critically important to slave descendants, it became a Divine calling for me. Reaching out over the centuries to touch slavery's descendants today through me, just in advance of ***"The 400th"***, its powerful magic made me its spill binders.

Lured here, by the lonesome wail of ***"Blues Masters,"*** like the howl of antediluvian specters in ancient ghost stories, they infused their haunting lament and spirits into the words of this narrative. Their dreich repine was the magnet that drew you into the open grave of poverty in the valley of dry bones to witness their unsung demised. Now you are as Ezekiel, facing God's question, *"Can these dry bones live?"* Making their reality an ever-present thought in any future you see is why they brought you here. Doubtlessly, after riding across the **"Middle Passage"** to the Western Hemisphere, you now understand that descendants of American slavery are the terminal end of the longest-running instant of genocide that stretches over the history of mankind. Think about that for a moment!!!!!!!!!!!!

First, before proceeding further with this recapitulation ask yourself, *"Have I ever really thought about* **'The 400th?'** *Had it ever been a thought that originated in my head?"* And, if so, *"How did it get there? What did I do in response to it?"* I ask now, before reading this summons, was slavery a subject you believed, you knew, but never thought about, at least, as a reality today?

When you began reading this narrative, did you know enough about the story of slaves and it's descendants' existence in America to have an independent thought? Was genocide one of the things you considered happened to African Americans? If you did, what did you do then? If not what do you do now that you know every descendant of American slavery today, no matter their condition or circumstances, are descendants, seeds, and survivors of those who endured the legacy you have read?

The corollary here is that white people living today are benefitting from the wealth; their ancestors robbed from slaves and descendants. Through their bondage, and the free labor extracted from enslaving free Africans to build Western culture, on which your life rest today. Consequently, if you are white, your white privilege is based on that wealth that you are reaping, as inherited wealth.

Through your whiteness, as an American or European, you are now conscious of their victimization and must chose to become opposition to the history of slavery or continue to turn blind eyes, as a party to the greed that started it all. Becoming part of commemorating and celebrating **"The 400th"**, you reject and devoice yourself from the terror, **"Dark Age"** *angry white men mob madness*, convict leasing, sharecropping, lynching, banishment, and racial cleansing. Otherwise, you knowingly embrace whiteness in Americans and cling to riches robbed from American slave descendants before, during and after slavery.

I repeat all African Americans you see before you today are part of the terminal end of the longest-running instant of genocide in the history of Homo sapiens. Denied *VOICE*, descendants of enslaved Africans, endure their degradation, desperation, and scarcity, though not silently—**_Slavery By Another Name: The Re-enslavement of African Americans from Slavery to WWII_** and **"We Charge Genocide,"** are their today **Blues!!!**

White people the world over did not see what they did to enslaved Africans, as genocide for them it was just a way of getting rich. After reading this narrative, if not genocide what do you call it? Germans did not consider what they did to Jews genocide either. They said, *"I was only doing my job,"* while Americans say, *"I was only making a living."* Still, the world forced Germany to recognize and acknowledge their crimes against humanity and atone. Now, facing ***"The 400th"*** whites in America will have to do as Germans, own up to the history they created, but will they begin to atone for their dirty deeds??????

Changing America has been a brutal and deadly battle for African Americans. Fighting, demonstrating and protesting—sit-ins, freedom rides, marches in the streets of Washington D.C., raising our black fists in defiance, supporting black power and kneeling to protest denial of *VOICE*—and now Black Lives Matter, the truth is we did not change America completely, we only pushed its racism back. That fact has never been clearer, as incidences like police murders of George Floyd, Breonna Taylor, Ahmud Arbery, Jacob Blake and so many others, then economic disparities, and COVID-19 preying on black Americans like a carnivore is the new normal revealing America's hypocrisy.

The reality is Dr. Martin Luther King, Jr. pointed his finger at the US Government as the culprit, not individual "bad" white people, as I thought before black power. Governments—federal, state and local—have kept black people lock in the grave of poverty in the valley of dry bones. Pres. Woodrow Wilson used the US government to structured racism and white supremacy into America's economy building in discrimination and disparate treatment for blacks Americans.

These policies limited slavery's descendants' access to America's bounty, and Pres. Wilson expressed his beliefs entering the White House this way, **"Self-preservation [forced whites] to rid themselves, by <u>fair means or foul</u>, of the intolerable burden of governments sustained by the votes of ignorant Negroes."** Then he went one sept further and unleashed the **"Dark Age"** *angry white men mob madness* era, to rein terror upon black people to force them to accept second class—separate but equal segregation and white supremacy—as a function of American government. He used lynchings, like NFL tailgate parties, which were not only about terrorizing black people they were wealth building enterprises for white people. Wilson created the atmosphere and environment young progressives are out in the streets today, insisting that "Black Lives Matter," responding to the lynching mentality he created. That hostile environment forced black people to bide their time, as *"second class"* and *"cheap labor"* in America's capitalistic genocidal system.

"The 400th" is a commemoration of those enslaved Africans who suffered America's horrendous genocide. Descendants of American slavery stand as the living rebuttal to all the negative stereotypes that fill history books, movies, legends, and political speeches. Whites claims that former slaves were dim witted, had poor work ethics, deserted families and showed total disregard for community to justify Woodrow Wilson's genocidal strategy. One of my goals writing **"The 400th"** is to speak to young white progressives, especially after showing their support and solidarity.

Speaking to all progressives as my great-grandfather talked with me, thus far your fight has been beating against the door, trying to get in. However, in 2020 you kick the door in, with votes. That is very important, because you took control of the political system in America with just the tip of the minority of the votes available. Your demography is the largest in the nation. Whether in America or elsewhere, *"The 400th"* is a time for you to make a personal statement about your past and what you see as an alternative future.

Those who understand the liberating impact of *"The 400th"* realize it signifies to artists, performers, entertainers, writers, filmmakers, dancers, producers, and other disciplines and expressions of creativity; you are the ones *"The 400th"* is for. You are the ones who must come together and make statements with your art to illustrate the future you see. This is a break out time for your imagination, and *"The 400th"* can be your release to live out your artistic dream.

The older generation can only draw on your inspiration, like Janus, looking back through their eyes, but simultaneously, looking forward through your young eyes as *"The 400th"* generation become the visionaries. You are the ones who will create the new normal your parents and grandparent can only marvel observing, because they could not envision what they are witnessing. If grandparents are going to be relevant, they must take their clues from your generation and allow you to show your visions of the new normal world Black Lives Matter and COVID-19 created.

For me, commemorating of *"The 400th"* is for those who have gone on before us, because we are now their *VOICE*. Definitely descendants of the **Trans-Atlantic Slave Trade**, that were not victims of American slavery, but are descendants of slavery from other places, should demand the right of *VOICE* also. They have the right and numbers, if they use them and take advantage of opportunities commemorating *"The 400th"* has created, they can become part of a world changing celebration of their arrival as a generation.

Just as they were part of the George Floyd/Black Lives Matter international movement and protest, which spread around the world, young progressives can push aside the old normal world that dominated their lives. Indigenous People are part of the genocide and are making their grievances know through telling their story as they commemorate and celebrate their ancestors in a new way. However, surviving America's genocide make slavery's descendants, people who have done something no other people have done to date. Enslaved African descendants have endured a system that was designed to turn them into animals. However, through our ancestors, who continued to make music, sing, dance, love, have babies, make families, and build communities, we emerged lovers, not haters, like characters in *"The WIZ."* I stated began this narrative, and the story of our survival *"is a love story!!!"*

African Americans are declaring—*"The 400th"*—an international celebration. Commemorating and celebrating *"The 400th"* it is going be like a dream birthday party, one has always hoped for but never had. Descendants of slavery around the world invite the world to join us in the biggest and longest family reunion ever. Young people who wanted to join George Clinton/Dr. Funkenstein aboard the *"The Mothership"* for a *"P-funk party cause a P-funk party never stops!!!!"* has only to get aboard **"The 400th"**. After 400 years, we can finally let our hair down, kick off our shoes, and boogie down!!!!! More importantly, it will be a rebirth for those who saw no reason to hope or dream.

"The 400th" will be a history-making period because nothing, like it has ever happened before. We will be the center of it all for the first time in history. No one can claim the spotlight or object to us filling the streets, having neighborhood shindigs, or claiming Central Park to throw down for a week. We will be the first generation ever to attempt such an audacious international celebration. Whatever we do will be historic, for as long as we chose to do it. The only question is, will you be part of that history?

Black Power Becomes Hip Hop

As I said beginning the previous section, the greatest trick of this narrative was getting you here. I repeat I was unprepared to write ***"The 400th"***, because I did not believe I possessed the knowledge base and skills set required to produce a clear, succinct, and unambiguous statement that would be informative enough to do justice to the struggle slave descendants waged reaching ***"The 400th"***. Sometimes, I know I probably overshot the mark regarding succinctness, if nothing else.

But, I was given a vision, and I believe it was divinely inspired, so I followed it like a beckon. I tried to establish and present a vision of the what, why, and how descendants of enslaved Africans followed, as they development their unique culture, which unlike any other became hip hop. Going from slavery to hip hop in this narrative, I presented individuals that played roles in events and developed ideas that became strategies and created technologies that descendants of enslaved Africans applied, creating this new culture.

Needing to understand the world the ***Trans-Atlantic Slave Trade*** created, I went to the edge of what was known. Then to understand hip hop, I had to take a real retro turn, like Eddie Griffin's hard U-turn in *"Under Cover Brother,"* getting readers headed in the right direction, so they would understand the world hip hop replaced; yes, replaced! Reading the history of how descendants of American slavery got to ***"The 400th"***, I realize I have finally arrived where I can present the development of hip hop and how it has become the highest level of development, as well as expression of African American Arts and culture.

Establishing my thesis, as fact, I had to retrace the process, telling my family's story, as they journeyed from slavery to now. Making the hard left turn out of the cotton fields of Mississippi, through the scarcity and desperation of Green Alley to the very outer edge of hip hop, it all began with the *"gas cap incident."* Explicating hip hop's beginning, development, and proliferation, of what seems a brief history to some, first like everything else connected to black people, nothing is as it seems.

Hip hop began with the first generation that embraced black power, as black activists threw off *"learned helplessness."* It seems, most people think or believe hip hop was and is only about rappers. But, when speaking of the growing international culture that is enveloping the world, you are talking about a technology that is a result of Black Arts development. So, to look at it as a totally new phenomenon is not only misleading, but misguided, similar to how I thought about communism.

Getting to know hip hop's true origin, I had to avoid getting caught up in traditions and folklore. An old school/soul music guy, generally, I slept through the birth, adolescence, and young adulthood of hip hop. Its expression and early

The 400th: From Slavery to Hip Hop   715

appearance was so different I didn't see it as a child I help bring into the world; I did not recognize my offspring. It's like the adage; "Victory has many fathers but defeat is an orphan." So as in real life, in such cases, I was so involved attending to my first born love—*black power*—trying to save it, I was not concerned with the bastard hip hop's struggle to survive. I was aware of efforts to undercut, even kill it, altogether, like a partial-birth abortion, it didn't look like my other child, in its infancy.

    I did not connect it to my affair with it mother, like a quickiey on a blind date or a one night stand, until John Gary Williams, STAX recording legend and *Invader*, pulled my coat to the resemblance in 1974. He said, *"John B, man R&B is on the way out, rap is taking over. You watch, and you'll see what I say. Ten years from now, it's going to be the big thing in black music."* John may have been off a decade or two, but he saw the lineage and resemblance almost immediately.

    So, as such, I was ignorant of this growing kid emerging into a giant, in our midst. Getting on the trail of hip hop in 2017 for **"The 400th"**, it was not the same as chasing down the roots of the **Trans-Atlantic Slave Trade.** Hip hop was like a back alley abortion that went bad, and the surviving fetus showed up on the doorstep, almost fully grown, before I noticed its existence. During the hunt for the beginnings of slavery, although there was no birth certificate, there was a christening (Popes Nicholas V issued the *Dum Diversas* on June 18, 1452), which left a historical records that provided stepping stones leading to ever-higher levels of knowledge. Each level added to the picture in my head that guided my assumptions.

    However, it was not that way with the bastard hip hop. I found myself in a situation, like looking in the rearview mirror at a reflection I thought I knew from back in the 1960s, but inheritance needed something more than the mother's word. Looking back through reflections, I could not be sure what I was seeing, while still trying to go straight ahead, on a crowded freeway.

    I looked for books, like a birth certificate but, found hip hop's beginnings were like the rest of the stories about black people, more she said he said word of mouth rumors, at best. Beyond a few books like Michael Eric Dyson **_Know What I Mean? Reflections on Hip-Hop_** (2007), though interesting, factual, and impressive, they were not DNA tests. Such books seemed to capture more of the episodic occurrences or developments, like how and where we meet, who was there, even the name of the place, but so many seemed involved in the act, with several births occurring simultaneously, who could say their hit or lick, made them the father of this particular offspring. Consequently hip hop grew up fatherless, that is until it became a toddler a child star, so you know everybody loves a child getting money!!!!

    When the lights came on, I was asleep in the corner, and was in the mix in the studio, so it was difficult to say whose dip put how much in the pot to justify claims on the star on the stage. I paint this picture that developed in my head, digging through the graveyard at the outer edges of mostly personal accounts of hip hop's wild orgies of creativity, like wife swopping and sharing, even gang-banging on a park bench that produced the hip hop child the world loves today.

Developing the portrait, I had in my head is a rendering more like a Floyd D. Tunson abstract. Its beauty lie in the use of lines, light, and shadows to give meaning, color and depth, creating a picture so black at birth it could look like anybody on the block. So hip hop seemed like just another black male screwing around at it birth, which is how the media made it seem when it got the story and the white moneyed class entered the picture.

I use what is known, as the balance between reports from those that say they were on the train when the child left the station but the mama was left standing on the platform. I can't say because I was sleep in the corner at the club. These actors or eyes witnesses are, like others in this narrative that dated the chick were not selected because of public success as hip hop pioneers, so they stood out. With only a few written reports, but their impact, as part of this expanding world culture gave me something I recognized, as connected to a past I was able to substantiate. It was not only their fame, which got the ones I discussed here into **"The 400th"** narrative, but where they fit into the story, serving as bridges connecting the many information gulfs I encountered.

My research revealed it was the particular type of people who saw real promise in hip hop, whereas others, were like me until I found it on my doorstep, but passed it by like I didn't notic. Anthropologically, I liken it to the early emergence or divergence of Homo sapiens from other mammals or primates in places like the *Olduvai Gorge*. Certain ones looked down from the trees and wondered what's down there and went down to check it out. Eons ago, some very early Homo sapiens saw sticks and stones as tools with which they cracked nuts.

Serendipitously, primitive individuals saw some things in totally new and different ways and decided or thought "what if I do this?" After seeing what happened, if it worked, they continued adding what they learned to the mix. This metaphor reflects the gulf hip hop technology has spanned since the 1960s, reaching its prominence today. The people I discuss, many were the ones whose ears heard or eyes saw something different and said, "what if?"

The road from slavery to hip hop began before emancipation, and the fight for education, which in reality were fights for survival. During those fights, slaves maintained the one thing master could not take away, the things going on inside their heads. Slaves' inner muse found ways of expressing itself, without other slaves noticing, as anything special, until master noticed and began asking them to do those improvised acts for his amusement. Minstrelsy was the result.

Notwithstanding Minstrelsy began with slaves during bondage, and northern whites loved it so much they were willing to pay to see it. Following emancipation, it became the first door through which former slaves pushed to participate in the technology based on what they did with their bodies. Doing

The 400th: From Slavery to Hip Hop

thing with their bodies became a theme in the lives of former slaves. Their movements, sounds, misspoken words, everything about them fascinated white people and became entertainment. Where white people saw something worth paying money to see, ambitious former slaves saw survival on another level. They viewed it as an exit from poverty, if they got knowledge of this technology—how businesses worked.

The thing that must be understood, looking at hip hop before black men could become entrepreneurs, they had to learn how to make money. I do not mean, make money in business, but make money doing anything. During slavery, whites allowed some slaves that had particular skills or talent to make pocket money. Some slaves were good enough at what they did, to buy their freedom.

On the other hand, there were blacks in the north that had businesses and some even got rich, but they were the exception. However, the vast majority could not read, neither count nor write. Education solved that problem for a very few, compared to the total population of former slaves.

Hip Hop: An Orphan Seed

The orphan legacy of hip hop is a concept I developed to emphasize the America recording/entertainment complex efforts to ignore it and when that strategy failed it tried to kill hip hop by shutting it off from main stream, because of it total African American origin. There were "NO" white people to any significant degree contributing talent or financing. More specifically, hip hop did not emerge, as an idea, it was not even hip hop; it was something young blacks in New York City began, doing because of their deprived communities' environments. Describing the situation as "neglect" is an upgrade, a nice word to indicate the cultural blight black and brown youngsters endured in large northern cities. Hallways, streets, sidewalks, and back alleys were their playgrounds, in most cases. Walls and other fixtures were their canvases and cans of spray paint were their brushes. Radios were their musical instruments, over which DJs gave voice to their misery and deprivation.

Former slaves' getting enough money to do anything was a bare knuckles battle with scarcity and desperation from eyes opening to closing, while hunger lurked like buzzards, in a generous mood, waiting for eyes to close. But, down South, slavery's descendants, before the death of sharecropping, saw those conditions in northern cities, as the Promised Land, if they could only get there. Their trips running northward were like "the children of Israel trek through the wilderness, to make it across the Mason-Dixon Line. However, down South for most blacks sidewalks and drugs didn't come along until black power made the South a melting pot of black liberation.

That story before descendant of slavery had money to do things—one would consider a business—with white people's eyeballing their every move, made that impossible for most. It took innovative engineering by tough, hard and mean devil may care, swashbuckling lone riders, like Sunbeam Mitchell, who would eventually built the *"Chitlin Circuit,"* the yellow brick road of American entertainment, to show the way to making money, without sponsors like the Church family. Before he hooked up with owners of chicken shacks, grease spoons, corn liquor dive, and gambling houses such operation had to be created, more than a century earlier.

Starting out, before hip hop was a glimmer in the eye of chance, small family operations were the only money-making efforts in the South. In most cases, money came to black families that found a way to owned land. These enterprises were family operations for several generations. Such operations fell within what white people allowed; they did not see them as competition. Even in cities, the best the vast majority of black man could do was a mom and pop neighborhood stand, or small store, a funeral operation in the backroom, or barbershop on the back porches and beauty shop in the kitchens; my mother had one.

The 400th: From Slavery to Hip Hop

The only other real hope was sending kids to school, getting professional training or opening a business. In terms of wealth creation, we are talking about arriving in the 1950s, where business in the black community was a barbershop, bar-b-que stand on weekends, beauty shop, funeral home, maybe burial policy salesman, and such. The very lucky families were able to produce a doctor, dentist, or lawyer. Business on this level is why I say black men like Sunbeam Mitchell and his crew were the first real black businessmen. They were the one that learned how to make money. They were the only ones that had enough money going through their hands to learn what it was to have it; next came bootleggers, drug dealers, gamblers, and other hustlers, all were Sunbeam's forte.

The fight for rights began, as slaves walked off plantations. Making families and building communities gave contrabands someplace to start, changing their economic status to give their efforts real meaning and a lasting impact. Former slaves' denial of rights made political awareness a major theme, in their desire to start a business. Marcus Garvey fired those hopes, like a torch, in the minds and hearts of former slaves. Hence, they moved up to mon-and-pop shops. The hope of having something someday gave them reasons to endure the pain or shame to gain knowledge. Carrying what they learned forward, as a beginning technology, entertainment became a major contributor to former slaves learning how to make money and build wealth, as families.

The new world of the 1960s was like being emancipated a second time for slavery's descendants. Although it was undeclared, there was a war then too. That war produced *black power* and a new radical mindset about everything, making money topped the list for some. Learning how to make money was why throwing off *"learned helplessness"* was so important.

With the advent of the Civil Rights Bill of 1964, politics, in and of the streets, gave *VOICE* to the voiceless, and a new type of black political speech was born. Defying white people was the first step for any aspiring black power activists, and one had to apply this attitude and show this fact in every way. Black power advocates condensed history, creating new terms and a new kind of delivery, based on catchy phrases. With this new technology, they dropped knowledge on a listening black world. Black power activists called this new organizing strategy or technology "rappin," which brings us back to hip hop.

The hip hop movement started at society's margins. Its origins are shrouded in mystery and filled with enigmas, as I pointed out earlier. People heard a confusing collection of names and read about mystical characters, while listening to R & B. They only saw such images in photographs or underground videos, even a few magazines; hip hop was like a myth to most, hence John Gary's statement. Many of those stories made hip hop seem a refuge for criminals, especially to the older generation. Old folks saw hip hop as the source of easy money, made skirting the law, and selling drugs. These Americans did not perceive hip hop as having any real intent or serious purpose, especially during its earliest development.

Most people are certain hip hop happened without design, forethought, or vision on any one's part. At best, they would say, it was *"an accidental occurrence, perpetrated by a hodgepodge of individuals without anything constructive in mind."* It seemed to them, I think, hip-hoppers were messing around with music between doing drugs and having sex. At worst, observers seemed convinced that in its beginnings, hip-hoppers were nothing more than a bunch of thieves and gangsters, stealing other people's hard work (music) and getting rich glorifying sex, drugs, and violence. If any of your considerations about hip hop fall into these categories, I would like to add a few real facts and events for your consideration, before closing the book on hip hop.

Research shows none of those statements have factual bases. I came to see hip hop as a process, an extension of the artistic development of slave descendants, which began during bondage with the roots of their **Blues**. Hip hop was not the overnight happening and success; many people today believe it was. I discovered during my research, hip hop had many origins, with one being the African griot tradition. That work supports the fact that in spreading the net of **The Trans-Atlantic Slave Trade,** slave catchers, snatched up any African they could and brought them to the Western Hemisphere (North America). Packng victims of all types aboard slave ships, griots were also victims, caught up, trapped, and kidnapped the same as other Africans.

A *griot*, also jali, or jeli (djeli or djéli French spelling), is a West African historian, storyteller, praise singer, poet, and musician. *Griots* functioned as repositories of oral tradition and other significant knowledge, while being advisors to royalty. Paul Oliver, in "*Savannah Syncopators: African Retentions in the Blues*" says, *"Though the griot has to know many traditional songs, without error, he must also have the ability to expound on current events, cultural changes and incidental happening of the day. Very witty, even comical, a griot's knowledge of local history is most formidable. Although they are sometimes known as praise singers, griots may use their vocal expertise for gossip, satire, or political commentary. Today, griots are still very much a part of African culture. They live in many parts of West Africa and are particularly present among the Mande peoples (Mandinka, Malinké, Bambara), Fulɓe (Fula), Hausa, Songhai, Tukulóor, Wolof, Serer, Mossi, Dagomba, Mauritanian Arabs, and many other smaller groups".*

The *griot* tradition was very important to the development of the American entertainment industry. Francis Bebey, writing about *griots* in African Music says, *"The West African griot is a troubadour, the counterpart of the medieval European minstrel... The griot knows everything that is going on... He is a living archive of the people's traditions... A virtuoso, griots talents command universal admiration.*

Their virtuosity is a culmination of long years of study, having worked under the tutorage of a teacher who is often a father or uncle. The profession is by no means a male prerogative.

The 400th: From Slavery to Hip Hop

There are many women griots whose talents as singers and musicians are equally remarkable." ("African Music, A People's Art," Francis Bebey, Brooklyn: Lawrence Hill Books),

Griots were no different from other Africans, caught up and kidnapped by slavers. They were brought to North America and other parts of the West Hemisphere and were most likely to use their talents to entertain master. *Master Juba* may have been trained by or been of *griot* lineage. Maybe, some black power activists, like H Rap Brown and Stokley Carmichael, were of griot lineage.

Moreover, Paul Oliver points out the *griot* connections to the **Blues,** as a link to America's only original musical creation. This narrative has presented the role of Minstrelsy, where white men took back North, what they saw slaves doing to entertain master down South. Emancipation gave slaves mobility, and slaves became minstrel performers. Many traveled on their own from town to town, singing and dancing on the street, as observers tossed coin like *medieval European minstrel.* **Blues** singers continued this tradition. Minstrelsy helped establish black people, as the foundation of entertainment in America.

The story of how black music and its many phases—**Blues**, ragtime, jazz, swing/Big band, R&B/soul, even rock n' roll—were part of the origin of America entertainment and has been discussed. Reaching the 1960s, we find hip hop's earliest and clearest origin. Hip hop, like other forms of entertainment, did not spring up out of nowhere; its foundations rested on a very solid foundation. Hip hop developed from the same tradition as other black music. Hip hop before it became a culture happening or even a phenomenon, was a process that took advantage of and commandeered things people were already doing. I saw hip hop as the **Trans-Atlantic Slave Trade**, *"It did not matter how much resources were available, how and what was done with those resources is what made the difference."*

Just a seed when it began growing in the late 1960 and early 1970s, no one was even thinking about what became hip hop. The talk was all about civil rights and then came *"Black Power."* Until Stokley Carmichael uttered those immortal words—*black power* (1966) from the Mississippi delta—black people had accepted being defined by whites, as colored people or Negros. It is at this point HBCUs (Historically Black Colleges and Universities) became incubators for **"The 400th"** and hip hop, in the late 1960s. Stokley Carmichael, H. "Rap" Brown and many other black students were trying to redefine who black people were and their relationship to America. Amidst protesting and demonstrating for their human rights, groups of students at HBCUs and other black colleges began coming together over the weekend, mostly at HBCUs, discussing these issues or what some called the *"black thang."*

Students from across the South on weekends gathered at HBCUs, trying to chart a path out of the colored/Negro box, whites created following slavery. They met in dorms and off-campus student apartments or in someone's cribs, who gave it up for the weekend to accommodate activists that came to these *"black power sleepovers."* The 1960s and 70s were a time, when young activists talked only *"black power."* The brothers and sisters who intensely study liberation politics and read books like <u>The Autobiography of Malcolm X, Black Skin White Masks, Before the Mayflower, Destruction of Black Civilization, The Wretched of the Earth</u> and communist literature on revolution, led these discussions.

These brothers and sisters were the ones developing black power philosophy and psychology. They interpreted political events and developed strategies to counter segregation. They were the ones that developed the quick-witted, catchy phrases, and new revolutionary speech that other copied and passed on to others. Black activists began calling their new speech "rappin." H. "Rap" Brown was one of, if not the best at this, hence his moniker "Rap" Brown.

These gatherings became known as "rap sessions" because that was what they did. Activists were really energetic and very passionate, while trying to make their point. While the discussions were going, music played in the background; some would dance or just chilled and listened. These gatherings were really parties but with a serious purpose (*"King" Khan's* **Black Power Tarot Exhibition** and **Invaders Screening** were conceived with this very ideas in mind).

I experienced this scene on weekends when I accompanied "Cab" to several of these black power "sleepover rap sessions" in Atlanta, South Carolina State and Jackson State. "Cab" was a graduate of Morehouse, so he had connections, and he knew "Rap" Brown and Stokley. I was just a tag-along picking up whatever I could, since I had no real experience, as an activist or real knowledge regarding black history. Those events were truly eye-opening for me. I was definitely a fish out of water. Sometimes black icons from the *Black Nationalist Movement* came to these black power "sleepovers" to talk and give direction to black power activists.

"Queen Mother" Moore was the first real radical leader, I met and heard speak. Audley Moore (1898–1997), was born into a very extraordinary life and lift a remarkable legacy. "Queen Mother" left behind a life of distinction with many disciples. She was one of the most revered figures helping to develop twentieth-century philosophies of Black Nationalism, Communism, and Pan-Africanism as movements. A life-long Garveyite and a leading personality in the World War II-era Harlem Communist Party, "Queen Mother," was a leader of black women across the African Diaspora. She was in the vanguard struggling for self-determination. The "Queen Mother" avoided the *Second Red Scare*, J. Edgar Hoover's destructive and deadly trap for communists by remaking herself.

Leaving the Communist Party in late 1950, she reinvented herself, as an ardent *Black Nationalist*. She created her philosophy of politics, by combining Garveyism, Marxism, Third Worldism, and feminism to become a central figure forging the 1960s- black power era and the modern reparations movement. Her life and activism show she was one of the most underappreciated black women that helped build radical black movements like the Diasporic movements. She continued the legacy of Marcus Garvey and reframed and refocused

Communism for black power activists. "Queen Mother" Moore refashioned the contours of twentieth-century black radicalism, black internationalism, and black women's activism.

These black power sleepover sessions took place at or around colleges in different southern states. However, because of its central location in the South with several colleges—Morris Brown, Clark College, Spelman College, and Morehouse University—were in Atlanta, so it became "Rap session central" for black power. The important point here for hip hop is, many students involved in black power were from northern cities, most particularly New York City.

Similar to whites who observed what slaves did down south, then took what they learned, back North to create Minstrelsy; black students did the same with black power and its new technology "rappin." They took the black power *"sleepover culture,"* they picked up down South, back home, and shared their education with their communities. Black power *"sleepovers"* harkened back to slave pens, where they developed the theme of teaching one another what they knew.

Their activism and what they learned became knowledge bases or repositories among their families, friends, associates, and communities. Sharing their experiences—*"word of mouth"*—at black power get-togethers, they transplanted "rap" sessions to New York City. Taking black activism back to New York City students' knowledge took on greater significance for hip hop than what they learned in college classes.

The Mothership Brings Funk to Hip Hop

Clarifying hip hop's beginning in the 1960s, with black power and rap, this narrative now shows how the use of catchy phrases and spoken word, after being transported north to New York City by students from HBCU in the South became a beginning technology. However, there was one more connection that began right next door in New Jersey that would become the vehicle on which those catchy phrases would ride. One artist stepped out of a cloud of smoke and lights aboard The Mothership, and create *"One Nation Under a Groove"* and make funk a hip-hop element, before DJ Kool Herc and Afrika Bambaataa scratched on their first turntable

George Edward Clinton (July 22, 1941) was born in Kannapolis, North Carolina, but grew up in Plainfield, New Jersey. An African American, he became a singer, songwriter, bandleader, and record producer, on the way to becoming Dr. Funkenstein. Inspired by Frankie Lymon & the Teenagers (a 1950 doo-wop group) inspired Clinton to form his own a doo-wop group called "The Parliaments." Clinton was part owner of a barbershop that specialized in conks (processed hair dos). It was also known as the "hangout for all the local singers and musicians" in Plainfield's 1950s and 60s doo-wop, soul, rock and proto-funk music scene, *("Parliament -Biography & History"*, Bush, John AllMusic).

In 1967, George had a major hit single, *"(I Wanna) Testify"* with the Parliaments. He created two different group names for performing Parliament and Funkadelic by the 1950s. George's Parliament-Funkadelic collective also performed as separate bands. Clinton was a major innovator of eclecto-funk musician, during the 1970s that drew on science fiction, outlandish fashion, psychedelic culture, and surreal humor. These two bands—Parliament and Funkadelic—combined the elements of musicians such as Jimi Hendrix, Sly and the Family Stone, Frank Zappa, and James Brown, while exploring various sounds, technology, and lyricism. Clinton and Parliament-Funkadelic brought a diverse style of music to the 1970s and had over 40 R&B hit singles (including three number ones) and three platinum albums. Funkadelic's title track *"One Nation Under a Groove"* (1978) spent six weeks at the top spot on the R&B charts that summer.

During the 1980s Clinton's career was marred by multiple legal problems, producing financial difficulties. That hullabaloo was due to royalty and copyright issues, notably with Bridgeport Music, who Clinton suit for fraudulently, obtained the copyrights to many of his recordings. Legal difficulties also arose with PolyGram's Records acquired Parliament's label, Casablanca Records.

Although Clinton recorded several solo albums during this period, all of these records featured contributions from P-Funk's core musicians. *("George*

Clinton Explains How Bridgeport Allegedly Faked Documents To Get His Music Rights", Mike Masnick, 2011Techdirt).

Clinton began his solo career with *"Computer Games"* in 1982. Then a few months later Clinton dropped the bomb *"Atomic Dog,"*. Hitting number one on the R&B charts, *"Atomic Dog"* stayed at the top spot for four weeks. However, it only reached number 101 on the pop charts. That's white folks for you; they never get it early.

The hip hop world, trying to develop an identity and get it legs beneath itself, began find its way to George's door. Nothing like Berry Gordy at Motown, but during the mid to late 1980s, many hip-hop and rap wanna-bes began following Clinton's lead, as a major influence. Rap producers sampled Clinton's songs with Parliament-Funkadelic, as well as James Brown. George said, *"Sure, sample my stuff..."* remarking in 1996, *"Ain't a better time than gettin paid than when you're my age, ("How George Clinton Made Funk a World View"*, Bob Gulla, 2008 The New Yorker).

In 1989, Clinton released *The Cinderella Theory* on Paisley Park, Prince's record label. This was followed by *Hey Man, Smell My Finger* in 1993. Clinton signed with Sony 550 and released T.A.P.O.A.F.O.M. (*The Awesome Power of a Fully Operational Mothership*) in 1996. George Clinton's: *"The Mothership Connection"* is the title of a DVD that features a concert performed by Parliament-Funkadelic at The Summit in Houston, Texas on October 31, 1976. The DVD documents the beginning of the famed *P-Funk Earth Tour*, which toured almost two years. *"The P-Funk Mothership,"* also known as *"The Holy Mothership,"* was a space vehicle that transported Dr. Funkenstein—alter ego of George Clinton. An integral part of the P-Funk mythology, *"The Mothership"* existed conceptually as a fictional vehicle of funk deliverance and as a physical prop central to Parliament-Funkadelic's concert universe, during the 1970s thru 1990s.

For many years, the landing of *"The Mothership"* was only alluded to at live concerts, due to the prohibitive cost of the elaborate stage-show George had in his mind. During their heyday of the 1970s, following the success of their platinum-selling album, 1975's *"Mothership Connection,"* George Clinton and his band Parliament Funkadelic-the Funk Mob-engaged in a series of high profile, no-expenses-spared stadium tours around the United States, culminating in the famous *"P Funk Earth Tour."* *"The Mothership,"* a full-scale model complete with lights, sound effects and pyrotechnics, was summoned by the vocal tones of P Funk singer/guitarists Glenn Goins and later Garry Shider.

"The Mothership" would land on stage amongst the band, as fans went wild watching Dr. Funkenstein disembark. George Clinton would emerge from the *"Mothership,"* as Dr. Funkenstein. The "cool ghoul" drop funk on the a listening world and audiences wet wild. In 1996, following the release of T.A.P.O.A.F.O.M. (*The Awesome Power of a Fully Operational Mothership*), George Clinton launched the *"Mothership Reconnection Tour"* with Bootsy Collins, Bernie

Worrell, and the latest incarnation of P Funk—"*P Funk All Stars*". *"The Mothership Reconnection Tour,"* which began in New York's Central Park, required a reconstruction of the 1970s *"Mothership,"* and the concerts included the landing of the Mothership. The last sighting of *"The Mothership"* was at Woodstock 1999. Since 1999, the landing of *"The Mothership"* has been strictly metaphorical. *"The Mothership"* has continued its legacy by finding an eternal docking port in the Smithsonian's National Museum of African American History and Culture in Washington, D.C.

The world began changing really fast for music, not only for R&B by 1999, as rapper like Dr. Dre sampled most of Clinton's beats to create his G-Funk music era. Clinton collaborated with Lil' Kim and Fred Durst for rap metal group Methods of Mayhem's single *"Get Naked."* Extending his influence further into rap and hip hop, Clinton also worked with Tupac Shakur on the song *"Can't C Me"* from the album *"All Eyez on Me"*; Ice Cube on the song and video for *"Bop Gun (One Nation)"* on the *"Lethal Injection"* album (which sampled Funkadelic's earlier hit *"One Nation Under A Groove"*); Outkast on the song *"Synthesizer"* from the album *Aquemini*; Redman on the song *"J.U.M.P."* from the album *Malpractice*; Souls of Mischief on *"Mama Knows Best"* from the album *Trilogy*: Conflict, Climax, Resolution; Killah Priest on *"Come With me"* from the album *Priesthood*; the Wu Tang Clan on *"Wolves"* from the album *8 Diagrams*, *("Funky George Clinton and Crew Are Back,"* Jonathan Gold, 1989, Los Angeles Times.)

All I can say is Dr. Funkenstein is one well sampled griot. He appeared on the intro to Snoop Dogg's *"Tha Blue Carpet Treatment"* album (2007). Clinton was also a judge for the 5th annual Independent Music Awards to support independent artists' careers. George's music became the soundtrack for the rap movement, as artists from MC Hammer, to LL Cool J to Snoop Doggy Dogg leaned heavily on the infectious grooves of Clinton productions, as the foundation of their recordings.

In April 2018, Clinton announced he would retire from touring in May 2019. *"Truth be told, it's never really been about me. It's always been about the music and the band. That's the real P-Funk legacy. They'll still be funkin' long after I gone."* Earlier in 2018, he told Rolling Stone that he had made a hologram, suggesting that the band could "have it to start performing in Vegas, *("Funk Icon George Clinton to Retire from Touring: Exclusive"*, Gail Mitchell, 2018, Billboard).

Clinton was inducted into the Rock and Roll Hall of Fame in 1997, alongside 15 other members of Parliament-Funkadelic. Also in 2009, Clinton was inducted into the North Carolina Music Hall of Fame. In May 2012, Clinton was awarded an Honorary Doctorate of Music from Berklee College of Music. That same year George Clinton and Parliament-Funkadelic were given Grammy Lifetime Achievement Awards (2019).

A New Technology is Born

Bringing black power sleepovers to New York City brought guys like DJ Kool Herc and Afrika Bambaataa into the mix; they became part of the process, and a new technology was born. Clive Campbell, an 18-year-old immigrant, introduced huge sound systems from his native Jamaica to inner-city party goers. Using two turntables, he melded percussion fragments from old records with popular dance songs to get a continuous flow of music. Becoming known as a hip hop deejays, Kool Herc drew other pioneers such as Grand Wizard Theodore, Afrika Bambaataa, and Grandmaster Flash into the new kind of party he was creating.

These brothers figured out how to isolated and extended the breakbeat (the part of a dance record where all sounds but drums drop out). Their intent was to stimulate improvisational dancing. Contests developed around breakbeats, and the best dancers created moves to match the breaks, hence break dancing. Although it was not New York based, "Soul Train" producer by Don Cornelius was instrumental in helping to develop a real interest in black dancing as a career. Young people developed styles and dance repertoires that included acrobatic and occasionally airborne moves with gravity-defying head-spins and back-spins. Their improvisational dancing became trademarks of what became hip hop—*do something with your body*.

Another process that began in the late 1960s and developed simultaneously in New York that hip hop commandeered was graffiti. For early pioneers, graffiti entered the game, as activists searched for way to give voice to their political aspirations and commentary. Their early expressions were statements of community pride.

They were part of groups, such as the Black Spades, Savage Skulls, La Familia, and Savage Nomads. These groups used graffiti to mark territory. Julio 204, a Puerto Rican was one of the first New York City graffiti artist. A member of the "Savage Skulls," he started writing his nickname in his neighborhood as early as 1968. The New York Times published an article *("Taki 183" Spawns Pen Pals")* about another graffiti writer TAKI 183, with similar form as JULIO 204.

According to the article, Julio had been writing for a couple of years when Taki, a Greek American teenager, began artistically writing his name. The term "tagging," was applied to this activity around the city. Taki also states in the article that Julio "got busted and stopped writing." Writers following in the wake of Taki and Tracy 168 added their street number to their nickname to "bomb" (cover) trains with their work.

Ingenuously, graffiti artist used subway trains to carry their message, and fame across the City. If the message was impressive or simply pervasive—"all New York" got the word. Although the elaborate Brooklyn style Tracy 168 dubbed "wildstyle" would come to dominate the art, bubble lettering initially held sway only among Bronx writers. The early trend-setters were joined in the 1970s by artists like Dondi, Futura 2000, Daze, Blade, Lee, Fab Five Freddy, Zephyr, Rammellzee, Crash, Kel, NOC 167 and Lady Pink, *(Rap Attack*, 3rd ed., David Toop: London: Serpent's Tail, 2000).

By 1975 young writers in the Bronx, Queens, and Brooklyn were clandestinely slipping into train yards, during the wee hours, to spray-paint colorful mural-size renderings of their names. Their imagery came from underground comics and television. They even planted Andy Warhol-like Campbell's soup cans on subway cars. Soon, influential art dealers in the United States, Europe, and Japan began displaying graffiti in major galleries. However, New York City's Metropolitan Transit Authority responded with dogs, barbed-wire fences, paint-removing acid baths, and undercover police squads to arrest offenders, like JULIO 204, while remove their work.

New York hip hop rose up out of the historic ruins of a post-industrial and ravaged South Bronx. Young urban black and Latino's, political expressions had been marginalized, as their community's discourse were written off. Teens began making public statements, speaking through hip hop. Coming to the fore, filling the voiceless vacuum for young people, DJ Kool Herc became their hip hop doorway. His first outreach was DJ-ing his sister's back-to-school party (8-11-1973).

Entering from stage left, DJ Kool Herc began extending the beat of records, as he played. He used two record players to isolate the percussion "breaks," by adding a mixer to switch between the two records. For hip-hoppers, this was like the "shot heard around the world" that got things moving. Herc's experiments, making music using record players, became known as breaking or "scratching." The first major hip-hop deejay to use two turntables, Herc melded percussive fragments from old records with popular dance songs to create a continuous flow of music. Kool Herc and other pioneering hip-hop deejays took the breaks of funk songs—the part most suited to dance, usually percussion-based—isolating the breaks for dancing at all-night parties.

Developing break-beat deejaying, deejays used hard funk and rock playbacks. Herc's style became the model and a basic element of hip hop music. Announcing and exhorting dancers with syncopated rhymes spoken by MCs or deejays to "get out on the floor," called forth the 1960s black power term "rappin" once again. DJ Kool Herc dubbed dancers "break-boys" and "break-girls," or simply b-boys and b-girls. According to Herc, "breaking" was also street slang for "getting excited" and "acting energetically," *("Kool Herc, in Israel (director), The Freshest Kids: A History of the B-Boy*," QD3, 2002.)

Taking the beat to a new level, Afrika Bambaataa (æfrɪkə bæmˈbɑːtə) born Lance Taylor (5-17-1957), a disc jockey, singer, songwriter and producer from the South Bronx, created a whole new language to give hip hop form and structure. Inspired by DJ Kool Herc, Afrika Bambaataa organized a street collective called the mighty Universal Zulu Nation. Bambaataa's Universal Zulu Nation was designed to draw hip hop teenagers out of gang life, drugs, and violence.

Bambaataa is responsible for outlining the five main elements of hip hop—"rapping" also called MC—microphone commander—with a rhythmic vocal rhyming style (orality); DJing (turntablism) making music with record players and DJ mixers (aural/sound and music creation); b-boying/b-girling/breakdancing (movement/dance); and graffiti art. The other elements of the hip hop subculture and arts movements beyond the main five are hip hop culture and historical knowledge of the movement (intellectual/philosophical), beatboxing, a percussive vocal style; street entrepreneurship; hip hop language; and hip hop fashion and style (*Can't Stop Won't Stop: A History of the Hip-Hop Generation*, Jeff Chang; DJ Kool Herc: (2005), Macmillan).

DJ Kool Herc's experimented with techniques of manipulating sounds, creating music and beats using two or more phonograph turntables (or other sound sources, such as tapes, CDs, or digital audio files) with a DJ mixer that is plugged into a PA system became known as DJing and turntablism. During the1970s, Kool Herc became so impressive, isolating and extending "breaks" (the parts of albums that focused solely on the percussion beat) Herc's techniques drew DJs, like Grandmaster Flowers, Grandmaster Flash, Grand Wizard Theodore, and Grandmaster Caz into his innovative universe. Kool Herc made "scratching" a hip hop staple and one of the key techniques associated with hip hop music.

Herc's house parties gained such popularity, they moved outdoors, to accommodate more people. Hosting venues in parks, these outdoor parties became an outlet for teenagers to express themselves artistically, "instead of running the streets, getting in trouble, teens now had a place to expend pent-up energy. Tony Tone, a member of the Cold Crush Brothers, said that *"hip hop saved a lot of lives."* For inner-city youth, hip hop provided a different way of dealing with the hardships of life, being minorities within America. The hip hop culture became an outlet that allowed them to avoid the ever-present risk of violence and the rise of the gang/thug culture in New York City. MC Kid Lucky mentions that *"people used to break-dance against each other instead of fighting."* (*"It's a Hip-hop World,"* Jeff Chang, 2007: Foreign Policy).

Grandmaster Flash and the Furious Five produced the seminal track *"The Message"* (1982), which pointed out the realities of life in housing projects of urban America. Hip hop lyrical content of many early rap groups was in the mode of *griots*. They focused on social issues, most notably, giving young African Americans voice by "rappin" about their issues.

Speaking about the reality of life for young African Americans was vigorously opposed by conservatives that claimed: "hip hop romanticized violence, law-breaking, sex, and gangs." The flip side of this white Americans' racist theme song from the 1930s was just as vigorously opposed by young blacks who brought their black power movement psychology into hip hop culture. Black power's children were very angry and rebellious, other black youths trapped in ghettos across America and locked in poverty, with no way out, they fought for *VOICE*. Their complaints were not answered by a hungover red necks world, still drunk on racism, spitting hatred out and throwing it up all over black people, like back during segregation in the1930s.

Rappers went on the attack with a wide variety of oracle epic styles. These styles reflected the connection to West African griot techniques, which merged from many black Americans lyrical styles, such as signifying, talking blues songs, jailhouse toasts (long rhyming poems recounting outlandish deeds and misdeeds), and the dozens (the ritualized word game based on exchanging insults, usually about members of the opponent's family). MCs and deejays also utilized the hipster-jive announcing styles of 1950s R&B deejays such as Jocko Henderson, Nat D. Williams, and Rufus Thomas. They also brought in other influences like the black power poetry of Amiri Baraka, "Nikki" Giovanni, Gil Scott-Heron, Oscar Brown, Jr., and the Last Poets. The black power term "rappin" kept alive the old school music that introduced new and different ways of using sections in recordings from artists like Isaac Hayes, James Brown, and George Clinton. They also reached into DJ Kool's heritage, adopting the Jamaican style of rhythmic speech, known as toasting, as hip hoppers pushed the growth of hip hop.

MCs and rappers continued innovating, commandeered "capping," the African American style of speech. "Capping" is when performers try to outdo each other in their originality of language, whereby gaining the favor of listeners. The basic elements of hip hop—boasting raps, rival "posses" (groups), uptown "throw-downs," and political and social commentary are elements that were present all along in African American music and speech. MCing and rap performers moved back and forth between the predominance of toasting songs packed with a mixture of boasting, "slackness" sexual innuendo, and a more topical, political, socially conscious style.

The role of the MC originally was a Master of Ceremonies for a DJ-ed dance event. The MC would introduce the DJ and try to pump up the audience. MCs spoke between the DJ's songs, urging everyone to get up and dance. MCs also told jokes and use their energetic language and enthusiasm to rev up the crowd, as in the *griot* tradition. Eventually, rhythmic wordplay, and rhyming, which became rapping, developed into longer sessions, (*"Hip hop: Origins, Characteristics and Creative Processes,"* Fredreich Neumann, 2000: The World of Music, 42 JSTOR).

Afrika Bambaataa is known for, along with being a major hip hop pioneer, releasing a series of genre-defining electro tracks in the 1980s that seriously influenced the development of hip hop culture. He is one of the originators of breakbeat DJing and is respectfully known as "The Godfather" and "Amen Ra of Hip Hop Kulture," as well as the father of electro-funk. Embracing the *Black*

Spades and bringing them into the music and the culture-oriented mighty Universal Zulu Nation, helped spread hip hop culture throughout the world, (*"Know What I Mean? Reflections on Hip-Hop,"* Michael Eric Dyson: 2007, Basic Civitas Books).

A major contributor to hip hop, the *Black Spades* developed a different scene in the Bronx in the mid-1970s. Established in the late 1960s, the *Black Spades* began throwing neighborhood block parties. They are an African-American group, described as a gang, a club, and a music group. Gaining popularity in the 1970s, the *Black Spades* expanded from the Bronx into Manhattan, Queens, Brooklyn, Staten Island, New Rochelle, New Jersey, and Connecticut by the late 1980s. During this period, Hispanic and white members were more common.

From Slavery to Hip Hop

From slavery to hip hop was not a short walk in the park for those trapped in it. Slavery was the most dominant backdrop for black people, until black power entered the picture in America in 1966, when Stokely Carmichael screamed it from the Mississippi Delta during James Meredith's March against Fear. Kidnapped and shanghaied from Africa to the Western Hemisphere, American slavery descendants reflected a subservience mindset—*learned helplessness*—until black power activists began to expose, reverse and eliminate *"learned helplessness"* among young black activists.

Black activists showed that it was possible to reverse or throw off *"learned helplessness,"* using a technique similar to Marcus Garvey, black power activists provided a model that gave slavery's descendants a new and dynamic view of themselves. Over the years, African Americans developed different attitudes and approaches to their existence in America.

No longer striving to be "good colored boys and girls," black activists expressed defiance against American racism and exploitation with their words—rappin—but their actions spoken even louder, as they took to the streets by the thousands, demanding respect and acknowledgement. Their defiance became the greatest peaceful and sustain defiance, until Black Lives Matter drew millions around the world into the streets, demanding to defund police department across America to stop police killing of innocent black men and women.

Returning home to northern cities, black students took "rappin" and black power back to New York. They used their new perspective and put a new spin on record players with their words. Giving the **Blues** culture a new base of operation, coming out of New York City, even before hip hop entered the vernacular; they changed the prevailing "good colored people" mindset of young black Americans.

Also, like jazz, when it hit the "Big Apple" in the 1920s into the 1930s, pioneers of this new technology—hip hop—blew it up, using DJs turntables for wheels. Rolling through New York neighborhoods, like East Coast dune buggies, DJs built everything on the beat. They used those catchy-phrases—rappin—instead of melodies entrenching hip hop. Blasting from huge speakers, heralding the entrance of the new genre, hip hop DJs took center stage and, anyone not aware of changes in the streets, got run down by this new world phenomenon. Destine to be an international shakers, and movers, wannabe rappers jumped aboard hip hop's dune buggy any way and place they could find.

The approach of **"The 400th"** brought descendants of enslaved Africans a clearer vision of their yesterday, which gives context to their present and a possible future. Blasting catchy phrases using huge speakers, which were like howitzers that allowed rappers blew huge holes in slave descendant's past. Bombing the world with hip hop, DJ's retrospectives of the past, as well as the present, opened up a future that was unimagined by black power activists, when they began spitting their catchy phrases at the world. By the 1990s music taste makers were blindsided by the Wu Tang Clan, as they karate chopped the music world into submission, with "Enter the Wu-Tang!"

My hope for ***"The 400th"***, now that it has arrived, is to create a new narrative that will provide descendants of enslaved Africans, with opportunities to build a future of their choosing. Seeing the world through the eyes of Janus, hip-hoppers can use their two-way vision to create a platform that diverges from their past, while opening new eyes to opportunities based on their new normal vision of the world. Hip hop moguls' current economic success shows they have gained more than enough entrepreneurial competence to stand proudly among the Wall Street crowd.

The vast majority of slaves leaving bondage and plantations 157 years ago were unable to read the written words or count. The amazing transformation of slavery's descendants, arriving in the present, following hip hop moguls' successes, has established that not only slavery's descendants had acquired the ability to read and write words, but speak them well enough and in ways that reflect economic competence, which garnered entrepreneurial success, while piling up billions of dollars in the international culture they created.

The ability and competence hip hoppers have acquired is only incidentally connected to the education and books they had as students. The information in those books made them dependent on what whites established for blacks in order to make money—*learned helplessness*. Their education worked well for whites but left black entrepreneurs on the edge of competition, as well as prosperity.

Hip hop is an extension of knowledge gained from the development of the *"Chitlin Circuit"* and similar ventures by black entrepreneurs. Moreover, hip hop is the second nationally developed economic system created and deployed entirely by black entrepreneurs. Marcus Garvey's UNIA was the first. Even though the *Chitlin Circuit* started out as a regional economic enterprise, it eventual grew to cover the North as well. My statement doesn't mean there were no white people involved, but they followed the trail, black entrepreneurs laid down, like Elvis Presley on Beale Street.

Hip hop developed and grew to prominence, right under the noises of the Wall Street crowd. Although, not clandestine, like the *"Chitlin Circuit,"* developed the record business, in spite of white men trying to control black entertainers' growth in popularity and prosperity. Hip hop is an extension of **Blues** magic, which was created by slaves in cotton, cane, and tobacco fields of the South. **Blues** magic came North with black students after being immersed in the southern **Blues** culture, during black power.

Building hip hop on the **Blues** culture, as I said opening this section, was not a short walk in the park. Establishing hip hop was far more complicated than running a numbers racket in the backroom. It required the same expertise that resided on Wall Street, even though hip-hoppers did not have access to "big bank money."

Hip hoppers continue changing the economic narrative for black communities today, and although it did not have the low interest rates, white start-up received out the gate, they still had to have financial geniuses like Sunbeam Mitchell, who were comparable to Wall Street expertise. The challenge for today's hip hoppers is to bring more benefits of the hip hop economy back to black communities' Main Street. The previous section opened up this area with a look at hip hop's beginnings. Now, based on the growth of hip hop, we look at how it was established and became the future in terms of an economic engine for the black community.

Hip hop artists drew on the magic of the **Blues** by commandeering *"rap"* from the South, as young black power activists carried the style H. "Rap" Brown and Stokley Carmichael, back to New York City as major developers. MCing or emceeing over "breakbeats" at house parties, in parks, and at neighborhood block parties thrown by hip hop groups like the *Black Spades and the Universal Zulu Nation*, kicked open the door, as the new genre strolled through. Groups in black communities made music a powerful instrument for social change and social justice. Hip hop gave *VOICE* to the ghetto and hip hoppers protested everything from the impact of legal institutions, particularly education, police, and prisons on minorities, to how the pop music industry tried to undercut and destroy hip hop.

I believe because the **Blues** originated in the souls of slaves, it gave all descendants of slavery a connection, only they understood. **Blues** magic became communal magic, and its spirit went North with black students, infusing itself into the music they created. *"Rap"* was the perfect entertainment vehicle for educating young inner-city dwellers because it was a technology developed by young blacks, during the mid-1960s, fighting for change against a system that refused to change. Young black inner-city dwellers commandeered *"rap"* bringing it North, like crusaders.

Rap Takes Center Stage

Previewing the 1980s as rap took center stage; it brought a total new crew of wordsmiths to the mic. The Sugarhill Gang, on the independent African American-owned label Sugar Hill, exploded on the scene, finding prominence in hip hop with the release of *"Rapper's Delight"* (1979). Within weeks, it became a chart-topping phenomenon, utilizing the 1960s black power magic of "rappin." It became the signature expression of the new genre. Grandmaster Flash and the Furious Five, Kurtis Blow, and the Cold Crush Brothers became drum majors in this new hit parade.

Female rappers became a real force in hip hop led by Queen Latifah and Salt-n-Pepa, who brought personal stands to rap's predominantly male, often misogynistic viewpoint. These woman like I said of Lorraine Hansberry, were like a spoon of sugar in a very vary strong cup of coffee, but they followed with a slap across the face of a man out of place. That did not change the bitter taste for women, but they added zest to hip hop's harsh savor. Queen Latifah brought more than words to hip hop's party; she unloaded U.N.I.T.Y, like a jab in the nose, before a fist to the gut. Doubling over, male hip hopers stepped back, giving her a wide berth.

Queen put her image of women in the face of music taste-makers. Establishing her perspective, Queen Latifah kicked the board room door in, putting the male-dominated genre on notice. She showed the guys she had real staying power, even in the clenches. Queen hooked and jabbed her way into the top echelon of hip hop over the years. Slipping punches she gained recognition not only in music, but film and television. Queen Latifah earned a Grammy, an Emmy, a Golden Globe, three Screen Actors Guild, two NAACP Image Awards, and an Academy Award nomination while selling over two million records.

Following those early beginnings, hip hop artists from places other than New York City, included more women began making their mark. "Rap" led a new parade of young blacks, now actually describing themselves as rappers, onto the scene. The new lineup was led by *DJ Jazzy Jeff* from Philadelphia, fronted this crew ushering in the first rapper that made it big in the movies from the hip hop stage, the *Fresh Prince,* Will Smith.

Will rapped his way to TV, turning his "red carpet" hip hop ride into a sliding board into the movies. Will gave Hollywood not only a new leading man, but one with humor, dramatic flair and poise with a little "macho" on the side. But the provocative *2 Live Crew* out of Miami became 'rap's" first "bad boys." The crew was so live, they sent white politicians screaming to the media, crying about the bad impact "Rap" was having on white children. M.C. Hammer from

Oakland, California, became one of the first big west coast rappers. Dropping *"U Can't Touch This"*, the Hammer got the Sunshine State out of rap's dark corner.

The mid-1980s opened with the next wave of hip hop artists, as Run-D.M.C. took "rappers" to a new school for word magicians. Crashing the party, fusing rap with hard rock, along with a new style of hip dress, they brought a commercial side to hip hop's developing technology. A trio of middle-class African Americans that came to prominence with Profile Records, one of several new charts busting labels, Run-D.M.C. raised the bar for hip-hoppers. Seizing the advantage, Run-D.M.C. pushed the envelope, growing the hip hop market for rap music with new appeal and apparel. Leading the assault on old established music trends, Run-D.M.C. became a staple on MTV. They broadened the hip hop genre, with a wider ride for mainstream audiences.

Rap continued growing in popularity causing a huge rumble, like an East coast earthquake, Def Jam shifted the tectonic plates causing a shift in hip hop's polarity. Shaking the very foundations of the new genre, pushing its way into the party, Def Jam after growing a whole new crop opened up with all new stars. Almost cornering the hip hop market in a single bound with innovator, Def Jam introduced LL Cool J, rap's first romantic superstar. LL really brought in the ladies, leaving wannabes, choking on trail dust. Then, on came the Beastie Boys, a trio of white guys, who also broadened rap's audience and market, by popularizing digital sampling (composing with music and sounds electronically extracted from other recordings).

A third element, on hip hop's chemical chart, following new recording companies, TV, new technology, and techniques was political and ideology radicalism. A new group brought an investment in blackness, blowing up turntables and sending them spinning like flying saucers, Public Enemy was like a new "mother ship" for hip hop. Bobbing through the door, Public Enemy landed hip hop back in the 1960, with black power rhetoric and themes. Public Enemy made social consciousness the sixth "element" of hip hop, for a while. This new path was like a hip-hop skateboard for Grandmaster Flash and the Furious Five, who brought *"The Message"* (1982) to a world confused about everything.

"The Message" brought not only popularity and money to hip hop, it introduced controversy as well. Melle Mel and Duke Bootee staked claims on *"The Message's"* message, claiming its lyrics, but came up empty, as official credit went to Grandmaster Flash and The Furious Five. That hubbub ignited a real hullaballoo over conscious statements. It also kicked up a storm of words, bringing new force to the socially conscious statements of Run-DMC's *"It's like That"* and Public Enemy doubled back with *"Black Steel in the Hour of Chaos."* ("*Black Noise: Rap Music and Black Culture in Contemporary America,"* Tricia Rose, 1994, Wesleyan University Press. Middletown, Connecticut).

The 400th: From Slavery to Hip Hop

After hiding out in his lair, like an ancient alchemist, Afrika Bambaataa had been laying in the cut, studying developments and trends in hip hop. After finally gathering enough fuel for his big launch, Bambaataa blasted the electro-funk track *"Planet Rock,"* into the stratosphere of hip hop with *Soulsonic Force*. Not content only rappin over disco beats, Bambaataa and producer Arthur Baker added new technology, sampling Kraftwerk to create an electronic sound using the Roland TR-808 drum machine.

Bambaataa fueled *"Planet Rock's"* ascent like it was sitting atop a Saturn V rocket. *"Planet Rock"* blasted hip hop into a new orbit around pop music. Bambaataa fused hip hop with electro for *"Planet Rock's"* launched and like *Sputnick* for aeronautics in 1957, became a new vector for a new hip hop trajectory, leading the international genre. It switched on the light for hip-hoppers, as it became a new beacon guiding the world to fun, partying, and fashions. All this party life and fun created a new hip hop cosmogony.

During the 1980s, hip hop also embraced another technological advance by creating rhythm using the human body (*do something with your body*), via the vocal percussion technique of "beatboxing." Pioneers, such as Doug E. Fresh, Biz Markie, and Buffy from the Fat Boys, made beats, rhythm, and musical sounds using their mouth, lips, tongue, voice, and other body parts. "Human Beatbox" artists also sang or imitated turntablism, scratching, or other instrumental sounds.

The fascination Bambaataa created with *"Planet Rock,"* gave music videos a seat at the table. Their appearance increased the reach of hip hop. Bambaataa's *"Planet Rock,"* brought such excitement to hip hop, he not only changed rap he induced musical videos, reshaping musical entertainment. It seems black producers' became soothsayers or gurus overnight.

Black producers' ears and eyes became windows of success for wannabe hip hop stars. New technologies coming into hip hop at this point was not a few showers, it was like, *"when it rained, it poured."* More than words, these videos necromancers took their lead from Afrika Bambaataa *"Planet Rock,"* as if it was the "Holy Grail." They put the spotlight on the ghetto, as never before. Visually glorifying urban ghetto life made black youth proud to say, *"I'm from there!"* or *"That's my hood."*

Beginning with Africa Bambaataa's music video *"Planet Rock,"* showcasing—black subculture, music, graffiti artists, and b-boys/b-girls—helped hip hop become the wave of the future. This new entertainment phenomenon introduced a whole new way of thinking and talking about black life in the ghetto, while revealing its harsh realities, as well as the splendor of its party life. Videos spawned several award-winning hip hop-related films between 1982 and 1985, among them *Wild Style, Beat Street, Krush Groove, Breakin,* and the documentary *Style Wars*. Hip hop films expanded its appeal beyond the boundaries of New York City and the East coast. By 1984, youth worldwide were embracing hip hop culture. Hip hop graffiti and "slang" of US urban communities quickly found their way to Europe, as its culture global appeal took root.

Hip hop's four traditional dances—b-boying/b-girling, rocking, locking, and popping—trace their origins back to the late 1960s or early 1970s. Many of these dances were first seen on *"Soul Train"*, which made Don Cornelius source-one for the moves black folks were doing. He built his fame bringing R&B—**Blues** magic—to TV weekly, followed by **"rap"** and hip hop. Don Cornelius with *"Soul Train"* brought hip hop into the spotlight, and living rooms before other entertainment outlets caught on.

Visually exposing "black dance" enabled hip hoppers to take their challenge to kid in unknown places, making them part of the hip hop culture. *("Hip Hop Dance,"* Joseph Schloss: Oxford Music Online, Oxford University Press. 2014). Although females were among the developers of hip hop dancing—B-girls' also called B-girling or breakdancing—faced the same challenges and disregard as female vocalists in hip hop. Many complained they were treated like *"second class"* or *"separate but equal"* and overlooked because of their gender.

Similarly, many aspects of the hip hop culture, females' presence in breakdancing involved navigating sexual politics in a masculine-dominated world, not just hip hop. Marked by limited access and lack of representation for females, few B-girls that participated in the genre found encouragement for women as participants. But despite facing gender discrimination, with models like Queen Latifah, woman carved out space, as leaders within the male-dominated genre, as well as break dancing community, and the numbers of B-girls continued increasing. *("From blues women to b-girls: performing badass femininity,"* Imani Kai Johnson, 2014; Women & Performance: A Journal of Feminist Theory).

Kurtis Blow, an early beatmaker, won producer of the year credits in 1983, 1984, and 1985. Known for his technological advance, creating sample and sample loops, Blow was considered the Quincy Jones of hip hop. One of the most influential beatmakers was producer/technician, J. Dilla from Detroit. He chopped samples by specific beats and combined them to create his unique sound.

Those who create these beats are known as either beatmakers or producers, but producers have more input and direction on the overall creation of a song or project. While a beatmaker only provides or creates the beat. Dr. Dre, one of the best, has said, *"Once you finish the beat, you have to produce the record."* The process of making beats includes sampling, chopping, looping, sequence the beat, recording, mixing, and mastering, (*Dr. Dre interview*, 2012).

By the late 1990s, hip-hop was artistically fully established, and the dominant group was the Wu-Tang Clan, which took the top spot on listeners list. A New York City Staten Island group, Wu-Tang evolved from a combination of street credibility, neo-Islamic mysticism, and kungfu lore. Wu-T was one of the most

The 400th: From Slavery to Hip Hop

complex groups in the history of rap and hip hop. Their debut album *"Enter the Wu-Tang"* (11-9-1993) is considered one of the greatest albums in hip hop history by most hip hop fans.

Sean "Puffy" Combs, aka Diddy, P Diddy and Puff Daddy, performer, producer, and president of Combs Enterprises—*Bad Boy Records*—is responsible for a series of innovative music videos by way of the Fugees. Puffy's technological advance was mixing pop music hooks with politics. P Diddy used this style to launch the solo careers of Wyclef Jean and Lauryn Hill.

Enter Gangsta Rap

The entrance of gangsta rap commercialized hip hop in a big way. One can say what happened in New York City did not stay in New York City. It spread to LA, and was comparable to African Americans, whites creating the computer in Simi Valley, California and white people. For me, "gangsta rap," although it was the biggest commercializing agent thus far in all of hip hop, at the same time, I saw it, as a case of, "the tail wagging the dog." My statement is not to controvert gangster rap's entrance into hip hop or even cast it in a negative light. Gangster rap is reflective of the slave environment in which most black men learned business acumen. This environment was unlike Robert R. Church, Sr.'s father teaching him business on his riverboat, and he taught his son.

Early black businessmen who pushed their way into entertainment management and production were not Harvard MBAs. Trying to attend Harvard as MBAs, these guys would have endured the same fate as Robert Delany and his three colleagues, entering Harvard medical school in the 1820s, they would not have been allowed through the door. I stated earlier, for black men, trying to enter any business was not a question of getting their hands dirty or keeping them clean. During the early rough and tumble times of the 1930s and 40s before civil rights and black power, a black man had to be hard and mean.

I reiterate, such men were the early backers of hip hop. They were hard-nosed self-made men, down for anything to make a dollar from any action. They refused to give white folks the inside track on making money. They were a breed of black men that believed, *"When money hits the table, it belonged to whoever picked it up."* Making money in their businesses depended on what was demand at the time.

The trick surviving in their business world was knowing how much skin to give up or keep to stay in a game—surviving in such games, with very little, if any control, when you can't win, you fold. Hustlers, numbers men, bootleggers, whiskey-runners, con artists, gangsters, dope pushers, and gamblers pick a suit; astute hard-driving businessmen traveling this route were not to be trifled with to boot. Reaching the early 1970s, these were the guys that became hip hop's venture capitalists; they were the only ones with money. Living on the edge in the real world of white supremacy, where white skin always held the dices, the best a black man could hope for was to cut craps on a losing roll.

These were the men who stepped up with cash, like a baby's bottle, at the birth of hip hop. These guys were not only money men; they were the muscle to make their word good. If necessary, they were like bounty hunters in this "wild wild west" that Kool MoDee rapped about. The beginning of hip hop was like Sunbeam Mitchell, trying to get money from a bank to start the *Chitlin Circuit*; you went to people with money you knew, who knew you. They were the wet nurses, cleaning up behind wannabe rappers doing dumb stuff. They took care of business when things went sideways, even when someone had to take the fall to throw the government off. They took the hit on the dodge-car ride when hip hop was a real gamble.

In the early-to-mid 1980s, there was no established hip hop music industry, as existed after 2000. Those "wild wild west" days in the 1980s world of hip hop, very few writers were around to record anything. Besides, that would have left a paper trail for the government to follow. Back then, hip hop did not have record labels, producers, managers, artists, and repertoire staff; that world was still more than 20 years away.

During the rough and tumble nescience days of hip hop in the 1970s and 80s, the new genre struggled, trying to get its legs beneath it. Politicians and businesspeople maligned or ignored hip hop's potential. Back then, most hip hop artists performed in their local communities and recorded in underground scenes. Everything was on the down-low or out the back door for those with the nerves to get aboard this wild train ride, hoping to achieve fame. However, in the late 1980s, based on the drive and talent of a few mega-stars, and some I have named, hip hop had arrived but was still basically a New York City game.

Opening the 1990s, a brash bunch of devil-may-care hood-rats from Compton, California crashed the party, and hip hop changed forever. These rambunctious irreverent in your face party crashers brought a new edge to hip hop—gangsta rap opened with a bang. This new gang of rowdies was more than an advance in new technology, and didn't just give hip hop a facial or change it style. These irreverent, devil-may-care hood-rats were not happy changing the look and sound of hip hop; they gave it a complete makeover. Their bravado and outrageousness in their lyrics to some sent the faint of heart, breaking for the exit, once they entered the scene. Kicking the door open, as they hit the market, they flipped the *American Establishment* a "bird," and never looked back to see if anyone was watching.

Their rough edge was so jagged it tore through the thin lines, tying hip hop to its consciousness roots. Gangsta rap became the most significant response to New York's conscious rap. NWA—*Niggaz With Attitude*—grabbed hip hop like a bride, leaving New York hip hop standing at the altar. They put LA rap on the map with, *'Boyz n the Hood'* by Eazy-E and NWA, which topped charts at number one for six weeks.

"Straight Outta Compton" (2016), the movie tells their story, but the album hit in 1988. LA gangsta rap caused trimers in New York, like a California earthquake. N.W.A.'s dynamic album shook hip hop all the way to the Brooklyn Bridge. Introducing this new crew of rowdy bad boys—Ice Cube, Eazy E, and Dr. Dre—they "mooned" everyone, who didn't like their style with a smile. They even made those who were pushing gangsta rap run for cover. Their graphic, frequently violent tales of real life in the inner city, showed society to be the bad

guy it really is. Joined by LA rapper Ice-T with *"Body Count,"* featuring *"Cop Killer"* (1992), West Coast rap took the led from the East Coast, as it grew in prominence in 1990.

Music industry executives realized, because of its message, they could capitalize "big time" on "gangsta rap" and began throwing money at gangsta rappers like confetti. They made it rain in January in Cali. These were the money bags most people believed were there all along, and thought the hard money bottle holders and wet nursing support from black entrepreneurs caused the bad image of hip hop. But no, that was not the way it was at all. It was the other way around, "good clean money" wearing Italian suits and shoes that stepped all over the conscious rappers that black hard money had previously supported.

The "good clean Wall Streeter type money" brought demands for a new image. The "good clean money" came with strings and formulas that created "a titillating buffet of hyper-masculinity that glorified violence and encouraged misogyny." "Good clean money" wanted to marketed rap to a new fan base: white males. They ignored the harsh reality revealed by socially conscious lyrics that brought hip hop out of the backwoods. They gave hip hop a new image that focused on sex, violence, and misogyny, pushing women to the margin. *("On Blackness, Humanity, and The Art of Rap,"* Gaye Theresa Johnson, 2012: TheHuffingtonPost.com.)

LA's Death Row Records doubled down and weathered a storm of criticism from *"Establishment taste-makers,"* while building an empire around Dr. Dre, Snoop Dogg, *"Doggystyle"* and N.W.A. Leaving the East Coast eating its dust, trying to catch up, with mid-speed *"Schoolly D."* However, LA went one better, kicking it in to overdrive with a charismatic, complicated rapper-actor *Tupac Shakur.*

It was the East coast turn to doubled down while doubling back, it answered with *Notorious B.I.G.* The media loved the back and forth, so they threw coals on sparks, hoping to make smoke into fire. The media called the jockeying to build fan bases a feud, trying to creating flames out of the smoldering economic rivalry. Media reports intensified the hot air and smoke blowing East to West and back again. *Death Row* and New York's *Bad Boy Records* were urged on by the stream of reports, as the East/West coast "squabbling" took on a life of its own, leaving lives hanging in the balance. Describing the hot air blowing from East to West and back again, as an East/West Coast "feud," the media-fueled a "feeding frenzy" that blew things up, and out of proportion, creating real hostility without a notion of what was coming. The war of words results in real bullets flying and leaving face down, the still-unsolved murders of Tupac Shakur and the gifted MC Notorious B.I.G. before rap got hip to the pop and hop back.

BET was the only television channel likely to show hip hop—rap videos—during the backwoods days of the late 1970s and early 80s. But the 1990s brought in VH1 and MTV, which significantly added to their playlist, not just hip hop, but gangsta rap took the top spot. Run DMC had brought MTV in, they were the first African American hip hop crew to appear on MTV's scene. The emergence of the Internet, with several online sites, was like a watershed, bringing a wave of hip hop, flooding white audiences in the burbs with videos, washing R&B out to sea.

With the commercialization of gangsta rap, success loomed large for hip hop in the late 1990s. "Good clean money" from Wall Street types came flowing into hip hop drowning consciousness lyrics in drugs, violence, and misogyny. With no way to pull the plug, shifting emphasis from consciousness, gangstrism the world watch consciousness go down for the third time, for hip hop money players, it was out of time. Wall Street open it money bag, washing rappers Ice-T on the playlist, even quicker up the charts, stunning East and West with the first gangsta rap record, *"6 N' the Mornin."*

But the main force behind LA hip hop was N.W.A, whose second album *"Niggaz4Life"* became the first gangsta rap album to enter the charts at number one. Their fan base exploded. Strangely enough, gangsta rap also played an important part in hip hop becoming a mainstream commodity. Considering albums such as N.W.A's *"Straight Outta Compton,"* Eazy-E's *"Eazy-Duz-It,"* and Ice Cube's *"Amerikkka's Most Wanted,"* which sold at amazingly high volume, Wall Street "good clean money" boys had a major role in replacing black teens, as hip hop's largest buying demographic, taking hip hop to suburbia.

White kid hiding out in the burbs, fantasizing about the gangsta life in ghettos, had cash registers ringing at such a fast clip, they sounded like AK47s. Gangsta rap became a platform for artists whose music spread political and social messages to parts of the US previously unaware or uninterested in conditions in ghettos. Media critics that totally disregarded, socially and politically conscious hip hop, now began arguing hip hop was damaging mainstream America, blaming black people rather than Wall Street.

Media attacks, trying to corner and corral hip hop and keep it from escaping the ghetto, rather than withering, white kids open door in their gated communities, allowing, gangsta rap to run naked wildly in the suburbs. Media critics and parents cried foul, complaining hip hop had sneaked into their children's bedrooms, which they were not allowed to enter, and was raping their children's pure white minds. Decrying hip hop's appeal, hoping to block its access to a broader white demographic, the older white population screamed daily, crying about hip hop's negative impact, but nobody cared what they thought, definitely not their children.

With the turn of the century (2000), fans discovered and downloaded or streamed hip hop music through social networking sites Web 2.0. Myspace began the rise of new media platforms, and websites like YouTube, Worldstarhiphop, SoundCloud, and Spotify join the party. Hip hop became far more portable. Hop-hoppers streaming music on cell phones put record stores on the endangered species list, like bookstores after the 2008 financial crisis.

However, the story for women artists remained the same. Even though women were at the forefront of hip hop's development in the Bronx, they were still riding in the back of the bus, when hip hop arrived at the new millennium. Hip hop followed "good clean money's" formula, producing many songs with misogynistic (anti-women) lyrics. The advent of music videos really put women in the spotlight, but the glare of drugs, sex, and misogynistic had conscious women wearing shades or blinders, looking for R-E-S-P-E-C-T—following Aretha Franklin's beat. Women's demands for self-respect made things even more challenging for women that gave *VOICE* to their displeasure, as hip hop's highly sexualized depictions of women flooded the market. Some women say their demands are why hip hop producers begin going to young hopefuls, who would follow taste-makers demands.

Gangsta rap became the dominant force in hip hop music, and in many cases, negated female voices and perspectives. Rappers misogynistic tendency defined mainstream hip hop music for many women. The recording industry, as a whole, has always shown an unwillingness to support female artists, as it does their male counterparts, and hip hop has not responded any differently thus far.

When it does support women, it seems, the emphasis is on their sexuality, more so than their musical virtuosity and other artistic abilities. Female hip hop artists have struggled to get mainstream attention, and even older artists like Queen Latifah and Salt N' Pepa struggled. Still, contemporary artists like Lil' Kim and Nicki Minaj have reached platinum status in far less time. Sexualized images and other issues are why it seems to me; this dog loves getting waged by its tail. (*"Where Did All The Female Rappers Go?"*, Erik Nielson: 2014 National Public Radio, NPR).

Hip Hop Reaches Around the World

I preference the next discussion by saying, most people do not have personal knowledge of hip hop, other than, as a participant in the general culture. Most people, I believe, around the world only have impressions of hip hop, and information in the general public is the bases of those impressions. Articles about people involved in hip hop or what they heard is similar to hearsay, and such information is all most people had for years.

I add this next section to provide a sort of "hip hop on the ground experience" without leaving your easy chair. Learning about hip hop's impact on the world is not a "one style or size fits all," and for many, that is its magic. Hip hop's greatest appeal is it gives expression to a wide range of perspectives across the world. One should find something in its characters, music, art, fashions, freestyle, venues, open access to innovation, and its spirit, which should reward one's patience during this read.

According to the U.S. Department of State, hip hop is *"now the center of a mega music and fashion industry around the world."* That culture crosses social barriers and cuts across racial lines. National Geographic recognized hip hop as *"The world's favorite youth culture, in which just about every country on the planet seems to have developed its own local rap scene."* Through its international travels, hip hop is now considered a *"global musical phenomenon."* According to *The Village Voice*, hip hop is *"custom-made to combat the anomie, (a condition in which society provides little moral guidance to individuals. It is the breakdown of social bonds between an individual and the community,) which preys on adolescents wherever nobody knows their name."* The current "Black Lives Matter" protest attest to the reach, power and influence of hip hop on the young generation of today, which most non-hip hoppers, white, black or in between no matter their country, were completely oblivious, but realized and became aware, because of the police murder of George Floyd.

Although long believed to be popular primarily with urban African American males, hip-hop became the best-selling genre of popular music in the United States in the late 1990s, among all sexes. Hip hop's impact is global, with formidable audiences and artist pools in cities such as Paris, Tokyo, Sydney, Cape Town, London, and Bristol, England, even New Zealand had huge "Black Lives Matter" protest. Hip hop also generates huge sales of products in fashion, liquor, electronics, and automobile industries that were popularized by hip-hop artists on cable TV stations such as MTV and The Box and in hip-hop-oriented magazines such as *The Source and Vibe*.

Hip-hop is currently the wellspring of several modern pop music techniques, using a canny blend of entrepreneurship and aesthetics, along with techniques, like digital drumming and sampling, to reach its current level of popularity. Through its technological innovations, it introduced rap listeners to the music of previous generations of performers, including Chic, Parliament-Funkadelic, and James Brown. Hip hop is simultaneously a new and old phenomenon. Most importantly, sampling tracks, beats, and basslines from old records into the art of today, the culture prides itself as a conduit for updating classic recordings, attitudes, and experiences for modern audiences. Sampling older cultural techniques and reusing them in new contexts or new format is called *"flipping"* in the new hip-hoppers culture.

Hip hop music has followed the footsteps of earlier African-American-rooted musical genres such as **Blues**, jazz, ragtime, funk, and disco to become the most practiced genre worldwide. It is the language of urban environments and youth cultures around the world. According to KRS-One, *"Hip hop is the only place where you see Martin Luther King Jr.'s 'I Have A Dream' speech."* He also notes that hip hop is beyond things such as race, gender, or nationality; it belongs to the world. (*"KRS-One's 40 Years of Hip Hop Documentary," 2014*). In 1990, while working on *Snap!*, Ronald "Bee-Stinger" Savage, the Zulu Nation, followed *Public Enemy's* message and created the *"Sixth element of the Hip Hop Movement," the Awarenesses—Consciousness Awareness, Civil Rights Awareness, Activism Awareness, Justice/Political Awareness, and Community Awareness in music.*

Hip hop music has spawned dozens of subgenres and incorporate them into hip hop production approaches, through sampling, creating beats, or rapping. However, some of the most creative aspects which affect hip hop's diversification are happening people to people. And, this is the most unquantifiable component in any interactive enterprise as freewheeling as hip hop, which is all about person to person.

The needs and desires of people to acquire means of expression, which allows them to *"tell their stories in their own words as they live,"* makes hip hop the perfect vehicle giving them *VOICE*. The appropriation of hip hop culture by other ethnic groups did not happen to fit hip hop's purposes, but to fit theirs. The varying social influences and cultures that have commandeered hip hop have strengthened its power, because they transmit their messages, which they are desperately trying to get out to the world. Unlike black Americans, trying to present **We Charge Genocide** to a closed world in 1951, such people today have hip hop, and the world is listening. It is clear young people have taken hip hop's musical entertainment aspirations and converted them into an instrument to further their nationalistic demand for political change and socioeconomic justice.

Hip Hop Movers and Shakers Who are Changing the World

Now we begin the **"Hip Hop World Tour!!"** The story of hip hop is not about its lyrics—conscious or gangsta—it is about its expressiveness, cultural adaptability, and *VOICE*, which created its prowess. Hip hop's success—beginning, development, and introduction to the world—although it began as a New York City story, now reaches around the world, giving *VOICE* to marginalized, oppressed, and downtrodden people. Had its success depended on another location in America—other than New York City—I fear it would have met the same fate as *"spoken word poetry"* in Atlanta—no money. The next section is not a romance with wealth, even though quite a bit of it comes from *Money's* report, <u>*"13 Hip-Hop Artists Who Make Millions as Successful Entrepreneurs,"*</u> by Brad Tuttle and Katy Osborn (8-24-2015), and it is not an exhaustive look at the subject. Although so much has changed since this article was written—COVID-19 is an example—time and events show, new individuals have moved up, while others have maintained, and still others are at lower levels, the individuals cited here are still very much in the mix and still have a path leading to things happening at the top of the hip hop mountain. Moreover, it is not only an effort to show how much money hip hop has generated for some of its more successful and well-connected entrepreneurs, it reflects this narrative's theme regarding wealth—*it is not how much money one has, but what is done with it that matters.*

My interest examining the impact of these individuals is their wealth-building strategies through the eight themes slaves began developing and pursued while still in slave pens and continued after walking off plantations, as they entered their contraband existence. Former slaves pursued eight specific categories. First making families and building communities, education and communication, entertainment and entrepreneurship, and political and cultural development are the strategies, I believe determined their survival and lead to hip hoppers ability to amass wealth todays. These concepts became the base of their survival, as former enslaved Africans. Presenting these categories getting here, I discussed former slaves and their descendants continued struggles and development, following their penniless emancipation beginning in 1863. The critical point I make, looking at the individuals mentioned here, created their wealth, during their lifetime, or the previous generation gave them only a point at which to start.

Unlike successful white Americans, those intricately involved in hip hop had to accumulate the knowledge necessary to achieve their level of power, position and success themselves, while moving up the ladder in the rough and tumble non-standardize world of hip hop. But readers must remember they also faced the same level of discrimination, disparate treatment and racism in the hostile environment in America, as former slaves faced. True, this is not an exhaustive collection, yet and still, it offers a significant slice of artists that garner the right combination of determination and experience, while being in the right place at the right time to reap great rewards.

Once hip hop got its leg beneath it, it did not matter where one was in the world. Those ingredients or characteristics, plus a whole lot of talent and business savvy, working for them, buttressed their efforts. With all of that going for artists, only gave these self-made businesspeople a chance to make it big.

I describe these individuals as self-made because none of them came from old money families or were tied to family success, like their white competition, which gave them an inside track to greater wealth. If they had relatives that were entertainers or in the business, these individuals still had to develop personal smarts and control over their personalities to survive the media traps and public relations boomerangs that brings destruction. And, this is where the curveball in the dirt and other rules of the game, called many out each time up at-bat.

My point is that only hip hop could have conjured conditions where an unheralded group of badasses (I will say in their lyrics) stepped up to the plate and drove the ball out the park their first time at bat, it seemed. While never looking back, as they circled the bases, after *"Straight Outta Compton"* hit the silver screen, these badasses today pulled in $60 million at the box office, the opening weekend. That movie—*Straight Outta Compton*—provides a blow-by-blow description of N.W.A.'s (*Niggers With Attitude*) battle for fame. *"Straight Outta Compton"* was America's #1 movie for three weekends in a row, making it one of the biggest-ever August releases. With a production cost of $29 million, the biopic of the group's road to the top reflects their life in an L A ghetto, on the way to making gangsta rap an America phenomenon. Spreading gangsta rap's message throughout the world, *"Straight Outta Compton"* crossed the $100 million ticket sales mark less than ten days after its debut.

Among other things, it allowed hip hop to add "blockbuster movie production" to the long list of major accomplishments and successful entrepreneurial endeavors it spawned. Such success in spite of the history of denial, discrimination, and disparate treatment black Americans entrepreneurs endured reaching **"The 400th"**, reflects the point of this section. Produced by Dr. Dre and Ice Cube, the leading creative members of N.W.A., are not only legends in the rap game, they have earned their larger than life persona, as super stars.

Cube and Dre are reflective of the phenomenal success many hip hop artists are enjoying outside music. Such artists have launched fashion lines, restaurant chains, luxury electronics, alcoholic beverage, and beverage brands. They have eclipsed many who had inside tracts from family, educational, and economic ties to America's white supremacy and white privilege system.

At first glance, it may seem odd that so many rap/hip-hoppers became entrepreneurs, but that has been the driving force behind the legacy introduced to slave descendants when Marcus Garvey landed in New York City (1914). He was the first black man to attempt to build an international business model for enslaved Africans. Garvey's vision showed former slave they had to rely on themselves, rather than government or what others promised.

Garvey pushed the idea *"If I can do it, you can do it too,"* giving black Americans in the Big Apple a vision of what the fruit tree of success looked like. Moreover he gave them a bite of the apple, and once they tasted that luscious fruit, they wanted more. The very thing that made rappers successful—carefully crafted words, style, swagger, and images to sell themselves to the masses—Garvey exemplify for former slaves that had only walked off plantations penniless just 52 years earlier. What Garvey showed black people had been denied slaves and was missing from their repertoire or mental picture of themselves—*the technology of salesmanship*.

By early 1950, descendants of American slavery had become experts at making *"Something from Nothing,"* as the title of the 2012 rap documentary by Ice-T put it. Knowing their audiences incredibly well, slave descendants like Ice-T worked tremendously hard, selling themselves and their music. Most found it fairly natural to crossover to marketing other products and lifestyle brands to their fans.

Hip-hoppers took advantage of what slave descendants learned entertaining master and found a way to make it an everyday job. No matter if we are talking song lyrics or the creation of a luxury brand of headphones, successful artists with roots in rap have demonstrated an uncanny ability to remain relentlessly focused on making money and "getting paid." Something the vast majority of newly freed slaves knew absolutely nothing about, walking off plantations just over 157 years ago.

In addition to being a gangsta rap pioneer with N.W.A., Dr. Dre is also the visionary who produced and called the world's attention to rap superstars like Snoop Dogg and Eminem. And he's been a hugely successful artist in his own right, starting with his multi-platinum solo debut album "The Chronic" and continuing with *"Compton: A Soundtrack,"* which was streamed 25 million times during the first week it was available on Apple Music.

Speaking of Apple, in 2014, the tech giant acquired Beats Music and Beats Electronics from Dr. Dre and Jimmy Iovine, co-founder of Interscope Records. The music subscription streaming service and maker of flagship $300 headphones, which they created, then reaped over $3 billion with its sell. Dre's net worth hit around the 800 million dollar mark, and that was before the release of *"Straight Outta Compton,"* the movie. Another indicator of the tremendous advance of slaves descendants in just over 157 years of freedom, Dre and Beyoncé were the only two black hip hoppers on Entrepreneur magazine's list of *"10 Entrepreneurs Who Defined 2014."*

I remind readers this narrative is not concerned with the lives of individuals. The object here is to examine hip hoppers' impact on the broader community. Some individuals are reflective of slavery's descendants' advances and success, with very favorable effect, while others not so much. Although some individuals were able to amass considerable wealth, their impact has been marginal on slave descendants' efforts to become one people. Black American faced haters throughout bondage and after emancipation on through their contraband existence. Attacked for exercising their constitutional right of speech, like Colin Kaepernick in 2017, hip-hoppers would not be muzzled.

Moreover, I will always defend the right of individual speech, whether I agree with what comes out of someone mouth or their actions. Kanye West is one person who exemplifies this statement. He has felt the vicious bite of haters for his words and actions. I will say, I will defend an individual's right to desire to be "king" or "conqueror," as well as "Jester," and black people have had more than their share of all three. However, I remind, even in the face of events like the current presidential campaign, descendants of slavery have survived by allowing such individuals to play the role they choose, no matter their charade.

Kanye is an individual imprisoned by his fan base, while amassing wealth catering to their whelms and demand. As a result, for others it comes down to what one sees when they look in the mirror each morning. I choose not to be, neither judge nor jury in such instances, I just vote my conscience. Kanye is one of the best-selling and most awarded artists in hip hop and has sold over 21 million copies of his six albums, not to mention having won 21 Grammys. He also has a record label, G.O.O.D. Music, while partnering with Jay Z, Kanye bought into Tidal a streaming service.

Kanye has also directed several short films. A New York Times story points out, his movement into the world of fashion, collaborating with A.P.C., Adidas, and Louis Vuitton to launch a, women's clothing label DW for the Paris Fashion Week 2011. He has "extended the hip hop genre by adding high-fashion and high-art to its dream list." Kanye reflects not only his and hip hop's reach but African American's extension into these areas, and as scuh make it a possibility for another black brothers and sisters to aspire to follow, whether Kanye open or close doors behind him or they kick it in after it closes. *"Judge not less ye be judged."*

Some people, it seems, would be successful at whatever they set as a task for themselves. "ICE-T" tops that list for me. He seems to be that hard cut guy, who may have been born a decade or two late, to be a character in his own time. I do not imply "ICE-T" is a fish out of water. He is my choice because he's adapted that character to the current time just the same. He is the man who made "hustling," a high art. "ICE-T," known mostly today for his starring roles in both the reality TV shows "Ice Loves Coco" and the 15-year-running cop drama "Law & Order: SVU," but he first entered from stage left, as a groundbreaking gangsta rapper with hot-selling tracks like "Colors."

Ice-T, however, has been many things beyond hustler, actor, and rapper. Before making a living from rap, he specialized in *"making something out of nothing,"* as a pimp, thief, and all-around street guy. A partial list of his non-rap ventures, once he laid the trick down, Ice created and fronted a metal band (Body Count). He founded an online music label back in the Napster era. He also launched a podcast. Ice has made multiple voice-overs for video games, while serving as a producer for 18 TV shows and movies.

T co-authored three books, and organized the first-ever Art of Rap Festival—a concert series that takes its name from the Ice-T-directed 2012 documentary, *"Something from Nothing: The Art of Rap."*

It's understandable, then, that the word most commonly associated with Ice-T is hustler. *"New Jack Hustler"* was one of Ice-T's most popular songs. It was used in the 1991 movie he also starred *"New Jack City."* But "hustle" has been part of the descriptive vernacular for Ice-T from his earliest beginnings. Reading about him, Ice-T reminds me of a very important, popular, and iconic character "Sunbeam" Mitchell, from Memphis, who invented the *"Chitlin Circuit"* back in the 1940s. Like everything else, hustlers during the 1980 and 90s talked about the game they picked up in the 1960s and 70s, getting to where they were. Their example shows, *"everybody is standing on somebody's shoulders,"* not the thin air.

In fact, instead of focusing on rap for its artistry and insights into urban culture, Ice-T has referred to it as just another way to get rich. *"Rapping is a hustle to me,"* he said on the VH1 documentary *"Behind the Music." "I'm not one of those guys that's like, 'Oh I love the music.' Nah, I love money."*

Trying to piece together a portrait of hip hop today, as the apex of slave descendants' advancement in all phases of entrepreneurial acumen, I wanted to gauge the impact of rising stars. I also wanted to assess females' ability to succeed in this male-dominated genre as an "up and comer" today. A new girl on the block compared to the guy and some women, Onika Tanya Maraj known professionally as Nicki Minaj, is an American rapper, singer, songwriter, actress, and model.

Born in Saint James, Port of Spain, Trinidad, and Tobago (6-8-1982), but she was raised in Queens, New York City. As such, she is not a victim of *learned helplessness*, as most American descendants of slavery. I believe, that explains to a large degree, her decidedly different mindset from most black American women. For some, even for me, when I began this narrative, I thought Nicki Minaj, may have come out of nowhere, but at the same time, Nicki was everywhere. She gained public recognition after releasing the mixtapes *Playtime Is Over* (2007), *Sucka Free* (2008), and *Beam Me Up Scotty* (2009) on her way to become one of the queens of social media with over 20 million social media followers on Twitter. Moreover, inside Madame Tussauds in wax, and soon, even a mobile game app—are only partially due to her rap music.

After signing with Young Money Entertainment in 2009, Minaj released her first studio album, *Pink Friday* (2010), which peaked at number one on the US Billboard 200 and was ultimately certified triple platinum by RIAA. Her sophomore album, *Pink Friday: Roman Reloaded* (2012), debuted at number one in several countries.

Minaj debuted in the animated film *Ice Age: Continental Drift* in 2012. Her third studio album was *The Pinkprint,* (2014), while subsequently playing supporting roles in *The Other Woman* (2014) and *Barbershop: The Next Cut* (2016). Throughout her career, Minaj has not focused entirely on music and movies; she has worked diligently building her brand. Nicki has extended her unique mix of smarts, flair, sex, and sassiness to perfume and beauty products (sold at HSN), a women's wear collection for Kmart, and a fizzy fusions Muscato wine called MYX.

These are just some of her many ventures that reflect her approach to business and why some see her as a paragon for how young people—women especially—should handle their role in the workplace. Her forte includes lessons on how to take charge at the office, how to rebrand oneself when switching careers or companies, and the necessity of being bold and assertive; as I said, all these traits defy *learned helplessness*.

Nicki's approach reflects my earlier remarks related to women in hip hop. Rap music has limited power and influence on how women are view in society—black or white. Hip hop cannot carry a full load of correcting this age-old societal problem. I must point out upfront America is a country in which **women get paid less than men**, who do the same job, and for me, that is where the problem starts.

Raising the issue of *"learned helplessness"* was not something related directly to Nicki but was to draw attention to its real impact on slavery's descendants because of their slave acculturation. Discounting women's ability is related to men, white and black, who are the greatest factor in reinforcing that mindset among women. The pay gap is another prime example. Black women get paid less than both white and black men, as well as white women that perform the same job.

Young women like Nicki are standing on the shoulders of women like Queen Latifah, who has always been a rock. Using her award-winning song "U.N.I.T.Y." to support other women and inform them of their power, Latifah showed again, *everyone is standing on black women's shoulders*. Queen and other women in hip hop and entertainment like Missy Elliott, Mariah Carey, Macy Gray, Jada Pinkett Smith, Mary J. Blige, Alicia Keys, Lauryn Hill, and many many others, have fought the battles in the trenches for years, creating a place of respect. They took on the issues of equality, representation, pay equity, language, and image of women in general in and outside hip hop.

I mentioned women icons above to indicate the success latter-day hip hop stars, Cardi B, Ava DuVernay, Rihanna, Ariana Grande, Nicki Minaj, Lil Kim, Solange, Zendaya, Yara Shahidi and many many others, owe Queen Latifah and her class of powerful women a real debt of gratitude for their stands in the early days, setting the standards for those that followed them.

I'm not one to try and tell a woman how to be a woman, but I do believe Nicki's mindset and her strategy will help counteract negative impulses that create self-doubt, and not only women must fight *"learned helplessness,"* black men need to take notice. *("The Psychology of Exploitation: Black Women In Entertainment,"* Ebony S. Muhammad: FinalCall.com, 2014).

I feel I need to clarify or at lease offer an example of what I am referring here. Back when I was working show production I help set up shows for such stars as Tina Turner, Diana Ross, Cher and Mary J. Blige to name a few. I worked shows for male artists also, but I mentioned only woman because my example is a woman, Alicia Keys. Our encounter occurred very early in her career, when *"Fallin"* and *"You Don't Know My Name"* were big. Alicia was playing a gig at Chastain Park in Atlanta, an outdoor amphitheater and I was working front of house. During sound check, Alicia walked by and stopped. She asked me several question, "How is it going? Are they treating you right? Do you need anything?" After answering, she asked "What do you think?" pointing toward her set. This was when she had the red telephone booth on stage right.

My answers are unimportant and my opinion probably is not important either. But I have been around long enough to have tried my theory, and my judgement has held up. Walking away I said to myself about Alicia, she's going to do alright. Entertainers, who see only themselves, tend to overlook people that can make their show go well or not care about how things go. It's best always to look out for people who look for you and acknowledge them and not look pass them.

It is easy to throw names around and claim they reflect this or that, but I noticed the career battles of women who have made valiant efforts fighting to hold their own. Those in the "know," know that only one female artist has won Best Rap album of the year at the Grammy Awards, since adding the category in 1995 (Shapiro 2007), Cardi B took home the Grammy award for Best Rap Album at the 61st Annual Grammy Awards, becoming the first solo female artist to win in that category and that speaks volumes, when one looks back down those 61 years and see only one when so many women who have given the world so much excellent music. That is why this writer is on the side of those complaining of gender bias. I believe, in most cases, "people see what they allow themselves to recognize."

Beginning with the films *"Friday,"* and *"Are We There Yet?"* which were a family-friendly affairs, Ice Cube's career in movies has been just as successful as his rap experiences. First, as a member of N.W.A. and later as a solo artist, in my opinion, both of Cube's worlds meld, producing *"Straight Outta Compton,"* the movie. Ice Cube not only served as producer on the movie, his son O'Shea Jackson Jr., plays the role of his dad on screen. Ice Cube's transition to film-making began while he was at the top of his rap game in 1991. Cast as *"Dough Boy"* in the critically acclaimed *"Boyz N the Hood,"* Ice Cube actually wrote a song with the same title a few years earlier.

Cube was also in the director's chair, for the 1998 film *"The Players Club"* and the ESPN documentary *"Straight Outta L.A.,"* about the period when the NFL Raiders were based in Los Angeles rather than Oakland. Hip hop offers some very unique male and female characters, which is why I reflected on the ways Ice-T is unique. A creature of street life—the world of drugs, gangsters, women, violence, and getting what you can while you can—gave hip hop this unique character, Curtis Jackson. Better known as 50 Cent, he started where Ice-T came from—hustling." Curtis followed in the foot prints of guys like Master P. He was one of the guys who brought that serious edge to hip hop, as well as some hard business savvy. In my opinion, such guys fought to establish the tradition of slave descendants holding on to the rights to what they created, as hip hop artists. This may seem a strange statement, but Ray Charles and James Brown fought hard as two of the first to fully claim that right.

Jackson went to the same school and fought the same fights Ray Charles and James Brown waged to own their musical production. Given he launched his music career with the nine-times-platinum album *"Get Rich or Die Tryin,"* 50 may be a surprise to some, but not to hip hop fans. Before he was worth 50 cent, he got his moneymaking, as a 12-year-old on the streets of Queens in the late '80s. Growing up in the street life, by the age of 18, he was raking in $5 grand a day from crack and heroin sales. I am not glorifying, but recognizing that a man does what a man has to do to survive, in a world without compassion for black skin, especially when it discounts those resembling 50 Cent.

Jackson's time on the street, as a dealer, put the people he loved most in harm's way. While outside his grandmother's home in 2000, Jackson was caught up in a shooting. The incident left him with a hole in his jaw, a bullet fragment lodged in his tongue and a new sound. He told *Rolling Stone* in 2003, *"Getting' shot just totally fixed my instrument,"* which was the birth of his hip hop money making sound.

His transition to music and the fame that followed, 50 cent became a protégé of Dr. Dre and Eminem in early 2000. Conjuring business success Jackson's magic continued in 2003; he established his record label and clothing company, both called G-Unit. He bought into Vitamin Water as a minority stakeholder, selling it he rapped on *"I Get Money."* *"I took quarter-water, sold it in bottles for two bucks. Coca-Cola came and bought it for billions buck. What the f***?"* 50 Cent's more recent ventures include a headphone competitor to Beats, a high-end vodka label, and patented technology for men's support underwear. It was no small blow when the rapper lost a high-profile lawsuit and filed for bankruptcy. Just two months after having ranked fourth on Forbes' Hip Hop's Five Wealthiest Artists 2015, 50 cent's net worth was still estimated above $155 million.

Although most people see him as a glamor boy and part of the penthouse set, he is one of the hardest working men in hip hop. Born Shawn Carter—Jay

The 400th: From Slavery to Hip Hop

Z has gone in and out of music retirement over the past decade and a half, but his status as an entrepreneur and entertainment mogul has not wavered.

In addition to having owned a nightclub, a vodka company and fashion line—Rocawear—which he sold in 2007 for over $200 million—Jay-Z also owned a lucrative share of the New Jersey Nets, which he later sold for a 135% gain. And in 2008, he founded the entertainment company Roc Nation, which in 2013 included a sports agency, new territory for the mogul.

Jay Z's net worth now sits somewhere around $550 million, but his investments haven't all exactly gone swimming: Tidal, a subscription-based music streaming service owned by media technology company Aspiro, which Jay Z acquired in March 2015, was served with a $50 million lawsuit last summer. The news has prompted "99 Problems" jokes galore. Although hip-hoppers are having fun laughing at Jay-Z's situation, most are praying for that problem, if they could get the rest of Jay-Z's life.

A sleeper for most when he debuted in the hip hop genre and hardly expected to do much, the man born Calvin Cordozar Broadus has come up big time. Recently becoming known as the "born again" Rastafarian Snoop Lion, Snoop Dogg boasts some of the most unique business ventures on our list. A major player in '90s West Coast gangsta rap's band of desperados, Broadus was ushered in from stage left by Dr. Dre. Featured on Dre first solo album following the break-up of N.W.A. in 1992, Snoop topped Billboard's 200 chart, with his album *"Doggystyle."* But Snoop's image wouldn't be complete without his ventures and adventures in filmmaking in the early 2000s—including the first hardcore porn video to make Billboard's music video sales charts and the Adult Video Network award-winning Snoop Dogg's Hustlaz: Diary of a Pimp. Personally, I can see Snoop Dog doing this and loving every minute. Founding a production company (2005) Snoopadelic films for Snoop-themed films.

In addition to having released his 13th studio album, Snoop Lion has become active in the world of venture capital. His estimated $135 million net worth includes a stake in Reddit, a high-end dog food company called DOG for DOG. A Lion in venture capital, Snoop also bought into Eaze, a California-based start-up that aims to deliver medical marijuana in 10 minutes or less, no "dog whistle." Dedicated Snoop lovers can also download his free sticker app Snoopify, complete with not-free stickers of joints or chicken and waffles with Snoop's face. According to the Wall Street Journal, the app was earning him $30,000 weekly in sales a month after its launch.

Going from Snoop and the edge of hip hop investing, I turn to a very mainstream William Adams—or Will.i.am. With all the originality, he spells his name—Will.i.am—had a couple of false starts before making it big as a founding member of the Black Eyed Peas. A debut album for Eazy-E's Ruthless Records got shelved in 1992 and later fell through altogether when Eazy-E tragically passed in 1995. There was also a stint in the "Black Eyed Pods" before a name change and the addition of Fergie to create the rave-inspired hip-hop group the world knows today. Will.i.am identifies himself primarily, as an entrepreneur and businessman, with music coming second.

However, out of the pod, this Black Eyed Pea has garnered enormous success—beyond selling over 76 million records to date—Adams is enjoying even more success in the world of innovation. His LA Fashion Institute of Design & Merchandising classes enabled him to create i.am +, a fashion tech start-up is most recently known for Puls, a competitor to the Apple Watch. He has partnered with Coke on Ekocycle, a project that promotes the use of recycled materials in the fashion world. He owned a founding share in Beats Electronics alongside Dr. Dre and reaped the rewards when Apple bought the company for $3 billion last year. He's also Intel's Director of Creative Innovation. And in 2012, he became the first artist ever to debut a song from another planet when he premiered *"Reaching for the Stars"* from the Mars Curiosity rover.

Coming back down to earth, Sean Combs has not topped the charts with songs like *"I'll Be Missing You,"* his 1997 tribute to the passing of friend and musical partner Notorious B.I.G. But Combs—a.k.a. Diddy, P. Diddy, Puff Daddy or Puffy— has been very busy. He has found other ways to stay on top. He currently has a net worth in the neighborhood, mind you this is a very small neighborhood, of $735 million, according to Forbes.

With his Sean John clothing line sold in mainstream outlets like Macy's, and with investments and partnership deals with huge companies like Diageo and upscale brands such as Aquahydrate and Ciroc vodka, one could say Combs is the quintessential rapper turned entrepreneur. As for his advice about being a successful businessman, Combs told Entrepreneur.com that *'It's essential to research and understand a company before getting involved. Above all, pay close attention to how the business will make a profit."* Puff Daddy's maxim is, *'If it doesn't make dollars, it doesn't make cents."*

"FLASH!!!!!" ***"The 400th"*** goes R&B. Puffy has become the first performing artist to commit to advancing the goal of **The 400th Performance Period** (2020-2030), which is building a platform to continue developing, as well as preserving American slavery descendants' first artistic development rhythm and Blues, which grew out of **Blues** magic. Puff Daddy, in a post to his fans, said he would, through REVOLT Media, lead a revival of R&B. Alone with all his many dynamic and impressive accomplishments, this may seem in and of itself of little consequence. However, Mr. Combs, like Floyd D. Tunson, who was the first visual artist to commit to creating a piece to commemorate ***"The 400th"***, made more than a statement, he offered a promise, not only to his devoted and admiring fans but to himself, which reflected a love of black music.

Diddy's post was not a news conference or a publicity campaign, but a declaration to correct a mistake, I belief black artists and the black community made letting R&B fad into the shadow of hip hop, like it was an episodic event.

The 400th: From Slavery to Hip Hop

"Blues," and later 1950s soul/R&B, as I have pointed out in this narrative, was the first technology slaves created and over the years has produced more economic wealth for the black community than any other technology. It is the hallmark of black culture, and with his declaration, Mr. Combs is putting his money and success where his mouth is, to use an overworked phrase. His statement indicates he recognizes the importance of preserving and cherishing the cultural heritage descendants of American slavery created. It is a legacy that our ancestor gave to black people and we owe it to them to always keep it alive and we must preserve it for the coming generations.

Mr. Combs' declaration is tremendous for *"The 400th"* and American slavery's descendants, which I wholeheartedly embrace and support because he did not simply commit to pushing *"The 400th"* but recognized the obligation to give back to a genre that has given him so much. Other cultures preserve and protect their artistic expressions and hold on to them. They do not walk away or drop them because of things like record sales or lack of popularity. They keep them alive as part of the community foundation, in the same manner, Mr. Combs has promised to undertake.

Puff Daddy is setting the example that is solely needy, at this point, to give *"The 400th"* substance and direction. I pray other artists will follow his example and take the lead in their area or field of expertise. When making his statement, Diddy spoke of his daughter not having the opportunity he had to experience and enjoy the L&H of R&B—the loneliness and happiness—R&B speaks to and celebrate for a people who knew only pain, scarcity, desperation and degradation. Black music is the one unifying endeavor that has always brought descendants of slavery together, during good times and bad. I welcome Mr. Combs aboard this fledging effort of *"The 400th"*. If you wondered why a "FLASH" that began this statement, it was to prepare you for the glaring rays of knowledge that would hit your brain and eyes.

When hip-hop began more than 30 years ago, corporate America ignored it, *"Big Mistake,"* according to Will Griffin, president and chief executive of Simmons Lathan Media Group (SLMG). Griffin makes that statement because hip hop now generates over $10 billion per year. It has moved beyond its musical roots to dominate and transform young people's ever-increasing lucrative lifestyle. World visionaries foresee hip-hop-inspired housewares, furniture, linen, foods, writing instruments, and even a special hip hop DVD section at Best Buy. They see publicly traded hip-hop companies and even a hip-hop entrepreneur rivaling Ralph Lauren or Oprah Winfrey on lists of the World's Richest People. *"It's not just music, but a culture,"* Griffin says, *"It's something you are, the way you look."*

Griffin's firm, which is a partnership with hip-hop entrepreneur Russell Simmons and television producer Stan Lathan, produces and distributes urban/hip-hop media content. Their works include "Def Poetry" on Broadway, The Steve Harvey Show, The Parkers on TV, and the Tupac Shakur movie Gridlock'd. Its most recent venture is a nationally syndicated radio show, "Russell Simmons' Hip Hop Laws of Success."

Hip hop has grown well beyond the urban market I talked about opening this section on hip hop. *"Rapper's Delight,"* released in 1979, opened the floodgates, and the green has not stopped flowing in to the beat. SLMG customer base is, *"the 45 million hip hop consumers between the ages of 13 and 34, 80 percent of whom are white."* According to SLMG's research, *"this group has $1 trillion in spending power."*

Griffin boastfully predicts *"Russell Simmons' empire places him in a position to garner a big chunk of that wealth."* The original hip hop mogul has his hand in every piece of the pie, from apparel to cell phones to videogames. He recently sold his apparel company, Phat Fashions, to Kellwood for $140 million, but will remain CEO. He and Rick Rubin founded Def Jam Recordings in 1984 in Rubin's New York University dorm room with a $5,000 investment. At that time, rap artists were selling music out of the trunks of cars, on street corners, in supermarket parking lots, and at parties, among other places. Entrepreneurs like Simmons are the ones that have come to dominate the industry. Griffin says, *"The reason why he [Simmons] is so successful is because of the arrogance of the established companies."*

Statements regarding women and their relevance or treatment as partners or targets within the hip hop genre are many. Although different assessments came forth, there is universal agreement that things could and should be far better than they presently are for women. My search for the following model, if you will, had to be someone that could show not just women, but the hip hop world culture, *"How it is done!"*

"Sean Combs represents the American dream, and that's a dream that's available for everyone," according to Dia Simms of Combs Enterprises. She made this statement opening an interview with Moira Forbes entitled' *"How Dia Simms Is Leading Sean "Diddy" Combs' Business Empire."* Although a mover and shaker today in hip hop, my next hip hop rising power broker was not steeped in the genre, and for me, that is what's so amazing about her level of success and rocket ship ride into the stratosphere of hip hop.

Dia Simms seems a woman on a mission, as President of Combs Enterprises. Her watchwords, *"bottom line success makes diversity far more than a buzzword,"* came through most clearly, during her interview with Moira Forbes. Simms has been with Combs Enterprises 12 years and appears to be a driving force behind Combs' continued success and growing empire. She talked confidently regarding her meteoric career rise, *"My being in the room makes all of us better. This is not a favor. You can look at any study, and it will continually reinforce the idea that more women actually make more money."*

Brought on as Comb's executive assistant in 2005, a quick study, Simms established herself across a diverse range of business ventures, working alongside the music, fashion, and beverage mogul. She credits her unconventional career experiences, a stint at the Department of Defense, as well as in the pharmaceutical and marketing industries, for helping hone her leadership skills. While identifying her professional passions, Simms says, her unconventional career experiences developed her work philosophy, *"I hire hard, and manage light."* These words underpin her efforts to bring together winning teams and talent. She emphasizes things that brought her success, *"The old school basics, come in early,"* and *"putting in the time upfront to find the right fit across an entire team."* Today, she oversees business ventures across a growing portfolio of lifestyle and consumer product brands, including Bad Boy Entertainment, CÎROC vodka, Revolt Media, and Sean John clothing line, to name a few.

With her experiences extending from Defense to hip hop, Dia bills herself as a *"quick learner."*

"The personal challenge of being the only woman in the room means I stand out. It's crucially important to make the right kind of first impression. You don't have twenty minutes to make an impact. You need to assert not only your confidence, but your excellence, your know-how, your prowess, and your conviction about your genuine value."

More than that, Simms insists she's *"a stickler for courtesy and respect"* and confesses that *"I always check to see how candidates treat the receptionist and will even test how helpful they are when something is dropped on the floor. Do they even move? Do they try to pick it up? I go out of my way to create an asshole-free, hater free, 'please and thank you' zone. I'm very old school about civility and thoughtfulness."* The following caveat was not part of the interview, but I believe women and men are paid "equally" for the same job by Simms.

When it comes to work-life balance, Simms says *"This is an unrealistic concept that should be 'deleted' from our expectations."* Simms goes on, *"It's my laser focus that allows me to maximize every second of the day, personally and professionally. Whatever I'm doing in that exact moment, I want to knock it the hell out of the park. If I'm with my daughter, I want to actually be engaged. I want to listen to actually hear what she says back and have an actual, engaged conversation. Conversely, if I'm in a boardroom negotiating something that is life changing for our organization, I want to be locked into that moment."*

In 2011, Dia was named one of Forbes *"40 Under Forty,"* and the same year, she was also named a Leader of the New School by Essence Magazine. Simms is actively involved with the Network for Teaching Entrepreneurship, which provides entrepreneurial training to High School students. She sits on the Board of the Boys and Girls Club of Harlem, (*"How Dia Simms Is Leading Sean "Diddy" Combs' Business Empire,"* Moira Forbes (2018), ForbesWoman).

Although he is not among the "Big Bucks Boys and Ladies" of hip hop, he is, for me, the quintessential artist among those who supported the main pillar of hip hop's early beginnings—*spoken word*. Lonnie Rashid Lynn. (3-13-1972), better known as "Common" or formerly "Common Sense," a rapper, actor, poet, and film producer, was part of hip hop's rise to prominence. He was a mainstay helped maintain hip hop's ties to "conscious lyrics."

Common was not a "lone rider" at this level; there were hundreds, if not thousands of sisters and brothers, who never made it to the top financial echelon of hip hop but were the ones who did the grunt work, building the structure after others laid the foundation. Without their dedication and perseverance through the 1980s and early 90s into the new millennium, in my opinion, hip hop would have lost its soul. That soul of consciousness is why I selected Common, as a major player and representative of thousand he reflect. His commitment to conscious lyric and spoken word set him apart from many up and coming hip hop artists of his day. Besides for me, he always looked so cool—unflappable!

Common Sense came to my attention in 1992 with the album *"Can I Borrow a Dollar?"* he was my son, Yohannes' favorite. Yohannes was part of the underground spoken word poetry scene with the *"Atlanta Vibe."* Maybe "underground" is not an accurate metaphor, because they were very much above ground and very public, but a lack of resources kept spoken word poetry in Atlanta on the "down low." Yohannes introduced me to Common and his art of "conscious lyrics."

The son of educator Dr. Mahalia Ann Hines and former basketball player, Lonnie Lynn Jr., Common didn't graduate from Ice-T or 50 Cent's school of hard-knock hip hop. But getting into hip hop wasn't any easier for Common than it was for thousands of wannabe rappers in the late 1980s. First trying regular school at Florida A&M University for two years, he dropped it, after dropping his first single *"Take It EZ."* The album *"Can I Borrow a Dollar?" (1992)* followed the single. Taking success in stride, Common maintained his underground connections, and consciousness stayed on his mind, if not in all his lyrics. After gaining mainstream success through his work with the Soulquarians, Common stayed very common even though he did not have Sense.

Starting as "Common Sense," he appeared on the Red Hot Organization's compilation CD, *"America Is Dying Slowly (A.I.D.S.),"* alongside Biz Markie, Wu-Tang Clan, and Fat Joe, among other prominent hip hop artists. The cut was heralded "a masterpiece" by *The Source Magazine* 1996. Following the release of *Resurrection*, "Common Sense" got lighter, he lost "Sense," but not his mind; he got smarter, not dumber. Showing his smarts, he ducked a beef with a UK group that thought fighting over the word "Sense" was smart. Then, as just Common (1997), he released his third album, *"One Day It'll All Make Sense."*

Hooking up with other conscious rappers and artists like Lauryn Hill, De La Soul, Q-Tip, Canibus, Black Thought, Chantay Savage, and Questlove, it seemed "consciousness" was in. Common won a Grammy Award for Best R&B Song with Erykah Badu on *"Love of My Life"* (2003) and a Grammy for Best Rap Performance by a Duo or Group, for *"Southside"* featuring Kanye West, from his album *"Finding Forever"* (2007). Getting into the movies, Common had roles in the crime thriller *American Gangster* (2007), *Smokin' Aces* (2010), the comedy *Date Night* (2010), AMC's *Hell on Wheels*, and the hitman in *Run All Night*.

Common is also part of the "Knowing Is Beautiful" movement, which supports HIV/AIDS awareness. He was also featured in the video *"Yes We Can,"* a song in support of Barack H. Obama's run for the White House (2008). Common has founded the Common Ground Foundation, a non-profit that seeks to empower underprivileged youth to be strong citizens of the world. His foundation is dedicated to programs of leadership, education, creative expression, and empowerment development, as well as a book club.

Common's movie roles were outstanding, and although those performances endeared him to his fans, they were not why he made this hip hop list. His early beginnings, as a "conscious rapper," stuck with me because I longed for the days when he and other conscious rappers kept hip hop in touch with its roots of spoken word. Holding on to consciousness also kept hip hop in touch with its **Blues** roots. I see hip hop as just another extension of the **Blues'** many iterations—ragtime, jazz, bebop, R&B/soul, rock & roll, and a few lesser genres in between, as it continues evolving, after all these years since slavery.

Music has physically and mentally sustained black people during good and bad times. It produced revenue and resources, once former slaves had to make it on their own. The course of black music's development has continually evolved to fit slave descendants' survival needs. The **Blues** gave expression to slaves and former slaves' misery and joy; as such, it kept changing, as black people and their times and circumstances changed. This process is considered innovations in art and other endeavors.

I bring innovation up, at this point, because I believe it was missed by many people in the early 1990s when gangsta rap came on the scene. Most hip hop listeners, who like me, loved conscious lyrics, acted as though music shouldn't change. For them, there was only one kind of rap or hip hop. They didn't see the rise of gangsta rap as innovation; rather, they saw it as degradation. I'm not defending the image or lyrics gangsta rap brought into hip hop, which many people believed represented violence, sex, misogyny, and drug. What I'm defending is the right of artists to give new expression to what exists, or can be imagined, as their innovation. As any genre or culture grows and matures, it will change or it will stagnate and lose relevance.

I think hip hop should be viewed as the highest expression of African American Art because it has consumed not only black culture, but it has become a world culture. It is the leading edge of economic development and growth, as well as advancement for black people presently. That fact is being recognized by more people each day around the world, as this narrative and other reports stress its socioeconomic prowess. I see it as the embodiment of Black Art today, however, not its totality. Black Arts are why I labored to explain the role of the communist party in the 1920 and 30s in Harlem, as they funded and created organizations that help develop black artists, more so than the US government.

For instance, Zora Neale Hurston, a Harlem Renaissance writer, took advantage of the communist writers' workshops in the 1920s and 30s. Zora Neale wrote the story of the Clotilda, in her novel *"Barracoon."* Her novel tells the story of the last ship of slaves brought to the United States. Their story has become part of African Americans' road to hip hop and *"The 400th",* not just in terms of history. Amazingly, today, Common plans to turn Zora Neale's novel, the story of the Clotilda, into a movie.

Common's new effort is why I feel the conscious side of hip hop is still very relevant and should be reflected, as part of hip hop's vision of the future. Relevance is certainly the issue when one considers that hip hop is the most powerful expression of Black Arts currently.

With the level of resources at hip hop's disposal, hip hop can bring stories like *"Barracoon"* alive, to commemorate and celebrate *"The 400th".* Rediscovering novels like *"Barracoon"* is a once in a lifetime opportunity for slave descendants, who are the first, hip hop generation to have an opportunity, to honor our survival, as one people. Also, bringing *"Barracoon"* back to life is part of hip hop's innovative technology of "flipping," updating things from the past for audiences today to experience.

Through Common's efforts, the story of the Clotilda and its cargo of 110 slaves has brought their story into our lives, after 157 years. So, at this time, descendants of American slavery can vicariously experience the callous and indifference of slave masters. The Clotilda is the dreadful account of one very rich white man, Timothy Meaher. A very wealthy Mobile slaver and shipyard owner, on a wager with a New England speculator (slaver trader), Meaher bet that he could successfully smuggle slaves into the US, despite the 1807 *Act Prohibiting the Importation of Slaves.*

Meaher built, outfitted and hired a crew for the ship, which sailed to Africa, kidnap the 110 Africans and brought them back to Mobil, Alabama, while dodging the Royal Navy's *West African Squadron.* After their arrival in 1859, slave masters worked these kidnapped Africans, as other slaves. Following emancipation, even though kidnapped and brought to America illegally, the US government refused to repatriate them back to Africa. Led by Cudjo Lewis, they built their settlement called Africatown, which still stands today.

Common's mindset here is why I think more of his type of consciousness is sorely needed in hip hop today. Common is a great example of giving *VOICE* to those unsung heroes by bringing these slaves' story to life, like Douglas Blackmon with his excellent treaties ***Slavery by Another Name: The Re-Enslavement of Africans Americans from the Civil War to World War II,*** and *"Be Free or Die"* starring Cynthia Erivo, directed and co-written by Kasi Lemmons ("Eve's Bayou") along with Gregory Allen Howard. Thanks to Zora Neale and now Common, the world will learn the story of the Clotilda and its cargo of 110 slaves.

Many have asked, what is the relevance of hip hop, other than, some black entertainers making lots of money? I would say hip hop through its resources can help tell the story; this narrative alone cannot give *VOICE*. Common is helping to tell the story of ***"The 400th"***, as part of Black Arts, and although he no longer has "sense," Common is so much wiser. Bringing such stories to life and asking questions of the American society will help hip-hoppers keep its longevity and relevance upfront in the futuristic thinking of those directing hip hop's course.

Giving Spoken Word a Second Look

The only thing our ancestors had were their dreams in their heads. Today while retracing **"The 400th"**, it is amazing that with everything they faced, along the way, their progenies have created a world culture, becoming their dreams fulfilled. Todays' hip hoppers are what they dreamed, not the physical representation seen today, but the psychological manifestation of a mental process they began, as former enslaved human beings struggling to hold on to self-love.

Their hope, thinking of conversations with my great great-granddaddy Burl Lee, was that their progeny would one day, make them part of "something" far greater than what they were, walking off plantations in 1863, because they survived bondage. That "something" began with millions of kidnapped Africans that were continually dragged aboard slave ships for 355 years (1452-1807) beginning the journey to the **Western Hemisphere** on the way to **"The 400th"**, as their progeny prepare to commemorate and celebrate their dream. Today as their progeny, we honor their dedication, endurance, commitment and fortitude, during the centuries of servitude that laid the foundation of their survival, and our emergence as one people.

I keep reiterating this point of fact, because after emerging from bondage, it still took 154 years, as their survival teetered on the brink of disaster, before we could declare **"The 400th"**. This fact deserves repeating time and again because former enslaved African Americans and their progeny are the first people to survived such bondage and genocide, then stand before the world as one people. Their endurance and dogged determination to hold on to self-love reflects and give credit to their strength and belief in their uniqueness. **"The 400th"** celebration will be enslaved Africans' rite of passage that officially acknowledges and establishes that fact.

Cerebrating their "word of mouth culture" they created, which sustained their progeny, reveals the relevance of "spoken word" and its role in hip hop. But, like R&B's relevance to the **"Blues,"** "spoken word", which came to its highest expression is reflected and best represented by one group **"The Last Poets."** They form the bridge to both—R&B and spoken word—in the 1960s. However, there is real confusion in the general public, as to who composed *The Last Poets?*

Although, there is no doubting the fact they were firebugs, using their lyrics to set the minds and hearts of young blacks ablaze with revolutionary hopes in the late 1960s and early 70s, no matter who made up the group. The name—*The Last Poets*—was taken from a revolutionary poem by South African poet Keorapetse Kgositsile, who believed he was living in *"the last era of poetry before guns took over."* And, we are experiencing that premonition today!!!

The 400th: From Slavery to Hip Hop

The confusion about membership in the group is because several groups of poets and musicians became affiliated with *The Last Poets*, making it a collective, like the *Wu-Tang Clan*. Nevertheless, like pyromaniac, they ignited flame that burned away black people's fears of what white folks thought about the black revolution. *The Last Poets* in 1968, became the voice of *Black Nationalism*. They made an indelible mark on the psyche of African-Americans fighting for human rights.

The version of the group led by Jalaluddin Mansur Nuriddin and Umar Bin Hassan had the greatest impact on popular culture. *The Last Poets'* energy gave a skateboard ride to hip-hop music, according to critic Jason Ankeny, who said, *"With their politically charged raps, taut rhythms, and dedication to raising African American consciousness, the Last Poets almost single-handedly laid the groundwork for the emergence of hip-hop,"* (*"Profile of Last Poets; Jason Ankeny,"* Allmusic.com, accessed 2-1-2007). The British music magazine NME stated, *"Serious spokesmen like Gil Scott-Heron, The Last Poets, and the later Gary Byrd, paved the way for many socially committed Black [emcees] a decade later."* With recordings like *"Niggers Are Scared of Revolution"* and *"When the Revolution Comes"* (1970), *The Last Poets* gave black power two seminal tracks that became theme songs of black activism. They made all black activists want to be poets, and many tried.

Reaching the US Top 10 chart with the successful debut album, *"The Last Poets"* their style of spoken word changed the nature of political discourse in the black community with poetry. They drew the ire of the Richard Nixon administration, which promptly placed them on his *"enemies list,"* along with "H." Rap Brown, Stokley Carmichael, the Invaders and the Black Panthers. Then, like the dark hand of death, J. Edgar Hoover's counter-intelligence program *"COINTELPRO,"* kicked into high gear, trying to kill anything that promoted *"Black Nationalism."* Their poetry and rhetoric inspired the generations of the 1970s through the 1990s to believe spoken word artists would lead the next revolution.

By the 1990s, Dot and I had become runners, trying to survive Co-Intel-Pro death hunt. Even after almost five years in prison, they continued birddogging me, until they killed my research efforts at Memphis State University. We settled in Atlanta in 1982 and began building new lives. That worked for a while, until Co-Intel-Pro realized it was working and got both of us fired (Dot from the IRS and me from the US Postal Service. Although, I transitions to show production as an independent stage hand(sound, lighting and audio) the FBI lurked in the shadows waiting for an opportunity to screw that up.

Disappointed that the black revolution had faltered, Dot and I looked out over the valley of dry bones with regrets. For the most part, black people were cutting off their afros, getting Jerri-curls and were only interested in humor; everything was funny. Giggling it up with *"All in the Family," "Good Times,"* and *The Jeffersons*, liberation for black people, became a thing of the past.

However our son Yohannes introduced us to, what seemed "a second coming for black power!" *"Spoken word"* had found new life with young blacks, as they developed a kind of underground scene and economy in the hood. Through their emergence, black power was seeing a rebirth. Young blacks were attempting to re-infuse black consciousness and a positive mindset among African Americans.

After the assassination of Dr. Martin Luther King, Jr. African Americans went into a "deep ghetto funk," like he had not taught them anything about America. Young black brothers and sisters in Atlanta created a vibe of positive black thought. With the second coming of black power, young black women and men were not laughing; they were growing afros or wearing braids. They had embraced spoken word, as an investment that would help shape their world. Trying to establish a foundation using the same strategy—making families and building communities former slaves' deployed, they banked on black consciousness, as the endeavor that would pay off for them in the future. Much like Dot and I in the late 1970s, they gave it their all, trying to *make something out of nothing*.

It was like "The Last Poets" had spawned a whole new generation of black power sibling that inherited their fire. So, I began this family narrative perspective by introducing my great-great-grandfather and great-grandfather and myself; now, I close out my family on my son, Yohannes Sharriff, and grandson Tyrus Chi Laster. Five generations, in terms of trying to build wealth, our family line is identical to most descendants of American slavery. Although, we have put in the work, the American system has continued finding ways of pulling my family back into the valley of dry bones in the graveyard of poverty.

My son's and grandson's worlds are a couple of decades apart. Yet and still, their prospects in life do not differ substantially from the first Burl Lee's. Yohannes, during his freshman year (1994), while attending Georgia Southern University, a predominately white school, fell in love with spoken word poetry. Back home in Atlanta, on summer break, Yohannes joined a group of spoken word artists, which Dot dubbed *"The Atlanta Vibe."*

Their spoken word vibe flourished during the 1990s, as spoken word was on the rise. Determined to make spoken word mainstream, much like CP-USA at its beginning, their new world envisioned through poetry, music, plays, and other educational efforts, fell short because, unlike the help CP-USA brought Black Arts in Harlem, they had no financial support from the arts community or government. Similarly to Harlem artists before CP-USA, trying to give life to their dreams, they maxed out credit cards, bank accounts, and family resources, breathing life into their spoken word dreams.

Their nearly 12-years working two or three jobs, with family commitments, their run grained slowly to a halt. The killing blow was the lack of any serious commercial endorsements or arts community support or sponsorship. Life took its toll on the spoken word scene and its young poets and Atlanta. Trying to make spoken word mainstream was too heavy a loud for poor black kids on the bottom of America's *"cheap Labor"* capitalistic economic system to lift spoken word to prominence.

Lack of support from the American Arts community is why the grassroots help from CP-USA for black people in Harlem (1910-1940) proved to be irreplaceable. Even though J. Edgar Hoover passed from the scene, his racist ghost still held sway, locking out black consciousness. There was no economic support for Black Arts at its most crucial beginnings in Atlanta. I speculate that if the Atlanta Vibe had received similar support as Rose McClendon, Langston Hughes, Richard Wright, Paul Robeson, William Patterson, Zora Neale Hurston, and many many others received in their early beginnings from CP-USA, things for the Atlanta Vibe would have yielded a different result. Put another way, had the Harlem Renaissance gotten the same response and support, as *the Atlanta Vibe*, there is no way to judge what would have resulted or whether there would even be black Arts, as we know it today?

Meanwhile, back in the real world of entertainment, hip hop was on the rise and sucked up all the interest and resources. Gangsta rap's commercial potential overpowered spoken word, as it took the world by storm. The arrested development of spoken word took its toll, as many spoken word artists became hip hop artists or returned to school and got degrees, as Yohannes. Paying to play, in a game where artists should get paid for their efforts on the rocky road to success, spoken word was a fast train ride that transported Atlanta poets to the valley of dry bones by 2010. More than lost opportunities in entertainment for young African Americans, I saw the black community losing valuable voices that were offering a conscious vision of the future.

Tyrus, my grandson, and Yohannes' dreams are symbolically as well as reflective of their struggles, trying to development their talent, while avoiding the grave of poverty. Although they did not follow the same path; they may, however, share similar dead-end realities, as a future, trying to escape the ghetto trap. Tyrus graduated high school, after four years of superior ratings in band, but no scholarship offers. He was still at square one. He enrolled at Georgia State University and became a business major, like Yohannes.

During his last two years of high school, Tyrus found he liked working out with the dance team. That summer (2016), after graduation, he stepped on the treadmill of the fast-food industry, as thousands of black children, trying to find an exit out of the graveyard of poverty. Ty entered a KFC intern manager program and was quickly promoted. Looking for an exit strategy, he joined a "stand battle" dance team and, again as Yohannes, "fell in love."

So, while attending school, he uses his KFC funds to pay his "stand battle" dance team's fees, reminiscent of so many icons, trying to get into entertainment. His start wasn't any different from what Sidney Poitier, Redd Fox, Malcolm X and many others went through in the 1930s and 40s, looking and hoping for an entry-level, trying to break into entertainment and break out of poverty. Again, the question is how far have blacks on the bottom, trapped in America's *"cheap labor"* economic strategy come, when they face the same conditions, as blacks over 8 or 9 decades ago?

Trying to *make something out of nothing*, young blacks today still have to "pay to play" on the bottom rung entry-level of entertainment and employment. I wonder if Tyrus will make it out before the ghetto trap door falls, leaving him without an exit. But, moving on, hoping to increase his chances, yet still unable to escape the fastfood treadmill, he moved to Dunkin Donut to maintain a job that allow him the time and flexibility to hold on to his first love—dancing. Full of hope he joined the 411 dance team and is very excited about his prospects.

Reacting similarly to "stand battle" as "spoken word," I see great potential in "stand battle" dancing, although "bottom rung," it is very very competitive in the mindset required for success. But, similar to spoken word, without any immediate or long-range economic promise, having to bankroll one's training and competition seems an instant replay of the fate spoken word artists in Atlanta experienced.

There should be a means of rewarding such an honest effort to succeed in America. I refer to stand battle dancing as "bottom rung" because it is so ghetto bound, just as spoken word in Atlanta, at its beginning. However, unlike spoken word, "stand battling" is overwhelmingly dominated by young girls, some as young as 3 or 4.

Usually, it is a total family effort, like sports begin at such young ages. They are the hopes of their family's advancement and thoughts of a better life for their progeny. Looking at the exposure and support for stand battle dancers, it resembles spoken word artists' run. The cost of regular dance classes at their economic level is prohibitive to such parents, but they find a way to make the investment for "stand battle" anyway. Families are hoping a modern dancer or ballerina will emerge from "stand battling" 10 or 15 years down the pike. For many families, the cost of "stand battling" is a case of "robbing Peter to pay Paul," trying to rise above their low-income status.

Tantamount to concrete sidewalks or hard courts for Althea Gibson or Venus and Serena Williams, even stickball for Willie Mays, these young "stand battlers," need support. They need a place to go to make their drive for success pay off. The drive to succeed is there, but "stand battling" needs visionaries, like Afrikaa Bambaataa, whose saw how, through the Almighty Universal Zulu Nation, his vision of B-Boying and B-Girling could come alive for youngsters in New York *"make something out of nothing."*

Talking with Ty about his choices, he said, *"Nobody knows what's going to happen. COVID-19 and Black Lives Matter protest following George Floyd murder has shown the world that. I came out of high school without a scholarship, which was what I based my entire educational future. Now four years later, I'm a top student in business, I've put my* education to work as a manager although it working in fast food, but that allowed me to compete against the best "stand battle" dance teams in the South. Now I'm with a modern dance group at 411.

Who knows what's going to happen. I'm so excited. Dancing has forced me to develop my body. I'm gaining dancing skills, and mental toughness and making the best out of what's available. 'Stand battling' taught me to dance with attitude. You are not just making moves; those moves are choreographed to express and communicate emotions and not allow your fears to intimidated you or be dominated by competition. I've learn to do things using my body I never dreamed possible. I love it."

"Stand battle" dancing can be compared to making statements dancers exhibit attitudes and efforts that sustained black people in their struggle to move forward, even when there did not seem a way. The idea of "stand battling" is to make a stand and refuse to allow anyone to push you back. Descendants of American slavery's stands have paid off because now we are commemorating and celebrating **"The 400th"**; there is no pushing slave descendants off of that stand!!!!

Promoters like Russel Simmons, who threw "spoken word," a lifeline with "Def Poetry Jam," is the kind of visionary needed now. Back in the 90s, *The Atlanta Vibe* gave *VOICE* to the struggles of real ordinary black people. My wife, Dot, designed a website to push what we saw as the rebirth of black consciousness and its positive mindset. Dot created *"The DISH.org" (Dot's Information Service Hotline)* an e-magazine. She began publishing before the advent of social media and blogs. We were trying to get the word out about the effort young black brothers and sisters were making with spoken word in Atlanta.

More than anything, we pushed back against the idea that our children all over America are lazy! They are struggling and searching, trying to find success. They need a hand up from those above who have gained success and know what it is to struggle without stepping stones that led someplace. The government has always refused or fought any effort that helped black people, as with CP-USA. If you have made this rough trek, look back at the road behind you. Is it empty or full?

AFROPUNK: Evolving as the Leading Edge of Hip Hop

Sustaining hip hop's torrid pace of production and innovations must be matched by innovative ways to delivers services to a very diverse audience and fan base. Most importantly, the demand for new products that provide variety in the types of genres available to address future needs should be at the top of the hip hop's genre's list. Thinking of innovation itself in new ways is the challenge for hip hop. The idea of marketing to particular demographics (white men) is a "bean counters" idea of art. Artists create and innovate, bean counters count, bottom line is their only concern.

My last comment brings this discussion to what I see as the leading innovation in hip hop—AFROPUNK. With the eyes of Janus this narrative readers looked back to whence slavery's descendants came. Now looking forward through the eyes of Janus, this section assesses hip hop's present efforts and possibly where the genre is headed. The fact that hip hop brought economic opportunity, political expression, and *VOICE* to the oppressed and downtrodden people across the world, begs the question, *"Where can hip hop go from its present level of success?"* For my money, *AFROPUNK* has already answered that question.

A newly evolving genre and model, *Afropunk* is a very different approach that is appealing to the futuristic international culture, which **"The 400th"** also hopes to appeal. I selected *Afropunk*, as a model, not only because of its successes over almost two decades, even though it struggled, getting its legs beneath it, this new genre has developed a real commitment to developing the type of community, I see through the eyes of Janus. Their beginning harkens back to the first commitments former slaves made as contrabands to make families and build communities.

The founders of *Afropunk* started with a documentary film in their effort to *"make something out of nothing."* It seems to me, they were not simply hoping to make money; they wanted to make their sense of community part of their innovative endeavor. What I offer to buttress my point comes from a Q&A conducted for **Afropunk Solution Sessions.** It is a conversation conducted by Bridget Todd and Yves Jeffcoat. They spoke with Matthew Morgan and Jocelyn Cooper founders of *Afropunk*.

This interview provides real insight into how these business partners developed their philosophical, and psychological, as well as community model. The point of presenting the list of people involved in hip hop is to show the necessity of continuing to innovate and reinvent successful entertainment endeavors. Entertainment has proven to be the most productive and successful enterprise for slave descendants, in my opinion. I will say music and related activities, taken as a whole, have produced more wealth for black communities, than all other sources of wealth black people have accumulated and managed to kept since emancipation.

Afropunk rose to significance in the caustic business environment, following the devastating 2008 financial crisis, which devastated the African Americans community. *Afropunk* founders took what already existed and re-envisioned new ways of updating their format—flipping. Led by a better vision of tomorrow, like the eyes of Janus, Jocelyn Cooper, and Matthew Morgan seem to embrace, as their philosophy, an idea I have offered previously in this narrative, *"not to change is to stagnate and die."*

That statement is not intended to steal their thunder, but to support the direction they carried *Afropunk*. Their efforts seem to anticipate the downward spiral of R&B's slide from prominence in the 1970s. Unless hip hop continues

The 400th: From Slavery to Hip Hop

its growth and innovation, it will be left without a future. However, as always, I look to innovation, and as Janus, looking at *Afropunk*, the future, very possibly, has arrived—that was before COVID-19. Now no one knows what the new normal holds for the world.

But I believe my assessment will hold, as I said I bank on innovation. I considered *Afropunk*, originally as a topic, when I began developing this narrative. But, I was unfamiliar with *Afropunk* and the weightiness, as well as expansive character of hip hop in general, which I knew very little, so it became my research topic. *Afropunk* seem a totally separate topic and a less important story. So, I put it off to concentrate on hip hop, but, then again, a strange turnabout demanded Afropunk's second look.

Prichard Smith director of the *Invaders* documentary was up against a deadline and needed help getting the doc licensed and ready for market. Ayanna Saulsberry came to his rescue, working very diligently and very impressively, pulling Prichard's *"fat out of the fire."* Ayanna possesses a skill set, which I believed could help **"The 400th"**, I wanted to ask her to be a volunteer. However, before I could ask, she climbed onboard *Afropunk's* dream ride. I was totally surprised Ayanna saw such security in this new genre to join the *Afropunk* family, so I took a second look before completing hip hop's review.

While researching *Afropunk*, I learned its beginnings were a fascinating ride from the outer edge of obscurity into the heart of hip hop. Many hip-hoppers see *Afropunk* and hip hop, as two totally different genres, but my research convinced me it was an extensions of the **Blues** entertainment culture created by slaves. I make the case *Afropunk* is only the latest innovation in entertainment for people of color, as part of the Hip hop culture, which sprang from the same source—the **"Blues."**

More precisely, *Afropunk* has become the leading edge of innovation in the new hip hop world culture. *Afropunk* has a very compelling story, and to tell it completely would require a book, as a few other topics I have discussed. So, what I share now is just a glimpse, in the rear view mirror to get a picture, *Afropunk* is painting of its future.

Listening to **Afropunk Solution Sessions,** reminded me of how my great-grandfather Burl Lee and Mama Laura, which I've talked about here, came together like other former slaves, with profound love and respect for building community. Similar to other former slaves, desperation and scarcity drove their development. Yet and still, they found the strength and character to throw off what slavery forced upon them, by taking advantage of slaves sense of commonality. My great-great-grandparent, the first Burl Lee and Mama Sarah's, decisied to come together and care about all that came to their communities with needs. Similarly, Matthew Morgan and Jocelyn Cooper insisted everyone is worthy of their concern.

Although their venture—*Afropunk*—is a business, the thoughts that Jocelyn and Matthew expressed said more about people than money to me. They reflected the entrepreneurial spirit I had endeavored to express here but had failed to capture thus far. However, through the vision of black entrepreneurial leadership they expressed, I feel I finally have it.

I will regretfully admit, only learning about *Afropunk* in 2017. And, although I keep up with its developments now, I have yet to attend an *Afropunk* event; 2020 was going to be my year. (However, COVID-19 put the world on hold, and like everything else, I will wait for the all clear.) So the **Afropunk Solution Sessions** are a very insightful and enlightening eavesdrop on how Morgan and Cooper see their enterprise, considering I was ignorant of *Afropunk's* mission and popularity when I began my look back. My education began with visiting the Afropunk webpage. It reminded me of Afrikaa Bambaataa, who defined hip hop's five basic elements. *Afropunk* needed the same defining philosophical and psychological intent.

Afropunk's history is posted on its website: *"Afro: as in, born of African spirit and heritage; see also black (not always), see also rhythm and color, see other, and underdog. Punk: as in, rebel, opposing the simple route, imbued with a DIY ethic,* (DIY refers to the ethic of self-sufficiency through completing tasks without paid experts. Literally, 'do it yourself,' the DIY ethic says anyone is capable of performing a variety of tasks rather than relying on paid specialists), *looking forward with simplicity, rawness and open curiosity, Afropunk defines culture by the collective creative actions of the individual and the group. It is a safe place, a blank space to freak out in, to construct a new reality, to live your life as you see fit while making sense of the world around you".* Copper and Morgan did the same thing with *Afropunk* that Afrikaa Bambaataa did with hip hop; they gave it a body and a soul.

Having moved around trying to find the right under-served community, Afropunk returned to Commodore Barry Park, Fort Greene, Brooklyn, in 2017. Matthew and business partner Jocelyn Cooper wanted to make a strong committed and connection to people in under-served communities, not only in New York City but across the globe (Paris, London, Atlanta, and Johannesburg). The New York Times called *AFROPUNK, "The most multicultural festival in the U.S."* Morgan responded:

"I can't say what that meant for the New York Times writer. Do I like it? Yeah, I love it. I love the idea that we're very multicultural. It's an interesting question because when looking at the audience, people may say, well, that's not multicultural (mostly black people). *But for me, that depends on how you look at blackness, and the whole point is; black people are not a monolith. And, although there are more people of color—they're Dominican, Puerto Rican, British, Nigerian, Ghanaian, French, Senegalese, Congolese, and American. That's pretty multicultural.*

The 400th: From Slavery to Hip Hop

I agree with Morgan in how they developed *Afropunk's* audiences. His statement on *Afropunk's* multicultural audiences is reminiscent of another theme of this narrative, *"white and black people can view or experience the same event or situation at the same time but come away with two totally different scenarios."* Copper and Morgan seems to be appealing to people where color does not mend everyone is from the same place. If white people from London, Paris, Poland, Sweden, Italy, and Germany are in the same space, they would consider that a multicultural event though they all have the same complexion.

I hope through ***"The 400th"*** people will start to see differences as strengths and embrace people of color as different, in the same way, white people are different. Beauty is in people, no matter their color. Afrpunk's founders' efforts came together as I hope ***"The 400th"*** will draw on the many different communities of slave descendants and descendants of those that did the enslaving, as a true reflection of unity. This particular festival (Brooklyn) brought acts like Raphael Saadiq, SZA, Solange, and Princess Nokia, among others, to the stage before an estimated 60,000 *Afropunkers*. The festival included visual arts, craft, and food vendors. Also, skates were the thing for the *"Battle for the Streets"* competition.

"The idea of an Afropunk festival began while we were screening the Afropunk documentary back in 2003," Morgan said. *"I was in the management business working with black artists that really didn't want to do R&B and Hip Hop. They were in punk bands, in rock n' roll bands, and there was not home for them. Growing a really engaged audience showing the film added a physical presence for their music around those notions. There wasn't a platform back then for kids of color to embrace something that looked like them and where they felt comfortable in a space that they could kind of feel a part of, to freely express themselves' in a way that wasn't currently available, made a lot of sense to us."*

Matthew put the next piece of the *Afropunk* puzzle in place when he put up a community page, where people could request to screen the documentary. Organically, people started coming to the community page, which turned into AFROPUNK.com. Cooper added,

"The documentary is very different from the community. But what resonated in the film, what resonated with Irish people and Latino people and Asian people, is that people feel different, and they feel like outsiders in a world that they want to be a part."

Again, the similarity between the beginning of *Afropunk* and what we are trying to do with the *Invaders* documentary is truly uncanny. The thing that struck me was Jocelyn and Morgan's concern for people, no matter their ethnicity. Jocelyn Cooper responded to questions about *Afropunk's* uniqueness,

> "Connecting people and promoting young artists, that is the heartbeat of AFROPUNK and our main business. The festivals themselves are just a celebration of that community. The festival is largely a big homecoming, and the artists who come and perform are part of that homecoming. If you feel the vibe behind the stage, as well as in front, it's about folks coming together to celebrate excellence and our culture. These are folks that think about the world differently and are outside the box individuals. In addition, we've got a big earned ticket component where people can earn a ticket by giving back to the community. We have a very low barrier ticket, where most festivals are charging as much as they can. Besides music, in New York, we have 100 local craft makers and young entrepreneurs we support. There's a huge visual art component. We do food as well. This year we'll have a lifestyle sports component, so skates are coming back to AFROPUNK."

Cooper's point about giving back by providing opportunities for fans to participate in and take ownership of a process built around them, as a community, is truly great. It is the kind of connectivity I hope to establish with *"The 400th"* narrative. I hope to connect with non-profits like Chance, the Rapper's *New Chance Arts & Literature Fund*. I plan to donate copies of *"The 400th"* to students in under-served communities. *"The 400th"* earned a ticket, and low ticket barrier will be a donation of 10% per book of *"The 400th"* for student causes in under-served community schools. Morgan followed with some personal reflections,

> "The way that I look at the world from where I grew up influences what we do and how we book bands. I'm an immigrant, and I grew up in London in a somewhat mixed environment. So I'm kind of free from a lot of the restrictions (learned helplessness) put upon people that were born here (in America) since I didn't grow up here (no learned helplessness). The way that we put music together I think, is a little different. Our approach to the people that we promote to is most certainly different. And when you put all of the elements together, it's not that it's completely and utterly novel, it's just a different approach within the same space".

Jocelyn offered her thoughts on the best part of being involved in Afropunk. "If I look at the broad scope of my career, what has always been frustrating for me at times is having, many years ago, to go through gatekeepers. To have folks who may not get a songwriter or a record or an artist, having to either try to convince them or getting rejected because it wasn't an appeal to their taste. What I am most proud of is the platform itself. It has taken those walls down and it's really just straight community. That is amazing for me. And, so many kids are interested in just authentically being themselves and they see Afropunk as a home and they identify with Afropunk in that way. That makes me really proud."

Cooper's thoughts, especially about gatekeepers, truly hit the bullseye with me, especially in the civil rights, social change and social justice communities. After civil rights, black Americans thought with the death of segregation, they would have access to better lives, but instead, America has become a nation of

The 400th: From Slavery to Hip Hop

gatekeepers. My gatekeeper example exemplifies today, although it comes from the past. It comes from my conversation with Dr. Martin Luther King, Jr. at the Lorraine Motel in Memphis, during his last hours. Dr. King told Cab and me about his struggles trying to get civil rights leaders to stop opposing black power activists joining the **Poor People's Campaign** coalition. He said,

"They felt they had gotten on the inside and had to keep black power activists out to protect what they believed they had gained." Dr. King went on, *"The point of all their complaining and opposition was the huge turnout you—the Invaders—produced. Civil rights leaders wanted that credit to make white people feel they were still in control."* He said he told civil rights leaders *"I embrace the Invaders because of the work they put in turning people out. I do not see this level of work from you. I was expecting this from you, but you are fighting the Invaders over prestige and position."* He said further, *"Rather than working to keep black power activists out; you need to go to work yourselves to maintain your place, and stop trying to bar the door, like gatekeepers."*

Refusing to support the **"Poor People's Campaign,"** they were helping white people keep poor black people locked on the bottom in poverty. Taking control of the liberation effort, after Dr. King's assassination, civil rights leaders began the gatekeeping tradition in earnest. The job of middlemen is keeping new and prospective opportunity seekers locked out; they decide who gets access. The only difference now is in the skin color of those keeping black people out. Morgan answered a question of legacy this way reflecting on his transition.

"When I first came to the U.S. from London, I came to be in a bigger space within the black music world. It was really stifling and small and provincial in the UK, and I came here, and it's sort of bigger and better. Really, what I came to were bigger boxes of the same thing. But what I didn't understand back then was why space for people of color is so important for them and growth and their perception of one another. We've never had a fight or an arrest at the festival, and that's an exceptionally unique atmosphere. That probably doesn't happen at any other festival in the county, and it probably doesn't happen at a lot of festivals around the world. The relevance of that, for me, is really about the perception of self and perception of one another. If we can actually get together and celebrate and still feel this unique sense of freedom, I think that reflects the way we interact within our community directly and outside of our community. Feeling good about oneself is really, really important, as you interact with other people. And coming from the UK, the idea of "historically black colleges" or "black music departments" or even a BET, seemed ludicrous. The whole idea of growing up in a mixed social environment was really, really important. I don't necessarily believe that in the same way as I once did. If I could leave something behind it would be a sense of community built and really inspiring young people to live beyond the narrow perceptions that were once perceived around them or thrust upon them."

Again, I agree wholeheartedly with Mathew's observation for the need for space, coupled with "black on black" aggression can be really problematic. And for *Afropunk* to have created a space that reduces the potential to zero is incredibly amazing. I could really identify with Morgan and Cooper's statements in response to a question about "doing something that one has never done before and their top three tips.

"Have absolute conviction in what you're doing in the face of complete and utter failure. Particularly if you want to create something new, stay away from people that did something before. I didn't start engaging folks until we were 12 or 13 years in on our purpose because I really didn't want anybody else's opinion. I wanted to try something, completely and utterly committed to it, and we went through extreme downs but persisted. If it makes sense to you, I think it can make sense to others. And spend the time. It takes a long while, depending on how big your dream is. It takes a very, very long time. Not everybody is meant to be successful from a financial standpoint. I would say perseverance, conviction, and the belief that you're doing something that can change the world."

Jocelyn added while championing Morgan's every word,

"Just do it. Find something that you're really passionate about, stay focused and work hard. I've been lucky enough in my life to find a profession that I love and life for me has been a roller coaster. When you're on that roller coaster ride when you're passionate about something, you hold on really tight and you keep going. You keep moving forward."

According to its website, *"Afropunk has become a radical act of self-care—a realized demand of safe spaces for people of color. In its 15 years of existence, Afropunk has created an environment that can only be described as an ethereal, momentary hideaway for black people from all corners and crevices of the Diaspora—and this year was no different. The festival explicitly invites folks to come and be who they are, wear whatever they wear, and dance how they dance. It was a blank space to freak out in—and freak out they did."*
"The musicians at Afropunk were there not just to sing and rap but to celebrate and give voice to communities of difference. That dual responsibility is exactly what separates AFROPUNK from other run-of-the-mill music festivals in America."

The following is a quote of a fan from *The New York Times;* it is not dated.

"It was our first time in New York. It was just such a beautiful experience to come to this festival that's for black people, by black people, about black people. I felt like I was falling in love every five seconds, just looking around. I have never been in this kind of beautiful space before, but it's such a surreal experience and I'm so glad that I can have it."

The 400th: From Slavery to Hip Hop

This quote is from *The Guardian* "*New heroes like Kaytranada, Sampha, Willow Smith and SZA sit alongside familiar names like Dizzee Rascal, Macy Gray, and Gary Clark Jr. in a lineup that challenges the idea of what "black music" was in 2017. With art installations and clothing markets, Afropunk offers a wholly novel and worthwhile perspective on the cultural role of a festival.*"

Hip Hop Gives Voice to the World

Some readers may wonder why I'm providing such detail on individuals that are obviously rich and do not need *"The 400"* to make them feel important. My desire is to show real people, slavery's descendants, built hip hop, not some favored and privileged group or class. Although rich now, they were not rich when they began making decisions that placed them at the top of the hip hop culture, along with Mathew Morgan and Jocelyn Cooper.

Hip hop became a megaphone that gave *VOICE* to African Americans, while providing a way out of the valley of desperation and scarcity—poverty. It became their pathway to freedom, justice and equality, even with racism dominating America. The affluence of such black people does not mean they have no difficulties; it simply means they do not need a civil rights protest to give *VOICE* to their problems.

Hip hop grew out of those volatile and rebellious times when almost all slave descendants needed protests and demonstrations to gain recognition and access, if not relief from their misery, once they reached the 1960s. Hip hop became the expression of African people fighting colonialism, racism, segregation, and other forms of socio-economic oppression. The voiceless around the world were inspired by Dr. Martin Luther King, Jr., who set the edge and drove the demands of poor people.

Giving up his life, Dr. King refused to yield on his demands for the poor, which drew black power activists out in support of his challenge—**the Poor People's Campaign**. Those issues and demands during those times gave conscious lyrics to rappers and spoken word artists, as they picked up on and seized Dr. King's new technology for placing black people's demands before the world. The success of those that help build hip hop listed here means today young African Americans do not have to actually become gangsters to be gangsta rappers.

Other cultures in places like the Caribbean islands, Japan, Great Britain, Islands of the Indian Ocean, and Africa picked up hip hop's beat of freedom, they merged it with their struggle for human rights. Talking about hip hop's impact on the world, South Africa offers the closest reflection of what developed in the US. The once conscious rap black people laid down in the US showed that their expressions—style, music, concepts of social and equal justice—tweaked the consciences of people internationally. The impact of hip hop reflects desires people other places and they adopted its music and style, as their expression.

South African hip hop is called Kwaito. It's a reflection of post-apartheid South Africa. US hip hop gave the voiceless in South Africa a way to express their demands in political terms. Kwaito is a lifestyle encompassing many aspects of American hip hop, including language and fashion. It is a political and party-driven genre. Their music expresses political views, while having a good time.

The 400th: From Slavery to Hip Hop

Ruled by foreigners, South Africans were oppressed and hated people. Kwaito's main consumers are young South Africans under 21; they constitute half the population, and hip hop is sweeping their nation. Their dominance is a trend sweeping the developing world.

Researcher and writer Tseliso Monaheng, in *"Hip-hop in South Africa,"* described the development of hip hop in South Africa for *musicinafrica.net/magazine*. Presenting the South African hip hop music scene Tseliso shares many interesting points on hip hop. According to Monaheng, South African hip-hop began in the 1980s long before it entered mainstream. The late bassist *Sipho Gumede* (1984) dabbled in hip hop, dubbing himself *"The Boogie Man,"* rapping in isiZulu with *'Jika Jika.' "Go Away,"* was *Senyaka's* hits in the 1980s. He bridged the gap between 80s bubblegum/disco, hip-hop, and the kwaito genre. Rapper *Taps* released albums such as *"Let's Go"* (1990) and *"Young Hip And African"* in 1991.

Then *Natano Braché* of Cape Town rose to prominence in the clubs and on the radio, as DJ *Natdog* with the maxi-single *"B-boys"* (1990). Then *I.N.T.R.I.B.E*, a group from Johannesburg, released *"Bubblegum In My Afro"* (1992). Their name stood for *Intelligent Natives Teaching Revolutionary Intellectual Black Education*. A wink and nod at *Public Enemy*. But the *Jungle Brothers*, *POC,* and *Black Noise* dropped their music, carring a message of self-awareness.

Credited, as the forerunner of South African hip-hop, *Prophets Of The City (POC)* formed in Cape Town in the1980s released the first album, *"Our World,"* in 1990. Founding member *DJ Ready D* recalled those early years in the documentary *"FedeFokol: 25 Years of South African Hip Hop"*, *"I was your typical Cape Flats kid, running around and doing what Cape Flats boys do. I didn't really think I would assume the role of an activist within our communities through music."* Today they are credited as the first hip-hop crew in South Africa to record and release an album. Led by the inimitable voice of *Shaheen Ariefdeen* on raps, *POC* came to international attention in the 1990s, performing at Nelson Mandela's inauguration in 1994.

Black Noise, another hip-hop crew with *Emile XY*, from Cape Flats, carved their own hip-hop path. *Black Noise* signed with Tusk (a local subsidiary of Warner Elektra Atlantic) releasing their debut album *"Pumpin' Loose Da Juice!"* in the 1980s. Emile champions the annual *African Hip Hop Indaba*, which showcases elements of hip hop—breakdancing, graffiti, MCing, and DJing—over three days.

South Africa hip-hop was aided by *YFM*, the Gauteng-based regional radio station (1997). *The Sprite Rap Activity Jam*, an hour-long weekly segment co-hosted by *Kalawa Jazmee* co-founder, *DJ Oskido* and *Rudeboy Paul*, heralded another phase in hip-hop, gaining an attentive audience for rappers. Picking up from where Cape Flats pioneers *POC* and *Black Noise* left off, *Brasse Vannie Kaap (BVK)* was one of the leading hip-hop crews in the 1990s with albums like *"BVK"* (1997), *"Yskoud"* (2000), *"Super Power"* (2004) and *"Ysterbek "* (2006). Rapping in Afrikaans and Flats slang set the trend for South African rappers to shed the

American influences and rapping in local vernacular languages they forged a uniquely South African sound. *BVK's* brand of socially conscious hip-hop addressed issues from the downtrodden communities of the Cape Flats. They kept all elements of the hip-hop culture alive, performing with B-boys, a DJ, and a MC, their imagery is heavily steeped in graffiti culture. BVK's was the first rap crews to transcending the "bedroom," rappers used to record and release music, they independently produced. *Red Antz,* grassroots movements on the Eastern Cape and others, focused on community development and less on commercial success.

Across the rest of South Africa, hip-hop gained momentum in 2002, Adam Haupt, Associate Professor of Media Studies at the University of Cape Town, sums up this early period of South African hip-hop in his book, <u>Stealing Empire</u>: *"Like POC and Black Noise has always aligned with black consciousness thinking, hence the crew's consistent reference to black—as opposed to coloured—identity. This, in part, is what the term 'conscious' hip-hop indicates, but it also alludes to the idea of raising critical consciousness via hip-hop as a lifestyle, philosophy and/or art form. It is in this area that POC and Black Noise had been active."*

The Cape Flats and the greater Western Cape also have a burgeoning Afrikaans rap scene. Influenced by the brazenness of *BVK,* the philosophy of *POC,* and the image of *Black Noise,* artists such as *Jitsvinger, Cream,* and *Jaak* are breathing new life into Cape hip-hop. Also, using Afrikaans in their lyrics is one of the most recognizable musical exports of the past few years: *Die Antwoord,* a rap-rave outfit consisting of *Ninja* and *Yo-landi Vi$$er. Ninja* is the alter ego of *Watkin Tudor Jones Jr.,* who honed his skills with hip-hop acts *The Original Evergreen* in the 90s and *Max Normal* in the early 2000s before deciding to take a new direction. The annual South African Hip Hop Awards were launch 2012. *Khuli Chana* is currently the biggest rapper in the country. His album *"Lost In Time"* earned him three South African Music Awards in 2013, including the coveted Artist Of The Year Award. In 2014, Hip-hop in South Africa was in a healthy state and Johannesburg drives the music industry; although Cape Town is making real moves with fresh and exciting new hip-hop. The coming years should be interesting in terms of media, record companies and decentralizing the movement.

AFROPUNK JOBURG 2018

Commercially, some *Kwaito* artists have sold more than 100,000 albums, in an industry where 25,000 albums sells are considered a gold record, which is a lot of cheese in any country. *Kwaito* gives a generation that lacked access and socially excluded from popular media, *("South African Music after Apartheid: Kwaito, the 'Party Politic,' and the Appropriation of Gold as a Sign of Success,"*

Bringing South African hip hop into 2020, as it is lived, I looked at *AFROPUNK JOBURG 2018, just* before COVID-19 began it deadly ride across the world. This look will not allow you to feel the music, free your mind, and enjoy the incredible lineup loaded with groundbreaking icons and emerging talents, but you will know a little about where African hip-hoppers are in the mix and where hip hop is headed. *AFROPUNK's Battle of the Bands* is the first expression of mentorship, support, and encouragement in its creative community. It is very competitive, in that winning new artists get a shot at the big stage at *AFROPUNK* festivals and other events. But it's more than that. It's an opportunity to show people *"what you got,"* and recognized by your audience, as well as your peers, since they are the ones picking winners. Some victors sign record-label deals and become famous, at least for a while. Others play a couple of big shows and fade away.

Encompassing the breadth of *AFROPUNK*, as a genre, would require a book of its own, I've said before. So, what I offer here is like a quick glance backward, through the rearview mirror, at high speed, while trying to keep one's eyes on the road ahead. This snap shot reveals only a very little of what can be seen, as well as what really happens at an *Afropunk* gig. Maybe, next time you and I will catch a show, without COVID-19 in the audience.

A peek at the lineup, *AFROPUNK Joburg 2018* featured some incredible acts. One was *Kaytranada,* who is experiencing an explosive rise in popularity over the past couple of years. He offers some exciting live sets, with great stage productions, after coming up the hard road. He became a true disciple of hip hop, after immersing himself in R&B. Touring the globe with his exciting tracks and mixes, while enjoying millions of online hits.

Also, *Azagaia* is an influential rising star and hip-hop artist from Mozambique. He offers major political views, rapping about the realities of post-colonial Mozambique and the continent of Africa, as a whole. He is backed up by the *Os Cortadores de Lenha,* featuring some of the finest musicians in the country.

What's a great party without great food? *AFROPUNK Joburg's Bites & Beats Food Festival* is an event within an event. It combines tastes from around the world. The idea is to try something hot, try something cold, spicy, or sweet. Try it all, your palate will love you for it.

Then there's "Activism Row" at *AFROPUNK*, an interactive educational installation that gives a platform to grassroots and non-profit organizations that solve urgent community problems. Getting involved and making a difference is what the community is all about. Alicia Garza is an Oakland-based organizer, writer, public speaker, and freedom dreamer. She is the *Director of the National Domestic Workers Alliance,* which is the US' leading voice for gaining dignity and fairness for millions of domestic workers. She is the Principal of the *Black Futures Lab*. It is an initiative aimed at transforming black communities into constituencies that build power in cities and states.

Art is central to the *AFROPUNK* aesthetic, and every year, it creates original murals, cutting edge works of art and art activations. *Ashley Akunna*, a filmmaker, is the host and creator of *The Grapevine* a talk show. She says, *"Whether it's the Bill Cosby, Colin Kaepernick's Nike Ad or the diaspora wars between Africans and African Americans, The Grapevine's panel-style discussions are by and for black millennials."*

Offering a different type of art, *DJ Coco.em* is a multi-talented artist based in Nairobi, Kenya. As part of an all femme DeeJay movement *FEKE* (Femme Electronic Key) in Uganda with *DJ Rachel,* fights for freedom, in the highly competitive industry. *Coco* wants equality and representation for her African female DJ sister.

AFROPUNK's Spinthrift Market showcases and celebrates the best makers and creators of products by community artists in its cities. It gives festival-goers and the DIY-minded, an array of one-of-a-kind and bespoken items inspired by African art and textiles. Jewelry, natural beauty products, apparel, housewares, books, prints, and more are all available for the glorification and aesthetic of the individual.

An idea whose time has truly come is *AFROPUNK Global Initiative (AGI)*. It leverages local, international, and social media influence to spotlight diverse perspectives in the *Afropunk* community. With the many unique voices behind the movement, *AGI* works to replace the narrow definitions and stereotypes of people, popularized by global media outlets. *Thokozani Ndaba* is an example of *Afropunk's AGI*. The Founder and Executive Director of the *Ntethelelo Foundation* in Johannesburg, *Ndaba,* work with different institutions and organizations in the Southern African Region, nationally and internationally, to tackle human rights violations.

Hip Hop in the Developing World

Looking at a few places outside of South Africa, despite the lack of resources, hip hop is making considerable inroads in the developing world, where artists are making real impacts socially in the developing world. Limited funds have made hip hop artists very creative and resourceful. Using very basic tools, they are expressing hip hop culture, and art, as artists take their special community based socio-economic and political agendas to a larger world. Telling their stories, minority artists have taken center stage, as many first-generation children come of age. One example is rapper *Awkwafina*, an Asian-American, who raps about being Asian and female. She "raps" to express her experiences as a minority *("Meet Awkwafina*," Jean Trinh, 2013: The Daily Beast, Newsweek/Daily Beast).

Hip hop artists that become international hip hop stars come to places like the US or UK, hoping to get mainstream access. Maya Arulpragasm *(aka, M.I.A.)* is a Sri Lanka-born Tamil artist that managed to get out of the developing world, she says, *"I'm just trying to build some sort of bridge, to create a third place, somewhere in between the developed world and the developing world.*

"Maya" is the daughter of a Tamil activist-turned-revolutionary-guerrilla, her father, Arul Pragasam, was born in London and supported Tamil efforts to win independence from the majority Sinhalese population. Maya was six months old, when her family moved back to their native Sri Lanka. Her father became politically known as Arular and was a founding member of *The Eelam Revolutionary Organization of Students (EROS)*. "M.I.A."—"Missing in Acton"—for "Maya" references to both her London neighborhood (Acton) and her politically tumultuous youth.

Another artist using hip hop to bring positive messages to young Africans is *Emmanuel Jal* a South Sudanese-Canadian artist, actor, former child soldier, and political activist. His autobiography, "*War Child: A Child Soldier's Story,*" was published in 2009. Jal believes his positive hip hop lyrics and message is a healing balm for children, trying to survive the almost constant state of war in many Africans nations.

Jamaican hip hop is a product of American and Jamaican influences. It is defined both through dancehall and reggae music. Jamaican DJ Kool Herc brought the sound system, technology, and techniques of reggae music to New York, during the 1970s. Almost single-handedly, he began laying the foundation of hip hop back in the 1960s. Similar to other international hip hop centers, Jamaican hip hop artists rap in both Brooklyn and Jamaican accents. They lay claim to their own special brand of hip hop by hanging on to internal influences of anti-colonialism sentiments and Rastafarians belief that marijuana or "ganja" bring them closer to God.

Hartwig Vens argues that hip hop can be viewed as *"a global learning experience."* Author Jeff Chang claims that *"The essence of hip hop is the cipher, born in the Bronx, where competition and community feed each other."* He adds, *"Thousands of organizers from Cape Town to Paris use hip hop in their communities to address environmental justice, policing, prisons, media justice, as well as education."* Hip hop allows the underprivileged and the mistreated to package their message in a way it will be heard and understood by the world. This narrative and review has shown that cultural translations cross borders, where music may be from a foreign country, the message is something many people can relate and accept as something not "foreign" at all, *("Hip-hop speaks to the reality of Israel,"* Hartwig Vens, WorldPress. 2003.)

Jamaica is a similar case. However, despite hip hop music produced on the island lacking widespread local and international recognition, artists such as *Five Steez* have defied the odds by impressing online hip hop taste-makers and even reggae critics. Hip hop, even when it's transplanted to other countries, retains its *"vital progressive agenda that challenges the status quo."*

Hip hop has played a small but distinct role as the musical face of revolution in the Arab Spring. I say it is very difficult to deal seriously with music while dodging bullets and bombs. Although the Arab Spring does not capture world attention as it once did, young activists continue fighting for *VOICE* in their culture, and I say "right on." For instance, Ibn Thabit, posing as an anonymous Libyan musician, there by setting the edge with hip hop, dropping anti-government songs, like bombs on his countrymen, supporting and fueling their rebellion. For young activists, the Arab Spring has turned into revolution's winter. (*"Libyan Rap Fuels Rebellion,"* Nadia Lane, (2011): CNN iReport. Cable News Network).

A slave's life amounted to a desperate voyage in treacherous tempest-tossed waters, chained and locked in the hold of a leaky ship. That's how I began this narrative, and even if a ship did not sink, slaves drown as water poured in upon them. Survivors had only unending servitude awaiting them and their descendants, as a life's endeavor. Perpetual bondage was enslaved Africans' only fate, after beginning that desperate odyssey some 400 years ago. Walking off plantations all over the South, approximately 58 years after the end of the **Trans-Atlantic Slave Trade (1807)**, former enslaved Africans were no longer slaves, but their penniless emancipation and *learned helplessness* made their survival a very tenuous, even doubtful proposition.

Slavery's descendants, over the last 157 years, faced a society without mercy and closed to them. White people kept black Americans locked on the bottom of society, as *cheap labor.* They used desperation, scarcity, convict leasing, sharecropping, **"Dark Age"** *angry white men mob madness*, segregation, and white supremacy to lock descendants of American slavery in second class status and poverty. Dorothy M. Smith's thesis and analysis **_Recession and Unemployment: A Retrospective Analysis of the Economic Welfare Loss_** established that government polices prevent slavery's descendants from changing their status and escaping the grave of poverty.

Douglas A. Blackmon's eye-popping book **_Slavery by Another Name: The Re-Enslavement of Black Americans from Civil War to World War II_** showed how the US government took on the role of protecting white culprits from their black victims. Blackmon picked up Smith's challenge, presenting the technology and chronology of how Southern governments re-enslaved black Americans, while imprisoning millions of African Americans on farms, in factories, mills and mines in the South for another 90 years after emancipation. He presented the what and how America's governments—federal, state and local—created the circumstances and conditions that continued the longest-running instance of genocide in the history of humankind, that did not end even with the advent of the cotton-picking machine and the death of sharecropping in the late 1960s.

Paul Robeson and William Patterson researched, published and presented the suffering and degradation of descendants of enslaved Africans to the United Nations—**We Charge Genocide**—petitioning it for a hearing of their grievances against America. However, the UN refused to grant a hearing, turning blind eyes and deaf ears to their pleas. The UN, while granting other exploited and oppressed people hearings, at the same time, no nation stood with African Americans against the United States' genocide. Black people in America stood alone in the world without defenders. Not one African Nation stood with us.

The US government threatened to withdraw and cut off funds going to the UN, if any nation acknowledged **_"We Charge Genocide"_** in anyway. America's genocide continues today, as a result of the UN's refusal to stand by its own definition of genocide: *"acts committed with intent to destroy, in whole or in part, a national, ethnic, racial or religious group, as such" including the killing of its members, causing serious bodily or mental harm to members of the group!!!*

Surviving those times, former enslaved Africans continued enduring to survive. Still, out of their denial, degradation, and exploitation in the US, slavery's descendants continued developing technologies base on their **Blues** culture through entertainment, which advanced their prosperity. Their efforts brought their enterprise to its highest level of socioeconomic and political development in the 21st Century as hip hop.

Hip hop has allowed descendants of American slavery to create a international culture. Having survived the physical trappings of chattel ownership, even though they continued struggling with the psychological impact of *"learn helplessness,"* African Americans today, for the most part, as reflected by the "BLACK LIVES MATTER" movement, are throwing off the ignorance that entrapped them, walking off plantations, penniless wretches 157 years ago. Not only have they survived the horrors of life, as descendants of American slavery, they are thriving, as the leaders of the world's new and dominate culture—HIP HOP. **_"The 400th"_** has shown this new revolution in international culture today is only beginning.

Previous discussions on hip hop explained how it developed. Those discussions presented some of the major players who led this "cultural revolution." It is true, a few bullets were fired, as far as revolutions go, but along the way, black music—**Blues**—became the technological weaponry black artists used to battle for space and prominence in America's economy. Hip hop has become an agent of social change and social justice the world over for descendants of slavery and other people of color, fighting oppression and exploitation.

Reading history books about the people who invented it, hip hop's creators are a side note, if mentioned at all, as white people claimed and commandeered everything slavery's descendants created, including hip hop, as part of their historical production. Beale Street is a classic example!!!

White historians disregarded the accomplishments of slavery's descendants, leaving them with only a "word of mouth culture" to attest to their presence and existence, as a testament to their life story. American history does not recognition black people created American entertainment—the "yellow brick road," of black American success.

Rising out of their penniless emancipation, black people rode entertainment like an HOV or express lane, transporting thousands to where they reap tremendous economic and cultural benefits, as successful mega-stars and entrepreneurs in today's hip hop culture. For me, this is why white people, in general and the media specifically, continue to malign the hip hop genre. They claim hip hop is only a refuge for criminals, who pervade drug use, gratuitous sex, senseless violence and misogyny. Their whole mantra presents hip hop as unworthy of acclaim. This narrative dispels such nonsense, presented hip hop's origin, development and movers and shakers.

The following discussion provides background for the statements made here about hip hop and those who built it from the ground up. The world has embraced what African Americans created, while others laid claim to its creation, but this time around because of hip hop's uniqueness and technological developments enslaved Africans claim hip hop in their name, without legitimate opposition.

Hip hoppers created technologies, as they stood against prevailing opinions, and brought about changes white Americans thought had no value or were impossible. Black artists struggle for relevance, as the hip hop genre fought for access and space in the entertainment marketplace, during 1970s and 1980s. Simultaneously, the white controlled media and music industry tried to undercut it; then to kill it.

The following list, which again is not, by any means, exhaustive, identifies just a few of those whose, through their careers surveyed and laid the foundation for, what I like to call, *"the yellow brick road of entertainment,"* that hip-hoppers have ridden to stardom. These African Americans were the first wave of devil-may-care swashbuckling lone riders that broke down barrier, ending Minstrelsy's "black face," and economy exclusion. The next wave, though "black face" was no longer a physical, but psychological barrier—attitudes—drew the color line that replaced "black face." Whites' Racial attitudes supporting segregation were stronger, even when sign came down, the walls remained in white people's heads, hanging on and lives in their minds. These attitudes still controlled black entertainers' access and progress well into the 1980s, for some even today. The most telltale sign of how those racist attitudes still nestle in white people's mind is their acceptance of murders of black men and women by police with impunity.

The idea here is to show hip hop is built on a solid foundation that has a clear lineage or pedigree. This list in no way represents all those who did the heavy lifting and grunt work, building the foundation upon which hip hop rest. I begin with icons, that were not buds on the rose before the first blossom on the bush of hip hop ever flowered and before the first word of rap ever passed H. "Rap" Brown's lips. I begin with someone no longer with us. She exemplifies many performers during her time, Rose McClendon (8-27-1884/7-12-1936).

Rose was among those who began the upward swing of black entertainment from the days of "blackface." Rose was a survivor of the foundation CP- CP-USA helped black artist eluded Minstrelsy by bringing them into CP-USA's to help create the foundation of Black Arts—*The Harlem Renaissance*. McClendon was a leading African American Broadway actress of the 1920s. She founded the

Negro People's Theatre in Harlem. McClendon also guided the creation of the *Federal Theatre Project* for African American theatre units nationwide, while co-directing the *New York Negro Theater Unit*.

Rose McClendon was born Rosalie Virginia Scott in Greenville, South Carolina. Her family became runners, joining the *"Great Migration,"* as my family. They relocated to New York City, while Rose was still a child. Rose married Dr. Henry Pruden McClendon. She began acting in church plays and won a scholarship to the American Academy of Dramatic Arts, where she became a professional actress in the 1920s.

McClendon's first notable role came in *Deep River*, a "native opera with jazz" by Karl Marlantes in 1926. Beyond acting, she also directed several plays at the *Harlem Experimental Theatre*. She appeared in the 1927 Pulitzer Prize-winning play *"In Abraham's Bosom"* by Paul Green. Rose appeared in another Paul Green play on Broadway, *"The House of Connelly,"* in 1931, which was the first production by the *Group Theatre*, directed by Lee Strasberg. The CP-USA was the sole supporter of Black Arts in America, during this time. Bankrolled by communist, "Black American Arts" began developing a systematic approach to cultural theater. Help provided by CP-USA gave African Americans an entry-level to American theatrics and was a foot-in-the-door for actors like McClendon *("Rose McClendon Scrapbooks,"* Manuscripts, Archives and Rare Books Division, The New York Public Library).

A very talented performer, Rose aspired, to direct, as well as act. Partnering with Dick Campbell in 1935, they co-founded the *Negro People's Theatre in Harlem*, and more than 4,000 people attended its first production. After an adaptation of Clifford Odets' *Waiting for Lefty*, the group was organized permanently in June 1935, *("As To a New Negro Stage,"* Rose McClendon, 1935; The New York Times).

The Negro People's Theatre directly inspired the *Negro Theatre Unit of the Federal Theatre Project,* created under McClendon's supervision in 1935. Through her determination and guidance, she created units in Seattle, Hartford, Philadelphia, Newark, Los Angeles, Boston, Raleigh, Birmingham, San Francisco, and Chicago, as well as New York. All these cities had very active CP-USA operations, which is why Memphis is not on this list. Rose served as liaison to numerous organizations and individuals who became involved in her theater projects, including Harry Edward, Carlton Moss, and Edna Thomas. McClendon believed success for the theater project depended on an experienced director and advised national director Hallie Flanagan to bring in John Houseman to co-direct the unit.

McClendon was a contemporary of Paul Robeson, Ethel Barrymore, Lynn Fontanne, and Langston Hughes. Hughes created a character for Rose in his 1935 play, *Mulatto*. However, McClendon left the cast of *Mulatto in December 1935*. She became critically ill with pleurisy *(Pleurisy results from inflammation of pleura tissue, which may result from infection, injury, autoimmune disorders, or cancer.) ("Run-Through: A*

Memoir," John Houseman, 1972; New York: Simon & Schuster). Countee Cullen working with producer John Houseman, composer Virgil Thomson and production designer Chick Austin, adaptation of Euripides' tragedy *Medea* as a showcase for McClendon. Although the sets and costumes had been ready for months, by the end of 1934, McClendon had fallen ill again, and the project never materialized.

Slated to portray Lady Macbeth in Orson Welles' *Federal Theatre Project* production of *Macbeth* (1936), McClendon's illness continued. Instead, Edna Thomas played the role. Rose McClendon's condition worsened, developing into pneumonia. She passed away at her home on July 12, 1936. (*"Rose McClendon, 51, Negro Actress, Dies,"* 1936; The New York Times).

Next, this review looks at another dearly departed, the man that took black music from night clubs to television. Although many stars rose during and after his stellar career, none eclipsed his brilliance and cosmopolitan charm. Born Nathaniel Adam Coles (3-17-1919/2-15-1965) in Montgomery, Alabama, people the world over came to love him as Nat "King" Cole. Best known for his soft, smooth, melodious baritone voice, on which crystalline articulated lyrics flowed, Nat "King" Cole, was the first African American performer to host a variety television show.

Nat "King" Cole was the first black man, many white families, welcomed into their living rooms via his television show. Throughout the late 1940s into the 1960s, Cole continued to record hits, in numbers that reached into the millions sold around the world. He maintained his international popularity, even after his death in 1965 (*"The Pittsburgh Courier Newspaper"* Pittsburgh, Pennsylvania on February 13, 1965).

Born in the South, where white supremacy was totally dominant, but even in the North segregation controlled black people's lives. Few people living today have memories, hence so it is difficult imagining the overall appeal he garnered, being a black man. Although black entertainers were losing "blackface" on stage by the late 1930s, everywhere else, they entered through the back door. Negros, activists, or actors did not confront white people about anything, especially regarding entertainment, before Nat began performing (1934).

Escaping the South, like other runners, Nathaniel's family moved to Chicago, Illinois, where his father, Edward Coles, became a Baptist minister. Nat was only four when he began his music career, as an organ man. His mother, Perlina, a church organist, taught him to play the organ. His first performance, at age four, was, *"Yes! We Have No Bananas".* In his early teens, Cole was given formal classical piano training, along with jazz and gospel. He eventually abandoned classical music for his first passion—jazz. Earl Hines, a leader of modern jazz (Universally known as Earl "Fatha" Hines, was a great American jazz pianist and bandleader. He was one of the most influential figures in the development of jazz piano. According to major sources, he is "one of a small number of pianists whose playing shaped the history of jazz") and was one of Cole's biggest inspirations.

When Nat was fifteen, his brother Eddie, a bassist, came home from touring with Noble Sissle. Nat left high school to pursue a career in music; the school's loss was the music world's gain. He joined Eddie sextet called *Eddie Cole's Swingsters*, and they began recording for Decca Records in 1936. During this period, the trio, also recorded radio transcriptions for Capitol Records. They performed on radio programs like *Swing Soiree*, *Old Gold*, *The Chesterfield Supper Club*, *Kraft Music Hall*, and *The Orson Welles Almanac*. They also performed in a revival of the musical *Shuffle Along*, and Nat Cole toured with that musical ("Capitol Transcriptions ad," 1948, (PDF), Broadcasting).

After *Shuffle Along*, Cole married Nadine Robinson (1937), when the show ended in Los Angeles, they settled there. Nat played piano in clubs around LA, where one owner wanted a band, and asked Nat to form one. Nat hired bassist Wesley Prince and guitarist Oscar Moore, to create a group called the *King Cole Swingsters*, after the nursery rhyme, *"Old King Cole was a merry old soul."* They changed their name to the *"King Cole Trio"* and began making radio transcriptions and recording for small labels.

The King Cole Trio toured extensively and finally hit the charts in 1943 with *"That Ain't Right,"* which Cole wrote. The 1944 hit, *"Straighten Up and Fly Right,"* was inspired by one of his father's sermons. Rising in fame, pop hits, like *"The Christmas Song,"* a holiday classic, and the ballad *"(I Love You) For Sentimental Reasons,"* put the trio on top.

Nat "King" Cole had many first, appearing in the first Jazz at the Philharmonic concerts (1944). The trio broadcast King Cole Trio Time, a fifteen-minute radio program (1946). It was the first radio program to be presented by a black musician. Cole began recording and performing pop-oriented material, and was often accompanied by a string orchestra. He cemented his stature as a popular star, during this period, with hits such as *"All for You"* (1943), *"(Get Your Kicks on) Route 66"*, *"There! I've Said It Again"* (1947), *"Nature Boy"* (1948), *"Frosty The Snowman,"* *"Mona Lisa"* (No. 1 song of 1950), *"Orange Colored Sky"* (1950), and *"Too Young"* (No. 1 song of 1951). Cole recorded *"The Christmas Song"* four times — on June 14, 1946, with the Nat King Cole Trio; on August 19, 1946, with an added string section; on August 24, 1953; and in 1961 for the double album The Nat King Cole Story.

Cole married singer Maria Hawkins Ellington in 1948. They had five children Natalie, Carole, Nat Kelly, and twin daughters, Casey and Timolin. By the 1950s, Nat King Cole was working with top talents, including Louis Armstrong and Ella Fitzgerald. Cole's presence on the record charts dwindled in the late 1950s. But, Nat King Cole was a big innovator, so he came up with another first to keep his magic alive.

The 400th: From Slavery to Hip Hop

"The Nat 'King' Cole Show" debuted on NBC on November 5, 1956. The variety show was another first for Cole and black people in general. The show started as a fifteen-minute spot but was increased to a half-hour in July 1957. Rheingold Beer was a regional sponsor, but NBC never found a national sponsor for the extended time. I believe, in places like Memphis, people never got an episode; we certainly never did. Jim Crow's reign in entertainment was aided by changing his look every time he showed up, so black entertainers never knew, whether whites were there to helped or hurt them.

NBC experienced financial problems when it did not get a national sponsor, but blamed Nat for not extending the time. Still, there was more to it than just money because, despite efforts by NBC, Harry Belafonte, Tony Bennett, Ella Fitzgerald, Eartha Kitt, Frankie Laine, Peggy Lee, and Mel Tormé, a sponsor still could not be found. If all of these individuals were truly helping, the show should have survived, one would think. My case in point is Melvin Van Peebles. When he was underwater with **"Sweet Sweetback's Badasssss Song,"** Bill Cosby showed up as himself, with $50 grand, which was real help, not lip service.

Cole decided to end the program. The last episode aired on December 17, 1957. Commenting on the lack of sponsorship, Cole said, *"Madison Avenue is afraid of the dark."* Black people had to speak in veiled tones and soft words. NBC said it was unable to secure a national sponsor for the show. NBC claimed further, it was afraid that Nat's show would be boycotted by disgruntled Southerners, which meant more to NBC than a successful Nat "King" Cole. The Nat "King" Cole facade foreshadowed Colin Kaepernick first kneel in 2016, and the NFL is still scared of not pleasing whites, whether in the dark or light.

Nat's show may have been brief, in terms of longevity, yet its lasting impact can be seen in music videos today. It is an important event in modern American history, but even more for African Americans advancement specifically. Cole was not only the highest-paid black person in America at the time, but he was also one of the most successful entertainers in the world. Another reason to speculate, regarding why a sponsor for Nat "King" Cole's show was such a problem for NBC, which is why I say the outcome was about more than the "color of money."

After a change in musical tastes, as entertainment entered the late 1950s, Cole's ballads held little appealed too young listeners. Similar to Dean Martin, Frank Sinatra, and Tony Bennett, Nat found the pop chart had been taken over by youth-oriented acts. However, smarter than he looked, like the scarecrow in **"The WIZ,"** Cole went to Havana, Cuba' and recorded *"Cole Español"* in 1958. Cole sang the entire album in Spanish. It was so popular in Latin America and the US he followed with two more Spanish-language albums: *"A Mis Amigos"* (1959) and *"More Cole Español"* (1962). Closing out the 1950s, Nat King Cole won a Grammy Award for Best Performance By a "Top 40" Artist for *"Midnight Flyer"* in 1959.

Nat "King" Cole's successful Latin albums made his brief hiatus in the late 1950s early 1960s, just a long-deserved vacation, from which he came roaring back in 1962 with *"Rambin' Rose."* The country-influenced hit reached number two on the Billboard pop charts. Modest successes, compared to his earlier career of number ones. Cole delivered two ballads—*"I Don't Want to Hurt Anymore"* and *"I Don't Want to See Tomorrow"*—in his signature smooth style. Cole performed in many films, sitcoms, and television shows. In the movie *"St. Louis Blues"* (1958) Cole played W. C. Handy, and starred in *"China Gate," "The Nat King Cole Story,"* and *"The Blue Gardenia"* (1953).

Nevertheless, Cole believed he still had a few good rolls left and "rattled the bones" a couple more times, recording several hit singles during the 1960s. Cole won the new music generation over with the light-hearted tune *"Those Lazy-Hazy-Crazy Days of Summer," "Let There Be Love"* with George Shearing in 1961, *"Dear Lonely Hearts"* and *"That Sunday, That Summer."* He made his last appearances on the pop charts in his lifetime in 1964, giving fans *"Send for Me,"* which peaked, at number 6, on the pop chart, which was not too shabby for anyone, except Cole.

Nat "King" Cole, similar to the vast majority of descendants of American slavery, struggled to find his place in a segregated America. "Colored" people in entertainment, as I said earlier, did not openly oppose Minstrelsy's "blackface" demands on black entertainers. When the smut came off, most Negros made accommodation with segregation, like Civil Rights leaders during the late 1960s. Their mindset was to "go along to get along." It wasn't until Sammy Davis, Jr., like James Brown, cut off their processed hair after Dr. Martin Luther King's assassination in1968, did big time entertainers begin giving up *"conks."*

However, unlike most, Nat King Cole encountered real and deadly racism firsthand, specifically while touring in the South. In 1956, Cole was attacked by white supremacists, during a mixed-race performance in Alabama. He was rebuked by Negro leaders, for what they considered "his less-than-supportive comments for racial integration," he made after the attack. Cole took the stance that he was *"an entertainer, not an activist."*

My statement during the previous discussion of "Jim Crow" residing in Hollywood was a reflection of incidents like the one Nat "King" Cole experienced when he purchased a house in the all-white Hancock Park neighborhood of Los Angeles in August 1948. I remember seeing pictures of his home in Ebony Magazine in the early 1950s. Members of the property-owners association told Cole they *"did not want any undesirables moving into the neighborhood."* Cole responded, *"Neither do I. And if I see anybody undesirable coming in here, I'll be the first to complain."* The Los Angeles Ku Klux Klan (1950s) promptly burning a cross on Cole front lawn.

Fast forward a couple years to 1956, while Nat "King" Cole performed in Birmingham, Alabama, as part of the Ted Heath Band, the Klan circulated photographs of Nat "King" Cole with white female fans draped all over him. If that was not enough, the picture had an incendiary boldface caption that read

The 400th: From Slavery to Hip Hop

"COLE and HIS WHITE WOMEN" and *"COLE and YOUR DAUGHTER."* While singing the song *"Little Girl,"* three white men, belonging to the North Alabama White Citizens Council, ran down the aisles and mounted the stage. Their invasion interrupted Cole's performance! An apparent attempt to kidnap Cole, but local law enforcement ended the mêlée, but not before Cole was thrown to the floor, as they dragged him from his piano bench. Cole received a severe back injury.

Even though, a native of Alabama, Cole was astonished, after Klan attacked him. He said, *"I can't understand it ... I have not taken part in any protests. Nor have I joined an organization fighting segregation. Why should they attack me?"* Cole, as most blacks in Americans in 1948, had accepted the customs and traditions of segregation. Cole's comments were reported in the press, which Negro civil rights leaders felt, he wanted to pretend the incident never happened. Cole said he *"could not change the situation in a day,"* which could have meant he was already under contract for such shows. With an international reputation, he probably, I would say was concerned that just walking away from contracts would have resulted in lawsuits. A rich black man, and no fair courts in America, whites would have loved to pluck Nat like a Christmas turkey.

Nat had contributed money to the Montgomery Bus Boycott and had himself, sued northern hotels that had hired him but refused to serve him. The upshot of it all was a hullaballoo with civil rights leaders that attacked Cole with hyperbole. Thurgood Marshall, the chief legal counsel of the NAACP, attacked Cole, calling him an Uncle Tom that should perform with a banjo.

Roy Wilkins, executive secretary of the NAACP, sent a telegram, *"You have not been a crusader or engaged in an effort to change the customs or laws of the South. That responsibility, newspapers quote you as saying, you leave to the other guys. That attack upon you clearly indicates that organized bigotry makes no distinction between those who do not actively challenge racial discrimination and those who do. This is a fight which none of us can escape. We invite you to join us in a crusade against racism".*

My hyperbole remark was to point the finger at the NAACP because, during this same time, they were supporting the US government cover up strategy against **_We Charge Genocide._** Members of the NAACP, Walter White, and Ralph Bunche, particularly, were sent to Europe to help speak against charges contained in **_We Charge Genocide,_** which helped hide American genocide against all black people.

The Chicago Defender said Cole's performances for all-white audiences were an insult to his race. The New York Amsterdam News said that *"thousands of Harlem blacks who have worshiped at the shrine of singer Nat King Cole turned their backs on him this week, as the noted crooner turned his back on the NAACP and said that he will continue to play to Jim Crow audiences."* A reporter for The American Negro wrote, *"To play Uncle Nat's discs would be supporting his 'traitor' ideas and narrow way of thinking,"* Deeply hurt by the criticism in the black press, Cole was chastened. He began emphasizing his opposition to racial segregation *"in any form,"* he joined other entertainers in boycotting segregated venues. He paid the $500 *"get on the good side of the NAACP"* fee and became a lifetime member in the Detroit branch. Until his death in 1965, Cole was an active and visible participant in the civil rights movement *("Did Success Spoil the United States," Warren Sussman, 1989, Lary (ed.) Recasting America, University of Chicago Press).*

It may seem I'm defending Nat, but that's not my purpose. I don't feel he needs defending any more than when historians offer statements like *"He was a man of his time,"* to explain why they still hold Woodrow Wilson, who an admittedly proud racist, in very high esteem. I say often, it is one thing to be a victim of one's times and circumstances, as black people trapped in poverty, but it is altogether different when someone like Wilson, spent his, life building a particular reputation and legacy of hate, while speaking and writing glowingly of the pain and anguish their racism caused others. I believe those are individuals who should be condemned universally by all humanity.

Cole sang *"That's All There Is to That"* at the 1956 Republican National Convention in support of President Dwight D. Eisenhower. He was also present at the Democratic National Convention in 1960 to support Senator John F. Kennedy for President. He was among the dozens of entertainers recruited by Frank Sinatra to perform at the Kennedy Inaugural gala in 1961. Cole consulted with President Kennedy and his successor, Lyndon B. Johnson, on civil rights. He also played an important role in planning the *March on Washington in 1963*.

In January 1964, Cole made one of his final television appearances on The Jack Benny Program. Benny introduced him as *"the best friend a song ever had."* He sang, *"When I Fall in Love." "Cat Ballou"* (1965) was his final film. He performed a duet with Stubby Kaye. The movie was released several months after he passed.

The magic of technology, one of the themes of this narrative, was demonstrated with great success by Nat "King" Cole's daughter Natalie. She used modern technology in a video that reunited father and daughter in a duet of the immortal *"Unforgettable."* In classic hip hop fashion, she *"flipped"* one of her father's greatest hits. Natalie introduced another generation of music lovers to her legendary father in 1991. The duet version rose to the top of the pop charts, almost forty years, after its original popularity, putting Nat "King" Cole on the charts one final time ("Nat King Cole," Terry Teachout, (1992), The American Scholar).

Comedy in America was a direct outgrowth of slaves entertaining master, because Minstrelsy grew out of that. Following its demise, black comedians adapted to the changing times. Most moved over to Vaudeville, as Minstrelsy slowly faded, they continued innovating, trying to *"make something out of nothing."* Many teamed up to develop duo comedy acts, if they stayed in show business. John Elroy Sanford was one of these fish out of water. He was born in Chicago (1922) and grew up to become the comedian and actor known as Redd Foxx.

The 400th: From Slavery to Hip Hop

Some may question the inclusion of such a raunchy and grungy character as Redd Foxx on such a prestigious list of notables, and that is their prerogative, but Redd Foxx help make telling jokes about far more than laughter.

Redd grew up in poverty, like me and many other blacks kids trapped in ghettos or on sharecropping plots, things only got worse, when his father abandoned the family. He left Redd, his mother, and brother to fin for themselves. Around age seven, John Elroy discovered his knack for telling jokes, while at the same time he never had much interest in school. According to the Los Angeles Times, he said, *"School meant nothing to me. Knowing that George Washington crossed the Delaware—how was that going to help me in a brick fight in St. Louis?"* Leaving home at the age of 13, young Sanford began performing with bands, and four years later, John Elroy was performing with his group called *the Bon Bons* in Chicago.

Adding an extra "d" to his nickname—Red, borrowing the trick from professional baseball player Jimmie Foxx, like magic, John Elroy became *"Redd Foxx."* Struggling to get by, Redd worked several jobs. He spent time in Harlem, where he met Malcolm X (then known as Malcolm Little). According to Redd's official website, Malcolm called him *"the funniest dishwasher on earth."* The pair became friends, sharing a ruddy complex coworkers in the restaurant started the joke, calling Malcolm "Detroit Red," and Foxx "Chicago Red," everyone else just laughed along.

Foxx and longtime friend Slappy White, (a comedian in his own right) joined forces and worked the *"Chitlin Circuit,"* (Originally the *"Chitlin Circuit"* was a string of black nightclubs, and juke joints first hooked up by Sunbeam Mitchell across the South, during the 1940s and 1950s. But, it grew to include spots up the East coast, across to Chicago and back down South through St. Louis). Creating his comedy routine, Redd did stand-up and became one of the best at it. Redd Foxx's comedy routines were considered too racy and raunchy for white audiences. However, laughing through it all, Redd Foxx built a fan base performing in African American clubs for years. He cultivated that fan base into an underground network by the 1950s. Bringing innovation to the Art of making people laugh, Redd hook up with a buddy, who worked for a recording studio, and they began "bootlegging" recording of his routines.

Redd and his friend parled their recordings from his shows into what became known as the *"party records"* genre. Redd's records were a big hit at house parties in the black community, during the 1950s and 1970s. But, "kids" had to leave the room; this was grown folks fun.

Over his career, Foxx sold more than 20 million copies of his comedy albums. Today, Redd's classic comedy records are available to all online; even kids can join the fun today. Other black comedians, like *"Pigmeat" Markham, Jackie "Moms" Mably, Niffity Russell, Dick Gregory, Slappy White, Dolomite*, and even very young comedians, like *Richard Pryor* and *Eddie Murphy* followed Redd Foxx's model and found success.

Redd became a successful stand-up comedian known for his willingness to tackle controversial topics such, as race and sex. He moved into what was a very risky business back then for blacks, TV comedy, on which white comedians had a lock. A trailblazer, pulling his assault on TV comedy off, Redd moved to Los Angles, where he pushed his way into television. Having come off the *"party records"* and *"Chitlin Circuit,"* venues, white producers thought white TV viewers would laugh themselves to death, watching Redd fall flat on his face. But no, Redd had other ideas. He made his first television appearance on the Today show in 1964. Redd continued innovating, becoming one of the first blacks to debut in a regular weekly sitcom series on NBC-TV. Today's hip-hoppers know him mostly as "Fred Sanford."

"*Sanford and Son*" hit the airwaves in 1972, and Redd Foxx did what Redd Foxx always did, left TV audiences rolling around on living room floors laughing. The show became a huge hit with black and white television audiences. Redd Foxx's crossover trick was using his real-life brother's first name, Fred. Setting up in Watts, El Segundo, South LA, California, Redd easily pulled off being a grumpy junk dealer. Demond Wilson played Sanford's son Lamont, and Redd made *"you big dummy"* an international rib. *Sanford and Son* became one of the first programs to feature an African American family, making it groundbreaking, like most things Redd Foxx did. According to the Los Angeles Times, Foxx said, *"The show is lighthearted, doesn't drive home a lesson, but it can open up peoples' minds enough for them to see how stupid every kind of prejudice can be."*

After five years, Foxx left NBC for ABC. He starred in *The Redd Foxx Comedy Hour*, but that show didn't last for long. Foxx spent his later years trying to cope with financial problems (Taxes are the way the federal government always attack successful black entertainers). Although they may have laughed at his joke, they didn't treat Redd tax problems like something to laugh about; he filed for bankruptcy in 1983.

Redd's career got a boost from his appearance in the 1989 film *Harlem Nights*. Eddie Murphy wrote, directed, and stars in this gangster style comedy movie, playing Quick, the protégé of the Harlem club owner Sugar Ray (Richard Pryor). Despite his TV career declined, Redd Foxx remained a popular live act, especially in Las Vegas.

Redd Foxx seemed to be on an upswing by the early 1990s. He landed a new sitcom called *The Royal Family* with Della Reese, which debuted in the fall of 1991. Foxx was working an episode of this series when he collapsed, during a rehearsal on October 11, 1991, and passed away from a heart attack. Foxx was 68 years old. Although Redd Foxx was one of the funniest comedians ever, he was a serious "lone rider." He opened doors for comedians, to truly be outrageous.

He made it possible for them to be scandalous, raunchy, and downright vulgar in some cases, yet make people laugh and pay to hear more. While best remembered for Fred Sanford, the real Redd Foxx (John Elroy) helped pave the way for many risqué comedians like Paul Mooney, George Carlin, and Lenny Bruce, pushing the boundaries of stand-up comedy.

Descendants of American slavery headed for *"The 400th"*, although they were unaware of its approach, getting there was not a one size fits all occasions or proposition, regarding survival strategies and individual pursuits undertaken. Entertainment was the major vehicle, which yielded the greatest economic reward for former slaves. It was also most reflective of African American's struggle to gain acceptance, thereby access to America's bounty. Looking inside entertainment, the motion picture industry reflected America's racism like a mirror.

Entertainment's social mirror, particularly movies, portrayed the mindset of white people's perception of blacks. Whether fantasy, myth, or stereotypes, they all played out on the silver screen, like burlesque. Movies, before black power and the demand for human rights by slave descendants in the 1960s, projected an image only whites had inside their heads of black people. Those stereotypes reflected, in terms of attitudes, what whites were willing, only grudgingly to concede regarding socioeconomic and political progress to black Americans.

Whites controlled everything that mattered in America's *"cheap labor"* economy for blacks, which determine their socioeconomic and political advancement. Whites projected, through movies, what whites consider progress for blacks. Playing out in African Americans real everyday lives, they were trapped in what mirrored a sick grade B sitcom farce. Whites grudgingly opening doors to African Americans, time, blacks bided their time, while having to laugh and play along, as though they were having a real party or get written out of the stripe altogether.

Waiting for changes that seemed would never come, although it was an individual undertaking, black entertainers were seen, as in all other endeavors, but more so in movies, like a group deal, by white people. The first major task for black performers coming out of the buffoonery of Minstrelsy and Vaudeville in the 1930s and 40s, was overcoming the general opposition the white mindset of black entertainers of bring not seriously prepared performers. That attitude was a hangover from Minstrelsy, which presented a very formidable challenge. Without seeming uppity or overly aggressive, black performers had to negotiate a minefield of hazards, countering and rejecting the *"blackface"* image that resided in white people's heads.

Simultaneously, they had to establish a definite and different persona, which they could not verbalize, but still be reflective of what blacks thought of themselves. White people verbalize is their racist demands on black people and revolt, especially when they for respect. Still, while carrying all that extra baggage, which white actors had no reason to consider, black actors had to fight self-effacing degradation, facing down the slave master's mindset that dominated Hollywood, as well as all America. Bearing that load, black actors had to appear dignified and culture in white people's eyes, while still exhibiting "grace and civility" in everything they did. Forever under the scrutinizing gaze of any and every white person, while doing this dance for life for any and every white person encountered, black entertainer and actors had to reflect calmness, deflecting the games white people played. Their agility avoiding such ambushes was a daily striving for not only entertainers but most blacks, whether preacher, teacher or domestic servants.

I believe there was not another performer, preacher, or teacher who mastered these skills and tasks, doing this dance of life with or without music, better than Sidney Poitier. Sidney, to all who observed him, seemed to be born in the lap of luxury and groomed to be Mr. Charley's man, but no. Sidney had to fight his way from the very outer reaches and backwashes of utter obscurity, without a model or mentor, but with the added complication of being born in the graveyard of poverty in the valley of dry bones in the island nation of the Bahamas, of all places.

Sidney began digging his way out of the graveyard of poverty on February 20, 1927. He was born to Evelyn (née Outten) and Reginald James Poitier, Bahamian farmers on Cat Island, which is about as far away from Hollywood one can get on this side of the world, unless one was born in Haiti. Sidney was the youngest son, in a brood of eight sons. His mother and father traveled to Miami to sell produce. While in Miami, like "Devin intervention," Sidney was born unexpectedly. Nevertheless, he grew up in the Bahamas, then a British Crown colony. However, because he was born in the US, Sidney automatically received American citizenship.

The Poitier family's history claimed that the Poitiers ancestors on his father's side were runners from Haiti, as runaway slaves. Maroons, runaway slaves, established communities throughout the Bahamas, including Cat Island *("Bio – Sidney Poitier,"* Archived from the original on 2014). Although the surname Poitier is French, there were no white Poitiers in the Bahamas. Slaves either were given or took the last name of whites or their owners at emancipation *("Sidney Poitier: Man, Actor, Icon,"* Aram Goudsouzian, 2004; Univ. of North Carolina Press).

Sidney, at age 15, was sent to Miami to live with a brother who had a large family. So, at 16, he moved on to New York City. Following the path of most immigrants, out of towners or low skilled blacks and fish out of water, which include Malcolm X and Redd Foxx, Sidney became a dishwasher. A waiter friend sat with him at night, teaching him to read from newspaper.

Lying about his age, Sidney enlisted in the US Army in 1943 during World War II. He only served briefly as a mental hospital orderly, but a quick study, Sidney learned to feign insanity and got an early discharge. Sidney was a great actor even then. After returning to his old job, Sidney was back to washing dishes. A fortuitous success at an audition landed Poitier a spot with *the American*

Negro Theater, which was supported by the CP-USA *("The Measure of a Man,"* Poitier Sidney, 2000; HarperCollins Publishers: New York).

Determined to refine his acting skills, while ridding himself of his heavy Bahamian accent, Sidney spent all his extra time and resources training to achieve theatrical success. Poitier gave the theater a second try and was given a leading role in the Broadway production *Lysistrata*. That success gained him an invitation to understudy for *Anna Lucasta*. By the end of 1949, he had to choose between leading roles on stage, or an opportunity offered by Darryl F. Zanuck, in the film *No Way Out* (1950). Sidney was a doctor, with a Caucasian bigot for a patient, played by Richard Widmark. Poitier received exceptional review and was projected the number one black actor.

His performance drew other leading roles; each role considerably more challenging, interesting, and prominent than those offered other African American actors. African American actor Canada Lee convinced Sidney to travel to South Africa with him for another very challenging role. He starred in the film version of *Cry, the Beloved Country* in 1951. However, *Blackboard Jungle*, casted as a member of an incorrigible high school class, many considered Poitier's breakout role (1955) *("Sidney Poitier Biography,"* 2015: at the Wayback Machine, AETN UK, The Biography Channel).

Sidney's next performance, for me, was one of his finest, especially for that particular time *The Defiant Ones'* (1958). Sidney was nominated for an Academy Award, becoming the first male Bahamian actor to receive such competitive recognition. He was also the first to win the Best Actor Academy Award for *"Lilies of the Field"* in 1963, five years later. Although tremendously successful, the Oscar honor brought Sidney trouble, according to his assessment, *"The industry was congratulating itself for having me as a token, and it inhibited me from demanding more substantive considerations thereafter."* ("Pictures at a Revolution: Five Films and the Birth of a New Hollywood," Mark Harris, 2008; Penguin Press).

Again, I say, white actors never had to deal with such extra baggage, as race appropriate roles and perceptions; which never enter their mines. However, as a result of such consideration, Poitier worked relatively little over the following year. Carrying that fully loaded backpack—the only major actor of African descent to win "Best Actor," among other considerations, he did typecast roles as—a soft-spoken appeaser (Sidney's characterization) became his only option.

An excellent example is *The Slender Thread* (1965). Though very suspenseful and dramatically challenging, and another splendid performance, Poitier played opposite Anne Bancroft, a white woman, which made the role too hot and psychologically challenging for critics, as well as white audiences. Statements, like *"I'm not sure movie goers are ready for those kind of scenes."* Characterizing critics assessments, if not audiences, critics were cold to the hot intimate and sexual context, as well as racial overtones implied from inside critics heads. The warm scenes had critics hot under the collier, seeing a black man connected, via telephone, to a white woman, with such emotions, left film critics cold to Poitier's performance. They may have been more receptive had the paring resembled *The Defiant Ones*.

The significance of Sidney's theatrical achievements bolstered and brought everything together for him in 1967, when he starred in three successful films. These 3 roles, though treading on racial stereotypes, for white people, they cemented Sidney's stature and status, as a leading man. They dealt with issues of race and race relations, in somewhat a sterile manner, but that was what white movie critics wanted, something where everything emotional happens in their heads not on the screen, but the implications keep white people on the edge of their seats. *To Sir, with Love; In the Heat of the Night;* and *Guess Who's Coming to Dinner,* fit the way white people think about race, and for them, were films that made Poitier the top box-office star of that era. In 1999, the American Film Institute named Poitier among the Greatest Male Stars of classic Hollywood cinema, (*"Top Ten MoneyMaking Stars,"* 2013: Quigley Publishing Co).

Critics claimed Poitier accepted typecasting, while portraying unrealistically characters, which did not permitted him to have sexuality or personality faults, much like his character in *Guess Who's Coming To Dinner*. Sidney admitted that, was all white people would pay him to do. And I add, Sidney had no control over any offers. Secondly, he showed real genius, deciding *"how much skin to give up or keep to remain in the game,"* that is what placed him among the greatest actor, black or white. Sidney was trapped like Nat "King" Cole!!!

Poitier said he felt obliged to set an example with his characterizations, while challenging old and new stereotypes, as he was the only major actor of African descent cast in leading roles in the American film industry, at that time. Those roles added to the bag Sidney already already carrying, when he left Cat Island. With his hands already filled and a loaded pack on his back, while white actors have porters to carry what Poitier "portered." Sidney's critics will always remain in the peanut gallery and not competitors, as Poitier. For instance, in 1966, Poitier turned down an opportunity to play the lead in an NBC television production of Othello. When it was all said and done, Sidney was just another black man caught up in white folk crap.

Poitier directed several films, including *A Piece of the Action, Uptown Saturday Night, Let's Do It Again,* with Bill Cosby; *Stir Crazy,* starring Richard Pryor and Gene Wilder; and *Ghost Dad,* also with Cosby. In 2002. Thirty-eight years after receiving the Best Actor Award, Poitier was chosen by the Academy of Motion Picture Arts and Sciences to receive an Academy Honorary Award, in recognition of his "remarkable accomplishments as an artist and as a human being," (*"Sidney Poitier awards: Academy of Motion Picture Arts and Sciences,"* Awardsdatabase.oscars.org. 2010).

Poitier, from his first movie roles, always reminded me of a young David struggling to remain pure, while on the run from Saul, where the American society was Saul. His big or make or break roles in my limited opinion were *The Defiant Ones' (1958)* and *A Raisin in the Sun* on Broadway and the move in 1959. Those roles to me, although he was acting, bore everyday significance, in that, his struggles in those roles were like a mirror, reflecting real-life challenges for a black man. They were reenactments of mental battles of young black men in America, trying to remain true to themselves and their communities, with little or no control over the situations that engulfed him.

Sidney was the most successful draw at the box office, during the commercial peak of his career. *Guess Who's Coming to Dinner; To Sir, with Love* and *In the Heat of the Night* were three of his most popular films. *"In the Heat of the Night"* is considered by critics Sidney's most successful characterization. He plays Virgil Tibbs, a Philadelphia detective, whose subsequent career was the subject of two sequels, *"They Call Me Mister Tibbs"* (1970) and *The Organization* (1971). Many of the films in which Poitier starred, during the 1960s, were later cited as social thrillers by both filmmakers and critics. *("TLA Film and Video Guide 2000–2001: The Discerning Film Lover's Guide,"* David Bleiler, (2013); St. Martin's Press.)

Queen Elizabeth II knighted Poitier in 1974. From 1997 to 2007, he served as the Bahamian Ambassador to Japan. On August 12, 2009, Poitier was awarded the Presidential Medal of Freedom, the United States' highest civilian honor, by President Barack H. Obama. In 2016, he was awarded the BAFTA Fellowship for outstanding lifetime achievement in film, (*"Sidney Poitier, Sen. Ted Kennedy Among 16 Who Receive Medal of Freedom,"* 2009; Washingtonpost.com). He was the ambassador of the Bahamas to UNESCO (2002 to 2007), *("Sir Sidney Poitier, best known Bahamian, honored,"* 2015).

However, only Sidney could have pulled off the real-life performance he did playing himself. It was truly a tough role, and he played it without flaws, never dropped a line or missed a cue. Truly, Sidney Poitier pulled off a hat trick, as a devil-may-care, swashbuckling, lone rider, always reflecting the persona of *"Mr. Right"* with dignity, yet rejecting subservience, while cleverly and successfully negotiating the hazardous shoals of race relations.

Yet and still, for Sidney's real-life performance to come through as genuine, whites need the counterpoint, and there was none better than his friend Harry Belafonte, who entered from stage left. In my observation, Harry Belafonte and Sir Sidney Poitier always seemed like sidekicks, each at opposite ends of the same continuum, like that of Marcus Garvey and Dr. Martin Luther King, Jr. They saw the same thing but came at it from opposite directions. For example, to me, neither seemed to be acting in *"Buck and the Preacher"* in the natural way they filled their roles.

I offer the following analysis not as a defense, but a statement of fact, which everyone knows, but never really thought about. I believe, Sir Sidney's and Harry's performances were done so well, critics missed the nuances and subtleties in this historical drama, as they fed off each other. Their performances were so complimentary, and their excellent interpretation, as well as recreation of character drew such little critical review because critics lack of exposure to black life and historial context for sucg characters.

Critics were oblivious to the fact that those were actual role drawn from the late 1800s into the early 1900s, when former slaves were on the move, trying to find sanctuaries from slave catcher, although slavery had ended, but whites were still trying to keep former slaves in the South. While on the other hand, they were victims of banishment and ethnic cleansing, chased out of places like Wilmington North Carolina, during those times, hold towns of black communities were driven out. Wagon trains like the one Sidney led were total victims of all kinds of thieves and con artists. Consequently, if you are totally unaware or simply choose to ignore the plight of former slave, Harry's and Sidney's performances, although they were in the West, they were not trying to portray cowboys. But against the true backdrop of history, they did an outstanding job filling those roles, without real models.

This is also why black actors and actresses have never received their just deserts the whites that populate the Academy have no appreciation for the struggles of black people, because of their top down view of everything. Sidney's sidekick, on the other hand, cast himself against a backdrop that only, a devil-may-care, swashbuckling, lone rider, the likes of Harry Belafonte, could pull off. Harry was not born in America, as Sidney. Consequently, neither was he subject to *"learned helplessness,"* as victims of America slavery.

Harold George Belafonte Jr. (3-1-1927) was nurtured by a culture that enabled him to become one of the most successful Jamaican-American pop stars in history. He was dubbed the *"King of Calypso"* by international audiences in the 1950s, as he popularized the Caribbean musical style (originating in Trinidad & Tobago). Harry's breakthrough album *Calypso* (1956) was the first million-selling LP by a single artist *("Harry Belafonte – Calypso,"* AllMusic (All Media Network).

Belafonte started his career in music, as a club singer, in New York City to pay for his acting classes. He broke into entertainment, as a pop singer. The first time he appeared in front of an audience, Charlie Parker's band, including Max Roach, and Miles Davis, among others was his backed up. Belafonte realized his love for folk music and studied folk material through the *Library of Congress' American folk songs archives*. With guitarist and friend Millard Thomas, Belafonte soon made his debut at the legendary jazz club *The Village Vanguard*. After launching his recording career on the Roost label in 1949, Harry was already very popular when he debuted, as a folk singer, which drew the attention of RCA Victor. Harry signed with them in 1952.

Belafonte's film debut was in *"Bright Road"* (1953), which was his first appearance with Dorothy Dandridge. The two subsequently starred in Otto Preminger's hit musical *Carmen Jones* (1954). Ironically, using his star clout, Belafonte took on several, then-controversial film roles. *Island in the Sun (1957)* was one such role. Media and critics saw hints of an affair between Belafonte's and Joan Fontaine due to their characterizations and the relaxed atmosphere, portraying scenes so realistically and the innuendos, drew a cold shoulder from critics, as with Sidney and Ann Bancroft.

In 1959, Harry starred in Robert Wise's produced, *Odds Against Tomorrow*, in which he played a bank robber uncomfortably teamed with a racist partner (Robert Ryan). He also co-starred with Inger Stevens in *The World, the Flesh, and the Devil*. Belafonte was offered the role of Porgy in Preminger's *Porgy and Bess*, where he would have starred opposite Dandridge once again, but refused the role because its racial stereotyping.

Dissatisfied with available film roles, Belafonte returned to music during the 1960s. He is perhaps best known for singing *"The Banana Boat Song,"* with its signature lyric *"Day-O."* Harry has recorded in many genres, including blues, folk, gospel, show tunes, and American standards. Early 1974, Belafonte appeared with Poitier in *Uptown Saturday Night*. In 1984, Belafonte produced and scored the musical film *"Beat Street,"* a story about the rise of hip-hop. Together with Arthur Baker, he produced the gold-certified soundtrack of the same name.

Harry didn't star in a major film again until the mid-1990s, appearing with John Travolta in the race-reverse drama *White Man's Burden* (1995); and in Robert Altman's jazz age drama *Kansas City* (1996), the latter of which garnered him the New York Film Critics Circle Award for Best Supporting Actor. He also starred as an Associate Justice of the US Supreme Court in the TV drama *Swing Vote* (1999). In 2006, Belafonte appeared in *Bobby*, Emilio Estevez's ensemble drama about the assassination of Robert F. Kennedy. Harry's last movie role was in Spike Lee's *BlacKkKlansman* (2018), as an elderly civil rights pioneer.

A major supporter of the Civil Rights Movement in the 1950s and 1960s, Belafonte was an early confidant of Dr. Martin Luther King Jr. Advocating throughout his career for political and humanitarian causes, Harry worked internationally, as well as with the *Anti-Apartheid Movement and USA for Africa*. While a UNICEF Goodwill Ambassador, beginning in1987, Harry was a vocal critic of Pres. George W. Bush's policies. Belafonte now acts as the American Civil Liberties Union celebrity ambassador for juvenile justice issues. He gave the keynote address at the ACLU of Northern California's annual Bill of Rights Day Celebration and received the Chief Justice Earl Warren Civil Liberties Award (2007).

Belafonte has won three Grammy Awards, including a Grammy Lifetime Achievement Award, an Emmy Award, and a Tony Award. In 1989, he received the Kennedy Center Honors. He was awarded the National Medal of Arts in 1994. Then in 2014, he received the Jean Hersholt Humanitarian Award at the Academy's 6th Annual Governors Awards. He followed that in March 2014, gaining an honorary doctorate from Berklee College of Music in Boston. *("Harry Belafonte – Calypso,"* AllMusic (All Media Network).

Mentored by Paul Robeson, Belafonte's political philosophy bore the heavy influences of the dynamic leader. Inspired by Robeson, a fellow singer, actor, and activist, who opposed not only racial prejudice in the United States but also western colonialism in Africa, Harry and Robeson stood shoulder to shoulder. However, Harry's success did not protect him from charges and criticism as a communist sympathizer, neither from racial discrimination, particularly in the American South. He refused to perform there from 1954 until 1961. He appeared in a campaign commercial for Democratic Presidential candidate John F. Kennedy in 1960. Kennedy later named Belafonte, a cultural advisor to the Peace Corps.

The 1960s proved to be Harry's finest hour, as he stood, like no other in Hollywood. He helped finance the *1961 Freedom Rides*, supported voter registration drives, and helped organize the *1963 March on Washington*. Harry was a Dr. Martin Luther King, Jr. supporter, as well as his family, because Dr. King made only $8,000 a year, as a preacher. Like many other civil rights activists, Belafonte was black-listed, during the anti-communist McCarthyism and *Second Red Scares*.

At the height of the civil rights movement in 1963, he bailed Dr. King out of jail in Birmingham and raised thousands of dollars for the release of other civil rights protesters. Only Harry would show up, like a devil-may-care, swashbuckling, lone rider, with $60,000 in cash to bankroll the Student Nonviolent Coordinating Committee's (SNCC) *"Mississippi Freedom Summer"* in 1964. Flying into Mississippi, like Batman and Robin, he and Sidney Poitier saved the day and stayed around to jam, entertain and talk with civil rights marchers in Greenwood.

Appearing on a Petula Clark primetime television special on NBC (1968) where, during a duet *"On the Path of Glory,"* Clark smiled and briefly touched Belafonte's arm *("Harry Belafonte with Petula Clark – On The Path Of Glory"* on YouTube). Her glancing look and incidental contact prompted complaints from Doyle Lott, the advertising manager of Plymouth Motors, the show's sponsor. (*"Tempest in TV Tube Is Sparked by Touch,"* 1968; Spokane Daily Chronicle). Lott demanded the segment be re-taped, but Clark, who had ownership of the special, told NBC that the performance would be shown intact, or she would not allow NBC to air it at all. Newspapers reported the controversy, and Lott was relieved of his responsibilities. The special aired and attracted high ratings, and probably no one, other than racists, noticed anything unusual.

When it came to controversy, Belafonte was truly prolific. He appeared on The Smothers Brothers Comedy Hour on September 29, 1968, performing a controversial *"Mardi Gras"* number intercut with footage from the 1968 Democratic National Convention Police riots, where police beat protestors in Chicago. CBS censors deleted the segments. The Smothers Brothers Hour broadcast (1993) the full unedited content.

Harry helped organize the Grammy Award-winning song *"We Are the World"'* a multi-artist effort to raise funds for Africa in 1985. He performed in the Live Aid concert that same year. In 1987, he received an appointment to UNICEF, as a goodwill ambassador. Following his appointment, Belafonte traveled to Dakar, Senegal, where he served, as chairman of the International Symposium of Artists and Intellectuals for African Children. He also helped raise funds—alongside more than 20 other artists—in the largest concert ever held in sub-Saharan Africa. In 1994, he went on a mission to Rwanda and launched a media campaign to raise awareness of the needs of Rwandan children.

Leaving acting but staying with music, this narrative extends its look at those who laid the foundation that became the *"yellow brick road"* of entertainment, which led to hip hop. Directly connected to what hip hop became, the next individual was a cornerstone laying the foundation of music, hip hop, and entertainment. His beginning was very unusual for one who achieved his level of success, as an entertainment entrepreneur. He had no real connection to any business, as a child or teenager, yet as a man, he became very successful, creating wealth for himself and others. What was his secret or magic formula? Did he somehow attract the attention of some sympathetic and generous benefactor, who gave him a start by bankrolling his dreams? No, not any of that, all he had was himself; Berry Gordy.

Born Berry Gordy, Jr., he founded Motown Records in 1959, which became the most successful black-owned music company in American history. He is the first self-made black man that surveyed the "yellow brick road" from a music producer's perspective and saw the super-highway it could become. His only model or guide as a prospector was the success of earlier planners, like Sunbeam Mitchell and his crew, which laid a major section starting the *"yellow brick road,"* as founders for the *Chitlin Circuit*. While laying it down, they dug gold out of black music, mostly in the South. Gordy recognized there was something magical hidden in what would become a gold mine, but how to tap into it and release the power and wealth buried there, he had no idea where to start. Trying to find success, Berry discovered the treasure by trying to *"making something out of nothing,"* starting the revolution that made black music far more than something to listen and dance to in clubs and at house parties.

Born at the start of the *Great Depression* in Detroit in 1929, as early as age 7, Berry had only one thought driving him, his love of music and his desire to make it. He was not a stellar student, so Berry struggled in school. His troubles mounted until he got kicked out of his high school music class. After that, he dropped school altogether.

A married man with a family to support (1953), Berry, like other black boys in Detroit, went to work for the automobile industry. Putting upholstery into cars on an assembly line, he retreated from the monotony of his work, composing songs in his head. Fortuitously that habit aided his dream when he met singer Jackie Wilson's manager. Gordy teamed up with him writing for Wilson. They produced his first hit, *"Reet Petite,"* in 1957.

Gordy continued co-writing for Wilson and hit the jackpot with Jackie's biggest hits *"Lonely Teardrops"* and *"To Be Loved."* Then *Money* came! *"Money, (That's What I Want),"* performed by Barrett Strong and co-written by Gordy, was one of the biggest hits in 1960. But with *"Money,"* Berry was still broke. It was like losing your first girl to your best friend, the love affair was over. Berry learned in the recording business white distributors, took sharks' bites out of record sales, leaving black artists, trying to hold onto their back pocket, with both hands. Without shark's teeth, and "Money" on the top ten but he was still broke, Gordy began thinking about music, as a business.

The fact that he wrote several big hits with not much economic success helped Berry face the one reality black entrepreneurs continually encountered. Whether up North or down South, trying to get money to start a business project, bank loans are for white folk. Aspiring black entrepreneurs do as Gordy, go to those they know that know them—family. A loan of $800 (that was like a few grand, back then), and Gordy was in business. He formed *Tamla Records* on January 12, 1959, and set up shop in a house on Detroit's West Grand Boulevard. Gordy chose the name *"Hitsville"* for his headquarters, following *Tamla's* inauspicious beginning. Berry went all in, incorporated the Motown Record Corporation in 1960; it embody the company's world image.

Watching his friend Smokey Robinson and *the Miracles*, sell more than a million copies of *"Shop Around,"* (1961) on the way to becoming No. 1 on the R&B charts and No. 2 on pops, Gordy knew they were making some white distributor rich. He convinced Smokey to let him handle his recordings and national distribution. Smokey Roberson and the Miracles were among Gordy's very early signees, but the Marvelettes, became the first *Motown* act to hit No. 1 on the pop charts with *"Please Mr. Postman."(1961)*

As the company took shape, Gordy brought on talent such as Marvin Gaye, who *"Hitch Hike"* (1962) to fame, riding Motown glory train. Mary Wells jumped aboard just before dropped the mega-hit *"My Guy"* (1964). Hitsville turned onto the "yellow brick road," picking up the Temptations, who wanted to strike gold. They stoked the engine, rising up the charts, singing, *"The Way You Do the Things You Do"* (1964). Stevie Wonder was like a kid in an amusement park, jumping board Motown's gory ride, just ahead of a hoard of singles artists lined up at Gordy's front door. Trying to catch Berry glory train, leaving the station three teenage girls—Mary Wilson, Florence Ballard, and Diana Ross caught the caboose, but worked their way up to the club car to reach Supremes stardom with *"Where Did Our Love Go"* (1964). They were not the only act in the caboose some were hanging out the windows, as Motown's glory ride pull out of the station. Motown dream ride became a magical trip; no one imagined in 1960.

Gordy's wizardry brought more and more popular artists to *Hitsville's* door, hoping to get their ticket punched for a place on Berry's magical ride to success. Chasing the train trying to get on board, the Four Tops were at the head of the

The 400th: From Slavery to Hip Hop

line, followed by the Chi-Lite, Brenda Holloway, The Isley Brothers, Gladys Knight & the Pips, Martha and the Vandellas, Jr. Walker and the All-Stars, Ashford & Simpson, and Billy Preston were among the last to catch the Motown express. The line waiting to get tickets aboard Hitsville USA's bullet train to stardom went around the corner and down the block, as Motown seemed to have the R&B tracks to fame on lockdown.

The 1960s Civil Rights Movement drew Gordy and Motown into the fray. Motown released Dr. Martin Luther King Jr.'s *Great March to Freedom* and *Great March to Washington* speeches. Back in 1965, Gordy's company earned $15 million in sales, more than tripling its 1963 receipts. The next year, 75% of Motown's releases made it onto the charts. In 1968 five of Motown's records climbed into the Top 10 on the pop charts. Then came, the Jackson 5 fronted by a young Michael Jackson, who climbed aboard Motown glory ride and changed music forever. The growth of black music and civil rights convinced Gordy that Motown's music was making African-American stars acceptable to white audiences, and abandoning the "Chitlin Circuit" to invade Las Vegas, chasing the "big dollar" by 1975.

It seemed as fate, time and the **Blues** magic would have it, Berry lost control of the whrilwend, like STAX in Memphis, during the late 1970s, as Motown tried to control **Blues** magic, but carry things too fast, too far and in too many directions. The whirlwind of change work differently on the other side of the Mississippi River, and Berry, like STAX, fell victim of his success, with he moved to LA. The whirlwind of change blew new tastes in music across America, as young hip-hoppers wanted to hear rap, as John Gary' predicted, catching Motown by surprise. The popularity of R&B declined, as all record sales dropped, except sales for hip hop, which sky rocketed. Gordy sold the company in 1988, and the world said goodbye to Hitsville express. Gordy was inducted into the Rock and Roll Hall of Fame that same year.

Shifting gears again but staying with music, another magic man had gotten his chops, before Berry Gordy got kicked out of music class. Quincy D. Jones, Jr. was just as unlikely to find success in music as Berry Gordy at birth. Born on Chicago's South Side (3-14-1933), the Jones family moved to Chicago, as part of the *Great Migration* (1910-1950s). The family fled the South, as most black families that became runners, looking for a better life. The son of runners, Quincy Jones inherited that trait like DNA, and would continue this legacy.

He was introduced to music by his mother, who sang gospel songs daily, as she worked around the house. But, it was their next-door neighbor, Mrs. Lucy Jackson, that kick-started everything musically for Quincy. Mrs. Jackson played stride piano, a special style created in Harlem during the 1920s. Quincy listened to her play through their apartment walls. When he was five or six, Mrs. Lucy recalled that *"After he heard me one-day, I let him try. I couldn't get him off my piano, if I tried, after that,"* ("Quincy Jones: The Story of an American Musician," Pbs.org. 2014).

Quincy's paternal grandmother was a slave in Louisville, Ky., so he knew what it meant to be black in America. Jones, in an interview, recalled his early childhood in Chicago:

"We were in the heart of the ghetto in Chicago during the Depression, and every block—it was probably the biggest black ghetto in America—every block—it also is the spawning ground probably for every gangster, black and white, in America too. So, we were around all of that. We saw that every day. There was a policeman named Two Gun Pete, a black policeman, who used to shoot teenagers in the back every weekend and everything happened there all the time. A gang on every street: the Vagabonds, the Giles HC, the Scorpions, and just on and on. In each gang they had the dukes and duchesses, junior and senior, which accommodated everybody in the neighborhood. That was the whole idea, for unity, really. Our biggest struggle every day was we were either running from gangs or with gangs. And it was just getting to school and back home. Because if your parents aren't home all day, you know, it's a notorious trek. I still have the medals here from the switchblade through my hand, pinned to a tree. I had an ice pick here in the temple one time. But, when you're young, nothing harms you, nothing scares you or anything. You don't know any better. And in the summertime—the schools were the roughest schools probably in America. I saw teachers getting hurt and maimed and everything every day, and it was everyday stuff," ("Quincy Jones Biography (1933–)" Filmreference.com, 2009).

Runners again, the Jones family moved from Chicago to Bremerton, Washington, in 1943, where his father worked at the Puget Sound Naval Shipyard, during WWII. After it ended, the Joneses were on the move again, relocating to Seattle. Quincy attended high school there and became friends with Charles Taylor. Charles' mother, Evelyn Bundy, had been one of Seattle's first society jazz-band leaders. Quincy's connection with the Taylor family exposed him to jazz and music history. Jones began playing trumpet while Taylor played the saxophone. By age 14, they were playing with a National Reserve band, (*"From his Great Depression childhood in Seattle, Quincy Jones dared to dream,"* Paul De Barros, 2013; Catholic.org). Jones said, *"I got much more experience with music growing up in a smaller city; otherwise, I would have faced too much competition."*

During that period, a very brash Quincy Jones introduced himself to an even brasher 16-year-old musician from Florida, Ray Charles. After watching Ray, who was playing a gig at the Elks Club, Jones cites Charles, as an early inspiration for his music career, noting that Charles *"overcame his disability (glaucoma blindness) to achieve his musical goals."* Also, he credits his father's sturdy work ethic, with guiding him to succeed, and his loving strength holding the family together. Jones said his father had a saying: *"Once a task is just begun, never leave until it's done. Be the labor great or small, do it well or not at all,"* (*"From his Great Depression childhood in Seattle, Quincy Jones dared to dream"* Paul De Barros, 2013; Catholic.org).

The 400th: From Slavery to Hip Hop

At 19, Jones traveled to Europe with Lionel Hampton's band. He said that his European tour with Hampton turned him upside down, altering his view of racism in the US.

"It gave you some sense of perspective on the past, present, and future. It took the myopic conflict between just black and white in the United States and put it on another level because you saw the turmoil between the Armenians and the Turks, and the Cypriots and the Greeks, and the Swedes and the Danes, and the Koreans and the Japanese. Everybody had these hassles, and you saw it was a basic part of human nature, these conflicts. It opened my soul; it opened my mind" ("Quincy Jones Interview," 2012, Academy of Achievement).

During the 1950s, Jones toured Europe with several jazz orchestras. As musical director of Harold Arlen,s jazz musical *"Free and Easy,"* Jones took to the road again. That European tour closed in Paris in February 1960. With musicians from the Arlen show, Jones very ambitiously, which was his stile, formed his own big band with eighteen artists. The band included double bass players Eddie Jones and fellow trumpeter Reunald Jones with Quincy Jones. So, it was called "The Jones Boys." Audiences responded enthusiastically, and received sparkling reviews, after touring North America, Jones headed back to Europe. However, the earnings could not support a band of that size, and things fell apart. The band dissolved, leaving Quincy in the hold.

"We had the best jazz band on the planet, and yet we were literally starving. That's when I discovered that there was music, and there was the music business. If I was to survive, I would have to learn the difference between the two" ("Conversations in Jazz: The Ralph J. Gleason Interviews," Ralph J Gleason and Ted Gioia, 2016; Yale University Press.)

In the 1960s, Jones worked as an arranger for some of the era's most important artists, including Billy Eckstine, Sarah Vaughan, Frank Sinatra, Ella Fitzgerald, Nana Mouskouri, Shirley Horn, Peggy Lee, and Dinah Washington. Jones' solo recordings also gained acclaim, including *Walking in Space, Gula Matari, Smackwater Jack, You've Got It Bad Girl, Body Heat, Mellow Madness,* and *I Heard That!*

After joining Mercury Records, Jones was promoted to vice-president in 1961, becoming the first African American to hold such a position. Jones turned to film scores, another musical arena long closed to African Americans. Director Sidney Lumet was so impressed with Jones' work he invited him to compose the music for *The Pawnbroker* (1964). It was the first of his nearly 40 major motion picture scores.

Following the success of *The Pawnbroker,* Jones became a runner, moving to Los Angeles. Settling there he was in constant demand, composing film scores for *Mirage* and *The Slender Thread* in 1965. Jones' film credits included *Walk, Don't*

Run, The Deadly Affair, In Cold Blood, In the Heat of the Night, Mackenna's Gold, The Italian Job, Bob & Carol & Ted & Alice, Cactus Flower, The Out-Of-Towners, They Call Me MISTER Tibbs!, The Anderson Tapes, $ Dollars, and *The Getaway*. He also composed *"The Streetbeater,"* which became the theme for the sitcom *Sanford and Son*, starring close friend Redd Foxx. He followed with other themes for TV shows, including *"Ironside," "Banacek," "The Bill Cosby Show,"* the opening episode of *Roots*, and the Mark Goodson-Bill Todman game show *"Now You See It."*

In 1968, Jones and his songwriting partner Bob Russell became the first African Americans nominated for an Academy Award for Best Original Song for *"The Eyes of Love"* for *Banning*. Jones was also nominated for an Academy Award for Best Original Score for *In Cold Blood (1967)*, making him the first African American to be nominated twice in the same year. Jones was the first African American director and conductor of music for the Academy Awards ceremony (1971). He was the first African American to receive the Academy's *Jean Hersholt Humanitarian Award* (1995). He and sound designer Willie D. Burton are tied for most Oscar-nominations by African Americans with 7 but Denzel Washington is first with 9 nominations.

Jones founded Qwest Productions (1975), which has produced hugely successful albums arranged for Frank Sinatra and other major pop figures. One of his greatest works, for me was the soundtrack for **The Wiz** (1978) and the feature film version starred Michael Jackson and Diana Ross. Jones produced Jackson's all-time best-selling album, Thriller (1982), *("Quincy Jones,"* 2014; Biography.com).

Jones's album *The Dude* (1981) yielded multiple hit singles, including *"Ai No Corrida," "Just Once,"* and *"One Hundred Ways."* The latter two songs featured James Ingram on lead vocals, which marked Ingram's first hits. The album also incorporated *Baby, Come to Me",* on which Ingram and Patti Austin were a duet. Jones co-produced and wrote the score for Steven Spielberg's film adaptation of Alice Walker's Pulitzer Prize-winning novel *"The Color Purple,"* (1985) which received 11 Oscar nominations. Additionally, through *"The Color Purple,"* Jones is credited with introducing Whoopi Goldberg and Oprah Winfrey to film audiences around the world, *("Home - Quincy Jones,"* Quincy Jones 2018).

Following the 1985 American Music Awards ceremony, Jones used his influence to draw most of the major American recording artists into the studio for a day to record *"We Are the World,"* to raise money for the victims of the famine in Ethiopia ("*Quincy Jones social activism"* Biography.com.) While working on the film *The Wiz,* Michael Jackson asked Jones to produce, *Off the Wall*, it ultimately sold about 20 million copies. *Off the Wall* made Jones the most powerful record producer in the industry at that time. Jones and Jackson's next collaboration, *Thriller,* sold 110 million copies and became the highest-selling album of all time. Jones also worked on Jackson's album *Bad,* which sold 45 million copies. *Bad* is their last project together, contains audio interviews of Jones (2001), as a special editions of *Off the Wall, Thriller,* and *Bad.*

Following Jackson's passing on June 25, 2009, Jones said:

> *"I am absolutely devastated at this tragic and unexpected news. For Michael to be taken away from us so suddenly at such a young age, I just don't have the words. Divinity brought our souls together on The Wiz and allowed us to do what we were able to throughout the '80s. To this day, the music we created together on Off The Wall, Thriller and Bad is played in every corner of the world and the reason for that is because he had it all...talent, grace, professionalism and dedication. He was the consummate entertainer and his contributions and legacy will be felt upon the world forever. I've lost my little brother today, and part of my soul has gone with him,"* ("Michael Jackson Dead at 50," Frank James, 2009); *The Two-Way, NPR.)*

Jones's social activism began in the 1960s with his support of Dr. Martin Luther King Jr. Jones is one of the founders of the Institute for Black American Music (IBAM); it hopes to create a national library of African-American art and music. Jones is also one of the founders of the Black Arts Festival in his hometown of Chicago. In the 1970s, Jones formed The Quincy Jones Workshops, which meets at the Los Angeles Landmark Variety Arts Center. The workshop educates, and hones skills of inner-city youth in musicianship, acting, and songwriting.

For many years, Jones has worked closely with Bono of U2 on several philanthropic endeavors. He is the founder of the Quincy Jones *Listen Up Foundation*, a nonprofit organization that built more than 100 homes in South Africa and which aims to connect youths with technology, education, culture, and music (*"Quincy Jones social activism,"* 2016; Biography.com). The Foundation's programs create intercultural exchanges that bring underprivileged youths from Los Angeles and South Africa together. Jones helped launch the *We Are the Future (WAF) project (2004)*, which gives children in poor and conflict-ridden areas a chance to live their childhoods and develop a sense of hope. The program is the result of a strategic partnership between the Global Forum, the Quincy Jones *Listen Up Foundation*, and Hani Masri, with the support of the World Bank, UN agencies and major companies. Jones launched the project with a concert in Rome, Italy, in front of an audience of half a million people.

Jones supports many other charities, including the NAACP, GLAAD, Peace Games, AmfAR, and the Maybach Foundation. He serves on the Advisory Board of HealthCorps. In 2001, Jones became an honorary member of the board of directors of the Jazz Foundation of America. He has worked with the foundation to save the homes and lives of America's elderly jazz and blues musicians, including those that survived Hurricane Katrina *("Humanity and the Nature of Man,"* William Amarteifio Ebsen, 2013); AuthorHouse).

There are many reasons I present the entertainers named here. I feel they are among the many that were part of laying the foundation for the hip hop culture. I selected them not only because of their professional and economic success, but they have endeavored to help build a sense of community, which include the poor and downtrodden people of the world.

"*The 400th*" effort looks at how successful individuals used their popularity, access, and economic power not only to "give back," but how others benefitted through their social change and social justice activities that provide access, opportunities and technologies that allowed them to help others with real needs around the world. The goal is to give young hip-hoppers models of how those, whose shoulders upon which they stand made vital contributions to building communities. More importantly, their efforts, as recipients give others real hope, and encouraged them to be even more generous as committed social change and social justice advocates.

Although his musical footprint is not as large as Barry Gordy or Quincy Jones', there's one music man who stole the hearts of black folks, as a child, and the love affair continued growing throughout his adult life. Having been amazed by him since I was a child, Stevie Wonder, to me, is the most inspiring and surprising artist to come out of all of Motown's successes, as well as all entertainment. He is unparalleled when considering his many challenges in life, yet he continues accomplishing and producing at an astonishingly highest level, which leaves him without peers. His production would be phenomenal for anyone, but his generosity makes him a world-class example of humanity at its best.

Born Stevland Hardaway Morris (5-131950), but beginning his astonishing life and career, he was known by his many adoring and loving fans the world over, as "Little" Stevie Wonder. The third of six children born to Calvin Judkins and Lula Mae Hardaway, "Little" Stevie arrived six weeks premature. Exposed to the oxygen-rich atmosphere in a hospital incubator, resulted in retinopathy of prematurity (ROP). That condition impairs the development of the eyes, causing the retinas to detach, leaving the victim without sight *("Transcript of interview: Larry King and Stevie Wonder,"* Larry King Live, 2010; CNN).

After his family became runners, moving to Detroit, Stevie, while still a child, began playing musical instruments—piano, harmonica, and drums. He formed a singing partnership with a friend; they called themselves Stevie and John. The duo played on street corners, and occasionally at parties and dances. He sang in the Whitestone Baptist Church choir also.

Stevie sang to anyone who would listen. One listener was Ronnie White of the Miracles. After hearing "Little" Stevie sing his composition, *"Lonely Boy,"* White arranged an audition at Motown with CEO Berry Gordy. Signing with Motown's *Tamla* label at age11, the label drew up a rolling five-year contract in which royalties would be held in trust until "Little" Stevie reached 21. He and his mother received stipends. Steve received a weekly amounts of $2.50

(equivalent to $20.47 in 2017) per week. Motown provided Wonder with private tutors when on tour.

At the end of 1962 and only 12 years old, "Little" Stevie joined the Motown Revue, touring on the *"Chitlin Circuit,"* the "yellow brick road" of entertainment success for black artists. Performing at the Regal Theater, Chicago, his 20-minute performance was recorded and released as an album in May 1963, *"Recorded Live: The 12-Year-Old Genius," ("Icons of R&B and Soul,"* Gulla, 2008); Greenwood Publishing Group). Released as a single, *"Fingertips,"* hit No. 1 on the Billboard Hot 100; simultaneously it was No. 1 on the R&B chart. Stevie is the youngest and only first artist to ever top both charts simultaneously at 13. Once he dropped *Fingertips*, the world recognized "Little" Stevie as a child prodigy. He is considered one of the most critically and commercially successful musical performers of the late 20th century (*"Blind Faith: The Miraculous Journey of Lula Hardaway, Stevie Wonder's Mother,"* Dennis Love; Stacy Brown, 2007; Simon & Schuster).

Wonder's mega-production include singles such as *"Signed, Sealed, Delivered I'm Yours," "Superstition," "Sir Duke," "You Are the Sunshine of My Life"* and *"I Just Called to Say I Love You"*; and albums such as *"Talking Book," "Innervisions"* and *"Songs in the Key of Life."* Stevie remained on or at the top of the R&B and pop charts into the 1990s. He has recorded more than 30 U.S. top ten hits and received 25 Grammy Awards, placing him among the most-awarded male solo artists. Not in a class unto himself, however, Wonder has sold over 100 million records worldwide, making him one of the top 60 best-selling music artists. Yet, "Little," Stevie Wonder grew with Motown in fame and fortune, as he continues performing and recording into the 2020-s. (*"The Sound of Stevie Wonder: His Words and Music,"* James E. Perone, 2006; Greenwood Publishing).

Stevie Wonder noted for his work as an activist for political and social justice is most noted for his 1980 campaign to make Dr. Martin Luther King Jr.'s birthday a holiday in the US. Wonder was named a UN Messenger of Peace, (*"Singer-songwriter Stevie Wonder designated UN Messenger of Peace,"* 2009; United Nations). Billboard magazine released a list of the Billboard Hot 100 All-Time Top Artists to celebrate the US singles chart's 55th anniversary in 2013, Stevie held down number six.

Reaching the 21st century, Wonder continues to record and perform occasional, while making guest appearances. He released one album of new material, 2005 *"A Time to Love."* His key appearances include the opening ceremony of the 2002 Winter Paralympics in Salt Lake City, the 2005 Live 8 concert in Philadelphia, the pre-game show for Super Bowl XL in 2006, Pres. Barack H. Obama's Inaugural Celebration in 2009, and the opening ceremony of the 2011 Special Olympics World Summer Games in Athens, Greece. He sang at Michael Jackson's memorial service in 2009, at Etta James' funeral in 2012, and a month later at Whitney Houston's memorial service (*"Michael Jackson Memorial Service: The Live Blog,"* 2009; mtv.com).

One of the most prominent and classic figures in popular music, during the latter half of the 20th century, Wonder received a Lifetime Achievement Award. He has also won an Academy Award for Best Song, *"I Just Called to Say I Love You,"* (1985) theme for *"The Woman in Red."* He was inducted into both the Rock and Roll and Songwriters halls of fame. Rolling Stone named him the ninth greatest singer of all time, and he received the Polar Music Prize. He also became the fourth artist to receive the Montreal Jazz Festival Spirit Award in June 2009.

Now I finally shift gears to climb out of the very deep and huge footprint of music. I leave this prolific genre behind, as my assessment turns to another big track, but not as deep, though just as wide, theater and movies once more. *"Grace becomes her"* is what I would call it if it was a movie, looking at the next icon. No matter her endeavor, Ruby Dee always exuded grace and quiet charm. Ruby Ann Wallace, (10-27-1922/ 6-11-2014) was born to Gladys and Marshall Edward Nathaniel Wallace in Cleveland, Ohio. Her father was a cook, waiter, and porter; they moved to Harlem, New York, where Ruby could get a better education. She attended Hunter College High School and received a degree in Romance languages in 1945 *("Ruby Dee, actress, and civil rights activist, dies at 91,"* Sarah Halzack, 1922); The Washington Post). Ruby married blues singer Frankie Dee Brown in 1941 and began using his middle name, as her stage name, even after devoice.

Another recipient of generous support from CP-USA provided in Harlem, Ruby joined the *American Negro Theater* and became part of the Leftist front, organized by CP-USA. Starting as an apprentice, working with Sidney Poitier, Harry Belafonte, and Hilda Simms, Ruby gained her bona fides in the theater. Appearing on Broadway, Dee's first performance was in *That Man of Mine* in 1946; then received national recognition for the 1950 film *The Jackie Robinson Story*. Dee performed in lead roles at the *American Shakespeare Festival* as Kate in *The Taming of the Shrew* and as Cordelia in *King Lear* (1965). Ruby Dee became the first black actress to perform in a leading role in the festival.

Sanders Dee's career crossed all major forms of media, which spanned eight decades, as an actress, poet, playwright, screenwriter, journalist, and civil rights activist. Ruby's break out roles includes the film *"A Raisin in the Sun."* She also played opposite Sidney Poitier also in *"Edge of the City."* Dee appeared in *"Gone Are the Days!"* and *"The Incident,"* during the 1960s. She also appeared in 20 episodes of Peyton Place in 1969. Ruby followed those roles, with more TV appears. First as Cora Sanders, a Marxist college professor, in the Season 1/Episode 14 of Police Woman, entitled *"Target Black"* in 1975. Her character as Cora Sanders, was based on the real-life of Angela Y. Davis. Ruby played Queen Haley in Roots: The Next Generations miniseries (1979).

Dee appeared in Spike Lee's 1989 film *Do the Right Thing*, and his 1991 film *Jungle Fever*. For her performance as Mahalee Lucas in *American Gangster* (2007), Dee was nominated as Best Supporting Actress Academy Award, and won the Screen Actors Guild Award for Female Actor in a Supporting Role. Ruby was nominated for eight Emmy Awards, winning once for her role in the 1990 TV film *Decoration Day*. Dee was a Grammy, Emmy, Obie, and Drama Desk winner. She also received a Screen Actors Guild Lifetime Achievement Award.

Dee married Ossie Davis, with whom she frequently performed until his death in 2005. Dee was awarded the National Medal of Arts in 1995. Ruby and Ossie narrated a series of WPA slave narratives in the HBO film directed by Ed Bell and Thomas Lennon *Unchained Memories* in 2003; they read the actual *Slave Narratives*. Dee also received the Kennedy Center Honor in 2004. Dee and Davis were winners of the Grammy Award for Best Spoken Word Album (2007) for "*With Ossie And Ruby: In This Life Together.*" ("*Ruby Dee marks 90th birthday with a new documentary about her illustrious life with late husband Ossie Davis*", 2012; New York Daily News). (*Oscar-Nominated Actress Ruby Dee Dies at 91*, Carmel Dagan, 2014; Variety).

Ruby met Ossie Davis while costarring in Robert Ardrey's 1946 Broadway play *Jeb*. Together, Dee and Davis wrote an autobiography in which they discussed their political activism and their open marriage (but later changing their views). Together they had three children: son, blues musician Guy Davis, and two daughters, Nora Day and Hasna Muhammad. Dee was a breast cancer survivor for more than three decades. She was a well-known activist in the Civil Rights Movement. Ruby had membership in the Congress of Racial Equality (CORE), the NAACP, the Student Nonviolent Coordinating Committee (SNCC), Delta Sigma Theta sorority, and the Southern Christian Leadership Conference SCLC).

In 1963, Dee emceed the March on Washington for Jobs and Freedom. Dee and Davis were both personal friends of Dr. Martin Luther King, Jr. Paul Robeson, William Patterson, and Malcolm X, with both Davis' giving the eulogy at Malcolm X's funeral in 1965. In 1970, she received the Frederick Douglass Award given by the New York Urban League. In 1999, Dee and Davis were arrested at 1 Police Plaza, the headquarters of the New York Police Department, protesting the police killing of Amadou Diallo (Diallo was a 23-year-old immigrant from Guinea, shot and killed by four New York City police 2-4-1999).

Seldom have two people come together, and their spirits aligned so closely that when I thinks or speaks about one, I automatically think of the other. It was that way for me with Ruby Dee and Ossie Davis. Both had their stellar careers, but their marital union, as far as I knew was so totally encompassing; it seemed they were a package deal. Ossie Davis was born Raiford Chatman Davis (12-18-1917/2-4-2005) in Cogdell, Georgia. He became a film, television and Broadway actor, director, poet, playwright, author, and civil rights activist. Davis experienced racism from an early age in Cogdell; the local KKK threatened to shoot his father, whose job they felt was too advanced for a black man to hold.

His parents got him out of the South, fearing for their son life in Georgia. They sent him to Howard University, but Davis left school in 1939 to fulfill his desire for an acting career in New York City. Ossie later attended Columbia University. Landing a spot with the Rose McClendon Players in Harlem in 1939, his acting career spanned eight decades. Ossie was another black actor that received the benefited from CP-USA's generous help. His break came in 1950 with his film debut in *"No Way Out"* also starring Sidney Poitier. He was the voice of Anansi, the spider on the PBS children's television series Sesame Street in its animation segments.

Davis encountered the usual roadblocks that black actors faced, pursuing theatrical careers, during the 1950s and early 1960s. Black actors were ask mostly to portray only stereotypical characters—Stepin Fetchit. Davis followed Sidney Poitier's example and played only distinguished characters. However, when he found it necessary to play a Pullman porter or a butler, he played those characters realistically, not as caricatures.

In addition to acting, Davis, along with Melvin Van Peebles, Sidney Poitier, and Gordon Parks, was one of the notable African-American directors of that generation: he directed movies such as *Gordon's War*, *Black Girl* and *Cotton Comes to Harlem*. Along with Bill Cosby and Poitier, Davis was one of a handful of African American actors able to find commercial success, while avoiding stereotypical roles before 1970.

Davis played a significant role in the 1965 movie *The Hill* alongside Sean Connery, where Davis' charater was in a British military stockade in North Africa. The plotline revolved around convicted soldiers forced to climb a rugged hill of sand daily, carrying a large sack in their hands. He also played significant roles in *The Cardinal* and *The Scalphunters*. As a playwright, Davis wrote *Paul Robeson: All-American*, which is performed frequently in theatre programs for young audiences.

Davis found recognition late in life by working in several of director Spike Lee's joints, including *Do The Right Thing*, *Jungle Fever*, *She Hate Me* and *Get on the Bus*. He also found work as a commercial voice-over artist and served as the narrator of the early-1990s CBS sitcom *Evening Shade*, starring Burt Reynolds, where he also played one of the residents of a small southern town. In 1989, the NAACP Image Awards Hall of Fame inducted Ossie Davis and Ruby Dee. Davis was presented the nation's highest honor the National Medal of Arts(1995), and was also a recipient of the Kennedy Center Honors (2004). Davis was an American Theater Hall of Fame inductee (1994).

Davis was a well-known Civil Rights activist and was close friends of Malcolm X, William Patterson, Paul Roberson, Martin Luther King, Jr., and other icons of that era. He helped organize the *1963 March on Washington* and served as one of its emcees. Davis, alongside Ahmed Osman, delivered the eulogy at Malcolm X funeral. *("Malcolm X's Eulogy,"* Ossie Davis, 1965; The Official Website of Malcolm X). Davis re-read part of his eulogy at the end of Spike Lee's film

Malcolm X. He also delivered a stirring tribute to Dr. Martin Luther King Jr, at a memorial in New York's Central Park the day after Dr. King's assassination.

A change in time requires not only a new approach but new and different personalities to fit the new time. Coming on the scene just before Stokely Carmichael screamed the immortal words *"black power"* from the Mississippi Delta, Bill Cosby was among the first African American to break the mold of the mumbling, bungling, fumbling, skinning and grinning "colored boy" image of black males on TV, in most movies and many other places. Paired with Robert Cult, who wasn't the smartest sidekick one could have, made Cosby's Ivy League mannerisms come across as cool and laid back, yet always ready with answers, in the nick of time. However, Cosby made the image of blacks working alongside whites in public acceptable to white folks. In the real world, Cosby was black people's devil-may-care swashbuckling lone rider.

William Henry Cosby Jr. was born on July 12, 1937, in Philadelphia, Pennsylvania. He was one of four sons of Anna Pearl (née Hite), a maid, and William Henry Cosby Sr., a mess steward in the U.S. Navy. Cosby was the class president, as well as class clown, the captain of both the baseball and track and field teams at Mary Channing Wister Public School in Philadelphia. Teachers even noticed Cosby's propensity for clowning it up instead of studying, he even described himself as the class clown *("Bill Cosby Biography,"* 2009; Filmreference.com).

Beginning as a stand-up comedian, before becoming an actor, musician, and author, Cosby attended Temple University in the 1960s and received his bachelor's degree in 1971. In 1973, he received a master's degree from the University of Massachusetts, Amherst, and earned a Doctor of Education degree in 1976, also from UMass. His dissertation discussed the use of Fat Albert and the Cosby Kids as a teaching tool in elementary schools.

Bill career began in stand-up at the *"Hungry I"* in San Francisco, during the 1960s. He landed the starring role in the television show *I Spy* espionage adventure in 1965. Cosby put a black face before America in the first weekly dramatic NBC television series, *("This Is How We Lost to the White Man': The audacity of Bill Cosby's black conservatism,"* Ta-Nehisi Coatesq 2008; The Atlantic Monthly).

NBC executives had similar concerns, as they did finding sponsors for *The Nat "King" Cole show*, eight years earlier. They feared some affiliates in the South would be unwilling to carry the series and stations in Georgia, Florida, and Alabama declined to air it. However, a confident Cosby insisted the show would work. Some say viewers responded to the show's exotic locales. Still, black viewers saw authentic chemistry between the two personalities, rather than the animosity reflected in roles, Sidney Poitier and Richard Widmark in *No Way out*, or Harry Belafonte against Robert Ryan in *Odd against Tomorrow*, casted opposite racists white guys.

I Spy became a hit, its first television season, and made seeing a black man in a professional capacity acceptable to white people. *I Spy* finished among the twenty most-watched shows that year, and Cosby received the Emmy Awards for Outstanding Lead Actor in a Drama Series three consecutive seasons *("The Eternal Paternal Bill Cosby's never-ending tour,"* Kelefa Sanneh, 2014; The New Yorker). When accepting his third Emmy for the show, Cosby told the audience: *"Let the message be known to bigots and racists that they don't count!"*

Bill's next stop was *"The Bill Cosby Show,"* which ran for two seasons from 1969 to 1971. Then in 1972, Bill used the Fat Albert character, which Cosby developed during his stand-up routines and his dissertation at UMass, in the animated series. Bringing the comedy series to television, Cosby produced and hosted *"Fat Albert and the Cosby Kids."* The show became the first TV series centering on a group of young black friends growing up in an urban ghetto. Throughout the 1970s, Cosby starred in about a half-dozen films, and occasionally returned to film later in his career

Beginning in the 1980s, Bill Cosby produced and starred in the television sitcom *The Cosby Show*, which aired from 1984 to 1992 and was rated as the number one show in America for 1984 through 1989. The sitcom highlighted the experiences and growth of an affluent African-American family—the Huxtables. He became known as "America's Dad." Cosby produced a spin-off sitcom *A Different World*, which aired from 1987 to 1993. He also starred in *The Cosby Mysteries* from 1994 to 1995, then starred in the sitcom *Cosby* from 1996 to 2000, and hosted *Kids Say the Darndest Things* from 1998 to 2000.

This narrative now moves from being in movies to making them. Shelton Jackson "Spike" Lee (3-20-1957) is a film director, producer, writer, and actor born in Atlanta, Georgia. The son of Jacqueline Carroll (née Shelton), a black arts and literature teacher, and William James Edward Lee III, a jazz musician, and composer, the family moved to Brooklyn, New York, when Shelton was a child. He enrolled in Morehouse College, a historically black college (HBCU), where he made his first film as a student, *"Last Hustle in Brooklyn."* He took film courses at Clark Atlanta University and graduated with a B.A. in mass communication from Morehouse. He did graduate work at New York University's Tisch School of the Arts, where he earned a Master of Fine Arts in film & television *("SHELTON 'SPIKE' LEE '79," 2012;* Morehouse College).

Spike enters the Hip hop picture from stage left, not only because he made films but because he linked the past with what was a shaky present for blacks in film making (1980s). Spike Lee answered the question, "Who would pick up the challenge of Oscar Micheaux, Sidney Poitier, Harry Belafonte, Ossis Davis, Melvin Van Peebles and Gordon Parks, who labored for years building expertise and credibility demanded by whites for an opportunity as directors. These forerunners left no doubt that a black man was capable of meeting the challenges. The question, however, was could he negotiate the minefield of Hollywood's Jim Crow system and be able to tell relevant stories about black life. Yet and still, Melvin Van Peebles' outrageousness with his independent film **"Sweet**

Sweetback's Badasssss Song," (1971) blew up the black film genre by crashed through the colored line. Van Peebles created a new mold white's labored **"blaxploitation films"/ "race films."** Spike and other young black filmmakers entered the scene freed to be truly creative, because of Van Peebles.

Lee's 1997 documentary *"4 Little Girls,"* about the children killed in the 16th Street Baptist Church bombing in Birmingham, Alabama in 1963, was nominated for the Academy Award for Best Feature Documentary. I have always wondered what was the name of the director and film that won? In October 2005, Lee responded to a CNN anchor's question as to whether the government intentionally ignored the plight of black Americans, during the Hurricane Katrina 2005 catastrophe, which we now know it did, he said, *"It's not too far-fetched. I don't put anything past the US government. I don't find it too far-fetched that they tried to displace all the black people out of New Orleans."* In later comments, Lee cited past government shenanigans, including its *Tuskegee Study of Untreated Syphilis in Male Negro (*"Clip of Lee expressing his views of the Hurricane Katrina and Tuskegee matters on, Real Time with Bill Maher,"* 2011; Youtube.com). Today Black Lives Matter protest points to the same possibility for black people with COVID-19.

Establishing his production company, *40 Acres and a Mule Filmworks*, Spike has produced over 35 films since 1983. He made his directorial debut with *"She's Gotta Have It"*(1986) and has directed such films as *"Do the Right Thing"* (1989), *"Malcolm X"* (1992), *"The Original Kings of Comedy"* (2000), *"Bamboozled* (2000)," *"25th Hour"* (2002), *"Inside Man"* (2006), *"Chi-Raq"* (2015), and *"BlacKkKlansman"* (2018). Lee has also acted in ten of his films.

Spike's films have examined race relations, colorism in the black community, the role of media in contemporary life, urban crime, and poverty, as well as other political issues. He has won numerous accolades for his work, including two Academy Award nominations, a Student Academy Award nominations, and an Honorary Award from the Academy of Motion Picture Arts and Sciences, two Emmys, two Peabodys, an honorary BAFTA, an Honorary César, the 2013 Gish Prize, and a Grand Prix award,

Forever a New York Knick, Spike remains part of the community from which he came. He did things with his "joints" that accentuated his unique stylistic approach to film making with such elements as dolly shots—portraying characters "floating" through their surroundings—in his filmography. After the 1990 release of *"Mo' Better Blues,"* starring Denzel Washington and Wesley Snipes, Lee was accused of antisemitism by the Anti-Defamation League and several film critics. They criticized the characters Josh and Moe Flatbush. Spike described these club owners, as "Shylocks." Lee denied the charge, explaining that he wrote those characters into his film to depict how black artists struggled against exploitation. Lee's films are referred to typically as "Spike Lee Joints," and the closing credits always include the phrases *"By Any Means Necessary,"* "Ya Dig," and *"Sho Nuff."* However, his 2013 film, *"Oldboy,"* used the traditional *"A*

Spike Lee Film" credit, after producers heavily re-edited it, *("Oldboy' Will Likely Be Trampled by New Releases in Thanksgiving Rush,"* Maane Khatchatourian, 2013); Variety).

My next lone rider, Rita Moreno, may seem strange to some, being cast among this crew, but this line up is about breaking down Jim Crow walls, which are to keep everybody except white people out. Rita came on the scene, a very young attractive and petite teenager with a soft voice. She reminds me of Lorraine Hansberry, quiet but a volcano on the inside or a caged tiger clawing to get free. Her complexion did not spear her, the indignities of discrimination, which is why she is an inductee into this *"hall of fame or shame,"* depending upon how one fell about discrimination and disparate treatment.

Rita Moreno was born (12-11-1931) in Puerto Rico to a teenage mother, Rosa Maria (17 years old), and spent her early life in nearby Juncos. Rosa moved to New York City, taking Rita with her in 1936. Rita adopted the surname of her first stepfather, Edward Moreno, *("Rita Moreno: A Memoir,"* 2013; Celebra, Penguin Group).

Soon after arriving in New York, she began her first dancing lessons with a Spanish dancer known as *"Paco Cansino."* Paco was a paternal uncle of film star Rita Hayworth. When she was 11 years old, Rita began lending her voice to Spanish language versions of American films. She played "Angelina" in her first Broadway role in *Skydrift*. Moreno received the attention of Hollywood talent scouts, as early as age 13. Moreno began acting steadily in films throughout the 1950s, usually in small roles, including *The Toast of New Orleans* (1950) and *Singin' in the Rain* (1952). In March 1954, Moreno appeared on the cover of Life Magazine with the chauvinistic, maybe even misogynistic caption *"Rita Moreno: An Actress's Catalog of Sex and Innocence."*

Moreno says she disliked most of her film work; during this period, she said: *"the roles offered were very stereotypical. The exception was the supporting role in the film version of "The King and I, as Tuptim."* In 1961, Moreno landed the role of Anita in Robert Wise and Jerome Robbins' film adaptation of Leonard Bernstein's and Stephen Sondheim's groundbreaking Broadway musical *West Side Story*, which was played by Chita Rivera on Broadway. Moreno won the Academy Award for Best Supporting Actress for that role *("Rita Moreno overcame Hispanic stereotypes to achieve stardom,"* 2008; The Miami Herald).

After winning the Oscar, Moreno thought, like Sidney Poitier, she would be able to perform in less stereotypical film roles, but was disappointed also, she said:

"Ha, ha. I showed them, but didn't make another movie for seven years after winning the Oscar.... Before West Side Story, I was always offered the stereotypical Latina roles; the Conchitas and Lolitas in westerns. I was always barefoot. It was humiliating, embarrassing stuff. But I did it because there was nothing else. After West Side Story, it was pretty much the same

thing. A lot of gang stories, ("Rita Moreno overcame Hispanic stereotypes to achieve stardom," 2008; The Miami Herald).

Again, like black actors, Morgan Freeman and Ossis Davis, Moreno became a cast member on the PBS children's series *The Electric Company* from 1971 to 1977. She screamed the show's opening line, *"Hey, you guys!"* Her roles included Millie the Helper, the naughty little girl Pandora, and Otto, a very short-tempered director.

Moreno's appearance on *The Muppet Show* earned her a Primetime Emmy Award for Outstanding Individual Performance in a Variety or Music Program in 1977. Another notable guest appearance includes a three-episode arc on *The Rockford Files* in 1977, as former call girl Rita Kapcovic. For her portrayal, Moreno won a Primetime Emmy Award for Outstanding Guest Actress - Drama Series. She was a regular on the three-season network run of 9 to 5, a sitcom based on the film hit (1980s).

Reaching the mid-1990s, Moreno provided the voice for Carmen Sandiego on Fox's animated series *Where on Earth is Carmen Sandiego?* In the late 1990s, a new generation of viewers came to know her as Sister Pete, a nun trained as a psychologist in the HBO series *Oz*. Rita won several ALMA Awards in that role. She made a guest appearance on The Nanny as Coach Stone, Maggie's tyrannical gym teacher.

Moreno's Broadway credits include *"Last of the Red Hot Lovers"* (1969), the very short-lived musical *"Gantry"* (1970), and *"The Ritz,"* for which she won the 1975 Tony Award for Best Featured Actress. She appeared in the female version of *"The Odd Couple"* that ran in Chicago, winning the Sarah Siddons Award in 1985. Moreno began performing a solo autobiographical show at the Berkeley Rep (theater) in Berkeley, California, in September 2011, *"Rita Moreno: Life Without Makeup,"* written by Berkeley Rep artistic director Tony Taccone. ("Rita Moreno's life laid bare in "Life without Makeup," 2011; Berkeleyside).

Moreno and Jennifer Lopaz, Camila Cabello, Luis Fonsi, and others contributed to Lin-Manuel Miranda's single *"Almost Like Praying."* The proceeds from the song went to benefit those affected by Hurricane Maria, which devastated the island of Puerto Rico. The relief program was sponsored by UNIDOS Disaster, the Hispanic Federation ("Lin-Manuel Miranda Releases Star-Studded 'Almost Like Praying' Song For Puerto Rico Hurricane Relief," Veronica Villafañe, 2017; Forbes).

Rita Moreno is one of the few artists to win all four major annual American entertainment awards: an Oscar, an Emmy, a Grammy, and a Tony ("Speakers on healthcare, 2013; the Wayback Machine). She is also one of 23 people that achieved what is called the Triple Crown of Acting, with individual competitive Academy, Emmy and Tony awards for acting; she and Helen Hayes are the only two woman who have achieved both distinctions, winning an Oscar (1962), a

Grammy (1972), a Tony (1975), and an Emmy (1977). She has won numerous other awards, including various lifetime achievement awards and the Presidential Medal of Freedom, America's highest civilian honor. ("*Rita Moreno: A Memoir,*" 2013; Celebra, Penguin Group).

The next mason on the yellow brick road is very familiar, and his circuitous journey to fame no one could have predicted, during his early life. However, he is the one person presented in this *"400ᵗʰ"* narrative on hip hop's foundation, whose life and art seems the same. His very doubtless future, even after reaching young adulthood, regarding success of any kind, definitely made him, a fish out of water. Reading about his life and family struggles—enduring brutality as a child—viewing his art, led me to conclude, not that it was easy or simple, Tyler Perry had only to master the techniques and psychology necessary to create the success his art brought him.

My statement, not by any means suggest that his road was something just anyone could have accomplished, which is why his selection is based, less on his success than his struggles, surviving childhood, mentally intact. Tyler Perry's road to success was definitely did not begin on easy street, his road will tax the most vivid imagination. His internalized experiences from his early life are not something most people would see, as a doorway to riches and greatness. Some people's lives fall apart sometimes while growing up or after they are grown up. Reading Perry's story, it is abundantly clear, Tyler's life was never together. It began in chaos and turmoil and went downhill from there, until reaching young adulthood. However, before reaching that point, the chaos in his environment consumed him totally.

Born Emmitt Perry Jr. to Willie Maxine and Emmitt Perry, Sr. (9-13-1969) in New Orleans, Louisiana, from the moment of his earliest memories, Tyler said of his father, *"His answer to everything was to 'beat it out of you."* Such harsh treatment, by his father, cast the relationship, with the man whose name he bore, in total negativity, so much so, rather than a source of strength and direction in his youth, young Emmitt, Jr. attempted suicide to escape his father's ascorbic treatment. Most psychologists would describe that act, as a desperate cry for help, in an attempt to escape his father's brutality.

Emmitt, Jr. turned all his affection toward the only other person in his environment capable of returning and extending the love and compassion he craved, his mother. She was his only refuge from his father's ferine ferocity. Recognizing his need for tenderness and affection, his mother carried him to church each week. His comments about her convey that her arms were his sanctuary. They filled his feral life with love and affection. Daily looking forward to Sundays, when he felt secure and enjoyed a certain sense of safety and contentment, Emmitt cherished those times.

I believe that relationship was the beginning of Tyler's belief that there was something in life beyond pain, degradation, and humiliation. Running from a kind of *"learned helplessness,"* Perry attempting suicide, at age 16, but beginning a self rescue, Emmitt legally changed his first name, and Tyler Perry was born a free spirit. (Biography.com, 2015 (FYI / A&E Networks) A new life, with that change, a new man was born. Escaping the psychological and physical domination of his father, a new Tyler Perry emerged.

An adage predicts, *time brings about a change*, and Tyler turned within to find strength, while developing a new self-concept. One day, while watching the film *Precious*, Perry says he had an epiphany. He found in that movie the motivation, which helped him face the horrible demons from his past and present that haunted his waking hours and nightly dreams. He found the freedom and strength to admit the molestation he suffered at the hands of his mother's friend at age 10. With that admission, for the first time, Tyler was able to look back at all the other times he was abused and defiled by people who should have been trustworthy.

There was the time three men molested him, and he also learned his father had molested his friend. Tyler wanted to devoice himself completely from such madness if possible, so he got a DNA test to learn, if he was biologically tied to the psychotic behavior that filled his life, through his father. Experiencing his first real taste of freedom and relief, the test revealed Emmitt Sr. was not his father, which for me explains his brutal and abusive treatment, *("Tyler Perry recounts childhood abuse on Web site,"* 2009 CNN).

I imagine that knowledge—Emmitt Sr. was not his father— was for Tyler, like the cage door swinging open, freeing his spirit to escape the prison he described, as his life. Although, relieved of the confused in his life was not within, however, his delusionary state prior to that knowledge had already caused real damage. Just the same, the DNA test gave Tyler what he needed to begin building a life base on his new mindset. After having given up on the whole enterprise of learning and dropping out of high school, Tyler decided to recoup and reconstruct his shattered life, one step at a time, and create a life of his choosing. I would say those recent events were the kind of shock therapy that reversed *"learned helplessness."*

First, that new life began with education and earning a GED in his early 20s. Looking at his life, which had been a series of disastrous consequences, Perry had another epiphany while watching *The Oprah Winfrey Show*. He learned writing, could have a therapeutic impact on people, trying to work through psychological problems and trauma. Perry concluded it may work for him also, and began writing a series of letters to himself. The impact of recanting his life enabled him to confront and defeat the demons from his past, which terrorizing him as a child and a young man. Inspired by his letters to himself, Perry began approaching his writing seriously, and as more than self-therapy, but as a possible career.

Tyler decided to try and turn his letters into a stage production. Relocating to Atlanta (1990), Perry struggle trying to transform his letters into what would become the musical *I Know I've Been Changed ("Speaker Bio: Tyler Perry,"* 2013, natpe.org). Bankrolling his dream of success, Perry sank $12,000, his life savings, on a go for broke roll of the dices, trying to win a career in entertainment. On his own and with a head full of titles—director, producer, playwright, and actor—the young inexperienced wanna-be, brought *I Know I've Been Changed* to a community theater for the first performance in 1998 ("A Showbiz Whiz," Brett Pulley, 2005, Forbes).

Relying on what he knew best—lessons with religious themes, forgiveness, dignity, and self-worth—he brought his dream to life on stage. But for me, his therapy, addressing the issues buried deepest in his subconscious—child abuse and dysfunctional families—freed him to really reconstruct his life through writing his play. These themes would become a fixture in Perry's work going forward. The fact that he did not roll craps on his first go for broke roll—"less than stellar" reviews and public reception of his play—left him still trying to *"make something out of nothing."* Even though a flop financially, it was better than craps. Tyler knew he had something to work with, which gave him a chance to make his point. He didn't allow his first roll to damper the titillating glow, I am sure he felt inside; Perry persisted.

Over the next six years, against the odds, even lackluster reviews, bankruptcy, even sleeping in his car did not deter him. Tyler Perry persevered, holding on to his dream; he knew he "had been changed." Continually rewriting the musical, Tyler fought the doubts of others, and his faith finally redeemed him, *("Tyler Perry holds on to his past,"* Scott Bowles, 2008, USA Today).

Undaunted by his lack of success through all his previous attempts to gain success, Perry relentlessly retooled *"I Know I've Been Changed."* He decided to give Atlanta one more shot, even though doubters abounded. Like a shooter coming out on his last dime, Tyler's *"I Know I've Been Changed"* maxed out the House of Blues. Based on the reworked play, Perry aimed for the largest theater venue in Atlanta—the Fox. Sure he had found a successful formula, after selling out the Fox, Perry took to the road, touring his play on the legendary *"Chitlin Circuit"* (also known as the "urban theater circuit" by northerners), *("How Tyler Perry rose from homelessness to a $5 million mansion",* Zondra Hughes, 2004, Ebony).

Some readers may feel I am providing far more detail on the personal life of Perry, but this narrative is about *"making something out of nothing,"* and Tyler and his life were definitely nothing starting out. My reason for this approach with Tyler is to show reader the importance of being able to separate what happens outside of an individual does not control what is going on inside of their head. Belief in one's ability to overcome adversity in one's life is an inner strength that can sustain, when all else fails. The pain and anguish Tyler Perry endured is similar to what slave masters put enslaved Africans through creating *"learned helplessness"* and Tyler Perry's life, as I present it, is an actual example of the resilience of the human spirit. But for me, more than anything it is that resilience, which enabled descendants of American slavery to make it to *"The 400th".*

Enduring to survive, Perry developed a devoted fan base among African-American audiences, which seemed to grow with each performance. In 2005, Forbes reported Perry sold *"more than $100 million in tickets, $30 million in videos of his shows, while raking in an estimated $20 million in merchandise,"* $150M all total. Even more impressive, Brett Pulley, in a *Showbiz Whiz* piece (2010), for Forbes said, *"The 300 live shows produced an average of 35,000 people a week each year to view them."*

Perry continued advancing at a very fast clip, raising $5.5 million mostly from ticket sales of his stage productions, which he used to fund his first movie, *"Diary of a Mad Black Woman."* That production went on to gross $50.6 million while scoring a 16% approval rating at the film review web site Rotten Tomatoes. On its opening weekend, February 24–26, 2006, Perry's film version of *Madea's Family Reunion* opened number one at the box office with $30.3 million. The film eventually grossed $65 million. Perry and his co-stars promoted the film on *The Oprah Winfrey Show* (*"Tyler Perry's Madea's Family Reunion,"* 2006; Boxofficemojo.com).

Director J. J. Abrams (2009) requested Perry play a small role, as the *Starfleet Academy* commandant Admiral Barnett in *"Star Trek."* It was Tyler's first film appearance in a project other than his own. Next, Perry wrote, directed, and starred in *"I Can Do Bad All By Myself"* (2009) and was Perry's eighth film. It also opened as a smash number one hit at the box office. Teaming up, as executive producer with Oprah Winfrey for the movie *"Precious,"* based on the novel **Push** by Sapphire, continued Perry's successful roll. *"Why Did I Get Married Too?",* the sequel to *"Why Did I Get Married?",* (2010), featuring Janet Jackson, Cicely Tyson, Louis Gossett, Jr., Jill Scott, and Malik Yoba grossed $60 million; it made $29 million on the opening weekend *("Tyler Perry's Why Did I Get Married Too?",* 2013; Boxoffice mojo).

Perry's films are co-produced and distributed by Lions Gate Entertainment; he retains full copyright ownership under the corporate name Tyler Perry Films and places his name in front of all titles. Perry's movies have seen very limited release outside North America, but in May 2010, Lionsgate began releasing his films in the United Kingdom.

Tyler Perry's *"For Better or Worse"* was based on his films *"Why Did I Get Married?"* and *"Why Did I Get Married Too?"* premiered on TBS (2011), but TBS dropped the series, canceling it in 2013. Meant to be a killing blow, I believe, however, it proved to be a blessing, Oprah Winfrey Network (OWN) picked it up and Tyler rolled 7 on his hot streak (2013). Perry struck an exclusive multi-year partnership with Oprah Winfrey on OWN (2012). The partnership brought scripted television to OWN, (*"Oprah Strikes Partnership with Tyler Perry,"* Oprah.com).

OWN features two other new television series of Perry's: the hour-long soap opera/drama series *"The Haves and the Have Nots"* premiered in 2013 and the sitcom *"Love Thy Neighbor"* also premiered in 2013 as well. *"The Haves and the Have Nots"* set a new 2013 record for OWN, scoring the highest ratings ever for a series premiere on the network, *("Solid Debut For Tyler Perry's 'The Haves And Have Nots' On OWN,"* Nellie Andreeva, 2013, Deadline Hollywood). *"Love Thy Neighbor"* scored the second-highest ratings ever for a series premiere on OWN, behind *"The Haves and the Have Nots."* However, *"Love Thy Neighbor"* has declined significantly in ratings, while *"The Haves and the Have Nots"* has continued to increase its ratings. *"The Haves and the Have Nots"* came in as the most-watched program in all of the cable television night programming 2014, *("OWN's 'Haves and the Have Nots' Surges to Series Highs,"* 2014, Rick Kissell @ratesrick Variety).

Continuing to soar, a *"Haves and the Have Nots,"* season 2 episode set an OWN 2014 scoring the highest ratings in the network's history. The record-breaking episode brought in 3.6 million viewers, surpassing the 3.5 million that tuned in for Oprah's *"Next Chapter"* interview with Bobbi Kristina, which was the previous highest-rated network viewing. Perry continued his partnership with OWN, the network ordered its fourth scripted series (and fourth series by Perry) based on the feature film, *"The Single Moms Club,"* which is called *"If Loving You Is Wrong"* (2014), the hour-long drama series premiered September 9, 2014.

"The 400th", as an event, reflects enslaved Africans struggle to become one people, despite slave masters efforts to make them haters of one another and that attitude is part of *"learned helplessness."* The idea here expresses itself in black people's willingness to attack each other publicly over personal issues or whatever! I feel about this, as Dia Simms and *"work-life balance,"* as an unrealistic concept and should be *"deleted"* from our behavior repertoire. Now that African Americans are presenting themselves to the world as one people "open public attacks" are destructive and demeaning to all.

I bring this up here because inevitably, after all the struggles in his early life to become a successful entrepreneur, Tyler has detractors. I present this controversy as a suggestion for why black people should handle such situations in a less public forum. Though few, sometimes the vociferous and shrill outcries from distractors seems to drown out other voices, which belie their sinister intent, in my opinion. Specifically, I present a controversy initiated by Journalist Jamilah Lemieux on National Public Radio and criticism by director Spike Lee of Perry in 2009. Director Spike Lee, after praising Perry's work in 2006, in 2009 stated, *'Each artist should be allowed to pursue their artistic endeavors,' but I still think there is a lot of stuff out today that is 'coonery buffoonery,'* (*"Our World with Black Enterprise,"* 2009, blackenterprise.com/tv-video). When asked if Perry's success among black audiences was a result of *"just giving black America what they wanted,"* Spike responded, *'The imaging is troubling."* What is troubling and confusing for me is Spike's comments since he wrote and directed *"Bamboozled,"* which was nothing but *"coonery buffoonery."* What's the difference?

Lemieux, despite praising Perry also, in her open letter on National Public Radio addressed to Perry, began with what seems, after reading it, a might disingenuous; *"I appreciate your commitment to giving black folk jobs in front of and behind the camera. Your films are known for their humor, and they also have positive messages about self-worth, love, and respect. For all of that, I thank you."* After accusing Perry of things, she does not bother to support with evidence; she launches what seemed to me, a diatribe base on personal taste. Her biting criticism about his shows, *"Meet the Browns"* and *"House of Payne,"* seem to sting like venom from a scorpion, *"Your shows are marked by old stereotypes of buffoonish emasculated black men and crass, sassy black women."*

Her caustic and philippic thrust, even after her declaimer, was only to reach for more fuel to throw on the pyre she built for Perry. Lemieux then threw motherhood under the bus, with her whetted offensive aimed at skewered Tyler with an extended thrush. Lunging she continued, *"Your most famous character, Madea, is a trash-talking, pistol-waving grandmother....The country has laughed at one of the most important members of the black community: Mother Dear, the beloved matriarch."*

Lemieux weakly tossed fig leaf, fail short of disguising, what Redd Foxx would call, *"a brick fight in St. Louis",* where her brick was aimed straight for Tyler's head, with a wink and nod at the white community. Lemieux may have thought she was teaching Perry a lesson. However, stretching to reach her point, struck me as signifying, maybe even playing the dozens, pretending her comments were defending motherhood, apple pie, and straight lace comedy. One should never stretch too far, trying to score points in a game out of one's league; one can lose their head to a spin move.

Presuming to speak for people in the black community, but simultaneously, denying Perry *VOICE* to tell the story he believes reflects the lives of black people he knew and grew up around, is to view African Americans as monolithic. It seems in her effort to represent the entire African Diaspora, or at least those in the US; her views are the only ones that have merit. Lemieux's backdoor attack is why I opened this discussion referencing to *"the vociferous and shrill outcries from distractors can drown out other voices, which belie their sinister intent."* So, I beg to differ totally with such sneak attacks, even when rapped in the cloak of objectivity.

I was unpersuaded that Lemieux protest was genuine *("An Open Letter to Tyler Perry,"* 2009, National Public Radio). I am not attempting to defend Perry; he has enough money to hire lawyers for that job. Again, I say, I will always step up to the plate and in such instance do as Dia Simms said, *"knock it the hell out of the park."* Even curveballs in the dirt can be lifted up over the fence for all to see, if one recognizes the pitch thrown. I will always ride to the defense of an artist's right to give *VOICE* to their vision, whether I agree with what they see or not!!!

When Tyler Perry decided to retire Madea, some may have thought; it was because of criticisms like those of Lemieux. I hope not, because I believe otherwise. This controversy reminds me of when Flip Wilson killed off Jeraldine. Flip said something to the effect that *"Jeraldine has become more popular than Flip Wilson and she is one of my characters."* I offer an exclamation point to his statement, because when I googled Flip Wilson, I got clips of *Jeraldine*.

Perry may have felt *Madea* was eclipsing her creator, as an image, and in such a case, she has outlived her usefulness. However, I will say, if Perry has decided to retire Madea truly, it should be done gracefully, rather than just dropping her, like a jilted spouse. The two have traveled the same road a long way together. *Madea* deserves a plot-line far better than an abusive lover.

Perry finally responded to his detractors, which came during a 60 Minutes interview (2009), he said of Spike Lee's comments about his work, *"I would love to read that [criticism] to my fan base. ... That pisses me off. It is so insulting. It's attitudes like that, that make Hollywood think that these people do not exist, and that is why there is no material speaking to them, speaking to us."* Perry also stated that *"all these characters are bait—disarming, charming, make-you-laugh bait. I can slap Madea on something and talk about God, love, faith, forgiveness, family, any of those."* In an interview with Hip Hollywood, Perry gave a different responded to Spike Lee's comments by telling him to *"go to hell"* (*"Tyler Perry Tells Spike Lee to 'Go To Hell!'"*, 2011 Hip Hollywood).

I believe this controversy speaks to something that is deeply rooted in the psyche and experiences of many black people and most have no idea of the source of their responses—*learned helplessness*. I will say, when Madea first appeared, I thought such thoughts about the character but to a much lesser degree. Contrarily, however, I would never call anyone out so brashly in writing before the world, based only on my personal views. My "mother" would be more embarrassed for me than Perry.

But my point here has real implications for African American unity after reaching **"The 400**th**"**. During my research on **"The 400**th**"**, I learned that during the years of struggle descendants of American slavery endured getting here, there were many different types of family situations and structures employed making families and building communities were multi-purpose. Trying to survive their penniless emancipation and the poverty that it produced, many family situations were forced upon people by necessity most times, choice was not one of the options, as in Perry early in life.

Also, I remind readers of the discussion on *"learned helplessness"* and how pain and terror by slave masters were intended to stripped away all sense of identity, pride, self-worth, values, love, and family structure for many many black people. The internal slave trade and breeding destroyed everything that had to do with the concept of the black family among people brought from Africa. Slavery and *"learned helplessness"* are reasons I believe black people today still struggle with family issues, as this Lemieux controversy exhibits.

Tyler's critics attack him because he did not enjoy the same middle-class upbringing and family environment, which their parents lavished on them. Their middle class up bringing controls how they think about others. For me, from the very beginning of his young life, Tyler Perry endured circumstances which makes him a poster child for brutality, abuse, scarcity, and desperation, all of which many black people continue experiencing, as a result from the impact of *"learned helplessness."* *Learned helplessness* was designed to make us haters, not lovers!!!!!!!!!!!!!!.

Similar to Oprah Winfrey, Tyler's physical and psychological abuse isolated them without defenders, and most crucially Tyler was estranged from the one person he wanted to love and be love by. Consequently, I think the abuse Tyler suffered, not only isolated and estranged him but seriously impacted his ability to know comfort and love, during his formative years. Overcoming his young life, he should be roundly applauded and resounding salute, not condemned, for any healthy vision he expresses as art. Moreover, he did not have the advantage of therapy; he had to figure out a therapy for himself, which was tantamount to a heart surgeon operating on himself. Then there is the Madea character, which seemed to draw the most vitriolic responses from critics. I think the interview Tyler gave Oprah is most revealing regarding the world that shaped Tyler during his young years. Oprah ask,

O: *I know you had great, deep love and affection for your mother. But what was your feelings about her when you were a child? Because you wanted your mother to stand up for you.*

TP: *Children love their mothers. Especially with a boy child and his mother, there's a bond that's unbreakable. I love my mother to this day. One of the most painful things I ever had to do was bury her, realizing that even though I was her hero, I couldn't help her with this last thing. I couldn't help her get better. All I wanted was to give her everything she wanted. Everything my father didn't give her, everything she never had.*

O: *You were never angry with her?*

TP: *Not as a child. I would never say this if she was alive, but there was a time when I was older when I was angry with her, yeah, sure. But my love would override that.*

O: *All right. But now, in the midst of all the physical abuse, you were also sexually abused. Was this by a neighbor, a friend of the family, somebody you knew?*

TP: *Neighbor, friend of the family, all of that. The first time, I was 6 or 7; it was a guy across the street. We built a birdhouse together and suddenly he's got a hand in my pants.*

O: *But you were molested by other people, too?*

TP: *Yes. One was a woman who lived in the apartment complex two doors down, when I was about 10 or 11. And there was a guy in church.*

O: *That must have been a lot for you to carry. A lot of hurt and anger and betrayal and confusion and shame. So how did all of this—all your experiences growing up—prepare you for the life you're now living? First of all, the aunt who came with the gun—the moment you said that, I thought, "Here comes Madea!"*

TP: *Yeah. The Bible says that all things work together for the good of those who love the Lord and are called according to his purpose. I believe that. Because I've seen it all work. I know for a fact if I had not been born to this mother, this father, this family, if I had not been born into this situation, then I wouldn't be here using my voice and my gifts to speak to millions of people.*

What broadened my perspective on the *Madea* movies happened while watching a rerun of *Madea's Family Reunion*. Coupled with my research, I saw *Madea* as someone fighting to hold families together and help others do the same. There have always been many strong black women that have played a *Madea* type role in black communities. Psychologically and physically, mothers and grandmothers have done this for centuries, like my mother. I shudder to think what some mothers have had to do to keep their families together.

The *Madea* series is a parody (A particular style of writing by an artist or a genre with **"deliberate exaggeration"** for comic effect), which disguises the lessons being taught. Calling Madea *"coonery or buffoonery"* misses the points I believe Perry makes in his movies, which reflects some periods I discuss at length in this narrative, beginning when slaves did whatever to "pleased master or tickled his fancy," as a means of survival, while white people turned it into Minstrelsy. They were not having fun, no matter how it is presented in history books today, through supposedly educated and enlightened eyes.

Today our problem is getting the attention of black people, old and young, long enough to teach them a positive lesson, about anything is not easy. Parodies have long been part of the effort to up-life black people. Redd Fox was one of the best. During his time, African Americans were so proud, appreciative and too happy to seeing a black face on TV for them to attack anything about *Sanford and Son*.

No one attacked Norman Lear. He did the same thing with *Good Times* and *The Jeffersons*. Lear put *"Amos and Andy"* to shame, making George the *"coonery or buffoonery"* champion of all times, but nobody complains about how that made black people look, and both Spike and Lemieux were around. Even more to this point, they are redoing *"The Jeffersons,"* with Jamie Foxx. What does that mean? Tyler Perry, at least, created his own *"coonery or buffoonery"* characters; he did not commandeer a white man's vision of black people. Tyler's life exemplifies the resiliency of the human spirit; anything can stop you if you allow it.

I beg readers indulgence to address a specific point in Lemieux's diatribe about *"crass, sassy black women….and a trash-talking, pistol-waving"* mother or grandmother. I offer Mrs. Willie May Gray and had Tyler Perry known her when he created the Medea character, I would swear, he modeled his Madea character, on my mother. During her life (now 101), although she was never a *"pistol packer,"* when we lived in Greens Alley, she intervened in domestic problems. Mudear chased abusive mates from their house, and would not allow them back in until they were ready to do right by their mate. She rescued her five-year-old cousin from a burning house just before it collapsed. And, although she was not a midwife, she delivered four babies without assistance, during her life, and they all lived. But, her coup de grace was, in her fifties, she chased a would-be purse snatcher through Riverside until he threw her purse down to get away from her.

There are a few more incidents I could recite about Mudear, but she would say I was bragging,' when she was only doing what needed to be done at the time to teach lessons or help people in desperate straits. So, unless one knows the story of the vast majority of black mothers across the African Diaspora, never think the things done by "Mudears" which is what we called my mother, are beyond their capacity when events call them to action.

The key lesson for me in *Madea's Family Reunion* came when the elder matriarchs called the family together with the ringing of the bell. Ringing the bell was very significant to slaves and descendants, especially if you were sharecroppers; it signaled the time to go to work. And the matriarchs went to work telling the family of their journey from slavery to **"The 400th"**. There was no laughter. I agree with Tyler, "It's time for black folks to get to work!!!!!!!!!!!!!!!!!!"

My last example considering those selected to reflect descendants of American slavery's progress, since arriving in North America, was even more unlikely, at birth, to rise to her present level of success, than Tyler Perry. She was not born (1-29-1954) destined to be the *"belle of the ball,"* but nevertheless, she reflects another adage, *"Cream rises to the top!"* An accident at birth gave us Oprah Winfrey, wiping Orpah Gail Winfrey out of existence shortly after opening her eyes. A spelling error, transposing the r, and p on her birth certificate, which made that error, a poison pen that did Orpah in. Eliminating Orpah from existence, Oprah Gail Winfrey is lucky to be here. An unintended person, like most unintended consequences, Oprah's stolen life, became descendants of American slavery's brightest star, as we reach **"The 400th"**. Maybe, without that trick of fate, the world would not have the media executive, actress, talk show host, television producer, and philanthropist, which has changed so many lives and made it a much better world for us all.

Her life from the beginning and the success that eventually resulted makes her life the most unusual of all on this list, especially since she's female and black.

These two points are most salient in the context of America's racist history. Now I discuss one of the most impactful individual that contributed mightily laying the *"yellow brick road of entertainment"* Oprah Winfrey. My effort here is to make clear her amazing accomplishment, surviving in the valley of poverty, while giving a hand up to millions, who are helping other is my goal.

Oprah, through her life, has redeemed the decision by descendants of American slavery to endure to survive for the next generation, now that we prepare to commemorate and celebrate **"The 400th"** for the very first time, is an accomplishment without words to explain how or why. Her talk show—*The Oprah Winfrey Show*—at the beginning of her career, is how she's best known. Her show is the highest-rated television program of its kind in history. Syndicated nationally in Chicago, Illinois, an unlikely place to achieve her level of fame, while logging 25 years, leading the talk show genre from the "Windy City" (1986 to 2011) is also amazing. Dubbed the "Queen of All Media," *("The World's Most Powerful Celebrities List,"* 2013; Forbes), by the media, she is the richest African American, of all times, as of 2019. She opened the 21st century as North America's first black multi-billionaire, *("The Wealthiest Black Americans,"* Matthew Miller, 2009; Forbes). Declared one of the greatest black philanthropists in American history, is only one of the many outstanding accolades showered on her. International publications dubbed her the *"most influential woman in the world", ("The most influential US liberals: 1–20,"* 2007; The Daily Telegraph, London).

How did such a thing happen to someone from Oprah Winfrey's meager beginnings in the grave of poverty in the valley of dry bones? First off, Oprah was born in the impoverished rural state of Mississippi to a teenage single mother, who moved to another impoverished area—the inner-city ghetto of Milwaukee, Wisconsin. At age 13, according to Oprah, after suffering an abusive childhood, she ran away from home and, at age 14, and became pregnant. Her son was born premature and died after birth. Poverty and postpartum depression alone would have devastated most women born in Oprah's circumstances, but even that could not count her out. *("Oprah Winfrey,"* 2008; The Biography Channel).

Oprah's amazing story of resilience and perseverance began after her mother moved to Milwaukee. There she attended Lincoln High School. Early success in the Upward Bound program, gained her a move up to an affluent suburban high school—Nicolet. Oprah confesses that *"Riding the bus to school with fellow African-Americans, my poverty was constantly rubbed in my face by some whose parents were servants of my classmates' families."* Trying to keep up with her free-spending peers, she admits, *stealing money from her mother.* Arguing with and lying to her regarding going out with older boys, their relationship deteriorated, (*Oprah Winfrey: Profile of a Media Mogul*, Jeanne M. Nagle, 2007; Rosen Publishing).

Frustrated, her mother sent her to live with Vernon, her biological father, in Nashville, Tennessee. Vernon was strict but encouraged Oprah to make her education her priority. She became an honor student and was voted *Most Popular Girl* at her school. She joined the East Nashville High School speech team and placed second in the nation in dramatic interpretation. At age 17, Winfrey won the *Miss Black Tennessee beauty pageant*. Her victory gained the attention of the local black radio station, WVOL, which hired her to do news part-time. She worked with WVOL, during her senior year of high school on through her first two years of college. While still in high school, Oprah began co-anchoring the local evening news at age 19.

Winning an oratory contest, Oprah was awarded a full scholarship to Tennessee State University (HBCU), where she studied communication. Her head filled with dreams of greatness, Winfrey stepped out on her own, relocating to Chicago in 1983. She became the host of WLS-TV's low-rated half-hour morning talk show, *AM Chicago*. Her emotional ad-lib delivery fit the daytime talk show format. After boosting the third-rated local Chicago talk show to first place, she launched her own production company, shortly after.

Movie critic Roger Ebert persuaded her to become syndicated. Ebert predicted she *"would generate 40 times the revenue of his television show, At the Movies,"* ("How I gave Oprah her start," Roger Ebert, 2005; Roger Ebert's Journal. Chicago). Winfrey signed a deal with *King World*. She is credited, by some, with creating a more intimate confessional form of media communication. It is said Oprah *"popularized and revolutionized the tabloid talk show genre,"* pioneered by Phil Donahue. According to a Yale University study, *"Winfrey broke 20th-century taboos by giving LGBT people voice in mainstream media."*

The first episode aired on January 2, 1984. Within months, after Winfrey debuted, the show moved out of last place in ratings to overtaking Donahue as the "highest-rated talk show in Chicago." The syndicated version was renamed *The Oprah Winfrey Show* and expanded to a full hour. Oprah began broadcasting nationally on September 8, 1986. Winfrey's syndicated show brought in double Donahue's national audience, *"replacing him as the number-one daytime talk show in America."* Their much-publicized contest was the subject of enormous scrutiny. TIME magazine wrote:

"Few people would have bet on Oprah Winfrey's swift rise to host of the most popular talk show on TV. In a field dominated by white males, she is a black female of ample bulk. As interviewers go, she is no match for, say, Phil Donahue ... What she lacks in journalistic toughness, she makes up for in plainspoken curiosity, robust humor and, above all empathy. Guests with sad stories to tell are apt to rouse a tear in Oprah's eye ... They, in turn, often find themselves revealing things they would not imagine telling anyone, much less a national TV audience. It is the talk show as a group therapy session," ("Oprah Winfrey: Lady with a Calling," 1988; Time Magazine).

By the mid-1990s, Winfrey had reinvented her show with a focus on literature, self-improvement, and spirituality. Many chided Oprah, criticizing her for "unleashing a confession culture, promoting controversial self-help ideas, and an overly emotion-centered approach." But and still, Oprah is often praised for "overcoming adversity in her life, while being a benefactor to others," *("Oprah Winfrey,"* Nelson Mandela, 2007; The TIME 100).

One estimate says, "Her endorsement of Barack H. Obama for president, delivered over a million votes in the closing days of the 2008 Democratic primary race," and became a major push in Obama winning the presidency. President Obama awarded her the Presidential Medal of Freedom. Duke and Harvard awarded her honorary doctorate degrees (*"The World's Most Powerful Celebrities List,"* Nelson Forbes, 2013; Forbes).

Winfrey's career choice in media would not have surprised her grandmother, who once said that *"Ever since she could talk, she was on stage. As a child, she played games interviewing her corncob doll and the cows at the fence on her family's farm."* Oprah later acknowledged her grandmother's influence, saying, *"It was Hattie Mae who encouraged me to speak in public and gave me a positive sense of myself,"* (*"Oprah: Talk Show Dynamo Treats the Audience Like a Friend,"* Mel Novit, 1986; Syracuse Post-Standard).

Returning to the question I opened with, *"How did such a thing happen to someone with Oprah's meager beginning in poverty?"* is not something that comes with a ready-made explanation. Born in the worse kind of poverty—in the belly of the beast in Mississippi—into a sharecropping family, which she shared with millions of descendants of American slavery, including this writer, means she was not unique in this regard.

She hung tough, even looking at the fact she was raised by a single mother dependent on government assistance in the poorest state in the union, was not unique either. Even after moving to an urban ghetto similar to or more impoverished than Mississippi and her aborted pregnancy, a common scenario millions of young slave descendant females, who shared her circumstances.

There has to be some unique undiscovered characteristics, unique to Oprah that explains her phenomenal success. I believe from my research, what sets Winfrey apart, elevating her to her current status and success, but even Oprah has not been able to articulate what that or those qualities are. That outcome is what I call the magic of the **Blues,** which she was born into in the Mississippi delta. Even conservatives agree, *"Oprah Winfrey is a phenomenon unto herself."* My assessment is based solely on the fact that she not only survived to obtain riches, but she also became one of the richest people in the world, even compared to "old money."

However, when one adds the remarkable fact that at age 32, Winfrey, in less than ten years, had just become a millionaire, with only her nationally syndication talk show, describing her as phenomenal is a tremendous understatement.

Winfrey negotiated ownership rights to the television program and started her own production company. At age 41, Winfrey had a net worth of $340 million. She joined Bill Cosby as the only African American on the Forbes 400. With a net worth of $800 million in 2000, 17 years after beginning her wild ride, it was believed, Winfrey had become the richest African American of the 20th century. Trying to understand this amazing entrepreneur, the University of Illinois offers a course focusing on Winfrey's business acumen, namely: *"History 298: Oprah Winfrey, the Tycoon,"* *("Oprah College Course,"* Race Matters. Marja Mills, 2001).

Winfrey became the highest-paid television entertainer in the United States in 2006, earning an estimated $260 million during that year, five times the sum earned by second-place music executive Simon Cowell. By 2008, her "yearly income" had increased another $275 million. Forbes' list of *The World's Billionaires* has Winfrey as the world's only black billionaire from 2004 to 2006 and as the first black woman billionaire in the world in 2003.

As of 2014, Winfrey had a net worth of over 2.9 billion dollars. That is an amazing accomplishment for anyone to earn $2.1 billion from 2000 to 2014, but for one from Oprah neck of the woods, that is beyond unprecedented. She has overtaken former eBay CEO Meg Whitman as the richest self-made woman in America. Forbes magazine (3-26-2007) says, *"There are only ten self-made women billionaires in the world, and Winfrey is the richest of the four listed as U.S. billionaires."*

I will now provide a basis for what may seem hyperbole to some. While pilling up her mammoth fortune, Winfrey has co-authored five books. At the announcement of a weight-loss book in 2005, co-authored with her trainer Bob Greene, her undisclosed advance fee broke former President Bill Clinton's record for the world's highest book advance fee. Her memoir, *The Life You Want*, was scheduled for publication in 2017.

Winfrey publishes *"O,"* *The Oprah Magazine*, and from 2004 to 2008, she also published a magazine called *"O At Home."* In 2002, Fortune called *"O,"* the *"most successful start-up ever in the industry."* Winfrey's company created the Oprah.com website to provide resources and interactive content relating to her shows, magazines, book club, and public charity. Oprah.com averages more than 70 million page views and more than six million users per month and receives approximately 20,000 e-mails each week. How does one manage such volumes? Winfrey initiated *"Oprah's Child Predator Watch List,"* through her show and website, to help track down accused child molesters. Within the first 48 hours, police captured two of the featured men.

On February 9, 2006, Winfrey had signed a three-year, $55-million contract with XM Satellite Radio to establish a new radio channel. The channel, Oprah Radio, features popular contributors from The Oprah Winfrey Show and *"O,"* including Nate Berkus, Dr. Mehmet Oz, Bob Greene, Dr. Robin Smith, and Marianne Williamson. Oprah & Friends began broadcasting at 11:00 am ET, September 25, 2006, from a new studio at Winfrey's Chicago headquarters. The channel broadcasts 24 hours a day, seven days a week, on XM Radio Channel 156. Winfrey's contract requires her to be on air 30 minutes a week, 39 weeks a year.

The Wall Street Journal coined the term "Oprahfication," meaning public confession as a form of therapy. Time magazine credits Winfrey with creating a new form of media communication known as "rapport talk," as distinguished from the "report talk" of Phil Donahue. Oprah's style of confessing intimate details about her weight problems, tumultuous love life, sexual abuse, and crying alongside her guests is the base of her "rapport talk." Time said, *"Winfrey saw television's power to blend public and private; while it links strangers and conveys information over public airwaves. TV is most often viewed in the privacy of our homes. As a family member, it sits down to meals with us and talks to us in the lonely afternoons."* Grasping this paradox, Oprah caused people to care because she cares. That is one part of Winfrey's genius and will be a major part of her legacy. Changes she has wrought in the talk show business continue to permeate our culture and shape our lives, *("The TV Host,"* 1998; Time).

Observers have also noted the "Oprahfication" of politics such as "Oprah-style debates" and Bill Clinton being described as *"the man who brought Oprah-style psychobabble and misty confessions to politics."*

Newsweek stated: *"Every time a politician lets his lip quiver or a cable anchor 'emotes' on TV, they nod to the cult of confession that Oprah inspired."* The November 1988 copy of Ms. observed that *"in a society where fat is taboo, she made it in a medium that worships thin and celebrates a bland, white-bread prettiness of body and personality [...] But Winfrey made fat sexy, elegant – damned near gorgeous – with her drop-dead wardrobe, easy body language, and cheerful sensuality."*

Oprah's reach around the world increased when she created *Oprah's Angel Network*, in 1998. Oprah's charity supports charitable projects and provided grants to nonprofit organizations around the world. *Oprah's Angel Network* raised more than $80,000,000. Winfrey personally covered all administrative costs associated with the charity, so 100% of all funds raised went to charity programs. In May 2010, with Oprah's show ending, the charity stopped accepting donations, and it shut down.

The power of Winfrey's opinions and endorsements to influence public choices, especially consumer purchasing decisions, has been dubbed *"The Oprah Effect."* The effect has been documented or alleged in domains as diverse as book sales, beef markets, and election voting. Late in 1996, Winfrey introduced the *Oprah's Book Club* segment to her television show.

The segment focused on new books and classics and often brought obscure novels to popular attention. The book club became such a powerful force that whenever Winfrey introduced a new book as her book-club selection, it instantly became a best-seller. For example, when she selected the classic John Steinbeck novel *East of Eden*, it soared to the top of the book charts. Being recognized by

Winfrey often means a million additional book sales for an author. In <u>Reading with Oprah: The Book Club that Changed America</u> (2005), Kathleen Rooney describes Winfrey as *"a serious American intellectual who pioneered the use of electronic media, specifically television and the Internet, to take reading – a decidedly non-technological and highly individual act – and highlight its social elements and uses in such a way to motivate millions of erstwhile non-readers to pick up books."*

When author Jonathan Franzen's book became a Book Club selection, he reportedly "cringed" and said selected books tend to be "schmaltzy." After James Frey's *A Million Little Pieces* experienced complaints of containing fabrications in 2006, Winfrey confronted him on her show over the breach of trust. In 2009, Winfrey apologized to Frey for the public confrontation.

During a show about mad cow disease with Howard Lyman (aired on April 16, 1996), Winfrey said she was *"stopped cold from eating another burger."* Texas cattlemen sued her and Lyman in early 1998 for "false defamation of perishable food" and "business disparagement," claiming that Winfrey's remarks sent cattle prices tumbling, costing beef producers $11 million. Attorney Chip Babcock represented Winfrey, and on February 26, after a two-month trial in an Amarillo, Texas, court, a jury found Winfrey and Lyman not liable for damages.

The viewership for *The Oprah Winfrey Show* was highest during the 1991–92 seasons when about 13.1 million U.S. viewers watched each day. Such phenomenal ratings gave Winfrey the ability to launch other successful talk shows such as Dr. Phil, Dr. Oz, and Rachael Ray. Media credits *"The Oprah Effect* for their success."* By 2003, ratings declined to 7.4 million daily viewers. Ratings briefly rebounded to approximately 9 million in 2005 and then declined again to around 7.3 million viewers in 2008, though it remained the highest-rated talk show.

In 2004, Winfrey and her team filmed an episode of *Oprah's Christmas Kindness*. Winfrey traveled to South Africa to bring attention to the plight of young children affected by poverty and AIDS. During the 21-day trip, Winfrey and her crew visited schools and orphanages in poverty-stricken areas, and distributed Christmas presents to 50,000 children—dolls for girls and soccer balls for boys and school supplies for everyone. Throughout the show, Winfrey appealed to viewers to donate money to *Oprah's Angel Network* for poor and AIDS-affected children in Africa. From that show alone, viewers around the world donated over $7,000,000.

Winfrey invested $40 million and some of her time establishing the *Oprah Winfrey Leadership Academy for Girls* in Henley on Klip south of Johannesburg, South Africa. The school is set on 22 acres, opened in January 2007 with an enrollment of 150 pupils (increasing to 450) and features state-of-the-art classrooms, computer and science laboratories, a library, theatre, and beauty salon.

Nelson Mandela praised Winfrey for overcoming her disadvantaged youth to become a benefactor for others. Critics considered the school elitist and unnecessarily luxurious. Winfrey rejected the claims, saying: *"If you are surrounded by beautiful things and wonderful teachers who inspire you that beauty brings out the beauty in you."* Winfrey, who has no surviving biological children, described maternal feelings towards her girls at *Oprah Winfrey Leadership Academy for Girls*. Winfrey teaches a class at the school via satellite.

In 2008, Winfrey's show was airing in 140 countries internationally and seen by an estimated 46 million people in the US weekly. According to a Harris poll, Winfrey was America's favorite television personality in 1998, 2000, 2002–06, and 2009. Winfrey was especially popular among women, Democrats, political moderates, Baby Boomers, Generation X, Southern Americans, and East Coast Americans.

Outside the U.S., Winfrey has become increasingly popular in the Arab world. The Wall Street Journal reported in 2007 that MBC 4, an Arab satellite channel, centered its entire programming around reruns of her show because it was drawing record numbers of female viewers in Saudi Arabia. In 2008, The New York Times reported that *The Oprah Winfrey Show*, with Arabic subtitles, was broadcast twice each weekday on MBC 4. Winfrey's modest dress, combined with her attitude of triumph over adversity and abuse, has caused some women in Saudi Arabia to idealize her.

In the wake of Hurricane Katrina, Oprah created the *Oprah Angel Network Katrina* registry, which raised more than $11 million for relief efforts. Winfrey personally gave $10 million to the cause. She built homes in Texas, Mississippi, Louisiana, and Alabama before the first anniversary of Hurricanes Katrina and Rita. Winfrey visited evacuees from New Orleans temporarily sheltered at the Reliant center in Houston following Hurricane Katrina. In 2004, Winfrey became the first black person to rank among the 50 most generous Americans, and she remained among the top 50 until 2010. By 2012, she had given away about $400 million to educational causes. As of 2012, Winfrey had also given over 400 scholarships to Morehouse College in Atlanta, Georgia.

Winfrey was the recipient of the first Bob Hope Humanitarian Award at the 2002 Emmy Awards for services to television and film. Celebrating two decades on national TV, and to thank her employees for their hard work, Winfrey took her staff and their families (1,065 people in total) on vacation to Hawaii in the summer of 2006. In 2013, Winfrey donated $12 million to the Smithsonian's National Museum of African American History and Culture.

For me, Oprah Winfrey is descendants of American slavery's *"Solomon."* As he—Solomon—was not only the richest man of his time, he is said to have been the smartest and wisest. There was no one who could be compared to him. I see Oprah as the quintessential entrepreneur, as *"Solomon* was the quintessential King." There is no counterpart to what Oprah has accomplished in "one lifetime." She has accomplished things that mere mortals have no reference. Her amazing fortune was accumulated over the last 40 years and places Oprah in a class unto herself.

The 400th: From Slavery to Hip Hop

From the cotton field to the board room, from slavery to hip hop, Oprah made her trek unassisted by family wealth or political/government connections. Against the current of racism, discrimination, and sexism, she swam upstream, like a salmon. Accomplishing such feats, placing her in a school of fish, like Forbes 400 and Fortune's 500, only defuses her brilliance, as well as minimizes the height of rapids she ascended reaching what black Americans hope is her spawning grounds.

Such comparisons ignore the fact that the rich fish in those schools—Forbes 400 and Fortune's 500—were not lone riders, they had families with a history of wealth built up over generations or were from a class with access to America's bounty. Whereas, Oprah was born into a sharecropper's family in the graveyard of poverty and was without benefactors for most of her young life.

The amazing fact about Winfrey's journey from a Mississippi cotton field to her corporate board room is her affluence did not begin until after the age of twenty-five, and she didn't make her first million until after the age of thirty. Consequently, she amassed her individual fortune in less than forty years.

I am not talking about someone born into a middle-class background, but someone who resided in the grave of poverty in the valley of dry bones until young adulthood before she knew what it was like to even make money. No one else on Forbes or Fortune's money list has come from the cotton field to the board room in *"one lifetime"* to join those exclusive schools. If one made a line of fish from those two schools and added the categories of sharecropping and descendant of American slavery to the poll, Oprah would be splashing around in the water by herself. This fact alone makes Oprah Winfrey the sparkling tip and the gleaming point of slave descendants' thrust in their 400-year drive to establish themselves as one people.

Oprah may not consider herself a hip-hopper, but she is the ultimate example of *making something out of nothing*. Once she began touching the world in her unique way, she made it a better place than it was before her embrace. Descendants of American slavery have struggled trying to overcome their penniless emancipation and had only their **Blues** to anesthetize their pain. Hip hop has firmly established *VOICE* for African Americans, as they claim their rights as one people. The sacrifices their ancestors made and the degradation suffered, reaching **"The 400th"** is a miraculous feat no one can deny.

Hip hop made it possible for young blacks to take old things and used them in new ways, and create innovative technologies, making *"something out of nothing."* That nothing now reigns as the new international culture. Hip Hoppers accomplished this without access to the socio-economic and political resources of the world slavery built. The same nothing, like the cotton field life that lay before Oprah Winfrey at birth, is hip hop's legacy at its beginning. Through hip hop, young black entrepreneurs have done as Oprah, beginning with nothing, they took what others had been doing for years and saw it in new ways and flip it.

Oprah's mindset, as well as the mindsets of all those on this list, used their unique vision to help lay the foundation for creating the new world culture—hip hop reflects.

The Grand Dame of Black Entertainment

Cicely L. Tyson was born in Harlem on December 19, 1924. Cicely was the daughter of Frederica and William Augustine Tyson, immigrants that came to America from Nevis in the West Indies. She became an actress and fashion model. Her career spans more than six decades, and her hallmark, as an actress, is portraying strong African-American women (Biography, A&E Television Networks, 2019).

An Ebony magazine photographer discovered Mrs. Tyson and helped her become a popular fashion model. Cicely's first acting role was on the NBC series *"Frontiers of Faith"* in 1951 and her first film role was *"Carib Gold"* in 1956. Her big chance in television came in the celebrated series *"East Side/West Side."* With that role she became the first African American to star in a television drama. Cecily also appeared on the soap opera *"The Guiding Light."*

Mrs. Tyson gained her acting bona fides appeared in the original cast of French playwright Jean Genet's *"The Blacks"* (1961), which became the longest-running off-Broadway non-musical of that decade, with 1,408 performances. The lights of motion pictures drew her to Hollywood, where she appeared with Sammy Davis Jr. in the film *"A Man Called Adam"* (1966). Cicely followed that with a starring role in the film version of Graham Greene's *"The Comedians"* (1967). Mrs. Cicely Tyson had a featured role in *"The Heart Is a Lonely Hunter" (1968)* to greet the 1970s.

Mrs. Tyson played the role of Rebecca Morgan in the critically acclaimed film *"Sounder"* in 1972. She was nominated for both the Academy Award and Golden Globe Award for Best Actress for her work in *Sounder,* and also won the NSFC Best Actress and NBR Best Actress Awards. Mrs. Tyson played the title role in the television film *The Autobiography of Miss Jane Pittman* (1974). Her portrayal of a young black slave won her a Primetime Emmy Award for Outstanding Lead Actress – Miniseries or a Movie and an Emmy Award for Actress of the Year – Special. Mrs. Tyson was also nominated for a BAFTA Award for Best Actress in a Leading Role for her work in television film.

The miniseries *"Coretta Scott King"* (1978) gained Mrs. Cicely a nomination for a Primetime Emmy Award for Outstanding Lead Actress. She appeared in *"Fried Green Tomatoes"* as Sipsey (1991). In the 1994–95 television series *"Sweet Justice,"* she portrayed a civil rights activist and attorney Carrie Grace Battle. She shaped her character by consulting with noted Washington, D.C. civil rights and criminal defense lawyer Dovey Johnson Roundtree. Other notable film roles include the dramas *"Hoodlum"* (1997) and *"Diary of a Mad Black Woman"* (2005), and the television films *Oldest Living Confederate Widow Tells All* (1994) (for which she received her third Emmy Award) and *"A Lesson Before Dying"* (1999).

The phenomenal Mrs. Tyson appeared in *"Why Did I Get Married Too?"* She narrated the Paul Robeson Award-winning documentary, *"Up from the Bottoms: The Search for the American Dream"* (2009). Willow Smith spotlighted Mrs. Tyson in her first music video in *"21st Century Girl"* (2011). That same year, she played Constantine Jefferson, a maid in Jackson, Mississippi, in the critically acclaimed period drama *"The Help."* Set against the backdrop of the Civil Rights Movement, the film won the Broadcast Film Critics Association Award for Best Acting Ensemble and the Screen Actors Guild Award for Outstanding Performance by a Cast in a Motion Picture (2011).

Mrs. Tyson won the 67th Tony Awards for Best Actress in a Play as Miss Carrie Watts in *"The Trip to Bountiful"*(6-9-2013). She also won the Drama Desk Award for Outstanding Actress in a Play and the Outer Critics Circle Award for Outstanding Actress in a Play for the role in *Andrew* (2013). ("Pippin Is Big Winner of 2012–13 Outer Critics Circle Awards", Playbill). Among the 96-year-old standard of excellence accolades are Screen Actor Guild, Tony, Emmy and Black Reel Awards.

Mrs. Tyson has received several other honors including, honorary degrees from Columbia University, Howard University, and Morehouse College, an all-male historically black college. In 1977, Mrs. Tyson became a Black Filmmakers Hall of Fame inductee. Mrs. Cicely Tyson was awarded the Women in Film Crystal Award given to outstanding women who, through their endurance and their excellence of work, have helped to expand the role of women within the entertainment industry. She received a Candace Award for Distinguished Service from the National Coalition of 100 Black Women 1988, *("CANDACE AWARD RECIPIENTS 1982-1990,"* National Coalition of 100 Black Women, 2003.)

Mrs. Tyson was an honoree at Oprah Winfrey's Legends Ball. She also became the NAACP's 2010 Spingarn Medal recipient for her modeling career, support of civil rights, and contributions to the entertainment industry ("NAACP Names Cicely Tyson 95th Spingarn Medalist", 2011www.naacp.org.) Mrs. Cicely was named a Kennedy Center honoree in 2015. She was also awarded the United States' highest civilian honor, the Presidential Medal of Freedom, by President Barack H. Obama in November 2016. Honorees also include philanthropists Bill and Melinda Gates, artist Maya Lin and Kareem Abdul-Jabbar. *("These Are The 21 People Receiving The Nation's Highest Civilian Honor", NPR 2016).*

In September 2018, the Academy of Motion Picture Arts and Sciences announced that Mrs. Tyson would receive an honorary Academy Award. On November 18, 2018, she became the first African-American woman to receive an honorary Oscar *(Cicely Tyson, Kathleen Kennedy break new ground with honorary Oscars, 2018).* **"The 400th"** is honored and proud to recognize and give voice to the two **"Grande Dames,"** of entertainment Mrs. Cicely at 95 and my Mudear Mrs. Willie May Gray at 101. Both are major women bricklayers on the *"yellow brick road of entertainment,"* on the way to hip hop. They give those of us today, excited

The 400th: From Slavery to Hip Hop

about commemorating and celebrating *"The 400th"* two of the longest living views of enslaved Africans trek and struggle to reach *"The 400th"*.

Assault on the Citadels of Racism

For those who truly believe lightning never strikes twice in the same place, try four times when dominance in World Gymnastic is hip hopper, Simone Biles. Simone captivated the world at the 2019 US Gymnastics Championships with her must-see performances the weekend of 8/16-18/2019 in Kansas City, Missouri. The 22-year-old earned a record-tying sixth all-around national title, which was highlighted by a double-double dismount from the balance beam Friday and a triple-double on floor exercises Sunday, neither of which had ever been performed by a woman.

Simone cruised through the US championships field, punching her express ticket to Rio de Janeiro 2020 Olympic Games. Biles, a 4-foot-8 package of dynamite, blew up the top scores over two nights of competition in the balance beam, floor exercise, and vault. She now has 11 national titles since joining the senior level in 2013. Named USA Gymnastics Athlete of the Year, after Sunday's performance, Simone became the first woman to win four US all-around titles in a row since Joan Moore Gnat in 1971-74. Simone, from Spring, Texas, outpaced not only her US counterparts but all of gymnastics over the past three years, *("Simone Biles First To Win Four Straight National Championships In 42 Years,"* Chrös McDougall, 6-26-2016, Red Line Editorial, Inc.).

An AP story *"Biles aims to write more history at gymnastics worlds!"* places "Miss Dynamite" on top of the world of champions, as her explosive moves vaulted her to another sure-fire record book designation. Stuttgart, Germany, will be Simone's, who already owns several records in gymnastics, chance to add still more in Stuttgart. At the upcoming world championships in Germany, Simone can break the record for most medals won by any gymnast. More than that, she can write herself into the sport's Code of Points forever. Biles showed off her triple-twisting double-flip — the triple-double for short—winning the US title in August. If she sticks it at the world games, it will go in the Code as "the Biles." The same goes for her double-double beam dismount. Taking everything in flips and bounces, Simone says:

"Getting the skills named after me is really exciting, to go out there and prove to myself that I can do them, especially under all the pressure that will be there that night. I feel like putting my name on a skill is really rewarding just because it'll be in the Code forever as well as the medals. It's something that I can hold onto just because I'm the one that did it first, so it's really exciting."

Simone already boasts two skills in the Code floor exercise element from 2013 and a vault from last year's world championships. She goes to the championships tied with Russian Svetlana Khorkina for the most medals won by a woman with 20, and could also surpass Vitaly Scherbo's record of 23 for the most medals by any gymnast. (Scherbo is one of the most successful gymnasts of all time. He is the only male gymnast ever to win a world title in all eight events. He was the most successful athlete at the 1992 Summer Olympics, winning 6 of 8 events—team, all-around, and 4 of 6 event finals).

Being placed among greats like track star Usain Bolt and swimming great Michael Phelps, both have retired since Tokyo, the last Olympics, making Simone odds on favorite at the Rio Games. Similar to her landings after her "triple-double," Simone said while giving one of her classic smiles:

"I feel like if I were to label myself as a superstar, it would bring more expectations on me. I would feel pressured, more in the limelight, rather than like now. A Monoymous person, Simone says, *I just go out there and compete, trying to represent Simone, not Simone Biles, whenever I go out there, because at the end of the day, I'm still a human being before I'm 'Simone Biles the Superstar.'"*

Simone is another living example of a major theme of this narrative, **"do something with your body."** She is an exclamation point for the discussion I began with "Dr. J," *"Once descendants of enslaved African push their way through barrier erected to keep them out, as Jackie Roberson showed, the game is never the same."* Game changers are no longer camping on the doorsteps of America's citadels of racism, patiently waiting for gatekeepers to decide to admit them. They are kicking in the door, and even if they were allowed in, they are bringing move into the game that gatekeepers never dreamed were possible for the human body to perform.

Game-changing athletes, such as Serena Williams, who closed the door on the thin pale, frail, fragile frames that once dominated the game, courts, mat, stage, or other performance venues. Back somersaults on ice skates by Surya Bonaly, double back-overs or double-double dismount from the balance beam and triple-double somersaults on floor exercise are flowing from them, like hip hop technological innovations. My last topic is about the assault on the last of these citadels of whiteness that has fallen, but the attitude of gatekeepers', as with Lorraine Hansberry, they still refuse to accept what they cannot stop.

The Two Lives of a Curvy Ballerina!

Ballet, since its beginning, as an art form, has been dominated by white females and males, and that story has not changed. During my early years because it was about what white people did for dance, it seemed dull and very uninteresting. I didn't know anyone who danced, and television was rare also, in my world, I had no exposure to ballet. Though my exposure increased over the years, it still was something white people did, that is until my niece Karen Smith-English began dancing in the 1970s and now her daughter Imani is a dancer in Chicago.

The other reason ballet bombed with me is, you couldn't do it at house parties, which may sound gross to some, but that was the nature of my environment and for most Africans Americans. I do not mean to give the impression I never saw ballet or that I don't appreciate it, because I love watching ballet, it's just that, it was not part of my life or world, to my regret. Thankfully, once I began researching **"The 400th"** ballet was one subject I decided to include because of the next person I discuss. She is so amazing and her dazzling performances, as well as her groundbreaking career is so inspiring, for more reasons than dancing. Without tragedy and resilience, which crush most people, I never would have encountered her amazing story for **"The 400th"**, which would have made it incomplete.

So, on my search to learned some of the inside story of ballet, I was introduced to many ballerinas of African heritage including Judith Jamison, Raven Wilkinson, Lauren Anderson, Aesha Ash, Janet Collins, Anne Benna Sims, Virginia Johnson, Thelma Hill and the amazing Katherine Dunham just to name a few that danced professionally as principal dancers with companies. I repeat, although I provide details about individuals cited here, this narrative is not concerned with providing biographies about them. It is the impact they had doing whatever they did as professionals to touch people and the human community at-large with their gifts that I include them in **"The 400th"**.

If this next section was a movie, book, or even a ballet, I would name this assault in a tutu, *"The Two Lives of a Curvy Ballerina!"* I've always been aware of ballet and ballerinas, as I said, but it was a world I was very unfamiliar. To make this point sharper, what I thought I knew, regarding ballet, but never thought about, I gained from movies, books, and TV. Ballerinas always looked very thin, shapeless, weak, and fragile; of course, they were all white girls, which makes curvy, a dead giveaway.

Digging around looking for information to bolster my appeal to the Arts/academic communities to support commemorating and celebrating **"The 400th"**, I encountered the term "curvy ballerina" for the first time. Unacquainted with ballet and ballerina terminology, I googled the term, lo and behold all I saw were young black girls dressed in tutus, looking like ballerinas. The research lit up my dim view, enlightening me, with a totally new perspective on ballerinas and ballet.

Tyde-Courtney Edwards, creator of *"Ballet After Dark" (BAD)* came up also, as an example of a curvy ballerina, so I read on. It said Edwards was a classically trained ballerina, art model, aspiring filmmaker, and a survivor of a very vicious and brutal sexual assault. Born and raised in Baltimore, Maryland, after her training, she remained there building a 20-year dancing career.

After graduating from the Baltimore School for the Arts, Edwards trained in various styles of dance, including classical and contemporary ballet, pointe, modern, lyrical, jazz, tap, and hip-hop. Edwards also trained with the Debbie Allen Dance Academy, the Dance Theatre of Harlem, Peabody Conservatory, Joffrey Ballet, Alvin Ailey American Dance Theater, other institutions and local dance pioneers such as Anton Wilson and Stephanie Powell.

With such credentials, one would not think she would be treated like a *"field nigger."* But this is America, even in ballet. *"Ballet After Dark: A Story of Resilience After Sexual Trauma"* is a story in several publications such as, MadameNoire and Nicole, which I was also unfamiliar. I assumed my unfamiliarity was because I'm not a female. However, they provided background on the struggles, trials and tribulations of this amazing person, trying to break into ballet, Tyde-Courtney Edwards.

No doubt, with thousands of young ladies desiring, as well as aspiring to be ballerinas, I realized the competition is furious. However, the reality is like a curveball in the dirt for curvy ballerinas. This whole dance game is call to favor the slender straight physique and shapeless image of white girls, rather than choreography, giving white girls' physique the advantage over black girls. This has been the barrier black girls could not change, because it resides in white people's heads, like Minstrelsy "black face," determining who can dance. White people only want to see white girls in tutus, and black girls cannot change their body type.

Detailing her struggles as a "curvy ballerina," clearly Edwards' experiences were typical and just another type of discrimination dressed up in a tutu. Tyde-Courtney opened her life up to the world in a piece by Victoria Uwumarogie in MadameNoire (2-9-2018) entitled *"Fitness Fridays: Tyde-Courtney Edwards Used Ballet to Heal after Being Raped, Now She's Helping Others Do the Same!"* Tyde-Courtney detailed her horror story and troubles trying to fit her voluptuous frame into the "straightjacket" ballet's demands of slender physical frame dancer must fit. The fact that she is a curvy ballerina was just the beginning of Tyde-Courtney's problems. First she faced the major taboo, but she embraced her natural hair, which made her road to ballerina-dom, very very knotty. But, Edwards refused to allow anything to keep her from her dreams.

"While searching for work and going on auditions, I was able to maintain my livelihood teaching and by finding different gigs. From time to time, I would be lucky enough to get some performance gigs, but it might be for only one day. It might pay $75 there, $50 on another. It was not stable and very, very difficult, being a black ballerina, trying to find something where I would not be cast on the back row or where I would not be encouraged to leave the ballet company altogether, and go for a modern company or a hip-hop company. I had all this training, grace and elegance. I knew what I could do, but there was nobody who was really willing to take a chance on me because I didn't look like everybody else. That hurt a lot."

Tyde-Courtney sounded like black baseball players before, during, and just after Jackie Roberson's day. Back then, baseball teams would allow uninvited black player to come to training camp year after year, but never sign them. They pretended black players had to have something special, whereas any-run-of-the-mill white boy could ride the bench for years getting experience and paid, while learning to play baseball. Edwards continued;

"Mainly, it was my physique and physicality. Most dancers, average ballet dancers, are about 5-foot-5. I'm 5-foot-1 1/2. Plus, I was always really, really proud of my 'nappy hair'. Auditioning with my hair in a pony puff, I would get bullied. I would get called names. I would get called 'ghetto.' My shoes would go missing at auditions. Also, because I am a "curvy woman," it was easy to stand out at auditions, but not in a good way.

There would be comments about how my wide hips compared to white dancers. But, I was always the one they call to demonstrate proper technique, mine is sound. So I would demonstrate at the bar or in the center, but at the end of the audition, I would get waitlisted. There were also times when I was younger and a lot curvier, ant thicker. I would have to wear two sports bras under my leotard. They would call me a "distraction" because I giggled too much, I know now that was a cover up. Some would even ask me to leave. My appearance wasn't "sleek" enough. I was doing all of this extra work to hide my curves and fit in, so they would consider me for a job. I did that for years and years and years until it got to a point where I was like, what am I doing?"

I will say giggling and laughing are classic signs of anxiety among black people, left over from slavery to cover up criticism from master and hide internal anger, when slave masters sanctioned slaves. This cover up continued in Minstrelsy "black face" and segregation. It was passed on like DNA from generation to generation. Moreover, it is a classic sign of *"learned helplessness,"* which white people look for as signals they have the advantage. Moreover, they know "this black person will not challenge me."

Everything fell apart, when Tyde-Courtney was attacked and raped. She was prepping for a big audition, a new beginning in a new apartment, and the completion of studies to earn a degree in pedagogy. The incident derailed her plans, crippled her confidence, and eclipsed her life with fear and shame. She said,

"I stayed in my home pushed people away I stopped taking care of myself, and was in a dark place for some time. Unexpectedly, it took an episode from a classic show and my love of dance to get me back out into the world and back to feeling comfortable in my own skin. I had to work for that. I had to fight for that. Sexual assault is a horrible, shaming act of violence. Most survivors are left deeply embarrassed with feelings of guilt, and often believe they brought the act upon themselves, by something they did. Often, survivors are left feeling helpless, trying to navigate through their pain and trauma. And, then one day I was watching Sex and the City, it was the episode where Charlotte suffered a miscarriage followed by depression. She was watching the E! True Hollywood Story of Elizabeth Taylor and how her life was up and down. What Charlotte gained from that episode was the way she landed on her feet every single time.

While Charlotte watched this episode, I could see her start to come to life. She would eventually reclaim her joy and sense of womanhood. I knew it was fictional, but you never know from where your inspiration will come. I was inspired by her moment of being down and her ambition not to be down any longer. It encouraged and inspired me to make little moves that would get me out of the house. When I was comfortable enough to make a move, I went to ballet. I just started to feel comfortable. I slowly started to remember what it was about ballet and dance that helped me reclaim my femininity."

Tyde-Courtney's epiphany was like, Tyler Perry's insightful awaking. Divine inspiration can come at the most unlikely of times, and from the most unlikely of places, especially when one has a prayer in their heart. Tyde-Courtney went on;

"I'm a hard worker. I'm a lover. I am a nurturer by nature. I am the mother of a movement right now. But besides all of that, I'm a strong black woman; that's who I am. That's exactly who I am. If nobody knew anything about me and they didn't know my name and didn't know my story; if they didn't know my educational level, and didn't know my level of talent and technique, what they would be able to take away, is the fact that I exude strength."

Although Edwards had become buried in her pain, humiliation, fear, and negative thought about herself and situation, I will say, the one thing slaves and their descendants held onto no matter the dire prospects facing them, as they endured to survive, was self-love. The inspiration of self-love, black folks in the Mississippi Delta called *"the magic of the **Blues!**"* Tyde-Courtney reiterated;

"Sexual assault is a horrible, shaming act of violence, I think the best thing I've discovered about myself, as a result of what happened, is how strong and resilient I actually am. Nothing can break me now! It really can't. I think that is most pleasing to me, with everything that I'm doing and with everything I'm trying to accomplish, I just want to change lives. That's all I want to do.

And it was that work, which inspired me to create 'Ballet After Dark.' It's an organization that provides ballet-based fitness classes, athletic conditioning programs, open dance classes, self-care workshops, mental health resources, self-defense classes, and a general space where survivors of sexual assault and domestic abuse, as well as all traumas, come together and practice self-care. They strengthen and heal their damaged bodies, and in turn, reclaim their lives. While ballet is a big part of the organization, 'it goes beyond learning plies,'" Tyde-Courtney said, banishing a hugely broad smile!!!!

Through *Ballet After Dark (BAD)*, women across the world have access to an international network of survivors of sexual assault and domestic abuse. They learn to heal and used the power of ballet. Women telling their stories of how they reprocessed, rebuilt, and reclaimed their lives to other women, while gaining a sense of empowerment. Their therapy begins during a five-day filmed workshop, which gives their self-confidence a real boost, women sharing stories of resilience and how to build life-long support systems, reminiscent of Oprah *"rapport talk."*

Too often, after assault, women feel helpless, less than human, and without a sense of familiarity and connection to their bodies, as they try to deal with psychological pain, following such abuse. At *BAD*, women share knowledge about "sexual assault" which is such a horrifically degrading and shame provoking act of violence." *Ballet After Dark* strives to help survivors, reconnect with their womanhood and sensuality. *BAD*, uses ballet to help women heal and reconnect with their femininity. *BAD*, through its workshop, is making ballet accessible to all women, without regard for ethnicity or physicality.

However, it has another major goal, which is to partner with organizations within the African Diaspora to educate women of color, many of whom are unfamiliar with the history of ballet and its benefits. *Ballet After Dark,* reaches out to not only women and organizations in the United States, but presently it is partnering with groups like *Woman's Inc* in Kingston, Jamaica, in Barbados with *Women of Purpose,* also in Belize with *Haven House,* at *The Bahamas Crisis Center* and in Kenya with *Agatha Amani House.*

Edwards says, *"My vision for Ballet After Dark is to create an internationally film-based program that brings dance fitness workshops to women who've had traumatic experiences and difficulties finding alternative ways to heal. Ballet After Dark's programs helps women regain comfort with their womanhood, following assault and abuse, so that they are gradually able to talk openly about reclaiming their sensuality and sexuality.*

A Curvy Ballerina's Rise to the Top

    Misty Danielle Copeland (9-10-1982) is an African American ballerina with the American Ballet Theatre (ABT), which is one of three leading classical ballet companies in the United States. Copeland became the first-ever African American woman to be promoted (2015) to principal dancer in ABT's 75-year history. *("Misty Copeland Is Promoted to Principal Dancer at American Ballet Theater,"* Michael Cooper, 2015, The New York Times). Although a late bloomer, Misty was considered a prodigy, almost from the first time she laced on ballet slippers. Copeland did not start ballet training until age 13 and then on a level where those guiding and coaching her, lacked sufficient prestige to raise an eyebrow among the highbrow.
    Ballet aficionados thought Misty would be, a fish out of water, flopping around, after her late beginning. Nevertheless, once Misty began leaping and bounding over obstacle, resembling a salmon ascending rapids, swimming upstream, she was viewed as a phenome destined for stardom. Her presence was not welcomed by all, in the pools of ballerina-dom. Copeland's meteoric rise elevating pass ballet's pools of aspiring small fries ballerina, with family and patrons serving as lifeguards, keeping them afloat in the many culture pools of ballet, *("Historic 1st for a ballet company".* Sheila Anne Feeley, A.M. New York 2015). All the small fry with lifeguards in these inner-pools of ballet's headwaters protecting small fry, bristle at the slightest suggestion that their help discriminate against "curvy ballerinas," which Misty certainly is. Porous as fish nets, their bristling responses are, *"We're just trying to keep ballet's stream free of trash."*
    Misty, like Tyde-Courtney Edwards, exemplifies the adage, no matter the container, *"cream always rises to the top."* Though not anything close to the traumatic struggles of Tyde-Courtney's horrible and potentially deadly attack, both ballerinas had problems, swimming upstream against the bitter current and dams opposing their success, in pools leading to ballet's headwaters. According to news stories, Misty's family circumstances were not always helpful, during her young years.
    Misty was born in Kansas City, Missouri to Sylvia DelaCerna and Doug Copeland, both of mixed heritage—mother Italian and African American, while her father is German and African American—yet and still Misty has always embraced her African American ancestry, before and after strapping on ballet slippers, *("Misty Copeland, American Ballet Theatre's First African-American Soloist in 20 Years, Talks Breaking Barriers with Aplomb,"* Meredith Turits, 2012, Glamour). Relocating to the San Pedro community of Los Angeles, California, and once there Misty began dancing, but it was not a smooth move at every turn. Her greatest distraction, according to media reports, was the custody battle between her

mother and custodial guardian. Calm and stoically, however, Misty ended the matter by filing for emancipation.

On the way to becoming the world's premier ballerina, Copeland has become a public speaker, celebrity spokesperson, and the most sought after stage performer in recent times. Misty has authored several books, and has produced and narrated a documentary about her career challenges, *"A Ballerina's Tale."* Time had Misty on its cover in 2015, recognizing her as one of *the 100 most influential people in the world.*

Copeland appeared on Broadway in *On the Town,* and was also a featured dancer with *Prince* (late R&B icon). Misty made appearances on reality television shows *"A Day in the Life,"* and *"So You Think You Can Dance."* She has endorsed diverse sponsors, like *T-Mobile, Coach, Inc., Dr. Pepper, Seiko, The Dannon Company, and Under Armour.* The Boys & Girls Clubs of America named Misty the *National Youth of the Year Ambassador* (2013). Pres. Barak H. Obama appointed her to his *Council on Fitness, Sports, and Nutrition(2014).* She was also awarded an *honorary doctorate* from the University of Hartford, for her contributions to classical ballet and helping to diversify the art form. Copeland was a *Dance Magazine Awardee* in 2014. After her promotion to principal dancer at ABT, Copeland was named one of Glamour's *Women of the Year for 2015*; (Leanne Italie, (2015), (*"Glamour's Women of the Year: Witherspoon, Jenner, Copeland,"* 2015Yahoo! Sports, Associated Press).

Budding late, like a rose in winter, Copeland did not study ballet or gymnastics formally, until her teenage years. However, as a youth, she enjoyed doing her own thing, choreographing flips and dance moves to Mariah Carey's music. ("5 Things Misty Copeland Knows for Sure", Jessica Winter, 2010, O: The Oprah Magazine). Though flowering without the glow of stag lights, Copeland endured ballet's harsh winter's breath, but her petals did not wither. Rather, Misty blossomed into a radiant African violet, as ballet's premier ballerina, curves and all. ("Where are our black ballerinas? Britain's ballet companies must start to look further than the white middle classes for their talent," Judith MacKrell, 2008); The Guardian).

Misty played a prominent role in *Don Quixote,* as Kitri, at the San Pedro Dance Center. She was also a featured performer in the L.A. Academy of Fine Arts, presentation of *The Chocolate Nutcracker,* an African American adaptation of that ballet, (like **The Wiz**), which was narrated by Debbie Allen. The role was modified especially for Copeland; she included some ethnic dances. An article, *"Misty Copeland: Should She Stay or Should She Go?"* in the L.A. Times, added to the drama surrounding Misty, which disturbed her mother. Bristling, she fired off this letter to the editor;

> *"As Misty Copeland's mother, I am greatly troubled by the misrepresentation of my family in your article "Solo in the City," by Allison Adato (Dec. 5). Misty is a loving yet strong young woman. She makes her own decisions with the caring guidance of our family and close friends. She is not the weak and easily manipulated person the article portrays. Misty is and*

has been, in charge of her own destiny. She has invested in her future by returning home to finish high school before accepting a contract offer and career with the American Ballet Theatre. Her maturity came through in her decision to return to her family, after material items were dangled in front of her.

She continues to excel academically with a 3.8 average at the end of her junior year and has continued to have an exceptional dance career and training under Diane Lauridsen of Torrance's South Bay Ballet. Misty's earnings are deposited in her bank account and used only as needed, for Misty and by Misty."

Under California ballet instructors, Copeland's star continued rising, but move eastward, as she joined the studio company of the American Ballet Theatre in 2000. Following several years of very very hard work, her effort paid big dividends, as Misty emerged a soloist. She starred in an array of productions, such as *The Nutcracker* and *Firebird*, on the way to becoming a principal dancer.

Although their—Misty's and Tyde-Courtney's—level of successes are entirely different, they shared the upstream challenges of all "curvy" ballerinas, which adds extra rapids, like Sidney Poitier breaking through as an actor, white girl do not have to content or surmount, trying to suceed at something they love. Tyde-Courtney remains on the outside looking in, while in contrast, Misty, on the inside, an international ballet star, if not looking in the mirror, has real difficulty find a reflection of anyone resembling her. However, news stories indicate, Misty is still an outsider, in a school unto herself, due to the responses of ballet's inner citadel of gatekeepers.

The public perception is that Misty is very much aware of the absence of black faces is the reflection of ballet's worldwide culture and not some figment, pirouetting in her head. According to those that write about ballet, they point to a lack of diversity in ballet culture as the culprit. These writers see the same discrimination that exists in the NFL and larger American society *("Where are the black ballet dancers?"* Olivia Goldhill, Sarah Marsh, 2012; The Guardian). The question **"The 400th"** ask is, *"When will it end? Is there a point, looking down the road as far as one can see, is there a point where discrimination and disparate treatment disappears or ends?"*

Copeland released a memoir, *"Life in Motion: An Unlikely Ballerina,"* co-authored with Charisse Jones in 2014. She offered her experiences, even detailing her cultural isolation. She followed that with a children's picture book, entitled *"Firebird,"* with illustrator Christopher Myers (2014). Copeland doubled down on black pride, with a message of empowerment for young people of color *("Firebird,"* Random House, 2014). Copeland released a third book, <u>Ballerina Body</u>, in 2017. A health and fitness guide for health enthusiasts, she said of that effort, *"I wanted to show that all athletes have to take care of themselves from the inside out."*

Definitely, a lone rider, fighting her way to the top in the white-dominated world of ballet, and with her devil-may-care stand for her heritage, no one can deny Misty is a swashbuckler, like William Patterson and Paul Robeson with ***"We Charge Genocide,"*** when taking on her critics. The screaming headline (4-1-2018) *"Everyone feels like they're a critic': Misty Copeland doubles down on her fiery response to those who slammed her after she failed to complete Swan Lakes famed 32 fouetté turns."* This "tempest in a tutu" highlights how quickly controversy can swirl about a black celeb, like Colin Kaepernick, especially when fans defend and are supportive of ballet's cultural bastion of white privilege.

Misty performed in Pyotr Ilyich Tchaikovsky's ballet *Swan Lake* in Singapore (4-29-2018), dancing the part of Odile. *Swan Lake* includes a famous sequence, during which Odile completes 32 fouetté turns, with one of her legs never touching the stage. While fans counted and expected Misty to complete the 32, she did 12, as part of an alternative choreography.

Similar to NFL fan, regarding Colin Kaepernick's refusing to stand, instead kneeling, during the national anthem, cultured ballet fans, *"went ghetto."* *"Some proceeded to slam her performance, branding it 'terrible,' with one person declaring it reflects 'very poorly' on the American Ballet Theatre, for which Misty's a "principal dancer,'"* according to *the Daily Mail* (5-29-2019). Ballet fans' reactions highlight my granddaughter Tahlia's point in her social study's project on lynching mentioned earlier, *"the media has become the lynch mob in the street, in the way they circle their wagons, supporting those who vociferously object to something a black person says or does."*

Clarifying her mindset about their attempted lynching, Copeland responded, *"As an artist, you have to be sensitive, and you have to be vulnerable, but at the same time, you can't let those things affect your performance, so I wanted to show that you can learn from these things, whether they're negative or positive and I wanted to show there's a positive way if you want to address these people, your critics, whoever say things about you that doesn't even know you."*

Again, like Colin, Misty did not allow herself to be cowed or drawn into a spitball fight with people who only came to see *"Swan Lake"* and not to see Misty Copeland dance her heart out. She told Cosmopolitan, *"Some viewers are bound to focus on technical prowess, rather than on the artistry of the performance. I just try not to get caught up in reviews and reading things on the internet because they don't know you and people don't know your journey. I think that, especially in America, especially in New York, when people come to see a ballet, I think everyone kind of feels like they're a critic. They're not just walking in to enjoy the beauty that we're trying to bring to them, but caught up in whether or not you're going to be perfect, and I think that's what's so beautiful about what we do, is that we're not [perfect]! You're coming to see live theater; it's not edited! Anything can happen in those moments."*

As a professional, Misty said she finds it's *"so exciting' learning how to bounce back from things that may go wrong in the moment."* Only after someone posted a video of her performance on YouTube did Misty chose to discuss the affair openly on social media, *"I thought it was important for me to set a positive example for young people when it comes to handling criticism."* A noteworthy aside on this *"tempest in a tutu,"* for disgruntled fans, some of the most famous ballerinas in history, including Anna Pavlova, chose to perform alternative moves to avoid the dreaded choreography, much like Misty did in Singapore, but ballet fans did not blow like Hurricane Katrina at Anna Pavlova for her alternative choreography. Could it have had anything to do with skin color?

Much of what I said previously commenting on this subject, I was mimicking Mark Twain satirizing *"The Gilded Age,"* which I cited earlier in this narrative. Poking fun at the pretentiousness of highbrow ballet culture, I had a serious point. Moreover, my comments did not have a humorous intended, as I pointed up the hurt and damage caused by discrimination and disparate treatment in the lives of black dancers, like Tyde-Courtney Edward and Misty. Though considered slight by those that cause pain, the impact can be devastating to some.

This statement is not only for ballet but the whole crowd of white overloads and gatekeepers, who feel America's society belongs to them and it is theirs to determine access to America's bounty for descendants of American slavery. Even in the face of Misty Copeland's astonishing performances to attain her level of recognition, talent, execution, and virtuosity, like Oprah Winfrey, when one adds African American to the category, she's splashing around in a pool by herself. No other ballerina in history has faced closed doors or extra-high hurdles and surmounted them to reach the top, like Misty. Overcoming cultural barriers, economic hurdles, most profoundly, after her delayed start, becoming exposed to the ballet culture in her early teens, Misty has shown character, facing lack of access that stops most African Americans, <u>but not all.</u>

Whatever the activity before African Americans participated, no matter the type, which was my point, beginning this section with Simone Biles, once they do, the activity changes, as ballet or Surya Bonaly on ice skates. The change Misty brought to Ballet means curvy ballerinas are in the house, so design some new tutus. Misty gave ballet a black face that is not like Minstrelsy; it will not wash off. Looking back over past endeavors, once African Americans gained access, their performances became standards, like "Dr. J."

Whether athletics, entertainment, or politics, white people band together to defend what they believe are their prerogatives. Even though whites justified discrimination by claiming, blacks did not have the ability, intellect, or vision to participate, once a Serena Williams, Jack Johnson, Wilma Rudolph, Surya Bonaly, Simone Biles, or Misty Copeland shows up, everything changed, and there is no going back.

Everyone whether they want to or not, are living in a world, which the death of George Floyd, Black Lives Matter and COVID-19 created. The new-normal deaths and protests have created is the world everyone will have to adjust; there is no going back. America's young progressives have taken charge, and they are deciding the kind of world they want to live in today, as they should.

The best example is style, hip hop's impact has changed everything about young people, and it is being determined by their preferences. Their mindset, dress and image is what the rest of society is adjusting, whether in the US or another country. There were millions of young progressives around the world marching in the street to serve notice, they are going to change this world, all the older generation can do is change with them or die of old age watching or fighting it. Either way, it doesn't matter to the hip hop generation, this is their world and they know it.

Check this out. The ways young people carry and present, as well as express themselves confuse even their parents, who would never think and act as they do. Whether performers or audience, whatever young hip-hoppers do with or to their bodies become trends, styles, dances, or the model for how something is done. The classic example is the sweatshirt. For old folks, it is just another garment, but once hip-hoppers like Trayvon Martin began wearing them, they became hoodies.

Today, young hip-hoppers are the "hoodie generation." Those who doubt my words need only look around at young people. Hoodies are their statements to the world. It symbolizes their defiance, in a world that tries to ignore, marginalize, or disregard them and their opinions. This is why the George Floyd and Black Lives Matter protests are so powerful. They have decided "Enough is Enough!!!!"

Hoodies are their covering that shuts the old world out. It is their way of telling the old world they do not care what it thinks, about what they do or how they look doing it. They are determined to create their own social standards. It is their way of saying they are done with hatred, racism, and white privilege, "the whole nine yards." Young hip-hoppers have changed styles around the world, giving *VOICE* to young people forced to live in silence. Like **"Blues"** once W. C. Handy played his blue note, music has never been the same. Entertainment and prospects for making money have definitely changed, as back then, things were never the same for "field niggers," once they found a downbeat.

The brutal truth is, young African American girls hoping to be dancers see Misty, are like black boys of my day that saw Jackie Roberson. Watching interviews of young girls and hearing their comments about Misty, they are so enamored, and awestruck in her presence. Most say they can't seem to find words to say anything, because they are so excited to be part of the same world she inhabits. They say things like, *"I can't do anything, but watch her and try to see myself trying to do things the way she does them."*

However, for me, in that regard, I see them like former slaves that watched Marcus Garvey and came to believe, *"If he can do it, I can do it too!"* Consequently, today's hip-hoppers have created an international culture, using the mindset Garvey preached from the street corners of New York City. That same magical process happened when Stokley Carmichael screamed "black power" from the

The 400th: From Slavery to Hip Hop

Mississippi delta. Even more to my point, when young black and white kids watched Pres. Barak H. Obama for eight years, they came to realize, as with Garvey, it was not a dream. What they witnessed is possible for them also.

My last example is four young women in Congress, dubbed the *"SQUAD"* —Alexandria Ocasio-Cortez, Ilhan Omar, Rashida Harbi Tlaib, and Ayanna Pressley—are standing up for the nation against the "Woodrow Wilson type rhetoric" pouring out of Donald Trump and his White House. I ask myself "Where are the young black and white men, when our women of color are kicking natural butt? It seems black young men have decided it is more fun standing on the side line being cheerleaders, as when Colin Kaepernick kneel, if that much.

I love women, of all colors and types, for the job they are doing; men use to do the heavy lifting. The women of the "SQUAD" are the kind of spokespersons former slaves did not have to speak out for them when Woodrow Wilson's segregated the federal government and organized the ***"Dark Age"*** *angry white men mob madness era*. Wilson madness came from the White House, MAGA is Donald Trump's do over.

Young progressives saw Pres. Barak H. Obama model a leaders standing up against racism for eight years. He showed that no matter what Trump spits out of his mouth, it is to control the world he leaves behind, like Woodrow Wilson. The ideas the *"SQUAD"* is pushing black, brown, red, yellow and white communities' to change the degradation, humiliation, and disregard old white people began showing people of color when white slavers dragged the first enslaved Africans aboard a slave ship in chains to begin ***"The 400th"***. Some people believe God created Misty Danielle Copeland for ballet, but no, I say, God created ballet in order for it to be available, so when Misty arrived, she could use ballet to help change the world from the top, during ***"The 400th"***.

We Are Here: Commemorating and Celebrating the 400th

    Finally, we have arrived in 2020, a destination long recognized as the arrival of ***"The 400th"***, but, like a black president, which no one thought consciously would happen, it has arrived. Never verbalized, as a consideration, it was just an idea that lurked in some slave descendants' minds, only marking our continued degradation. However, coronavirus and Black Lives Matter has rewritten the future, creating the new-normal of ***"The 400th"*** and has allowed me to imagine **The 400th Performance Period.** I took on this effort because it seemed no one else was taking or even thinking about it, as a personal challenge, in order to facilitate it.

    No more than a question, not expressed openly, or asked aloud, after all these years descendants of enslaved Africans are finally ask, *"How is it we are still here, and what does it mean in the larger context of slavery's descendants survival?"* Young black, brown, red, yellow and white progressives across the world are answering that question by standing shoulder to shoulder with black Americans. Older blacks are asking, *"What about a time 400 years ago, makes it important enough to black folks today that they should feel connected to those unknown individuals that arrival in the Western Hemisphere centuries ago that makes it important today?"* Those questions, in reality, are the answer, in that, arriving 400 years ago, our progenitors were individuals. But, yet and still, today's young slave descendants stand before the world, through their protests, demanding recognition as "ONE PEOPLE!!!"

    "The 400th" detailed in this narrative, you have just read, is an amazing journey of struggle, pain and death, endured to reaching—their descendants the new normal of today. Surviving that story, those who endured that long desperate night, I believe, hoped their effort would produce a generation that would be able to do exactly what ***"The 400th"*** generation is currently doing. Descendants of American slavery today, after their saga, became Janus on January 1, 2020. Now that ***"The 400th"*** is here descendants of American slavery have their story laid out before them, for the first time, as one people. This narrative gives their progeny the ability to read the same sentence, in the same paragraph, on the same page and in the same book at the same time. That understanding will allow today's descendants of slavery to be of one mind about how we go forward from this point.

    Prior to ***"The 400th"***, everyone had a story in their head, based on hearsay or some word of mouth story passed around, maybe through their family, which made one story, as good as another. Now with ***"The 400th"*** descendants of American slavery can learn the what, why and how we became one people. The facts they learned explain that we are a unique people because we have done something no other people the world over have done. For those who missed it: American slavery descendants were brought to America, as individuals, kidnapped from all along the West African coast, but today after 400 years of bondage, we emerged one people.

Reading *"The 400th"* every black person, who love their blackness can join the effort to commemorate the sacrifices and struggles of those who got us here to celebrate the love we being here. Before *"The 400th"*, there was never an occasion that prompted such thoughts, which young black minds are contemplating today, now that they have reached *"The 400th"*. Knowing their story in words they understand for the first time, *"The 400th"* establishes everything they believed was part of their history, but never thought about. The only thing left is to develop an action plan to obtain the goals we set for *"The 400th."*

Dr. Martin Luther King, Jr. said, *"Once the light of knowledge is received, one has to choose to remain in darkness."* I am not a magician! I cannot turn darkness into light, so I cannot make *"The 400th"*, a reality that will materialize from the thoughts in my head for others to experience. For *"The 400th"* to materialize, descendants of enslaved Africans must think and act as one people. If such thoughts are ever to become a reality for African Americans, they must embrace *"The 400th"*, as the last step in their rite of passage and establish those facts before the world that we are truly one people.

"The 400th" acknowledges slave descendants' capacity, as productive people, having built the present world white people enjoy, which black people are not a part. The preceding statements are why *"The 400th"* Committee believes the Arts and academic communities will play an important role and will support *"The 400th"* network descendants of American slavery are organizing. The efforts to redefine themselves through various artistic expressions, artists of all types will bring *"The 400th"* live in our joint effort to give substance and solidity to the views African Americans have of themselves and want the world to share.

It is through the Arts, other people around the world, express who they are and what they are about to the world. My previous statements reflect the ultimate goal **The 400th Performance Period** will bring to the world. African Americans' new narrative is the new-normal young slave descendants are creating for themselves, and their world through hip hop. They are hopeful that the world will responded with empathy and support as partners in this vision they bring to the world. I will say they are bringing hope at a time when the world truly needs hope.

Now that descendants of American slavery have their story—*"The 400th"*—detailed, as their ancestors lived it, the Arts will allow artists to bring that story alive to illustrate its significance, using whatever medium they choose. Ferreted out and presented here, for the first time, the very broad picture created by *"The 400th"* is a new and different image of descendants of American slave's struggles to survive the last 400 years in America and is also presented for the world's consideration.

The first part of this new consideration, no matter what you thought you knew about American slavery's descendants, but never thought about, the knowledge **"The 400th"** provides, makes clear we are survivors of the longest running genocide against any people in the history of mankind. Slavery's descendants the world over will be presenting artwork to tell a story to an unaware world.

Today, as events have transpired, since the murder of George Floyd, the vast majority of white people are asking black people to tell them a story, words alone are inadequate to clearly convey. This is why the Arts and academic community can play a crucial role facilitating an understanding of this new normal the world faces. Social change and social justice for American slavery's descendants is that goal, because change is the goal of life, as well as ***"The 400th"***. Never changing is to stagnate and die. ***"The 400th"*** offers life to America and the world through its ability to transform America's lifeless promises of the last 400 years.

"The 400th" will be the first time the world will have to recognize the real potential descendants of enslaved Africans possess, as something other than machines. This new vision will replace present perspectives of African Americans, which is why the double vision of Janus is so appropriate. Artists can provide an empathic view, which will give guidance to all humans, like Janus, to see and recognize the past for what it truly was for enslaved Africans the world over, while they endeavor to show the future through eyes of ***"The 400th"***.

All those who presently supporting ***"The 400th"*** have enthusiastically begun this audacious challenge, looking at what we have to build upon, things have never looked better. First, our Janus vision looks back over all previous major mass organizing efforts black people have mounted. Beginning with the *UNIA*, *March on Washington (1963)*, the *"Poor People's Campaign"* the *Million Man March (1995)*, *USA for Africa*, making *Dr. Martin Luther King, Jr.'s birthday a holiday*, and other mobilization efforts black people make around gaining freedom, justice, and equality. However, today we look forward with anticipation at the new normal our votes have produced electing Pres. Joe Biden and flipping the US Senate by Gerogia Votes. All the previous movements mentioned above were one-day affairs or short-lived projects. There weren't any follow up activities that sustained the unity those projects achieved. But black voters have changed the political culture in America, if we use **The 400th Performance Period** to bring on the political changes that will create economic changes through the Arts, we can bring the nation in to this new normal.

Even with the exception of—***The Poor People's Campaign (1968)***—which Dr. King gave his life, lasted only three months. Many believe—***The Poor People's Campaign***—was an aborted effort, but no, the Invaders remained committed to Dr. King last dream, as we promised Dr. King, we continue to support his effort to help poor people. This narrative has presented the efforts of many progressives today that are pushing social change and social justice as supporters of ***The Black Power Tarot Card Exhibition and Invaders Documentary Screening,*** which is the leading edge of what became **"The 400th" Performance Period.** Arish Khan and I have been touring the world since 2017 getting the truth out in order to bail the truth out of jail in America.

Even though Dr. King had a huge image, as a civil rights leader, he and George Floyd shared the same fate in the end. Freeing the truth in America is bringing people together around the world not just to help poor people with the ***"Poor People's Campaign"*** but to free exploited and oppressed people everywhere.

Dreams Are Possible: Ideas Do Live

"The "Poor People's Campaign" of Dr. Martin Luther King, Jr. is proof dreams do live on after the Dreamer has passed on. The important thing here is that during my research into hip hop's beginnings and development, I learned, among other things, most artists and businesses that helped build the hip hop culture, also built foundations/501(c)(3)s, and are currently working in communities across America. Consequently, *"The 400th"* does not have to start from stretch and "reinvent the wheel!!!" Hip hoppers, athletes, entertainers and entrepreneurs did that already. They have done the heavy lifting so all **The 400th Performance Period** needs to do is plug into them.

"The 400" Committee will partner with these established organizations to give descendants of American slavery a hand up getting started. *"The 400th"* Committee will have access to groups capable of designing, developing, mounting, and presenting productions to commemorate and celebrate *"The 400th".* Moreover, there are numerous community-based social networks that have been around since the 1960s and 70s and many of those can do the same thing all that is needed is to plug in to them to have a national functioning system across the Black community headed into 2021, as the COVID-19 pandemic recedes.

African Americans, in the past, had to build each movement as they were needed to address problems. Today descendants of American slavery have advanced for beyond that stage. With foundations/501(c) 3s of hip hop icons and other artists and organizations, adopting *"The 400th"* and its **Performance Period,** these groups and organizations will put *"The 400th"* celebration head of all the mass movements black Americans mounted in the past. With this effort, we will not have to rally the black community and mobilize with protest or demonstrated.

Today, with the expressions of love and concern expressed by "Black Lives Matter," black, brown, red, yellow and white young progressives are showing that Americans and people around the world can come together on social justice and social change issues. Hip-hoppers can lead the way with their foundations. Through their resources, they can establish, facilitate, organize, develop and present how and why even though American entertainment grew out of what slaves did to "tickle master fancy," their progeny will have the last laugh making their efforts into an international cultural effort, which makes *"The 400th"* a reality of unity and love.

Hip hop icons, entertainers and other artists should adopt **The 400th Performance Period** and use their foundations/501(c)(3)s to augement and aid *"The 400th"* committee's leadership getting community involved. *"The 400th"* Committee adopted this approach because it has no paid staff, at this point, we are a totally volunteer effort, and to get up and running we need to utilize existing foundations, community networks, and other support systems to help developed a platform to support our dreams. Cooperating with and supported by talent and expertise of these foundations, other groups, and organizations have at their disposal descendants of American slavery can launch performances, colloquiums, symposiums, movies, plays, ballets, and any number of activities to express the new normal we all see.

"The 400th" Committee understands this is a huge undertaking, which is why **The 400th Performance Period,** will extend from 2020 through 2030 the Quadricentennial year. One may think this is an unnecessarily long period, however, everyone should understand, this is something no people have ever attempted. More importantly, descendants of Americans will need time to learn work together in this fashion. For us in many ways this will be a reenactment of slaves walking off plantations in 1865, in terms of knowing what to expect and how to do what we have never done. We will draw on their example, as they decided to make families and build communities. They began with what they knew and what they had to begin with.

The hip hop generation did the same thing creating their culture. They can share and exchange knowledge, expertise, skills, and access as they partner with *"The 400th"* Committees as it sets up across America. Today social responsibility is the key to being a good corporate citizen. My example is Viva con Agua's nonprofit effort to get clean drinking water to people in poor countries. With eyes like Janus, looking back, this narrative has revealed; numerous examples of how hip hop foundations and other types of non-prophet groups are presently educating, eradicating and elevating those trapped in ignorance and poverty. They are helping relieve deprivation, discrimination, exploitation, and political domination around the world through such programs.

My best examples are efforts like Quincy Jones helping launch with the *"We Are the Future (WAF) project."* That project *"gave children in poor and conflict-ridden areas a chance to live their childhoods and develop a sense of hope."* It was the result of *"a strategic partnership"* between *the Global Forum*, the Quincy Jones' *Listen Up Foundation*, and Hani Masri, with the support of *the World Bank*, *UN agencies* and *major companies*. Quincy Jones and his network launched that project with a concert in Rome, Italy, before an audience of half a million people. Imagine the impact if such an effort is undertaken on behalf of *"The 400th" Performance Period*.

Children of *"The 400th"* are no less needy than those children. Millions reside in America's ghettos, and Black Lives Matter's protests have shown America's ghettos are one of the deadliest environments of any place on earth. They have a legacy of trying to escape the graveyard of poverty in the valley of dry bones. The penniless emancipation of enslaved Africans, after the end of legal slavery of their progenitors, placed their progeny among those most susceptible to conflict, violence, and police brutality, as well as murder in America, with stand your ground laws, as any children any place in the world.

"The 400th" was conceived as a program that could help America's neglected children with education, opportunities, and upward bound programs. Needing help and generosity of humanitarians that have resources and access, the hope is they will play a huge role in *"The 400th"* efforts. I am talking about an effort like those in the past by caring people, like Harry Belafonte and Sidney Poitier rode to the rescue of the "Mississippi Freedom Summer" (1964), back in the 1960s, with $60,000 cash for SNCC. There wasn't any concern about what will happen regarding contributed funds, and without flack or fallout, Harry even stayed around and entertained activists in Greenwood.

The world has myriad examples I could cite, but the question is will the world open its heart to slave descendants? Also, after his appointment as a goodwill ambassador for UNICEF, Belafonte traveled to Dakar, Senegal, as chairman of an International Symposium of Artists and Intellectuals to help African children. Raising funds alongside more than 20 other artists, Harry participated in the largest concert ever held in sub-Saharan Africa. Following that, he went on a mission to Rwanda and launched a media campaign to raise awareness about the needs of Rwandan children (1994). I ask will hip hop artists step up, like Harry?

These are the types of efforts and commitments; I hope hip-hoppers will undertake for the commemoration and celebration of *"The 400th"*. Over the entire 400 years, enslaved Africans have endured in America; no individual, group, organization, or company on behalf of slave descendants has attempted such an effort. Driven by fears created by segregation, white supremacy, and memories of the *"Dark Age" angry white men mob madness,* black people were forced to come together in the 1960s and 70s in solidarity to break the back of legal segregation in America. That kind of unity is needed now and can breathe life into the efforts to commemorate and celebrate *"The 400th"*.

Just imagine the response to *"The 400th"*, if those benefitting from the hip hop culture led an effort similar to the one Steve Wonder single-handedly led campaigning to make Dr. Martin Luther King Jr.'s birthday a holiday in the United States. This celebration should be an international holiday because the benefitted from the enslavement of Africans, even in the Indian and Pacific Oceans. *"The 400th"* is African American's birthday and although we arrived in North America as individuals in 1619 and emerged in 2019 one people, still residing in the same nation that enslaved us, other Africans were taken around the horn of Africa as slaves as early as 14th century. What's miraculous after such an outcome is slavery's descendants are not talking about launch their own *"Dark Age" angry black men mob madness era* to avenge their outrage.

Looking at just the list of hip hop moguls discussed here, it is clear, their foundations and non-profits can kick off *"The 400th"* and lead the effort on a very high level. No one needs permission to start a project; it is your birthday as well. Everyone can make it up as they go along; the idea is to make it a real celebration. African Americans have moved beyond the days when leadership came from the streets, after the 1990s, where radicals led efforts, shouting demands and throwing bricks at buildings. Now, for such large social undertakings, outlined here, leadership resides at the corporate level.

Expertise for creating teams, garnering resources, developing goals, implementing programs, and assessing results are best handled by those in corporate broad rooms. Descendants of American slavery occupy seats in most board rooms today, which they did not during the 1960s. They meet face to face with other corporate types daily. Previously, before the Black Lives Matter movement took to the streets around the world, corporate types would not listen to voices in the street. They claim not to understand what street people, especially black voices were saying, why they are upset or what they are seeking.

"The 400th" is not a protest but a demonstration of slavery's descendants desire to create a new narrative to give focus to the new normal hip hoppers are trying to establish. It is an expression of the determination of black people to build upon the legacy descendants of American slavery's progenitors established over the last 400 years. African Americans have established, through hip hop and now *"The 400th"*, that America can no longer denying its legacy of slavery, which locked black people on the bottom in the grave of poverty. Their progeny have established **The 400th Performance Period** as a marker that claims our place and future in America, as free spirits, and we are not going back, this is the new normal.

African Americans in the corporate and entertainment world can provide leadership through their positions in the corporate world. They have access to resources, street activists did not have in the 1960s nor do they have now. Corporate types have contacts with leaders that can sponsor and guide programs in underserved communities. Such individuals should lead *"The 400th"* effort. I make these statements because of my education, not because I am abdicating responsibility to guide *"The 400th"*.

It is clear from my research and experience on the streets, those with access to corporate board rooms in America and around the world can form *"strategic partnerships"* capable of designing and mounting major projects. They possess the expertise, knowledge, and support to launch such projects with efficiency in much less time than any street person; they can maximize this opportunity to make *"The 400th"* an event the world will remember.

The corporate world can envision projects that will leave an indelible mark on the world's conscience and help change the image of black people the world over. I am not saying street organizers are of no use; we have our roles and will play them when appropriate. I believe *"The 400th"* commemoration and celebration can take advantage of what black groups have already developed over the decades, since the 1960s. Their support and assistance will allow descendants of American slavery to accomplish far more than what is imagined presently.

Today, because of their presence in broad rooms, black Americans do not have to break into the conversation to engage corporate America and enlist support for commemorating and celebrating *"The 400th"*. I relate my last comment to Dia Simms' declaration, *"I'm a stickler for courtesy and respect,"* and she confessed, "I *always check to see how candidates treat the receptionist and will even test how helpful they are when something is dropped on the floor. Do they even move? Do they try to pick it up? I go out of my way to create an asshole-free, hater free, 'please and thank you' zone. I'm very old school about civility and thoughtfulness.*"

There should be a reciprocal response on the part of corporate America, just as it is when they seek support from the black community for their social and economic causes. More precisely, when America celebrated its Bicentennial, even though America treated African Americans shamefully, as I have reflected throughout this narrative, the black community supported that celebration just the same.

When United Way, St. Jude Hospital, the Heart Foundation, Easter Seal, Muscular Dystrophy, Cancer Society and many other charities come to the black community for support, we give. *"The 400th"* is aimed at addressing the debilitating effects of *learned helplessness* and its psychological impact on descendants of American slavery, which is one of the major reasons many slave descendants are still trapped in prisons and poverty today.

The controversy in sports today smacks of the effort to reestablish a *"white boy"* mentality that denies black athletes *VOICE*. It is a backward step to *"make America great again,"* which harkens back to the "Dark Age angery white men mob madness era's horrifically brutal and deadly life black people endured when things were great for white people. Black athletes have the right to *VOICE*, their **First Amendment** rights, when supposedly they have the same rights white have to express their opposition.

It would be a game-changer, in my opinion, for black communities, if large professional sports organizations and other entities joined forces with eleemosynary efforts by hip-hoppers and others supporting *"The 400th"*. I would love to see wives and husbands of athletes and sports entities like the NFL, NBA, Major League Baseball, the Soccer federation and athletes in other professional sports like tennis, golf, WNBA, track and field teams and leagues; even the Olympic Committee embrace this effort and form committees to become part of commemorating and celebrating *"The 400th"*. By forming committees, they can develop programs and overseeing their administration in supporting *"The 400th"*.

Through league and federation programs they could develop year-round programs, during league play and the offseason, with after schools, recreational, and upward bound type programs. The wives, husbands, and children of professional athletes have the expertise to do it. They are college-educated, were cheerleaders, dancers, majorettes, sorority sisters, fraternity brothers, athletes, and are business owners, so there is no doubt they could set up such committees for the communities their teams represent. They do not need to be micro-managed by street people!!!!!

Then there are entertainment groups and organizations that maintained *"white only policies"* for decades that deprived African Americans of opportunities. Their records, awards, and other recognition remain tainted because of their policies of discrimination. Coming on board ***"The 400th"***, they can acknowledge once and for all, their contrition, while addressing their unfairness. It is a time everyone, every group, and organization publicly put racism behind them and join the effort to create a new normal in America.

"The 400th" can be that time, over the coming years Americans can truly come together and heal divisions of the past, while creating an inclusive environment for all in America. As I said earlier, ***"Being mad about the past is not going to change the future."*** Presently, most talk, as though this is the case, but Black Lives Matter's and the insurrection in Washington D.C. at the Nation's Capital have written a new chapter to the new normal story COVID-19 washed upon America's shores. These events have pulled the hood off America's racist face showing it for a country dedicated to "whiteness." Now everyone knows the the reality for most non-white groups in America, particularly for Native people and descendants of slavery.

At this very moment, America is building a "wall of division" and has thousands of children imprisoned because their patents crossed the board, looking for a better life. Hatitians, can not find peade, stability or love in a world where they are being put on by nature and men. Descendants of American slavery should help and support them, as Canadians and Mexicans helped runways slaves on the *Underground Railroad*. Standing together will send the message that we reject walls that divide to make America a nation where only white voices matter.

During my travels, I have encountered many attitudes and actions of Americans reminiscent of South Africa under Apartheid. ***"The 400th"*** commemoration and celebration is a result of the mindset of white people that kidnapped and enslaved free Africans, as a normal course building wealth. Building wealth for white people is how this whole thing started, which created a need to commemorate and celebrate ***"The 400th"***. Using the Arts, which should be "colorblind," artists can create statements that reflect the one-world society on this one planet that hip hop now dominates, as a culture.

Museums, art galleries, concert venues, Broadway theaters, and other major Arts facilities and venues should mount shows, commission artists, and send out calls for artists to create exhibitions, also offer competitive challenges/prizes to create various types of artwork. Theaters should offer prizes for plays—dance, musical, and dramatic productions—based on the theme of *"The 400th"*. The idea is to let the Arts, all types, speak for *"The 400th"*, with thoughts of pushing the present bounds of artistic standards and concepts to open up access to those shut out. The goal should be to express a vision of hip hop and where artists of all types see the culture headed.

Libraries and educational institutions should commission seminars, symposiums, colloquiums, conferences, and panel discussions featuring some of the writers, scholars, and professors whose works are presented or cited herein *"The 400th"* to provided extended views of *"The 400th"* period. School boards across the nation should do the same to get *"The 400th"* discussions down to where it will do the most good, to children, while they are forming their views of the world. The earlier children get honest reflections of their world; less re-education is necessary later in life. The institutions mentioned above should be the ones to bring government into their efforts; this time, the government can make amend for it past actions undermining, sabotaging, and organizing to stop black leaders, like Dr. Martin Luther King, Jr.'s efforts to help the poor.

In the meantime, I envision *"The 400th"* committee presently being organized, as playing the role of a clearinghouse to communicate, coordinate, facilitate and register all those interested in becoming part of *"The 400th"* commemoration and celebration. Presently, we are simply trying to get the word out and draw attention to the fact that it's here. There has not been any preparation or preplanning before *"The 400th"* arrived. There is no national organization with resources, access, or personalities volunteering to take a leadership role and be responsible for directing this massive effort. My hope is several individuals like Reggie Van Lee, for instance, a patron of the Arts with access and positions in the Arts community will fill liaison roles for the black community, facilitating access to large institutions, foundations, corporations and others that sponsor cultural events with the idea of partnering with *"The 400th"*.

"The 400th" has no budget, office, or paid staff, Divine inspiration has gotten us this far.. I see us in the same position as Dr. Martin Luther King, Jr., when he announced the *"Poor People's Campaign"* on 12-4-1968. He didn't know what would happen once he did, but he knew something would happen. And it did. It drew me into the fight, as a black activist. Along the way, the *"Poor People's Campaign"* has become *"The 400th"* for me. Today, the hip-hop generation has become the new activists.

The Strength of Granite

Considering all the icons presented in ***"The 400th"***, the last stone I will lay on the *"yellow brick road of entertainment,"* and because of his prolific, dynamic and impactful career his stone was the most difficult to place. My problem was that almost everyone has an opinion and something to say about his work, genius, professionalism, and command of the tools of his trade. Their voluminous expressions regarding his accomplishments, not even a book, could fully enlighten readers of his production, which would require a library. So, I will not attempt to tell his story. What I offer is just a few facts about him as a preface for the statement I will make about the image in my mind's eye when I see him or hear his name.

The image James Earl Jones evoked (1-17-1931) through his many great characterizations or voice-overs like Othello, Hamlet, Jack Jefferson (Jack Johnson: they even favored), Thulsa Doom, Darth Vader, Mufasa or King Jaffe Joffer in *"Coming to America"* left indelible impressions on people the world over. Descriptions abound of James Earl Jones, such as *"one of America's most distinguished and versatile actors"* or *"one of the greatest actors in American history"* (*"James Earl Jones Biography,"* Rebecca Flint Marx, All Movie Guide).

Admirers of Jones say he possesses *"one of the best-known voices in show business, a stirring basso profundo that has lent gravel and gravitas"* to his projects, including live-action acting, voice acting, and commercial voice-overs (*"James Earl Jones: A voice for the ages, aging gracefully,"* Ann Hornaday, 9-25-2014; Washingtonpost.com). According to Richard Ouzounian, theatre critic, "the deep, staccato tones, *O Iago, the pity of it, Iago!,* is the finest Othello I've seen to this very day. I share his assessment.

For all of James Earl Jones' successes, one would think he was an upper-middle-class kid who received dramatic lessons from an early age, which provided access to Broadway theatrics, right, but no. James Earl, like several individuals listed here, including Oprah Winfrey, and Rufus Thomas, was born (1-17-31) "in the belly of the beast" in Arkabutla, Mississippi. He was the son of Ruth (Williams) Jones (1911–1986), a teacher and maid, and Robert Earl Jones (1910–2006), a boxer, butler, and chauffeur. Again, like numerous other descendants of American slavery, his father walked away, leaving the family to struggle on their own. However, unlike Oprah, leaving the South only made things worse for James Earl.

At the age of five, James went to live with his maternal grandparents, John Henry and Maggie Williams, on their farm in Jackson, Michigan. They were runners leaving Mississippi, during the Great Migration (1910-1960). Once he arrived in Michigan, Jones says he felt, *"The move there was so traumatic, I developed a severe stutter, during the trip to my grandparents."* James Earl refused to speak for several years and remained functionally mute for eight years, until he entered high school. According to Jones,

"It wasn't that I stopped talking, it's that I resolved that talking was too difficult. You see, in the move from Mississippi to Michigan, you would think it would be a jubilant journey for a young boy of — I was then five years old — going to the Promised Land, you know. For me though, it was leaving the soil that I had touched with my bare feet, and I didn't know if I'd ever touch soil with my bare feet again, and that was traumatic for me. I was leaving a Huck Finn world. Forget social problems; I was leaving the earth of Mississippi, the clay soil along the banks of the Mississippi River. And that was a trauma for me.

I was an adopted child of my grandparents, and I don't know how I can ever express my gratitude for that because my parents would have been a mess. And there were considerations about that, where should I go, and that began to bother me when I'd hear those discussions at night. "Where should James Earl go?" But it was the journey itself that I really feel, the being ripped from the soil is what set me into a state of trauma. So by the time I got to Michigan, I was a stutterer. I couldn't talk. So my first year of school was my first mute year, and then those mute years continued until I got to high school."(James Earl Jones Biography — Academy of Achievement (February 26, 2010).

Having a similar experience, transferring from Mississippi to Memphis, joining my family, I believe that move, even though, I wanted it, had a similar impact, but in a different way. Memphis was totally different from my life in Mississippi. There I knew people and things, but in Memphis, other than my family, I knew nothing or no one. Trying to adjust to all the newness, school, people and neighborhood, the vastness of the place, my adjustment was a blur.

Now, reading about James Earl's problem, I understand my lack of progress in school those first years until high school. My first real help came in the fourth grade. Mrs. Cargile, my teacher, was the first to make me feel I could learn that stuff, if I tried. I also had teachers that challenged me in high school, Mrs. Charlotte Brooks, and Commander of NDCC (ROTC for whites) Mr. McCray helped turn my life around.

Although James Earl Jones' stutter lasted for several years, he said during an interview on Biography, he overcame the affliction through poetry, public speaking, and acting. He gives credit to his English teacher, who discovered he had a gift for writing poetry, and challenged his end his silence. Mr. Crouch lured him out of his silence. *"I was a stutterer. I couldn't talk. So my first year of school was my first mute year, and then those mute years continued until I got to high school,"* ("James Earl Jones Biography and Interview – Academy of Achievement," www.achievement.org).

After debuting on Broadway in *"The Great White Hope"* (1957), Jones became a two-time Tony Award winner for his work in 1969's *"The Great White Hope"* and 1987 for *"Fences"* as Best Actor in a Leading Role, as well as a Tony Lifetime

Achievement award. Jones received an Academy Award nomination *"The Great White Hope"* (1971) and an Honorary Award 2012. He received four Golden Globes nominations, winning Most Promising Newcomer – Male for *"The Great White Hope"* (1970). He received Primetime Emmy Awards 1964 and 2004, he received five nominations and won two for Outstanding Lead Actor in a Drama Series *"Gabriel's Fire"* (1990) and Outstanding Supporting Actor in a Miniseries or a Special for *"Heat Wave"* (1990).

Then, of course, there is the *VOICE* category; Behind the Voice Actors Awards and Jones was nominated four-time, winning three for Best Male Vocal Performance in a Feature Film in a Supporting Role *"Rogue One"* (2016) *"Star Wars."* He also won a Grammy Award, Best Spoken Word Recording (1977). I have always been a huge fan of James Earl even before learning we had similarities in our young lives and our grounding connection to the land in Mississippi. I had, as he, to learn what the real connection was, and not to think of it as odd. James Earl Jones explained it this way,

"I didn't realize that until I went back for a family reunion when I was 40 years old. I got back to the old homestead, and I felt such warmth. Not temperature, not heat warmth, but such sucking warmth hit me that I was back to that land again. That choo-choo train journey from Mississippi to Michigan was a trauma. There were other things that happened along the way that one might pin it to, family things."

As I said beginning this discussion of James Earl Jones, *I present just a few facts about him as a preface for the statement I make about the image in my mind's eye when I see him or hear his name.* The image of James Earl is a huge price of granite sitting in the middle of an open area, sticking up out of the earth. If in a field, rows go around it. If a highway ran that way, there would be a curve. No one dared try and move it, for fear it is like an iceberg; much more beneath the surface than what meets the eye. Undisturbed by children climbing on it, even their graffiti does not diminish its hulking presence. James Earl, always reflecting such solidity, his strength, power, and stability in an immovable kind of way, which would tell a farmer, looking at it, it is easier and more productive to go around. My point in presenting James Earl Jones last is because his persona is the kind of image ***"The 400th"*** needs reflected by a "grand marshal." Although ***"The 400th"*** will be ceremonial and celebratory events, I long to have an image like that James Earl reflected and projected, as King Jaffe Joffer in *Coming to America*.

The Stone Awards Go Invaders

Psalm 118:22 says *"The stone the builders refused is become the headstone of the corner."*

On October 2, 2019, the Memphis City Council passed a historic resolution designating the Month of October *"Stone Awards Month."* The Stone Awards honors outstanding but unheralded community leaders, entrepreneurs, entertainers, and activists in the Memphis Metropolitan area, as well as America. Consider this, a rock, when designed for a particular purpose or specific function, becomes a stone, mostly when building. My best example is a diamond, which is nothing but a rock that is designed for adornment. Stone is also a unit of weight; the official British unit is equal to 14 pounds. Some even consider the hard central core of drupaceous fruit stones, like a hard as rock pit or seed, which is a source of growth and development (progeny).

Mr. Terry Campbell Sr. and Mrs. Thelma Campbell-Brownlee planted nine "mustard seeds"—Terry "YaYa"Campbell Jr., Doris Campbell-Mabry, Linda Campbell-Branch, Pastor Jerry Campbell, Annie Campbell-Glenn, Pastor Melvin Campbell, Minister Larry Campbell, Emma Boatman-Campbell and Stanley "Cam MTenzi" Campbell in the rock hard soil of the Riverside community of South Memphis. Hard little nothings, they shaped them into stones. Now, looking back over almost 30 years of growth and harvesting such stones/seeds, as himself "Cam MTenzi" presented **The 24th Annual Stone Awards** on October 19, 2019. Creator and director of the continuing effort to recognize collections of stones, Cam brought from what was once cotton fields in Memphis and surrounding area or those facing similar circumstances in other parts of the US to receive the coveted and venerable signification. **The Stone Awards** acknowledges individuals that have spent their lives, turning all kinds of rocks into cornerstones or jewels of leadership, innovation, entrepreneurial, and community developers. Their commitment and professionalism, as well as accomplishments, have shaped them into "community cornerstones." During their shaping, they were taught all rocks were not created to become diamonds. Cutting and buffing gives particular rocks their value.

The incredible thing in all of this is Cam selected me to be among 2019's *Stone Awards* recipients. **The Stone Awards** are among the most prestigious and coveted accolades I've received, because of Cam's ongoing effort to commemorate and recognize the Invaders. Consequently, I accepted the honor for the unheralded black power group, with great pride and humility, as a grateful seed and son.

Beyond the personal recognition, **The Stone Awards** served as the finale of the inaugural year, closing out a very successful and exciting beginning for **"The 400th."** **The Stone Awards** weekend left supporters of **"The 400th"** eagerly anticipating 2020, as an even more exciting and spectacular year. However, as I have said previously here, COVID-19 placed the world on lockdown, so *"The 400th"* is socially distenting and looking forward to the new normal that will developing in 2021.

Cam Mtenzi didn't only honor me through ***The Stone Awards*** but honor all Invaders, particularly those that have passed on. The amazing weekend began with a "meet and greet" that brought together awardees, staff, volunteers, and past recipients of the obeisant distinction. The gathering provides an opportunity to mingle with previous celebrities, icons and friends.

Friday night was very special; it was an Invaders night. It began with a panel discussion that included other awardees that gave their histories and spoke about what ***The Stone Awards*** recognition meant to them. The panel discussion was a prelude to a commemorative candlelight visual and balloon release for Invaders afterwards.

The tandem of Darryl Buford and Sharon Davis conducted the ardent and emotional roll call honoring departed Invaders and families. It brought everyone into the same mental space by giving everyone a name of a departed Invader and a candle. Darryl placed a lit candle in the distance, about thirty yards away from the group. The light in the distance symbolized Africa; He said:

Let the light in the distance represent Africa, the land where our slave journey began. Let us never forget the ones that paid the price, past, and present whose shoulders on which we stand today. As painful as our history has been, we must embrace their struggle. So let us commemorate and celebrate the journey that God has set and launched us upon.

Following Darryl's words, Invaders' family and supporters offered silent prayers. After prayers, those with names called them aloud. Entreating their spirit to rise, I released a bundle of ten huge balloons, with a flashing light and their names attached, into the heavens. I gave a remembrance salute, *"These balloons carry forth our prayers and symbolically free their spirits, lifting them from their earth-bound bondage into a hopeful universe. We commemorate these unsung heroes, though they are gone, they are not unremembered."* The balloons carried their names and our prayers a loaf. We acknowledged and recognized Charles "Cab" Cabbage, Charles Ballard, Charles "Izzy" Harrington, Richard Kirksey, Juanita "mule train" Thornton, Janice Lewis-Payne, Maurice Lewis, "Big" John Smith, John Gary William, John Ferguson, Verdell "Gee" Brooks, Ben Cauley, Wendell Withers, and his father Dr. Ernest C. Withers and others. *"The Stone the builders refused is become the headstone of the corner."*

Saturday morning began with a breakfast with the men's group from Pilgrim Rest Baptist Church. The once-a-month gathering is a tradition that began with the passing of a family member Jeffery Smith, my nephew, son of Tommy C. Smith. The gathering has grown from personal loss to a general concern for bringing black men together to work on community problems. Terry and Darryl Buford are founders and moderators, along with Stanley and Barry Springfield. Although starting as a family project, it has grown to include men from other churches and communities. I was so proud to be among these younger members of my family, who have assumed such an important role in a community in desperate need of black men to stand up and provide responsible leadership.

The Stone Awards itself is important for many reasons, but its focus on black heritage and community, which is unprecedented to me, in this regard, in Memphis. The evening began with a *"Red Carpet* meet and greet" for recipients and attendees. I thoroughly enjoyed talking and taking pictures and selfies with attendees, before the show. Again the audience was treated to more than individuals walking across the stage receiving accolades. There were skits; one of which combined video footage of Marcus Garvey's life, presented by, Deon Bates, a freelance videographer. Deon portrayed Mr. Garvey, uniform, plumed hat and all, for a very lifelike reenactment of the iconic character. Deon projected a resemblance truly reminiscent of the iconic leader, as he spoke of Marcus Garvey's life and impact.

"Be Free or Die," the trailer for the Academy Award nominated biopic on the life of Harriet Tubman, starring Cynthia Erivo, was shown two weeks before the movies hit theaters. Also, the trailer for the 2016 movie on the life of Nat Turner was shown. Though the biopic seemed interesting and entertaining, it's confusing title—*"The Birth of a Nation"*—gave me real problems separating it from D. W. Griffith's racist film by the same name. I like what I saw in the trailer, but I believe the name confusion, leave most Africans Americans cold and unable to separate the two and understand there is a difference in the two movies before viewing them.

I was so grateful that Cam showed the trailer to clear up my confusion. Nate Parker, I remembered from *"The Great Debaters"* director by Denzel Washington, even with the name confusion, Nate seemed to give another excellent performance, from what I could see and learn from the trailer. Without that confusion, Nat Turner may have garnered as much notoriety, as Harriet Tubman at the box office and award nominations. However, that may have been the plan—confusion—since Nate Turner is such a hated figure in American history.

Surrounding the presentation of awards with such a cultural backdrop gave context and even more relevance to **The 24th Annual Stone Awards** for me. Plus, my favorite MC Drew McCraven kept things moving and lively; even his jokes had cultural significance. There were dancers, models, artwork and vocalists. One of my favorite groups "The Temprees" were honored and gave a quick sample of their virtuosity, which capped a very entertaining and enlightening evening.

Cam Mtenzi has created a program that recognizes the symbolic power of what descendants of American slavery can gain by commemorating unsung individuals and groups development that helped get us to *"The 400th"*. Seeds that grew in unfertile soil but their struggle to endure to survive got enslaved Africans here. By honoring me at *The 24th Annual Stone Awards,* it has become the cornerstone of the inaugural year of commemorating and celebrating *"The 400th"*. It is the second major event of 2019. *The TD International Vancouver Jazz Festival* June 21-July1, 2019 was the first. That festival kicked off the inaugural year of reminding the world that 1619 is the year American historians offer to mark the arrival of the first enslaved Africans in North America. However, descendants of enslaved Africans are claiming more than one year for such a huge occasion for us. Honoring me at *The 24th Annual Stone Awards,* Cam Mtenzi becomes the first annual awards show to recognize, commemorating, celebrating and honoring *"The 400th*. The plaques and certificates bore *"The 400th"* logo. No matter how many awards shows may come after, none will ever come before *The Stone Awards!!!!*

New Normal VII: Where Today Began

Reviewing descendants of American slavery's sojourn in North America, beginning with **The Trans-Atlantic Slave Trade,** descendants of American slavery struggling to reach the **"The 400th"**, a reoccurring question followed that theme; *"Why isn't there a plan to extend the same rights and freedom to descendants of American slavery that white people have and presently enjoy?"* The other side of this warped coin is the same question asked another way. *"When will slave descendants be accorded the same rights, as people today, who came to America from other countries that arrive aboard ship, on airlines or in boat flotillas, maybe even trek across the desert, receive upon request for citizenship?"* The downside of that coin shows slave descendants, since landing in chains in North America, have jumped through hoops, kneel in protest, stood against incredible odds, and continually laid their lives on the line defending America in wars, still remain in the second class status they received at emancipation 157 years ago.

Now that descendants of enslaved Africans have reached **"The 400th"**, such questions must be asked aloud. *"Why do descendants of American slavery still bear the 3/5 Compromise stigma of being treated as though they are less than white men, perpetually locked on the bottom of America's socioeconomic structure, as cheap labor?"* No other Americans citizens bear this second class stigma. Why is that? What does that mean today in 2021? Will there ever come a time, when the US Government acknowledge that it maintains discrimination against black people, while not accepting the fact that America is violating their human right, as well as "The Civil Rights Bill of 1866, also their right of *VOICE?*

I had planned to end **"The 400**th*"* with the Stone Awards, as the grand finale for the inaugural year of 2019. However, as time, events and Divine intervention would have it, the coronavirus created a totally unimagined scenario for the world, when it escaped China, like a runaway freight train in late 2019. It hopscotched its way across the world, reaching the United States in January 2020. America was absolutely unprepared, as the coronavirus pandemic invade from both shores.

Coronavirus was not like illegal aliens, where a border wall was seen, as the first line of defense to keep invaders out. But, unlike threats from illegal aliens, Donald Trump took to the rose garden and railed at COVID-19, but like his wall against illegal aliens, his efforts only amount to huffing and puffing, but didn't cowed it. Coronavirus turned cold shoulder of indifference to Trump's hot air. His bombastic pronouncements only spread COCID-19's. Trump's bolster did not keep it bottled up at the border like illegal immigrants, or in wire cages like immigrant children, his travel ban was a sieve.

So, Trump went with his gut instinct, he denied the pandemic was a threat, declaring it would magically blow away. Hoping to keep his sputtering economy

The 400th: From Slavery to Hip Hop

going, he called it the Democratic Party's *"new hoax."* Similar to most Americans, I was totally ignorant of coronavirus, so I searched available information and came across a video by Dr. Abdul Alim Muhammad that provided the most intelligent review of COVID-19 at the time. Basically, he gave advice, like my grandmamma, she called it winterizing us against colds. We goggled mornings and nights before bed, drank lots of liquids, and ate vegetables and fruit preserves to build up our immune system with vitamin C.

By now most people not only know the drill, they lived through it, except those that followed Trump example. The lockdown closed schools and then another phenomenon happened, I never imagined. Those who could, begin working from home. Can you imagine "slave picking cotton in their living rooms?" With those decisions my daughter, Liquitta, her four kids, Tyrus, Toi, Tahlia and Tristyn hunkered down for the duration.

Thinking I had seen it all, but no, the Federal Reserve began printing money, like paper was going out of style and Congress, Trump and Republicans began throwing money at big corporations, like they were in a spitball fight. However, when it came down to poor people and cities loaded with them, Republicans recoiled, as though they had run out of paper and spit. So thus far there is no help for the same people, who are always at the end of the line, except when people are going to jail or getting murdered by police, they are pushed up front of that line. As per usual, poor folks got crumbs, if anything at all.

Then another plague, joined COVID-19, and struck black people disproportionally. While coronavirus was killing 3 blacks to every one white person, white men, whether in street clothes or police uniforms began killing black men, like even death was going out of style. I could have missed the one white killed, if there was one, but during that time, it seemed every day or two a black man was murdered by police, but not one white person was even beaten up, unless they were protesting police killings.

The strange thing is, when dealing with black people, white police act as though to do anything but slavishly follow their every word, make a black person guilty of a capital crime, which put white men in fear for their lives. But in a crowded Michigan Capitol building, facing "white nationalists," carrying assault rifles, Donald Trump's favorite people, invaded the state house, and stood nose to nose, and stared police down. Screaming and spitting in their faces, police stood, calm and cool as cucumbers, not one was made to fear for their life. Unflappable, police showed absolutely no anxiety and exhibited no signs of feeling threatened, while giving white rebel and Nazi flag waving renegades free rein. Some even took selfies, with what seemed to me terror is not peaceful protesters.

Simultaneously, state capitol employees were wearing bulletproof vests. I repeat, these are what Trump called "very fine people!!!!" No one got jacked-up or accosted with questions. No body went to jail, no police pulled a gun, everyone to a man, stood calmly, like statues or cigar store Indians. This incident, along with those I present, reflect this narrative's theme, white and black people can witness the same event at the exact same time from the same perspective, yet see two totally different scenarios.

Then, like a seismic tremor, the video of an American lynching, George Floyd murder, by the knee of a policeman on his neck for 8 minutes and 46seconds suffocating him went viral. If the video of Ahmud Arbery, who was hunted down, by 3 KKK, on the street, in broad daylight, in rural Georgia, didn't wake up the world, George Floyd's "snuff" film popped eyes, waking the world from its deep sleep. George Floyd's lynching revealed a level of hatred some white people, particularly those on police forces across America, harbor for black skin. It was such a horrific sight, watching the 8 minutes and 46 second lynching, while the policeman looked into the cameras, as though he was auditioning for the celebrity "Apprentice."

Never were the eyes of the whole world fixed on a human being suffered such an excruciating death of one police, while 3 other either helped or calmly watch, like police at the Michigan Capitol. The world watched a white policeman kneel with the whole force and weight of his body on George Floyd's neck, as he called for his mother with his last breath, as other officers on the scheme assisted in the lynchings. Absolutely no one attempted to stop this obvious police murder.

Although, the video is horrible, no one with real human empathy watching, in total disbelief, could look away. What America thinks of black life was on display for 8 minutes and 46 seconds, for the world to see and no one with a ounce of humanity could deny what they were seeing. The horror of it all brought young black, brown, red, yellow and whites progressive minded people into streets across America, behind one idea *"Black Lives Matter,"* in numbers I never imagined for protests over the death of a black man. Watching in amazement, their protests not only spread across the US but around the world, as thousand in large and medium size cities, as well as small towns join the protest. London, Paris, The Netherlands, Germany, Japan, Africa, and even in faraway places like New Zealand held massive protests. *"Black Lives Matter"* became the largest mass action in the world, in just a matter of days, faster than any movement ever around the world wide.

This massive upheaval of humanity truly inspired me and as always words began flowing, as never before, not even back during the 1960 did I become so motivated. Once I began writing, it was like having one foot in the 1960s and one in 2020, and my reflections, gave me a new understanding and appreciation for the work of a man few think about, if they remember him at all—Edward R. Murrow. Murrow was a CBS correspondent during WWII that report nightly via radio on the "Battle of Britain," as the Nazis rained buzz bombs and other highly inflammatory explosives on London.

I did not see myself in such an iconic role but what I related to from that time was the need for people in the United States to know what some human beings were enduring, at the hands of merciless, uncaring and powerful people, just because they could. I wanted, in my writings to reveal what it was and possibly meant to people, who cared enough about others to step into the breach, so that others understand and vicariously have a model of what carrying looks like, especially whites.

This was the first time such visual examples of American racism were clearly on display on American soil, as it happened. For the first time the death of a black man—George Floyd—and COVID-19 impact seemed to create an alternate universe, where people show who they truly are and what they truly think of black people. I offer what this time gave me, and I share it with the world to show how young progressives protesting Americans hatred means without any doubt. I felt very fortunate and privileged to be the world's window to such madness in 2020.

It is obvious, having been enslaved in America for 400 year the older white population still view descendants of American slavery, as less than human beings. Even after a bloody Civil War, whites still refused to give up their "slave master mindset." After Civil War, Abraham Lincoln inspired Republican, called "radicals," to pass and stand behind the Civil Rights Act of 1866, enacted April 9. COVID-19 has uncovered America racist face and revealed its legacy of hatred, murder, lynching and total degradation of black people out today. So, I wanted the world to know how America got here. Coronavirus revealed things about Americans, no other event had been able to touch and bring out their humanity, as their children have embraced black people, and see them as they are.

I believe, their parents were totally unaware, having such empathy existed for black people. Shocked and appalled by their children's lack of open racism, they could not understand how that happened. They did not realize, their children are fully invested in the hip hop generation. It is the one thing they own, as members, that the "old America" cannot claim or stop. With racism, so engrained in their personalities and completely dominate their psychology, older Americans were surprised that their children divorced themselves from America's history of racism and many parents are losing contact with their progeny. The depth of racism among white people and is so prominent it impacts everything involved in human relations.

Basically, TV and cell phones became the window to the world for most people over the last two decades. The ***"Black Lives Matter"*** protests have presented a world white people cannot run away from because it is their children, who are helping fuel the demands for social justice and social change being made.

Now I give readers a literary view of how events impact people and the kind of thoughts their behavior prompted, relative to the history I knew. This is not an effort to justify or provide an ultimate answer to what the new normal will bring, regarding their current demands for justice. What I relay is an episodic perspective based on the historic and psychosocial diversion from what Americans told themselves before coronavirus invaded America.

Also, I will remind readers my views are those of a shut in, with only a view through Facebook and other social media analysis. I am not out in the street with my grandchildren. But I am reminding older white people of the United States federal law—the Civil Rights Act of 1866—which defined citizenship for newly freed slaves and affirmed that all citizens were equally protected under the law. It was passed and intended to protect the civil rights of newly freed slaves and descendants born in or brought to the US.

What Happened After Emancipation of Slaves?

The United States Government has been lying to black Americans since 1866, in order to deny them access to America's bounty. These are the facts I have presented in the history that followed its passage of **The Civil Rights Bill of 1866.** This narrative has detailed what white people in government—federal, state and local—did to deny formal slaves their human, as well as civil rights. I will reiterate!

Everything you have read since **"The Gilded Age,"** the lynching, robbery, denial, banishment, ethnic cleansing, segregation, white supremacy and **"Dark Age"** *angry white men mob madness* were all to force former slaves and their descendants to accept the "second class" status white people demand. The creation of the United Nations pointed out here, made it possible for William Patterson and Paul Robeson to challenge America's treatment of slavery's descendants with ***"We Charge Genocide"*** in 1952. Their challenge is why the US Congress, doubled back in 1954 and pass a second Civil Rights Bill, to give the world the impression America was changing it racist regime. That is why America's streets today are filled with our children, demanding justice and equality for all Americans because the US Constitution and civil rights law grant that to all, not just white people. The refusal to recognize those laws is why a white policeman kneeled on George Floyd's neck for 8 minutes and 46 second. The open act of murder, my law enforcement, symbolized America's total disregard for the lives of descendants of American slavery.

I also want readers to know and understand that white people, over the last 157 years, which followed the passage of **"The Civil Rights Act of 1866"** continually lied and denied African Americans all the civil rights every other US citizens are accorded by the US Constitution. While at the same time, whites have spent this same period—157 years—using the US Supreme Court, to deny black people access to fair courts, simply refusing to hear their just complaints.

Again, as I have shown, throughout **"The 400th"**, white politicians, educators, lawyers, judges, religious leaders, businesses leaders and everyday white person agreed to re-enslaved black Americans with—convict leasing, sharecropping, discrimination, lynching, segregation, and white supremacy— that culminated in the police-state that exist today and hostile environment of police murders are permitted against black people to prevent descendants of American slavery from exercising the rights given by **"The Civil Rights Act of 1866"** and the Constitution of the United States.

In other words, the only reason Africans Americans cannot exercise first class rights in America is that white people, like Donald Trump and Mitch McConnell, uses the power of the federal government and the Supreme Court to illegally block their access. This is a very important point, they are violating laws on the book, in other words, they are criminals, according to *The Civil Rights Bill of 1866*, a legal act that has never been repealed or overturned by the US Supreme Court. So the United States has created an Apartheid state the same as South Africa, which is why the atmosphere for African Americans is so caustic and deadly.

Here is the history and the law itself, which reveals why the United States is currently in violation of the US Constitution. This explanation begins before *The Civil Rights Bill of 1866* became law. US President Andrew Johnson of Tennessee vetoed this legislation—*The Civil Rights Bill of 1866*—twice, but each time a two-thirds majority vote in each chamber of Congress to override Johnson's vetoes. *"The Civil Rights Bill of 1866"* became the law of the land without a presidential signature. *"The Civil Rights Bill of 1866,"* protected *"the Civil Rights of all Persons in the United States, and furnishes the Means of their vindication, by declaring that all people born in the United States who are not subject to any foreign power are entitled to be citizens, without regard to race, color, or previous condition of slavery or involuntary servitude."* A similar provision (called the Citizenship Clause), was written into *the Fourteenth Amendment* to the United States Constitution from *The Civil Rights Bill of 1866*. The Fourteenth Amendment is what is used in place of *The Civil Rights Bill of 1866*, because of it limits the scope regarding of discrimination, this is why *The Civil Right Bill of 1866* is not taught in Law Schools. I believe judges are completely ignorant of *The Civil Rights Bill of 1866*.

The Civil Rights Bill of 1866 declared among other things that *"any citizen has the same right that a white citizen has to make and enforce contracts, sue and be sued, give evidence in court, and inherit, purchase, lease, sell, hold, and convey real and personal property."* Additionally, the act *guaranteed to all citizens the "full and equal benefit of all laws and proceedings for the security of person and property, as is enjoyed by white citizens, like punishment, pains, and penalties... Persons who denied these rights on account of race or previous enslavement were guilty of a misdemeanor and upon conviction faced a fine not exceeding $1,000, or imprisonment not exceeding one year, or both.*

I repeat, *The Fourteenth Amendment* incorporated the same language in the *Equal Protection Clause* from *The Civil Rights Bill of 1866*. In particular, the act discussed the need to provide *"reasonable protection to all persons in their constitutional rights of equality before the law, without distinction of race or color, or previous condition of slavery or involuntary servitude."* This is why police murders and other disparate treatment is a violation of the law and black people should file suits against police for the slightest violation of a black person rights.

That is why when police deviate from the law in their treatment of a black person they are *"guilty of a misdemeanor and upon conviction faced a fine not exceeding $1,000, or imprisonment not exceeding one year, or both.*

Today penalties are much greater. Again, I say, this is current law of the United States and why Donald Trump is a criminal and is currently violating the law with his discrimination and disparate treatment of Black Lives Matter protesters, while favoring white nationalists, among other things. This open violation began with Woodrow Wilson. And, similarly Donald Trump, is using Woodrow Wilson's strategy. Wilson developed his plan, during his White House screenings of the movie ***"The Birth of a Nation."*** This narrative has shown, Woodrow Wilson screened that movie over 30 times in the While House for Supreme Court Justices, members of Congress, captains of industry, moguls of finance, the press and other politicians. He is the president that illegally segregated the federal government, beginning with the US Postal Service. Wilson follow that by sponsoring white supremacy from the White House, as Donald Trump is attempting to do presently, and if he is re-elected he will go full court press on black people. It is that legacy, which young Americans are out in the streets fighting with ***"Black Lives Matter"*** protests.

Since 1866, "it has been illegal in the US to discriminate in employment and housing on the basis of race." So black people continue to be discriminated against and denied their legal right because the Supreme Court refuses to allow **The Civil Rights Bill of 1866** to be enforced, which businesses, schools, the Federal Reserve, Wall Street all institutions are operating illegally denying and violating African American Constitutional rights. The US Supreme Court currently makes slavery's descendants victims of discrimination without recourse. Since the latter half of the 20th century and passage of related civil rights legislation, there have been an increasing number of remedies provided, including the landmark Jones v. *Mayer* and *Sullivan v. Little Hunting Park, Inc.* decisions, and the **1964 Civil Rignt Act** but none of these actions have mattered because white people refuse to follow the law. However, all that is needed is to defeat Donald Trump on November 3, 2020.

An Open Letter in The New Tri-State Defender to Candidate Joe Biden

Sir,

All indications point to you, as the presumptive Democrat Party Nominee for President of the United States of America, and with that, I offer my congratulations. Following a long grueling, and even bitter contest at times, now the Democratic Party must turn to the job of "binding up its wounds." Following another long bitter and deadly fight among the American family, Pres. Abraham Lincoln used that theme "binding up the nation's wounds" in his re-election message to the nation. The President's theme reflected America's greatest need and the proper therapy for a broken nation.

I believe President Lincoln designed his prescription to get ahead of and undercut those forces that would "use the moment to keep hatred and division alive." Sir, I believe, metaphorically, as well as symbolically, presently, you are standing in his shoes, and as such, I hope your actions, in the eyes of future generations, cast a shadow as long as Pres. Lincoln's back then. I say this because the same issuers that racked America back then are present today, as America faces emeries within and without. The need is clear for most Americans; the question is will the Democrats be the party that will step forth to provide leadership to guide the nation out of the present morass?

My credibility in offering the following assessment comes with credentials that began with my mother, Mrs. Willie May Gray. Mrs. Gray's involvement with the Democratic Party which began in 1948 in Memphis, Tennessee, as a supporter of Pres. Harry S. Truman for election. I remember walking door to door with her, as a 9-year-old, campaigning for Adlai Stevenson in 1952. My history of support for the Democrat Party transitioned, as I became a black power activist and founding member of the Invaders (1967). Through the Invaders' support for the Memphis sanitation workers, during their strike (1968), I became one of the last two people (Charles "Cab" Cabbage was the other) to meet with Dr. Martin Luther King, Jr. in a strategy meeting less than an hour before his assassination.

I became a political activist in 1972, as a campaign coordinator for former Congressman of the 9th District of Tennessee, Harold E. Ford. I was also the campaign manager Dedrick "Teddy" Withers (1974), youngest state representative ever elected in Tennessee at age 22. "Teddy" represented the 85th District in South Memphis.

But the political milestone that means most was Rep. Shirley Chisholm's 1972 campaign for President. Rev. Hosea Williams inspired Rep. Chisholm's candidacy during the first "Black Political Convention (1972)" since 1864. During the Democratic Presidential Nominating Convention, Rep. Shirley

Chisholm's helped organize the first-ever "Black Political Caucus (1972), within in the Democrat Party.

Following that convention, two years later, the "Black Political Caucus met at the 1974 Democratic Party's Mini-Convention in Kansas City. A progressive coalition of blacks, Native People, women, Latinos, and poor whites through the Black Caucus broke the stranglehold "Dixiecrats" had on the party's nomination process. These progressives opened the delegate selection process for further Presidents, while giving those groups representation in the party. They also increased representation for progressive members on the Rules Committee and limited the number of uncommitted special and super delegates. That progressive coalition made it possible for insurgent candidate Jimmy Carter to become President, and I was part of that campaign, through Rep. "Teddy" Withers re-election campaign in 1976.

The Democratic Party's concerns today should be keep Sen. Bernie Sanders supporters, which I am one, from walking away. It is evident you have elderly Democratic voters locked in and those that consider themselves moderates, but by anyone's count that gets you only half-way. I spoke about the type of leadership needed because of this dilemma. You have committed to selecting a woman as your vice-presidential running mate, which I agree is the kind of essential step needed, but it is your next decision that will either seal the deal or widen the breach.

Consequently, since the VP is your offering, as the other half of your effort to unite the party behind your candidacy, I throw Mrs. Michelle Obama's hat in the ring. I offer her name, as a unity candidate for the other half of the Democratic Party's unity ticket to end the bloodletting. Some may question my analysis or my presumptuousness in putting Mrs. Obama's name forth before gauging her willingness to accept such a challenge. Offering the former First Lady, I believe, gives renewed hope to not only Sen. Sander's supporters, but fence-sitting African Americans trust in your candidacy.

Moreover, we can lay qualifications aside because Mrs. Obama's credentials are impeccable. Her broad experience is more extensive, regarding the White House, than any woman in America. It is clear the Constitution gives no role in the performance of the office of President to the First Lady, but "pillow talk" goes both ways. So, the former First Lady has a perspective, on the office of President and Vice President, no other woman, under consideration has. Indubitably, as the other half of this unity ticket, designed to seal the breach, adding a proven asset, like Mrs. Obama, would bring luminescence and glamour to what black voters see, as a lack luster campaign.

However, in her own right, before entering the White House, the former First Lady served her community, as a lawyer and community advocate. But, more importantly, after leaving the White House, she continued building a very loyal and dedicated following. Mrs. Obama not only has admirers among black women but women and men of all races, as well as young people, which many are not presently part of Sen. Sanders' supporters. These voters would overwhelmingly accept half-a-loaf, with the former First Lady, making the cut. Again, however, for black people, it would amount to a full loaf, because beyond Pres. Obama, descendants of American slavery have not been full partners with any administration since they gained the vote.

Now, we come down to the major sticking point if there is a deal-breaker, and that is, will she accept? I believe, first and foremost, Mrs. Obama is a "patriot" of the first order. One of the most lucid thinkers regarding America's current problems, and she knows this is one of the most critical moments in history for America's descendants of slavery. She is very much aware we, as a people, reached this juncture before back in 1912, then Woodrow Wilson entered the White House. Pres. Wilson used the federal government to initiate segregation, beginning with the federal government, while supporting lynching, mayhem, banishment, and ethnic cleansing against descendants of American slavery, which lasted into the 1960s.

Looking at that history, the former First Lady understands these times, even this moment, was made for her. God is never wrong when He puts someone in a place, He has prepared for them, and events in their life brought them there. Therefore, I believe if you ask, Mrs. Obama will not refuse. Sen. Sanders supports, and many young progressives that are not involved in this process will accept and support half-a-loaf, rather than nothing.

How Important Are African American Votes?

The 24th Annual Stone Awards was the last event of 2019 for *"The 400th"*. The dawning of 2020 was a new day for *"The 400th"* committee, we began the year, elated following the totally unexpected level of success, we experienced in 2019. The reception in 2019 showed that *"The 400th"* was a proper vehicle for commemorating and celebrating this momentous occasion. With that reality frashing in our minds, we believed descendants of American slavery had finally arrived where our survival, as one people, was no longer in doubt. I wanted to put the importance of African American voting power into proper perspective by stating with crystalline clarity that for the first time, descendants of American slavery's votes can determine who will occupy the White House. And, as history, time and events would have it, African Americans could make the decision that will determine the destiny of *"The 400th"* Generation.

The fact that 2020 is an election year, I am pushing the point, the future of African Americans would ride upon the strength at the ballot box. For the first time, based on the strength of African American voting power, they have the opportunity to demand the Vice President position on the Democrat Party ticket for President, given the potential of their political support. The election of Pres. Barak H. Obama moved descendants of American slavery from politics in and of the street to where they were establishing political priorities, heading into the 2020 election. Therefore, I put forth a "patriot," Mrs. Michelle Obama, who in previous service to America had established that she has the knowledge, experience, expertise, insight, and courage to lead this divided nation. This time around, black Americans deserve a real choice, a leader, totally different from the past.

America, in 2020, has arrived at a place of decision and change. Its citizens are facing the prospect of losing their democratic process, as established under constitutional government through the vote. That loss will lead to a decline in democracy for all but the wealthiest Americans. Descendants of American slavery have endured the injustices and degradation of the second-class status forced upon them by the system of segregation and white supremacy, even under its so-called democratic system. After breaking the back of segregation, which lasted into the 1960s, today, the threat is on our doorstep once again.

The 2020 election will present the most significant challenge to slavery's descendants' progress since the 1930s. However, simultaneously, the 2020 election will be the best opportunity for slavery's descendants to create a full partnership in a coalition government.

By selecting Mrs. Michelle Obama, as the other half of the Democrats unity ticket, Mr. Biden, will show his commitment to creating a new America. Mrs. Obama's selection will give descendants of American slavery a spokesperson at the highest levels of government that can help shape this new world enveloping in America. Mr. Biden's choice will indicate how important he feels the votes of African Americans are to him becoming President, and the revitalization of America.

Happy Birthday, Maya.

I began this long look backward at black icons in *"The 400th"* with a woman no longer with us, Rose McClendon. She was at the head of the line of those who laid stones on the *"yellow bricks road of entertainment."* McClendon along with her brothers and sisters laid the foundation for hip hop. Though not planned in the way this narrative developed, I continue finds information about particular descendants of American slavery, after I thought my list was complete, another icon pops up, who must be included without them, and my effort would be diminished.

Marguerite Annie Johnson (4-4-1928/5-28-2014), better known to her adoring and admiring fans as Maya Angelou was a tremendously successful writer, poet, singer, memoirist, civil rights activist, cook, sex worker, nightclub dancer, performer, and mentor, which are among only some expressions of this multi-talented icon. Although Mrs. Angelou had millions of loving and appreciative fans, I believe Oprah Winfrey is one of the more vociferous among them. Maya's life was filled with far too many accomplishments to try and detail them here. For instance, Mrs. Angelou enjoyed a beautiful life that included becoming a journalist in Egypt and Ghana, during the decolonization of Africa. She directed, as well as produced plays, movies, and public television programs in the late 1960s.

Then there is Broadway and her fight for human rights. Mrs. Angelou met novelist John O. Killens in 1959 and he convinced her to move to New York City, where she could concentrate and fully develop as a writer. She joined the Harlem Writers Guild, where she met and worked with several major African American authors, including John Henrik Clarke, Rosa Guy, Paule Marshall, and Julian Mayfield. In 1960, she met civil rights leader Rev. Martin Luther King Jr., and she and Killens organized the legendary *"Cabaret for Freedom"* which was a benefit for *the Southern Christian Leadership Conference (SCLC)*. Later, she was named SCLC Northern Coordinator. In 1961, Mrs. Angelou performed in Jean Genet's play *"The Blacks,"* which had an outstanding cast of notable icons including Abbey Lincoln, Roscoe Lee Brown, James Earl Jones, Louis Gossett, Jr., Godfrey Cambridge, and Cicely Tyson. That was truly one hell of a cast.

While in Accra, Ghana, she became close friends with Malcolm X, during his visit in the early 1960s. When Mrs. Angelou returned to the US, she worked with Malcolm, as he began building his *Black Nationalist* organization, the *Organization of Afro-American Unity* (OAU), just before he was assassinated.

Mrs. Angelou received dozens of awards and more than 50 honorary degrees before reaching the 1990s, where she, in 1993, recited her poem *"On the Pulse of Morning"* at Bill Clinton's presidential inauguration. US President Barack H. Obama presented the Presidential Medal of Freedom (2011) to Mrs. Angelou.

Reading all her honors, one might think Mrs. Angelou lived a life of ease and gaiety, however, that was definitely not the case. According to Mrs. Angelou, *"I had many hard struggles, but that is life, struggle."* I first met Mrs. Angelou through *"I Know Why the Caged Bird Sings"* (1969). I read that autobiography while in jail in 1971. I learned, as with so many black men and women detailed here, she was abused during childhood by her mother's boyfriend. When she told her uncles, unlike many other abusers, later, the culprit was found dead. The rumor was the culprit had been kicked to death. The boomerang for Maya was she became so frightened by the power of her words, at age eight; she became mute, refusing to speak for the next five years.

Again, like many other black children, including this writer, a concerned teacher found a way to draw her out of her closed off world. However, Mrs. Angelou's influence did not end with her passing, the impact of her words continued reaching out from the grave, like a healing balm, to inspire today. Consider this. I received a post on Facebook that illustrates her truly amazing power. The clip was posted by L. BrooklynPhenix Smith from Great Britain. While showing Meghan Markle's courage facing her latest travails, including the backstabbing from the so-called British "royal circle."

The post featured Mrs. Angelou reciting her iconic poem *"And still I Rise"* (1978). Brilliantly produced, the clip showed Mrs. Angelou giving a live performance interspaced with video clips of Meghan Markle, poised as always, going about her life with Harry and their baby. The post was accompanied by a Youtube.com piece entitled, *The Story about Maya Angelou that you have never heard in her own word!*

Mrs. Angelou's message is not just for Meghan, but for all black women. Mrs. Angelou made the point in her poem and the video that, if you are a black woman and though you may be hated, verbally abused, attacked unjustly, ostracized and lynched upon the scaffold of ridicule, you should never feel alone or ashame, because that has always been the lot of black women. Black women can never afford to show weakness or to be fragile in the face of such assaults from those bent on their destruction. You must stand tall, as a proud vessel of life.

Bearing that burden with pride and grace is the beauty you reflect, which drives those jealous of your femininity, womanly powers and strength that defies incredible odds to gain victory. Mrs. Angelou's clarion call is to stand forth when haters try to push you down, and even when they manage to cover you with their lies and plots, still as a black woman, you must rise!!!

That is the demand before all enslaved Africans descendants, women, and men. We must always reach deep to bring forth the self-love that got slavery's descendants to **"The 400th"**.

Mrs. Angelou and Meghan Mackle were both touched by the **Trans-Atlantic Slave Trade**, which Great Britain was a major pillow and its Crown rest atop the graves it filled with slaves. The attitude that supported that monster—

slavery—still lives in the hearts of people who see former enslaved Africans as people they once owned. The world will never change, if attitudes remain the same.

The New Normal: A Referendum on Donald Trump

The United States, for most of its existence, claimed to be a relatively egalitarian, liberal middle-class democracy, with structures in place that supported the aspirations of ordinary people. The illusion, on the part of its people, was that a basic deal existed between America's government and the people. They believed that if one worked hard, follow the rules, and educated their children, one would be rewarded, not only with a decent existence, but a safe and secure life, during retirement. Also, that the government could be trusted to guard the nation's core values and protect its citizens from enemies foreign and domestic. However, over the years southern racists and northern conservatives, basically on behalf of rich people, added a series of riders and clauses to this unwritten contract that excluded large numbers of Americans, black people in particular and other minorities—women, Hispanics, Native People, the gay community (LGBT)—leaving them without even a backdoor to enter unto this so-called democracy, where in May 2020, gun carrying protestors held state governments hostage.

However, April also saw the beginning of sheltering in place, social distancing, high unemployment, recession, the rise of armed white nationalists intimidating state governments, and police killing black people reached epidemic proportions, like Covid-19. Deaths from coronavirus overtook Vietnam War fatalities, which were unimaginable 2 months earlier, even if one awoke from a drunken or drug laced stupor. I support my forgoing statement with the fact that in January I celebrated my 77th birthday with my daughter Liqutta and four grandchildren—Tyrus, Toi, Tahlia and Tristyn. Astonishingly, today I love calling their names because I can still hear them answer. This new normal gave me a deeper appreciation for a reality, I never dreamed of losing. The realization which came with that thought is, I have completely lost the sense of safety I had just 3 months ago. That reality prompts the question, "Will I ever have it again?"

Any American who has asked themselves that or a similar question can charge it off to Donald Trump. Parsing out blame is totally unnecessary because the buck stops at the Oval Office. Watching daily White House briefings, Americans have endured a display of utter incompetence, total lack of empty, infantile arrogance, annoying intemperance, and absolute disregard for truth, as the coronavirus body count raises daily. Leadership from the current administration was the first causality of COVID-19.

This November will not only be a referendum on Donald Trump; it is a referendum on democracy and demand for truth from those who lead America. If you are happy with a liar in the White House and accept his kind of abdication of leadership, as well as feel he is doing a great job, as president, vote for him. You know exactly what you are getting. Any American that is of two minds regarding Donald J. Trump need only replay US Rep. Adam Schiff's impeachment summation. Rep. Schiff told the world that Trump is a man without a moral compass, therefore he will never find his way to truth. Mitch McConnell and Senate Republicans are even more at fault, because they had truth before their eyes and accepted lies from Trump in order to maintain their partisan advantage. They could have spared the nation much of the pain, death, and loss of Americans' sense of safety, but instead voted to support lies and American citizens are paying the cost in lives.

If this nation makes it to November with its democracy still intact, without a coup d'état, there is only one man standing between Donald Trump and 4 more years of what the American people are experiencing presently is Joe Biden. First, I will admit, Joe Biden was not my choice, even more to the point, he may not even be the best candidate possible for president, but Joe is the only American standing in the breach, at this moment, when America needs a patriot to defend it. A vote for Joe is the only thing that can save America's democracy. So, Joe Biden is not the problem, he is the solution, unless you are a Trump loyalist.

COVID-19 has eliminated all alternatives. America's young progressives are filling its street demanding an end to unjust and senseless killings of black people of all types, genders, ages and locations by police. There are no other issues that Joe Biden can put forth that can undercut Trump clearer and more decisively than his performance over the last 3 months. Consequently, if you are a Trump loyalist, I ask, are you willing to leave your grandchildren a far lesser democracy than your parents left you? If you want to leave them at least what you received, Joe is your guy!!!!

The next issue is the integrity of the American electoral process. Congress must act to ensure the safety and sanctity of the electoral process. John Bolton, although he refused to be a patriot and testify before the impeachment committee, and later is better than never, what he described in his book, Republicans knew, but refuse to accept. If the American people lose control of its democratic process, nothing will stand between Trump becoming an American Adolf Hitler or Benito Mussolini. Those are the only options beyond Joe Biden.

Let me be clear about this, if one looks at what is happening with the brazen willingness of gun carrying white nationalists in confronting legal state authority, what will stop them from surrounding the White House and defying the election results.

Trump will not "Go gently into that goodnight." He must be driven from power at the ballot box.

This nation must gear up for the first and largest vote by mail election, while it has time to make sure voters in certain states will not be intimidated at the polls by Trump's white nationalists gun carrying thugs. Democrats must gear up to produce a turnout and protection for voters willing to brave COVID-19 and white Republican poll workers. Trump's strategy is to suppress the vote so his tiny base will be large enough to steal the election, as in 2016, with Russian help. Americans must understand that this election is a referendum on whether they want to save America's democracy or accept Apartheid like South Africa. Let us put all the cards on the table and take off the gloves!!!! This is a fight to the political death of Donald Trump or America's democracy, which side are you on??

How White TV Writers Decide the Stories Hollywood Tells America about COVID-19

Major media outlets routinely present a distorted picture of black families—portraying them as dependent and dysfunctional—while white families are more likely to be depicted as sources of social stability. According to a report released by Color of Change, a racial justice organization, and Family Story in 2017, *"black families exhibit very diverse family situations."*

America's media present stereotypes that fueled political rhetoric that support and undergird public policies, which say just the opposite. Such contrary reports provided conservatives in Congress with support to "gut the social safety net, which supported the "poorest Americans." These efforts insisted on stricter work requirements, drug testing, and other restrictions on welfare recipients, which are more likely to be supported by a public inundated with inaccurate portrayals of black families. Legislators often point to media coverage of black families in their zeal to further limit welfare programs, with statements like, "It is their fault." The poor "just need to get their ducks in a row," as justification for their actions. Travis L. Dixon, a communications professor, at the University of Illinois at Urbana-Champaign, who studied this welfare problem said, *"Such baseless claims are readily accepted,"* by white law makers.

Poverty and welfare have not always been stigmatized in the media, as a predominantly black issue. The report explained, "White men who benefited from anti-poverty programs in the 1920s and 1930s were thought of typically, as having *'run into hard luck'* and just needed support to *'help them through the tough times.'"* Nicole Rodgers, the founder of Family Story, said, *"Over time, however, political leaders and the media have worked to make the problems black families face, seem pathological in American's imagination to justify and dismiss the severity of the economic problems American descendants of slavery suffered. Jim Crow, mass incarceration, widespread economic inequities, and urban disinvestment, as well as gaining and maintaining political and social power,"* whites use these themes to create the illusion of black family as dysfunction.

These researchers reviewed more than 800 local and national news stories and commentaries published or aired between January 2015 and December 2016. They randomly sample the most highly rated news programs for each of the major broadcast and cable networks, which included ABC, CBS, NBC, CNN, Fox News, and MSNBC. These researchers report also included newspapers of national influence such as The Washington Post, Wall Street Journal, New York Times, USA Today, Los Angeles Times and the Chicago Tribune, as well as regional newspapers, conservative websites like Breitbart, and Christian news sources like the Christian Post.

The study concluded that both newspapers and broadcasts are ideologically driven news sources, as well as advanced traditional false narratives about black families. They help shape public opinions and assumptions about black families that they are *"uniquely and irrevocably pathological"* and are *"an undeserving lot,"* Dixon said. The Color of Change report examined the statistics on how attitudes trump reality. According to their analysis, *"Black families represent 59 percent of the poor that are portrayed in the media but only account for 27 percent of Americans in poverty. White families makeup just 17 percent of the depiction of the poor by news media but comprise 66 percent of the American poor,"* the study showed.

"African Americans are nearly three times more likely to be depicted, as dependent on welfare, than whites," by such news stories. Also, these news reports show *"black fathers spent time with their kids half as often as white fathers."* Those offering such statistics, regarding crime, ignore the fact that *"American blacks constitute only 26 percent of those arrested on criminal charges but represent 37 percent of those portrayed as criminals in newscasts."* In contrast, news media portray *"whites as criminals only 28 percent of the time,"* whereas FBI crime reports *"show whites make up 77 percent of criminal suspects,"* the report pointed out.

There are dire consequences for black people when these outlandish archetypes rule the day. Rashad Robinson, executive director of Color of Change, added that *"abusive treatment by police, less attention from doctors, and harsher sentences from judges,"* also contribute to the dire outcomes for descendants of American slavery. And, Dixon added that such racial tropes as the *"absentee black father or family dysfunction"* were frequently invoked, during new shows featuring political commentary. Moreover, *"pundits were often allowed to spout inaccurate generalizations about black families without being challenged by hosts."*

Considering these *"outlandish archetypes, racial tropes, trumped-up pathological claims,"* as well as *"an undeserving lot"* stereotype, give such allegation dire implications for African Americans when actual and real-life situations, as the coronavirus struck America. Presently there is no better example than Chicago, Illinois (April 2020), where more than half the people who have contracted COVID-19 reside in the black community and are causing havoc for the elderly poor. On Monday (4-6-2020), according to Mayor Lori Lightfoot and health officials, currently, *"over 70% of those who have expired due to COVID-19 are African Americans. Black Chicagoans make up only 30% of the citys population but constitute 70% of the fatalities"* data shows. Information provided by the city on Sunday shows *"98 people in Chicago have died from COVID-19, and of those 98 deaths, 67 were African American."* Dr. Allison Arwady, Chicago Public Health Department Commissioner, said: *"Most strikingly Fifty-two percent of our cases or 72% of deaths have been black Chicagoans."*

"Seventy-one percent of Chicago's COVID-19 deaths were people over 60," Arwady said *"while adding that people with underlying conditions such as chronic lung disease, diabetes, and hypertension continue to be most at-risk. Statistically, men in Chicago are more affected by COVID-19 than women."* She attributed this fact primarily to their *"habits"* and

"underlying conditions. Men, as compared to women, have higher rates of deaths from chronic disease." Commenting further, *"men are less likely to seek medical help, are more likely to smoke and actually are less likely to wash their hands and use soap."* Dr. Monica Peek studies health disparities at the University of Chicago told CBS News, *"African Americans are more likely to have underlying health conditions and still be working."*

Today the system and conditions during and after slavery in America have real-life and death implications and consequences for descendants of American slavery. White people deny any responsibility and shift all blame from slavery to black people as *"their fault"* historically. Dr. Peek poignantly points out that *"When the city puts out orders for people to shelter in place ... the grocery stores are open ... public transit is still open, and people that work such jobs are primarily and disproportionately black or ethnic minorities."* Also, *"both race and socioeconomic status contribute to this trend. But since testing hasn't been comprehensive, city health officials say the real problem is likely worse."*

On Monday, Chicago mayor and eight of the city's professional sports teams—the Bears, Blackhawks, Bulls, Cubs and White Sox, along with the WNBA's Sky, MLS' Fire and National Women's Soccer League's Red Stars—announced a 'We Are Not Playing" campaign. Joining forces urging residents, remain home to stem the coronavirus outbreak, they are promoting compliance with the state's stay-at-home order.

Such programs and activities are well and very necessary. But, after this feel-good-session, my question is, *"where is this same level of agreement and concern, and the "we are all in this together"* mindset, when black Chicagoans need good jobs, food stores in their "food deserts" neighborhoods, decent housing, livable incomes, not to mention having liquor stores on every corner, as well as the dire need of health care assistance? Related to these underlying causes suffered by many black Chicagoans is their history of denial and degradation, began in slaves with their progenitors penniless emancipation in 1863.

Chicago was also a significant sight of the **"Red Summer"** white riots of 1919 that killed hundreds of black and destroyed property they owned on the Southside. Chicago was the *"Promised Land"* for black sharecroppers, escaping the South, during the "Great Migration," These events contributed to the level of poverty black Chicagoans presently endure. Pres. Donald Trump is not the only politician/businessman that sticks his head in the sand and refuses to see and accept responsibility; these underlying causes Americans created for descendants of slavery.

April 8, 2020—in states such as Michigan and Louisiana, as well as in cities like Chicago and Milwaukee—African Americans made up a disproportionately number of COVID-19 cases and deaths, officials say. In Michigan, *"African Americans account for only 14% of the population but makeup 33% of the state's confirmed COVID-19 cases and 40% of deaths,"* according to the most recent figures. *"African Americans in Louisiana are only 32% of the state population but account for over 70% of*

COVID-19 deaths." In Milwaukee County, WI, *"African Americans comprised 40 deaths of the 652 confirmed cases, compared to 362 cases and 15 deaths of whites. African American residents make up 27% of the county population (which is an undercount), while white residents account for 64%."*

Health care, which has produced the high COVID-19 mortality rates among African Americans, heads seems stuck in sand like Trump's. President Donald Trump called the impact on African Americans a "real problem" at a White House Coronavirus Task Force briefing, but beyond talks, he has done nothing. A new report from the Kaiser Family Foundation found that although some states, counties, and cities were reporting data by race and ethnicity, that information was not widely available. Also, the CDC was not reporting data by race and ethnicity to date. There is absolutely no accounting of the number of elderly black people that are dying in their homes because they could not afford to go to a doctor, so they are not reflected in any COVID-19 statistics. The report said that COVID-19 might disproportionately affect communities of color and compound underlying health and economic disparities, less health coverage and health care access, and other socioeconomic factors. But even though black American are dying at a higher rate than other groups, the CDC is not collecting data by race and ethnicity, which is crucial for planning responses to health care needs and access, as well as economic relief, the report states.

Cities should have been a category in the massive three trillion-dollar stimulus package, before Corporations and airlines. Cities and counties employ have far more people than either. Who will take the blame for that?

The New Normal and New Leadership

I said earlier that, "The election of President Barak H. Obama moved descendants of American slavery from politics in and of the street to where they are establishing political priorities, heading into the 2020 election. Therefore, I put forth the name of Mrs. Michelle Obama, a "patriot," whose "previous service to America has established she has the knowledge, experience, expertise, insight, and courage to lead this divided nation." Another advance for slavery's descendants occurred on April 9, 2020.

Sean "Diddy" Combs held a virtual town hall meeting on his REVOLT Media U-tube platform. This gathering was groundbreaking because Diddy brought together a dozen panelists to brainstorm the growing problem of poverty among descendants of American slavery, which was highlighted in the previous section. The deadly threat of the coronavirus to black people was revealed in that report. Watching the town hall meeting, I was reassured, and it is also fitting that the hip hop generation has matured and gained sufficient courage to embrace a major role of community leaders.

There are no doubts today's young hip hoppers have acquired an uncanny ability to generate enormous amounts of economic resources. Moreover, combining that with the political savvy black people have gained over the years, as reflected by the "Squad" and other developments, as an example, 2020 has become the year African Americans are beginning to claim the relevance they rightfully have earned. This is also reflected by the post on Democratic Party politics discussing the upcoming presidential campaign for 2020.

Going back to the assassination of Dr. Martin Luther King, Jr., the mantle of leadership in the black community has languished in the gutter of mediocrity, for any fly-by-night or shyster opportunists to pick up, and attempts over the years since his assassination has been detrimental to African Americans. I offered the following discussion, as a heads up to young leaders involved in Mr. Combs' new effort. I share the wisdom Dr. Martin Luther King gave Charles Cabbage and me, during his last hours at the Lorraine Motel on April 4, 1968.

I bring this tragic time into the present discussion because, during our meetings, Dr. King spoke a great deal and at length, about the disastrous impact of division that resulted, once he launched ***"The Poor People Campaign"*** in Atlanta on December 4, 1967. First, he told us *"infighting and concern for personal recognition by some within the civil rights community hampered the progress of **"The Poor People's Campaign."** Civil rights leaders across America refused to work with and accommodate black power activists."* That fight left both civil rights and black power leaderless in many ways. After Dr. King's assassination, the black community has suffered immensely, as a result.

Most people today are unaware that Dr. King spent January into early February on the road, trying to drum up support among civil rights leaders, who had been at his side in the past. According to Dr. King, *"they were not interested in fighting the federal government on behalf of the poor."* He explained that *"integration,"* meant to them, *"achieving middle-class status and make gains for middle-class Negros."* He explained further that, *"They saw themselves as 'go-betweens,' managers of segregation, spokesmen for Negros, delivering their demands to white people."* Also, as spokespersons, *"They should be first in line to receive whatever whites conceded to black people."* Describing how they turned on him, Dr. King said, civil rights leaders charged, *"I was betraying the middle class by taking the spotlight off them and putting it on the poor."*

Black power activists responded with demands for a place at the leadership table. Black power activists wanted to tear down the whole racist and discriminatory system because to us, segregation was just another name for slavery, but without chains. Our goal was to destroy it, not maintain it through accommodation waiting on the crumbs that fell from the white man table.

The coronavirus in 2020 has created a parallel between 1968 and today by pulling the covering off American racism with black people's deaths outnumbering white deaths, as **"The Poor People's Campaign"** brought the division in the black community out in the open in 1968. The sanitation strike brought this division to a head, early in February 1968. Beginning on a stormy afternoon in Memphis, a malfunctioning compactor crushed two sanitation workers, killing Echols Cole 35 and Robert Walker 29 on February 13th.

The Memphis sanitation workers went out on strike; they were among the poorest of the poor, earning only $1.75 an hour. Not only did most sanitation workers receive food stamps/welfare, but they worked under very unsafe conditions, as the death of those two workers indicated. A major concern for sanitation workers, because the City of Memphis refused to repair broken equipment and denied any responsibility for injuries and deaths really compounded the problem.

While trying to convince the Invaders to serve as marshals for his second march, following the police roit on March 28th, as well as join **"The Poor people's Campaign,"** Dr. King told us in his last meeting with Charles and me, *"The Invaders are my last chance to hold The Poor People's Campaign together. Civil rights leaders, I counted on in the past, are not raising money, providing facilities and food for marchers along the way to Washington D.C., neither are they recruiting volunteers to serve as marshals."* Dr. King sounded virtually alone in the effort to help the poor, except for Reverends Ralph Abernathy, Hosea Williams, and James Orange.

Over the last 52 years, that day created a dilemma for me, especially if it was, as some believe Dr. King had a premonition of his fate, reflected in his *"Mountain top Speech"* the previous night. I have asked myself over the years, if their speculation had real relevance, *"Why did he spend the last hours of his life, talking with the Invaders?"* However, only now, watching Mr. Combs and his colleagues grappling with the complete uncertainty brought upon African Americans by COVID-19, and the many-headed monster of poverty, the answer to that question became clear.

I now believe Dr. King did the one thing he thought would help future generations by passing on to us what he considered most important, if we were able to use it. Continuing the parallel between today and 1968, black leaders today must understand the dynamics in the battle against poverty, back then it was called *"The War on Poverty,"* but it was fought without bullets. Racism was like COVID-19, in terms of black people's understanding of poverty and the kind of offensive needed to defeat such a many headed monster.

The one thing Dr. King had come to realize those around him did no, as he was tried to point out with **"The Poor People's Campaign"** was the federal government and the Supreme Court were the culprits, as I have pointed out in this narrative with the research of Dot M. Smith—**Recession and Unemployment: A Retrospective Analysis of the Economic Welfare Loss—**, as well as Douglas A Blackmon **Slavery by Another Name: The Re-enslavement of Black Americans from the Civil War to WWII (2008),** in support of Dr. King's analysis. He said *"the federal government had written 'black people a check' that had come back stamped 'insufficient funds.'"* Descendants of American slavery gave democrats their votes but got only lip service regarding poverty, even until today. Responding to democrats, unfulfilled promises young blacks took to the streets, trying to burn poverty out of the black community, like young hip hoppers with "Black Lives Matter," using street protests.

COVID-19 has pushed the lessons from 1968 and **"The Poor People's Campaign"** to the fore, once again. The coronavirus pandemic is killing black people today, like lynching, banishment, ethnic cleansing, convict leasing, and sharecropping did from 1900 through the 1950s. Calling for a bold and daring plan to address the myriad problems that are ravishing black, red and brown communities today, Mr. Combs' coalition see the new poor filling America's ghettos. The poor today are drivers of all types, health care workers, grocery store clerks, restocking workers, butchers, city, and county maintenance workers of all kinds, but they are trapped on the bottom of today's pay scale hierarchy. Addressing the problem of black, yellow, red and brown communities; even Native people must, join Mr. Combs and not only stand with him but lift his efforts to show the world we know how to treat benefactors.

Data on the coronavirus shows black Americans are dying far in access to their percentage in the American population than white people. Experts say their high mortality rate is due to their poor health and underlying conditions that develop because of their diet and lack of access to affordable health care. These health conditions developed as a result of poverty. Consequently, poverty is the killer, and COVID-19 is merely taking advantage of America's neglect. Reducing the death rate among African Americans, during such pandemics means the federal government must address poverty among slavery's descendants as a real priority or remain vulnerable to pandemics and poverty issues.

Again, that is the rub. After having brought black people into the streets over poverty, demanding justice, and equality for descendants of American slavery, Dr. King was assassinated 52 years ago. Along the way getting to today, President Barak H. Obama inspired slavery's descendants to advance beyond politics in and of the streets. Now in 2020, African Americans realize they have not moved beyond 1968, regarding poverty among black Americans.

African Americans today, as in 1964, are faced with electing a candidate that is only making promises, as descendants of slavery's face COVID-19. Donald Trump is doing absolutely nothing to address their poverty and deaths. Joe Biden is waffling, while hoping black people will favor him with their votes. I favored Mrs. Michelle Obama, who to me had the best credentials and experience, second only to him. But, Kamala Harris is his choice and her choice has the potential to benefit slavery's descendant, if black votes are counted, which Trump is trying everything to suppress.

So, Mr. Biden has black people where we must "trust me first," but black voters are witnessing Donald Trump's incompetence and total insensitivity. I am convinced without a democrat in the White House poverty will only grow, like the deaths of black people at the hands of police. With Donald Trump, not even a *"Poor People's Campaign"* will move African Americans beyond begging for crumbs, we may as well have Trump; we know what it is like to kiss his hand to get crumbs.

Black people need someone we can trust that understands issues that affect them, from their perspective, and as they exist currently in the black community. Mr. Biden has select someone with the potential, if black, brown, red, yellow and other progressives put their power behind their votes, can chase Donald Trump from the White House and vindicate the new leadership waiting in the wings. Mr. Combs, along, with his colleagues, are looking beyond this election as *"The 400th"* committee prepares for the "new normal" where prosperity replaces poverty.

Ode to Ahmaud Arbery: A Lynching in 2020 America

Ahmaud Marquez Arbery was a very handsome, outgoing, active young African American and by all accounts he had an exciting and hopeful future awaiting. But his life was cut short by a group of white racist, father, son and a friend, vigilante team. They chased him down and shot him dead in Brunswick, Georgia (2-23-20). Many Americans and people around the world responded with horror, shock and even disbelief regarding the incident. Under Pres. Barak H. Obama's US Justice Department, AG Eric Holder would have sent agents to investigate the matter, during the first weeks of the Trump DOJ's inaction. Even Pres. George W. Bush would not have turned a blind eye to such an obvious lynching. But with Trump's demoralizing impact on the Department of Justice, black people have lost the only government watchdog for civil rights. African Americans should brace themselves for a return to the days of J. Edgar Hoover, who used of the FBI to attack black activists.

I will not try to recreate the situation or describe the circumstances surrounding Mr. Arbery murder (news videos does that), I simply want to acquaint readers with a little of Georgia's history regarding lynching. For sceptics, in terms of those who believe, first that lynching is a thing of the past, and secondly even back then it was over blown, I offer several sources to allay concerns, regarding the history of which I speak. First, Ralph Ginzburg's book **_One Hundred Years of Lynching_** presents an account of thousands of lynchings from newspaper reports of such murders in real time. Ginzburg explores the lynching phenomenon, as it stretched across the US, which such an epidemic did not occur in other civilized nations. I call this period the **_"Dark Age" angry white men mob madness_** era. Although lynching began in the 1880s and lasted until 1950, however, lynching didn't end, it simply evolved.

For those who are unable to muster the courage to read page after page describing the monstrous time when lynching was like a tailgate party, following a college or NFL football game in America, James Allen offers a pictorial exposé. Allen's book **_Without Sanctuary: Lynching Photography in America_** is an excellent source. It exhibits and gives concreteness to many lynching scenes, which took place in America. Ginzburg pictorial exposé provides scenes from lynching photographs, which were made into postcards, vendors sold to lynching participants and others in attendance as souvenirs.

These horrific images were cherished, as mementos spawned by the postcard industry, which supplied pictures of the invidious cruelty of hanging, burning, roasting and mutilating a black human being. These atrocious photographers' were also peddled to the general public long after the "picnic" was over.

Photographs of these brutal murders are physical evidence of the terrorism, brutality and viciousness that federal, state and local government inspired, sanctioned, condoned and promoted, "as the only means to protect *'white woman'* from black men." James Allen tells this shocking pictorial story in his book "***Without Sanctuary: Lynching Photography in America***" and exhibit. Allen collected over one hundred such images of original pictures that remind the world that Pres. Woodrow Wilson led and inspired, supposedly enlightened white American, in what was a crusade of gruesome blood lust rituals and murders, for almost one hundred years in America.

My last source for skeptics is Jacqueline Battalora's thesis ***Birth of a White Nation: The Invention of White People.*** Battalora also has a video lecture (on u-tube) detailing the process that created the concept of white people in America, as we know them today. She explains how the concept of whiteness and white privilege began and development. Woodrow Wilson entrenched white supremacy as a function of government, after his election in 1912. Woodrow Wilson biographers, Ray S. Baker and William E. Dodd (eds.) in ***The Public Papers of Woodrow Wilson***, described him as follows, *"Wilson never presented his racist face to the world, but Pres. Woodrow Wilson's first act, after his election in 1912, was to begin segregating the US federal government."* Wilson justified his actions this way, **"Self-preservation [forced whites] to rid themselves, by fair means or foul, of the intolerable burden of governments sustained by the votes of ignorant Negroes."**

The adage, *as the President leads, the nation follows*, truly exemplifies Woodrow Wilson's leadership of America, the same as Donald Trump today. Wilson's election marks the point at which the US government became the instrument of the darkest force of racism in America. Wilson implemented his racist views through government policies and edits. He mandated segregation throughout the federal government. Wilson pushed thousands of black workers off federal jobs, particularly those in the US postal service. Some former slaves had held their positions since the contraband period (1865 to 1880s), following the Civil War (1860-1865). Wilson spread segregation throughout the federal government, denying black Americans access to America's socioeconomic and political benefits based solely on skin color.

The topic of lynching is relevant to Ahmaud Arbery's murder because Georgia led America in overall lynchings for 31 years (1900-1931) with 302 known lynchings. During this period, "lynch mobs or lynch law" became the legal system for anyone whose death, whether black or white, served the purposes of white supremacy. According to the Tuskegee Institute, Florida led the nation in lynchings per capita from 1900-1930, when Georgia took the lead there too. Moreover, a five-year study published by the *Equal Justice Initiative (EJI)*, Montgomery, Alabama (2015) found over 4,075 black men, women, and children were lynched in the twelve southern confederate states over that period.

These hate-filled years were about demonstrating how virulent, humiliating, and painful white people could make dying for a black person. Striped of all legal protection, by the US Supreme Court with ***Plessy v. Ferguson***—separate but equal—black men's lives hung on the whim of any white man or group that was imbued with blood lust. For whatever reason or for no reason, if whites desired the life of a black man, his life was forfeited. If he fought back, he was charged with murder, by law a black man could not resist, in any way, what a white person wanted.

Now I offer a couple of examples of the lynch mob mindset that still dominates Georgia, and Ahmaud Arbery is exhibit A today. The scourge of lynching was well underway in 1899 when Sam Hose, (c. 1875/4-23-1899), an African American farm laborer, requested time off to visit his sick mother. Alfred Cranford, his white boss, pointed his gun at Hose and threatened to shoot him. Knowing Cranford was going to shoot him, Hose in fear of his life, and while chopping wood, swung the ax in his defense, killing Cranford.

After his capture, a mob took Hose out of the hands of law enforcement, the following Sunday morning (4-23-1899). Hose was brought to the Newman, Georgia town square, where over two thousand excited onlookers awaited. They had been ferried by train from Atlanta to celebrate the lynching, which had been announced in advance in Atlanta's newspapers.

Amidst celebrating, vendors sold whiskey, food and souvenirs before, during and after the lynching. Hose was marched to the Cranford home for the big attraction. There Hose was stripped bare. While still alive, mobsters cut off ears, fingers, and genitals and skinned his face, while the crowd cheered wilily. Then the mob burned him on a pyre. Souvenir hunters fought over his organs, bones and other remaining body parts.

Georgia did not reserve lynching exclusively for black men. Three events that occurred in 1915, although widely dispersed, were closely related in more than their temporal connection. Release of the film ***The Birth of a Nation*** (1914), the reorganization of the Ku Klux Klan (1915) with a new emphasis on violence against immigrants, Jews, and Catholics, and the lynching of Leo Frank (1915) in Georgia, proved to be preludes to one of the darkest times for justice in America for such groups.

During the early to mid-1900s, black writers characterized the period—***"Dark Age"*** *angry white men mob madness"*—in America, as the most violent and murderous times for slavery's descendants in American. Those events named above reflected the open disregard for legal authority, justice, and life, if one was not white. Pres. Woodrow Wilson established the consensus that America was a nation for only white people. Pushing white supremacy, as the philosophy and psychology of the federal government and America, murdering black men became entertainment for whites on all levels of society

Lynching, as I said, was a spectator sport for white people. Huge crowds with a craving for blood gathered to watch while feeding their appetite for black men's blood. This lustful craving grew wildly among whites, like the coronavirus pandemic. Thousands of white men, women, and children flocked to participate or simply witness, such grotesquely loathsome events.

Leo Frank, a factory superintendent, was convicted of murdering 13-year-old, Mary Phagan in Atlanta, Georgia (1913). Leo's trial, conviction and lynching (1915) attracted national and international attention. While in Milledgeville prison farm, the Georgia Governor pardoned Frank. A group, *"Knights of Mary Phagan"* prominent citizens of Marietta, appeared at the prison and Frank was given over to them.

The mob drove him to Marietta, where they lynched him the next morning. Many Georgians denounced Leo Frank and Jews in general for "using their money to undermine justice in Georgia." His murder was the social, political, and racial focus around the world regarding anti-Semitism. Needless to say, evidence emerged later that proved Frank' was innocent!!! (*The betrayal of the Negro: From Rutherford B. Hayes to Woodrow Wilson*. Logan, R.W. New York: Macmillan (1965).

The years from 1889 to 1923, saw 50 to100 lynchings of human beings each year. Death by lynch mobs no longer occurred in the dead of night in some dark and deathly swamp; they were no longer anomalies or unusual shocking events. Spectacle lynchings became terror parties and big business for some whites.

During lynching's heyday (1889-1918), 3,224 individuals were lynched; 2,522 or 78% were black. One account (1882-1968), showed approximately 4,742 individuals lynched; 3,445 or 73% were black. These statistics highlight the variance in lynching statistics. Typically, the victims died at the hands of white vigilantes led by civic leaders frequently in front of thousands of spectators (*Lynching in the new South: Georgia and Virginia, 1880-1930;* W. F. Brundage, 1993, University of Illinois Urbana Press).

The first American president to take a visible stand against lynching was Harry S. Truman in 1946. Shocked by a lynching in Moore's Ford (Monroe, Georgia), in which four black people—one a WWII veteran and hero, George Dorsey, his pregnant wife, May Murray, a friend Robert Malcolm and his wife, Dorothy—were brought by the sheriff to a waiting mob, where the mob shot them dozens of times and then cut the baby out of the mother.

Pres. Truman launched a campaign to guarantee civil rights for blacks, including a push for federal anti-lynching laws, but the US Congress refused to put a stop to the heinous act of lynching, the same as Republicans refused to convict Donald Trump, after his impeachment. Although unsuccessful, for the first time since Abraham Lincoln, there was a President in the White House that spoke out against the injustice and terror black Americans endured.

The 400th: From Slavery to Hip Hop

Fast forward to *"The 400th"*, recently, historic legislation (2/26/20), which will make lynching a federal hate crime, passed the House Representatives by near-unanimous consent. Only three Republicans voted against the measure: GOP members Ted Yoho of Florida, Louie Gohmert of Texas, Thomas Massie of Kentucky and the lone Independent, Justin Amash of Michigan—who switched from Republican to Independent after his support for impeaching President Donald Trump. Sixteen members did not vote.

The proposal, however, received broad bipartisan support and passed 410-4. Republicans accused Democrats of "legislative overreach" and federal government encroaching on states' rights. The legislation, if enacted, would add lynching to the list of current criminal civil rights violations. There is no word whether Mitch McConnell's Republican senate will even take up the Legislation. Lynching is another case where black people needlessly died, and Republicans do not give a damn!!!!!

A Look Back at Today's Yesterday

There is a reality in America that white people on all levels of society refuse to accept. Essentially that reality is "white people and black people can observe and experience the very same event or reality at the exact same moment under the same conditions yet come away with two totally different scenarios. My example is the socioeconomic and political events following the riots of 1966-67 and the assassination of Dr. Martin Luther King, Jr. (4-41968).

Responding to the impact of black power, whites saw something entirely different in black people's demand for equality and justice than blacks and young white progressives. Two incidents, one bloody in Mayor Richard Daily's Chicago, and the other, Tommie Smith and John Carlos' black-gloved fist salute in Mexico City. These intrepid devil-may-care African American lone riders—Tommie Smith and John Carlos—showed the kind of courage no African American athletes showed until Colin Kaepernick.

These acts were viewed in totally different ways by whites and blacks. The two groups gave totally different responses. Symbolic of the time, like hearing the scream of "fire" in a dark theater, the majority of white people saw the acts and demands for equality and justice by black people as terrifying. Whites responded with force—the National Guard and active duty military troops—as African Americans totally rejected the second-class status whites demanded, since refusing to honor the **Civil Rights Act of 1866**.

Following the rebellions of the 1966 and 67, the reality of the demands for social change and social justice, sent white people, with their tax dollars, running for the exits. They burned rubber heading to what became suburbia, abandoning inner cities. Whites left smog in their wake, but in escaping hollowed-out inner cities, they sucked up the wealth, as white politicians redirected tax revenues from inner cities to the suburbs. Called ghettos, a euphemism for slave pens, whites left dying and decaying hulks, boarded-up storefronts and empty promises behind, getting away from black people. Inner cities became *"Raisins in the Sun."*

However, today, they are back, leaving suburbia running from drive time and skyrocketing gas prices. Similar to their exit, they are supported by government and banks in this new transfer of wealth again. Government and banks are facilitating their return, with low interest loans and tax cuts. Whites are reclaiming neighborhoods black people stayed behind and saved.

With low-interest rates, government is helping whites take back neighborhoods they abandoned in the 1970s and 80s. After eviscerating *"The Fair Housing Act of 1968,"* governments and banks have a new term, for whites' displacement of blacks in neighborhoods they abandoned is "gentrification." *"The Fair House Act of 1968 protected black people from discrimination when renting or buying a home, getting a mortgage, seeking housing assistance, or engaging in other housing-related activities. Additional protections applied to federally-assisted housing."* Government calls whites evacuating cities *"white flight,"* but now instead, the reclaiming process is another euphemism called *"gentrification."* This process is the "new" racism for the same old reason. Black people see this process as an attempt to lure black people to the Suburbs with low home prices, but will face drive time woes and high gas prices, whites are trying to escape. For Trump this is like another tax cut for whites. Whites are losing the big price tag of living in the burbs, ducking drive time and high gas prices. But their children want to get closer to entertainment, while escaping driving problems, after drinking and partying, as well as sports events. However, some African American voters questioning what will Mr. Biden do?

Black people are facing the same "old red neck, red lining mentality" Woodrow Wilson's use following his **Birth of a Nation** pogrom to entrenched racism, segregation, and white privilege in the 1920s. Today in Trump's America an instant replay is on full view with "Black Lives Matter" protest dominating the news. And as such, America's governments pretend it is doing black people a favor saving inner-city. They claim *"gentrification"* the return of whites to innercities is bringing money back to urban areas." But, in reality, whites are sucking up the tax dollars black people paid these same cities to keep them solvent and livable, after *"white flight."*

And, as during *"white flight,"* blacks could not get any money for anything. Government, black or white, claims the tax money black people paid before, during, and after whites abandoned inner-cities, is now being given returning whites for *"revitalization,"* however these same city governments refused to spend money to revitalize or improve anything in cities, once white ran to the "burbs."

White people always have a term for what they do, when they screw black people around. This is part of the ongoing denial of black people's rights, because government spends so much on policing to keeping black people on lockdown in ghettos and prisons across America. There are no redevelopment for the black community, only retail establishments and houses, and even with that banks only provide money to whites. When blacks remained in inner cities, they were the only tax base cities had. Now bringing back the same white people that ran to suburbs, they are now touting them as saviors of urban life. Again, black people are in the back of the bus, even though black Mayors are in the drivers' seat, like here in Atlanta and DeKalb County.

The Old Normal: Powerful Hand of Government

There was a high level of disbelief regarding the preceding topic, "A Look Back at Today's Yesterday!" So, to show I was not fudging or creating fake statistics to make my point about *"gentrification,"* I provide readers another view with those responses in mind. I offer a lengthy explanation of the wealth gap and other disparities African Americans face, trying to escape poverty in America.

Declining homeownership reflects dire consequences for African Americans as retirement looms. Today *"Black people are moving into homeownership at a much 'slower rate' than at any time in the past,"* says Laurie Goodman, co-director of the Urban Institute's Housing Finance Policy Center and the co-author of its May 2017 report, *"Are Gains in Black Home Ownership History?"* Homeownership among African Americans has declined to levels not seen since before the passage of the *Fair Housing Act of 1968*. The long-term impact is an ever-present concern of black economists, who paints a very grim picture this looming crisis foretells.

Researchers see disaster for the retirement hopes of African Americans in terms of homeownership. Looking back to the passage of the *Fair Housing Act*, discrimination has erased black homeownership gains. According to the Urban Institute's report, the black homeownership rate in America rose by nearly six percentage points but the black homeownership rate dropped to roughly 41% from 2000 to 2015 erasing gains. By contrast, the homeownership rate among white Americans was virtually unchanged at 71%, a 30% bulge.

"Gains in black homeownership were hard-won, which amplifies the concern that over the last 15 years, black homeownership rates declined to levels not seen since the 1960s, when 'private race-based discrimination' was made illegal," the report states. The black community got hit hardest by the housing crisis—2008—compared to other groups. In general, *"African Americans bought homes at the 'peak of the housing bubble,' paying higher rates than whites. They were offered costly subprime loans, even though they qualified for lower prime loans interest rates,"* also black families did not benefit as much as white families, overall, from the post 9/11 recovery.

This huge homeownership declines for black households was for all age groups, especially young adults. The homeownership rate for blacks 35 to 44 year-olds fell from 45% in 1990 to 33% by 2015, half the level for whites of the same age. Moreover, it dropped lower than the black homeownership rate in 1960. Homeownership also fell from 1990 to 2015 for whites, Hispanics, and others in that same age group, but not by nearly as much as the hourly pay gap, which has widened to its worst disparity in the last 40 years, according to the *Economic Policy Institute (EPI)*. This gap amounted to roughly a 27% difference in 2015. Whites earned an average $25.22 an hour vs. $18.49 for blacks. Looking at the wage gap, it doesn't seem freighting, but let us go inside the disparity. First

$25.22 amounts to $6.73 more than $18.49 and after an 8 hour day that's only $53.84. Over a 5 day week the bump is $269.2, times 52 weeks it is 13,998.4. This picture turns into a horror story, after 30 years of regular work exploding to $419,952. Here is where the heavy hand of government takes its greatest toll. For a two wage earner family $839,904 is lost to black families. Failure to raise the minimum wage and failure to enforce anti-discrimination laws the government has contributed enormously to the growing black-white wage gap, according to the EPI.

Maya Rockeymoore of the Center for Global Policy Solutions, a Washington, DC-based nonprofit. She is former adjunct professor in the Women in Politics Institute at American University. Maya has also served as the vice president of research and programs at the Congressional Black Caucus Foundation (CBCF), senior resident scholar at the National Urban League, chief of staff to Congressman Charles Rangel (D-NY), professional staff on the House Ways and Means Committee, and as a CBCF legislative fellow in the office of Congressman Melvin Watt (D-NC) said,

"Blacks are earning less than whites, and it is not a reflection of talents or skills. It is a reflection of discrimination in the labor market. We talk about the gender-pay gap, but we need to talk about the "racial-pay gap." We need to be having forums addressing labor-market discrimination and decisions." Next, **the wealth gap is growing**. On average white families wealth in 2013 was more than $500,000 higher than African American families ($95,000).

In 1963, the year of the **March on Washington** (1-28-1963), the average wealth of white families was $117,000 higher than that for black families. This difference is compounded by the fact that white families accumulate more wealth over their lives than African American families, on average, which means the wealth gap is also a factor of age, in that it widens with age. Whites have an average of $140,000 more in wealth in their 30s than African Americans (three times as much). Obscenely, whites have over $1 million more in wealth than African Americans (11 times as much) by their 60s. The wealth gap is also a reflection of the years of banishment and ethnic cleansing, from 1900 through the 1940s. During that period, white took wealth from blacks to get what they have, while pushing black people back deeper into poverty.

Furthermore, the Federal Reserve reported that *"whites are five times more likely to receive large gifts and inheritances than blacks, and the amounts receive by whites tend to be much larger."* Nick Abrams of AJW Financial Partners in Columbia, Md., a financial planner, says, *"That is one of the main issues. We [African Americans] are starting at ground zero every generation."* Rockeymoore agrees as she points to disparities between blacks and whites regarding employer-sponsored retirement plans. *"The wealth gap is serious. A significant number of us [blacks] are in jobs where we do not have access to pre-tax preferred retirement vehicles like 401(k) or 403(b) accounts."* Many blacks work in small businesses where such plans frequently are not available. If we do work in jobs *that offer tax-preferred vehicles, we tend not to contribute at rates similar to whites (This also reflects the pay gap). And loans we take out are offered at the highest rate."*

The use of credit scores and arrest records are used to deny or push blacks into the highest interest rates, which is totally discriminatory. Blacks pay more for everything, which is like a "ghetto tax." The thing white will not admit is the use of interest rates and credit, in general, discriminates against blacks. Credit scores are manipulated specifically to push blacks toward "pay day loans, where they pay obscene interest rates. Considered in tandem, these are why whites and blacks pay different rates for everything. Banks, lenders, credit card issuers, and other financial instruments use the prime verse subprime game to the disadvantage of black people, who pay more.

That point brings us back to Homeownership. It plays a big role in the wealth gap. The typical white household aged 47 to 64 has housing wealth of $67,000; the typical household of color in this age group has zero home equity, according to the December 2016 report by the National Academy of Social Insurance which says "Social Security is also part of the racial gap in retirement wealth."

New Normal XVIII: Echoing Economic Disgrace

Dorothy May Smith (1950-2013), the author of the groundbreaking thesis ***Recession and Unemployment: A Retrospective Analysis of the Economic Welfare Loss*** was published on August 2, 1982 it challenged the prevailing view of, why descendants of American slavery remain trapped in poverty 400 years, after the first enslaved Africans began arriving in North America and 157 after their emancipation from slavery in the United States of America. White economists railed against her revolutionary statement, as revisionist history. Challenging the prevailing view of why poverty has entrapped slavery's descendants Dot's sought to giving substance to Dr. Martin Luther King, Jr.'s speculation that "The federal government is the culprit and root cause of poverty among Negros. The federal government has written Negros a check that has come back stamped 'insufficient funds.'" However, economists and political leaders ignored Dot Smith's findings, once she published her ground breaking results. No one wanted to examine her theory that *poverty among descendants of American slavery is a function of how government—federal, state and local—structured the American economy.* Everyone resisted reexamining the status quo assumptions about poverty among descendants of American slavery.

Dot Smith began at the point where large scale poverty among descendants of American slavery began 413 years ago with the creation of the **Trans-Atlantic Slave Trade.** Following it demise, enslaved Africans remained trapped in America's internal slave trade and breeding system another 58 years throughout the "antebellum period" until the end of Civil War (1865). Contrarily, during this entire period, white people were free and were paid for working, as well as built their wealth on the backs of enslaved Africans. Smith compared the socioeconomic welfare loss between enslaved Africans and white people, as she rendered poverty accessible to statistical analysis for the first time, based on specific variables, using a mathematical function she developed called the *"chasm of inequality analysis."*

Dot's "chasm of inequality analysis" revealed that US Government policies and procedures exert a negative impact on blacks relative to whites. Smith's research proved that federal, state and local governments orchestrate external forces and manipulate outcomes for black Americans relative to whites, through programs, like unemployment, level of income, homeownership, interest rates, credit, insurance, convict leasing, sharecropping etc....which determines black people's level of general welfare compared to whites. Victims of discrimination and disparate treatment in the hostile environment whites created (policing in the black community), blocking process and locking black Americans on the bottom of its "capitalistic cheap labor system," as wage slaves. The most important point here is the US Government maintains poverty, as an economic outcome for slave descendants by manipulating those external variables mentioned above. How does that work?

Data from the US Labor Department, which is where Smith obtained her information, allowed her to zeros in on the gap between blacks and whites unemployment and median family income. These two variables—unemployment and median family income—are the most reliable indicators of economic welfare gains and losses in the American system. The economic welfare loss for descendants of American slavery began during bondage and continued after **emancipation, Civil War, 13th, 14th, and 15th Amendments, the Civil Rights Act of 1866, Brown v. Board of Education (1954), 1964 Civil Rights Bill** and **1965 Voting Rights Acts,** hence the socioeconomic and political conditions black people face today, attest to the fact nothing has change for African Americans relative to the socioeconomics and wealth white Americans have accumulated since slavery.

I now bring all of this together with an article from someone who spent most of her career in government with one of its most important agencies—the Federal Reserve. Claudia Sahm held a very impactful position, as former principal economist, at the Federal Reserve Board of Governors, and from her personal blog Macromom, in an article by Megan Cerullo *"Former Fed Economist Calls Profession A Disgrace"* for Bloomberg, Sahm criticized the economics profession at large, while naming prominent economists that have sullied the field. Claudia Sahm attacked the Fed and economists for their help maintaining discrimination and racism in America. A former senior economist at the Federal Reserve, Sahm mounted a scathing attack on her blog *"The economics profession suffers from systemic issues of racism, sexism and elitism that stymie young professionals' careers and compromise the quality of our economic policy. The lack of diversity and inclusion degrades our knowledge and policy advice, leading to incidences of harassment against me and other female colleagues while working in the male-dominated field of economics is a disgrace."*

Sahm says *"A male 'tormentor' that routinely sabotaged my work, was part of the culture that routinely went out of the way to degrade women. A female colleague, then new to the Fed, was asked by male colleagues during lunch, if she 'satisfied' her husband. Also, Nonwhite men are also subject to rampant harassment. We drive away talent; we mistreat those who stay; and we tolerate bad behavior."* Sahm said underscoring her frustration, *"My experience is not unique at the Federal Reserve, all the women I know at the Board have had their expertise and accomplishments devalued. So, I am not special."*

Responding to questions, regarding Sahm's, Fed Chairman Jerome Powell, at a press conference, while denying he read Sahm post said Wednesday, *"There's been a lot of pain and injustice and unfair treatment women have experienced in the workplace, not just among economists but among economists at the Fed,"* which to me means he knew and tolerated such behaviors, if he was not a party to it. *"That's been going on for far too long,"* which to me is an admission he knew about the treatment Sahm and her colleagues have endured. *"And, you know,"* he continued, like a baseline, *"like every other organization, the Fed could have done more and should have done more."*

But he leaves out "I" while admitting discrimination and disparate treatment occurred and is rampant at the Fed.

Now come the usual self-servicing platitudes, CEOs like Powell offer to cover over, if not excuse racism and sexism, while claiming to have ended the matter in their male dominated enterprise, which continues to dominate, because Powell supported sexism, owing to the fact, we know he can see, if he cannot hear. But, the Fed will make the same speech when another woman steps forward. Powell excused the Board's pass negligence, as he turned blind eyes toward racism, discrimination, disparate treatment and sexism. He sounded like Donald Trump about coronavirus accepting "no responsibility." He claims the Fed is, *"doing a 'lot' to foster a respectful climate, particularly for women, but for all people, so it's a 'very high' priority for us, as an organization."* "Bull!!!"

How many times has the public heard this same speech, and saw crocodile tears offered to symbolize remorse, only to have a similar charge levied before the smoke clears? Exercises, like Powell's, are what keep systemic racism intact. But then the Fed Chair, again like Donald Trump, when the issues of systemic racism are raised, offered on specifics policies he had introduced at the Fed to address the facts in Sahm's complaint. No different from "_every other organization, the Fed could have done more and should have done more,_" is the trapdoor through which Powell and CEOs like him use to escape responsibility again, like Donald Trump.

Sahm not only pointed an accusatory finger at the Fed, but "German economist Harald Uhlig, as a major culprit that continues to exacerbate the "race problems" in economics, and there are many. Uhlig is the lead editor at the Journal of Political Economy from the University of Chicago Press and recently Uhlig drew fire for criticizing the "Black Lives Matter" movement. Sahm also levied an attack on economist William Dudley, the former president of the Federal Reserve Bank of New York, who tried to devalue her expertise by claiming she did not deserve credit for her eponymous *"Sahm Rule,"* which signals the start of a recession by measuring changes in the unemployment rate which Dot Smith's thesis addresses.

But, now Dudley said he believes Sahm deserves full credit for the *"Sahm Rule,"* which he called *"insightful and noteworthy,"* while simultaneously, pointing out that *"economists at Goldman Sachs had identified another empirical regularity that plays an important role that is part of the Sahm Rule earlier."* Not impartial, Dudley glossed over his true attitude because, you see, he was one of those Goldman Sachs economists. The controversy is reminiscent of Dot M. Smith's *"Chasm of inequality analysis."*

Sahm concluded her blog by announcing her resignation from the field of economics. *"Until we make progress, I will no longer identify as a member of the American*

Economic Association or the economics profession." Sahm is currently the director of macroeconomic policy at the Washington Center for Equitable Growth, a non-profit organization that promotes economic growth and stability.

Arriving at this point, I can admit Sahm's treatment is why I began this discussion as I did, introducing my wife Dot. Once she published her groundbreaking research, as a graduate student at the University of Memphis, she became persona non grata. Just six months away from receiving her PhD, the male dominated economics department, rose up and began launching challenges. They harassed and attempted to bullied her , as she prepared to release her finding, like Sahm, she walked away from a profession that refused to shed its racism and sexism, which continues to stick its head in the sand or some other dark place.

However, the economic data and conclusions related to black Americans socioeconomic welfare loss, today is based on her groundbreaking research, even though she does not receive credit for her "chasm of inequality analysis." But, I celebrate her for being one of the many black power activists that study the problem and developed solutions that explain poverty among descendants of American slavery. But, however, now as in 1982, white economists still pretend not to hear, also civil rights and so-called black leaders continue accepting white folk answers to black people's problems. Instead of throwing their racist claptrap and tropes back in their faces. A very recent example is Bill Clinton's ill-tempered remark about Kwame Ture, at John Lewis' Memorial!!!! Who asked him to critique black power anyway??

New Normal IV: Your Vote is Your Voice

On the Evening of April 4, 1968, Charles Cabbage and I sat with Dr. Martin Luther King, Jr. in his Lorraine Motel room. We were there because he invited us, and we were hoping during his remark could be trusted, while recruiting our black power group—the *Invaders*—to support his **"Poor People's Campaign."** He turned to the *Invaders*, during his last desperate hour, he said, *"I am trying to hold the* **"Poor People's Campaign"** *effort together. I am facing opposition and division within the ranks of the civil rights movement."*

Most old-line civil rights leaders were fighting to keep young black activists from becoming part of black leadership. I believe now, their opposition was from division caused by those against including social change and social justice activists at the center of black people's organizing efforts. Black power activists were pushing to open up American society, while J. Edgar Hoover was determined to stop Dr. King's **"Poor Peoples' Campaign."** Hoover believed that, *if they cut off the head of that movement, the body would die.* And, unfortunately, his assessment did not proved accurate: the Invaders are still here fighting.

Today, America is back there again, where protest is the only way dissident voices are heard. Dr. King's major point to us in his last hours was about the importance of Voice, he said, *"I believe the police riot against sanitation marchers and supporters here in Memphis, was a denial of Negro's right of VOICE. That march was a reflection of their right to express their attitudes about their condition as a people. Negros ability to tell their story, in their own words, and in their own way, as they live it, is a human right all people have and is a basic right of life. If Negros cannot tell the story of what is happening to, them to the world, they are denied the most basic right of human beings."*

Less than an hour after those words, Dr. King was dead from an assassin's bullet. I believe Dr. King spent his last minutes of life, talking to protesters, which we were, because he wanted to leave a message to future generations that the right of protest, as he said at Mason Temple, *"the greatness of America is the right to protest for rights."* I speak to young progressives, as Dr. King spoke to us. You have shown your commitment and determination to get justice in the lynching of George Floyd, Ahmaud Arbery, Breonna Taylor and countless others. You have raised your voices, but to give your efforts real impact, you must consolidate your gains. Young progressive have gained the attention of the world, so what I hope you are learning is that *"politic is the art of the possible."* If you are among those leading this effort, and there are many, you must turn your *"street protest into street politics"* action. Political action becomes power, only at "the ballot box."

I repeat *"politics is the art of the possible"* because your vote will make those in power respond, and with enough vote whatever your demands, they become possible. Based on how many votes you can put into ballot boxes across

America, it is possible for you to become leaders in American politics. If young progressive leaders can put as many votes in ballots boxes, as you put into the streets across America, you will drive Donald Trump from the White House. Your votes can give you the kind of revenge against him he cannot resist. His plan is to make the election a close vote, so he can clench to power, while claiming the election was rigged. If you turn the acrimony you are facing into votes, you deny him that opportunity. That does not mean he will not try every trick to hang on to the White House, but the system will be on your side. And again, why *"politics is the art of the possible,"* you represent that possibility.

What do you want? What is at stake? I believe America wants the same thing you want. Looking at the electorate, older white people are evenly split between Donald Trump and Vice President Joe Biden. For the first time ever, young progressives are the balance of power in the coming election. The question is, *"have young progressives matured sufficiently to step up to the plate and drive Trumps' spitball out of politics and save America from a fate, no patriot imagined back in January?"* Voting in numbers your potential reflects is possible. If you are among leaders of young progressives, you must convince your comrades to build networks and use those networks to help register your comrades and get them to the polls to vote. Pulling that off you will have your revenge, by showing Trump that voters run America not a clown in the White House or his thugs in the street. Trump's Republicans enablers in the Senate and House are all committed to circling their wagons around Trump, as they did during impeachment. Senate Republicans could have saved America much pain and deaths from COVID-19, but they accepted lies rather than the truth before their eyes. That was treason and they do not deserve to spend another second enjoying the blessing of liberty in America, since they stood up for partisan politics, rather than the Constitution.

America needs you. If you want a *"Green New Deal"* put it in the ballot box. You want changes in policing and a fair justice system put your demand in the ballot box. Your votes, as no other group, can rescue America from the grasp of tyranny and dictatorship. Progressives have at their fingertips, what they have been fighting for and dreaming of, since the 1940s. Now is the time to show your maturity more than anything by voting. If you bring your voting power to the ballot box, you will show you can be trusted to stand up for America in times of her greatest need, as Trump has shown he will not. Raise Your Voices and Vote!!!!!!

New Normal V: Ballot or the Bullet

On April 3, 1964 Malcolm X opined *"The Ballot or the Bullet."* He posed this dichotomy to juxtapose the position and condition American descendants of slavery had as choices facing and contending with, after almost 400 hundred years of bondage and wage slavery in America. Malcolm, like Dr. Martin Luther King, Jr., could not see **"Black Lives Matter"**, waiting in the wings, just over fifty years later. They could not see, waiting around the corner of history, not thousands, but millions of young black, white, brown, red and yellow progressives from all across America and around the world, standing in solidarity behind one idea **"Black Lives Matter!!!!!"**

Although, their—Malcolm and Dr. King—times were dark and unyielding, as racism dominated black people, their stalwart leadership provided continuity, trying to make blackness no longer the divide, but a point of unity. Following Malcolm, even after his death, I found Dr. King and my social change and social justice activities, as a community organizer, took on a new perspective. Working with the Memphis sanitation worker strike, I thought we did what seemed impossible, when we put over 50,000 marchers on Beale Street for Dr. King's last march in Memphis.

However, I take my hat off, as well as salute all the young leaders who pulled together and produce this international outpouring of love and support for the struggle of downtrodden people everywhere. Connecting the world, you have out done us all. Prior to you, Marcus Garvey was the only black man able to pull off such an international feat. Watching nights and daily, the unfolding of history in real time, I became an eyewitness to a never before historical happening, as you move black Americans beyond our "word of mouth legacy."

So, with all that amazing history transpiring, I was truly taken aback by the president of the United States' remarks two mornings ago, during his news conference. I never thought my comments in my last post, urging young people to participate in the electoral process, as voters, would draw ridicule. Most definitely, I never thought a US president would belittle my efforts to encourage young potential voters to register and use their votes to help clean up the environment, by supporting a "green new deal."

The simple fact that his policies have dump more toxic substances into the environment and the atmosphere, is no reason for him to make jokes, because his policies are causing African Americans to breathe foul air. COVID-19 has made it abundantly clear, black people already cannot breathe. Turning such a serious issue into a foil—getting young people to vote to clean up the environment, Trump made himself a laughing stock, poking fun at the need for clean air. In times past, no President would reach out of the White House with such a heavy ham-handed scoff, rather than encouraging young people, as I was, to vote.

Obviously, the president's disdain for the environment, maybe a laughing matter to him, but with his deprecating remarks, he seems to discount, how dirty air make it very difficult for people with "underlying conditions," and racism is one, which black people are at greater risk. His foul environmental policies and callous attitude toward "a green new deal" make young people victims of his dirty environment. It seems, while black people are suffering and cannot breathe, like his knee on their necks, the president is chuckling it up in the safety of the White House, bunker and all, while those recovering from coronavirus struggle with damaged lungs.

I never imagined such sarcasm, flowing from the White House, like some polluted waterway, from which, some American communities draw water. On top of his total disregard for the health of vulnerable citizens, I suffered through a litany of pompous and bellicose "fake" claims of how great his administration has handled the coronavirus and the economy. The president's diatribe certainly did not encouraged young potential voters whose support reduces global warning, as part of America's future political initiatives, will not take heart and see registering to vote and voting, will improve their chances of enjoying a better and healthier life.

New Normal VI: Young Progressives the Face of America's Future

Beginning in March 2020, there was little doubt former Vice President Joe Biden would out poll Sen. Bernie Sanders for the Democratic nomination for president. A progressive, I believe "politics is the art of the possible." So, I saw supporting Joe Biden, as the next best options, because Donald Trump has shown himself to be an enemy of African American on all levels. I directed an open letter to Mr. Biden, because I have no direct communication with him, and as of today, I still do not. My aim was to present what I thought progressive voters are willing to accept, if Mr. Biden was interested in gaining their support. I repeat again, I believe "politics is the art of the possible," an at that point, sealing the possible breach between Bernie's supporters and the candidacy of Mr. Biden would be the best move, following their bitter primary.

Frist, I wanted to put the importance of African American voting power into proper perspective and state with crystalline clarity that for the first time, descendants of American slavery's votes will determine who will occupy the White House. And, as history, the times and events would have it, African Americans occupy a controlling position in determining the destiny of America because of their potential voting power, as the *"The 400th"* Generation. I remind again, for the first time, based on the strength of African American voting power, and the fact that white voters are evenly split, young progressives, also make up a large part of the black vote, which Mr. Biden does not see as distinct. This is very important because the Biden camp seem to discount the importance of their voting power.

Young people, in past elections, have not been very active except for Pres. Barak H. Obama, as older black voters. However, their fight in the streets of America demanding just for George Floyd is showing their developing political power. The fact that they, not the older generation, took to the streets to make their demands known, supports their lack of trust in American politicians will speak to their needs

My second reason, for addressing the open letter to Mr. Biden, was the leadership young progressives have showed, mounting the current protest, without any "adult supervision." No one can deny the power of young progressives, they brought, not only millions of people of all colors into the streets of America, but around the world in support of one idea *"Black Lives Matter."* Such an occurrence has not been witnessed by any generation in American or world history. The problem they are attacking existed when Mr. Biden and his generation were part of the problem.

I make this statement because I was out in the streets, leading the Invaders in support of Dr. Martin Luther King, Jr.'s *"Poor People's Campaign."* Many of the older civil rights leaders and politicians of that day condemned black power activists, as they did ten years ago condemning ***"Black Lives Matter."*** They also refused to support the ***"Poor People's Campaign."*** They discount young people's political motives and power. Similarly today, even though young progressives are presently changing America, in ways the older generation has never been able to do, they still refuse to see and admit that these leadership are working to correct what politicians, like Joe Biden help create.

My reason for making such statements is my third point. The behavior of the older generation is very predictable, and it reminds me of their behavior during the 1960s. They rushed in when TV cameras showed up and news shows want spokespersons. Now, that young people organized the mass protest with only young people and brought millions into the streets, the older generation has shown up again to take over the spotlight.

The older generation was not first in line to march, but they ran over young progressives getting to the mic. Taking over, making speeches, even kneeling with them before the camera, the older generation loves the spotlight not the "black out." Rather than showing deference to these young leaders and their work, the old "civil right leaders are up to their old tricks gain." Just ten years ago, every civil rights leader attacked ***"Black Lives Matter***," including Mr. Biden. They disparaged their organization and the need for them, as an organizing effort.

My point here becomes a question, "How can young progressives trust the older generation to fight for their issue, when they do not respect them as leaders? Once in power, they will return to the old-normal they created, and black men will continue dying in the streets, once ***"Black Lives Matter"*** is drowned out by all "the Johnny come late-lies."

That is what "older civil rights leaders" did in 1968, which helped J. Edgar Hoover use Co-Intel-Pro to jail and kill black power activists. That was how the federal government killed the black power movement. I make this statement because I was one that police railroaded into jail for five years. Presently, police are identifying all young black actives and when the smoke settles and the TV cameras go away, young black leaders will become targets of law enforcement. Moreover, those old grandfathers will go back to during what they were doing before the cameras showed up.

My last point was in a post, dated 3-24-2020, and presented what I believed young progresses would accept, as a "good faith" effort on the part of Mr. Biden entitled, *"How Important are African Americans Votes??????"* I believe older black voters will accept Mr. Biden as is, but they will only get him half-way and any fall off in elderly black voters—coronavirus or voter suppression—will result in a close outcome. Such a prospect is frightening to me, because everyone know Trump will "not go quietly into that good night!!!"

I offered what I believe will close the door on any such proposition, if Mr. Biden has the courage to do what America needs most, at this juncture. If he is the leader for these times, he will ask, implore even, Mrs. Michelle Obama to become his running mate. Young progressives have trust for both the former First Lady and the President, which Mr. Biden does not command. I support her not wanting to get into a lottery with other women with less potential for healing this nation's division. Progressives see potential as the problem, and demand someone in which we have complete trust.

Mrs. Obama eliminates any concern for a learning curve; "she's "been there done that." There is nothing in her closet, if there were the Republicans would have found it. Anyone under consideration for the VP slot will have to be guessed about and are a potential booby trap. Stated bluntly, there is no other woman in America, white or black that can come up to Mrs. Obama's waist, when measuring prospects that can step into the job of president from day one, which is what the *Founding Fathers* had in mind, when they created the position of Vice President, and not simply a means of entice votes.

America is at a crossroads and it needs its best and brightest patriots up on the line, for if that line falters, its democratic experience may very well be over. This is the time when patriots put everything, personal and professional, aside. We are trying to save our nation, so in the future young people can rise up, as our children and grandchildren are today, and save America's future, if the need ever arises again. I raised the issue of courage earlier, because the real truth comes out when a white man has to go, "hat in hand," and ask a truly qualified black woman to help save him and our country. But, that is what separates true leaders from the Donald Trumps of the world. As I said opening, I believe "politics is the art of the possible" and this is possible, if Mr. Biden is the man for the job?

New Normal VII: The Price of Peace

My post on April 3, 2020 referenced a 1964 speech *"The Ballot or the Bullet"* by Malcolm X. His opine posed a dichotomy that juxtaposed a reality America is approaching again today, which it faced in real time in 1964. Once his statement reached out of the ghetto to touch white American's ears, my brother Malcolm X became a target. America's white leaders reacted predictably, anytime a black person stepped outside of the image they created for black people. His deadly sin was explaining black people's circumstances, similar to David Walker with his ***Appeal, in Four Articles; Together with a Preamble, to the Coloured Citizens of the World, but in Particular, and Very Expressly, to Those of the United States of America*** in 1828. They understood Malcolm's explanation as to why they were trapped in poverty. His speeches detailed how their slave ancestor's penniless emancipation made them the base of America's *"cheap labor"* socioeconomic capitalistic system.

Today that system has not changed and is why black, brown, red, yellow and white young progressives, by the thousands, are filling the streets of America and kneeling in remembrance of George Floyd. The other side of Malcolm's dichotomous proposition is what really sent white people off the cliff in 1964. Malcolm raised the prospect of revolution.

Malcolm X offered the bullet, if the ballot did not produce real change. White America saw black people as J. Edgar Hoover and supported his CO-Intel-Pro solution, as the best way to keep black people lock on the bottom of America's *"cheap labor"* capitalistic economic system. They did not see military troops in the streets against America's children, as a total rejection of *VOICE*. Assassination was seen as a viable option for maintaining white privilege and stop social change and social justice form creating and negotiating real changes in public policy. Sadly to them, however, that would make Malcolm a prophet.

Although, many Americans were around the last time young progressive were pushed to the wall by federal, state and local law enforcement's drive to prevent change, so most Americans probably have no memory of the huge rip in the American fabric the rise of the "counterculture and black power" caused. For those who were in the streets then, the scares and stiches are clearly reflective of today for those who know what they are seeing. Again, for most, progressive wave began with the "hippies/flower children." Peace loving at their beginnings, next the *"antiwar movement"* rose up, which combined with the *"free speech movement"* on college campuses. Demonstrations rocked college campuses, presidents' offices were takeover, and students fought to keep military recruiters off campuses with class boycotts. Then, out of the smoke of protest emerged the *"Weather Underground",* which brought a revolutionary edge to campus protests in support of young progressives' demands. Bombings completely radicalized

The 400th: From Slavery to Hip Hop

America's educational system, as teachers were pulled, first one way then the other by campus radicals. The radical left grew until it began attacking international targets, like the WTO in Seattle, Washington in 1999.

This time around, the lynching, on video of one black man—George Floyd—in broad daylight, made the world witnesses and relive those 8 minutes and 46 seconds. Inundating Americans with their history while on lockdown, many white people were reminded of the time when they acted a total racist, and their act could have started all of this. George Floyd's lynching repeated itself moment by moment, reoccurring hourly throughout the day and night in the lives of black people, and kept repeating itself, but no one cared because it was not them. However, like Malcolm X's ghostly haunting even though it was not in American history books, nevertheless it brought everyone to the same place at the same time in America's slave history once again. Americans must ask itself, how many time does it have to be dragged here, before Malcolm's alternative hypothesis becomes the reality staring them in the face.

Such an outcome is not anything America wants to see again, because with it behavior in the face of coronavirus and facing protest, it resembles "a deer in the headlight." Young progressives in the streets protesting today are not us. Today's young people are far smarter, more energetic, dedicated and super tech savvy, which means they can be far more dangerous. Having been part of many protests, I will say their stamina is amazing. They walk and stand until late at night, but are up early the next morning ready to go, without pay, unlike police. Military people will tell you what that mean in a scenario, like that Malcolm X posited.

America needs only to put racism, oppression, voter suppression, and its *"cheap labor"* socioeconomic capitalistic system behind it or prepare to militarize society, as it did against it children, during the 1960s. Is that a price mothers and fathers want to pay with the future of their children for peace? For instance, conceding to young progressives' demand for a *"Green New Deal"* has been rejected out of hand. However, young progressives have laid it on the table, as their proposition going forward. Their proposition today is reminiscent of the scatting rebuke James Baldwin laid on the table in *"Fire Next Time"* in 1963. I believe that politics is the art of the possible, so a more productive approach is to accept young progressives initiatives like a "Green New Deal" Medicare for All and increasing the minimum wage to $15 an hour immediately and an increase to $20 over five years as *"good faith"* effort and a starting points with the goal of increased specificity each year to get there.

Expose: Law Enforcement, LA County Terroism?

"Black Lives Matter" protests have made the "Fugitive Slave Act of 1850" a today concern for African Americans. Law enforcement is a deadly plague for America's slavery's descendants and other brown, red and yellow people. The demand to defund police is to addresses brutality and murder by law enforcement. Whether it is termed defunding or reforming policing must change.

Recent reports discussing law enforcement across America are very disturbing, because they identify police criminal enterprises and good old boy networks that are hidden within policing operations and media fails to expose sham investigations disguising police gangs from the public. A series of eye opening exposés on Los Angeles County, California, reflect the depth of the problem. Deputy Austreberto Gonzalez, a decorated Marine veteran, with the Compton Sheriff Department (2007), filed a whistleblower complaint charging, "A gang of deputies, 'Executioners,' terrorized me and other deputies. Deputies opposed to this gang of 'Executioner' deputies' demands are harassed, beaten, intimidated and denied promotions."

Deputy Gonzalez was targeted, after reporting a fellow deputy, Thomas Banuelos, was beaten by an "Executioner," outside the patrol station. Now he says, "I'm afraid for my safety and the safety of my family." His attorney, Alan Romero, told EyewitnessNews, "He should be. These are very violent people, in a very violent gang, you know; violence, shooting, and beating people. They celebrate shooting citizens with 'tattoo parties.' They also set illegal arrest quotas and control duty assignments."

Compton city leaders sent a letter to U.S. Attorney General William Barr and California Attorney General Xavier Becerra requesting civil rights investigations into the Compton sheriff station, but received "no response." Days after deputy Banuelos was assault by an "Executioner," Gonzalez filed an anonymous report with internal affairs. However, "My text was posted at the parking lot entrance saying: 'ART IS A RAT.' This was the first direct 'Executioners' retaliation against me."

"Executioners' sport matching tattoos and are celebrated throughout the LA Sheriff Department." Gonzalez continued, "Executioners,' wield tremendous power, commanding obedience at Compton station. The 'Executioner' tattoo has a skull with Nazi imagery and an AK-47. The tattoo signifies a deputy has been 'inked' for shooting a citizen, which they received during 'inking parties.' 'Executioners' set illegal arrest quotas and threatening work slowdowns anytime their power is threatened. They ignore or respond very slowly to calls for help, if they are not given preferred assignments, promotions or other advancements," according to Gonzalez.

Gonzalez detailed this surreal tragedy, "Deputy Jaime Juarez an inked 'shot-caller' for the 'Executioners,' and enforces illegal work slowdowns. They stopped performing their duties to 'impose their will' on CPT. Juarez attempted to flex the gang's muscle with Captain Larry Waldie, pressuring him to change Training and Scheduling for deputy positions. Captain Waldie assigned shifts, a very desirable position for the gang, which would allow their members to receive preferential shifts assignments. Capt. Waldie refused, Deputy Juarez signaled 'Executioners' to stage a work slowdown."

'Inked' deputies with monikers like—Spartans, Regulators, Grim Reapers and Banditos—are the source of long-standing concerns; such groups currently operate at several sheriff stations, constituting criminal enterprises within law enforcement. Such ruthless groups have sparked multiple internal investigations, but despite recent FBI probes, these groups remain entrenched, leading civil liberties advocates to accuse the Sheriff's Department of complicity and turning a blind eye.

Att. Romero, who represents Gonzalez proclaimed, "We have a gang that has grown so powerful it dominates every aspect of life at the Compton station. It essentially controls scheduling, the distribution of informant tips, and assignment preferences for gang members." Contrarily, Sheriff Alex Villanueva say, "I have ordered an investigation. But I know there is no gang of any deputies running any station. But, I am disturbed by the allegations in Gonzalez's claim and swift administrative action is being taken."

Sounding like Donald Trump, disclaiming "no responsibility for COVID-19 deaths," Villanueva said, "I take these allegations very seriously and recently enacted a policy specifically addressing illicit groups, deputy cliques, and sub-groups, and I instituted measures in February that prohibit deputies from participating in cliques." However, Inspector General Max Huntsman contradicted Villanueva's rosy scenario, "I am not aware of no implementation whatsoever of the policy. My office has not been able to effectively investigate these secret societies because of obstruction by the Sheriff's Department. It's in writing, but has not been implemented, no investigations have been conducted," Huntsman told the Civilian Oversight Commission. Moreover," state government seems complicit."

Gonzalez's complaint states, "Gangs at Compton station numbers about 20 deputies, while 20 more are prospects or associates. Most work at night and communicate through WhatsApp. Black and female deputies are not allowed in these gangs. Nearly all CPT Deputies involved in high-profile shootings and out-of-policy beatings at CPT have been 'inked' members of the 'Executioners.' Roughly 1/5 of the 100 deputies at the Compton Station are part of the 'Executioners gang,'" his filing says. "Some 20 other deputies are closely associated with the gang, awaiting 'Executioners inking.' Members become 'inked' as 'Executioners' after executing members of the public or committing acts of violence to further gang power. Deputies refused to partner with me, while a dispatcher, an "inked" deputy, dumped excessive calls on me. 'Executioner' retaliation against me forced my resignation from a field training officer position," Gonzalez explained.

The subculture of matching tattoos is not a new phenomenon. Deputy gangs are deeply rooted in the LA County Sheriff's Department. Secret societies are blamed for glorifying brutal policing. Sean Kennedy, member of the Civilian Oversight Commission, a professor at Loyola Law School, stated "My students and I have identified at least 17 department gangs." Although Sheriff Villanueva claims gangs do not exist, defenders say "gangs represent hard work, boost morale and camaraderie." Moreover, last year the FBI interviewed deputies about gangs falsely reporting violence, while violating civil rights of the public, but no report has surfaced. The Rand Corporation, a nonprofit research agency, studied gang culture at CPT, its report was due in January, but was not released." Maybe, "Executioners" also dominate "The Rand".

While flooding media with disclaimers, CPT still face extra scrutiny over high-profile uses of force allegations. The arrest and beating of Dalvin Price in May is an example. Three deputies beat Dalvin severely. Also, Andres Guardado, an 18-year-old, was shot fatally in the back five times in Gardena by a deputy. Such beatings and shootings sounds like "inking parties." Compton police gangs were first revealed in the civil case of Donta Taylor, 31, killed by a deputy, during a foot chase in 2016. Another LA County 'inking party' possibly that was settled for $7 million. A deputy, Samuel Aldama, admitted under oath to having ink, a calf tattoo, depicting a skull with a rifle, a military-style helmet in flames and "CPT" for Compton. Att. Romero said, this is the same image found posted at 'the station's parking lot entrance saying: 'ART IS A RAT.' A top jail official stated that, 'gangs of deputies' at Men's Central Jail 'earned ink' by breaking inmates' bones.

Once gang revelations exploded in the press, Sheriff Villanueva condemned Gonzalez's claim, like Donald Trump blamed his predecessor, "I implemented reforms to stop abuse and corruption committed by former Sheriff Lee Baca and his Undersheriff Paul Tanaka, tattooed members of the Vikings." Again however, two deputies complained in 2017 that they were improperly punished with undesirable assignments for not meeting illegal arrest quotas and were told by a sergeant: "Yes, you should have known that by now." Illegal arrest quotas allow deputies to double arrest numbers each month, which also means hundreds of citizens' civil rights" were violated.

According to Att. John Sweeney, who represented the Taylor family, "This is an atomic bomb dropped on law enforcement and it reflects Gonzalez's claim." Sweeney's firm represents another excessive-force case involving the same deputies from the Taylor case. Deputies beat Sheldon Lockett and used racial slurs at him, during an incident in 2016, LA County denied allegations. Today, Lockett's attorneys are citing Gonzalez's claim in their court filing to reopen discovery, seeking to depose several deputies again and examine their WhatsApp accounts.

Compton is now considering defunding the Sheriff's Department, and believed that will save $7 of the $22-million it spends for policing. Sheriff's deputies have been operating like a 1920s mob of gangsters. Deputies fired 120 rounds at an unarmed man in a moving vehicle, wounding him four times in 2005. In 2009, a 16-year-old boy was fatally shot in the back by a Compton deputy, who claimed the boy pointed a gun at him. The family's attorney said the deputy planted a "drop weapon." These shootings fit Gonzalez's description of "inking" requirements of the "Executioners."

Deputy Thomas Banuelos said, "I endured five years of 'bullying and intimidation' from 'Executioners,' at the Compton station. I received a very violent vicious and bloody beating that nearly killed me, at the hands of an 'Executioner.' He had me on the ground and just bashed my head with his elbow over and over and over again. I suffered injuries to my head, but did not report the beating because 'Executioners' told me 'not to cooperate with investigators and to lie about the violent attack. They threatened even 'more violence,' so I had to meet with Deputy Eugene Contreras, an 'enforcer' of the gang.

Deputy Contreras told me 'if you open your mouth, you'll be labeled no good,' this meant I would be open to sudden retaliatory attacks at the station by all members of the gang." Att. Romero told EyewitnessNews, "Banuelos was also ordered by the department not to talk about the matter until they complete their investigation." However, Banuelos spoke up by filing his complaint.

Gangs of deputies like the "Vikings," "Regulators," "Jump Out Boys," "3000 Boys," "Banditos" and now the "Executioners" have infested the LA County Sheriff's Department for decades. A county document obtained by EyewitnessNews lists dozens of cases since the 1990s related to deputy gangs leading to nearly $55 million in court judgments and settlements. Many lawsuits, including one related to the "Banditos," are still pending.

Although this may read like an action novel, it reflects a real very very deadly situation for black residents of Compton. Derrick Cooper, founder of the L.A. City Wildcats Youth Academy in Compton said, "I was arrested last Thanksgiving while preparing a meal for my group. I wasn't told why I was arrested. At the county jail, I was locked butt naked in a shower, with over 200 other men.

Deputies said, 'I fit the description of someone they were looking for.' Deputies hauled me off, as young black men looked on. Then, I was released without charges. They apologized, but that did not change what happened or erase the incident from my kids' minds. Maybe showing black people's rights are not respected is the point!

Jermelle Henderson, who city officials, call a community partner, and contributes toys and food in the community, said, "A deputy pulled me over at gunpoint. They grabbed my arms, pulling me out of the car, and put me in handcuffs. I asked why she was doing this. She said, 'Oh, this is what we do in Compton.' I was handcuffed and detained in the back of a patrol car, before I was released with no explanation. The deputy recognized me as owner of Taco Mell, saying she had come by 'for a care package.'" Henderson's attorney, Walter Mosley said, "He's not a gang banger, and not a drug dealer... he makes food for our community. But, the way things are in Compton, he didn't know if he would make it home from a traffic stop."

Compton's City Council was outraged again on August 6, 2020 when Mayor Aja Brown was forced from her car and humiliatingly searched by LA County deputies. The Council called on the State of California to investigate allegations of violence, intimidation, terrorism, false arrests, excessive force and other corruption charges against the Compton Sheriff's Department and deputies gangs like "The Executioners." Jasmyne A. Cannick of CNN detailed Mayor Aja Brown's appealing and degrading encounter, during a "traffic stop." She called for state AG Xavier Becerra and the U.S. Justice Department to investigate deputy gangs in the LA County Compton Sheriff's Department. Police use of excessive force, discriminatory policing, improper stops, searches, arrests and murders of citizens in Compton; but neither commented, as though they supported the Sheriff, rather than Mayor Brown.

Mayor Aja Brown said, "I was driving through the city, when a Compton sheriff's deputy made a hard u-turn in traffic to pull me over. I was with my husband and baby daughter. I rolled my window down and asked why was I being pulled over? Within seconds nine sheriff deputy vehicles arrived on the scene. They ordered me out of my car, while demanding I spread-eagle with my hands on the squad car." The Mayor should have been recognizable by people she employs, which indicates deputies open disregard for black people's rights, no one spoke up or questioned her treatment.

While manhandling Mayor Brown, deputies claimed she ran a red light, which she adamantly denies, but didn't seem to matter. "Although deputies claimed they stop me for running a red light, they immediately began looking for drugs, of course none were found. They frisked me down, as if I was a criminal.

"Mind you, I was accompanied by my husband and my infant daughter in her car seat. I did not look like a drugs trafficker. My infant daughter was screaming at the top of her lungs, as deputies pulled her father from the car to search him and the car." A watch commander arrived, after Mayor Brown was manhandled and degradingly searched, he released her before they hauled her off to Jail.

"Although I filed an official complaint with the LASD, the response was totally unsatisfactory. I plan to file a lawsuit against the LA County Sheriff; that is the only thing they understand. They will remember who I am and how I look, after that. And, even though deputies gave me a ticket, they tore it up without explanation." I believe the Mayor was right, they realized they did not dare show up in court to defend the ticket and violating her, and her family's civil rights, not to mention humiliating and degrading her in front of her husband, who had to watch, deputies run their hands all over her. Thank God they did not demand a cavity search, as other black women!

Consider the psychological anguish inflicted upon her, an infant child, and husband, during that entire episode. This was an insult to her constituents, who are embarrassed for the Mayor, not to mention the mental trauma, seeing their leader treated in that manner. Following that disgusting displays of contempt and disregard suffered by Mayor Brown, as a city official, the painful and deadly truth of police gangs on the innocent is never considered. Politicians across America should be outraged, while expressing total indignation and revulsion, that a city Mayor was treated with such disregard by police. Where is Gov. Gavin Newsom's support for Mayor Aja Brown's fight against police gangs in Compton?

I truly feel Aja Brown's husband's rage and anguish, as both women he cares most about were degraded and humiliated before his eyes. But, a black man in America knows in such situations any show of outrage could get him, as well as his family killed, while police claim she and he were angry over the traffic ticket. More importantly, with "qualified immunity" no one would pay. Black Lives Matter only if white Americans watch black people die for 8 minutes and 46 seconds, like a "snuff" film.

In fact, I believe, those cops recognized Mayor Brown, which is why they made the u-turn. Defunding the Sheriff Department by Compton will put all those deputies out of cushy jobs, which was the point of the charade. They were putting Mayor Aja Brown in her place. They run Compton!! My question is without a federal motorcade, would deputies recognize Sen. Kamala Harris, who has been labored angry, would she be made to spread-eagle and get patted down, as Mayor Aja Brown?

Winning Georgia

Penniless slaves walking of plantations did not mean slaves could leave it behind. That statement is as true for descendants of American descendants of slavery today as back then; leaving the fight to end legal racism, segregation white supremacy, convict leasing, and sharecropping in the 1970s did not mean black Americans left them behind. Today, due to Donald Trump's four years, those dreaded outcomes have worsened and are staring all Americans in the face because of COVID-19. Americans are adrift in a whirlpool of potentially disastrous consequences and are like fish; they do not realize they are wet.

Change always takes place in the present; nothing ever happens in the past because it results from the old normal that makes their present. The future differs from the past when the new normal pushes the old normal aside. Consequently, this is why America is where it is today. Having faced massive protests worldwide, following George Floyd's lynching, and as COVID-19's scorecard has topped 250,000 deaths, America is only getting promises of a virus vaccine from Donald Trump. And there is even less being done to secure a reliable antidote for the social and economic threats hovering over pandemic stricken states and a recoiling economy because so many ststes refuse to issue mask mandates. Echoes from the past, like voices trying to call back the old normal, like Donald Trump, are reinforcing the idea that a slave's life does not matter.

America is slowly emerging, states like Georgia, from the long dark winter of Donald Trump's Grinch-like reign. The ashes of the Republican Party are still smoldering, but the fire is extinguished, with Pres. Joe Biden's victory in Georgia. The President's 306 Electoral votes sealed Trump's fate for all times as a petulant, obnoxious, and very selfish bore. As president, Trump's tenure was identical to an awful opera, although the music ended, and even after the curtain ring down, the sound lingers, like the screech from a sharp object across a mirror. My following remarks are not an attempt at mirror scrying, but a post mortem for the Republican ghost from the past that continues to divide America as their only strategy for maintaining power.

Democrats winning Georgia signaled the death knell of Trumpism, which began with his impeachment trial in the US Senate. Although Republicans cowed before the world, accepting lies, and to a man, save one, rejected truth to save a "petite dictator" in the eyes of the world. Impeachment manager Rep. Adam Schiff (D-CA) courageously stated that "Trump was a man without a moral compass and as such, would never find his way to the truth." Dragged before the bar of justice kicking and screaming, Republicans had an opportunity to spare America the pain and needless deaths (150,000 at the time, now 250,000), and their COVID-19 deaths are on their hands. They choose to stand against justice and the US Constitution to maintain a partisan advantage. Their cowardice back then has yield the present disgraceful spectacle Trump is staging before the world, as he cries foul against the American people's vote.

Republicans continued their ridiculous post-election charade, led by Sen. Mitch McConnell. He summoned Mark Zuckerberg president of Facebook, and Jack Dorsey of Twitter to come before his inquisition to answer accusations their companies censor conservative content, after several of Trump's social media posts were labeled false and misleading because they claimed voter fraud. The session is likely to focus on their companies' statements about the electoral process and outcome, many of which were labeled as false or misleading. Even worse, Senators are fuming over the treatment of a New York Post story on Hunter Biden, which was supposed to be Donald Trump's big "October surprise," as the "Hilary Clinton emails." The chief executive officers of the social networks are scheduled to testify before the Senate Judiciary Committee on Tuesday in their second congressional appearance in a month to defend themselves against charges of silencing conservatives.

America has reached a point of reckoning as a result of Republican leadership. Voters must hold them accountable for their decisions and actions that are tearing at America's fundamental structures and foundation or they will lose the very freedom patriotic Americans prize. However, my point in this old normal Republican slide downhill is to point out that David Perdue and Kelly Loffler had front seats aboard Trump's bandwagon. They are offering Georgian's voters their record to justift re-election. Perdue and Loffler underscored their low bar by leading the chorus trying to force Georgia's Republican Secretary of State Brad Raffensperger to resign for lack of support for Donald Trump's false claims of election fraud. Secretary of State Raffensperger said Monday that Republican leaders such as Sen. Lindsey Graham (R-S.C.) have been trying to pressure him to exclude legal ballots and declare Trump the winner of Georgia's sixteen electoral votes.

Georgia's double-talking, double-dealing, and double-tongued Senators doubled down, going even lower during interviews, both refused to acknowledge Georgia's voters choice of President-elect Joe Bien over Trump, warning that retaining the two Georgia Senate seats serve as "the last line of defense against this liberal socialist agenda the Democrats will perpetuate." Instead, Georgia voters must hold Perdue and Loffler accountable for their record of supports for Trump, as he continues playing golf, doing nothing to stop COVID-19's rampage, as it kills thousands of Americans daily. Trump cares nothing about the unnecessary pain and agony his do-nothing attitude allows coronavirus to cause Georgia families.

Beyond threatening Georgia voters with the prospect of Democrats flipping control of the Senate in Washington, Perdue and Loffler have no accomplishments as Senators. So Georgia voters' concerns like protecting the Port of Savannah, trade policies to help Georgia farmers, jobs for the state's stagnant economy, as well as solar and wind farms on some of Georgia's vacant farmland and Georgia student debt. Young activists and elderly Georgians worked and elect President Biden because he promised to address student debt and low-income student aid. These are issues neither Purdue nor Loffler supports.

Taking the offensive on Monday, Reverend Raphael Warnock led off tossing the gauntlet before Senator Kelly Loeffler, challenging her to three televised debates ahead of the January 5th runoff election. Although it is highly unlikely Loffler will brave the media spotlight and accept the Democrat's, come on out and fight invitation. While simultaneously, Warnock said Sunday, "Schumer is not on the ballot in the Georgia Senate race. A very high-profiled runoff, Warnock is aware of the national implication of his race with Loffler but wants Georgians to know he is more concerned with serving them and concentrating on their need than being part of the national battle for the US Senate. "I will tell you what is on the ballot that concerns Georgian voters health care is on the ballot—access to affordable health care. We have got 500,000 Georgians in the Medicaid gap. We have got 1.8 million Georgians with preexisting conditions. That what I'm concerned about for the people of Georgia and not the fight to control the Senate."

"We finished in a strong position." Doubling down on his commitment to running on local issues, rather than talking about taking the Senate, Warnock said, "There is no question in my mind, once Georgians learn of my commitment for affordable health care, and the work I have done for years, fighting for ordinary people, we will prevail come Jan. 5." Warnock said I'm not worried. We galvanized thousands of voters in the runoffs; we received unwavering support from Georgia voters, who are an influential sector of the Biden coalition and make up a third of the state's electorate. "This was the closest Senate race in the country. It really reflected the power of first-time voters here and the determination of Black voters in Georgia to make a change in this country."

Democrat Jon Ossoff—who is in a runoff with Sen. David Perdue— is also redirecting attention away from the national stage and focusing on Georgia voters' needs and their health care. "I finished first, handily, far ahead of a candidate who is the wealthiest member of Congress, who poured millions of dollars into this race. Georgia Republican Sen. David Perdue has declined an invitation to debate Democratic challenger Jon Ossoff ahead of the January runoff election for his seat, CNN has learned. Perdue has declined to debate his Democratic rival on December 6th, according to Mary Lynn Ryan, the chairwoman of the Atlanta Press Club, the host of two separate debates for both Senate runoffs. Ossoff's campaign told CNN they accepted the Press Club's invitation, and Ossoff tweeted Sunday, "Looks like Sen. David Perdue is too much of a coward to debate me again. Come on out, Senator, and defend your record. I'm ready to go." The Georgia Senator drew fire for withdrawing from the debate to attend a Trump rally in northwest Georgia just before Election Day. Ossoff blasted

Perdue for profiting off of inside information, as Kelly Loffler. Ossoff branded Perdue a "crook," and said he refused to debate because Perdue could not defend making money by representing the State of Georgia in the Senate.

The LA Times Op-Ed: What broke the Republican Party? by Seth Masket indicated everything might not be rosy for Republicans Purdue and Loffler. The Reagan/Bush GOP that ranged from 1980 to 2008 embraced so-called economic conservatism (low taxes, reduced business regulation) and international engagement (willingness to use force abroad) as governing philosophy. It also generally embraced democratic values—acknowledging its opponents' legitimacy, demonstrating some forbearance in the use of its powers, supporting American democratic elections, but regime change was on the table. But Christian conservatives pushed the GOP toward regulating personal behavior, especially abortion and sexual preference. Neo-cons pushed aggressive and often disastrous foreign escapades to gain votes.

GOP Neo-cons preached fiscal responsibility under Democratic administrations while running up record deficits once in power. Newt Gingrich, a demagogue, smeared opponents and employed extreme tactics, while encouraging its ranks to look away not at bigotry, used dog whistles to procure the white racist vote. The GOP over immigration, individual liberties, and other vital issues, while trying to appear it adhered to democratic values, free and fair elections.

What changed? "Race" became the central issue of the GOP. White Americans, especially white Republicans, increasingly identify themselves as white people, and today many see that white identity as under threat. Barack Obama's presidency, which he indicated in his recent memoir, magnified that threat in most conservative voters' minds. The Democratic Party's candidates threatened whites atop the social order. Suddenly, the old rules of political engagement were out. White privilege was being challenged for them as the top racial group. This change produced a no-holds-barred competition for power within the Republican Party and the nation. Good governance and democratic values were cast off. An example of how this played out in the Trump administration came from a federal judge Saturday (11-4-2020) Chad Wolf, chief of Homeland Security, acted unlawfully for Donald Trump, and ruled his suspension of protections for migrants brought to the US illegally, as children, is invalid.

Today in America and Georgia, we are experiencing the New Normal COVID-19 brought upon the world. In its deadly ride across the United States, the coronavirus has revealed what no other occurrence in its history had been able to show, not even "Civil War." Most readers may ask, what is that? My answer is that "We need each other more today than ever before." Looking back over Georgia's history of racial hatred and slavery has dominated its socio-economic and political development, giving it a legacy of the Ku Klux Klan's lynching, burning, and murder. Today on the face of Stone Mountain, there is a memorial to those that inspired and instigated that gruesome and loathsome heritage.

However, today in Georgia, lightning out of a clear blue sky to most across America, leaders like Stacey Abrams turned Georgia blue to match that sky. For me, she epitomizes Alicia Key's mega-hit, "Girls on Fire," and the blue flame of change is burning across Georgia. Stacey is carrying the banner that "We need each other more today than ever before." She is the leader for these times like no other and serves as a model for aspiring political and civic leaders that reflect this "new normal" Americans need to embrace.

Denied the governorship of Georgia in 2018, with similar tactics Republicans are presently trying to use to deny President-elect Joe Biden, rather than whine, like the outgoing President of the United States, even though she had just cause, Stacey went to work, showing Georgians how a real leader looks and performs. Stacey showed America the kind of progressive organizing leadership young Democrats deploying to unify America. Stacey is inspiring Georgians of all types, races, and ethnicities to believe they have real power when they work together and believe in their effort. That effort turned Georgia blue for the first time since 1996 when almost no one other than she thought it was possible.

Stacey and other volunteers brought first-time voters to the polls in overwhelming numbers. She did not run away from Black Lives Matter; instead, she ran to young black and white BLM supports and embraced their cry to change policing or redirect funding and practices of police in the black community. Unlike, moderates or neo-cons, she felt the pain and fear black families have and are expressing, as their children die at the hands of police without cause and for crimes that do not carry the death penalty, even if a shooting victim is guilty. Black Lives Matter says that police cannot continue to be "judge and jury" on the streets and not be held accountable for needless and preventable deaths because they have" qualified immunity" to kill without personal responsibility.

Why DONALD TRUMP LEAD THE THE U.S. CAPITOL INSURRECTION

"Black Lives Matter" and an 8 minutes and 46 seconds video of George Floyd's horrendous death scene, has African Americans fighting a war of words, about why black people are still locked in poverty. The fault line in this war of words began with slavery. Most involved in these verbal fisticuffs on both sides are beset by ignorance because their weapons are hearsay. The major reason I present is *"The 400th" From Slavery to Hip Hop* is to lay out the stepwise course of descendants of American slavery's journey, which has lasted more than 400 years in America.

I wanted to construct a narrative that showed their slow but continuous slough across time, the question is asked and answered about how they found purpose along their journey. Their survival struggles were assuredly far more difficult than their lives in slavery, in many ways. Slavery would be a piece of cake compared to the challenges of learning to live on their own, after generations of forced dependency, domination, dreary, pain and death. I asked myself, was there a formula that could provide a matrix, which organized the hundreds of years filled with toil, sweat and death that would flow out of the words and descriptions I gathered into streams that explained how I got here. The what, why and how of my alchemy has produced a narrative, that not only black children can understand but as a result, they are able to stand before the world upon a solid information foundation that clearly state their claims, as one people.

It is impossible to create one story that includes everyone and every event, which opposed or aided former slaves' survival struggles. Beginning as individuals forced to live in slave pens, enslaved Africans developed societies, which served their needs, under such total domination and oppression. Slaves by the millions structured those societies on thousands of plantations, and it was that knowledge they brought with them into their penniless emancipation. Put another way, it was what they had in their heads, which allowed former slaves to survive amidst confusion, mayhem and death that civil war wrought all about them without any real concern or refuge for them.

I had accumulated a head filled with information but haphazardly picked up that I came to understand, as a family story, beginning this project. Some information I received, as a child from my great-grandfather, Burl Lee, Jr. He was the first Lee born free. My family name came from Burl Lee, Sr. my Great great-grandfather, who was the last Lee born in slavery. His son Burl talked with me until age 11. He told me stories of his father's times, as well as his. Although, most of those stories faded over time, however this research reawakened them when I began trying to fill in the blanks of my matrix with real people and events. My wife Dot had a maxim, regarding telling stories, *"It must be a love story, why else bother?"* That was her way of saying our lives are always about the next generation—our children.

Those thoughts revealed eight themes upon which I construct and filled in my matrix. Consequently, following emancipation, former slaves decided, not formally and not all at the same instance, to pursue eight lines of development, which began back in those slave pens because that was what they knew. I saw those categories as: making **families and building communities; education and communication; entertainment and entrepreneurship, and political and cultural involvement.** Those themes began as individual thoughts or actions slaves engaged, which developed not as conscious choices, but what they had and what their needs forced upon them, while sharing what they learned with one another.

Their strategies were productive and gave former slaves what I envisioned, as those eight distinct areas. Newly freed slaves used that knowledge to sustain them, as they endure to survive, no matter what white people threw at them. Even though descendants of American slavery were affected negatively by their penniless emancipation, it was white people's use of the legal system and terror to dominate former slaves which caused the greatest problems. White people relegated former slaves on bottom of America's capitalistic economic system in poverty, as "cheap labor."

The one thing most African Americans were not taught in school or in the street is they are in the place they are today because of their ignorance of what really happened and why, after Republicans in Congress passed **"The Civil Rights Act of 1866.** Those Republicans were a different breed from those that fill the US Senate and those that instigated the insurrection on Capitol Hill on 1-6-2021. A United States federal law—**The Civil Rights Act of 1866** defined citizenship for newly freed slaves and affirmed that all citizens were equally protected under the law. It was mainly intended to protect the civil rights of newly freed slaves and descendants born in or brought into the US, as slaves. That point is the reason behind the insurrection of 1/6.

However, before becoming law, US President Andrew Johnson of Tennessee vetoed this legislation twice, but each time a two-thirds majority vote in each chamber of Congress, overrode Johnson's vetoes. Johnson was actually a Republicans like today. **"The Civil Rights Act of 1866"** became the law of the land without a president's signature. **"The Civil Rights Act of 1866,"** protected **"the Civil Rights of all Persons in the United States, and furnished the Means of their vindication. It declared that all people born in the United States who are not subject to any foreign power are entitled to be citizens, without regard to race, color, or previous condition of slavery or involuntary servitude."** A similar provision (called *the Citizenship Clause*), was written into the Fourteenth Amendment to the United States Constitution also.

The *Civil Rights Act of 1866* declared that, *"any citizen has the same right that a white citizen has to make and enforce contracts, sue and be sued, give evidence in court, and inherit, purchase, lease, sell, hold, and convey real and personal property."* Additionally, the act *guaranteed to all citizens the "full and equal benefit of all laws and proceedings for the security of person and property, as is enjoyed by white citizens, like punishment, pains, and penalties… Persons who denied these rights on account of race or previous enslavement were guilty of a misdemeanor and upon conviction faced a fine not exceeding $1,000, or imprisonment not exceeding one year, or both.*

The Fourteenth Amendment incorporated the same language in the Equal Protection Clause that is in the *Civil Rights Act of 1866*. In particular, the act discussed the need to provide *"reasonable protection to all persons in their constitutional rights of equality before the law, without distinction of race or color, or previous condition of slavery or involuntary servitude."*

So, here I will use media personality Roland Martin's favorite expression, "let me help y'all out" to clarify why *"The Civil Rights Act of 1866"* has been treated as though it is not the law on the books by Congress, the US Supreme Court and Presidents of the United States of America. First, it is *"currently"* and has always been a federal law passed by the Congress of the United States in 1866 and has *"never been overturned by the US Supreme Court"* or *repealed by the Congress of the United States*, which is why it is current law today. That means descendants of Americans have always had every legally right white people current have!!! Think about that for a moment. So, black people have been fooled and intimidated into believing they did not have those rights by the US Supreme Court when in established *Plessy v Ferguson*. That ruling was a trick, a charade concocted by former slaveholders of the court and reinforced by Woodrow Wilson, with the *"Dark Age" angry white men mob madness* era of lynching—the same as police murders today—to compel former slaves to accept "second class" status white people demanded. That is the only reason why "we as slavery's descendants are forced to accept less than our full rights. Allow that to sink in for a moment!!!

The *"Dark Age" angry white men mob madness* era was a massive *"learned helplessness"* experiment, a pogrom conducted by the United States government to convince Descendants of slavery to submit to second class or die. Think about that for a moment. In other words descendants of American slavery were "hoodwinked," bamboozeled, flimflammed and conned into believing or intimidated into accepting white people had the right to deny them first class rights.

How did it happen? Ignorance was governments' tool. Never ever having real knowledge of how they ended up in the position they found themselves and their ignorance was compounded by their *"learned helplessness"* to pull this con game off. It took the entire American society's cooperation. How were descendants of American Slavery to know?

Southern Democrats employing what they termed "interposition" and "nullification" to crafted a facetious legal theory that they enforced as laws. That theory denied former slaves access to fair courts—***Plessy v Ferguson***—as plaintiffs. Using their made up justification—interposition and nullification—whites in the South claimed they had the right to void, based on this made-up concept, the ***Civil Rights Act of 1866*** and further claimed, southern states had the right the stand between—interposition—the US Constitution and former slaves and nullify any law that deprived white people of their heritage, as slave masters; states' rights (the Capitol insurrection.)

Based on that absurdity alone, southerners denied former slaves access to all rights granted by the ***Civil Rights Act of 1866***. That is why black lawyers, even though they attended law school and got degrees, are kept, by their education from thinking beyond what they are taught learned helplessness. This is accomplished through the Bar Associations and is the threat of disbarment.

For southern states claim to work, southerners needed someone in the White House, like Andrew Johnson, who vetoed the Civil Rights Bill twice) and that person was Woodrow Wilson. Five years after ***Plessy v. Ferguson***—separate but equal—Wilson, in 1912, entered the White House and used the power of government to make these fictitious legal claims work. Wilson's organizing principle was *"Birth of A Nation,"* which he screened, over 30 times at the White House. He invited Supreme Court judges, politicians, businessmen, industrialists, educators, financiers, preachers and the press. Everyone agreed to support his plan to use segregation to rob black people—*an undeserving lot*—of their rights.

But more importantly, Donald Trump was useing the same strategy to get white people to agree to repeat Wilson's strategy, as MAGA "Make America Great Again." Like Wilson, it did not start out, looking like what it came to be, but once instituted it became segregation throughout the federal government and the rest of America. What most people do not understand is Woodrow Wilson had lots of black people as Trump supporting him when he began.

I did not present ***The Civil Rights Act of 1866*** at this point, only because I wanted readers to know and understand that newly freed slaves and descendants were actually given all rights white people had in 1866, but to make sure they know they have them now and have always had them. White people used "interposition and nullification," as legal theories, which the Supreme Court in ***Plessy v. Ferguson*** used to justify what came after that ruling. Justice John Marshall Harlin was the only justice that spoke for the US Constitution. Woodrow Wilson claimed southerners had a legal right to nullify the ***Civil Rights Act of 1866—white people were forced by "fair means or foul" to rid themselves of the intolerable position of government sustained by votes of*** *ignorant Negros*—with the support of federal, state and local governments engineering poverty black people endure today.

However as time, events and Divine intervention would have it, in March of 2020 the US Supreme Court finally reaffirmed that **The Civil Rights Act of 1866** is and has always been the law, as it currently exist in the United States. News headlines stated it this way *"Supreme Court Sides with Comcast, Sets Higher Burden for Byron Allen to Win Racial Bias Suit."* The unanimous ruling sent the case back to the 9th U.S. Circuit Court of Appeals in San Francisco. It seemed for many that black people had lost again, especially considering Comcast's statement, *"We are pleased the Supreme Court unanimously restored certainty on the standard to bring and prove civil rights claims. The well-established framework that has protected civil rights for decades continues. The nation's civil rights laws have not changed with this ruling; they remain the same as before the case was filed."* That is my point, *"The nation's civil rights laws remain the same as before the case was filed."*

That is what I wanted black people to understand, and maybe they will believe it now that it has come out of white people's mouths. The Supreme Court, the same US Supreme Court that established **Plessy v Ferguson**, and supported "interposition and nullification," actually "unanimously restored" the integrity of **The Civil Rights Act of 1866** for black people in America, whether they understood what they did or not. The same US Supreme Court that had undermined the US Constitution for 123 years supporting Woodrow Wilson and the South, with **Plessy v. Ferguson**—separate but equal—segregation and white supremacy, since the end of Reconstruction in 1876, did an about face. This same Supreme Court admitted that white people and government in the United States of America, never had the right to deny slavery's descendants first class rights and that discrimination and disparate treatment was a violation of the **Civil Rights Act of 1866**. I was told in school that the **Civil Rights Act of 1866** was outlawed by **Plessy v. Ferguson,** which is why segregation was legal in the United States. Nothing could be further from the truth!!!!! Segregation was never legal!!!!

Moreover, it is obvious that all the years of *"second class"* treatment by southern states and white people in them was a con-game and Paul Robeson and William L. Patterson's **We Charge Genocide** was on point 68 years ago. Black people in American are owed damages for the 144 years the civil rights violations of African Americans rights by federal, state and local government, according to the penalties in the law, not to mention the businesses and institutions across America. This also vindicates Dot M. Smith groundbreaking research and thesis **Recession and Unemploment: A Retrospective Analysis of the Economic Welfare Loss** and her "chasm of inequality analysis." Stated in a different manner, black people in the United States have been *"hoodwinked,"* by segregation in the South. They were *"sold a bill of goods"* by all governments and lawyers "white and black," in order to help white people build wealth at the expense of African Americans.

Federal, state and local governments, created this illegal system to force black people to accept *"second class status"* on the bottom of American society. The federal government was a full partner with southern states in violating the US Constitutional rights of black people. They used the pogrom of segregation, white supremacy, lynching, banishment, ethnic cleansing, and the **"Dark Age"** *angry white men mob madness* for over 144 years to keep descendants of American slavery in poverty.

All of the denials, restrictions and discrimination imposed on African Americans beginning after the 1876 election and the withdrawal of federal troops, set black people up for a murderous pogrom led by Woodrow Wilson and the US Federal Government. This re-enslavement period of black people has been painstakingly and expertly presented by Douglas A. Blackmon in his eye opening book **_Slavery by Another Name: The Re-Enslavement of Black Americans from the Civil War to World War II_**.

The Washington D.C. insurrection was what white people in America do when ever Descendants of American slavery organize theirselves in to a political force and use the vote to achieve equality. The first time was following 1876 election when Republican nominee Rutherford B. Hayes lost to Democrat Samuel J. Tilden. But Hayes supported slavery and southerners engaged in a similar process and used the US Congress to deny Tilden the election and give it to Hayes. Hayes promised he would end Reconstruction and pulled Union troops out of the South and leave the so-called *"Negro problem"* to the South to solve as it please.this was Trumps goal on 1/6/21.

Descendants of American slavery was never able to gain enough political power until after the passage of the Civil Rights Bill of 1964 and the Voting Rights Bill of 1965 to begin to build a political coalition that challenge the status quo in America. That effort was derailed with the assassination of Dr. Martin Luther King, Jr. and J. Edgar Hoover's death hunt for black power activists. As I said earlier in this narrative "Black Lives Matter" protest showed me what could be the rebirth of the 1960 black power movement and the political coalition we created, but this time around it would be led by our grandchildren. They were not afraid to take to the streets in far greater numbers than the Invaders produced for Dr. King's last March for the Memphis sanitation workers. Young progressives were drawing more than our 50,000 to each march from Minnesota to New Zealand.

I decided if I could help them understand they need to **"turn their street protest into street politics,"** they could establish a coalition that could take power in America. The hardest part of bringing this coalition together was convincing Former Vice-President Joe Biden to reach out and bring progressive into his campaign. I will admit his effort was not a wholehearted embrace, he refuse to kiss on the first date. However, I knew the courtship was with a young "hot" partner that would be here after he is gone and their children, children will be like our grandchildren.

Progressive are in Congress and their numbers are growing. The only remaining problem is, as with civil rights leader refused to bring black power activists into leadership, so when they lose relevance or pass on, the move was left leaderless!!!!!!!

Stevie Wonder Leads the Call for: A Truth Commission

"The Rolling Stone" broke the story of Stevie Wonder's "Calls for A Truth Commission" with a video letter on Dr. Martin Luther King, Jr.'s Birthday. Spearheading the national effort, after leading the congress to declare Dr. King's Birthday a national holiday, Stevie's open letter is the ultimate honor for Dr. King!" His appeal was a very strong and heartfelt statement, "I am calling on President Biden and Vice President Harris **<u>to launch a formal, government investigation to establish the truth regarding inequality in this country. This truth will validate the history, and this commission will recommend reconciliation.</u>**" Listening to Stevie's plea tears filled my eyes, as my memories raced back to that last day at the Lorraine Motel (4-4-1968), as Charles Cabbage and I listened to Dr. King's desires for his ***"Poor People's Campaign,"*** hopes for the poor, unity between black power activists and civil rights leaders, as well as racial justice and equality across America.

Watching Stevie's video my though also return to that room in the Nation's Capitol hearing room where Charles and I testified before the Congressional Committee investigating Dr. King's assassination and conversation with committee staffers that express such happiness that the nation would finally know the truth about FBI Director J. Edgar Hoover's role in Dr. King's death. But again, from back then, tears continued filling my eyes, thinking about how the House of Representatives voted to seal their report before the public knew what was in it for 25 years; so the truth would not be known even today!!!

So, back in the 1970s truth tellers and other voices like mine were overshadowed and drowned out by those who did not want the truth of Dr. King's assassination known. Many today, for whatever reason, still after 52 years still fight to keep those lies from back then alive. Again I say Stevie's call for "A Truth Commission" renews Dr. King's favorite quote ***"Truth forever on the scaffold, wrong forever on the throne."*** Stevie is leading a chorus of artists, including Alicia Keys and Khalid, who are calling on the Biden-Harris administration to establish a "Commission On Racial Justice." In June 2020, Rep. Barbara Lee (D-CA) proposed legislation for forming a Truth, Racial

Healing and Transformation Commission following the killing of George Floyd and in the wake of Covid-19

I sent a letter entitled "Truth Forever on the Scaffold" 11/10/2020 to the Chairperson of the Congressional Black Caucus, US Representative Karen Bass, requesting Speaker of the US House of Representatives Nancy Pelosi schedule a vote to unlock the investigation report from the House of Representatives investigation of Dr. Martin Luther King, Jr.'s assassination which convened in 1978. However, there has been no response or action from either Chairwoman Bass or Speaker Pelosi. I made this request to the Congressional Black Caucus because it comprises every representative elected from the majority of African American communities across the United States. However, it seems and great that someone of pubic statue and acclaim, like Stevie Wonder and others, are saying out load things I have advocated since I testified before the US House of Representatives hearings into the Assassination Investigation in 1978 is fallen on deaf ears and cold hearts.

It was truly heartwarming as Stevie said of Dr. King, "For 36 years we've had a national holiday honoring your birthday and principles; yet you would not believe the lack of progress." He referred to first meeting Dr. King at age 14, "You became an inspiration, and a true hero!" But then Stevie drew attention to, "It is painful to know that the needle has not moved one iota….. It makes me physically sick, and yet you would not believe the lack of progress…. More than any award that I have ever received, I want you to know that I am thankful how you influenced my place of love, which allowed me to try to push the needle of love and equality forward."

I will say and hope in establishing "A Truth Commission" we do not make the same mistake as Pres. Bill Clinton with his Presidential Commission—Dialogue on Race," (1997). Prompted by the 1995 Oklahoma City bombing by Timothy McVeigh, which were another white supremacist militias and other hate groups respond to demand of equality and justice by descendants of American slavery. Pat Buchanan at the 1992 Republican National Convention pandered to racism, similar to Donald Trump, attacked changes in American culture.

Also, 24 years earlier The National Advisory Commission on Civil Disorders or Kerner Report was released on February 29, 1968, after seven months of investigation. However, even though it was published like a novel, the government paid no attention to its findings. The Kerner Commission's analysis—which argued that the nation was moving towards two separate and unequal, communities, and that billions in dollars was needed to rectify these problems—preceded the assassination of Dr. King just over a month 4-4-1968 later. Many believe that report brought white politicians to J. Edgar Hoover's side and his opinion that "Dr. King Martin Luther King, Jr. is the most dangerous Negro in America," and support for his solution.

With this new "Truth Commission" the nation needs to designate young new voices to lead it, like Rep. Jamaal Bowman, Rep. Cori Bush, Rep. Alexandria Ocasio-Cortez, Rep. Ayanna Pressley, and BLM activists like Tamika Mallory, Alicia Garza, Patrisse Cullors and Opal Tometi. The tendency is to fill such efforts with older individuals who need to retire and go somewhere and sit down. It is long past their usefulness. They all have bought into the system and gotten rich milking it. They were part of creating the problem that needs addressing today, and will only protect their legacy of thievery and lies. They will never look for truth and real change, because they are invested in the system. If this "Truth Commission" will be about truth telling, select people who have no reason to protect the old lies.

This is why the *Rock and Roll Hall of Fame* alum and icon Stevie Wonder cited "being sick of lies and deceit," and rebukes people who use "God for convenience" alongside politicians 'trying to find an easy solution to a 400 year problem' while 'truth is struggling to be heard and defended.' 'Until we turn our mouth movement into righteous action, we are doing our nation, God and your (Dr. King) memory an injustice!" He concluded, "Until what we say is what we do, there is no truth. It is just repeating and rewriting history, just as we have for the last 400 years.... Without truth we cannot have accountability. Without accountability we cannot have forgiveness. Without forgiveness, we cannot heal!!!!!!

My Family's Last Word

The following three poems by Yohaness Shariff Smith's are ***"The 400th"*** last offerings. They are from his book T.H.I.N C. (Teaching Humanity in New Consciousness) The Chrysalises of Evolution!!! T.H.I.N.C. is an underground anthology from the Atlanta Vibe during the 1990s.

ENDURE TO SURVIVE: An American Hell!!!
"Dear God make me a bird, so I can fly far...far away."
From the field I saw the Klan...
Hoods, horses, torches moving thru the twilight
Dear God, what am I going to do?
Running...running...running toward the back door...
They already in the house!
Dear God, my woman... my children!
"Nigger, where are you?
We heard you been stirring up some trouble around here."
Dear God, what am I going to do?
Running thru the backdoor half crazy, I'm tackled by three white sheets.
He...he...he touching my woman!
He putting his filthy hands...
Dear God, help me! My son lying on the floor bloody!
Bleeding black and blue,
What am I going to do?
Shaking and shivering, I know she needs me, but I can't think.
This son of a bitch is standing over me with a gun.
Teaching a lesson he brought his son.
Trembling with rage, as they made me watch.
Blind rage as they take turns.
I fight...fight...fight!!!!
Dear God, help me!!
She is begging me...not to die.
Begging me to stay down...to stay alive!
She screams at me...
"Baby, we need you here...alive!
You ain't no good to us dead."
I can't breathe. Dear God, help me!
He's on top of her, raping her!
Still trying to fight! A knife is at her neck.
She cries out, "This ain't the first time!"
Quiet tears stream down her tortured face

And, I... I bury my eyes in the floor.
Screams for help in a silent protest, as the pig grunts, she gasps for death...
Breath... straining for a breath free of death... free of pain... free of his stench
With fists clinched she pleads,
"Please...please...Let my babies leave.
They don't need to see this! "
Sweating and breathing heavily he quickly finishes.
Standing over her, he spits in her face and calls her a whore.
He turns to me and says,
"Nigger, you're a lucky Nigger.
You better thank your merciful Master that this is picking season,
Or me n' the boys we would beat you bloody,
But this way you and your bitch can still pick, the fields a'waiten."

A SLAVE REMEMBERS!

(Swosh...Crack!!!)
I can still hear that fine crisp, crackle of whips splitting thick July air.
(Swoosh...Crack!!!)
Hot leather ripping into flesh... Beaten to within an inch of death.
Those tortured screams, the silence of unbearable pain...
Hideous beads of salty sweat creeping into wounds...
Ropes so tight hands grow purple and numb.
Forced to live a lie, watching friends and family die.
Feeling helpless!!!
Powerless!!!
Running... running... running away... barefoot
Through the forest towards freedom
A freedom... I ain't ever known!
You see, I was born a slave!
We could hear dogs in the swamp.
Men and their horses... that terrified look in Jo-Jo eyes as I choked him to death.
"I won't go back, we either escape or die trying!"
He was so afraid, but I eased his pain.
I can still feel those greedy hands groping at my ass, spreading my cheeks...
Examining my teeth!
Degraded on the auction block! Sold!
(Swoosh...Crack!!! Swoosh...Crack!!!)
Lesson 1: Massa's secret sessions with those young slave boys...with me...with my son!
I can still feel his white hands shaking with excitement...
His penis ripped thru my rectum.
I remember...
My momma teaching me how to please Massa, teaching me how to survive hell.
See, I remember the overseer cutting out my momma's tongue!
The sight of beautiful Black women forced to breast feed li'l pink babies
While theirs starved to death during that harsh winter of '43
I can still see those soulless eyes.
Young and old come to celebrate hatred, as they gathered around the lynching tree.
That stabbing pain as my li'l brother struggled for breath!
Eyes bulging out of his electrified body dangling...gasping for life!

Noose digging into skin... His neck collapsing under the weight of his thrashing body!

I remember my life spent in hell!
The devil strapped me down... I begged and screamed.
I remember that blade and them greedy faces.
A sweaty hand holding my penis... That quick stroke slicing!
I remember working like a beast until my back broke
'Cause I didn't want to remember what they stole!
I remember the revolt of '46'.
Hot metal ripping thru my chest!
The peace of dying a warrior
I remember it all!
Dear God! I remember.

BEAUTIFUL BLACK CHILD !!!

Beautiful black child fill the world with wonder,
breathe life into exhausted hopes.
Your pure innocent nature,
not yet hindered by the evils of this world,
can forever change those you touch.
Help us to honor the love still living in slave quarters.
The bloodshed and pride fed to European insecurities.
Whips struck lashes like lightening
Across the horizon of shackled African bodies.
Field hands wounded and bleeding running North to freedom.
Escaping the Klan, communing with natives in swamplands.
Recaptured stretched necks suspended in midair from southern trees.
Nooses dangled strange fruit burned bare.
Blistered ebony backs frying in the Mississippi sun.
Crisping while picking cotton, crying a soulful moan,
As bolls pricked over worked fingertips.

With impunity that master bastard raped your queens forcing fathers to watch.
All endured 'cuase da baby cain't go hungry.
Do not let fear rob you of your gift!
You are special!
Lead the way to the future for those who follows.
Defy the odds and let your light shine in defiance.
Sheer brilliance blinding the faithless and guiding the believers.
An ever-glowing tribute to your people.

Beautiful black child
The inhumane condition you have endured
For thousands of generations transformed you.
Glory belongs to our ancestors' sacrifices.

Beautiful black butterfly,
Rise as the sun with your dreams firmly in hand.
Boldly place them among the stars,
Ever burning spectacles for the world to gaze upon.

Beautiful black people,

Let our audacious ascension emulate the Nile River.
It began as a few struggling drops.
As time passed its surging growth overcame obstacles,
defeating whatever lay in its path.
Refusing to allow the world to define it,
Our existence instead defines the world.
We are an unstoppable force, shaping the universe.
All lips shall utter these words,
"Beautiful Black Child."
Beautiful Black Child,
This is my prayer for you!

About the Author

John Burl Smith is a native Memphian who now lives in Atlanta, Georgia. A veteran of the United States Air Force and magna cum laude graduate of the University of Memphis with a B.A. in psychology, he has spent his entire adult life advocating for social justice. In high school, Burl was a founding member of the Invaders, an organization most noted for its elevation of African-American injustice during the Civil Rights Movement. Later, he served as Chair of the Black Organizing Project (1967-1977). He was also the publisher What's Trump and the Founder of Men in Progress (1973) at LeMoyne Owen College. Burl has been a change agent for the African-American political landscape in the south serving as the grassroots organizer and delegate coordinator for Shirley Chisholm's Presidential Campaign and the author of a class-action lawsuit against the 8th Congressional district lines that paved the way for Rep. Harold Ford's election to Congress in 1976. He was also the chairman of the First Tennessee Draft for Ted Kennedy (1978), and delegate on the Summit on Africa from Georgian (1988). Among other positions, he was also a writer for *Dot's Information Service Hotline (The DISH)*, an E-magazine for the Dialogue on Race (1997-2012).

Burl is the author of three books *Archangel: A Hip Hop Vision of Love and the Battle of Good Verse Evil, Dr. Martin Luther King, Jr.'s Last Strategy Meeting: The Invaders Story*, and *The 400th: From Slavery to Hip Hop*.

To contact him, email jbsmith908@gmail.com.

www.ingramcontent.com/pod-product-compliance
Lightning Source LLC
Chambersburg PA
CBHW030511230426
43665CB00010B/594